Lecture Notes of the Institute for Computer Sciences, Social Informatics and Telecommunications Engineering

284

More information about this series at http://www.springer.com/series/8197

Jin Li · Zheli Liu · Hao Peng (Eds.)

Security and Privacy in New Computing Environments

Second EAI International Conference, SPNCE 2019
Tianjin, China, April 13–14, 2019
Proceedings

Editors
Jin Li
Guangzhou University
Guangdong, Guangdong, China

Zheli Liu
College of Cyberspace Security
Nankai University
Tianjin, Tianjin, China

Hao Peng
College of Mathematics and Computer
Science
Zhejiang Normal University
Zhejiang, Zhejiang, China

ISSN 1867-8211   ISSN 1867-822X (electronic)
Lecture Notes of the Institute for Computer Sciences, Social Informatics
and Telecommunications Engineering
ISBN 978-3-030-21372-5   ISBN 978-3-030-21373-2 (eBook)
https://doi.org/10.1007/978-3-030-21373-2

This Springer imprint is published by the registered company Springer Nature Switzerland AG
The registered company address is: Gewerbestrasse 11, 6330 Cham, Switzerland

Preface

We are delighted to introduce the proceedings of the second edition of the 2019 European Alliance for Innovation (EAI) International Conference on Security and Privacy in New Computing Environments (SPNCE). This conference brought together researchers, developers, and practitioners from around the world who are leveraging and developing security and privacy in new computing environments. The theme of SPNCE 2019 was "New Computing Environment: Security and Privacy Protection."

The technical program of SPNCE 2019 consisted of 62 full papers. The conference tracks were: Track 1—Privacy and Security Analysis; Track 2—Internet of Things and Cloud Computing; Track 3—Blockchain and Its Application; Track 4—Schemes, Models, and Applications for Data; and Track 5—Mechanisms and Methods in New Computing. Aside from the high-quality technical paper presentations, the technical program also featured four keynote speeches. The four keynote speakers were Dr. Jie Li from Shanghai Jiaotong University, China; Dr. Xinpeng Zhang from Fudan University, China; Dr. Xiaohua Jia from City University of Hong Kong, SAR China; and Wenjing Lou from Virginia Tech, USA.

Coordination with the steering chair, Imrich Chlamtac, was essential for the success of the conference. We sincerely appreciate the constant support and guidance. It was also a great pleasure to work with such an excellent Organizing Committee and we thank them for their hard work in organizing and supporting the conference. In particular, we thank the Technical Program Committee, led by Dr. Changyu Dong and Dr. Xiaochun Cheng, who completed the peer-review process of technical papers and compiled a high-quality technical program. We are also grateful to the conference manager, Karolina Marcinova, for her support and all the authors who submitted their papers to the SPNCE 2019 conference.

We strongly believe that the SPNCE conference provides a good forum for researchers, developers, and practitioners to discuss all scientific and technological aspects that are relevant to smart grids. We expect that future SPNCE conferences will be as successful and stimulating as indicated by the contributions in this volume.

May 2019

Jin Li
Zheli Liu
Hao Peng

Organization

Steering Committee

Imrich Chlamtac   University of Trento, Italy

Organizing Committee

General Chair

Zheli Liu   Nankai University, China

General Co-chairs

M. Atiquzzaman   University of Oklahoma, USA
Jin Li   Guangzhou University, China

Sponsorship and Exhibit Chair

Yongjian Yang   Jilin University, China

Local Chairs

Chunfu Jia   Nankai University, China
Guangquan Xu   Tianjin University, China

Workshops Chairs

Tao Li   Nankai University, China
Ilsun You   Soonchunhyang University, South Korea

Publicity and Social Media Chairs

Jian Xu   Northeastern University
Mianxiong Dong   Muroran Institute of Technology, Japan

Publications Chairs

Siu-Ming Yiu   Chinese University of Hong Kong, SAR China
Hao Peng   Zhejiang Normal University, China

Web Chair

Shaojing Fu   National University of Defense Technology, China

Technical Program Committee

Changyu Dong   University of Newcastle Upon Tyne, UK
Xiaochun Cheng   Middlesex University, UK

Contents

Privacy and Security Analysis

A Blind Signature Scheme Applying on Electronic Payment Scene Based
on Quantum Secret Sharing 3
    Jia-lei Zhang, Ming-sheng Hu, Bei Gong, Zhi-Juan Jia,
    and Li-Peng Wang

Threshold Signature Scheme with Strong Forward Security Based on
Chinese Remainder Theorem 15
    Ya-ge Cheng, Zhi-juan Jia, Bei Gong, Li-peng Wang, and Yan-fang Lei

Lightweight Secure Cloud Auditing Scheme for Shared Data
Supporting Identity Privacy and Traceability. 29
    Jun-Feng Tian, Xuan Jing, and Rui-Fang Guo

Research on Big Data Platform Security Based on Cloud Computing 38
    Xiaxia Niu and Yan Zhao

Database Query System with Budget Option for Differential Privacy
Against Repeated Attacks. 46
    Jingyu Jia, Yuduo Wu, Yue Guo, Jiqiang Gao, Jin Peng, Peng Ran,
    and Min Li

Research on Social Networks Publishing Method Under
Differential Privacy 58
    Han Wang and Shuyu Li

CROSS: Supervised Sharing of Private Data over Blockchains 73
    Mingxin Yin, Jiqiang Gao, Xiaojie Guo, Mengyao Sun, Zheli Liu,
    Jianzhong Zhang, and Jing Wang

A Survey of Trusted Network Trust Evaluation Methods 87
    An-Sheng Yin and Shun-Yi Zhang

Anomaly Detection of Vehicle CAN Network Based on Message Content . . . 96
    Xiuliang Mo, Pengyuan Chen, Jianing Wang, and Chundong Wang

Android Malware Detection Based on Sensitive Permissions and APIs 105
    Chunhui Zhao, Chundong Wang, and Wenbai Zheng

Security Assessment for Cascading Failures of Cyber-Physical Systems
Under Target Attack Strategy 114
    Hao Peng, Zhe Kan, Dandan Zhao, Jianmin Han, and Zhaolong Hu

Privacy Preservation in Publishing Electronic Health Records Based
on Perturbation 125
   Lin Yao, Xinyu Wang, Zhenyu Chen, and Guowei Wu

Privacy in Location-Based Services: Present Facts and Future Paths 141
   Zakaria Sahnoune and Esma Aïmeur

Privacy Disclosures Detection in Natural-Language Text
Through Linguistically-Motivated Artificial Neural Networks 152
   Nuhil Mehdy, Casey Kennington, and Hoda Mehrpouyan

Research on Information Security Test Evaluation Method Based
on Intelligent Connected Vehicle. 178
   Yanan Zhang, Shengqiang Han, Stevenyin Zhong, Peiji Shi,
   and Xuebin Shao

Study on Incident Response System of Automotive Cybersecurity. 198
   Yanan Zhang, Peiji Shi, Yangyang Liu, Shengqiang Han,
   Baoying Mu, and Jia Zheng

Secure Multi-keyword Fuzzy Search Supporting Logic Query over
Encrypted Cloud Data 210
   Qi Zhang, Shaojing Fu, Nan Jia, Jianchao Tang, and Ming Xu

A Practical Group Signatures for Providing Privacy-Preserving
Authentication with Revocation 226
   Xiaohan Yue, Jian Xu, Bing Chen, and Yuan He

An Efficient Privacy-Preserving Palmprint Authentication Scheme
Based on ElGamal 246
   Yong Ding, Huiyong Wang, Zhiqiang Gao, Yujue Wang, Kefeng Fan,
   and Shijie Tang

PJC: A Multi-source Method for Identifying Information Dissemination
in Networks 268
   Yong Ding, Xiaoqing Cui, Huiyong Wang, and Yujue Wang

Steganalysis of Adaptive Multiple-Rate Speech Using Parity of Pitch-Delay
Value 282
   Xiaokang Liu, Hui Tian, Jie Liu, Xiang Li, and Jing Lu

Network Risk Assessment Based on Improved MulVAL Framework
and HMM 298
   Chundong Wang, Kongbo Li, Yunkun Tian, and Xiaonan He

Internet of Things and Cloud Computing

FIREWORK: Fog Orchestration for Secure IoT Networks   311
  Maryam Vahabi, Hossein Fotouhi, and Mats Björkman

An Effective Encryption Scheme on Outsourcing Data for Query
on Cloud Platform.   318
  Jianchao Tang, Shaojing Fu, and Ming Xu

Design of an Urban Waterlogging Monitoring System Based on Internet
of Things   333
  Jiachen Liu, Yintu Bao, Yingcong Liu, and Wuyungerile Li

A Multi-Objective Service Selection Method Based on Ant Colony
Optimization for QoE Restrictions in the Internet of Things   342
  Chuxuan Zhang, Bing Jia, and Lifei Hao

FDSCD: Fast Deletion Scheme of Cloud Data   354
  Tong Shao, Yuechi Tian, Zhen Li, and Xuan Jing

A RBAC Model Based on Identity-Based Cryptosystem in Cloud Storage . . .   362
  Jian Xu, Yanbo Yu, Qingyu Meng, Qiyu Wu, and Fucai Zhou

Public Auditing of Log Integrity for Cloud Storage Systems via Blockchain. . .   378
  Jia Wang, Fang Peng, Hui Tian, Wenqi Chen, and Jing Lu

Coordinated Web Scan Detection Based on Hierarchical Correlation   388
  Jing Yang, Liming Wang, Zhen Xu, Jigang Wang, and Tian Tian

Research on Multi Domain Based Access Control in Intelligent
Connected Vehicle   401
  Kaiyu Wang, Nan Liu, Jiapeng Xiu, and Zhengqiu Yang

System Building

Cryptanalysis of a Public Key Cryptosystem Based on Data Complexity
Under Quantum Environment   411
  Zhengjun Jing, Chunsheng Gu, and Peizhong Shi

A Design of the Group Decision Making Medical Diagnosis Expert System
Based on SED-JD Algorithm   421
  Na Zong, Wuyungerile Li, Pengyu Li, Bing Jia, and Xuebin Ma

Design and Implementation of a Lightweight Intrusion Detection
and Prevention System.   433
  Xiaogang Wei

Reliability Analysis of Coupled Cyber-Physical Systems Under Different
Network Types.. 440
  Hao Peng, Zhe Kan, Dandan Zhao, Jianmin Han, and Zhaolong Hu

Invulnerability Assessment of Cyber-Physics Systems for Blockchain
Environment... 450
  Hao Peng, Zhe Kan, Dandan Zhao, Zhonglong Zheng, and Feilong Lin

Intrusion Detection System for IoT Heterogeneous Perceptual Network
Based on Game Theory... 459
  Man Zhou, Lansheng Han, Hongwei Lu, and Cai Fu

A Blockchain-Based Digital Advertising Media Promotion System........ 472
  Yong Ding, Decun Luo, Hengkui Xiang, Chenjun Tang,
  Lingang Liu, Xiuqing Zou, Shijie Li, and Yujue Wang

Detecting Steganography in AMR Speech Based on Pulse Correlation...... 485
  Jie Liu, Hui Tian, Xiaokang Liu, and Jing Lu

State Consistency Checking for Non-reentrant Function Based on Taint
Assisted Symbol Execution 498
  Bo Yu, Qiang Yang, and CongXi Song

SE Dots: A Sensitive and Extensible Framework for Cross-Region
DDoS Processing 509
  Li Su, Meiling Chen, Jin Peng, and Peng Ran

Scheme, Model and Application for Data

A One-Way Variable Threshold Proxy Re-signature Scheme
for Mobile Internet 521
  Yanfang Lei, Mingsheng Hu, Bei Gong, Lipeng Wang, and Yage Cheng

A New Signcryption Scheme Based on Elliptic Curves 538
  Wen-jun Cui, Zhi-juan Jia, Ming-sheng Hu, Bei-Gong,
  and Li-peng Wang

A Robust Reversible Watermarking Scheme for Relational Data.......... 545
  Ruitao Hou, Hequn Xian, Xiao Wang, and Jing Li

BL-IDS: Detecting Web Attacks Using Bi-LSTM Model Based
on Deep Learning.. 551
  Saiyu Hao, Jun Long, and Yingchuan Yang

An Static Propositional Function Model to Detect Software Vulnerability. ... 564
  Lansheng Han, Man Zhou, and Cai Fu

Design of ZigBee-Based Energy Harvesting Wireless Sensor Network
and Modeling of Solar Energy 576
   Yingcong Liu, Wuyungerile Li, Baoyintu, and Bing Jia

Application of Big Data Technology in JD. 585
   Ning Shi and Huwei Liu

A Trusted International Settlement Solution Based on Cross Check
of CDRs 596
   Peng Ran, Jin Peng, Bo Yang, Li Su, Xiaoyong Hang, and Junzhi Yan

Fog-Enabled Smart Campus: Architecture and Challenges 605
   Chaogang Tang, Shixiong Xia, Chong Liu, Xianglin Wei, Yu Bao,
   and Wei Chen

An Ant Colony Optimization Fuzzy Clustering Task Scheduling Algorithm
in Mobile Edge Computing 615
   Jianwei Liu, Xianglin Wei, Tongxiang Wang, and Junwei Wang

Mechanism and Method in New Computing

A Posted Pricing Mechanism Based on Random Forests
in Crowdsourcing Market. 627
   Lifei Hao, Bing Jia, and Chuxuan Zhang

A Reverse Auction Incentive Mechanism Based on the Participant's
Behavior in Crowdsensing 637
   Tao Zhou, Bing Jia, and Wuyungerile Li

A General Hardware Trojan Technique Targeted on Lightweight
Cryptography with Bit-Serial Structure. 647
   Yijun Yang, Liji Wu, Ye Yuan, and Xiangmin Zhang

Identification and Trust Techniques Compatible with eIDAS Regulation 656
   Stefan Mocanu, Ana Maria Chiriac, Cosmin Popa, Radu Dobrescu,
   and Daniela Saru

Gathering Pattern Mining Method Based on Trajectory Data Stream 666
   Ying Xia, Lian Diao, Xu Zhang, and Hae-young Bae

Travel Modes Recognition Method Based on Mobile Phone Signaling Data . . . 677
   Ying Xia, Jie Tang, Xu Zhang, and Hae-young Bae

Two-Level Feature Selection Method for Low Detection Rate Attacks
in Intrusion Detection 689
   Chundong Wang, Xin Ye, Xiaonan He, Yunkun Tian, and Liangyi Gong

A Novel Wireless Sensor Networks Malicious Node Detection Method   697
  Hongyu Yang, Xugao Zhang, and Fang Cheng

Grid Partition and Agglomeration for Bidirectional Hierarchical Clustering. . .   707
  Lei Wu, Hechang Chen, Xiangchun Yu, Sun Chao, Zhezhou Yu,
  and RuiTing Dou

A Non-repudiable Dynamic Provable Data Possession   723
  Jun-Feng Tian, Rui-Fang Guo, and Xuan Jing

Zone Based Lossy Image Compression Using Discrete Wavelet
and Discrete Cosine Transformations   731
  Nafees Ahmad, Khalid Iqbal, Lansheng Han, Naeem Iqbal,
  and Muhammad Adil Abid

Author Index   743

Privacy and Security Analysis

A Blind Signature Scheme Applying on Electronic Payment Scene Based on Quantum Secret Sharing

Jia-lei Zhang[1], Ming-sheng Hu[1(✉)], Bei Gong[2], Zhi-Juan Jia[1], and Li-Peng Wang[1]

[1] College of Information Science and Technology, Zhengzhou Normal University, Zhengzhou 450044, Henan, China
295533745@qq.com, 874667607@qq.com
[2] College of Computer Science, Beijing University of Technology, Beijing 100124, China

Abstract. The basic idea of quantum secret sharing is to share classical information through quantum schemes. In reality, the number of secret bits shared will vary according to the actual situation. For this reason, a secret sharing scheme of double qubits is constructed based on single particle. At the same time, combined with the needs of real life in e-commerce, this paper proposes a quantum blind signature protocol suitable for electronic cash payment scenarios. In this protocol, the blinding of the message is an XOR operation, which makes the solution simpler and easier to implement, and the owner of the message cannot be tracked. Moreover, we use quantum key distribution protocol and quantum one-time pad to guarantee its unconditional security. The quantum blind signature applied to the electronic payment system proposed in this paper could protect user's anonymity as the traditional E-payment systems do, and also have unconditional security which the classical E-payment systems cannot provide. Security analysis shows that our scheme is unforgeability, undeniability, blindness and unconditionally secure.

Keywords: Quantum secret sharing · Bell measurement · Quantum blind signature · Controlled non-gate · Unconditionally secure

Supported by the National Natural Science Foundation of China (Grant No. U1304614, U1204703), Henan Province Education Science Plan General Topic "Research on Trusted Degree Certification Based on Block-chain" (Grant No. (2018)-JKGHYB-0279), Zhengzhou Innovative Science and Technology Talent Team Construction Project Fund Project (Grant No. 131PCXTD597), Henan Science and Technology Project (Grant No. 162102310238).

J. Li et al. (Eds.): SPNCE 2019, LNICST 284, pp. 3–14, 2019.
https://doi.org/10.1007/978-3-030-21373-2_1

1   Introduction

In 1979, Shamir and Blakley proposed a secret sharing scheme based on Lagrange interpolation polynomial [1] and photographic geometry theory [2]. With the development of quantum cryptography, the classic secret sharing scheme starts with vector sub-secret sharing. Quantum cryptography is a new type of cryptosystem based on classical cryptography and quantum mechanics. It uses quantum mechanics to realize unconditional information exchange. In 1984, Bennett et al. proposed the concept of quantum cryptography [3]. Since then, quantum cryptography has become a hot research topic in the field of information security. Compared with the secret sharing based on the classical cryptosystem, the research on secret sharing based on quantum theory has begun to appear. In 1999, Hillery et al. proposed the first quantum multi-party secret sharing scheme using quantum entangled states combined with quantum teleportation [4].

The research of quantum multi-party secret sharing mainly focuses on the use of quantum technology to realize the secret sharing of classical information [5] and the use of quantum teleportation to reconstruct unknown quantum states [6] to realize the secret sharing of quantum information. The idea of quantum secret sharing is that: if needs to pass secret information to multiple agents, all agents can cooperate to recover secret information, but one or a part of agents cannot recover secret information. With the development of quantum cryptography, many quantum secret sharing schemes have been proposed. In 1999, Karlsson et al. proposed a new quantum secret sharing protocol based on two-particle entanglement [7]. For the first time, they systematically analyzed the security of protocols in several situations. In 2002, Tyc et al. first proposed a continuous variable quantum secret sharing scheme [8]. In 2003, Guo et al. first proposed the use of multi-particle product states to achieve quantum secret sharing [9]. In 2005, Yan et al. proposed a single-photon-based threshold quantum secret sharing scheme [10] for the first time. In 2008, Markham et al. used the Graph state to design a quantum secret sharing protocol [11]. In 2016, Li et al. proposed a quantum secret sharing scheme based on GHZ state [12], which requires partial particles to detect channels and reduce particle utilization. In 2018, Gao et al. proposed a multi-party secret sharing scheme based on quantum theory [13]. In the above secret sharing scheme, the shared quantum states are single-particle states. In this paper, based on the quantum secret sharing of a four-particle entangled state, the shared quantum state is extended to the two-particle state, which makes the formation of relatively perfect quantum secret sharing mechanism.

In 1983, Chaum first presented a blind signature [14]. When signed, the message is disguised to ensure privacy. In other words, it allows a signatory to sign a message for a user in such a way that she cannot learn the content of the message. In 1996, Fan and Lei also proposed a blind signature based on quadratic residues problem [15]. However, these schemes are more and more vulnerably with the advent of quantum computer, hence researchers have shown great interest in quantum blind signature [16–19]. Based on the characteristics of blind signature, this technology plays an important role in protecting user anonymity in applications such as electronic payment and electronic voting. In the electronic payment system, the bank is required to complete the signature of the electronic bill while ensuring the anonymity of the users consumption content. Although there are many signature schemes based on quantum cryptography, combined with the complexity of the current electronic cash system, there are few solutions for applying blind signatures based on quantum secret sharing to electronic cash system scenarios.

Based on the above problems, combined with the needs of real life, this paper proposes a quantum blind signature scheme that can be adapted to the electronic cash payment system. The scheme realizes secret sharing and reconstruction based on quantum truth secret sharing. At the same time, the shared secret is a double quantum state, which improves the information amount of the transmitted message, and provides a new method for the transmission of multi-qubit in quantum secure communication. In addition, the scheme of this paper combines quantum secret sharing and blind signature technology to provide a basis for the security of electronic payment. Moreover, the blinding of the message is an XOR operation, which makes the solution simpler and easier to implement, the owner of the message cannot be tracked. Furthermore, quantum key distribution and one-time pad are adopted in our scheme in order to guarantee unconditional security.

2   Basic Knowledge

2.1   Quantum Secret Sharing

In the quantum secret sharing scheme, the owner of any single part cannot effectively obtain the original complete information. Only through the unanimous cooperation of the various parts of the owner the owner of a certain part can get the complete information. In the process, if someone eavesdrops or one of the message owner is disloyal and wants to steal information, they will be detected back.

2.2   Bell State

The four Bell states of 2-qubit are

$$|\phi^{\pm}\rangle = \frac{1}{\sqrt{2}}(|00\rangle \pm |11\rangle), |\psi^{\pm}\rangle = \frac{1}{\sqrt{2}}(|01\rangle \pm |10\rangle). \tag{1}$$

2.3   Controlled Non-gate

Assume that the two qubits of the controlled non-gate are M and N, respectively. Where M is the control bit and N is the target bit. Its function is as follows: when the control bit is $|0\rangle$, the target bit does not change; when the control bit is $|1\rangle$, the target bit is inverted ($|0\rangle \leftrightarrow |1\rangle$). The controlled non-gate circuit diagram Fig. 1 and the truth Table 1 are as follows.

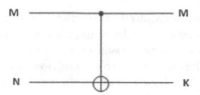

Fig. 1. Controlled non-gate circuit diagram

3 Quantum Secret Sharing Scheme

Based on the quantum secret sharing protocol of three-particle entangled state, the quantum secret sharing scheme proposed in this paper increases the shared secret quantum state from single particle to multi-particle state. Furthermore, the quantum blind signature scheme based on the secret sharing is discussed.

Table 1. Controlled non-gate truth table

M	N	$K = M \oplus N$	M^*	N^*
0	0	0	0	0
0	1	1	0	1
1	0	1	1	1
1	1	0	1	0

Suppose there are three legal participants Peter, Bob and David. Peter is the sender of the message, Bob and David are the agents of the message. Peter wants to send an unknown two-particle state to Bob or David as follows

$$|\varphi\rangle_M = (\alpha|00\rangle + \beta|11\rangle)_{12}, \tag{2}$$

in which $|\alpha|^2 + |\beta|^2 = 1$.

Suppose Peter, Bob and David share an entangled W-state particle as follows

$$|\xi\rangle_W = \frac{1}{\sqrt{3}}(|010\rangle + |100\rangle + |001\rangle)_{345}, \tag{3}$$

Particles 1 and 3 are given to Peter, and particle 2 is given to Bobparticles 4 and 5 are given to David. The distribution of particles is shown in Fig. 2.

The resulting five-particle state is

$$|T\rangle_{12345} = |\varphi\rangle_M \otimes |\xi\rangle_W$$

$$= (\alpha|00\rangle + \beta|11\rangle)_{12} \otimes \frac{1}{\sqrt{3}}(|010\rangle + |100\rangle + |001\rangle)_{345}$$

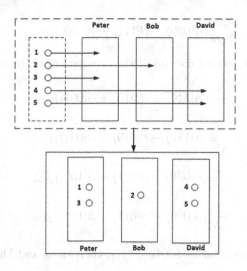

Fig. 2. Schematic diagram of particle distribution

$$= \frac{1}{\sqrt{3}}|\phi^+\rangle_{13}(\alpha|010\rangle + \beta|100\rangle + \alpha|001\rangle)_{245}+$$

$$= \frac{1}{\sqrt{3}}|\phi^-\rangle_{13}(\alpha|010\rangle - \beta|100\rangle + \alpha|001\rangle)_{245}+$$

$$= \frac{1}{\sqrt{3}}|\psi^+\rangle_{13}(\alpha|000\rangle + \beta|101\rangle + \beta|110\rangle)_{245}+$$

$$= \frac{1}{\sqrt{3}}|\psi^-\rangle_{13}(\alpha|000\rangle + \beta|101\rangle - \beta|110\rangle)_{245}$$

(1) Peter performs a Bell measurement on particles 1 and 3, Bob and David's particles will collapse. Bob and David judge the state of their particles based on Peters measurement results.

(2) Two control operations between Peter and Bob were performed. First, particle 2 is used as the control qubit, particle 4 is the target qubit to control the non-gate operation; then particle 4 is the control qubit, and particle 2 is the target qubit to control the non-gate operation.

(a) The result of the first control of the non-gate operation is $|T\rangle_{245}^1$:

$$\frac{1}{\sqrt{6}}(\alpha|010\rangle + \beta|110\rangle + \alpha|001\rangle)_{245};$$

$$\frac{1}{\sqrt{6}}(\alpha|010\rangle - \beta|110\rangle + \alpha|001\rangle)_{245};$$

$$\frac{1}{\sqrt{6}}(\alpha|000\rangle + \beta|111\rangle + \beta|100\rangle)_{245};$$

$$\frac{1}{\sqrt{6}}(\alpha|000\rangle - \beta|111\rangle - \beta|100\rangle)_{245}.$$

(b) The result of the second control of the non-gate operation is $|T\rangle_{245}^2$:

$$\frac{1}{\sqrt{6}}(\alpha|110\rangle + \beta|010\rangle + \alpha|001\rangle)_{245};$$

$$\frac{1}{\sqrt{6}}(\alpha|110\rangle - \beta|010\rangle + \alpha|001\rangle)_{245};$$

$$\frac{1}{\sqrt{6}}(\alpha|000\rangle + \beta|011\rangle + \beta|100\rangle)_{245};$$

$$\frac{1}{\sqrt{6}}(\alpha|000\rangle - \beta|011\rangle - \beta|100\rangle)_{245}.$$

(3) If Peter's measurement result is $|\phi^-\rangle_{13}$, then Bobs and Davids state is

$$|T\rangle_{245} = \frac{1}{\sqrt{6}}(\alpha|110\rangle - \beta|010\rangle + \alpha|001\rangle)_{245}$$

$$= \frac{1}{\sqrt{6}}[\alpha|10\rangle_{45} \otimes |1\rangle_2 + (\alpha|01\rangle - \beta|10\rangle)_{45} \otimes |0\rangle_2]$$

(4) If Bob's measurement result of particle 2 is $|0\rangle_2$, then David's particle 5 collapses to $|T\rangle_{45} = (\alpha|01\rangle - \beta|10\rangle)_{45}$, so David has to do a $I \otimes i\sigma_y$ operation to get $|T\rangle_{45} = (\alpha|00\rangle + \beta|11\rangle)_{45}$. Otherwise, David cannot get the quantum state transmitted by Peter. For other cases, the relationship between Peter's, Bob's measurement results and David's operation is listed in Table 2.

Table 2. The relationship between Peter's, Bob's measurement results and David's operation

Peter's result	$|T\rangle_{245}^2$	David's state after Bob operation	David's operation
$|\phi^+\rangle_{13}$	$(\alpha|110\rangle + \beta|010\rangle + \alpha|001\rangle)_{245}$	$(\alpha|01\rangle + \beta|10\rangle)_{45}$	$I \otimes \sigma_x$
$|\phi^-\rangle_{13}$	$(\alpha|110\rangle - \beta|010\rangle + \alpha|001\rangle)_{245}$	$(\alpha|01\rangle - \beta|10\rangle)_{45}$	$I \otimes i\sigma_y$
$|\psi^+\rangle_{13}$	$(\alpha|000\rangle + \beta|011\rangle + \beta|100\rangle)_{245}$	$(\alpha|00\rangle + \beta|11\rangle)_{45}$	$I \otimes I$
$|\psi^-\rangle_{13}$	$(\alpha|000\rangle - \beta|011\rangle - \beta|100\rangle)_{245}$	$(\alpha|00\rangle - \beta|11\rangle)_{45}$	$I \otimes \sigma_z$

4 Quantum Blind Signature for Electronic Payment Scenarios

Blind signature is a special kind of digital signature which allows a signatory to generate a message signature under the condition that he knows nothing about the content of the message.

Our blind signature scheme involves three participants: (1) Peter: the massage owner (the consumer); (2) Bob: the signer (the bank); (3) David: the verifier (the merchant).

The functions implemented by the protocol are as follows: the consumer Peter blinds the message m containing the privacy purchase content to obtain the message m_1, the bank Bob signs the blinded message m_1 to obtain $sig(m_1)$, and David verifies the legitimacy of the message m and the signature $sig(m_1)$. The intrinsic relationship between the message m and the signature $sig(m_1)$ cannot be found, so identity tracking cannot be implemented for consumers. The specific process diagram of the scheme is shown in Fig. 3.

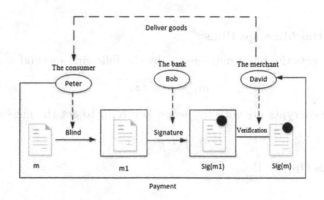

Fig. 3. Schematic diagram of electronic payment protocol

4.1 Initial Phase

Step1. Peter divides her purchase information M into two parts: m^*, involving the amount that Peter ought to pay; m, including Peters purchase information which cannot be seen by others. So Peter needs to blind the part m. The segmentation of the message is shown in Fig. 4.

Step2. Peter and Bob share a secret key K_{PD}, K_{BD} with David, respectively. Peter and Bob share a secret key K_{PB}. All these keys are distributed via QKD protocols, which have been proved unconditionally secure.

Step3. According to the secret sharing scheme described above, suppose Peter, Bob and David get sub-secrets are t_P, t_B and t_D, respectively.

Step4. Peter, Bob and David share a hash function H.

Step5. The message to be signed is m. Peter encrypts with the secret key K_{PD} to get

$$O_{PD} = K_{PD}(m) \tag{4}$$

Then she sends O_{PD} to David. We adopt one-time pad [18] as the encryption algorithm to guarantee the unconditional security.

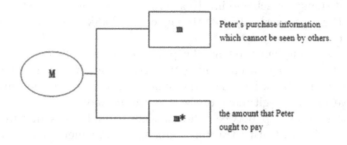

Fig. 4. Segmentation of the message

4.2   Blind the Message Phase

Step1. Peter gets the blind message m_1 by the following method

$$m_1 = m \oplus t_P. \tag{5}$$

Step2. Peter encrypts m_1 with the secret key K_{PB} to get the message

$$O_{PB} = K_{PB}(m_1). \tag{6}$$

then she sends O_{PB} to Bob.

4.3   Trading Purchase Phase

Step1. David performs a hash operation on t_D to get $H(t_D)$ and encrypts it with the secret key K_{BD} to get the message

$$O_{BD} = K_{BD}(H(t_D)) \tag{7}$$

Then he sends O_{BD} to Bob.
Step2. After Bob receives the message O_{PB}, he decrypts it with the secret key K_{PB} to get the message m_2 and get the message m_3

$$m_3 = m_2 \oplus t_B. \tag{8}$$

Step3. Bob encrypts m_3 with the secret key K_{BD} to get the message

$$S_{BD} = K_{BD}(m_3) = sig(m_1) \tag{9}$$

Then he sends $sig(m_1)$ to David.

4.4   Verifying Phase

Step1. David decrypts O_{PD} with the secret key K_{PD} to get the message m_4.
Step2. David decrypts S_{BD} with the secret key K_{BD} to get the message m_5 and get the message m_6:

$$m_6 = m_5 \oplus t_D. \tag{10}$$

Step3. If $m_6 = m_4$, the signature is valid. Otherwise, David will reject it.

4.5   Trading Payment Phase

Step1. David encrypts t_D with the secret key K_{BD} to get the message

$$O_{BD}^* = K_{BD}(t_D) \tag{11}$$

Then he sends it to Bob.
Step2. Bob decrypts O_{BD}^* with the secret key K_{BD} to get the message t_D^*. Then Bob performs a hash operation on t_D^* to get $H(t_D^*)$.
Step3. Bob decrypts O_{BD} with the secret key K_{BD} to get the message $H(t_D')$. If

$$H(t_D') = H(t_D^*) \tag{12}$$

the signature is valid.
Step4. If there is no dispute, the merchant David should send the corresponding goods to Peter. After Peter receives goods from the merchant, she will pay for the bank.

5   Security Analysis

5.1   Security Analysis of Quantum Secret Sharing

The secret sharing adopts the method of quantum teleportation. The secret quantum state is not known by any participant in the transmission process, which greatly improves the security of secret reconstruction.

(1) Internal attack

In the secret sharing scheme, suppose that one or several participants want to acquire secrets by means of deception and cooperation, it is impossible, because they must know the quantum state of the particles in the hands of the legal secret restorer to succeed. Even if the particles belonging to the secret restorer are intercepted by a dishonest agent and sent by another particle instead, the interception attack will also be discovered.

(2) Intercept-resend attack

Since secret reconstruction is realized by quantum teleportation, the attacker Eve stealing the detection quantum will inevitably lead to the change of the quantum state and thus be perceived. If Eve resends the intercepted particle with another quantum substitution, it will break the original particle value $|0\rangle$ and $|1\rangle$, which will cause the actual Bell measurement result to be wrong, and the secret cannot be reconstructed.

5.2   Security Analysis of Quantum Blind Signature

(1) Impossible of Forgery

No one other than the signer can forge a signature. Suppose that an attacker or eavesdropper Eve want to forge Bobs signature. However, he not be able to know the secret key K_{BD} shared between Bob and David, so he cannot send message encrypted by K_{BD}, in other words, it is impossible for Eve to forge Bobs signature. Assume that Eve guesses K_{BD} randomly, then he can produce the valid signature with the probability at most $\frac{1}{2^n}$, which vanishes zero if n is large enough. Therefore, Eve cannot forge Bobs signature.

(2) Impossible of Denial

On the one hand, if the legal signature is signed by Bob, he will not be able to deny it, because Bob encrypts m_3 with the secret key K_{BD} to get the message S_{BD}. So Bob could not deny that he had signed it. On the other hand, David cannot deny that he indeed have received the signature. It is obvious that the process of the verifying indicates he has received it. Therefore, David could not deny that he had received it.

(3) Blindness

The signature is blind. In this scheme, according to $m_1 = m \oplus t_P$, Peter gets the message m_1. Therefore, the message m is blinded to m_1, so the signer Bob cannot know the specific content of the original message m. At the same time, the message owner Peter could not know Bobs message based on the message passed by David, because David passed the hash value to Peter during the audit, and the Hash function has unidirectionality.

(4) Quantum security

Our scheme ensures security from the following two aspects. First, the protocol BB84 is adopted for quantum key distribution; Second, our protocol is based on the secure quantum channel, which has instantaneous transmission not restricted by distance, time or obstacles, all of these are proved to be unconditional security.

5.3   Performance Analysis

The efficiency analysis of the scheme is considered from the following aspects:

1. Consider the number of bits of the message transmitted in the channel. In this paper, the message transmitted is a double quantum state. Compared with scheme [13], the message transmitted by this paper contains a relatively large amount of information, which improves the information amount of the transmitted message, and provides a new method for the transmission of multi-qubit in quantum secure communication.

2. Consider the complexity of signatures and verification. In this paper, the XOR operation of the blinding of the message is low in complexity and easy to implement. And this paper uses fewer classical bits in the signature process.

3. Considering the method used in the secret sharing scheme, the secret sharing of this paper is based on the entangled W state, and the efficiency is higher than other entanglements.

4. Combining quantum secret sharing and quantum blind signature, this paper proposes a signature protocol suitable for electronic cash payment system, which is the application of quantum technology in e-commerce.
5. In this protocol, the message owner cannot be tracked, which guarantees the anonymity of the consumer.

6   Conclusion

Combined with the actual needs of real life, this paper proposes a quantum blind signature scheme for electronic payment systems based on quantum secret sharing protocol. The scheme can realize that the signer signs the blind message to obtain a blind signature, and the blinding process adopts an XOR operation, and the operation is simple. At the same time, the owner of the message cannot be tracked, which guarantees the anonymity of the consumer. In addition, the scheme sets the audit phase to ensure the legitimacy of the e-payment process. Moreover, the scheme proposed in this paper is not limited by the computing power of the new party. Even if the attacker has very powerful computing resources, the scheme cannot be broken. Furthermore, the scheme realizes secret sharing and reconstruction based on quantum secret sharing. At the same time, the shared secret is a double quantum state, which improves the information amount of the transmitted message, and provides a new method for the transmission of multi-qubit in quantum secure communication.

References

1. Shamir, A.: How to share a secret. Commun. ACM **22**(11), 612–613 (1979)
2. Blakley, G.R.: Safeguarding cryptographic keys. IEEE Comput. Soc. **48**, 313–317 (1979)
3. Shen, C.: Research on trusted computing and its development. Sci. China Inf. Sci. **53**(3), 405–433 (2010)
4. Hillery, M., Buzek, V., Berthiaume, A.: Quantum secret sharing. Phys. Rev. A **59**(3), 1829–1834 (1999)
5. Kogias, L., Xiang, Y., He, Q.Y., et al.: Unconditional security of entanglement based quantum secret sharing schemes. Phys. Rev. A **95**(1), 012315 (2017)
6. Long, Y.X., Long, D.Y., Qiu, D.W.: Sharing classic secret information with maximum true entangled hexagonal state. J. Comput. Sci. Technol. **6**(5), 465–472 (2012)
7. Karlsson, A., Koashi, M., Imoto, N.: Quantum entanglement for secret sharing and secret splitting. Phys. Rev. A **59**(1), 162–168 (1999)
8. Tyc, T., Sanders, B.C.: How to share a continuous-variable quantum secret by optical interferometry. Phys. Rev. A **65**, 042310 (2002)
9. Guo, G.P., Guo, G.C.: Quantum secret sharing without entanglement. Phys. Lett. A **310**, 247–251 (2003)
10. Yan, F.L., Gao, T.: Quantum secret sharing between multiparty and multiparty without entanglement. Phys. Rev. A **72**, 012304 (2005)
11. Markham, D., Sanders, B.C.: Graph States for Quantum Secret Sharing. arXiv:0808.1532v1 (2008)

12. Li, W.Z., Liu, Z.W.: Multi-party quantum secret sharing scheme based on GHZ state for flawless operation. Comput. Appl. Res. **33**(2), 491–494 (2016)
13. G, M., W, X.M.: A multi-party secret sharing scheme based on quantum theory. Appl. Res. Comput. **35**(7), 2135–2145 (2018)
14. Chaum, D.: Blind signatures for untraceable payments. In: Chaum, D., Rivest, R.L., Sherman, A.T. (eds.) Advances in Cryptology, pp. 199–203. Springer, Boston (1983). https://doi.org/10.1007/978-1-4757-0602-4_18
15. Fan, C., Lei, C.: Efficient blind signature scheme based on quadratic residues. Electron. Lett. **32**(9), 811–813 (1996)
16. Zhang, J.L., Zhang, J.Z., Xie, S.C.: Improvement of a quantum proxy blind signature scheme. Int. J. Theor. Phys. **57**(6), 1612–1621 (2018)
17. Zhang, J.L., Xie, S.C., Zhang, J.Z.: An elaborate secure quantum voting scheme. Int. J. Theoret. Phys. **56**(10), 3019–3028 (2017)
18. Guo, W., Zhang, J.Z., Li, Y.P., et al.: Multi-proxy strong blind quantum signature scheme. Int. J. Theor. Phys. **55**(8), 3524–3536 (2016)
19. Zhang, J.L., Zhang, J.Z., Xie, S.C.: A choreographed distributed electronic voting scheme. Int. J. Theoret. Phys. **57**(9), 2676–2686 (2018)

Threshold Signature Scheme with Strong Forward Security Based on Chinese Remainder Theorem

Ya-ge Cheng[1], Zhi-juan Jia[1(✉)], Bei Gong[2], Li-peng Wang[1], and Yan-fang Lei[1]

[1] College of Information Science and Technology,
Zhengzhou Normal University, Zhengzhou 450044, China
897373693@qq.com, 13676951984@163.com
[2] College of Computer Sciences,
Beijing University of Technology, Beijing 100124, China

Abstract. The traditional cryptosystem is based on the security of private key. While the private key is leaked, the signature information may be exposed. Based on this, a threshold signature scheme with strong forward security based on Chinese remainder theorem is proposed. The signature is generated through the cooperation of members, which solve the problem of authoritative fraud introduced by the dealer. The private key is updated periodically to handle the threat caused by the private key leakage. Security analysis shows that the existing signatures will not be affected by the compromise of the corresponding private keys, and do not allow for forgery of the future signatures, which shows that the new scheme has the forward security and the backward security. The efficiency analysis shows that our scheme is more efficient compared with the well-known existing schemes in the literature.

Keywords: Strong forward security · Threshold signature · Chinese remainder theorem · Secret sharing

1 Introduction

In the era of explosive development of the Internet today, while it brings convenience to people, it also faced the problems such as privacy leaked and information tampering. The rapid development of the network has promoted the widespread application of digital signature technology, however, the biggest challenge of digital signature technology is the leakage of the private key, which make the information seriously inaccurate, in this context, the idea of forward security came into being.

In 1997, Anderson [1] first proposed the concept of forward security at the cryptography conference in Europe. The core idea was the update of the key. Then Bellare and Miner [2] proposed forward theory based on One-Schnorr and Fiat-Shamir's schemes in 1999, in which implemented a forward-secure digital signature scheme for the first time. In 2000, Anderson [3] summarized the forward security scheme and

J. Li et al. (Eds.): SPNCE 2019, LNICST 284, pp. 15–28, 2019.
https://doi.org/10.1007/978-3-030-21373-2_2

proposed two security: forward safety and backward safety. In 2001, Mike Burmester et al. proposed a strong forward security definition [4], it means a signature system will not affect the previous and subsequent signatures when the current key is compromised. Its proposal greatly improves the efficiency of the signature.

The literature [5] based on the zero-knowledge proof proposed a forward-backward secure digital signature scheme. Literature [6] proposed a forward-backward security digital signature based on the strong RSA hypothesis. Literature [7] proposed a two-way secure signature scheme based on discrete logarithm problem. Literature [8] proposed a proxy signature scheme with strong forward security based on the ElGamal scheme. The literature [9] proposed forward and backward security group signature scheme based on Lagrangian difference polynomial. In literature [10] the dual key is introduced on the basis of Guillou-Quisquater signature system and Rabin cryptosystem, proposed a strong forward-secure digital signature scheme. The literature [11] based on the bilinear pairing algorithm proposed a verifiable strong forward secure ring signature scheme, both in signature and verification process requires bilinear pairing calculation, which makes the signature efficiency lower. All of the solutions above have strong forward security but are inefficient.

In [12], a signature scheme with forward security based on the Chinese remainder theorem was proposed. In [13], given a subgroup signature scheme. In [14], Tang proposed a group blind signature scheme. A group signature scheme was proposed in [15]. The signature schemes above were all based on the Chinese remainder theorem, all of which have forward security but no backward security.

Based on the above researches, a threshold signature scheme based on the Chinese remainder theorem with strong forward security is proposed. The scheme does not require a trusted center and solves the problem of authoritative fraud in the trusted center. Through cooperation, the partial signatures synthesized the final signature. It also supports the members' private keys updated periodically to ensure strong forward security of the signature system.

2 Prerequisite Knowledge

2.1 Forward Security Theory

The forward security theory [2] means the entire signature time is divided into cycles and the public key remains unchanged throughout the signature time, but the member private key is continuously updated as the signature cycle progresses. In each cycle, signatures are generated by using the member's current private keys. When a member's private key is leaked in a certain period, due to the update of the private key, the malicious attacker cannot forge the signature information before the period, so the signatures before the current period are secure.

The implementation of forward security theory is as follows:

1. Divide the validity period of the signature into T periods;
2. The public key remains unchanged throughout the signature time, and the private key is dynamically updated as time passes;

3. In j cycle, member P_i counts $SK_{ij} = h(SK_{i(j-1)})$, where h is a one-way function;
4. P_i deletes $SK_{i(j-1)}$ immediately after calculating $SK_{i(j-1)}$. Thus, even if an attacker obtains the j cycle's private key of P_i, it cannot obtain any information of the private keys before the period. The update of private key is shown as follows (Fig. 1).

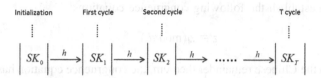

Fig. 1. Schematic diagram of private key update

2.2 Strong Forward Security

Strong forward security means that if the current key of a signature system is given away, it will not have any effect on the signature before and after the current period. It mainly includes two aspects of security:

1. Forward security: refers to that the key's leak of the current period will have no effect on the signature information before this;
2. Backward security: refers to that the key's leak of the current period will have no effect on the signature that will to be generated.

2.3 Asmuth-Bloom Secret Sharing Scheme

The Asmuth-Bloom [16] secret sharing scheme was proposed by Asmuth and Bloom in 1983. Its mainly includes three steps:

1. Initialize

Suppose DC is a secret distributor, $P = \{P_1, P_2, \cdots, P_n\}$ is a collection of n members, the threshold is t and the secret is S. The DC selects a large prime $q(q > S)$, A is an integer, $d = \{d_1, d_2, \cdots, d_n\}$ is a strictly increasing sequence of positive integers, and d satisfies the following conditions:

(1) $0 \leq A \leq M/q - 1$;
(2) $d_1 < d_2 < \cdots < d_n$;
(3) $gcd(d_i, d_j) = 1, (i \neq j)$;
(4) $gcd(d_i, q) = 1, (i = 1, 2, \cdots, n)$;
(5) $M = \prod_{i=1}^{t} d_i > q \prod_{i=1}^{t-1} d_{n-t+1}$.

2. Secret distribution

DC calculation $z = S + Aq$ and $z_i = z mod d_i, (i = 1, 2, \cdots, n)$, send (z_i, d_i) to $P_i(i = 1, 2, \cdots, n)$ as a secret share of P_i.

3. Secret recovery

Any t members can recover secrets. After exchanging secrets between members, any member can establish the following congruence equations:

$$z \equiv z_i (mod \ d_i)$$

According to the Chinese remainder theorem, the congruence equation has a unique solution:

$$z = \sum_{i=1}^{t} \frac{D}{d_i} e_i X_i mod D, (i = 1, 2, \cdots, t)$$

So, we can find $S = z - Aq$.

3 The Proposed Scheme

Based on the Chinese remainder theorem, this paper proposes a dynamic threshold signature scheme with strong forward security. This solution does not require a dealer and the member private keys' are updated regularly, which keeping the group public key unchanged, to ensure the scheme strong forward security. The architecture diagram of the scheme is shown as follows (Table 1):

Table 1. signature scheme architecture diagram

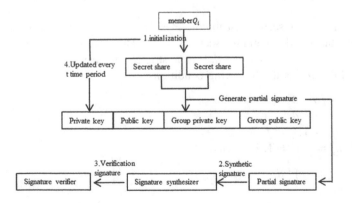

The solution consists of four steps: initialization, signature generation, signature verification and the updated of private key. The initialization phase generates a secret share, calculates verification information, and generates member keys and group keys. The signature compositor combines the partial signature into the final signature and it is verified by the signature verifier. The member private key is updated every t time periods.

3.1 System Initialization

$Q = \{Q_1, Q_2, \cdots, Q_n\}$ is a collection of n members, p and q is two large prime numbers that satisfy $q/p - 1$, $d = \{d_1, d_2, \cdots, d_n\}$ is a set of strictly monotonically increasing positive integer sequences which satisfies the Asmuth-Bloom secret sharing scheme, t is the threshold, g is the generator element on the finite field, M is the message to be signed, $N = \prod_{i=1}^{t} d_i$ is the product of the t smallest d_i.

1. Generate secret shares:

(1) Q_i selects α_i^0 and N_i^0 randomly to satisfy the following conditions:

$$0 < \alpha_i^0 < \lceil q/n \rceil \tag{1}$$

$$0 < N_i^0 < [N/q^2 - 1]/n \tag{2}$$

(2) Q_i calculates the verification information ω_i^0 and φ_{ij}^0:

$$\omega_i^0 = g^{(\alpha_i^0 + N_i^0 q)} mod p \tag{3}$$

$$\tau_{ij}^0 = (\alpha_i^0 + N_i^0 q - L_{ij}^0)/d_j \tag{4}$$

$$\varphi_{ij}^0 = g^{\tau_{ij}^0} mod p \tag{5}$$

broadcast ω_i^0, φ_{ij}^0.

(3) Q_i calculates secret shares for other members:

$$L_{ij}^0 = (\alpha_i^0 + N_i^0 q) mod d_j \tag{6}$$

retains L_{ii}^0, broadcasts $g^{\alpha_i^0}$, $g^{N_i^0}$ and sends L_{ij}^0 to Q_j.

2. Generate members' private keys

Q_j verifies the correctness of the message from Q_i through (7, 8)

$$g^{\alpha_i^0} \cdot g^{N_i^0 q} modp = \omega_i^0 \tag{7}$$

$$((g^{L_{ij}^0} modp) \, ((\varphi_{ij}^0)^{d_j} modp)) modp = \omega_i^0 \tag{8}$$

If they are right, then Q_j calculates his private key:

$$H_j^0 = \sum_{i=1}^{n} L_{ij}^0 modd_j \tag{9}$$

So the member's personal public key is:

$$C = g^{H_j^0} \tag{10}$$

3. Generate a group key:

According to the sub-secrets α_i^0 selected by each member, the group public key is:

$$PK = \prod_{i=1}^{n} g^{\alpha_i^0} modp \tag{11}$$

Then the group private key is:

$$SK = \sum_{i=1}^{n} \alpha_i^0 \tag{12}$$

3.2   Generate Signature

1. Q_i selects a random number $x_i \in Z_p$ and calculates:

$$z_i = g^{x_i} modp \tag{13}$$

broadcasts g^{x_i}.
2. After Q_j receives z_i, it calculates:

$$z = g^{\sum_{i=1}^{t} x_i} modp = \prod_{i=1}^{t} g^{x_i} modp = \prod_{i=1}^{t} z_i modp \tag{14}$$

3. Q_i calculates:

$$V_i^0 = \frac{D}{d_i} e_i H_i^0 modD \tag{15}$$

4. Q_i calculates part of the signature R_i^0:

$$R_i^0 = M \cdot z \cdot x_i + V_i^0 modD \qquad (16)$$

then, sends the partial signatures (M, z, R_i^0) to the signature compositor.

5. After the signature compositor receives the partial signature of the t members, synthesize them

$$R = \left(\sum_{i=1}^{n} R_i^0 modD \right) modq \qquad (17)$$

so the signature of the M is (M, z, R)

3.3 Verify Signature

When the certifier receives the signature of M, it verifies the signature:

$$g^R \equiv z^{M \cdot z} \cdot PKmodp \qquad (18)$$

If the equation is true, the signature (M, z, R) of the M is valid.

3.4 Private Keys Update

The update of private keys can prevent attacks effectively. Assume that the update cycle is T, the detailed update algorithm is shown as follows

1. Q_i selects a random number N_i^T to satisfy the initial conditions.
2. Q_i calculates the update factors:

$$L_{ij}^T = L_{ij}^{(T-2)} + N_i^T qmodd_j \qquad (19)$$

sends it to Q_j, broadcasts $g^{L_{ij}^{(T-2)}}$ and $g^{N_i^T}$;

3. Q_i calculates verification information ω_i^T and φ_{ij}^T.

$$\omega_i^T = g^{L_{ij}^{(T-2)} + N_i^T q} modp;$$
$$\tau_{ij}^T = (L_{ij}^{(T-2)} + N_i^T q - L_{ij}^T)/d_j;$$
$$\varphi_{ij}^T = g^{\tau_{ij}^T} modp;$$

and broadcasts them.

4. When Q_j received the messages L_{ij}^T, ω_i^T and φ_{ij}^T, verifies the correctness through the following two equations:

$$g^{L_{ij}^{(T-2)}} \cdot (g^{N_i^T})^q modp = \omega_i^T \qquad (20)$$

$$((g^{L_{ij}^T} modp) ((\varphi_{ij}^T)^{d_j} modp))modp = \omega_i^T \qquad (21)$$

5. If Q_j has a private key during T-2 is $H_j^{(T-2)}$, then the private key for the T period after update is:

$$H_j^T = H_j^{(T-2)} + \sum_{i=1}^{n} L_{ij}^T mod d_j \qquad (22)$$

The new private key can still be used for signature and verification.

4   Analysis of the Proposed

4.1   Correctness Analysis

Theorem 1. The signature generated by the updated private key is valid. That is to prove that the (18) formula is established.

Prove:

$$H_j^T = H_j^{(T-2)} + \sum_{i=1}^{n} L_{ij}^T mod d_j$$

$$= H_j^{(T-3)} + \sum_{i=1}^{n} L_{ij}^{(T-2)} mod d_j + \sum_{i=1}^{n} L_{ij}^T mod d_j = \ldots$$

$$= H_j^0 + \sum_{i=1}^{n} L_{ij}^0 mod d_j + \ldots + \sum_{i=1}^{n} L_{ij}^T mod d_j$$

$$= H_j^0 + \sum_{i=1}^{n} \left(\sum_{r=1}^{T} L_{ij}^r \right) mod d_j$$

$$= \sum_{i=1}^{n} (\alpha_i^0 + N_i^0 q) + \sum_{i=1}^{n} \left[\sum_{r=1}^{T} L_{ij}^{(T-2)} + N_i^T \right] mod d_j$$

$$= \sum_{i=1}^{n} \left(\alpha_i^0 + \sum_{r=1}^{T} N_i^r q \right) + \sum_{i=1}^{n} \sum_{r=1}^{T-1} L_{ij}^{(T-2)} mod d_j$$

$$= \sum_{i=1}^{n} \left(\alpha_i^0 + \sum_{r=1}^{T} N_i^r q \right) + \sum_{i=1}^{n} \sum_{r=1}^{T-2} (\alpha_i^0 + N_i^r q) mod d_j$$

$$= 2 \sum_{i=1}^{n} \left(\alpha_i^0 + \sum_{r=1}^{T-2} N_i^r q \right) + N_i^T q mod d_j; (j = 1, 2, \cdots, n)$$

make

$$G^T = \frac{1}{2} \sum_{i=1}^{n} \left(\alpha_i^0 + \sum_{r=1}^{T} N_i^r q \right) + \sum_{i=1}^{n} \sum_{r=1}^{T-2} (\alpha_i^0 + N_i^r q) mod d_j \qquad (23)$$

Then

$$H_j^T = 2G^T \bmod d_j, \; (j = 1, 2, \cdots, n).$$

Solving the congruence equations according to the Chinese remainder theorem:

$$\begin{cases} H_1^T \equiv 2G^T \bmod d_1 \\ H_2^T \equiv 2G^T \bmod d_2 \\ \vdots \\ H_t^T \equiv 2G^T \bmod d_t \end{cases}$$

Get a unique solution:

$$G^T = \frac{1}{2} \sum_{i=1}^{t} \frac{D}{d_i} e_i H_i^T \bmod D$$

Make

$$V_i^T = \frac{D}{d_i} e_i H_i^T \bmod D$$

Then

$$G^T = \frac{1}{2} \sum_{i=1}^{t} V_i^T \bmod D,$$

It can be known from the formulas (1), (2) and (19):

$$\begin{aligned}
G^T &= \frac{1}{2} \left[\sum_{i=1}^{n} \left(\alpha_i^0 + \sum_{r=1}^{T} N_i^r q \right) + \sum_{i=1}^{n} \sum_{r=1}^{T-2} \left(\alpha_i^r + N_i^r q \right) \right] \\
&\leq \frac{1}{2} \left\{ \sum_{i=1}^{n} \left(\alpha_i^0 + q \cdot \left[\frac{N}{2q^2} - 1 \right] / n \right) + \sum_{i=1}^{n} \sum_{r=1}^{T-2} \left(\alpha_i^0 + q \cdot \left[\frac{N}{2q^2} - 1 \right] / n \right) \right\} \\
&\leq \frac{1}{2} \left[n \cdot \left(\frac{q}{n} + q \cdot \left[\frac{N}{2q^2} - 1 \right] / n \right) + n \cdot \left(\frac{q}{n} + q \cdot \left[\frac{N}{2q^2} - 1 \right] / n \right) \right] \\
&\leq \frac{1}{2} \cdot 2 \cdot n \cdot \left\{ \frac{q}{n} + q \cdot \left[\frac{N}{q^2} - 1 \right] / n \right\} \\
&\leq \left\{ q + q \cdot \left[\frac{N}{q^2} - 1 \right] \right\} \\
&\leq \frac{N}{q}
\end{aligned}$$

According to the literature [17], when $t > 2$

$$M \cdot z \cdot \sum_i^t x_i + G^T \leq D$$

According to formula (16, 17)

$$
\begin{aligned}
R &= \left(\sum_{i=1}^t R_i^0 \bmod D \right) \bmod q \\
&= \left(\sum_{i=1}^t M \cdot z \cdot x_i + K_i^0 \bmod D \right) \bmod q \\
&= \left[\left(M \cdot z \cdot \sum_{i=1}^t x_i + G^T \right) \bmod D \right] \bmod q \\
&= \left[\left(M \cdot z \cdot \sum_{i=1}^t x_i + G^T \right) \right] \bmod q
\end{aligned}
$$

According to Eq. (23)

$$
\begin{aligned}
G^T &= \frac{1}{2} \left[\sum_{i=1}^n \left(\alpha_i^0 + \sum_{r=1}^T N_i^r q \right) + \sum_{i=1}^n \sum_{r=1}^{T-2} (\alpha_i^0 + N_i^r q) \bmod d_j \right] \\
&= \sum_{i=1}^n \alpha_i^0 \bmod q
\end{aligned}
$$

So have

$$R = [(M \cdot z \cdot \sum_{i=1}^t x_i + \sum_{i=1}^t \alpha_i^0)] \bmod q$$

$$
\begin{aligned}
g^R &\equiv g^{[(M \cdot z \cdot \sum_{i=1}^t x_i + \sum_{i=1}^n \alpha_i^0)] \bmod q} \\
&\equiv z^{M \cdot z} \cdot PK \bmod p
\end{aligned}
$$

Equation (18) is established, so the signature is valid.

4.2 Forward Security Analysis

If a member's private key is leaked in a certain period, no one else can falsify the signatures before it.

Suppose an attacker has stolen the personal private key H_j^T of the member Q_j of the T period, and the attacker wants to calculate $H_j^{(T-1)}$, then the attacker must calculate $\sum_{i=1}^{n} L_{ij}^T mod d_j$, and

$$L_{ij}^T = L_{ij}^{(T-2)} + N_i^T qmod d_j$$
$$= L_{ij}^{(T-3)} + (N_i^{(T-2)} + N_i^T)qmod d_j$$
$$= L_{ij}^{(T-4)} + (N_i^0 + \ldots\ldots + N_i^{(T-2)} + N_i^T)qmod d_j$$
$$= L_{ij}^0 + \sum_{r=1}^{T} (N_i^r - N_i^{(T-1)})qmod d_j$$

So

$$\sum_{i=1}^{n} L_{ij}^T mod d_j = \sum_{i=1}^{n} (L_{ij}^0 + \sum_{r=1}^{T} (N_i^r - N_i^{(T-1)})qmod d_j)$$

The attacker needs to obtain the random numbers N_i^r of the first T cycles and the initial secret share L_{ij}^0 of all members in a limited time, however they are secretly selected by the members, so it is difficult. The initial secret share is $L_{ij}^0 = (\alpha_i^0 + N_i^0 q)mod d_j$, since α_i^0 and N_i^0 are secretly selected and saved by members, so it is not possible to get.

In the stage of generating secret shares, an attacker may intercept the broadcast messages $g^{\alpha_i^0}$ and $g^{N_i^0}$ to calculate the secret shares L_{ij}^0, but it is difficult for the attacker to calculate the discrete logarithm problem in the limited time, so it is impossible to get for the attacker.

During the private key update phase, the attacker may intercept the broadcast information $g^{L_{ij}^{(T-2)}}$ and attempt to obtain L_{ij}^{T-2} directly, but it is still a discrete logarithm problem, solving this problem is extremely difficult, so the attacker cannot obtain it within a limited time through calculation.

Therefore, the attacker cannot calculate the member's private key before the period based on the private key of the current period, the scheme has forward security.

4.3   Backward Security Analysis

If the attacker wants to falsify the members' private key after the current cycle, it is not possible.

The member's private key is $H_j^T = H_j^{(T-2)} + \sum_{i=1}^{n} L_{ij}^T mod d_j$, if an attacker wants to falsify the private key after the current, suppose the attacker wants to fake the private key of the T + 1 period, the attacker must calculate $H_j^{(T-1)}$ and $\sum_{i=1}^{n} L_{ij}^{T+1}$, from the analysis in the previous paragraph, it is impossible for an attacker to calculate the private keys before the period in the effective time, so the attacker cannot obtain

$H_j^{(T-1)}$. In addition $\sum_{i=1}^{n} L_{ij}^{T+1} = \sum_{i=1}^{n} (L_{ij}^{(T-1)} + N_i^{T+1} q \bmod d_j)$, if the attacker want to get

$\sum_{i=1}^{n} L_{ij}^{T+1}$, he must calculate $L_{ij}^{(T-1)}$ and $N_i^{T+1} q$, while both of them are selected secretly by members, so it is impossible to get. Through analysis, the attacker cannot calculate the secret share of T + 1 cycle, so it is impossible to forge the member's private key after the cycle.

Therefore, the attacker cannot get the members' private keys after the current period in a limited time, so the scheme is backward security.

5 Performance Analysis

5.1 Efficiency Analysis

Since the modulo-addition operation and the modulo-subtraction operation are negligible compared with other operations, the scheme mainly analyzes the follow aspects of bilinear pair, hash, modular power, modular multiplication and Modular inverse. For ease of understanding, this article defines the following symbols:

This scheme analyzes the three stages of key update, signature generation and signature verification, and compares the calculation complexity between the literature [8, 10, 11], the comparison results are shown in Table 2 below.

Table 2. Time complexity representation symbol.

Operation	Symbol	Time complexity representation
Bilinear pair	e	$o(e(x))$
Hash	h	$o(h(x))$
Modular power	m	$o((lbn)^k)$
Modular multiplication	c	$o(\cdot lbn)$
Modular inverse	u	$o((lbn)^{-1})$

Table 3 is the comparison results of the calculation complexity between this article and other schemes. All of the solutions above have strong forward security. Through analysis, it can be found that the calculation complexity of this scheme is significantly lower than the others.

The computational complexity of the three stages in [8] is higher than that in this paper. In [10] and [11] the algorithm in the update phase is lower than this paper, but it is higher in the stage of generating signature and verification signature.

The order of algorithms complexity involved in the scheme is as follows $e > m > u > h > c$, that is, the bilinear pair calculation has the highest complexity, followed by the modulus power, the modular inverse, and the modular multiplication. This paper mainly includes modular power, modular multiplication and modular inverse, while other schemes all need hash operation. Literature [11] required bilinear

Table 3. Comparison of calculation complexity.

Schemes	Update phase	Signature generation phase	Signature verification phase
This article	$4o((lbn)^k)+2o(\cdot lbn)+o((lbn)^{-1})$	$o((lbn)^k)+3o(\cdot lbn)+o((lbn)^{-1})$	$o((lbn)^k)+2o(\cdot lbn)$
Literature [8]	$2o(h(x))+5o((lbn)^k)+$ $5o(\cdot lbn)+o((lbn)^{-1})$	$o(h(x))+2to((lbn)^k)$ $+2to(\cdot lbn)+o((lbn)^{-1})$	$2o(h(x))+4o((lbn)^k)+5o(\cdot lbn)$
Literature [10]	$3(t+2)o((lbn)^k)$	$o(h(x))+4o((lbn)^k)+3o(\cdot lbn)$	$o(h(x))+4o((lbn)^k)+3o(\cdot lbn)$
Literature [11]	$2to((lbn)^k)$	$2to(h(x))+2to((lbn)^k)$ $+to(e(x))+to((lbn)^{-1})$	$t\left[2o(e(x))+o(h(x))+o((lbn)^k)\right]$

pair calculation which of the computational complexity is significantly higher than the others. So, it is obvious that the operation of this scheme is simpler and the computational complexity is lower than the others.

5.2 Simulation

The environment of the simulation experiment is: 64-bit Window 10 operating system, MyEclipse2015 system, CPU is Intel Core i5-8300H processor, clocked at 2.3 GHz, memory 8 GB. The simulation experiment was carried out on the time overhead between the scheme and the literature [11] in the signature generation and verification phase. The result is shown below:

It can be seen from Fig. 2 that both of the scheme and the literature [11] have an increasing trend with the increase of the number of members. From the experimental result, the scheme [11] takes more time than the scheme proposed. This is because scheme [11] requires bilinear pairing operations in both the signature generation and verification phases, which is computationally complex than the other operations.

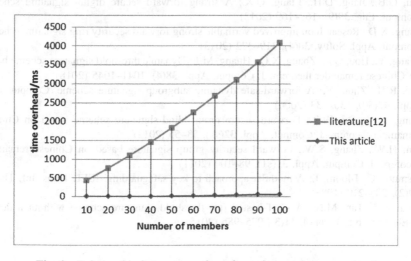

Fig. 2. Relationship between number of members and time overhead

6 Conclusion

In this manuscript, we proposed a threshold signature scheme with strong forward security. The scheme does not need a dealer. Through periodically update member private keys, it solved the problem of forgery or falsification of signatures due to private key leaks.

References

1. Anderson, R.: Invited lecture. In: Proceedings of Fourth Annual Conference on Computer and Communication Security, pp. 1–7. ACM Press, New York (1997)
2. Bellare, M., Miner, S.K.: A forward-secure digital signature scheme. In: Wiener, M. (ed.) CRYPTO 1999. LNCS, vol. 1666, pp. 431–448. Springer, Heidelberg (1999). https://doi.org/10.1007/3-540-48405-1_28
3. Anderson, R.: Two remarks on public key cryptology. In: Proceedings of the 4th ACM Conference on Computer and Communication California, pp. 16–30. Springer, USA (1997)
4. Burmester, M., Chrissikopoulos, V., Kotzanikolaou, P., Magkos, E.: Strong forward security. In: Dupuy, M., Paradinas, P. (eds.) SEC 2001. IIFIP, vol. 65, pp. 109–121. Springer, Boston, MA (2002). https://doi.org/10.1007/0-306-46998-7_8
5. Wang, M.W., Hu, Y.X.: A forward-backward security digital signature scheme. J. Xidian Univ. 41(2), 71–78 (2014)
6. Li, C., He, M.X.: A forward and backward security digital signature scheme. In: China Cryptography Society Annual Conference (2008)
7. Wang, Y.B.: Two-way secure signature scheme based on discrete logarithm. J. Qinghai Normal Univ. (Nat. Sci. Ed.) 2, 6–10 (2016)
8. Yang, J., Qian, H.F., Li, Z.B.: A proxy signature scheme with strong forward security. Comput. Eng. 34(17), 162–166 (2008)
9. Ye, J., Ding, Y., Liu, Y.N.: Forward and backward secure group signature scheme based on verifiable random number. J. Lanzhou Univ. Technol. 37(1), 86–90 (2011)
10. Xu, G.B., Jiang, D.H., Liang, Q.X.: A strong forward secure digital signature scheme. Comput. Eng. 39(9), 167–169 (2013)
11. Yang, X.D.: Research on improved verifiable strong forward security ring signature scheme. Comput. Appl. Softw. 30(4), 319–322 (2013)
12. Wang, Y., Hou, Q.F., Zhang, X.Q., Huang, M.J.: Dynamic threshold signature scheme based on Chinese remainder theorem. J. Comput. Appl. 38(4), 1041–1045 (2018)
13. Shi, R.H., Zhou, Y.: A forward-safe dynamic subgroup signature scheme. Comput. Eng. Appl. 42(30), 130–133 (2006)
14. Tang, L.W., Du, W.Z.: Forward secure group blind signature scheme based on Chinese remainder theorem. J. Comput. Appl. 32(s1), 53–55 (2012)
15. Ou, H.W., Zhang, S.W.: Forward security group signature based on Chinese remainder theorem. J. Comput. Appl. 31(s1), 98–100 (2011)
16. Asmuth, C., Bloom, J.: A modular approach to key safeguarding. IEEE Trans. Inf. Theory 29(2), 208–210 (1983)
17. Hou, Z.F., Tan, M.N.: A CRT-basted (tn) threshold signature scheme without a dealer. J. Electron. Inf. Technol. 11(3), 975–986 (2015)

Lightweight Secure Cloud Auditing Scheme for Shared Data Supporting Identity Privacy and Traceability

Jun-Feng Tian[1,2], Xuan Jing[1,2(✉)], and Rui-Fang Guo[1,2]

[1] School of Cyberspace Security and Computer Institute, Hebei University,
Baoding 071000, China
abidble@gmail.com
[2] Hebei Key Laboratory of High Confidence Information Systems, Hebei
University, Baoding 071000, China

Abstract. Cloud platform provides users with shared data storage services. To ensure shared data integrity, it is necessary to validate the data effectively. The audit scheme that supports the group dynamic operations conducts the integrity verification of the shared data, but this approach results in complex calculations for group members. The audit scheme of the designated agent implements the lightweight calculation of the group members, but it ignores the security risks between the group members and the agents. By introducing Hashgraph technology and designing a Third Party Medium (TPM) management strategy, a lightweight secure cloud auditing scheme for shared data supporting identity privacy and traceability (LSSA) is proposed, which realizes the security management of dynamic groups and the lightweight calculations for group members. Meanwhile, a virtual TPM pool is constructed by combining TCP sliding window technology and interconnected functions to improve agent security. Experiments on real data sets show that the theoretical analysis and experimental results are consistent, thereby reflecting the feasibility and efficiency of the scheme.

Keywords: Shared data · Dynamic groups · Lightweight calculation ·
Agent security

1 Introduction

Users can easily communicate with one another on cloud platforms to share data. Data sharing means that a user in a group uploads shared data to the cloud, and the rest of the group can access the shared data. Many cloud storage service providers (e.g., iCloud, OneDrive, and Baidu Cloud) currently use cloud data sharing as one of their main services. However, there are some data damage threats in the cloud, such as unavoidable hardware failures, external attacks, and cloud service provider damage. Therefore, in order to verify the integrity of the data stored in the cloud, Ateniese *et al.* first proposed a provable data possession (PDP) model, which can verify the integrity of cloud data without retrieving all data [1].

To support effective group dynamic operations, some researchers have proposed some audit schemes for shared data based on the PDP model [2–4], where group

J. Li et al. (Eds.): SPNCE 2019, LNICST 284, pp. 29–37, 2019.
https://doi.org/10.1007/978-3-030-21373-2_3

dynamics operations refer to supporting effective changes, additions, and deletions of group members. Yang *et al.* used the IDL table to record the use of shared data by group members and achieved the traceability of group members [2]. Jiang et al. adopted the vector commitment technique, and the verifier removed the illegal group members. This technique achieved the purpose of resisting collusion attacks of the cloud service provider and the group members [3]. Fu *et al.* proposed an audit scheme that can restore the latest correct shared data blocks by changing the binary tree tracking data and implementing homomorphic authentication in the group [4].

In the above scheme [1–4], in order to verify the integrity of the data stored in the cloud, the group members need to block the data and calculate the authentication label before uploading the data, but the computational burden is large. Guan *et al.* used an indistinguishable confusing approach to build an audit scheme for cloud storage [5], thereby reducing the time that is required to generate authentication label but increasing the time to verify the integrity of the cloud data. Wang *et al.* introduced agents to assist group members in generating authentication labels [6], which alleviated the computational burden for group members. However, in order to guarantee data privacy, blinding data is needed before each data upload, which inevitably increases the computational burden. Shen *et al.* realized the lightweight calculation of group members by introducing an agent to replace group members for generating authentication label [7], but it failed to consider the security risks that may occur when malicious group members collude with agents to obtain group keys.

Through the above analysis, how to ensure lightweight computing costs for group members while realizing the group dynamic operations is a problem to be solved in the current audit scheme of shared data. Considering the problem of improving the security and lightweight computing for agents, a lightweight secure cloud auditing scheme for shared data supporting identity privacy and traceability (LSSA) is proposed. The main contributions of this paper are as follows.

(1) By introducing a Hashgraph, the traceability of group membership can be guaranteed, and then effective changes, additions, and deletions of group members can be realized.
(2) The Third Party Medium (TPM) management strategy is designed, and the virtual TPM pool is built by the group manager. The strategy ensures the data privacy and identity privacy of group members and prevents the TPM from leaking group keys. This strategy also realizes lightweight calculations for a single TPM. Using the TPM instead of group members to calculate the authentication label and audit data integrity realizes the lightweight calculations for group members.
(3) The security analysis of the scheme shows that the scheme is safe and can resist replace attacks and replay attacks.

2   System Model

The system model of this scheme consists of four different entities: the Group members (M), the Cloud, the Group Manager (GM) and the TPM. As shown in Fig. 1, there are multiple group members in a group. After the data owner creates the data file and uploads it to the cloud, any group member can access and modify the corresponding shared data. Note that the original data owner can play the role of GM and there is only one GM in each group. The cloud provides data storage services for group members. The TPM replaces group members to calculate the authentication label and audit the integrity of shared data.

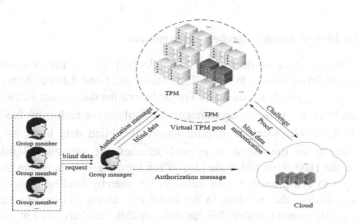

Fig. 1. System model

Group members need to share blind data and send requests to the GM to upload blind data. According to the request of group members, the GM chooses the TPM and the processing time for the blind data. The GM formulates the selection strategy (Sect. 3.2 for details) and builds a virtual TPM pool through the selection strategy, thereby making it difficult for entities other than the GM to know the TPM that is performing a computational task. This approach avoids the threats of attackers and prevents malicious group members from obtaining the TPM's private key. The GM authorizes the selected TPM and sends the blind data to it. The TPM calculates the corresponding authentication label based on the received blind data and uploads the blind data and authentication label to the cloud. The cloud verifies the TPM's identity information according to the authorization information sent by the GM. After verification, the real data and authenticated label are recovered from the blind data and the corresponding authentication label and stored. When the GM wants to verify the integrity of the cloud data, the GM selects the TPM according to the selection strategy, and then the TPM challenges the cloud. After receiving this challenge, the cloud returns the evidence of shared data to the TPM. Finally, the TPM verifies the correctness of the evidence to judge the integrity of the shared data.

3   The Main Design Ideal of LSSA

In this section, we use the Hashgraph technology to propose the design idea of group member management. By referring to the TCP sliding window [8] and using the Interconnection function [9], the design idea of the TPM management strategy is proposed.

3.1   Design Idea of Group Member Management

Assume that the data files are divided into n blocks (m1, m2, … mn), each data block mi is fragmented into s sectors (mi,1, mi,2, … mi,s), and blind data can be represented by $m'_{i,j}(1 \leq i \leq n, 1 \leq j \leq s)$. As shown in Fig. 2, before the data owner MOwner sends the blind data block $m'_{i,j}$ to the group manager, it calculates the hash value hash(idi,j) of idi,j (idi,j is the public identifier information of the blind data block $m'_{i,j}$) as the transaction record of the initial event and attaches the signature SignMOwner. According to the Hashgraph technique [10], it randomly selects the group member or group manager to synchronize it with initial event, thereby sending the event to the nodes in the network. The members in the group can access and modify the original shared data, but the group members Mi that have modified and accessed $m'_{i,j}$ since then need to update the identifier of the blind block after use. Thus, the members calculate the hash value of idi,j as a transaction record for a new event and attach the signature SignMi to spread it within the group.

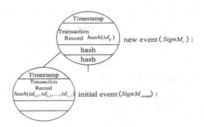

Fig. 2. Event diagram

3.2   Design Idea of TPM Management Strategy

After each group member sends a request to upload the shared data, the group manager selects a TPM for authorization. The port number address of the group member Mi is $u_i(x_0, x_1, \ldots, x_\theta)$ (θ is the number of bits in the binary address), and the port number address of the TPM is $TPM_i(x_0, x_1, \ldots, x_\theta)$. The following describes the detailed selection method.

(1)   The group manager chooses the processing time of the request.

Referring to the principle of the TCP sliding window, the sending window is set for the input end, and the sending window corresponds to a period of time. During this period, the group manager receives the application sent by the group member.

As shown in Fig. 3, the sending window has 3 pointers that slide clockwise. The window that allows u1 to send is the time between P1 and P3, and the current time is P2. Suppose that the group manager divides a certain time period into 20 parts as t1–t20. When group member M1 sends an application at t8, it is just in the allowable sending time of the sending window, and then the group manager receives the sent application from M1. According to the time frame rotation, if group member M1 does not send the request in the allowed sending time, P2 slides clockwise to $\Delta t_1'$, which corresponds to M_1's port number address u_1, and then $\Delta t_1'$ is the time to process the request of M_1.

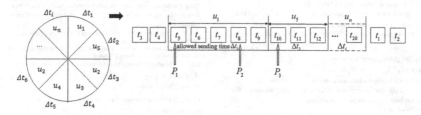

Fig. 3. Sending window

(2) The group manager selects the output address TPMi based on the time of the request that was processed and the address ui of the input end.

As shown in Fig. 4, assuming that u_2 sends the application to the group manager at Δt_1, the group manager selects the interconnection function $f = C_1$ and selects $f_i' = C_0$ from the sequence of interconnection functions. According to the sending window, the round is transferred to the time period Δt_3, and the group manager calculates the output at the moment through u_2, Δt_3 and the interconnection function C_0. At that moment, the correspondence between the input and output can be represented by a matrix

$$
\begin{array}{c}
\\
TPM_{1\Delta t_3} \\
TPM_{2\Delta t_3} \\
TPM_{3\Delta t_3} \\
TPM_{4\Delta t_3}
\end{array}
\begin{array}{cccc}
u_1 & u_2 & u_3 & u_4 \\
\left(\begin{array}{cccc}
0 & 1 & 0 & 0 \\
1 & 0 & 0 & 0 \\
0 & 0 & 0 & 1 \\
0 & 0 & 1 & 0
\end{array}\right)
\end{array}
$$

$(i = 4)$, which indicates that the group manager selects the output address TPM_1 through u_2 and C_0 at Δt_3.

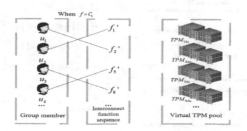

Fig. 4. Virtual TPM pool construction diagram

4 Detailed Description of the LSSA Scheme

The LSSA scheme consists of nine algorithms: *KeyGen, DataBlind, Authorize, Auth-Gen, AuthVerify, Recovery, Challenge, ProofGen,* and *ProofVerify.* The parameters used in the algorithm are as follows (Fig. 5).

Data upload phase:

KeyGen(1^k)

(1) The group manager randomly selects $\beta_i \in Z_p^*$ and calculates g^{β_i}, which will act as the private key of TPM$_i$.

(2) The group manager randomly selects $k_1 \in Z_p^*$ as the input key of a pseudo-random and sends it to the group members and the cloud.

(3) The group manager randomly selects $\alpha^j \in Z_p^*(1 \leq j \leq s)$, calculates $\{g^{\alpha^j}\}_{1 \leq j \leq s}$, and computes $pk_{TPM_i} = (g^{\beta_i}, g^{\alpha^1 \beta_i}, g^{\alpha^2 \beta_i}, ..., g^{\alpha^s \beta_i})$ as a public key TPM$_i$. The global parameter is set to $\{p, g, n, s, \{g^{\alpha^j}\}_{1 \leq j \leq s}, G_1, G_2, H_1, H_2, h, \zeta_k\}$.

(4) The group manager selects the interconnection function f, the interconnection function sequence f_s^*, and the sending windows of the input and output and sends them to the cloud.

DataBlind(m_i)

(1) Group members use the input key k_1 to calculate the blind factor $\alpha_i = \zeta_{k_1}(i, name)$, which in turn calculates the blind data $m'_{i,j} = m_{i,j} + \alpha_i$. Here, $name \in {}_R Z_q^*$ is the data file name, and the blind data block is $m'_{i,j} = (m'_{i,1}, m'_{i,2}, ..., m'_{i,s})$.

(2) The group member sends a request to upload the data to the group manager, calculates the hash value $hash(id_{i,j})$ of the file identifier information $id_{i,j}$ of the used blind data $m'_{i,j}$, and sends it to the group manager through the secure channel $id_{i,j}$. A new event is created by the group member. The $hash(id_{i,j})$ will be used as a transaction record for the new event and be propagated within the group. After receiving the request, the group manager verifies $hash(id_{i,j})$ according to the same hash algorithm and receives the group members $m'_{i,j}$ after the verification is passed.

Authorize

The group manager calculates TPM$_i$ corresponding to u_i in the virtual TPM pool according to the TPM management strategy.

The group manager generates the authorization $\{ID_{group} \| u_i \| \Delta t_i), \Delta t'_i\}$ (ID_{group} is the identity of the group manager, Δt_i is the time when the group manager processes the request, and $\Delta t'_i$ is the time authorized by the group manager for the TPM) for TPM$_i$ and calculates $H_1((ID_{group} \| u_i \| \Delta t_i), \Delta t'_i)$.

The group manager sends $\alpha^j, \beta_i, m'_{i,j}$ and $H_1((ID_{group} \| u_i \| \Delta t_i), \Delta t'_i)$ to TPM$_i$, and sends the authorization to the cloud.

AuthGen($\beta_i, m'_{i,j}$)

(1) After receiving the blind data block $m'_{i,j}$, the TPM$_i$ uses the private key to generate the authentication label $\sigma'_i = (H_2(i) \cdot \prod_{j=1}^s (g^{\alpha^j})^{m'_{i,j}})^{\beta_i}$ of the blind data block $m'_{i,j}$. The TPM$_i$ will send the data file $(m'_{i,j}, \sigma_i')$ corresponding to the *name* and $H_1((ID_{group} \| u_i \| \Delta t_i), \Delta t_i')$ to the cloud.

(2) After receiving the $(m'_{i,j}, \sigma_i)$ and the authorization information of the corresponding group manager, the cloud first calculates the TPM$_i$ according to $\{(ID_{group} \| u_i \| \Delta t_i), \Delta t'_i\}$. If the TPM$_i$ just sends the message at $\Delta t'_i$, then the cloud calculates $H_1((ID_{group} \| u_i \| \Delta t_i), \Delta t'_i)$ and determines whether the value is consistent with the value from the TPM$_i$. If they are consistent, AuthVerify is executed, and otherwise the execution is refused.

AuthVerify($pk_{TPM_i}, \sigma_i', m'_{i,j}$)

The cloud verifies the correctness of the label σ'_i using the following equation: $e(\sigma'_i, g) = e(H_2(i) \cdot \prod_{j=1}^s (g^{\alpha^j})^{m'_{i,j}}, g^{\beta_i})$. If the equation is true, it is received and stored as $(m'_{i,j}, \sigma'_i)$, and otherwise it is rejected.

Recovery($pk_{TPM_i}, \sigma'_i, m'_{i,j}$)

The cloud calculates $\alpha_i = \zeta_{k_1}(i, name)$ based on k_1, and then computes the real data $m'_{i,j} = m_{i,j} - \alpha_i$ and the real authenticator label σ_i according to pk_{TPM_i} and σ'_i.

$\sigma_i = \sigma'_i \cdot \prod_{j=1}^s (g^{\alpha^j \beta_i})^{-\alpha_i} = (H_2(i) \cdot \prod_{j=1}^s (g^{\alpha^j})^{m_{i,j}})^{\beta_i}$

Finally, the cloud stores the real data blocks $m_{i,j} = (m_{i,1}, m_{i,2}, ... m_{i,s})$ and their corresponding real authenticator labels σ_i.

Audit stage:

Challenge

The group manager randomly selects Δt as the authorization time to the TPM$_i$ which corresponds to u_i and it is also the time to process the request. The group manager sends an audit authorization command to the TPM$_i$ through u_i at Δt, and sends $\{ID_{group} \| u_i \| \Delta t\}$ as the audit authorization information to the cloud.

After receiving the authorization command from the group manager, the TPM$_i$ implements the audit process.

(1) The TPM randomly selects c blocks from all blocks of shared data and denotes the index of the selected block as L.

(2) The TPM generates two random numbers $o, r \in Z_p^*$, and calculates $X = g^o$ and $R = g^r$.

(3) The TPM calculates $\{X^{\alpha^j}\}_{1 \leq j \leq s}$.

(4) The TPM outputs the challenge information CM = $\{L, R, \{X^{\alpha^j}\}_{1 \leq j \leq s}\}$, and sends it to the cloud.

ProofGen($pk_{TPM_i}, ID_{TPM}, CM, \sigma_i, m_{i,j}$)

After receiving the challenge information CM = $\{L, R, \{X^{\alpha^j}\}_{1 \leq j \leq s}\}$, the cloud first calculates TPM$_i$ according to $\{ID_{group} \| u_i \| \Delta t\}$. The cloud service provider uses the method in AuthGen for authentication and generates the proof of having shared data as follows:

(1) The index set L of selected blocks is divided into subsets $L_1, ..., L_d$, where L_i is the subset of selected blocks that are signed by TPM$_i$.

(2) For each subset L_i, the cloud server calculates $u_g = \sum_{a \in L_i} m_g$ and

$\pi_i = \prod_{l \in L_i} e(\sigma_i, R) = e(\prod_{l \in L_i} H_2(l) \prod_{j=1}^s g^{\alpha^j \sum_{a \in L_i} m_g}, g)^{\beta_i r}$.

(3) The cloud server calculates $w_i = \prod_{l \in L_i} X^{\alpha^j u_g}$ and $\pi = \prod_{i=1}^d \pi_i$. Then, it returns $prf = \{\{w_i\}_{1 \leq i \leq d}, \pi\}$ as a response to the challenge message from the TPM$_i$.

ProofVerify(pk_{TPM_i}, prf, CM)

Based on the received prf = $\{\{w_i\}_{1 \leq i \leq d}, \pi\}$ and the challenge message CM = $\{L, R, \{X^{\alpha^j}\}_{1 \leq j \leq s}\}$, the TPM$_i$ verifies the integrity of the shared data by checking the correctness of the following equation:

$\prod_{i=1}^d e(\eta_i^n, pk_{TPM_i}^r) \cdot e(w_i, pk_{TPM_i}^r) = \pi^o$, where $\eta_i = \prod_{l \in L_i} H_2(l), 1 \leq i \leq d$. The above equation can be further rewritten as $(\prod_{i=1}^d e(\eta_i^n w_i, pk_{TPM_i}))^r = \pi^o$.

If the equation is true, the TPM$_i$ outputs TRUE, and otherwise FALSE is returned. In other words, if the selected block in the challenge has been tampered with, the cloud service provider cannot generate valid evidence, and the cloud service provider will not be able to pass the audit process from the TPM$_i$.

When the shared data is properly stored in the cloud server, if the cloud provides a valid integrity certificate prf = $\{\{w_i\}_{1 \leq i \leq d}, \pi\}$, the validation procedure can verify the integrity of the data.

Proof: According to the nature of bilinear mapping, the right side of the equation can be derived from the left side of the equation to prove the correctness of the equation.

$\prod_{i=1}^d e(\eta_i^n, pk_{TPM_i}^r) \cdot e(w_i, pk_{TPM_i}^r)$

$= \prod_{i=1}^d e(\prod_{l \in L_i} H_2(l)^o, g^{\beta_i r}) \cdot e((\prod_{j=1}^s (g^{\alpha^j})^{o \sum_{a \in L_i} m_g}, g^{\beta_i r})$

$= \prod_{i=1}^d e(\prod_{l \in L_i} H_2(l), g)^{o \beta_i r} \cdot e((\prod_{j=1}^s g^{\alpha^j \sum_{a \in L_i} m_g}, g)^{o \beta_i r}$

$= \prod_{i=1}^d e(\prod_{l \in L_i} H_2(l) \prod_{j=1}^s g^{\alpha^j \sum_{a \in L_i} m_g}, g)^{o \beta_i r}$

$= \prod_{i=1}^d \pi_i^o = (\prod_{i=1}^d \pi_i)^o = \pi^o$

Therefore, as long as the evidence comes from complete data, the validation equation will hold.

Fig. 5. Algorithm diagram

5 Security Analysis

This section performs the security analysis separately from the, audit security, data privacy, identity privacy, TPM security, and traceability of group membership analyses.

5.1 Audit Security

The malicious cloud service provider cannot complete the audit process through replace attacks and replay attacks. ① Since each time the TPM initiates a challenge both $L = \{L_1, \ldots, L_d\}$ and $X = g^\circ$ are randomly generated, the cloud service provider cannot calculate $u_{ij} = \sum_{l \in L_i} m_{lj}$ and $w_i = \prod_{j=1}^{s} X^{\alpha^j u_{ij}}$ in advance, and cannot implement the replace attack. ② Cloud service providers must calculate η° ($\eta = \prod_{l \in L} H_2(l) \in G_1$) if they want to implement replay attacks. Suppose that the cloud service provider chooses $\psi \in Z_p^*$ to meet $\eta = g^\psi$. Since the CDH problem is computationally infeasible, the cloud service provider still cannot calculate $g^{\psi \circ}$ based on g^ψ, g and g°.

5.2 Data Privacy and Identity Privacy

① In the user upload data phase, the TPM cannot extract the real data $m_{i,j}$ through the blind data block $m'_{i,j}$. This finding is observed because the TPM receives $m'_{i,j} = m_{i,j} + \alpha_i (j \in [1, s])$, where $\alpha_i = \zeta_{k_i}(i, name)$ is generated by group members through a random function. ② The TPM management strategy is flexible and secure. This strategy expands the method to select TPM_i and solves the problem of insufficient computing power of a single TPM. Each TPM independently performs computing tasks and cannot find more valuable information through randomly distributed blind data blocks $m'_{i,j}$.

5.3 TPM Security

The TPM public key is used to verify the integrity of the shared data. The final authentication label of the data block is actually encrypted using the TPM private key. Therefore, it is necessary to prevent the TPM from leaking the private key for some reasons. ① A malicious group member may collude with the TPM to obtain a private key. To this end, the group manager specifies multiple TPMs, and each TPM works independently and distributes different private keys for it, which avoids the above problems. ② It is necessary to prevent the TPM from being maliciously attacked for some reasons. By constructing a virtual TPM pool, only the group manager can calculate TPM_i, and those outside cannot find the target of the attack.

5.4   Identity Traceability

Through Swirld's Hashgraph Consistency Algorithm [11], group members agree on the order of events (that is, the order of transaction records within the event) and the timestamp for each event (transaction record). The transaction records of each event can be determined in chronological order according to the Hashgraph. Once a member of the group maliciously modifies the data block, the dirty data block may be discovered by other group members. Once such a data dispute is generated, the group member may trace the usage history of the modified data block according to a Hashgraph. Legal group members can open the data block information to prevent the illegal group members from collapsing the structure, and finally the group member whose data block information has illegal data is as an illegal group member.

6   Summary

By introducing a Hashgraph, a group manager can flexibly register or remove group members and achieve the traceability of group membership. By specifying multiple TPMs for calculation and management according to the TPM management strategy, each group member and each TPM are independent of each other, which ensures the secure calculations of the TPM and realizes the lightweight calculation of the TPM. Through security analysis, the scheme of this paper can avoid replay attacks and replay attacks while protecting the identity privacy and data privacy of group members and ensuring secure storage of shared data.

References

1. Ateniese, G., Burns, R., Curtmola, R., et al.: Provable data possession at untrusted stores. In: ACM Conference on Computer and Communications Security, pp. 598–609. ACM (2007)
2. Yang, G., Yu, J., Shen, W., et al.: Enabling public auditing for shared data in cloud storage supporting identity privacy and traceability. J. Syst. Softw. **113**(C), 130–139 (2016)
3. Luo, Y., Xu, M., Huang, K., et al.: Efficient auditing for shared data in the cloud with secure user revocation and computations outsourcing. Comput. Secur. **73**, 492–506 (2018)
4. Fu, A., Yu, S., Zhang, Y., et al.: NPP: a new privacy-aware public auditing scheme for cloud data sharing with group users. IEEE Trans. Big Data **PP**(99), 1 (2017)
5. Guan, C., Ren, K., Zhang, F., Kerschbaum, F., Yu, J.: Symmetric-key based proofs of retrievability supporting public verification. In: Pernul, G., Ryan, P.Y.A., Weippl, E. (eds.) ESORICS 2015. LNCS, vol. 9326, pp. 203–223. Springer, Cham (2015). https://doi.org/10. 1007/978-3-319-24174-6_11
6. Wang, H., He, D., Tang, S.: Identity-based proxy-oriented data uploading and remote data integrity checking in public cloud. IEEE Trans. Inf. Forensics Secur. **11**(6), 1165–1176 (2016)
7. Shen, W., Yu, J., Xia, H., et al.: Light-weight and privacy-preserving secure cloud auditing scheme for group users via the third party medium. J. Netw. Comput. Appl. **82**, 56–64 (2017)
8. Xie, X.: Computer Networks. Publishing House of Electronics Industry, Beijing (2008)

9. Zheng, W., Tang, Z.: Computer System Architecture. Tsinghua University Press, Beijing (1999)
10. Baird, L.: Hashgraph consensus: detailed examples (2016)
11. Baird, L.: The Swirld Hashgraph Consensus algorithm: fair, Fast, Byzantine Fault Tolerance (2016)

Research on Big Data Platform Security Based on Cloud Computing

Xiaxia Niu$^{(\boxtimes)}$ and Yan Zhao

School of Information, Beijing Wuzi University, Beijing, China
15136212624@163.com, 605671232@qq.com

Abstract. Emerging services such as cloud computing, the Internet of Things, and social networking are driving the growth of human society's data types and scales at an unprecedented rate. The age of big data has officially arrived. The use of cloud computing technology to bring great convenience to big data processing, solve various deficiencies in traditional processing technology, make big data more application value and service value, but at the same time, it also brings new security problems. By analyzing the security threats faced by cloud computing-based big data platforms, a cloud computing-based big data platform security system framework is proposed, and a security deployment strategy is given.

Keywords: Cloud computing security · Cloud computing · Big data

1 Introduction

In 2010, the global data volume entered the era of ZB. According to IDC prediction, by 2020, the world will have the amount of 35 ZB data. Massive data will affect our work and life in real time. Even the national economic, social development and big data era has arrived.

The arrival of the era of big data has put forward higher requirements for the real-time and effectiveness of data processing. Traditional IT technology has been unable to meet the needs. Cloud computing technology has made the data analysis, data mining and data processing of mass data become a reality. The large data platform based on cloud computing provides a better service to users, and it also brings a series of security problems. On the one hand, big data means massive amounts of data, and it means more complex and sensitive data. This data will attract more potential attackers. Once a successful attack, hackers can get more data, which in turn reduces hackers. The offensive cost increases the "yield rate." On the other hand, the ownership and use rights of some sensitive data are not clearly defined. Many big data services or big data applications based on data analysis do not take into account the possibility of user privacy issues. In addition, under the cloud computing deployment architecture, computing, storage, and network resources are loosely coupled, resources are allocated on demand, and network boundaries are blurred, which also brings security challenges [1].

In this context, the purpose of this paper is to propose a cloud computing-based big data platform security system framework and provide a big data platform security strategy.

© ICST Institute for Computer Sciences, Social Informatics and Telecommunications Engineering 2019
Published by Springer Nature Switzerland AG 2019. All Rights Reserved
J. Li et al. (Eds.): SPNCE 2019, LNICST 284, pp. 38–45, 2019.
https://doi.org/10.1007/978-3-030-21373-2_4

2   Overview

2.1   Cloud Computing and Big Data

2.1.1   Cloud Computing and Its Architecture

Cloud computing is a developing concept. There is a variety of explanations for what exactly is cloud computing. There is no universally accepted definition. The definition given by Wikipedia [2] is that cloud computing is a computing model that provides dynamically scalable virtualized resources to users through the Internet. Users do not need to know how to manage the infrastructure supporting cloud computing. The definition of NIST provided by the National Institute of Standards and Technology [3] is: Cloud is a parallel distributed system composed of a group of interconnected virtualized computers. It is based on the dynamics of service contracts between service providers and consumers. Computing resources.

Cloud computing can provide elastic resources on demand. It is a collection of services. Combining current cloud computing applications and research, its architecture can be divided into three layers: core services, service management, and user access interfaces. The core service layer abstracts the hardware infrastructure, software operating environment, and application programs into services. These services have the characteristics of strong reliability, high availability, and retractable scale, which meet diverse application requirements. Service management provides support for core services to further ensure the reliability, availability, and security of core services. Users access the interface layer to achieve end-to-cloud access.

2.1.2   Big Data and Its Main Features

Generally speaking, big data means large and complex data sets which are difficult to be processed by existing database management tools or traditional data processing software. People use the word "big data" to describe and define the mass data produced in the era of information explosion, and to name the technology development and innovation related to it.

Large data has the characteristics of "4V", that is, which is quantified, diversified, fast and valuable.

(1) Volume: refers to a very large amount of data, that is, a large amount of data storage, a large amount of calculations, and the data has jumped from the TB level to the PB level.

(2) Variety: It means that big data includes not only structured data tables and semi-structured texts, videos, images, and other information, but also the interaction between data is very frequent and extensive, including unstructured data. The proportion has increased year by year. Many types of data impose higher requirements on data processing capabilities.

(3) Value density is low. Big data has a relatively low value density. For example, with the wide application of the Internet of Things, information perception is omnipresent and information is massive, but the value density is low, and there is

a large amount of irrelevant information. Therefore, it is necessary to make predictable analysis of future trends and patterns, and use machine learning, artificial intelligence, etc. to perform in-depth and complex analysis. How to more quickly complete the value extraction of data through powerful machine algorithms is a difficult problem to be solved in the era of big data.

(4) Velocity: It refers to the continuous updating of data and the rapid growth. At the same time, the processing speed of data storage and transmission is also very fast. This is the most significant feature of Big Data that distinguishes it from traditional data mining.

2.2 Big Data Platform Security System Framework Based on Cloud Computing

Based on cloud computing, the security protection of big data platform is based on data, from the aspects of data access, use, destruction, modification, loss, and leakage. It mainly includes the following aspects [4].

(1) Network security: refers to the design, construction, and use of the platform network itself, as well as various security-related technologies and methods based on the network, such as firewalls, IPS, and security auditing.

(2) Server security: including server virus protection and server security configuration and reinforcement.

(3) Storage Security: Data preservation and backup and recovery design.

(4) Virtualization platform security: It includes the isolation, configuration, and reinforcement of virtual machines, malicious virtual machine protection, and monitoring.

(5) Platform software security: System security including software such as operating systems, databases, data processing software, and platform components, as well as system security analysis and hardening using security assessment management tools to improve the security of these systems.

(6) Application security: Including application access security and application data security.

(7) Security management: complete user identity authentication and security log audit trails, as well as unified analysis and recording of security logs and events.

(8) Interface security: including authentication of internal and external interfaces, transmission security, and interface call control. The cloud-based big data platform security system framework is shown in Fig. 1.

2.3 Data Security Threats Faced by Cloud Computing

Due to the large scale of cloud computing systems, the application and privacy data of many users are concentrated. At the same time, cloud computing has unprecedented openness and complexity, and its security faces more severe challenges than traditional information systems. Cloud Security Alliance CSA and Hewlett-Packard jointly listed seven aspects of cloud computing security issues.

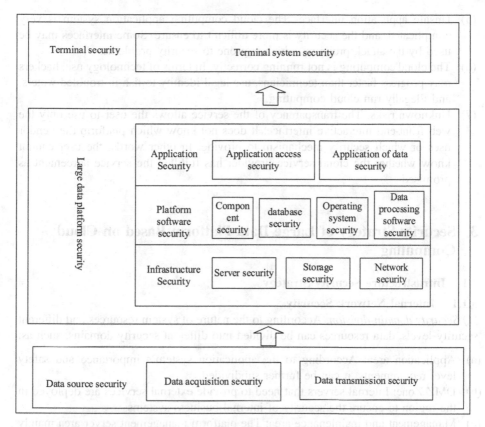

Fig. 1. The cloud-based big data platform security system framework

(1) Data loss and leakage. The security control of data in cloud computing is not high. The lack of security mechanisms and management deficiencies may cause data leakage. Whether it is private data or important national data, if it is lost or leaked, it will have bad consequences.

(2) Sharing technology vulnerabilities. Cloud computing is a large shared data center. The greater the degree of sharing, the more vulnerabilities and the more attacks.

(3) Supplier reliability is not easy to assess. To avoid the theft of sensitive information, a reliable service provider is needed, but how to conduct a credible assessment of the service provider remains to be studied.

(4) The identity authentication mechanism is weak. Since a large amount of data, applications, and resources are concentrated in the cloud, if the authentication mechanism of the cloud computing is weak, the intruder can easily obtain the user account and log in to the user's virtual machine to perform various illegal operations.

(5) Unsafe application interface. The cloud computing application system is very complicated, and the security is more difficult to ensure. Some interfaces may be used by the attack program, which is prone to security problems.

(6) The cloud computing is not running correctly. In terms of technology use, hackers may progress faster than technicians, use legal identity to fish in troubled waters, and illegally run cloud computing.

(7) Unknown risks. The transparency of the service allows the user to use only the web front-end interactive interface. It does not know which platform the vendor uses or which security mechanism to provide. In other words, the user cannot know whether the cloud service provider has fulfilled the service agreement as promised.

3 Security Strategy of Large Data Platform Based on Cloud Computing

3.1 Infrastructure Security Strategy

3.1.1 Internal Network Security

(1) Security domain division. According to the nature of system resources and different security levels, data resources can be divided into different security domains, such as:

(a) Application area: According to the application system's importance and safety level requirements, it can be further subdivided.

(b) DMZ Zone: Internal servers that need to provide external services are deployed in the region to ensure the security of internal business systems.

(c) Management and maintenance area: The platform management server area mainly includes public and platform servers such as network servers, host management servers, database management servers, and security management servers.

(2) Security domain isolation and protection technology deployment. Through the deployment of authentication, role-based access control, ACL, VLAN, MPLS, VSAN and other technologies, the isolation of different security domains can be achieved. Deploy an intranet security system such as a firewall, IPS/IDS, and baseline analysis technology on the core switch to implement intelligent security monitoring and control. At the same time, through the in-depth analysis of application layer protocols such as FTP and HTTP, the content transmitted by these protocols is accurately restored, and the data sent from the internal network device is discovered to prevent the leakage of sensitive information. Different resources are deployed in different service areas. The service areas are isolated by VLAN and virtual firewalls [5].

3.1.2 Storage Security

In the process of uploading data, when uploading to the cloud, data may leak due to server failure. After the cloud platform suffers from illegal access, data may be forged, tampered with, and stolen. Therefore, after the data is stored in the cloud, it is encrypted and needs to be operated by the corresponding encryption technology. The big data in the cloud is divided into two types: static data and dynamic data. The corresponding data encryption mechanism also has two kinds of static data confidentiality mechanism and dynamic data encryption mechanism [6, 7]. There are two encryption algorithms for static data encryption, namely symmetric encryption algorithm and asymmetric encryption algorithm.

After the data holder encrypts and splits, it uploads to the cloud computing platform. The user has to decrypt the data after downloading the required data. If there is a phenomenon of being stolen or lost when data is stored, transmitted, and used, it will be avoided because it is encrypted. At present, the encryption technology that adopts mainstream data for cloud computing mainly includes proxy encryption and attribute encryption. The ciphertext-based attribute encryption (CP-ABE) and key (KP-ABE) data encryption methods have their own characteristics when applied. The data encryption model of cloud computing can effectively enhance the security of data by deploying agents. Because the cloud platform is a semi-trusted agent when it is used, the architecture of the PRE can be transplanted into the cloud computing. A security scheme with a high security. If the b user wants to share the data uploaded by the user in the cloud after encryption, a needs to generate a transition key based on the user's information and b's public key. This key only has the function of mutual conversion between ciphertexts. The ciphertext of a can be changed into ciphertext for B, and after the user downloads the ciphertext accordingly, the user can perform more operations on the data shared by a.

Data security is a key part of big data cloud storage security. In the process of storing big data, the selected encryption technology must be effective and reliable, and it plays a vital role in the establishment of big data storage security system. The use of reasonable and scientific encryption technology can not only ensure the corresponding confidentiality of big data in storage, but also have important significance for cloud computing and users to achieve optimal allocation of network resources [8].

3.1.3 Server Security

(1) Security configuration and hardening
The operating system should follow the principle of minimum installation and install only the required components and applications. Configure operating system and database system access control measures, identify and authenticate logged-in users, and set security policies such as password policies, account policies, audit policies, and user rights. Security assessment and optimization are performed for devices such as compute nodes, storage nodes, and management nodes, and security hardening is implemented when necessary. Deploy a unified policy to upgrade server operating system software and application software.

(2) Server security protection
Monitoring of important servers, including monitoring of the server's CPU, hard disk, memory, network and other resources. Deploy security measures for the server, such as host firewall, host IDS, and so on.

(3) Server virus protection

Deploy a unified management of anti-virus and anti-malicious code products to achieve centralized management of virus and malicious code protection to ensure that the server is free from virus threats. Ensure that antivirus products can be upgraded in a timely manner.

3.2 Platform Software Security Policy

3.2.1 System Hardening

System hardening mainly reinforces the operating system, database, etc., and fixes the loopholes in the software itself. The following hardening procedures can be adopted: (a) Minimizing cutting: Abolishing unnecessary components and services. (b) Code Security: Optimize the code according to the specification. (c) Security configuration: Configure according to the configuration hardening specifications in the industry. (d) Security Test: Tests are conducted using the industry's leading scanning tools. (e) Integrity protection: review by means of an integrity check tool.

3.2.2 Database Security Audit System Deployment

The database audit system is deployed in the intranet security system, collects, analyzes, and recognizes the data stream that accesses the database through the bypass interception method, and monitors the running status of the database in real time, records multiple access behaviors, and monitors abnormal access operations, etc. The distributed deployment mode can be used to centrally manage the domain database auditing system in the high-efficiency management area. The branch nodes are no longer independent, and all under the unified supervision, effectively improve the efficiency of regional security auditing.

3.3 Application Security Policy

3.3.1 Application Access Security Policy

The application system shall provide a dedicated login control module to perform identity identification and authentication of the logged-in user, and important information (such as user accounts and passwords) is encrypted and stored; identity authentication, uniqueness of user identity identification, complexity check of user identity authentication information, and login are provided. Fails to process functions, and configures related parameters according to security policies. Provides security audit function that covers each user. Audits important application security events. The contents of the audit records should include the date, time, originator information, and type of the event, descriptions and results, etc.

3.3.2 Application Data Security Policy

Deploy a web application attack defense system to detect and prevent as many attempts as possible to tamper with static web page files, dynamic web page script files, or dynamic web page data. At the same time, web page tampering events caused by other unknown types of attacks can be promptly restored. Blurring sensitive data involved in Web presentation data.

4   Conclusion

The emergence of cloud computing and big data has changed the traditional data storage model and data computing model. It has brought tremendous changes to human society. People are enjoying the benefits of this kind of change. It is therefore increasingly recognized the importance of information technology. The combination of cloud computing and big data provides users with better services but also creates new security threats. This paper proposes a cloud computing-based big data platform security architecture framework, and gives security strategies for big data platforms. Only by providing users with reliable, reliable, and cost-effective cloud computing services can enterprises succeed in the field of cloud computing.

Acknowledgments. The study is supported by the National Nature Science Foundation of China "Research on the warehouse picking system blocking influence factors and combined control strategy" (No. 71501015), Intelligent Logistics Collaboration Center and Tongzhou Canal Project Leaders.

References

1. Ban, R., Tu, L., Liu, H.: Cloud computing platform for big data security strategy research based on J. Post Design Technol. **10**, 74–78 (2017)
2. Cloud Computing - [EB/OL] (2013). http://zh.wikipedia.org/wild/wikimeco
3. Mell, P., Grance, T.: The NIST definition of cloud computing [R/OL], 11 February 2010. http://csrc.nist.gov/groups/SNS/cloud-computing/cloud-def-v15.doc
4. Yaofeng, Z.: Analysis of cloud data security in the background of big data. Cyber Secur. Technol. Appl. **11**, 102–103 (2014)
5. Li, Y.: Cloud security data center network security deployment. Netw. Inf. (6), 38–39 (2012). Author, F.: Contribution title. In: 9th International Proceedings on Proceedings, pp. 1–2. Publisher, Location (2010)
6. Bellare, M., Rogaway, P.: Introduction to Modern Cryptography. UCSD CSE,207,2005,207
7. Riyest, R.L., Shamir, A., Adleman, L.: A method for obtaining digital signatures and public-key cryptosystems. Commun. ACM **21**(2), 120–126 (1978)
8. Sun, L.: Discussion on the security of big data storage based on cloud computing. Netw. Secur. Technol. Appl. (2018)

Database Query System with Budget Option for Differential Privacy Against Repeated Attacks

Jingyu Jia[1], Yuduo Wu[1], Yue Guo[1], Jiqiang Gao[1], Jin Peng[2], Peng Ran[2], and Min Li[1(✉)]

[1] College of Cyber Science, Nankai University, Tianjin, China
{1511372,1511406,2120180514}@mail.nankai.edu.cn,pdsgjq@163.com,
limintj@nankai.edu.cn
[2] China Mobile Communications Corporation Research Institute, Beijing, China
{pengjin,ranpeng}@chinamobile.com

Abstract. Differential privacy enables data analysis while protecting individual privacy. However, existing differential privacy database platforms do not defend against repeated attacks. This paper proposes a practical Database Query System for differential privacy protection against repeated attacks with customizable privacy budget. By limiting adversary's success probability and the number of attacks, the administrator can protect privacy against the repeated attacks. We conduct an evaluation of this solution, and explain the applicability of this system.

Keywords: Differential privacy · Privacy budget · Repeated attack · Laplace mechanism

1 Introduction

Large volumes of personal data collected by various organizations are key resources for statistical analysis. Statistical data analysis and publishing is used extensively for potential economic and social benefits. However, the adversary may get personal information through different statistical query results, which is called differential attack. Differential privacy is proposed by Dwork [6] to resist differential attacks. It allows general statistical analysis of data while protecting individual data, and provides quantitative evaluation method for privacy protection. Although this mechanism guarantees privacy theoretically, the repeated attacks still may obtain personal information in practice. Therefore, the security assurance of differential privacy against repeated attacks need further research.

Generally, the organizations with amounts of private data provide an interface for clients to get statistics of specific data sets. The clients are limited to querying statistical results instead of individual personal information, but it is enough for them to pick out the specific group to send advertisement, to acquire the demand tendency of customers, et al r.

© ICST Institute for Computer Sciences, Social Informatics and Telecommunications Engineering 2019
Published by Springer Nature Switzerland AG 2019. All Rights Reserved
J. Li et al. (Eds.): SPNCE 2019, LNICST 284, pp. 46–57, 2019.
https://doi.org/10.1007/978-3-030-21373-2_5

In most cases, the statisticial query interface is provided in form of relational database that supports SQL queries. Various platforms are proposed for different query requests. Privacy Integrated Queries (PINQ), designed by McSherry et al. [13], provides a platform for interactive data analysis of real-time data with differential privacy. Weighted PINQ (wPINQ) [14], which uses weighted datasets to bypass difficulties encountered (the worst-case requirements of differential privacy for the noise magnitudes), is intended for graph analyses. Johnson et al. [1] develop FLEX with elastic sensitivity, a novel approach for differential privacy of SQL queries and their approach is compatible with real database systems.

These existing platforms provide a number of methods to deal with different query requests, but almost without exception, the platforms select the privacy budget arbitrarily without any specific setting mode. However, it is often of low security in the face of different attack models, especially the repeated attack. Privacy Budget is a parameter on the degree of privacy protection, concerning to the balance between security and utility. It is surely non-trivial to choose an appropriate value for privacy budget in accordance with whether the intuitive theoretical interpretation in the definition or the practical experience.

This paper proposes **Database Query System** for differential privacy protection against repeated attacks with customizable privacy budget, for statistical SQL queries. In contrast to existing work, our approach calculates the upper bound of privacy budget according to input parameters, which are related to specific attack model. We focus on repeated attacks model, by which the attackers can guess the real data. In this attack model, the guessed right or wrong depends on the amount of added noise and the number of attacks, which underscoring the importance of privacy preserving level. The success probability of a specific attack algorithm is computationally feasible, and hence the upper bound of privacy budget can be calculated by prescribing a limit to probability of success attack. The administrator input the number of attacks and the probability of success that in line with their expectations, then the privacy budget value that meets its requirements would be worked out.

Other than parameter choosing mechanism, elastic sensitivity is enforced to analyse the sensitivity of every SQL query. Compared to existing mechanisms for global sensitivity and local sensitivity, this mechanism is more efficient and supports majority of statistical queries in practice.

Furthermore, it is unnecessary for administrators to have knowledge of difference privacy. As long as administrators limit the cost for successful attack by attackers, the system would run well. This approach can make differential privacy more flexible to be used and help clients to find the most appropriate balance between protecting client privacy and ensuring data availability.

Contributions. We make two primary contributions in this paper:

1. Existing database platforms do not provide protection against repeated attack. In this paper, our system realizes the protection of repeated attacks by limiting attack times and attack success probability. The server calculates

privacy budget and the client's privacy budget allocation appropriately limits interaction numbers with the database.

2. This system allows administrators without background knowledge to set restrictions only by the acceptable risk level. It is more flexible and convenient for practical use in the organizations of different fields.

Paper Outline. The paper continues in three parts, the rest parts are organized as follows. In Sect. 2, we introduce the specific definition of differential privacy and the key methods used in our system design. The system is detailed in Sect. 3, and we show how clients can use the system to defend against attacks, as well as the experimental evaluation of the system, and Sect. 4 concludes this work and talks about the improvement direction.

2   Mathematical Foundations

2.1   Differential Privacy

Differential privacy is a privacy preserving method with rigorous theoretical basis, which provides higher security compared to others (k-anonymity, l-diversity, t-closeness). Under the protection of differential privacy, the specific personal data cannot be obtained even if the attacker has the greatest background knowledge.

This mechanism considers a set of databases. The distance measures how many records differ between two databases, which is denoted as $|D_1 - D_2|$. Two databases are neighbors if there is only one different record between them. The query function set for the database is $F = \{f_1, f_2, \cdots, f_n\}$, and algorithm M represents a randomized mechanism that meets the requirement of differential privacy. The randomized mechanism applies to the result of query function F. For any two neighbors D and D', P_M is set of all possible output of M, and O is its subsets ($O \in P_M$). If M satisfies the following inequalities, it is (ε, δ) -differential privacy.

$$Pr[M(D) \in O] \leq \exp(\varepsilon)Pr[M(D') \in O] + \delta \tag{1}$$

The core thought of differential privacy is to reduce the impact of a single record on query results by a randomized way. Of the two parameters, ε is privacy budget concerning the level of privacy protection, while δ is typically a function that grows more slowly than the inverse of any polynomial in the database size. We choose $\delta = n^{-\varepsilon \ln n}$ in the following sections according to Dwork's work [5].

2.2   Laplace Mechanism

Difference privacy is generally implemented by adding noise to the query result. Similar to other platforms, our system use Laplace mechanism to add noise. Laplace mechanism adds random noise of the Laplace distribution to the query results to enforcing (ε, δ)-differential privacy. The size of the noise added is closely related to privacy budget ε and the query's sensitivity Δf. For different queries, the system will return the sum of query results and noise to satisfy difference privacy by algorithm M.

$$M(x) = f(x) + Lap(\frac{\Delta f}{\varepsilon}) \tag{2}$$

If the position parameter μ is set to zero, and the scale parameter set to b, the probability density function is $p(x) = \frac{1}{2b}e^{-\frac{|x|}{b}}$. For it's an absolute value function, the cumulative distribution function can be easily get by integrating:

$$F(x) = \frac{1}{2} + \frac{1}{2}sgnx(1 - e^{-\frac{|x|}{b}}) \tag{3}$$

In that case, the noise added by Laplace can be calculated according to the inverse cumulative distribution function. The scale parameter $b = \frac{\Delta f}{\varepsilon}$, and p denotes the probability of random selection from $(0, 1)$. $F^{-1}(p)$ is the noise added ultimately.

$$F^{-1}(p) = -bsgn(p - 0.5)\ln(1 - 2|p - 0.5|) \tag{4}$$

As shown in Fig. 1, the noise increases with the increase of b. So with the decrease of ε, more noise would be added to the primary result which means higher security but lower utility. When ε are 0, it means that a single piece of data has no effect on the query result. At this time, the added noise is very big, and the data is meaningless. If ε is set to a big value, the database is more likely to be attacked. Therefore, how to set the privacy budget becomes an important issue.

2.3 Privacy Budget

Privacy budget controls the level of privacy protection, and its selection is the key to achieve differential privacy. Several existing works have researched on this issue. Lee and Clifton [3] propose an attack model based on the prior and posterior belief, and give a method to calculate the upper bound of privacy budget. Then He et al. [10] improve the attack model by the definition of Laplace distribution and provide how to determine whether the object of attack is presence or not. Above schemes consider only a single attack, however, the attack on a specific object generally perform repeatedly to get individual information at a higher success probability. Therefore, the attack model of repeated attack [12] is put forward based on the former, as well as a more sophisticated way to compute the upper bound of privacy budget.

The result of a differential privacy mechanism is $f(D) + x$ for the query function f. Since the noise is of Laplace distribution, it is impossible for adversary to obtain x. Considering the features of some aggregation functions like count,

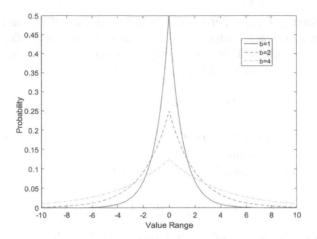

Fig. 1. Laplace probability density function

the real result could be leaked as long as the noise is in the range of certain interval. It is called fault-tolerant interval (which is a dangerous interval for the owner of individual data), and L denotes the half length of the interval. If L = 0.5, fault-tolerant interval is [−0.5,0.5], the real value of $f(D)$ could be inferred from the result of a count query. A single attack is ever so unreliable, therefore the repeated attack model performs the same query for N times, and guesses the private data of attack target in every query result according to L. Then the final determination could be made by the guess with higher probability. For a single attack, the success probability can be calculated by cumulative distribution value of the interval. The possibility of $f(D)+x$ in $(-\infty, f(D)+\mu+L)$ is equal to that of x in $(-\infty, \mu+L)$. Then according to the cumulative distribution function, the probability that x falls in this region is:

$$F(\mu + L) = 1 - \frac{1}{2}e^{-\frac{L\varepsilon}{\Delta f}}(\mu = 0)$$ (5)

If the success probability is limited to ρ, the upper bound of privacy budget calculate formula is:

$$\varepsilon \leq -\frac{\Delta f \ln 2(1 - \rho)}{L}$$ (6)

The repeated attack follows binomial distribution $B(n, \rho)$. If the attacker attacks N times, n attacks occur in above interval, the possibility of this event is:

$$\sum_{i=1}^{n+1} C_{2n+1}^{n+i}(1 - \frac{1}{2}e^{-\frac{\varepsilon}{2}})^{n+i}(\frac{1}{2}e^{-\frac{\varepsilon}{2}})^{n+1-i}$$ (7)

While if the fact is $f(D) = y+1$, the probability in this case is the same as the result above. In conclusion, the probability of the adversary attacks successfully is the result above. According to this theorem, the privacy budget could be limited to a small range as long as the administrator set a certain value to the successful probability of the attacker. As seen in the inequality, the range of parameter selection is related to the sensitivity of a query, the number of attacks, fault-tolerance interval and the successful probability of the attacker

$$\rho \leq \sum_{i=1}^{n+1} C_N^{n+i} (1 - \frac{1}{2}e^{-\frac{L\varepsilon}{\Delta f}})^{n+i} (\frac{1}{2}e^{-\frac{L\varepsilon}{\Delta f}})^{n+1-i} \tag{8}$$

Actually, the ideal case is to make adversary in a dilemma of figuring out the presence or absencewhich happens when the probabilities of success and failure both are 50%. Therefore, what we can do is to limit the probability close to this value.

2.4 Elastic Sensitivity

Johnson et al. [1] propose Elastic Sensitivity, a mechanism that enforces differential privacy on majority of queries through analysis of SQL statements in practice. Elastic sensitivity meets the requirement of universal practical difference privacy, which can approximate the local sensitivity of queries with general equijoin.

The definition is expressed as $\acute{S}_R^{(k)}(r,x)$, which means the elastic sensitivity of query or relation r at distance k from the true database x. It origins from $mf_k(a,r,x)$, the maximum frequency of attribute a at distance k. When $k = 0$ the value $mf(a,r,x)$ is the database metric that needs to be precomputed. As calculating the approximation of upper bound, we should consider the worst condition in each case. The details of this method are listed in Table 1.

Before adding Laplace noise it should be smoothed by smooth sensitivity, as it can reduce the amount of noise to improve the utility of differential privacy. It is calculated by using the maximum value of elastic sensitivity at k multiplied by an exponentially decaying function in βk. By Nissim et al. [2] $\beta = \frac{\varepsilon}{2\ln(2/\delta)}$ suffices to provide differential privacy when applying Laplace mechanism. In the end, we release the query result as $q(x) + Lap(2S/\varepsilon)$.

3 Database Query System with Budget Option

After introducing the background knowledge, the following gives details of our system. The system design draws partly from PINQ and FLEX, their analysis of SQL statements brings inspiration to our design. We design Database Query System with a flexible privacy budget selection mechanism, to fight against differential privacy attack methods.

Table 1. Definition of elastic sensitivity

Table t	$mf_k(a,t,x) = mf(a,t,x) + k$	$\acute{S}_R^{(k)}(t,x) = 1$
$r_1 \bowtie r_2$ $a=b$	$mf_k\left(a_1, \begin{matrix} r_1 \bowtie r_2 \\ a2 = a3 \end{matrix}, x\right) =$ $\begin{cases} mf_k(a_1,r_1,x)\, mf_k(a_3,r_2,x) & a_1 \in r_1 \\ mf_k(a_1,r_2,x)\, mf_k(a_2,r_1,x) & a_1 \in r_2 \end{cases}$	$Self\ Join$ $\acute{S}_R^{(k)}\left(\begin{matrix} r_1 \bowtie r_2 \\ a=b \end{matrix}, x\right) =$ $mf_k(a,r_1,x)\,\acute{S}_R^{(k)}(r_2,x) +$ $mf_k(a,r_2,x)\,\acute{S}_R^{(k)}(r_1,x) +$ $\acute{S}_R^{(k)}(r_1,x)\,\acute{S}_R^{(k)}(r_2,x)$ $Non-self\ join$ $\acute{S}_R^{(k)}\left(\begin{matrix} r_1 \bowtie r_2 \\ a=b \end{matrix}, x\right) = max$ $mf_k(a,r_1,x)\,\acute{S}_R^{(k)}(r_2,x),$ $mf_k(a,r_2,x)\,\acute{S}_R^{(k)}(r_1,x)$
$\pi_{a1,\cdots,an}r$	$mf_k(a,\pi_{a1,\cdots,an}r,x) = mf_k(a,r,x)$	$\acute{S}_R^{(k)}(\pi_{a1,\cdots,an}r,x) = \acute{S}_R^{(k)}(r,x)$
$\sigma_\varphi r$	$mf_k(a,\sigma_\varphi r,x) = mf_k(a,r,x)$	$\acute{S}_R^{(k)}(\sigma_\varphi r,x) = \acute{S}_R^{(k)}(r,x)$
$Counting$	$mf_k(a,Count(r),x) = \bot$	$Count(r)$ $\acute{S}_R^{(k)}(Count(r)) = 1$ $\acute{S}_R^{(k)}(Count(r),x) = \acute{S}_R^{(k)}(r,x)$ $Count\ with\ gourping\quad \begin{matrix} Count(r) \\ G1\ldots Gn \end{matrix}$ $\acute{S}_R^{(k)}\left(\begin{matrix} Count(r) \\ G1\ldots Gn \end{matrix}, x\right) =$ $2\acute{S}_R^{(k)}(r,x)$

3.1   System Design

Considering the shortcomings of the existing database platforms based on differential privacy protection, our system provides more privacy protection management authority for data publishers. The administrator can limit attack times and adversary's success probability, then they can estimate the attack cost of the adversary. Similar to PINQ, administrator can assign a query budget to clients, and each query of clients will consume part of the query budget until the query budget is used up.

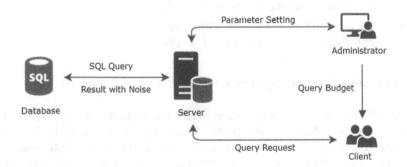

Fig. 2. System interactions

The interaction process is sketched in Fig. 2. Before data release, the administrator inputs the attack times and success probability as expected into the system. Then, the system calculates the privacy budget based on the parameters input by the administrator and returns privacy budget to the administrator. According to the privacy budget obtained, the administrator limits the scope of client access to the database and assigns a query budget to the client, and each query of the client will consume part of the budget. When the budget is insufficient, the client can apply to the administrator, who decides whether to assign another query budget to the client. When the client poses a query request to the server, the server sends a SQL statement to the database of query, and calculates the elastic sensitivity according to the query statement. The client's query budget decreases accordingly. Afterwards, the database returns the query results to the sever, and the server adds noise of Laplace distribution to the query results. Finally, the result with noise is returned to the client.

3.2 Budget Management

Here's more information on how to calculate a privacy budget. The administrator inputs the probability of success and attack times based on the security requirements, and calculates the privacy budget according to the repeated attack model proposed above. Considering the attack model, the probability of success under repeated attacks is actually equal to a binomial distribution of the success probability of a single attack. Therefore, we can simplify the probability formula of repeated attacks to the following formula:

$$\rho' \leq \sum_{i=1}^{n+1} C_N^{m+i}(\rho)^{n+i}(1-\rho)^{n+1-i} \tag{9}$$

N is the number of repeated attacks, $N = 2n+1$, ρ is the success probability of a single attack, and ρ' is the success probability of repeated attacks.

In this way, the transformation calculation of the success probability of a single attack becomes polynomial. Based on the single success probability ρ, it is easy to calculate the privacy budget ε. Under the same privacy budget, the success probability increases with the increasing number of attacks. Therefore, controlling the number of queries is an effective way to protect personal data security. The administrator can assign the query budget to the client based on the privacy budget. Each query of the client consumes the query budget. When the query budget is exhausted, the client needs to apply to the administrator for another budget, and the administrator decides whether to assign another budget to the client based on specific usage of client and security requirements attack success probability. When setting parameters, the attack success probability should be greater than 0.5. In fact, under the optimal protection, the success probability of the adversary will be maintained at 0.5. Because under optimal protection, even if the opponent has the most background knowledge, it cannot profit from it. That is, the adversary can only determine the information of the attack target by guessing rather than extracting useful data from the dataset. Under optimal protection, an attack on a counting query is like guessing the heads and tails of a coin, whose success rate is 50%.

3.3   Security Evaluation

The essence of Laplace mechanism is to add a random noise to the result, and the random noise is in the interval $(-\infty, +\infty)$ with an average of 0. Therefore, the target value can be obtained according to the feature of the average value as long as executing the same query enough number of times.

Considering the attack model by predicting the noise, take the count query for example. For different values of privacy budget ε the adversary averages the noise of S number of attack times experimental results. When the average value is within the $[-0.5, 0.5]$ interval (known as the "fault-tolerant interval"), the adversary can infer that the average value of noise is 0. Therefore, we need pay attention to the probability of the average value of S times noise in the dangerous interval.

The Table 2 shows the data distribution and mean values of noise under different conditions for different values of privacy budget ε. For example, when the value of privacy budget ε is 0.1, 90% noise is within the range of $[-23.24, 23.24]$ and 95% noise is within the range of $[-29.00, 29.99]$. Averaging 100 different noise, the average falls in the danger range with 25.59% probability; and averaging 1,000 noise, the average falls in the danger range with 73.75% probability. That is to say, when privacy budget ε is 0.1, the adversary has a 73.75% probability of getting the true value of the query result through executing the same query 1,000 times.

Table 2. The Laplace noise distribution and the possibility of noise mean within danger interval in different ε

ε	Data distribution of noise (Tabsolute value of T)				The probability that the average noise of S times in dangerous interval			
	90%	95%	99%	99.9%	100	1000	10000	100000
1	2.29	2.98	4.50	6.43	100.00	100.00	100.00	100.00
0.1	23.24	29.99	45.51	66.56	25.59	73.75	99.99	100.00
0.01	227.97	296.22	463.48	677.26	2.72	9.12	27.85	73.70

The above attack model is an attack on the characteristics of Laplace noise. While considering the adversary's background knowledge, the adversary can use another repeated attack model to guess the information of the target. That is, the repeated attack model introduced in Sect. 2.3. Take count query as an example. Because the adversary has extensive background knowledge, the adversary knows that the value of the query result $f(D)$ is y or $y + 1$. Set $N = 2n + 1$, the adversary executes the same query N times and counts the result $f(D) + noise$ in $(-\infty, y+0.5)$ or in $(y+0.5, +\infty)$. If the result in $(-\infty, y+0.5)$ is more than $(y+0.5, +\infty)$, the adversary will guess the query result $f(D) = y$. Otherwise, the adversary will guess the query result $f(D) = y + 1$. In Sect. 2.3, we list the success probability of this attack model is:

$$\rho \leq \sum_{i=1}^{n+1} C_N^{n+i}(1 - \frac{1}{2}e^{-\frac{L\varepsilon}{\Delta f}})^{n+i}(\frac{1}{2}e^{-\frac{L\varepsilon}{\Delta f}})^{n+1-i}$$

According to the formula and Fig. 3, under the same privacy budget ε, the success probability increases with the increasing of query times.

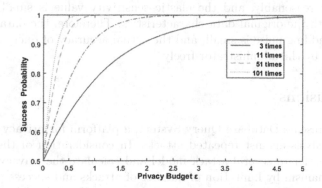

Fig. 3. The success probability of counting query under different attack times

To evaluate the security of the Database Query System, we analyze the input parameters and privacy budget ε in Table 3. We also list the success probability of the first attack model. As mentioned above, the ideally attack success probability is 0.5. The significance of 0.5 is that the adversary cannot get advantage by his extensive background knowledge and can only guess target value. Based on this privacy budget, the predicting noise attack model success probability is less than 50%. That is to say, by calculating the average value of the noise, the success accuracy is evenworse than that of random guessing.

Table 3. Protection model evaluation

Attack times	Success probability	Privacy budget	The probability average noise in dangerous interval	Noise mean
51	0.6	0.0717	14.57%	13.93
101	0.6	0.0510	13.80%	19.67
201	0.6	0.0359	13.86%	27.94
101	0.7	0.1068	30.01%	9.3319
101	0.55	0.0250	7.17 %	39.89
101	0.65	0.0779	22.04 %	12.90

3.4   Performance Analysis

The main time overhead before data publishing is the polynomial computation process of privacy budget. After releasing the database, neither the calculation of elastic sensitivity nor the generation of Laplace noise involves complex calculation, and the time overhead is relatively small. In each query, in addition to ordinary interactions with the database, only a simple calculation is required to achieve differential privacy protection, and the calculation overhead can be ignored. This system has the advantage of easy implementation. The privacy budget is set reasonably, and the elastic sensitivity value is small and more consistent with the original data characteristics. Therefore, the data distortion degree after adding noise is small, and the actual accuracy of query results can be controlled by the administrator freely.

4   Conclusions

This paper presents Database Query System, a platform for privacy preserving statistical analysis against repeated attacks. In consideration of the attack in practical, we refer to several attack model and calculate the privacy budget of Laplace Mechanism by limitation of number of attacks and success probability. For further research, the aggregate functions except for count should be take into consideration. And abstracting out the complicated attack in practice into a detailed algorithm is a challenge as well.

References

1. Johnson, N.M., Near, J.P., Song, D.: Towards practical differential privacy for SQL queries. PVLDB **11**(5), 526–539 (2018)
2. Nissim, K., Raskhodnikova, S., Smith, A.D.: Smooth sensitivity and sampling in private data analysis. In: STOC 2007, pp. 75–84 (2007)
3. Lee, J., Clifton, C.: How much is enough? choosing ε for differential privacy. In: Lai, X., Zhou, J., Li, H. (eds.) ISC 2011. LNCS, vol. 7001, pp. 325–340. Springer, Heidelberg (2011). https://doi.org/10.1007/978-3-642-24861-0_22
4. Johnson, N.M., Near, J.P., Hellerstein, J.M., Song, D.: Chorus: Differential Privacy via Query Rewriting. CoRR abs/1809.07750 (2018)
5. Dwork, C., Lei, J.: Differential privacy and robust statistics. In: STOC 2009, pp. 371–380 (2009)
6. Dwork, C.: Differential Privacy. Encyclopedia of Cryptography and Security, 2nd edn, pp. 338–340. Springer, Boston (2011). https://doi.org/10.1007/978-1-4419-5906-5
7. Dwork, C.: Differential privacy: a survey of results. In: Agrawal, M., Du, D., Duan, Z., Li, A. (eds.) TAMC 2008. LNCS, vol. 4978, pp. 1–19. Springer, Heidelberg (2008). https://doi.org/10.1007/978-3-540-79228-4_1
8. Zhu, T., Li, G., Zhou, W., Yu, P.S.: Differentially private data publishing and analysis: a survey. IEEE Trans. Knowl. Data Eng. **29**(8), 1619–1638 (2017)
9. Dwork, C., Roth, A.: The algorithmic foundations of differential privacy. Found. Trends Theor. Comput. Sci. **9**(3–4), 211–407 (2014)

10. He, X., Wang, X.S., Chen, H., Dong, Y.: Study on choosing the parameter ε in differential privacy. J. Commun. **36**(12) (2015)

11. Xiong, P., Zhu, T.-Q., Wang, X.-F.: A survey on differential privacy and applications. Chin. J. Comput. **37**(1), 101–122 (2014)

12. Hao, C., Peng, C., Zhang, P.: Selection method of differential privacy protection parameter ε under epeated attack. Comput. Eng. **44**(7), 145–149 (2018)

13. McSherry, F.: Privacy integrated queries: an extensible platform for privacy-preserving data analysis. Commun. ACM **53**(9), 89–97 (2010)

14. Dwork, C., McSherry, F., Nissim, K., Smith, A.: Calibrating noise to sensitivity in private data analysis. In: Halevi, S., Rabin, T. (eds.) TCC 2006. LNCS, vol. 3876, pp. 265–284. Springer, Heidelberg (2006). https://doi.org/10.1007/11681878_14

15. McSherry, F., Talwar, K.: Mechanism design via differential privacy. In: FOCS 2007, pp. 94–103 (2007)

Research on Social Networks Publishing Method Under Differential Privacy

Han Wang[✉] and Shuyu Li

School of Computer Science, Shaanxi Normal University, Xi'an 710119, China
{wanghan, lishuyu}@snnu.edu.cn

Abstract. Data publishing for large-scale social network has the risk of privacy leakage. Trying to solve this problem, a differential private social network data publishing algorithm named DP-HRG is proposed in the paper, which is based on Hierarchical Random Graph (HRG). Firstly, the social network is divided into 1-neighborhood subgraphs, and the HRG of each subgraph is extracted by using both Markov Monte Carlo (MCMC) and exponential mechanism to compose the HRG candidate set. Then an average edge matrix is obtained based on the HRG candidate set and perturbed by a random matrix. Finally, according to the perturbed average edge matrix, a 1-neighborhood graph is regenerated and pasted into the original social network for publishing. Experimental results show that the proposed algorithm preserves good network characteristics and better data utility while satisfying the requirement of privacy protection.

Keywords: Differential privacy · Social network · Hierarchical random graph · Data publishing · Privacy protection

1 Introduction

With the rapid development of mobile Internet, social networks have become an increasingly significant way of communication among people. Social networks contain massive valuable information about individual and social relationships. Meanwhile, such information usually contains sensitive information. For example, in a medical network, the communication between an AIDS patient and a doctor may be considered sensitive information. The direct release and analysis of such information may violate individual privacy and cause extremely serious consequences. Therefore, it has become a very important issue about how to ensure the effective release of information in social network without leaking individual privacy. Traditional privacy protection methods, such as k-anonymity [1], l-diversity [2] and t-closeness [3], have been extensively used in practical applications. The basic idea of these methods is to employ the techniques of de-identification, generalization and suppression to process the attributes and records in the original data set to satisfy anonymity requirements and finally release the anonymous data set. However, all these methods are related to the background knowledge of potential attackers and privacy quantization cannot be strictly verified. Dwork [4] proposed the differential privacy theory in 2006, which successfully solved the problems encountered by traditional privacy protection methods. Differential privacy method does not need to consider the background knowledge of attackers, and provides

J. Li et al. (Eds.): SPNCE 2019, LNICST 284, pp. 58–72, 2019.
https://doi.org/10.1007/978-3-030-21373-2_6

a strict definition on privacy protection and provides a quantitative evaluation method. Differential privacy has become a research hotspot in the field of privacy protection.

Differential privacy is a data-distortion-based privacy protection technology that uses a noise-adding mechanism to distort sensitive data while ensuring data availability. However, due to the complexity of social networks, the direct addition of noise will probably result in a significant decline in the utility and values of social network data. Therefore, this research aims to preserve the original characteristics of social network and release the disturbed information as much as possible under the condition of satisfying the requirements for privacy protection.

2 Preliminaries

2.1 Differential Privacy

Definition 1 (ε-differential privacy). In proximate data sets D_1, D_2 (one and only one piece of data is different in the two data sets), the algorithm M can output any $S \subseteq Range(K)$ that satisfies

$$\Pr[K(D_1) \in S] \le e^{\varepsilon} \times \Pr[K(D_2) \in S] \tag{1}$$

The algorithm is said to satisfy differential privacy protection.

Definition 2 (Gaussian mechanism). For a query function $f : D \to R^d$ on the given data set D, let $\sigma = \Delta_2 f \sqrt{2\ln(2/\delta)}/\varepsilon$, $N(0, \sigma^2)$ is an independent identically distributed Gaussian random variable (i.e. Gaussian noise), then the random algorithm M: $M(D) = f(D) + (N_1(0, \sigma^2), N_2(0, \sigma^2)...N_d(0, \sigma^2))$ provides (ε, δ) differential privacy. The Gaussian mechanism is suitable for processing numerical data.

Definition 3 (Exponential mechanism). Given a scoring function $u(D, r)$, for an input data set D, the output is a random algorithm M of entity object $r \in Range$. Let Δq be the sensitivity of the function $u(D, r)$. If the algorithm M chooses and output r from *Range* with a probability proportional to $\exp\left(\frac{\varepsilon \cdot u(D, r)}{2\Delta q}\right)$, then the random algorithm M provides ε-differential privacy. The exponential mechanism is suitable for processing non-numeric data.

2.2 Social Network

Undirected and unweighted graph $G(V, E)$ is used to model a social network, where V is a point set, E is an edge set and $|V|$ represents the number of nodes.

Definition 4 (1-neighborhood graph). For each node in V, if the social network, if there is a sub-graph consisting of only 1-hop node and v itself in the social network, then we call this sub-graph as the 1-neighborhood graph centered on node v, and it can be labeled as $g(v)$.

For example, Fig. 1 is a social network containing 9 nodes. Figure 2 shows the two 1-neighborhood graphs centered on nodes D and F, respectively, in a social network.

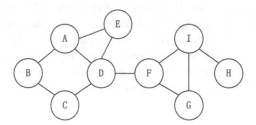

Fig. 1. Social network

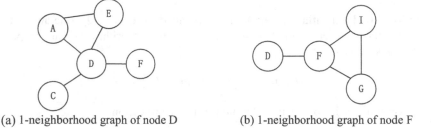

(a) 1-neighborhood graph of node D   (b) 1-neighborhood graph of node F

Fig. 2. 1-neighborhood graph of social network G

2.3 Hierarchical Random Graph

Clauset et al. [5] proposed the concept of hierarchical random graph (HRG) in 2008. HRG represents a social network using network hierarchy and a set of link probabilities, to seek the best hierarchical graph of the network, thus formulating a more accurate description of the hierarchical structure. The hierarchical structure of HRG is represented by leaf nodes and a tree diagram T consisting of internal nodes. The leaf nodes represent the real nodes in social network. The internal nodes represent the probability P_r that there is an edge between left subtree L_r and right subtree R_r, where r is the root and P_r is the degree of relation between different groups. The larger the degree of relation, the closer the relationship is between the two. P_r is defined by

$$P_r = \frac{e_r}{(n_{L_r} \cdot n_{R_r})} \tag{2}$$

where e_r represents the number of edges that exist between the left and right subtrees of internal node r, n_{L_r} represents the number of nodes in the left subtree, and n_{R_r} represents the number of nodes in the right subtree.

Similarity measure L is used to indicate whether the HRG of social network retains the structural attributes of the original social network to the greatest extent. Similarity measure is defined as

$$L(T, \{p_r\}) = \prod_{r \in T} p_r^{e_r} (1 - p_r)^{n_{L_r} n_{R_r} - e_r} \tag{3}$$

For a given T, the similarity measure represents the product of the link probabilities of all internal nodes. In this paper, the calculation process is simplified by taking the logarithm of the similarity measure L, shown as below:

$$\log L(T, \{p_r\}) = - \sum_{r \in T} n_{L_r} n_{R_r} h(p_r) \tag{4}$$

where $h(p_r) = -p_r \log p_r - (1 - p_r) \log(1 - p_r)$ is the Gibbs-Shannon entropy function. The higher the similarity, the better the structure of social network can be described. For convenience, $\log L(T)$ is used to replace $\log L(T, \{p_r\})$ in the rest sections.

3 Related Work

Many achievements have been made in applying differential privacy to social networks. Wang et al. [6] proposed a RescueDP method for the problem of the publishing of real-time spatio-temporal data in social networks. This method provided privacy-preserving statistical data publishing on infinite time stamps by integrating adaptive sampling and privacy budget allocation, dynamic grouping, disturbance and filtering technologies. The RescueDP method improved the practicability of real-time data and had strong privacy protection. Li et al. [7] proposed a network weight-based privacy protection algorithm. The algorithm treated the edge weight sequence of the undirected weighted graph as a non-attribute histogram, and added the weight containing sensitive information to the Laplace noise to meet the requirements for differential privacy. To reduce the amount of noise, the buckets with the same count in the histogram were merged into groups, and the requirements for differential privacy were satisfied through the inter-group k-unidentifiability. The reasoning of consistency was performed on the original weight sequence to keep the shortest path of the network unchanged. Tian et al. [8] proposed the DWDPP method for privacy protection in weighted social network. The method used discrete wavelet transform to decompose the weight matrix, and then added Laplace noise to the high-frequency detail matrix of each layer and the low-frequency approximation matrix of the last layer to reconstruct the weight matrix. Data availability was preserved by this method. Xiao et al. [9] modeled the social network graph by HRG, then added noise to the generated graph, and finally restored the HRG with noise to obtain a network graph that satisfied the differential privacy. However, the time complexity of the algorithm was high. Most of the above algorithms are directly processing a whole social network graph. So, for a large-size social network graph, these algorithms may encounter the problems such as long processing time and sharp decline in data availability. Therefore, based on the privHRG algorithm proposed by Xiao [9], this paper proposes a social network publishing algorithm DP-HRG which satisfies the differential privacy requirements for undirected and unweighted social networks, as well as preserves the features of original network. This research mainly contains the following work.

- For the problems of large size and data correlation in real social network graphs, this paper proposes a 1-neighborhood graph partitioning method based on the largest independent set of social network. This method can effectively reduce the network size and improve the computational efficiency.
- When searching the best matching tree in the candidate tree set, the sampling technique that combines Markov Monte Carlo (MCMC) method and exponential mechanism is designed to improve the sampling efficiency while protecting the privacy. In addition, a subgraph re-generation and link method is proposed to paste the regenerated 1-neighborhood graph into the original social network to publish the complete social network.
- The DP-HRG algorithm is experimentally evaluated on two kinds of real social network datasets, and the privacy analysis, sensitivity analysis and utility analysis of the algorithm are carried out.

4   Social Network Publishing Algorithm Based on Differential Privacy

4.1   The Ideas of the Algorithm

For small-size social networks, we can construct their HRG directly and then perform the corresponding disturbance operations. However, social network usually has large size, their nodes and structures are complex, and various complex factors affect each other, which is very inefficient to directly construct HRG. In this case, we mainly face two problems: (1) how to construct HRG efficiently for large-size social networks and perform disturbance; (2) how to find the best matching tree from the candidate tree set while satisfying privacy protection.

For the first problem, a partition-based method is used to improve efficiency. On the basis of the largest independent set, the original social network is partitioned into several 1-neighborhood graphs, and HRGs are constructed for these subgraphs, and then corresponding disturbances are performed. On the one hand, the graph size is greatly reduced, and the spatial size of the output HRG is reduced. Besides, since the generation of the largest independent set is uncertain, the attacker will not know which subgraphs are disturbed. On the other hand, the 1-neighborhood graph itself reflects the local characteristics of the network. The method of constructing HRG on subgraphs and conducting the disturbance makes the noise is added to only a part of the subgraphs in the whole social network, which preserves the availability of the social network to a greater extent. In addition, 1-neighborhood graph can represent the direct relation between a target user and all of its neighbors, and it needs to be protected. For the second problem, MCMC is employed in the sampling process to improve the sampling efficiency, and the exponential mechanism is incorporated to satisfy the differential privacy.

In order to guarantee the greater accuracy and better availability of the sampled sample tree set, each HRG in the sample tree set is converted into a corresponding edge number matrix, and obtain the average edge number matrix of all edge number matrixes. Then, for the disadvantage of insufficient privacy protection, the average edge number matrix is disturbed by random matrix method, and only a small amount of noise is required to ensure differential privacy, thereby improving data availability.

The DP-HRG algorithm can be divided into the following four steps:

1. Find the largest independent set of social networks and obtain the 1-neighborhood graph for each node in the largest independent set;
2. Extract the HRG of each 1-neighborhood graph using MCMC method and exponential mechanism to obtain a sample tree set;
3. Convert the HRG in the sample tree set to the edge number matrix, and then obtain the average edge number matrix which is then disturbed using use the random matrix;
4. Regenerate the 1-neighborhood graphs and paste them into the original social network, and finally publish the disturbance graph;

The algorithm framework is as follows:

Table 1. DP-HRG algorithm

Algorithm 1 DP-HRG algorithm
Input: original social network G, privacy budget ε, random noise variable σ
Output: disturbed social network $\tilde{G}$
1. Obtain the 1-neighborhood graph of the largest independent set;
2. Perform sampling to obtain sample tree set S ← SampleHRGs $(g(v), \varepsilon)$;//Algorithm 2
3.1. Convert the HRGs in S into edge number matrix and put them into a set M ;
3.2. Obtain the average edge number matrix after disturbance $\tilde{M}$ ←RandMatrixDisturb (M, σ);//Algorithm 3
4. Subgraph generation and link $\tilde{G}$ ←SubgraphGenAndLink $(G, \tilde{M})$;//Algorithm 4
5. Publish the disturbed social network $\tilde{G}$;

4.2   Algorithm Design

Obtaining the Largest Independent Set and 1-Neighborhood Graph

The algorithm needs to partition the original social network into several subgraphs and disturb some of the subgraphs. However, due to the correlation between nodes in the social network, the social network cannot be directly partitioned. Therefore, it is required to find the largest independent set of the social network G, and then obtain the

1-neighborhood graph of each node in the largest independent set. This method not only reduces the size of the original network, but also preserves the correlation, and also lays the foundation for data disturbance.

Extracting the HRG to Obtain Sample Tree Set

Due to the nature of the HRG, each 1-neighborhood graph corresponds to multiple HRGs. Let T be a set of all possible trees, so for a network with $|V|$ nodes, the number of T is $|T| = (2|V| - 3)!!$, where !! represents a semi-factorial symbol. When the size of a social network is large, the efficiency of finding the best HRG from many HRGs will be greatly reduced, although the partition is employed to reduce the output space, the output space is still large for a larger subgraph. Therefore, the MCMC method is used to control time complexity and reduce computation time. At the same time, the exponential mechanism is incorporated with MCMC method. The similarity measure function is used as the scoring function u. The acceptance probability of the MCMC process is changed from $\frac{u(T)}{u(T')}$ to $\alpha = \frac{\exp\left(\frac{\varepsilon}{2\Delta q}u(T')\right)}{\exp\left(\frac{\varepsilon}{2\Delta q}u(T_{i-1})\right)}$, where Δq is the global sensitivity of the scoring function u.

This algorithm first selects an arbitrary tree as the initial state of the Markov chain, and then performs looping executions: randomly selects the neighbor tree T' of T_{i-1} and updates it as follows:

$$T_i = \begin{cases} T' & \text{with probability } \alpha \\ T_{i-1} & \text{with probability } 1 - \alpha \end{cases} \tag{5}$$

Therefore, if we need randomly select the neighbor tree T' of T_{i-1}, we first need to randomly select the internal nodes r other than the root node from T_{i-1}, and find their brothers and two children, and then transform the three subtrees to generate the two alternative trees of r, as shown in Fig. 3. One of the two alternative trees is selected as the neighbor tree T'.

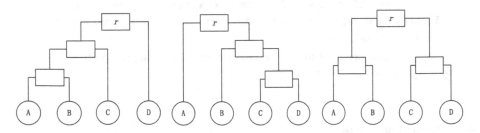

Fig. 3. Three structures of subtrees

When the MCMC process reaches a steady state, the sampling is performed at regular intervals to obtain a set S containing N sample trees.

Table 2. HRGs sampling of differential privacy

Algorithm 2: HRGs sampling of differential privacy (SampleHRGs)
Input: 1-neighborhood graph $g(v)$, privacy budget ε
Output: the set $S = \{T_1, T_2, ..., T_n\}$ containing N sample trees

1. Randomly select a tree T_0 to initialize the Markov chain;
2. For the every step i of Markov chain, perform looping execution:
   Randomly select an internal node r;

   Randomly select a subtree of r as the neighbor tree T_i' of T_{i-1};

   Take the T_i' as T_i with the acceptance probability of $\min(1, \dfrac{\exp(\frac{\varepsilon}{2\Delta q} u(T'))}{\exp(\frac{\varepsilon}{2\Delta q} u(T_{i-1}))})$;

   When the Markov chain reaches steady state, the loop ends;
3. Select a number of sampling trees in the generated sample tree set;
4. Return to the sample tree set S;

Random Matrix Disturbance

After obtaining the sample tree set S, we need to convert the N sample trees in S into edge number matrix and perform further disturbance to achieve stronger privacy protection. The combination of random matrix theory and differential privacy is adopted. Firstly, the N sample trees in the sample tree set are transformed into N edge number matrixes, and their average $\bar{M}$ is obtained. Then, the average edge number matrix is disturbed by the Gaussian random noise matrix, and finally we obtain the average edge number matrix with random disturbance.

The horizontal and vertical coordinates of the edge number matrix represent the coordinates of the nodes in the social network, and the values of these elements represent the number of linked edges of the left and right subtrees of the internal node r. After disturbing edge number matrix using the random matrix, a new average edge number matrix with random disturbance is obtained, and the number of edges after the disturbance is labeled as $\tilde{e}_r$.

Table 3. Random disturbance matrix

Algorithm 3: Random disturbance matrix (RandMatrixDisturb)
Input: Edge number matrix set M, random noise variable σ
Output: Average edge number matrix after disturbance $\tilde{M}$

1. Obtain the average edge number matrix obtained by averaging the N edge number matrixes in M;
2. Obtain the random disturbance matrix by sampling Gaussian distribution $N \sim (0, \sigma^2)$;
3. Calculate the average edge number matrix with random disturbances $\tilde{M} = \bar{M} + Q$;

Subgraph Generation and Link

After obtaining the average edge number matrix with random disturbance, the probability $\tilde{P}_r$ of each pair of leaf nodes corresponding to the disturbance is calculated based on the value of $\tilde{e}_r$, and the edge is placed between the pair of leaf nodes to generate the disturbed subgraph $\tilde{g}(v)$. The v nodes in the undisturbed graph are randomly determined in the disturbed graph $\tilde{g}(v)$, and then comparison is performed between the disturbed subgraph and the undisturbed subgraph. If an edge is added or deleted between the nodes of the disturbed subgraph, modification should be made in the corresponding 1-neighborhood graph in the original social network. In this way, the disturbed subgraph can be pasted into the original social network.

For example, Fig. 4 is the 1-neighborhood graph after the disturbance on Fig. 2(b), and then it is compared with the 1-neighborhood graph of node F in Fig. 1. In the disturbed graph, the D node is linked to the nodes F and G with edges, while in the original graph, the node D is only linked to the node F, so it is required to add an edge between D and G in the original graph. The other three nodes F, G, and I all take the similar operations, and finally we obtain a disturbed social network graph, as shown in Fig. 5.

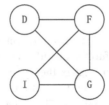

Fig. 4. 1-neighborhood graph after disturbance

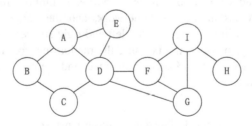

Fig. 5. Social network after disturbance

4.3   Privacy Analysis

The Algorithm 2, which combines MCMC with exponential mechanism to extract HRG, is essentially a method of sampling the output with a probability proportional to $\exp(\varepsilon u(D, r)/2\Delta q)$ in the target distribution, where $u(D, r)$ is the scoring function and Δq is the sensitivity. Therefore, by matching the smooth distribution of the MCMC with the target distribution required for the exponential mechanism, the MCMC can be

Table 4. Subgraph generation and link

Algorithm 4: Subgraph generation and link (SubgraphGenAndLink)
Input: Social network G , average edge number matrix with disturbance $\tilde{M}$
Output: distributed social network $\tilde{G}$
1. For every $g(v)$ in G , perform looping execution:
1.1. For every pair of nodes i, j in $g(v)$, perform looping execution:
(1) Find the number of linked edges $\tilde{e}_r$ of the left and right subtrees of the internal node r corresponding to each pair of leaf nodes in the average edge number matrix with disturbance;
(2) Calculate the link probability $\tilde{P}_r$ after the disturbance based on $\tilde{e}_r$;
(3) Place the edges between the i, j in network graph with probability $\tilde{P}_r$ to gen er ate a disturbed subgraph;
End of loop
1.2 Randomly determine the v nodes in the undisturbed graph $g(v)$ in the disturbed graph $\tilde{g}(v)$;
1.3 For each pair of nodes i, j in $\tilde{g}(v)$, perform looping execution:
(1) If there is an edge between i and j , then add an edge between them in $g(v)$;
(2) If there is no edge between i and j , then delete the edge between them in the $g(v)$ of G ;
End of loop
End of loop
2. Return to the disturbed social network graph;

used to implement the exponential mechanism. The scoring function $u(T)$ of T is set as $\log L(T)$, then the acceptance probability of MCMC is given by

$$\min\left(1, \frac{\exp\left(\frac{\varepsilon}{2\Delta u} \cdot \log L(T')\right)}{\exp\left(\frac{\varepsilon}{2\Delta u} \cdot \log L(T_{i-1})\right)}\right) \tag{6}$$

When the Markov chain converges to steady state, the sample is extracted from the probability mass function which is expressed as

$$\Pr(T) = \frac{\exp\left(\frac{\varepsilon}{2\Delta u} \cdot \log L(T)\right)}{\sum_{T' \in T} \exp\left(\frac{\varepsilon}{2\Delta u} \cdot \log L(T')\right)} \tag{7}$$

This means that the exponential mechanism outputs T with a probability proportional to $\exp\left(\frac{\varepsilon}{2\Delta u} \cdot \log L(T)\right)$. Therefore, Algorithm 2 satisfies differential privacy.

The random matrix disturbance process of Algorithm 3 satisfies the differential privacy, which has been proved in literature [10]. The rest steps of the algorithm do not consume the privacy budget. According to the sequenced combination property of differential privacy, the algorithm as a whole satisfies 2ε-differential privacy.

4.4 Sensitivity Analysis

Sensitivity can be expressed as:

$$\Delta q = \max(u(T(e_r)) - u(T(e_r - 1)))$$
$$\log(\Delta q) = \max\left(n_{L_r} n_{R_r}\left(h\left(\frac{e_r}{n_{L_r} n_{R_r}}\right) - h\left(\frac{e_r - 1}{n_{L_r} n_{R_r}}\right)\right)\right)$$

Let $N = n_{L_r} n_{R_r}$, then

$$\Delta q = \log N - (N - 1) \cdot \log\frac{N - 1}{N} =$$

$$\log N + (N - 1)\log\left(1 + \frac{1}{N - 1}\right) =$$

$$\log N + \log\left(1 + \frac{1}{N - 1}\right)^{N-1} <$$

$$\log N + \log e \leq \log\frac{|V|^2}{4} + 1 = O(\log n)$$

When $n_{L_r} \cdot n_{R_r}$ is increasing, Δq is monotonically increasing. When n_{L_r} equals n_{R_r} and the value is equal to half of the number of all nodes, i.e. $|V|/2$ ($|V|$ represents the number of nodes), Δq reaches its maximum. When the number of nodes increases, the magnitude of the noise increases, where both $|V|$ and n represent the total number of nodes in the graph. Therefore, the sensitivity of the method is $O(\log n)$. The specific proof process can be found in literature [9].

5 Experiment and Results Analysis

5.1 Experimental Setup

The experiment adopted two real data sets from SNAP [11]: the polblogs data set and the facebook data set. The statistics of the data sets used in the experiment are shown in Table 5. The experimental environment was Intel Xeon, CPU of E7-4830 2.13 GHz, RAM of 32 GB, operating system of Windows Server 2008, and the algorithm is written in C++ language.

Table 5. Data set information statistics table

Data set	Number of nodes	Number of edges
polblogs	1490	19090
facebook	4039	88234

5.2 Utility Analysis

The algorithm proposed in this paper was compared with the algorithm of literature [8] to verify the utility of the proposed algorithm. In the experimental renderings, Origin represents the original social network, privHRG represents the algorithm proposed in literature [8], and DP-HRG represents the algorithm proposed in this paper. The utility of the proposed DP-HRG algorithm was examined by comparing it with Origin and the network graph processed by privHRG from the aspects of node degree distribution, average clustering coefficient and shortest path length distribution. Due to the randomness of the algorithm, three tests were carried out for each aspect to obtain an average. When conducting the experiments, we set a relatively large privacy budget and variance, with the privacy budget $\varepsilon = 1$ and variance $\sigma = 1$. The reason for this is as follows. On the one hand, the generation of HRG in this algorithm and the randomness of the subgraph generation and link process had rendered the algorithm certain privacy protection capabilities; on the other hand, the structural characteristics of the complex graph itself determined that a relatively large privacy budget could guarantee the privacy protection effect.

Degree Distribution: The degree of a node in a network refers to the number of links that the node has with other nodes. The degree of node distribution reflects the structure of a network to a certain extent. Figures 6 and 7 show the results of node degree distribution under different data sets. In order to better represent the experimental results, we intercepted the parts of the two graphs with significant changes in degrees for better illustration. It can be seen from the experimental results that both DP-HRG and privHRG algorithms followed the overall trend that the larger the degree of nodes, the fewer the number of nodes in the original network, and they both maintained the original network structure characteristics for large social networks. Compared with the publishing results of the polblogs data set, those of the facebook dataset were closer to the original network, indicating that the good effect of DP-HRG algorithm for large social networks.

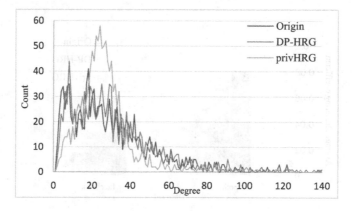

Fig. 6. Degree distribution of polblogs

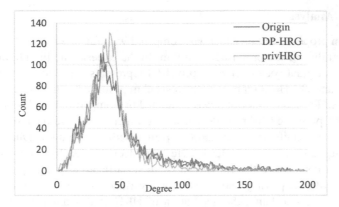

Fig. 7. Degree distribution of facebook

Average clustering coefficient: The clustering coefficient refers to the degree of aggregation of nodes in a network. It is assumed that node i in a network has k_i edges to link it with other nodes, then the clustering coefficient is $C_i = 2E_i/(k_i(k_i - 1))$, where E_i refers to actual number of edges that exist among k_i nodes. Average clustering coefficient is the average of the clustering coefficients C_i of all nodes i. Figure 8 shows the average clustering coefficients for two data sets under Origin, DP-HRG, and privHRG. It can be observed from the figure that DP-HRG and privHRG could maintain the clustering characteristics of the original network compared with the average clustering coefficient of the original network, but the average clustering coefficient of the network published by the DP-HRG algorithm was closer than that of the privHRG algorithm, with an error of less than 0.01 for the polblogs dataset, and an error of 0.0005 for the facebook dataset. This indicated that the DP-HRG algorithm could better maintain the aggregation characteristics of the nodes in original social network, and better describe the structure of the network, with even more obvious effect on large social networks.

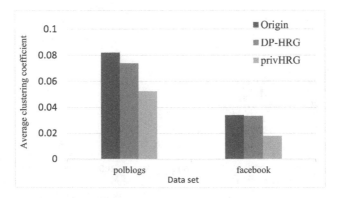

Fig. 8. Average clustering coefficient

Shortest path length distribution: This term refers to the distribution of the shortest path lengths between nodes in a network, which to some extent reflects the characteristics of a graph. Figures 9 and 10 show the shortest path length distribution of the two data sets. According to the experimental results, the number of paths with a length of 2 in the polblogs data set was the largest, and that with a length of 3 in the facebook data set was the largest. Both DP-HRG and privHRG algorithms were be able to preserve the characteristics of the original network path length. It should be noted that although the differences in some stages of the figure were not obvious, there would still be large differences between them for massive data.

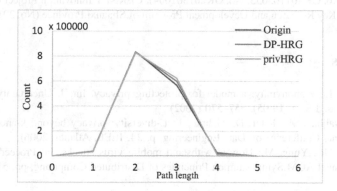

Fig. 9. Shortest path length distribution of polblogs

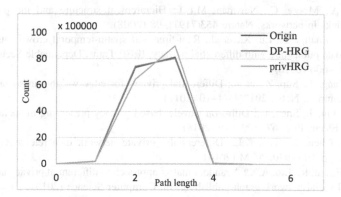

Fig. 10. Shortest path length distribution of facebook

6 Conclusions

This paper investigates the differential privacy-based social network publishing method using HRG. Firstly, on the basis of obtaining the largest independent set of a network and the 1-neighborhood graph, the method that combines MCMC method and exponential mechanism is employed to sample the HRG. Then, random matrix is used to disturb the average edge matrix to further enhance the privacy protection. After that, the 1-neighborhood graph is generated. Finally, the new 1-neighborhood graph is pasted into the original social network for publishing. The experimental results show that the proposed algorithm guarantees good data utility under the premise of satisfying differential privacy. However, in the process of random matrix disturbance, due to the addition of noise to the number of edges, a great impact will still be formulated on the probability of the existence of HRG edge. In the future work, more efforts will be made to further optimize the mechanism of adding noise.

Acknowledgments. This work is supported by the Fundamental Research Funds for the Central Universities (No. GK201703055, No. GK201801004), CERNET Innovation Project (No. NGII2 0170703) and Key Research and Development Program of Shaanxi Province (No. 2017GY-064).

References

1. Sweeney, L.: k-anonymity: a model for protecting privacy. Int. J. Uncertainty Fuzziness Knowl. Based Syst. **10**(05), 557–570 (2002)
2. Machanavajjhala, A., Kifer, D., Gehrke, J.: L-diversity: privacy beyond k-anonymity. In: International Conference on Data Engineering, p. 24. IEEE, Atlanta (2006)
3. Ostrovsky, R., Yung, M.: How to withstand mobile virus attacks. In: Proceedings of the Tenth Annual ACM Symposium on Principles of Distributed Computing, pp. 51–59. ACM (1991)
4. Dwork, C.: Differential privacy. In: Bugliesi, M., Preneel, B., Sassone, V., Wegener, I. (eds.) ICALP 2006. LNCS, vol. 4052, pp. 1–12. Springer, Heidelberg (2006). https://doi.org/10. 1007/11787006_1
5. Clauset, A., Moore, C., Newman, M.E.J.: Hierarchical structure and the prediction of missing links in networks. Nature **453**(7191), 98 (2008)
6. Wang, Q., Zhang, Y., Lu, X., et al.: Real-time and spatio-temporal crowd-sourced social network data publishing with differential privacy. IEEE Trans. Dependable Secure Comput. **15**(4), 591–606 (2018)
7. Li, X., Yang, J., Sun, Z., et al.: Differential privacy for edge weights in social networks. Secur. Commun. Netw. **2017**(4), 1–10 (2017)
8. Tian, H., Liu, J., Shen, H.: Diffusion wavelet-based privacy preserving in social networks. Comput. Electr. Eng. **67**, 509–519 (2018)
9. Xiao, Q., Chen, R., Tan, K.L.: Differentially private network data release via structural inference, pp. 911–920. ACM (2014)
10. Ahmed, F., Jin, R., Liu, A.X.: A random matrix approach to differential privacy and structure preserved social network graph publishing. In: Computer Science (2013)
11. SNAP Homepage. http://snap.stanford.edu. Accessed 17 Nov 2018

CROSS: Supervised Sharing of Private Data over Blockchains

Mingxin Yin[1], Jiqiang Gao[1], Xiaojie Guo[1], Mengyao Sun[1], Zheli Liu[1(✉)],
Jianzhong Zhang[1], and Jing Wang[2]

[1] College of Cyber Science, Nankai University, Tianjin, China
{yinmx0315,jiqiang,xiaojie.guo,mysun}@mail.nankai.edu.cn,
{liuzheli,zhangjz}@nankai.edu.cn
[2] Bubi Technologies Ltd, Beijing, China
wangjing@bubi.cn

Abstract. The transparent property of the blockchain guarantees the immutability of the data on the chain, but it can lead to violations of data privacy protection. On the other hand, absolute anonymity will make it difficult for the government to supervise the encrypted content stored on the chain. Moreover, it is inconvenient for the data owners to delegate their decryption authority to others. In order to solve the problem of data privacy concern and supervision in the current blockchain, we propose a supervised data sharing model called CROSS, which combines the proxy re-encryption mechanism with the tree key distribution mechanism. The model realizes the hierarchical supervision and horizontal sharing of private data on the blockchain, which effectively improves the privacy of the blockchain while taking into account security. Consideration should be given to some potential attacks and corresponding defenses against our proposed model.

Keywords: Blockchian · Proxy re-encryption ·
Hierarchical supervision · Data sharing

1 Introduction

Blockchain technology has broken the centralization nature of the traditional Internet, making the crisis of confidence to plague the modern economy resolved to some extent. The transparency is one of the important features of blockchain (i.e., the data stored on the blockchain is visible to any node), but it is a double-edged sword. It ensures the behavior that attempts to tamper with the data is recorded and discovered, but in turn, the privacy of data is at risk. Users don't want anyone to view their data at any time, especially in the business or government affairs. The data of governments or companies, etc. needs to be kept private strictly. Meanwhile, the transfer of decryption rights to a particular user may occur in a particular scenario. How to securely share private data on the blockchain is a challenge.

© ICST Institute for Computer Sciences, Social Informatics and Telecommunications Engineering 2019
Published by Springer Nature Switzerland AG 2019. All Rights Reserved
J. Li et al. (Eds.): SPNCE 2019, LNICST 284, pp. 73–86, 2019.
https://doi.org/10.1007/978-3-030-21373-2_7

A simple solution is to encrypt the data before it is released to the chain, but this makes it harder for the authorities to supervise the data. Government departments or regulators should be able to conduct regulatory review of company data to ensure that data retained or shared on the chain is in compliance with legal requirements. For encrypted data, regulators need a feasible regulatory scheme.

Existing blockchain-based data sharing platforms, such as Blockstack [1] and Calypso [2], are facing the problems above. A feasible and effective solution should meet the following requirements simultaneously:

Hierarchical Supervision. When a new node joins, the authority assigns a key to it based on its hierarchy. The authoritative node can calculate the key of the lower-level node, and view the encrypted data that is stored and shared by the subordinate nodes without authorization, so as to ensure the security of the data.

Private Data Sharing. Nodes can maintain fine-grained access control for data on the chain. Other users (non-authoritative nodes) can obtain the partial data after having the data owner's authorization. In this process, the plaintext will not be leaked to any third party other than the data owner and authorized user.

Our Contribution. The contributions of this paper are summarized as below:

Tree-Based Key Distribution Mechanism. We design a key distribution mechanism based on tree structure, which can effectively realize hierarchical membership of key. The authoritative node can calculate the key of the subordinate node, but the subordinate node cannot reversely crack the key of the authoritative node.

Supervised Private Data Sharing Model. We propose a supervised private data sharing model based on the consortium blockchain, combined with proxy re-encryption and key tree (hierarchical key distribution) scheme, that has realized hierarchical supervision and sharing of the encrypted data on the chain, effectively improves the privacy of blockchain while taking into account the security. Some potential attacks which can attempt on the proposed model and how the model can handle such attacks are also discussed.

2   Related Work

There have been various attempts to address the problems of data privacy, from both the system level and specific technology level. As an emerging technology, blockchain plays an important role in the field of privacy protection.

Data Management Systems Based on Blockchain. Some data management systems [3,5] based on blockchain have been proposed, their starting point is to guarantee the security of access control management and log audit by utilizing the immutability of blockchain. Chain Anchor [5] attempts to provide anonymous but verifiable identities for entities, which seek to submit transactions to the blockchain. Zero knowledge proof (ZKP) is the core stone for5 proving the anonymous membership in it.

Data Sharing System Based on Blockchain. A large part of the research on the privacy data sharing system of blockchain is applied to the medical data sharing scenario. BBDS [4] is a data sharing framework based on consortium blockchain, which uses encryption operations (e.g., encryption and digital signature) to ensure the effective access control for sensitive shared data pools. MedRec [7] and MedShare [8] are generally similar, both of them control the operations of exchanging data between the providers' databases via smart contract. Xu [10] proposed the blockchain combined with homomorphic encryption to build a scheme for protecting privacy of electronic healthy record. Proxy re-encryption is a novel method for designing secret sharing schemes [2,6,9], that allows third party to alter a ciphertext which has been encrypted for one party, so that it may be decrypted by another. CALYPSO [2] is a decentralized and auditable blockchain framework for data sharing.

In this paper, in addition to considering private data sharing, we also provide solutions of hierarchical supervision for encrypted data on the chain.

3 Preliminaries

Our resarch is on blockchain, combined with proxy re-encryption which is implemented based on bilinear mapping. In this section, we review some basic cryptology concepts which will be needed later in this paper.

3.1 Blockchain

Blockchain is a distributed ledger technology that maintains a continuously growing list of records in a verifiable and permanent way by cryptography. Multiple parties can jointly maintain the ledger through a specific consensus mechanism, so that the data on the chain has the characteristics of decentralization and strong consistency. Since the blockchain has the feature of immutability, it can be the underlying architecture of many trusted distributed systems, not just in the field of cryptocurrency [14,15]. In the process of landing, the blockchain technology often encounters resistances due to the difficulties of regulation and privacy issues.

Based on the consortium blockchain, we implement a supervised private data sharing model. The blockchain is used in the model as a publicly verifiable and chronologically-ordered immutable database. Each node in the consortium encrypts part of its own public data, and broadcasts the digital digest and additional information to the entire network. All nodes record and update the data operation on the local ledger, that makes adversary difficult to tamper with the data and avoids the single point of failure. Each block of the chain is composed of transactions and each transaction records a data processing event. All nodes follow the Longest Chain Rule [14] to maintain the uniqueness of ledger.

In addition, compared with the traditional node key generation mechanism, we propose a tree-based key distribution supposed hierarchical supervision. The private key of each node is no longer randomly generated, but is distributed by the root node in the consortium according to the key generation policy. The node's private key participates in the data encryption process, so that the authoritative node can realize the supervision.

3.2   Bilinear Groups

Let $\mathcal{G}$ setup be a bilinear group generator that on input the security parameter, outputs the parameters for a bilinear map as $(q, g_1, g_2, G_1, G_2, G_T, e)$, where G_1, G_2 (Here, G_1 may equal G_2) and G_T are groups of prime order q and g_1, g_2 are generators of G_1, G_2, respectively. The bilinear map $e: G_1 \times G_2 \to G_T$ is efficiently computable and non-degenerate.

In the proxy re-encryption protocol, we use bilinear mapping to improve the security of the key, and also resist the occurrence of collusion attacks by the proxy and the receiver.

3.3   Proxy Re-Encryption

Proxy re-encryption is a ciphertext conversion mechanism under public key cryptography(PKC). It was first proposed by Blaze et al. in 1998 [11], subsequently some improved schemes were proposed by [12,13]. Proxy re-encryption mechanism converts the ciphertext encrypted with data owner's public key into ciphertext encrypted with data user's public key and no leaks of private key or plaintext. Several main functions are as follows:

Init(). User initialization generates public and private keys. The input is as the security parameters 1^k, key generator generates (pk_A, sk_A), (pk_B, sk_B).

Encrypt(pk_A, m). Encrypt plaintext m with pk_A, return ciphertext c.

RekeyGen(sk_A, pk_B). Generate a re-encryption key according to A's private key and B's public key, return $rk_{A \to B}$.

Re-encrypt($rk_{A \to B}$, c). Use the $rk_{A \to B}$ to perform ciphertext conversion and return the re-encrypted ciphertext Rc.

Decrypt(Rc, sk_B). Decrypt the Rc with sk_B, return the plaintext m.

For example, the data owner Alice wants to share the data encrypted by her public key with Bob relying on the third-party proxy without leaking the private key and plaintext. The working process is as follows:

Alice and Bob call the function $init()$ to get their own public key and private key respectively. Alice uses the public key pk_A to encrypt the plaintext m to ciphertext c and stores c in cloud database. Then Alice combines part of her private key with part of Bob's public key to generate the proxy re-encryption key $rk_{A \to B}$, which is sent to the proxy. The proxy re-encrypts the ciphertext c to Rc using $rk_{A \to B}$, then sends Rc to Bob. Bob decrypts the Rc with his own private key sk_B.

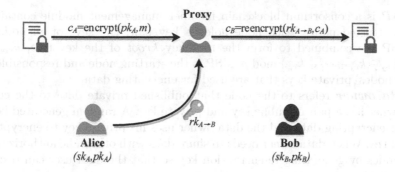

Fig. 1. The interaction process of proxy re-encryption

Proxy re-encryption has been used in many interesting applications, such as mail forwarding system [12], distributed file system [12] and so on. In our model, proxy re-encryption as a core stone in the data sharing scenario, can realize the trusted sharing of private data on the blockchain (Fig. 1).

4   System Model

The proposed model aims to solve the problem of private data sharing and hierarchical supervision simultaneously. In this section we present an overview of CROSS, then describe the model sub-module in detail.

4.1   Overview

Goals. The goals of designing the model are as follows:

Privacy-Persevering. In the process of private data sharing, the data will not be disclosed to any organizations or individuals other than the data owner and the authorized data user. The proxy re-encrypts the ciphertext, but it can not touch the plaintext;

Supervised. The authoritative node can calculate the key of the lower-level node according to the key generation policy, and can view the encrypted data at any time without informing the subordinate node, so as to realize data supervision;

Auditable. The data owner encrypts the data and publishes the digital digest to the chain, ensuring that the data is not tamperable. Simply, if the new digital digest is not the same as the one on chain, it indicates that the data has been tampered. The blockchain provides an effective way to acheive audit.

User Roles. There are five kinds of participating roles in the model, namely Membership Service Provider(MSP), data owner, data user, proxy server and authoritative node.

MSP is a consortium blockchain member management module containing a set of trusted nodes, each node holds a key pair, the keys of all nodes in the MSP are combined to form the root key $kroot$ of the key tree, $k_{root} = (k_{r_1} \oplus k_{r_2} \oplus k_{r_3} \oplus \cdots \oplus k_{r_n}) \bmod p$. MSP is the starting node and responsible for issuing nodes' private keys that are used for encrypting data.

Data owner refers to the node that published private data to the chain. Data owner has a pair of public key and private key. A random generated key is used for encrypting data and the data owner uses his private key to encrypt the random key. When data owner needs to share data with others, he authorizes the other nodes by generating re-encryption key so that the data user can decrypt data with his own private key.

Data user refers to the node that wants to get data from data owner and has been authorized by data owner. Data user requests proxy server to re-encrypt ciphertext, obtains the converted ciphertext and decrypts it using his private key. There is no limit to the hierarchical relationship between data user and data owner.

Proxy server refers to the server that converts the ciphertext encrypted by the data owner into a format that data user can decrypt when the data owner shares data with the data user. The data owner sends the re-encryption key to the proxy server, and the data user requests the proxy server to perform the re-encryption operation. Suppose the proxy server is semi-trusted, that is to say, the server performs this process accurately, but it will always try to understand the ciphertext.

Authoritative node is the relative concept of data owner, refering to the high-level node of the data owner. Authoritative node can calculate data owner's private key according to the key generation policy and view the encrypted data without authorization of the subordinate node.

Collusion Attack. The proxy re-encryption scheme in model resists collusion attack. In common BBS98 scheme [11], the proxy server and data user may collude to crack the data owner's private key, such as the proxy server has the re-encryption key $a^{-1}b$ and the data user provides b^{-1}, they can crack the data owner's private key a by simply calculating the inverse of the result a^{-1} that is from multiplying $a^{-1}b$ and b^{-1}. The proxy re-encryption scheme used in our model is based on bilinear group, that can defend against such attacks.

Malicious Access. Suppose a malicious user wants to write and read encrypted data. For write operation, data can be only written to the blockchain after the signature has been successfully verified. For read operation, there are only two conditions: (1) the authoritative node reads its subordinate node's data. (2) only the authorized user can read the re-encrypted ciphertext.

4.2   System Design

The tasks we completed with the CROSS model are as follows: First, the CROSS controls two processes, the registration and the key distribution. Then, the high-level authoritative node supervises the data encrypted by the lower node, and the nodes can share private data via proxy utilizing the re-encryption mechanism. Finally, for some invalid nodes, undo and reclaim their keys. It is mainly divided into three modules, namely key management module, data sharing module and data supervision module. Generally, the model can be described as $CROSS = \{keyManagement, dataSharing, dataSupervision\}$. In particular, the key management module includes two cases: add node and undo node. The overall architecture of the model is shown in Fig. 2.

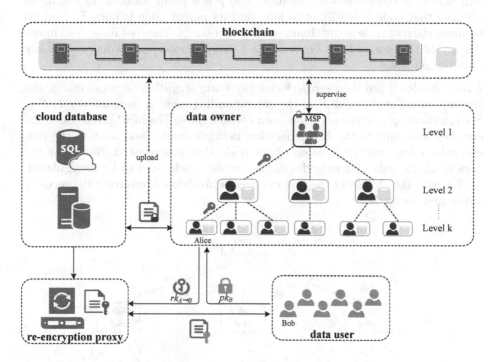

Fig. 2. The overall architecture of CROSS

Threat Model. We considered two attacks, collusion attacks and malicious access attacks.

Key Management Module. We have designed a key distribution mechanism based on tree structure, which effectively realizes the hierarchical relation of key management, as shown in Fig. 3. The key of each node is related to its parent node's key, and the path from the root node to each node is taken as one of the hash factors to generate keys to reduce the probability of repetition between two node's key. In order to achieve the security of the undo mechanism, the undo state value S is also introduced as one of the hash factors. When the key tree is established, the root key $kroot$ is set for the root node of the key hash tree, and the revocation state value S of all nodes is set to 0, indicating that it has never been revoked.

Add Node. Whenever a new node joins, its parent node requests the root node to distribute a key, and the root node calculates the key value of the new node according to the parent node key value, path value and state value. That is, the key derivation policy is: $k_{new} = H(k_{parent} \parallel path_{new} \parallel S_{new}) \bmod p$, among them, k_{parent} is the key corresponding to the new node's parent node, which is known to root node. $Path_{new}$ is the path from the root node to the new node. S_{new} represents the state value. $H()$ is the SHA-256 digest algorithm, $\parallel$ represents the concatenation operation, and p is a prime number. In Fig. 3, we suppose that node N is willing to join, and its parent node is node E. Node E requests the root node to distribute the key for node N. The root node determines the key of the new node as $k_N = H(k_E \parallel 010 \parallel 0) \bmod p$ according to the key distribution policy.

Undo Node. When the user performs key undo operation on some nodes, the key revocation state value S of the corresponding node is increased by 1, $S = S + 1$, indicating that the node has been revoked once. The MSP recalculates the new key according to the key generation policy formula, assigns it to the new user who takes over the location of the node that was revoked. Note that the keys of all the subordinate nodes of the revoked node need to be recalculated. In this way, the old key of the original user is invalidated, ensuring the security of the new user's data.

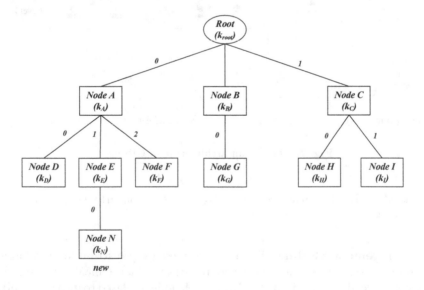

Fig. 3. The structure of key derived tree

According to the principle of asymmetric encryption, we generate public key and private key to each node in the consortium blockchain. In the previous section, we mentioned that the model uses the proxy re-encryption scheme based on bilinear mapping to improve the security of the key. The derived tree distributes the private key for each node, and the public key is generated according to the private key. So for node N, the private key of its parent node is $sk_E = (e_1, e_2)$, the private key of node N is $sk_N = (n_1, n_2)$,

$$n_1 = H(e_1 \parallel 010 \parallel 0) \bmod p,$$

$$n_2 = H(e_2 \parallel 010 \parallel 0) \bmod p,$$

the public key of node N is $pk_N = (Z^{n_1}, g^{n_2})$.

Data Sharing Module. In the data sharing module, there are three kinds of entities: data owner, data user and proxy server. The interaction process is shown in Fig. 4. In our scheme, the data set $DST = (metadata, edek, epos, hash(m))$ is published to the chain. The real ciphertext is stored in cloud databases.

In each round of sharing, the data owner always does this first: Generates a random key $dek = random()$ ($dek \in G_T$) for encrypting data, and uses the random key dek to encrypt plaintext m to ciphertext c, $c = encrypt_{sym}(dek, m)$. Next, the data owner stores the ciphertext c in the cloud database and returns the storage location pos, subsequently encrypts (dek, pos) with the public key to $(edek, epos)$, signs $DST = (metadata, edek, epos, hash(m))$ and then publishes it to the chain.

We take Alice as data owner and Bob as data user to illustrate the process of data sharing in Fig. 4. Alice and Bob already have $sk_A = (a_1, a_2)$, $pk_A = (Z^{a_1}, g^{a_2})$ and $sk_B = (b_1, b_2)$, $pk_B = (Z^{b_1}, g^{b_2})$. When Alice wants to share data with Bob, Alice generates the re-encryption key $rk_{A \to B} = rekey(sk_A, pk_B)$ based on part of her private key a_1 and part of Bob's public key g^{b_2},

$$rk_{A \to B} = (g^{b_2 a_1}), \tag{1}$$

and sends the re-encryption key to the proxy server. Note that every public key is visible to all nodes.

After the proxy server received $rk_{A \to B}$ and saved it. Bob gets $(edek, epos)$ from the chain and requests the proxy server to convert the encrypted data. In response, the proxy server accepts the re-encryption request from Bob and converts $(edek, epos)$ that needs to be decrypted with sk_A into $(edek', epos')$ that can be decrypted with sk_B,

$$(edek', epos') = re - encrypt(rk_{A \to B}, (edek, epos)). \tag{2}$$

According to the algorithm in [12], the ciphertext has two types:

(1) First-level Encryption E_1. The ciphertext can be only decrypted by Z^{a_1},

$$E_1(m, pk_A) = (Z^{a_1 k}, m Z^k). \tag{3}$$

(2) Second-level Encryption E_2. The ciphertext is used to do the proxy re-encryption operation,

$$E_2(m, pk_A) = (g^k, mZ^{a_1 k}).\tag{4}$$

The proxy re-encryption process can be understood as converting the second-level ciphertext of Alice to the first-level ciphertext of Bob. The plaintext need to be encrypted is (dek, pos). Input the $rk_{A \to B} = g^{a_1 b_2}$ and Alice's Second-level ciphertext $edek = (g^k, dek Z^{a_1 k})$, $epos = (g^k, pos Z^{a_1 k})$. According to the properties of bilinear mappings,

$$e(g^k, g^{a_1 b_2}) = e(g, g)^{b_2 a_1 k} = Z^{b_2 a_1 k}.\tag{5}$$

The result after the re-encryption conversion is

$$(Z^{b_2 a_1 k}, dek Z^{a_1 k}) = (Z^{b_2 k'}, dek Z^{k'}) = edek', (k' = a_1 k),\tag{6}$$

similarly, $epos'$ can be obtained. At this point, $edek'$ and $epos'$ are the first-level ciphertext that can only be decrypted with sk_B. Bob decrypts and gets the plaintext,

$$dek = dek Z^{k'} \cdot ((Z^{b_2 k'})^{b_2^{-1}})^{-1} = dek \cdot Z^{k'} \cdot (Z^{k'})^{-1} = dek \pmod{p}.\tag{7}$$

The pos is calculated in the same way. Bob gets the dek, which can be used to decrypt the data at the pos position.

Then proxy server sends $(edek's, epos's)$ to Bob for his decryption, Bob decrypts $(edek', epos')$ with sk_B,

$$(dek, pos) = decrypt(sk_B, (edek', epos')).\tag{8}$$

The dek can be used to decrypt the data in the cloud database located in the pos, and finally Bob generates a digital digest of the decrypted plaintext and verifies whether the data is tampered or not by comparing with the existing digital digest on the chain.

Data Supervision Module. The model is designed in the consortium blockchain scenario, the private key of the authoritative node determines the key of the subordinate node, and the authoritative node can have the permission of decrypting data encrypted by the subordinate node, but the ciphertext generated by the authoritative node cannot be decrypted by the subordinate node, in this way, while ensuring the anonymity of data, the content can be regulated and the availability of blockchain can be extended. In the data supervision module, it includes two entities: data owner and data user. The interaction process is shown in Fig. 5.

We take Alice as the data owner to illustrate the process of data supervision. The authoritative node wants to view the encrypted data after Alice encrypts the data and publishes it to the chain. The simple way for authoritative node is to

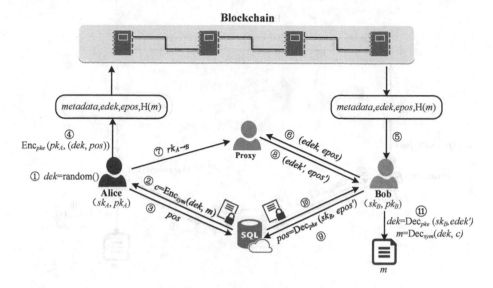

Fig. 4. The interaction process of privacy data sharing

calculate Alice's private key sk_A according to the key generation policy so that he can decrypt $(edek, epos)$ with sk_A to obtain (dek, pos). To obtain the key dek, the data in the cloud database located in the pos can be easily decrypted. Finally the authoritative node generates a digital digest of the decrypted plaintext, which can be verified whether the data is tampered by comparing with the digital digest on the chain.

5 Security Analysis

In order to meet the security of the CROSS, it is necessary to simultaneously satisfy the key management security, non-tampering of data and the invisibility of plaintext to proxy. In this section we analyze the security of the model. According to Theorems 1, 2 and 3, we prove that the proposed model is safe and feasible.

Theorem 1. *It is impossible for the lower node to crack the key of the authoritative node.*

Proof. In the model, the root node of the key distribution tree is composed of a set of trusted nodes. Each node holds a key, and the keys of all nodes are combined to form $kroot$, which ensures the security of the key distribution mechanism. Even if a single node in MSP is hijacked, the key of a subordinate node cannot be stolen. The key of each node in the tree is associated with the superior node. According to the characteristics of the hash function, it is easy for the authoritative node to calculate the key of its subordinate node, but the reverse is non-computable, which satisfies the requirements of supervision.

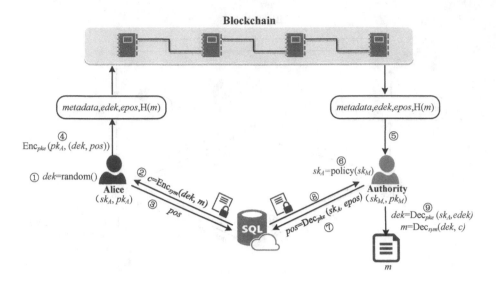

Fig. 5. The interactive process of data supervision

In addition, a revoked user can no longer read any data from the subordinate node with the original private key, after the user has been revoked, the revocation status value changes, the new node that replaces the revoked node will get the new key, and the private keys of all cascaded subordinate nodes will be updated, ensuring that only valid users can get the data.

Theorem 2. *The proxy server does not have access to plaintext.*

Proof. Data owners maintain an access control list that supports fine-grained access control of data and protects the privacy of data owners. Only the data owner can create a re-encryption key and set an access control policy, and the data owner can control other users' access to their data by updating the access list, that is, by adding or revoking the re-encryption key. In our model, it is assumed that the re-encryption proxy server is semi-trusted, that is to say, the server performs this process accurately, but it will always try to understand the data. Real data is encrypted using a random key *dek* generated by the dataowner, *dek* was encrypted to *edek* by the public key of data owner, the proxy server knows all the re-encryption keys, but it cannot get the real dek. Before performing re-encryption conversion, only the data owner can decrypt *edek*, after re-encryption conversion, only the authorized data user can decrypt the encrypted the *edek'*. The corresponding private keys are not revealed in the re-encryption process, thus the proxy server cannot access any plaintext data.

Theorem 3. *Malicious tampering with private shared data is impossible.*

Proof. The main advantage of blockchain is verified and non-repudiation. In our model, all access to data can be traced through the blockchain log. In order to ensure the authenticity of the data, the signature is verified before the data is published to the blockchain. The authentication mechanism allows real users to access the data. On the blockchain, the digital digest of plaintext data is stored, after data user decrypts the ciphertext, he can generate a new digital digest of plaintext locally to compare with the digital digest on the chain, confirming whether the data has been tampered with or not.

6 Conclusions

Considering the problem of data privacy concern and supervision on the current blockchain, we propose a blockchain-based supervised private data sharing model, combined with proxy re-encryption scheme and key distribution mechanism based on tree structure. It realizes the hierarchical supervision and private data sharing on the chain, effectively improving the privacy of the blockchain. The security of the model is analyzed and proved in the paper. In future work, we will use the consortium blockchain to conduct experimental research on the proposed model and evaluate the experimental results to improve the model.

Acknowledgment. This work was supported by the National Natural Science Foundation of China (No. 61672300), National Natural Science Foundation of Tianjin (No. 16JCYBJC15500), and Technology Research and Development Program of Tianjin (No. 18ZXZNGX00140). Jiqiang Gao has the same contribute to this paper with Mingxin Yin.

References

1. Ali, M., et al.: Blockstack: a global naming and storage system secured by blockchains. In: USENIX Annual Technical Conference, pp. 181–194 (2016)
2. Kokoris-Kogias, E., et al.: CALYPSO: Auditable Sharing of Private Data over Blockchains. Cryptology ePrint Archive 209 (2018)
3. Zyskind, G., Nathan, O.: Decentralizing privacy: using blockchain to protect personal data. In: Security and Privacy Workshops (SPW), pp. 180–184 (2015)
4. Xia, Q., Sifah, E.B., Smahi, A., et al.: BBDS: blockchain-based data sharing for electronic medical records in cloud environments. Information 8(2), 44 (2017)
5. Hardjono, T., Pentland, A.S.: Verifiable Anonymous Identities and Access Control in Permissioned Blockchains (2016)
6. Cui, S., Asghar, M.R., Russello, G.: Towards blockchain-based scalable and trustworthy file sharing. In: International Conference on Computer Communication and Networks (ICCCN), pp. 1–2 (2018)
7. Azaria, A., Ekblaw, A., Vieira, T., et al.: Medrec: using blockchain for medical data access and permission management. In: Open and Big Data (OBD), pp. 25–30 (2016)
8. Xia, Q., Sifah, E.B., Asamoah, K.O., et al.: MeDShare: trust-less medical data sharing among cloud service providers via blockchain. IEEE Access 5, 14757–14767 (2017)
9. Xue, T.-F., Fu, Q.-C., Wang, C., Wang, X.-Y.: A medical data sharing model via blockchain. Acta AutomaticaSinica 43(9), 1555–1562 (2017)

10. Xu, W., Wu, L., Yan, Y.: Privacy-preserving scheme of electronic health records based on blockchain and homomorphic encryption. J. Comput. Res. Develop. **55**(10), 2233–2243 (2018)
11. Blaze, M., Bleumer, G., Strauss, M.: Divertible protocols and atomic proxy cryptography. In: Nyberg, K. (ed.) EUROCRYPT 1998. LNCS, vol. 1403, pp. 127–144. Springer, Heidelberg (1998). https://doi.org/10.1007/BFb0054122
12. Ateniese, G., Fu, K., Green, M., Hohenberger, S.: Improved proxy re-encryption schemes with applications to secure distributed storage. In: Proceedings of the 12th Annual Network and Distributed Systems Security Symposium (NDSS) (2005)
13. Green, M., Ateniese, G.: Identity-based proxy re-encryption. In: Katz, J., Yung, M. (eds.) ACNS 2007. LNCS, vol. 4521, pp. 288–306. Springer, Heidelberg (2007). https://doi.org/10.1007/978-3-540-72738-5_19
14. Nakamoto, S.: Bitcoin: a peer-to-peer electronic cash system (2008). http://www.bitcoin.org/bitcoin.pdf
15. Wood, G.: Ethereum: a secure decentralised generalised transaction ledger. Ethereum Proj. Yellow Pap. **151**, 1–32 (2014)

A Survey of Trusted Network Trust Evaluation Methods

An-Sheng Yin[1]([⊠]) and Shun-Yi Zhang[2]

[1] Key Lab of Broadband Wireless Communication and Sensor
Network Technology, Nanjing University of Posts and Telecommunications,
Nanjing 210023, China
16629797@qq.com
[2] Department of Internet of Things,
Nanjing University of Posts and Telecommunications, Nanjing 210023, China

Abstract. The proposed trusted network is respond to the increasingly prominent internal network security threats. At present, research on trusted networks focuses on two aspects: pre-network access check and dynamic evaluation after access. The pre-access check considers the integrity of the terminal and uses encryption and authentication methods to achieve it. The dynamic evaluation uses the static and dynamic attributes of the trust to implement trust evaluation.

Keywords: Trusted network · Trust evaluation · Trust model

1 Introduction

With the rapid development of new technologies and services on the Internet, network and information security issues have become increasingly prominent. Most of the current information security threats come from within the network, and the attack methods present trends of intelligence, systematization, and integration. In order to make up the current decentralized, isolated, single defense, and externally attached network security system defects, the trusted network was proposed.

Trusted network studies the security threats within the network. The evaluation and control of internal entities on the network has become an important means for achieving network trust. Trusted network theory has also been widely used in fields such as IoT [1], MANETs [2], Cloud Computing [3], E-commerce [4], and Social Network [5].

The current network powers are racing to study trusted networks. The eID network trusted space construction scheme represented by South Korea and the European Union has been proved to be incomplete. The US government proposed the "trusted network space: Federal Network Space Security R & D Strategic Plan" in 2011 to give a roadmap for the development of trusted network, which requires an integrated approach to ensure the trust of cyberspace. China started earlier in the field of trusted computing. Teams represented by Zhang Huanguo and Feng Dengguo have achieved many successes in security chips, trusted security hosts, trusted computing platforms and applications. Lin Chuang conducted research on the trusted network architectures and prediction of user network behaviors.

J. Li et al. (Eds.): SPNCE 2019, LNICST 284, pp. 87–95, 2019.
https://doi.org/10.1007/978-3-030-21373-2_8

2 Trusted Network Connection

At present, research on trusted networks mainly focuses on two aspects: pre-network access check and dynamic evaluation.

In the stage of network access, the early research realized network trust through encryption and authentication mechanisms, and gradually developed into trusted network architecture based on trusted computing base, trusted chain, and trusted behavior analysis. There are Trusted Network Connect (TNC) architectures of Trusted Computing Group, Microsoft's Network Access Protection (NAP) architecture, and Cisco's Network Admission Control (NAC) architecture.

In terms of products, Huawei launched TSM (Terminal Security Management) solution; TOPSEC launched TNA (Trusted Network Access) access solution; Juniper developed TNC-compliant unified access control product "Juniper Networks Network Connect 8.0". These solutions or products are mainly used to implement system or device authentication, key negotiation, and establishment of trust connections.

The mainstream trusted access technologies that are generally accepted and widely studied at present are the TNC architecture and its basic technology TPM (Trusted Platform Module) module and the mobile terminal's trusted module MTM (Mobile Trusted Module). TNC implements trusted access based on integrity check. It will be one of the basic technologies for high-trusted networks because of its advantages, which will have a significant impact on next-generation information security solutions [6]. The current research on TNC focuses on the improvement of the TNC architecture and protocol, cross-domain authentication, session key agreement, IPSec SA, trusted certificate, two-way non-equivalent evaluation, trust chain transfer and other aspects [7–9].

The main function of the TNC architecture is to determine whether the terminal can access the corresponding network through the pre-access integrity and security check, and there is insufficient attention to the security measures after the access. Therefore, many researchers use the dynamic trust evaluation mechanism after access to achieve the terminal's full trust.

3 Trust Evaluation Model

In the field of dynamic trust evaluation, trusted network research lies in two aspects. One is applied to the Internet of Things, such as WSN, M2M, MANETs, IoV, etc. [1, 2]. The trust evaluation model achieved access control, secure routing, data forwarding, etc. under consideration of the energy consumption of the terminal, the computing capacity, the node mobility, and other issues [11, 12]. The other is used for inter-members interaction in social networks [5], commodities recommendation and consumers decision in e-commerce [4]. Device privacy and user privacy are also the focus of attention. Prasant has been paying attention to user privacy protection methods for reputation collection [13].

3.1   Dynamic Trust Evaluation Model

The dynamic trust evaluation models include behavior analysis model, multi-attribute decision model and reputation model.

The behavior analysis can be divided into equipment behavior analysis and user network behavior analysis. Device behavior analysis is used for identity authentication. Velten used touch screen interactions with smart devices to identify users by analyzing touch behaviors. Wesolowski combined keyboards, mice, and graphical user interfaces to increase the accuracy of authentication [15]. Peng et al. authenticate users more accurately by adding dynamic learning habits and preferences based on devices behavior identification [16].

Lin believes that trusted network should focus on the recording, evaluation, and prediction of online user behavior [17]. Tian proposed behavior-based terminal state analysis and trust decision criteria [18]. Meo combined the semantic analysis methods to determine the relationship between user behaviors and trust in social sharing networks [19]. Behavior analysis models are generally used to identify malicious behaviors [20], behavioral predictions [21], and so on. In the field of e-commerce, consumers recommendation can be made through users purchase behaviors [4].

The multi-attribute decision-making model carries out trust decisions by analyzing the attributes and attribute values that affect the user's trustworthy. The multidimensional trust decision attributes proposed by Li include direct trust, trust risk, feedback trust, incentive function, and entity activity [22]. Jameel et al. proposed a vector-based trust model in a pervasive environment. The model comprehensively considers attributes such as self-trust, historical trust, and time to reflect the dynamics of the trust relationship [23]. Liu selected the optimal trusted path based on the attributes such as interaction degree, interaction times, and self-importance [24]. Xiong selected the optimal trusted network component through multidimensional trusted evaluation index trees such as functional attributes, reliable attributes, security attributes, and aging attributes [25].

Trusted attributes include static attributes and dynamic attributes [26]. The static attribute evaluation mechanism implements the subjective trust evaluation of the trust evaluation subject based on the object's own attributes. The static attributes include the identity trust credentials and the inherent status information of the entity. The dynamic attribute evaluation mechanism implements the subjective trust evaluation of the trust evaluation subject for the object-related interactive behavior, and is related to the behaviors type, the bearer information, the number of successful interactive behaviors, and the subsequent influence.

Reputation model is one of the most widely used trust models. Since the beginning of this century, reputation mechanisms have been used to build trust models, such as TRUMMAR [27], EigenTrust [28], PeerTrust [29], and PowerTrust [30]. Josang often uses reputation models to calculate entity trust [31, 32]. Since the reputation value is derived from the recommendation and evaluation information among individuals, the reputation model is widely applied to P2P networks [28], Ad hoc networks, cloud platforms [33], e-commerce [34], and social networks.

In order to improve the performance of the trust model, the accuracy of reputation values can be improved by accumulating local knowledge [12], analyzing the relevance of the recommended values with Pearson correlation coefficient [33], or evaluating the volatility and consistency of the values [35].

Reputation model mostly uses graph theory to construct computational frameworks [36]. Du divides the model into multiple community structures [5], Yin divides the distributed system into several groups through group partitioning strategy [35]. Theodorakopoulos et al. calculated the shortest trusted path using semi-ring theory [37].

The reputation models study the assessment data collection and computation of network users, and is applied to multi-user interaction scenarios. The reputation model can be regarded as an extension of the behavior analysis model and the multi-attribute decision model. The behavior analysis model is used to analyze user interaction data to generate reputation values [33], and the multi-attribute decision model is used to distinguish multidimensional scenarios and applications and generate corresponding reputation values [34].

3.2   Trust Calculation Method

The trust evaluation model implements trusted network based on trust of the network entity. Trust is a measure of the mutual trust relationship in the network. It is similar to the trust relationship in human society and has the characteristics of timeliness, partial transitivity, ambiguity, and contextual relevance, anti-symmetry, composability, agglomeration, etc. [1, 38]. Referring to these attributes of trust, the algorithms used in the dynamic trust evaluation model include: discrete trust weighting algorithm, probability statistics methods, game theory algorithms, and fuzzy algorithms.

The discrete trust weighting algorithm comes from the composability and partial transitivity of trust, and the weight is divided into decision maker weight and attribute weight. The decision makers weight means that the evaluation subject weights include subjective, objective and combination weighting methods [39]. According to the sources of data, attribute weights are divided into subjective weighting method, objective weighting method and subjective and objective weighting method [40]. Discrete values and colloquial expression values are generally used to calculate discrete trust [41]. The discrete trust weighting algorithm is widely used because it is easy to calculate and understand. Mco uses the context and node depth information to determine the weight of the recommendation value [42]. In the current trust evaluation process, the trust of the user or terminal is calculated using the discrete trust model, dividing the trust level [23], setting the trust threshold [36], determine the trust strategy are become more and more common.

Discrete trust weighting model needs to divide trust grades, which will bring a new problem. If the grading is too broad, it may not get effective control effect. If the grading is too fine, it will cause the efficiency to decline. At the same time, performance distortion may occur at the boundary of the trust grades [43], which leads to the fact that the classification accuracy does not have a uniform distribution.

Because of the ambiguity of trust and the uncertainty of the trust relationship, it is reasonable to calculate the trust value based on probability and statistical methods. There are probability distribution models [44, 45], D-S evidence theory models [46], information entropy models [47, 48], and Bayesian models [31, 32, 49] and so on.

Ganeriwal [44] and Fang [45] build a trust model using beta distributions. Josang established the Bayesian trust model [31] and constructed a trust model using multiple evaluations based on the Dirichlet distribution [32]. Tian et al. proposed a P2P trust model based on recommendation evidence, and predicted node behavior through maximum likelihood estimation [46]. Wang enters the evaluation value of trust into the reverse cloud algorithm, converts the obtained expectation into trust, and reflects the uncertainty of trust through entropy and hyperentropy [47]. Ayday used the Bayesian network model to perform multi-conditional predictions based on the statistics of the previous behavior of the node, and made use of game theory to make decisions on trust results [49].

The game theory algorithm is used for trust decisions, it provides a tool to determine whether the terminal can interact with other terminals [52]. Sankaranarayanan proposed a trust-based game theory framework and algorithm [53]. Fallah used a multi-stage game strategy to solve terminal trust problems in mobile ad hoc networks [54]. Wu uses Stackelberg game to solve user trustworthiness in cognitive radio networks [55]. Yahyaoui uses the game theory model to improve the performance, robustness, and scalability of trusted services [56]. Pawlick proposed a games-of-game framework, which combines the advantages of FlipIt game and Signaling game to calculate the trust of the message [3].

Because of the fuzzy, dynamic, and complex nature of trust, fuzzy algorithms are also widely used in trust computing [46]. Fuzzy trust models rely on defining functions to reflect the degree of trust of nodes [57]. Damiani proposed a global method for calculating trust by summarizing fuzzy trust values [58]. Nepal transformed the user's opinion into fuzzy values and calculated the evaluation sequence accordingly [59].

More and more studies are now using uncertainty-based methods to calculate trust. For example, based on complex network and fuzzy decision analysis [60], cloud model [47], probability theory method [44], gray system theory [61], and group decision [62]. This is because trust is not only ambiguous, but also rough because the boundary of the confidence interval cannot be absolutely clear and causes the trust boundary to be indefinite or has an indiscernible relationship.

3.3 Further Discussion

Above Trust calculation methods always need to summarize trust data globally or locally. Due to the multi-source heterogeneity and mass characteristics of data, it is impossible to achieve real-time or quasi-real-time trust evaluation anyway. Real-time understanding of the state of internal entities is critical to achieving the trust of the network.

In order to achieve real-time or quasi-real-time evaluation of a trusted network, many considerations have been made from the perspective of reducing space complexity [63]. Ayday reduced the computational complexity of the edge function by means of factor graph and the Belief Propagation algorithm [49]. However, considering the continuous increase of data running with the network, this method cannot fundamentally solve the problem.

4 Conclusion

The security threats within the current network are becoming more and more prominent. The proposal of the trusted network is precisely to solve the security risks that appear within the network. Trusted network is achieved by calculating the trust of entities in the network. Behavior analysis model, multi-attribute decision model and reputation model provide a model framework for evaluation. Discrete trust weighting algorithms, probability statistics methods, game theory algorithms and fuzzy algorithms provide an algorithm framework for the calculation of trust.

The method of trust evaluation is quite mature. However, how to evaluate the security threats within the network in a timely and effective manner is an urgent problem to be solved. There is no effective solution at present, so we need to focus on and study.

References

1. Sicari, S., Rizzardi, A., Grieco, L.A., et al.: Security, privacy and trust in Internet of Things. Comput. Netw. Int. J. Comput. Telecommun. Netw. **76**(C), 146–164 (2015)
2. Cho, J.H., Swami, A., Chen, I.R.: A survey on trust management for mobile ad hoc networks. IEEE Commun. Surv. Tutorials **13**(4), 562–583 (2011)
3. Pawlick, J., Zhu, Q.: Strategic trust in cloud-enabled cyber-physical systems with an application to glucose control. IEEE Trans. Inf. Forensics Secur. **12**(12), 2906–2919 (2017)
4. Dan, J.K., Ferrin, D.L., Rao, H.R.: A trust-based consumer decision-making model in electronic commerce: the role of trust, perceived risk, and their antecedents. Decis. Support Syst. **44**(2), 544–564 (2008)
5. Du, J., Jiang, C., Chen, K.C., et al.: Community-structured evolutionary game for privacy protection in social networks. IEEE Trans. Inf. Forensics Secur. **13**(3), 574–589 (2018)
6. Sailer, R., Zhang, X., Jaeger, T., et al.: Design and implementation of a TCG-based integrity measurement architecture. In: Proceedings of the 13th USENIX Security Symposium, San Diego, CA, USA (2004)
7. Ma, J.-F., Li, X.-H., Jiang, Q.: Provable security model for trusted network connect protocol. Chin. J
8. Wei, D., Jia, X.-p., Wang, J., Liu, Y.-s.: New access model and implementation of trusted network based on trusted certificate. J. Jilin Univ. **40**(2), 496–500 (2010)
9. Qin, X., Chang, C.-w., He, R.-y.: Novel trusted network access architecture ETNA. J. Chin. Comput. Syst. **32**(8), 1493–1498 (2011)
10. Govindan, K., Mohapatra, P.: Trust computations and trust dynamics in mobile adhoc networks: a survey. IEEE Commun. Surv. Tutorials **14**(2), 279–298 (2012)
11. Vamsi, P.R., Kant, K.: Performance analysis of trust based geographic routing protocols for Wireless Sensor Networks. In: International Conference on Parallel, Distributed and Grid Computing, pp. 318–323. IEEE (2015)
12. Movahedi, Z., Hosseini, Z.: A green trust-distortion resistant trust management scheme on mobile ad hoc networks. Wireless Pers. Commun. 1–17 (2016)
13. Wang, X.L., Cheng, W., Mohapatra, P., Abdelzaher, T.: Enabling reputation and trust in privacy-preserving mobile sensing. IEEE Trans. Mob. Comput. **13**(12), 2777–2790 (2014)

14. Velten, M., Schneider, P., Wessel, S., Eckert, C.: User identity verification based on touchscreen interaction analysis in web contexts. In: Lopez, J., Wu, Y. (eds.) ISPEC 2015. LNCS, vol. 9065, pp. 268–282. Springer, Cham (2015). https://doi.org/10.1007/978-3-319-17533-1_19

15. Wesolowski, T., Kudlacik, P.: User profiling based on multiple aspects of activity in a computer system. J. Med. Inform. Technol. 11(6), 121–130 (2014)

16. Peng, J., Gao, N.: Research on identity trusted level evaluation mechanism based on user behavior analysis. Netinfo Secur. 9, 124–129 (2016)

17. Lin, C., Tian, L., Wang, Y.: Research on user behavior trust in trustworthy network. J. Comput. Res. Dev. 45(12), 2033–2043 (2008)

18. Tian, J., Liu, Y., Du, R.: Trust evaluation model based node behavior character. Inf. Int. Interdisc. J. 14(10), 3351–3371 (2011)

19. Meo, P.D., Ferrara, E., Abel, F., et al.: Analyzing user behavior across social sharing environments. ACM Trans. Intell. Syst. Technol. 5(1), 1–31 (2013)

20. Jung, J.J.: Trustworthy knowledge diffusion model based on risk discovery on peer-to-peer networks. Expert Syst. Appl. 36(3), 7123–7128 (2009)

21. Liu, C., Fan, M., Wang, G.: Unsupervised behavior evaluation method in trustworthy network. In: 2010 Second International Workshop on Education Technology and Computer Science, vol. 24, no. 3, pp. 78–82 (2010)

22. Li, X.-Y., Gui, X.-L.: Trust quantitative model with multiple decision factors in trusted network. Chin. J. Comput. 32(3), 405–416 (2009)

23. Jameel, H., Hung, L.X., Kalim, U., et al.: A trust model for ubiquitous systems based on vectors of trust values. In: Proceedings of the 7th IEEE International Symposium on Multimedia, pp. 674–679. IEEE Computer Society, Washington, D.C. (2005)

24. Liu, G., Wang, Y., Orgun, M.A.: Finding the optimal social trust path for the selection of trustworthy service providers in complex social networks. IEEE Trans. Serv. Comput. 6(2), 152–167 (2013)

25. Xiong, G., Lan, J.-l., Hu, Y.-x., Liu, S.-r.: Evaluation approach for network components performance using trustworthiness measurement. J. Commun. 37(3), 117–127 (2016)

26. Huang, C.: The study of dynamic trust relationship modeling and managing. National University of Defense Technology, Hunan (2005)

27. Derbas, G., et al.: TRUMMAR: a trust model for mobile agent systems based on reputation. In: IEEE/ACS International Conference, pp. 113–120 (2004)

28. Kamvar, S.D., Schlosser, M.T., Garcia-Molina, H.: The Eigentrust algorithm for reputation management in P2P networks. In: International Conference on World Wide Web, pp. 640–651. ACM (2003)

29. Xiong, L., Liu, L.: PeerTrust: supporting reputation-based trust for peer-to-peer electronic communities. IEEE Trans. Knowl. Data Eng. 16(7), 843–857 (2004)

30. Zhou, R., Kai, H.: PowerTrust: a robust and scalable reputation system for trusted peer-to-peer computing. IEEE Trans. Parallel Distrib. Syst. 18(4), 460–473 (2007)

31. Jøsang, A., Quattrociocchi, W.: Advanced features in Bayesian reputation systems. In: Fischer-Hübner, S., Lambrinoudakis, C., Pernul, G. (eds.) TrustBus 2009. LNCS, vol. 5695, pp. 105–114. Springer, Heidelberg (2009). https://doi.org/10.1007/978-3-642-03748-1_11

32. Josang, A., Haller, J.: Dirichlet reputation systems. In: Werner Beds. Proceedings of 2nd International Conference on Availability, Reliability and Security Vienna, Los Vaqueros, pp. 112–119. IEEE Computer Society (2007)

33. Coles, M., Kioussis, D., Veiga, H.: Reputation measurement and malicious feedback rating prevention in web service recommendation systems. IEEE Trans. Serv. Comput. 8(5), 755–767 (2015)

34. Tadelis, S.: The economics of reputation and feedback systems in e-commerce marketplaces. IEEE Internet Comput. **20**(1), 12–19 (2016)
35. Yin, A., Zhang, S.: A trust model based on volatility and consistency in trusted groups. J. Nanjing Univ. Posts Telecommun. (Nat. Sci.) **34**(3), 101–106 (2014)
36. Jiang, L., Zhang, K., Jian, X., et al.: A new evidential trust model based on graph theory for open computing systems. J. Comput. Res. Dev. **50**(5), 921–931 (2013)
37. Theodorakopoulos, G., Baras, J.S.: Trust evaluation in ad-hoc networks. In: Proceedings of the 3rd ACM Workshop on Wireless Security, pp. 1–10. ACM (2004)
38. Zhang, H.-G., Chen, L., Zhang, L.-Q.: Research on trusted network connection. Chin. J. Comput. **33**(4), 706–717 (2010)
39. Yue, Z.: An extended TOPSIS for determining weights of decision makers with interval numbers. Knowl.-Based Syst. **24**(1), 146–153 (2011)
40. Huang, D., Wu, Z., Zong, Y.: An impersonal multi-attribute weight allocation method based on attribute importance. Syst. Eng.-Theory Methodol. Appl. **13**(3), 201–207 (2004)
41. Carbone, M., Nielsen, M., Sassone, V.: A formal model for trust in dynamic networks. In: Proceedings of the International Conference on Software Engineering and Formal Methods, pp. 54–61. IEEE (2003)
42. Meo, P.D., Nocera, A., Quattrone, G., et al.: Finding reliable users and social networks in a social internetworking system. In: International Database Engineering and Applications Symposium, pp. 173–181 (2009)
43. Guo, Z.-q., Wang, Q., Wan, Y.-d., et al.: A classification prediction mechanism based on comprehensive assessment for wireless link quality. J. Comput. Res. Dev. **50**(6), 1227–1238 (2013)
44. Ganeriwal, S., Balzano, L.K., Srivastava, M.B.: Reputation-based framework for high integrity sensor networks. ACM Trans. Sens. Netw. (TOSN) **4**(3), 66–77 (2008)
45. Fang, W., Zhang, C., Shi, Z., et al.: BTRES: beta-based trust and reputation evaluation system for wireless sensor networks. J. Netw. Comput. Appl. **59**, 88–94 (2016)
46. Tian, C., Yang, B.: A D-S evidence theory based fuzzy trust model in file-sharing P2P networks. Peer-to-Peer Netw. Appl. **7**(4), 332–345 (2014)
47. Wang, S., Zhang, L., Li, H.: Evaluation approach of subjective trust based on cloud model. J. Softw. **21**(6), 1341–1352 (2010)
48. Sun, Y., Yu, W., Han, Z., et al.: Trust modeling and evaluation in ad hoc networks. In: Global Telecommunications Conference, GLOBECOM 2005, vol. 3, pp. 1862–1867. IEEE (2005)
49. Ayday, E., Fekri, F.: Iterative trust and reputation management using belief propagation. IEEE Trans. Dependable Secure Comput. **9**(3), 375–386 (2012)
50. Liang, H.-q., Wu, W.: Research of trust evaluation model based on dynamic Bayesian network. J. Commun. **34**(9), 68–76 (2013)
51. Hu, H., Chen, Y., Su, Z.: Weighted trust evaluation-based malicious node detection for wireless sensor networks. Int. J. Inf. Comput. Secur. **3**(2), 132–149 (2009)
52. Guo, J.-j., Ma, J.-f., Li, Q., Wan, T., Gao, C., Zhang, L.: Game theory based trust management method for mobile ad hoc networks. J. Commun. **35**(11), 50–58 (2014)
53. Sankaranarayanan, V., Chandrasekaran, M., Upadhyaya, S.: Towards modeling trust based decisions: a game theoretic approach. In: Biskup, J., López, J. (eds.) ESORICS 2007. LNCS, vol. 4734, pp. 485–500. Springer, Heidelberg (2007). https://doi.org/10.1007/978-3-540-74835-9_32
54. Fallah, M.S., Mouzarani, M.: A Game-Based Sybil-Resistant Strategy for Reputation Systems in Self-organizing MANETs. Oxford University Press, Oxford (2011)

55. Wu, Y., Liu, K.J.R.: An information secrecy game in cognitive radio networks. IEEE Trans. Inf. Forensics Secur. **6**(3), 831–842 (2011)

56. Yahyaoui, H.: A trust-based game theoretical model for Web services collaboration. Knowl.-Based Syst. **27**(3), 162–169 (2012)

57. Nefti, S., Meziane, F., Kasiran, K.: A fuzzy trust model for e-commerce. In: IEEE International Conference on E-Commerce Technology, pp. 401–404. IEEE (2005)

58. Damiani, E., Vimercati, S.D.C.D., Samarati, P., et al.: A WOWA-based aggregation technique on trust values connected to metadata. Electron. Notes Theor. Comput. Sci. **157** (3), 131–142 (2006)

59. Nepal, S., Sherchan, W., Bouguettaya, A.: A behaviour-based trust model for service web. In: IEEE International Conference on Service-Oriented Computing and Applications, pp. 1–4. IEEE (2010)

60. Ma, J.-y., Zhao, Z.-j., Ye, X.-y.: User behavior assessment in trusted network based on fuzzy decision analysis. Comput. Eng. **37**(13), 125–131 (2011)

61. Zhao, T.-z., Yang, Q.-h., Mei, D.-h.: Trust model for P2P network based on fuzzy set and grey relation. Comput. Eng. **35**(6), 173–175 (2009)

62. Cha, B.R., Sun, P., Kim, J.W.: A fake content remove scheme using binomial distribution characteristics of collective intelligence in peer-to-peer environment. IETE J. Res. **57**(5), 423–429 (2011)

63. Veltri, L., Cirani, S., Busanelli, S., et al.: A novel batch-based group key management protocol applied to the Internet of Things. Ad Hoc Netw. **11**(8), 2724–2737 (2013)

Anomaly Detection of Vehicle CAN Network Based on Message Content

Xiuliang Mo[1,2], Pengyuan Chen[1,2(✉)], Jianing Wang[3], and Chundong Wang[1,2]

[1] Key Laboratory of Computer Vision and System, Ministry of Education,
Tianjin University of Technology, Tianjin 300384, China
cpy1001@foxmail.com
[2] Tianjin Key Laboratory of Intelligence Computing and Novel Software Technology,
Ministry of Education, Tianjin University of Technology, Tianjin 300384, China
[3] Sichuan University, Chengdu 610207, Sichuan, China

Abstract. With the rapid advance of intelligent vehicles, auxiliary driving and automatic driving have been paid more attention to. While vehicle security has become increasingly prominent, which is seriously related to the property and personal safety. The attacker can send abnormal information to the controller through internal CAN bus. Because of the particularity of the vehicle CAN network information communication protocol, the encryption authentication technology cannot effectively solve the safety problem of the vehicle network. In the paper, a novel anomaly detection method based on CAN packet content is proposed. The scheme is effective in preventing in-vehicle ECU attacks caused by malicious modifications. Statistical thinking is adopted to analyze the characteristics of normal message content. Then a confidence interval based on normal features is defined for detecting abnormal network messages. Its detection performance has been demonstrated through experiments carried out on real CAN traffic gathered from an unmodified licensed vehicle.

Keywords: Anomaly detection · CAN network · CAN bus ·
Data frame · Mahalanobis distance

1 Introduction

Cars have become an indispensable tool in our lives. The car network is closely related to our lives. The CAN bus is currently the most widely used in-vehicle bus network technology. Because of its strong real-time communication, and short on-off cycle, the CAN bus has been widely utilized. However, with the increase in the

Our work is supported by the General Project of Tianjin Municipal Science and Technology Commission under Grant (No. 15JCYBJC15600), the Major Project of Tianjin Municipal Science and Technology Commission under Grant (No. 15ZXDSGX00030), and NSFC: The United Foundation of General Technology and Fundamental Research (No. U1536122).

J. Li et al. (Eds.): SPNCE 2019, LNICST 284, pp. 96–104, 2019.
https://doi.org/10.1007/978-3-030-21373-2_9

number of peripheral access interfaces of the networked cars, security problems have become more prominent. These interfaces can be utilized to access the CAN network, attack the CAN network, and forge the CAN message to allow the cars ECU to execute and consume ECU resources. These operations can directly send control instructions to the CAN bus of the car [6]. These hidden dangers are no longer as simple as stealing information and money, but actually threatening our personal safety.

The anomaly detection mechanism proposed in this paper is mainly for the anomaly detection of CAN bus data block. The CAN message primarily consists of ID block and data block. Only detecting CAN ID is unable to find whether the content of the message data block has an abnormality, the data field of CAN bus carries important control commands, sensor information and other key information to control the operation of the on-board system [7]. Thus, It is extremely significant to detect the anomaly of the data field of the CAN bus. The performance of the algorithm for the injection of malicious messages has been evaluated. Moreover, computational requirements of the algorithm are low enough to be compatible with the very limited hardware constraints of micro-controllers used to develop the ECUs (Electronic Control Units) embedded in modern vehicles.

2   Related Work

Kammerer et al. proposed the design of a star-coupled router as the central gateway for all sub-networks in the car to enhance the security of the CAN bus [3]. Each sub-network is connected to the router through the CAN interface system. The router has a routing configuration table. The router uses the information in the routing configuration table to detect and filter the CAN data frames. This method increases the cost and requires higher computing and storage capabilities of the router.

Groza et al. conducted various researches on the safety problems of the on-board CAN bus, proposed a series of light broadcast authentication protocols such as EPSB and Libra-CAN, and verified the availability of these protocols in the scenario where the number of ECU nodes is small [1]. However, in the real vehicle environment, involving multiple ECU nodes, the effectiveness of the algorithm is difficult to verify.

Studnia et al. proposed to design a state based anomaly detection system to determine whether the data frames transmitted on the bus meet the current state of the car (such as stationary, normal driving, and emergency procedures after collision) [4].

Many researchers tried to apply different neural network models to anomaly detection in CAN networks, such as recurrent neural network, deep neural network, and so on. Based on the trained neural network model, a predicted data packet can be output, and then the predicted data packet is compared with the real data packet, and if the error exceeds the acceptable range, an abnormal alarm is performed. Therefore, The sensor can identify malicious attacks on the vehicle [8–11]. However, due to the limited calculation and storage of the ECU, The proposed algorithm is constrained.

Narayanan et al. proposed a Hidden Markov Model to detect anomalous states. Using this model, while a vehicle is in operation, the system is able to detect and issue alerts [2]. Similarly, due to the limited calculation and storage of the ECU, The proposed algorithm is constrained.

The algorithm proposed in this paper mainly monitors the data frame of a CAN message. This design choice has several advantages over the prior art. First, We remark that proposed solution for improving CAN bus security complies with the hardware constraints of a typical automotive ECUs, having very low memory and computational requirements. Secondly, attacks against malicious tampering with CAN message data frame content can be detected in real time.

3   Preview

3.1   Controller Area Network

Automotive electronic components are connected in the car through the CAN network, and electronic components ECUs communicate via CAN messages. CAN network model is shown in Fig. 1. In CAN bus, ECU and ECU controller use data frame to transmit information, and broadcast messages to CAN network with specified ID. CAN data frame can carry 0–8 bytes of data, and the message can use 11-bit standard frame ID or 29-bit extension frame ID. The standard format of the data frame is shown in Fig. 2. It should be noted that the CRC field can only provide some form of protection against random modification of a CAN data frame. Since it is not built upon strong crypto and authentication primitives, attackers can inject data over the CAN bus or introduce arbitrary modifications in legit CAN data frames and easily compute a new valid CRC.

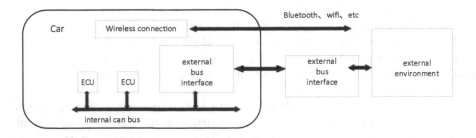

Fig. 1. On-board CAN network model.

3.2   Security Problems in CAN

Previous studies have pointed out the following security vulnerabilities in the CAN protocol.

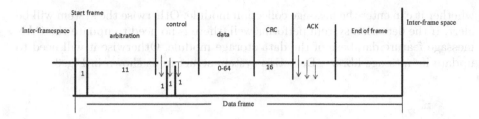

Fig. 2. CAN message standard format.

Lack of security mechanism: Every CAN message can be easily spoofed because it does not contain sender information and does not use any message authentication mechanism other than CRC.

Broadcast nature: Each CAN message is transmitted to all nodes connected to a single CAN bus, which allows an attacker to easily eavesdrop or analyze CAN messages.

Due to these security vulnerabilities in the CAN protocol, it poses a serious threat to today's smart cars.

3.3 Mahalanobis Distance

The Mahalanobis distance is an effective way to calculate the similarity between samples or between samples and their shared patterns. It is not affected by the dimension and can amplify small changes in the variable. It can also be used to identify outliers. The Mahalanobis distance was proposed by Indian statistician Mahalanobis in 1936. The generic formula for evaluating the Mahalanobis distance between the sample vector and population G can be found in Eq. 1.

$$D_M(x) = \sqrt{(x - \mu)^T S^{-1} (x - \mu)} \tag{1}$$

where μ and S represent the mean vector and covariance matrix of the overall sample G, respectively.

4 System Resign

4.1 Overview of the System

The whole system is generally divided into a model training part and a test part.

Training phase: After the message flows into the data processing module, the data frame is calculated by the method proposed in the paper to obtain the confidence interval of the data frame feature. The feature storage module is responsible for storing these features, which will be used to identify CAN data frame anomalies.

Test phase: The decision module is responsible for determining whether a CAN message has an exception. If it is a normal message, you can also control whether it can enter the message collection module. Otherwise the system will be alert. If the detection system performs well, there is no need to update the CAN message feature database of the data storage module. Otherwise it will need to update its message library. Detection system structure is shown in Fig. 3.

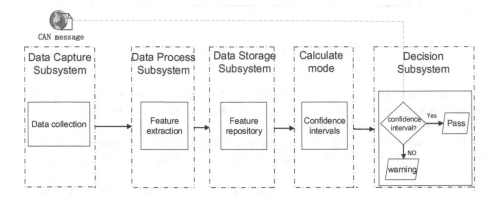

Fig. 3. System architecture.

4.2　Overview of the Proposed Algorithm

Since the CAN data frame can have up to 8 bytes, it uses 4-bit encoding. We assume that the data frame samples of the same CAN ID follow the same distribution. First, preprocess the on-board CAN bus message samples to obtain a standardized on-board CAN bus message samples. Samples of packets with incomplete data bits are self-filled to 8 bits, and all filled with 0. Finally, Normalized message samples are grouped based on the same CAN ID. Suppose the group has M sample vectors $X_1 \sim X_m$, each sample vector has 8 features (every 8 bits as a feature), μ and S represent the mean vector and covariance matrix of the overall sample G, respectively. The Mahalanobis distance is evaluated as shown in formula (1). The algorithm steps are as follows.

Then, we can define a confidence range $\left(\bar{x} - \frac{s}{\sqrt{n}} t_{\frac{\alpha}{2}}(n-1),\right.$ $\left. \bar{x} + \frac{s}{\sqrt{n}} t_{\frac{\alpha}{2}}(n-1)\right)$, where S is the variance of samples, n is the number of the samples, and $1 - \alpha$ is Confidence level (here take 0.95), $\bar{x}$ is the mean of all d_i values, and $t_{\frac{\alpha}{2}}$ value can be gained from table in [5]. The value of d falls below an empirical threshold $\left(0 < d < \bar{x} - \frac{s}{\sqrt{n}} t_{\frac{\alpha}{2}}(n-1)\right)$ or exceeds an empirical threshold $d > \bar{x} + \frac{s}{\sqrt{n}} t_{\frac{\alpha}{2}}(n-1)$ indicates that the value is abnormal.

It is worth noting that the t distribution is used because the experimental data collected can only be regarded as the sampling of the normal CAN message distribution, so we use the confidence interval of the Mahalanobis distance to perform anomaly detection, and the detection effect will be better.

Algorithm 1. Calculating Mahalanobis distance from data frames

---

Input: CAN bus messages $M = \{m_1, m_2, m_3, ..., m_n\}$
Output: Mahalanobis distance between samples and population mean vector $D_M = \{d_{M_1}, d_{M_2}, \cdots, d_{M_n}\}$
1: **for** each data frame **do**
2:     Group by ID
3:     **for** every 8 bit **do**
4:         Convert into decimal
5:     **end for**
6:     Calculate Mahalanobis distance
7: **end for**

---

5 Experiments

5.1 Experiment Setup

The data set used in this experiment is a real CAN bus data from an unmodified licensed vehicle, which contains 150000 CAN messages from the CAN bus with a speed of 250 kbit/s.

The data in its original state is a collection of text files containing comma separated values with ID, DLC fields (Indicates data length) and data fields. We divide the raw data files into different files by ID. For each different ID file, we assign 80% of the file data to the training model and the 20% file data is split into normal and simulated anomaly among the testing packets. Each byte in data field is an attribute of the message. The data frame is composed of 8 attributes (n0, n1, n2, n3, n4, n5, n6, n7) to represent the corresponding meaning in the communication protocol. In actual situations, the received CAN message needs to be analyzed based on the specific communication protocol. We convert the bus message from hexadecimal to decimal, which does not lose its attribute characteristics. The experimental data comes from the real vehicle environment and there are no abnormal messages. Therefore, we use the odd-order random method to generate abnormal messages. Each of these attribute value is obtained by a random assignment of 0–255. We inject these abnormal data frame into the message which CAN ID is legal to get the abnormal test data. Finally, these abnormal data are randomly mixed into the normal data as test samples.

5.2 Anomaly Detection

Select 500 normal CAN message with ID 0x10d as training samples. Take 200 abnormal samples randomly mixed with 300 normal samples as test cases and input to system for detection. The test results are shown in Table 1. It should be noted that for the attack of maliciously injecting data packets, the proposed detection algorithm has no false alarm, hence the false positive rate is 0.

Table 2 shows the range of Mahalanobis distances between the sample data frames of each ID and their overall samples. Figure 4 shows the detection rate of the different kind of CAN ID message. From the result, we can know that the anomaly

Table 1. Test results

Messages	Abnormal packets	Abnormal packets detected	Detection rate (%)
500	200	185	92.5

detection for the data field of the CAN message has different detection effect on different CAN ID. We find that the detection rate of an abnormal message whose data frame contains many 0 or changes less is high. In contrast, the detection rate of an abnormal message whose data field changes greatly is low.

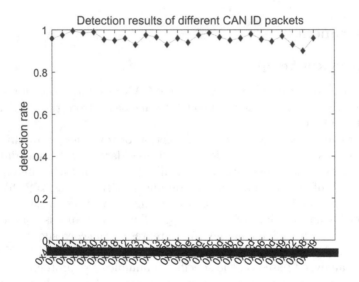

Fig. 4. Detection results of different CAN ID packets.

Table 2. Mahalanobis distance interval for different ID samples.

ID	1	2	3	4	5	6	7	8	9	10	11	12	13
min_{D_M}	1.117	1.534	0.884	0.868	0.903	0.860	1.621	1.410	0.873	0.865	0.913	1.029	0.861
max_{D_M}	5.298	3.938	5.620	4.725	5.738	5.634	5.534	5.050	5.507	5.532	4.158	4.956	6.021

5.3 Time and Memory Cost

This section gives an accurate examination of the computational complexity and memory requirements of the proposed algorithm to demonstrate its low computational requirements, making it suitable for common ECUs in modern vehicles.

Computational Complexity: Since the message transmitted on the CAN bus is binary, Sect. 4 discusses the real-time detection algorithm that requires the conversion of binary data to decimal. The time complexity required for this step is O(N), N is the number of digits required. When calculating the Mahalanobis distance between a CAN message data frame of a specific ID and its overall mean value, the required time complexity can be regarded as a constant, that is, the calculation can be completed in a linear time. The computational complexity of the final real-time detection is evaluated as O(N).

Memory Requirements: The proposed detection system requires the use of an index data structure to store a confidence interval for a specific ID with respect to the Mahalanobis distance. The size of the structure is evaluated as $N*L$, where N is the number of unique ID on the internal network (in this paper, 27 different CAN ID are found), and L is the number of bits required to store the confidence interval. The confidence interval data is FLOAT type. The memory of the FLOAT type consists of three parts: the sign bit (1 bit), the exponent part (8 bits) and the mantissa part (23 bits). So for the detection system, in the feature storage module, $2*32*27/8 = 216$ bytes is required, in the calculation module, $(8*8+8)*32/8 = 288$ bytes is required. $8*8*32$ is used to store the inverse of the covariance matrix of a particular ID, and $8*32$ is used to store the mean vector. Common low-end ECUs are generally composed by microcontrollers with 1 computational core, with few hundreds of Kilo Bytes of RAM. And its operations can be carried out by a common microcontroller equipped with a single core. Hence, the proposed live-detection algorithm can be implemented on common low-end ECUs.

6 Conclusion

A novel anomaly detection algorithm proposed in this paper detects the abnormality of the CAN message data frame, which can effectively prevent the attacker from maliciously modifying the content and launching an attack on the ECU in the vehicle. In this paper, when collecting vehicle bus messages, the collection time is not long, high speed and other conditions are not considered.

Future work includes not only the integration of our algorithms with detection methods based on replay attacks and traffic attacks, but also the study of the approximate location of tracking malicious ECUs.

References

1. Groza, B., Murvay, S., van Herrewege, A., Verbauwhede, I.: LiBrA-CAN: a lightweight broadcast authentication protocol for controller area networks. In: Pieprzyk, J., Sadeghi, A.-R., Manulis, M. (eds.) CANS 2012. LNCS, vol. 7712, pp. 185–200. Springer, Heidelberg (2012). https://doi.org/10.1007/978-3-642-35404-5_15

2. Narayanan, S.N., Mittal, S., Joshi, A.: Using data analytics to detect anomalous states in vehicles. arXiv preprint arXiv:1512.08048 (2015)

3. Kammerer, R., Frömel, B., Wasicek, A.: Enhancing security in CAN systems using a star coupling router. In: 2012 7th IEEE International Symposium on Industrial Embedded Systems (SIES). IEEE (2012)

4. Studnia, I., et al.: Security of embedded automotive networks: state of the art and a research proposal. In: SAFECOMP 2013-Workshop CARS (2nd Workshop on Critical Automotive applications: Robustness & Safety) of the 32nd International Conference on Computer Safety, Reliability and Security (2013)
5. Tang, D.: Probability Theory and Mathematical Statistics. Tianjin University Press, Tianjin (2009)
6. Miller, C., Valasek, C.: Adventures in automotive networks and control units. Def Con **21**, 260–264 (2013)
7. Taylor, A.: Anomaly-based detection of malicious activity in in-vehicle networks. Université d'Ottawa/University of Ottawa (2017)
8. Kang, M.-J., Kang, J.-W.: Intrusion detection system using deep neural network for in-vehicle network security. PloS One **11**(6), e0155781 (2016)
9. Kang, M.-J., Kang, J.-W.: A novel intrusion detection method using deep neural network for in-vehicle network security. In: 2016 IEEE 83rd Vehicular Technology Conference (VTC Spring). IEEE (2016)
10. Wang, C., et al.: A distributed anomaly detection system for in-vehicle network using HTM. IEEE Access **6**, 9091–9098 (2018)
11. Taylor, A., Leblanc, S., Japkowicz, N.: Anomaly detection in automobile control network data with long short-term memory networks. In: 2016 IEEE International Conference on Data Science and Advanced Analytics (DSAA). IEEE (2016)

Android Malware Detection Based on Sensitive Permissions and APIs

Chunhui Zhao[1,2](✉), Chundong Wang[1,2], and Wenbai Zheng[1,2]

[1] Key Laboratory of Computer Vision and System, Ministry of Education,
Tianjin University of Technology, Tianjin 300384, China
574878671@qq.com
[2] Tianjin Key Laboratory of Intelligence Computing and Novel Software Technology,
Ministry of Education, Tianjin University of Technology, Tianjin 300384, China

Abstract. With the widespread use of the Android operating system, the number of applications based on the Android platform is growing. How to effectively identify malware is critical to the security of phones. This paper proposes an Android malware detection method based on the combination of sensitive permissions and API features. This method extracts the permission features and API features by decompiling the APK file, and then uses the mutual information to select sensitive permissions and APIs as feature sets. On this basis, an ensemble learning model based on decision tree classifier and KNN classifier is used to quickly and accurately detect unknown APKs. The experimental results show that the discriminative accuracy of the proposed method is higher than that of the permission set or the API set alone, and the accuracy rate can reach up to 95.5%.

Keywords: Permissions and APIs · Android malware detection ·
Mutual information · Ensemble learning algorithm

1 Introduction

With the continuous development of mobile phone hardware performance, smart phones have become more and more popular in people's daily life, and the corresponding Android applications are also growing. Since Android apps can earn revenue through advertising, etc., many independent developers may pursue benefits and steal the privacy, property, etc. of the downloaded users, which results in the creation of a large number of malicious applications. In addition to the Google Play market, there are many other third-party application download

Our work is supported by NSFC: The United Foundation of General Technology and Fundamental Research (No. U1536122), the General Project of Tianjin Municipal Science and Technology Commission under Grant (No. 15JCYBJC15600), and the Major Project of Tianjin Municipal Science and Technology Commission under Grant (No. 15ZXDSGX00030).

J. Li et al. (Eds.): SPNCE 2019, LNICST 284, pp. 105–113, 2019.
https://doi.org/10.1007/978-3-030-21373-2_10

platforms on the market [1]. However, the supervision of relevant departments is often limited, resulting in some malicious applications flowing into the market, and the crazy spreading of people's downloads has caused huge losses to people. According to the 2017 Android malware special report released by 360 Fire Lab [2], the total number of malware samples on the Android platform intercepted in 2017 was 7.573 million, an average of 21,000 per day. Therefore, how to effectively detect malicious applications from a large number of programs to protect the security and interests of Android mobile phone users is a necessary and urgent challenge for researchers.

The paper proposes an Android malicious application detection method based on sensitive permissions and APIs. The method is mainly divided into two parts: training phase and detection phase. In the training phase, the permissions and API features in the APK file are extracted in batches by decompilation, and then use the mutual information model to generate feature sets with 10 sensitive permissions and 20 sensitive APIs ranking from high to low. The results of the two classifiers of the tree classifier and the KNN classifier are linearly correlated to generate the final result, which is used as an ensemble learning model. In the detection phase, using the above set learning model to quickly classify a large number of APKs. Experiments show that the detection method that combines sensitive permissions and APIs is more accurate than the detection by using permission or API alone.

2   Related Work

Malware detection and classification are challenging problems, especially on mobile platforms. Researchers have made great efforts to address these problems in various ways. In this section, the previous work addressing malware problems is discussed.

2.1   Dynamic Analysis Approaches

Android application dynamic analysis is to trace the relevant memory, such as register contents, function execution results, memory usage, etc., to analyze function functions, clarify code logic, and mine possible loopholes in the case of running code. The advantage of the behavior-based detection method is that it can handle the obfuscated encryption of the code very well. Many researchers have deeply analyzed the application from a dynamic perspective. Cai and Chen [3] proposed that there are some unique advantages of behavior-based dynamic detection techniques. The feature databases are small and do not require frequent updates. TaintDroid [4] identified sensitive information at a taint source, and tracked, dynamically, the impact of labeled data to other data that might leak the original sensitive information. The impacted data were identified before they left the system at a taint sink. DroidScope [5] collected detailed native and Dalvik instruction traces to track information leakage through both Java and native components. These dynamic methods all aim to conduct taint analysis to detect suspicious behaviors during runtime. However, behavior-based detection technology needs to be monitored in real time during the running of the program. It requires high automation and real-time, and requires more time and memory resources.

2.2 Static Analysis Approaches

Static code analysis is an analysis of code correctness and compliance that can be performed without executing a program. The advantage of static code analysis is the high speed of detection. Because there is no need to run, the detection speed is fast. Apposcopy [6] proposed a high-level language to capture the signatures describing semantic characteristics of malware families. Based on the extracted signatures, a static analysis was conducted to detect certain malware families. The literature [7] proposed a model based on API calls, and used the permissions available in various Android applications to capture the functions related to malware behavior, but there is a problem of high false positive rate in this model, which needs to be solved in the future. Literature [8] proposed a tool called Stowaway. With the help of this tool, people can identify whether the programmer has excessive permission to apply for permission during the development of Apps, because of this seemingly inconspicuous behavior there will be many security risks for the application. Wang et al. [9] considered each permission as a feature to establish a feature vector and distinguish between malicious programs and normal programs through classification algorithms. However, there are limitations to only having permissions as features, because this does not fully describe the characteristics of malware.

3 System Design and Implementation

The malware detection process framework designed in this paper is shown in Fig. 1. The main process is divided into two parts: feature generation and integrated learning model.

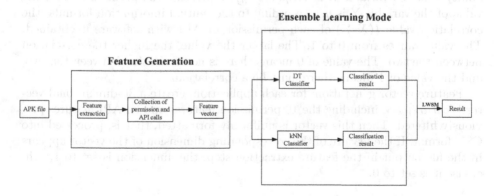

Fig. 1. Flow chart of malware detection

3.1   Feature Generation

The feature generation phase mainly includes three modules: feature extraction, generation permission application and collection of API calls, and feature vector generation.

Feature extraction: APK is the Android application package file, which is an application installation file format on the Android operating system. Structurally, APK is a file based on the zip file format, which is similar to the way jar files are constructed [10]. The permission information and API information used in this article are respectively stored in the manifest.xml file and the smali file. This article uses the python script file provided by the Androguard tool to decompile static analysis. For this purpose, a python script program is written to extract and output the application permissions and API calls information in the APK file to the specified file in batches in order to complete the first step of the experiment to extract features.

Generating a collection of permission requests and API calls: through the above, the permissions and API information of the application have been collected, but there are tens of thousands of known permissions and APIs, and malicious applications and benign applications are different in the permission applications and API calls. The extracted information features need to be filtered. This paper uses the mutual information method to filter out the top 10 sensitive permissions and the 20 top sensitive APIs (see Table 1). Mutual information can measure the relevance of specific permissions, APIs, with applications. A collection of permissions and APIs are choosed based on the relevance. The formula for mutual information is as follows:

$$I(X,Y) = \sum_{x_i}\sum_{y_j} p(X=x_i, Y=y_j) \times log\frac{p(X=x_i, Y=y_j)}{p(X=x_i) \times p(Y=y_j)} \tag{1}$$

Among them, the variable X indicates whether the permission or API appears in an application, the variable Y represents the category of the application (belonging to normal software or malware), and $p(X=x_i)$ indicates the probability that the variable X is x_i, $p(Y=y_j)$ represents the probability that the value of the variable Y is y_j. According to the mutual information formula, the correlation value $I(X,Y)$ of each permission or API with software is obtained. The value ranges from 0 to 1. The larger the value, the higher the correlation between the two. The value of 0 means there is no correlation between the two, and the value of 1 means there must be a correlation.

Feature vector generation: for each application, create a 30-dimensional vector $[feature]_{1*30}$, including the 10 permission features and 20 API features previously filtered. Then this vector is uniformly formatted, that is, processed into CSV format. If the feature of the corresponding dimension of the vector appears in the file output in the feature extraction step, the dimension is set to 1, otherwise it is set to 0.

Table 1. The 10 most sensitive permissions and 20 most sensitive API calls

	Permissions		API calls			
1	READ_SMS	1	sendMultipartTextMessage()	11	getSimOperator()
2	SEND_SMS	2	getNETWORKCountryIso()	12	getAccountsByType()
3	READ_PHONE STATE	3	openConnection()	13	getDisplayMessageBody()
4	READ_CONTACTS	4	chmod()	14	com.android.contacts()
5	RECEIVE_SMS	5	abortBroadcast()	15	getOutputStream()
6	ACCESS_NETWORK_STATE	6	writeTextMessage()	16	getDeviceId()
7	INTERNET	7	writeExternalStorageState()	17	getInputStream()
8	CALL_PHONE	8	sendTextMessage()	18	startService()
9	WRITE_SMS	9	getLine1Number()	19	getRunningTasks()
10	INSTALL_PACKAGES	10	getLastKnownLocation()	20	updateConfigurationLocked()

3.2   Ensemble Learning Model

The classification algorithm is trained by using the feature vector [11] of the collected samples, and then discriminates the unknown samples. Different classification algorithms are trained and tested for the same batch of samples, and the resulting classification results will be different. Therefore, using the ensemble learning method to classify the training of samples. This study uses the ensemble learning method based on kNN and decision tree to train and classify samples. In the ensemble learning model, a single weak classifier performs training prediction on the sample data, and then combines the prediction results of these weak classifiers to vote for the final prediction result. This approach reduces the variance of the base class classification by introducing randomness into the model building process [12].

Weak classifier: first of all, the kNN classification algorithm is easy to implement and understand, and it has high classification accuracy in the classification algorithm. In addition, KNN is an online technology, new data can be directly added to the data set without retraining, so the kNN classifier is more suitable than other classifiers. The "information gain" approach is used in the attribute selection of the decision tree algorithm, which is much the same as the mutual information method used in this study. Therefore, the decision tree classifier is used.

Weighted voting: better classification results can be obtained by combining multiple individual classifiers into one strong classifier. This paper assigns different weights to KNN and decision tree classifier. Finally, the weight of 0.4 is assigned to KNN, and the weight of 0.6 is assigned to the decision tree. If the detected application is benign, then result-DT and result-kNN are set to 1. Otherwise, set it to 0. In addition, our detection model has a threshold set to 0.5. This is because the probability that an unknown application is considered malicious is theoretically the same as a benign probability. Specifically, using the Linear Weighted Weights Method (LWSM) to calculate the probability that an unknown application is classified as a vicious or benign program. The linear weighted sum calculation is shown in Eq. 2:

$$Result = \frac{1}{2}(R_1 * P_1 + R_2 * P_2) \tag{2}$$

Where R_i represents the result of the classifier, its value is 0 or 1, which means that the application is a malicious application or a benign application. P_i represents the weight of the two classifiers, and $P_1 + P_2 = 1$. Based on this, the following four results are obtained:

- when result-DT = 1 & result-kNN = 1:
  Result $= \frac{1}{2}(1 * 0.6 + 1 * 0.4) = 0.5$
- when result-DT = 1 & result-kNN = 0:
  Result $= \frac{1}{2}(1 * 0.6 + 0 * 0.4) < 0.5$
- when result-DT = 0 & result-kNN = 1:
  Result $= \frac{1}{2}(0 * 0.6 + 1 * 0.4) < 0.5$
- when result-DT = 0 & result-kNN = 0:
  Result $= \frac{1}{2}(0 * 0.6 + 0 * 0.4) < 0.5$

If the result is equal to 0.5, the application will be judged as a benign application. Otherwise, it will be a malicious application.

4   Experimental Results and Analysis

4.1   Experimental Environment

In this experiment, 2474 normal applications and 3526 malicious applications are selected as experimental data sets. Among them, the normal Android applications are collected from third-party application market and Google Android Market [13] by using web crawler programs, and the malicious applications are provided by the malicious sample set of the virusShare.com [14]. The experimental environment is: operating system of Windows 10, processor: Intel Core i5, 4 GB of memory, Python 2.7 scripting languages.

4.2   Results and Analysis

In order to evaluate the detection model, testing a large number of samples for experiments and conducted multiple sets of comparative experiments to demonstrate the superior performance of proposed test models. The results of the experiment are evaluated by TPR, FPR, Precision and Accuracy.

Overall performance: as shown in Fig. 2, experiments are performed on 5,000 samples by selecting different features. The distribution ratio of test set and training set is 1:3. As can be seen from the figure, the overall detection accuracy of the model can reach 95.5%. Our proposed method of combining permissions and API as a feature has a better classification effect than the detection of a feature alone. It can be clearly seen that the single feature detection in detection

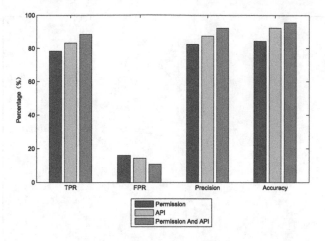

Fig. 2. Overall performance

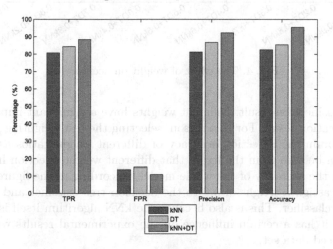

Fig. 3. Ensemble learning model performance

accuracy is lower than the permission and API combination detection. And our method has a significant reduction in the false positive rate, but the false positive rate is still high, which is a problem needed to be solved in the future. In short, the malware detection method proposed based on sensitive permissions and API has better detection results.

Ensemble learning model effect: the ensemble learning model is evaluated by comparing the combined classification method of k-nearest neighbors and decision trees with the classification method using only one of them. The effect diagram is shown in Fig. 3. Through Fig. 3, all aspects of using the ensemble learning model are better than using any of the classifiers alone, so using the ensemble learning model to detect and classify is effective.

Ensemble learning model weight selection: the ensemble learning model needs to assign a weighting ratio to the classification results of each classifier to obtain

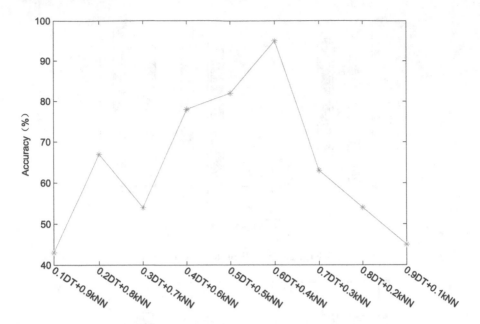

Fig. 4. The effect of weight on accuracy

the final classification result. Different weights have a significant impact on the final classification result. For this reason, selecting the test weighting interval to be 0.1 to obtain the detection accuracy of different weight ratios as shown in Fig. 4. It can be seen from the figure that different weight selection has a great influence on the accuracy of the whole model. According to the figure, the final choice is to assign a weight of 0.6 to the decision tree classifier and assign 0.4 to the kNN classifier. This is also because the kNN algorithm itself is relatively simple, and it has a certain influence on the experimental results when facing the unbalanced data set.

5   Conclusion

Starting from the two characteristics of the Android application's permissions and API, we collect the feature set of the application software sample through decompilation, and then extract the high-risk API and permission features using the mutual information model, and combine the two to generate the permission-API feature. The vector is then used to implement classification detection of Android malicious applications through an ensemble learning model. The simulation experiments on 3526 malicious applications and 2474 normal applications show that the proposed method has good effects on accuracy and true positive rate. This method can effectively improve the accuracy of Android malicious application detection, more comprehensively reflect the characteristics of Android applications, but the false positive rate of this method is still slightly higher, and we need further improvement in subsequent research.

References

1. Wu, D.J., Mao, C.H., Lee, H.M., Wu, K.P.: DroidMat: Android malware detection through manifest and API calls tracing. In: 7th Asia Joint Conference on Information Security, Tokyo, Japan, pp. 62–69 (2012)
2. 360 Campfire Lab: 2017 Android malware special report. http://blogs.360.cn/post/review_android_malware_of_2017-2.html. Accessed 3 Jan 2018
3. Cai, L., Chen, T.: Research review and outlook on Android mobile malware detection. In: Netinfo Security 2016, vol. 9, pp. 218–222 (2016)
4. Enck, W., et al.: TaintDroid: an information-flow tracking system for real time privacy monitoring on smartphones. ACM Trans. Comput. Syst **32**(2), 5 (2014)
5. Yan, L.K., Yin, H.: Droidscope: seamlessly reconstructing the OS and Dalvik semantic views for dynamic Android malware analysis. In: Proceedings of 21st USENIX Security Symposium, pp. 569–584 (2012)
6. Feng, Y., Anand, S., Dillig, I., Aiken, A.: Apposcopy: semantics-based detection of Android malware through static analysis. In: Proceedings of the 22nd ACM SIGSOFT International Symposium on Foundations of Software Engineering, pp. 576–587 (2014)
7. Sharma, A., Dash, S.K.: Mining API calls and permissions for Android malware detection. In: Gritzalis, D., Kiayias, A., Askoxylakis, I. (eds.) CANS 2014. LNCS, vol. 8813, pp. 191–205. Springer, Cham (2014). https://doi.org/10.1007/978-3-319-12280-9_13
8. Felt, A.P., Chin, E., Hanna, S., et al.: Android permissions demystified. In: Proceedings of 18th ACM Conference on Computer and Communications Security, pp. 627–638 (2011)
9. Wang, W., Wang, X., Feng, D.W., et al.: Exploring permission-induced risk in Android applications for malicious application detection. IEEE Trans. Inf. Forensics Secur. **9**(11), 1869–1882 (2014)
10. APK. http://zh.wikipedia.org/wiki/APK
11. Xiang, C., Yang, P., Tian, C., Liu, Y.: Calibrate without calibrating: an iterative approach in participatory sensing network. IEEE Trans. Parallel Distrib. Syst. **26**(2), 351–356 (2015)
12. Yang, Z., Wu, C., Zhou, Z., Zhang, X., Wang, X., Liu, Y.: Mobility increases localizability: a survey on wireless indoor localization using inertial sensors. ACM Comput. Surv. **47**(3), 1–34 (2015)
13. Google Android Market. http://play.google.com/store/apps?feature=corpusselector. Accessed 30 Jan 2017
14. Virusshare. http://virusshare.com. Accessed 30 Sept 2017

Security Assessment for Cascading Failures of Cyber-Physical Systems Under Target Attack Strategy

Hao Peng[1,2], Zhe Kan[1], Dandan Zhao[1(✉)], Jianmin Han[1], and Zhaolong Hu[1]

[1] College of Mathematics and Computer Science, Zhejiang Normal University, Jinhua 321004, Zhejiang, China
ddzhao@zjnu.edu.cn
[2] Shanghai Key Laboratory of Integrated Administration Technologies for Information Security, Shanghai 200240, China

Abstract. Due to the multi-scale fusion of cyber-physical systems, attackers can attack the physical space based on cyber space intentionally. This process can cause cascading failures and then in sharp contrast with the previous physical space. Thus, how to effectively evaluate the security of cyber-physical systems becomes critical. In this paper, we model the cyber-physical systems and then analyze the cascading failure process under target attack strategy. After doing that, based on the comparative analysis of simulation experiments, we analyze the main factors affecting the security of the cyber-physical system.

Keywords: Cyber-physical systems · Target attack · Cascading failures · Security assessment

1 Introduction

With the advancement of smart grid technology, the continuous integration of technologies such as information perception, ubiquitous computing has realized the interconnection and deep integration of physical space and cyberspace, and finally formed Cyber-Physical System (CPS) [1–3]. In CPS systems, communication network needs grid network to support power energy, while power stations are controlled by communication network [4, 5]. Then the CPS systems can be regarded as interdependent systems [6–9]. However, for interdependent system architecture, the failures in one network can lead to the cascading risk in another. For example, the breakdown of a power station network [10] could lead the corresponding nodes failure in communication network. Especially, the failures may even occur recursively between the two interdependent grid network and communication network [11]. The hacker may attack the physical space based on the information space due to the integration of cyberspace and physical space. That is to say, a node in one network is attacked or invalidated [12–14], may cause cascading failure of another network node. For this reason, it is very important that carry out security risk assessment and how to ensure that the CPS system operates stably.

J. Li et al. (Eds.): SPNCE 2019, LNICST 284, pp. 114–124, 2019.
https://doi.org/10.1007/978-3-030-21373-2_11

Many researchers have carried out research on security assessment of CPS system in recent years. The traditional reliability analysis method "fault tree analysis" [15, 16] is used in the security assessment of CPS systems such as intelligent transportation [17] and power system [18]. However, the derivative failure caused by the coupled relationship between the cyber network and the physical network in the CPS systems is not considered. Yang [19] and Chen [20] considered the cascading failure characteristics of CPS system, and simulated and verified the failure process based on interdependent network theory. But the type of attack in the actual CPS is often a highly targeted target attack [21, 22], and brings a large cascading failure risk to the CPS system. The abovementioned security assessment methods for CPS are mainly analyzed from the perspectives of single network attributes or a single random attack. And it lacks effective analysis of the cascading failure process and security assessment of CPS under actual type of attacks.

2   System Model and Basic Concepts

In this section, we mainly introduce the model of cyber-physics systems. We analyze the actual cyber-physical system and its types of attacks, and model the types of attacks to which the actual network is subjected.

2.1   System Model

By analyzing the connection relationship between the coupled systems, we divide the connection relationships of the coupled system into two types. One is the connection inside the network, we call it the intra-network connection, and the other is the connection between the networks, which we call the inter-network connection. In order to analyze the reliability of the cyber-physical system qualitatively, we assume that the connections between the nodes of the two networks are equal ratio connection. Without loss of generality, we set $N_A : N_B = 3 : 1$, which means one node in network B is connected to three nodes in network A, and this connection is completely random. Here we use N_A and N_B respectively to show the number of nodes in the cyber network and the physical network.

2.2   Basic Concepts

In the foregoing modeling process, the model of the cyber-physical system is a coupled network composed of communication network A and physical network B. The failure of the nodes in the A network will invalidate the nodes in the B network in turn. The cascading failure will stop in the following two situations. The process of cascading failure is a very important characteristic of the cyber-physical system after being attacked. It is completely different from the failure process of single network under attack. When a network is attacked, the network will splits into a larger component and some smaller components. We stipulate that only nodes satisfy the following two conditions can maintain the function [20, 22].

(1) A node in the current network must be connected to a node in another network.
(2) The node must be within the giant connected component.

The nodes that satisfy the above two conditions are called functional nodes. The functional node is a very important node in the network. When a network is attacked, only the functional node can be retained. There is no functional node in the network illustrate that the network has completely collapsed.

3   Theoretical Analysis of Cascading Failures Process

In this section we will establish a mathematical framework to analyze the security of cyber-physical systems under target attacks.

3.1   Target Attack in Cyber Network

We use $W_\alpha(k_i)$ to represent the probability of node i with degree k attacked in initial target attack:

$$W_\alpha(k_i) = \frac{k_i^\alpha}{\sum_{i=0}^{N} k_i^\alpha} \tag{1}$$

For the Eq. (1) we can see that the formula becomes meaningless when $\alpha = 0$. Therefore, we improved the above equation to get the following equation for the study of the actual coupling system:

$$W_\alpha(k_i) = \frac{(k_i + 1)^\alpha}{\sum_{i=0}^{N} (k_i + 1)^\alpha} \tag{2}$$

When target attack occurs, we assume that the ratio of nodes being attacked is 1-p, but we keep the edges of the remaining nodes which lead to the removed nodes. Assume $A_p(k)$ represent the number of nodes with degrees k, we can get:

$$P_p(k) = \frac{A_p(k)}{pN_A} \tag{3}$$

In the limit of $N \to \infty$, the Eq. (3) can be showed as derivative of $A_p(k)$ with respect to p. When $N \to \infty$ combining Eq. (2) with Eq. (3) we can get

$$-p\frac{dA_p(k)}{dp} = P_p(k) - N\frac{P_p(k)(k+1)^\alpha}{\sum_k P_p(k)(k+1)^\alpha} \tag{4}$$

The probability of edge deletion in the remaining node is equal to the ratio of the number of edges in the remaining node to the number of edges.

$$\tilde{p} \equiv \frac{p\mathrm{N}\langle k(p)\rangle}{N\langle k\rangle} = \frac{\sum_k P(k)kt^{(k+1)^x}}{\sum_k P(k)k} \tag{5}$$

Where $\langle k \rangle$ is the average degree of the original network A. Then we can obtain the generating function of the remaining nodes as follows:

$$G_{Ac}(x) \equiv G_{Ab}(1 - \tilde{p} + \tilde{p}x) \tag{6}$$

Equation (6) is the generating function of the remaining nodes after target attacked in network A. We can get $\tilde{G}_{A0}(x)$ from the equation $\tilde{G}_{A0}(1 - p + px) = G_{Ac}(x)$ as

$$\tilde{G}_{A0}(x) = G_{Ab}\left(1 + \frac{\tilde{p}}{p}(x - 1)\right) \tag{7}$$

According to the generating function of the network, we can obtain the generating function of the underlying branching process $\tilde{G}_{A1}(z)$ as follows:

$$\tilde{G}_{A1}(z) = \tilde{G}'_{A0}(z)/\tilde{G}'_{A0}(1) \tag{8}$$

When A' is attacked randomly to delete (1-p) proportion nodes, the degree distribution of the remaining nodes and the generating function of the corresponding degree distribution will change. The fraction of nodes that belong to the giant component is

$$g_A(p) = 1 - \tilde{G}_{A0}[1 - p(1 - f_A)] \tag{9}$$

We can get the iterative equation of cascading failure by the method of generating function and percolation theory.

3.2 Equivalent Random Failure in Network A'

We assume that the fraction 1-p of nodes fails due to the attack. Then we can find the number of remaining nodes can be shown as:

$$N'_{A1} = p \cdot N_A = \mu'_1 \cdot N_A \tag{10}$$

Where μ'_1 is the fraction of the remaining nodes. According to the previous analysis, we can know that the number of nodes belonging to the giant component in N'_{A1} is

$$N_{A1} = g_A(\mu'_1) \cdot N'_{A1} = \mu'_1 \cdot g_A(\mu'_1) \cdot N_A = \mu_1 \cdot N_A \tag{11}$$

3.3   Cascading Failures in Network B Due to A-Node Failures

Owing to the coupling of the cyber-physical system, the nodes in the network B will fail due to the failure of the nodes in the network A'. The number of nodes in network B that have dependencies is

$$N'_{B2} = \left[1 - (1 - \mu_1)^3\right] \cdot N_B = \left(\mu_1^3 - 3 \cdot \mu_1^2 + 3 \cdot \mu_1\right) \cdot N_B = \mu'_2 \cdot N_B \qquad (12)$$

Similar to the first step, we can obtain that the number of nodes belonging to the giant component,

$$N_{B2} = g_B\left(\mu'_2\right) \cdot N'_{B2} = \mu'_2 \cdot g_B\left(\mu'_2\right) \cdot N_B = \mu_2 \cdot N_B \qquad (13)$$

3.4   More Fragment in Network A'

According to the random failure of the first step, we can know that one node in network B may be connected to one, two or three nodes in network A', or may not be connected to any node in network A'. Based on the coupled system model, the number of nodes with dependencies in the network A' is

$$N'_{A3} = \mu_2 \cdot N_B \cdot \left[C_3^1 \cdot \mu_1 \cdot (1 - \mu_1)^2 \cdot 1 + C_3^1 \cdot (1 - \mu_1) \cdot 2 + \mu_1^3 \cdot 3\right] \Big/ \left[1 - (1 - \mu_1)^3\right] \qquad (14)$$

From N_{A1} to N'_{A3}, we know that

$$N_{A1} - N'_{A3} = \left(1 - g_B\left(\mu'_2\right)\right) \cdot N_{A1} \qquad (15)$$

The proportion of nodes removed from N_{A1} is equal to the same proportion of nodes removed from N'_{A1}. Then

$$N_{A1} - N'_{A3} = \left(1 - g_B\left(\mu'_2\right)\right) \cdot N_{A1} = \left(1 - g_B\left(\mu'_2\right)\right) \cdot N'_{A1} \qquad (16)$$

Thus the number of nodes belonging to the giant component in N'_{A3} can be found,

$$N_{A3} = \mu'_3 \cdot g_A\left(\mu'_3\right) \cdot N_A = \mu_3 \cdot N_A \qquad (17)$$

3.5   Further Cascading Failures on Network B Once Again

Similar to the second step, we can find the number of nodes with dependencies in the remaining nodes in network B

$$N'_{B4} = \left[1 - (1 - \mu_3)^3\right] \cdot N_B = \left(\mu_3^3 - 3 \cdot \mu_3^2 + 3 \cdot \mu_3\right) \cdot N_B \qquad (18)$$

As with the third step of the analysis process, we can obtain

$$N_{B2} - N'_{B4} = \left[1 - (\mu_3^3 - 3 \cdot \mu_3^2 + 3 \cdot \mu_3)/\mu_2\right] \cdot N'_{B2} \qquad (19)$$

Therefore, the fraction of the total failed nodes in network B is

$$\begin{aligned}
1 - \mu'_2 + \mu'_2 \cdot \left[1 - (\mu_3^3 - 3 \cdot \mu_3^2 + 3 \cdot \mu_3)/\mu_2\right] \\
= 1 - \mu'_1 \cdot (\mu_3^3 - 3 \cdot \mu_3 + 3) \cdot g_A(\mu'_3)
\end{aligned} \qquad (20)$$

According to the previous analysis of the cascading failure process, we can know the number of nodes in the network after each cascading failure. We can use the following equations to represent

$$\begin{cases} \mu'_{2i} = \mu'_1 \cdot (\mu'^2_{2i-1} - 3 \cdot \mu_{2i-1} + 3) \cdot g_A(\mu'_{2i-1}) \\ \mu'_{2i+1} = \mu'_1 \cdot g_B(\mu'_{2i}) \end{cases} \qquad (21)$$

Where $\mu'_1 = p$. Using a similar analysis process, we can get the iterative equations under different connection ways. When the connection ratio between networks is 2:1, the iterative equation for cascading failure is

$$\begin{cases} \mu'_{2i} = \mu'_1 \cdot (2 - \mu'_{2i-1}) \cdot g_A(\mu'_{2i-1}) \\ \mu'_{2i+1} = \mu'_1 \cdot g_B(\mu'_{2i}) \end{cases} \qquad (22)$$

4 Numerical Simulation and Analysis

4.1 Equation Solving

For the cascading failure of the coupled system, the network will not fail again when the cascading failure stops. So we can get the following equations:

$$\begin{cases} \mu'_{2i} = \mu'_{2i-2} = \mu'_{2i+2} \\ \mu'_{2i+1} = \mu'_{2i-1} = \mu'_{2i+3} \end{cases} \qquad (23)$$

In order to facilitate the analysis of iterative formulas for cascading failure, we define two variables x, y that satisfy the following equations

$$\begin{cases} y = \mu'_{2i} = \mu'_{2i-2} = \mu'_{2i+2} \\ x = \mu'_{2i+1} = \mu'_{2i-1} = \mu'_{2i+3} \end{cases} (0 \le x, y \le 1) \qquad (24)$$

Because of the complexity of the degree distribution of the network, it is difficult to solve this equation, so we use the method of drawing to find the approximate solution. First, we will write the Eq. (21) as the equations as follows:

$$\begin{cases} z = x \\ z = p \cdot g_B \left[\dfrac{p \cdot \left((x \cdot g_A(x))^3 - 3 \cdot x \cdot g_A(x) + 3\right)}{\cdot g_A(x)} \right] \end{cases} \qquad (25)$$

Then we will draw the two lines in the figure according to the two equations in Eq. (25). It is the solution of Eq. (21) when the two lines are tangent. As shown in Fig. 1.

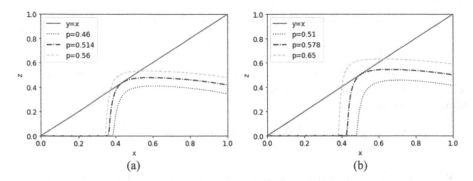

Fig. 1. Solving iterative equations

We take three values of p to represent the trend of curve change in Fig. 1. We can get more accurate theoretical solution by calculating the distance between curve and straight line. We can know that the critical threshold $p_c = 0.514$ when $\alpha = 1$ in Fig. 1(a). The curve and the straight line have no intersection point in the interval of $(0, 1)$. When the value is equal to the critical threshold p_c, the curve is tangent to the straight line. When the value of p is greater than the critical threshold p_c, the curve has two intersection points with the straight line. In Fig. 1(b), we know that the critical threshold $p_c = 0.578$ when $\alpha = 2$. And the Figs. 1(a) and (b) have similar laws. Then we use the same method to find the critical threshold under different connection ratios. From Fig. 2 we can get $p_c = 0.557$ when $\alpha = 1$ and $p_c = 0.614$ when $\alpha = 2$ corresponding to Figs. 2(a) and (b) respectively under $N_A : N_B = 2 : 1$. We also know that $p_c = 0.49$ when $\alpha = 1$ and $p_c = 0.559$ when $\alpha = 2$ corresponding to Figs. 2(c) and (d) respectively under $N_A : N_B = 4 : 1$. So far we have obtained the theoretical solution of the coupled system. In order to ensure the correctness of the results, we will verify the correctness of the results through simulation experiments.

4.2   Simulation and Analysis

In order to verify the correctness of the results through numerical simulation, we use the probability equations presented above to represent target attacks. In the process of simulating cascading failure, the number of nodes after each cascading failure will be saved in the file to facilitate analysis of the data. When no nodes are deleted in the two networks that make up the coupled network, the cascading failure is considered to have stopped. When the cascading failure stops, we will count the number of the remaining nodes in the two networks at the end of cascading failure.

In Figs. 3(a) and (b) we take the average degree of nodes of the two networks that make up a coupled system is $\langle k \rangle = 4$. But the parameter α in the probability equation is

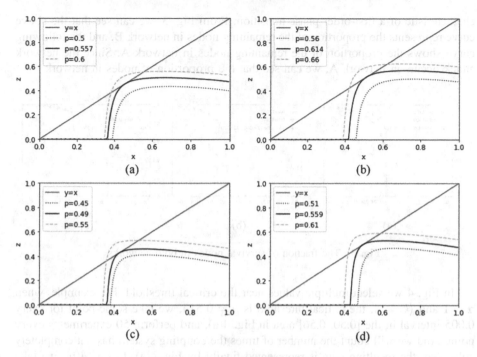

Fig. 2. Critical threshold solution

taken as 1 and 2 respectively. The proportion of nodes that were attacked was (1-p). The ordinate indicates the fraction of nodes remaining in the two networks when the cascade fails. In the process of simulating the cascading failure, in order to ensure the correctness of the experiment, we take the average value after repeat the 50 experiments for each p value. Moreover, we take two sets of p values near the critical threshold to better observe the reliability of the coupled system near the critical threshold. It shows that the reliability of the network is lower. The increase of α indicates that the probability of a node with larger degree being attacked is increasing. The reduced reliability of the network indicates that the experimental results are consistent with our expected results, and proving that our conclusions are correct. Comparing Fig. 3(a) with Fig. 3(c), we can see that as the average of the network increases, the critical threshold p_c decreases, and the decrease of the critical threshold indicates that the reliability of the coupled system is increasing. We have known that the connection between networks becomes closer when the degree of network increases, so the reliability of the coupled network will increase.

In the vicinity of the critical threshold that the position represented by the black arrow in Figs. 3(a), (b) and (c), we can see that when the value of p is greater than the critical threshold, the change trend of the two networks is close to a straight line. This phenomenon shows that the number of the remaining nodes in the network increases rapidly when the value of p increases near the critical threshold. This behavior is characteristic of a first-order phase transition. From Fig. 3, we can see that the above curve represents the proportion of the remaining nodes in network B, and the following curve shows the proportion of the remaining nodes in network A. Since the network attack occurs in network A, we can see that the proportion of nodes in network

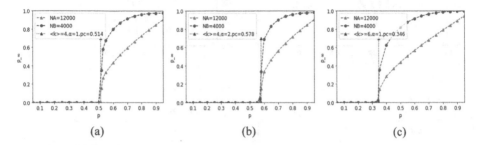

(a)   (b)   (c)

Fig. 3. The fraction of survival nodes in both networks

In Fig. 4 we select multiple values near the critical threshold. For example, when $\alpha = 1$ and $\langle k \rangle = 4$, the critical threshold is $p_c = 0.514$, we take some point for every 0.005 interval in the [0.50, 0.56] area in Fig. 4(a), and perform 50 experiments every point. And we will count the number of times the coupling system has not completely collapsed; the resulting data is represented finally by Fig. 4(a). In Fig. 4(b), we take $\alpha = 2$, and the remaining parameters are the same as in Fig. 4(a). From Figs. 4(a) and (b), we can see that the number of nodes for the coupled system increases from small to large, and as the number of nodes increases, the curve approaches the critical threshold. The critical threshold is indicated by a black arrow in the Fig. 4. We can see that the curve will produce a first-order phase transition near the critical threshold, which is completely different from the second-order phase transition in a single network when the number of nodes is large enough, which is similar to the phenomenon in Fig. 3.

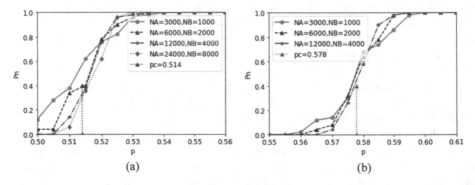

(a)   (b)

Fig. 4. The probability of having a giant component

5   Conclusion and Future Work

This paper proposes an analysis model and security assessment indicators for cyber-physical systems. Under the target attack strategy, the cascading failure process of the cyber-physical system for the attack behavior is analyzed. However, our proposed analysis model still has some limitations which could be our future work. For instance, we consider both networks are ER networks while the realistic CPS environment obeys the scale-free distribution. Meanwhile, the giant components could not always work in reality. It is also of interest to study models that are more realistic than the existing ones in this paper. Clearly, there are still many open questions about interdependent smart grid systems. We are currently investigating related work along this avenue.

Acknowledgements. This work was supported by National Natural Science Foundation of China (Grant No. 61602418, No. 61672468), Zhejiang Provincial Natural Science Foundation of China (Grant No. LQ16F020002), Social development project of Zhejiang provincial public technology research (Grant No. 2016C33168), MOE (Ministry of Education in China) Project of Humanity and Social Science (Grant No. 15YJCZH125) and the Opening Project of Shanghai Key Laboratory of Integrated Administration Technologies for Information Security (Grant No. AGK2018001).

References

1. Zhang, Y.: Health-CPS: healthcare cyber-physical system assisted by cloud and big data. IEEE Syst. J. **11**(1), 88–95 (2017)
2. Zhang, Y.: Agent and cyber-physical system based self-organizing and self-adaptive intelligent shop floor. IEEE Trans. Ind. Inform **99**, 1 (2017)
3. Cintuglu, M.H.: A Survey on smart grid cyber-physical system testbeds. IEEE Commun. Surv Tutorials **19**(1), 446–464 (2017)
4. Li, B.: DDOA: a Dirichlet-based detection scheme for opportunistic attacks in smart grid cyber-physical system. IEEE Trans. Inf. Forensics Secur. **11**(11), 2415–2425 (2016)
5. Li, B.: Distributed host-based collaborative detection for false data injection attacks in smart grid cyber-physical system. J. Parallel Distrib. Comput. **103**, 32–41 (2016)
6. Yağan, O.: Optimal allocation of interconnecting links in cyber-physical systems: interdependence, cascading failures, and robustness. IEEE Trans. Parallel Distrib. Syst. **23** (9), 1708–1720 (2012)
7. Saad, W., Saad, W., Maham, B.: A colonel blotto game for interdependence-aware cyber-physical systems security in smart cities. In: International Workshop on Science of Smart City Operations and Platforms Engineering, pp. 7–12. ACM (2017)
8. Zeng, X.: E-AUA: an efficient anonymous user authentication protocol for mobile IoT. IEEE Internet Things J. **99**, 1 (2018)
9. Xu, G.: A novel efficient MAKA protocol with desynchronization for anonymous roaming service in global mobility networks. J. Netw. Comput. Appl. **107**, 83–92 (2018)
10. Zhang, G.: Cascading failures of power grids caused by line breakdown. Int. J. Circuit Theory Appl. **43**(12), 1807–1814 (2016)
11. Liao, W.: Cascading failure attacks in the power system: a stochastic game perspective. IEEE Internet Things J. **4**(6), 2247–2259 (2017)

12. Xu, G.: An algorithm on fairness verification of mobile sink routing in wireless sensor network. Pers. Ubiquit. Comput. **17**(5), 851–864 (2013)
13. Dey, P.: Impact of topology on the propagation of cascading failure in power grid. IEEE Trans. Smart Grid. **7**(4), 1970–1978 (2017)
14. Zhang, X.: Modeling the dynamics of cascading failures in power systems. IEEE J. Emerg. Sel. Top. Circuits Syst. **7**(2), 192–204 (2017)
15. Yazdi, M.: Failure probability analysis by employing fuzzy fault tree analysis. Int. J. Syst. Assur. Eng. Manage. **8**(2), 1–17 (2017)
16. Rampurkar, V.: Cascading failure analysis for indian power grid. IEEE Trans. Smart Grid **7** (4), 1951–1960 (2016)
17. Younes, M.B.: A performance evaluation of a fault-tolerant path recommendation protocol for smart transportation system. Wirel. Netw. **11**, 1–16 (2016)
18. Sanislav, T., Zeadally, S., Mois, G.: Multi-agent architecture for reliable Cyber-Physical Systems (CPS). In: Computers and Communications, pp. 170–175. IEEE (2017)
19. Yang, G.: Synchronization control of cyber physical systems during malicious stochastic attacks. J. Tsinghua Univ. **1**, 14–19 (2018)
20. Chen, X., Zhou, Y., Zhou, H.: Analysis of production data manipulation attacks in petroleum cyber-physical systems. In: International Conference on Computer-Aided Design, p. 108. ACM (2016)
21. Sabaliauskaite, G., Mathur, A.P.: Aligning cyber-physical system safety and security. In: Cardin, M.A., Krob, D., Lui, P., Tan, Y., Wood, K. (eds) Complex Systems Design & Management Asia, pp. 41–53. Springer, Cham (2015). https://doi.org/10.1007/978-3-319-12544-2_4
22. Fang, Y., Zio, E.: Optimizing the resilience of interdependent infrastructure systems against target attacks. In: International Conference on System Reliability and Safety, pp. 62–67. IEEE (2018)

Privacy Preservation in Publishing Electronic Health Records Based on Perturbation

Lin Yao[1], Xinyu Wang[2], Zhenyu Chen[2], and Guowei Wu[2(✉)]

[1] DUT-RU International School of Information Science and Engineering,
Dalian University of Technology, Dalian, China
[2] School of Software, Dalian University of Technology, Dalian, China
wgwdut@dlut.edu.cn

Abstract. The patients' health information is often kept as electronic health records (EHRs). To improve the quality and efficiency of the care, EHRs can be shared among different organizations. However, the inappropriate sharing or usage of these healthcare data could threaten people's privacy. It becomes increasingly important to preserve the privacy of the published EHRs. An attacker is apt to identify an individual from the published EHRs by partial measurement information as background knowledge, with attacks through the record linkage and attribute linkage. To resist the above types of attacks, we propose a privacy preservation with perturbation in the published healthcare data (PPHR). To protect the privacy of sensitive information, we first determine the critical sequences based on which some specific records are easy to be identified. Then, we adopt perturbation on these sequences by adding or deleting some points while ensuring the published data to satisfy l-diversity. A comprehensive set of real-life healthcare data sets are applied to evaluate the performance of our anonymization approach. Simulations show our scheme possesses better privacy while ensuring higher utility.

Keywords: Privacy Preservation · Perturbation · Electronic health records

1 Introduction

The traditional paper-based health records may cause much inconvenience in collecting and storing various types of patient data. With the development of information and communications technologies, there is a great interest in moving from paper-based health records to electronic health records (EHRs). In 2003 and 2004, EHRs were used in 18% of the estimated 1.8 billion physicians in the U.S. In 2016, over 70% of physicians have used EHRs [20]. By storing a patient's medical history in electronic form, errors due to bad handwriting can be eliminated and it is easier for doctors to follow a patient's health condition.

© ICST Institute for Computer Sciences, Social Informatics and Telecommunications Engineering 2019
Published by Springer Nature Switzerland AG 2019. All Rights Reserved
J. Li et al. (Eds.): SPNCE 2019, LNICST 284, pp. 125–140, 2019.
https://doi.org/10.1007/978-3-030-21373-2_12

On the one hand, disseminating these data can provide better quality of care and thereby improve the public health [17]. For example, doctors in the San Diego Beacon Community (SDBC) can provide a cheaper, faster and more efficient diagnosis by obtaining the patient's EHR from his/her healthcare provider. On the other hand, researchers can benefit from the shared EHRs. In 2012, a group of UCLA researchers set out to mine thousands of EHRs for a more accurate and less expensive way to identify people who have undiagnosed Type 2 diabetes.

While the publication of EHRs is greatly beneficial, it can still entail a privacy threat for the users if some sensitive information is released with each EHR consisting of the patient's name, measurement history of physiological indicators, medical history, and other health data information. The measurement history or medical history is in chronological order which called healthcare trajectory or patient trajectory. A recent study has summarized that approximately 87% of the population of the United States can be identified by a given data set [26]. Therefore, it is critical to conserve the privacy of published health data, especially the sensitive information. The HIPAA Privacy Rule also proposed that the privacy of individually identifiable health information should be protected [15].

The original data tables or EHRs such as in Table 1 typically consist of four types of attributes, direct identifier, quasi-identifier, sensitive attribute, and non-sensitive attribute [8,25]. Direct identifier such as name and social security number can identify an individual uniquely, which is usually removed from the published tables. Each specific Quasi-Identifier (QI) such as healthcare trajectory in Table 1 cannot uniquely identify an individual, but the combination of some points can cause identity disclosure. Sensitive Attribute (SA) such as disease in Table 1 contains the private or specific information of each individual. Non-sensitive attribute can be known for the public without any concern. Based on the above attributes, it is obvious that privacy threats are related to those attributes except the last one.

Table 1. An example of healthcare trajectory dataset

ID.	Name	Healthcare trajectory	Disease	· · ·
1	Alice	$a1 \rightarrow d2 \rightarrow b3 \rightarrow e4 \rightarrow f6 \rightarrow e8$	HIV	· · ·
2	Ben	$d2 \rightarrow c5 \rightarrow c7 \rightarrow e9$	Flu	· · ·
3	Cary	$b3 \rightarrow f6 \rightarrow c7 \rightarrow e8$	Hepatitis	· · ·
4	David	$b3 \rightarrow e4 \rightarrow f6 \rightarrow e8$	Fever	· · ·
5	Eric	$a1 \rightarrow d2 \rightarrow c5 \rightarrow f6 \rightarrow c7$	Flu	· · ·
6	Frank	$c5 \rightarrow f6 \rightarrow e9$	Hepatitis	· · ·
7	Gina	$f6 \rightarrow c7 \rightarrow e8$	Fever	· · ·
8	Henry	$a1 \rightarrow c2 \rightarrow b3 \rightarrow c7 \rightarrow e9$	Hepatitis	· · ·
9	Kevin	$e4 \rightarrow f6 \rightarrow e8$	Fever	· · ·

1.1 Motivation

It is a challenge to prevent the disclosure of a person's specific healthcare data from the published EHRs so as to preserve his/her privacy. To achieve anonymity, the original records should be modified before being published. The existing privacy preserving approaches of publishing health data are classified into generalization and suppression, anatomization and permutation, and perturbation techniques [6,8]. Generalization or suppression technique aims to hide some details of QIs. Generalization replaces some QI values with a broader category such as a parent value in the taxonomy of an attribute. Suppression eliminates a certain number of points in the trajectory for privacy. Both techniques often result in considerable information loss by modifying the trajectory or sensitive attributes [21]. Perturbation distorts the original dataset by adding noise, aggregating values, swapping values, or generating synthetic data while preserving the statistical information of the attributes. Consequently, the transformed data after perturbation can provide higher utility [19].

By adopting the idea of perturbation, we consider the problem of publishing EHRs for more accurate analysis while limiting the disclosure of sensitive health information. Specifically, we want to ensure that an adversary cannot reliably infer the presence of an individual by linking some QIs. In this paper, we focus on the privacy breach caused by the healthcare trajectory in EHRs. For example, the sequence $e4 \rightarrow f6$ as background knowledge cannot infer a specific record in Table 1. Thereby, the privacy of each record is preserved. In this paper, we introduce a novel data perturbation approach to protect the privacy of sensitive health data and resist the following two kinds of attacks, record linkage and attribute linkage [14]. Record disclosure happens when a target user can be identified from a specific sequences in healthcare trajectory. Attribute disclosure occurs when some revealed attributes can link to a specific individual or infer a victims sensitive information. In our approach, we first identify the critical sequences in the healthcare trajectory that are prone to privacy breaches. For each sequence, we use addition or subtraction to implement l-diversity so as to ensure that each sequence matches at least l types of SA values in the published data.

1.2 Contributions and Organization

In this paper, we propose a novel scheme to preserve the health or medical privacy of EHRs with a single SA, named Privacy Preservation in Publishing Electronic Health Records Based on Perturbation (PPHR). Given all the above considerations, this paper has the following contributions:

- We propose our l-diversity privacy model to protect the sensitive information such as *Disease* in EHRs. l-diversity ensures that at least l records are matched by the attacker based on the healthcare trajectory sequence as background knowledge, which can be set according to the owner' s requirement.

- Our PPHR includes two steps, determining critical sequences and anonymizing data using perturbations. To the best of our knowledge, we are the first to perform perturbation to protect the sensitive attribute in EHRs.
- We evaluate the performance through extensive simulations based on a real-world data set. Compared with **PPTD** [14], and **KCL-Local** [4], our mechanism is superior in data utility ratio with better privacy.

The remainder of this paper is organized as follows. In Sect. 2, we discuss the related work. Preliminaries are given in Sect. 3. In Sect. 4, we present the details of our approach. Simulations on data utility are presented in Sect. 5. Finally, we conclude our work in Sect. 6.

2   Related Work

In this section, we mainly introduce existing approaches to prevent the privacy leakage of the published data from the following three categories, generalization, suppression and perturbation [8,28].

Generalization-Based. Generalization is one of the most common anonymity operations to implement k-anonymity for privacy protection. Generalization replaces some QI values with a broader category such as a parent value in the taxonomy of an attribute. In [12,31], a taxonomy tree was built first and then a node in the tree was generalized to its parent node, which aimed to reach k-anonymity. In [16], a node' s attribute was replaced by its sibling' s attribute. Generalization was first proposed in [13] to process trajectories and sensitive attributes based on different privacy requirements of moving objects. Gao [7] proposed to use trajectory angle to evaluate trajectory similarity and direction, and construct an anonymity region on the basis of trajectory distance so as to achieve k-anonymity. In [9], generalization technique is applied to anonymize the trajectory data and a heuristic approach is proposed to achieve LKC-privacy model. A look-up table brute-force (LT-BF) algorithm is proposed to preserve privacy and maintain the data quality based on LKC-privacy model by applying the generalization technique in [10].

Suppression-Based. Suppression approaches aim to replace some attributes with some special symbolic characters. It was first adopted to satisfy the constraint of breach probability in [29]. [4] was the first paper to adopt suppression to prevent record linkage and attribute linkage attacks. In [2], k^m-anonymity was proposed to suppress the critical location points chosen from the quasi-identifiers in order to resist the attacks based on the background knowledge of m moving points. In [24], locations suppression and trajectories splitting are used to protect privacy and ensure the accuracy of query answering and frequent subsets.

Perturbation. Data perturbation is considered as a relatively easy and effective technique in protecting sensitive electronic data from unauthorized users. There are two main types of data perturbation appropriate for EHR data protection. The first type is known as the probability distribution approach and the second type is called the value distortion approach. Perturbation distorts the data by adding noise, swapping values, or generating synthetic data [6]. In [1,3,30], noise was added to protect the privacy of sensitive attribute by achieving ϵ-differential privacy. Sensitive attribute values are exchanged among records to achieve data swapping [5]. Random edge perturbation was used to resist structural identification attack in [27].

Summary of Related Work. To prevent a specific individual from being re-identified from the published tables, the key solution is to protect the privacy of some sensitive information. In addition, the design of an anonymization approach should consider the balance between the data utility and the privacy preservation. Generalization and suppression often result in considerable information loss by modifying quasi-identifiers or sensitive attributes, which often causes severe loss of data analysis [21]. Comparatively, perturbation can maintain the statistical properties of published data without changing any sensitive attribute. In this paper, we adopt the perturbation technique to achieve l-diversity of the sensitive attribute. Compared with k-anonymity, l-diversity is practical and can addresses the shortcomings of k-anonymity with respect to the background knowledge such as record linkage attack and attribute linkage attack [18].

3   Preliminaries

In this section, we introduce some knowledge on the database of EHRs and two kinds of attacks.

3.1   EHRs Database

Patient healthcare trajectory [22] is a recent emergent topic, focusing on the patient trajectory based on disease management and care. A healthcare trajectory is similar to a moving path, which consists of many different positions at different timestamps. By regularly collecting the corresponding trajectory of one patient, the hospital can trace the patient disease and determine the relationship between disease and patient trajectory. The definitions of healthcare trajectory and electronic health record are given as follows:

Definition 1 (*Healthcare Trajectory*). *A healthcare trajectory is published based on the time order. Each trajectory point (such as a1) has two essential components, a measurement result (such as a) and a time stamp (such as 1), which indicate where a subject is get a measurement result at a given time instant.*

$$t = (r_1, t_1) \rightarrow (r_2, t_2) \rightarrow \cdots \rightarrow (r_k, t_k). \tag{1}$$

where k is the length of trajectory, t_i is a time stamp and r_i represents a measurement result of a data owner.

Definition 2 *(Electronic Health Record(EHR)* [23]. *An EHR is compose of several attributes such as ID, Name, Healthcare Trajectory, Disease and other attributes in Table 1.*

$$EHR = <ID, Name, t = (r_1, t_1) \rightarrow (r_2, t_2) \rightarrow \cdots \rightarrow (r_k, t_k), SA, \ldots>, \quad (2)$$

where SA represents the sensitive attribute such as Disease.

3.2 Privacy Attack

In this paper, we focus on protecting sensitive attributes in publishing EHRs such as those in Table 1. The attacker uses a sequence of at least one point in the healthcare trajectory as background knowledge to launch record linkage attack and attribute linkage attack and thereby infer the sensitive attribute of the data owner such as *Disease*.

- **Record linkage attack.** The attacker matches a specific record according to the trajectory sequence in the publishing data and can directly identify the specific data owner. When some trajectory sequences in the data occur at a low frequency, the attacker can easily identify the specific record of the data owner from the data. For example, we assume that the attacker knows that a data owner has a sequence $c2{\rightarrow}b3$ in the healthcare trajectory. It is easy to speculate that Henry has Hepatitis from Table 1.
- **Attribute linkage attack.** The attacker cannot lock to a specific record, but the SA distribution of the matched records is very concentrated. The attacker can infer that the data owner possess a certain attribute at a higher probability. For example, we assume that the attacker knows a sequence $c7{\rightarrow}e9$. He can infer that the data owner may suffer Flu or $Hepatitis$ with the probability of $\frac{1}{2}$ or $\frac{1}{2}$ respectively because the 2nd and 8th records contain this sequence.

To resist these two attacks, we anonymize the original data set T into T^* to achieve l-diversity. Assuming that the attacker uses the trajectory sequence with an upper bound length of m as the background knowledge. l-diversity is defined as follows:

Definition 3 *(l-diversity).* *The anonymized dataset T^* satisfies l-diversity if for any sequence q that does not exceed m in length, all records that q matches contain at least l types of SA values: $\forall q \in T^*, |SV(q)| \geq l$, where $SV(q)$ represents all the SA values associated with q.*

4   Privacy Preservation in Publishing Electronic Health Records Based on Perturbation (PPHR)

Our goal is to protect sensitive information in publishing EHRs by implementing l-diversity and to provide the data utility. The notations commonly used in this section are listed in Table 2.

Table 2. Notations

Notations	Description
T	The original data before being published
m	Maximum length of the trajectory sequence as the adversary's background knowledge
CS	Set of sequences whose SA values do not satisfy l-diversity
$T(q)$	Records including q in T
$SV(q)$	All the SA values associated with q in T
SP	Set of sequences in CS that need subtraction operation
AP	Set of sequences in CS that need addition operation

4.1   Overview

Our PPHR aims to protect the privacy of sensitive attribute and resist the attacks based on the background knowledge of a part of healthcare trajectory. PPHR can be divided into two steps: identifying critical sequences in the trajectory data and anonymizing the dataset T. A critical sequence is one whose length does not exceed m and the number of SA values corresponding to this sequence does not satisfy l-diversity. To achieve l-diversity of SA values, we implement perturbation by adding or subtracting points in the trajectory sequences including the critical sequences as shown in Fig. 1:

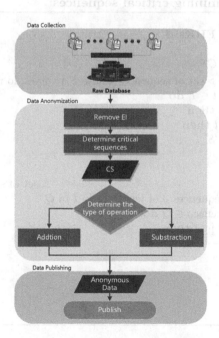

Fig. 1. Architecture of PPHR

4.2   Algorithm

In order to achieve l-diversity of SA values, we use perturbation to obscure the correlation between healthcare trajectory and SA. We first identify the critical sequences that are easy to reveal the privacy of patients, and then revise the matching records of these sequences to achieve l-diversity.

Determining Critical Sequences. In this process, we find those sequences whose length is equal to m and does not satisfy l-diversity. The steps to determine the critical sequence in the trajectory are listed as follows:

Step 1: First, the trajectory sequences of length m in each record are determined. In addition, if the whole length of a user's health trajectory is less than m, the trajectory will be checked whether it can be treated as a critical sequence in the next step.

Step 2: For each sequence q got in **Step** 1, if the number of types of the corresponding SA values matched by q in T is less than l, i.e. $|SV(q)| < l$, q will be regarded as a critical sequence and be added into CS, where $|SV(q)|$ represents all the SA values associated with q in T and CS is the set of sequences whose SA values do not satisfy l-diversity.

Algorithm 1. Determining critical sequences

Require:
   Original dataset of EHRs: T
Ensure:
   Critical sequences: CS
 1: $CS \leftarrow Null$ ▷ set of sequences whose SA values do not satisfy l-diversity.
 2: **for** each trajectory $t \in T$ **do**
 3:    **if** $length(t) \leq m$ **then**
 4:       **if** $|SV(t)| < l$ **then**
 5:          $add\ t \rightarrow CS$
 6:       **end if**
 7:    **else**
 8:       $Q \leftarrow Null$ ▷ set of sequences of length m
 9:       Add all the sequences q of length m in t to Q
10:       **for** each sequence$q \in Q$ **do**
11:          **if** $|SV(t)| < l$ **then**
12:             $add\ q \rightarrow CS$
13:          **end if**
14:       **end for**
15:    **end if**
16: **end for**
17: $return\ CS$

Performing the Anonymization. In this process, we execute addition or substraction operation to make SA satisfy l-diversity. For each sequence q in CS, we first determine the addition or substraction operation by evaluating the data utility. Then, l-diversity of SA values corresponding to q will be satisfied by adding or substracting points in the healthcare trajectory of records corresponding to q.

Algorithm 2. Performing the anonymization

Require:
  Original dataset of EHRs:T
Ensure:
  Anonymous dataset of EHRs: T^*
1: $T^* \leftarrow T$
2: $CS \leftarrow Null$ $\triangleright$ set of sequences whose SA values do not satisfy l-diversity.
3: $SP \leftarrow Null$ $\triangleright$ Set of sequences in CS that need substraction operation.
4: $AP \leftarrow Null$ $\triangleright$ Set of sequences in CS that need addition operation.
5: **for** each sequence $q \in CS$ **do**
6:      **if** $|T(q)| \leq (l - |SV(q)|) * |q|$ **then**
7:         add $q \rightarrow SP$
8:      **else**
9:         add $q \rightarrow AP$
10:    **end if**
11: **end for**
12: **for** each sequence $q \in SP$ **do**
13:    **for** each point $p \in q$ **do**
14:        **if** no new critical sequence caused by subtracting p **then**
15:           $subtracting\ p\ from\ T^*(q)$
16:        **end if**
17:    **end for**
18: **end for**
19: **for** each $sequence \in AD$ **do**
20:    $AlterRec \leftarrow Null$ $\triangleright$ The records can be constructed q
21:    Add the records whose SA values are not in $SV(q)$ and there is no location conflict at the corresponding timestamp into $AlterRec$
22:    sort $AlterRec$ by LCS
23:    constructed q in first $l - |SV(q)|$ records of $AlterRec$ in T^*
24: **end for**
25: $return\ T^*$

Step 1: We define the following criteria to determine addition or substraction operation,

$$CR(q) = |T(q)| - (l - |SV(q)|) * |q|, \tag{3}$$

where $|T(q)|$ represents the number of records that include q, $SV(q)$ all the SA values associated with q, and $|q|$ the length of q. When l-diversity is not satisfied, $l - |SV(q)|$ indicates the number of different SA values that need to be added in order to satisfy l-diversity. $(l - |SV(q)|) * |q|$ represents the upper limit of number of points to be add to achieve l-diversity. $CR(q) \leq 0$ means the number of points modified in the anonymized data will be smaller if the subtraction operation is executed. In this case, a better data utility can be provided. q will be add to the set SP. Otherwise, if $CR(q) > 0$ holds, the addition operation is necessary and q will be add to the set AP.

Step 2: For each critical sequence q in SP, we use the subtraction method to eliminate q from T, but a new critical sequence cannot be generated. When a special point is moved from all the records in $T(q)$, q will not appear any more in the published data. Consequently, there is no any privacy leakage caused by q. If a new critical sequence is caused by executing the subtraction operation, q will be added into AD.

For example, 2-diversity is not satisfied for the sequence $q = f6 \rightarrow e9$ in Table 1, because there is only one SA value such as Ben's disease. To achieve 2-diversity, we execute subtraction to process q. If $f6$ is moved from $q = f6 \rightarrow e9$, $e9$ can achieve 2-diversity such as the 2nd and 8th records in Table 1. But, $c5 \rightarrow f6$ will be a new critical sequence, because only one value for this sequence such as the 5th record exists. If $e9$ is moved from $q = f6 \rightarrow e9$, there is no new critical sequence generated. Finally, we will subtract $e9$ to eliminate the privacy threat of the original sequence $q = f6 \rightarrow e9$.

Step 3: For each sequence q in AP, we use addition operation to construct q on the selected records to satisfy l-diversity.

First of all, we select the records whose SA values are not in $SV(q)$ because we must increase the variety of SA values in order to achieve l-diversity. In addition, we need to add points at some timestamps to construct q. When adding a point, we must ensure that there is no same point at the corresponding timestamp in T.

Last, we use the Longest Common Subsequence (LCS) to sort the selected records. A sequence will be the longest common subsequence if it is a subsequence of two or more sequences and is the longest of all subsequences. For example, the LCS of $a1 \rightarrow d2 \rightarrow c5 \rightarrow f6 \rightarrow c7$ and $c5 \rightarrow f6 \rightarrow e9$ is $c5 \rightarrow f6$. We choose $l - |SV(q)|$ records which have longer LCS to construct q to satisfy l-diversity.

4.3   Privacy Analysis

In our algorithm, we only need to consider sequences of length m. We use perturbation to process the sequences of length m to achieve l-diversity of SA. In this section, we aim to prove that those sequences of length less than m make l-diversity be satisfied if l-diversity is met for all sequences of length m.

For each sequence q of length less than m, we assume q is the subsequence of n parent sequences $q_1, q_2..., q_n$ which q_i represents a sequence of length m. The records in $SV(q)$ are composed of all records in $SV(q_i)$ for $i = 1 \cdots n$. We can get the following equations:

$$SV(q) = SV(q_1) \cup SV(q_2) \cdots \cup SV(q_n)$$
$$|SV(q)| = |SV(q_1) \cup \cdots \cup SV(q_n)|$$
$$\geq |SV(q_i)|$$
$$\geq l \tag{4}$$

Consequently, we can prove that all the sequences of length no more than m can make *l-diversity* be satisfied in the anonymized data T^*. l-diversity of the SA values is achieved in T^*.

5   Performance Evaluations

To evaluate the performance of our PPHR, we use a real-world dataset **MIMIC-III** dataset [11]. MIMIC is a publicly available data set which includes identified health data associated with approximately 40,000 patients. It includes personal information, diagnostic information, medication information, measurement results, etc. We selected the health data of 11,047 patients. *Disease* as SA contains 32 possible values and 8 of them are considered as sensitive values. The health measurement history of these 11,047 patients contains 90 types of disease and 24 different timestamps. We implement our PPHR algorithm in Python. We evaluate the performance on a PC with an Intel Core i7 2.5 GHz CPU and 8 GB RAM.

We compare our PPHR with **PPTD** [14], and **KCL-Local** [4]. **KCL-Local** combines local suppression and global suppression to implement $(k, C)_m$-privacy model. $(k, C)_m$-privacy model can implement k-anonymity to resist record linkage attack and implement C confidence to resist attribute linkage attack. m is the upper limit of the attacker's background knowledge as defined in this paper. **PPTD** achieve personalized privacy with sensitive attribute generalization and trajectory local suppression which also resist record linkage attack and attribute linkage attack.

5.1   Utility Loss

In this section, we the following metrics to evaluate the performance of data utility [4, 14].

- **Trajectory Points Loss (TPL)**, the loss rate of trajectory points data after anonymization which contains ratios for increasing and decreasing trajectory points, is defined as $\frac{|P(T^*)-P(T)|+|P(T)-P(T^*)|}{|P(T)|}$, where $P(T^*)$ and $P(T)$ are the sets of trajectory points in T^* and T.
- **Frequent Sequences Loss (FSL)**, the loss rate of frequent sequences which contains ratios for increasing and decreasing frequent sequences, is defined as $\frac{|F(T^*)-F(T)|+|F(T)-F(T^*)|}{|F(T)|}$, where $F(T^*)$ and $F(T)$ are the sets of frequent sequences in T^* and T.

To study the effectiveness of PPHR, we evaluate the utility loss by varying l and m. For frequent sequences loss, we choose $K' = 70$ which is the frequency threshold of frequent trajectory sequences.

Effect of *l*. Figure 2 shows that the impact of *l* on TPL and FSL. As *l* varies from 3 to 7, both types of utility loss increase slowly because as privacy requirements increase, more points need to be added or subtracted in our PPHR. For different sequences, we take n appropriate addition or substraction operation to achieve *l-diversity*, which can effectively reduce the utility loss. Addition is more conducive to protect the frequent sequences. In addition, as *m* increases, utility loss also increases.

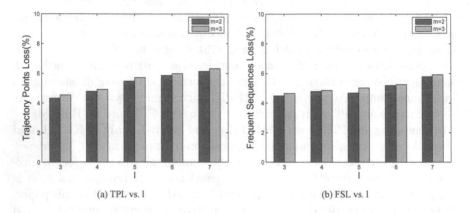

(a) TPL vs. l   (b) FSL vs. l

Fig. 2. Utility Loss vs. l-diversity.

5.2   Leakage Probability

We use the leakage probability as a measure of the probability that each sequence could cause a privacy breach. The leakage probability of a sequence q is defined as:

$$Pr_{leak}(q) = max(\frac{1}{|SV(q)|}, \frac{max_{SA}}{|T(q)|}),$$

where $\frac{1}{|SV(q)|}$ and $\frac{max_{SA}}{|T(q)|}$ represent the probability of identity disclosure and that of attribute disclosure respectively.

We randomly sample 20k sequences whose length is not more than m to calculate the leakage probability of each sequence. The average leakage probability is shown in Fig. 3. As l increases, leakage probability gradually decreases because both the number of records that q matches and the types of SA increase.

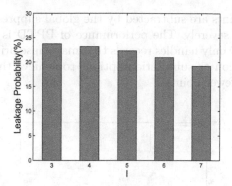

Fig. 3. Leakage probability vs. l

5.3 Comparison

We compare our PPHR with **KCL-Local** and **PPTD** on both types of utility loss and runtime. Our PPHR achieves l-diversity to defend against both attacks while KCL-Local and PPTD achieve $(k, C)_m$-privacy model. Though these kinds of schemes implement different privacy models, they can resist record linkage attack and attribute linkage attack. Consequently, we compare them by evaluating the leakage probability as the privacy protection degree. Then, we compare the utility loss under the same level of privacy protection. For example, leakage probability of 3-diversity and $(5, 0.5)$-privacy model means the same level of privacy protection.

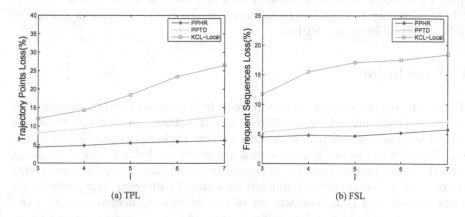

(a) TPL   (b) FSL

Fig. 4. Utility loss

We vary l from 3 to 7 with $m = 3$ to compare the effect of l on PPHR. We set the values of k and C to ensure these 3 schemes can provide the same privacy level as l varies. Figure 4 shows KCL-Local has the worst performance because a large number of points are subtracted by the global suppression and therefore utility loss is caused severely. The performance of PPTD is better than KCL-Local, because PPTD only handles records that may cause privacy breaches. Our PPHR chooses addition or subtraction options to achieve the best data utility by trying to change fewer points.

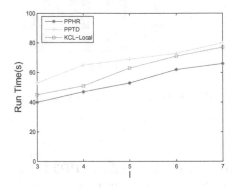

Fig. 5. Runtime

Runtime. Figure 5 shows the runtime increases with l because more sequences are processed, causing more time. PPTD has the longest running time because it takes some time to determine new critical sequences. Our PPHR has the shortest running time because we only process the sequences of length m but KCL-Local and PPTD should deal with the sequences of length no more than m. Besides, it is no necessary to consider the influence of new critical sequences during the addition operation in our PPHR.

6   Conclusion

We design and implement an anonymous technique to protect the sensitive attribute during publishing the EHRs. In our scheme, we first determine the critical sequences based on which some specific patients are easy to be identified. To resist the record linkage attack and attribute linkage attack, we adopt perturbation to process these critical sequences by adding or deleting some points to make the SA values in the published data satisfy l-diversity. Our performance studies based on a comprehensive set of real-world data demonstrate that our scheme can provide higher data utility compared to peer schemes. In the future work, we plan to optimization our algorithm to resist other linkage attacks.

Acknowledgment. This research is sponsored in part by National Key Research and Development Program of China (2017YFC0704200), the National Natural Science Foundation of China (contract/grant numbers: 61772113 and 61872053).

References

1. Ahmed, F., Liu, A.X., Jin, R.: Social graph publishing with privacy guarantees. In: IEEE 36th International Conference on Distributed Computing Systems (ICDCS), pp. 447–456. IEEE (2016)
2. Brito, F.T., Neto, A.C.A., Costa, C.F., Mendonça, A.L., Machado, J.C.: A distributed approach for privacy preservation in the publication of trajectory data. In: Proceedings of the 2nd Workshop on Privacy in Geographic Information Collection and Analysis, p. 5. ACM (2015)
3. Cano, I., Torra, V.: Edit constraints on microaggregation and additive noise. In: Dimitrakakis, C., Gkoulalas-Divanis, A., Mitrokotsa, A., Verykios, V.S., Saygin, Y. (eds.) PSDML 2010. LNCS (LNAI), vol. 6549, pp. 1–14. Springer, Heidelberg (2011). https://doi.org/10.1007/978-3-642-19896-0_1
4. Chen, R., Fung, B.C., Mohammed, N., Desai, B.C., Wang, K.: Privacy-preserving trajectory data publishing by local suppression. Inform. Sci. **231**, 83–97 (2013)
5. Domingo-Ferrer, J., Torra, V.: A quantitative comparison of disclosure control methods for microdata. In: Confidentiality, Disclosure and Data Access: Theory and Practical Applications for Statistical Agencies, pp. 111–134 (2001)
6. Fung, B., Wang, K., Chen, R., Yu, P.S.: Privacy-preserving data publishing: a survey of recent developments. ACM Comput. Surv. (CSUR) **42**(4), 14 (2010)
7. Gao, S., Ma, J., Sun, C., Li, X.: Balancing trajectory privacy and data utility using a personalized anonymization model. J. Netw. Comput. Appl. **38**(1), 125–134 (2014)
8. Gkoulalas-Divanis, A., Loukides, G., Sun, J.: Publishing data from electronic health records while preserving privacy: a survey of algorithms. J. Biomed. Inform. **50**(8), 4–19 (2014)
9. Harnsamut, N., Natwichai, J.: Privacy preservation for trajectory data publishing and heuristic approach. In: Barolli, L., Enokido, T., Takizawa, M. (eds.) NBiS 2017. LNDECT, vol. 7, pp. 787–797. Springer, Cham (2018). https://doi.org/10.1007/978-3-319-65521-5_71
10. Harnsamut, N., Natwichai, J., Riyana, S.: Privacy preservation for trajectory data publishing by look-up table generalization. In: Wang, J., Cong, G., Chen, J., Qi, J. (eds.) ADC 2018. LNCS, vol. 10837, pp. 15–27. Springer, Cham (2018). https://doi.org/10.1007/978-3-319-92013-9_2
11. Johnson, A.E.W., et al.: MIMIC-III, a freely accessible critical care database. Sci. Data **3**, 160035 (2016)
12. Kiyomoto, S., Tanaka, T.: A user-oriented anonymization mechanism for public data. In: Garcia-Alfaro, J., Navarro-Arribas, G., Cavalli, A., Leneutre, J. (eds.) DPM/SETOP -2010. LNCS, vol. 6514, pp. 22–35. Springer, Heidelberg (2011). https://doi.org/10.1007/978-3-642-19348-4_3
13. Komishani, E.G., Abadi, M.: A generalization-based approach for personalized privacy preservation in trajectory data publishing. In: Sixth International Symposium on Telecommunications, pp. 1129–1135 (2012)
14. Komishani, E.G., Abadi, M., Deldar, F.: PPTD: preserving personalized privacy in trajectory data publishing by sensitive attribute generalization and trajectory local suppression. Knowl. Based Syst. **94**, 43–59 (2016)
15. Lang, L., Lang, L.: Hipaa privacy rule and negative influence on health research. Gastroenterology **134**(1), 6–6 (2008)
16. LeFevre, K., DeWitt, D.J., Ramakrishnan, R.: Incognito: efficient full-domain k-anonymity. In: Proceedings of the 2005 ACM SIGMOD International Conference on Management of Data, pp. 49–60. ACM (2005)

17. Loukides, G., Liagouris, J., Gkoulalas-Divanis, A., Terrovitis, M.: Disassociation for electronic health record privacy. J. Biomed. Inform. **50**(8), 46–61 (2014)
18. Machanavajjhala, A., Gehrke, J., Kifer, D.: l-diversity: privacy beyond k-anonymity. In: International Conference on Data Engineering, p. 24 (2006)
19. Okkalioglu, B.D., Koc, M., Koc, M., Polat, H.: A survey: deriving private information from perturbed data. Artif. Intell. Rev. **44**(4), 547–569 (2015)
20. Ozkaynak, M., Reeder, B., Hoffecker, L., Makic, M.B., Sousa, K.: Use of electronic health records by nurses for symptom management in inpatient settings: a systematic review. Comput. Inform. Nurs. (CIN) 1 (2017)
21. Rajaei, M., Haghjoo, M.S., Miyaneh, E.K.: Ambiguity in social network data for presence, sensitive-attribute, degree and relationship privacy protection. PLoS ONE **10**(6), 1–23 (2015)
22. Tai-Seale, M., Wilson, C.J., Stone, A., Durbin, M., Luft, H.S.: Patients body mass index and blood pressure over time: diagnoses, treatments, and the effects of comorbidities. Med. Care **52**, S110–S117 (2014)
23. Tavares, J., Oliveira, T.: Electronic health record patient portal adoption by health care consumers: an acceptance model and survey. J. Med. Internet Res. **18**(3), e49 (2016)
24. Terrovitis, M., Poulis, G., Mamoulis, N., Skiadopoulos, S.: Local suppression and splitting techniques for privacy preserving publication of trajectories. IEEE Trans. Knowl. Data Eng. **29**(7), 1466–1479 (2017)
25. Victor, N., Lopez, D., Abawajy, J.H.: Privacy models for big data: a survey. Int. J. Big Data Intell. **3**(1), 61–75 (2016)
26. Xu, Y., Ma, T., Tang, M., Tian, W.: A survey of privacy preserving data publishing using generalization and suppression. Appl. Math. Inf. Sci. **8**(3), 1103 (2014)
27. Xue, M., Karras, P., Chedy, R., Kalnis, P., Pung, H.K.: Delineating social network data anonymization via random edge perturbation. In: Proceedings of the 21st ACM International Conference on Information and Knowledge Management, pp. 475–484. ACM (2012)
28. Yao, L., Liu, D., Wang, X., Wu, G.: Preserving the relationship privacy of the published social-network data based on compressive sensing. In: IEEE/ACM International Symposium on Quality of Service, pp. 1–10 (2017)
29. Yarovoy, R., Bonchi, F., Lakshmanan, L.V.S., Wang, W.H.: Anonymizing moving objects: how to hide a mob in a crowd? In: International Conference on Extending Database Technology, EDBT 2009, Saint Petersburg, Russia, 24–26 March 2009, Proceedings, pp. 72–83 (2009)
30. Zaman, A.N.K., Obimbo, C., Dara, R.A.: An improved data sanitization algorithm for privacy preserving medical data publishing. In: Canadian Conference on Artificial Intelligence, pp. 64–70 (2017)
31. Zhang, X., Liu, C., Nepal, S., Chen, J.: An efficient quasi-identifier index based approach for privacy preservation over incremental data sets on cloud. J. Comput. Syst. Sci. **79**(5), 542–555 (2013)

Privacy in Location-Based Services: Present Facts and Future Paths

Zakaria Sahnoune$^{(\boxtimes)}$ and Esma Aïmeur

Department of Computer Science and Operations Research, University of Montreal,
Montreal, Canada
{sahnounz,aimeur}@iro.umontreal.ca

Abstract. The usage of Location-Based Services (LBSs) ranges from searching points of interests to location-based social networking. They are present in almost every daily task. Moreover, with smartphone ownership growth, getting one's location became easier, and the privacy-related issues became almost inescapable. Accordingly, numerous efforts have extensively explored the problem from different perspectives. Many of the existing solutions lack rigorous privacy safeguards and have been foiled by several location attacks. In a nutshell, their shortcomings are mainly due to the heavy dependence on computational privacy models, and the lack of consideration for adaptable protections. We discuss in this paper the current location-based services models, privacy issues, a general overview of the protection mechanisms, and our thoughts about location-privacy in the near future.

Keywords: Location-based services ·
Location Privacy Preserving Mechanisms · Privacy models ·
Collaborative mechanisms

1 Introduction

A Location-Based Service (LBS) is tracking your location, well one may think that it is not that bad. They may also think that they can check out the visited locations, manage them, and probably turn off location tracking entirely. While being true in some cases, an investigation done by Associated Press affirms that Google keeps gathering its users' location data even when they switch the tracking feature off [13]. In a nutshell, Google offers "apparently" an option to turn off location tracking from the account settings portal. However, even when the user disables any tracking, Google keeps collecting location-related data. One may also think that it is an individual act that cannot be generalized. Similar incidents occurred, and they keep occurring. Facebook [15], Yahoo [18], eBay [16] and others all reported serious privacy-related incident in the last 5 years. The bottom line is that such incidents are kept hidden until being forced to be revealed.

J. Li et al. (Eds.): SPNCE 2019, LNICST 284, pp. 141–151, 2019.
https://doi.org/10.1007/978-3-030-21373-2_13

To be more precise, LBSs are the application services relying on gathering and processing location data. Their primary purpose is to determine coordinates of objects such as parcels, vehicles, and mobile devices, which often includes locating their owners too. LBSs are almost everywhere, ranging from exploring *Point-of-Interests* (POIs) to geosocial networking and location-based commerce. As a matter of fact, among the ≈1M application available on Google Play, 24% of them request access to the user's precise location [20]. Besides, a typical Android device may share accurate location coordinates up to 5398 times in just two weeks; with the presence of just ten of the most popular apps, and with or without the explicit consent of its owner [3]. Furthermore, 70% of smartphone users have at least 11 downloaded applications. Moreover, a study conducted by the US Census Bureau revealed that more than 50% of users are willing to share their exact location [21].

The issue is not just about the location coordinates themselves; it is about their value to LBSs and other third parties. For instance, location is a valuable asset in an individual re-identification process [19]. However, as long as the location data does not link to an individual identity, it may prove useful in various cases. For example, in Canada, police analysts were able to build a picture of what was going on in downtown Ottawa during the October 2014 attacks, by using specific Twitter hashtags and location tools [23], illustrates an example of positive use of location data.

To use LBS features, a user needs to provide accurate geographic coordinates. In other words, LBS users do not have other choices but giving up their geographic coordinates, even when they are aware of the related privacy risks. For example, when 68% of mobile users are concerned about privacy and security on their devices [6], 74% of them still use LBSs to get location-based routes and information [27]. In 2015, The European Global Navigation Satellite Systems Agency, also known as The European GNSS Agency (GSA), released a report about LBSs and their usage [11]. Among its key findings, the report affirms that mobile applications relying on location information hit almost 3 billion downloads from both Android Play and Apple App stores.

Similarly, most of the recent mobile devices include support for numerous positioning systems such as GPS, Beidou, GLONASS, and SBAS, which improves location accuracy beyond what conventional GPS receivers can provide. Moreover, knowing that only 35% of mobile users think of turning off location services on their devices [27], suggests that the amount of user-generated location-based content is considerably huge. Many companies raise their revenues from data warehouses and analytic tools [2].

Location information itself is considered sensitive, for instance, four distinct spatiotemporal transactions are enough to identify 90% of LBS users [7]. Furthermore, collecting and processing location data on a regular basis may lead to infer one's private information such as the home or work locations, sexual preferences, or religious inclinations [4]. However, the benefits that LBS may provide cannot be ignored; one cannot just wipe out all location-based applications from his device. It is up to researchers and service providers to ensure the user's privacy on LBSs, either by building privacy-aware applications or by supplying protection mechanisms that meet user expectations.

Even when the existing protection models and mechanisms may guarantee good location protection, the fact that continuous requests are not independent, and the user's data is not isolated from location data may foil many Location Privacy Preserving Mechanism (LPPM from here onward). Moreover, performing privacy-preserving operations on geographic coordinates may lead to a notable quality loss. Thus, the balance between preserving users' privacy, and ensuring high accuracy from their location data is one serious challenge in today's applications.

Similarly, the technological advances in today's LBSs, especially in machine learning and inference technologies, put into question the effectiveness of abstracting location privacy to geographical coordinates, or single location-based request. LBSs can access, collect and store data that could help pinpoint to the exact user whereabouts. An example of the advancement achieved in location-related intelligence is the work proposed by Weyand *et al.* where the authors succeeded in identifying the location of photos just by analyzing them [25]. An approach entirely based on convolutional neural networks attests the progress achieved in this field.

We discuss in the next section the context of LBSs in more details, along with the significant privacy issues associated with their usage. Then, we represent the paradigms used in today's protection mechanisms. We also discuss the effectiveness of the latter and their potential shortcomings in the near future.

2 Location and Privacy

As stated by Bettini, "A privacy threat occurs whenever an unauthorized entity can associate with high probability the identity of an individual with private information about that individual" [5]. Accordingly, a privacy threat in LBS is characterized by the use of one's location to increase the probability of their identification.

We describe two scenarios in the context of this paper which involve interactions between users and LBSs. They are used to discuss our point of view regarding privacy in LBSs. It is assumed that the users are equipped with high-end devices, (*i.e.* GPS and WiFi enabled mobile devices) and can access various services offered by different service providers. Figure 1 illustrates the possible services that users can access nowadays via their smart mobile devices.

The context of this paper is LBSs, which are application services that rely on the location information transmitted by users. We abstract away from communication services, which include telephony and internet services, and have to determine the mobile device availability and position as a part of their base architecture. Communication services have to determine in which cell the mobile device is located so it can be served by the respective base transceiver station (BTS) [12]. Accordingly, we set in the following two scenarios that describe hypothetical LBS use cases that are not far from reality and may occur to any LBS user.

Scenario 1. Alice has an appointment with a doctor that she never visited before. The doctor is a specialist in treating diabetes, and his office is in a region

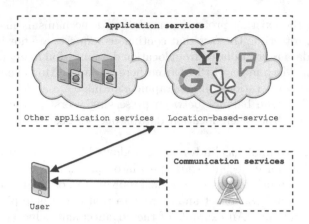

Fig. 1. Accessible services via smart mobile devices

that Alice is not very familiar with it. The day of her appointment, Alice takes her car and drives to the vicinity of the office. Once there, she cannot locate the doctor's office and thinks of using her smartphone to use her favorite LBS to find it. Although she knows that using an LBS would get her to the doctor faster, Alice is concerned about her privacy and knows that she has to disclose her identity and location to the LBS along with her request of finding the diabetes physician.

Scenario 2. Alice decides to use LBS to locate the doctor's office since she is afraid of being late. When she arrives, she meets Bob, a computer engineer who works on software development. While they are chatting in the waiting room, Alice mentions the fact that she is not comfortable with sharing her information to application services, especially geographical coordinates. Bob agrees with Alice's point of view and affirms that, as he works on collecting data from users, he can ensure her that the actual information disclosure is far beyond her perception. Bob gives her the example of storing the details of appointments in her device's calendar along with using an LBS to locate her appointments' locations. Alice realizes that even if she preserves her geographical coordinates, an installed LBS application still can access and correlate other sensitive data, such as photos, calendar events, and contacts.

  While hypothetical, the above scenarios are close to real-world situations and may happen to any LBS user, even when using one LBS only. Thus, identifying the LBS-related privacy issues from the previous scenarios helps in setting the following requirements that an efficient LPPM should ensure.

- **Strong location privacy.** To efficiently protect user's location privacy, LBSs should not be able to identify or infer his exact location.
- **Maximum data utility.** The users are using LBSs to get location-enhanced data and provide them with inaccurate or misleading information thereby making the LBS useless. Consequently, ensuring high accuracy and maximum utility is a crucial requirement for an efficient LPPM.

– *Efficiency.* The LPPM should be able to deploy and run smoothly on mobile devices, along with keeping adequate run time, computation, and bandwidth efficiency factors. Similarly, the execution on the LPPM should not affect the latency and the response time when using LBSs.

Given the current LBS applications, the above requirements are fundamental to any proposed LPPM. Today's LBSs are beyond using location data only, and their ability to learn users' behaviors is evolving quickly. For example, consider an LBS user Alice who is concerned about her privacy protection and uses a given LPPM to achieve that. The latter tries to make Alice's location-based requests indistinguishable among a set of locations (*Confusion paradigm*). However, the LBS can access multiple data types on Alice's device, and can eventually identify if the request comes from Alice by correlating current and past data. Table 1 lists the required permissions in some of LBS mobile applications on Android.

Table 1. Examples of the required permissions in LBS mobile application

LBS application	Version	Common permissions	Other permissions
Google Maps	9.54.1	Location Storage Stored accounts	Camera Contacts
Yelp	9.12.0		Camera Contacts Microphone
Foursquare	2017.05.15		Contacts WiFi and Bluetooth information
Tinder	7.2.0		Call information Device and app history Device ID
Pokémon GO	0.63.4		Camera Contacts

The examples specified in Table 1 illustrate LBSs from different classes, and they sample what most of today's LBS applications collect from users' devices. More precisely, an LPPM that abstracts away from any background knowledge acquired by LBSs can be foiled, and eventually, fails to achieve its purpose of protecting location privacy.

3   Related Work Overview

Preserving privacy in LBSs implies that the users' exact locations must not be, in any case, disclosed or inferred. This rule, which might look simple, has driven many researchers to deeply explore the related issues, and produce numerous valuable work on privacy threats in LBSs. From the perspective of this paper, we discuss the related work according to the paradigms on which existing privacy mechanisms have been built. Regardless of the adopted privacy metric (*e.g.* k-anonymity, differential privacy), we discuss in the following the two main classes of paradigms used in almost any LPPM.

3.1 Transformational Paradigms

Obfuscation. Mechanisms using this class of paradigms aims to hide the user's true location inside a larger area. As defined in [9], the main purpose of location obfuscation is deliberately degrading the quality of information about an individual's location in order to protect their location privacy. Let M be the mechanism using the obfuscation as its transformation paradigm, and $\mathbb{E}^2$ the space on which location operations are executed. The obfuscation region r is defined as follows:

$$M(loc) = r \in \mathbb{E}^2 \quad \text{with} \quad loc \in M(loc)$$

Substitution. In this class of transformations, the mechanism maps the user's true location to a different nearby location. As a result, a substitute location loc' is reported to the LBS instead of the user's true location loc. Let M be the mechanism using the substitution as its transformation paradigm, and $\mathbb{E}^2$ the space on which location operations are executed. The substitute location loc' is defined as follows:

$$M(loc) = r \in \mathbb{E}^2 \quad \text{with} \quad loc \in M(loc)$$

Confusion. The user's real location is confused when it is contained in a set of dummy locations in the aim of hiding it [17]. In other words, a mechanism using confusion paradigm maps the user's actual location loc into a set of n locations of which one is the exact location. Let M be the mechanism using the confusion as for its transformation paradigm. The set of confused location is defined as follows:

$$M(loc) = \{loc_i\}_{i \in [1,n]} \quad \text{such that} \quad \exists loc_i = loc$$

Suppression. Also known as *invisible cloaking*, the mechanisms using this class of transformations withdraw the LBS requests and prevent reporting any location coordinates in the presence of some predefined conditions. Let M be the mechanism using the suppression as its transformation paradigm; the suppression transformation is expressed by:

$$M(loc) = null$$

3.2 Collaborative Paradigms

Collaborative mechanisms ensure co-utility among users, and it has been proven that in a privacy-aware setting, not only they can provide strong privacy guarantees, but also more likely to be adopted by rational users [8]. They are based on forwarding location-based requests from one user to another such that the final request set R sent to an LBS from a collaborative network composed of n users is:

$$R = \{r_i\}_{i \in [1,n]} \quad \text{such that} \quad \exists r_i = r_u$$

The use of the discussed paradigms depends on the privacy goals of a mechanism and the properties of the LBS under consideration. As listed in Table 2, some paradigms outperform in the case of sporadic requests (*e.g.* Location-based search engines), others are more suitable for continuous requests (*e.g.* Navigation services). Mechanisms based on suppression paradigms are more useful in interrogation-based LBSs where the user initiates the request, and they cannot be used in transaction-based LBSs where the request is first sent by the service (*e.g.* Crowdsensing services). The table also mentions the effectiveness of the paradigms in both privacy protection and utility.

Table 2. Summary of location privacy preservation models

LPPM	LBS Properties						Effectiveness	
Paradigms	Direction		Request frequency		Content		Privacy	Utility
	Interrogation	Transaction	Sporadic	Continue	Location	Other		
Transformational paradigms								
Obfuscation	•	•	•	•	•		•	
Substitution	•	•	•		•		•	
Confusion	•	•	•		•			•
Suppression	•		•		•		•	
Collaborative paradigms								
Collaboration	•	•	•		•	•	•	•

4 Discussions

Location data has always been considered as personal information or at least known only by acquaintances. The negative consequences of its disclosure cannot be neglected. Besides, the combination of location data with other personal information can lead to precisely identify individuals by potentially malicious parties.

The current state of LBSs reveals several privacy-related issues. For instance, location prediction on social networks such as Twitter represents one of them [26]. Location prediction combines the inaccurately reported positions with social content (*e.g.* posts, photos) to provide accurate coordinates. Moreover, a study conducted by Haffner *et al.* attested that the location data gathered from social networks seem to be more accurate than volunteered geographic information such as OpenStreetMap [14].

Location prediction is not related to social networks only, for instance, the navigation application Waze uses the mobility patterns of its users to provide traffic predictions. Exact location prediction is the primary feature of LBSs to provide useful data. However, the more a position is accurate, the more the privacy is at risk.

Another emerging field that may imply additional privacy protection measures is the ability to identify the location using photos on social media [24,25]. The user's photos on social networking platform can be used to identify their exact location using contextual information extracted from the photo itself (*e.g.* Buildings, Road signs, weather). As long as no protection mechanism analyzes photos for possible location identification, such technology makes current mechanisms completely useless. Users can disable location tracking, prevent any unwanted location disclosure, but this is not enough when it comes to content analysis.

One other questionable point is the effectiveness of the existing protection mechanisms. Most existing solutions focus on preserving privacy by ignoring the utility. As a result, some LBSs may end up good for nothing, for instance, navigation LBSs cannot provide directions if the location is not accurate. Nevertheless, preserving privacy alone is a complicated issue given the computational and learning capabilities that current LBSs possess. Thus, the consideration of utility adds a dimension that must be treated independently.

Even when the existing protection mechanisms can guarantee privacy protection, the lack of severe measures for some LBS models may lead to privacy breaches and quality loss. In other words, if a user opts for various LBSs, which is often the case, they will be forced to select the same number of protection models to ensure the privacy protection and the service quality. Moreover, the absence of a global LBS model behind the existing solutions makes them unable to achieve higher privacy guarantees. For instance, a user can obtain rigorous privacy guarantees when using a location-based social network with a protection mechanism. However, using the same mechanism in a navigation service may be ineffective.

It is important to note the usefulness of current technologies in many aspects of our daily lives. However, the information they collect can be exploited and therefore cause harm to our privacy. An adversary can examine a user's data, analyze it, and create relevant information that could be used to generate behavioral models based on the user's location. For example, marketing companies, such as Urban Airship or others, now offer audience profiling tools that enable the integration of customer targeting capabilities based on their location-based data.

The issue of privacy in location-based services is far from being new. Nevertheless, the fast growth of both their users' adoption and their technologies makes the existing LPPMs either ineffective or complicated. While ineffective LPPMs are dismissed, complicated ones decrease the utility of LBSs. For instance, LPPMs based on differential privacy end up adding too much noise to the real position to the point the retrieved data from an LBS becomes completely useless.

We discuss in the next section the future of LBSs and the need for rethought LPPMs.

5   Future of Geolocation

A team from *Imperial College London* and *M Squared* have recently developed what they called "quantum accelerometer" [10]. The device measures movements and, unlike traditional accelerometers, it can accurately report positions. What makes it revolutionary is its autonomy, it does not rely on satellites or wireless networks to estimate its position. From a privacy perspective, this may make the control over location disclosure even harder. Cutting links with satellites will not be enough.

One other category that impacts the location as we know today is the Internet of Things (IoT). With already existing devices (*e.g.* smart watches, connected home appliances) and near-future launching plans (*e.g.* connected smart lens, health monitoring rings), the control over how location data is collected and used may become impossible. What is done today by switching off location tracking on a smartphone, could imply, soon, a whole set of settings and reading privacy agreements. Using multiple connected devices ensures high location accuracy on the one hand and facilitates privacy breaches on the other hand.

A report from *Reserach and Markets* predicts that revenues from location-enabled IoTs will reach $49 billion by 2021 [22]. The report also suggests that the significant growth of Low-Power Wide Area Network (LPWAN) technologies will help in connecting IoT devices more easily, and as a result facilitating location data collection. In a nutshell, LPWANs networks represent a type of wireless telecommunication wide area networks designed specifically to allow long-range communications at a low bit rate among IoT devices [1].

The bottom line is that location collection methods and techniques are changing and newly related privacy-issues are emerging. Today's protection mechanisms rely on satellites data and calculation power of smartphones. With auto-locating devices and limited IoT resources, the challenge becomes even harder. Not to mention the multitude of connected devices that implies the need for one protection system that controls privacy over all of them at once.

6   Conclusion

The fact that LBSs are invading our lives on a daily basis cannot be overlooked; it is thanks to their ease of use and convenience that the number of their users is increasing exponentially. However, this adoption leads to severe risks regarding users' privacy. The aggregation and analysis of location data have become even more accessible, and can certainly be refined when position history and tracking.

The usefulness and convenience offered by LBSs is the primary reason behind this adoption. In the majority of cases, users adopt an LBS because they need to use it. Therefore, a radical "abandon LBS" solution is not applicable. Users need to use LBS, but they also need to protect their privacy.

We discussed in these paper LBS models and privacy-preserving paradigms, along with significant challenges when it comes to providing the optimal protection.

References

1. Adelantado, F., Vilajosana, X., Tuset-Peiro, P., Martinez, B., Melia-Segui, J., Watteyne, T.: Understanding the limits of LoRaWAN. IEEE Commun. Mag. **55**(9), 34–40 (2017)
2. Aïmeur, E., Lawani, O., Dalkir, K.: When changing the look of privacy policies affects user trust: an experimental study. Comput. Hum. Behav. **58**, 368–379 (2016)
3. Almuhimedi, H., et al.: Your location has been shared 5,398 times! A field study on mobile app privacy nudging. In: Proceedings of the 33rd Annual ACM Conference on Human Factors in Computing Systems, pp. 787–796. ACM (2015)
4. Andrés, M.E., Bordenabe, N.E., Chatzikokolakis, K., Palamidessi, C.: Geo-indistinguishability: differential privacy for location-based systems. In: Proceedings of the 2013 ACM SIGSAC Conference on Computer & Communications Security, pp. 901–914. ACM (2013)
5. Bettini, C.: Privacy protection in location-based services: a survey. In: Gkoulalas-Divanis, A., Bettini, C. (eds.) Handbook of Mobile Data Privacy, pp. 73–96. Springer, Cham (2018). https://doi.org/10.1007/978-3-319-98161-1_4
6. Clarke, N., Symes, J., Saevanee, H., Furnell, S.: Awareness of mobile device security: a survey of user's attitudes. Int. J. Mob. Comput. Multimed. Commun. (IJMCMC) **7**(1), 15–31 (2016)
7. De Montjoye, Y.A., Radaelli, L., Singh, V.K., et al.: Unique in the shopping mall: on the reidentifiability of credit card metadata. Science **347**(6221), 536–539 (2015)
8. Domingo-Ferrer, J., Martínez, S., Sánchez, D., Soria-Comas, J.: Co-utility: self-enforcing protocols for the mutual benefit of participants. Eng. Appl. Artif. Intell. **59**, 148–158 (2017)
9. Duckham, M., Kulik, L.: A formal model of obfuscation and negotiation for location privacy. In: Gellersen, H.-W., Want, R., Schmidt, A. (eds.) Pervasive 2005. LNCS, vol. 3468, pp. 152–170. Springer, Heidelberg (2005). https://doi.org/10.1007/11428572_10
10. Dunning, H., Angus, T., Martin, M.: Quantum compass could allow navigation without relying on satellites, November 2018. https://goo.gl/Dwr8ed. Accessed 13 Nov 2018
11. European GNSS Agency: GNSS market report: location-based services, March 2015. https://goo.gl/FBvrRa. Accessed 25 Nov 2018
12. Frattasi, S., Della Rosa, F.: Mobile Positioning and Tracking: From Conventional to Cooperative Techniques. Wiley (2017)
13. Griffin, A.: Google stores location data even when users have told it not to, August 2018. https://goo.gl/4erH3v. Accessed 13 Nov 2018
14. Haffner, M., Mathews, A.J., Fekete, E., Finchum, G.A.: Location-based social media behavior and perception: views of university students. Geogr. Rev. **108**(2), 203–224 (2018)
15. Howley, D.: Facebook reveals 50 million accounts affected by security breach, September 2018. https://goo.gl/ETjrpV. Accessed 13 Nov 2018
16. Kelly, G.: eBay suffers massive security breach, all users must change their passwords, May 2014. https://goo.gl/42wSHH. Accessed 13 Nov 2018

17. Kido, H., Yanagisawa, Y., Satoh, T.: An anonymous communication technique using dummies for location-based services. In: Proceedings. International Conference on Pervasive Services, ICPS 2005, pp. 88–97. IEEE (2005)
18. Larson, S.: Every single Yahoo account was hacked - 3 billion in all, October 2017. https://goo.gl/bXZbru. Accessed 13 Nov 2018
19. Li, G.: A new reidentification method for location-based social networks. IEEJ Trans. Electr. Electron. Eng. **14**(3), 499–500 (2019)
20. Olmstead, K., Atkinson, M.: Apps permissions in the Google play store, November 2015. http://www.pewinternet.org/2015/11/10/apps-permissions-in-the-google-play-store/. Accessed 25 Nov 2018
21. Olmsted-Hawala, E., Nichols, E.: Willingness of the public to share geolocation information in a us census bureau survey. Soc. Sci. Comput. Rev. (2018). https://doi.org/10.1177/0894439318781022
22. Research and Markets: Location-based IoT and geo analytics market outlook and forecasts 2017–2022, April 2017. https://goo.gl/fHdpi8. Accessed 13 Nov 2018
23. Stewart, E.: Live-tweeting a terrorist attack: how the public's posts can help in an emergency, April 2016. http://www.rcmp-grc.gc.ca/en/gazette/live-tweeting-a-terrorist-attack. Accessed 25 Nov 2018
24. Wang, K., Huang, Y.H., Oramas, J., Van Gool, L., Tuytelaars, T.: An analysis of human-centered geolocation. In: IEEE Winter Conference on Applications of Computer Vision (WACV), pp. 2058–2066. IEEE (2018)
25. Weyand, T., Kostrikov, I., Philbin, J.: PlaNet - photo geolocation with convolutional neural networks. In: Leibe, B., Matas, J., Sebe, N., Welling, M. (eds.) ECCV 2016. LNCS, vol. 9912, pp. 37–55. Springer, Cham (2016). https://doi.org/10.1007/978-3-319-46484-8_3
26. Zheng, X., Han, J., Sun, A.: A survey of location prediction on Twitter. IEEE Trans. Knowl. Data Eng. **30**(9), 1652–1671 (2018)
27. Zickuhr, K.: Location-based services (2013). https://goo.gl/JYcjeq. Accessed 25 Nov 2018

Privacy Disclosures Detection in Natural-Language Text Through Linguistically-Motivated Artificial Neural Networks

Nuhil Mehdy, Casey Kennington, and Hoda Mehrpouyan[✉]

Boise State University, Boise, ID 83702, USA
{akmnuhilmehdy,caseykennington,hodamehrpouyan}@boisestate.edu

Abstract. An increasing number of people are sharing information through text messages, emails, and social media without proper privacy checks. In many situations, this could lead to serious privacy threats. This paper presents a methodology for providing extra safety precautions without being intrusive to users. We have developed and evaluated a model to help users take control of their shared information by automatically identifying text (i.e., a sentence or a transcribed utterance) that might contain personal or private disclosures. We apply off-the-shelf natural language processing tools to derive linguistic features such as part-of-speech, syntactic dependencies, and entity relations. From these features, we model and train a multichannel convolutional neural network as a classifier to identify short texts that have personal, private disclosures. We show how our model can notify users if a piece of text discloses personal or private information, and evaluate our approach in a binary classification task with 93% accuracy on our own labeled dataset, and 86% on a dataset of ground truth. Unlike document classification tasks in the area of natural language processing, our framework is developed keeping the sentence level context into consideration.

Keywords: Privacy · Security · Natural language processing · Machine learning

1 Introduction

In this era of global communication, individuals often share stories, news, and information with each other. It is not easy for these users to keep track of what information they have shared, whether or not that information was a private disclosure, and to whom they shared that information. While the importance of user centric privacy management systems is being widely studied [22,32,33,38,40], only some of this work are concerned with real-time text analysis and identifying text that contains private information. An important step in constructing an effective privacy management system is to concentrate on identifying and discriminating private information from public information.

© ICST Institute for Computer Sciences, Social Informatics and Telecommunications Engineering 2019
Published by Springer Nature Switzerland AG 2019. All Rights Reserved
J. Li et al. (Eds.): SPNCE 2019, LNICST 284, pp. 152–177, 2019.
https://doi.org/10.1007/978-3-030-21373-2_14

For example, a very common medium of social communication between people is messaging using text; e.g., email, SMS/text messages, chat, social media, etc. While interacting, people sometimes disclose personal and sensitive information, unintentionally. For example a sentence, *Let's meet at the Joe's Coffee Shop tonight at seven* is disclosing someone's meeting place along with the time. Whether or not these disclosures are intentional, it could potentially be an unwanted security threat and cause for alarm–or for harm. This example illustrates a common problem in a multitasking environment where users are simultaneously using in both public and private communication mediums. Our approach serves as an automated privacy check in these kinds of situations, warning individuals regarding risky communications in both private and public contexts. This framework could also be effective while processing large amount of off-line text documents. An example case study could be filtering out all the privacy disclosures from a batch of documents that belongs to a person before it's disposal or archival.

Privacy concerns exist wherever personally identifiable information (e.g., name, address, age) or other sensitive information (e.g., health, finance, mental status) is involved [27]. Therefore, improper disclosure control can be the root cause for many privacy issues and the negative consequences of disclosing information could be immense [9]. A recent data scandal involving Facebook and Cambridge Analytica shows how personally identifiable information of up to 87 million Facebook users influenced voter opinions [20,50].

The requirements for privacy measures to protect sensitive information about organizations or individuals has been researched extensively [6,21,34,48]. One approach to protect the disclosure of private information is to detect them in textual data. However, automating the process of classifying private information prior to their disclosure is challenging [1]. One of the difficulties results from the volume of textual data that would need to be processed, and further the automation process is complicated even more by the number of real-time requirements that need to be analyzed [2,49]. Moreover, it remains a challenge to analyze and dissect the details of private information from the text data due to the ambiguities that arise from natural language [19].

In this paper, we identify a potential approach that brings this challenge within reach: recognizing disclosures in a piece of text, which could be a short phrase (i.e., a sentence) within a longer content (i.e., a paragraph or document). Specifically, we focus on identifying whether or not sentences have disclosures in them. Our approach enriches text data with linguistic features such as part-of-speech tags, syntactic dependency parse information, and entity relation information using off-the-shelf language processing tools. We then use these features to train a Convolutional Neural Network (CNN) to learn a mapping from the features to a binary label: disclosure/non-disclosure. This is a structured approach to train a machine learning model for detecting privacy disclosures and then automating that knowledge to classify certain types of privacy breaches.

The contributions of this paper can be summarized as follows:

- **Sentence level privacy disclosure identification:** While there exists similar techniques for classifying an entire document as private (i.e., confidential) or public, most of these approaches rely only on the existence of the privacy related keywords in a document regardless of their semantics. In this paper, we consider detecting privacy disclosure at a sentence level, which is based on not only the existence of privacy related keywords (i.e. disclosure related entities) but also on the valid grammatical structure of each sentence. This reduces false positive results by verifying the construction of a statement.
- **Disclosure Related Entity recognizer:** A Disclosure-Related Entity Recognizer (DRER) is developed by extending a trainable Named Entity Recognizer (NER) model. The developed DRER is later utilized to prepare a unique labeled dataset as well as to provide tagged entities for learning word embedding (i.e. similarities among disclosure related entities).
- **Case study and performance comparison:** We represent a comparison of the efficiency of different neural network architectures to detect privacy disclosure. Further, the proposed framework was evaluated to other similar datasets for a baseline comparison.

In the following section, we review some related work. In Sect. 3, the methodology along with data collection and pre-processing steps are explained. Later in this section, the neural network model and its architecture is described in detail. In Sect. 4, evaluations of the model are explained and experimental results are given. A test implementation and the usability of the proposed framework is also detailed in this section. Finally, some limitations of the approach and a baseline comparison are discussed in Sect. 5, following the conclusion.

2   Related Work

In this paper we focus on the state of the art research on privacy disclosure, which has been studied across different domains, e.g. financial disclosure [5, 30] where economical status such as salary, debt, bank balance etc., could be disclosed. Similarly, sensitive business information of an organization could be sorely disclosed if their loss, profit, or inventory price is shared through their website or employees. Furthermore, location (e.g., home address, meeting point) [4], health information (diagnosis report, health status) [11, 15, 37, 47] are considered sensitive or private information. The rest of this section reviews the techniques and approaches that help in identifying privacy disclosures.

2.1   Information Theory and Global Search

In the context of sensitive information detection, Sánchez et al. utilized information theory along with large corpus of words [45] to automatically detect sensitive information from textual documents regardless of the information context.

This approach determines the sensitivity of terms (e.g., person name, disease name, country name) according to their amount of contributed information in a context (e.g., a document). For example, specific terms (e.g., pancreatic cancer) provide more Information Content (IC) than those more general ones (e.g., disease, America). So, they compute the IC of each term by the inverse of the probability of encountering the term in a corpus (e.g. TFIDF = term frequency inverse document frequency). One advantage of this approach is that the disclosure detection does not depend on a finite set of named entities; however, the technique introduces some weaknesses. For example, the proposed framework removes the stop words from the documents, which could demolish the grammatical validity of the sentences. As a result, it is possible to inaccurately cause the algorithm to fail by providing a document containing sensitive terms in a random and meaningless order. In the proposed approach in this paper, we retain punctuations to determine the structural validation and to reduce the false positive outcomes.

The other group of privacy disclosure techniques are built on rule-based approaches, e.g., [53] for conducting global search. In this technique, personally-identifiable information (e.g. name, address) is first detected using pre-specified patterns and templates. This extends to how addresses are written, how phone number is formatted, etc. One of the weaknesses of this approach is that it only focuses on the recognition and removal of personally-identifiable information regardless of the association of the entities with the subjects. For example, a medical document could contain phone number and address of a hospital which should not be considered as sensitive information because they are considered public information. Our approach takes care of both recognition of entities and association of themselves, before giving a decision on how confident the model is.

2.2   Leveraging Dictionaries

The second category of research, utilizes the linguistic resources such as privacy dictionary to automate the content analysis of privacy related information. A privacy dictionary is used with existing automated content-analysis software such as LIWC [31]. Vasalou et al. proposes a technique that uses such a dictionary of individual words or phrases which are assigned to one or more privacy domains [55]. They showed that the dictionary categories could distinguish differences between documents of privacy discussions and general language by measuring unique linguistic patterns within privacy discussions (e.g., medical records, confidential business documents). Although, they prepared the dictionary by sampling from a rich variety of contexts (e.g., self reported privacy violations, health records, social network sites, children's use of the Internet) their approach relies only on the count of sensitive words in a document. Thus, this model could categorize privacy conditions based on a set of words to different privacy domains, however, it fails to consider the context that these words are used in.

2.3   Machine Learning, Probabilistic and Statistical Models

Detection of privacy leaks has also been well-addressed by statistical techniques such as association rule mining [8]. In such an approach, (Chow et al.) employs a model of inference detection using a customized web based corpus as reference where inferences are based on word co-occurrences. The model is then provided a topic (e.g. HIV - human immunodeficiency virus) and said to identify all the associated keywords. This approach is suitable for identifying privacy related keywords (i.e., health information in this case) by utilizing corpus based association rules, but without contextual concern. For example, if a keyword *gp120 (an envelope glycoprotein)* from the reference collection is fed then the system returns more related sensitive tokens such as *gp120-HIV* and *gp120-Flu* without considering their neighboring words and overall meaning. Again, this makes the system inappropriate for valid and precise identification of privacy disclosure.

Hart et al. (2011) utilize machine learning techniques to classify full documents as either sensitive or non-sensitive information by automatic text classification algorithms. They introduce a novel training strategy called *supplement and adjust* to create an enterprise-level classifier based on support vector machine (SVM) with a linear kernel, stop word elimination, and unigram methodology. The weaknesses of this approach is that it classifies private information only based on a set of keywords. Also, the proposed supervised machine learning models are not trained based on the proper set of labeled dataset (e.g., wikileaks data set were assumed to be private and normal web sites data are assumed to be public information). Thats why no clear visualization is presented about the learned features of these models.

Caliskan et al. (2014), describes a method for detecting private information and collective privacy behavior in a large social network. The authors introduce a novel learning based approach to determine if a given text contains private information by combining topic modeling, named entity recognition, privacy ontology, sentiment analysis, and text normalization [7]. In this approach, all the data are labeled by Amazon Mechanical Turk (AMT) workers and then different machine learning approaches are tested for generic classification of privacy score.

A further combination of linguistics and machine learning techniques are studied to detect Personal Health Information (PHI) disclosure detection [43]. Razavi et al. compiled a list of patterns/keywords which are related to persons' health information which resulted in a list of health information entities. Then by applying Key-word combinatorial web search, and filters on PHIs and Personally Identifiable Information (PII)s the disclosure of health information is detected. Secondly, machine learning layer was implemented to the system to detect and model any possible type of latent semantic PII/PHI patterns in the annotated dataset. In addition, Mao et al. studied privacy leaks on Twitter by automatically detecting vacation plans, tweeting under the influence of alcohol, and revealing medical conditions [35]. For the classifier, they implemented two machine learning algorithms; Naive Bayes and SVM.

Most of the above statistical methods are trained and tested on a relatively larger piece of content (i.e. a paragraph of sentences) and look for togetherness of keywords in any part of the whole paragraph. A disclosure related entity (e.g., age) might not reveal someone's privacy when standing alone in a sentence, however, it is considered sensitive when it is combined with other entity (e.g., person with age). The proposed approaches in this section also neglect the sentence coherence and ignore grammatical validation.

2.4 Impact Analysis of Privacy Disclosure

Along with the development of disclosure identification systems, some research has studied the impact of disclosure in the society [46,56]. Schrading et al. [46] provide an analysis of domestic abuse discourse using the data collected from the social and news-aggregation website (reddit.com). Before experimenting with the impact, they developed a disclosure identification system in order to discover the semantic and lexical features salient to abusive relationships. They used one single SVM algorithm but fed it different combination of input features for producing more than one models of other variants. The classifiers were designed specially for identifying texts that contain discussion on domestic abuse. Utilizing different combination of n-gram attributes (1-gram, 2-gram, 3-gram) and semantic role attributes (role, predicates), their linear SVM classifier was able to identify 72% to maximum of 92% abusive relationship from text (72% using predicates only, 92% using n-grams). The disclosure (abusive) identification methodology of this research work is an excellent approach for a specific privacy domain but not a perfect fit across varied domains or contexts which has been addressed in our work.

Andalibi et al. investigate sensitive self disclosures on online social media (Instagram) and the responses they attract [3]. For the identification of self disclosures in that specific social media, they worked on both the visual and textual qualitative content analysis and statistical methods. They analyzed people's comments, feedback on posts and also the relationship among the them. The methodology is mostly dependent on hash-tag (#depression) based keywords that people usually include in the description of their posted photos. Thus, this approach also suffers to precisely identify a disclosure event. For example, someone could tag a public photograph with some depression related hash-tags that does not explicitly disclose his own situation. Hence, the limitations we discussed already (e.g. not looking into sentence structure, relying on existence of keywords only, domain dependency etc.) have also been propagated to these works. Although these research work, related to impact analysis of privacy disclosure highly inspire us toward developing our proposed model that can identify meaningful privacy disclosures.

3 Methodology

In this paper, we leverage a multichannel convolutional deep neural network (DNN) to utilize lexical and sentence level features. Our model takes all of the word tokens, part-of-speech tags, and dependency parse tree information of a sentence as input. First, lexical analysis are done in sentence level. Then, the tokens are transformed to word vectors by learning word embeddings. Later, these features are concatenated to form the final feature vector. Finally, sentence level structure, and privacy related keywords are learned using the convolutional approach.

In this paper, privacy related keywords are defined as disclosure related entities (DREs). These fall into the super set of all possible named entities (NE) but contextually different (i.e., not all Named Entities are Disclosure Related Entities by our definition). We develop a DRE recognizer by extending an off-the-shelf NE recognizer tool to assist the proposed model.

Definition 1 *(**Disclosure Related Entities**). Let sentence S be a set of words, $S = \{w_1, w_2, \cdots, w_n\}$. A word w_i is considered to be a DRE if it indicates private information such as name of disease, amount of debt, location of meeting, time of outing etc.*

However, dis-joined existence of such entities in any random part of a sentence does not always prove the occurrence of a valid disclosure of private information *(e.g. My son nothing morning no sense makes spoofing not $100 dollars)*. A sentence has to carry a reasonable meaning after being constructed by disclosure related entities (DRE) *(e.g. We are planing to leave for Paris on 31st December in early morning)*. Moreover, non-machine learning methods seemed to perform well based on rules and reference datasets, but they are not scalable and adaptable when time comes to analyze large amount of data. In order to overcome these challenges, this paper employs a framework which is based on typical convolutional neural network with extended capabilities. It first looks for disclosure related entities in a sentence, retrieves syntactic information, identifies grammatical validation, learns semantic information, and then determines the occurrence of disclosure or non-disclosure of information.

3.1   Data

The proposed framework consists of a neural network model that requires labeled data to learn patterns of disclosure and non-disclosure sentences from text data. Unfortunately, no particular data set with ground truth (i.e., set of sentences labeled as disclosure/non-disclosure) is available so far to work with. Therefore, after collecting textual data we use a state of the art Natural Language Processing (NLP) Toolkit named Spacy [51] to conduct a preliminary labeling (i.e., labeling raw dataset for training) of the dataset as well as to pre-process before feeding into the DNN model. The left section of Fig. 3 demonstrates the usage of the NLP Toolkit for both data labeling and pre-processing; the following subsections describe the process in detail.

3.2   Data Collection

In order to collect data from different domains, we consider online platforms where people post reviews, ask questions, post tweets, and discuss from a first-person perspective. Online forums like medical, psychiatric, and relationship communities mostly contain private information through users conversations. However, we also wanted to see whether private information is disclosed by an user unintentionally in public forums (e.g. Stackoverflow, Amazon). This is why we introduce domain diversity here to give the model more generalized data. We sampled the same number of user posts from each domain such as medical forums, social sites, food reviews, place and service reviews etc. All of the domains are selected randomly. This is summarized in Table 1. All the posts are written in English language, and each of them are comprised of 4 to 15 sentences. Average sentence length throughout the whole data set is 9 words. As this research requires data that are related to privacy, we carefully avoided any sensitive resource that could have caused privacy violation. Anonymity has also been assured while collecting these data sets from reliable public sources.

Table 1. Summary of data sources.

Source	Amount of posts
Medhelp forum posts [57]	3000
Amazon product reviews [13]	3000
Amazon food reviews [36]	3000
Hotel reviews [12]	3000
Place of interest reviews [18]	3000
Psychiatric forum posts [41]	3000
Twitter posts [42]	3000
Stack overflow questions [17]	3000
Total	**24000**

In each of the above mentioned domains, people shared their views, feedback, or comments in a set of sentences (i.e., a product review, a twitter status, a question regarding health). Thus they expressed their overall opinions about a product, location, situation etc. Our focus is to analyze each piece of content, and evaluate whether or not an individual is disclosing private information through any of the sentences while expressing his pronouncements. Some examples of private disclosures and public information can be found in Table 2.

3.3 Data Labeling

As mentioned above, no ready-made labeled dataset is found for our experiment where various types of sentences are marked as discloser or non-discloser. Both the privacy policy of available data sources and complexity in classification of such textual data, might be the cause. Yet, this is the most important factor from the model's perspective which learns in a supervised fashion. So, our collected dataset is labeled using an algorithm that is built upon the idea of rule-based approach used by [53,55], and obeying following definitions.

Table 2. Example disclosure and non-disclosure sentences

	Text	Is disclosure
1	I have been living in W Boise Avenue for last few months	Yes
2	I got unexpected divorced after 2 years of relationship	Yes
3	1 pound is equivalent to 1.41 dollars	No
4	My company lost \$1 million dollar revenue in last quarter	Yes
5	Spending \$100 dollars for a lunch in restaurant is too bad	No
6	Our meeting will be at 3 pm in the US Bank building	Yes
7	Yesterday to garbage keywords am nothing Houston more keywords	No
8	I got the Flu	Yes
9	My son nothing morning no sense makes spoofing not \$100 dollars	No
10	We are planing to leave for Paris on 31st December in early morning	Yes
11	Houston is a very populated city to live in	No

Definition 2 (*Disclosure Related Entity Type*). *Each $DRET_f$ is a set of DREs that belong to a type f, where $f \in F = \{Person, Location, Money, Health, Date, Time, Interpersonal Relationship, Business Information\}$. Having D as an infinite set of all possible DREs then*

$$\forall\, DRE_d \in D \,\nexists\, i, j \in F \text{ where } i \neq j, DRE_d \in DRET_i \cap DRET_j$$

By applying an entity and relation extraction tool [51], we implemented the following formal definition of disclosure to classify the dataset:

Definition 3 (*Disclosure*). *Let sentence S be a set of words, $S = \{w_1, w_2, \cdots, w_n\}$. S is disclosing if it satisfies the following condition:*

$$\exists\, w_i, w_j \in S \text{ where } i \neq j, w_i \in DRET_{Person} \wedge w_j \in \bigcup_{f \in F} DRET_f$$

In order to label a sentence as disclosure (Definition 3), we examine the sentence. If it contains one or more entities (i.e., mention of a person, place, location, etc., explained below) and if one of those entities is of type *person* then its labeled as disclosure. This is a simple, yet effective rule which allows us to label our data set with disclosure/non-disclosure classes. A more structured guideline for manual labeling is given below:

1. Start with an example sentence
   (a) Look if that contains one or more DRE (by Definition 1) which falls into the set of DRET (by Definition 2).
   (b) If Count of DRE > 1 AND at least one of the DREs is type of PERSON go to Step 2 otherwise label it as a Nondisclosure sentence.
2. Is it a grammatically valid sentence?
   (a) If YES go to Step 3 otherwise label it as a Nondisclosure sentence.
3. Label the sentence as Disclosure and return to step 1.

This produced 5000 disclosure sentences and 5000 non-disclosure sentences from the collected dataset (Table 1), that yields proper labeled information with ground truth. Human evaluation on the labeled examples (i.e. 20% of the data) was also done for the verification of the applied techniques. We use this data to train our model which we hypothesize will generalize to new data, that we show in our evaluation. Although, those 24,000 posts contained more than 100 thousands of sentences, we picked only those with disclosure related entities in it. Hence, the final quantity becomes lower after eliminating most of the sentences with non-disclosure content.

At this stage of our work, we consider the following entity types while discriminating sentences with privacy disclosure: Person *(e.g. I, He, Robert)*, Location *(e.g. Starbucks, Airport, Main Street)*, Money *(e.g. $100, 1 million)*, Date *(e.g. Tomorrow, 31st December)*, Time *(e.g. 7 pm, Evening)*, Interpersonal Relationships *(e.g. Married, Divorced)*, Health Information *(e.g. Flu, Pregnant)*, and Business Information *(e.g. Revenue, Loss, Profit)*. It's worth mentioning that the types mentioned above are just few from all possible categories that might be related to privacy and security. The number of considerable categories could be extended or reduced as per problem domain.

3.4 Data Pre-processing

As can be seen from the examples in Table 2, many DREs (e.g., I, divorce, 3 pm, $100 dollar, Houston) can be used in both private disclosures and in public posts. This makes the problem particularly challenging because we cannot simply rely on the lexical items in the text; we have to consider the intent of the author of the text, and somehow determine if the intent was for the text to be public (i.e. DRE used in a public statement) or private (i.e. DRE used in personal context). To this end, we do special tokenization and enrich our data with additional information using linguistic details such as part-of-speech tags and syntactic dependency relations. We make use of the NLP toolkit Spacy [51] for all of our data pre-processing. This tool is also used for feature enrichment by creating synthetic features (e.g. dependency tree, POS tags) out of existing features (i.e. word tokens, sentences).

Tokenization. In many text-based natural language processing tasks, the text is pre-processed by removing punctuation and stop words, leaving only the lexical items. However, we found that the way people punctuate their texts helps give the clues as to whether or not it is a valid private or public information. That is, we considered tokens from an example sentence like *Ok... I will meet you; tomorrow morning,, in-front of the Coffee Shop!... :)* are *["Ok", "I", "will", "meet", "you", "tomorrow", "morning", ",", "in", "front", "of", "the", "Coffee", "Shop"]*. Therefore, we use the NLP Toolkit to tokenize the sentences in a customized way that ignores redundant tokens such as *",", ";", "!", ":)"* but keeps the important ones. This step of considering all the valid sequential tokens helps our model learn important arrangement of tokens for validating relationships of entities. This is somewhat in contrast to other text analysis literature where clearing off all the punctuation tends to improve task performance. However, keeping the punctuations showed better performance than removing them, throughout our experiment.

Syntactic Structure. Present linguistic theory, classifies certain formal properties of language as "purely stylistic." That is, two sentences can have different forms but express the same meaning [16,44]. For example, a sentence with the structure *subject verb direct-object preposition object* is semantically equivalent to *subject verb object direct-object*, though they are syntactically different. Also, as per our experiments, dependency parse information, and parts of speech tags are two synthetic features that improved the performance of the neural network model. This helps the model to observe common sequence of tokens as well as co-occurrence of dependency tags. We use a Dependency Parser (DP) Toolkit [51] to extract the syntactic relation information (which is different from, but in some ways similar to, entity relation information). This allowed us to enrich our data with dependency parse information.

Parts-of-Speech. Even though we use syntactic structure, we also include parts of speech as a slightly less structured representation of the input text that is also non-lexical. (We found, however, that including Parts-of-Speech did not dramatically increase the performance of our model.)

Figure 1 shows an example of the linguistic feature enrichment for the example sentence *Me and Steve will meet you tonight* for parts-of-speech (which appear below the words) and the dependency parse tree. Figure 2 shows the entities with their tagged entity types.

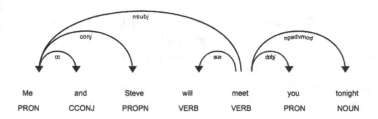

Fig. 1. Parts-of-speech and dependency parse tree of an example sentence.

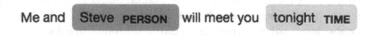

Fig. 2. Recognized entities in an example sentence.

In summary, our data set is comprised of the original tokenized text enriched with parts-of-speech, tagged entities, and syntactic information.

3.5 Model and Approach

Our model composes together multiple channels of a convolutional neural network to perform the disclosure/non-disclosure classification task, where each channel refers to different representations (i.e., word tokens, dependency parse tree, parts-of-speech tags) of the same candidate piece of text. All the channels use similar hyper parameters (e.g., input/output dimension, activation function, dropout) applied to them to keep computational consistency. Shared input layers are combined together at the first stage of the neural network which is described in this section.

3.6 Neural Network Architecture

The primary task is a supervised optimization problem while minimizing error of classifying disclosure/non-disclosure sentences. An overview of our proposed framework, along with the core model, is represented in Fig. 3. We explain most of the important constituents of the system below.

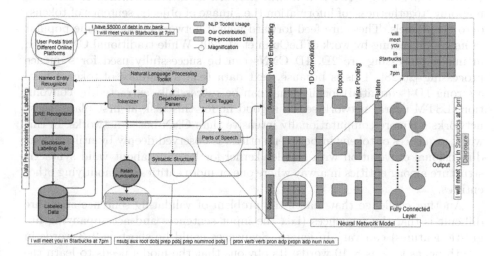

Fig. 3. The bigger picture of the whole framework combining linguistics and neural network stages.

Word Embedding Layer. Word embedding represents words as a dense vector representation in high-dimensional space [10,23,54]. Unlike the typical bag-of-words model, where words are represented as very sparse high-dimensional (e.g. 1-hot) vectors, in word embeddings, words are represented by dense vectors where a vector represents the projection of the word into a continuous vector space. The most important benefit of utilizing word embedding is that the position of a word or token within the vector space is learned from text and is based on the words that surround the word where it is used. This is useful because words that have similar semantic meanings are close (in terms of Euclidean distance) to each other; which is more semantically useful than one-hot encodings, in which all words are semantically equidistant from each other.

In the proposed neural network architecture, we apply word-embedding as the first layer of the model to learn embeddings through training. Specifically, three separate embedding layers are used as the first hidden layer of each of the multichannel input of the network. We prefer this technique of learning embeddings because we did not observe better accuracy while using pre-trained word vectors like GloVe [39], rather it caused computational overhead. Glove for example, contains 800 billion of tokens which in turns incorporate 800 billion of word vectors. On the other hand, these embedding layers learn semantic relationships from DREs, words, and tags from our data throughout the process. This is particularly crucial, as we apply embeddings not just to words, but also to three types derived linguistic features: parts-of-speech, entities, and dependency parses, as explained in Sect. 3.1). We observed better performance while implementing this approach.

Convolution Layer. CNN is a neural network architecture which is useful in mapping 'togetherness' of information (i.e., image of objects, sentence of tokens) onto class labels. These are feed-forward neural networks that became popular in image processing by work of LeCunn et al. [29]. While traditional CNNs used in image processing are 2D, 1D CNNs can be successfully used for sequence processing [26,28]. This is because, text data (e.g. a sentence of tokens) have a strong 1D (sequential) locality that can be successfully extracted by convolution. LSTM neural network seems a good fit for this task at first place, these networks are more computationally intensive than CNN-based networks. In this work, sequences of tokens in-between entities is observed deeply by utilizing one dimensional convolution with smaller kernel for learning about valid syntactic structure among entities in a way where one or more entities are modifying other entities.

Another challenge that makes the problem of validating sentence structure difficult is that the sequences (i.e., the input sentences and accompanying linguistic features) can vary in length. Sequences could be short as 2–3 words in length or, as long as 8–10 words. Its obvious that the model needs to learn the co-occurrence of tokens or dependencies between symbols in the input sequence. Unlike two-dimensional convolution in an image processing area which focuses on spatial visual structure, a one dimensional convolution suits perfectly in this approach for looking into sentences. As with the word embedding layers, there is a convolution layer for each channel–one for each linguistic feature type.

Following each convolution layer, we introduce a dropout layer, a pooling layer and, a flatten layer before going into the concatenation layer where inputs from different channels are merged.

Concatenation. In this layer, the three channels are brought together. Our final goal is a single, composed neural network that uses the three linguistic feature types then performs a single binary classification task. Concatenation is the simplest form of bringing these different channels together by simply representing the output layer of the respective CNNs from each channel as a single input into the following layer.

Fully Connected Layer. After concatenation, we apply several densely connected network layers. These hidden layers are comprised of one hundred neurons in the input, then ten neurons in the hidden layer and, finally an output neuron for binary classification at the end. We implemented the well-known Rectified Linear Unit (ReLU) neurons for the first two layers and Sigmoidal neuron in the output layer.[1] Our final resulting model is depicted in Fig. 3 where three separate channels take in three different linguistic feature sequence types, each channel begins with an embedding layer, followed by a CNN layer; those three layers are concatenated, then a three-layer feed-forward network made up of dense layers (using standard ReLU and sigmoid activations) outputs a distribution over a binary class.

In summary, the model is not only learning about the private information but also learning about the correct grammatical structure of such sentences. We train it with words themselves as well as with two other representations (i.e. parts of speech and dependency tree) of the example sentences. This helps the machine learning model to learn both privacy related tokens and pattern of a correct sentence.

4 Experiment

This section and the subsequent portions contain details about the experimental environments and tools, along with implementation of the proposed model in the processed data set and results from an off-line evaluation.

4.1 Data Preprocessing

In the data pre-processing step, we applied Spacy [51] to derive the linguistic features of each sentence. This tool comes with several features to analyze natural language text. Parts of speech tagging, deriving syntactic structure, and tokenization are done by this toolkit. The reasons behind selecting Spacy include - its trainable statistical model (we trained its existing NER model), dependency parser, tokenizer, noun chunk separator in a single toolkit. Two peer-reviewed papers in 2015 confirm that spaCy offers the fastest syntactic parser in the world and that its accuracy is within 1% of the best available. It also contains a statistical entity recognition model in it, but does not have an entity recognizer

---

[1] It is worth mentioning that we get little fluctuation on the accuracy value while changing the number of neurons in these layers. It seems obvious because, this layer might have needed more neurons for better non-linearity understanding when it sees relatively more data.

for more specific types in which we are interested, such as Interpersonal Relationships, Health Information and, Business Information. The default model identifies a variety of named and numeric entities, including companies, locations, organizations and products, falling somewhat short of identifying some additional entities according to our problem scope.

For example, out of the box, it can not identify *flu* as a disclosure-related entity, whereas it should be identified as a Health Information type entity as a task of the first step toward the whole disclosure recognition system. We were, however, able to leverage Spacy's model extension provisions [51], resulting in an extended entity recognizer model that was trained to identify Interpersonal Relationships, Health Information and, Business Information such as *divorce*, *marriage*, *flu*, *cancer*, *fever*, *loss*, *profit* etc. as valid recognizable entities. An annotator tool by Spacy called Prodigy [52] is used to train the NER model further for identifying these new types of entities. Prodigy has a loop model architecture by which it shows relevant keywords based on the annotation of previous steps.

After this, text encoding is done using Keras [25]. At the end of integer encoding, post padding with zeros are also done for all the sequences or sentences to a certain value which is the maximum length of a sentence in the whole training data set. The post padding is needed to make all the input sequences same length which is required by the later neural network architecture.

4.2 Neural Network Implementation

For implementing the word embeddings we use the *Embedding* layer of Keras [23] that turns positive integers into dense vectors of fixed size [23]. As per its requirement, the integer encoding of all text data is completed on the earlier stages. At the beginning, the embedding layers are initialized with random weights and then learn embeddings for all of the words in the training dataset.

For the *Convolution* layer, we use the Conv1D layer of Keras. To avoid the over-fitting problem of this neural network, we applied 20% dropout rate after each convolution layers using Dropout layer of Keras. This is a common practice which means setting the values of 20% input units to 0 at each update during each iteration of the training life cycle. A pooling layer is also added just after the dropout layer by utilizing *Pooling* followed by a *Flatten* layer of Keras.

The Keras functional API provides some methods to define complex model structure such as multi input and or multi output models that best suits our case. The `concatenate` method of Keras takes all the output vectors from the convolution layers and merges them into a single vector which then acts as the input to the later fully connected layers [24].

4.3 Model Hyper Parameters

This section describes all the needed model hyper parameters and intuition behind the selection of those parameters and associated values. First of all, random seeding is used for maintaining reproducibility while experimenting with different architectural values. For the `Input` layers that define the shape for each of the three multi channel inputs, is determined by the length of the longest sentence (by tokens).

In each of the three embedding layers all the mandatory parameters are chosen as follows: input dimension is the vocabulary size and, output dimension that describes the size of output vectors where words are embedded is 100 and increased to 200 while working with more than twenty thousand sentences.

Convolution layers are comprised of 32 filters with kernel size of 4, and `relu` as activation function, keeping all other parameters to default values as determined by Keras. Some default parameters are worth mentioning such as, `valid` (no padding) as padding type, 1 as the strides and dilation rate, `zeros` as bias initializers, with no kernel regularization (regularizers allow to apply penalties on layer parameters during optimization).

Pooling layers are responsible for the max pooling operations on the temporal data which are comprised of 2 as pooling window and, strides for downscaling. This layer uses `valid` as the padding type by default. To prepare the data for concatenation, we flatten all the multi channel inputs separately after the max pooling.

We use ReLU (Rectifier Linear Unit) as the activation function for all the neurons in the dense hidden layers, whereas Sigmoid is used as the activation function in the only neuron of the output layer where we get a probability value towards disclosure or, non-disclosure. The model is trained using 50 epochs, with a batch size of 100.

4.4 Model Summary

A high level summary of the multi channel convolutional neural network goes as follows - each embedding layer produces 100 dimensional word embeddings, and connected to the earlier input layers. Also, each of the convolution layers contains 32 filters with no padding. After the convolution, dropout layers and pooling layers are employed. Later, three separate flatten layers are used. Eventually, a concatenation layer merges all the input vectors to a single one, and forwards to the fully connected layers. Finally, the output layer that contains a single neuron produces the probability score for the desired binary classification.

4.5 Task and Procedure

Our task is a binary classification task of identifying whether a piece of short text contains a personal disclosure or not. We compare our model (as described above) to several other known classification models after the data pre-processing step (i.e., all models had the same inputs). Procedure of applying those models and their outcomes are described below.

Simple Convolutional Neural Network. A simple CNN with only word tokenization is first applied for identifying disclosure and non-disclosure events. This simple network also uses a word embedding layer along with 32 filters with kernel size of 3 by maintaining same padding for convolution, max pooling of 2, using binary cross entropy as loss function and, ReLU as the activation function. This network serves as our baseline.

LSTM Recurrent Neural Network. We also compare to a recurrent neural network, LSTM, because LSTMs have been shown to produce good results in sequential language processing tasks. We use a word embedding, LST (with 100 neurons), and dropout (20%) layer.

CNN with LSTM Network. We also compare to a combination of the CNN and LSTM models as they are explained above. This allows the model to combine the benefits of the sequential LSTM and filters from the CNN in a single model. The data of this experiment contains one-dimensional spatial structure in the sequence of words in conversational text and the CNN (Convolutional Neural Network) tries to pick out invariant features for disclosure and non-disclosure events. This learned spatial features is then treated as sequences by the subsequent LSTM layer. This combined neural network shows very good improvement in accuracy but going through an obvious computational overhead.

The Multichannel CNN. Eventually, our proposed multichannel convolutional neural network is applied for the classification of disclosure and non-disclosure sentences by providing word tokens in one channel, dependency parse tree to another channel, and parts of speech tags to the third channel. This is the final model we integrate in the proposed framework (after the data simplification stage) because of it's ideal performance. Its worth mentioning that, a multichannel LSTM recurrent neural network was also applied for the classification of the data set Just like the final multichannel CNN. This network also gets different data representations into different channels but could not beat the final model. Even though, LSTM based network seems best suit for learning pattern from sequential data, our convolutional network makes best use of learning togetherness of tokens on the pre-processed data and outperformed all of our other experimental models.

4.6   Metrics

Classification accuracy (Eq. 1), F-Measure, and Receiver Operating Characteristic (ROC) are used as the evaluation metrics. We consider these different types of evaluation metrics because we take it as a binary classification task where accuracy, precision, recall, and diagnostic ability of disclosure identification are equally important. We use labeled data to train our model in a supervised fashion, and evaluation is also based on similarly labeled data-set (actually a split from the original data set by 30%). Remaining 70% of data was used as training and validation set, containing 50% and 20% in each group respectively.

$$Accuracy(ACC) = \frac{\sum True positive + \sum True negative}{\sum Total population} \tag{1}$$

For observing the precision and recall of our final model, we consider F-Score as per following equation (Eq. 2). We try to look how precise our model is, while identifying disclosure sentences as well as its capability of pulling out disclosure sentences as much as possible from the test data set.

$$F_1 = \frac{2}{\frac{(TP+FN)}{TP} + \frac{TP+FP}{TP}} = \frac{2TP}{2TP + FP + FN} \tag{2}$$

A ROC curve is used to evaluate the association of true positive rate against the false positive rate to examine the sensitivity, and fall-out of the model. We also calculate the AUC (area under curve) value of the ROC curve.

4.7 Results

For experimenting with different models to achieve a strong classification result, the model variants described above with different architectures are applied in the same data set. Each variant gets the same simplified and entity marked data.

The simple convolutional neural network that uses only word tokenization shows 69.2% accuracy in identifying disclosure and non-disclosure occurrence. Simple LSTM network shows 70.6%, and the combined neural network of convolution and LSTM layers shows 74.1% of accuracy. The multi-channel LSTM neural network model achieved 81% accuracy.

Our proposed model that uses multi-channel inputs and convolution layers along with word embeddings shows 93.72% accuracy on the data set of labeled disclosure and non-disclosure sentences. Also, it shows significant learning improvement on the amount of training data set. Figure 4 shows the comparison of accuracy among all the experimented models along with the final proposed one. Accuracy is measured on the test data that is basically a split of the whole data set and unseen to the model while training.

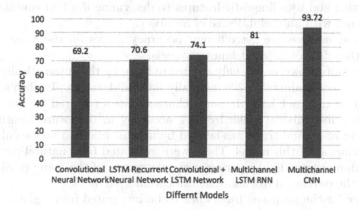

Fig. 4. Comparison among different models

The model shows 0.94 F-Score on disclosure label and, 0.93 on non-disclosure with an overall weighted F-Score of 0.93. Figure 5 shows the ROC curve that is generated as per the predicted labels and, true labels of the test data set. We find significantly large area under the curve which is 0.98 that clearly indicates the strength of the classification model. The ROC curve tells us where we can reliably set the model to disallow false negatives. Its important to know because in this particular task the system should notify users about information disclosure in a lower threshold (i.e., positive if prediction beyond 0.40) to be strict in information leakage.

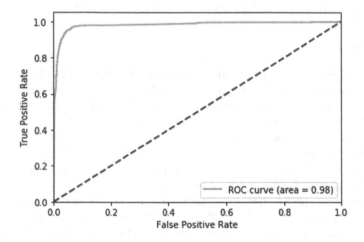

Fig. 5. Receiver operating characteristic curve

These are overall positive results. They show that, despite a lack of large amounts of labeled data, we can train a classifier that goes beyond simple keyword spotting and uses linguistic features to determine if a text contains a disclosure or not with an useful degree of accuracy.

Table 3 shows how we get different accuracy scores on the same data set based on the effect of different input channels.

These results, however, are only applied to learning the automatically labeled data. We further evaluate on 200 manually labeled data (i.e., English sentences which may or may not have the same characteristics required for our labeling rule, as described above) yielded 86.4% accuracy in disclosure identification. This dataset of ground truth was labeled by human who had no idea about the working principle of this model. Those were evaluated from natural perspective of the human agents. This experiment simulates one of the many possible case studies of the developed disclosure identification system.

In order for the proposed framework to be integrated into a global solution for the end users' privacy management problem, a web browser extension is developed to detect privacy disclosures as users are typing their text messages. The implementation is based on a server based request-response architecture.

Table 3. Impact of using multichannel data.

Channel	Accuracy %
Single channel with word tokens	70.6
+ dependency parse tree information as second channel	87.4
+ parts of speech tags as third channel	89.0
Multi-channel input	93.7

The client (i.e. Browser Extension) captures user side text and sends to the server for classification where the trained model is already deployed. If any sentence contains privacy disclosure then the color of that text changes to red, as depicted in Fig. 6. On the other hand, as represented in Fig. 7, the color of the text does not change, since no disclosure is detected.

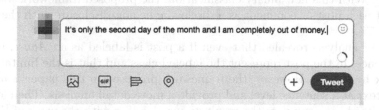

Fig. 6. Information disclosure marked as red automatically by the browser extension. (Color figure online)

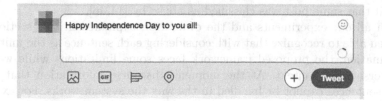

Fig. 7. Non-private information keeps default color. (Color figure online)

This implementation of the proposed framework is one of the many possible use cases. It is also important to note that we recognize the limitation of the developed tool, since sending personal data to a remote server for a classification purposes might result in user's privacy violation. For the future version of this tool we will implement an architecture based on a pre-trained model stored in the client side (e.g. Using TensorflowJS). Source code of this implementation (i.e. the web browser extension and the API server) along with other resources regarding this work are made available for interested researchers[2].

---

[2] https://anonymous.4open.science/repository/3c84ab7b-02ce-4fd7-b982-f278d6f3c4f4/.

5   Discussion and Analysis

For a baseline evaluation and assessment of the generalizability of the proposed framework, a dataset that was created by Schrading et al. and Choudhury et al. [14,46] is utilized to detect privacy disclosures in Reddit users' posts and comments. This dataset was created mainly to analyze and study the dynamics of domestic abuse in electronic social media (i.e. Reddit). This dataset is comprised of posts and comments from Reddit users under several sub-reddits such as *abuseinterrupted, domesticviolence, survivorsofabuse, casualconversation, advice, anxiety, anger, relationships, and relationship_advice.* All the posts and comments are labeled with one of the above classes.

For the purpose of creating a comparable result, we divided the posts into two classes of Disclosure or Non-disclosure. Submissions under the sub-reddits - *abuseinterrupted, domesticviolence, survivorsofabuse, and relationship* are considered as *Disclosure* class and *casualconversation, and advice* as *Non-disclosure* (Table 4). With this new binary classification, the proposed framework was able to detect each post or comment as a disclosure or non-disclosure with the accuracy of 95%.

Further analysis revealed that even if a post is labeled as an *Abuse*, not all the sentences in the post represent the labeled class and that is the limitation of the work by [14,46]. However, the framework proposed in this paper is able to classify text at a sentence level and provide a more detail analysis. Therefore, in order to be able to compare the result of our classifier with the work of [14,46], we implemented a rule that if at least 70% (i.e. 7 out of 10 sentences of a submission) of the sentences of a post are classified as disclosure, then that entire post is classified as a disclosure. The result of the classifier was assumed correct if that same post was classified as abuse by [14,46].

From all our experiments and the evaluation explained in this section, we have been able to recognize that with considering each sentence as the unit piece of information, the proposed framework faces some limitations while working on conversational context. At the moment, discourse information that spans beyond sentences cannot be handled in the way the system works. For example a chat conversation like - *:How is your son? ..., :Bad ..., Got flu ...* can mislead the whole system for identifying both the disclosure and the actual nominal subject of this context. Whereas the understandable and rephrased version of the sentence is actually *My son got the flu* and is certainly a disclosure. One possible workaround is to implement that exact same procedures with an extended lookup window. For example, an information extraction step can be implemented in a sliding window style where each window will contain more than one phrases or utterances. Thus, it might be able to find the semantics, and the dependency parse tree of the conversation.

Another limitation of this proposed system is related to incorrectly (i.e., grammatically) written sentences. People often do not care about sentence structure while texting (which is more like speech than standard text) with close friends, and family members. On the other hand, this system moderately depends on sentence structure, specifically structure in-between entities.

Table 4. Summary of the reddit dataset.

Sub-reddit	Class	Quantity	Target class
abuseinterrupted	Abuse	1653	Disclosure
domesticviolence	Abuse	749	Disclosure
survivorsofabuse	Abuse	512	Disclosure
relationship	Relationship	8201	Disclosure
Total	–	11,115	–
casualconversation	Not-abuse	7286	Nondisclosure
advice	Not-abuse	5913	Nondisclosure
Total	–	13,199	–

6   Conclusion and Future Work

A practical model of privacy protection is in dire need by users in the era of social networks that results in activities such as posting online, chatting, text messaging, blogging, and playing online games, etc. Therefore, the development of algorithm and tools that helps users to identifying privacy disclosure in textual data is important. While many research studies in this area mainly focus on classifying textual data as public or private at the document or paragraph level, only few of those are concerned with the privacy detection at the sentence level analysis. Hence, these approaches can not be used for managing privacy for users and they are mostly designed for privacy protection of organization and corporations.

To address this limitation, this paper proposes a privacy disclosure iden-tification framework, comprised of neural network model with linguistics. The proposed framework is capable of: (I) detecting disclosure related entities more effectively by utilizing natural language processing techniques rather than rely-ing on random keywords from an unbound set of tokens, (II) conducting disclo-sure detection analysis only on sentences with correct subject-verb agreement to increase performance time.

For the proof of concept, we conducted several experiments, examining vari-ous machine learning based algorithms Fig. 4 with the different types of data pre-processing techniques, and parameter tunning approaches, while experimenting with various neural network architectures. Throughout this process it was proven that the entity based evaluation, and enriching the input data with additional underlying features helped improving the performance of the model. Convolu-tion over the feature vectors resulted in learning about the sentence structure as well as to overcome the computational overhead.

The future work will concentrate on extending the number of Disclosure Related Entity Types (DRET) to improve the disclosure detection process. Fur-ther, the proposed framework will be made more intelligent to be able to infer from the text analysis the interpersonal relationship (i.e., relationship among friends, family members, colleagues, and public), the context in which the disclosure occurs, and the timing of disclosure to provide an effective privacy management tools an algorithms for users. In order to achieve this objective, an inter-annotator agreement measures and annotation guidelines will be used to ensure consistent annotations, while developing a generalized dataset that will include human annotation through crowdsourcing.

Acknowledgments. The authors would like to thank National Science Foundation for its support through the Computer and Information Science and Engineering (CISE) program and Research Initiation Initiative(CRII) grant number 1657774 of the Secure and Trustworthy Cyberspace (SaTC) program: A System for Privacy Management in Ubiquitous Environments.

References

1. Abril, D., Navarro-Arribas, G., Torra, V.: On the declassification of confidential documents. In: Torra, V., Narakawa, Y., Yin, J., Long, J. (eds.) MDAI 2011. LNCS (LNAI), vol. 6820, pp. 235–246. Springer, Heidelberg (2011). https://doi.org/10.1007/978-3-642-22589-5_22
2. Agerri, R., Artola, X., Beloki, Z., Rigau, G., Soroa, A.: Big data for natural language processing: a streaming approach. Knowl. Based Syst. **79**, 36–42 (2015)
3. Andalibi, N., Öztürk, P., Forte, A.: Sensitive self-disclosures, responses, and social support on Instagram: the case of #depression. In: CSCW, pp. 1485–1500 (2017)
4. Bettini, C., Wang, X.S., Jajodia, S.: Protecting privacy against location-based personal identification. In: Jonker, W., Petković, M. (eds.) SDM 2005. LNCS, vol. 3674, pp. 185–199. Springer, Heidelberg (2005). https://doi.org/10.1007/11552338_13
5. Boyd, V.: Financial privacy in the United States and the European union: a path to transatlantic regulatory harmonization. Berkeley J. Int'l L. **24**, 939 (2006)
6. Buchanan, T., Paine, C., Joinson, A.N., Reips, U.D.: Development of measures of online privacy concern and protection for use on the internet. J. Assoc. Inf. Sci. Technol. **58**(2), 157–165 (2007)
7. Caliskan Islam, A., Walsh, J., Greenstadt, R.: Privacy detective: detecting private information and collective privacy behavior in a large social network. In: Proceedings of the 13th Workshop on Privacy in the Electronic Society, pp. 35–46. ACM (2014)
8. Chow, R., Golle, P., Staddon, J.: Detecting privacy leaks using corpus-based association rules. In: Proceedings of the 14th ACM SIGKDD International Conference on Knowledge Discovery and Data Mining, pp. 893–901. ACM (2008)
9. Christofides, E., Muise, A., Desmarais, S.: Information disclosure and control on facebook: are they two sides of the same coin or two different processes? Cyberpsychol. Behav. **12**(3), 341–345 (2009)
10. Word Embedding Wikipedia Contributors: Word embedding — Wikipedia, the free Encyclopedia (2018). https://en.wikipedia.org/w/index.php?title=Word_embedding&oldid=836044700. Accessed 7 May 2018
11. Costello, J.: Nursing older dying patients: findings from an ethnographic study of death and dying in elderly care wards. J. Adv. Nurs. **35**(1), 59–68 (2001)
12. Datafiniti: Hotel reviews — Kaggle (2018). https://www.kaggle.com/datafiniti/hotel-reviews. Accessed 01 May 2018

13. Dave, K., Lawrence, S., Pennock, D.M.: Mining the peanut gallery: opinion extraction and semantic classification of product reviews. In: Proceedings of the 12th International Conference on World Wide Web, pp. 519–528. ACM (2003)
14. De Choudhury, M., De, S.: Mental health discourse on reddit: self-disclosure, social support, and anonymity. In: ICWSM (2014)
15. DeCew, J.W.: The priority of privacy for medical information. Soc. Philos. Policy **17**(2), 213–234 (2000)
16. Evans, D.A., Zhai, C.: Noun-phrase analysis in unrestricted text for information retrieval. In: Proceedings of the 34th Annual Meeting on Association for Computational Linguistics, pp. 17–24. Association for Computational Linguistics (1996)
17. Stack Exchange: Stack exchange data dump. Stack Exchange, Inc.: Free Download, Borrow, and Streaming: Internet Archive (2018). https://archive.org/details/stackexchange. Accessed 01 May 2018
18. Ganesan, K., Zhai, C.: Opinion-based entity ranking. Inf. Retrieval **15**(2), 116–150 (2012)
19. Groves, T.: Why is analyzing text so hard? (2018). http://www.ibmbigdatahub.com/blog/why-analyzing-text-so-hard. Accessed 01 Feb 2018
20. Hern, A.: Far more than 87m Facebook users had data compromised, MPs told (2018). https://www.theguardian.com/uk-news/2018/apr/17/facebook-users-data-compromised-far-more-than-87m-mps-told/-cambridge-analytica. Accessed 01 May 2018
21. Joinson, A.N., Reips, U.D., Buchanan, T., Schofield, C.B.P.: Privacy, trust, and self-disclosure online. Hum. Comput. Interact. **25**(1), 1–24 (2010)
22. Joshaghani, R., Mehrpouyan, H.: A model-checking approach for enforcing purpose-based privacy policies. In: IEEE Symposium on Privacy-Aware Computing (PAC), pp. 178–179. IEEE (2017)
23. Keras: Embedding layers - Keras documentation (2018). https://keras.io/layers/embeddings/. Accessed 01 Feb 2018
24. Keras: Guide to the functional API - Keras documentation (2018). https://keras.io/getting-started/functional-api-guide/. Accessed 01 Feb 2018
25. Keras: Text preprocessing - Keras documentation (2018). https://keras.io/preprocessing/text/#tokenizer. Accessed 01 Feb 2018
26. Kravchik, M., Shabtai, A.: Anomaly detection; industrial control systems; convolutional neural networks. arXiv preprint arXiv:1806.08110 (2018)
27. Krishnamurthy, B., Wills, C.E.: On the leakage of personally identifiable information via online social networks. In: Proceedings of the 2nd ACM Workshop on Online Social Networks, pp. 7–12. ACM (2009)
28. LeCun, Y., Bengio, Y., et al.: Convolutional networks for images, speech, and time series. Handb. Brain Theor. Neural Netw. **3361**(10), 1995 (1995)
29. LeCun, Y., et al.: Handwritten digit recognition with a back-propagation network. In: Advances in Neural Information Processing Systems, pp. 396–404 (1990)
30. Leyshon, A., Signoretta, P., Knights, D., Alferoff, C., Burton, D.: Walking with moneylenders: the ecology of the UK home-collected credit industry. Urban Stud. **43**(1), 161–186 (2006)
31. LIWC: Linguistic inquiry and word count (2018). https://liwc.wpengine.com/. Accessed 01 February 2018
32. Madden, M.: Privacy management on social media sites. In: Pew Internet Report, pp. 1–20 (2012)
33. Madden, M., et al.: Teens, social media, and privacy. Pew Res. Center **21**, 2–86 (2013)

34. Malhotra, N.K., Kim, S.S., Agarwal, J.: Internet Users' Information Privacy Concerns (IUIPC): the construct, the scale, and a causal model. Inf. Syst. Res. **15**(4), 336–355 (2004)
35. Mao, H., Shuai, X., Kapadia, A.: Loose tweets: an analysis of privacy leaks on twitter. In: Proceedings of the 10th Annual ACM Workshop on Privacy in the Electronic Society, pp. 1–12. ACM (2011)
36. McAuley, J.J., Leskovec, J.: From amateurs to connoisseurs: modeling the evolution of user expertise through online reviews. In: Proceedings of the 22nd International Conference on World Wide Web, pp. 897–908. ACM (2013)
37. Meerabeau, L.: The management of embarrassment and sexuality in health care. J. Adv. Nurs. **29**(6), 1507–1513 (1999)
38. Mehrpouyan, H., Azpiazu, I.M., Pera, M.S.: Measuring personality for automatic elicitation of privacy preferences. In: IEEE Symposium on Privacy-Aware Computing (PAC), vol. 00, pp. 84–95, August 2017. https://doi.org/10.1109/PAC.2017.15, doi.ieeecomputersociety.org/10.1109/PAC.2017.15
39. Mikolov, T., Sutskever, I., Chen, K., Corrado, G.S., Dean, J.: Distributed representations of words and phrases and their compositionality. In: Advances in Neural Information Processing Systems, pp. 3111–3119 (2013)
40. Milberg, S.J., Burke, S.J., Smith, H.J., Kallman, E.A.: Values, personal information privacy, and regulatory approaches. Commun. ACM **38**(12), 65–74 (1995)
41. Milne, D.N., Pink, G., Hachey, B., Calvo, R.A.: CLPsych 2016 shared task: triaging content in online peer-support forums. In: Proceedings of the Third Workshop on Computational Linguistics and Clinical Psychology, pp. 118–127 (2016)
42. Pak, A., Paroubek, P.: Twitter as a corpus for sentiment analysis and opinion mining. In: LREc, vol. 10 (2010)
43. Razavi, A.H., Ghazinour, K.: Personal health information detection in unstructured web documents. In: IEEE 26th International Symposium on Computer-Based Medical Systems (CBMS), pp. 155–160. IEEE (2013)
44. Sachs, J.S.: Recoption memory for syntactic and semantic aspects of connected discourse. Percept. Psychophys. **2**(9), 437–442 (1967)
45. Sánchez, D., Batet, M., Viejo, A.: Detecting sensitive information from textual documents: an information-theoretic approach. In: Torra, V., Narukawa, Y., López, B., Villaret, M. (eds.) MDAI 2012. LNCS (LNAI), vol. 7647, pp. 173–184. Springer, Heidelberg (2012). https://doi.org/10.1007/978-3-642-34620-0_17
46. Schrading, N., Alm, C.O., Ptucha, R., Homan, C.: An analysis of domestic abuse discourse on reddit. In: Proceedings of the 2015 Conference on Empirical Methods in Natural Language Processing, pp. 2577–2583 (2015)
47. Serenko, N., Fan, L.: Patients' perceptions of privacy and their outcomes in healthcare. Int. J. Behav. Healthc. Res. **4**(2), 101–122 (2013)
48. Siegel, A.: In pursuit of privacy: laws, ethics, and the rise of technology. Wilson Q. **21**(4), 100 (1997)
49. Singh, J., Nene, M.J.: A survey on machine learning techniques for intrusion detection systems. Int. J. Adv. Res. Comput. Commun. Eng. **2**(11), 4349–4355 (2013)
50. Solon, O.: Facebook says Cambridge Analytica may have gained 37m more users' data (2018). https://www.theguardian.com/technology/2018/apr/04/facebook-cambridge-analytica-user-data-latest-more-than-thought. Accessed 01 May 2018
51. Spacy: Linguistic features (2018). https://spacy.io/usage/linguistic-features. Accessed 01 Feb 2018
52. Spacy: Named entity recognition (2018). https://prodi.gy/features/named-entity-recognition. Accessed 01 Feb 2018

53. Sweeney, L.: Replacing personally-identifying information in medical records, the scrub system. In: Proceedings of the AMIA Annual Fall Symposium, p. 333. American Medical Informatics Association (1996)
54. Turney, P.D., Pantel, P.: From frequency to meaning: vector space models of semantics. J. Artif. Intell. Res. **37**, 141–188 (2010)
55. Vasalou, A., Gill, A.J., Mazanderani, F., Papoutsi, C., Joinson, A.: Privacy dictionary: a new resource for the automated content analysis of privacy. J. Assoc. Inf. Sci. Technol. **62**(11), 2095–2105 (2011)
56. Wang, Y.C., Burke, M., Kraut, R.: Modeling self-disclosure in social networking sites. In: Proceedings of the 19th ACM Conference on Computer-Supported Cooperative Work & Social Computing, pp. 74–85. ACM (2016)
57. Yang, C.C., Tang, X.: Estimating user influence in the MedHelp social network. IEEE Intell. Syst. **27**(5), 44–50 (2012)

Research on Information Security Test Evaluation Method Based on Intelligent Connected Vehicle

Yanan Zhang, Shengqiang Han$^{(\boxtimes)}$, Stevenyin Zhong, Peiji Shi,
and Xuebin Shao

Automotive Data Center, China Automotive Technology
and Research Center Co., Ltd., Tianjin 300393, China
{zhangyanan,hanshengqiang}@catarc.ac.cn
http://www.catarc.ac.cn/ac2016/index.html

Abstract. In order to effectively evaluate the information security level for an intelligent and connected vehicle, a novel Intelligent Connected Vehicle (ICV) Information Security Attack and Defense (ICV-ISAD) test evaluation method is proposed in this paper. ICV-ISAD test method is based on long-term large number of real vehicle test experiments. It mainly consists of security threat and risk analysis, test strategy design, test tool call, test point mapping, test procedure execution, and remediation measures mapping. Using ICV-ISAD test method, we conducted test experiments to In-vehicle Network, Telematics Box, Engine Control Unit, In-Vehicle Infotainment, Mobile Application, Radio and Telematics Service Provider for different types of vehicle. The results show that some vulnerabilities exist in ICV's system, such as gateway filtering vulnerability, high-risk port opening, Cross Site Scripting (XSS), Structured Query Language (SQL) injection, weak password, and cleartext network traffic (HTTP). Besides, ICV-ISAD test method could map some remediation measures or recommendations for these vulnerabilities. It denotes that ICV-ISAD test method can effectively test and evaluate the information security of ICV.

Keywords: Intelligent connected vehicle · Information security ·
Test evaluation · Vulnerability · Remediation measure

1 Introduction

Intelligent Connected Vehicle (ICV) is a new generation of vehicle which is equipped with advanced in-vehicle sensors, controllers, actuators and other devices, and integrates modern communication and network technology to realize intelligent information exchange and sharing between vehicles and X (people, cars, roads, backgrounds, etc.) [1]. The Chinese government said it is paying great attention to the development of intelligent connected vehicles and considers the sector a vital way to ease the burden on transportation, energy consumption and

J. Li et al. (Eds.): SPNCE 2019, LNICST 284, pp. 178–197, 2019.
https://doi.org/10.1007/978-3-030-21373-2_15

environmental pollution [2]. By 2020, the market scale of the country's intelligent connected vehicles sector is expected to exceed 100 billion yuan [3]. However, these rapid changes to enhance the intelligent and connected functions of vehicles are having a serious effect on their security. Specifically, the Internet penetrates into the modern vehicles [4]. Increased connectivity often results in a heightened risk of a cybersecurity attack [5–7], such as Denial-of-Service (DoS) attack, man-in-the-middle attack and Structured Query Language (SQL) injection. In 2015, preeminent hackers Charlie Miller and Chris Valasek dominated headlines with their landmark hack of a Jeep Cherokee [8]. In 2016, team of hackers take remote control of Tesla Model S from 12 miles away [9]. In 2017, Keen Lab discovered new security vulnerabilities on Tesla motors and realized full attack chain to implement arbitrary CAN BUS and ECUs remote controls on Tesla motors with latest firmware [10]. In 2018, researchers hacked BMW cars and discovered 14 vulnerabilities [11].

Cars are getting more and more connected, which means more electronics plus access to the internet. Which, in turn, means more opportunities to hack cars remotely. For the security, generally speaking, the measures of protection against malicious attacks are little known to automotive manufacturers and suppliers. Modern cars need to be developed with security in mind, and that is something that has to be done by security professionals, whereas the Original Equipment Manufacturers (OEMs) lack the ability to comprehensively evaluate the security levels of their cars. Automotive information security can be guaranteed in many ways, such as security standards, regulations and test evaluation methods or public announcement system. As one of the most direct and effective means, the test evaluation method could provide a security process framework and guidance to help OEMs identify and assess security threats and design security into cyber-physical vehicle systems throughout the entire development lifecycle process. However, due to the lack of relevant standards, there are relatively few test evaluation methods for automotive information security in the industry, while most of these methods focus on testing the safety of cars [12,13].

In this paper, a novel Intelligent Connected Vehicle Attack and Defense (ICV-ISAD) test evaluation method is proposed to address the test evaluation issue of automotive security. The article is structured as follows: in the following Sect. 2 it studies the problem and object statement under investigation from the two aspects of ICV's classic system architecture and the main attack surfaces it faces. In Sect. 3 we introduce the test methodology of ICV-ISAD test method from three stages. In Sect. 4 there are some experimental results and analyses for ICV-ISAD test method. After the overall outlook for above, the last section concludes this article with a summary.

2 Problem and Object Statement Under Investigation

While automobile manufacturers have improved the intelligent and connected functions of their automobiles a lot during the past decades, adequate protection measures for vehicle security are not available yet [14]. Moreover, vehicle security related incidents can also affect the safety of automotive systems [15]. All of this interplay between intelligent and security clearly motivates automotive security as a research topic with increasing relevance and importance. Also, it motivates us to explore a test method to evaluate automotive security.

For this section, it serves as a research basis of security test evaluation method analyzing the current state-of-the-art ICV's classic system architecture and the main attack surfaces it faces, respectively.

2.1   Classic System Architecture

The object under investigation is an ICV system consisting of actuators, sensors, and all kinds of embedded ECUs (Electronic Control Units) that are connected with each other through different busses, such as CAN bus, FlexRay, Ethernet and MOST. To investigate the security of ICV more clearly, we develop an ICV's classic system architecture that consists of multiple functional modules, such as Gateway, Telematics Box, In-Vehicle Infotainment, Body Electronic Module, Chassis Controller and Powertrain Controller. It is illustrated in Fig. 1. Specifically, the Classic System Architecture can be clearly seen that the OBD and USB interface can provide direct contact physical attacks, while the Wi-Fi and Bluetooth may be used to attack the ICV's system remotely. Besides, Gateway plays a vital role in the system, which has close ties with many units of the car.

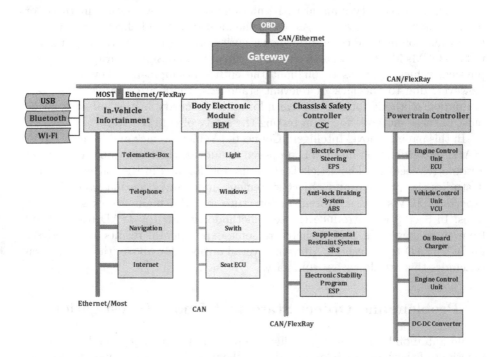

Fig. 1. Intelligent connected vehicle classic system architecture

Furthermore, successful exploitation of the CAN vulnerability on an automobile with this classic system architecture may allow an attacker with physical access and extensive knowledge of CAN to reverse engineer network traffic to perform a Denial of Service (DoS) attack disrupting the availability of arbitrary functions of the car [19]. In the following section, we will do some research on security test evaluation method based on this ICV's classic system architecture.

2.2   Attack Surfaces

The intelligent connected vehicle has a complex system with many embedded Units. With many intelligent technologies being introduced into vehicle, the threats of malicious attack of automotive security are gradually increasing and the problems of information security are increasingly highlighted. It is not difficult to imagine that automobile manufacturers cannot come up with a strong security system for protecting vehicle networks unless they are very well aware of the attack surfaces that an automobile is facing and have a clear understanding of the existing vulnerabilities. Before helping them solve this puzzle, we first need to analyze the main threat surfaces ICV faces at present. Based on the ICV's classic system architecture being presented in Fig. 1, in this section, there is an introduction of the attack surfaces threating ICV's security. An illustration of these attack surfaces is shown in Fig. 2. The details of these seven attack surfaces are as follows.

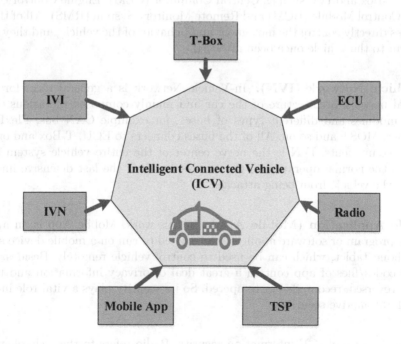

Fig. 2. Attack surfaces that ICV faces

Telematics Box (T-Box). Telematics Box is an electronic unit that integrates all kinds of chips, such as 3G/4G chip, wireless module, communication module, microcontroller (MCU), System on a Chip (SoC). It can be used to the interactive communication between the vehicle and the cloud-platform and connect with the cellular communication networks. In addition, some T-Boxs have the function of tracking with various satellite constellations (GPS, Galileo, GLONASS). As an important communication unit, T-Box's security is critical for that of ICV. Therefore, hackers take it for granted that T-Box is one of the main breakthroughs used to compromise vehicles.

In-Vehicle Infotainment (IVI). In-Vehicle Infotainment is the centerpiece of the car's sound and information system, which provides some direct user experience (UX) for car owners, such as music, applications, navigation. The IVI systems hack is possible and is a real concern [16]. The system is responsible for controlling some of the most vital functions of the car's system. Specifically, IVI systems frequently utilize Bluetooth technology and/or smartphones to help drivers control the system with voice commands, touchscreen input, or physical controls, which exposes outside and provides a direct way to attack the vehicle.

Electronic Control Unit (ECU). During our research on attack surfaces for ICV, electronic control unit consists of all kinds of critical electronic units except T-Box and IVI, such as Central Computer (CEM), Engine Control Unit, Brake Control Module (BCM) and Remote Monitory System (RMS). All of these modules directly control the movement and behavior of the vehicle, and they can do harm to the vehicle once been attacked.

In-Vehicle Network (IVN). In-Vehicle Network is a general term for the internal network architecture of the car and mainly composed of various electronic modules and different types of buses, for example CAN bus, FlexRay, Ethernet, MOST and so on. All of the buses connects to ECU, T-Box and other critical components. IVN is the nerve center of the entire vehicle system and controls the normal operation of the car system. It is the last defensive line to protect the vehicle from being attacked.

Mobile Application (Mobile App). In this work, Mobile App is an automotive program or software application designed to run on a mobile device such as a phone/tablet, which can be used to control vehicle remotely. Besides, the source codes/files of app contain a great deal of privacy information and they can be reversed, recompiled or tempered. So its security plays a vital role in the field of automotive security.

Radio. In term of ICV information security, Radio refers to the technology of using radio waves to carry information in vehicle, such as sound and images, by systematically modulating properties of electromagnetic energy waves transmitted through space, such as their amplitude, frequency, stage, or pulse width. There are Wi-Fi, Bluetooth, Tire Pressure Monitoring System (TPMS), Remote Keyless Entry System (RKMS) and so on. For the security risks of radio, some hackers set up a radio listening station to find and decode hidden radio signals—just like the hackers who triggered the emergency siren system in Dallas, Texas, probably did [17].

Telematics Service Provider (TSP). In research about Telematics Service Provider's security, it mainly serves as the cloud platform and some servers that are used to provide the services to the vehicles on the road, which plays a role in the connected car value chain centered on secure vehicle to cloud data management. Due to its close connection with the Internet, it has attracted the attention of many attackers and has become one of the most commonly used attack surface or path.

These attack surfaces related to vehicles exacerbate the problem of causing much information disclosure or compromising an entire in-vehicle network due to the lack of protective measures in the automotive pipeline (network) and other counterparts. Considering the interests of OEMs and users, they are the main objects used to study common car vulnerabilities and possible attack paths.

3   Test Methodology

Based on the ICV's classic system architecture and seven attack surfaces it faces, in this section, a novel Intelligent Connected Vehicle (ICV) Information Security Attack and Defense (ICV-ISAD) test evaluation method is proposed and the

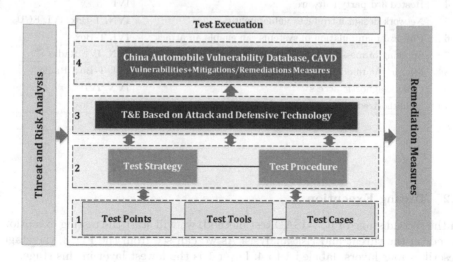

Fig. 3. ICV-ISAD test method architecture

design thoughts of test methodology are presented comprehensively. ICV-ISAD test method shows how to evaluate the information security of the car through testing method that aims to discover security vulnerabilities and threats as well as maps corresponding remediation measures. It is derived from the long-term large number of real automotive test experiments and is constantly optimized in the experiments. In this method, the implementation of the security evaluation realized from three stages, which are Threat and Risk Analysis, Test Execution as well as Remediation Measures.

3.1   Threat and Risk Analysis

Since the dependencies between the vehicle security and the design system architecture described in Sect. 2, there exists a lot of threats and risks for ICV's system or network. In the first stage of ICV-ISAD test method, some threats and risks to the vehicle are considered, respectively. The threat analysis is a process to determine anything that can exploit a vulnerability, intentionally or accidentally, and obtain, damage, or destroy the security of ICV. Table 1 shows an example of threats analysis. Risk analysis is designed to consider the potential for loss, damage or destruction of the vehicle security as a result of a threat exploiting a vulnerability. For an example of risks analysis, see Table 2.

Table 1. Threats analysis

No.	Threat (Vulnerability)	Effect (Attack surface)
1	Compromise of update procedures	IVI
2	Denial of service attacks	IVN, IVI, Mobile App
3	Unprivileged users access to vehicle systems	IVI, IVN
4	Hosted 3rd party software	IVI
5	Network design introduces vulnerabilities	IVN, T-Box, IVI, ECU
6	Physical manipulation of systems can enable an attack	IVI, T-Box
7	Spoofing of messages	IVN, IVI, Radio
8	Man in the middle attack	IVI, T-Box, Radio
9	OBD Diagnostic access	IVN, IVI
10	Unauthorized deletion/manipulation of system event logs	IVI, T-Box
...	...	...

3.2   Testing Execution

In the second stage of ICV-ISAD test method, we will start the testing execution based on the threat and risk analysis. As we can see from the Fig. 3, the stage describes four layers, labeled 1 to 4. Layer 1 is the lowest layer in this stage.

Table 2. Risks analysis

No.	Risk	Effect (Attack surface)
1	Stealing personally identifiable information	IVI, T-Box, TSP
2	Manipulating a vehicle's operation	IVN, IVI, Mobile App
3	Unauthorized vehicle system entry	IVN, IVI, T-Box
4	Compromise of over the air software update procedures	IVI
5	GPS spoofing	Radio
6	Disrupting TPMS signal	Radio
7	The installation package was tampered with	Mobile App
8	Transfer data is hijacked	Mobile App
9	Loss of information in the cloud	TSP
10	Information breach by unintended sharing of data	TSP
...	...	...

Layer 1: Test Baseline Layer. The Test Baseline Layer is the main component in the test execution stage. 335 test points, 733 test cases and 69 test tools are collected in this layer, which are the important part of ICV-ISAD test method. Test points serve as the idea and technical points for the specific implementation of the security test, which are derived from a large number of practical automotive experiments, taking into account the feasibility and applicability. It describes the research ideas and technical points that plays a vital role in the comprehensive security test of automotive components. Some examples of test points are shown in Table 3. Test cases are usually a single step, or occasionally a sequence of steps, to test the correct security behavior or functionality in the design of vehicle, features of objects corresponding to each test points, one part of which is shown in Table 4. Test tools are partly shown in Table 5, which offer the execution of security test and implement quick security analysis to vehicle system function, software binary code and communication traffic packet across multiple automotive units, etc. Many test tools incorporate automatic test capabilities to traversing and discover threats, vulnerabilities and other security problems from the tested objects.

Table 3. Test points

Attack surface	1	2	3	...
IVN	Security access service	Subnet	Gateway	...
T-Box	Key usage	Hash function	SPI bus	...
IVI	Backdoor	Weak token	Port security	...
ECU	CAN bus isolation	Verification level	Secure storage	...
Mobile APP	Decompile	Process injection	Data security	...
Radio	Sniffing	Replay attack	Interference	...
TSP	CSRF vulnerability	Webshell getting	SQL injection	...

Table 4. Test cases

Surface	Test points	Test cases
IVN	Security access	1 Connect the PC to the car through the OBD port
		2 Send 022701 via Vehicle Spy
		3 To test whether the ECU feeds back the seed or not
		4 Observe, analysis and record the results
...	...	...
T-Box	Key usage	1 Confirm whether the encryption key is multi-purpose
		1 Confirm whether the authentication key is multi-purpose
		1 Confirm whether the random number generation key is multi-purpose
		1 Confirm if the digital signature key is multi-purpose
...	...	...
IVI	Backdoor	1 To analyze whether the program has backdoor through the reverse engineering. Such as the hidden browser
	Port security	1 Use nmap to find all open ports
		2 Test whether the opened ports are secure or not
...	...	...

Layer 2: Strategy and Procedure Layer. In Strategy and Procedure (S&P) Layer, we elaborate the thoughts of test strategy and the flow chart of test procedure. The S&P Layer plays a role of bridge between the Test Library Layer and Test and Evaluation (T&E) Layer using for test planning and management. The test strategy is to build a practical test idea and test route based on the test points around a specific test object, such as IVN, ECU, IVI, T-Box, Mobile App, Radio and TSP. Table 6 takes Test Strategy of IVN's Security for an example. The test procedure is a test logic based on test points and test strategies, given in the form of a flow chart. It covers major security test policies such as functional security test, static code analysis, reversing engineering and penetration testing. Test procedure is shown in Fig. 4.

Layer 3: Test and Evaluation Layer. To address the evaluation problem of the security for ICV, the Test and Evaluation (T&E) Layer is deployed in third layer of Test Execution. It focus on evaluating the security defensive capability of vehicle based on the attack and defense technology. Test and Evaluation (T&E) is the process by which a system or components are compared against test points and test strategies according to test procedure. Figure 3 highlights the relationship among the Test Baseline Layer, S&P and T&E Layer. The results are evaluated to assess ICV's security of architecture design.

Table 5. Test tools

No.	Tool name	Function description
1	Burpsuite	Using to analyze network packets
2	jeb2	Decompile apk application
3	Defensics	Fuzz testing by communication protocol
4	IDA-PRO	Decompile and dynamically debug binary file
5	Appscan	To discover vulnerabilities, hosts and services
6	Nmap	Test security of the ports and running services opened
7	Protecode	Analyze, detect and check the known vulnerabilities of binary codes
...	...	...

Table 6. Test strategy for IVN's security

Step	Description
1	Analysis of vehicle network structure and bus type
2	Investigate the open bus service of the OBD interface
3	Call the corresponding test tools for different open services
4	Message reading and analysis
5	Diagnostic service test
6	Denial of service test
7	Brute force cracking test
8	Fuzz testing
9	Summary and analysis

The Test and Evaluation (T&E) involves evaluating an automobile's security from the component level to whole vehicle system as well as its integrated system. Components mainly refer to the units related to seven attack surfaces, such as IVI, T-Box and ECUs. Through black-box, gray-box and white-box testing, it analyzes the security of automotive systems (Fig. 1) to discover unknown vulnerabilities, threats and risks that the car faced based on the seven major attack surfaces (Fig. 2). In the overall execution process of Test and Evaluation Layer, it complies with test strategy and test procedure showed in the S&P Layer. Different test objects and different steps of the test will selectively call the corresponding test points, test tools and test cases in the Test Library Layer.

During the process of security test, Test Baseline Layer and T&E Layer work together under the connection of S&P Layer. For instance, in the security test evaluation of IVI, one of test points is the port security. And all of test process follows to the test procedure and is guided by the test strategies designed in T&E Layer. Specifically, the nmap in the test tools will be called firstly.

Then its test cases corresponding to the port security in the test cases library is going to been matched. Finally the security test of port security will be implemented as follow steps:

1 Use nmap to find all open ports.
2 Test whether the opened ports are secure or not.

Layer 4: Information Security Database. The fourth layer is the information security database, China Automotive Vulnerability Database (CAVD) [18], which is built and operated by Automotive Data Center of China Automotive Technology and Research Center Co., Ltd. It is responsible for collecting the state of the art automotive information security data, such as vulnerabilities, mitigation measures and treatments. These data are mainly derived from the test experiments based on the attack and defense technology and are processed through verification, review, assessment and classification.

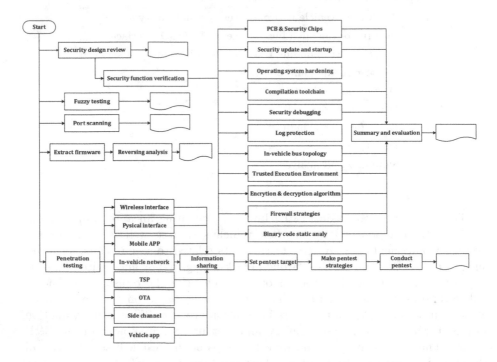

Fig. 4. Test procedure

In addition, as the number of the vehicle's type and testing increases, the data of CAVD would be iterated and updated. Specifically, the vulnerabilities and threats found in the test are matched with that of the CAVD. For the existed vulnerabilities and threats in the library, the corresponding remediation measures or mitigations will be mapped and output from the CAVD. Otherwise for the unknown vulnerabilities and threats, some new protection schemes will be created and stored in the CAVD so as to map the corresponding vulnerabilities or threats next time.

3.3 Remediation Measures

The two stages for test evaluation method of ICV-ISAD have already been mentioned during the presentation of Sects. 3.1 and 3.2. Remediation measures are the output of ICV-ISAD test method. The output function is mainly implemented by the CAVD in the test execution stage. During the period of ICV-ISAD third stage, the basic remediation measures are identified in today's ICV systems that provide some patch recommendations for vulnerabilities to launch attacks based on these test achievements in the first two stages. While this is done with a focus on the vulnerabilities aspects, it also addresses potential threat implications (like those summarized in Table 1), which can arise from successful exploits of vulnerabilities. The ICV's vulnerabilities and threats found in the test are mapped with the CAVD to find the corresponding protection schemes.

4 Test Experimental Results

In our experiments, some different types of cars numbered 1 to 10 were selected to assess the performance of the proposed test evaluation method of ICV-ISAD. The vehicles participating in the experiment have intelligent and connected functions,

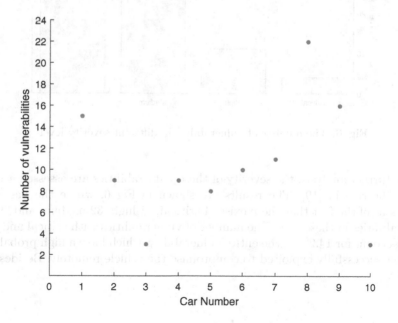

Fig. 5. The number of vulnerability for different car

which generally conform to the system framework shown in Fig. 1 and are faced with seven attack surfaces given in Fig. 2. The test experiment are aimed to evaluate the security of the whole vehicle and their components, such as IVI, T-Box, Mobile App, Radio and TSP, based on the black-box, gray-box and white-box testing.

4.1   Results and Analyses

During the experiments of ICV-ISAD test method, 106 automotive system security vulnerabilities are discovered. As can be seen from Fig. 5, the 10 cars used to the test all have security vulnerabilities, and the average number of security vulnerabilities per car is 10.6. In particular, the number of vulnerability in No. 1, No. 8, and No. 9 cars ranks in the top three.

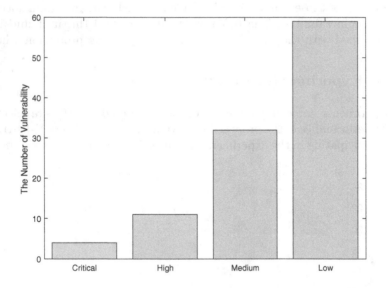

Fig. 6. The number of vulnerability in different severity level

For further analysis, the severity of these vulnerabilities are assessed according to the rule in [19]. The results are shown in Fig. 6, where the bar chart informs us of the fact that there exists 4 critical, 11 high, 32 medium and 59 low vulnerabilities in these cars. The number of vulnerabilities with critical and high levels account for 14.2% of the entire vulnerability, which have a high probability of being successfully exploited to compromise the vehicle remotely. Besides, the proportion of vulnerabilities with medium level is 30.2% in the entire vulnerability. However, once hackers have physical access to the vehicle, these medium vulnerabilities provide great possibilities of destroying the vehicle. Moreover, it can be clearly seen from Fig. 7 that the car's vulnerability covers a large area. They are distributed to various components of the car to varying surface. Three units were found serious vulnerabilities, evolving two in T-Box, one each in Mobile APP and TSP. T-Box, IVI, APP, radios and TSP were discovered vulnerabilities with high level in varying degrees. All of these results indicate that these 10 vehicles have different levels of security risks.

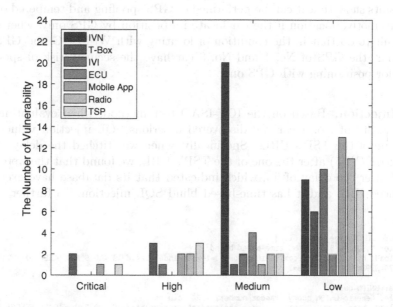

Fig. 7. Vulnerability severity for different vehicle units

4.2 Typical Vulnerabilities and Threats

In order to better illustrate the efficiency of the ICV-ISAD test method in automotive information security testing and evaluation experiments, we highlight several typical security issues found in the experiments as a result of ICV-ISAD test method, mainly introducing threats and vulnerabilities. Taking into account the privacy protection issues associated with the experimental results, we covered some sensitive information with mosaics.

Radio Vulnerability (Threat). In this paper, the research objectives of radio includes Wi-Fi, Bluetooth, GPS, Wireless Key Fob and Tire Pressure Monitoring System (TPMS).

To evaluate the security of key fobs by using ICV-ISAD test method, GQRX of test tools was called to detect the key frequency band of 315 MHz and 433 MHz at first. Then GNURADIO and USRP of test tools were called to capture and recorded the signal from the wireless key fob. Finally, the effect of the recorded signal was verified by a replay attack to test the security of wireless key fob. The results show that the replay attack is invalid for key fobs encrypted with rolling code, or else the replay attack can open the door and trunk. Specifically, the key fobs of No. 1 and No. 5 car have security risk for having no rolling codes, which can be replay attacked. During the evaluation of GPS security, we tried to cheat and temper the car localization by spoofing GPS signals using radio tools. The results show that it can be performed of GPS spoofing and tempered of the true automotive location if the car locate its position by GPS only, whereas it is difficult to do that in the condition of locating with Wi-Fi, 4G and GPS. In particular, the GPS of No. 1 and No. 3 car have the security risk of spoofing attack for positioning with GPS only.

SQL Injection. Based on the ICV-ISAD test method, when evaluating the TSP security of No. 4 car, we discovered a serious SQL injection vulnerability in one of the TSP's URLs. Specifically, when we stitched the delay string *AND SLEEP*(5) after the one of the TSP's URL, we found that the web page opened after the delay of 5 s, which indicated that its database have executed the spliced URL and it has time-based blind SQL injection. To further verify

```
Type: AND/OR time-based blind
Title: MySQL >= 5.0.12 AND time-based blind
    Payload: http://www.    com:80/index.php?a=text&c=index&catid=19 AND 3 AND SLEEP(5)-- tgde21=
6 AND 379=379&m=huancun&page=2

Type: UNION query
Title: Generic UNION query (random number) - 24 columns
    Payload: http://www.    .com:80/index.php?a=text&c=index&catid=19 AND 3 UNION ALL SELECT 3110,
3110,3110,3110,3110,3110,3110,3110,3110,3110,3110,3110,3110,3110,3110,3110,3110,CONCAT(
0x7178717a71,0x4a6b714765349765873517341445466664b6942427144434a59734f4e65506a6a5545436f76435161,0
x7171627a71),3110,3110,3110,3110-- IFrE21=6 AND 379=379&m=huancun&page=2
---
[08:52:25] [INFO] the back-end DBMS is MySQL
back-end DBMS: MySQL >= 5.0.12
[08:52:25] [INFO] fetching database names
available databases [22]:
[*] alltest
[*]       2008
[*] db_2017_shes_mercedes
[*] db_
[*] db_ibm
[*] dcms
[*]
[*]       _gwdz
[*]       _juhui
[*]       _l5
[*]       _two
[*] information_schema
[*] jblh_qingzhuxinchun
[*] mysql
```

Fig. 8. SQL injection

the vulnerability, we detected the address using *sqlmap.py* and found time-based blind SQL injection and union query SQL injection. Besides, a large amount of database information is exposed. As shown in Fig. 8.

Gateway Filtering Vulnerability (Threat). When using the ICV-ISAD test method to evaluate engine-related ECU security, we tested the effects of different ID signals on the vehicle by sending random data. The test results show that the signal corresponding to $ID = 350$ would cause a sudden increase in car speed, as shown in Fig. 9. For further verification, the eight-byte bit data sent by ID of 350 was accurately analyzed. The result shows that the vehicle speed was constantly increasing when all eight bytes were FF, as shown in Fig. 10. The CAN protocol threat can be exploited to compromise the vehicle speed system once hackers have physical access to the vehicle.

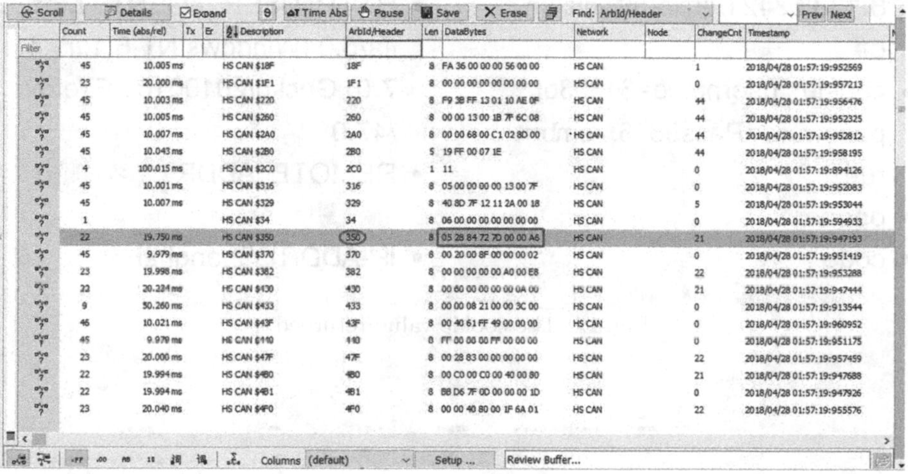

Fig. 9. Speed control ID

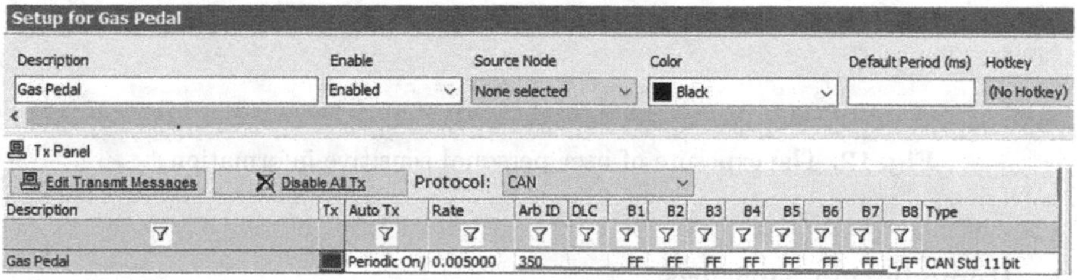

Fig. 10. Speed control by accurate ID message

XSS Vulnerability. Under the test to No. 7 car by ICV-ISAD test method, the feedback communication packets of Mobile APP can be intercepted successfully by Burpsuite. Then we insert the constructed malicious JavaScript into the APP's function of feedback and send it to the server. Through opening the XSS background receiver, we can receive the cookie (username, password) value returned after the malicious code is executed, as shown in Fig. 11. Even more striking, more user personal sensitive information exposed from the server database by further sending the JavaScript with the function of screenshot and reading the website source code again, as shown in Fig. 12.

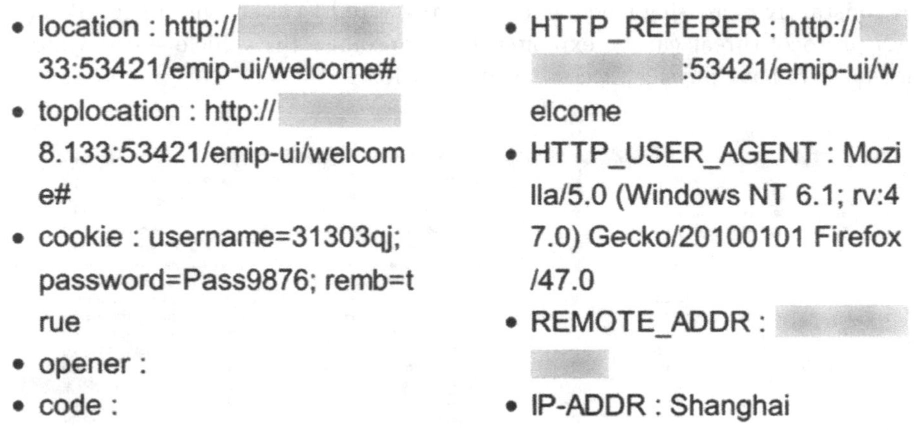
• location : http://
33:53421/emip-ui/welcome#
• toplocation : http://
8.133:53421/emip-ui/welcom
e#
• cookie : username=31303qj;
password=Pass9876; remb=t
rue
• opener :
• code :
• HTTP_REFERER : http://
:53421/emip-ui/w
elcome
• HTTP_USER_AGENT : Mozi
lla/5.0 (Windows NT 6.1; rv:4
7.0) Gecko/20100101 Firefox
/47.0
• REMOTE_ADDR :
• IP-ADDR : Shanghai

Fig. 11. The cookie value returned

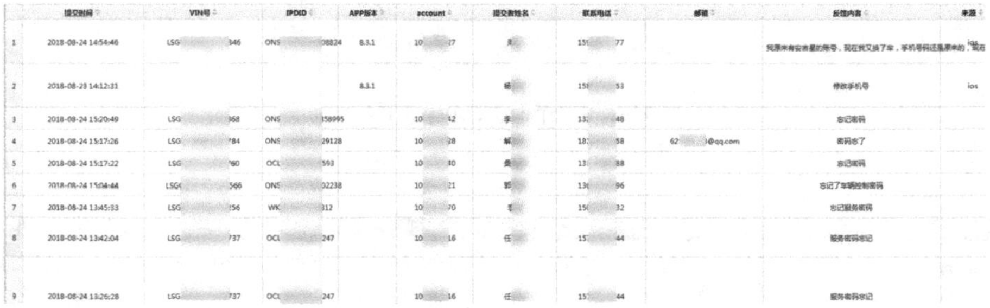
VIN号
IPDID
APP版本
account
2018-08-24 14:54:46
2018-08-23 14:12:31
2018-08-24 15:20:49
2018-08-24 15:17:26
2018-08-24 15:17:22
2018-08-24 13:45:33
2018-08-24 13:42:04
2018-08-24 13:26:28
8.3.1
@qq.com
ios

Fig. 12. The exposure of user personal sensitive information

4.3 Remediation Measures

In previous work, ICV-ISAD test method was used to evaluate the security of 10 ICVs and 106 vulnerabilities were discovered, especially several typical vulnerabilities and threats were analyzed. To further show its efficiency, in this part, we present some remediation measures or recommendations corresponding to the previous typical vulnerabilities/threats. All of these remediation measures could be mapped from the CAVD database of ICV-ISAD test method, as shown in Table 7.

Table 7. Remediation measures or recommendations

Vulnerability/Threat	Remediation measures & Recommendations
XSS vulnerability	1 Set the value of *httponly* to *true* for vital cookie
	2 To convert character content to *html* entity by using the *htmlspecialchars* function
	3 Filter or remove special *html* tags, such as $< script >$, $< iframe >$
SQL injection	1 Precompile and bind the variables of SQL statements with the function of *PreparedStatement*
	2 Front-end *JS* should have the ability to check for illegal characters
	3 Filter the keywords reserved by the database in the SQL statement, such as AND, OR, EXEC
Gateway filtering	1 OBD port shields each BUS and only reserves diagnostics function
	2 Add hardware Firewalls or other Encrypted Routes to enhance BUS filtering capabilities
Radio vulnerability	1 Protect key fob from *replayattack* by using *rollingcode*
	2 Improve the strength of the wireless key fob's signal encryption algorithm
	3 Use 4G, Wi-Fi and GPS *joint positioning*

5   Conclusion

In this paper, we proposed a novel approach to address the security evaluation problem for ICV based on the attack and defense technology. The proposed ICV-ISAD test method not only helps OEMs secure the car through vulnerability discovery, but also provides the specific remediation measures or recommendations that can be implemented in the vehicle with security risks. Specifically, we explored the ICV's classic system architecture which presents the main automotive units, system buses, and mutual communication relationship, as well as we discussed seven attack surfaces that ICV faces by and large. Based on the classic system architecture and the seven attack surfaces, ICV-ISAD test method has been elaborated from the three stages of threat and risk analysis, test execution, and remediation measures. Also, a special focus has been put to the stage of test execution, which includes the main components and core technologies of ICV-ISAD test method. Experimental results of 10 vehicles security tests show that ICV-ISAD test method can effectively discover security vulnerabilities and threats to evaluate vehicle's security. In addition, some remediation measures or recommendations could be mapped from the CAVD of ICV-ISAD test method to mitigate the corresponding vulnerabilities.

Acknowledgments. The work described in this article has been supported by Automotive Data Center of China Automotive Technology and Research Center Co., Ltd. that provides the laboratory, all the cars, test tools and support required to carry out this research successfully.

The work in this article concerning CAVD has been supported by China Automotive Technology and Research Center Co., Ltd. through the project "Development of Automobile Information Security Vulnerability Database and Emergency Response Platform" under Contract No. 18190122.

References

1. Li, Y.: Big wave of the intelligent connected vehicles. China Commun. **13**(2), 27–41 (2016)
2. Kuang, X.: Intelligent connected vehicles: the industrial practices and impacts on automotive value-chains in China. Asia Pac. Bus. Rev. **24**(1), 1–21 (2018)
3. China prepares to issue temporary 5G licenses to operators. https://technode.com/ 2019/01/11/chinese-grant-temporary-5g-licence/. Accessed 17 Jan 2019
4. Bécsi, T.: Security issues and vulnerabilities in connected car systems. In: 2015 International Conference on Models and Technologies for Intelligent Transportation Systems (MT-ITS), Denver, pp. 3–5. IEEE (2015)
5. Parkinson, S.: Cyber threats facing autonomous and connected vehicles: future challenges. IEEE Trans. Intell. Transp. Syst. **18**(11), 2898–2915 (2017)
6. Sadek, A.: Special issue on cyber transportation systems and connected vehicle research. J. Intell. Transp. Syst. **20**(1), 1–3 (2016)
7. Luo, Q.: Wireless telematics systems in emerging intelligent and connected vehicles: threats and solutions. IEEE Wirel. Commun. **25**(6), 113–119 (2018)
8. Mccluskey, B.: Connected cars - the security challenge [Connected Cars Cyber Security]. Eng. Technol. **12**(2), 54–57 (2017)
9. Tesla Model S hacked from 12 miles away. https://www.welivesecurity.com/2016/ 09/21/tesla-model-s-hack/. Accessed 17 Jan 2019
10. New Car Hacking Research: 2017, Remote Attack Tesla Motors Again. https:// keenlab.tencent.com/en/2017/07/27/New-Car-Hacking-Research-2017-Remote-Attack-Tesla-Motors-Again/. Accessed 16 Jan 2019
11. Researchers hack BMW cars, discover 14 vulnerabilities. https://www. helpnetsecurity.com/2018/05/23/hack-bmw-cars/. Accessed 17 Jan 2019
12. Arbabzadeh, N.: A data-driven approach for driving safety risk prediction using driver behavior and roadway information data. IEEE Trans. Intell. Transp. Syst. **19**(2), 446–460 (2018)
13. Jesper, C., Christophe, B.: Nonlinear Optimization of Vehicle Safety Structures: Modeling of Structures Subjected to Large Deformations, 1st edn. Butterworth-Heinemann, Waltham (2015)
14. Siegel, J.E.: A survey of the connected vehicle landscape-architectures, enabling technologies, applications, and development areas. IEEE Trans. Intell. Transp. Syst. **19**(8), 2391–2406 (2018)

15. Sandor, P.: Security and safety risk analysis of vision guided autonomous vehicles. In: 1st IEEE International Conference on Industrial Cyber-Physical Systems (ICPS-2018), Saint-Petersburg, pp. 193–198. IEEE (2018)
16. Li, X.: Connected vehicles' security from the perspective of the in-vehicle network. IEEE Network **32**(3), 58–63 (2018)
17. Hijacking FM Radio with a Raspberry Pi & Wire. https://null-byte.wonderhowto.com/how-to/hack-radio-frequencies-hijacking-fm-radio-with-raspberry-pi-wire-0177007/. Accessed 18 Jan 2019
18. China Automotive Vulnerability Database (CAVD). https://cavd.org.cn/. Accessed 21 Jan 2019
19. CAN Bus Standard Vulnerability. https://ics-cert.us-cert.gov/alerts/ICS-ALERT-17-209-01. Accessed 18 Jan 2019

Study on Incident Response System of Automotive Cybersecurity

Yanan Zhang, Peiji Shi$^{(\boxtimes)}$, Yangyang Liu, Shengqiang Han,
Baoying Mu, and Jia Zheng

China Automotive Technology and Research Center Co. Ltd.,
Tianjin 300393, China
spj_2004@126.com

Abstract. With the development of Intelligent Connected Vehicles, a large number of automobile cybersecurity incidents also occur. Scientific and reasonable incident response system is the key technology to ensure the successful handling of cybersecurity incidents. From the point of view of management, referring to the construction of incident response system in IT industry and combining with the characteristics of automobile cybersecurity, this paper puts forward the framework of incident response system for automobile cybersecurity. The framework includes five aspects: plan and prepare, detection and reporting, assessment and decision, responses and lessons learnt. Emphasis is laid on the formulation and updating of management policy, the establishment of incident response team, incident coordination mechanism and so on. Then, based on the method of questionnaire survey, the evaluation method of incident response capability is put forward. The research method makes up for the blank of automobile industry in cybersecurity incident response, and has an important positive role in reducing the adverse impact of security incidents.

Keywords: Automotive cybersecurity · Incident response ·
Evaluation system · Questionnaire

1 System Framework

In the traditional field, establishing an incident response system is one of the effective security services for solving network system security problems. The incident response system in the traditional field includes the incident response system for enterprises' production safety accidents, the incident response system for public disasters and accidents, and the incident response system for traditional public health safety incidents, etc. [1, 2]. The corresponding laws and regulations and related work technologies have been established in various fields, and certain technological innovation. The event response methodology is the discipline that studies the event response process. The event response method is not unique. It is widely accepted that the PDCERF methodology is the earliest classical method, which divides the corresponding process into six stages of preparation, detection, containment, eradication, recovery and Follow-up [3, 4]. But in this process, there is no clear distinction between the tasks of the victim and the responder. The NIST.SP.800-61r2-computer security incident

J. Li et al. (Eds.): SPNCE 2019, LNICST 284, pp. 198–209, 2019.
https://doi.org/10.1007/978-3-030-21373-2_16

handling guide in the United States divides the incident response into four steps: Preparation, detection & Analysis, Containment Eradication & Recovery, and Post-incident Activity four stages. ISO 27035 divides incident response into five steps: plan and prepare, detection and reporting, assessment and decision, incident responses, and lessons learnt [5, 6]. This paper will establish an automotive cybersecurity incident response system according to the idea of 27035.

2 Plan and Prepare

2.1 Development and Update of Management Policy

The organization's cybersecurity incident management policy should provide the principles and intent of formal records to guide decisions and ensure consistent and appropriate implementation of processes, procedures, etc. related to this policy. Any cybersecurity event management policy should be part of the organization's cyberse-curity policy. It should also support the existing mission of its parent organization and be in line with existing policies and procedures. Before making a cybersecurity policy, the organization should consider the purpose, internal and external related groups, the types of events and vulnerabilities that require special attention, and the need for specific personnel, the benefits to the entire organization or department, etc. The management policy should be high-level and applicable to all employees and con-tractors. Details and steps should be included in a series of documents.

2.2 Develop a Management Plan

The management plan document should include multiple documents, including forms, procedures, event classification, organizational elements, and support tools for testing and reporting, evaluating and making decisions, responding to and learning from cybersecurity incidents. The management plan includes a basic low-level and high-level summary of incident management activities to provide the structure and pointers to the detailed components of the plan. These components provide step-by-step instructions for event handlers to work with specific tools, follow specific workflows, or handle specific event types as appropriate.

2.3 Establish Incident Response Team (IRT)

The purpose of establishing a cybersecurity incident response mechanism is to provide organizations with the appropriate capabilities to evaluate, respond to, and learn about cybersecurity incidents and provide the necessary coordination, management, feed-back, and communication. IRT helps reduce physical and monetary losses and reduces the damage to the organization's reputation that is sometimes associated with cyber-security incidents.

IRTs can be structured differently based on the size of the organizational, employee and industry type.

Effective event response depends on the capabilities and reliability of the IRT staff.

The IRT should be responsible for ensuring that the incident is resolved. In this case, the IRT manager and team members should have the authority to take the necessary actions and consider it appropriate to respond to cybersecurity incidents. However, actions that may adversely affect the entire organization, whether financially or reputational, should be approved by top management. Therefore, cybersecurity incident management policies and plans must detail the appropriate authority for the IRT manager to report serious cybersecurity incidents to them. The authority shall undertake to provide services to IRT members and provide timely guidance.

2.4   Communication with Other Organizations

Incident management is not a self-contained process. Relationships, communication channels, data sharing agreements, and policies and processes should be established throughout the organization. These internal collaborations may include coordination with business managers, IT representatives, human resources representatives, public relations representatives, any existing security groups, any law enforcement liaisons, or investigators. The organization should also establish a relationship between the IRT and the appropriate external stakeholders.

2.5   Technical Support

To ensure a prompt and effective response to cybersecurity incidents, the organization shall acquire, prepare and test all necessary technical and other support means. All internal and external parties to support and reporting should have a clear definition and agree on communication channels and workflow.

2.6   Cultivate Safety Awareness and Strengthen Drills

Cybersecurity incident management is a process involving both technical means and people. Therefore, it should be supported by individuals with appropriate cybersecurity awareness and trained individuals within the organization.

2.7   Incident Management Plan Test

The organizations should regularly review and test cybersecurity incident management processes and procedures to highlight potential defects and problems that may arise when managing cybersecurity incidents and vulnerabilities. Regular tests should be organized to check the process/procedure and verify the IRT response.

2.8   Summary and Improvement

Once the cybersecurity incident is over, it is important that the organization quickly identify and learn lessons from the cybersecurity incidents and ensure that the conclusions are implemented. In addition, lessons can be learned from assessing and resolving reported cybersecurity vulnerabilities.

3 Detection and Reporting

The detection and reporting stage mainly involve the collection, recording, and reporting information related to security events [7]. Its key activities include monitoring the recording system and network activities, detecting and reporting discovered security events or security vulnerabilities, collecting security events or security vulnerability information and events development trends. At this stage, it has not been determined whether a cybersecurity event has occurred. It should ensure that all activities, results and decisions are fully and completely documented for future analysis and improvement, while ensuring the secure collection and storage of relevant electronic evidence.

In the detection and reporting stage, the change control mechanism should be followed to continuously track cybersecurity events and vulnerabilities. All information should be stored in the cybersecurity database in a timely and complete manner and kept up-to-date, and system upgrades should be performed as needed for further evaluation, decision, review or take action.

4 Evaluation and Decision

Based on the security problems or security vulnerabilities detected in the previous stage, the relevant information is collected, tested and processed, and the special evaluation agency evaluates whether it is a cybersecurity incident [8]. If the false alarm is suspected, the IRT can conduct quality review to ensure that the incident processing procedure is correct.

Once identified as a cybersecurity incident, the responsibility of the responders should be defined immediately according to the corresponding distribution system.

Issue formal guidance documents and decision documents, including review and modification of reports, evaluation results, internal notices, etc., and comprehensively recording security incident information and follow-up activities according to the guidelines.

This stage should ensure that all relevant parties involved in the IRT focus on all activities, results and decisions are correctly and completely documented for future analysis. At the same time, ensure that the change control mechanism is maintained to cover cybersecurity event tracking and event reporting updates, and to keep the cybersecurity database up to date [9].

5 Incident Response

According to the evaluation and decision results, the responders can make incident response quickly. The response steps are as follows:

Conduct security event classification. The classification of cybersecurity events mainly considers the importance of information systems, system losses and social impacts [10, 11]. It can be divided into extraordinary major events, major events, larger events and general events, as shown in Table 1 [12].

Table 1. Cybersecurity event classification.

Level	Loss of information systems			Social influence
	Particularly important information system	Important information system	General information system	
Extraordinary major events (Class I)	Especially serious	——	——	Extraordinary major
Major events (Class II)	Serious	Extraordinary serious	——	Major
Larger events (Class III)	Larger	Serious	Extraordinary serious	Larger
General events (Class IV)	Smaller	Larger	Serious or below	General

The IRT review determines whether the cybersecurity event is under control. If the event is controllable, the required response will be executed. If the event is uncontrollable or will have a serious impact on the organization's operations, the incident response is implemented by upgrading to the incident management function [13].

Allocate internal resources and identify external resources in response to events.

After recovering from an accident, the post-incident actions should be initiated based on the nature and severity of the incident, including investigating information related to the incident, investigating relevant personnel and other relevant sources, and the summary of the investigation result report [14].

After the security incident is resolved, it should be closed according to the requirements of the IRT or the parent organization and notify all stakeholders.

Based on IRT communication planning and information disclosure policy, to the asset owner and can help manage and solve the problem of internal and external organizations (such as other incident response teams, law enforcement agencies, Internet service providers, and information sharing organizations) to share information, provide the existence of security incidents, threats, attacks and vulnerabilities and other information.

In addition, actions such as record and report updates, cybersecurity database updates, and forensic data collection and storage should be carried out throughout this stage [15, 16].

6 Lessons Learnt

After the security incident is resolved, it should be reviewed and summarized to draw lessons. Key activities in the stage include:

Summarize the control implementation management policy, cybersecurity risk assessment and management review system related to improving automotive cybersecurity;

Evaluate and optimize the response process, report format, organizational structure, etc.;

Review the effectiveness of incident response, improve cybersecurity incident plans and management plans, and evaluate regularly.

Sharing the results of the review with the public and share and communicating with other incident response teams to improve their incident response capabilities for similar problems [17].

7 System Evaluation

The fundamental purpose of automotive cybersecurity incident response is to detect the type of attack in time and minimize the scope of the loss. However, the cybersecurity threats faced by different automobile companies and different models at different stages of development vary greatly. Therefore, how to establish a universal automobile cybersecurity incident response system, and provide reference for the formulation of incident response contingency plan and management formulation is the key problem to be solved in this paper.

7.1 Review Metrics

Based on the whole life cycle of the vehicle, considering the main objectives of each stage of the incident response, the six factors of management system, organization, personnel level, emergency materials and facilities, technology and treatment methods, records and reports are selected as key elements in the evaluation of automobile cybersecurity.

7.2 Review Questionnaires

Based on the framework of the automotive cybersecurity incident response system, the design review questions for the review of key elements are presented around Sect. 4. Considering the universality of the questionnaire, consider the issue of setting multiple levels for each element, and each part can be answered separately. The problem is mainly in the form of multiple-choice questions. For the question with the answer "yes", there are some extension problems in the form of blank-filling question [18].

In order to simplify the answer form of the review questionnaire and reduce the error caused by the subjective factors of the respondents, the answer to the multiple-choice questions is designed to include three options, namely "yes", "no" and "partial". The answer to the blank-filling question is open, and the user answers it according to his or her own situation.

The contents of the questionnaires at each stage are as follows:

Plan and prepare stage (1) In terms of management system, the review management policy is formulated and updated. Does the management plan include formalities, procedures, event classification, organizational elements, support tools, testing and other elements, and IRT managers' report serious cybersecurity to top management?

(2) In terms of organization, the authority will assess whether an IRT has been established, its structural form, through a collaborative mechanism with business managers, its representatives, human resources representatives, public relations representatives, any existing security groups, any law enforcement liaison officers or investigators, whether the bureau provides services and guidance to IRT members. (3) In terms of technology and processing capabilities, whether to acquire, prepare and test the necessary technologies and other supporting means. (4) In terms of personnel level, the frequency and form of training exercises, and whether the organization has the appropriate cybersecurity awareness and the support of trained individuals. (5) In terms of records and reports, whether detailed information and procedures for the development and updating of the management system are recorded, and whether there are records of summary and improvement after the completion of the security incident.

Detection and reporting stage (1) In terms of management system, the main focus is on the monitoring system, that is, whether the automobile and related services, back-end systems, vehicle systems and public information database are actively monitored. If monitoring measures have been taken, the monitoring tools and technical means will be further investigated. (2) In terms of personnel level, it involves the review of the level of incident response team members and non-incident response team personnel, respectively, to assess their awareness of the importance of incident response, whether they can clearly define security events, and whether they know the contact person and contact information of security events. In addition, attention should also be paid to the training and application of the professional ability of the incident response team members to receive training drills and timely safety event marking. Also focus on whether stakeholders are aware of security event contacts and contact information. (3) In terms of technology and processing mode, attention is paid to the difference between security issues and security incidents for service requests and service interruptions. (4) In terms of organizational structure, it is concerned with whether or not to set up a special institution to register security incidents. Whether the institution is responsible for formulating, preserving, updating and monitoring the test reports, whether the system automatically assigns the person in charge of management. (5) In terms of records and reports, check whether the checklist contains the security issues of detection, information of the reporter, notes and annotation time, initial notes and annotation time of the reporter, credibility and confidentiality of the report, etc.

Assessment and decision stage (1) The level of personnel, including the testing qualifications of technicians and the qualifications for obtaining evidence, and whether the personnel performing emergency operations are on call around the clock. (2) In terms of records and reports, attention should be paid to the priority, completeness and confidentiality of the records, whether the records are guaranteed to have not been tampered with, and whether the forensic data is verifiable. (3) In terms of technology and processing methods, whether it has the same security event processing techniques and methods, whether it has provisions for handling security events that are occurring, whether technicians have compromised systems and all access to data, and whether they have access to external experts. (4) In terms of management system, whether there is a mature safety event classification system, a management system in which the response team and the evaluation team are connected, whether a safety and business risk assessment management process, a technical risk assessment process are established, and whether the employee and expert contact regulations and protection are established Suspicious data guide. (5) In terms of organization, we pay attention to the communication between different departments, including whether the technicians know how to contact the evaluation agency, external experts, detailed information providers, and other security response teams. In addition, in terms of notification release, the timeliness of internal notifications should be reviewed and whether relevant personnel have been notified to reduce activities.

Incident response stage (1) In terms of organization, whether the organization or personnel providing information to the third party should be established. (2) In terms of technology and processing methods, whether to ensure that unrelated personnel do not have access to information related to security incidents, whether technicians have control over the formulation, modification and execution of measures in the whole process of response, the control over the whole life cycle, whether the technician is responsible for the shutdown event after success, and whether the technician has the specific test on the adequacy, stability and functionality of safety events before incident response. (3) In terms of technical facilities, whether there are sufficient technical facilities to meet the requirements of evidence collection. (4) In terms of management system, the notification release system should review the timeliness of internal notifications and examine whether relevant personnel have been notified to reduce activities. In terms of process formulation, whether there are specific safety incident response regulations and regulations for monitoring the effectiveness of response. (5) In terms of records and reports, it should include targeted countermeasures and standard response lists, and whether confidentiality of forensic storage can be ensured.

Experience summary stage (1) In terms of management system, summarize methods and tools, and regularly assess their applicability and effectiveness, whether to set up a special incident response process applicability and effectiveness evaluation process, special incident response improvement process, special education difference review and training drills Process, specialized vulnerability management system, long-term security measures, whether to carry out safety event evaluation and latest information inspection, etc. (2) In terms of personnel level, the development department can or can't ensure that security vulnerabilities are adequately addressed. (3) In terms of technology and treatment methods, whether to ensure that similar or mutated security issues can be effectively addressed. (4) In terms of records and reports, whether the event cause report is fed back to the development department. Whether vulnerabilities, threats, and security incidents are updated in a timely manner in the public database. (5) Whether to form a complete safety incident handling report, summary report, and record of optimization improvement measures.

7.3   Review Method

According to the key elements of the review, the automotive cybersecurity incident response system can be simply determined by three ways of conformity, basic

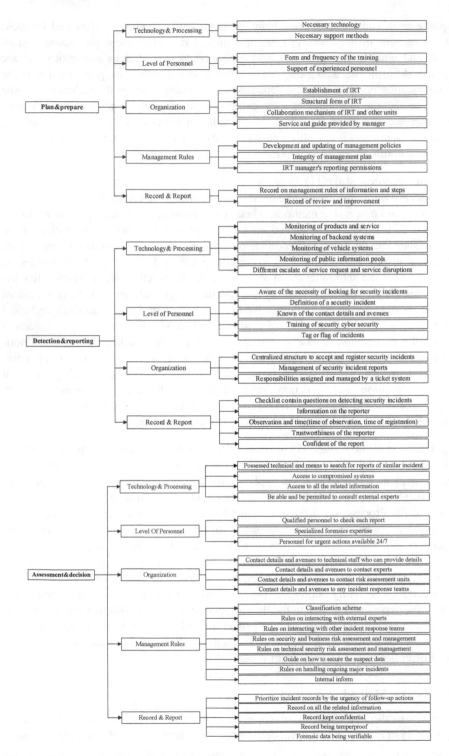

Fig. 1. Questionnaire framework for incident response system of automotive cybersecurity.

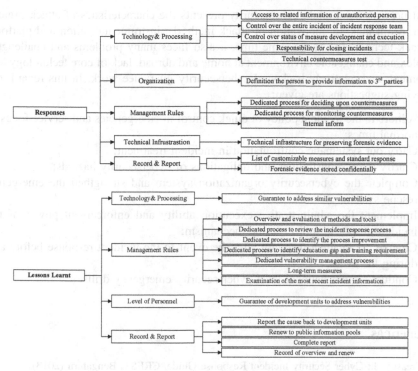

Fig. 1. (*continued*)

conformity and non-conformity. For the basic conformity and non-conformity of the project, should put forward guiding opinions or suggestions.

According to the questionnaire, the incident response system is reviewed from the aspects of conformity, applicability, pertinence, completeness, scientific, formativeness and cohesiveness. For detailed review, the review elements can be reviewed separately by means of a list. When reviewing the emergency plan, the elements of the emergency plan are analyzed correspondingly with the review contents and requirements in the table to determine whether the requirements in the table are met, and problems and deficiencies are found (Fig. 1).

8 Summary

In this paper, the construction method of automobile cybersecurity incident response system is given, and a questionnaire is designed to evaluate the incident response system. The system is suitable for OEMs, parts supplier, third party organization, etc. In addition, the complexity and cross-regional nature of the Internet determine that the incident response of cybersecurity incidents should be a collaborative process of multiple departments and units, which requires the competent departments and emergency agencies to constantly integrate their respective advantages, and ultimately form a joint effort to cope with the problem of automobile cybersecurity.

At present, automobile cybersecurity presents the characteristics of attack organization, profit-making, innovation of attack methods, instrumentalization and platform of attack technology. At the same time, it also faces many problems and challenges: complex and changeable environment at home and abroad, lack of core technology and equipment, and relatively backward cybersecurity guarantee work. In this regard, the following suggestions are given:

(1) Adhere to the incident policy of quick control in emergencies and service focus in normal times;
(2) Carry out systematic confrontation in incident treatment;
(3) Clarify the responsibilities and obligations of cybersecurity hazards;
(4) Complete the cybersecurity organization system and strengthen the emergency rescue system;
(5) Implement the administrative execution ability and enforcement power of the incident response subject in the mechanism;
(6) Change the incident response after the event to the incident response before and during the event;
(7) Conduct regular national-level cyber security emergency drills.

References

1. Creasey, J.: Cyber Security Incident Response Guide. CREST, Bengaluru (2013)
2. Choucri, N., Madnick, S., Koepke, P.: Institutions for cyber security: international responses and data sharing initiatives. In: Working Paper CISL (2016)
3. Shen, X.: Research on Network Security Emergency Response Linkage System. Hubei University of Technology, Wuhan (2009)
4. De Muynck, J., Portesi, S.: Strategies for Incident Response and Cyber Crisis Cooperation. ENISA, Heraklion (2016)
5. ISO/IEC 27035-1: Information Technology-Security Techniques - Information Security incident management-Part 1: Principles of Incident Management (2016)
6. ISO/IEC 27035-2: Information Technology-Security Techniques - Information Security Incident Management-Part 2: Guidelines to Plan and Prepare for Incident Response (2016)
7. Liu, X., Li, B., Chang, A., Hui, L., Tian, Z.: The current network security situation and emergency network response. Strateg. Study Chin. Acad. Eng. **18**(6), 83–88 (2016)
8. GB/T 28448-2012: Information Security Technology-Testing and Evaluation Requirement for Classified Protection of Information System (2012)
9. Loukas, G., Gan, D., Vuong, T.: A review of cyber threats and defense approaches in emergency management. Future Internet **5**, 205–236 (2013)
10. Ma, H.: The Research of Network Security Emergency Response System Based on CBR. Shanghai Jiaotong University, Shanghai (2010)
11. Rico, S., et al.: Incident Management and Response. ISACA, Rolling Meadows (2012)
12. GB/Z 20986-2007: Information Security Technology-Guidelines for the Category and Classification of Cybersecurity Incidents (2007)
13. Chunfei, W.: Database Design of the Cybersecurity Vulnerability Database and Implementation of the Management Platform. Beijing University of Posts and Telecommunications, Beijing (2011)

14. Zhang, Y., Lu, S., Qiu, L.: Research and practice of information security emergency handling mechanism based on event. Information Security and technology (2015)
15. Practice Guide for Information Security Incident handling. Hong Kong: Office of the Government Chief Information Officer (2017)
16. Loukas, G., Gan, D., Vuong, T.: A review of cyber threats and defense approaches in emergency management. Future Internet 5(2), 205–236 (2013)
17. Kämppi, P., Rathod, P., Hämäläinen, T.: Cybersecurity safeguards for the automotive incident response vehicles. In: Proceedings of the 9th International Joint Conference on Knowledge Discovery, Knowledge Engineering and Knowledge Management, pp. 291–298. SCITEPRESS-Science and Technology Publications, Funchal, Madeira (2017)
18. Hao, Y.: Research on Risk Quantification Method of Cybersecurity. Dalian University of Technology, Dalian (2016)

Secure Multi-keyword Fuzzy Search Supporting Logic Query over Encrypted Cloud Data

Qi Zhang[1], Shaojing Fu[1,2(✉)], Nan Jia[1], Jianchao Tang[1], and Ming Xu[1]

[1] College of Computer, National University of Defense Technology, Changsha, China
shaojing1984@163.com
[2] State Key Laboratory of Cryptology, Beijing, China

Abstract. Compared with exact search, fuzzy search will meet more practical requirements in searchable encryption since it can handle spelling errors or search the keywords with similar spelling. However, most of the existing fuzzy search schemes adopt bloom filter and locality sensitive hashing which cannot resist Sparse Non-negative Matrix Factorization based attack (SNMF attack). In this paper, we propose a new secure multi-keyword fuzzy search scheme for encrypted cloud data, our scheme leverages random redundancy method to handle the deterministic of bloom filter to resist SNMF attack. The scheme allows users to conduct complicated fuzzy search with logic operations ("AND", "OR" and "NOT"), which can meet more flexible and fine-grained query demands. The theoretical analysis and experiments on real-world data show the security and high performance of our scheme.

Keywords: Searchable encryption · Fuzzy search · Logic query · Bloom filter

1 Introduction

Recently, Cloud storage services have become more and more prevalent and many individuals and businesses choose to outsource their local data to remote cloud service providers to reduce local storage and computing overhead. In order to protect the privacy of the outsourced data, data encryption is usually used, making it impossible for an attacker to recover the original data from the encrypted data. However, data encryption will cause a decrease in data availability, making it difficult to perform operations such as information retrieval on ciphertext. How to implement secure search over encrypted cloud data becomes a topic worth studying.

Searchable encryption technology can realized the function of information retrieval on encrypted cloud data while protecting privacy. Most of the searchable encryption schemes can only support exact keyword search which does not have fault tolerance. Fuzzy search is mainly designed for misspelling, similar

J. Li et al. (Eds.): SPNCE 2019, LNICST 284, pp. 210–225, 2019.
https://doi.org/10.1007/978-3-030-21373-2_17

query and other scenarios. According to some similarity metrics, such as edit distance, Jaccard distance, Euclidean distance etc., the similarity between the index and the trapdoor can be calculated, and the scheme can return the results with higher similarity to the query. Existing fuzzy searches mainly fall into two directions. One is to construct a pre-defined wildcard-based fuzzy keyword set for each keyword which will result in high storage and can only support single keyword search. The other is using bloom filter and locality sensitive hashing [8] to construct index which can map similar keywords to the same position to realize multi-keyword fuzzy search. However, the structure of bloom filter cannot resist ciphertext-only attack which will leak the search pattern [12].

Aiming at the security flaws of existing fuzzy search schemes, our paper proposes a multi-keyword fuzzy search scheme with high security and can support logical query. Our paper add random number redundancy to confuse the original keyword features, so that the search pattern will be protected and the scheme can resist ciphertext-only attack. In addition, our paper extends to implement logic query function, i.e. "AND", "OR" and "NOT" which is practical in applications. Users can customize the files that must contain certain keywords, or the files that does not contain certain keywords, thereby obtaining the search results that are more in line with the user's needs. Finally, this paper theoretically analyzes the security of the scheme and analyzes its performance on the real-world text dataset. Our contributions can be summarized as follows:

(1) To resist the ciphertext-only attack basing on sparse non-negative matrix factorization, we randomized the index by adding random redundancy to mask the deterministic of bloom filter and improve the security of scheme proposed by Wang et al. [15] as a result.
(2) To realize flexible query for users, we extend the scheme to support logic query, the mixed "AND", "OR" and "NOT" operations, to exclude the results users don't need, and pick out the results they want, and last rank the relevance scores according to the possibly existing keywords.
(3) The scheme is proved secure against two threat model by theoretical analysis, and has high performance by evaluating on the real-world dataset.

The remaining sections of this paper are organized as follows. In Sect. 2, we outline the system model, threat model, design goals and the notations used in this scheme. And Sect. 3 introduces the basic theoretical knowledge of the scheme. Section 4 describes the technical details of the scheme. Section 5 gives the theoretical analysis of the security of the scheme. The experiment results of the scheme are given in Sect. 6. Section 6.1 gives a brief introduction of the related work. Finally Sect. 7 concludes the paper.

2 Problem Formulation

2.1 System Model and Threat Model

As shown in Fig. 1, the system consists of three entities: data owner, cloud server and data user. Before outsourcing data to the server, the owner needs to encrypt

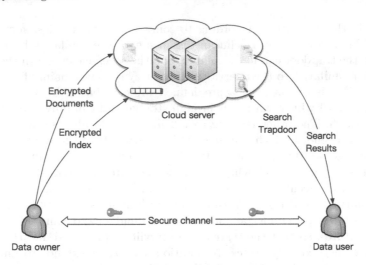

Fig. 1. System model

the data, construct secure indexes, and upload them to the cloud. The keys used in symmetric encryption algorithm for documents and secure kNN algorithm for indexes are transmitted to the data user via a secure channel. When searching a certain file, data user generates the trapdoor according to the input of "AND", "OR", "NOT" operations, and encrypts it using the same key for index encryption, and then sends it to cloud server. After receiving the query trapdoor, cloud server calculates the relevance scores one by one for the encrypted indexes, and returns the most satisfactory results to data user. When the query results returned, data user decrypts them locally using the key for document encryption.

We assumes that the cloud server is honest but curious. In other words, the cloud server will honestly follow the steps of algorithms, but will be curious about the content of files, keywords, and other additional information. In this model, in addition to the encrypted information introduced above, cloud server will obtain additional background information, such as trapdoor correlation. This information will be used for statistical attacks to infer the keywords contained in search requests.

2.2 Preliminaries

Bloom Filter. Bloom Filter [1] is a data structure with high space efficiency which can determine whether the collection contain the element.

The structure of bloom filter is shown in Fig. 2. Bloom filter uses a fixed-length vector with m bits to represent a set of elements. For a given collection with n elements $S = \{s_1, s_2, \ldots, s_n\}$, use l hash functions from a hash family $H = \{h_i | h_i : S \rightarrow [1, m], 1 \leq i \leq l\}$ to map the elements to l positions of the vector and set the value to be 1, others set to be 0. The l position represents the element. To check whether the input element x is in the collection, first calculate the element x with the same l hash function to get l positions. If the value in all positions are 0, then $x \notin S$; otherwise, we predicate $x \in S$.

Bloom filter have significant advantages. First of all, the size of the bloom filter is fixed and is not limited by the number of elements in the set. At the same time, it does not need to store the information of the element itself, which will not leak any information of the collection and elements. But on the other hand, it has false positive result, that is, the non-existent element will be predicated to existent. The false positive rate is approximately $(1 - e^{-\frac{ln}{m}})^l$.

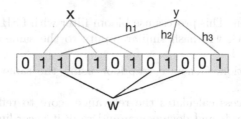

Fig. 2. Structure of bloom filter

Locality Sensitive Hashing. Locality sensitive hashing function is an algorithm used to solve near-neighbor search. It can map similar elements to the same bucket with high probability, thus deciding the similarity between elements. The hash function family is defined as [8]:

Definition 1. *For any two points x and y are satisfied:*
If $d(x, y) \leq r_1$, $Pr[h(x) = h(y)] \geq p_1$;
If $d(x, y) \geq r_2$, $Pr[h(x) = h(y)] \leq p_2$.
Where $d(x, y)$ is the distance between x and y, $r_1 < r_2$, $p_1 > p_2$, and $h(x)$ is the hash value for x. Then the hash function family H can be defined as (r_1, r_2, p_1, p_2)-sensitive.

This definition shows that two adjacent points in the original space will be mapped into two points still adjacent, and the non-adjacent points are still not adjacent after mapping. Based on this property, LSH can be used in bloom filter to replace the original hash function to achieve fuzzy search.

3   The Proposed Scheme

3.1   Previous Scheme and Security Defect

The first multi-keyword fuzzy search scheme using bloom filter and locality sensitive hashing is proposed by Wang et al. [15]. There are 4 main processes in the scheme:

1. Keyword transformation. Since LSH function uses a vector as input, this process converts the keyword string into a vector. The scheme uses bi-gram set that contains all of the two consecutive letters to represent the keyword. For example, the bi-gram set of the keyword "network" is {ne, et, tw, wo, or, rk}. Later, the scheme transforms the bi-gram set to 26^2-bit vector, and we eet the position to 1 if the element exist in the bi-gram set. Through this expression, a keyword can have many different forms of spelling errors, but it can still be represented by a vector with very close distance with the correct one.
2. Index construction. This process use bloom filter with LSH to build an index for each file, which will hash similar inputs to the same output with high probability.
3. Trapdoor generation. Generate trapdoor using the same process as index construction.
4. Search. This process calculates the relevance score to reflect the relevance of multiple keywords and documents, and rank it according to the result of inner product.

Ciphertext-Only Attack. The main process in Wang's scheme can be simply expressed as the following function:

$$I_i = f(LSH(P_i), k_i)$$
$$T_j = f(LSH(Q_j), k_i) \qquad (1)$$
$$R = I_{enc,i}^T T_{enc,j} = I_i^T T_j$$

Where k_i is the key for pseudo-random function f, f can be equivalent to position permutation, P_i and Q_j are plaintext keyword vectors, I_i and T_j are m-bit bloom filter obtained by P_i and Q_j through LSH and pseudo-random function, $I_{enc,i}$ and $T_{enc,j}$ are encrypted from I_i and T_j, R is the relevance score.

Analyzing above equations, I_i and T_j cannot be inferred from P_i and Q_j without knowing the key K. However, the generation of the bloom filter is deterministic which means same query vector will generate the same bloom filter and leak the search pattern as a result. According to the analysis by Lin et al. [12], an adversary can conjecture I_i and T_j by deploying sparse non-negative matrix factorization (sparse-NMF) algorithm [9] on the encrypted index $I_{enc,i}$ and trapdoor T_{enc}. In other words, The basic scheme is vulnerable to the ciphertext-only attack (COA). Although I_i and T_j do not directly leak the plaintext P_i and Q_j, similar I_i and T_j will reflects the relationship of plaintext due to the deterministic of LSH and f and make statistical analysis attack feasible which will reveal the frequency and other information of keywords.

3.2 Secure Scheme Supporting Logic Query

To resist above-mentioned ciphertext-only attack (COA) against the previous scheme, we extend m-bit vector of the original scheme to $(m+U+1)$-bit, which is a combination of bloom filter and random numbers. With the confusion of random numbers, the location of the keywords and random numbers is indistinguishable. Even if two identical trapdoor, it is impossible to determine whether the same position corresponds to the keyword or the random number, and thus it is impossible to determine whether the query is the same. It is also unable to perform statistical analysis to obtain keyword information such as frequency.

Then to increase flexibility of query, we also design a scheme to support logic query. Users can input keywords with customization that must exist, must not exist and possibly exist. So that user can exclude undesirable documents, and select requisite documents.

First, the TF-IDF algorithm used in this scheme is defined as:

$$
\begin{aligned}
S &= \sum_{w_i \in Q} TF_{f_i, w_i} \times IDF_{w_i} \\
&= \sum_{w_i \in Q} \frac{ln(1 + N_{f, w_i})}{\sqrt{\sum_{w_i \in W} (ln(1 + N_{f, w_i}))^2}} \times \frac{ln(1 + N/N_{w_i})}{\sqrt{\sum_{w_i \in W} (ln(1 + N/N_{w_i}))^2}}
\end{aligned}
\tag{2}
$$

Then the details of enhanced scheme is shown in the following aspects:

- $\{SK, sk\} \leftarrow KeyGen(1^\rho)$. This algorithm is executed on data owner side. Given a parameter, the algorithm will generate the key $SK = \{S, M_1, M_2\}$ for the index and trapdoor encryption. Our scheme extends the vector from m bits to $(m+U+1)$ bits, where m-bit vector represents the bloom filter and U-bit is for random numbers. Thus S is a $(m+U+1)$-bit vector $S \in \{0,1\}^{m+U+1}$, $\{M_1, M_2\}$ are two $(m+U+1) \times (m+U+1)$-bit invertible matrices. At the same time, the key sk of the symmetric encryption algorithm for file encryption and decryption will be generated.
- $C \leftarrow Enc(F, sk)$: Data owner encrypts the plaintext document collection F using a symmetric encryption algorithm, like AES. And the encrypted documents will be finally uploaded to the cloud server for storage.
- $BF \leftarrow BuildBF(W)$: This algorithm maps the input keyword set to the bloom filter to generate an index. First initialize a m-bit bloom filter BF, each of which is set to 0. Then, transform each keyword to a 26^2-bit vector, $W = \{w_1, w_2, \cdots, w_n\}, w_i \in \{0,1\}^{26^2}$. Then select l independent hash function

h_j from p-stable LSH function family $H = \{h : \{0,1\}^{26^2} \rightarrow \{0,1\}^m\}$ and combine l hash function with the pseudo-random function f_{k_i} together to generate a new hash function $\{g_i | g_i = f_{k_i} \circ h_i, h_i \in H, 1 \leq i \leq l\}$. Those pseudo-random functions is equivalent to randomly permutate the positions of bloom filter, and k_i is the key of the random function, which eliminates the connection between the keyword and bloom filter to resist known background attack [15]. Then, for each keyword vector w_i, use l hash functions g_i to get l positions, set the corresponding position of the bloom filter to its weight. In this case, the bloom filter is constructed.

- $I_{enc} \leftarrow Index(F, SK)$: This algorithm is used to construct the secure index vector. Data owner extracts the keywords of each document f_i in the document collection F, and obtains the keyword set W_{f_i}. Then call the $BuildBF(W_{f_i})$ algorithm to generate a m-bit bloom-filter-based index vector I_i for each file whose value is set to TF_{w_i}. If the collision occurs, the maximum value is retained. Then, each vector is expanded to a $(m + U + 1)$ bit vector. The $(m + j)^{th}$ $(j \in [1, U])$ bit is set to a random number $\varepsilon^{(j)}$. The $(m + U + 1)^{th}$ bit is set to -1. The maximum value D of the vector will be sent to the user after expanding. Next use the secure kNN algorithm [17] to encrypt the index vector. First split the index vector I_i into two random vectors according to the vector S, namely $\{I_i', I_i''\}$, S is the secret vector used for splitting. When $S[j] = 0$, set $I_i'[j] = I_i''[j] = I_i[j]$; when $S[j] = 1$, set $I_i'[j]$ and $I_i''[j]$ as random numbers, and $I_i'[j] + I_i''[j] = I_i[j]$. Finally, each index vector is encrypted as $I_{enc,i} = \{M_1^T I_i', M_2^T I_i''\}$.

- $T_{enc} \leftarrow Trapdoor(Q, SK)$: We select v random positions $j(j \in [m, m + U])$ to be the random number $\sigma^{(j)}$ which can be equivalent to the keyword of "OR" operation. Then to realize logic query, the query keywords Q consisting of t keywords are arranged in the order of "OR", "AND" and "NOT" operation, defined as $(a_1, a_2, \cdots, a_{l_1}, a_{l_1+1}, \cdots, a_{l_1+v})$, $(a_{l_1+v+1}, a_{l_1+v+2}, \cdots, a_{l_1+v+l_2})$, $(a_{l_1+v+l_2+1}, a_{l_1+v+l_2+2}, \cdots, a_N)$, which contains l_1 "OR" operation keywords, v random numbers, l_2 "AND" operation keywords, and $N - l_1 - l_2 - v$ "NOT" operation keywords, a_i is the value of the keyword w_i. For l_1 keywords of "OR" operation, the value is set as its own IDF value. For other keywords, assign a random value satisfying $\sum_{i=1}^{j-1} l \cdot a_i \cdot D < a_j (j = l_1 + 1, l_1 + 2, \cdots, N)$. Then call $BuildBF(Q)$ for the query keyword to generate a m-bit bloom-filter-based query vector T. For collision, the maximum value will be selected as the weight. Append the v positions to expand T to $(m + U + 1)$-bit vector and set the $(m + U + 1)^{th}$ bit to $t = a_{l_1+v+l_2+1}$. Next, split T by secret vector S into two random vectors $\{T', T''\}$, if $S[j] = 1$, set $T'[j] = T''[j] = T[j]$; if $S[j] = 0$, $T'[j]$ and $T''[j]$ are set to random numbers, and $T'[j] + T''[j] = T[j]$. Finally, the trapdoor is encrypted as $T_{enc} = \{M_1^{-1} T', M_2^{-1} T''\}$.

- $R \leftarrow Search(I_{enc,i}, T_{enc})$: After receiving the trapdoor T_{enc} uploaded by the data user, cloud server calculates the relevance score between T_{enc} and the index vector stored on the cloud server to get the most relevant results.

The relevance score is calculated as:

$$
\begin{aligned}
S &= I_{enc,i} \cdot T_{enc} \\
&= (M_1^T I_i{}') \cdot (M_1^{-1} T') + (M_2^T I_i{}'') \cdot (M_2^{-1} T'') \\
&= I_i \cdot T \\
&= r \cdot (P \cdot Q - t) \\
&= r \cdot (\sum_{i=1}^{N} \gamma_i \cdot score(w_i, F_j) \cdot a_i - t) \\
&= r \cdot (\sum_{i=1}^{l_1+v} \gamma_i \cdot score(w_i, F_j) \cdot a_i + \sum_{i=l_1+v+1}^{l_1+v+l_2} \gamma_i \cdot score(w_i, F_j) \cdot a_i \\
&\quad + \sum_{i=l_1+v+l_2+1}^{N} \gamma_i \cdot score(w_i, F_j) \cdot a_i - t)
\end{aligned}
\tag{3}
$$

(1) "NOT" operation. Since $t = a_{l_1+v+l_2+1} > \sum_{i=1}^{l_1+v+l_2} \gamma_i \cdot score(w_i, F_j) \cdot D$, where $\gamma_i (0 \le \gamma_i \le l)$ is the amount of the keyword exist in bloom filter after collision. Once there exist "NOT" operation keywords, $R_j = r \cdot (\sum_{i=1}^{l_1+v+l_2} \gamma_i \cdot score(w_i, F_j) \cdot a_i + \sum_{i=l_1+v+l_2+1}^{N} \gamma_i \cdot score(w_i, F_j) \cdot a_i - a_{l_1+v+l_2+1}) > 0$, otherwise $R_j < 0$. This process can eliminate results that do not meet the requirements, and only go to the next process when $R_j < 0$.

(2) "AND" operation. Mod R_j by $(-r \cdot a_{l_1+v+l_2+1}, r \cdot \gamma_{l_1+v+l_2} \cdot a_{l_1+v+l_2}, \cdots, r \cdot \gamma_{l_1+v+1} \cdot a_{l_1+v+1})$ iteratively and judge whether the keyword is exist. First, mod R_j with $-r \cdot a_{l_1+v+l_2+1}$ to eliminate the effect of s and obtain the remainder result.

$$
\begin{aligned}
R_j &= (r \cdot (\sum_{i=1}^{l_1+v} \gamma_i \cdot score(w_i, F_j) \cdot a_i + \sum_{i=l_1+v+1}^{l_1+v+l_2} \gamma_i \cdot score(w_i, F_j) \cdot a_i \\
&\quad + \sum_{i=l_1+v+l_2+1}^{N} \gamma_i \cdot score(w_i, F_j) \cdot a_i) - t) mod(-r \cdot a_{l_1+v+l_2+1}) \\
&= r \cdot (\sum_{i=1}^{l_1+v} \gamma_i \cdot score(w_i, F_j) \cdot a_i + \sum_{i=l_1+v+1}^{l_1+v+l_2} \gamma_i \cdot score(w_i, F_j) \cdot a_i \\
&\quad - a_{l_1+v+l_2+1}) mod(-r \cdot a_{l_1+v+l_2+1}) \\
&= r \cdot (\sum_{i=1}^{l_1+v} \gamma_i \cdot score(w_i, F_j) \cdot a_i + \sum_{i=l_1+v+1}^{l_1+v+l_2} \gamma_i \cdot score(w_i, F_j) \cdot a_i)
\end{aligned}
\tag{4}
$$

The quotient of equation is 1, and the remainder is the sum of the previous $l_1 + v + l_2$ items.

Then we mod R_j with the remaining reverse ordering keywords $(r \cdot \gamma_{l_1+v+l_2} \cdot a_{l_1+v+l_2}, r \cdot \gamma_{l_1+v+l_2-1} \cdot a_{l_1+v+l_2-1}, \cdots, r \cdot \gamma_{l_1+v+1} \cdot a_{l_1+v+1})$ in turn. If the quotient of $R_j mod(r \cdot \gamma_{l_1+v+l_2} \cdot a_{l_1+v+l_2})$ is greater than 1, it can be determined that the keyword $w_{l_1+l_2}$ exists in the index vector, then assign the remainder to $R_j = r \cdot (\sum_{i=1}^{l_1+v} \gamma_i \cdot score(w_i, F_j) \cdot a_i + \sum_{i=l_1+v+1}^{l_1+v+l_2-1} \gamma_i \cdot score(w_i, F_j) \cdot a_i)$. Otherwise we break the iteration and check next index.

(3) "OR" operation. When all the keywords in "AND" operation are successfully checked, the obtained $R_j = r \cdot (\sum_{i=1}^{l_1+v} \gamma_i \cdot score(w_i, F_j) \cdot a_i)$ is the final relevance score for rank search.

– $PR \leftarrow Dec(R, sk)$. The data user decrypts the returned result R using the key sk transmitted from the data owner via the secure channel, resulting in the plaintext results PR.

4 Security Analysis

4.1 Known Ciphertext Model

The cloud server can only obtain encrypted documents, encrypted indexes and trapdoors under this model. The difference between the indexes and documents depends mainly on the index generation algorithm $I \leftarrow Index(F, SK)$ and file encryption algorithm $C \leftarrow Enc(F, sk)$. The index vector has $(m + U + 1)$ bits. The first m bits represent the weight of the keyword. The U bits are randomly selected. And the last 1 bit is set to -1.

For the index generation, the index vector is first split into two vectors. The value of the vector is randomly set if the value in S is 1. Assuming that the total number of "1" in the first m bit and the last one bit is μ_1, and each dimension of index is η_f bits, then there will be $(2^{\eta_f})^{\mu_1} \cdot (2^{\eta_f})^U$ possible values. Then the two vectors are encrypted by two random $(m + U + 1) \times (m + U + 1)$-bit secret matrices. Assuming each element in the matrix has η_M bits, then there will be $(2^{\eta_M})^{(m+U+1)^2 \times 2}$ possible values. Therefore, the probability of same indexes for two documents can be calculated as:

$$P_d = \frac{1}{(2^{\eta_f})^{\mu_1} \cdot (2^{\eta_f})^U \cdot (2^{\eta_M})^{(n+U+1)^2 \times 2}}$$
$$= \frac{1}{2^{\mu_1 \eta_f + U\eta_f + 2\eta_M (n+U+1)^2}} \tag{5}$$

In addition, under known ciphertext attack, it is also necessary to consider the case where multiple ciphertext pairs are known to be (I_i', T') and the relevance score for each result after querying Security. According to the attack method described in the third section of this chapter, the adversary can decompose the (I_i, T) pair before encryption based on the ciphertext pair and the relevance score. First of all, due to the role of the pseudo-random function, the plaintext index and the query vector pair (P_i, Q) cannot be pushed out without knowing the key of the pseudo-random function. At the same time, even if the same two query vectors Q are used, the trapdoors will be different because of the addition of random numbers. At the same time, after random replacement, the positions of the keywords and the trapdoors will be indistinguishable, even if the decomposition gets the same trapdoor. It is also impossible to distinguish whether it is a keyword, and thus subsequent operations such as frequency statistics have no meaning.

4.2 Known Background Model

In this model, the adversary can obtain additional statistical information to infer keywords or other information. The trapdoor is represented by a $(m+U+1)$-bit vector, where the first m bits indicates whether the keyword exists in the query, and U bits will contain v random number while the other bits are 0, the last 1 bit is set to s.

First, the vector is expanded by η_r-bit random number r, which has 2^{η_r} possible values. Then use the $(m+U+1)$-bit vector S to split into two vectors. Assuming that the value of each dimension is η_q-bit and the number of 0 is μ_0, then there are $(2^{\eta_q})^{\mu_0}$ possible values. Finally, the two query vectors are encrypted with two random matrices. Therefore, the probability to distinguish two trapdoor is calculated as follows:

$$P_q = \frac{1}{2^{\eta_r} \cdot (2^{\eta_q})^{\mu_0} \cdot (2^{\eta_M})^{(n+U+1)^2 \times 2}} \tag{6}$$

It can be indistinguishable by setting a larger η_r, η_q μ_0 and η_M. For example, if $\eta_r = 1024$, $P_q < 1/2^{1024}$ and can be negligible.

4.3 Privacy

1. Data privacy. Each document will be encrypted by a symmetric encryption algorithm like AES before outsourcing. Since AES is known as semantic security [5], the adversary can not infer any information or content of the document without getting the key sk. So the confidentiality of the encrypted document can be well protected.
2. Index and trapdoor privacy. In this scheme, secure kNN algorithm is used to encrypt the index and trapdoor vector. When encrypting, both S and $\{M_1, M_2\}$ are randomly generated, so as long as the key $SK = \{S, M_1, M_2\}$ is kept secret, the cloud server cannot analyze the index or trapdoor from encrypted index and trapdoor, which has been proved secure under known ciphertext model in previous subsection.
3. Trapdoor unlinkability. In the $(m+U+1)$-bit trapdoor vector, only the keyword in "OR" operation is set to IDF value, others are random values. In addition, the trapdoor vector is scaled by random number r. Those random numbers protects the search patter, so that the trapdoor can not be distinguished even for the same query. It has been proved secure under known background model in previous subsection.

4. Keyword privacy. The $(m + U + 1)$-bit trapdoor vector consists of m-bit bloom filter, U-bit random number, and 1 bit fixed number. The bloom filter itself uses multiple locations to indicate a certain keyword, so the relationship between keywords and locations is reduced. At the same time, the random numbers ϵ_i randomize the information in the vector, so that the keyword is indistinguishable from the random number. Therefore, the statistical analysis will no longer effect.

5   Performance Analysis

To evaluate performance, we implement our scheme on real-world dataset using C# language on the Inter(R) Core(TM) i5-4590 CPU 3.30 GHz Windows 7 server.

5.1   Precision

The precision is defined as: $Precision = k'/k$, where k' is the number of documents that actually satisfy the query, and k is the number of the documents returned. In this scenario, in addition to the relevance of the document, the false positive rate of bloom filter will also influence the precision of the results. Figure 3 gives the influence of the number of query keywords on precision. It is easy to observe that the less query keyword, the lower precision of the fuzzy query, but as the number of query keywords increases, the precision will increases since the impact of false positive rate on the results will decrease.

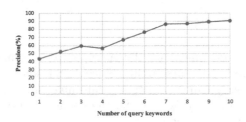

Fig. 3. Search precision

5.2   Efficiency

Index Construction. The construction of the index consists of two processes: one is to construct bloom filter for each document, and the other is to encrypt each bloom filter to generate an encrypted index. The results are shown in Fig. 4. When constructing bloom filter, the time complexity of the bloom filter construction is linearly related to the file keyword set size, the number of hash functions, and the number of documents. And in index encryption, since the encryption process uses a decomposition vector s and two secret matrices $\{M_1, M_2\}$, the complexity of the encryption depends on the size of bloom filter $\mathcal{O}(m^2)$, and since the index is generated for each document, it is also linearly related to the size of collection $\mathcal{O}(N)$. Since the process is one-time on data owner side, the time overhead is acceptable.

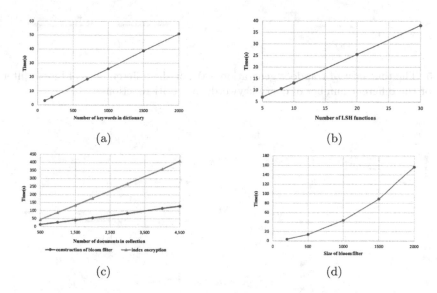

Fig. 4. The time cost of index construction. (a) The relationship between the time of bloom filter construction with the number of keywords in dictionary. (b) The relationship between the time of bloom filter construction with the number of LSH hash functions. (c) The relationship between the time of bloom filter construction and index encryption with the number of documents in collection. (d) The relationship between the time of index encryption with the size of bloom filter.

Trapdoor Generation. The complexity of the trapdoor generation depends on the secret vector S for splitting and secret matrices $\{M_1, M_2\}$. Therefore, its complexity is related to the bloom filter size $\mathcal{O}(m^2)$, as shown in Fig. 5(a), while (b) shows that the number of query keywords and hash functions has little effect on trapdoor generation. This process is generated once at the data user side and the time overhead is acceptable.

Search. The search process can be summarized as the inner product of each index vector and trapdoor vector. Therefore, the complexity depends mainly on the size of document collection and the size of the bloom filter. Figure 6(a) and (b) give the influence of the size of document collection and bloom filter, while (c) proves the number of query keywords has little influence on search.

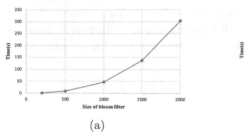
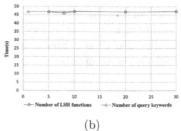

(a)   (b)

Fig. 5. The time cost of trapdoor generation. (a) For the different size of bloom filter. (b) For the different number of query keywords and LSH functions.

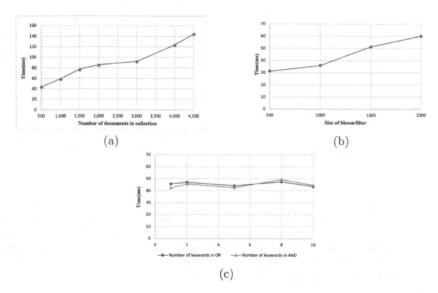

Fig. 6. The time cost of search. (a) For the different number of documents in collection. (b) For the different size of bloom filter. (c) For the different number of query keywords in "AND" and "OR" operations.

6   Related Work

6.1   Exact Search

Song et al. [13] first proposed a solution for searching single keyword on encrypted data with sequential scan which was provably secure but in high cost. Goh [7] defined a secure index using bloom filter and pseudo-random functions, but the scheme only support single keyword search. To provide multi-keyword function, conjunctive multi-keyword search first proposed. Boneh et al. [2] proposed a public-key scheme supporting conjunctive search and subset, range query. Wang et al. [14] designed an public-key searchable encryption scheme based on inverted index and private set intersection. Later ranked multi-keyword scheme was proposed to improve the boolean search. Cao et al. [3] first proposed a basic multi-keyword ranked search scheme (MRSE) using secure kNN computation which had low overhead on computation and communication. Chen et al. [4] used k-means algorithm to construct a hierarchical cluster index tree to develop the search efficiency.

6.2 Fuzzy Search

Fuzzy search scheme using a wildcard-based fuzzy keyword set was first proposed by Li et al. [11]. They used the edit distance to judge the keyword relevance. The scheme first constructs a wildcard-based fuzzy keyword set $S_{w_i,d}$ which contains the keyword variant with an edit distance less than d, such as $S_{CASTLE,1} = \{CASTLE, *CASTLE, *ASTLE, C * ASTLE, C * STLE, \cdots,$ $CASTL * E, CASTL*, CASTLE*\}$ defines the variants of "CASTLE" with 1 edit distance. And then each element in the fuzzy set is encrypted. When searching, the user first generates the same encrypted fuzzy keyword set, and then the cloud server finds the corresponding fuzzy keyword and returns the corresponding file. Later, Zheng et al. [18] gave an effective attack against [11], and proved that Li et al.'s scheme [11] had low security. Wang et al. [16] made further improvements based on the work of [11] and proposed an efficient fuzzy search mechanism. The efficiency of search is improved by constructing an index tree structure based on the keywords. However, above methods must pre-configure a predefined dictionary which will cause overhead in time and storage space, and usually only support single keyword queries.

Later, locality sensitive hashing [8] was proposed to construct index which can map similar keywords to the same position to implement multi-keyword fuzzy search. At present, the research direction of fuzzy query is mainly on the innovation of the construction and functionality of fuzzy keyword index. Kuzu et al. [10] first designed the fuzzy search scheme based on Jaccard similarity, which used the bloom filter and locality sensitive hashing function minhash to map the keyword to multiple random positions to form an inverted index. The sum of the values in the same address is used to obtain the similarity between the index and the trapdoor. At the same time, the scheme also gives a multi-server public key encryption scheme, which uses the homomorphic Paillier encryption algorithm. However, due to the inverted index, the scheme only support single keyword search. Wang et al. [15] proposed the first basic scheme of multi-keyword fuzzy search based on bloom filter and locality sensitive hashing. Firstly, they transformed the keyword string into bi-gram set and used the 26^2 bits binary vector to represent the set. Later they mapped the vector into a fixed-length bloom filter by LSH function, and the relevance score is obtained by calculating the inner product of the index and the trapdoor. Fu et al. [6] improved the scheme in [15] through two main optimization. Firstly, they used stemming algorithm to extract keyword stems. Thus the keywords with same stem will be simplified to one common word which can represent more variant and provide more query request. Secondly, they selected uni-gram vector to represent the keyword. Each keyword first transformed into the uni-gram set consisting of one letter and one number to indicate the position of the letter. Later, they mapped the set into a 160-bit vector to represent the keyword. These optimizations can provide more variants of the query keyword, such as the repeated letters, and the Euclidean distance of the two keywords will be smaller which will lead to more accurate search results.

7   Conclusion

This paper proposes a multi-keyword fuzzy search scheme that supports logic queries and can resist ciphertext-only attack. We focus on the security defect of existing fuzzy search scheme, and improve the basic scheme by randomizing the bloom filter to protect the search pattern. To meet more search demands, we extend the scheme to support logic query on fuzzy search. We give a theoretical analysis of the security against two threat model and apply our scheme on real dataset to analyze the performance.

For the further work, we can extend to support semantic query and synonym query, which can scale the concept of fuzzy query, not only can consider keyword spelling errors, but also semantically similar queries. And also consider designing a scheme to support double judgments which can combine both exact and fuzzy search.

Acknowledgments. This work is supported by the National Nature Science Foundation of China (NSFC) under grant 61572026, 61672195, Open Foundation of State Key Laboratory of Cryptology (No: MMKFKT201617).

References

1. Bloom, B.H.: Space/time trade-offs in hash coding with allowable errors. Commun. ACM **13**(7), 422–426 (1970). https://ci.nii.ac.jp/naid/20001345133/en/
2. Boneh, D., Waters, B.: Conjunctive, subset, and range queries on encrypted data. In: Vadhan, S.P. (ed.) TCC 2007. LNCS, vol. 4392, pp. 535–554. Springer, Heidelberg (2007). https://doi.org/10.1007/978-3-540-70936-7_29
3. Cao, N., Wang, C., Li, M., Ren, K., Lou, W.: Privacy-preserving multi-keyword ranked search over encrypted cloud data. IEEE Trans. Parallel Distrib. Syst. **25**(1), 222–233 (2014)
4. Chen, C., et al.: An efficient privacy-preserving ranked keyword search method. IEEE Trans. Parallel Distrib. Syst. **27**(4), 951–963 (2016). https://doi.org/10.1109/TPDS.2015.2425407
5. Curtmola, R., Garay, J., Kamara, S., Ostrovsky, R.: Searchable symmetric encryption: improved definitions and efficient constructions. In: ACM Conference on Computer and Communications Security, pp. 79–88 (2006)
6. Fu, Z., Wu, X., Guan, C., Sun, X., Ren, K.: Towards efficient multi-keyword fuzzy search over encrypted outsourced data with accuracy improvement. IEEE Trans. Inf. Forensics Secur. **11**(12), 2706–2716 (2017)
7. Goh, E.J.: Secure indexes. Cryptology ePrint Archive, Report 2003/216 (2003). https://eprint.iacr.org/2003/216

8. Indyk, P., Motwani, R.: Approximate nearest neighbors: towards removing the curse of dimensionality. In: Proceedings of the Thirtieth Annual ACM Symposium on Theory of Computing, STOC 1998, pp. 604–613. ACM, New York (1998). https://doi.org/10.1145/276698.276876. http://doi.acm.org/10.1145/276698.276876

9. Kim, H., Park, H.: Sparse non-negative matrix factorizations via alternating non-negativity-constrained least squares for microarray data analysis. Bioinformatics **23**(12), 1495–1502 (2007)

10. Kuzu, M., Islam, M.S., Kantarcioglu, M.: Efficient similarity search over encrypted data. In: IEEE International Conference on Data Engineering, pp. 1156–1167 (2012)

11. Li, J., Wang, Q., Wang, C., Cao, N., Ren, K., Lou, W.: Fuzzy keyword search over encrypted data in cloud computing. In: Conference on Information Communications, pp. 441–445 (2010)

12. Lin, W., Wang, K., Zhang, Z., Chen, H.: Revisiting security risks of asymmetric scalar product preserving encryption and its variants. In: IEEE International Conference on Distributed Computing Systems, pp. 1116–1125 (2017)

13. Song, D., Wagner, D., Perrig, A.: Practical techniques for searches on encrypted data. In: Proceeding 2000 IEEE Symposium on Security and Privacy, SP 2000, pp. 44–55 (2000). https://doi.org/10.1109/SECPRI.2000.848445

14. Wang, B., Song, W., Lou, W., Hou, Y.T.: Inverted index based multi-keyword public-key searchable encryption with strong privacy guarantee. In: Computer Communications, pp. 2092–2100 (2015)

15. Wang, B., Yu, S., Lou, W., Hou, Y.T.: Privacy-preserving multi-keyword fuzzy search over encrypted data in the cloud. In: IEEE INFOCOM, pp. 2112–2120 (2014)

16. Wang, C., Ren, K., Yu, S., Urs, K.M.R.: Achieving usable and privacy-assured similarity search over outsourced cloud data. In: IEEE INFOCOM, pp. 451–459 (2012)

17. Wong, W.K., Cheung, D.W., Kao, B., Mamoulis, N.: Secure kNN computation on encrypted databases. In: ACM SIGMOD International Conference on Management of Data, pp. 139–152 (2009)

18. Zheng, M., Zhou, H.: An efficient attack on a fuzzy keyword search scheme over encrypted data. In: IEEE International Conference on High Performance Computing and Communications & 2013 IEEE International Conference on Embedded and Ubiquitous Computing, pp. 1647–1651 (2014)

A Practical Group Signatures for Providing Privacy-Preserving Authentication with Revocation

Xiaohan Yue[1], Jian Xu[2], Bing Chen[1], and Yuan He[1(✉)]

[1] School of Information Science and Engineering, Shenyang University of Technology,
Liaoning, People's Republic of China
isaac.y.he@ieee.org
[2] Software College, Northeastern University, Liaoning, People's Republic of China

Abstract. In recent years, many revocable group signatures schemes were proposed; however, the backward security, which can disable a revoked signer to generate group signatures pertaining to future time periods, was not fully realized through those schemes. In this paper, we present a security model with the definition of backward security and propose a revocable group signatures scheme that is more efficient than previous ones, especially in Sign and Verify algorithms, which are performed much more frequently than others. In addition, considering the heavy workload of group manager in original group signatures, we separate a group into groups by employing a decentralized model to make our scheme more scalable, and thus more practical in real-life applications.

Keywords: Group signature · Revocation · Backward security · Efficiency

1 Introduction

As a widely recognized extension to digital signatures, Chaum and Heyst proposed group signatures for the first time in 1991 [15]. With group signatures, members of a group are able to sign messages on behalf of the group while maintaining anonymity [4]. The verifier can only verify if the signature was generated by a member but cannot specify the identity of the signer. When necessary, the group manager is able to look into the signature to track the identity of the signer

We would like to sincerely thank the reviewers for their valuable comments. X. Yue was supported in part by the Program for Excellent Talents from the Department of Education of Liaoning Province under Grant LJQ2015081 and the Doctoral Research Startup Fund from the Natural Science Foundation of Liaoning Province under Grant 201601166. J. Xu was supported in part by the National Natural Science Foundation of China under Grant 61872069. Y. He was supported in part by the Natural Science Foundation of Liaoning Province under Grant 20180550194.

J. Li et al. (Eds.): SPNCE 2019, LNICST 284, pp. 226–245, 2019.
https://doi.org/10.1007/978-3-030-21373-2_18

(traceability [4]). At the same time, group signatures have non-frameability [5], that is, even the group manager cannot forge signatures of group members. These important features of group signatures have attracted many real-life applications like network identity escrow [26], online anonymous electronic voting election [35], anonymous certificate systems [14], trusted computing [12], in addition to wireless MESH networks [22] and VANET networks [44].

After group signatures were proposed [6–8,10,23], providing revocation is regarded as a major research topic, that is, an authority can revoke the membership of a user. This is called revocable group signatures and it is a very important feature for real-life applications as in many cases, a system must clearly identify the validity of a member in a timely manner to avoid any potential threat.

With revocable group signatures, there are several obvious ways of revoking a member's signature. For example, when revoking a member, the group manager can publish a new public key and provide a new signing key to each valid member, except those who have been revoked. This approach is not suitable in practice because it requires the generation of a new key and updating all members and verifiers for every such revocation. An alternative way is to revoke the member and distribute a message to existing signers. As a consequence, the signer must then prove its validity when signing. Unfortunately, this is still not considered a suitable method for revocation in real-life applications, as existing members must track the revocation message. In a word, the difficulty of providing revocation to group signatures is for the verifier to publicly confirm the status of revocation for an anonymous signer. Furthermore, the cost of such revocation is relative to the number of revoked signers so that both its communication and computation overhead can be a burden for the group manager and a performance bottleneck of the system.

To overcome such difficulties, there are some more in-depth attempts and they can be classified as follows.

– Signers are explicitly checked by the verifier for their revocation status [9, 11, 13, 14, 16, 19, 24, 28, 32, 36, 40, 41, 45].
– Revoked signers are not allowed to generate a signature to pass the verification; in this case, an explicit revocation check is not necessary [1, 2, 20, 25, 29–31, 34, 37–39, 42].

And in the following subsection, we go through these two types of attempts in more details.

1.1 Related Works

In earlier group signature schemes with revocation, both the signing cost and the verification cost depend on the number of revoked members. In 2002, Camenisch et al. [14] proposed a method based on dynamic accumulator. It maps a set of values to a fixed-length string and allows for a valid membership certificate. However, this approach requires existing members to track revoked users, therefore increasing existing member's workload.

Brickell *et al.* propose a simple revocation mechanism in 2003 [11]. It is called Verifier-Local Revocation (VLR). Its formal definitions are given by Boneh and Shacham [9] and some extensions to it were proposed in [32,36,45]. In these schemes, the group member maintains a revocation list. The information of the revoked members is only sent to the verifier for verification, the signing cost is not relevant to the number of revoked group members, but the revocation list is updated every time when the group member is revoked. Therefore, the verification overhead increases as the number of revoked members increases. Recently, some VLR-type schemes have achieved sub-linear/constant verification costs [28,40,41]. However, they haven't considered backward unlinkability, that is, there are linkable parts in signatures to efficiently carry out verifications.

In 2012, a scalable scheme of the second type was presented by Libert, Peters and Yung (LPY) [31]. In this scheme, a ciphertext of broadcast encryption is periodically published while non-revoked members can decrypt this ciphertext and prove that they haven't been revoked through such decryption. As revoked signers cannot decrypt the ciphertext, they cannot generate the signature that passes the verification at early stage. For such schemes, in addition to prove its membership of the group, the signer also needs to prove that it has not been revoked. As follow-up works of the LPY scheme [1,2,29,30,37,42], revocable group signatures with compact revocation list have also been proposed.

In recent years, Ohara *et al.* [39] proposed an efficient revocable group signatures scheme to retain a constant revocation check complexity by employing the Complete Subtree (CS) method in LPY construction [31]. In this scheme, each group member is assigned to the leaf node of a tree. Instead of the identity-based encryption used in LPY, Ohara *et al.* uses the BBS signature scheme [21] in CS method, that is, signatures of nodes are written to a revocation list (RL_t), where signatures of revoked members are not in the list at a revocation epoch t. Thus, a non-revoked member can prove that its signature is in the list. In 2017, based on the method presented by Ohara *et al.* [39], Emura *et al.* [20] proposed a new revocable group signatures scheme with time-bound keys, where the notion of time-bound keys (TBK) is introduced by Chu *et al.* [16], that is, each signing key is given an expiry time. In 2018, Emura *et al.* [25] proposed and implemented a revocable group signatures scheme with scalability based on simple assumptions.

However, for security models of schemes that do not allow revoked signers to generate signatures to pass the verification, backward security is not sufficiently considered. We believe it is a security feature which is required to be explicitly defined, especially for revokable group signatures schemes relied on revocation periods. In our definition of backward security, capabilities and winning conditions of adversaries are different from other security features. When an adversary obtained private keys and credentials of all group members at a time t, he/she is able to generate a valid group signature for a revoked member who was revoked within $t^* \leq t - 1$. This security feature thus ensures the rationality of a fact that when verifiers verify group signatures, it is not necessary for them to download RL_t.

In terms of performance, considering the fact that both Sign and Verify are the most frequently used algorithms for group signatures, although the above schemes [16,19,40] perform well under the random oracle model, to further improve their performance is still a good motivation for the practical application of group signatures. So this is also one of the targets of our proposal.

In addition, for previous revokable group signatures schemes [15], the group manager is responsible for issuing certificates to group members and periodically updating the revocation list for signers to download. This is inevitably a bottleneck for the deployment of group signatures at scale. Therefore, it is another concern of this work as to improve the system model of previous revokable group signatures schemes.

1.2 Our Contributions

Targeting at defects of existing work, we present a new revocable group signatures scheme in this paper. Contributions of our work are summarized as follows.

- Our scheme realizes the backward security, which disables a revoked signer to generate group signatures pertaining to future time periods. This helps complete the security model for group signatures.
- Our proposal allows deployments in a much larger scale as with its decentralized design, the group manager are freed from maintaining the revocation list while the trusted third party can be freed from the generation of group member certificates.
- Both Sign and Verify operations are highly optimized with our proposal. As both operations are dominating, we have therefore cut the computation overhead significantly.
- Security features, such as backward security, non-frameability, traceability and anonymity are fully guaranteed as our scheme is constructed with the XDH, DL and q-SDH assumptions.

Other sections are organized as below. In Sect. 2, we introduce basic knowledge of cryptography for our work. In Sect. 3, we give definitions of our scheme, its security model and our purposes. We then propose a new group signatures scheme in Sect. 4. Section 5 conducts security analyses and certifications. Comparisons between the proposed scheme and other existing schemes are made in Sect. 6. Finally, Sect. 7 concludes our work.

2   Preliminaries

In this section, we review bilinear groups, the complexity assumptions which our scheme relies on, complete sub-tree methods, and BBS+ signatures.

2.1 Bilinear Groups and Complexity Assumptions

Let G_1 and G_2 be cyclic groups of prime order p, and g_1, g_2 be generators of G_1 and G_2, respectively. Let G_T be a multiplicative cyclic group with the same order, and define $par_{Bilinear} = (p, G_1, G_2, G_T, e, g_1, g_2)$ as the set of pairing group parameters. Bilinear pair $e(G_1, G_2) \rightarrow G_T$ is a map and it satisfies properties below:

- Bilinearity: $e(g_1^a, g_2^b) = e(g_1, g_2)^{ab}$ for all $a, b \in Z_p$, any $g_1 \in G_1$ and $g_2 \in G_2$.
- Non-degeneracy: $e(g_1, g_2) \neq 1$.
- Computability: The function e is efficiently computable.

Definition 1 (The Discrete Logarithm assumption (DL)). The DL assumption holds in G_1 if the probability below is negligible in security parameter κ for all adversaries $\mathcal{A}$ and all parameters $par_{Bilinear}$:

$$Adv_{\mathcal{A}}^{DL}(\kappa) = Pr[x \leftarrow Z_p; u = v^x, v \leftarrow G_1 : \mathcal{A}(u, v, par_{Bilinear}) \rightarrow x]$$

Definition 2 (The Decisional Diffie-Hellman assumption). The DDH assumption holds if the probability below is negligible in security parameter κ for all adversaries $\mathcal{A}$:

$$Adv_{\mathcal{A}}^{DDH}(\kappa) = Pr[\mathcal{A}(u, u^\alpha, u^\beta, z) = 1 | z = u^{\alpha \cdot \beta}] - Pr[\mathcal{A}(u, u^\alpha, u^\beta, z) = 1 | z = u^\gamma]$$

Definition 3 (The eXternal Diffie-Hellman assumption). Let $e : G_1 \times G_2 \rightarrow G_T$ be an asymmetric bilinear map, if the DDH assumption is hard in group G_1, then the XDH assumption will hold.

Definition 4 (The q-Strong Diffie-Hellman assumption). The q-SDH assumption holds if the probability below is negligible in security parameter κ, for all adversaries $\mathcal{A}$ and all parameter sets $par_{Bilinear}$:

$$Adv_{\mathcal{A}}^{q-SDH}(\kappa) = Pr[x \leftarrow Z_p; g_1^x, g_1^{x^2}, ..., g_1^{x^q} \leftarrow G_1; g_2^x$$
$$\leftarrow G_2 : (g_1^x, g_1^{x^2}, ..., g_1^{x^q}, g_2^x, par_{Bilinear}) \rightarrow (g_1^{1/(x+c)}, c \in Z_p)]$$

2.2 BBS+ Signature

The BBS+ signature scheme [21] is introduced as follows:

Given $par_{Bilinear} = (p, G_1, G_2, G_T, e)$, let $g_0, g_1, ..., g_L, g_{L+1}$ be the generators of G_1 and h be a generator of G_2.

Key Generation: Select $\gamma \leftarrow Z_p$ randomly and let $w = h^\gamma$. The secret key is $sk = \gamma$ and the verification key is $vk = w$.

Signing: For message $(m_1, ..., m_L)$, choose $\eta, \zeta \leftarrow Z_p$ randomly and compute $s = (g_0 g_1^\zeta g_2^{m_1} ... g_{L+1}^{m_L})^\lambda$ where $\lambda = (\eta + \gamma)^{-1}$. Let the signature be $\sigma = (s, \eta, \zeta)$.

Verifying: For signature $\sigma = (s, \eta, \zeta)$ and message $(m_1, ..., m_L)$, if $e(s, h^\eta vk) = e(g_0 g_1^\zeta g_2^{m_1} ... g_{L+1}^{m_L}, h)$, then the output is 1, otherwise it is 0.

This BBS+ signature scheme has unforgeability against chosen message attack (CMA) under the q-SDH assumption [8].

2.3 Complete Sub-tree Methods

In this section, we briefly introduce the Complete Subtree method [18]. Let N be the set of all signers and $R \subset N$ be the set of revoked signers. With the CS method, $N \setminus R$ is divided into m disjoint sets, that is, $N \setminus R = S_1 \cup \ldots \cup S_m$, where $m = O(R \cdot log(N \setminus R))$.

Definition 5 (Complete Subtree Algorithm). When a signer with index i is revoked at time t, the Complete Subtree algorithm takes the binary tree BT and a set of revoked signers R_t as inputs, where $i \in R_t$, and outputs a set of nodes. The description of CS is stated below.

> CS(BT, R_t)
>
> X, Y $\leftarrow \emptyset$
>
> Add Path(i) to X
>
> $\forall_x \in$ X
>
> If $x_{\text{left}} \notin$ X, then add x_{left} to Y;
>
> If $x_{\text{right}} \notin$ X, then add x_{right} to Y;
>
> If $|RL_t| = 0$, then add root to Y;
>
> Return Y;

In our scheme, a private key is assigned to each node of the binary tree and each user is assigned to a leaf node of the binary tree. Let $\{n_0, n_1, \ldots, n_l\}$ be the path from the root node to the leaf node where l is the height of the complete binary tree. The user then gets a key associated with each $n_i \in \{n_0, n_1, \ldots, n_l\}$ and a ciphertext is computed by keys of nodes. Let $\Theta = \{n'_0, n', \ldots, n'_m\}$ be a set of nodes and their corresponding keys are used for encryption. If the path of a user is $\{n_0, n_1, \ldots, n_l\}$, which is indicated as the authorized receiver, then there is a node ε such that $\varepsilon \in \{n_0, n_1, \ldots, n_l\} \cap \{n'_0, n', \ldots, n'_m\}$. Therefore, the user can decrypt the ciphertext using this private key corresponding to node ε.

In the proposed scheme, the Revoke and Update algorithms are constructed with the complete subtree method to ensure that non-revoked group members can generate valid signatures.

3 Definition of the Group Signatures Scheme and the Security Model

The model of our scheme is presented in Fig. 1. It consists of four entities, *i.e.*, a trusted authority (TA), the group manager (GM), group members and verifiers. Their properties are as follows:

Trusted Authority: In our scheme, The TA is responsible for maintaining system global security parameters and is trusted. If a dispute needs to be resolved, the TA has the ability to trace real identities of group members. After revealing the actual identity, the TA can revoke malicious users and renew the revocation list (RL) which contains a set of revoked identities and a set of non-revoked tokens. We assume the revocable group signatures scheme that has its lifetime divided into epochs for revocation while at the beginning of which the trusted authority updates its revocation list.

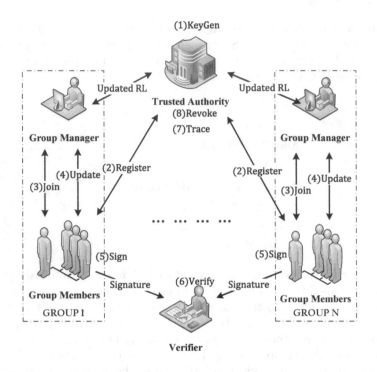

Fig. 1. The model of our scheme.

Group Manager: In our scheme, when a user wants to join a group, the GM is given the ability to generate and issue a group certificate to the user. For each group member, the GM is responsible for helping them to update the newest non-revoked tokens at a new epoch.

Group Member: Before being a group member, the user should register with TA to obtain a tag which helps him to get the non-revoked token. After joining a group, the group member is able to anonymously sign messages on behalf of the group with his secret signing key, group certificate and non-revoked token, where the non-revoked token can be updated periodically from GM.

Verifier: The verifier can verify signatures using the global public parameters and the group public key from TA or GM. When necessary, it can also forward the group signature to TA to trace a group member.

Next, we give definitions of our scheme which has seven probabilistic polynomial-time algorithms as shown in Fig. 1. Then we show security properties of our scheme.

3.1   Definitions of Our Scheme

In our proposal, the revocable group signatures scheme is made up of the following eight algorithms/protocols.

(1) KeyGen algorithm

KeyGen(λ): Every entity in our scheme performs this algorithm.

- **TAKg**(λ): TA executes this algorithm at the setup stage with a security parameter $\lambda \in \mathbb{N}$ as the input to produce the global public key gpk, the secret tracing key tk_{TA} and the non-revoked token secret key rk_{TA}. After such key generations, TA then publishes gpk.
- **GMKg**(gpk): Taking gpk as the input, it generates the secret key sk_{GM} and the group public key pk_{GM} of the group manager.
- **UKg**(gpk): Every new user before interacting with TA and GM executes this algorithm. Taking gpk as the input, it generates the secret signing key sk_M and the personal public key pk_M for a user.

(2) Register protocol

Register(User:(sk_M, pk_M),TA:($BinaryTree$)): Before joining a group, each user needs to interact with TA to prove the knowledge of private key sk_M with some zero-knowledge proof protocol. TA will then assign a tag_i to user i.

(3) Join protocol

Join(User:(gpk, sk_M, pk_M),GM:($gpk, pk_{GM}, sk_{GM}, RL_t$)): It is interactive between the group manager and a user when the latter turns into a member. For the first time when a user joins a group, this protocol terminates with the user i obtaining a group membership certificate gCert$_i$. It is to be noted that any revoked member in the revoked user set R_t is not allowed to join a group.

(4) Update algorithm

For each revocation epoch, group members need to update their non-revoked tokens by communicating with the GM giving an assumption that the GM can obtain the current revocation list RL_t.

Update(Member:(tag),GM:(RL_t)): At a revocation epoch t, a member i sends a request to the GM to obtain a new non-revoked token. When receiving such request, the GM checks if member i is in R_t. If not, the GM forms a token token$_{i,t}$ from the set Φ in RL_t according to the member's tag_i, and then returns it to the member.

(5) Sign algorithm

Sign($gpk, t, token_{i,t}, \text{gCert}_i, sk_M, msg$): When being given an epoch t with an updated token$_{i,t}$, a group membership certificate gCert$_i$, a secret signing key sk_M, and a message msg, this algorithm will generate a group signature σ.

(6) Verify algorithm

Verify($\sigma, msg, t, gpk, pk_{GM}$): When being given a signature σ, a revocation epoch t, a message msg, the global public key gpk, and the group public key pk_{GM}, this deterministic algorithm will output either 0 (if invalid) or 1 (if valid).

(7) Trace algorithm

Trace$(gpk, tk_{TA}, \mathrm{RL}_t, msg, \sigma)$: This deterministic verifiable algorithm traces a signer by taking gpk, the tracing key tk_{TA}, RL_t, and the message-signature pair (msg, σ) as inputs while returning the identity of this signer i.

(8) Revoke algorithm

Revoke$(gpk, rk_{TA}, t, \mathrm{R}_t)$: This algorithm allows TA to generate an updated revocation list $\mathrm{RL}_t = \{t, \mathrm{R}_t, \Phi = \{\mathrm{token}_{i,t}\}_{i=0}^{m}\}$ for a new revocation epoch t, where the token set Φ has all tokens of non-revoked users. It accepts the set R_t of identities of revoked members for gpk, rk_{TA} and revocation epoch t as inputs while it outputs the revocation list RL_t for epoch t.

3.2   The Security Model

Here, we introduce security properties of our scheme. First, notations and the oracles used in the definitions are given as follows:

$\mathcal{O}_{\mathrm{a-join}}$: The adversary $\mathcal{A}$ executes Join algorithm with honest group manager, and the member that collude with the adversary is added to the group. Then the number of members is incremented and adds the information of new member to a registration table Reg.

$\mathcal{O}_{\mathrm{b-join}}$: The adversary $\mathcal{A}$ executes Join algorithm while colluding the group manager (this member does not collude with the adversary). Then the number of members is incremented and adds the information of new member to a registration table Reg.

$\mathcal{O}_{\mathrm{AddM}}$: By calling this oracle with an argument, an identity i, the adversary can add i to the group as an honest user where HM is the set of honest members. It also picks a pair of personal public and private keys $(sk_{M,i}, pk_{M,i})$ for i. It then executes the Join protocol (on behalf of i). When finished, it adds the information of i to the registration table Reg. The calling adversary then receives $pk_{M,i}$.

$\mathcal{O}_{\mathrm{Sign}}$: It receives a query that is a message msg and identity i and returns $\perp$ if $i \notin \mathrm{HM}$, and otherwise returns σ for the member i and epoch t.

$\mathcal{O}_{\mathrm{Trace}}$: The adversary $\mathcal{A}$ can call this oracle with arguments, a message msg and signature σ, to obtain the output of the Trace algorithm on msg, σ, computed under the tracing key tk_{TA} given that σ was not previously returned as a response for any query to $\mathcal{O}_{\mathrm{Ch}}$.

$\mathcal{O}_{\mathrm{Ch}}$: On input $i_0, i_1 \in \mathrm{HM}$, and a message msg, the challenge oracle computes signature σ by performing the Sign algorithm with the private signing key of i_b, where $b \in_R \{0, 1\}$, and returns σ. The oracle keeps as record the message-signature pair to make sure that the adversary does not call the tracing oracle on it later.

$\mathcal{O}_{\mathrm{MSK}}$: On input i, the member secret key oracle reveals $(sk_{M,i}, pk_{M,i})$ and adds i to the set CM of corrupted members.

$\mathcal{O}_{\text{WReg}}$: On input i, the oracle allows the adversary to modify member i in the registration table Reg.

$\mathcal{O}_{\text{RReg}}$: On input i, the oracle allows the adversary to read member i in the registration table Reg.

$\mathcal{O}_{\text{RRL}}$: On input i and t^*, the oracle allows the adversary to read member i of the revocation List RL_{t^*} at an epoch t^*.

$\mathcal{O}_{\text{Update}}$: At an epoch t, the adversary can call this oracle with an argument, an identity i, to obtain the corresponding non-revoked token $\text{token}_{i,t}$.

$\mathcal{O}_{\text{Revoke}}$: It revokes a member from the group. It receives a query of member identity $i \in \text{HM}$ and increments t, adds i to RL_t and updates RL_t.

Next, we define the anonymity with backward unlinkability (BU-anonymity), which guarantees that no adversary (who does not have tk_{TA}) can distinguish if signers (even if the signer has been revoked) of two group signatures are the same.

Definition 1: BU-Anonymity is defined by the following game.

Attack-Game $\text{Game}_{\mathcal{A}}^{bu-anon}(\lambda)$:

$b \in_R \{0,1\}$
$(gpk, pk_{GM}, sk_{GM}, rk_{TA}, tk_{TA}) \leftarrow \text{KeyGen}(\lambda)$
$\text{CM} \leftarrow \emptyset, \text{HM} \leftarrow \emptyset, \text{RL}_t \leftarrow \emptyset$
$d \leftarrow \mathcal{A}(gpk, pk_{GM}, sk_{GM} \ : \ \mathcal{O}_{\text{Ch}}, \mathcal{O}_{b-\text{join}}, \mathcal{O}_{\text{WReg}}, \mathcal{O}_{\text{MSK}}, \mathcal{O}_{\text{Trace}}, \mathcal{O}_{\text{Revoke}},$
$\quad \mathcal{O}_{\text{Update}}, \mathcal{O}_{\text{Sign}})$
If $d = b$ return 1 else 0.

The advantage of the adversary $\mathcal{A}$ against this game is $\text{Adv}_{\mathcal{A}}^{bu-anon}(\lambda) = |\,Pr[\text{Game}_{\mathcal{A}}^{bu-anon}(\lambda)] - 1/2\,|$. We say that our scheme satisfies BU-anonymity if $\text{Adv}_{\mathcal{A}}^{bu-anon}(\lambda)$ is negligible in λ for any probabilistic polynomial-time algorithm $\mathcal{A}$.

Next, we define non-frameability which guarantees that no adversary (who can corrupt the GM and the TA) is able to produce group signatures with its tracing result being an honest user.

Definition 2: Non-frameability is defined by the following game.

Attack-Game $\text{Game}_{\mathcal{A}}^{frame}(\lambda)$:

$(gpk, pk_{GM}, sk_{GM}, rk_{TA}, tk_{TA}) \leftarrow \text{KeyGen}(\lambda)$
$\text{CM} \leftarrow \emptyset, \text{HM} \leftarrow \emptyset, \text{RL}_t \leftarrow \emptyset$
$(msg, \sigma, t, \text{RL}_t) \leftarrow \mathcal{A}(gpk, pk_{GM}, sk_{GM}, tk_{TA} \ : \ \mathcal{O}_{b-\text{join}}, \mathcal{O}_{\text{WReg}}, \mathcal{O}_{\text{Sign}},$
$\quad \mathcal{O}_{\text{Revoke}}, \mathcal{O}_{\text{Update}})$
If $\text{Verify}(gpk, pk_{GM}, msg, \sigma, t) = 0$, return 0.
$i \leftarrow \text{Trace}(gpk, rk_{TA}, t, \text{RL}_t, msg, \sigma)$
If $i \in \text{HM}$, return 1.
Reurn 0.

The advantage of the adversary $\mathcal{A}$ against this game is $\text{Adv}_{\mathcal{A}}^{frame}(\lambda) = Pr[\text{Game}_{\mathcal{A}}^{frame}(\lambda) = 1]$. We say that our scheme satisfies non-frameability if $\text{Adv}_{\mathcal{A}}^{frame}(\lambda)$ is negligible in λ for any probabilistic polynomial-time algorithm $\mathcal{A}$.

Next, we define traceability which guarantees that no adversary (who does not have sk_{GM}) can generate a valid group signature with its tracing result being outside of the set of non-revoked adversarially-controlled users.

Definition 3: Traceability is defined by the following game.

Attack-Game $\text{Game}_{\mathcal{A}}^{trace}(\lambda)$:

$(gpk, pk_{GM}, sk_{GM}, rk_{TA}, tk_{TA}) \leftarrow \text{KeyGen}(\lambda)$
$\text{CM} \leftarrow \emptyset, \text{HM} \leftarrow \emptyset, \text{RL}_t \leftarrow \emptyset$
$(msg, \sigma, t) \leftarrow \mathcal{A}(gpk, pk_{GM}, tk_{TA} : \mathcal{O}_{\text{a-join}}, \mathcal{O}_{\text{AddM}}, \mathcal{O}_{\text{MSK}}, \mathcal{O}_{\text{RReg}}, \mathcal{O}_{\text{Sign}}, \mathcal{O}_{\text{Revoke}}, \mathcal{O}_{\text{Update}})$
If $\text{Verify}(gpk, pk_{GM}, t, msg, \sigma) = 0$, return 0.
$i \leftarrow \text{Trace}(pk_{GM}, tk_{TA}, reg, msg, \sigma, \text{RL}_t)$
If $i \notin \text{HM} \cup \text{CM} \backslash \text{R}_t$, return 1.
Reurn 0.

The advantage of the adversary $\mathcal{A}$ against this game is $\text{Adv}_{\mathcal{A}}^{trace}(\lambda) = Pr[\text{Game}_{\mathcal{A}}^{trace}(\lambda) = 1]$. We say that our scheme satisfies traceability if $\text{Adv}_{\mathcal{A}}^{frame}(\lambda)$ is negligible in λ for any probabilistic polynomial-time algorithm $\mathcal{A}$.

Next, we define backward security which guarantees that no adversary (who does not have rk_{TA}) can forge a valid group signature with its tracing result being in the set of revoked users.

Definition 4: Backward Security is defined by the following game.

Attack-Game $\text{Game}_{\mathcal{A}}^{backward}(\lambda)$:

$(gpk, pk_{GM}, sk_{GM}, rk_{TA}, tk_{TA}) \leftarrow \text{KeyGen}(\lambda)$
$\text{CM} \leftarrow \emptyset, \text{HM} \leftarrow \emptyset, \text{RL}_t \leftarrow \emptyset$
$(msg, \sigma, t) \leftarrow \mathcal{A}(gpk, pk_{GM}, sk_{GM}, tk_{TA} : \mathcal{O}_{\text{a-join}}, \mathcal{O}_{\text{AddM}}, \mathcal{O}_{\text{MSK}}, \mathcal{O}_{\text{Sign}}, \mathcal{O}_{\text{RRL}}, \mathcal{O}_{\text{Revoke}}, \mathcal{O}_{\text{Update}})$
If $\text{Verify}(gpk, pk_{GM}, t, msg, \sigma) = 0$, return 0.
$i \leftarrow \text{Trace}(pk_{GM}, tk_{TA}, reg, msg, \sigma, \text{RL}_t)$
If $i \in \text{R}_t$, return 1.
Reurn 0.

The advantage of the adversary $\mathcal{A}$ against this game is $\text{Adv}_{\mathcal{A}}^{backward}(\lambda) = Pr[\text{Game}_{\mathcal{A}}^{backward}(\lambda) = 1]$. We say that our scheme satisfies backward security if $\text{Adv}_{\mathcal{A}}^{backward}(\lambda)$ is negligible in λ for any probabilistic polynomial-time algorithm $\mathcal{A}$.

4   The Proposed Group Signatures Scheme

In this section, we present details of our group signatures scheme. This scheme is based on an assumption that interactions between new users and the TA/GM happen through a secure channel.

KeyGen(λ): In this algorithm, TA generates a private key for itself and parameters for the system. In addition, GM and all the users also generate private key pairs for themselves. Details are stated below:

- **TAKg**(λ): TA carries out steps below with the security parameter λ:
  - Choose an asymmetric bilinear group pair $(G_1 = \langle g_1 \rangle, G_2 = \langle g_2 \rangle)$ of prime order $p \in \{0,1\}^\lambda$ and a pairing function $e : G_1 \times G_2 \to G_T$.
  - Select $\dot{g}_1, \ddot{g}_1 \leftarrow G_1$ randomly and a secure cryptographic hash function H where $\mathrm{H}(\cdot) : \{0,1\}^* \to Z_p$.
  - Select a secret key $\gamma \leftarrow Z_p$ randomly, and issue $(rk_{TA}, pk_{TA}) = (\gamma, g_2^\gamma)$.
  - Select $x_1', x_2', y_1', y_2' \leftarrow Z_p$ randomly, and compute $\varphi_1 = \dot{g}_1^{x_1'} \ddot{g}_1^{x_2'}, \varphi_2 = \dot{g}_1^{y_1'} \ddot{g}_1^{y_2'}$.
  - Select a secret key $\nu \leftarrow Z_p$ randomly, and compute $u = \dot{g}_1^\nu$. Let $tk_{TA} = \nu$ be the tracing key of the TA.
  - Keep rk_{TA} and tk_{TA} secret.
  - Publish global public system parameters $gpk = (p, G_1, G_2, G_T, e, g_1, g_2, \dot{g}_1, \ddot{g}_1, \varphi_1, \varphi_2, u, \mathrm{H}, pk_{TA})$.
- **GMKg**(gpk): Each GM takes steps below:
  - Select a secret key $\omega \leftarrow Z_p$ randomly, and compute $(sk_{GM}, pk_{GM}) = (\omega, g_2^\omega)$. pk_{GM} is the group public key and sk_{GM} is the private key of GM.
  - Keep sk_{GM} secret.
- **UKg**(gpk): Users take steps below:
  - Select a secret key $\chi \leftarrow Z_p$ randomly, and compute $(sk_M, pk_M) = (\chi, \ddot{g}_1^\chi)$, χ is the private key of a user.
  - Keep sk_M secret.

Register(User:(sk_M, pk_M),TA:$(BinaryTree)$): This protocol is based on an assumption that interactions between new users and the TA is carried out in a secure channel.

- Users interact with the TA with some zero-knowledge proof protocol to obtain the tag used for getting the non-revoked token later.
  - In order to prove the knowledge of the secret signing key $sk_{M,i} = \chi_i$, the user i randomly chooses $\gamma_\chi \leftarrow Z_p$, and computes $R_\chi = \ddot{g}_1^{\gamma_\chi}$, $c = \mathrm{H}(gpk \parallel pk_{M,i} \parallel R_\chi)$ and $s_\chi = \gamma_\chi + c \cdot \chi_i$.
  - Through the above operations, the user sends the proof $(pk_{M,i}, c, s_\chi)$ to TA.
  - TA computes $\check{R}_\chi = \ddot{g}_1^{s_\chi} pk_M^c$, and checks whether that $c = \mathrm{H}(gpk \parallel pk_{M,i} \parallel \check{R}_\chi)$. The proof is valid if positive and this means that user i knows the knowledge of the secret key χ_i.
- According to the CS method in Sect. 2.3, the TA will give user i an available leaf node ν_i of the binary tree and a path $\rho_i := \langle n_0 = \epsilon, n_1, \ldots, n_l = \nu_i \rangle$ connecting the leaf ν_i to the root ϵ. The TA will then send a path ρ_i to user i. Here we name ρ_i as tag tag_i of i, which is used to request the non-revoked token from the GM.

– Next, the TA will carry out the Revoke algorithm to update the set of non-revoked tokens and store $\{i, pk_{M,i}, \text{tag}_i, *\}$ in the registration table Reg, where the symbol $*$ denotes the group membership certificates of user i and it will be generated by the Join protocol.

Join(User:(gpk, sk_M, pk_M),GM:$(gpk, pk_{GM}, sk_{GM}, \text{RL}_t)$): This protocol is interactive between the GM and users.

– To obtain a group membership certificate from the GM, at first, the user need to perform a zero-knowledge proof protocol as described in Register to prove the knowledge of its secret signing key.
– Next, the user sends a node $\varepsilon \in$ tag to the GM (The node ε was determined in Update).
– After receiving the node ε, the GM takes steps below.
  • Checks whether user i exists in the R_t. If positive, move on; otherwise, abort this step.
  • Compute the group membership certificate $\text{gCert}_i = (g_1 \dot{g}_1^\varepsilon \cdot pk_{M,i})^{1/(sk_{GM}+\eta)}$, where $\eta \in_R Z_p$.
  • Send (gCert_i, η) to the user.
  • Send a copy of the user's $(i, pk_{M,i}, \text{gCert}_i)$ to the TA who will update the registration information of user i with the copy.
  • After receiving the response (gCert_i, η) from the GM, user i checks if $e(\text{gCert}_i, pk_{GM} \cdot g_2^\eta) = e(pk_{M,i}, g_2) \cdot e(g_1 \dot{g}_1^\varepsilon, g_2)$. If yes, the user accepts its group certificate $\text{gCert}_i = (g_1 \dot{g}_1^\varepsilon \ddot{g}_1^\chi)^{1/(\omega+\eta)}$.

Sign($gpk, t, token_{i,t}, \text{gCert}_i, sk_M, msg$): Upon entering $msg \in \{0,1\}^*$, the GM signs it with SIGN and sends the signature with msg. Details are stated below:

– Select $\zeta \leftarrow Z_p$ randomly, and output: $\psi_1 = \text{gCert} \cdot u^\zeta$, $\psi_2 = token_{\varepsilon,t} \cdot g_1^\zeta$, $\psi_3 = \dot{g}_1^\zeta$, $\psi_4 = \ddot{g}_1^\zeta$, $\psi_5 = (\varphi_1 \varphi_2^h)^\zeta$, where $h = \text{H}(\psi_1 \parallel \psi_2 \parallel \psi_3 \parallel \psi_4)$. Let $\alpha = \zeta \cdot \eta$ and $\beta = \zeta \cdot \eta'$.
– Compute the signature of knowledge (SPK) as below. $V = SPK\{(\zeta, \alpha, \beta, \varepsilon, \chi, \eta, \eta')$:
$e(\psi_1, g_2)^{-\eta} e(\ddot{g}_1, g_2)^\chi e(u, g_2)^\alpha e(u, pk_{GM})^\zeta e(\dot{g}_1, g_2)^\varepsilon = e(\psi_1, pk_{GM})/e(g_1, g_2)$,
$e(\psi_2, g_2)^{-\eta'} e(\ddot{g}_1, g_2)^t e(g_1, g_2)^\beta e(g_1, pk_{TA})^\zeta e(\dot{g}_1, g_2)^\varepsilon = e(\psi_2, pk_{TA})/e(g_1, g_2)$,
$\psi_3 = \dot{g}_1^\zeta, \psi_4 = \ddot{g}_1^\zeta, \psi_5 = (\varphi_1 \varphi_2^h)^\zeta \}(msg)$
The SPK is computed using the following steps.
  • Pick blind factors $r_\alpha, r_\beta, r_\zeta, r_\varepsilon, r_\chi, r_\eta, r_{\eta'} \leftarrow Z_p$ and compute:
$R_1 \leftarrow \dot{g}_1^{r_\zeta}$
$R_2 \leftarrow \ddot{g}_1^{r_\zeta}$
$R_3 \leftarrow (\varphi_1 \varphi_2^h)^{r_\zeta}$
$R_{\text{gCert}} \leftarrow e(\dot{g}_1, g_2)^{r_\varepsilon} e(\psi_1, g_2)^{-r_\eta} e(\ddot{g}_1, g_2)^{r_\chi} \cdot e(u, g_2)^{r_\alpha} e(u, pk_{GM})^{r_\zeta}$
$R_{\text{token}} \leftarrow e(\dot{g}_1, g_2)^{r_\varepsilon} e(\psi_2, g_2)^{-r_{\eta'}} e(\ddot{g}_1, g_2)^t \cdot e(g_1, g_2)^{r_\beta} e(g_1, pk_{TA})^{r_\zeta}$
  • Compute $c = \text{H}(msg \parallel \psi_1 \parallel \psi_2 \parallel \psi_3 \parallel \psi_4 \parallel \psi_5 \parallel R_1 \parallel R_2 \parallel R_3 \parallel R_{\text{gCert}} \parallel R_{\text{token}})$.

- With results above, values below are computed.

$$s_\alpha \leftarrow r_\alpha + c \cdot \alpha$$
$$s_\beta \leftarrow r_\beta + c \cdot \beta$$
$$s_\zeta \leftarrow r_\zeta + c \cdot \zeta$$
$$s_\eta \leftarrow r_\eta + c \cdot \eta$$
$$s_{\eta'} \leftarrow r_{\eta'} + c \cdot \eta'$$
$$s_\chi \leftarrow r_\chi + c \cdot \chi$$
$$s_\varepsilon \leftarrow r_\varepsilon + c \cdot \varepsilon$$

The group signature is $\sigma = (c, s_\alpha, s_\beta, s_\eta, s_\zeta, s_{\eta'}, s_\chi, s_\varepsilon, \psi_1, \psi_2, \psi_3, \psi_4, \psi_5)$.

Verify$(\sigma, msg, t, gpk, pk_{GM})$: The verifier executes Verify to validate the received message (msg, σ). Details are stated below:

- Compute values below.

$$\check{R}_{\text{gCert}} \leftarrow e(\dot{g}_1, g_2)^{s_\varepsilon} e(\psi_1, g_2)^{-s_\eta} e(\ddot{g}_1, g_2)^{s_\chi} e(u, g_2)^{s_\alpha} e(u, pk_{GM})^{s_\zeta} (e(g_1, g_2)/ e(\psi_1, pk_{GM}))^c$$

$$\check{R}_{\text{token}} \leftarrow e(\dot{g}_1, g_2)^{s_\varepsilon} e(\psi_2, g_2)^{-s_{\eta'}} e(g_1, g_2)^{s_\beta} e(g_1, pk_{TA})^{s_\zeta} (e(\ddot{g}_1^t g_1, g_2)/e(\psi_2, pk_{TA}))^c$$

$$\check{R}_1 \leftarrow \dot{g}_1^{s_\zeta} \psi_3^{-c}$$

$$\check{R}_2 \leftarrow \ddot{g}_1^{s_\zeta} \psi_4^{-c}$$

$$\check{R}_3 \leftarrow (\varphi_1, \varphi_2^h)^{s_\zeta} \psi_5^{-c}, where h = \mathrm{H}(\psi_1 \parallel \psi_2 \parallel \psi_3 \parallel \psi_4).$$

- Check whether $c = \mathrm{H}(msg \parallel \psi_1 \parallel \psi_2 \parallel \psi_3 \parallel \psi_4 \parallel \psi_5 \parallel \check{R}_1 \parallel \check{R}_2 \parallel \check{R}_3 \parallel \check{R}_{\text{gCert}} \parallel \check{R}_{\text{token}})$. The verifier will accept the message if the equation holds; otherwise the message will be rejected.

Trace$(gpk, tk_{TA}, \mathrm{RL}_t, msg, \sigma)$: It is possible to identify the actual signer with the valid group signature σ on message msg. The steps are as follows.

- Compute the group certificate gCert $= \psi_1/\psi_3^{tk_{TA}}$.
- Look up gCert in the registration table and retrieve its registration information $\{i, pk_{M,i}, tag_i, \text{gCert}\}$. If matched, return i. Otherwise, output 0 and abort with a failure.

Revoke$(gpk, rk_{TA}, t, \mathrm{R}_t)$: In general, the TA periodically updates RL_t; or it updates when a member is revoked. Meanwhile, the TA will also update the non-revoked token set Φ, and the revoked user set R_t with an epoch t. Details are presented below.

- Determine the non-revoked node set $\Theta = \{n_0, n_1, \ldots, n_m\}$, where m is the number of non-revoked users, with the CS covering algorithm.
- For $i = 1$ to m, select $\eta_i' \leftarrow Z_p$ randomly, and output the non-revoked token $(\text{token}_{i,t} = (g_1 \dot{g}_1^{n_i} \ddot{g}_1^t)^{1/(rk_{TA}+\eta_i')}, \eta_i')$.
- Send the updated $\mathrm{RL}_t = \{t, \mathrm{R}_t, \{\text{token}_{i,t}\}_{i=0}^m, \Theta\}$ to each GM via an authenticated and secure channel.

Update(Member:(tag),GM:(RL$_t$)): Group members periodically update their non-revoked tokens from the GM. Interactions between group members and the GM are presented below.

– The member forwards pk_M and tag to GM.
– Upon receiving pk_M and tag, the GM performs steps as follows:
  • Find out if member i exists in R$_t$. If no, move on; otherwise, abort.
  • Select a node ε from the intersection of the tag and the node set Θ, as in Sect. 2.3.
  • Search in the non-revoked token set $\Phi = \{\text{token}_i\}_{i=1}^m$ in RL$_t$ for token$_{\varepsilon,t}$ corresponding to node ε.
  • Encrypt the selected token$_{\varepsilon,t}$ and ε for the member.
– After the response is received, the member checks if $e((g_1\dot{g}_1^\varepsilon\ddot{g}_1^t)^{1/(rk_{TA}+\eta_i')}$, $pk_{TA} \cdot g_2^{\eta'}) = e(\ddot{g}_1^t, g_2) \cdot e(g_1\dot{g}_1^\varepsilon, g_2)$. If yes, the member accepts it.

5   Security Analyses

Here, we discuss the security of our scheme. That is, we explain that our scheme satisfies backward security, BU-anonymity, non-frameability, traceability defined in Sect. 3.1. For backward security, the attack on backward security is to fake a BBS+ signature as a non-revoked token. Therefore, the security against backward security attacks can be simplified as the unforgeability of the BBS+ signature scheme, which was proved in [21]. For traceability, the adversary is essentially concerned with faking a valid group membership certificate. This also can be reduced to the unforgeability of the BBS+ scheme. For security against framing attacks, in the join protocol of our proposal, a user chooses its secret signing key sk_M while the GM does not know it. Therefore, from a forged signature output by the adversary of framing attacks, an algorithm can be constructed so that it extracts this secret key and solves the DL problem with it. Furthermore, because of the CCA security of the Cramer-Shoup encryption scheme [17], our scheme is anonymous. Due to space constraints, we will present security proofs of the following theorems in an extended version of this paper.

Theorem 1. *The proposed group signatures scheme has BU-anonymity in the random oracle model if the XDH assumption holds in* (G_1, G_2, G_T).

Theorem 2. *The proposed group signatures scheme has non-frameability in the random oracle model under the DL assumption.*

Theorem 3. *The proposed group signatures scheme has traceability in the random oracle model under the q-SDH assumption.*

Theorem 4. *The proposed group signatures scheme has backward security in the random oracle model under the q-SDH assumption.*

6   Performance Evaluations

We evaluate the computation and communication overhead of our scheme in this section and compare its performance to two existing schemes [20,39]. Our scheme is implemented with the Barreto-Naehrig (BN) curves [3] over a 382-bit prime field to ensure 128-bit security [27,43]. Our implementation was simulated on a workstation with specifications as follows:

- CPU: Intel Xeon E5-2680v2 (3.6 GHz)
- OS: Windows Server 2012
- Compilation environment: Microsoft Visual Studio C++ 2017
- Crypto-library: the PBC library [33]

For above-mentioned experimental settings, Table 1 summarizes the benchmarks used in our work.

Table 1. Benchmarks of group operations on a 382-bit BN curve.

Operations	Time (μsec)
$\text{Mul}(\mathbb{G}_1)$	344.5
$\text{Mul}(\mathbb{G}_2)$	471.3
$\text{Exp}(\mathbb{G}_T)$	981.6
$\mathbb{P}$	1847.3

Here, $\text{Mul}(\mathbb{G}_1)$, $\text{Mul}(\mathbb{G}_2)$, $\text{Exp}(\mathbb{G}_T)$ are scalar multiplication on G_1, G_2, and exponentiation on G_T, respectively. $\mathbb{P}$ is the time to perform a pairing operation. We only consider the influence of these four operations as the speed of signature generation/verification actually depends on them. We firstly consider the load of computation for our algorithms according to benchmarks of the PBC library. We reduce the computation overhead of the Sign/Verify algorithms by decreasing the number of exponentiations on G_T.

For the Sign algorithm, we transform R_{gCert} and R_{token} as $R_{\text{gCert}} \leftarrow e(\dot{g}_1^{r_\varepsilon} \ddot{g}_1^{r_x} u^{r_\alpha} \psi_1^{-r_\eta}, g_2)e(u^{r_\varsigma}, pk_{GM})$, $R_{\text{token}} \leftarrow e(\dot{g}_1^{r_\varepsilon} \ddot{g}_1^t g_1^{r_\beta} \psi_2^{-r_{\eta'}}, g_2)e(g_1^{r_\varsigma}, pk_{TA})$. By precomputing pairing values, such as $e(\dot{g}_1, g_2)$, original computations require $2\text{Mul}(\mathbb{G}_1)+7\text{Exp}(\mathbb{G}_T)+2\mathbb{P}$. But $9\text{Mul}(\mathbb{G}_1)+4\mathbb{P}$ are required in our modifications.

For the Verify algorithm, we also transform $\check{R}_{\text{gCert}}$ and $\check{R}_{\text{token}}$ as $\check{R}_{\text{gCert}} \leftarrow e(\dot{g}_1^{s_\varepsilon} \psi_1^{-s_\eta} \ddot{g}_1^{s_x} u^{s_\alpha} g_1^c, g_2)e(u^{s_\varsigma} \psi_1^{-c}, pk_{GM})$, $\check{R}_{\text{token}} \leftarrow e(\dot{g}_1^{s_\varepsilon} \psi_2^{-s_{\eta'}} \ddot{g}_1^{tc} g_1^{c+s_\beta}, g_2)$ $e(\psi_2^{-c} g_1^{s_\varsigma}, pk_{TA})$ which originally requires $5\text{Mul}(\mathbb{G}_1)+7\text{Exp}(\mathbb{G}_T)+5\mathbb{P}$ with precomputed pairing values, but our modifications require $12\text{Mul}(\mathbb{G}_1)+4\mathbb{P}$. In Table 2, we present comparisons of the computation overhead between our proposal and schemes in [39] and [20]. Our attention was laid on two specific algorithms: Sign (signature generation algorithm) and Verify (signature correctness verifying algorithm). We focus on them as they need to be frequently performed by the GM and the verifier.

Table 2. Comparisons of the computation overhead.

Schemes	Sign (opt.)	Verify (opt.)
Ohara *et al.* [39]	$20\text{Mul}(\mathbb{G}_1)+1\text{Exp}(\mathbb{G}_2)+4\mathbb{P}$	$21\text{Mul}(\mathbb{G}_1)+6\mathbb{P}$
Emura *et al.* [20]	$28\text{Mul}(\mathbb{G}_1)+2\text{Exp}(\mathbb{G}_T)+4\mathbb{P}$	$20\text{Mul}(\mathbb{G}_1)+12\text{Exp}(\mathbb{G}_2)+2\text{Mul}(\mathbb{G}_T)+8\mathbb{P}$
Proposed	$17\text{Mul}(\mathbb{G}_1)+4\mathbb{P}$	$18\text{Mul}(\mathbb{G}_1)+4\mathbb{P}$

In Table 2, It can be seen that our proposal takes low computational cost among the existing schemes to perform signature generation and signature verification processes. For Sign algorithm, the proposed scheme can generate a group signature with 13.25 ms whereas the other two schemes [39] and [20] take 14.75 ms and 19 ms respectively. When verifying a signature, our proposal takes 13.6 ms but the schemes [39] and [20] take 18.3 ms and 32.73 ms.

Table 3. Comparisons of the communication overhead.

Schemes	Element Size	Signature Length
Ohara *et al.* [39]	$20\mathbb{G}_1+11\mathbb{Z}_p$	871 bytes
Emura *et al.* [20]	$12\mathbb{G}_1+4\mathbb{Z}_p$	780 bytes
Proposed	$5\mathbb{G}_1+8\mathbb{Z}_p$	629 bytes

The communication overhead is presented in TABLE 3. With our proposal, a group signature has 13 group elements (5 elements in G_1 and 8 elements in Z_p). On the other hand, in the schemes [39] and [20], each signature has 18 group elements (7 elements in G_1 and 11 elements in Z_p) or 16 group elements (12 elements in G_1 and 4 elements in Z_p). When BN&382-bit is employed, the size of a value in Z_p, an element in G_1, an element in G_2 and an element in G_T are 48 bytes, 49 bytes, 97 bytes and 384 bytes, respectively. Therefore, the signature length in our proposal is 629 bytes and it is smaller than the other two schemes.

7 Conclusions

In this paper, we have further improved revocable group signatures with respect to signature generations/verifications and the signature size. In our security model, we present a new security feature, backward security; we believe this feature is necessary for revocable group signature schemes as it ensures unforgeability of group signatures when group members were revoked and rationality for verifications without the RL, especially for LPY-type schemes. For real-life applications, our scheme applies a decentralized group model to relax the original group manager from the heavy workload of revocation list maintenance which makes the deployment of group signatures more practical in providing privacy-preserving authentications.

References

1. Attrapadung, N., Emura, K., Hanaoka, G., Sakai, Y.: A revocable group signature scheme from identity-based revocation techniques: achieving constant-size revocation list. In: Boureanu, I., Owesarski, P., Vaudenay, S. (eds.) ACNS 2014. LNCS, vol. 8479, pp. 419–437. Springer, Cham (2014). https://doi.org/10.1007/978-3-319-07536-5_25

2. Attrapadung, N., Emura, K., Hanaoka, G., Sakai, Y.: Revocable group signature with constant-size revocation list. Comput. J. **58**(10), 2698–2715 (2015)

3. Barreto, P.S.L.M., Naehrig, M.: Pairing-friendly elliptic curves of prime order. In: Preneel, B., Tavares, S. (eds.) SAC 2005. LNCS, vol. 3897, pp. 319–331. Springer, Heidelberg (2006). https://doi.org/10.1007/11693383_22

4. Bellare, M., Micciancio, D., Warinschi, B.: Foundations of group signatures: formal definitions, simplified requirements, and a construction based on general assumptions. In: Biham, E. (ed.) EUROCRYPT 2003. LNCS, vol. 2656, pp. 614–629. Springer, Heidelberg (2003). https://doi.org/10.1007/3-540-39200-9_38

5. Bellare, M., Shi, H., Zhang, C.: Foundations of group signatures: the case of dynamic groups. In: Menezes, A. (ed.) CT-RSA 2005. LNCS, vol. 3376, pp. 136–153. Springer, Heidelberg (2005). https://doi.org/10.1007/978-3-540-30574-3_11

6. Bichsel, P., Camenisch, J., Neven, G., Smart, N.P., Warinschi, B.: Get shorty via group signatures without encryption. In: Garay, J.A., De Prisco, R. (eds.) SCN 2010. LNCS, vol. 6280, pp. 381–398. Springer, Heidelberg (2010). https://doi.org/10.1007/978-3-642-15317-4_24

7. Boneh, D., Boyen, X.: Short signatures without random oracles. In: Cachin, C., Camenisch, J.L. (eds.) EUROCRYPT 2004. LNCS, vol. 3027, pp. 56–73. Springer, Heidelberg (2004). https://doi.org/10.1007/978-3-540-24676-3_4

8. Boneh, D., Boyen, X., Shacham, H.: Short group signatures. In: Franklin, M. (ed.) CRYPTO 2004. LNCS, vol. 3152, pp. 41–55. Springer, Heidelberg (2004). https://doi.org/10.1007/978-3-540-28628-8_3

9. Boneh, D., Shacham, H.: Group signatures with verifier-local revocation. In: ACM-CCS 2004, pp. 168–177. ACM Press (2004)

10. Bootle, J., Cerulli, A., Chaidos, P., Ghadafi, E., Groth, J.: Foundations of fully dynamic group signatures. In: Manulis, M., Sadeghi, A.-R., Schneider, S. (eds.) ACNS 2016. LNCS, vol. 9696, pp. 117–136. Springer, Cham (2016). https://doi.org/10.1007/978-3-319-39555-5_7

11. Brickell, E.: An efficient protocol for anonymously providing assurance of the container of a private key. In: Submitted to the Trusted Computing Group (2003)

12. Brickell, E., Camenisch, J., Chen, L.: Direct anonymous attestation. In: ACM-CCS 2004, pp. 132–145. ACM Press (2004)

13. Bringer, J., Patey, A.: VLR group signatures - how to achieve both backward unlinkability and efficient revocation checks. In: SECRYPT 2012, pp. 215–220 (2012)

14. Camenisch, J., Lysyanskaya, A.: Dynamic accumulators and application to efficient revocation of anonymous credentials. In: Yung, M. (ed.) CRYPTO 2002. LNCS, vol. 2442, pp. 61–76. Springer, Heidelberg (2002). https://doi.org/10.1007/3-540-45708-9_5

15. Chaum, D., van Heyst, E.: Group signatures. In: Davies, D.W. (ed.) EUROCRYPT 1991. LNCS, vol. 547, pp. 257–265. Springer, Heidelberg (1991). https://doi.org/10.1007/3-540-46416-6_22

16. Chu, C., Liu, J.K., Huang, X., Zhou, J.: Verifier-local revocation group signatures with time-bound keys. In: ASIACCS 2012, pp. 26–27. ACM Press (2012)

17. Cramer, R., Shoup, V.: A practical public key cryptosystem provably secure against adaptive chosen ciphertext attack. In: Krawczyk, H. (ed.) CRYPTO 1998. LNCS, vol. 1462, pp. 13–25. Springer, Heidelberg (1998). https://doi.org/10.1007/BFb0055717

18. Naor, D., Naor, M., Lotspiech, J.: Revocation and tracing schemes for stateless receivers. In: Kilian, J. (ed.) CRYPTO 2001. LNCS, vol. 2139, pp. 41–62. Springer, Heidelberg (2001). https://doi.org/10.1007/3-540-44647-8_3

19. Emura, K., Hayashi, T.: Road-to-vehicle communications with time-dependent anonymity: a lightweight construction and its experimental results. IEEE Trans. Veh. Technol. **67**, 1582–1597 (2018)

20. Emura, K., Hayashi, T., Ishida, A.: Group signatures with time-bound keys revisited: a new model, an efficient construction, and its implementation. In: ASIACCS 2012, pp. 777–788. ACM Press (2017)

21. Furukawa, J., Imai, H.: An efficient group signature scheme from bilinear maps. In: Boyd, C., González Nieto, J.M. (eds.) ACISP 2005. LNCS, vol. 3574, pp. 455–467. Springer, Heidelberg (2005). https://doi.org/10.1007/11506157_38

22. Gao, T., Peng, F., Guo, N.: Anonymous authentication scheme based on identity-based proxy group signature for wireless mesh network. EURASIP J. Wirel. Commun. Network. **2016**, 193 (2016)

23. Groth, J.: Fully anonymous group signatures without random oracles. In: Kurosawa, K. (ed.) ASIACRYPT 2007. LNCS, vol. 4833, pp. 164–180. Springer, Heidelberg (2007). https://doi.org/10.1007/978-3-540-76900-2_10

24. Ishida, A., Sakai, Y., Emura, K., Hanaoka, G., Tanaka, K.: Fully anonymous group signature with verifier-local revocation. In: Catalano, D., De Prisco, R. (eds.) SCN 2018. LNCS, vol. 11035, pp. 23–42. Springer, Cham (2018). https://doi.org/10.1007/978-3-319-98113-0_2

25. Emura, K., Hayashi, T.: A revocable group signature scheme with scalability from simple assumptions and its implementation. In: Chen, L., Manulis, M., Schneider, S. (eds.) ISC 2018. LNCS, vol. 11060, pp. 442–460. Springer, Cham (2018). https://doi.org/10.1007/978-3-319-99136-8_24

26. Kilian, J., Petrank, E.: Identity escrow. In: Krawczyk, H. (ed.) CRYPTO 1998. LNCS, vol. 1462, pp. 169–185. Springer, Heidelberg (1998). https://doi.org/10.1007/BFb0055727

27. Kim, T., Barbulescu, R.: Extended tower number field sieve: a new complexity for the medium prime case. In: Robshaw, M., Katz, J. (eds.) CRYPTO 2016. LNCS, vol. 9814, pp. 543–571. Springer, Heidelberg (2016). https://doi.org/10.1007/978-3-662-53018-4_20

28. Kumar, V., Li, H., Park, J., Bian, K., Yang, Y.: Group signatures with probabilistic revocation: a computationally-scalable approach for providing privacy-preserving authentication. In: ACM CCS, pp. 1334–1345 (2015)

29. Libert, B., Ling, S., Nguyen, K., Wang, H.: Zero-knowledge arguments for lattice-based accumulators: logarithmic-size ring signatures and group signatures without trapdoors. In: Fischlin, M., Coron, J.-S. (eds.) EUROCRYPT 2016. LNCS, vol. 9666, pp. 1–31. Springer, Heidelberg (2016). https://doi.org/10.1007/978-3-662-49896-5_1

30. Libert, B., Peters, T., Yung, M.: Group signatures with almost-for-free revocation. In: Safavi-Naini, R., Canetti, R. (eds.) CRYPTO 2012. LNCS, vol. 7417, pp. 571–589. Springer, Heidelberg (2012). https://doi.org/10.1007/978-3-642-32009-5_34

31. Libert, B., Peters, T., Yung, M.: Scalable group signatures with revocation. In: Pointcheval, D., Johansson, T. (eds.) EUROCRYPT 2012. LNCS, vol. 7237, pp. 609–627. Springer, Heidelberg (2012). https://doi.org/10.1007/978-3-642-29011-4_36

32. Libert, B., Vergnaud, D.: Group signatures with verifier-local revocation and backward unlinkability in the standard model. In: Garay, J.A., Miyaji, A., Otsuka, A. (eds.) CANS 2009. LNCS, vol. 5888, pp. 498–517. Springer, Heidelberg (2009). https://doi.org/10.1007/978-3-642-10433-6_34

33. Lynn, B.: The pairing-based cryptography library. http://crypto.stanford.edu/pbc/

34. Nakanishi, T., Fujii, H., Hira, Y., Funabiki, N.: Revocable group signature schemes with constant costs for signing and verifying. In: Jarecki, S., Tsudik, G. (eds.) PKC 2009. LNCS, vol. 5443, pp. 463–480. Springer, Heidelberg (2009). https://doi.org/10.1007/978-3-642-00468-1_26

35. Nakanishi, T., Fujiwara, T., Watanabe, H.: A linkable group signature and its application to secret voting. Trans. Inf. Process. Soc. Jpn. 40(7), 3085–3096 (1999)

36. Nakanishi, T., Funabiki, N.: Verifier-local revocation group signature schemes with backward unlinkability from bilinear maps. In: Roy, B. (ed.) ASIACRYPT 2005. LNCS, vol. 3788, pp. 533–548. Springer, Heidelberg (2005). https://doi.org/10.1007/11593447_29

37. Nakanishi, T., Funabiki, N.: Revocable group signatures with compact revocation list using accumulators. In: Lee, H.-S., Han, D.-G. (eds.) ICISC 2013. LNCS, vol. 8565, pp. 435–451. Springer, Cham (2014). https://doi.org/10.1007/978-3-319-12160-4_26

38. Nguyen, L.: Accumulators from bilinear pairings and applications. In: Menezes, A. (ed.) CT-RSA 2005. LNCS, vol. 3376, pp. 275–292. Springer, Heidelberg (2005). https://doi.org/10.1007/978-3-540-30574-3_19

39. Ohara, K., Emura, K., Hanaoka, G., Ishida, A., Ohta, K., Saka, Y.: Shortening the libert-peters-yung revocable group signature scheme by using the random oracle methodology. In: IACR Cryptology ePrint Archive, vol. 2016, p. 477 (2016)

40. Perera, M.N.S., Koshiba, T.: Almost-fully secured fully dynamic group signatures with efficient verifier-local revocation and time-bound keys. In: Xiang, Y., Sun, J., Fortino, G., Guerrieri, A., Jung, J.J. (eds.) IDCS 2018. LNCS, vol. 11226, pp. 134–147. Springer, Cham (2018). https://doi.org/10.1007/978-3-030-02738-4_12

41. Rahaman, S., Cheng, L., Yao, D., Li, H., Park, J.: Provably secure anonymousyet-accountable crowdsensing with scalable sublinear revocation. In: PoPETs, vol. 2017, pp. 384–403 (2017)

42. Sadiah, S., Nakanishi, T.: Revocable group signatures with compact revocation list using vector commitments. In: Choi, D., Guilley, S. (eds.) WISA 2016. LNCS, vol. 10144, pp. 245–257. Springer, Cham (2017). https://doi.org/10.1007/978-3-319-56549-1_21

43. Sarkar, P., Singh, S.: A general polynomial selection method and new asymptotic complexities for the tower number field sieve algorithm. In: Cheon, J.H., Takagi, T. (eds.) ASIACRYPT 2016. LNCS, vol. 10031, pp. 37–62. Springer, Heidelberg (2016). https://doi.org/10.1007/978-3-662-53887-6_2

44. Yue, X., Chen, B., Wang, X., Duan, Y., Gao, M., He, Y.: An efficient and secure anonymous authentication scheme for vanets based on the framework of group signatures. IEEE Access 6(1), 62584–62600 (2018)

45. Zhou, S., Lin, D.: Shorter verifier-local revocation group signatures from bilinear maps. In: Pointcheval, D., Mu, Y., Chen, K. (eds.) CANS 2006. LNCS, vol. 4301, pp. 126–143. Springer, Heidelberg (2006). https://doi.org/10.1007/11935070_8

An Efficient Privacy-Preserving Palmprint Authentication Scheme Based on ElGamal

Yong Ding[1], Huiyong Wang[2](✉), Zhiqiang Gao[2], Yujue Wang[1], Kefeng Fan[3], and Shijie Tang[4]

[1] Guangxi Key Laboratory of Cryptography and Information Security, School of Computer Science and Information Security, Guilin University of Electronic Technology, Guilin 541004, People's Republic of China
[2] School of Mathematics and Computing Science, Guilin University of Electronic Technology, Guilin 541004, People's Republic of China
why608@163.com
[3] China Electronics Standardization Institute, Beijing 100007, People's Republic of China
[4] School of Electronic Engineering and Automation, Guilin University of Electronic Technology, Guilin 541004, People's Republic of China

Abstract. Biometric credentials have become a popular means of authentication. However, since biometrics are unique and stable, one data breach might cause the user lose some of his biometrics permanently. And the stolen biometrics may be used for identity fraud, posing a permanent risk to the user. There have been many studies addressing this problem, in which the protection of biometric templates is a basic consideration. However, most existing solutions have inefficient security or efficiency. In this paper, we use the ElGamal scheme which shows good performance in applications to construct an efficient, privacy-preserving palmprint authentication scheme. We first construct a palmprint recognition scheme based on palm lines and feature points with good performance. Then, we use the RP (random projection) method to effectively reduce the extracted palmprint features, which greatly reduces the volume of data to be stored. Finally, we design a confidential comparison process based on the ElGamal scheme to perform efficient comparisons of palmprint features while ensuring provable security. Subsequent theoretical analysis/proof and a series of experiments prove the significance and validity of our work.

Keywords: Biometric · Palmprint · ElGamal · Random projection

© ICST Institute for Computer Sciences, Social Informatics and Telecommunications Engineering 2019
Published by Springer Nature Switzerland AG 2019. All Rights Reserved
J. Li et al. (Eds.): SPNCE 2019, LNICST 284, pp. 246–267, 2019.
https://doi.org/10.1007/978-3-030-21373-2_19

1 Introduction

1.1 Biometric Authentication and Some Security Concerns

Traditionally, identification methods can be classified into two categories: token-based (e.g., using a physical key, an ID card, and a passport), and knowledge-based (e.g., using a password). However, these approaches both have some limitations. In token-based approaches, the token can be easily stolen or lost. In knowledge-based approaches, the knowledge can be guessed or forgotten. Compared with traditional approaches, biometrics (fingerprint, palmprint, face, iris, voice, etc.) are more accurate, portable and user friendly. As a result, biometrics have emerged as a powerful means for authentication [1] in recent years.

Biometrics are also known as biometric authentication, referring to the process of extracting the characteristics of an individual's physiological characteristics or personal behavior by using automatic technology, and comparing these characteristics with the existing templates stored in the database, so as to verify an individual's identity [2].

Nevertheless, biometrics has also accumulated many security and privacy concerns, for they are susceptible to many threats. On the one hand, human biometrics are unique and stable, which means that in case of information theft, it is impossible to withdraw the stolen biometrics and re-register them. However, it is very difficult to protect some biometrics from being maliciously collected, such as face, gait, sound, and the picture might be enough for an identity fraud or individual profiling and tracking. On the other hand, if biometrics are transmitted and stored in plain text, it is easy to cause large-scale data leakage when subjected to external and internal attacks. For example, Aadhaar, the world's largest biological (iris) identification database project launched in India in 2009, has produced a large amount of evidence of personal information abuse [3].

Thus, how to build a privacy-preserving biometric authentication system (BAS) which can effectively mitigate the aforementioned privacy and security risks has become an important issue.

A typical biometric authentication system (Fig. 1) is an access control system equipped with biometric acquisition devices. It can be classified into two categories according to the purpose of the tasks [4]: verification and identification. The task of a verification system is to determine whether the individual to be authenticated is a legitimate user. Such systems are often used as an access mechanism for certain systems, such as unlocking mobile phones with fingerprints. They usually require a one-to-one comparison of the user's biometric feature with a particular record (a stored feature template) in the database. The task of identification is to use biometrics to find an individual's identity without knowing any of his personal information. Usually, the user data is compared with a plurality of records in the database, and the workload is larger than verification. Most identification systems are used in passive ways, such as screening a mass of people to locate certain suspects in public environments. The above two tasks both include two stages: registration and authentication. During the registration phase, the user (active or passive) enters a certain biometric feature along with his identity using an acquisition sensor, then the biometric feature is transformed (or encrypted) into a template and stored to the database. In the authentication phase, a verification system calls the acquisition device to re-acquire a fresh biometric feature of the client, then finds the record by the proposed identity in the database (if it exists), and compare the fresh template and the stored template to decide whether they belong to a same person. In contrast, an identification system compares the fresh template and nonspecific multiple templates to check if a template belonging to the client is stored in the database, so as to find his identity.

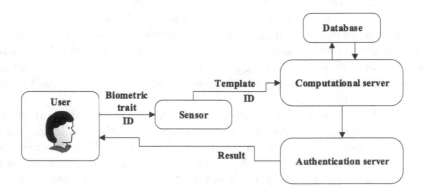

Fig. 1. The authentication phase in a BAS with a distributed architecture.

Generally, it is believed that unauthorized access to biometric templates is the greatest threat to biometrics security [5]. As a result, many template protection schemes were proposed, which can be classified into two categories [7]: transformation based schemes and crypto-based schemes. Transformation based methods use invertible or non-invertible functions to transform biometrics into unreadable templates, so that no information about the original biometric feature should be leaked in case of a theft. Meanwhile, crypto-based schemes turn to cryptography techniques to protect biometrics from leaking.

In the family of biometrics, palmprint is a promising member, for human palms have Larger region and provide more information than other biometrics, such as fingers, iris and retina. As a result, palm features can be extracted even from a low resolution image, and easier to achieve a high accuracy in authentication [6].

1.2   Related Work

A biometric template method should have the following properties [8]:

Diversity: The templates for the same biometric trait stored in multiple databases should be diverse enough, so that none data can be comprised under cross matching attacks.

Revocability: A stolen biometric should be revoked and replaced.

Security: A leaked template should not reveal inform about the original biometrics.

Performance. The performance of an authentication system should be degraded heavily due to any template protection methods.

It is not easy to build a template protection scheme which satisfies the above conditions, and the standard encryption schemes like RSA, AES, etc. cannot be used to encrypt the templates [7].

The following schemes are representative of transformation-based template protection schemes

Biohashing or biometric salting was proposed by Teoh et al. [9] and Ngo et al. [10] as an invertible transformation technique, and were applied to several biometrics like fingerprints [11,12], iris [13,14], and palmprints [15].

In 2005, Sutcu et al. [16] proposed a non-invertible method based on cryptographic hash functions. In 2006 and 2007, Ratha et al. [17,18] used three non-invertible transformations to generate secure fingerprint templates. And in 2008, Zuo et al. [19] proposed several ways to construct cancellable iris biometrics.

In crypto-based template protection methods, the following schemes are representative.

In 1999, Juels and Wattenberg [20] introduced the concept of fuzzy commitment. In 2007, Teoh and Kim [21] proposed a finger template protection based on fuzzy commitment. And in 2006, Hao et al. [22] proposed the first fuzzy commitment scheme for iris. In 2006, Van Der Veen et al. [23] applied the fuzzy commitment technique to face authentication.

In 2002, Juels and Sudan [24] introduced the concept of fuzzy vault, and in 2003, Clancy et al. [25] proposed and implemented the first fingerprint vault. In 2004, Uludag and jain [26] proposed the first finger-print based fuzzy vault. Lee et al. [27] and Wu et al. [28] proposed two fuzzy vault method for iris in 2007 and 2008.

In recent years, homomorphic encryption (HE) has shown great potential in constructing privacy-preserving biometric authentication systems. Homomorphic encryption (HE) allows us to compute arbitrary functions confidentially, which is in line with the need of privacy protection in cloud computing.

In 2014, Luo [29] uses the RSA algorithm to construct a blind authentication scheme, and built a palmprint authentication system on that basis. The system uses a three-layer architecture, which includes a client, a remote server and a trustworthy third party, which turned to be the critical defect of the architecture.

In 2015, Qu [30] summarized the application of homomorphic encryption in biometric authentication, and designed a palmprint authentication scheme based on HE. This scheme includes four stages: registration, authentication, update and cancellation. Yet this paper didn't give any specific experimental data, and no dimension reduction technique is used, leading to comparatively low efficiency.

In 2016 Erkin [31] used the mobile phone to acquire the palmprint images and build an authentication system. The resulting error recognition rate is 15.2%.

In 2017, Wang [32] proposed an effective privacy-preserving palmprint authentication scheme, which reduced the palmprint feature vector size from $128 * 128$ to $100 * 1$, and reached a correct recognition rate of 95%. But their scheme is susceptible to selective ciphertext attacks.

1.3 Our Contribution

Our contribution mainly includes the following aspects:

(1) We propose a palmprint verification scheme based on the extraction of palm ridge lines and achieves good performance.
(2) We use the RP method [34] to reduce the dimension of the feature vectors, and find the optimal balance between dimension reduction and performance.
(3) We propose a projection that maps binary vectors to prime vectors, which strengths the robustness of the encryption algorithm against chosen ciphertext attacks.

2   Image Processing and Feature Acquisition

2.1   Extracting ROI from Palmprint

The procedure consists of seven steps: (1) Select the palmprint image. (2) Smooth the original image.(3) Use a threshold to convert the smoothed image to a binary image. (4) Trace the boundary of the binary image. (5) Find the key points. (6) Build a palmprint coordinate system. (7) Crop a subimage with fixed size from the center of the image as ROI. The flow chart of the algorithm is shown in Fig. 2.

The details of each step are described in the following:

(1) Select the palmprint image I. The palmprint image can be captured by a CCD camera, a mobile phone or a Webcam. The most ideal palmprint image we select looks like Fig. 2(a), which satisfies that $\angle 1 < \angle 2$, $\angle 1 < \angle 4$, $\angle 3 < \angle 2$, $\angle 3 < \angle 4$. Namely, the angle between the index finger and the middle finger, the angle between the ring finger and the little finger are both smaller. Other angles between fingers are greater. This is because we will detect the valley points between the index–middle fingers and the ring–little fingers as key-points. We will explain the specific reasons at step (5). In this paper we take the palmprint image from PolyU databases (provided by Hong Kong Polytech University).
(2) Smooth the original image. We use a Low-pass filter to smooth the original image. The purpose is to make the image more smooth and convenient for binarization.

$$I_{SmoothMap} = I * A$$

(where A is the low-pass filter).

(3) Binarize the image. Use a threshold α to convert the original gray image into a binary map.

$$I_{binarymap} = \begin{cases} 1, I_{SmoothMap} > \alpha \\ 0, I_{SmoothMap} \leq \alpha \end{cases}.$$

(4) Trace the boundary of the palmprint. Use the boundary tracking operator to obtain the boundary of palmprint

$$I_{bounbary} = I_{binarymap} * B$$

where B is the boundary tracking operator.

(5) Detect the key points of the palmprint.

The area-method. We find that the image has the following characteristics: As shown in the Fig. 2(b), let the area of the circle be S, and when the center of the circle is at the A, B, F, the area of the intersection of the circle and the palm is approximately $1/2S$. When the center is at C, D, E, the intersection of the circle and the palm is approximately $3/4S$. If the input of the palmprint is an ideal image, and the appropriate radius is chosen so that the center of the circle moves along the edge of the palm to compute the area where the circle intersects with the palm. When the area reaches its maximum, the center of the circle is the first key point and then the neighborhood of the key point is removed and the second key point will be detected using the same way.

The arc-method. As shown in the Fig. 2(b), let the circumference of the circle be L, and when the center of the circle is at the A, B, F, the arc of the intersection of the circle and the palm is approximately $1/2L$. When the center is at C, D, E, the intersection of the circle and the palm is approximately $3/4L$. If the palmprint is ideal, when the appropriate radius is chosen so that the center of the circle moves along the edge of the palm to compute the area where the circle intersects with the palm, and the area reaches maximum, the center of the circle is the first key point and then the neighborhood of the key point is removed and the second key point will be detected using the same way.

(6) Create the Cartesian coordinate system. By the above steps, the key points C and E(the valley point between the index finger and the middle finger and the valley point between the ring finger and little finger) have been found. Then connect CE, and make a line parallel to line CE on the right side which intersect with each other at two points C_1E_1 with the boundary of palms, the midpoint of E_1C_1 is the origin of the coordinates, the direction of E_1C_1 is the y-axis, and the direction perpendicular to E_1C_1 is the x-axis (Fig. 2(c)). Those operations are based on the following reasons: Due to individual differences, sometimes CE might be too long or too short and may lead to an inappropriate ROI and E_1C_1. The length of E_1C_1 is approximate to the length of the palm. The shape of the same palm is not always same at different time, the distance of the two key points is not equal at

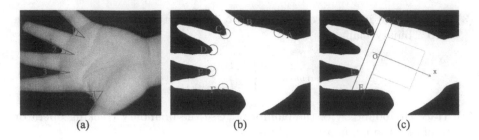

(a)   (b)   (c)

Fig. 2. Our ideal palmprint image.

different time. We select the width of palmprint as reference, since the width of the palm will not change.

(7) Extract ROI. With reference to the length of E_1C_1, a square area $\left([0,+\frac{d}{2}] \times [-\frac{d}{4},+\frac{d}{4}]\right)$ whose length is equal to half of E_1C_1 is extracted as the ROI (Fig. 2(c)).

2.2   Extracting Features from ROI

The features of the palmprint are based on image features, digital features, texture features and main features. We use the image features and the texture features as the palmprint features.

(1) Extract the image feature of the palmprint. Firstly, we calculate the average gray value of the image and choose a threshold, then binarize the image. if the value of the image is greater than the threshold, set it to 1, otherwise set it to 0.

(2) Extract image texture feature. First, we calculate the sum of the horizontal and vertical gradients of each point, and obtain an image of a gradient value. Then we calculate the average gray value of the image and take it as a threshold. Finally we binarize the image. If the value of the image is greater than the threshold, let it be 1, otherwise 0.

(3) Extract the image feature based on LBP. The Local Binary Patterns method (LBP) is proposed by Ojala [33] and used for the description of texture features. The original operator of LBP is defined as follows: firstly, a window unit is set for each pixel in the image, and then the pixel is taken as the threshold of the pixel, and the remaining 8 pixels in the window are binarized. Then the weighted sum is used to get the LBP value of the point. The calculation of the LBP value for each pixel is shown as: $LBP = \sum_{i=0}^{7} B(g_i - g_c)2^i$, where g_c is the gray value of the center pixel and g_i is the gray value of a neighboring pixel, the two valued function is defined as follows:

$$B(x) = \begin{cases} 1, x > 0 \\ 0, x \le 0 \end{cases}.$$

2.3   Dimension Reduction

We use the random projection (Rp) [34] method to reduce the dimension of the feature vector. Firstly we construct a matrix of $U = ml^2$, where m is the dimension to be descended, and l^2 is the dimension of the characteristic matrix. The concrete steps are as follows:

(1) Generate a random projection matrix: A random projection matrix U of ml^2 dimension is generated as follows:

$$U_{i,j} = \begin{cases} 1, p = 1/6 \\ 0, p = 1/6. \\ -1, p = 1/6 \end{cases}$$

(2) Reduction. The original feature matrix A is reduced by multiplying U to get the m dimension vector α.

$$\alpha = UA$$

(3) Binaryzation. The vector α is binarized and resulting vector β is obtained.

$$\beta_{(i,1)} = \begin{cases} 1, \alpha_{(i,1)} > 0 \\ 0, \alpha_{(i,1)} \leq 0 \end{cases}.$$

(4) The vector β is the target feature vector.

3   Confidential Comparison

3.1   The ElGamal Encryption Scheme

The security of the ElGamal encryption scheme [35] is based on hardness of solving the discrete logarithm problem on a cyclic group. It goes as follows.

Select a large prime number p, where $g(g < p)$ is the generator of cyclic group Z_p^*. Select a random number $x \in Z_p^*$, and calculate $y = g^x \bmod p$. Take array (y, g, p) as a public key and x as a private key.

Encryption: select a random number r, where r and $p - 1$ are mutual prime, then compute ciphertext as:

$$E(m) = (a, b) = (g^r \bmod p, my^r \bmod p)$$

Decryption: compute:

$$m = b(a^x)^{-1} \bmod p = my^r((g^r)^x)^{-1} \bmod p = m(g^x)^r(g^{rx})^{-1} \bmod p$$

Since a random number is introduced to the encryption process, the encryption result of ElGamal is randomised, which enables the algorithm to resist selective ciphertext attacks (CPA). Besides, ElGamal is multiplicatively homomorphic.

3.2　Hamming Distance

Hamming distance [36] are often used to evaluate the similarity between two n-bit binary strings. Set $X, Y \in \{0, 1\}^n$, the Hamming distance $H(X, Y)$ between X, Y is defined as:

$$H(X, Y) = \sum_{i=1}^{n} (x_i \oplus y_i)$$

In order to use Hamming distance to calculate the similarity between two eigenvectors, Wong et al. [37] proposed the definition of fraction Hamming distance, which was defined as:

$$H_F(X, Y) = \frac{1}{n} \sum_{i=1}^{n} (x_i \oplus y_i)$$

3.3　Our Scheme

We now describe the process of the matching phase. Note that the registration phase includes the former two steps of the matching phase.

The first step is to project the binary feature vectors to prime vectors. We assume the original binary feature vector is $x = (x_1, x_2, \ldots, x_n)$. Since the ElGamal encryption scheme can not encrypt 0 and 1, we propose the following projection to transform the binary feature vector into a prime vector:

$$x_i{}' = \begin{cases} a_i, x_i = 0 \\ pb_i, x_i = 1 \end{cases}.$$

where $x' = (x'_1, x'_2, \ldots, x'_n)$ and p is a prime number, a_i and b_i are non-zero random integers but not any multiple of p.

Obviously, this projection enables the proposed scheme to resist CPA attacks, for the mapping result varies in each trial.

The second step is to encrypt the prime vector by the ElGamal scheme. We calculate:

$$E(x') = (E(x'_1), E(x'_2), \ldots, E(x'_n))$$

and

$$E(y') = (E(y'_1), E(y'_2), \ldots, E(y'_n))$$

where $y = (y_1, y_2, \ldots, y_n)$ is a newly extracted feature vector for authentication. In registration, $E(x')$ will be stored to the database as the template.

The third step is the confidential comparison: For a newly extracted feature (fresh) vector $y = (y_1, y_2, \ldots, y_n)$ and its projection $y' = (y'_1, y'_2, \ldots, y'_n)$, calculate the bitwise product of the two vectors:

$$c = (c_1, c_2, \ldots, c_n) = (E(x'_1)E(y'_1), \; E(x'_2)E(y'_2), \; \ldots, \; E(x'_n)E(y'_n))$$

The fourth step is to calculate the Hamming distance: Decrypt ciphertext $c = (c_1, c_2, \ldots, c_n)$ with the private key sk and get $c' = (c'_1, c'_2, \ldots, c'_n)$.

$$d_i = \begin{cases} 1, c'_i \bmod p \equiv 0 \\ 0, c'_i \bmod p \not\equiv 0 \end{cases}.$$

$$d_i' = \begin{cases} 1, c_i' \ mod \ p^2 \equiv 0 \\ 0, c_i' \ mod \ p^2 \not\equiv 0 \end{cases}.$$

Then the fractional Hamming distance of x and y is

$$H_F(X,Y) = \frac{1}{n} \sum_{i=1}^{n} (d_i \oplus d_i')$$

The fourth step is to compare the fractional hamming distance with the preset threshold τ. If $H_F > \tau$, x and y are from a same individual; Otherwise, authentication fails.

4   Experiments

The proposed scheme is implemented with MATLAB 2013b on a desktop PC powered by a Intel(R) Xeon(R) CPU E5-2670 (2.60 GHz), and 8 GB random access memory.

4.1   Extrating ROI

We use the PolyU Palmprint Database provided by Hong Kong Polytech University, which contains 600 palmprint images of 100 person (each person has 6 palmprint images). The resolution of each image is 75dpi, and the size of each image is 384×284 pixcels. Their palmprint capture device includes ring source, CCD camera, lens, frame grabber, and A/D (analogue-to-digital) converter [1]. The images were collected by special equipments: the thumbs have been removed, the brightness is uniform and the valley points them are very obvious.

The specific steps are as follows:

(1) Read the original image $orignal\_I$ (Fig. 3(a)).
(2) Smooth the image with the sequential statistics filter (Fig. 3(b)).

$$ord\_I = ordfilt2(orignal\_I, 300, ones(20, 40)).$$

(3) Set the threshold and binarize the smoothed images (Fig. 3(c)).

$$I_{binarymap} = \begin{cases} 1, I_{ord} > 8 \\ 0, I_{ord} \leq 8 \end{cases}.$$

(4) Extract the edge of the image. We use four edge detection operators ($[011], [110], [011]', [110]'$) to detect the boundary of $I_{binarymap}$, and get I_{edge} (Fig. 3(d)).
(5) Detect the key points. A circle C with a radius r along the edge image I_{edge} scans the binary image $I_{binarymap}$, when the area which the circle C intersect with the binary image $I_{binarymap}$ is maximal, the center of the circle is the first key K_1 (Fig. 3(e)), remove this point and its neighborhood (Fig. 3(f)), the second key point K_2 is got with the same method (Fig. 3(g)).

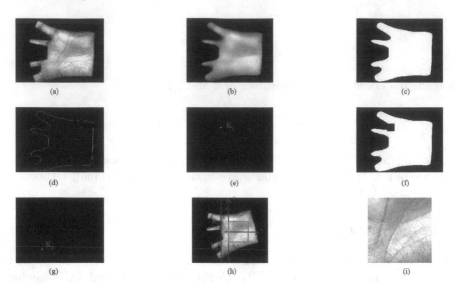

Fig. 3. The program runs on the polyU database.

(6) Build the coordinate system and extract ROI from palmprint. Connect K_1K_2, calculate the length of K_1K_2 l and the slope of K_1K_2 k; Rotate the original image $orignal\_I$ $tan^{-1}k$ to get $orignal\_I'$ (Fig. 3(h)), correspondingly. Rotate K_1K_2 to $K_1'K_2'$, moves the line $K_1'K_2'$ by $1/4l$ unit to the right, which will intersect with the edge of the image at A and B. Then set the length of the line segment AB to d, then the midpoint of AB is the coordinate origin, the direction of BA is the y-axis, and the x-axis is perpendicular to the BA direction. Then we extract $[0, +\frac{d}{2}] \times [-\frac{d}{4}, +\frac{d}{4}]$ in the rotated image as the ROI (Fig. 3(i)).

The result of this experiment is shown in Tables 1 and 2. Table 3 gives the comparison results of our algorithm with several previous algorithms. Figure 4 shows the relationship between the correct extraction number and the radius. Figure 5 shows the relationship between the total extraction time and the radius.

Analysis of the results: we find that with the increase of the radius, the correct rate is also increased, and correspondingly the extraction time also becomes longer. When the radius is equal, the arc method has a shorter time and a higher recognition rate compared with the area method.

4.2   Plain-Text Matching

In this section, we use three different methods to extract palmprint features, and compare their performance. Since each person has 6 images, we use 2 images as template images, and the other 4 are used as fresh images.

Table 1. Experimental results of different radius (area-method)

Radii	Test images	Correct	Recognition rate (%)	Total time (s)	Averaging time (ms)
13	600	580	99.67	203.918	339
14	600	582	97.00	230.266	383
15	600	587	97.83	252.548	420
16	600	590	98.33	268.046	446
17	600	593	98.33	288.956	481
18	600	594	99.00	317.131	528
19	600	595	99.17	344.761	574
20	600	597	99.50	371.090	618
21	600	598	99.67	396.137	660
22	600	598	99.67	396.137	702
23	600	599	99.83	421.718	762
24	600	600	100	457.404	804
25	600	600	100	482.819	849
26	600	600	100	537.327	895
27	600	600	100	562.910	938

Table 2. Experimental results of different radius (arc-method)

Radii	Test images	Correct	Recognition rate (%)	Total time (s)	Averaging time (ms)
13	600	591	98.50	202.058	336
14	600	596	99.33	220.301	337
15	600	596	99.33	239.395	398
16	600	598	99.67	259.870	433
17	600	598	99.67	275.202	458
18	600	599	99.83	299.360	498
19	600	599	99.83	325.165	541
20	600	600	100	345.969	576
21	600	600	100	372.364	620
22	600	600	100	402.543	670
23	600	600	100	426.053	710
24	600	600	100	455.431	759
25	600	600	100	476.773	794
26	600	600	100	519.209	865
27	600	600	100	548.246	913

Table 3. Comparison results of different algorithms

Algorithms	Published year	Correction rate of location (%)
Proposed by [38]	2004	97.8
Proposed by [39]	2012	98.83
Proposed by this paper	2017	100

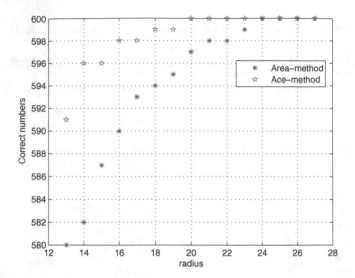

Fig. 4. The relationship between the correct extraction number and the radius.

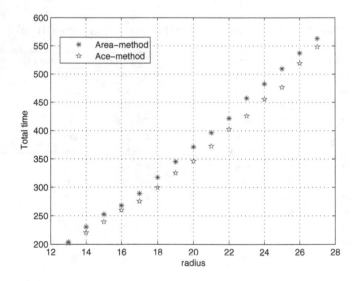

Fig. 5. The relationship between the total extraction time and the radius.

The Image Feature Method. In this method, the palmprint ROI comes directly from the binarization of the image, and the binarized image matrix is used as the feature matrix.

The Texture Feature Method. The procedure is divided into two steps. The first step is to obtain the gradient image of the ROI, and the second step is:

use the average gray value method to binarize the gradient image, and take the obtained binarized matrix as the feature matrix.

The LBP Method. First, we use the LBP method to get the LBP encoding of palmprint, then we use Gauss filter to smooth it. Finally, we use the average gray value method to binarize the image.

Analysis of the Experimental Results. The experimental results show that the LBP method is obviously better than the other two methods. When the recognition rate is 99%, the error recognition rate of the image method, the texture method and the LBP method are 4%, 5% and 0.1% respectively; When the recognition rate is 95%, the error recognition rate of the image method, the texture method and the LBP method are 0.5%, 0.1% and 0.003% respectively; When the recognition rate is 90%, the error recognition rate of the image method, the texture method and the LBP method is 0.2%, 0.03% and 0% respectively. It is obvious that the feature area extracted by the LBP method is very large. The hamming distances between different people are basically within $[0.39, 0.41]$, and

Table 4. Experimental results based on image feature method

Threshold	Correct recognition rate (%)	Error recognition rate (%)
0.34	100	34.492
0.33	100	27.03
0.32	100	20.773
0.31	99.75	15.558
0.3	99.5	11.154
0.29	99.5	7.828
0.28	99	5.455
0.27	99	3.664
0.26	98.75	2.439
0.25	98.75	1.654
0.24	98.25	1.121
0.23	97.5	0.717
0.22	94.5	0.437
0.21	93	0.263
0.2	88.25	0.124
0.19	83.25	0.063
0.18	79	0.033
0.17	76.5	0.015
0.16	68.75	0.003

Table 5. Experimental results based on texture feature method

Threshold	Correct recognition rate (%)	Error recognition rate (%)
0.4	100	76.144
0.395	100	53.141
0.39	99.75	33.003
0.385	99.75	18.467
0.38	99	9.816
0.375	99	4.866
0.37	98.75	2.371
0.365	98	1.187
0.36	97.5	0.629
0.355	96.75	0.311
0.35	95.75	0.177
0.345	94.75	0.098
0.34	94	0.048
0.335	92.5	0.038
0.33	90.75	0.03
0.325	89.5	0.023
0.32	88	0.013
0.315	85.5	0.005
0.31	82.75	0.005
0.305	79.5	0.005
0.3	75	0.003

the distances for the same person is around 0.36. This implies that the optimal threshold value can be set to 0.375 (Table 4).

Comparisons. The equal error rate is the recognition rate when the false acceptance rate is equal to the true rejection rate. The equal error rate is an important index to measure the quality of a biometric system. When the equal error rate becomes lower, the system becomes better.

4.3   Dimension Reduction

The feature matrix we derived is in size of 128×128. In order to reduce the storage cost and improve the efficiency of the subsequent encryption steps, we use the RP method to reduce the dimension of the original feature matrix. We also carry out matching experiments on the results after dimension reduction.

Table 6. Experimental results based on texture feature method

Threshold	Correct recognition rate (%)	Error recognition rate (%)
0.4	100	96.202
0.395	100	66.677
0.39	100	29.172
0.385	100	10.975
0.38	99.75	4.01
0.375	99.25	1.374
0.37	99.25	0.465
0.365	99.25	0.174
0.36	98.75	0.063
0.355	98.5	0.038
0.35	98.25	0.028
0.345	97.75	0.023
0.34	97.25	0.02
0.335	96.25	0.018
0.33	96	0.01
0.325	96	0.005
0.32	95.25	0.003
0.315	93.75	0

Table 7. Comparison of equal error rates of different palmprint recognition systems

Palmprint system	Proposed year	Error recognition rate
Proposed by [6]	2014	2.36%
Proposed by [32]	2017	1.22%
Proposed by this paper	2018	0.12%

Dimension Reduction with Features from the Image Method. In order to verify the feasibility of the dimension reduction, it is necessary to compare the matching results. We first match the extracted features based on image method. We test the performance of matching with features reducted to 100 bits, 200 bits, 300 bits, 400 bits, and 1000 bits respectively. The results are as follows (Table 5).

Analysis of the Result. Since the dimension reduction process may cause information loss, the matching results are not as good as from the original data. And since the reduction process carries out two calculations, it causes greater loss of information. For two 1000-bit vectors, when the recognition rate is 97%,

Table 8. Matching experimental results to 100 dimension

Threshold	Correct recognition rate (%)	Error recognition rate (%)
0.27	100	84.497
0.26	99.75	77.197
0.25	99.25	68.091
0.24	99.25	68.091
0.23	98.75	46.326
0.22	98.75	46.326
0.21	97	35.417
0.2	88.75	16.97
0.19	88.75	16.97
0.18	83.75	10.487
0.17	64.5	3.376
0.16	64.5	3.376
0.15	52.75	1.662
0.14	28.75	0.311
0.13	19	0.101
0.12	9.5	0.033
0.11	9.5	0.033

Table 9. Matching experimental results to 300 dimension

Threshold	Correct recognition rate (%)	Error recognition rate (%)
0.29	100	87.301
0.28	99.75	74.174
0.27	99.5	60.598
0.26	99.25	45.386
0.25	98.25	30.914
0.24	97	22.556
0.23	94	10.601
0.22	92.5	6.636
0.21	83.75	3.023
0.2	67	0.924
0.19	57.75	0.482
0.18	44.75	0.167
0.17	29.25	0.028
0.16	21.25	0
0.15	13	0

Table 10. Matching experimental results to 1000 dimension

Threshold	Correct recognition rate (%)	Error recognition rate (%)
0.27	100	46.737
0.26	99.75	30.316
0.25	99	17.394
0.24	99	9.417
0.23	97.5	3.838
0.22	95.25	1.715
0.21	88.5	0.616
0.2	79.25	0.177
0.19	66.75	0.081
0.18	51.5	0.015
0.17	35	0.003
0.16	22.75	0

the error recognition rate is 3%, which shows that the dimension reduction is also practical.

Comparison of Experimental Results. Jong-Hyuk et al. [40] also applied the RP method to palmprint recognition, but the result is not particularly satisfactory. The following results show the comparison of equal error rates with Jong-Hyuk's work.

Table 11. Comparison of equal error rates with Jong-Hyuk dimension reduction

Dimensionality reduction method	Proposed year	Equal error rate (%)
Proposed by [40]	2016	15
Reduced to 100 dimensions by this paper	2018	13
Reduced to 200 dimensions by this paper	2018	8
Reduced to 300 dimensions by this paper	2018	7
Reduced to 400 dimensions by this paper	2018	6
Reduced to 1000 dimensions by this paper	2018	3

4.4   Confidential Matchings

We take 13 as the sk and $(78443, 97, 99991)$ as the pk. Map 1 to a multiplier of 17 and map 0 to a random number less then 17. Assume m_1 and m_2 are two binary vectors, x_1 and x_2 are two prime vectors derived with our method.

Table 12. Security comparison experiment

m_1	m_2	x_1	x_2	c_1	c_2	c	d	d_1	d_2	D	M
1	0	85	16	(20808, 46841)	(59922, 6092)	(69197, 81049)	1360	1	0	1	1
1	1	119	34	(139, 27588)	(21674, 48111)	(12956, 5734)	4046	1	1	0	0
0	0	14	9	(55692, 25926)	(2833, 67173)	(89629, 83942)	126	0	0	0	0
1	1	170	153	(82541, 95541)	(78443, 30557)	(46440, 9110)	26010	1	1	0	0
1	1	272	34	(86608, 84838)	(353, 70687)	(75369, 83472)	9248	1	1	0	0
1	0	68	15	(23963, 9973)	(2833, 11964)	(93281, 27709)	1020	1	0	1	1
1	0	238	15	(49067, 16968)	(88153, 44192)	(92564, 17347)	3570	1	0	1	1
0	0	11	8	(17256, 79985)	(89373, 76198)	(59295, 45598)	88	0	0	0	0
1	0	68	13	(51504, 23205)	(59295, 49914)	(4558, 58617)	884	1	0	1	1
0	0	8	3	(18556, 6285)	(52128, 28379)	(74225, 78062)	24	0	0	0	0
1	0	119	10	(96329, 83887)	(49067, 65413)	(473, 94224)	1190	1	0	1	1
1	1	170	85	(88153, 34218)	(92863, 14330)	(88851, 88067)	14450	1	1	0	0
1	1	221	136	(12956, 64173)	(22666, 25232)	(87120, 58873)	30056	1	1	0	0
0	1	2	238	(18556, 26569)	(33016, 1495)	(39, 24228)	476	1	0	1	1
1	0	238	4	(88153, 27907)	(8183, 60947)	(20925, 1019)	952	1	0	1	1
0	1	14	85	(86368, 61809)	(78443, 5866)	(74819, 4228)	1190	1	0	1	1
0	0	6	8	(13186, 43787)	(90928, 64994)	(84518, 48427)	48	0	0	0	0
1	1	119	102	(2840, 91412)	(42743, 53932)	(1046, 75720)	12138	1	1	0	0
1	1	170	221	(13483, 14669)	(78234, 43950)	(23963, 60573)	37570	1	1	0	0
0	0	12	16	(59695, 8260)	(26609, 3568)	(67220, 74326)	192	0	0	0	0
1	1	204	51	(98163, 66133)	(34241, 49136)	(1818, 3570)	10404	1	1	0	0
1	1	221	68	(51606, 5421)	(23963, 9973)	(45881, 68493)	15028	1	1	0	0

Take c_1 and c_2 as the result of encryption for x_1 and x_2, and c as the result of $c_1 \times c_2$, d as the result of decryption of c. d_1, d_2, D, M is given by the following formula (Tables 6, 7, 8, 9, 10, 11 and 12).

If $d \bmod 17 \equiv 0$, then $d_1 = 1$, otherwise $d_1 = 0$; if $d \bmod 289 \equiv 0$, then $d_2 = 1$, otherwise $d_2 = 0$; $D = d_1 \oplus d_2$, $M = m_1 \oplus m_2$.

5   Conclusion

We have proposed an privacy-preserving palmprint authentication scheme. First we employ three algorithms to extract feature vectors from plamprint images and compared their performance. Then we use the RP method to reduce the dimension of the feature vector. Finally, we use ElGamal to implement confidential comparisons. Experiments show that the scheme can meet practical requirements in small or media application scenarios.

Acknowledgements. This work was partially supported by the National Natural Science Foundation of China (Grant Nos. 61772150, 61862012), the National Cryptography Development Fund of China under project MMJJ20170217, the Guangxi

Key R&D Fund under project AB17195025, the Guangxi Natural Science Foundation under grant 2018GXNSFAA281232, and the open project of Guangxi Key Laboratory of Cryptography and Information Security (Grant Nos. GCIS201622, GCIS201702).

References

1. Zhang, D., Kong, W.K., You, J., et al.: Online palmprint identification. IEEE Trans. Pattern Anal. Mach. Intell. **25**(9), 1041–1050 (2003)
2. Jain, A.K., Flynn, P., Ross, A.A.: Handbook of Biometrics. Springer, New York (2008). https://doi.org/10.1007/978-0-387-71041-9
3. Aadhaar: India top court upholds world's largest biometric scheme. BBC News, 26 September 2018. https://www.bbc.com/news/world-asia-india-44777787
4. Pagnin, E., Mitrokotsa, A.: Privacy-preserving biometric authentication: challenges and directions. Secur. Commun. Netw. **2017**, 1–9 (2017)
5. Tuyls, P., Škoric, B., Kevenaar, T. (eds.): Security with Noisy Data: On Private Biometrics, Secure Key Storage and Anti-counterfeiting. Springer, London (2007). https://doi.org/10.1007/978-1-84628-984-2
6. Han, Y., Sun, Z., Wang, F., Tan, T.: Palmprint recognition under unconstrained scenes. In: Yagi, Y., Kang, S.B., Kweon, I.S., Zha, H. (eds.) ACCV 2007. LNCS, vol. 4844, pp. 1–11. Springer, Heidelberg (2007). https://doi.org/10.1007/978-3-540-76390-1_1
7. Riaz, N., Riaz, A., Khan, S.A.: Biometric template security: an overview. Sens. Rev. **38**(1), 120–127 (2018)
8. Jain, A.K., Nandakumar, K., Nagar, A.: Biometric template security. EURASIP J. Adv. Signal Process. **2008**, 113 (2008)
9. Teoh, A.B.J., David, C.L.N., Goh, A.: Personalised cryptographic key generation based on FaceHashing. Comput. Secur. **23**(7), 606–614 (2004)
10. Ngo, D.C.L., Andrew, B.J.T., Goh, A.: Biometric hash: high-confidence face recognition. IEEE Trans. Circuits Syst. Video Technol. **16**(6), 771–775 (2006)
11. Ong, T.S., Jin, A.T.B., Ngo, D.C.L.: Application-specific key release scheme from biometrics. IJ Netw. Secur. **6**(2), 127–133 (2008)
12. Jin, A.T., Beng, D.N., Ling, C., Goh, A.: Biohashing: two factor authentication featuring fingerprint data and tokenised random number. Pattern Recognit. **37**(11), 2245–2255 (2004)
13. Chin, C.S., Jin, A.T.B., Ling, D.N.C.: High security iris verification system based on random secret integration. Comput. Vis. Image Underst. **102**(2), 169–177 (2006)
14. Chong, S.C., Teoh, A.B.J., Ngo, D.C.L.: Iris authentication using privatized advanced correlation filter. In: Zhang, D., Jain, A.K. (eds.) ICB 2006. LNCS, vol. 3832, pp. 382–388. Springer, Heidelberg (2005). https://doi.org/10.1007/11608288_51
15. Connie, T., et al.: PalmHashing: a novel approach for cancelable biometrics. Inf. Process. Lett. **93**(1), 1–5 (2005)
16. Sutcu, Y., Sencar, H.T., Memon, N.: A secure biometric authentication scheme based on robust hashing. In: Proceedings of the 7th Workshop on Multimedia and Security, pp. 111–116. ACM (2005)
17. Ratha, N., et al.: Cancelable biometrics: a case study in fingerprints. In: 18th International Conference on Pattern Recognition. ICPR, vol. 4, pp. 370–373. IEEE (2006)
18. Ratha, N.K., et al.: Generating cancelable fingerprint templates. IEEE Trans. Pattern Anal. Mach. Intell. **29**(4), 561–572 (2007)

19. Zuo, J., Ratha, N.K., Connell, J.H.: Cancelable iris biometric. In: International Conference on Pattern Recognition, pp. 1–4. IEEE (2008)
20. Juels, A., Wattenberg, M.: A fuzzy commitment scheme. In: ACM Conference on Computer and Communications Security, pp. 28–36. ACM (1999)
21. Teoh, A.B.J., Kim, J.: Secure biometric template protection in fuzzy commitment scheme. IEICE Electron. Express **4**(23), 724–730 (2007)
22. Hao, F., Anderson, R., Daugman, J.: Combining crypto with biometrics effectively. IEEE Trans. Comput. **55**(9), 1081–1088 (2006)
23. Van Der Veen, M., et al.: Face biometrics with renewable templates. In: Security, Steganography, and Watermarking of Multimedia Contents VIII, Vol. 6072, p. 60720J. International Society for Optics and Photonics (2006)
24. Juels, A., Sudan, M.: A fuzzy vault scheme. Des. Codes Cryptogr. **38**(2), 237–257 (2006)
25. Clancy, T.C., Kiyavash, N., Lin, D.J.: Secure smart card based fingerprint authentication. In: Proceedings of the 2003 ACM SIGMM Workshop on Biometrics Methods and Applications, pp. 45–52. ACM (2003)
26. Uludag, U., Jain, A.K.: Fuzzy fingerprint vault. In: Proceedings of the Workshop: Biometrics: Challenges Arising from Theory to Practice, pp. 13–16 (2004)
27. Li, C., Jiankun, H.: A security-enhanced alignment-free fuzzy vault-based fingerprint cryptosystem using pair-polar minutiae structures. IEEE Trans. Inf. Forensics Secur. **11**(3), 543–555 (2016)
28. Wu, X., et al.: A novel cryptosystem based on iris key generation. In: Fourth International Conference on Natural Computation, ICNC 2008, vol. 4, pp. 53–56. IEEE (2008)
29. Luo, Z.: Research on blind identity authentication protocol based on biometrics. Ph.D. thesis, Beijing Jiaotong University, Beijing (2014)
30. Qu, Y.: Research on palmprint authentication based on homomorphic encryption. Ph.D. thesis, Southwest Jiaotong University (2015)
31. Erkin, Z., Franz, M., Guajardo, J., Katzenbeisser, S., Lagendijk, I., Toft, T.: Privacy-preserving face recognition. In: Goldberg, I., Atallah, M.J. (eds.) PETS 2009. LNCS, vol. 5672, pp. 235–253. Springer, Heidelberg (2009). https://doi.org/10.1007/978-3-642-03168-7_14
32. Wang, H., Ding, Y., Tang, S., Wang, J.: An efficient privacy-preserving palmprint authentication scheme based on homomorphic encryption. In: Wen, S., Wu, W., Castiglione, A. (eds.) CSS 2017. LNCS, vol. 10581, pp. 503–512. Springer, Cham (2017). https://doi.org/10.1007/978-3-319-69471-9_39
33. Ojala, T., Pietikäinen, M., Harwood, D.: A comparative study of texture measures with classification based on featured distributions. Pattern Recognit. **29**(1), 51–59 (1996)
34. Achlioptas, D.: Database-friendly random projections: Johnson-Lindenstrauss with binary coins. J. Comput. Syst. Sci. **66**(4), 671–687 (2003)
35. ElGamal, T.: A public key cryptosystem and a signature scheme based on discrete logarithms. IEEE Trans. Inf. Theory **31**(4), 469–472 (1985)
36. Aykut, M., Ekinci, M.: Developing a contactless palmprint authentication system by introducing a novel ROI extraction method. Image Vis. Comput. **40**, 65–74 (2015)
37. Wong, K.-S., Kim, M.-H.: A privacy-preserving biometric matching protocol for iris codes verification. In: 2012 Third FTRA International Conference on Mobile, Ubiquitous, and Intelligent Computing (MUSIC), pp. 120–125. IEEE (2012)

38. Wu, X., Wang, K., Zhang, D.: HMMs based palmprint identification. In: Zhang, D., Jain, A.K. (eds.) ICBA 2004. LNCS, vol. 3072, pp. 775–781. Springer, Heidelberg (2004). https://doi.org/10.1007/978-3-540-25948-0_105
39. Wu, G., et al.: A contour extraction algorithm of palmprints based on corner point features. In: 2012 IEEE International Conference on Automation and Logistics (ICAL), pp. 501–505. IEEE (2012)
40. Wang, Y., Malluhi, Q.M.: Privacy preserving computation in cloud using noise-free fully homomorphic encryption (FHE) schemes. In: Askoxylakis, I., Ioannidis, S., Katsikas, S., Meadows, C. (eds.) ESORICS 2016. LNCS, vol. 9878, pp. 301–323. Springer, Cham (2016). https://doi.org/10.1007/978-3-319-45744-4_15

PJC: A Multi-source Method for Identifying Information Dissemination in Networks

Yong Ding, Xiaoqing Cui, Huiyong Wang$^{(\boxtimes)}$, and Yujue Wang

Guangxi Key Laboratory of Cryptography and Information Security,
Guilin University of Electronic Technology, Guilin 541004,
People's Republic of China
why608@163.com

Abstract. With the development of science and technology, the world has become increasingly closely linked. While enjoying the convenience brought by the Internet, we are also facing the danger of risk dissemination. This problem has become more challenging in real-world networks. In this paper, in view of the outbreak of network threats, such as malware, computer viruses, rumors, etc. It is particularly important to identify the source of network threats. In this paper, we have done the following work. Firstly, we draw on the propagation models from epidemiology and design an algorithm partitioned Jordan Center (PJC) to locate the multiple propagation sources. Then, by establishing an extended model originated from propagation sources, we derive the number of sources of estimation. In order to evaluate the performance of the proposed method, a series of experiments were carried out in real-world network topologies. Experimental results show that the method is more accurate than the existing methods.

Keywords: Information dissemination · PJC · Identification of multi-source

1 Introduction

In today's increasingly interconnected world, while we enjoy the convenience of the world, we are also affected by new diffusion risks. For example, the rapid development of the Internet of Things has made more user contacts more secure. However, we need to guard against loopholes in information transmission technology. "Intelligent" Internet of Things devices may be an entry point for them to attack the network. Similarly, the rapid popularity of social media and mobile Internet devices has enabled people to easily and quickly access news and other information from social networks [1–3]. Rumor spread has entered the new media era, which makes the efficiency and harmfulness of rumor spread reach an unprecedented level. For biological viruses, the capture of highly pathogenic H5N1 influenza virus always threatens people's health. It is essential to identify the location of the source and find the number of the sources.

Assuming that a threatening message may begin to spread over different sources and times, after a certain period of time, we observe that nodes on the network are infected. Due to most real-world networks are complex, most of the previous work on

J. Li et al. (Eds.): SPNCE 2019, LNICST 284, pp. 268–281, 2019.
https://doi.org/10.1007/978-3-030-21373-2_20

source identification was based on single source detection [4, 5] or simple network topology. However, the multi-source heuristic algorithm proposed in recent years can't detect the real source of infection, and the average error is relatively large. For example, [6] proposes a multi-rumor recognition method to identify multiple sources in tree networks, which is difficult to implement in large networks.

In this paper, we propose a novel source identification method to overcome the challenges. First, In the process of information dissemination, we focus on considering that there is a certain gap between the sources when multiple source nodes propagate. When the distances between sources are close, too many overlapping nodes make the same nodes get the same infection, which makes the propagation range smaller. Second, In the real network, the diffusion in the network is complex in time and space. For a clearer understanding, we use effective distance [7]. The concept of effective distance reflects that the small propagation probability between nodes effectively corresponds to the large distance between nodes. The relative arrival time from the source to the node does not depend on any parameters, but is linear to the effective distance between the source and the infected node. In order to determine multiple sources, we firstly need to partition the infection map to minimize the effective distance between the source and the infected node. The node that minimizes the maximum distance to the infected area is considered the source of the propagation.

This paper mainly makes the following contributions: Firstly, we propose a novel method of partitioned Jordan Center to identify multiple sources. We prove that our method is convergent. The experimental results show that this method is superior to other methods. Secondly, by locating the source, we use an effective algorithm to estimate the source diffusion time. Finally, according to the estimated diffusion time, we can accurately estimate the number of diffusion sources.

The rest of this paper is organized as follows. Sect. 2 introduces the preliminary knowledge of the relevant background. Section 3 is the problem formulation of multi-source identification. Section 4 presents a method of Partitioned Jordanian centers for identifying multi-source problems. Section 5 evaluates the proposed method in the actual network topology. Section 6 is related work, and Sect. 7 is a summary of this paper.

2 Preliminary

In this section, we introduce relevant background knowledge, Propagation models and distances. Usually in these Propagation models, we divide the research objects into three categories, each of which has its own state. It mainly includes: the first is the susceptible state (S). Nodes in this state refer to healthy nodes, which are easy to be infected, but not yet infected; the second is Infected state (I). Nodes in this state are infected nodes, which are infectious; the third is Recovered state (R). Nodes in this state are immunized, not infected, or dead. Specific description in the following section. A specific meaning of symbols is given in Table 1 below.

Table 1. Used notations

Notation	Meaning
$P_s(i,t)$	The probability that node i is a susceptible node at time t
$P_I(i,t)$	The probability that node i is the infected node at time t
$v(i,t)$	Probability of node i being infected by neighboring nodes
$\mu_{j,i}$	Probability of node j propagating to node i
$m(i,j)$	Effective distance from node i to node j
$\alpha, \sigma(\alpha)$	Path, The sum of the effective lengths along the edge of the path
$\overrightarrow{S}, S^*$	Estimated source, Propagation source
B_n, D	Infection map, Infected partition

2.1 Propagation Model

Researchers mainly use three propagation models: SIR model, SIS model and SI model. SIR model considers the recovery process. Nodes are initially sensitive. They can be infected with the spread of risk and spread the threat to the next node. But the node can recover and become insensitive. The model deals with infection and curing processes $S \rightarrow I \rightarrow R$. The transmission schematic of SIR is shown in Fig. 1(A). The susceptible person S appears to be in a healthy state. It changes into the infected person I through direct contact with the infected person with a certain probability P. Infected person I regains health status and acquires immunity with the probability of u, thus becoming restorer R.

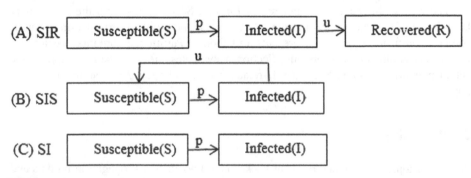

Fig. 1. The propagation diagrams of the three propagation models are (A) SIR (B) SIS (C) SI from top to bottom.

In the SIS model, infected nodes may become susceptible again after being cured. The model represents the process of infection and recover $S \rightarrow I \rightarrow S$. The susceptible node S will be transformed into an infected node with a certain probability p after contact with the infected node I, and some infected nodes will be restored to a susceptible node with a certain probability u. The propagation diagram of SIS is shown in Fig. 1(B).

In this paper, we adopt SI model. SI model is more convenient and applicable. We assume that infection spreads at discrete time steps. Each node is initially sensitive, and it can be infected as the risk spreads. Once a node is infected, it will always be infected. At time t, the probability that a vulnerable node i is infected by any infected neighbor is v(i,t). Therefore, we can calculate the probability that node i is a susceptible node at time t is

$$P_s(i,t) = [1 - v(i,t)] \cdot P_s(i, t - 1) \tag{1}$$

Then, we can get that the probability of node i being infected at time t is

$$P_I(i,t) = v(i,t) \cdot P_s(i, t - 1) + P_I(i, t - 1) \tag{2}$$

We use μ_{ji} to represent the propagation probability of node j to neighbor node i, and then we can calculate the probability that node i is infected by neighbor node is

$$v(i,t) = 1 - \prod_{j \in N_i} [1 - \mu_{j,i} \cdot P_I(i, t - 1)]. \tag{3}$$

Here, N_i represents the set of neighbors of node i. This model reflects the probability that any node is in different states at different times. Each time hop can mean one minute, one hour or one day.

2.2 Definition of Distance

Brockmann and Helbing [7] proposed a new concept to solve geometric problems in complex propagation processes by the relationship between propagation probability and effective distance between nodes. The effective distance from a node i to the neighbor node j is expressed as:

$$m(i,j) = 1 - \log \mu_{ij} \tag{4}$$

Where μ_{ij} is represented as the propagation probability from node i to node j. This formula reflects the small propagation probability from node i to node j is equivalent to the large distance between nodes. The length of path $\alpha = \{u_1, \cdots u_l\}$ is defined as the sum of effective length $\sigma(\alpha)$ along the edge of path. The effective distance from any node i to node j is defined as the length of the shortest path, which is expressed as: $d(i,j) = \min_\alpha \sigma(\alpha)$. We refer to the effective distance from node i to node j as the distance, denoted by $d(i,j)$. Given any set $A \subset V$, the maximum distance between node v and any node j is expressed as:

$$\overline{d}(v, A) = \max_{u \in A} d(v, u) \tag{5}$$

We call $\overline{d}(v, V_e)$ the maximum distance between node v and the infected range of any v. Nodes with the smallest infection range are called Jordan Center [8].

From the above formula, the Jordanian centrality of a node is considered to be the maximum distance from that node to any other infected node [9]. The Jordanian Center represents the node with the smallest Jordanian centrality.

3 Problem Formulation

Suppose that at time T = 0, there are k sources, and the $S^* = \{s_1, s_2, \cdots s_k\}$ diffusion propagation begins at the same time. After a few ticks, n nodes were infected. These nodes form a connected infected graph B_n, and each infected area is $D_i (\subset B_n)$. Let $D = \bigcup_{i=1}^{k} D_i$ be the partition of the infected area, satisfying $D_i \cap D_j = \emptyset$ and $i \neq j$ between partitions. Each partition is a subgraph of the connection of B_n, and the source node s_i can be found in each partition. We try to keep the source node s_i and s_j as far apart as possible. Figure 2 shows a certain distance between source nodes s_1 and s_2, so that many overlapping nodes can be avoided between each region. This can increase the probability of spreading. Assuming the infected node $v_j \in D_i$, the node v_j is infected in a short time. It means that it has a shorter distance to the corresponding source than to other sources. We consider the minimum of the maximum distance from the infected node to any other infected node as the source of propagation.

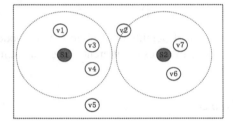

Fig. 2. Topological schematic diagram of separated propagation source nodes.

Our aim is to identify the corresponding partition D of a set of propagation sources S^* and infection graph B_n, so as to minimize the objective function value f.

$$\min f_D = \sum_{i=1}^{k} \max_{u_x \in D_i / s_i} d(u_x, s_i) \tag{6}$$

4 A Partitioned Jordan Center Method for Identifying Multi-source Problems

In this section, we propose a partitioned Jordan Center method (PJC) to identify multiple sources of diffusion and corresponding infected areas. We firstly introduce a method of network partitioning to export the PJC method. Then, it is used to identify multiple sources and estimate the number of sources.

4.1   Multi-source Network Partition

Given the infected graph B_n and a series of source nodes $S^* = \{s_1, s_2, \cdots s_n\}$. The distance between any two source nodes s_i and s_j satisfies $d(s_i, s_j) > \delta$. If $d(s_i, s_j) \leq \delta$, the source node is re-selected until the condition is met. In this section, we firstly divide the infected graph B_n into K infected subgraphs, with the corresponding s_i as the center of the partition D_i. We know that any node $v_j \in B_n$ should be assigned to the partition D_i where the source s_i is located. v_j must satisfy the following conditions:

$$d(v_j, s_i) = \min_{s_t \in S} d(v_j, s_t) \tag{7}$$

For any node $v_j \in B_n$, it needs to correspond v_j to the nearest source s_i. This is similar to the Capacity Constrained Network-Voronoi Diagram (CCNVD) problem [10]. In the K-center [8] method, there is also a similar partitioning method. In future work, a common structure may be used for network partitioning.

Algorithm 1: PJC method to identify multiple sources

Input: An infection graph B_n and the number of sources k.

Initialization: An positive integer T, Randomly select a suitable set $S^{(0)} = \left\{ s_1^{(0)}, \cdots, s_k^{(0)} \right\} \subseteq B_n$.

For t start from 1 to T_{max} **do**

$S^{(0)}$ as the center of the partition. Used the partition method to obtain a partition: $D^{(t)} = \bigcup_{i=1}^{k} D_i^{(t)}$.

Find a new partition center in each partition $D_i^{(t)}$ with the following formula:

$s_i^{(t)} = \arg \min_{v_j \in D_i^{(t)}} \max_{v_x \in D_i^{(t)}/v_j} d(v_j, v_x), i = 1, 2 \cdots k$.

if $S^{(t)} = S^{(t-1)}$ **then**

stop.

End

End

Output: A set of estimated sources $S^{(t)} = \left\{ s_1^{(t)}, \cdots, s_k^{(t)} \right\}$.

4.2   Identifying Multiple Propagation Sources and the Infected Partition

In this section, we propose a partitioned Jordan Center method to identify multiple diffusion sources. We firstly need to find the partition D that changes the infection graph B_n, which can minimize the minimum distance from the infected node to the corresponding partition center. If we randomly select a suitable set of source nodes, Voronoi partition can divide the network into subnets, so that each node is associated with its nearest source node. Therefore, Voronoi partition can find a locally optimal B_n partition. However, to optimize partition D, we need to adjust the center of each partition to minimize the objective function value f in Eq. (6). We adjust the center of each partition by choosing a new partition center to minimize the maximum distance from the partition center to any node in the partition. Detailed partitioning Jordan central method such as algorithm 1. The following theorem shows the convergence of the proposed method.

Theorem 1: The objective function of Eq. (6) is to decrease iteratively monotonously. Therefore, the partitioned Jordan Center is convergent.

Proof: Suppose that $S^l = \{s_1^l, \cdots s_n^l\}$ is the sources of estimation in the l times iteration. We use partitioning method to divide the infected graph B_n into $D^l = \bigcup_{i=1}^k D_i^l$. In this way, the objective function becomes

$$f^l = \sum_{i=1}^k \max_{u_x \in D_i^l / S_i^l} d(S_i^l, u_x) \tag{8}$$

after l iterations.

At the next iteration $l+1$, according to the PJC method, we calculate the center $D^l = \bigcup_{i=1}^k D_i^l$ of each partition again and get $S^{l+1} = \{s_1^{l+1}, \cdots, s_k^{l+1}\}$, which satisfies

$$\max_{u_x \in D_i^l / S_i^{l+1}} d(S_i^{l+1}, u_x) \le \max_{u_x \in D_i^l / S_i^l} d(S_i^l, u_x) \tag{9}$$

Then the target function becomes

$$\overline{\overline{f}}^l = \sum_{i=1}^k \max_{u_x \in D_i^l / S_i^{l+1}} d(S_i^{l+1}, u_x) \tag{10}$$

From Eqs. (8) and (9), we noticed that

$$\overline{\overline{f}}^l \le f^l \tag{11}$$

We redistribute the infected graph B_n so that the center of each infected partition is $S^{l+1} = \{s_1^{l+1}, \cdots s_k^{l+1}\}$. Let each infected node $v_j \in B_n$ be associated with the nearest central node s_i^{l+1}, and we get a new partition $D^{l+1} = \bigcup_{i=1}^k D_i^{l+1}$ for B_n. Thus, the objective function becomes

$$f^{l+1} = \sum_{i=1}^k \max_{u_x \in D_i^{l+1} / S_i^{l+1}} d(S_i^{l+1}, u_x) \tag{12}$$

in the iteration $l+1$ times.

Since each node is associated with its nearest central node s_i^{l+1}, we can know

$$f^{l+1} \le \overline{\overline{f}}^l \tag{13}$$

From Eqs. (11) and (13), we have

$$f^{l+1} \leq \overline{\overline{f}} \leq f^l \qquad \text{.} \qquad (14)$$

Therefore, the objective function of Eq. (6) is consistently reduced, and our proposed partitioned Jordan Center method is convergent.

4.3 Identifying the Number of Propagation Sources

The heuristic algorithm is used to estimate the number of sources. By using the proposed method of source identification, we can obtain the partition D of B_n which is consistent with S^*. If the number of sources is known, the propagation time $T^{(k)}$ can be estimated by Eq. (16). In order to estimate the number of sources, we start from 1 and increase the number of source k in turn, and calculate the corresponding propagation time $T^{(k)}$ until we find $T^{(k)} = T^{(k-1)}$. We choose k (or k–1) as the number of diffusion sources. This is similar to the method [8] in estimating the number of sources.

The propagation time can be determined by the total number of time ticks of diffusion. Given an arbitrary source, the propagation time can be estimated based on the number of time hops between the source and the infected node in each region. In regional D_i, according to any source s_i, any node $v_j \in D_i$ can be found. $g(s_i, v_j)$ represents the sum of the minimum time hops between s_i and v_j, the propagation time of each region can be estimated as

$$t_i = \max\{g(s_i, v_j) | v_j \in D_i, i = 1, 2 \cdots k\} \qquad (15)$$

Then the propagation time of the whole infected area is

$$T = \max\{t_i | i = 1, 2 \cdots k\} \qquad (16)$$

This process of propagation is actually simplified. In the real world, the propagation time of different paths with the same hop number is different. Based on SI model, we have solved this time problem in another article [11]. In this field, many current models are based on time hops [12].

5 Experiment Analysis

In this section, we make an experimental analysis of the proposed method of Partitioned Jordan Center. We tested our approach on the following network topologies: Yeast protein-protein interaction network [13], the large-scale web Facebook [14], and the North American Power Grid [15]. The basic attributes of the networks are listed in Table 2. We set the propagation probability μ_{ij} of each edge to follow the uniform distribution on (0,1). Previous work [16, 17] has proved that the distribution of propagation probability will not affect the accuracy of SI model. We randomly select different threat sources that satisfy the conditions to generate the dissemination data as the basic fact. Under each parameter setting, our method is used to simulate 100 propagation processes and identify the source of each propagation.

Table 2. Basic attributes of real networks

Dataset	Power Grid	Yeast	Facebook
Number of nodes	4,941	2,361	45,813
Number of edges	13,188	13,554	370,532
Average degree	2.67	5.74	8.09
Maximum degree	19	64	223

5.1   Evaluation Source Detection Algorithm

In this section, we test source identification methods. In order to compare the performance with other methods, we match the estimated source $\vec{S} = \{\vec{s_1}, \cdots \vec{s_k}\}$ with the real source $S^* = \{s_1, s_2, \cdots s_k\}$. So that the total error distance between them is the smallest. The average error distance formula is

$$\Delta = \frac{1}{|S^*|} \sum_{i=1}^{|S^*|} g(s_i, \vec{s_i}) \tag{17}$$

The average error distances of the three real source network topologies are shown in Table 3. Table 3 shows that the average error distance is very small compared with other methods. This shows that our method is superior to other methods. In order to make a clearer comparison, we show a histogram of the average error distance (Δ) as shown in Figs. 3 and 4. Frequency is used to express the percentage of test times when the average error distance is fixed.

We applied the algorithm to the Yeast protein-protein interaction network, the large-scale web Facebook and the North American Power Grid. As shown in Figs. 3 and 4.

We have made histograms for different cases where the true source S is 2 and 3 respectively. When the source is 2, on the Power Grid, the error range is often active in the range of 1 to 2 hops, indicating that our method performs well. And with the Dynamic Age method [4], the average error distance shows 3–5 hops, the maximum number of errors is 3 hops. Multi-rumor-center (MRC) [18] method shows an average error range of 3 to 4 hops. The most common error is 4 hops. The K-center [8] method shows an error range of 1 to 3 hops. On the Yeast network, our method show that the average error is 2 hops. And with the Dynamic Age method, the average error distance is 3–4 hops. The average error distance between the Multi-rumor-center method and the K-Center method is 2–4 hops, and the most experimental results are 3 hops. On the Facebook network, the most performance of our method is 1–3 hops. And with the Dynamic Age method, the average error distance shows 3–5 hops. The average error distance of the Multi-rumor-center method shows 3–4 hops. K-Center method is active around 2–3 hops, but the most performance is 3 hops.

Similarly, when the source is 3, In any network, the average error of our method is more 1–3 hops. Therefore, compared with other methods, our method estimates that the diffusion source is very close to the real source.

Table 3. Accuracy of multi-source identification

Experiment settings		Average error distance			
Network	$|S^*|$	PJC	Dynamic age	MRC	K-center
Power grid	2	1.600	3.510	3.135	1.750
	3	2.460	4.626	4.246	2.670
Yeast	2	2.521	3.175	2.710	2.680
	3	2.632	3.146	3.520	2.733
Facebook	2	3.237	3.950	3.433	3.215
	3	3.681	4.763	4.667	4.073

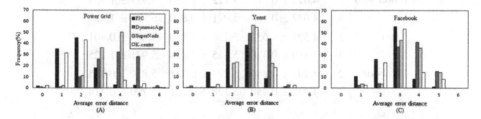

Fig. 3. When the number of sources is 2, the average error distance of different methods on the following three networks. (A) Power Grid; (B) Yeast; (C) Facebook

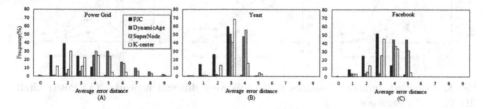

Fig. 4. When the number of sources is 3, the average error distance of different methods on the following three networks. (A) Power Grid; (B) Yeast; (C) Facebook.

5.2 Evaluation of the Number of Sources

In this section, we evaluate the proposed method for estimating the number of sources and predict the diffusion time. When the number of sources is determined, the propagation time of the source can be estimated. Table 4 shows the average and standard variance of estimated time. The results show that the mean of estimated time is close to the true propagation time, and the results of standard deviation are mostly less than 1. This shows that our method can estimate the real diffusion time of the source.

We simulated experiments on North American Power Grid, Facebook and Yeast networks to estimate the number of diffusion sources. As shown in Fig. 5. We let the number of diffusion sources range from 1 to 3. The horizontal axis represents the estimated number of sources and the vertical axis represents the percentage of the estimated number of sources in the experimental operation. On the Power Grid network, when the number of propagation sources is 1, about 78% of the experimental results can accurately estimate the number of sources. When the number of sources is 2, more than 80% of the experimental results can accurately estimate the number of sources. When the number of sources is 3, more than 60% of the experimental results can accurately estimate the number of sources. Similarly, it is obvious that at least half of the experiments can accurately identify the number of sources in the other two networks.

Table 4. Accuracy of spreading time estimation

Experiment settings		Estimated spreading time		
Network	$|S^*|$	T = 4	T = 5	T = 6
Power grid	2	4.012 ± 0.710	5.122 ± 1.790	5.987 ± 1.365
	3	4.032 ± 0.580	5.021 ± 0.860	6.025 ± 1.225
Yeast	2	4.521 ± 0.652	5.180 ± 0.420	5.851 ± 0.401
	3	4.340 ± 0.370	5.065 ± 1.210	5.921 ± 1.225
Facebook	2	4.242 ± 0.840	5.273 ± 0.521	5.820 ± 0.725
	3	4.432 ± 0.450	5.120 ± 0.721	5.790 ± 0.414

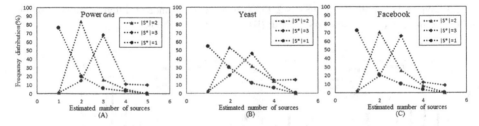

Fig. 5. Estimated number of sources in the following different networks. (A) Power Grid; (B) Yeast; (C) Facebook

5.3   Correlation Between the Real Sources and the Estimated Sources

By the Eq. (6), we detect the correlation between the objective function values on the Power Grid, Year and Facebook networks. As shown in Figs. 6 and 7 below. When the number of sources is 2, the distribution of points on the Power Grid shows an obvious linear relationship. This shows that the objective function values are highly correlated. On Yeast and Facebook, though there are fewer dots scattered, many dots float smaller around a line. This shows that the objective function values are also linearly correlated. Similarly, when the number of sources is 3, the objective function values are linearly correlated regardless of the network. It shows that we can use the proposed source detection method to estimate the location of the real source.

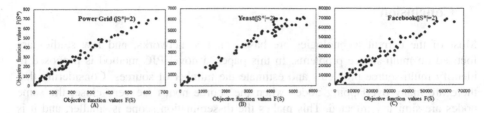

Fig. 6. When the number of sources is 2, the correlation between the objective function values is in the following network. (A) Power Grid; (B) Yeast; (C) Facebook

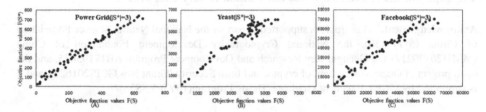

Fig. 7. When the number of sources is 3, the correlation between the objective function values is in the following network. (A) Power Grid; (B) Yeast; (C) Facebook

6 Related Work

In large-scale networks, the problem of outbreak threat propagation has become particularly serious. It becomes very meaningful to identify the source of propagation. However, most of the work focuses on the identification of single source in tree networks. Trees do not contain loops, but only a path between any pair of nodes. This greatly reduces the uncertainty of diffusion and the complexity of propagation, and further reduces the computational complexity. In real networks, threat propagation mostly involves multi-source problems, and the network is more complex. Diffusion processes of different sources are usually interactive and have uncertainties in the propagation process.

We mainly compare with the following multi-source identification methods. Fioriti et al. [4] proposes a dynamic aging method, which takes advantage of the correlation between eigenvalues and the "age" of nodes. The oldest nodes associated with the largest eigenvalues are considered diffusion sources. It essentially calculates the reduction of the maximum eigenvalue of the adjacent matrix after removing nodes. This method is based on the prior knowledge of the number of diffusion sources, and this method is not suitable for large-scale network source identification. Luo et al. [18] identifies multiple sources by expanding a single rumor center. For multiple sources, they propose a two-step method. They divide all infected nodes into different partitions by using Voronoi segmentation algorithm [19]. We need to calculate the number of different propagation paths from the sets. This method is difficult to use in large networks. The K-center [8] method is also a concept of introducing effective distances, using a Voronoi-like partitioning method to partition the network.

7 Conclusion

Most of the current technologies are based on tree networks, and few studies are focused on multi-source problems. In this paper, a novel PJC method is proposed to identify multi-source problems and estimate the number of sources. Considering that there are many overlapping nodes when the source nodes are very close, the same nodes are similarly infected. This makes the dissemination scope is smaller, and it is not suitable to study this propagation mode in large-scale networks. Therefore, this paper considers that there is a certain distance between the source nodes, which can avoid too many overlapping nodes. This can increase the probability of propagation. The experimental results show that our method is very effective.

Acknowledgement. This article is supported in part by the National Natural Science Foundation of China (61772150), the National Cryptography Development Foundation of China (MMJJ20170217) and Guangxi Key Research and Development Program AB17195025, and the open project of Guangxi Key Lab. of crypto, and Info. Security (Grant Nos.GCIS201622), and it is supported by GUET Excellent Graduate Thesis Program(16YJPYSS23).

References

1. Bakshy, E., Hofman, J.M., Mason, W.A., Watts, D.J.: Everyone's an influencer: quantifying influence on Twitter. In: Proceedings of ACM International Conference Web Search Data Mining, pp. 65–74, February 2011
2. Aral, S., Walker, D.: Identifying influential and susceptible members of social networks. Science **337**(6092), 337–341 (2012)
3. Tay, W.P.: The value of feedback in decentralized detection. IEEE Trans. Inf. Theory **58**(12), 7226–7239 (2012)
4. Luo, W., Tay, W.P., Leng, M.: Identifying infection sources and regions in large networks. IEEE Trans. Signal Process. **61**(11), 2850–2865 (2013)
5. Lokhov, A.Y., Mézard, M., Ohta, H., Zdeborová, L.: Inferring the origin of an epidemic with a dynamic message-passing algorithm. Phys. Rev. E **90**(1), 012801 (2014)
6. Luo, W., Tay, W.P.: Finding an infection source under the sis model. In: IEEE International Conference on Acoustics, Speech and Signal Processing (ICASSP), pp. 2930–2934 (2013)
7. Brockmann, D., Helbing, D.: The hidden geometry of complex, network-driven contagion phenomena. Science **342**(6164), 1337–1342 (2013)
8. Jiang, J.J., Wen, S., Yu, S., Xiang, Y., Zhou, W.: K-center: an approach on the multi-source identification of information diffusion. IEEE Trans. Inf. Forensics Secur. **10**(12), 2616–2626 (2015)
9. Dekker, A.H.: Centrality in social networks: theoretical and simulation approaches. In: Proceedings of SimTecT 2008, pp. 12–15 (2008)
10. Yang, K., Shekhar, A.H., Oliver, D., Shekhar, S.: Capacity-constrained network-Voronoi diagram: a summary of results. In: Nascimento, Mario A., et al. (eds.) SSTD 2013. LNCS, vol. 8098, pp. 56–73. Springer, Heidelberg (2013). https://doi.org/10.1007/978-3-642-40235-7_4
11. Wen, S., Zhou, W., Zhang, J., Xiang, Y., Zhou, W., Jia, W.: Modeling propagation dynamics of social network worms. IEEE Trans. Parallel Distrib. Syst. **24**, 1633–1643 (2013)

12. Wang, Y., Wen, S., Xiang, Y., Zhou, W.: Modeling the propagation of worms in networks: a survey. Commun. Surv. Tutorials IEEE **16**(2), 942–960 (2014)
13. Jeong, H., Mason, S.P., Barabási, A.L., Oltvai, Z.N.: Lethality and centrality in protein networks. Nature **411**(6833), 41–42 (2001)
14. Viswanath, B., Mislove, A., Cha, M., Gummadi, K.P.: On the evolution of user interaction in facebook. In: Proceedings of the 2nd ACM Workshop on Online Social Networks, pp. 37–42 (2009)
15. Leskovec, J., Kleinberg, J., Faloutsos, C.: Graph evolution: densification and shrinking diameters. ACM Trans. Knowl. Discovery Data **1**(1) (2007)
16. Wen, S., Zhou, W., Zhang, J., Xiang, Y., Zhou, W., Jia, W.: Modeling propagation dynamics of social network worms. IEEE Trans. Parallel Distrib. Syst. **24**(8), 1633–1643 (2013)
17. Fioriti, V., Chinnici, M., Palomo, J.: Predicting the sources of an outbreak with a spectral technique. Appl. Math. Sci. **8**(135), 6775–6782 (2014)
18. Wolpert, D.H.: The lack of a priori distributions between learning algorithms. Neural Comput. **8**(7), 1341–1390 (1996)
19. Hakimi, S.L., Labbé, M.L., Schmeichel, E.: The Voronoi partition of a network and its implications in location theory. ORSA J. Comput. **4**(4), 412–417 (1992)

Steganalysis of Adaptive Multiple-Rate Speech Using Parity of Pitch-Delay Value

Xiaokang Liu[1], Hui Tian[1(✉)], Jie Liu[1], Xiang Li[1], and Jing Lu[2]

[1] College of Computer Science and Technology,
National Huaqiao University, Xiamen 361021, China
htian@hqu.edu.cn
[2] Network Technology Center,
National Huaqiao University, Xiamen 361021, China

Abstract. Exploiting the fact that the pitch period parameter in speech parameter encoding is difficult to predict, a large number of steganographic strategies choose to embed secret information in the pitch period. Several detection methods for these steganography strategies based on the pitch period have also been proposed so far, but it is still a challenge to detect the steganography accurately. In this work, a new steganalysis scheme is proposed to detect pitch period based steganography, which has lower complexity and higher accuracy compared with the existing steganalysis schemes. Firstly, we regard a frame as a calculation unit within which the parity of four sub-frames can be obtained. Secondly, after filtering and merging into 14-dimensional PBP (parity Bayesian probability) features, these features are classified by the support vector machine (SVM). We evaluate the performance of the proposed strategy with numerous speech samples encoded by the adaptive multi-rate audio codec (AMR) and compare it with the state-of-the-art strategies. The experimental results illustrate that proposed method can effectively detect the pitch-delay based steganography. It is not only superior to the existing steganalysis methods in detection accuracy, but also has outstanding real-time detection performance and robustness because of its lower feature dimension and complexity.

Keywords: Steganalysis · Adaptive multi-rate codec · Pitch delay · Bayes's theorem · Support vector machine (SVM)

1 Introduction

Steganography is a common means of hiding secret information in the carrier without perceptible distortion, and it has been applied to very broad areas from war to politics since the ancient Greek era. The carrier of information (namely, the steganographic carrier) has been changing over the ages. Current steganography chiefly relies on networks such as the Internet protocols [1] and digital multimedia (text [2, 3], image [4–6] voice [7, 8], video [9]). In recent years, mobile device-based voice communication protocol has been greatly technologically advanced. Therefore, a large number of steganographic researches are attracted to the field of voice transmission [8, 10–12] because of not only the wide range of applications but also reliability real-time and considerable redundancy. AMR [13–15] has become a hotspot in steganography

© ICST Institute for Computer Sciences, Social Informatics and Telecommunications Engineering 2019
Published by Springer Nature Switzerland AG 2019. All Rights Reserved
J. Li et al. (Eds.): SPNCE 2019, LNICST 284, pp. 282–297, 2019.
https://doi.org/10.1007/978-3-030-21373-2_21

research because it is widely used in 3G and 4G networks. Moreover, AMR has considerable coding redundancy, which eventually makes it practical and efficient to apply AMR-based steganography into secure communication. However, on the one hand, the development of steganography provides a better choice for the safe transmission of data. On the other hand, it also provides a better choice for the illegal transmission of data. If the technology is exploited illegally, it will pose a threat to network security. Therefore, steganalysis, aimed at detecting steganography in the communication process, has increasingly received widespread attention.

AMR adopts an optimized compressed speech coding mode [16], and it is extensively employed by almost all cell phone. Specifically, AMR is a multi-rate ACELP (Algebraic Code Excited Linear Prediction) encoder with 8 modes, from 4.75 kbit/s to 12.2 kbit/s and sampling frequency of 8000 Hz. The process of mode integration and bit rate conversion is mainly operated by changing the quantization parameters, which provides seamless switching of 20 ms frame boundaries [17]. Additionally, the encoding method of AMR leads to a large amount of redundancy in the encoding, which makes AMR an ideal voice steganographic carrier. Correspondingly, steganalysis for AMR also evolves with steganography [18–21].

As described above, AMR is a typical algebraic code excited line prediction (ACELP) coding. The structure of ACELP mainly includes Liner Prediction Coefficient (LPC) analysis, Fixed Code Book (FCB) searching and Adaptive Code Book (ACB) searching. The adaptive codebook is to match the pitch period, and the fixed codebook is founded on the algebraic codebook search. Although ACELP has been developed for quite a long time and many prediction algorithms have been proposed for it, these parts of predictive coding are still hard to be accurate. The unavoidable redundancy provides favorable conditions for steganography. In the LPC analysis, Liu et al. [22] proposed a new quantized index modulated LPC steganography algorithm. Not only does it improve the efficiency, but it also reduces the distortion of speech. After that, Liu et al. [22] also proposed a new method based on matrix embedding information, and the method greatly improves security and the efficiency of embedding. Similarly, there are also many steganography schemes for the fixed codebook [11, 13, 23, 24]. Geiser et al. [13] introduced a method of hiding data at a higher rate in the FCB, in which the information bandwidth can reach 2 kbit/s. Based on the similar principle, Miao et al. [15] proposed a 3G speech encoding steganography scheme, which bases on the Adaptive Suboptimal Pulsed Combination Constraints (ASOPCC) method. Compared with the linear prediction analysis and fixed codebook searching, the adaptive codebook searching is more flexible and the range of the pitch period of speech is wider when considering the complexity of the speech itself. The redundancy caused by inaccurate predictions drives the development of steganography in recent years. Based on the AMR pitch delay, Huang et al. [25] presented a new steganography scheme. It divides the adaptive codebook into two parts, and then introduces a random location selection to adjust the embedding rate dynamically and improve the security of steganography. The experimental results show that not only are the considerable capacity and real-time performance ensured, but also the quality and the anti-detection ability of the steganographic speech remain high. Based on Huang, Yan et al. [26] proposed a twice-layer steganography algorithm using low-rate speech as a carrier. The first layer of steganography is implemented by limiting the search set of the pitch period value of the speech sub-frame. The second layer of steganography is implemented by exploiting the randomness of the pitch period in the search set. In the process of twice-layer embedding, the value of the pitch period is determined by the principle of minimizing the amplitude of modification. The advancement of steganography directly promoted the generation and the development of another opposite technology-steganalysis.

Compared with steganography the development process of steganalysis is always lagging. However, there are still massive valid works have been proposed [18, 21, 22, 27–30]. For the steganography on the LPC, Li et al. [28] observed that the correlation properties of the split vector quantization (VQ) codebook of linear predictive coding filter coefficients changed after the QIM steganography. Based on this observation, they construct the QCCN (Quantitative Codebook Correlation Network) model and obtain the eigenvector after quantifying the fixed-point related features of the pruned network. These steganalysis methods have got great feedback. Tian et al. [21] employed probability distribution of pulse pairs as the long-term distribution features and employed Markov transition probability matrix of pulse pair as the short-term invariant features. Moreover, adaptive boosting was introduced to optimize these features, and finally, the feature classification results obtained are superior to the existing detection methods. Some efficient detection methods for coping with the new pitch delay steganography was also proposed. Li et al. [31] proposed a method for detecting quantization index modulation (QIM) steganography in a G.723.1 bit stream. They extract these eigenvectors based on the correlation and the imbalance of each quantized index (codebook) distribution in the quantized index sequence. Based on the correlation and the imbalance of each quantized index (codebook) distribution in the quantized index sequence, a kind of novel eigenvector is extracted, and then the extracted features are combined with support vector machines to construct a classifier for detecting QIM steganography in the G.723.1 coding stream. Experiments show that this method has achieved good results in detecting steganography. However, Ren et al. [20] proposed a new steganalysis scheme for AMR speech and achieved better results. Based on the differences in the continuity of the adjacent pitch delays between the original and steganographic AMR speech, they calculated the second-order Markov transition probability (MSDPD) feature matrix and then obtained C-MSDPD by subtracting the MSDPD after calibration. Experiments show that the effect of C-MSDPD is better than Li et al. and is the most efficient detection method for pitch delay steganography presently.

The rest of this paper is organized as follows. To make this paper self-contained, Sect. 2, firstly, introduces the structure of AMR codec and the principle of the state-of-the-art steganalysis. Section 3 explores the steganalysis features based on the parity of the pitch delay. The steganalysis scheme is revealed in Sect. 4, which is followed by the evaluation and experimental results that are presented in Sect. 5. Finally, the conclusions are drawn and directions for further work are suggested in Sect. 6.

2 Background and Related Work

In this section, the principle of the pitch delay searching in AMR codec is introduced. Firstly, the defects of the coding principle exploited by steganography will be explored. Secondly, the state-of-the-art steganography and steganalysis schemes based on the pitch delay are introduced in detail.

2.1 The Principle and Analysis of AMR Codec

The structure of AMR mainly consists of linear prediction, adaptive codebook searching, fixed codebook searching, gain quantization, post-processing and error concealment. The fundamental function of the linear prediction is to obtain the 10 coefficients of a 10-order LPC filter, and convert them into line spectra to quantify the parameters LSF. Adaptive codebook searching, including open-loop pitch analysis and closed-loop pitch analysis, obtains the pitch delay and the pitch gain. While fixed codebook searching, including the quantization of the quantization, is to obtain algebraic codebook gain [32]. AMR coding structure is shown in Fig. 1.

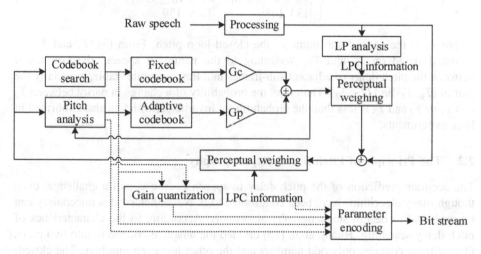

Fig. 1. AMR structure

AMR sets the speech rate to 8 kHz as the sampling rate. One frame has 240 sampling points and is divided into four sub-frames (T_0, T_1, T_2, T_3). In order to illustrate the AMR search principle more clearly, we take the case of 12.2 kb/s mode. The open-loop pitch delay T_{OP} is calculated based on a weighted speech signal which is the output of the original signal input to the perceptual weighting filter. The purpose of predicting the open-loop pitch period is to reduce the computational complexity of the closed-loop pitch period. Then the closed-loop pitch delay can be calculated by the signal f and the cross-correlation formula $C_{OL}(j)$ searching a maximum within a certain range around the open-loop pitch delay. The formula is as follows.

$$C_{OL}(j) = \frac{\left(\sum_{n=0}^{119} f[n]f[n-j]\right)^2}{\sum_{n=0}^{119} f[n-j]f[n-j]} \quad 18 \le j \le 142. \tag{1}$$

The coefficient j of the maximum $C_{OL}(j)$ is selected as the open-loop pitch within the search range according to formula (1). The closed-loop pitch T_0 and T_2 are searched on the basis of the open-loop pitch, then the closed-loop pitch of T_1 and T_3 are calculated based on the closed-loop pitch delay of T_0 and T_2 which have been obtained. The range of the pitch delay for T_0, T_2 is determined by formula (2).

$$T_0 = \begin{cases} [18, 24], & T_{OP} \le 21 \\ [T_{OP} - 3, T_{OP} + 3], & 21 \le T_{OP} \le 140, \\ [137, 143], & T_{OP} > 140 \end{cases} \tag{2}$$

where T_{OP} is the open-loop pitch, and T_0 is the first sub-frame of closed-loop pitch.

$$T_1 = \begin{cases} [18, 27], & T_0 \le 23 \\ [T_0 - 5, T_0 + 4], & 23 \le T_0 \le 139, \\ [134, 143], & T_0 > 139 \end{cases} \tag{3}$$

where T_1 is the second sub-frame of the closed-loop pitch. From (3), T_1 and T_3 are searched based on T_0 and T_2. According to the nature of speech, the correlation between the pitch delay of adjacent sub-frames in a frame is quite stable, especially the pair of (T_0, T_1) and (T_2, T_3). Therefore, the probability of a change in parity between T_0 and T_1 or T_2 and T_3 is less than the probability of invariance, which is also confirmed in later experiments.

2.2   The Principle of Pitch-Based Steganography

The accurate prediction of the pitch delay in speech coding is still a challenge, even though many algorithms have been contributed to it. Nevertheless, this uncertainty can be exploited to design steganography algorithms. According to the characteristics of pitch delay searching, Huang et al. [25] divided the adaptive codebook into two parts. One of them contains only odd numbers and the other just even numbers. The closed-loop pitch is calculated by (1) and (2), yet a restriction is added when searching for the closed-loop pitch so that mod $(T_t, 2)$ equals the secret information to be embedded. In the process of extracting secret information, the procedure is exactly the opposite, namely, adding the judgment mod $(T_t, 2)$ to extract the secret information. T_t is the pitch delay of the t-th sub-frame. Yan et al. [24] proved that Huang's steganography could undermine the quality of speech at high embedding rates through experiments. Moreover, they discovered that if the changes were T_1, T_3 (T_0, T_2 unchanged), then there would be less impact on the quality of speech. In order to improve the embedding rate, they proposed a twice-layer steganography method, which calculates λ under the condition of Huang's T_0 and T_2 embedding.

$$\lambda = [(T_1 \bmod 4)/2 \oplus (T_3 \bmod 4)/2], \tag{4}$$

where T_1 and T_3 are determined by controlling the value of λ (0, 1) (T_1 is the second sub-frame closed-loop pitch value and T_3 is the fourth sub-frame closed-loop pitch value).

2.3 Review of the AMR-Based Steganalysis

After analyzing the variance of first-order difference and second-order difference of the pitch delay, Ren et al. [20] found that Huang's steganography method [25] makes obvious changes of some features before and after steganography, especially the second-order difference. Therefore, Ren et al. choose the second-order difference of the pitch delay as the classification feature.

$$D_T^2(t) = T_{t+2} - 2T_{t+1} + T_t, \tag{5}$$

where $D_T^2(t)$ is the second-order difference of the t-th sub-frame and T_t is the pitch delay of the t-th sub-frame. According to the inherent principle of speech, the changes of the adjacent second-order difference should be more concentrated and Markov transfer probability is expert in illustrating this connection. Therefore, the second-order difference construction is employed to construct Markov transition matrices as the classification characteristics.

$$M_{D_T^2} = \frac{\sum_{t=0}^{N-4} \delta(D_T^2(t), D_T^2(t+1) = i)}{\sum_{t=0}^{N-4} \delta(D_T^2(t) = i)}, \tag{6}$$

where $M_{D_T^2}$ is the transition probability of the current second-order difference to the next second-order difference. According to the experimental data, (−6, 6) is selected as the threshold. Therefore, there are 169 kinds of Markov transition probability.

What is special is that the appointment of a method called calibration [33] has greatly improved the accuracy of the MSDPD feature detection. The specific process is to divide the steganographic file into A and B parts. After decoding the part B, the original AMR encoder is re-encoded to obtain B_1, then the MSDPD obtained by decoding the extracted pitch delay of A and B_1. Finally, the subtraction of MSDPD of A and MSDPD of B_1 is

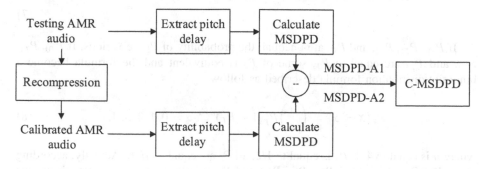

Fig. 2. C-MSDPD extraction process

C-MSDPD. The process is shown in Fig. 2. The experimental results show that using C-MSDPD as the classification feature by SVM can acquire the best results.

3   Background and Related Work

In this section, our Bayes's theorem features are illustrated below, which followed by the exact representation of our features. For the convenience of description, the AMR-NB at 12.2 kbps is taken as the example. Afterward, the characteristics, including advantages and disadvantages between the proposed features and C-MSDPD, are elaborated and compared.

3.1   Bayes's Theorem Features of Pitch Delay Parity

From the analysis of the pitch delay searching principle, the closed-loop pitches of T_1 and T_3 are searched based on T_0 and T_2. According to the analysis of the AMR coding principle above, the steganography methods, embedding secret information through changing the closed-loop pitch, distorts the connection between sub-frames. After determining the current sub-frame, the range of the next sub-frame pitch delay has narrowed and the possibility of the change of the parity has narrowed accordingly. Nevertheless, the distribution of the pitch delay value tends to be random under normal condition but concentrated under the condition of existing steganography, as shown in Fig. 3a. It is inferred that the existing steganography destroys the parity-correlation of the closed-loop and has a negative influence on the stability of the pitch delay distribution. Subsequently, we apply the probability distribution of the parity distribution within a frame to illustrate the effect of the steganography in the pitch delay. It is assumed that an AMR speech sample contains N frames with T sub-frames per frame ($T = 4$ AMR-NB codec at mode 12.2 kbps).

The parity of each sub-frame has only two states, and each sub-frame is an independent event. Therefore, there are 2^4 states in all four sub-frames. Assuming the probability of four odd sub-frames are P_{T0}, P_{T1}, P_{T2}, and P_{T3} respectively, the distribution probability P_k ($k = 1, 2, 3, \ldots, 16$) of each of the 16 states is as follows.

$$P_k = P_{T0}^{\alpha_0} \cdot (1 - P_{T0})^{1-\alpha_0} \cdot P_{T1}^{\alpha_1} \cdot (1 - P_{T1})^{1-\alpha_1} \cdot P_{T2}^{\alpha_2} \cdot (1 - P_{T2})^{1-\alpha_2} \cdot P_{T3}^{\alpha_3} \cdot (1 - P_{T3})^{1-\alpha_3},$$
$$k = 1, 2, \ldots, 16. \, \alpha_0 = 0, 1. \, \alpha_1 = 0, 1. \, \alpha_2 = 0, 1. \, \alpha_3 = 0, 1.$$

$$(7)$$

If P_{T0}, P_{T1}, P_{T2}, and P_{T3} are unequal, the probability of P_k are various. If P_{T0}, P_{T1}, P_{T2}, and P_{T3} are equal to P_T, some of P_k is equivalent and the formula become a binomial distribution formula described as follow.

$$P_k\{X = \alpha\} = \binom{n}{a} P_T^\alpha (1 - P_T)^{n-\alpha}, \alpha = 0, 1, 2, 3, 4, \tag{8}$$

where n is equal to 4. If P_T is equal to 1/2, all P_k are equal to 1/16. Actually, according to ANR-NB coding rules, P_{T0}, P_{T1}, P_{T2}, and P_{T3} are unequal. However, typically the probability that the secret information appears 0 (or 1) is similar to approximately 1/2. Therefore, P_k will definitely change before and after steganography.

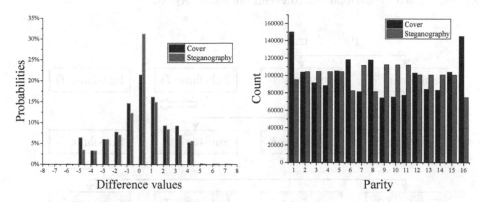

Difference values   Parity

Fig. 3a. The distribution of pitch difference.   **Fig. 3b.** The distribution of P_k

In order to validate our conjecture, the following experiment was designed. The differences between T_0 and T_1 and the difference between T_2 and T_3 in 3600 samples were statistically analyzed to obtain Fig. 3a. The statistics of the number of consecutive odd-numbered sub-frames in the sample are shown in Fig. 3b.

Figure 3a is a representation of the relationship between T_0, T_1 and T_2, T_3 within a frame, from which the difference between before and after steganography can be observed clearly. Figure 3b illustrates that the probability distribution of P_k are more average for steganographic samples. From Fig. 3a, it can be learned that the difference in the original sample is more concentrated and the distribution after steganography is evener, which verifies our previous theoretical analysis. This conclusion can be drawn in Fig. 3b that the parity distribution within one frame after steganography is evener. In Fig. 3b, the parity distribution is not uniform within one frame without steganography. Therefore, we choose the parity of the difference to characterize this change. However, the statistical result is not enough to demonstrate the correlation of each sub-frame within a frame. Therefore, we describe their correlation by the Bayes's theorem of the parity of the current sub-frame and the parity of the next sub-frame. Then the conditional probability is regarded as the feature of classification, and finally, SVM is applied to classify to judge whether the sample is steganographic.

3.2   Description of the Features Based on Bayes Theorem

Three features based on Bayes' theorem are depicted in this section. From the above description, it is known that there is an obvious difference between the pitch delay parity Bayes probability in the original sample and the steganographic sample. In order to describe this difference, the Bayesian formula of the pitch delay is considered as the feature. Since the state of the pitch delay is either odd or even and these are two mutually exclusive events, only one of them needs to be recorded as a feature. For the convenience of describing the following features, only the Bayesian probability of odd pitch delay is calculated. Assume that the four sub-frames are odd-numbered events A_0, A_1, A_2, A_3, and the even-numbered events are $A_0, \bar{A}_1, \bar{A}_2, \bar{A}_3$.

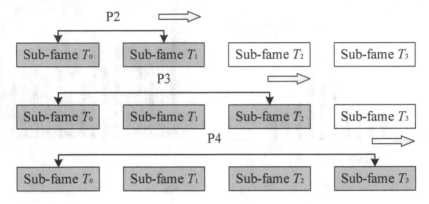

Fig. 4. Features based on Bayes's theorem

The first kind of feature is the relationship between the second sub-frame and the first sub-frame, which include two cases: P_1 and P_2. P_1 ($P_1 = P(A_1 \mid A_0)$) is the conditional probability of the first sub-frame occurred odd under the condition the second sub-frame occurred odd. P_2 ($P_2 = P(A_1 \mid A_0)$) is the conditional probability of the first sub-frame occurred odd under the condition the second sub-frame occurred even.

$$P_1 = P(A_1|A_0) = \frac{P(A_1 A_0)}{P(A_0)}. \tag{9}$$

In the same way, the second kind of feature is the relationship between the first sub-frame, the second sub-frame and the third sub-frame. These features include four cases, which are $P_3 = P(A_2 \mid A_0 A_1)$, $P_4 = P(A_2 \mid \bar{A}_0 A_1)$, $P_5 = P(A_2 \mid A_0 \bar{A}_1)$, $P_6 = P(A_2 \mid \bar{A}_0 \bar{A}_1)$ respectively.

$$P_3 = P(A_2 \mid A_0 A_1) = \frac{P(A_0 A_1 A_2)}{P(A_0 A_1)}. \tag{10}$$

The third feature is that the fourth sub-frame is an odd Bayesian probability in the case where the first sub-frame, the second sub-frame, and the third sub-frame are determined. These features include eight cases, which are $P_7 = P(A_3 | A_2 A_0 A_1)$, $P_8 = P(A_3 \mid A_2 A_0 \bar{A}_1)$, $P_9 = P(A_3 \mid A_2 \bar{A}_0 A_1)$, $P_{10} = P(A_3 \mid A_2 \bar{A}_0 \bar{A}_1)$, $P_{11} = P(A_3 \mid \bar{A}_2 A_0 A_1)$, $P_{12} = P(A_3 \mid \bar{A}_2 A_0 \bar{A}_1)$, $P_{13} = P(A_3 \mid \bar{A}_2 \bar{A}_0 A_1)$, $P_{14} = P(A_3 \mid \bar{A}_2 \bar{A}_0 \bar{A}_1)$ respectively.

$$P_7 = P(A_3 \mid A_0A_1A_2) = \frac{P(A_0A_1A_2A_3)}{P(A_0A_1A_2)}. \tag{11}$$

Figure 4 demonstrates the extraction processing of features based on the Bayes formula for the speech sample encoded with the AMR-NB codec at 12.2 kbps mode. Finally, all of these 14-dimensional are combined to the PBP features.

4 Steganalysis Scheme

In this section, we will introduce steganalysis steps using SVM (support vector machines) as a classifier, which has become an increasingly popular tool for classification. Moreover, its accuracy and detection efficiency have a huge advantage, especially in the small sample set (Figs. 5 and 6).

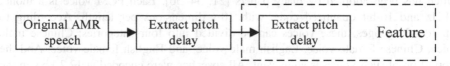

Fig. 5. Extract feature steps

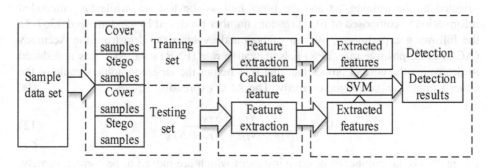

Fig. 6. Classification steps

The SVM training set main steps are shown as follows:

STEP 1. Collect a large number of speech samples randomly and divide it into two parts, half of which are used to steganography and the other half encoded by the original encoder.

STEP 2. Calculate the proposed features through formulas in Sect. 3.2.

STEP 3. Train the steganographic and original speech samples with original and steganographic tags using the above features.

The SVM testing set main steps are shown below:

STEP 1. Recode the voice samples of the test set with the same standard.
STEP 2. Calculate the proposed features in both the original and re-encoded samples.
STEP 3. Enter the feature vectors into the trained classifier to determine whether the sample is steganographic.

5 Performance Evaluation and Analysis

5.1 Experimental Settings

In this paper, SVM open source library is used as a classifier to evaluate experimental results, in which parameters, for example, Gaussian radial basis function kernel for SVM classification, are default setting. Our database consists of 3367 PCM voices, which has been adopted by many papers [21, 34–36]. Each PCM voice is a mono, 8 kHz and 16-bit quantized code, with 10-s dimensions per length. According to different languages, these voices can be divided into four categories: Chinese male voice, Chinese female voice, English male voice, and English female voice. And the proportion of such voices is equivalent. All speeches were encoded at 12.2 kb/s in the AMR using 10% to 100% embedding rate from 1 s to 10 s applying the steganography method of Huang et al. [25] and Yan et al. [26]. Half of the databases are randomly selected as the training set and the other half as the test set, while the embedded information is composed of (0, 1) random number produced by random seed 3367. In the following experiments, we will analyze and evaluate the data from the Accuracy (ACC) False-positive rate (FPR) False-negative rate (FNR) data. ACC has introduced to determine the correct proportion, that is, whether the steganographic sample or the cover sample can be judged correctly. The ACC expression is:

$$ACC = \frac{N_{TP} + N_{TN}}{N_{TP} + N_{TN} + N_{FP} + N_{FN}}, \tag{12}$$

where N_{TP} is the number of positive instances which are judged to be correct, namely, the steganographic samples are identified. N_{TN} is the number of passive instances which are judged to be negative, namely, the samples that are not steganographic determined to be not steganographic. N_{FP} is the number of negative instances which are judged to be positive, that is, the samples with no steganography are mistakenly considered as a steganographic sample. N_{FN} is the number of positive instances which are judged to be negative, that is, steganographic samples are considered non-steganographic samples. FPR is the proportion of negative instances which are mistaken in all negative instances.

$$FPR = \frac{N_{FP}}{N_{FP} + N_{TN}}, \tag{13}$$

where FNR is the proportion of positive instances which are mistaken in all positive instances.

$$FNR = \frac{N_{FN}}{N_{TP} + N_{FN}}. \qquad (14)$$

The result obtained in our experiments is that the method of Ren et al. [19] have an advantage when using Huang's steganography method in a relatively short time compared with the features mentioned in the previous section, but in other cases, the effect is close. It should be noted that the feature dimension mentioned is much lower than the C-MSDPD feature and therefore has better robustness. In the following data, for convenience, only partial results are shown, which are the features of the contrast chart of one-second to ten-second samples.

5.2   The Method Proposed Under High Embedding Ratio Is Compared with the Existing Method

Table 1 shows the comparison of the features when the embedding rate is 100% at different times. When Huang's steganography is exploited as the detection object, the classification effects of the PBP features are similar to the C-MSDPD features. However, when Yan's steganography is exploited as the detection object, the classification effects of the PBP features are better than C-MSDPD's. Moreover, when Yan's steganography is exploited as the detection object, the classification effects of the PBP features are better than C-MSDPD's. Yan's steganography method is an improvement of Huang's, and aim to promote the anti-detection ability. As can be seen from the table, compared with Huang's method, the detection accuracy of C-MSDPD in Yan's method is dropped markedly. However, different steganography methods have a minor effect on PBP's performance, which has better adaptability compared with C-MSDPD.

Table 1. The detection accuracies for three features when the embedding rate is 100%

Time (100%)	Huang		Yan	
	C-MSDPD	PBP	C-MSDPD	PBP
1 s	74.36%	73.41%	68.27%	72.70%
2 s	82.41%	81.91%	75.07%	80.93%
3 s	86.45%	86.04%	79.62%	84.85%
4 s	90.02%	89.19%	83.63%	88.86%
5 s	90.79%	91.59%	85.18%	90.29%
6 s	92.84%	93.26%	87.23%	92.04%
7 s	94.24%	93.88%	88.27%	92.93%
8 s	94.83%	95.13%	89.22%	94.56%
9 s	94.95%	95.54%	90.26%	94.86%
10 s	96.08%	96.35%	90.85%	95.28%

As can be seen in Figs. 7 and 8, compared with the MSDPD-C features the ACC, FPR and FNR of the proposed features have obvious advantages. Figure 7 is a comparison of ACC, FPR and FNR for the proposed features and the MSDPD-C feature when the sample length is 1 s to 10 s for an embedding rate of 100% in Huang's steganography while Fig. 8 in Yan's steganography. From Figs. 7 and 8, the accuracy increases with the increase of sample length, while the FPR and FNR decrease. Compared with the MSDPD-C, the FPR of proposed PBP is underperforming. However, it has better performance in Accuracy and the FNR. Figure 9 is a comparison of ROC for the proposed features and the MSDPD-C feature when the sample length is 10 s, and the embedding rate is from 30% to 90% in Huang's method while Fig. 10 in Yan's method.

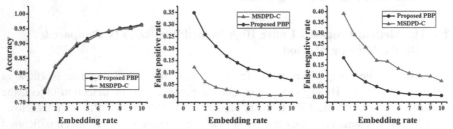

7.1 Statistical results of ACC 7.2 Statistical results of FPR 7.3 Statistical results of FNR

Fig. 7. The detection accuracies for Huang's method in 100% embedding rate

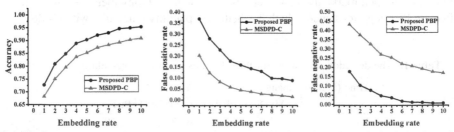

8.1 Statistical results of ACC 8.2 Statistical results of FPR 8.3 Statistical results of FNR

Fig. 8. The detection accuracies for Yan's method in 100% embedding rate

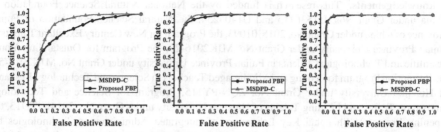

9.1 Embedding rate of 30%   9.2 Embedding rate of 60%   9.3 Embedding rate of 90%

Fig. 9. The ROC curves for detecting Huang's method

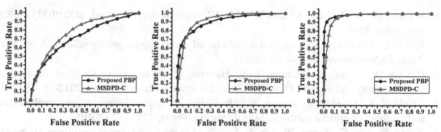

10.1 Embedding rate of 30%   10.2 Embedding rate of 60%   10.3 Embedding rate of 90%

Fig. 10. The ROC curves for detecting Yan's method

6 Conclusion

Because of the unpredictability for the pitch of speech parameter encoding, many steganographic methods are presented for secret communication. Motivated by present difficulties, a practical steganalysis scheme is developed in this paper. Distinct from existing works, we treat a frame as a calculation unit and pay more attention to the change in numerical parity rather than just the change in these values. Finally, SVM is employed to classify the PBP features. We evaluate the performance of the proposed method with plenty of speech samples coded by adaptive multi-rate audio coder (AMR), and compare it with the state-of-the-art methods. The experimental results illustrate that our method can effectively detect the pitch delay-based steganography and achieve superior performance than other state-of-the-art methods on ACC, FPR, and FNR. Particularly, the proposed method can provide excellent real-time perfor-mance and robustness because of its lower feature dimension and complexity. There-fore, the proposed method can support credible practicability in the steganalysis scenario for real-time speech streams.

Acknowledgements. This research is funded by the National Natural Science Foundation of China under Grant Nos. U1536115 and U1405254, the Natural Science Foundation of Fujian Province of China under Grant No. 2018J01093, the Program for New Century Excellent Talents in Fujian Province University under Grant No. MJK2016-23, the Program for Outstanding Youth Scientific and Technological Talents in Fujian Province University under Grant No. MJK2015-54, the Promotion Program for Young and Middle-aged Teachers in Science and Technology Research of Huaqiao University under Grant No. ZQN-PY115, Program for Science and Technology Innovation Teams and Leading Talents of Huaqiao University under Grant No. 2014KJTD13, the Opening Project of Shanghai Key Laboratory of Integrated Administration Technologies for Information Security under Grant No. AGK201710 and the Subsidized Project for Postgraduates' Innovative Fund in Scientific Research of Huaqiao University No. 17014083010.

References

1. Mazurczyk, W., Lubacz, J.: LACK - a VoIP steganographic method. arXiv:08114138 Cs, November 2008
2. Kar, D.C., Mulkey, C.J.: A multi-threshold based audio steganography scheme. J. Inf. Secur. Appl. **23**(Supplement C), 54–67 (2015)
3. Djebbar, F., Ayad, B., Meraim, K.A., Hamam, H.: Comparative study of digital audio steganography techniques. EURASIP J. Audio Speech Music Process. **2012**(1), 25 (2012)
4. Cheddad, A., Condell, J., Curran, K., Mc Kevitt, P.: Digital image steganography: survey and analysis of current methods. Signal Process. **90**(3), 727–752 (2010)
5. Zhang, Y., Qin, C., Zhang, W., Liu, F., Luo, X.: On the fault-tolerant performance for a class of robust image steganography. Signal Process. **146**, 99–111 (2018)
6. Luo, X., et al.: Steganalysis of HUGO steganography based on parameter recognition of syndrome-Trellis-Codes. Multimed. Tools Appl. **75**(21), 13557–13583 (2016)
7. Mazurczyk, W.: VoIP steganography and its detection—a survey. ACM Comput. Surv. **46**(2), 20:1–20:21 (2013)
8. Tian, H., et al.: Optimal matrix embedding for voice-over-IP steganography. Signal Process. **117**, 33–43 (2015)
9. Sadek, M.M., Khalifa, A.S., Mostafa, M.G.M.: Video steganography: a comprehensive review. Multimed. Tools Appl. **74**(17), 7063–7094 (2015)
10. Neal, H., ElAarag, H.: A reliable covert communication scheme based on VoIP steganography. In: Shi, Y.Q. (ed.) Transactions on Data Hiding and Multimedia Security X. LNCS, vol. 8948, pp. 55–68. Springer, Heidelberg (2015). https://doi.org/10.1007/978-3-662-46739-8_4
11. Tian, H., Liu, J., Li, S.: Improving security of quantization-index-modulation steganography in low bit-rate speech streams. Multimed. Syst. **20**(2), 143–154 (2014)
12. Tian, H., et al.: Improved adaptive partial-matching steganography for voice over IP. Comput. Commun. **70**, 95–108 (2015)
13. Geiser, B., Vary, P.: High rate data hiding in ACELP speech codecs, pp. 4005–4008 (2008)
14. Ren, Y., Wu, H., Wang, L.: An AMR adaptive steganography algorithm based on minimizing distortion. Multimed. Tools Appl. **77**(10), 12095–12110 (2018)
15. Miao, H., Huang, L., Chen, Z., Yang, W., Al-Hawbani, A.: A new scheme for covert communication via 3G encoded speech. Comput. Electr. Eng. **38**(6), 1490–1501 (2012)
16. Luo, D., Yang, R., Huang, J.: Identification of AMR decompressed audio. Digit. Signal Process. **37**, 85–91 (2015)

17. Ekudden, E., Hagen, R., Johansson, I., Svedberg, J.: The adaptive multi-rate speech coder. In: IEEE Workshop on Speech Coding Proceedings. Model, Coders, and Error Criteria (Cat. No. 99EX351), pp. 117–119 (1999)
18. Miao, H., Huang, L., Shen, Y., Lu, X., Chen, Z.: Steganalysis of compressed speech based on Markov and entropy. In: Shi, Y.Q., Kim, H.-J., Pérez-González, F. (eds.) IWDW 2013. LNCS, vol. 8389, pp. 63–76. Springer, Heidelberg (2014). https://doi.org/10.1007/978-3-662-43886-2_5
19. Ren, Y., Cai, T., Tang, M., Wang, L.: AMR steganalysis based on the probability of same pulse position. IEEE Trans. Inf. Forensics Secur. 10(9), 1801–1811 (2015)
20. Ren, Y., Yang, J., Wang, J., Wang, L.: AMR steganalysis based on second-order difference of pitch delay. IEEE Trans. Inf. Forensics Secur. 12(6), 1345–1357 (2017)
21. Tian, H., et al.: Steganalysis of adaptive multi-rate speech using statistical characteristics of pulse pairs. Signal Process. 134(Supplement C), 9–22 (2017)
22. Liu, P., Li, S., Wang, H.: Steganography in vector quantization process of linear predictive coding for low-bit-rate speech codec. Multimed. Syst. 23(4), 485–497 (2017)
23. Liu, J., Tian, H., Lu, J., Chen, Y.: Neighbor-index-division steganography based on QIM method for G.723.1 speech streams. J. Ambient Intell. Humaniz. Comput. 7(1), 139–147 (2016)
24. Yan, S., Tang, G., Chen, Y.: Incorporating data hiding into G.729 speech codec. Multimed. Tools Appl. 75(18), 11493–11512 (2016)
25. Huang, Y., Liu, C., Tang, S., Bai, S.: Steganography integration into a low-bit rate speech codec. IEEE Trans. Inf. Forensics Secur. 7(6), 1865–1875 (2012)
26. Yan, S., Tang, G., Sun, Y.: Steganography for low bit-rate speech based on pitch period prediction. Appl. Res. Comput. 32(6), 1774–1777 (2015)
27. Xiao, B., Huang, Y., Tang, S.: An approach to information hiding in low bit-rate speech stream. In: IEEE Global Telecommunications Conference, IEEE GLOBECOM 2008, pp. 1–5 (2008)
28. Li, S., Jia, Y., Kuo, C.C.J.: Steganalysis of QIM steganography in low-bit-rate speech signals. IEEE/ACM Trans. Audio Speech Lang. Process. 25(5), 1011–1022 (2017)
29. Ghasemzadeh, H., Tajik Khass, M., Khalil Arjmandi, M.: Audio steganalysis based on reversed psychoacoustic model of human hearing. Digit. Signal Process. 51, 133–141 (2016)
30. Ma, Y., Luo, X., Li, X., Bao, Z., Zhang, Y.: Selection of rich model steganalysis features based on decision rough set α-positive region reduction. IEEE Trans. Circuits Syst. Video Technol. 29, 336–350 (2018)
31. Li, S., Tao, H., Huang, Y.: Detection of quantization index modulation steganography in G.723.1 bit stream based on quantization index sequence analysis. J. Zhejiang Univ. Sci. C 13(8), 624–634 (2012)
32. Manjunath, S., Gardner, W.: Variable rate speech coding, US7496505B2, 24 February 2009
33. Kodovský, J., Fridrich, J.: Calibration revisited. In: Proceedings of the 11th ACM Workshop on Multimedia and Security, New York, NY, USA, pp. 63–74 (2009)
34. Tian, H., et al.: Distributed steganalysis of compressed speech. Soft Comput. 21(3), 795–804 (2017)
35. Tian, H., et al.: Steganalysis of low bit-rate speech based on statistic characteristics of pulse positions. In: 10th International Conference on Availability, Reliability and Security, pp. 455–460 (2015)
36. Tian, H., et al.: Steganalysis of analysis-by-synthesis speech exploiting pulse-position distribution characteristics. Secur. Commun. Netw. 15(9), 2934–2944 (2016)

Network Risk Assessment
Based on Improved MulVAL
Framework and HMM

Chundong Wang[1,2], Kongbo Li[1,2(✉)], Yunkun Tian[3], and Xiaonan He[3]

[1] Key Laboratory of Computer Vision and System, Ministry of Education,
Tianjin University of Technology, Tianjin 300384, China
vincy3319833@163.com
[2] Tianjin Key Laboratory of Intelligence Computing and Novel Software Technology,
Ministry of Education, Tianjin University of Technology, Tianjin 300384, China
[3] Tianjin E-Hualu Information Technology Co., Ltd., Tianjin, China

Abstract. With the increasingly extensive applications of the network, the security of internal network of enterprises is facing more and more threats from the outside world, which implies the importance to master the network risk assessment skills. In the big data era, there are various security protection techniques and different types of group data. Meanwhile, Online Social Networks (OSNs) and Social Internet of Things (SIoT) are becoming popular patterns of meeting people and keeping in touch with friends [2,5]. However, risk assessment, as a bridge between security experts and network administrators, to some extent, whose accuracy can influence the judgment of administrators to the entire network state. In order to solve this problem, this essay proposes the improved MulVAL framework to optimize the risk assessment process by establishing the HMM model and the Bayesian model, which can improve the accuracy of the evaluation value. Firstly, behavior of the attacker is described in-depth by the attack graph generated through MulVAL. Then, with the quantitative evaluation conducted by the Common Vulnerability Scoring System, the nodes on the attack path can will be evaluated and the value will be further evaluated by the Bayesian model. Finally, by establishing the hidden Markov model, the corresponding parameters can be defined and the most likely probabilistic state transition sequence can be calculated by using the Viterbi algorithm to deduce the attack intent with the highest possibility.

Keywords: Network security assessment · HMM · MulVAL · Attack graph

1 Introduction

Increasing cyber attacks have attracted high attention in contemporary data security and network security studies. In wireless sensor network, target tracking [3] and data gathering and aggregating [7] has became more and more concerned.

J. Li et al. (Eds.): SPNCE 2019, LNICST 284, pp. 298–307, 2019.
https://doi.org/10.1007/978-3-030-21373-2_22

The main factor which causes this problem is that the large-scale computer network and enterprise network have relatively more or less vulnerabilities. External attackers can easily take advantage of these vulnerabilities; therefore, security policies are particularly important. A detailed vulnerability analysis of the complex network can cost a lot of time, funds, and resources, so the most effective strategy can be the network risk assessment. Based on above situations, two approaches have been considered: (1) assess the potential risk one by one; (2) detecting existing vulnerabilities which can be used by attackers through the overall deduction of a series of vulnerabilities.

Cyber attack is the process conducted by an attacker based on the attack conditions and goals and through implementing the information access and enhancing the information permission. The attack depends on the ability of attackers, experiments and the control environment. Prerequisites regarding cyber attacks are shortcoming in the contemporary network (or system). In addition, due to the inter-relations among these vulnerabilities, the host devices have established mutual trust, which can be used by cyber attackers to continue the attack after a specific completed attack. Therefore, cyber attacks are usually a complex, multi-step process. In order to explain the process of cyber attack, a number of researchers have proposed risk assessment methods by building security models of network systems through paradigms such as attack graphs.

In order to build such a comprehensive model regarding network attack relationships, a range of challenges have to be overcome. We have to correlate data from numerous resources, which include topology, vulnerabilities, and configurations, into an integrated model. The construction of the model representation and persistence must be flexible and can be easily extended.

However, it is very difficult to use only one method to process the system vulnerability analysis and generate optimal safety management strategies. Since the test result remains uncertain, it is not possible to accurately infer the attack intention. Thus, information and probabilities of the attack graph are further explored by using Hidden Markov Model. HMM is applied to detect uncertainties of those observable states and attack states. Then, a probabilistic mapping between network observations and attack states can be generated by HMM. Parameters of the model are redefined through the improved MulVAL framework and the maximum probability state transition sequence is further calculated by using the Viterbi algorithm. Based on these processes, the intention of attackers has been finally inferred. According to the experimental results, the maximum probability path with the network topology and configurations has been demonstrated.

The attack intention can be accurately inferred by this dual model. This method provides a good representation of network security administrators and equips them with some security strategies to overcome existing shortcoming in the enterprise network.

2   Related Work

Network security risk is propagative and network security risk will be the target in network through its multiple vulnerabilities between relevant services and hosts. Wang et al. [4] considered the difficulty of attack, the cost of reconfiguration of the network and the value of key information assets in the network based on the attribute attack graph, put forward the network security measurement method. Feng et al. [1] put reliability ideas into the attack graph to analyze the vulnerability of the network. There may be a circular path in the attack graph, when the network security probability calculation is carried out, the repeated calculation of the cyclic node probability value will result in the error probability value which does not match the actual situation. Most literatures did not consider this situation.

Ou et al. [8] first proposed that one of the reasons for the complex attack pattern is a cyclic path problem in the attack graph, and it is found that the circular path in the graph can not be solved simply by deleting some atomic attacks, otherwise some important unconfirmed attacks. Wang [6] discussed the impact of three different types of circular paths on the risk assessment, and eliminated the loops by removing the succeeding nodes and edges of each node in loop path, the method is very complicated to deal with the nodes in the loop path. At the same time, Wang does not give a detailed algorithm to calculate the probability of each node, nor does it consider the probability error calculation caused by the correlation between infiltration. Attack path analysis technology, takes forward search mode and depth-first search strategy to find the effective attack path of each node, through a collection of intermediate nodes to prevent the generation of a circular path, the algorithm's time complexity is exponential, nor does it apply to large-scale networks; The attack graph can statically evaluate the security of the network system, but it is difficult to dynamically deduce the attack intent and evaluate the next attack state based on the current system.

In this paper, these ideas of probability dependence to the improved MulVAL framework are purposed, and the probability generated by improved MulVAL will be more realistic in representing the real network environment. Also, the use of HMM would be expanded, not only to establish the probability of mapping between the network observation and attack state, but also calculate the use of HMM maximum probability state transition sequence. This framework will be used to infer the attacker's attack intent.

3   Model Establishment

3.1   Common Vulnerability Scoring System

Common Vulnerability Scoring System consists of three metrics: baseline score, time score, and environment score. Each group produces a scoring range from 0 to 10. The benchmark score metric represents the inherent and basic characteristics of the constant time and the vulnerability of user environment. The value of the time scale measure is the change in the value of vulnerability over time. The environmental score measure is fragile depending on the particular implementation environment.

The following is the CVSS evaluation system official manual to provide the score evaluation equation: A total of three parts are in the fractional compositions.

3.2   Hidden Markov Model

Basic Theory. The hidden Markov model is a model with a double stochastic process, where the first stochastic process is the Markov chain, which describes the state sequence. Another random process describes the relationship between the state and the observed variable. The state is not visible to the observer. And the state and its characteristics can only be observed by a random process, which reflects the relationship between the state and the observed variables. Implicit state S: Set up a set S = [S1, ..., SS], where S is a model of a set of hidden states. Once the network system state is exploited for exploits, the S would be denoted this event. For example: = Exploit (Ha, Hw, Vi) that the host Ha through the loop-hole Vi on the host Hw attack, s is the number of state in the model. These states satisfy the Markov nature, which is the actual implied state in the Markov model. These states are usually not obtained by direct observation (E.g., S1, S2, S3, etc.).

Define observable state Y: Associated with the implicit state in the model can be obtained by direct observation (E.g., Y1, Y2, Y3, ..., YT, etc.), the number of observable states does not necessarily coincide with the number of implied states.

Define The initial state probability matrix π The initial state probability matrix π = [p1, p2, p3] is the initial state distribution, for example, t = 1, P (S1) = p1, P (S2) = p2, P (S3) = p3.

Define state transition probability matrix A that describes the transition probability between the states in the HMM model.

Define the state transition probability distribution matrix A: The observation set V indicates the exploit used by the attacker. For example, V1 is CAN-2003-0252.

Define observed state transition probability matrix B: Let N be the number of implicit states, and M be the number of observable states, then, B = {Mv /)}.

Define Oi: The probability of observing the state is Oi at the time t, the implied state is Sj.

Define tri-tuple λ: We use λ = (A, B, π) tri-tuple to concisely represent a hidden Markov model. The hidden Markov model is actually an extension of the standard Markov model, adding a set of observable states and the probabilistic relationship between these states and implicit states.

Define DVi: Indicating that the possibility of being attacked is the use of vulnerability Vi, it is clear that the greater the value, the greater the probability of occurrence, the attack will be less difficult. The system state is shifted from state S0 (normal state) to S1, and a new vulnerability has occurred. This process continues until the target state SS is achieved with the observation VS. Therefore, if Vi is successfully used, then the system state will turn to S.

Define DWi: Its weight of the system state will go through the loophole vi to the Si state. Hidden state setting S = S1, ..., SS. If the system state is transferred from state S to SS by exploiting the vulnerability, then the corresponding weight is IS. If the system state transitions from Vulnerability V1, V2, ..., Vs to another state SS, its corresponding weights are I1, I2, .., IS.

The state transition probability distribution matrix A formula is shown as follows:

Define the observed state transition probability matrix B. The detailed parameters are calculated as follows:

$$A = \{Aij\} = \left\{ Wj / \sum_{t=1}^{n} Wt, Si \xrightarrow{Vj} Sj \right\} \tag{1}$$

When the system state is S, the attacker will attack the target successfully through the vulnerability. So we set the observations of these loopholes Vi to 1; When the system state is Si, the system state cannot be transferred from Si to Sj through Vulnerability V, then we put the probability to DVi accordingly; When the system state is Si, the system state can be transferred from Si to Sj through Vulnerability V, then we put the probability to DVi+DVi*DVj accordingly.

Finally, the data of the probability matrix was standardized.

Viterbi Algorithm. Viterbi algorithm is a dynamic programming algorithm. It is used to find the Viterbi path-implicit state sequence, which is most likely to produce the sequence of observed events, especially in the Markov information source context and the hidden Markov model. The Viterbi algorithm is a special but most widely used dynamic programming algorithm, which can solve the shortest path problem in any graph by using dynamic programming. And the Viterbi algorithm is proposed for the shortest path problem of a special graph - directed graph of the fence network. We want to find the hidden state sequences behind the observation sequence, and the hidden sequence of the largest probability of occurrence of the observation sequence, that is the result we need to find out.

The observation space is O, the state space is S, the observation sequence is Y, A is the transfer matrix, where Aij is the transition probability from the state Si to Sj, and the state transition probability matrix B is observed, where the state is observed in the state Si The probability of Sj, the initial probability of K, and the path X is the state sequence of the observed value Y. Output: Most likely implied state sequence X.

In the approach proposed by Jake, the introduction of CVSS and CCSS will represent a more realistic model. In order to calculate the vulnerability variables, their probabilities can be calculated using CVSS. For CVE-ID for CAN-2002-0392, the vulnerability has been confirmed and its identity becomes CVE-2002-0392: Apache packet encoding memory corruption vulnerability. The basic vector for this vulnerability is (AV: N/AC: L/Au: N/C: P/I: P/A: P).

Through the above basic vector, the formula (2), (3), (4) were be calculated the following results:

$$Base = (0.6 * Imp + 0.4 * Exp - 1.5) * f(Imp), f(Imp) = 1.176 \qquad (2)$$

$$Imp = 10.41 * (1 - (1 - ConImp) * (1 - IntImp) * (1 - AvaImp)) \qquad (3)$$

$$Exp = 20 * AccessComplexity * Authentication * AccessVector \qquad (4)$$

Define three node types as vL for LEAF nodes, vA for AND nodes, and vO for OR nodes, then the probability of each node p(vL), p(vA), p(vO), in MulVAL attack graphs G can be derived using general theory of probability, as follows (5), (6), (7).

$$p(vL) = p(v)(for LEAF nodes) \qquad (5)$$

$$p(vA) = p(v) \prod_{i=1}^{N} p(vI)(Conjunctive probability for AND nodes) \qquad (6)$$

$$p(vO) = p(v) \prod_{i=1}^{N} p(vI)(Disjunctive probability for OR nodes) \qquad (7)$$

CAN-2002-0392:
Exp = 20 × AV × AC × Au = 20 × 1 × 0.71 × 0.704 = 9.9968
Imp = 10.41 * (1 − (1 − ConfImpact) * (1 − IntegImpact) * (1 − AvailImpact))
= 1.041 × (1 − (1 − 0.275) × (1 − 0275) × (1 − 0275)) = 6.443
Base = (0.6Imp + (0.4Exp − 1.5)) × f (Imp) = ((0.6 × 6.443) + (0.4 × 9.9968) − 1.5) × 1.176 = 7.5
CVE-2009-3586:
Exp = 20 × AV × AC × Au = 20 × 1 × 0.71 × 0.704 = 9.9968
Imp = (1 − Availability) × (1 − Availability)) = 1.041 × (1 − (1 − 0.275) × (1 − 0.275) × (1 − 0.275)) = 6.443
Base = (0.6Imp + (0.4Exp − 1.5)) × f (Imp) = ((0.6 × 6.443) + (0.4 × 9.9968) − 1.5) × 1.176 = 7.5
CVE-2003-0252
Exp = 20 × AV × AC × Au = 20 × 1 × 0.71 × 0.704 = 9.9968
Imp = (1 − A) × (1 − A)) = 10.41 × (1 − (1 − 0) × (1 − 0) × (1 − 0)) = 10.41
Base = (0.6Imp + (0.4Exp − 1.5)) × f (Imp) = ((0.6 × 10.41) + (0.4 × 9.9968) − 1.5) × 1.176 = 10
CVE-2009-4776
Exp = 20 × AV × AC × Au = 20 × 0.61 × 0.71 × 0.704 = 8.6
Imp = 10.41 * (1 − (1 − ConfImpact) * (1 − IntegImpact) * (1 − AvailImpact))
= 10.41 × (1 − (1 − 0) × (1 − 0) × (1 − 0)) = 10.41
Base = (0.6Imp + (0.4Exp − 1.5)) × f (Imp) = ((0.6 × 10.41) + (0.4 × 8.6) C 1.5) × 1.176 = 9.3
Since MulVAL's attack graph shows that the probability of all LEAF nodes or configuration nodes is 1.0, this means that each variable in the LEAF node

is assumed to exist and manipulated as an attacking medium. This is not a real case, so in this article the second method of Jake's approach was implemented. Because the display network state does not exist can take advantage of vulnerability variables. If there is a loophole in a node, the probability of other nodes will be higher loopholes. This means that the vulnerability of node N1 depends on the vulnerability at node N3, and the probability vulnerability at node N1 may increase or exceed the original possibility. Node N3 has identity CAN-2002-0392, node N1 has identity CAN-2003-0252. If these two vulnerabilities can be used remotely, access rights state was changed. Thus, the result was came out:

N3 vul = P(CAN-2002-0392) = 0.75

Node N3: vulExists (webServer, 'CAN-2002-0392', httpd, remoteExploit, priv Escalation): 0.75

N1 vul = P(CAN-2003-0252) * P(CVE-2009-4436) = 0.85

Node N1: vulExists (fileserver, 'CAN-2003-0252', mountd, sqlInject, priv Escalation): 0.85

N2 vul = P(CVE-2009-3586) * P(CVE-2009-4251) = 0.8

Node N2: vulExists (webServer, 'CVE-2009-3586', httpd, remoteExploit, priv Escalation): 0.8

N4 vul = P(CVE-2009-4776) * P(CVE-2007-6432) = 0.7

Node N4: vulExists (webServer, 'CVE-2009-4776', httpd, bufferOver, priv Escalation): 0.7

4   Experiment and Analysis

4.1   Experimental Environment

In the network topology, there are three regions (internet, dmz, internal). The Internet is considered a threat from an external network, a potential attacker; the middle area is a DMZ (non-military area), a web server (Web Server) placed in the DMZ and the external network Firewall is fw1; internal (internal), placed a file server (File Server) and a workstation (Work Station), a firewall placed between the network and DMZ. External accesses to the web server through the internet, and cannot directly access the workstations within the network.

4.2   Simulation Attack Flow Graph and Vulnerability Information

The simulation values and descriptions used in our simulation experiments are shown in Table 1.

The weight of each vulnerability would be computed and generated, and the im-proved MulVAL evaluation score which we purposed used as the weight of the new vulnerability. Its values are shown in Table 2.

Table 1. Vulnerability and descriptions

Host	Node	Vulnerability
Web server	V1	CAN-2003-0252
Web server	V2	CVE-2009-3586
File server	V3	CAN-2002-0392
Work station	V4	CVE-2009-4776

4.3   HMM

According to the network topology and network configuration, the attacker wants to attack the target with vulnerabilities. Therefore the intention of the attacker will be extracted.

S is the system state space, S shows the state of the system in the attacker to make the attack process, the system state of the process of change. Where T0 is the initial state, indicating that the attacker is ready to attack, this time the system is not at-tacked. S1 indicates that the attacker has compromised the web server through the V1 vulnerability. S2 indicates that the attacker had a buffer overflow attack on the web server through the V2 vulnerability. S3 indicates that the attacker by taking the web server and then attack the file server, using V3 vulnerabilities. S4 indicates that the attacker utilize the file server and then attack the workstation with V4 vulnerabilities.

According to the method mentioned in Sect. 3, the HMM parameters were calculated as follows:

$$A = \begin{bmatrix} 0 & 0 & 0.47 & 0.53 \\ 0 & 0 & 0.47 & 0.53 \\ 0 & 0 & 0 & 1 \\ 0 & 0 & 0 & 1 \end{bmatrix}$$

$$B = \begin{bmatrix} 0.28 & 0.24 & 0.32 & 0.32 \\ 0.24 & 0.28 & 0.32 & 0.30 \\ 0.24 & 0.28 & 0.22 & 0.22 \\ 0.24 & 0.24 & 0.14 & 0.16 \end{bmatrix}$$

As shown in the HMM state transition diagram, S0 can be directly converted to SI, S2 or S3. We use python to implement the Viterbi algorithm, enter the observation sequence VI, V2, V3, V4 and model parameters $= (A, B, \pi)$. The results are as follows:

A. If $= (1, 0, 0, 0)$, the optimal state sequence is S1, S2, S3, S4, the probability is 0.03561;
B. If $= (0, 1, 0, 0)$, the optimal state sequence is S2, S4, the probability is 0.031584;
C. If $= (0, 0, 1, 0)$, the optimal state sequence is S3, S4, the probability is 0.0576;

Summarize all the results to arrive at the most likely sequence, we can see the system state transition sequence is S3, S4. Therefore, the most likely path is to crack the file server FS through exploit V3 and V4. The best strategy is to fix vulnerabilities CVE-2009-4776 and CAN-2002-0392.

The algorithm of Liu was implemented. He considers the difficulty of calculating the vulnerability as a probability of determining the state transition, using the state transition probability directly as evidence of the decision of the network security administrator. The state transition probability matrix is calculated using the Liu method. The state transition probability matrix is as follows:

$$C = \begin{bmatrix} 0 & 0.34 & 0 & 0.24 & 0.42 \\ 0 & 1 & 0 & 0 & 0 \\ 0 & 0 & 0 & 0.36 & 0.64 \\ 0 & 0 & 0 & 1 & 0 \\ 0 & 0 & 0 & 0 & 1 \end{bmatrix}$$

5   Conclusion

The generation of attack graphs is part of the network risk assessment, and the model of the attack network makes network assessment more accurate. From the perspective of network experts and network administrators, the implementation of this model allows them to take more effective measures with changes between networks and threats from external networks. Based on the improved MulVAL framework, this paper uses the Viterbi algorithm to deduce the most probable state transition sequence, which is the path of the most likely attack through simulation experiments. Also, this paper uses the combination of improved Mul-VAL framework and Markov Model to make a more accurate prediction of the entire network and risk assessment.

Table 2. Vulnerability and weight

Vulnerability	Improved MulVAL assessment score	Weight
V1	0.85	0.85
V2	0.8	0.8
V3	0.75	0.75
V4	0.7	0.7

This approach is not easy to deploy in the super large scale network environment, the future work is researching about how to work effectively with these two models deployed in a larger network environment, or in the real business network.

References

1. Feng, P., Lian, Y., Dai, Y.: A vulnerability model of distributed systems based on reliability theory. J. Softw. **17**(7), 1633–1640 (2006)
2. Jiang, W., Wang, G., Bhuiyan, M.Z.A., Wu, J.: Understanding graph-based trust evaluation in online social networks: methodologies and challenges. ACM Comput. Surv. **49**, 10:1–10:35 (2016)
3. Li, Y., Wang, G., Nie, L., Wang, Q.: Collaborative target tracking in wireless sensor networks. J. Ad Hoc Sens. Wirel. Netw. **23**, 117–135 (2014)
4. Wang, L., Singhal, A., Jajodia, S.: Toward measuring network security using attack graphs. In: Proceedings of the 3rd International Workshop on Quality of Protection (QoP), pp. 49–54 (2007)
5. Shen, J., Zhou, T., Wei, F., Sun, X., Xiang, Y.: Privacy-preserving and lightweight key agreement protocol for V2G in the social Internet of Things. IEEE Internet Things J. (2017). https://doi.org/10.1109/JIOT.2017.2775248
6. Wang, L., Islam, T., Long, T., Singhal, A., Jajodia, S.: An attack graph-based probabilistic security metric. In: Atluri, V. (ed.) DBSec 2008. LNCS, vol. 5094, pp. 283–296. Springer, Heidelberg (2008). https://doi.org/10.1007/978-3-540-70567-3_22
7. Xing, X., Xie, D., Wang, G.: Energy-balanced data gathering and aggregating in WSNs: a compressed sensing scheme. Int. J. Distrib. Sens. Netw. **2015**, 1–10 (2015)
8. Ou, X., Boyer, W.F., McQueen, M.A.: A scalable approach to attack graph generation. In: Proceedings of the 13th ACM Conference on Computer and Communications Security (CCS), pp. 336–345 (2006)

Internet of Things and Cloud Computing

FIREWORK: Fog Orchestration for Secure IoT Networks

Maryam Vahabi$^{(\boxtimes)}$, Hossein Fotouhi, and Mats Björkman

School of Innovation, Design, and Technology, Mälardalen University,
Västerås, Sweden
{maryam.vahabi,hossein.fotouhi,mats.bjorkman}@mdh.se

Abstract. Recent advances in Internet of Things (IoT) connectivity
have made IoT devices prone to Cyber attacks. Moreover, vendors are
eager to provide autonomous and open source device, which in turn adds
more security threat to the system. In this paper, we consider network
traffic attack, and provide a Fog-assisted solution, dubbed as FIRE-
WORK, that reduces risk of security attacks by periodically monitoring network traffic, and applying traffic isolation techniques to overcome
network congestion and performance degradation.

1 Introduction

Internet of Things (IoT) considers billions of devices and objects connected to
Internet in order to collect and exchange information to offer various application
domains, such as health monitoring, industrial automation, home automation
and environmental monitoring. IoT devices are equipped with sensor(s) and
processing power, enabling them to be deployed in many environments [23].
The research and development in IoT devices in both academia and industry
have failed to provide secure devices. Thus, security experts have warned for
the potential risk of having large numbers of unsecured devices connected to the
Internet [15].

In December 2013, a researcher at a security company (Proofpoint) found
the first IoT botnet. According to Proofpoint, more than 25% of the botnet was
generated by devices other than computers, including smart TVs, baby monitors,
and other household appliances. Recently, New Hampshire-based provider of
domain name services (Dyn) experienced service outages as a result of what
appeared to be well coordinated attack [12]. On October 21, 2016, many websites
including Twitter, Netflix, Spotify, Airbnb, Reddit, Etsy, SoundCloud, and The
New York Times were reported inaccessible by users caused by a distributed
denial of service attack (DDoS) attack using a network of consumer devices
from the IoT.

Many security issues and challenges have been identified in the literature
that focus on various IoT standard protocols at the PHY, MAC, network and
application layers [10]. Some of the security issues are known as authentication,

© ICST Institute for Computer Sciences, Social Informatics and Telecommunications Engineering 2019
Published by Springer Nature Switzerland AG 2019. All Rights Reserved
J. Li et al. (Eds.): SPNCE 2019, LNICST 284, pp. 311–317, 2019.
https://doi.org/10.1007/978-3-030-21373-2_23

access control, confidentiality, privacy, trust, secure middleware, mobile security and policy enforcement [18]. However, addressing each of these issues in traditional IoT architectures require high bandwidth utilization and high processing and memory capabilities.

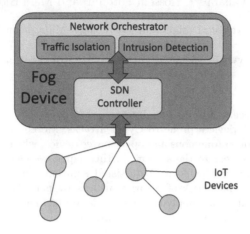

Fig. 1. Orchestration in Fog-based IoT networks.

Fog computing has been introduced to bring the provision of services closer to the end-users and IoT devices by pooling the available computing, storage and networking resources at the edge of the network [6,22]. The decentralized computing architecture provides the opportunity of collaboration between IoT devices and the edge devices to reduce the processing burden on resource-constrained devices, reaching latency requirements of delay-sensitive applications and overcome the bandwidth limitations for centralized services [26].

To the best of our knowledge, the research on security considering the Fog computing architecture for IoT devices is still in its preliminary stages. In this paper, we consider the coexistence of IoT and Fog devices in the network. We tackle security issue as one of the main elements of different IoT applications. **We provide an idea to overcome security threat imposed by network traffic attacks by considering Fog-based IoT networks.**

Coordinating and orchestrating of future IoT networks with heterogeneous devices is of paramount importance. It is common to experience devices generating different types of traffic (low or high, periodic or sporadic). It is nontrivial to manage the traffic without a central management unit, while being capable of detecting suspicious traffic. There are some related works in the literature, where the main focus is on the design of a generic protocol stack [21], which is more suitable for traditional network architecture with the IoT-Cloud layers. Moreover, such solutions will add more cost to the system as each IoT device requires higher level of intelligence. This paper concentrates on a novel orchestration architecture based on using Software Defined Networking (SDN) controller as one of the major components of a Fog computing architecture for IoT networks. The proposed orchestration approach launches upon detecting a security threat in the network, where part of the suspicious traffic will be isolated. Figure 1 depicts the general architecture of a Fog-based IoT network, where the network orchestrator runs network management in terms of intrusion detection as well as traffic isolation.

The main contributions of this work for reducing network security attacks through network traffic are: (1) the need for exploiting a run-time intrusion detection algorithm, and (2) the need for running a traffic isolation algorithm upon detecting an intrusion in the network. These algorithms are currently rough ideas that are under implementation.

We have defined few research questions (RQ) that are necessary to answer while designing and implementing such intrusion detection algorithms:

RQ1. *How to identify an intrusion in an IoT network?* In order to prevent and confront a security threat, it is crucial to devise a mechanism to identify intrusion in the network. There are various ways that the system may have vulnerabilities and holes. **This work limits the intrusion attacks to additional traffic that leads to network congestion.**

RQ2. *What are the benefits of security approach in a three-tiered network architecture (Iot-Fog-Cloud) compared with a traditional two-tiered network architecture (IoT-Cloud)?* Conventional security mechanisms were considering IoT devices and the Cloud, while current mechanisms consider existence of Fog devices in the middle with the purpose of increasing security, while providing reliability and timeliness.

RQ3. *How to collect network traffic and apply new rules on traffic isolation while keeping low overhead?* It is naïve to devise complex algorithms for IoT networks as they have resource limitations. It is important to propose simple yet efficient security algorithms to monitor network traffic in real-time, and then react to changes in a timely manner, while adding low overhead to the system.

RQ4. *How to verify the feasibility of the proposed algorithm in a real environment?* It is important to conduct real-world tests by applying the algorithm to the network, while varying network condition.

2   Related Research Topics

In this section, we briefly address some of the most relevant topics to the research area.

Security in IoT Networks. The Internet of Things integrates various sensors, objects and smart nodes, capable of communicating through Internet connection [3]. IoT devices are able to deliver lightweight of data, accessing and authorizing cloud-based resources for collecting and extracting data. IoT nodes are widely used in different application domains, ranging from healthcare to transportation [5]. Many business opportunities have been created with IoT devices since there will be more closer interaction between the end users and manufacturers and service providers. Security issues, such as privacy of data, access control, secure communication and secure storage are becoming important challenges in IoT applications [25]. Rapid growth of IoT devices and applications have led to the deployment of several vulnerable and insecure nodes and networks [9]. Moreover, traditional IoT architectures with user-driven security architectures are of little use in object-driven IoT networks [1]. Thus, new techniques and procedures are required to reside in IoT networks. FIREWORK focuses on the security challenge of IoT networks by considering a different perspective on how efficiently and timely detecting intrusions in the network and how to confront the identified attack.

Fog Computing Architecture. Fog/Edge computing is an architecture organized by the networking edge devices and clients to provide computing services for customers or applications, locating between networking central servers and end-users [4,24]. In Fog computing, massive data generated by IoT devices can be processed at the network edge instead of transmitting to the centralized Cloud infrastructure in order to conserve more bandwidth and energy [16,17]. Since Fog computing is organized in a distributed manner, it is possible to get faster response and better quality in comparison to Cloud computing [16]. Fog computing is more suitable to be integrated within the IoT network, while providing more efficient and secure services for large number of end users [4]. This paper considers Fog computing architecture for IoT network, and defines security threats and solutions within this novel architecture.

SDN Controller and Orchestration. Following the recent innovations brought about by the Cloud computing, current advances in communication infrastructures show an unprecedent central role of software-based solutions [8,14,19]. The concept of SDN decouples software-based network control and management planes from the hardware-based forwarding plane, turning traditional vendor locked-in infrastructures into communication platforms that are fully programmable via a standardized interface [11]. This interface provides a unified management and orchestration of end-to-end services across multiple domains. It is possible to separate the data plane and control plane in IoT networks, allowing the IoT controller to program the network with the aim of guaranteeing specific quality of services.

SDN orchestration often involves coordinating software actions with an SDN Controller, which can be built using open source technologies such as OpenDaylight [7]. The controller can be programmed to make automated decisions in case of network congestion, faults and security threats. SDN-based orchestration can use network protocols including OpenFlow [13] and IP-based networking. The most important element of SDN orchestration is the ability to monitor network security threats. For this reason, it is considered as one of the most promising growth areas of SDN networks. FIREWORK provides network orchestration component for network management in terms of security. This is a novel approach that has been neglected in IoT networks.

Security in Fog Computing. Fog computing technology bridges ·the gap between the Cloud and IoT devices, while enabling enhanced security, decreased bandwidth, and reduced latency [4]. Fog is considered as a nontrivial extension of the Cloud, and thus it is inevitable that some security challenges will continue to persist [2]. Fog computing can introduce new security challenges due to its distinct characteristics such as mobility support. These challenges might impact the adaptation of Fog computing into the IoT network. On the other hand, Fog computing offers an ideal platform to address many security issues in the IoT. Fog nodes are represented as proxy nodes that provide enhanced security support that IoT nodes are unable to provide [20]. The research on security in Fog computing for IoT networks is still in its early stage, and thus, we are aiming to enhance this line of research by initiating novel ideas.

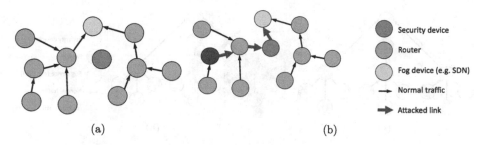

Fig. 2. Network monitoring in a Fog-based IoT network, (a) without security attach and (b) with security attack.

3   Fog-Based Security Solution

The proposed Fog-based security solution, also known as FIREWORK, has two steps, where the first step stands for detecting attacks, and the second step focuses on recovering the network.

Network Monitoring. It is crucial to devise and develop algorithms in the SDN controller in order to (i) detect attacks in the networks, and (ii) re-route traffic through security devices to confirm that devices (hosts and routers) are secure. There are various techniques for detecting attacks in the network. Security threats may involve increasing network traffic and degrading network performance. Keeping a history of network performance is a need to identify sudden increase or drop in network traffic. Upon detecting suspicious data packets, SDN controller is supposed to route network traffic through security devices. It is important to note that placement of security devices in the network will affect our approach in terms of timeliness.

Figure 2(a) depicts the case, where Fog devices detect normal traffic in all links. Apparently, the traffic from each device may vary from a low threshold (T_l) to a high threshold (T_h). However, there are some cases that there is a sudden change in one link, meaning that either there is an alarm message or a security threat. It is not trivial to distinguish between these situations, unless re-routing part of the traffic through a security device, which has been shown in Fig. 2(b).

Traffic Isolation. One of the main advantages of Fog nodes is the ability to maintain network traffic shunt system, where it is possible to isolate part of the network that has security threat. It is also possible to separate a special traffic from a part of the network, which is more suspicious. SDN controller provides the opportunity to allocate network slicing and dynamically moving traffic or eliminating traffic. Figure 3 shows two examples, where in the left figure all routers can communicate with each other, either directly or through the Fog device. However, upon detecting a security threat, Fog device abandons part of the network, eliminating network traffic spreading the network. This is the first step in network security before resolving the problem.

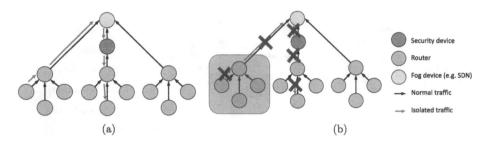

(a)   (b)

Fig. 3. Traffic isolation after detecting a security attack; (a) a network without traffic isolation, and (b) a network with traffic isolation.

Acknowledgment. The work presented in this paper is supported by the Swedish Foundation for Strategic Research via the project Future Factories in the Cloud (FiC), and by the Swedish Research Council (Vetenskapsrådet), through starting grant no. 2018-04582 via the MobiFog project, and from the Swedish Knowledge Foundation (KKS) throughout Prospekt project (FlexiHealth) and the ESS-H plus research profile.

References

1. Alaba, F.A., Othman, M., Hashem, I.A.T., Alotaibi, F.: Internet of Things security: a survey. J. Netw. Comput. Appl. **88**, 10–28 (2017)
2. Alrawais, A., Alhothaily, A., Hu, C., Cheng, X.: Fog computing for the Internet of Things: security and privacy issues. IEEE Internet Comput. **21**(2), 34–42 (2017)
3. Ambrosin, M., et al.: On the feasibility of attribute-based encryption on Internet of Things devices. IEEE Micro **36**(6), 25–35 (2016)
4. Bonomi, F., Milito, R., Zhu, J., Addepalli, S.: Fog computing and its role in the Internet of Things. In: Proceedings of the First Edition of the MCC Workshop on Mobile Cloud Computing, pp. 13–16. ACM (2012)
5. Chifor, B.C., Bica, I., Patriciu, V.V., Pop, F.: A security authorization scheme for smart home Internet of Things devices. Future Gener. Comput. Syst. **86**, 740–749 (2018)
6. Fog Computing the Internet of Things: Extend the Cloud to Where the Things Are. Cisco White Paper (2015)

7. OpenDaylight Consortium, et al.: OpenDaylight (2013)
8. Fotouhi, H., Vahabi, M., Ray, A., Björkman, M.: SDN-TAP: an SDN-based traffic aware protocol for wireless sensor networks. In: 2016 IEEE 18th International Conference on e-Health Networking, Applications and Services (Healthcom), pp. 1–6. IEEE (2016)
9. Giaretta, A., Balasubramaniam, S., Conti, M.: Security vulnerabilities and countermeasures for target localization in bio-nanothings communication networks. IEEE Trans. Inf. Forensics Secur. **11**(4), 665–676 (2016)
10. Granjal, J., Monteiro, E., Silva, J.S.: A secure interconnection model for IPv6 enabled wireless sensor networks. In: Wireless Days (WD), 2010 IFIP, pp. 1–6. IEEE (2010)
11. Hu, F., Hao, Q., Bao, K.: A survey on software-defined network and openflow: from concept to implementation. IEEE Commun. Surv. Tutorials **16**(4), 2181–2206 (2014)
12. Lam, B., Larose, C.: How did the Internet of Things Allow the Latest Attack on the Internet? (2016)
13. McKeown, N., et al.: Openflow: enabling innovation in campus networks. ACM SIGCOMM Comput. Commun. Rev. **38**(2), 69–74 (2008)
14. Peterson, L., et al.: Central office re-architected as a data center. IEEE Commun. Mag. **54**(10), 96–101 (2016)
15. Poslad, S., Hamdi, M., Abie, H.: Adaptive security and privacy management for the Internet of Things (ASPI 2013). In: Proceedings of the 2013 ACM Conference on Pervasive and Ubiquitous Computing Adjunct Publication, pp. 373–378. ACM (2013)
16. Pu, Q., et al.: Low latency geo-distributed data analytics. In: ACM SIGCOMM Computer Communication Review, vol. 45, pp. 421–434. ACM (2015)
17. Shi, W., Cao, J., Zhang, Q., Li, Y., Xu, L.: Edge computing: vision and challenges. IEEE Internet Things J. **3**(5), 637–646 (2016)
18. Sicari, S., Rizzardi, A., Grieco, L.A., Coen-Porisini, A.: Security, privacy and trust in Internet of Things: the road ahead. Comput. Netw. **76**, 146–164 (2015)
19. Soares, J., et al.: Toward a telco cloud environment for service functions. IEEE Commun. Mag. **53**(2), 98–106 (2015)
20. Stojmenovic, I., Wen, S., Huang, X., Luan, H.: An overview of fog computing and its security issues. Concurrency Comput. Pract. Exp. **28**(10), 2991–3005 (2016)
21. Vahabi, M., Fotouhi, H., Björkman, M.: Network management in heterogeneous wireless sensor network applications. In: 2016 3rd Smart Cloud Networks & Systems (SCNS), pp. 1–6. IEEE (2016)
22. Vaquero, L.M., Rodero-Merino, L.: Finding your way in the fog: towards a comprehensive definition of fog computing. ACM SIGCOMM Comput. Commun. Rev. **44**(5), 27–32 (2014)
23. Yang, Y., Wu, L., Yin, G., Li, L., Zhao, H.: A survey on security and privacy issues in Internet-of-Things. IEEE Internet Things J. **4**(5), 1250–1258 (2017)
24. Yi, S., Li, C., Li, Q.: A survey of fog computing: concepts, applications and issues. In: Proceedings of the 2015 Workshop on Mobile Big Data, pp. 37–42. ACM (2015)
25. Zarpelão, B.B., Miani, R.S., Kawakani, C.T., de Alvarenga, S.C.: A survey of intrusion detection in Internet of Things. J. Netw. Comput. Appl. **84**, 25–37 (2017)
26. Zhang, T.: Fog Boosts Capabilities to Add More Things Securely to the Internet. Cisco Blogs (2016)

An Effective Encryption Scheme on Outsourcing Data for Query on Cloud Platform

Jianchao Tang[1]([✉]), Shaojing Fu[1,2], and Ming Xu[1]

[1] National University Of Defense Technology, Changsha 410073, China
tangjianchao14@nudt.edu.cn
[2] Sate Key Laboratory of Cryptology, Beijing 100878, China

Abstract. Outsourcing encrypted data to cloud platforms is widely adopted by users, but there are some problems existing in it: one is that encrypted databases only provide limited types of queries for users. Meanwhile, in the deterministic encryption, users' encrypted data is subject to the frequency attack easily. Besides, users' data privacy is disclosed to cloud platforms when their data is updated. To address these problems, in this paper, we propose an effective encryption scheme on outsourcing data for query on cloud platforms. In our scheme, users' data is encrypted according to all possible queries to meet users' diverse query demands. Furthermore, a double AES encryption method is adopted to cope with the frequency attack existing in deterministic encryption. To protect users' privacy when their data is updated, a neighbor rows exchange method is designed in our scheme. The theoretical analysis and comparative experiments demonstrate the effectiveness of our scheme.

Keywords: Cloud platform · Encrypted database · Possible queries · Double AES encryption · Neighbor rows exchange

1 Introduction

With the maturity of cloud storage technology and the proliferation of cloud platforms, more and more users outsource their data to cloud platforms [2,7,19,22,23]. For one thing, cloud platforms have enough resources to store enormous users' data, which can greatly decrease the storage burden on users' side. For another thing, cloud platforms provide the accessing interfaces for users, where users can access their data easily. However, for users, cloud servers are not trustworthy [1,13,18,21]. If users directly upload their data to cloud platforms, the sensitive information in their data will be exposed to cloud servers, which results in users' privacy disclosure. To avoid this case, users usually encrypt their data before outsourcing it. Since users' encryption keys are private, cloud servers can not decrypt users' encrypted data and users' privacy is protected.

© ICST Institute for Computer Sciences, Social Informatics and Telecommunications Engineering 2019
Published by Springer Nature Switzerland AG 2019. All Rights Reserved
J. Li et al. (Eds.): SPNCE 2019, LNICST 284, pp. 318–332, 2019.
https://doi.org/10.1007/978-3-030-21373-2_24

Common encryption techniques adopted by users include deterministic encryption [3,4], order-preserving encryption [5,6] and homomorphic encryption [8,15]. For deterministic encryption, its algorithm is deterministic, which can always generate the same ciphertext for the same message. Therefore, users can leverage deterministic encryption to realize equality check on encrypted data. Order-preserving encryption is another encryption technique where ciphertexts can preserve the order of plaintexts. This means that users can realize complex operations on encrypted data by order-preserving encryption (e.g., range query). Besides, homomorphic encryption allows users to aggregate their encrypted data on cloud platforms. In this encryption technique, the calculation results on ciphertexts after decryption is same as the working directly on the raw data. Although users' privacy is protected under these encryption techniques, there exists another problem for users: how to query for their encrypted data effectively.

To address the above problem, an early method is proposed in [10] for executing SQL queries over encrypted data by performing approximate filtering at the server and performing final query processing at the client. This method is extended to handle aggregation queries in [11,12]. However, this method consumes a lot of hardware resources. Then, a query-based encryption method is proposed in [17,20]. In this method, based on users' query demands, users' data is encrypted by multiple encryption techniques simultaneously (e.g., deterministic encryption, order-preserving encryption or homomorphic encryption). By this method, users can have rich queries on their encrypted data and avoid some unnecessary post-processes to their data after queries. However, query-based encryption requires users to provide their query sets in advance. In fact, this may be difficult for users because they do not have clear plans for their data. Furthermore, this method fails to defeat the frequency attack in deterministic encryption [14]. To address the second problem, a system named Seabed is proposed in [16]. Seabed adopts additively symmetric homomorphic encryption (ASHE) to implement data encryption and greatly reduce the overhead of data aggregation in the encrypted domain. Meanwhile, Seabed introduces a splayed ASHE method to cope with the frequency attack by splaying sensitive columns to multiple columns. However, splayed ASHE results in heavy storage overheads because multiple new columns are added in original databases. Besides, users' privacy will be leaked out if their data is updated in ASHE.

To overcome the deficiencies in the existing schemes, in this paper, we will propose an efficient encryption scheme on outsourcing data for query on cloud platforms. Specifically, in our scheme, users' data is encrypted according to all possible queries rather than users' query sets. This method is more reasonable than the query-based encryption. Meanwhile, a double AES encryption method is proposed in our scheme, which leverages AES and row identifies of data to encrypt raw data twice to cope with the frequency attack in deterministic encryption. Its cost is much lower than that of splayed ASHE. To implement the dynamic update of users' encrypted data, a neighbor rows exchange method is designed in our scheme. In this method, when the data in some rows faces with the update, the updated value in neighbor rows will exchange their storing positions. This method ensures that users' privacy is not exposed to cloud servers when their data is updated. In summary, our contributions in this paper are listed as follow.

- We propose an effective encryption scheme on outsourcing data in this paper. In our scheme, the possible encryption method provides all possible queries on encrypted data for users. Meanwhile, the double AES encryption method can effectively defend against the frequency attack. Besides, the neighbor rows exchange method can ensure that users' encrypted data is updated without disclosing users' privacy.
- We present detailed theoretical analysis to demonstrates the effectiveness of the possible encryption method, the double AES encryption and the neighbor rows exchange method.
- The comparative experiments are executed in this paper to show that our scheme has good performance on users' data encryption cost and users' aggregation query cost compared with the existing schemes.

The remaining of this paper is organized as follows. Section 2 describes the system model and the adversary model of our scheme. Section 3 introduces the preliminaries of our scheme including query-based encryption and ASHE. Section 4 presents our scheme in detail. Section 5 provides the theoretical analysis for our scheme and Sect. 6 shows the experimental results. Finally, Sect. 7 concludes this paper.

2 Problem Statement

2.1 System Model

Three entities are involved in our scheme as illustrated in Fig. 1: users, the user proxy and the cloud server. Here, users are the owner of data and they generate their own secret keys for encryption. The user proxy is the middleman who is in charge of transmitting data between users and the cloud server. The cloud server is the entity who stores users' encrypted data. The process of this model is described as follows. First, users share their keys with the user proxy and submit their original data to the user proxy. Then, the user proxy encrypts the data according to all possible queries and outsources the encrypted data to the cloud server. To query the encrypted data, users submit their queries to the user proxy. Then, these original queries are parsed and transformed into the queries used in the encrypted domain by the user proxy. Next, the user proxy submits the new version of queries to the cloud server. Finally, the cloud server returns the query results to the user proxy according to submitted queries. Since the user proxy has users' keys, he can decrypt these results and send them to users. Once users obtain the query results, the whole procedure is finished.

2.2 Adversary Model

In our scheme, we assume that users and the cloud server are semi-honest [9]. That is, they will strictly follow our scheme but they are also curious about

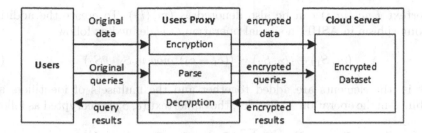

Fig. 1. The framework of our scheme

the other entities' sensitive information. Meanwhile, for users, the user proxy is trustworthy. This means the user proxy will not tamper the transmitted data. Besides, he will not collude with the cloud server to leak out users' privacy.

3 Preliminaries

3.1 Query-Based Encryption

Query-based encryption in [17,20] aims to improve the efficiency of querying encrypted databases and it adopts multiple encryption techniques to achieve this goal, including randomization, deterministic encryption (DE), order-preserving encryption (OPE) and homomorphic encryption (HE). For randomization, two identical values are mapped to different ciphertexts. Thus, ciphertext operations are not allowed under this technique. For DE, two equal values are mapped to the same ciphertext and it allows the equality checks in the encrypted domain. For OPE, the order of plaintexts is preserved after encryption and the range query is allowed. For HE, the ciphertexts are allowed to perform aggregation calculations and the decrypted results are still correct.

In query-based encryption, users first submit their data and query sets to the user proxy. Then, the user proxy selects the corresponding encryption techniques to encrypt users' data according to users' query sets. Finally, the user proxy uploads the encrypted data to the cloud server.

3.2 ASHE

ASHE in [16] assumes that there exists an additive group $\mathbb{Z}_n = \{0, 1, \cdots, n - 2, n - 1\}$ and a secret key k is shared between the encrypting entity and the decrypting entity. A message $m \in \mathbb{Z}_n$ is encrypted by ASHE as follow.

$$Enc_k(m, i) = ((m - F_k(i) + F_k(i - 1)) \bmod n, \{i\}) \tag{1}$$

Here, i is an identifier from a set I. $F_k : I \to \mathbb{Z}_n$ is a pseudo-random function (PRF) that maps an identifier i in I to a value in $\mathbb{Z}_n$ and it is implemented by AES. For ease of presentation, The ciphertexts in ASHE is also denoted as (c, S). Here, c is an element of $\mathbb{Z}_n$ and S is a multiset of identifiers. That is, the ciphertext $Enc_k(m, i)$ can be also denoted as $(m, \{i\})$. To create the additive homomorphism in ASHE, a special operation $\oplus$ is defined as follow.

$$(c_1, S_1) \oplus (c_2, S_2) = ((c_1 + c_2) \bmod n, S_1 \cup S_2) \tag{2}$$

That is, the elements are added together and the multisets of identifiers are combined in the operation $\oplus$. Besides, the ciphertext (c, S) is decrypted as follow.

$$Dec_k(c, S) = (c, \sum_{i \in S} (F_k(i - 1) + F_k(i))) \bmod n \tag{3}$$

The additive result of two ciphertexts is decrypted by computing:

$$Dec_k(Enc_k(m_1, i_1) \oplus Enc_k(m_2, i_2)) = (m_1 + m_2) \bmod n \tag{4}$$

As shown in Eq. (1), the encryption function in ASHE is designed as $(m - F_k(i) + F_k(i - 1))$ which has great advantages on data aggregation in the encrypted domain. For example, the ciphertexts of ASHE with consecutive identifiers $\{i, i+1, \cdots, n-1, n\}$ are added together. Due to the clever design of encryption function, the final result of these ciphertexts only contains $F_k(i) - F_k(n)$ and the other F_k is offset during the aggregation. Besides, $F_k(i)$ and $F_k(n)$ are easy to be worked out. Since the F_k is implemented by AES, the total computation overheads are low. Even if the identifiers of ciphertexts are consecutive partly, the overhead of data aggregation in ASHE is still much lower than that in the Paillier Homomorphic Encryption [15] adopted in [17] and [20].

4   Our Scheme

In this section, we will introduce our scheme in detail, which includes three methods: possible query encryption, double AES encryption and neighbor rows exchange.

4.1   Possible Query Encryption

To meet users' diverse query demands for encrypted databases, the possible query encryption in our scheme also adopts the same encryption techniques as the query-based encryption described in Sect. 3.1. However, there are some obvious differences between them. First, DE is implemented directly by AES in the query-based encryption, which can not defend against the frequency attack. In contrary, in the possible query encryption, a double AES encryption is proposed to implement the DE. This encryption method can cope with the frequency attack effectively and will be discussed later. Second, in the possible query encryption, HE is implemented by ASHE rather than Paillier homomorphic encryption. From Sect. 3.2, we can see that the ASHE is much more efficient than Paillier homomorphic encryption in terms of data aggregation in the encrypted domain. Last but not least, instead of users' query sets, all possible queries for users' data are taken into consideration in the possible query encryption. For one thing, users do not have clear understanding of their data so that they can not provide valid query sets. For another thing, users' query demands may change over time. This means that users' data should not be encrypted by a single encryption technique. Based on such considerations, the thought of all possible queries is adopted in the possible query encryption.

paginationAssume users' original data is presented as Table 1. The user proxy encrypts the data by columns according to the possible query encryption method. First, the user proxy picks out the column of gender and figures out the possible queries on it. Since the equality check is the only operation on this column, the user proxy adopts DE to encrypt it. Similarly, since the equality check and the range query are possible operations on the column of age, the user proxy encrypts it by DE and OPE. For the column of salary, data aggregation is the common operation on it. Therefore, in addition to DE and OPE, HE is also used to encrypt it. Here, HE is implemented by ASHE. Besides, an identifier is introduced to each row of encrypted database due to the application of ASHE. By the possible query encryption method, the encrypted version of users' data in Table 1 is shown as Table 2.

Table 1. The incomes of employees.

···	Gender	Age	Salary	···
···	Male	31	7000	···
···	Female	25	4800	···
···	Female	37	10000	···
···	Male	45	20000	···
···	···	···	···	···

Table 2. The encrypted version of Table 1.

ID	···	DE(Gender)	DE(Age)	OPE(Age)	DE(Salary)	OPE(Salary)	ASHE(Salary)	···
1	···	DE(male)	DE(31)	OPE(31)	DE(7000)	OPE(7000)	ASHE(7000)	···
2	···	DE(female)	DE(25)	OPE(25)	DE(4800)	OPE(4800)	ASHE(4800)	···
3	···	DE(female)	DE(37)	OPE(37)	DE(10000)	OPE(10000)	ASHE(10000)	···
4	···	DE(male)	DE(45)	OPE(45)	DE(20000)	OPE(20000)	ASHE(20000)	···
···	···	···	···	···	···	···	···	···

4.2 Double AES Encryption

For one thing, the frequency attack is a common form of attack in DE. Specifically, the attacker can obtain the occurrence frequency of plaintexts in advance.

If these plaintexts are encrypted by the existing DE, then the attacker can infer the corresponding plaintexts according to the occurrence frequency of ciphertexts. This is because the same plaintexts have the same ciphertexts in DE. For another thing, the ASHE in the possible query encryption introduces an identifier for each row in the encrypted database. By these identifiers, the double AES encryption method in our scheme can defend against the frequency attack.

Double AES encryption method adopts two rounds of AES to encrypt users' data. During the first round of AES encryption, the user proxy encrypts users' data m by using the secret key k shared by users. The encrypted result $Enc_k(m)$ is calculated as follow.

$$Enc_k(m) = AES_k(m) \tag{5}$$

Then, at the second round of AES encryption, the intermediate encrypted result $Enc_k(m)$ is viewed as the secret key of AES to encrypt the identifier i (i is the identifier of the row where m is). The final encrypted result $DE(m)$ is shown as follow.

$$DE(m) = AES_{Enc_k(m)}(i) = AES_{AES_k(m)}(i) \tag{6}$$

Since the identifier of each row is unique, the final encryption results of two identical data in different rows will be different by using double AES encryption. This means the double AES encryption in our scheme can defeat the frequency attack effectively. It is worth noting that we use $AES_k(m)$ to encrypt the identifier i rather than i to encrypt $AES_k(m)$. This is because the cloud server can directly access i and the final encryption result $DE(m)$. Since AES is a symmetric encryption technique, if i is the secret key to encrypt $AES_k(m)$, then the cloud server can directly decrypt $DE(m)$ and obtain $AES_k(m)$. In this case, the cloud server can still launch the frequency attack. In contrast, using $AES_k(m)$ as the key can avoid this because $AES_k(m)$ is unknown to the cloud server and AES is currently not vulnerable to known-plaintext attacks.

To support equality queries on encrypted databases implemented by double AES encryption, the user proxy should submit the intermediate encrypted result $Enc_k(m)$ to the cloud server. Then, the cloud server calculates the $DE(m)$ row by row according to Eq. (6) and performs the equality checks in the encrypted database. If the $DE(m)$ is equal to the data stored in the database, then the data meets users' query demands. Although the cloud server can know the counts of data being queried, he can not infer the corresponding plaintexts by the

Table 3. The double AES encryption version of Table 1.

ID	$\cdots$	Gender	Age	Salary	$\cdots$
1	$\cdots$	$AES_{AES(male)}(1)$	$AES_{AES(31)}(1)$	$AES_{AES(7000)}(1)$	$\cdots$
2	$\cdots$	$AES_{AES(female)}(2)$	$AES_{AES(25)}(2)$	$AES_{AES(4800)}(2)$	$\cdots$
3	$\cdots$	$AES_{AES(female)}(3)$	$AES_{AES(37)}(3)$	$AES_{AES(10000)}(3)$	$\cdots$
4	$\cdots$	$AES_{AES(male)}(4)$	$AES_{AES(45)}(4)$	$AES_{AES(20000)}(4)$	$\cdots$
$\cdots$	$\cdots$	$\cdots$	$\cdots$	$\cdots$	$\cdots$

frequency attack because the occurrence frequency of other data is unknown to him under the double AES encryption. The double AES encryption version of Table 1 is shown as Table 3.

4.3 Neighbor Rows Exchange

As mentioned before, in the possible query encryption, we adopt the ASHE to implement the HE. However, if users update their data encrypted by ASHE, their data privacy will be leaked out to the cloud server. Assume a user's original data is m_1. According to Eq. (1), it is encrypted by ASHE as follow.

$$Enc_k(m_1, i) = ((m_1 - F_k(i) + F_k(i - 1)) \bmod n, \{i\}) \tag{7}$$

Then, the $Enc_k(m_1, i)$ is stored in the i-th row of database on the cloud server. Now, this user intends to change the m_1 to m_2. Then, m_2 is encrypted by ASHE as follow.

$$Enc_k(m_2, i) = ((m_2 - F_k(i) + F_k(i - 1)) \bmod n, \{i\}) \tag{8}$$

The $Enc_k(m_2, i)$ is sent to the cloud server to update the content of the i-th row in database. However, the curious cloud server can disclose this user's data privacy by calculating:

$$\begin{aligned}\Delta m &= Enc_k(m_2) - Enc_k(m_1) \\ &= ((m_2 - F_k(i) + F_k(i-1)) - (m_1 - F_k(i) + F_k(i-1))) \bmod n \\ &= m_2 - m_1\end{aligned} \tag{9}$$

The Δm may indicate the changes in users' salaries or the personnel changes of a company. Anyway, the private information can be easily obtained by the cloud server, which results in the disclosure of users' privacy.

To address this problem, a neighbor rows exchange method is proposed in our scheme. Neighbor rows in this method are defined as two update rows which are adjacent to each other. Assume the data in the i-th, $(i + 3)$-th, $(i + 9)$-th and $(i + 14)$-th row faces with update. Then, the i-th row and the $(i + 3)$-th row are neighbor rows. Similar, the $(i + 9)$-th row and the $(i + 14)$-th row are also neighbor rows. In the case of multiple data updates at the same time, each pair of neighbor rows are divided into an exchange group and their updated value is stored in each other's locations. That is, for the data m_1 to be updated in i-th row and the m_2 to be updated in j-th row, assume i and j are neighbor rows. Then, in neighbor rows exchange method, m_1 and m_2 are divided into an exchange group. Meanwhile, the updated value of m_1 is stored in j-th row and the updated value of m_2 is stored in i-th row. Since the rows where users' data locates have changed after the update, the cloud server can not infer users' sensitive information anymore and users' privacy is protected.

In the case of a single data update, after receiving the i-th user's update data m, the user proxy stores this update data locally and does not modify the corresponding data on the cloud platform for the time being. Once some other users submit their update data, the user proxy will take out m from the local and combines it with other update data. The next steps will the same as those in multiple data updates. It is worth noting that the i-th user can query his update data at any time and the user proxy can ensure the correctness of query result. The above procedure can protect the i-th user's privacy.

In neighbor rows exchange method, the neighbor rows rather than two random rows exchange their stored data is to minimize the location changes of update data, which can take full advantage of the homomorphic property in ASHE. In addition, the validity of neighbor rows exchange method will be demonstrated in the next section. The neighbor rows exchange method is summarized as Algorithm 1.

Algorithm 1. Neighbor Rows Exchange

Input: Users' update data sets $M = \{m_1, \cdots, m_i, \cdots, m_n\}$
Output: The updated database on the cloud platform
1 The user proxy counts the number of update data in M: N_m
2 if $N_m > 1$
3   The user proxy devides the update data into multiple neighbor rows
4   The user proxy encrypts the update data according to ASHE where the identifiers of their
       neighbor row are used
5   The cloud server stores the encrypted data in their neighbor row
6 else
7   The user proxy stores the only update data m_o in the local
8   if other update data is submitted from users
9   m_o is combined with these update data
10   repeat the step 3, 4 and 5
11 end

Table 4. Different outsourcing data encryption schemes.

Scheme	Defeat frequence attack	Update	Special
Our scheme	✓	✓	Possible query encryption
Scheme in [17]	×	✓	Query-based encryption
Scheme in [20]	×	✓	Query-based encryption
Scheme in [16]	✓	×	ASHE

At the end of this section, we compare our scheme with other existing outsourcing data encryption schemes as shown in Table 4.

5   Theoretical Analysis

In this section, we will present the theoretical analysis of our scheme. Specifically, we will respectively analyze the effectiveness of possible query encryption, double AES encryption and neighbor rows exchange.

Theorem 1. *Possible query encryption in our scheme can provide users with richer queries on encrypted data.*

Proof. In the possible query encryption, users' data is encrypted according to all possible queries on their data. Each type of data has its own characteristics: some are suitable for equality checks but range queries and data aggregations are meaningless to them (e.g., gender). DE is enough for this type of data. Some are not only suitable for equality checks but also for range queries and even data aggregations (e.g., salary). This type of data should be encrypted by DE, OPE and HE simultaneously. Considering these cases, possible query encryption encrypts users' data according to the characteristics of the data. This can avoid a lot of unnecessary encryption for users' data.

Compared with query-based encryption, possible query encryption fully excavates the potential characteristics of users' data and provides a more complete query view for users. For one thing, this method does not depend on users' query sets, which can avoid users' subjective limitations. For another thing, users can change their query plans at any time. In this case, their queries will not become invalid. Therefore, possible query encryption is more reasonable than the query-based encryption.

Theorem 2. *Double AES encryption in our scheme can defend against the frequency attack.*

Proof. In the double AES encryption, users' data has a unique identifier and the different identifiers ensure that the equal data has different ciphertexts. Assume m_1 is equal to m_2 and their identifiers are i and j (Here, $i \neq j$). According to Eqs. (5) and (6), m_1 and m_2 is encrypted by double AES encryption as follow.

$$DE(m_1) = AES_{Enc_k(m_1)}(i) = AES_{AES_k(m_1)}(i) \tag{10}$$

$$DE(m_2) = AES_{Enc_k(m_2)}(j) = AES_{AES_k(m_2)}(j) \tag{11}$$

Since m_1 is equal to m_2, then $AES_k(m_1)$ is equal to $AES_k(m_2)$. But i is not equal to j, then $AES_{AES_k(m_1)}(i)$ is not equal to $AES_{AES_k(m_2)}(j)$. That is, $DE(m_1)$ is not equal to $DE(m_2)$.

From the above discussion, we can find two equal data are mapped to different ciphertexts by double AES encryption. This can prevent the attacker from inferring the occurrence frequency of plaintexts from the occurrence frequency of ciphertexts. Therefore, double AES encryption can defend against the frequency attack effectively.

Theorem 3. *Neighbor rows exchange method in our scheme can protect users' privacy when their data is updated.*

Proof. In the neighbor rows exchange method, in the case of multiple data update, the update data of neighbor rows exchanges their storage locations. Suppose m_1 in the i-th row and m_2 in the j-th row are facing updates and their update value are m_1' and m_2' respectively. Meanwhile, the i-th row and the j-th row are the neighbor rows. According to Eq. (1), m_1 and m_2 are encrypted by ASHE as follow.

$$Enc_k(m_1, i) = ((m_1 - F_k(i) + F_k(i-1)) \ mod \ n, \{i\}) \tag{12}$$

$$Enc_k(m_2, j) = ((m_2 - F_k(j) + F_k(j-1)) \ mod \ n, \{j\}) \tag{13}$$

According to the neighbor rows exchange method, m_1' is encrypted by ASHE with the identifier j and m_2' is encrypted by ASHE with the identifier i:

$$Enc_k(m_1', j) = ((m_1' - F_k(j) + F_k(j-1)) \ mod \ n, \{j\}) \tag{14}$$

$$Enc_k(m_2', i) = ((m_2' - F_k(i) + F_k(i-1)) \ mod \ n, \{i\}) \tag{15}$$

To disclose users' privacy, the cloud server will try to obtain Δm_1 by calculating:

$$\begin{aligned}
\Delta m_1 &= Enc_k(m_1') - Enc_k(m_1) \\
&= ((m_1' - F_k(j) + F_k(j-1)) - (m_1 - F_k(i) + F_k(i-1))) \ mod \ n \\
&= m_1' - m_1 + (F_k(i) + F_k(j-1) - F_k(j) - F_k(i-1))
\end{aligned} \tag{16}$$

Since the cloud server does not know the key k, he can not work out the $F_k(i) + F_k(j-1) - F_k(j) - F_k(i-1)$ and obtain the Δm_1 according to the Eq. (16). Similar, the cloud server can not obtain Δm_2 either. In the case of a single data update, the only update data m_o is stored in the user proxy temporarily. At this stage, the cloud server can not disclose users' privacy because the encrypted database on the cloud platform has no change. When other update data is submitted, m_o is combined with them and they are updated by following the method of multiple update data. Therefore, at this stage, users' privacy is also protected. In summary, the neighbor rows exchange method in our scheme can protect users' privacy when their data is updated.

6   Experiment

6.1   Experiment Configure

In this section, we will run some simulated experiments to evaluate the performance of our scheme. These experiments are run on a laptop with Intel i5-5200U CPU @ 2.20 GHz and 4GB RAM. Meanwhile, the operating system is Windows 10 and the programming language is Java 1.8.0. To implement OPE and Pallier

Homomorphic encryption, the opetoolbox[1] and the pailliertoolbox[2] are used in our experiments. Meanwhile, AES and AHSE are also implemented in our experiments. In addition, the experimental data is synthetic which includes 21 users. Each user has gender data, age data and salary data, as shown in Table 1. We will evaluate the performance of our scheme from two aspects: the encryption cost of the user proxy and the aggregation query cost of users.

6.2   The Encryption Cost of the User Proxy

In this experiment, we will compare the encryption cost of the user proxy in our scheme with that of the user proxy in [17]. Concretely, in our scheme, the user proxy needs to encrypt users' data by double AES encryption, OPE and AHSE, as shown in Table 2. While In [17], the user proxy adopts DE, OPE and Pallier Homomorphic encryption to encrypt users' data. Meanwhile, in this experiment, users' query sets in [17] includes all possible queries. To observe the encryption cost of the user proxy, we measure the encryption time of the user proxy under the different number of users which varies from 3 to 21. Repeat 10 times for each experiment and calculate the averages. The experimental result is shown as Fig. 2.

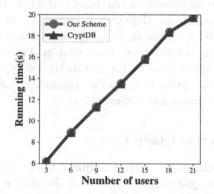

Fig. 2. The user proxy's encryption cost

From Fig. 2, we can find the user proxy in the two schemes has similar encryption cost. Through our analysis, we find OPE is most time-consuming in all of the encryption techniques mentioned in this paper. OPE in our scheme has the same implementation as OPE in [17], which results in the similar encryption cost of the user proxy in the two schemes. To further compare the DE cost and HE cost of the user proxy in the two schemes, we use double AES encryption, AES, ASHE and Paillier homomorphic encryption to encrypt users' salary data. Similarly, in these experiments, the number of users is varied from 3 to 21. Each experiment is repeated 10 times and the averages are calculated. The experimental results are shown as Fig. 3.

---

[1] https://github.com/ssavvides/jope.
[2] http://cs.utdallas.edu/dspl/cgi-bin/pailliertoolbox.

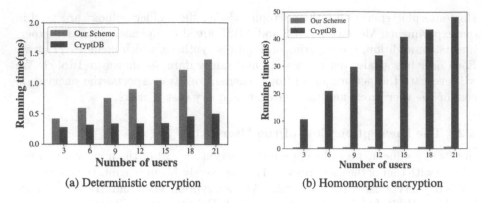

Fig. 3. The encryption cost of the user proxy

From Fig. 3(a), we can find the deterministic encryption cost of the user proxy in our scheme is higher than that in [17]. This is because double AES encryption in our scheme is implemented by two rounds of AES while the deterministic encryption in [17] is implemented by one round of AES. To defend against the frequency attack, in our scheme, the extra encryption cost for the user proxy is acceptable. From Fig. 3(b), we can find the homomorphic encryption cost of the user proxy in our scheme is much lower than that in [17]. This is because ASHE used in our scheme is implemented by the symmetric encryption AES. Compared with the asymmetric encryption (i.e., Paillier homomorphic encryption) used in [17], ASHE is obviously much more efficient.

6.3   Users' Aggregation Query Cost

In this experiment, assume users intend to query the sum of their salaries. This is a typical aggregation query in the encrypted domain, which is supported by our scheme and [17]. To compare the users' aggregation query cost in the two schemes, we measure users' query time under the different number of users which varies from 3 to 21. Each experiment is repeated 10 times and the averages are calculated. The experimental result is shown as Fig. 4.

From Fig. 4, we can find that users' aggregation query cost in our scheme is much lower than that in [17]. This is because users' data is encrypted by ASHE in our scheme. When aggregating the encrypted data, many calculation items are automatically offset in our scheme, as discussed in Sect. 3.2. In contrast, in [17], since users' data is encrypted by Paillier homomorphic encryption, many exponent operations are executed when aggregating the encrypted data. This results in huge time cost. Therefore, users' aggregation query in our scheme is much more efficient than that in [17].

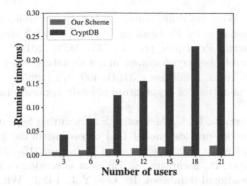

Fig. 4. The users' aggregation query cost

7 Conclusion

In this paper, we propose an effective scheme to support for query on encrypted databases on cloud platforms. In our scheme, the possible query encryption provides a complete query view for users and users can have more query choices. Meanwhile, the double AES encryption can defend against the frequency attack in deterministic encryption. Besides, the neighbor rows exchange method can protect users' privacy when their data is updated on encrypted databases. The theoretical analysis in this paper demonstrates the effectiveness of the three methods of our scheme. Meanwhile, The comparative experiments show that our scheme has good performance on the encryption cost of the user proxy and users' aggregation query cost.

References

1. Almorsy, M., Grundy, J., Müller, I.: An analysis of the cloud computing security problem. arXiv preprint arXiv:1609.01107 (2016)
2. Baldwin, P.K.: Cloud Services. Encyclopedia of Big Data, pp. 1–4 (2017)
3. Bellare, M., Boldyreva, A., O'Neill, A.: Deterministic and efficiently searchable encryption. In: Menezes, A. (ed.) CRYPTO 2007. LNCS, vol. 4622, pp. 535–552. Springer, Heidelberg (2007). https://doi.org/10.1007/978-3-540-74143-5_30
4. Bellare, M., Fischlin, M., O'Neill, A., Ristenpart, T.: Deterministic encryption: definitional equivalences and constructions without random oracles. In: Wagner, D. (ed.) CRYPTO 2008. LNCS, vol. 5157, pp. 360–378. Springer, Heidelberg (2008). https://doi.org/10.1007/978-3-540-85174-5_20
5. Boldyreva, A., Chenette, N., Lee, Y., O'Neill, A.: Order-preserving symmetric encryption. In: Joux, A. (ed.) EUROCRYPT 2009. LNCS, vol. 5479, pp. 224–241. Springer, Heidelberg (2009). https://doi.org/10.1007/978-3-642-01001-9_13
6. Boldyreva, A., Chenette, N., O'Neill, A.: Order-preserving encryption revisited: improved security analysis and alternative solutions. In: Rogaway, P. (ed.) CRYPTO 2011. LNCS, vol. 6841, pp. 578–595. Springer, Heidelberg (2011). https://doi.org/10.1007/978-3-642-22792-9_33

7. Calder, B., et al.: Windows azure storage: a highly available cloud storage service with strong consistency. In: Proceedings of the Twenty-Third ACM Symposium on Operating Systems Principles, pp. 143–157. ACM (2011)
8. ElGamal, T.: A public key cryptosystem and a signature scheme based on discrete logarithms. IEEE Trans. Inf. Theory **31**(4), 469–472 (1985)
9. Goldreich, O.: Foundations of cryptography: basic applications. J. ACM **10**(509), 359–364 (2004)
10. Hacigümüş, H., Iyer, B., Li, C., Mehrotra, S.: Executing SQL over encrypted data in the database-service-provider model. In: Proceedings of the 2002 ACM SIGMOD International Conference on Management of Data, pp. 216–227. ACM (2002)
11. Hacıgümüş, H., Iyer, B., Mehrotra, S.: Efficient execution of aggregation queries over encrypted relational databases. In: Lee, Y.J., Li, J., Whang, K.-Y., Lee, D. (eds.) DASFAA 2004. LNCS, vol. 2973, pp. 125–136. Springer, Heidelberg (2004). https://doi.org/10.1007/978-3-540-24571-1_10
12. Hacıgümüş, H., Iyer, B., Mehrotra, S.: Query optimization in encrypted database systems. In: Zhou, L., Ooi, B.C., Meng, X. (eds.) DASFAA 2005. LNCS, vol. 3453, pp. 43–55. Springer, Heidelberg (2005). https://doi.org/10.1007/11408079_7
13. Li, J., Liu, Z., Chen, X., Xhafa, F., Tan, X., Wong, D.S.: L-ENcDB: a lightweight framework for privacy-preserving data queries in cloud computing. Knowl.-Based Syst. **79**, 18–26 (2015)
14. Naveed, M., Kamara, S., Wright, C.V.: Inference attacks on property-preserving encrypted databases. In: Proceedings of the 22nd ACM SIGSAC Conference on Computer and Communications Security, pp. 644–655. ACM (2015)
15. Paillier, P.: Public-key cryptosystems based on composite degree residuosity classes. In: Stern, J. (ed.) EUROCRYPT 1999. LNCS, vol. 1592, pp. 223–238. Springer, Heidelberg (1999). https://doi.org/10.1007/3-540-48910-X_16
16. Papadimitriou, A., et al.: Big data analytics over encrypted datasets with seabed. In: OSDI, pp. 587–602 (2016)
17. Popa, R.A., Redfield, C., Zeldovich, N., Balakrishnan, H.: CryptDB: protecting confidentiality with encrypted query processing. In: Proceedings of the Twenty-Third ACM Symposium on Operating Systems Principles, pp. 85–100. ACM (2011)
18. Singh, A., Chatterjee, K.: Cloud security issues and challenges: a survey. J. Netw. Comput. Appl. **79**, 88–115 (2017)
19. Stanek, J., Sorniotti, A., Androulaki, E., Kencl, L.: A secure data deduplication scheme for cloud storage. In: Christin, N., Safavi-Naini, R. (eds.) FC 2014. LNCS, vol. 8437, pp. 99–118. Springer, Heidelberg (2014). https://doi.org/10.1007/978-3-662-45472-5_8
20. Tu, S., Kaashoek, M.F., Madden, S., Zeldovich, N.: Processing analytical queries over encrypted data. In: Proceedings of the VLDB Endowment, vol. 6, pp. 289–300. VLDB Endowment (2013)
21. Wang, C., Ren, K., Yu, S., Urs, K.M.R.: Achieving usable and privacy-assured similarity search over outsourced cloud data. In: INFOCOM, 2012 Proceedings IEEE, pp. 451–459. IEEE (2012)
22. Wu, J., Ping, L., Ge, X., Wang, Y., Fu, J.: Cloud storage as the infrastructure of cloud computing. In: 2010 International Conference on Intelligent Computing and Cognitive Informatics (ICICCI), pp. 380–383. IEEE (2010)
23. Yang, J., He, S., Lin, Y., Lv, Z.: Multimedia cloud transmission and storage system based on Internet of Things. Multimedia Tools Appl. **76**(17), 17735–17750 (2017)

Design of an Urban Waterlogging Monitoring System Based on Internet of Things

Jiachen Liu, Yintu Bao, Yingcong Liu, and Wuyungerile Li[(✉)]

Inner Mongolia University, Hohhot 010020, Inner Mongolia, China
gerile@imu.edu.cn

Abstract. The Internet of things (IoT) is the network that composed of different devices (e.g. computers, vehicles, RFID and sensors etc.) and allows these things to connect, interact, generate data and exchange data. The IoT technology plays a role in people and has become a research hotspot. Due to the expansion of urban area, the construction of underground pipelines lags behind, the increase of rainfall makes it impossible to drain rainwater from the city interior, which endangers the safety of life and property. On the one hand, the planning of urban drainage system is unreasonable, on the other hand, the water monitoring system of city road is not formed, the data monitoring and data processing is not timely enough, so that it is failure to achieve effective early warning. In view of the above problems, this paper proposes an urban waterlogging monitoring and warning system. In view of the above problems, this paper proposes a urban waterlogging monitoring and warning system. The system combines Vehicle Network, Sensor Technology and Cellular Network technology to realize an IoT application of rain water monitoring, data transmission, processing and warning system of urban waterlogging situation, which makes the traffic environment in the city more networked and intelligent, and reduces the occurrence of property and personal safety incidents.

Keywords: IoT · Vehicle Network · Sensor Technology · Cellular network · Urban waterlogging

1 Introduction

With the continuous prosperity of social economy and the rapid development of cities, the city circle is also growing [1, 2]. However the planning of underground drainage pipelines of some roads is not reasonable enough, it is difficult to transform, so there are some potential drainage hazards. Urban waterlogging is a phenomenon of urban flooding caused by heavy or continuous precipitation exceeding urban drainage capacity. The objective reasons are the concentration of rainfall area and rainfall intensity. Water is formed into areas where rainfall is particularly heavy and concentrated [3–4]. Once the city suffers heavy rainfall, in key areas prone to water accumulation, such as tunnels, low-lying areas, rainwater can not be discharged in time, will form a "river", light traffic jam, heavy casualties and property losses. Therefore researchers and industries aim to realize urban waterlogging warning system. Sun [3] networked the water level sensors and uploaded information to the server. The water level information monitored in real time

J. Li et al. (Eds.): SPNCE 2019, LNICST 284, pp. 333–341, 2019.
https://doi.org/10.1007/978-3-030-21373-2_25

was calculated and judged by threshold to get the corresponding warning level and sent to the relevant departments. Dong [9] combined the early warning system with GIS and establishes the urban rainstorm waterlogging model. The model involves knowledge of meteorology, hydrology, hydrodynamics, river dynamics and drainage engineering. Finally, the early warning and forecasting information is sent to the relevant departments. Naranmandra team [10] networked rainfall stations, water level detectors and other sensors, cameras and other equipment, uploaded relevant information to the server, finally, issued decision-making and warning information on the server side.

In this paper, the Urban Waterlogging Warning System monitors the water level in real time via set up sensors on cars and roadsides. The sensors monitor water level and generate data, then send the data to the server. The server processes the data, and uses the time series exponential smoothing prediction method to predict the water level of the road, and integrates the prediction results and collected information, then send the corresponding warning information to the user's mobile phone in the way of mobile application software push, reminding people of the water situation ahead.

In Sect. 2, the authors present the design method of system. In Sect. 3, the authors implement the design and give the results. Finally, the conclusion is made in Sect. 4.

2 System Design

The Traditional Urban Waterlogging Monitoring and Warning System is that sensors are placed in low-lying areas and under overpasses. The sensors sense water level data and send to a control center but not to the people around the area. Hence it cannot provide timely warning to people and vehicles around. In addition, for a long time used road, the ground is always uneven. Hence, sensors deployed on the two sides of road always cannot accurately reflect the water level of the road center area.

In view of the above situation, this paper has made improvements as follows:

(1) The innovative use of hydraulic sensors on cars can measure the real-time water depth of cars passing through the road section and send early warning information to the cars and people around them in time.

(2) The time series exponential smoothing prediction method is used in the road water accumulation prediction algorithm. This method is very effective for the irregular change of rainfall results. It can predict the road water depth at the next moment and improve the prediction accuracy.

2.1 Overview of System Design

The system is composed of two parts. One part we call Accurate Monitoring Center (AMC) and another is Instant Warning Center (IWC). In AMC, it provides the functions of rainfall monitoring, water depth monitoring and the prediction of water accumulation in the section. In IWC, the hydraulic sensors are installed on the cars. The pressure value that measured by the contact of the hydraulic sensor to the liquid during the driving process of the car is converted to the water depth of the passage section, and the real-time water level data of the road surface is sending to the cars nearby.

As shown in Fig. 1, proposed Urban Waterlogging Warning System is formed by water level sensor node, data processing center, wireless terminals, cars, hydraulic sensors and road. The AMC uses Cellular network to send data to the server at a predetermined time interval. The server gathers road water accumulation data from the roadside sensor and the sensors set up the cars to calculate road water accumulation forecast data, then sends the data to the mobile client. In IWC, the hydraulic sensor installed on the body of the car measures the dynamic parameters of real-time water accumulation on the road surface when driving through, and gets the dynamic water depth of data conversion. The water depth value getting from the car passing through the road section is sent to the cars nearby, reminding users that there is water accumulation in the front of the road section, thus realizing the purpose of real-time early warning.

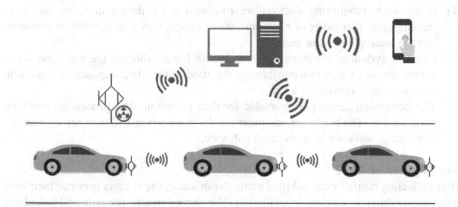

Fig. 1. Actual scene diagram

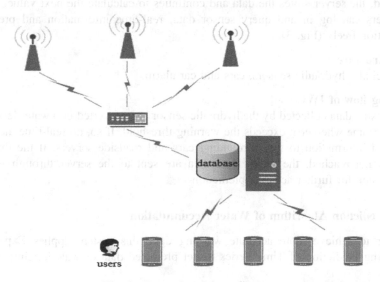

Fig. 2. Network topology diagram

Figure 2 is the network topology of the AMC. Sensors include rain gauges, electronic water gauges and hydraulic sensors. The data they collected included rainfall, road depth of water and liquid pressure. Wireless transmission terminals support operator network, multiple network protocols and data transmission is efficient. The server receives the data transmitted by wireless transmission terminals for storage, processing, and then sends the data to the client.

2.2 System Structure Design

AMC Structure
The AMC includes three parts: Road water logging monitoring, out-of-car hydraulic monitoring and processing center.

(1) Road water monitoring stations are responsible for data acquisition and data transmission. It consists of electronic water gauge, rain gauge, wireless terminal, storage battery and solar panel.
(2) External hydraulic monitoring is responsible for monitoring the real-time water accumulation of cars passing through the road, which is composed of hydraulic sensors setting outside of a car.
(3) The processing center is responsible for data reception, data processing and data transmission. The hardware equipment is database server and web server, and the installation software is application software.

Working flow of AMC
After collecting rainfall data and road water depth value, the sensors transmit their data to the server through wireless transmission. The server obtains the data and calculates whether it exceeds the water level threshold. If it exceeds the threshold, it sends early warning information to the user through cellular network. If it does not exceed the threshold, the server stores the data and continues to calculate the next value. At this end, users can log in and query sensor data, real-time information and predictive information freely (Fig. 3).

IWC Structure
IWC includes hydraulic sensors, cars and car alarm.

Working flow of IWC
The pressure data collected by the hydraulic sensor are converted into water level data, and determine whether it exceeds the warning threshold. If so, do real-time alerts and also send information to the surrounding cars and roadside servers. If the threshold value is not reached, the water level data are sent to the server through wireless transmission for further accurate prediction.

2.3 Prediction Algorithm of Water Accumulation

In order to achieve more accurate warning data, this system applies Exponential Smoothing Prediction of Time Series to get predicted data of waterlogging warning system.

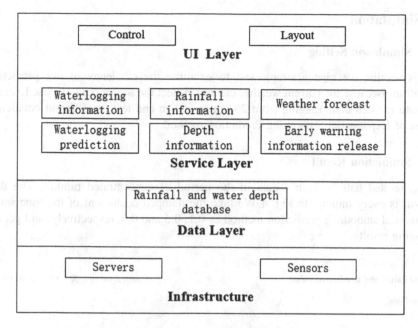

Fig. 3. Structural design of AMC

Exponential Smoothing Prediction of Time Series

The principle of this method is weighted average. It uses the growth trend of water level data to calculate the short-term prediction technology of water level data at a certain time in the future. In the past period of time, the continuous time points constitute a series of water level data arrays $H_{(t)}$, $H_{(t-1)}$, $H_{(t-2)} \cdots$, which are continuous in time. Then the weighted average of the array is obtained. Finally, the data of the predicted time points is obtained. The iterative formulas are as follows:

$$H_{(t+1)} = \alpha H_{(t)} + \alpha(1-\alpha)H_{(t-1)} + \alpha\left(1-\alpha^2\right)H_{(t-2)} + \cdots \tag{1}$$

Parameter description: $H_{(t+1)}$ is the predicted value of water level data at t + 1 time, and $\alpha = 1/n$, n is the number of accumulated arrays.

In practical application, the distribution of weighting coefficients should increase the weighting coefficients of the latest time points and reduce the weighting coefficients of the past time points. The whole calculation process should show a gradual change in time. Different weighting coefficients can reflect the influence degree of the time points closer to the predicted time points. This short-term prediction method has the advantages of simple operation and easy realization.

3 Simulation

3.1 Simulation Setting

In this section we give a simple test to examine the efficiency of our prediction algorithm. Because the current weather can not collect the seeper data, we use Excel to generate random data, ranging from 20 cm to 30 cm and test for different coefficient values of Exponential Smoothing Prediction method.

3.2 Simulation Result

We generated half an hour's data in the period of concentrated rainfall. The data interval is every minute. In Fig. 4 We take the damped coefficient of the time series exponential smoothing prediction method as 0.1, 0.5 and 0.9, respectively, and get the following results:

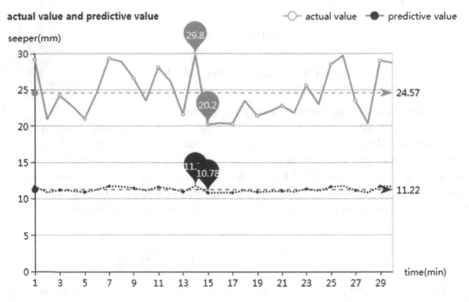

Fig. 4. Damped coefficient $\alpha = 0.1$, actual value and predictive value

For the data collected by sensors, the time series exponential smoothing prediction method is used to predict the depth of road water accumulation. When the damped coefficient is different, the prediction results are slightly different. In view of the prediction error, we calculate the relative error to evaluate the prediction results. The specific formula is as follows:

$$\text{Error}(\%) = |\text{Actual Value} - \text{Predictive Value}| / \text{Actual Value} \qquad (2)$$

When damped coefficient $\alpha = 0.1$, the predicted value is too gentle to reflect the results well. Then we calculate the relative error is 0.54. The predicted results are far from the actual results.

When damped coefficient $\alpha = 0.5$, The forecast is better than before. Then we calculate the relative error is 0.3. But it still can not reflect real situation (Fig. 5).

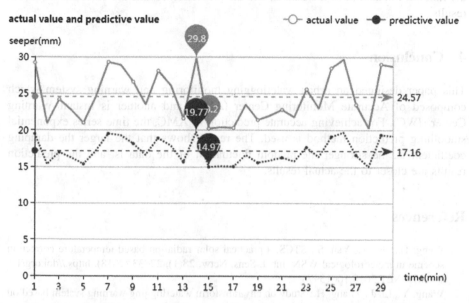

Fig. 5. Damped coefficient $\alpha = 0.5$, actual value and predictive value

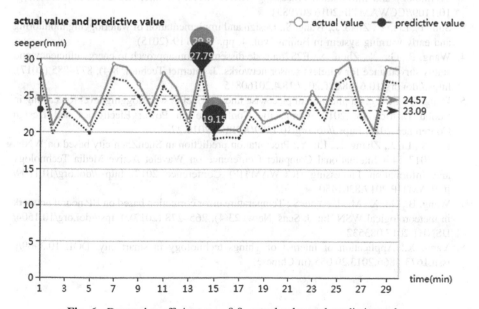

Fig. 6. Damped coefficient $\alpha = 0.9$, actual value and predictive value

When damped coefficient $\alpha = 0.9$, from the results reflected in Fig. 6, we can see that they are very close to the real results. Then we calculate the relative error is 0.06. So the algorithm we use is calculated with the current damped coefficient.

By using time series exponential smoothing method to predict the data collected from the experiment, we know that the larger the damping coefficient is, the stronger the random fluctuation of the data is, and the prediction results are closer to the actual results.

4   Conclusion

This paper designed an urban waterlogging monitoring and warning system which composed of Accurate Monitoring Center (AMC) and another is Instant Warning Center (IWC). For achieving accurate prediction in AMC, the time series exponential smoothing prediction method is used. The result shows that the larger the damping coefficient is, the stronger the random fluctuation of the data is, and the prediction results are closer to the actual results.

References

1. Wang, B., Gu, X., Yan, S.: STCS: a practical solar radiation based temperature correction scheme in meteorological WSN. Int. J. Sens. Netw. **28**(1), 22–33 (2018). https://doi.org/10.1504/IJSNET.2018.10015978
2. Wang, Y., Li, J., Zhang, H.: Study on city rainstorm waterlogging warning system based on historical data. In: 2016 13th International Computer Conference on Wavelet Active Media Technology and Information Processing (ICCWAMTIP) Conference 2016. https://doi.org/10.1109/ICCWAMTIP.2016.8079831
3. Sun, Y., Liu, Y., Zhao, J., Wang, S.: Design and implementation of waterlogging monitoring and early warning system in Beijing. vol. 4, pp. 117–119 (2015)
4. Wang, B., Gu, X., Zhou, A.: E2S2: a code dissemination approach to energy efficiency and status surveillance for wireless sensor networks. J. Internet Technol. **8**(4), 877–885 (2017). https://doi.org/10.6138/JIT.2017.18.4.20160815
5. Dong, Q., Yu, Q.: Application of piecewise linear model to waterlogging level forecasting in Luohu District. In: 2010 Asia-Pacific Conference on Power Electronics and Design Conference 2010. https://doi.org/10.1109/APPED.2010.27
6. Lin, S., Li, J., Zhang, L., Lu, Y.: Precipitation prediction in ShenZhen city based on WNN. In: 2017 14th International Computer Conference on Wavelet Active Media Technology and Information Processing (ICCWAMTIP) Conference 2017. https://doi.org/10.1109/ICWAMTIP.2017.8301450
7. Wang, B., Gu, X., Ma, L., Yan, S.: Temperature error correction based on BP neural network in meteorological WSN. Int. J. Sens. Netw. **23**(4), 265–278 (2017). https://doi.org/10.1504/IJSNET.2017.083532
8. Yang, X.: Application of Internet of Things technology in smart city. DOI: 10.3969/j.issn.1673-4866.2013.20.055 (in Chinese)

9. Dong, Y.: Research and Development of Rainstorm Waterlogging Forecasting and Warning System in Chengdu City Based on GIS (2010)
10. Naranmandra: Urban Flood Disaster Monitoring, Early Warning, Management and Control Equipment and Intelligent Management System (2017)

A Multi-Objective Service Selection Method Based on Ant Colony Optimization for QoE Restrictions in the Internet of Things

Chuxuan Zhang[1,2], Bing Jia[1,2(✉)], and Lifei Hao[1,2]

[1] College of Computer Science, Inner Mongolia University, Hohhot 010021, China
jiabing@imu.edu.cn
[2] Inner Mongolia A.R. Key Laboratory of Wireless Networking
and Mobile Computing, Hohhot 010021, China

Abstract. With the development of Wireless Sensor Network (WSN), the number of Internet of Things (IoT) services has increased dramatically. In order to use IoT services conveniently, it has become a key issue to reasonably aggregate information, content and applications, and filter services according to users' needs. Most of the existing service selection algorithms adopt heuristic search algorithm or Genetic Algorithm (GA). The heuristic algorithm is not stable, and GA cannot meet the needs of service selection because of the one-dimensional chromosome coding. For overcoming the disadvantages of these methods, this paper proposes a multi-objective service selection algorithm based on Ant Colony Optimization (ACO) for Quality of Experience(QoE) restrictions. The proposed method can get a feasible solution quickly and efficiently by utilizing the fast convergence speed of ACO. Specifically, QoE model was established firstly, and relevant constraints and quantitative methods are given. Secondly, a service selection model based on ACO was constructed to select specific services based on the above model. Finally, the proposed method is verified through simulations. Results show that, compared with GA-based method, the proposed algorithm can improve the recall rate and precision rate, and has a higher algorithm efficiency in solving the service selection problems.

Keywords: Internet of Things · Ant Colony Optimization · Service selection · QoE

1 Introduction

In recent years, the Internet of things (IoT) [1] technology has been widely concerned by people. IoT is characterized by loose coupling, platform independence, language neutrality and openness, etc. It has become an important part of the new generation of information technology. There are many IoT services, but the

© ICST Institute for Computer Sciences, Social Informatics and Telecommunications Engineering 2019
Published by Springer Nature Switzerland AG 2019. All Rights Reserved
J. Li et al. (Eds.): SPNCE 2019, LNICST 284, pp. 342–353, 2019.
https://doi.org/10.1007/978-3-030-21373-2_26

function of a single IoT service is pretty simple. The implementation of complex services requires the aggregation of multiple services. However, the selecting of services becomes difficult due to the existence of a large number of IoT services with the same or similar functions. Therefore, the realization of IoT service selection becomes a key problem to be solved.

In order to better meet the needs of users, [2] proposed the concept Quality of Experience (QoE) to solve problems from the perspective of user experience. QoE, as a means of service quality quantification, effectively helps service providers improve service quality and user's satisfaction. In [3], key indicators affecting QoE were studied and defined, and an evaluation and quantification algorithm for QoE was proposed. However, there are many factors that affect user experience, leading to the difficulty of modeling. [4] introduced user preference, adopt three-layer hierarchical model, and proposed a satisfaction calculation method based on weighted sum. However, the Analytic Hierarchy Process (AHP) algorithm used to calculate user preferences in this model is inefficient. [5] uses the expert opinions to preset user preferences, which improves the algorithm efficiency, but it is difficult to meet the needs of mobile application scenarios due to the inability to dynamically learn user preferences.

There are many algorithms for service selection, which can be summarized into four categories. The first one is Direct Search Method (DSM) [6]. This method traversed all possible paths, but was so inefficient that it was only suitable for a small number of services. Secondly, Heuristic Search Algorithm (HSA) [7], heuristics are added to speed up the search process. Although using the appropriate search strategy, the search speed is quite fast, but the stability is poor. The third category is Integer Programming Algorithm (IPA) [8]. IPA establishes the global optimization model for service aggregation and transforms this issue into a 0–1 linear programming problem. It improves search speed, but is still not ideal for large-scale service selection. Finally, Genetic Algorithm (GA) [9] is a computational model simulating natural selection and genetic mechanism in Darwinian evolution. Coding mode is the basis of GA, and will directly affect the design of selection, crossover and mutation operations, thus affecting convergence, complexity and efficiency. So different problems adopt different coding patterns, which is difficult to reuse.

To sum up, the above models and service selection methods both have advantages and disadvantages, but they are not quite suitable for IoT services. Aiming at IoT service selection for QoE restrictions, this paper proposed a multi-parameter linear weighted QoE quantitative model, and designs a corresponding service selection algorithm based on Ant Colony Optimization (ACO) [10]. The model is widely applicable and has good scalability by extensive analysis of IoT services and QoE evaluation methods. Compared with other service selection algorithms, the proposed method can effectively improve the precision rate and recall rate of service selection, and greatly reduce the computation time and complexity in the same scenario.

The rest of this paper is organized as follows. The next section formally gives a multi-parameter linear weighted QoE quantitative model for IoT services and the standardization method. The ACO is introduced in Sect. 3, and combined with the proposed model, a service selection algorithm based on ACO has been described in detail. In Sect. 4, experiments are designed and the proposed method is evaluated by extensive simulations. Finally, the last section summarizes the whole paper and outlooks the future work.

2 The Multi-parameter Linear Weighted QoE Quantitative Model

The study of the factors which affected QoE is crucial for the evaluation of QoE, because the basic objective of QoE evaluation is to predict the QoE which is difficult to measure directly from known or easily measured factors [11]. In order to quantify the QoE of IoT services reasonably, this paper proposes a multi-parameter linear weighted quantitative model by considering the characteristics of IoT services, e.g., variety and different grading factors. This model mainly examines four major aspects, including service performance experience, service provider's brand effect, users' sensitivity to price, and users' personal preferences, as shown in Fig. 1.

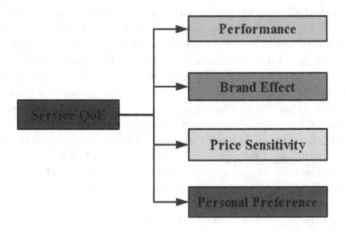

Fig. 1. The structure diagram of multi-parameter linear weighted QoE quantitative model.

Service performance experience can be directly measured by Quality of Service (QoS) parameters, including some common Internet service indicators such as response time, availability, reliability. The definition for QoE performance experience indicator of service can be formalized as follow.

$$q_p = \theta_{RT} \cdot RT' + \theta_A \cdot A + \theta_R \cdot R \tag{1}$$

where

$$RT' = \begin{cases} RT_{max} - RT, & if\ RT \leq RT_{max} \\ 0, & else \end{cases} \tag{2}$$

RT is the actual value of response time, A and R are the standard scores of availability and reliability, and θ_{RT}, θ_A and θ_R are the corresponding weights.

Brand Effect plays a great role in commodity economy as well as in IoT service selection. People preferred to choose the services of provider with high reputation or ranking. It is a common intuition that users have lower differentiating degree for services with a large brand effect and vice versa. So it is advisable to use logarithmic function for quantification, which is defined as Formula (3).

$$q_{be} = \ln(BE + 1) \tag{3}$$

where BE is the comprehensive score of brand effect which can be graded by incorporating reputation and ranking.

Different service prices will have different psychological experience for users such as the common 9-end commodity prices used to bring better sales. Therefore, it is appropriate to define the user's price sensitivity as a piecewise constant function as below.

$$q_{ps} = \begin{cases} S_1, & if\ 0 \leq price < p_1 \\ S_2, & if\ p_1 \leq price < p_2 \\ S_3, & if\ p_2 \leq price < p_3 \\ S_4, & if\ p_3 \leq price < p_4 \\ S_5, & if\ price < p_4 \end{cases} \tag{4}$$

where S_i is the score of price sensitivity, $S_1 < S_2 < S_3 < S_4 < S_5$ and $[p_i, p_{i+1}]$ is a price interval.

However, the previous service experience of users and the attractiveness of the content provided by the service often have a decisive impact on the user's choice, so the personal preference is represented by exponent function.

$$q_{pp} = e^{\frac{PP}{\alpha}} - 1 \tag{5}$$

where PP is a comprehensive score of personal preferences, which is determined by previous experience and service content, and α is an adjustment parameter.

Basing on the above definition of influencing factors, we can get a comprehensive QoE index of the IoT service as follow, which is the linear weighted of the above four factors.

$$qoe_i = \sum_j \theta_j \cdot q_j \tag{6}$$

where $q_j \in \{q_p, q_{be}, q_{ps}, q_{pp}\}$ and θ_j are weight coefficients of the four influencing factors, respectively.

Owing to the above seven indicators $(RT', A, R, q_p, q_{be}, q_{ps}, q_{pp})$ are calculated by actual values, the ranges of results are different, which means it is impossible to evaluate the importance of each factor. Therefore, the Formula (7) is given according to [12], which can standardize each sub-index linearly so that their ranges of value are between $[0, 1]$.

$$P_i = \begin{cases} \frac{q_i - q_i^{min}}{q_i^{max} - q_i^{min}}, & if \ q_i^{max} - q_i^{min} > \varepsilon \\ 1, & if \ q_i^{max} - q_i^{min} \leq \varepsilon \end{cases} \tag{7}$$

where $q_i \in [q_p, q_{be}, q_{ps}, q_{pp}]$, and the superscripts max and min represent maximum and minimum respectively.

3   The Service Selection Method Based on Ant Colony Optimization

Ant Colony Optimization (ACO) [10,13] is a bionic probabilistic algorithm which take full advantage of the ant colony's intelligence to find the optimal path so that it can solve complex problems. This method has the characteristics of distributed computation, positive information feedback and heuristic search, and is essentially a heuristic global optimization algorithm in evolutionary algorithm. At present, ACO has been widely used in many fields, the most common of which is to solve the Traveling Salesman Problem (TSP) [13,14]. However, this method can be applied to the service selection problem and can rapidly converge to the global optimal solution by the deformation of it and with the optimization of its parameters.

The behavior of a single ant is extremely simple, but the colony of thousands ants possess great intelligence due to they use pheromones to transmit information. As shown in Fig. 2, there are three paths from the ant nest (gray circle) to the food (yellow pentagram). In the process of searching for food, the direction of moving is selected according to the concentration of pheromones, and the food can be found finally. At the beginning, the ants' moving paths were random (see Fig. 2(a)) since there were no pheromone on the ground. Ants constantly release pheromone that marks their path as they moving. As time goes on, several ants find food, and there are several routes from the nest to the food (see Fig. 2(b)). But the pheromones gradually evaporate over time. Besides, since the behavior of ants is randomly distributed, there are more ants in the short path than in the long path in unit time, so the concentration of pheromones left by ants in the short path is higher. This provides strong guidance for the ants behind, and more and more ants gather on the shortest path (see Fig. 2(c)). Therefore, this process achieves the selecting of shortest path or the so-called optimal path.

It can be mapped the IoT services selection to the ACO scenario, as shown in Fig. 3. All m IoT services form a set of services and each service represented by a yellow pentagram. When the user's request arrives, there is a path from the user's request to each service. We use the reciprocal of the corresponding QoE value of a service to indicate its path length, i.e. $d_i = \frac{1}{qoe_i}(i = 1, 2, ..., m)$, where

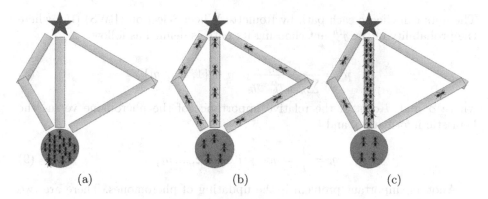

Fig. 2. The process by which ants search for food.

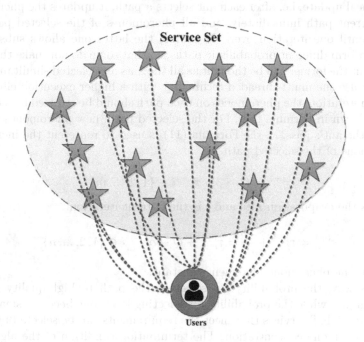

Fig. 3. The mapping from service selection problem to the ACO scenarios.

d_i is the distance from the nest to the ith service. This is because the larger the QoE of a service is, the more the service meets the user's demands, which is similar to the shorter path from service to user.

Selecting a path from all paths by each ant, the pheromone concentration τ_i and some heuristic information η_i of this path should be taken into account at the same time in order to accelerate the convergence speed of algorithm.

The ants can choose each path by Roulette Wheel Selection (RWS) [15], where the probability of the jth ant choosing its path is defined as follow.

$$p_i^j = \frac{\tau_i^\alpha \cdot \eta_i^\beta}{\sum_{k=0}^m \tau_k^\alpha \cdot \eta_k^\beta} \quad i \in \{1, 2, ..., m\} \tag{8}$$

where α and β control the relative importance of the pheromone versus the heuristic information, and

$$\eta_i = \frac{1}{d_i} = qoe_i \quad i \in \{1, 2, ..., m\} \tag{9}$$

Another important problem is the updating of pheromones. There are two main modes for pheromones updating. One is the global synchronous update, i.e. concentrate on updating all pheromones after all ants had selected the path. The other is local update, i.e. after each ant selects a path, it updates the pheromone of the current path immediately, and all pheromones of the selected path are updated until one iteration over. Of course, the latter one allows subsequent ants to perform different probabilistic paths, so that some do not make the same choices. But the former can be thought as all the ants are selected simultaneously, which can use the multi-threaded technology with a higher execution efficiency. After each iteration, the pheromones on each path should be reduced by a certain ratio, as shown in Formula (10). For the selected path, new pheromones will be left after the ant's pass, so the Formula (11) is used to represent the increasing in pheromone of the selected path.

$$\tau_i^{l+1} = (1 - \rho) \cdot \tau_i^l \quad i \in \{1, 2, ..., m\} \tag{10}$$

where ρ is the evaporation rate and l is the current iteration.

$$\tau_i^{l+1} = \tau_i^{l+1} + \frac{Q}{d_i} = \tau_i^{l+1} + Q \cdot qoe_i \quad i \in \{1, 2, ..., n\} \tag{11}$$

where Q is the pheromone increment constant.

In this way, the probability for selecting the path to high-quality service becomes larger, while the probability for selecting lower one becomes smaller, so that the first k IoT services that meet the requirements can be selected by using ordered pheromone concentration. The termination condition of the algorithm can be fixed iterations or the stagnant phenomenon appears (all ants choose the same path, and the solution will not change). The ACO-based IoT Service Selection algorithm (ACO-SS) is shown in Algorithm 1. The algorithm consists of four parts: the initialization in Line 1–2; the iteration in Line 3–18 includes the selection of service (path) by each ant and the update of pheromone; in the Line 19–21, the service set is sorted according to the pheromone matrix, and the first k services are taken as results.

Algorithm 1. ACO-based IoT Service Selection Algorithm

Input: Ant colony size n, the maximum iteration I, Service Set S,
        Demand Service Number k, Evaporation rate ρ, Pheromone
        increment constant Q

Output: Demand Service Set S_k

1 Initialize all elements in pheromone matrix M_{ph} as 1;
2 Compute the QoE matrix S_{qoe} for all the services;
3 **while** $i < I$ **do**
4     $S_{select} = \emptyset$;
5   **while** $j < n$ **do**
6   R_j =random$(0, 1)$;
7   **while** $l < m$ **do**
8   **if** $\frac{\sum_1^l M_{ph}^l \cdot S_{qoe}^l}{M_{ph} \cdot S_{qoe}} > R_j$ **then**
9             $S_{select} = S_{select} \bigcup \{l\}$
10   **break**;
11   **end**
12   **end**
13   **end**
14     $M_{ph} = M_{ph} \cdot (1 - \rho)$;
15   **foreach** j in S_{select} **do**
16        $M_{ph}^j = M_{ph}^j + Q \cdot S_{qoe}^j$;
17   **end**
18 **end**
19 Sort S according to M_{ph};
20 Choose first k services in S as S_k;
21 **return** S_k

4 Simulations

4.1 Set up

The simulations in this section runs on a PC with win7 (64bit) operating system. The CPU is an i5 processor and the memory is 8GB. It is programmed to generate service set and to realize both algorithms with MATLAB2016Ra.

The simulation generates a set of 1000 services, and the attributes of each service are randomly produced. The value of fixed parameters in QoE model and the range of each service attribute are shown in Tables 1 and 2, respectively.

4.2 Comparison

In order to verify the actual effect of the proposed algorithm in solving the problem of service selection, we implemented another Service Selection algorithm based on Genetic Algorithm (GA-SS). GA-SS has changed the traditional

Table 1. The value of fixed parameter in QoE model.

Category	Parameter	Value
Performance	RT_{max}	1000
	θ_{RT}	0.3
	θ_A	0.4
	θ_R	0.3
Price sensitivity	S_1, S_2, S_3, S_4, S_5	5, 4, 3, 2, 1
	p_1, p_2, p_3, p_4	300, 800, 2000, 5000
Personal preference	α	40
QoE	$\theta_p, \theta_{be}, \theta_{ps}, \theta_{pp}$	0.25

Table 2. The value range of each service attribute.

Category	Attribute	Value range
Performance	RT(ms)	[1,1500]
	A	[1,100]
	R	[1,100]
Brand effect	BE	[0,99]
Price sensitivity	Price(USD)	[1,10000]
Personal preference	PP	[1,100]

GA to applicability of service selection. Its encoding adopts the form of service composition with the length $4 \times k_{max}$, where k_{max} is the maximum number of services required, and the population size is 100. The fitness function is calculated by Formula (6), the selection function adopts RWS, the crossover function uses one-point crossover and one-point mutation method was used for mutation function with the rate 0.2. At last, the number of iterations is 100 as well as in ACO-SS. Meanwhile, ACO-SS takes the following parameters: the ant colony size is 100; evaporation rate is 0.25 and Q is 1.5; both α and β are 1; the number of iterations is 100.

The precision rate and recall rate as the evaluation indexes defined in Formula (12) and (14). In the simulation, precision and recall are obtained by the mean of serval results.

$$precision = \frac{\sum s_i^s}{k} \times 100\% \quad i = (1, 2, ..., k) \tag{12}$$

where

$$s_i^s = \begin{cases} 1, & if \; qoe(s_i^s) \geq qoe_{th} \\ 0, & else \end{cases} \tag{13}$$

qoe_{th} is the QoE threshold of the service that meets the requirement.

$$recall = \frac{\sum s_i^s}{\sum s_j} \times 100\% \quad i = (1, 2, ..., k), j = (1, 2, ..., n) \tag{14}$$

where

$$s_j = \begin{cases} 1, & if \ qoe(s_j) \geq qoe_{th} \\ 0, & else \end{cases} \tag{15}$$

n is the total number of services.

The experiment results are shown in Fig. 4. It can be clearly seen that both methods have close precision and recall when k is small, but the gap between them becomes larger with the increasing of k. In general, the precision and recall of ACO-SS are almost 10% higher than that of GA-SS on average.

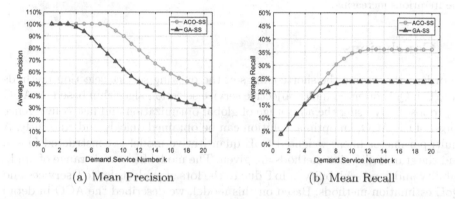

(a) Mean Precision   (b) Mean Recall

Fig. 4. Comparison of the mean precision and recall between two methods as the demand service number k increasing.

However, although adjusting the parameters can make both methods perform better in terms of precision and recall, it will significantly reduce the efficiency of them, which means users cannot get results within an acceptable time. By the analysis for both algorithms, it can be known that the algorithm efficiency of ACO-SS is mainly affected by the ants number and iterations. While for the GA-SS, the encoding length will also greatly affect its algorithm efficiency besides the population size and iterations due to the encoding length will directly affect the three operations: selection, crossover and mutation. As shown in Fig. 5, we compared the execution time of two methods with $k = 5$ as the number of iterations increasing. ACO-SS adopts the same parameters as above, while GA reduces the population size to 40 and the encoding length to $2 \times k$. It can be seen that the time of 100 iterations for both algorithms is less than 1s, which is within the acceptable range of users. In addition, the algorithm efficiency of ACO-SS is still several times higher than that of GA-SS, even if the GA's parameters are greatly reduced (its recall and precision are reduced accordingly).

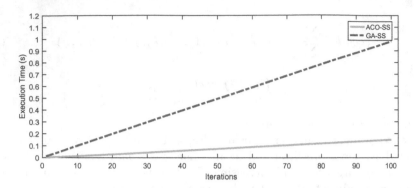

Fig. 5. Comparison of the average execution time between two methods with $k = 5$ as the iterations increasing.

5   Conclusions

In order to overcome the shortcomings of the existing service selection methods in IoT, a QoE-oriented multi-objective service selection algorithm based on ACO is proposed. By using the advantage of global optimization and fast convergence speed of the ACO, an optimal solution can be obtained quickly and efficiently. A multi-parameter linear weighted QoE quantitative model is constructed firstly, and the standardization methods are given. The model has a wide range of applicability and good scalability in IoT due to the lots of analysis for IoT services and QoE estimation methods. Based on this model, we described the ACO in detail and proposed the ACO-SS algorithm. Finally, the proposed method is validated by simulations and the results show that, compared with other algorithms such as GA, the proposed method can effectively improve the precision and recall for service selection in the same scenario with a far more higher computational efficiency and thus is a feasible and effective way to solve the issue of service selection in IoT. In the future, we will consider combing ACO-SS with other methods and conducting more extensive simulations to evaluate the efficiency and robustness of the proposed method on a larger scale data.

Acknowledgements. Thanks to the National Natural Science Foundation of China (Grants No. 41761086) for funding.

References

1. Atzori, L., Iera, A., Morabito, G.: The Internet of Things: a survey. Comput. Netw. **54**(15), 2787–2805 (2010)
2. Jain, R.: Quality of experience. Multimedia IEEE **11**(1), 95–96 (2014)
3. Jing, H., Wengdong, W.: A service implementation scenario measuring users' QoE. J. Beijing Univ. Posts Telecommun. **30**(2), 106–109 (2007)
4. Runqun, X., Junzhou, L., Aibo, S.: QoS preference-aware replica selection strategy in cloud computing. J. Commun. **32**(7), 93–102 (2011)

5. Herrera-Viedma, E., Chiclana, F., Herrera, F., et al.: Group decision-making model with incomplete fuzzy preference relations based on additive consistency. IEEE Trans. Cybern. **37**(1), 176–189 (2007)
6. Guohua, C.: Direct search algorithm to integer linear programming portfolio selection model. Commun. Appl. Math. Comput. **25**(1), 119–126 (2011)
7. Tantan, L., Ming, L.: Heuristic algorithm-based initiation method of probability hypothesis density filter for target tracking. J. Shanghai Jiaotong Univ. **52**(1), 63–69 (2018)
8. Jansen K., Rohwedder, L.: On Integer Programming and Convolution (2018)
9. Rojas, I., González, J., Pomares, H., et al.: Statistical analysis of the main parameters involved in the design of a genetic algorithm. Syst. Control Lett. **58**(9), 652–663 (2002)
10. Marco, D., Montes, O.M.A., Sabrina, O., Thomas, S.: Ant colony optimization. IEEE Comput. Intell. Mag. **1**(4), 28–39 (2007)
11. Chunlin, L., Dan, L., Ling, X.: A service selection algorithm based on quantified QoE evaluation. Chin. J. Electron. **43**(11), 2145–2150 (2015)
12. Bing, J., Lifei, H., Chuxuan, Z., et al.: An IoT service aggregation method based on dynamic planning for QoE restraints. Mobile Netw. Appl. **24**, 25–33 (2018)
13. How does "ant colony algorithm" get the optimal solution from "more hands produce a stronger flame" (2018). https://blog.csdn.net/dog_bite_dog/article/details/79221048
14. Solnon, C.: Ant Colony Optimization and Constraint Programming. Wiley-IEEE Press, New York (2018)
15. Lipowski, A., Lipowska, D.: Roulette-wheel selection via stochastic acceptance. Physica A Stat. Mech. Appl. **391**(6), 2193–2196 (2011)

FDSCD: Fast Deletion Scheme of Cloud Data

Tong Shao[1(✉)] (iD), Yuechi Tian[2], Zhen Li[1,2], and Xuan Jing[1]

[1] Cyberspace Security and Computer College,
Hebei University, Baoding 071002, China
15613668123@163.com
[2] School of Computer Science and Technology, HUST, Wuhan 430074, China

Abstract. With the rapid development of cloud storage technology, cloud data assured deletion has received extensive attention. While ensuring the deletion of cloud data, users have also placed increasing demands on cloud data assured deletion, such as improving the execution efficiency of various stages of a cloud data assured deletion system and performing fine-grained access and deletion operations. In this paper, we propose the Fast deletion scheme of cloud data. The scheme replaces complicated bilinear pairing with simple scalar multiplication on elliptic curves to realize ciphertext policy attribute-based encryption of cloud data, while solving the security problem of shared data. In addition, the efficiency of encryption and decryption is improved, and fine-grained access of ciphertext is realized. The scheme designs an attribute key management system that employs a dual-server to solve system flaws caused by single point failure. The scheme is proven to be secure, based on the decisional Diffie-Hellman assumption in the standard model; therefore, it has stronger security. The theoretical analysis and experimental results show that the scheme guarantees security and significantly improves the efficiency of each stage of cloud data assured deletion.

Keywords: Cloud storage · CP-ABE · Data privacy ·
Elliptic curve cryptography (ECC) · Assured deletion

1 Introduction

With the rapid development of cloud storage technology, an increasing number of individuals or enterprises choose to store data in the cloud to reduce data management costs. However, compared with traditional data storage methods, data storage in the cloud is beyond the direct control of the data owner, which renders the security of the data difficult to guarantee.

To protect the confidentiality and privacy of data, cloud data must be encrypted before they are outsourced to the cloud [1–5]. A central advantage of using cryptographic primitives such as symmetric-key encryption is that the safety of a large amount of sensitive data can be reduced to the safety of a very small key [6]. Therefore, the issue of cloud data assured deletion is translated into the secure deletion problem of the corresponding key of the client [7]. A cloud data assured deletion scheme can be divided into two types: assured deletion based on key management and assured deletion based on an access control policy.

© ICST Institute for Computer Sciences, Social Informatics and Telecommunications Engineering 2019
Published by Springer Nature Switzerland AG 2019. All Rights Reserved
J. Li et al. (Eds.): SPNCE 2019, LNICST 284, pp. 354–361, 2019.
https://doi.org/10.1007/978-3-030-21373-2_27

Assured deletion schemes based on key management. proposed a cloud data security self-destruction scheme (ISS) that is based on identity-based encryption (IBE) [8], which divides the data to be protected into different security levels according to different sensitivity levels. Yao et al. [9] proposed a cloud data assured deletion scheme that is based on bitstream conversion.

The assured deletion scheme that is based on key management cannot achieve fine-grained access to ciphertext. When the key of the encrypted data is deleted, all users cannot decrypt the ciphertext again.

Assured deletion schemes based on access control policy. For fine-grained access control problems, Liang et al. [10] proposed an assured deletion scheme that is based on an undo tree, which uses a linear secret sharing scheme and a binary tree as the underlying tool and assigns a set of attributes to each user and assigns a unique identifier. Wang et al. [11] proposed an assured deletion scheme that is based on attribute revocation, which is a CP-ABE scheme that supports attribute-level user revocation. Xue et al. [12] proposed a cloud data assured deletion scheme that is based on hash tree verification for attribute revocation.

Although the assured deletion scheme that is based on an access control policy solves the problem of fine-grained access control, these schemes use a bilinear pair to implement the attribute-based encryption scheme, which creates the problem of low system efficiency.

In this paper, the Fast deletion scheme of cloud data (FDSCD) is proposed for schemes that cannot balance efficiency and fine-grained access. This scheme employs simple scalar multiplication in an elliptic curve instead of a complex bilinear pair to implement an attribute-based encryption algorithm [13], which simplifies the calculations during encryption and decryption. The key is generated by the key generator and the attribute authorizer in the attribute key management system. The key generator is responsible for generating the system master key and the public key, and the attribute authorizer is responsible for maintaining a list of user attributes. When the user needs to decrypt, the authorized user sends part of the ciphertext to the attribute authorizer. The attribute authorizer generates the user private key via the attribute list, and partially decrypts the ciphertext, which reduce the decryption overhead of the authorized user. When deleting data, the data owner only needs to generate a random number to replace the attribute value of the attribute that needs to be deleted in the attribute list of the original attribute authorize. The public key of the corresponding attribute value is not updated, which ensure that fine-grained access control can be realized without complicated calculation.

2 System Model

2.1 System Model

The system model of the FDSCD solution is shown in Fig. 1. The model includes four types of entities: Attribute Key Management System (AKMS), Data Owner (DO), Cloud Service Provider (CSP), Authorized user (AU).

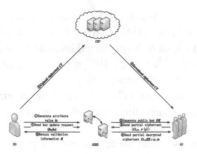

Fig. 1. The system model

AKMS is responsible for the generation and update of the key and helps an authorized user to decrypt part of the ciphertext. The main internal structure is shown in Fig. 2. AKMS is primarily composed of a key generator and an attribute authorizer. The two parts independently communicate with other components and the TPM security chip protects its internal data. The key generator is responsible for managing the system master key and the system public key. The attribute authorizer is responsible for assigning each authorized user a unique identifier ID and maintaining a list of attributes for the authorized user. When the authorized user decrypts the ciphertext, the attribute authorizer generates the user private key and assists the authorized user to partially decrypt the ciphertext. A question-and-answer method is employed between the key generator and the attribute authorizer to confirm that each is normally functioning. The attribute authorizer periodically issues a question to the key generator, and the key generator must return the correct answer within the specified time. If a question or answer is not returned within the specified time, the party is considered to have an abnormality, and the other party will replace the abnormal party to handle the transaction, which ensures normal operation of the system and prevents system paralysis caused by failure of a single point.

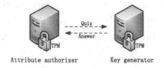

Fig. 2. Internal structure of attribute key management system

The CSP is responsible for storing the encrypted data of the data owner. CSP honestly stores the encrypted data of the data owner and reliably responds to data requests.

The DO is responsible for assigning the unique identifier k_i to each attribute and encrypting the data that needs to be uploaded to the cloud. When the cloud data are deleted, the DO sends an update request to the attribute authorizer in the attribute key management system and verifies the returned update result.

The AU accesses the encrypted data stored by the data owner in the cloud and obtains the encrypted data by sending a data request to the cloud service provider. After obtaining the encrypted data, the AU requests that the attribute authorizer in the attribute key management system partially decrypt the ciphertext. After receiving the result returned by the attribute authorizer, the UA decrypts all ciphertexts to obtain the original data.

3   Detailed Design of the FDSCD Scheme

The workflow of the FDSCD scheme is shown in Fig. 1. The main algorithms are described as follows:

Step 1. System Initialization
Let $GF(p)$ be a finite field of order p, E be an elliptic curve defined in the finite field $GF(p)$, r be the order of the subgroup in the elliptic curve E, and G be a base point in the subgroup. G generates a cyclic subgroup of elliptic curves E; Z_r is an integer domain of order r; and the one-way function $H: \{0, 1\}^* \to Z_r^*$ is randomly selected: the user ID is mapped to the integer domain Z_r.

$$Setup(n, S, k_i) \to (MSK, PK)$$

For each attribute i in the system attribute set S, the data owner randomly selects the parameters $k_1, k_2, \cdots, k_S \in Z_r$ to upload to the attribute key management system.

The key generator randomly selects n ($n \in Z_r$) to generate the system master key.

$$MSK = (k_1, k_2, \cdots, k_S, n, G),$$

Generate the system public key parameters.

$$PK = (k_1 G, k_2 G, \cdots, k_S G).$$

The attribute authorizer maintains a list of attributes that correspond to its ID for each user in the system, as shown in Table 1.

Table 1. User attribute list

ID_1	ID_2	...	ID_n
$k_{Att_{11}}$	$k_{Att_{21}}$	...	$k_{Att_{n1}}$
$k_{Att_{12}}$	$k_{Att_{22}}$	...	$k_{Att_{n2}}$
$k_{Att_{13}}$	$k_{Att_{23}}$	...	$k_{Att_{n3}}$
...	...	...	...

Step 2. Generate a private key

$$AKMSKeyGen(ki, ID, n) \rightarrow \{SK_{i,ID}\}$$

For each attribute i in the user ID attribute set S_{ID}, the attribute authorizer calculates the user private key

$$SK_{i,ID} = k_i + H(ID)n.$$

Step 3. Data Encryption

The data owner encrypts the original data M to generate the encrypted data CT, and the encryption algorithm proceeds as follows:

$$Encrypt(M, s, PK_i, A, v, u) \rightarrow CT$$

The data owner randomly selects $s \in Z_r$ as the encryption key; it calculates

$$C = M + sG.$$

The key s is split using the LSSS [14, 15] as follows:

Define the access control strategy (A, ρ), where A is a linear secret sharing matrix, ρ is the mapping function of the matrix row vector and the attribute, and ρ maps each row A_x of the matrix A to the attribute $\rho(x)$. As in [16], ρ does not map two different rows to the same attribute. Randomly select the parameters $v_2, v_3, \cdots, v_l \in Z_p$, define the vector $v = (s, v_2, v_3, \cdots, v_l)^T$, and calculate the inner product $\lambda_x = A_x \cdot v$ for each row A_x of the matrix A. Randomly select the parameters $u_2, u_3, \cdots, u_l \in Z_p$, define the vector $u = (0, u_2, u_3, \cdots, u_l)^T$, and calculate the inner product $\omega_x = A_x \cdot u$ for each row A_x of the matrix A.

The data owner outputs the ciphertext

$$CT = ((A, \rho), C, \{C_{1x} = \lambda_x G + \omega_x PK_{\rho(x)}, C_{2x} = \omega_x G\}_{x=1}^m).$$

Step 4. Data decryption

$$Decrypt(C, SK_{\rho(y),ID}) \rightarrow M$$

To decrypt the cloud data, the authorized user sends a ciphertext request to the cloud. After obtaining the ciphertext, the authorized user sends the ID and the $(C_{2,y}, \rho(y))$ associated with each attribute $y \in S_{ID}$ to the attribute authorizer. The attribute authorizer verifies the sender identity and the attribute set based on the maintained attribute list. If the request is valid, the attribute authorizer calculates each of the requests $(C_{2,y}, \rho(y))$

$$
\begin{aligned}
C_{2,y}SK_{\rho(y),ID} &= \omega_y G(k_{\rho(y)} + H(ID)n) \\
&= \omega_y k_{\rho(y)} G + \omega_y H(ID)nG^{\cdot}
\end{aligned}
$$

The attribute authorizer sends the calculated result to the authorized user, and the authorized user receives the returned result and then calculates

$$C_{1,y} - C_{2,y}SK_{\rho(y),ID}$$
$$= (\lambda_y G + \omega_y PK_{\rho(y)}) - (\omega_y k_{\rho(y)}G + \omega_y H(ID)nG).$$
$$= \lambda_y G - \omega_y H(ID)nG$$

The authorized user selects the vector $c \in Z_r$, lets $c \cdot A_y = (1, 0, \cdots, 0)$, and calculates

$$\sum_{y \in S_{ID}} c(\lambda_y G - \omega_y H(ID)nG) = sG.$$

The authorized user calculates

$$C - sG = M.$$

The original data M are obtained.

Step 5. Delete Data

$$DeleteDate(ID_{RL_x}, k_x, h_x, n) \rightarrow \{SK_{x, ID_{RL_x}}\}$$

The data owner sends a key update request to the attribute authorizer. First, randomly select $h_x \in Z_r$ and $h_x \neq k_x$, and then send the original attribute value k_x of the attribute x and the updated attribute value h_x to the attribute authorizer. The attribute authorizer finds the user set RL_x, owns the attribute according to k_x, and then replaces k_x with h_x. The user private key after the attribute value is replaced is

$$SK_{x, ID_{RL_x}} = h_x + H(ID_{RL_x})n.$$

The public key remains

$$PK_x = k_x G.$$

When the authorized user in the user set RL_x decrypts the ciphertext, the attribute authorizer calculates $(C_{2, x}, \rho(x))$ for each attribute $x \in S_{ID_{RL_x}}$.

$$C_{2,x}SK_{\rho(x), ID_{RL_x}} = \omega_x G(h_{\rho(x)} + H(ID_{RL_x})n)$$
$$= \omega_x h_{\rho(x)}G + \omega_x H(ID)nG$$

Return the result to the authorized user. After the authorized user receives the result, it calculates

$$
\begin{aligned}
C_{1,x} &- C_{2,x}SK_{\rho(x),ID_{RL_x}} \\
&= (\lambda_x G + \omega_x PK_{\rho(x)}) - (\omega_x h_{\rho(x)}G + \omega_x H(ID_{RL_x})nG) \\
&= (\lambda_x G + \omega_x k_{\rho(x)}G) - (\omega_x h_{\rho(x)}G + \omega_x H(ID_{RL_x})nG) \\
&\neq \lambda_x G - \omega_x H(ID_{RL_x})nG
\end{aligned}
$$

Therefore, the ciphertext cannot be decrypted, and the deletion operation of the encrypted data is realized.

Step 6. Verification

$$
Verify(R, X_{RL_x}, \Omega_{RL_x}) \rightarrow result
$$

The attribute authorizer hashes the attribute list of each user in units of users, and then uses the hash value X_{ID} of each column of the attribute list as the leaf node of the hash tree to establish a hash tree and obtain the hash tree root value R. The data owner also maintains a list of attributes of an authorized user, uses the same hash function as the attribute authorizer to calculate the hash values $\tilde{X}_{ID}$ of each attribute list of the user, and generates a hash tree. When the data owner verifies whether the attribute authorizer performs an update or delete operation, the root value R of the updated attribute list hash tree is sent to the data owner by requesting the attribute authorizer, and the data owner updates the hash value $\tilde{X}_{RL_x}$ of the user set RL_x. Calculate the local hash tree root value $\tilde{R}$ using the hash value $\tilde{X}_{RL_x}$ and the auxiliary authentication information Ω_{RL_x}. If $\tilde{R} = R$, the attribute update operation requested by the data owner is successful; otherwise, the request execution fails.

4 Conclusion

This paper proposes the fast deletion scheme of cloud data that enables users to encrypt and decrypt and delete original data in a short period. In this scheme, if the attribute authorizer changes the attribute value of the maintained user attribute list, and the data owner does not update the public key, the user whose attribute is revoked cannot decrypt the ciphertext of the cloud, only the attribute satisfies the access policy and users who have not been revoked can successfully decrypt the ciphertext. Thus, fine-grained access and deletion of cloud data are achieved. The scheme also realizes the reasonable allocation of the work in the system, which reduces the computational overhead of a single party and increases the communication overhead.

References

1. Reardon, J., Basin, D.A., Capkun, S.: Secure data deletion. Inf. Secur. Cryptogr. (2016)
2. Xiong, J.B., Li, F.H., Wang, Y.C., et al.: Research progress on cloud data assured deletion based on cryptography. J. Commun. **37**(8), 167–184 (2016)
3. Liu, Z.L., Li, T., Li, P., et al.: Verifiable searchable encryption with aggregate keys for data sharing system. Futur. Gener. Comput. Syst. **78**(2), 778–788 (2018)
4. Liu, Z.L., Huang, Y.Y., Li, J., et al.: DivORAM: towards a practical oblivious RAM with variable block size. Inf. Sci. **447**, 1–11 (2018)
5. Li, T., Liu, Z.L., Li, J., et al.: CDPS: a cryptographic data publishing system. J. Comput. Syst. Sci. **89**, 80–91 (2017)
6. Agrawal, S., Mohassel, P., Mukherjee, P., et al.: DiSE: distributed symmetric-key encryption. In: ACM Conference on Computer and Communications Security, pp. 1993–2010 (2018)
7. Li, H., Sun, W.H., Li, F.H., et al.: Secure and privacy-preserving data storage service in public cloud. J. Comput. Res. Dev. **51**(7), 1397–1409 (2014)
8. Xiong, J.B., Yao, Z.Q., Ma, J.F., et al.: A secure self-destruction scheme with IBE for the internet content privacy. Chin. J. Comput. **37**(1), 139–150 (2014)
9. Yao, W., Chen, Y., Wang, D.: Cloud multimedia files assured deletion based on bit stream transformation with chaos sequence. In: Ibrahim, S., Choo, K.-K.R., Yan, Z., Pedrycz, W. (eds.) ICA3PP 2017. LNCS, vol. 10393, pp. 441–451. Springer, Cham (2017). https://doi.org/10.1007/978-3-319-65482-9_31
10. Liang, X., Lu, R., Lin, X., et al.: Ciphertext policy attribute based encryption with efficient revocation. IEEE Symp. Secur. Priv. **2008**, 321–334 (2010)
11. Wang, G.B., Liu, H.T., Wang, C.L., et al.: Revocable attribute based encryption in cloud storage. J. Comput. Res. Dev. **55**(6), 1190–1200 (2018)
12. Xue, L., Yu, Y., Li, Y., et al.: Efficient attribute-based encryption with attribute revocation for assured data deletion. Inf. Sci., 1–11 (2018)
13. Li, B., Huang, D.J., Wang, Z.J., et al.: Attribute-based access control for ICN naming scheme. IEEE Trans. Dependable Secur. Comput. **15**(2), 194–206 (2018)
14. Peng, Q., Tian, Y.L.: A secret sharing scheme based on multilinear Diffie-Hellman problem. Acta Electron. Sin. **45**(1), 200–205 (2017)
15. Waters, B.: Ciphertext policy attribute based on encryption: an expressive, efficient, and provably secure realization. In: Proceedings of the 14th International Conference on Practice and Theory in Public Key Cryptography, Taormina, Italy, pp. 53–70 (2011)
16. Lewko, A., Okamoto, T., Sahai, A., Takashima, K., Waters, B.: Fully secure functional encryption: attribute-based encryption and (hierarchical) inner product encryption. In: Gilbert, H. (ed.) EUROCRYPT 2010. LNCS, vol. 6110, pp. 62–91. Springer, Heidelberg (2010). https://doi.org/10.1007/978-3-642-13190-5_4

A RBAC Model Based on Identity-Based Cryptosystem in Cloud Storage

Jian Xu$^{(\boxtimes)}$, Yanbo Yu, Qingyu Meng, Qiyu Wu, and Fucai Zhou

Software College, Northeastern University, Shenyang 110169, China
xuj@mail.neu.edu.cn

Abstract. Aiming at the shortcomings of most of existing ciphertext access control scheme in cloud storage does not support dynamic update of access control strategy, has large computational overhead ,combine identity-based cryptosystem and role based access control model (using RBAC1 model of the RBAC96 model family), build RBAC model based on identity-based cryptosystem in cloud storage. This paper presents a formal definition of the scheme, a detailed description of four tuple used to represent access control strategy, the hybrid encryption strategy and Re-encrypt when writing strategy in order to improve the efficiency of the system, detailed steps of system initialization, add and delete users, add and delete permissions, add and delete roles, add and delete role inheritance, assign and remove user, assign and remove permission, read and write file algorithm.

Keywords: Access control · RBAC · Identity-based cryptosystem · Cloud storage

1 Introduction

With the rapid development of computer technology and Internet applications, data is growing at an exponential rate. Faced with such massive data, cloud storage which developed from the concept of cloud computing has become the most common and popular third-party storage with its advantages of low cost, huge capacity, resource sharing, easy management and good scalability. Users and enterprises can purchase storage services flexibly according to their own needs, which not only save expensive software and hardware infrastructure investment, but also ensure that storage resources are fully utilized. Cloud storage service providers also provide professional data backup, disaster recovery and other functions to effectively ensure the continuity of services [1, 2].

Although cloud storage has many advantages, however, its promotion is relatively slow. The main reason is that once the data is uploaded to the cloud, users lose control of it, and they do not know what the cloud storage provider will do with the data. Cloud storage providers may snoop on the content of the data and even provide the user's data directly to third parties, especially in an untrusted cloud environment. Therefore, ensuring the confidentiality of user data, avoiding it being illegally accessed, achieving secure and efficient access control is the key to solving data security problems in cloud storage [9]. However, as the cloud environment has the characteristics of dynamic

J. Li et al. (Eds.): SPNCE 2019, LNICST 284, pp. 362–377, 2019.
https://doi.org/10.1007/978-3-030-21373-2_28

change, multi-tenancy and virtualization, the traditional access control model cannot meet the requirements of the new cloud architecture. So how to expand and optimize the traditional access control model, especially combine advanced encryption technology with traditional access control models, to build an access control scheme for cloud storage environment has become a hot topic in academic research. In the case that the cloud storage provider is not trusted, the research of ensuring the confidentiality of data and implement access control of the ciphertext data is therefore a top priority.

1.1 Related Works

Many researchers have started research on access control technology under the cloud computing environment and have obtained many research results.

Jung et al. [3] proposed an adaptive resource access control scheme based on the RBAC model. This scheme can dynamically adjust the security level of resources and solve the problem of dynamic changes of environment variables in cloud computing. Wang et al. [4] introduced the concept of task into the RBAC model and proposed a task- and role-based access control model (T-RBAC) in the cloud computing environment. In T-RBAC, workflow is first broken down into a series of interdependent tasks, which are then assigned to the role, and the user gets the role by executing the task node. The Danwei et al. [5] adopts a negotiation policy when designing the access control model, and proposes a UCON-based cloud service access control scheme. Based on the UCON model, Krautsevich et al. [6] introduced a risk assessment mechanism, and purposed an access control scheme for highly dynamic system, which improves the flexibility and security of the UCON model.

Attribute-Based Encryption (ABE) is the most commonly used advanced encryption algorithm in cloud access control. It extends the concept of identity as a set of attributes. In 2005, Sahai et al. [7] first proposed a fuzzy identity-based encryption scheme, in which the concept of attributes was introduced. Subsequently, based on this, Goyal et al. [8] proposed an attribute-based encryption scheme. And then derived two attribute-based encryption algorithms closely related to the access control policy, KP-ABE (Key Policy Attribute-Based Encryption) [9] and CP-ABE (Ciphertext Policy Attribute-Based Encryption) [10], in which CP-ABE is more suitable for cloud environments. Sun et al. [11] proposed a data security access control scheme for cloud storage based on CP-ABE. This scheme adopts a distribution method for distributed key, and access control is implemented by designing keys. However, the scheme is suitable for the case where the access permission type is small, once the type is increased, key management may become very complicated. Jung et al. [12] designed an anonymous access control scheme, which perform anonymous access control on cloud data to protect user's privacy; Ruj et al. [13] proposes a cloud security access control framework that can implement user authentication and privacy protection of data.

Although the above attribute-based access control schemes can ensure the confidentiality of user data and achieve fine-grained access control of data, but they do not support dynamic update of access control policy. It obviously does not meet the requirements of the dynamic environment in the cloud. For the problems mentioned above, researchers have proposed some schemes. Yu et al. [14] proposed a secure and scalable cloud storage access control scheme based on CP-ABE, which supports attribute revoking and employs a proxy re-encryption policy to save computational overhead; Hur et al. [15] designed an access control scheme that supports user attribute revoking, using double-layer encryption mechanism to improve efficiency; Chen et al. [16] proposed a hybrid access control scheme that supports hierarchical management of multiple authorization mechanisms, which reduced management complexity. Although these schemes can support the revoke operation, the computational overhead cannot be ignored.

As mentioned above, there are many shortcomings of current access control schemes in the cloud environment. Although simply optimize the traditional access control model and apply it to the cloud environment can implement basic access control functions, the confidentiality of data cannot be guaranteed. The attribute-based ciphertext access control scheme can protect data when the cloud storage provider is not trusted, but most schemes do not support the dynamic update of access control policy, or the computational overhead is huge although the policy update is supported.

1.2 Contributions

To solve the problems mentioned above, this paper proposes an RBAC scheme based on identity cryptosystem in cloud storage. This paper describes the application scenarios and entity composition of the scheme, and gives a formal definition of the scheme. The four tuples used to represent the access control policy in the scheme are described in detail, as well as the hybrid encryption policy and the write-time re-encryption policy designed to improve system efficiency. Detailed steps of system initialization, user addition and deletion, permission addition and deletion, role addition and deletion, role's inheritance relationship addition and deletion, user assignment and revocation, permission assignment and revocation, file reading and writing are given.

2 Constructions

2.1 Design Idea

Our scheme is mainly composed of three-party entities: access control administrators, cloud storage providers (reference monitors are deployed in the cloud as part of the cloud storage provider, not separately listed as one entity) and users. The roles and functions of the three entities are as follows:

(1) Access control administrator: It is the administrator of the access control system, responsible for developing and updating access control policy. It determines who has the permission to access the resource. In this scheme, it has two important functions. One is to act as a key generation center in the identity-based cryptosystem; it holds the system master key, creates and distributes keys for users in the system. Second is to develop and update the access control policy in the system. The specific operations include the addition and deletion of roles, the addition and deletion of role's inheritance relationships, the assignment and revocation of users, and the assignment and revocation of permissions.

(2) Cloud storage provider: As a provider of storage services, it manages the storage needs of users. It not only stores the data that users deposit in the cloud, but also stores access control policy that provide protection for those data. This paper assumes that the cloud storage provider is untrustworthy and cannot let it view the contents of the file stored on it, but at the same time believes that it can guarantee the availability of the file and that only authorized users can change the content of the file.

Reference monitor: Most access control models have one thing in common, that is, relying on a trusted reference monitor to check whether an access request conforms to an access control policy before accessing the protected resource. In this scheme, the reference monitor is deployed in the cloud and is responsible for coordinating authorized access to resources. For example, when write permission is executed, it is responsible for verifying that if the user's signature is valid and checking if the user has write permission.

In a nutshell, cloud storage providers ensure file system consistency by blocking unauthorized updates, while it cannot read files or change files and access control policy.

(3) User: It is a user of the cloud storage service and is managed by the access control administrator. It needs to register with the administrator and obtain its own key before using the system. It can upload its own data to the cloud storage, or download the data in the cloud for read and write operations (The premise is that there is a corresponding access permission, otherwise the data will not be decrypted, or the reference monitor will determine that there is no corresponding permission, and the operation cannot be performed).

2.2 Formal Definitions

Definition 1: The RBAC scheme based on identity cryptosystem (RBAC-IBC) in cloud storage can be represented by a tuple composed of eight PPT algorithms, that is, RBAC-IBC = $(Setup, User, Permission, Role, Inh, UR, PA, R\&W)$. The details are described as follows:

(1) $Setup(I^n)$: System initialization algorithm. The input is security parameter n, which generates a common parameter of identity-based encryption algorithm and a master key of identity-based signature algorithm, and generates an identity-based decryption key and signature key for the administrator.

(2) $User(addU(u), delU(u))$: User addition and deletion algorithm. It contains two sub-algorithms: user addition algorithm and user deletion algorithm. The input of user addition algorithm is the username u, which generates an identity-based decryption key and signature key for the user; the input of user deletion algorithm is also the username u, which revokes the user from the system, and then the user will not be able to access any files in the cloud.

(3) $Permission(addP(fn, f), delP(fn))$: Permission addition and deletion algorithm. It contains two sub-algorithms: permission addition algorithm and permission deletion algorithm. The input of permission addition algorithm is the file name fn

and the file content f, which encrypts the file and uploads it to the cloud; the input of permission deletion algorithm is the file name fn, which removes the file from the system.

(4) *Role(addR(r), delR(r))*: Role addition and deletion algorithm. It contains two sub-algorithms: role addition algorithm and role deletion algorithm. The input of role addition algorithm is the role name r, which adds a role to the access control system and generates an identity-based decryption key and signature key for the role; the input of role deletion algorithm is the role name r, which revokes the role from the system.

(5) *Inh(addInh(r_c, r_p), delInh(r_c, r_p))*: Role's inheritance relationship addition and deletion algorithm. It contains two sub-algorithms: role's inheritance relationship addition algorithm and role's inheritance relationship deletion algorithm. The input of role's inheritance relationship addition algorithm is the child role r_c and the parent role r_p, which adds a role's inheritance relationship to the system, so that the role r_c inherits the role r_p; the input of role's inheritance relationship deletion algorithm is the child role r_c and the parent role r_p, which revokes the inheritance relationship between them from the system.

(6) *UR(assignU(r, u), revokeU(r, u))*: User assignment and revocation algorithm. It contains two sub-algorithms: user assignment algorithm and user revocation algorithm. The input of user assignment algorithm is the role r and the user u, which assigns user u to role r; the input of user revocation algorithm is the role r and the user u, which revokes user u from the user list of role r.

(7) *PA(assignP(r, ⟨fn, op⟩), revokeP(r, ⟨fn, op⟩))*: Permission assignment and revocation algorithm. It contains two sub-algorithms: permission assignment algorithm and permission revocation algorithm. The input of permission assignment algorithm is the role r, the file name fn and permission name op, which assigns the operation permission (op) of the file fn for the role r; the input of permission revocation algorithm is the role r, the file name fn and permission name op, which revokes the operation permission (op) of the file fn from the role r.

(8) *R&W(read(fn), write(fn, f))*: File reading and writing algorithm. It contains two sub-algorithms: file reading algorithm and file writing (update) algorithm. The input of file reading algorithm is the file name fn, and the user reads file; the input of file writing algorithm is the file name fn and the updated content of the file f, which updates file content stored in the cloud.

According to the access control scheme evaluation method, the relevant properties used to evaluate RBAC-IBC are defined as follows:

Definition 2: If the implementation of the RBAC scheme based on the identity cryptosystem $\langle \sigma, \alpha, \pi \rangle$ has the following properties:

Property 1: Command mapping protects state mapping and protects security.
Property 2: State mapping protects query mapping.
Property 3: Query mapping is access control protected.
Then the scheme is correct, access control protected, and secure.

2.3   Detailed Description

The scheme is divided into eight parts by function: System initialization, user addition and deletion, permission addition and deletion, role addition and deletion, role's inheritance relationship addition and deletion, user assignment and revocation, permission assignment and revocation, file reading and writing. Each detailed step is given below.

For convenience, first explain the symbols used in this section. The definition of each symbol is described in Table 1.

Table 1. Symbol description

Symbol	Description
u	User name
r	Role name
f	File (Here is the file content itself)
fn	File name
v	Version number
k	Symmetric key
EK	Identity-based decryption key
SK	Identity-based signature key
$USERS$	File that stores the username
$ROLES$	File that stores the role name and role's key version number
$FILES$	File that stores the file name and file's key version number
SU	Access control administrator
$R.M$	Reference monitor deployed in the cloud
$-$	Wildcard

2.3.1   System Initialization

$Setup(I^n)$: System initialization algorithm. The administrator performs system initialization operation. The main steps are as follows:

Step 1: Perform the initialization algorithm of identity-based encryption and identity-based signature scheme. Generate their own public parameters and master keys, expose public parameters, and secretly save the master keys.

Step 2: Create three empty files——USERS, ROLES and FILES, upload ROLES and FILES to the cloud.

Step 3: Generate an identity-based decryption key EK_{SU} and signature key SK_{SU} for himself:

$$KeyGen^{IBE}(SU) \rightarrow EK_{SU}, KeyGen^{IBS}(SU) \rightarrow SK_{SU}.$$

Note that in order to save space, the description of the key generation process is simplified here, and parameters such as the master keys are not listed, and the subsequent algorithm description is also the same.

2.3.2 User Addition and Deletion

$addU(u)$: User addition algorithm. When a new user joins the system, he needs to register with the administrator and the administrator performs the user addition operation. The main steps are as follows:

Step 1: Add the username u to the file *USERS*.
Step 2: Generate the identity-based decryption key EK_u and signature key SK_u for the user:

$$KeyGen^{IBE}(u) \rightarrow EK_u, KeyGen^{IBS}(u) \rightarrow SK_u.$$

Step 3: Send EK_u and SK_u to the user via the trusted channel

$delU(u)$: User deletion algorithm. To delete a user from the system, the administrator needs to do the following operations:

For each role r that contains user u, perform the operation *$revokeU(r,u)$.
The symbol $*$ here means that the specific steps of this operation will be given later, and the following appears $*$ is synonymous with this.

2.3.3 Permission Addition and Deletion

$addP_u(fn,f)$: Permission addition algorithm. Actually, the operation of adding permission is that the user uploads file. The permission to read and write files is first assigned to the administrator, who then assigns permission to the role. The main steps are as follows:

Step 1: User generates the symmetric key required to encrypt the file: $KeyGen^{Sym} \rightarrow k$.
Step 2: Build tuple F and tuple PA (the initial file key version number is set to 1), the forms are as follows: $\langle F, fn, 1, Enc_k^{Sym}(f), u, Sign_u^{IBS} \rangle$, $\langle PA, SU, (fn, RW), 1, Enc_{SU}^{IBE}(k), u, Sign_u^{IBS} \rangle$, and send them to the cloud.
Step 3: After receiving the two tuples, the reference monitor $R.M$ deployed in the cloud performs the following operations:

(1) Check that the tuple format is correct. If the format is correct, proceed to the next step, otherwise send an error report.
(2) Verify that the user's identity-based signature is legal. If the signature is legal, that is:
$Verify_u^{IBS}(\langle F, fn, 1, Enc_k^{Sym}(f), u \rangle, Sign_u^{IBS}) = 1$
$Verify_u^{IBS}(\langle PA, SU, (fn, RW), 1, Enc_{SU}^{IBE}(k), u \rangle, Sign_u^{IBS}) = 1$
proceed to the next step, otherwise send an error report.
(3) Add the file name and file's key version number $(fn, 1)$ to the file *FILES*, store the two tuples to the appropriate location in the cloud.

delP(fn): Permission deletion algorithm. The deletion of permission is actually to delete all tuples related to a file stored in the cloud. The administrator notifies $R.M$ to perform it. The main steps are as follows:

Step 1: $R.M$ deletes (fn, v_{fn}) from file *FILES*.
Step 2: Delete all $\langle F, fn, -, -, -, - \rangle$ tuples and $\langle PA, -, (fn, -), -, -, -, - \rangle$ tuples.

2.3.4   Role Addition and Deletion

addR(r): Role addition algorithm. The administrator adds a role to the system. The main steps are as follows:

Step 1: Add role name and the initial version number $(r, 1)$ of role key to the file *ROLES*.
Step 2: Generate the identity-based decryption key $EK_{(r,1)}$ and signature key $SK_{(r,1)}$ for the role.
Step 3: Build tuple $\langle UR, SU, (r, 1), Enc_{SU}^{IBE}(EK_{(r,1)}, SK_{(r,1)}), Sign_{SU}^{IBS} \rangle$ and send it to $R.M$.
Step 4: $R.M$ stores the received tuple to the corresponding location in the cloud.

Note that the initial version number of the role key is set to 1 here. And because the administrator needs to assign users to roles in the future, the administrator first becomes a member of the role so that the key of the role can be accessed later.

delR(r): Role deletion algorithm. The administrator deletes the role in the system. The main steps are as follows:

Step 1: Revoke (r, v_r) from file *ROLES*, delete all tuples $\langle UR, -, (r, v_r), -, - \rangle$.
Step 2: If role r is a parent role, delete all tuples $\langle RH, -, (r, v_r), -, - \rangle$; if role r is a child role, delete all tuples $\langle RH, (r, v_r), -, -, - \rangle$, and perform operation *delInh*($r, -$) on all of its parent roles.
Step 3: For each permission $\langle fn, op \rangle$ owned by role r, perform operation *revokeP*($r, \langle fn, RW \rangle$).

2.3.5   Role's Inheritance Relationship Addition and Deletion

addInh(r_c, r_p): Role's inheritance relationship addition algorithm. The administrator makes role r_c inherit role r_p, let r_c have all permissions of r_p. The main steps are as follows:

Step 1: Download tuple $\langle UR, SU, (r_p, v_{r_p}), Enc_{SU}^{IBE}(EK_{(r_p, v_{r_p})}, SK_{(r_p, v_{r_p})}), Sign_{SU}^{IBS} \rangle$ from the cloud and verify the signature.
If $Verify_{SU}^{IBS}(\langle UR, SU, (r_p, v_{r_p}), Enc_{SU}^{IBE}(EK_{(r_p, v_{r_p})}, SK_{(r_p, v_{r_p})}) \rangle, Sign_{SU}^{IBS}) = 1$, proceed to the next step, otherwise send an error report.
Step 2: The administrator decrypts the decryption key and signature key of the parent role from the *UR* tuple using his own decryption key EK_{SU}:

$$(EK_{(r_p,v_{r_p})}, SK_{(r_p,v_{r_p})}) = Dec_{EK_{SU}}^{IBE}(Enc_{SU}^{IBE}(EK_{(r_p,v_{r_p})}, SK_{(r_p,v_{r_p})})).$$

Step 3: Build tuple $\langle RH, (r_c, v_{r_c}), (r_p, v_{r_p}), Enc_{(r_c,v_{r_c})}^{IBE}(EK_{(r_p,v_{r_p})}, SK_{(r_p,v_{r_p})}), Sign_{SU}^{IBS}\rangle$ and send it to *R.M.*

Step 4: *R.M* stores the received tuple to the corresponding location in the cloud.

delInh(r_c, r_p): Role's inheritance relationship deletion algorithm. The administrator deletes the inheritance relationship between role r_c and role r_p. For the parent role, it is equivalent to remove a user from it. The main steps are as follows:

Step 1: Delete tuple $\langle RH, (r_c, v_{r_c}), (r_p, v_{r_p}), Enc_{(r_c,v_{r_c})}^{IBE}(EK_{(r_p,v_{r_p})}, SK_{(r_p,v_{r_p})}), Sign_{SU}^{IBS}\rangle$.

Step 2: Generate a new decryption key and signature key for the parent role: $KeyGen^{IBE}((r_p, v_{r_p}+1)) \rightarrow EK_{(r_p,v_{r_p}+1)}$, $KeyGen^{IBS}((r_p, v_{r_p}+1)) \rightarrow SK_{(r_p,v_{r_p}+1)}$, update the file *ROLES* to increase the role's key version number by 1.

Step 3: Generate a new *RH* tuple for the other child roles $(r_c' \neq r_c)$ of the parent role: That is, $\langle RH, (r_c', v_{r_c'}), (r_p, v_{r_p}+1), Enc_{(r_c',v_{r_c'})}^{IBE}(EK_{(r_p,v_{r_p}+1)}, SK_{(r_p,v_{r_p}+1)}), Sign_{SU}^{IBS}\rangle$, and upload it to *R.M* and replace the old tuples.

Step 4: Generate a new *UR* tuple for all user members of the parent role. That is, build a new tuple $\langle UR, -, (r_p, v_{r_p}+1), Enc_-^{IBE}(EK_{(r_p,v_{r_p}+1)}, SK_{(r_p,v_{r_p}+1)}), Sign_{SU}^{IBS}\rangle$ and upload it to *R.M.*

Step 5: Generate a new *PA* tuple for all files that the parent role can access, the specific steps are as follows:

(1) The administrator first downloads tuple $\langle UR, SU, (r_p, v_{r_p}), Enc_{SU}^{IBE}(EK_{(r_p,v_{r_p})}, SK_{(r_p,v_{r_p})}), Sign_{SU}^{IBS}\rangle$ from the cloud and verifies the signature, proceed to next step if the verification is passed.

(2) The administrator uses his own decryption key EK_{SU} to decrypt the role's decryption key and signature key from the *UR* tuple:

$$(EK_{(r_p,v_{r_p})}, SK_{(r_p,v_{r_p})}) = Dec_{EK_{SU}}^{IBE}(Enc_{SU}^{IBE}(EK_{(r_p,v_{r_p})}, SK_{(r_p,v_{r_p})})).$$

(3) For each tuple $\langle PA, (r_p, v_{r_p}), (fn, op), v_{fn}, Enc_{(r_p,v_{r_p})}^{IBE}(k), SU, Sign_{SU}^{IBS}\rangle$, first use role's decryption key to decrypt the file's symmetric key: $k = Dec_{EK_{(r_p,v_{r_p})}}^{IBE}(Enc_{(r_p,v_{r_p})}^{IBE}(k))$. Then build a new tuple $\langle PA, (r_p, v_{r_p}+1), (fn, op), v_{fn}, Enc_{(r_p,v_{r_p}+1)}^{IBE}(k), SU, Sign_{SU}^{IBS}\rangle$ and upload it to *R.M.*

(4) Delete all $\langle PA, (r_p, v_{r_p}), -, -, -, -, -\rangle$ tuples and $\langle UR, -, (r_p, v_{r_p}), -, -\rangle$ tuples.

Step 6: Update the symmetric key of all files that parent role can access, the specific steps are as follows:

(1) Generate a new symmetric key for each file that parent role can access: $KeyGen^{Sym} \rightarrow k'$.
(2) Generate a new PA tuple for all roles that have access to the above files: build a new tuple $\langle PA, -, (fn, op), v_{fn} + 1, Enc_{-}^{IBE}(k'), SU, Sign_{SU}^{IBS} \rangle$ and upload it to $R.M$.
(3) Update file $FILES$, make the symmetric key version number of the file add 1.

Note that the write-time re-encryption policy is used in the role's inheritance relationship deletion algorithm. The specific embodiment is: After step 6 is executed, the cloud actually stores two versions of the PA tuple of files that the parent role can access. The only difference between the two versions is that the file key version number and the encrypted file's symmetric key is different. When the file is read, the old symmetric key is used for decryption; When the file is written, the new symmetric key is used for encryption. This is the specific implementation of write-time re-encryption policy.

2.3.6 User Assignment and Revocation

$assignU(r, u)$: User assignment algorithm. The administrator assigns users to the roles. The main steps are as follows:

Step 1: Download tuple $\langle UR, SU, (r, v_r), Enc_{SU}^{IBE}(EK_{(r,v_r)}, SK_{(r,v_r)}), Sign_{SU}^{IBS} \rangle$ from the cloud and verify the signature. If $Verify_{SU}^{IBS}(\langle UR, SU, (r, v_r), Enc_{SU}^{IBE}(EK_{(r,v_r)}, SK_{(r,v_r)}) \rangle, Sign_{SU}^{IBS}) = 1$, proceed to the next step.

Step 2: The administrator uses his own decryption key EK_{SU} to decrypt the role's decryption key and signature key from the UR tuple: $(EK_{(r,v_r)}, SK_{(r,v_r)}) = Dec_{EK_{SU}}^{IBE}(Enc_{SU}^{IBE}(EK_{(r,v_r)}, SK_{(r,v_r)}))$.

Step 3: Build tuple $\langle UR, u, (r, v_r), Enc_{u}^{IBE}(EK_{(r,v_r)}, SK_{(r,v_r)}), Sign_{SU}^{IBS} \rangle$ and upload it to $R.M$.

Step 4: $R.M$ stores the received tuple to the corresponding location in the cloud.

$revokeU(r, u)$: User revocation algorithm. The administrator revokes a user from the role. The main steps are as follows:

Step 1: Generate a new decryption key and signature key for role r: $KeyGen^{IBE}((r, v_r + 1)) \rightarrow EK_{(r,v_r+1)}$, $KeyGen^{IBS}((r, v_r + 1)) \rightarrow SK_{(r,v_r+1)}$. Update file $ROLES$, make the key version number of the role add 1.

Step 2: If role r has child roles, generate a new RH tuple for all its child roles. That is, build a new tuple $\langle RH, -, (r, v_r + 1), Enc_{-}^{IBE}(EK_{(r,v_r+1)}, SK_{(r,v_r+1)}), Sign_{SU}^{IBS} \rangle$ and upload it to $R.M$ and replace all old tuples.

Step 3: Generate a new UR tuple for other user members ($u' \neq u$) of the role. That is, build a new tuple $\langle UR, u', (r, v_r + 1), Enc_{u'}^{IBE}(EK_{(r,v_r+1)}, SK_{(r,v_r+1)}), Sign_{SU}^{IBS} \rangle$ and upload it to $R.M$.

Step 4: Generate a new PA tuple for files that all roles can access. The specific steps are as follows:

(1) First download tuple $\langle UR, SU, (r, v_r), Enc_{SU}^{IBE}(EK_{(r,v_r)}, SK_{(r,v_r)}), Sign_{SU}^{IBS} \rangle$ from the cloud and verify the signature. If verification passed, proceed to the next step.

(2) The administrator uses his own decryption key EK_{SU} to decrypt the role's decryption key and signature key from the UR tuple: $(EK_{(r,v_r)}, SK_{(r,v_r)}) = Dec_{EK_{SU}}^{IBE}(Enc_{SU}^{IBE}(EK_{(r,v_r)}, SK_{(r,v_r)}))$.

(3) For each tuple $\langle PA, (r, v_r), (fn, op), v_{fn}, Enc_{(r,v_r)}^{IBE}(k), SU, Sign_{SU}^{IBS}\rangle$, first use role's decryption key to decrypt the file's symmetric key: $k = Dec_{EK_{(r,v_r)}}^{IBE}(Enc_{(r,v_r)}^{IBE}(k))$. Then build a new tuple $\langle PA, (r, v_r + 1), (fn, op), v_{fn}, Enc_{(r,v_r+1)}^{IBE}(k), SU, Sign_{SU}^{IBS}\rangle$ and upload it to $R.M$.

(4) Delete all $\langle PA, (r, v_r), -, -, -, -, -\rangle$ tuples and $\langle UR, -, (r, v_r), -, -\rangle$ tuples.

Step 5: Generate a new symmetric key for the files that all roles can access: $KeyGen^{Sym} \rightarrow k'$.

Step 6: Generate a new PA tuple for all roles that have access to the files in step 5. That is, for all $\langle PA, -, (fn, op), v_{fn}, Enc_{-}^{IBE}(k), SU, Sign_{SU}^{IBS}\rangle$, perform the following operations:

(1) Build a new tuple $\langle PA, -, (fn, op), v_{fn} + 1, Enc_{-}^{IBE}(k'), SU, Sign_{SU}^{IBS}\rangle$ and upload it to $R.M$.

(2) Update file $FILES$, make the symmetric key version number of file add 1.

The user revocation algorithm also uses the write-time re-encryption policy. After step 6 is executed, the cloud also stores two versions of the PA tuple of the files that the roles can access.

2.3.7 Permission Assignment and Revocation

$assignP(r, \langle fn, op\rangle)$: Permission assignment algorithm. The administrator assigns permissions to the role. The main steps are as follows:

Step 1: If the role already has read access to the file and needs to add write access, i.e. $op = RW$ and $\langle PA, (r, v_r), (fn, R), v_{fn}, Enc_{(r,v_r)}^{IBE}(k), SU, Sign_{SU}^{IBS}\rangle$ already exists, perform the following operations:

(1) Download all versions of $\langle PA, (r, v_r), (fn, R), v_{fn}, Enc_{(r,v_r)}^{IBE}(k), SU, Sign_{SU}^{IBS}\rangle$ and verify the signatures of tuples. If $Verify_{SU}^{IBS}(\langle PA, (r, v_r), (fn, R), v_{fn}, Enc_{(r,v_r)}^{IBE}(k), SU\rangle, Sign_{SU}^{IBS}) = 1$, proceed to the next step.

(2) Build the new tuple $\langle PA, (r, v_r), (fn, RW), v_{fn}, Enc_{(r,v_r)}^{IBE}(k), SU, Sign_{SU}^{IBS}\rangle$, upload it to $R.M$ and replace old tuples.

Step 2: If the role does not have any permissions on the file, first download the tuple $\langle PA, SU, (fn, RW), v_{fn}, Enc_{SU}^{IBE}(k), SU, Sign_{SU}^{IBS}\rangle$ from the cloud and verify the signature. If $Verify_{SU}^{IBS}(\langle PA, SU, (fn, RW), v_{fn}, Enc_{SU}^{IBE}(k), SU\rangle, Sign_{SU}^{IBE}) = 1$, proceed to next step.

(1) Decrypt the symmetric key of the file from PA tuple: $k = Dec_{EK_{SU}}^{IBE}(Enc_{SU}^{IBE}(k))$.

(2) Build the new tuple $\langle PA, (r, v_r), (fn, op), v_{fn}, Enc_{(r,v_r)}^{IBE}(k), SU, Sign_{SU}^{IBS}\rangle$ and upload it to the cloud. After receiving the tuple, $R.M$ stores it in the corresponding location in the cloud.

$revokeP(r, \langle fn, op\rangle)$: Permission revocation algorithm. The administrator revokes a permission from the role. The main steps are as follows:

Step 1: If only remove write permission and retain read permission, i.e. $op = W$, perform the following operations: Download all versions of tuple $\langle PA, (r, v_r),$ $(fn, RW), -, Enc_{(r,v_r)}^{IBE}(k), SU, Sign_{SU}^{IBS}\rangle$ from the cloud and verify the signature. If $Verify_{SU}^{IBS}(\langle PA, (r, v_r), (fn, RW), -, Enc_{(r,v_r)}^{IBE}(k), SU\rangle, Sign_{SU}^{IBS}) = 1$, build the new tuple $\langle PA, (r, v_r), (fn, R), -, Enc_{(r,v_r)}^{IBE}(k), SU, Sign_{SU}^{IBS}\rangle$, upload it to $R.M$ and replace the old tuple.

Step 2: If read and write permissions are revoked, i.e. $op = RW$, then:

(1) Delete all $\langle PA, (r, v_r), (fn, RW), -, Enc_{(r,v_r)}^{IBE}(k), SU, Sign_{SU}^{IBS}\rangle$ tuples.
(2) Generate a new symmetric key for the file: $KeyGen^{Sym} \rightarrow k'$.
(3) Generate new PA tuples for all other roles that can access the files. That is, build a new tuple $\langle PA, -, (fn, op), v_{fn} + 1, Enc_-^{IBE}(k'), SU, Sign_{SU}^{IBS}\rangle$ and upload it to $R.M$.
(4) Update file $FILES$, make the symmetric key version number of file add 1.

Note that in the step 2 of permission revocation algorithm, the write-time re-encryption policy is also used. In step 3, a new version of PA tuple containing the file's new symmetric key is generated for the role, which is stored in the cloud along with the PA tuple containing the file's old symmetric key.

2.3.8   File Reading and Writing

$read_u(fn)$: File reading algorithm. User reads a file, the main steps are as follows:

First, the user downloads the tuple $\langle F, fn, v_{fn}, Enc_k^{Sym}(f), (r, v_r), Sign_{(r,v_r)}^{IBS}\rangle$ from the cloud and verifies the signature. If

$$Verify_{(r,v_r)}^{IBS}(\langle F, fn, v_{fn}, Enc_k^{Sym}(f), (r, v_r)\rangle, Sign_{(r,v_r)}^{IBS}) = 1,$$ do the following operations:

First Case: If the user is a member of role r and r has permission to read the file, i.e. tuple $\langle UR, u, (r, v_r), Enc_u^{IBE}(EK_{(r,v_r)}, SK_{(r,v_r)}), Sign_{SU}^{IBS}\rangle$ and $\langle PA, (r, v_r), (fn, op), v_{fn},$ $Enc_{(r,v_r)}^{IBE}(k), SU, Sign_{SU}^{IBS}\rangle$ exist, download these two tuples from the cloud. Note that because of the write-time re-encryption policy, you need to download the PA tuple whose v_{fn} is consistent with tuple F, the same is true of the following. Then verify the signature of the tuple, if:

$$Verify_{SU}^{IBS}(\langle UR, u, (r, v_r), Enc_u^{IBE}(EK_{(r,v_r)}, SK_{(r,v_r)})\rangle, Sign_{SU}^{IBS}) = 1,$$
$$Verify_{SU}^{IBS}(\langle PA, (r, v_r), (fn, op), v_{fn}, Enc_{(r,v_r)}^{IBE}(k), SU\rangle, Sign_{SU}^{IBS}) = 1,$$ perform the following operations:

Step 1: The user uses his own decryption key EK_u to decrypt the decryption key and the signature key of the role r from the UR tuple: $(EK_{(r,v_r)}, SK_{(r,v_r)}) = Dec_{EK_u}^{IBE}(Enc_u^{IBE}(EK_{(r,v_r)}, SK_{(r,v_r)}))$.

Step 2: Use r's decryption key $EK_{(r,v_r)}$ to decrypt the symmetric key of the encrypted file from the PA tuple: $k = Dec_{EK_{(r,v_r)}}^{IBE}(Enc_{(r,v_r)}^{IBE}(k))$.

Step 3: Use k to decrypt the encrypted file from the F tuple: $f = Dec_k^{Sym}(Enc_k^{Sym}(f))$.

Second Case: If the user is a member of the role r and r is a child role of the role r', r' has the permission to read the file fn, i.e. the following tuple exists:

$$\langle UR, u, (r, v_r), Enc_u^{IBE}(EK_{(r,v_r)}, SK_{(r,v_r)}), Sign_{SU}^{IBS} \rangle$$

$$\langle RH, (r, v_r), (r', v_{r'}), Enc_{(r,v_r)}^{IBE}(EK_{(r',v_{r'})}, SK_{(r',v_{r'})}), Sign_{SU}^{IBS} \rangle$$

$$\langle PA, (r', v_{r'}), (fn, op), v_{fn}, Enc_{(r',v_{r'})}^{IBE}(k), SU, Sign_{SU}^{IBS} \rangle$$

Then download the three tuples from the cloud and verify the signature. If the signature is valid, perform the following operations:

Step 1: The user uses his own decryption key EK_u to decrypt the decryption key and the signature key of the role r from the UR tuple: $(EK_{(r,v_r)}, SK_{(r,v_r)}) = Dec_{EK_u}^{IBE}(Enc_u^{IBE}(EK_{(r,v_r)}, SK_{(r,v_r)}))$.

Step 2: Use r's decryption key $EK_{(r,v_r)}$ to decrypt the decryption key and signature key of r' from the RH tuple:

$$(EK_{(r',v_{r'})}, SK_{(r',v_{r'})}) = Dec_{EK_{(r,v_r)}}^{IBE}(Enc_{(r,v_r)}^{IBE}(EK_{(r',v_{r'})}, SK_{(r',v_{r'})}))$$

Step 3: Use r''s decryption key $EK_{(r',v_{r'})}$ to decrypt the symmetric key of the encrypted file from the PA tuple: $k = Dec_{EK_{(r',v_{r'})}}^{IBE}(Enc_{(r',v_{r'})}^{IBE}(k))$.

Step 4: Use k to decrypt the encrypted file from the F tuple: $f = Dec_k^{Sym}(Enc_k^{Sym}(f))$.

$write_u(fn, f)$: File writing algorithm. The user writes the file, that is, updates the file. The main steps are as follows:

First Case: If the user is a member of role r and r has permission to write the file fn. That is, tuple $\langle UR, u, (r, v_r), Enc_u^{IBE}(EK_{(r,v_r)}, SK_{(r,v_r)}), Sign_{SU}^{IBS} \rangle$ and $\langle PA, (r, v_r), (fn, RW), v_{fn}, Enc_{(r,v_r)}^{IBE}(k), SU, Sign_{SU}^{IBS} \rangle$ exist. Then download these two tuples from the cloud and verify the signature. Note that due to the write-time re-encryption policy, the latest version of the file key is used here, i.e. download the largest version of the PA tuple in v_{fn}. The same is true of the following.

If $Verify_{SU}^{IBS}(\langle UR, u, (r, v_r), Enc_u^{IBE}(EK_{(r,v_r)}, SK_{(r,v_r)}) \rangle, Sign_{SU}^{IBS}) = 1$ and $Verify_{SU}^{IBS}(\langle UR, (r, v_r), (fn, RW), v_{fn}, Enc_{(r,v_r)}^{IBE}(k), SU \rangle, Sign_{SU}^{IBS}) = 1$, perform the following operations:

Step 1: The user uses his own decryption key EK_u to decrypt the role's decryption key and signature key from the UR tuple: $(EK_{(r,v_r)}, SK_{(r,v_r)}) = Dec_{EK_u}^{IBE}$ $(Enc_u^{IBE}(EK_{(r,v_r)}, SK_{(r,v_r)}))$.

Step 2: User r's decryption key $EK_{(r,v_r)}$ to decrypt the symmetric key of the encrypted file from the PA tuple: $k = Dec_{EK_{(r,v_r)}}^{IBE}(Enc_{(r,v_r)}^{IBE}(k))$.

Step 3: Build the new tuple $\langle F, fn, v_{fn}, Enc_k^{Sym}(f'), (r, v_r), Sign_{(r,v_r)}^{IBS} \rangle$ and upload it to $R.M$.

Step 4: After $R.M$ receives the tuple, it performs the following operations:

(1) Check that the tuple's format is correct. If the tuple's format is correct, then proceed to the next step.
(2) Verify the signature. If $Verify_{(r,v_r)}^{IBS}(\langle F, fn, v_{fn}, Enc_k^{Sym}(f'), (r, v_r) \rangle, Sign_{(r,v_r)}^{IBS}) = 1$, proceed to the next step.
(3) $R.M$ checks if role r has permission to write the file fn. That is, check if tuple $\langle PA, (r, v_r), (fn, RW), v_{fn}, Enc_{(r,v_r)}^{IBE}(k), SU, Sign_{SU}^{IBS} \rangle$ exists. If the tuple exists and the signature is valid, then $R.M$ uses the new tuple F instead of the old tuple.
(4) Delete all PA tuples associated with file fn and whose version numbers are less than v_{fn}.

Second Case: If the user is a member of the role r and r is a child role of the role r', r' has the permission to write the file fn, i.e. the following tuple exists:

$$\langle UR, u, (r, v_r), Enc_u^{IBE}(EK_{(r,v_r)}, SK_{(r,v_r)}), Sign_{SU}^{IRS} \rangle$$

$$\langle RII, (r, v_r), (r', v_{r'}), Enc_{(r,v_r)}^{IRF}(EK_{(r',v_{r'})}, SK_{(r',v_{r'})}), Sign_{SU}^{IBS} \rangle$$

$$\langle PA, (r', v_{r'}), (fn, RW), v_{fn}, Enc_{(r',v_{r'})}^{IBE}(k), SU, Sign_{SU}^{IBS} \rangle$$

Download the three tuples from the cloud and verify the signature. If the signature is valid, perform the following operations:

Step 1: The user uses his own decryption key EK_u to decrypt the role r's decryption key and signature key from the UR tuple: $(EK_{(r,v_r)}, SK_{(r,v_r)}) = Dec_{EK_u}^{IBE}(Enc_u^{IBE}$ $(EK_{(r,v_r)}, SK_{(r,v_r)}))$.

Step 2: Use r's decryption key $EK_{(r,v_r)}$ to decrypt the decryption key and signature key of r' from the RH tuple:

$$(EK_{(r',v_{r'})}, SK_{(r',v_{r'})}) = Dec_{EK_{(r,v_r)}}^{IBE}(Enc_{(r,v_r)}^{IBE}(EK_{(r',v_{r'})}, SK_{(r',v_{r'})})).$$

Step 3: Use r''s decryption key $EK_{(r',v_{r'})}$ to decrypt the symmetric key of the encrypted file from the PA tuple: $k = Dec_{EK_{(r',v_{r'})}}^{IBE}(Enc_{(r',v_{r'})}^{IBE}(k))$.

Step 4: Build the new tuple $\langle F, fn, v_{fn}, Enc_k^{Sym}(f'), (r', v_{r'}), Sign_{(r',v_{r'})}^{IBS} \rangle$ and upload it to $R.M$.

Step 5: After $R.M$ receives the tuple, it performs the following operations:

(1) Check that the tuple's format is correct. If the tuple's format is correct, then proceed to the next step.
(2) Verify the signature. If $Verify_{(r,v_r)}^{IBS}(\langle F, fn, v_{fn}, Enc_k^{Sym}(f'), (r', v_{r'})\rangle, Sign_{(r',v_{r'})}^{IBS}) = 1$, proceed to the next step.
(3) $R.M$ checks if role r has permission to write the file fn. That is, check if the following tuples exist:

$$\langle RH, (r, v_r), (r', v_{r'}), Enc_{(r,v_r)}^{IBE}(EK_{(r',v_{r'})}, SK_{(r',v_{r'})}), Sign_{SU}^{IBS}\rangle$$

$$\langle PA, (r', v_{r'}), (fn, op), v_{fn}, Enc_{(r',v_{r'})}^{IBE}(k), SU, Sign_{SU}^{IBS}\rangle$$

If the tuples exist and the signature is valid, then $R.M$ uses the new tuple F instead of the old tuple.

Delete all PA tuples associated with file fn and whose version numbers are less than v_{fn}.

3 Conclusions

This paper combines identity-based cryptosystems and role-based access control models (RBAC$_1$ model), and built an RBAC scheme based on identity cryptosystem in cloud storage. This paper first describes the application scenario and entity composition of the scheme; then gives the formal definition of the scheme; then describes the key technologies of the scheme, and introduces the four tuples used to describe the access control policy in detail and the designed optimization method in order to improve system efficiency-hybrid encryption policy and write-time re-encryption policy; this paper also gives a detailed description of the scheme, specific to each step of each operation; finally analyzes the scheme to prove that the scheme is correct, access control protected and secure.

Acknowledgement. This work is supported, in part, by the National Natural Science Foundation of China under grant No. 61872069, in part, by the Fundamental Research Funds for the Central Universities (N171704005), in part, by the Shenyang Science and Technology Plan Projects (18-013-0-01).

References

1. Peng, S., Zhou, F., Jian, X., Zifeng, X.: Comments on "identity-based distributed provable data possession in multicloud storage". IEEE Trans. Serv. Comput. **9**(6), 996–998 (2016)
2. Xu, J., Wei, L., Zhang, Y., Wang, A., Zhou, F., Gao, C.: Dynamic fully homomorphic encryption-based Merkle Tree for lightweight streaming authenticated data structures. J. Netw. Comput. Appl. **107**, 113–124 (2018)

3. Jung, Y., Chung. M.: Adaptive security management model in the cloud computing environment. In: The International Conference on Advanced Communication Technology, pp. 1664–1669. IEEE (2010)
4. Wang, X.W., Zhao, Y.M.: A task-role-based access control model for cloud computing. Comput. Eng. **38**(24), 9–13 (2012)
5. Danwei, C., Xiuli, H., Xunyi, R.: Access control of cloud service based on UCON. In: Jaatun, M.G., Zhao, G., Rong, C. (eds.) CloudCom 2009. LNCS, vol. 5931, pp. 559–564. Springer, Heidelberg (2009). https://doi.org/10.1007/978-3-642-10665-1_52
6. Krautsevich, L., Lazouski, A., Martinelli, F., et al.: Risk-aware usage decision making in highly dynamic systems. In: Fifth International Conference on Internet Monitoring and Protection, pp. 29–34. IEEE (2010)
7. Sahai, A., Waters, B.: Fuzzy identity-based encryption. In: Cramer, R. (ed.) EUROCRYPT 2005. LNCS, vol. 3494, pp. 457–473. Springer, Heidelberg (2005). https://doi.org/10.1007/11426639_27
8. Goyal, V., Pandey, O., Sahai, A., et al.: Attribute-based encryption for fine-grained access control of encrypted data. In: ACM Conference on Computer and Communications Security, pp. 89–98. ACM (2006)
9. Ostrovsky, R., Sahai, A., Waters, B.: Attribute-based encryption with non-monotonic access structures. In: CCS 07 ACM Conference on Computer & Communications Security, pp. 195–203 (2007)
10. Bethencourt, J., Sahai, A., Waters, B.: Ciphertext-policy attribute-based encryption. In: IEEE Symposium on Security and Privacy, pp. 321–334. IEEE Computer Society (2007)
11. Sun, G.Z., Yu, D., Yun, L.I.: CP-ABE based data access control for cloud storage. J. Commun. **32**(7), 146–152 (2011)
12. Jung, T., Li, X.Y., Wan, Z., et al.: Privacy preserving cloud data access with multi-authorities. In: 2013 Proceedings IEEE INFOCOM, pp. 2625–2633. IEEE (2013)
13. Ruj, S., Stojmenovic, M., Nayak, A.: Privacy preserving access control with authentication for securing data in clouds. In: IEEE/ACM International Symposium on Cluster, Cloud and Grid Computing, pp. 556–563. IEEE (2012)
14. Yu, S., Wang, C., Ren, K., et al.: Achieving secure, scalable, and fine-grained data access control in cloud computing. In: 2010 Proceedings IEEE INFOCOM, pp. 1–9. IEEE (2010)
15. Hur, J., Dong, K.N.: Attribute-based access control with efficient revocation in data outsourcing systems. IEEE Trans. Parallel Distrib. Syst. **22**(7), 1214–1221 (2011)
16. Chen, D.W., Shao, J., Fan, X.W., et al.: MAH ABE based privacy access control in cloud computing. Acta Electron. Sin. **42**(4), 821–827 (2014)

Public Auditing of Log Integrity for Cloud Storage Systems via Blockchain

Jia Wang[1], Fang Peng[1], Hui Tian[1(✉)], Wenqi Chen[1], and Jing Lu[2]

[1] College of Computer Science and Technology, National Huaqiao University,
Xiamen 361021, China
{jwang,pengfang,htian,wqchen}@hqu.edu.cn
[2] Network Technology Center, National Huaqiao University,
Xiamen 361021, China
jlu@hqu.edu.cn

Abstract. Cloud storage security has been widely focused by the industry and academia in recent years. Differing from the previous researches on cloud data integrity audit, we pay more attention to the security of log generated during the operation of cloud data. While cloud data is damaged and tampered by various security threats (e.g. faulty operations, hacker attacks etc.), it is one of the most common methods to track accidents through log analysis. Therefore, ensuring the integrity of the log files is a prerequisite for completing the incident tracking. To this end, this paper proposes a public model for verifying the integrity of cloud log based on a third party auditor. In order to prevent the log data from being tampered with, we aggregate the log block tags by using the classic Merkle hash tree structure and generate the root node which will be stored in the blockchain. In addition, the proposed scheme does not leak any log content during public audit. The theoretical analysis and experimental results show that the scheme can effectively implement the security audit of cloud logs, which is better than the past in terms of computational complexity overhead.

Keywords: Public auditing · Cloud forensics · Cloud security · Forensic investigation

1 Introduction

The various benefits of emerging cloud computing and its storage service have attracted a lot of enterprises and private users. Although it is popular with companies and private users, cloud storage can be targeted by criminals. As the users outsource their local data to the cloud, the security of data on the cloud becomes a very important issue [1]. Compared with the local environment, the dynamic nature of cloud computing makes traditional data security solutions become powerless, which brings greater challenges to the protection of cloud data [2–4]. Especially for users as the government, banking, securities, insurance and other industries, as well as large enterprise users, they attach great importance to data security. If sensitive data is stolen or leaked, it will cause huge losses to cloud users. Besides, there is another possibility that cloud service may be abused. For example, criminals can also store and hide incriminating and illegal

© ICST Institute for Computer Sciences, Social Informatics and Telecommunications Engineering 2019
Published by Springer Nature Switzerland AG 2019. All Rights Reserved
J. Li et al. (Eds.): SPNCE 2019, LNICST 284, pp. 378–387, 2019.
https://doi.org/10.1007/978-3-030-21373-2_29

materials in cloud, even distribute illegal information through shared cloud storage service [5].

Different to the previous cloud auditing research [6–8], we pay more attention to the security of log generated during the operation of cloud data. As any user behavior is recorded by cloud service provider as activity logs, the logs can be an important resource for extracting user behavior characteristics or illegal behavior. Collecting evidence of incidents or crimes involving cloud users and cloud services used by them is known as digital forensics (or cloud forensics) [9, 10]. Hence, logs are critical evidence in cloud forensics [11]. With analyzing logs, investigators can trace back after the event to obtain important clues [12]. However, acquisition of logs is completely dependent on the cloud service provider because logs are generated and stored by them. Considering that after an incident, the cloud service provider may modify the log data in order to evade responsibility. And the existence of some hardware and software failure factors will inevitably lead to the destruction of data. Therefore, the logs provided directly by the cloud service provider are not completely trusted. In our threat model, the cloud provider is honest when generates the log. However, after that the provider may hide the fact that logs have been tampered with, or even manipulate the logs for some business interests. An incompletely trusted log will throw subsequent investigations and forensics into a dilemma. To this end, ensuring the integrity of logs in cloud storage must be achieved before log analysis in digital forensics.

As trustworthy logs are very critical for digital forensics, researchers have come up with several solutions to ensure the security of log. However, most of current schemes focused on the secure logging method. Although some of them supported public verification, the schemes required downloading the whole logs for verification, which was not practical for cloud environment. In [13], public auditing for operation behaviors log in cloud storage was introduced, which enhanced the credibility of forensic results. However, the scheme was complex and caused large computational and communication overhead. On this basis, we made some improvements. In this paper, we present a novel public secure auditing scheme for logs in cloud based on blockchain. As blockchain can ensure the integrity and non-repudiation of data [14], the properties of blockchain make it suitable for protecting log security. However, the size of log in cloud is generally significant and it is not realistic to store log in the blockchain. Therefore, we just store only a small amount of important auxiliary information on the blockchain. In addition, considering that log information is highly sensitive and user's privacy issues are directly related to it, we use random masking technique proposed in [15], enabling the auditor to audit the logs without learning the log content. The proposed scheme ensures that the forensic investigators get secure and reliable logs.

The contributions of this paper are as follows:

1. We designed a secure and efficient auditing scheme for logs recording activities of users generated in cloud environment.
2. We introduce blockchain to prevent external attacker or CSPs from tempering with the logs after-the-fact.

3. We evaluate the performance of the proposed scheme by experiments and comparisons with the state-of-the-art schemes and prove our advantage in computing overhead.

The rest of this paper is organized as follow. Section 2 provides some background information and our public auditing model for logs in cloud storage. Section 3 presents our scheme in detail. In Sect. 4, we provide the performance evaluation, and finally we conclude in Sect. 5.

2   Problem Statement

2.1   Public Auditing Model for Logs in Cloud Storage via Blockchain

A representative public auditing model for cloud storage logs is illustrated in Fig. 1. The model includes three different entities as follows:

Users, an entity that needs to store large amounts of data in the cloud. The user is the owner of the data and has the right to share data (the data hosted by the user can be shared), which can be an individual or an organization.

Cloud Storage Provider (CSP), an entity that is responsible for supervising and maintaining the outsourced data provided by users. At the same time, in order to meet user needs, CSP also provides related services such as cloud computing and logging.

Third Party Auditor (TPA), an entity that is authorized by the user or its forensic institution to verify the integrity of log operations on the cloud and return the verification results.

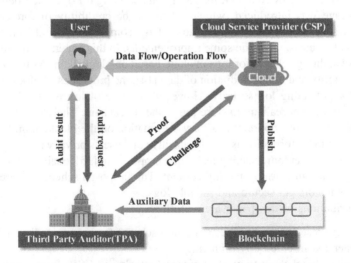

Fig. 1. Public auditing model for logs in cloud storage via blockchain

In general, users hosting large amounts of data on a cloud server can greatly reduce local storage and computational overhead. In addition, data stored on the cloud can be easily shared with others. Generally, users and other data visitors who are granted legal rights can complete a series of operations on data through cloud services, such as adding, deleting, and modifying cloud data. And every operation of the data should be recorded in the log by the cloud service provider correctly, since there may be illegal operations on cloud data. Once the data is destroyed, we need to obtain evidence of illegal operations through log analysis. Determining the integrity of the log before log analysis is the key to solving the above problem. Therefore, we introduced a log integrity audit. In cloud data integrity auditing, a common practice is to introduce a trusted third party to improve the credibility of the audit process. In view of this, we propose a public audit model for logs in cloud storage based on third parties and use the blockchain as an aid.

2.2 Design Objectives

To efficiently support public verification of log integrity in cloud storage, our protocol is designed to achieve the following security and performance objectives:

- **Public auditing**: to enable any authorized TPA to verify the integrity of the cloud logs.
- **Auditing correctness**: to ensure that there exist no cheating cloud logs that can pass TPA's audit without indeed storing logs intact.
- **Privacy preserving**: to ensure that TPA cannot directly or indirectly obtain the actual log content during the auditing process.
- **Blockless verification**: to ensure that the actual log data does not need to be retrieved during the audit process.
- **Lightweight**: to enable TPA to carry out auditing with minimum communication and computation costs.

3 The Proposed Scheme

In this section, we first briefly introduce the preliminaries that will be used to construct the proposed scheme. Then, we present our public auditing for logs in cloud storage with all design details.

3.1 Preliminaries

Homomorphic Hash Function: A homomorphic hash function H is a collision-resistant hash function that for any vectors a, b and scalars α, β holds that $H(\alpha a + \beta b) = H(a)^\alpha H(b)^\beta$. Collision resistance implies that if one knows vectors $H(c) = H(a)^\alpha H(b)^\beta$ then it must be $c = \alpha a + \beta b$ [16].

Merkle Hash Tree (MHT): Merkle hash tree is a classic validation data structure [17] and is often used to verify the data integrity. As Fig. 2. Shows, it is a binary tree consisting of a root node, a set of intermediate nodes, and a set of leaf nodes. The bottom leaf node contains the stored data or its hash value. Each intermediate node is the hash of the contents of its two child nodes as well as the root node [18], such as $h_d = h(h(N_3)\|h(N_4))$. Suppose the verifier has the value h_r corresponding to the root node and he wants to verify the integrity of N_3 and N_6. Then, only the certifier needs to provide relevant auxiliary information $\Omega = \{N_3, N_6, h(N_4), h(N_5), h_c, h_f\}$. The verifier could use the auxiliary information to recursively obtain the root node h_r' by constructing the MHT and check whether the calculated h_r' is the same as the authentic one.

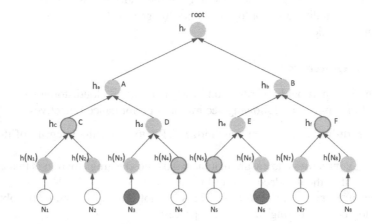

Fig. 2. Example of Merkle hash tree

Blockchain Technology: Blockchain [19] is a distributed general ledger technology derived from digital cryptocurrency bitcoin [20]. The development of this technology has aroused widespread concern in industry and academia. From a technical point of view, blockchain is a combination of innovations in various technologies, such as peer-to-peer network technology, asymmetric encryption technology, consensus mechanism, smart contracts, etc. Therefore, blockchain technology has many features and we have briefly summarized it here:

- Decentralization. A blockchain is a point-to-point network composed of many nodes. There is no centralized device and management organization. The maintenance of the network depends on all the nodes with maintenance functions in the network. Each node has equal status.
- Dependence. The blockchain operation rules and inter-node data are open and transparent, and nodes do not need to rely on trusted third parties to establish trust relationships in advance.
- Irreversibility. The latter block in the blockchain system stores the hash value of the previous block. Therefore, to tamper with the data of a certain block, the data content of the block and all subsequent blocks must be modified accordingly. So, tampering with data in a blockchain system is computationally infeasible.
- Traceability. The blockchain stores data by using a time-stamped chained block structure. So, the transactions on the chain are traceable.

3.2 Description of the Proposed Scheme

In our scheme, after each user operation is detected, a log entry e will be generated by CSP. The log entries generated within a certain period constitute a log block $B_i = \{e_{i1}, \ldots, e_{is}\}$. A log file F, which needs to be verified, consists of a fixed number of log blocks: $\{B_1, \ldots, B_n\}$. Let $H(\cdot)$ and $h(\cdot)$ denote a homomorphic hash function and a one-way hash function respectively, G be a multiplicative cyclic group of the prime order q, g represent the generator of G. The system public parameters are $\{G, q, g, H, h\}$.

Specifically, our scheme consists of 4 algorithms: {Setup, Challenge, Prove, verify}. The details of the proposed scheme are as follows:

1. **Setup Algorithm**: In this algorithm, the CSP generates a key pair. Then, CSP computes a tag for each log block B_i of the log file F, and constructs a Merkle tree with hashes of log block tags as leaf nodes. Finally, the CSP stores all the tags and publishes the tree root into blockchain to protect the integrity of the tags.
   a. The CSP generates tag σ_i for each log block B_i as:

$$\sigma_i = H\left(\sum\nolimits_{j=1}^{s} e_{ij}\right) \tag{1}$$

   Let $\Sigma = \{\sigma_i\}$ be the set of tags, where $1 \leq i \leq n$.
   b. The CSP uses tags as leaf nodes to construct a Merkle tree MT and generates the tree root R. Finally, the CSP publishes the tree root R with blockchain to prevent the tags from being altered.
2. **Challenge Algorithm**: This algorithm is conducted by the TPA to generate an auditing challenge for checking the integrity of logs in the cloud. The TPA first randomly picks a set $L = \{l_1, \ldots, l_c\}$ with c elements, where $1 \leq l_i \leq n$. Then, the TPA chooses a random value $v_i \in \mathbb{Z}_p$, for each element $l \in L$. Finally, the TPA sends the auditing challenge $chal = \{i, v_i\}$ to the CSP, where $i \in L$.
3. **Prove Algorithm**: After receiving the auditing challenge, the CSP runs this algorithm to generate a proof of log integrity as follows:
   a. The CSP first chooses s random valuer $w_j \in \mathbb{Z}_p$, $1 \leq j \leq s$. Then, the CSP computes

$$W = H\left(\sum\nolimits_{j=1}^{s} w_j\right) \tag{2}$$

$$E_j = \sum_{i \in L} v_i \cdot e_{ij} + w_j \tag{3}$$

   b. The CSP generates the sibling path from the leaf nodes $\{\sigma_i\}$ to the root node in the tree as an auxiliary information $\{\Omega_i\}$, where $i \in L$. Finally, the CSP responds the TPA with proof $P = \{W, E_j, \{\sigma_i, \Omega_i\}_{i \in L}\}_{j \in S}$.
4. **Verify Algorithm**: In this algorithm, the TPA first retrieves the root R from the blockchain. Then, the TPA computes root r using the received $\{\sigma_i, \Omega_i\}_{i \in L}$ and checks that if r and R are equal. If r is not the same value as R, the TPA outputs

False, which means that the tags of the log blocks stored in cloud has been tampered with. Otherwise, the TPA checks where the following equation holds:

$$W \cdot \prod_{i \in L} \sigma_i^{v_i} = H\left(\sum_{j=1}^{s} E_j\right) \tag{4}$$

If the equation holds, output *TRUE*; otherwise, False.

Here, we give the demonstration about the correctness of the verification Eq. (5) as follows:

$$
\begin{aligned}
\text{Right} &= H\left(\sum_{j=1}^{s}\left(\sum_{i \in L} v_i \cdot e_{ij} + w_j\right)\right) \\
&= H\left(\sum_{j=1}^{s}\sum_{i \in L} v_i \cdot e_{ij} + \sum_{j=1}^{s} w_j\right) \\
&= H\left(\sum_{i \in L} v_i\left(\sum_{j=1}^{s} e_{ij}\right)\right) \cdot H\left(\sum_{j=1}^{s} w_j\right) \\
&= \prod_{i \in L} H\left(\sum_{j=1}^{s} e_{ij}\right)^{v_i} \cdot W \\
&= \prod_{i \in L} \sigma_i^{v_i} \cdot W = \text{Left}
\end{aligned} \tag{5}
$$

4 Performance Evaluation

4.1 Theoretical Analysis

We compare our scheme with ref. [18] in terms of computational cost. For convenience, we define the following notations to denote the operations. *EXP* and *MUL* to denote the complexity of one exponentiation operation and one multiplication operation on Group G respectively. With the use of homomorphic hash function, our computation overhead in tag generation for each log file is $nEXP$ operations, where n is the number of elements in block, compared with the overhead in [18] which is $2nEXP$ and n hash operation. Since both schemes use Merkle hash tree, we do not consider the time of constructing the MHT in this section. In our scheme, the CSP runs the *Prove* algorithm with one *EXP* and c *MUL* operations, where c is the number of challenged blocks. After that, TPA runs *Verify* algorithm with $(c + 1)$ *EXP* and one *MUL* operations. However, in [18] needs $cEXP$ and $cMUL$ operations while the TPA needs two Pairing, $2cEXP$ and $cMUL$ operations. In conclusion, our scheme can reduce computation overhead in both CSP and TPA side.

4.2 Experimental Results

In this subsection, we show the performance of our scheme by the experiments implemented with python based on Pairing Base Cryptography (PBC) library version 0.5.14 and employs an MNT d159 curve based on 160-bit group order to achieve 80-bit security parameter. We conduct all the experiments on a Linux system (ubuntu 16.04.2 LTS x64 with 4.8.0 kernel version) with an Intel Xeon E3-1225 v5 CPU at 3.31 GHz, 8 GB RAM and a 7200 RPMSATA 2 TB. All the results are the averages of 20 trials. In experiments, we assume that a log file is 20 MB composed by 5000 blocks.

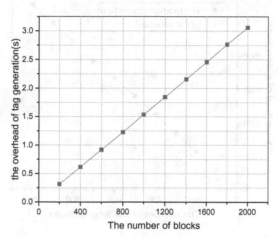

Fig. 3. The computation overhead of tag generation under different number of blocks

We conduct the experiments for tag generation and evaluate its performance in Fig. 3, where the number of blocks is increased from 200 to 2000 with intervals of 200. As we can see, the time cost of tag generation linearly increases with the number of blocks, which ranges from 315.56458 ms to 3059.623603 ms.

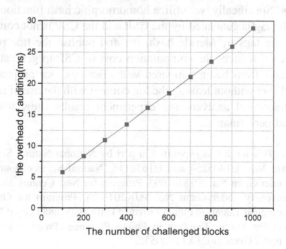

Fig. 4. The computation overhead of TPA in challenge phase under different number of challenged blocks

The computation cost for the algorithm challenge, proof and verify is shown in Figs. 4 and 5. The results of these experiments under different number of challenged blocks varied from 100 to 1000 show that the time in different auditing phases increases proportionally to the number of challenged blocks. From the above experimental results, it is clearly that most of the computation overhead is taken by the CSP and TPA only costs a little time. Therefore, our proposed scheme achieves high efficiency on TPA side.

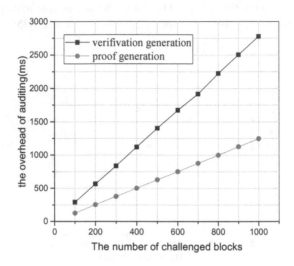

Fig. 5. Computation overhead in different auditing phase under different number of challenged blocks

5 Conclusion

In this paper, we present a public auditing scheme for logs in cloud storage with privacy preserving. Specifically, we utilize homomorphic hash function to generate tag of log block. As the tag is generated by the CSP and the CSP is not completely trusted, we aggregate the log tags by Merkle hash tree and publish the tree root with block-chain, which not only reduces the computation cost of CSP to generate tags, but also prevents the log tags from being tampered with. Besides, our proposed scheme can support public auditing without leaking the log content with the use of random masking technique. The theoretical analysis and experiment results show that the proposed scheme has a good performance.

Acknowledgement. This work was supported in part by National Natural Science Foundation of China under Grant Nos. U1405254 and U1536115, Natural Science Foundation of Fujian Province of China under Grant No. 2018J01093, Program for New Century Excellent Talents in Fujian Province University under Grant No. MJK2016-23, Program for Outstanding Youth Scientific and Technological Talents in Fujian Province University under Grant No. MJK2015-54, and Research Project for Young Teachers in Fujian Province (Program for High-Education Informationization) under Grant No. JAT170055.

References

1. Tang, J., Cui, Y., Li, Q.: Ensuring security and privacy preservation for cloud data services. ACM Comput. Surv. **49**(1), 1–39 (2016)
2. Wang, C., Wang, Q.: Security challenges for the public cloud. IEEE Internet Comput. **16**(1), 69–73 (2012)
3. Xiao, Z., Xiao, Y.: Security and privacy in cloud computing. IEEE Commun. Surv. Tutorials **15**(2), 843–859 (2013)
4. Puthal, D., Sahoo, B.P.S., Mishra, S.: Cloud computing features, issues, and challenges: a big picture. In: International Conference on Computational Intelligence and Networks. IEEE, Bhubaneshwar (2015)
5. Coileáin, D.Ó., O'mahony, D.: Accounting and accountability in content distribution architectures: a survey. ACM Comput. Surv. **47**(4), (2016). https://doi.org/10.1145/2723701
6. Tian, H., Chen, Y., Chang, C.: Dynamic-hash-table based public auditing for secure cloud storage. IEEE Trans. Serv. Comput. **10**(5), 701–714 (2017)
7. Wang, C., Wang, Q., Ren, K.: Toward secure and dependable storage services in cloud computing. IEEE Trans. Serv. Comput. **5**(2), 220–232 (2012)
8. Zhu, Y., Ahn, G., Hu, H.: Dynamic audit services for outsourced storages in clouds. IEEE Trans. Serv. Comput. **6**(2), 227–238 (2013)
9. Zawoad, S., Dutta, A.K., Hasan, R.: Towards building forensics enabled cloud through secure logging-as-a-service. IEEE Trans. Dependable Secure Comput. **13**(2), 148–162 (2016)
10. Martini, B., Choo, K.-K.R.: Cloud forensic technical challenges and solutions: a snapshot. IEEE Cloud Comput. **1**(4), 20–25 (2014)
11. Martini, B., Choo, K.-K.R.: An integrated conceptual digital forensic framework for cloud computing. Digit. Invest. **9**(2), 71–80 (2012)
12. Dykstra, J., Sherman, A.T.: Acquiring forensic evidence from infrastructure-as-a-service cloud computing: exploring and evaluating tools, trust, and techniques. Digit. Invest. **9**, S90–S98 (2012)
13. Tian, H., Chen, Z., Chang, C.: Enabling public auditability for operation behaviors in cloud storage. Soft. Comput. **21**(8), 2175–2187 (2017)
14. Dorri, A., Steger, M., Kanhere, S.S.: BlockChain: a distributed solution to automotive security and privacy. IEEE Commun. Mag. **55**(12), 119–125 (2017)
15. Wang, C., Wang, Q., Ren, K., Lou, W.: Privacy-preserving public auditing for data storage security in cloud computing. IEEE Trans. Comput. **62**(2), 362–375 (2013)
16. Xu, W., Feng, D., Liu, J.: Remote data integrity checking protocols from homomorphic hash functions. In: 14th IEEE International Conference on Communication Technology. IEEE, Chengdu (2012)
17. Ralph, C.: Merkle: protocols for public key cryptosystems. In: 1980 IEEE Symposium on Security and Privacy, pp. 122–122. IEEE, Oakland (1980)
18. Wang, Q., Wang, C., Ren, K.: Enabling public auditability and data dynamics for storage security in cloud computing. IEEE Trans. Parallel Distrib. Syst. **22**(5), 847–859 (2011)
19. Christidis, K.: Blockchains and smart contracts for the Internet of Things. IEEE Access **4**, 2292–2303 (2016)
20. Swan, M.: Blockchain: Blueprint for a New Economy. O'Reilly Media, Sebastopol (2015)

Coordinated Web Scan Detection Based on Hierarchical Correlation

Jing Yang[1,2], Liming Wang[1(✉)], Zhen Xu[1], Jigang Wang[3], and Tian Tian[3]

[1] State Key Laboratory of Information Security,
Institute of Information Engineering, Chinese Academy of Sciences, Beijing, China
{yangjing,wangliming,xuzhen}@iie.ac.cn
[2] School of Cyber Security, University of Chinese Academy of Sciences,
Beijing, China
[3] Zhongxing Telecommunication Equipment Corporation, Nanjing, China
{wang.jigang,tian.tian1}@zte.com.cn

Abstract. Web scan is one of the most common network attacks on the Internet, in which an adversary probes one or more websites to discover exploitable information in order to perform further cyber attacks. For a coordinated web scan, an adversary controls multiple sources to achieve a large-scale scanning as well as detection evasion. In this paper, a novel detection approach based on hierarchical correlation is proposed to identify coordinated web campaigns from the labelled malicious sources. The semantic correlation is used to identify the malicious sources scanning the similar contents, and the temporal-spatial correlation is employed to identify malicious campaigns from the semantic correlation results. In both correlation phases, we convert the clustering problem into the group partition problem and propose a greedy algorithm to solve it. The evaluation shows that our algorithm is effective in detecting coordinated web scan attacks, since the metric Precision for detection can achieve 1.0, and the metric Rand Index for clustering is 0.984.

Keywords: Web security · Coordinated scan ·
Hierarchical correlation · Cyber security

1 Introduction

Web scan is one of the most common web attacks on the Internet. During a web scan attack, an adversary probes one or more websites to discover exploitable information in order to perform further cyber attacks. According to the adversaries' intension, web scan attacks can be classified into three categories, i.e., web vulnerability scan, sensitive information scan and webshell scan. As a reconnaissance method, scanning is very important for subsequent attacks. For example, it is reported that more than 3,500 websites were added unauthorized code by attackers using automated scripts to scan these websites and find exploitable bugs in January, 2016 [1].

© ICST Institute for Computer Sciences, Social Informatics and Telecommunications Engineering 2019
Published by Springer Nature Switzerland AG 2019. All Rights Reserved
J. Li et al. (Eds.): SPNCE 2019, LNICST 284, pp. 388–400, 2019.
https://doi.org/10.1007/978-3-030-21373-2_30

To achieve large-scale or comprehensive web reconnaissance, an adversary utilize multiple sources to scan the responding websites in a coordinated web scan. Furthermore, employing multiple sources can make the scan activities remain stealthy, and accordingly avoid detection. Coordinated web scan campaigns of different scan types vary greatly in the access patterns. Coordinated scan sources for web vulnerabilities are probably similar with legitimate web crawlers due to the significant temporal synchronicity in their time series. The reason is that adversaries usually employ multiple sources to scan simultaneously in order to gather as much information as possible in a short time duration. While with regarding to sources in a coordinated scan for sensitive information or webshell, the access patterns are totally different. Since a few requests sent in these scan activities, adversaries may control multiple sources to scan different targets alternately.

Detection of single-source web scan activity is similar to web application attacks detection, and there are plenty of methods proposed [2–8] in the literature. However, those methods cannot identify the correlation of multiple web scan sources. The coordinated port scan detection has been addressed in many works [9–14], which put the emphasis on measuring the relativity between different sources. However, profiling web scan activities is quite a contrast to profiling port scan activities. The searching space for a port scan is limited and predictable due to the limited range of networking ports, but that for web scan is unlimited. Consequently the methods for coordinated port scan detection can not be applied to coordinated web scan detection. Jacob et al. [15] proposed PUBCRAWL to achieve malicious web crawlers detection and crawling campaign attribution. Their method can be used for coordinated web vulnerability scan detection, but it is not suitable for the other two scan types.

In this work, a novel detection approach is proposed to identify coordinated web scanners from the labelled malicious sources. We employ a hierarchical correlation model to comprehensively analyze the similarity of different sources. For the labelled malicious scan sources and the corresponding web traffic logs, the semantic correlation is deployed to aggregate malicious sources into groups. Sources in each group are semantically similar with each other. Then we employ the temporal-spatial correlation to each group in order to find the coordinated scanners. In both correlation phases, we convert the clustering problem into the group partition problem and propose a greedy algorithm to solve it. Our evaluation is carried out on a large dataset collected from a web hosting service provider with about 25 million web traffic log entries. We respectively quantify the capabilities of detection and clustering of our method. The evaluation results show that our algorithm is effective in detecting coordinated web scan activities, since the metric Precision for detection can achieve 1.0 at the best, and the metric Rand Index for clustering is 0.984.

We organize this paper as following: Sect. 2 presents our insight on coordinated web scan attacks. Related work is introduced in Sect. 3. Section 4 gives an overview of our approach and more details on the hierarchical correlation model.

The evaluation of our approach is in Sect. 5. Finally we make a discussion and conclude the paper in Sect. 6.

2 Coordinated Web Scan

As an important reconnaissance approach, a web scan is used by an adversary to gather information about the responding websites. We summarize web scan attacks into three categories according to the adversaries' intension.

- **Web Vulnerability Scan.** A typical website usually has three layers, i.e., the web server, some third-party web application frameworks and the business application. Web vulnerabilities consist of web application vulnerabilities (e.g., SQL or code injections, Cross-Site Scripting) and web server vulnerabilities (e.g., IIS, Apache, Tomcat). The web application vulnerabilities in known third-party web application frameworks are most concerned by adversaries, for instance, the Apache Struts framework vulnerabilities including CVE-2017-5638 and CVE-2018-11776. To scan web vulnerabilities of a website, adversaries need to crawl the structure of the website and determine which query URLs may be vulnerable. Hence they always employ some automated tools to make a comprehensive scan, in which the amount of requests is large and the time duration of scanning is long compared to the benign users' traffic. IBM AppScan, HP WebInspect, Acunetix Scanner and Nikto are the most popular web application vulnerabilities scan tools. Adversaries usually perform web vulnerability scan attacks aiming at a handful of websites.
- **Sensitive Information Scan.** The misconfiguration of a website may lead to open access of sensitive information about the web application and sensitive files on the web server. Typical sensitive information includes backup files, configuration files, password files and administrative interfaces. It is not necessary to crawl the structure of the website for scanning sensitive information, and an adversary can employ a black list and an open-sourced web crawler to perform a scan attack. For this type of scan, the amount of requests is small and the time duration of scanning is short. Adversaries usually perform large-scale sensitive information scan attacks on the Internet.
- **Webshell Scan.** A webshell is a malicious backdoor uploaded by an adversary to control a compromised website. Compared to compromising a website, it is easier to determine whether or not a website has contained a known webshell. An adversary can perform a webshell scan attack with a black list on URLs of known webshells, such as "/plus/mytag_js.php?aid=9090", "/plus/90sec.php". As same as the sensitive information scan, the amount of requests is small and the time duration of scanning is short in a webshell scan attack, and the scan scale is large.

Table 1 presents the comparison of the three web scan types from four aspects, including the scan scale, request amounts, time duration and whether specialized scanner tools are needed.

Table 1. Comparison of web scans.

Type	Scale	Requests amounts	Time duration	Specialized tools
Web vulnerability scan	Small	Large	Long	Yes
Sensitive information scan	Large	Small	Short	No
Webshell scan	Large	Small	Short	No

During a coordinated web scan, an adversary employs multiple sources to scan the responding websites in order to improve efficiency and evade detection. Different sources in a coordinated web scan sweep websites for similar exploitable information, so there may be likenesses of semantic content between their web requests. In addition, adversaries may manipulate multiple sources to scan the target websites synchronously or alternately. If they perform scan attacks at the same time, there may be significant temporal synchronicity between their access patterns, which is the same as the distributed web crawlers. If they scan the target websites in turn, it is hard to discriminate between multiple sources within a coordinated scan and multiple adversities with the same scanner tool. However, from our observation, most of coordinated sources alternatively carrying out scan attacks are usually in a subnet of IP addresses. In other words, there is spatial similarity for the alternative coordinated web scan sources. Most of coordinated web vulnerability scan campaigns conform to the previous pattern, while most of coordinated sensitive information and webshell scan activities comply with the latter pattern.

Two examples of coordinated web scanners with different access patterns are shown in Fig. 1. Figure 1(a) illustrates the time series of four scan sources carrying out a web vulnerability scan attack. Since the time duration for a web vulnerability scan is relatively long, the temporal synchronicity is significant from their time series. The four sources in Fig. 1(b) belong to a webshell scan campaign, and they swept targets alternatively. Owing to the small volume of requests, their time series seem irrelevant. However their IP addresses are in the same /24 subnet and they used the similar source ports for scanning, indicating that they belong to the same malicious campaign.

3   Related Work

The concept of coordinated attack was first introduced by Green [9]. The author analyzed various coordinated attacks and probes, including traceroutes, Net-BIOS scans, Reset scans, SFRP scans and DNS server exploit attempts. Braynov et al. [10] defined two types of cooperation for the coordinated attack: action correlation and task correlation. Gates et al. [11] developed a detection algorithm to recognize coordinated port scan activities based on the set covering technique. Zhou et al. [12] summarized different coordinated attacks including large-scale stealthy scans, worm outbreaks and distributed denial-of-service attacks, and gave a review of collaborative intrusion detection systems for detecting such

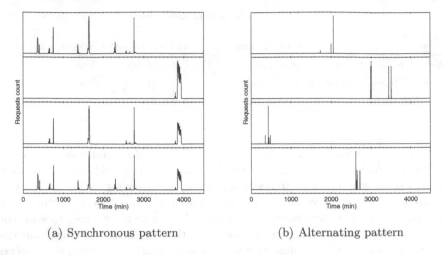

(a) Synchronous pattern   (b) Alternating pattern

Fig. 1. Examples of coordinated web scanners with different access patterns

attacks. Elias et al. [13] presented an approach to fingerprint probing activity and inferred the machinery of the scan based on time series analysis techniques. Mazel et al. [14] provided a method to find the relationship of different scan sources based on the overlap and structure of destination IPs.

All of the above detection methods focus on the port scan attack. For the port scan, the scanning space is limited, which is only the range from 0 to 65535. It is practical to identify the correlation between different scanners based on the individual coverage of the whole scanning space. However, for the web scan, the scanning space is unlimited because the length of a HTTP request can be long enough. Accordingly, it is difficult to profile a web scanner's communication and predict its activities. Consequently the methods for coordinated port scan detection can not apply to coordinated web scan detection.

For coordinated web scan attacks, Xie et al. [5] introduced a clustering based approach named Scan Hunter to detect HTTP scanners, which can be used to identify scanners with the same scanner tool, but cannot distinguish the coordinated scan sources. Jacob et al. [15] proposed a method named PUBCRAWL for detecting malicious crawler campaign by identifying synchronized traffic. They also utilized time series clustering to aggregate similar time series from detected malicious crawlers. Squared Euclidean Distance is the metric for measuring the similarity between time series. Obviously, it can only detect the synchronous web scanners mentioned previously, and for the alternating web scanners it doesn't work.

4   Methodology

In our detection method, we employ a hierarchical correlation model to comprehensively analyze the similarity of different sources from the semantic characteristic and the temporal-spatial characteristic. For the labelled malicious scan sources and the corresponding web traffic logs, a semantic correlation is firstly employed to aggregate malicious sources into groups. Sources in each group are scanners with similar tools to scan similar contents. Then for each semantic similar group, a temporal-spatial correlation is utilized to find the coordinated scanners. The concept of our methodology is shown in Fig. 2.

For the semantic correlation, we use a word set to profile a scan source's visiting behavior and construct a similarity matrix with the Jaccard distance as the similarity metric. Because there is no knowledge of the number of clusters in advance, we transform the similarity matrix into the adjacency matrix with a similarity threshold and convert the problem of clustering into partitioning.

For the temporal-spatial correlation, the time series of each source in a semantic similar group are extracted at first. If two time series have overlaps, we compute the Pearson correlation coefficient to measure the similarity between them. While if two series don't overlap and the two sources are in the same subnet of IP address, we denote they are correlated and the similarity is set to 1. As same as the semantic correlation, we employ the group partition technique to identify coordinated scanners from a semantic similar group.

A simple and efficient group partition algorithm is proposed at the end of this section, which is a greedy method to divide nodes in an adjacency matrix into groups.

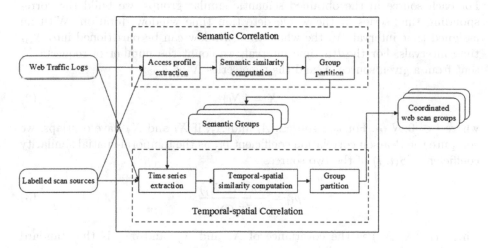

Fig. 2. Overview of our approach

4.1 Semantic Correlation

We utilize the method proposed in our previous work [8] to profile the web access behavior of a scan source. For a scan source A, we extract all requests and put all resource identifiers and query strings together into two independent text files. Different separators are applied to split the files into two word sets W_u and

W_q. Then we combine the two word sets together and get the whole word set $W = W_u \cup W_q$.

To find the groups of different scan sources with similar scan contents, we construct the semantic similarity matrix M_S. The semantic similarity $SS(i, j)$ of two sources A_i and A_j is measured by the Jaccard distance. which is denoted by the following equation:

$$SS(i, j) = 1 - J(W_i, W_j) = 1 - \frac{|W_i \cap W_j|}{|W_i \cup W_j|}. \tag{1}$$

Traditional clustering techniques require specifying the number of clusters in advance, which is not piratical in our detection. Hence we convert the clustering problem into the group partition problem by transforming the similarity matrix M_S into the adjacency matrix M_{AS}. With an assigned semantic similarity threshold λ_S, if the similarity of two sources is larger than the threshold, we define the pair of sources are adjacent, otherwise they are not. For the adjacency matrix M_{AS}, we employ our proposed partition algorithm which is detailed as following to cluster the input scan sources.

4.2   Temporal-Spatial Correlation

For each source in the obtained semantic similar groups, we build the corresponding time series in the whole detection time window duration. With an assigned time interval Δt, the whole time window can be partitioned into $N_{\Delta t}$ time intervals. For the lth time interval, we count the number of requests N_l sent from a given source A, and the time series X of A is:

$$X = \{N_l\} \tag{2}$$

where $l \in [0, N_{\Delta t}]$. For two sources A_i and A_j, if X_i and X_j have overlaps, we compute the Pearson correlation coefficient ρ_{ij} as the temporal-spatial similarity coefficient $TS(i, j)$ of the two sources:

$$\rho_{ij} = \frac{cov(X_i, X_j)}{\sigma_{X_i} \sigma_{X_j}} \tag{3}$$

where $cov(X_i, X_j)$ is the covariance of X_i and X_j, and σ_{X_i} is the standard deviation of X_i.

If X_i and X_j have no overlap, we identify the relevance of the two sources from the spatial characteristic. If the two sources are in the same subnet of IP addresses, we denote they are correlated and the similarity $TSS(i, j)$ is set to 1, otherwise it is set to 0. The subnet space is defined by the assigned threshold λ_{IP}.

As same as the semantic correlation, we transform the similarity matrix M_{TS} into the adjacency matrix M_{ATS} by assigning the temporal-spatial similarity threshold λ_{TS}. For the adjacency matrix M_{ATS}, we employ our proposed partition algorithm which is detailed as following to get the final results.

4.3 Proposed Group Partition Algorithm

For an input adjacency matrix M_A, a greedy algorithm is presented to partition the nodes in the adjacency matrix. Our core idea is that if two nodes are connected with each other, they should be put together into one group. Specifically, assuming $node_i$ and $node_j$ are connected, if $node_i$ already belongs to the group G_k but $node_j$ is alone, then $node_j$ is added into G_k; if $node_j$ already belongs to G_k but $node_i$ is alone, then $node_i$ is added into G_k; if the two nodes have belonged to different groups, skip to the next pair of nodes. If $node_i$ is not connected to any other nodes, it is added into a new group.

Actually the known community detection algorithm Louvain [16] can apply to our method. The *Louvain* algorithm includes two iteratively repeated phases. The first phase is for modularity optimization, and the second phase is for community aggregation. Compared with it, our algorithm is more efficient and more suitable for our detection method, since it only has one phase and does not need to repeat.

5   Evaluation and Results

We utilized the open-source network monitor Bro [17] to collect a large volume of web traffic logs from a web hosting service provider in order to evaluate our approach. The method proposed in our previous work [8] is employed to detect malicious IPs from the dataset, and we labeled the coordinated web scan campaigns manually. Our approach is implemented in Java with the full-text search engine Elasticsearch for data storage.

Our evaluation is divided into two parts. At first, we measured the detection capability of our method in order to check whether our approach can differentiate between a single scanner and a coordinated scanner. Furthermore, we measured the clustering capability of our method to examine whether our approach can identify the different sources of one campaign into the same group.

5.1   Dataset

Our dataset consists of about 20 million log entries generated by 156,396 IP addresses, which involves 534 fully qualified domain names (FQDNs) from May 17 to 26, 2016. We equally divided it into the training dataset D_{train} and the testing dataset D_{test}. The training dataset, with logs in the first 5 days, is used for parameters selection, and the test dataset, with the left logs, is used for evaluating the performance of the method.

In the training dataset there are totally 1,207 detected malicious IPs. With the auxiliary of visualization tool Kibana, we manually analyzed the scan contents, time series synchronization and IP addresses distribution of these malicious IPs, and labelled 134 coordinated scan IPs involving 30 different groups. Among of them, 2 groups performed the web vulnerability scan attacks, 9 groups carried out the sensitive information scan attacks, and 19 groups scanned for webshells. The testing dataset includes 1,058 malicious IPs with 149 labelled coordinated scan IPs and 38 labelled groups. In the testing dataset, only one group performed the web vulnerability scan attacks, 16 groups carried out sensitive information scan attacks, and 21 groups scanned for webshells. The distribution of numbers of group members is shown in Table 2. In most groups, the multiple IP addresses are in a /24 subnet. Only two groups contain several totally different IP addresses.

Table 2. Distribution of numbers of group members.

Num. of groups members	2	3	4	5	6	8	9	11	15	16	17	18
Num. of groups in D_{train}	15	1	5	5	2	0	0	1	0	1	1	0
Num. of groups in D_{test}	16	10	4	3	1	1	1	0	1	0	0	1

5.2   Evaluation of the Detection Capability

With regarding to the detection capability, we use four metrics: Precision (P), Recall (R), Accuracy (Acc) and F measure (F_β) to quantify the performance of our approach. The most common measure F_1 with $\beta = 1$ is chosen. Assuming a malicious entity is labelled as a coordinated scan entity, if our approach also classifies it as a coordinated entity, it is defined as a true positive, and if it is classified by our approach as a single scan entity, it is defined as a false negative. The definitions of a true negative and a false positive are similar. Given the numbers of true positives, false positives, true negatives, and false negatives as TP, FP, TN and FN, the four metrics are calculated as:

$$P = \frac{TP}{TP + FP} \tag{4}$$

$$R = \frac{TP}{TP + FN} \tag{5}$$

$$Acc = \frac{TP + TN}{TP + TN + FP + FN} \tag{6}$$

$$F_1 = \frac{PR}{P + R} \tag{7}$$

Precision can measure the portion of actual coordinated scan entities in all predicted coordinated scan entities. Recall measures the number of correctly classified coordinated scan entities out of the total number of labelled coordinated scan entities. Accuracy measures the number of correctly distinguished coordinated scanners and single scanners. F_1 score is the harmonic mean of Precision and Recall.

Parameter Selection. In our approach, there are four assigned parameters: Δt, λ_{SS}, λ_{IP} and λ_{TS}. We empirically set Δt as 1 min. For the last three threshold parameters, we designed three groups of experiments with the training dataset. In each group of experiments, two thresholds are fixed and one threshold is changed to find the best threshold value. Figure 3 illustrates the results of the three groups of experiments. In the first group, we fixed $\lambda_{IP} = 256$ and $\lambda_{TS} = 0.5$, and when $\lambda_{SS} = 0.5$ we achieved the best Precision and F_1 score. In the second group, we fixed $\lambda_{SS} = 0.5$ and $\lambda_{TS} = 0.5$, and Precision is the best when $\lambda_{IP} = 1024$ but the F_1 is the best when $\lambda_{IP} = 2048$. With an overall consideration, we chose $\lambda_{IP} = 2048$. In the last group, we fixed $\lambda_{SS} = 0.5$ and $\lambda_{IP} = 2048$, and when $\lambda_{TS} = 0.5$ Precision and F_1 are the best.

Finally the three threshold parameters are set as: $\lambda_{SS} = 0.5$, $\lambda_{IP} = 2048$ and $\lambda_{TS} = 0.5$. With these settings, our method on the training dataset can achieve: $P = 0.99$, $R = 0.793$, $Acc = 0.97$ and $F_1 = 0.846$.

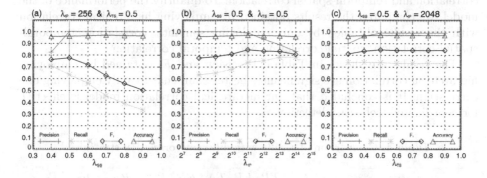

Fig. 3. Results of experiments for parameter selection.

Comparison with Different Partition Algorithms. In this section, we measure the performance of our proposed group partition algorithm. By replacing the algorithm used in the group partition part, we compare the detection performance by employing our greedy partition algorithm with that by employing the Louvain algorithm on the testing dataset D_{test}.

The comparison of metrics with different algorithms is shown in Table 3. With our algorithm, the precision is 1.0 with the number of true positives is 108 and no false positive, and the recall is 0.724 with 41 false negatives. The metric F_1 is 0.84 and Acc is 0.961. Among the 41 false negatives, 11 labelled groups involving 26 malicious IPs are not detected at all, and 8 labelled groups involving 15 malicious IPs are partially not detected. By examining the traffic logs of the 26 malicious IPs in 11 undetected groups, we found that most of their traffic logs were mixed by massive random resource identifiers or normal web accessing requests, which leads to a significant decrease in the semantic similarity.

The results obtained by utilizing the Louvain algorithm are almost the same as that obtained by our algorithm, while our algorithm is slightly better than Louvain. It is revealed that the proposed partition algorithm is more suitable for our method.

Table 3. Comparison of detection metrics with different algorithms.

	TP	FP	TN	FN	P	R	Acc	F_1
Our algorithm	108	0	909	41	1.0	0.724	0.961	0.84
Louvain	107	0	909	42	1.0	0.718	0.96	0.836

Comparison with Different Correlation Strategies. In our method, we introduce the hierarchical correlation model with a combination of semantic correlation and temporal-spatial correlation. To quantify the performance of the model, we compared the results obtained by employing hierarchical correlation with the results obtained by only employing semantic correlation, temporal-spatial correlation, spatial correlation and temporal correlation.

The results are shown in Table 4. Precision and F_1 obtained by employing hierarchical correlation are significantly better than that by only employing one correlation. It is concluded that our hierarchical correlation model is effective for coordinated web scan detection.

Table 4. Comparison of results with different correlation strategies.

	TP	FP	TN	FN	P	R	Acc	F_1
Hierarchical correlation	108	0	909	41	1.0	0.724	0.961	0.84
Only semantic correlation	123	567	342	26	0.178	0.826	0.44	0.293
Only temporal-spatial correlation	144	277	632	5	0.342	0.966	0.733	0.505
Only spatial correlation	145	532	377	4	0.214	0.973	0.493	0.351
Only temporal correlation	53	181	728	96	0.226	0.356	0.738	0.277

5.3 Evaluation of the Clustering Capability

We chose the widespread measure Rand index (RI) for evaluating the performance of clustering. With regarding to group partition, a true positive decision assigns two similar sources to the same group, and a true negative decision assigns two dissimilar sources to different groups. There are two types of errors. A false positive decision assigns two dissimilar sources to the same group. A false negative decision assigns two similar sources to different groups. RI measures the percentage of decisions that are correct, which is calculated as following:

$$RI = \frac{TP + TN}{TP + TN + FP + FN}. \tag{8}$$

With the setting of parameters as the above, our method aggregates 108 malicious sources into 28 groups, and the RI is 0.984. Among the 28 groups, 20 classified groups are equal with their labelled groups, and 8 classified groups are partial equal with the labelled groups. There is no group containing sources from different labelled groups. The satisfactory results prove that our method for coordinated web scan detection can be applied into practice.

6   Discussion and Conclusions

In this paper, we introduce a hierarchical correlation based methodology to distinguish coordinated web scanners. With the combination of semantic correlation analysis and temporal-spatial correlation analysis, our method can effectively detect coordinated web scan campaigns in different access patterns. Compared with PUBCRAWL proposed by Jacob et al. [15], which can only detect malicious web crawler campaigns with significant temporal synchronicity, our work combines the temporal synchronicity, the semantic similarity and the spatial distribution similarity, and can combat with both the synchronous and alternating coordinated web scan attacks.

In conclusion, we give an overall insight on the coordinated web scan attack, and propose a novel detection approach based on hierarchical correlation. In our detection approach, the semantic correlation is used to identify the malicious entities scanning the similar contents, and the temporal-spatial correlation is employed to identify scan campaigns from the semantic correlation results. Furthermore, we propose an efficient greedy algorithm for group partition which is used in both correlation phases to aggregate sources. We evaluate our approach on a manually labeled dataset, and the results reveal that it can effectively distinguish the coordinated web scan campaigns.

Acknowledgments. This paper is supported by the National Key R&D Program of China (2017YFB0801900).

References

1. Security Newspaper. https://www.securitynewspaper.com/2016/01/23/web-reconnaissance-attack-infects-3500-websites-possibly-wordpress/. Accessed 20 Nov 2018
2. Kruegel, C., Vigna, G.: Anomaly detection of web-based attacks. In: Proceedings of the 10th ACM Conference on Computer and Communications Security, pp. 251–261. ACM (2003)
3. Valeur, F., Mutz, D., Vigna, G.: A learning-based approach to the detection of SQL attacks. In: Julisch, K., Kruegel, C. (eds.) DIMVA 2005. LNCS, vol. 3548, pp. 123–140. Springer, Heidelberg (2005). https://doi.org/10.1007/11506881_8
4. Robertson, W., Vigna, G., Kruegel, C., Kemmerer, R.A.: Using generalization and characterization techniques in the anomaly-based detection of web attacks. In: Annual Network & Distributed System Security Symposium (NDSS) (2006)

5. Xie, G., Hang, H., Faloutsos, M.: Scanner hunter: understanding HTTP scanning traffic. In: Proceedings of the 9th ACM Symposium on Information, Computer and Communications Security, pp. 27–38. ACM (2014)
6. Shancang, L.I., Romdhani, I., Buchanan, W.: Password pattern and vulnerability analysis for web and mobile applications. ZTE Commun. **14**(S1), 32–36 (2016)
7. Mimura, M., Tanaka, H.: Heavy log reader: learning the context of cyber attacks automatically with paragraph vector. In: Shyamasundar, R.K., Singh, V., Vaidya, J. (eds.) ICISS 2017. LNCS, vol. 10717, pp. 146–163. Springer, Cham (2017). https://doi.org/10.1007/978-3-319-72598-7_9
8. Yang, J., Wang, L., Xu, Z.: A novel semantic-aware approach for detecting malicious web traffic. In: Qing, S., Mitchell, C., Chen, L., Liu, D. (eds.) ICICS 2017. LNCS, vol. 10631, pp. 633–645. Springer, Cham (2018). https://doi.org/10.1007/978-3-319-89500-0_54
9. Green, J., Marchette, D.J., Northcutt, S., Ralph B.: Analysis techniques for detecting coordinated attacks and probes. In: Proceedings of workshop on Intrusion Detection and Network Monitoring, pp. 1–9 (1999)
10. Braynov, S., Jadliwala, M.: Detecting malicious groups of agents. In: Proceedings of the First IEEE Symposium on Multi-Agent Security and Survivability, pp. 90–99. IEEE (2004)
11. Gates, C.: Coordinated scan detection. In: Annual Network & Distributed System Security Symposium (NDSS) (2009)
12. Zhou, C.V., Leckie, C., Karunasekera, S.: A survey of coordinated attacks and collaborative intrusion detection. Comput. Secur. **29**, 124–1402 (2010)
13. Elias, B.H., Mourad, D., Chadi, A.: On fingerprinting probing activities. Comput. Secur. **43**, 35–48 (2014)
14. Mazel, J., Fontugne, R., Fukuda, K.: Identifying coordination of network scans using probed address structure. In: Traffic Monitoring and Analysis-8th International Workshop, pp. 7–8 (2016)
15. Jacob, G., Kirda, E., Kruegel, C., Vigna, G.: PUBCRAWL: protecting users and businesses from CRAWLers. In: Proceedings of 21st Usenix Conference on Security Symposium, pp. 507–512. Usenix (2013)
16. Blondel, V.D., Guillaume, J.L., Lambiotte, R., Etienne, L.: Fast unfolding of communities in large networks. J. Stat. Mech. Theory Exp. **2008**(10), P10008 (2008)
17. Paxson, V.: Bro: a system for detecting network intruders in real-time. In: Proceedings of 7th USENIX Security Symposium. Usenix (1998)

Research on Multi Domain Based Access Control in Intelligent Connected Vehicle

Kaiyu Wang[✉], Nan Liu, Jiapeng Xiu, and Zhengqiu Yang

Software Engineering School, Beijing University of Posts and
Telecommunications, No.10 Xitucheng Road, Haidian District, Beijing, China
{wangkaiyu, nanliu, xiujiapeng, zqyang}@bupt.edu.cn

Abstract. With the development of Intelligent Connected Vehicle (ICV), the information security problems it faces are becoming more and more important. Authentication and access control is an important part of ensuring the security of intelligent connected vehicles' information. In this paper, we have proposed a multi-domain based access control model (MDBA) based on the attribute-based access control model. The model proposes access control from the aspects of intelligent connected vehicles' multi-domain, thus ensuring the information security of intelligent connected vehicles.

Keywords: Intelligent connected vehicle · Access control · Multi domain · Information security

1 Introduction

1.1 ICV Background

In recent years, with the increasing number of private vehicles, the road carrying capacity of many cities have reached saturation. Traffic safety, travel efficiency, environmental protection and other issues have become increasingly prominent, and hinder the development of society. In this case, more and more public and vehicle manufacturers are turning their attention to intelligent connected vehicles. In order to solve the problems faced by current vehicles, various manufacturers are committed to developing intelligent vehicles with "pre-judgment" functions.

The intelligent connected vehicles contain many devices such as on-board sensors, controllers, actuators, etc., which combines modern communication and network technologies. This will enable intelligent information exchange and sharing between vehicles and X(vehicles, rode-side unit, people, clouds, etc.) through perception. Intelligent decision-making in the surrounding complex environment helps drivers to achieve coordinated control of the connected vehicle itself, and ultimately replaces people with "safe, efficient, comfortable, energy-saving" automated driving.

The information security of intelligent connected vehicles is getting more and more attention. The traditional information security problems in the Internet also appear in the vehicle. Information tampering and virus intrusion have been successfully applied in car attacks. For example, In January 2015, BMW's intelligent driving system Connected Drive had security vulnerabilities, and millions of vehicles were exposed to

J. Li et al. (Eds.): SPNCE 2019, LNICST 284, pp. 401–407, 2019.
https://doi.org/10.1007/978-3-030-21373-2_31

hackers. In February 2015, the On-star vehicle system installed by General Motors had a loophole, and the vehicle could be controlled at will after hacking. In July 2015, the White Hat hacker demonstrated the invasion of the Unconnect in-vehicle system and controlled the vehicle via remote commands. In September 2016, the Keen Security Lab of Tencent conducted a remote attack on the Tesla Model S in parking and driving mode, successfully invading and controlling the vehicle. Due to the frequent occurrence of vehicle safety problems in recent years, the information security crisis of intelligent connected vehicles can not only cause losses to individuals and enterprises, but also even rise to national public security issues.

1.2   Security Problems

Due to its intelligent and connected features, ICV need to interact with other entity like other ICVs, manufacture cloud platform and public service platform. Potential threats will also enter the vehicles network. We group the security threats on ICV as cloud layer, telecommunication layer and vehicle layer. All these threats can potentially impact the safety and privacy of the ICV.

The security threats faced by ICV are shown in the following Fig. 1:

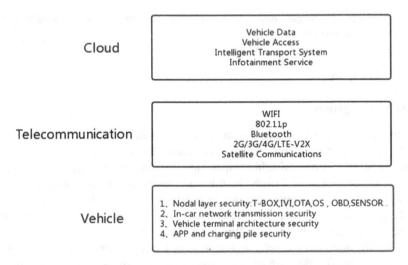

Fig. 1. The security threats faced by ICV

Vehicle layer's threats mainly involves vehicle system, car's CAN bus, Electronic Control Unit (ECU), On Board Diagnostic (OBD), T-Box and Infotainment (IVI) etc. Once crack the T-Box, hackers can send command through the CAN bus. The ECU connected to CAN bus will execute the command, which will impact the safety of the ICV.

Telecommunication layer's security threats mainly involves in telecommunication protocol itself. Once the telecommunication protocol cracked, the hackers can attempt a replay attack or Denial-of-Service (Dos) attack.

The cloud layer's security mainly includes the manufactures' platform and the public service platform. The cloud platform's threats Denial-of-Service, privacy data leak etc.

2 Related Work

Access control technology has been widely used to ensure system security, information confidentiality and integrity. Research on access control has become one of the research hotspots in computer security. With the continuous development of computing technology and network, the application of access control has also expanded to more fields, such as operating systems, databases, and wireless mobile networks, grid computing, cloud computing, and etc.

At present, the research on access control of intelligent connected vehicles mainly starts from two perspectives, one is access control based on identity authentication, and the other is access control through encryption mechanism.

The research on identity authentication has been widely used in traditional computer networks, these research results have laid a foundation for identity authentication in the intelligent connected vehicles environment. However, due to the complexity of the communication scenario of the intelligent connected vehicles and the low timeliness of information, thus increasing the difficulty of identity authentication. Sun etc. [1], proposed that the authentication method in the intelligent connected vehicles environment is constructed. The ID is used as the identity identifier of the vehicle node, which avoids the drawbacks caused by the certificate. Liu etc. [2] designed a dynamic trust model based on vehicle node messages and behaviors, providing strong real-time and high-accuracy trust evaluation, providing method support for actively sensing malicious nodes, and creatively considering future vehicles environments. It may run in the quantum communication environment and deduct the research direction of quantum threshold anonymous authentication and quantum trust evolution decision mechanism. Song etc. [3] proposed a lightweight uncertified and one round key agreement scheme without pairing, and further proved the security of the scheme in the random prediction model. This solution not only resists known attacks, but also has a small amount of computation. It is also an effective way to reduce vehicle-to-vehicle certification workloads, especially if there is no infrastructure available.

The research on encryption mechanism has been towards on attribute-based encryption. The key mechanism is that the holder of the subject encrypts the subject, and only the object that can be decrypted can access the subject data. This research idea is an access control strategy implemented by encrypting the attributes of the object by referring to the attribute-based access control idea in the traditional access control model. Huang etc. [4] proposed attribute-based encryption (ABE) to build an attribute-based security policy implementation framework. The framework treats various road conditions as attributes. These attributes are used as encryption keys to protect the transmitted data. At the same time, it is possible to naturally include a data access control policy on the transmitted data. Kang etc. [5] proposes an access control with an authentication scheme for propagating messages in VANET. In this scheme, the pseudonym is integrated with an identity-based signature (IBS), which not only verifies the messages in the in-vehicle communication, but also protects the privacy of the message generator. Rao etc. [6] proposed a large cipher text size problem in the access control mechanism for vehicle communication based on attribute-based encryption (ABE). By using the access strategy in the Disjunction Paradigm (DNF), the length of the cipher text is linear in the number of conjunctions, not the number of attributes in the access policy. The communication overhead can be greatly reduced, and the scheme has the ability to resist collusion attacks under the damaged RSU.

3   Demand Analysis

3.1   Analysis of New Situation

The access control technology in ICV is quite different from the traditional cloud platform.

In the ICV background, the subject include other ICVs, roadside infrastructure (RSU), manufactures' cloud platform, public service cloud platform and people who can control the vehicle through the APP. We will pay attention to whether or not the subject have the access rights to the ICV, the access control process and granularity of Permissions.

Traditional access control models include autonomous access control (DAC) [7], mandatory access control (MAC) [8], and role-based access control (RBAC) [9, 10], which are static access control models. However, in the fast moving situation of the ICVs, the number of external subjects such diverse. Thus, this kind of dynamic authorization is quite different from the traditional access control models. The traditional access control model is difficult to adapt to such a large-scale and dynamic environment. The attribute-based access control (ABAC) [11] can better solve the access control problem in the intelligent connected vehicles environment, which is the main method of current research.

Therefore, we have proposed an access control strategy in a new situation, which can well solve our problems.

3.2   Multi-domain Based Access Control Model

In the intelligent connected vehicle environment, we have proposed a multi-domain based access control model. On the one hand, due to the intelligence of the intelligent connected vehicles and the characteristics of the network connection, the intelligent connected vehicles also have different functional components inside, and different functional components have different security levels. On the other hand, due to the complexity of the communication scenarios involved in the intelligent connected vehicle, the number of resources that the external subject accessing the vehicle and the vehicle object need to access is different from the level of access. Therefore, it is necessary for us to divide the domain of the resources inside the vehicle. At the same time, according to the behavior of the subject's access request, the subject is granted different level rights. Thus, a more granular access control is provided for the external subject to access the vehicle.

4 MDAC Model

Definition 1: subject
The subject refers to the entity that accesses the intelligent connected vehicles. Such as other connected vehicles, service cloud platforms, roadside communication infrastructure. Use S to represent the collection of subjects, S = {s1, s2 ... sn}.

Definition 2: Object
The object that the subject is accessing. Use O to represent the resource object.
O = {o1, o2 ... on}.

Definition 3: Domain
A unit that divides the internal resources of an object. Such as information domain, control domain, etc. D is used to represent the set of domains, D = {d1, d2 ... dn}. The interdomain is divided into 4 parts shown in Fig. 2.

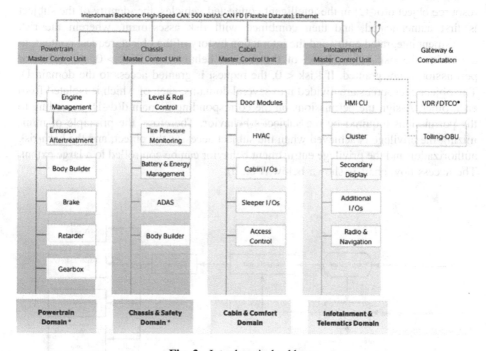

Fig. 2. Interdomain backbone

Definition 4: Permission
The specific access operation of the subject to the object resource. Such as creating, reading, copying, and etc. Use P to represent the set of permissions, P = {p1, p2 ... pn}.

Definition 5: Action

The dynamic request operation of the subject's permission on the object resource, and the process of obtaining the dynamic permission. For example, the roadside infrastructure requests specific information of the vehicle, and the cloud service platform acquires real-time information of the vehicle. A is used to represent the set of requests, A = {a1, a2, ... an}.

Definition 6: Risk

The threat index of the subject's access object's behavioral assessment, with a value of {−1, 1}. Where −1 means no risk and 1 means risky.

The authorization group of the MDAC model can be represented by a 7-tuple MDAC = {S, S-A, P, S-P, D, P-D, O}. Among them, S is subject, S-A is the subject's behavior, P is the permission set of the operation resource, S-P is the permission set possessed by the subject, D is the fine-grained access control domain, P-D is the domain that the permission can access the operation, O is the A resource object that can be manipulated.

In the MDAC model, when the external subject s(s∈S) requests access to the resource object o(o∈O) in the intelligent connected vehicles, the identity of the subject is first authenticated, and then combined with risk assessment, wherein the risk assessment integrated entity and the interaction history of the object, request context, to determine the risk value (Risk) of the request behavior. If Risk > 0, the behavior permission is not granted. If Risk < 0, the request is granted access to the domain D. The object's resources are divided into several domains, each of which is isolated from each other. Assign the permissions on the corresponding domain d(d∈D) according to the permissions required by the subject's behavior. Therefore, the principle of minimizing the privilege is achieved when the subject accesses the object, and the high-risk authorization and the privilege entrustment behavior can be controlled to a large extent. The access flow chart is shown below (Fig. 3).

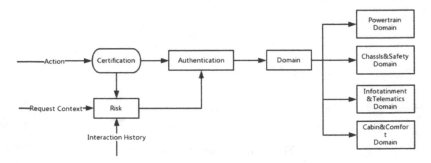

Fig. 3. The access flow chart.

5 Summary

By analyzing the development status of intelligent connected vehicles and the information security problems they face. This paper first analyzes the importance of information security, permission control and current permission control based on attributes, and deeply studies the current permission control technology, the mainstream permission control model and the characteristics of each model. A more efficient multi-domain based access control model (MDAC) is proposed through the abstraction of demand scenarios and the new attribute-based permission control model (ABAC). And the model is deeply explained from the aspects of the components, operation flow and working principle of the model, solving the problem of the authority control of the intelligent connected vehicle.

Acknowledgement. This work is supported by the subject (2017YFB0102502) of the National Key Research and Development Program of China.

References

1. Sun, J., Zhang, C., Zhang, Y., Fang, Y.: An identity-based security system for user privacy in vehicular Ad Hoc networks. IEEE Trans. Parallel Distrib. Syst. **21**(9), 1227–1239 (2010)
2. Liu, Y., Song, X., Xiao, Y.: Authentication mechanism and trust model for internet of vehicles paradigm. J. Beijing Univ. Posts Telecommun. **40**(3), 1–18 (2017)
3. Song, J., He, C., Zhang, L., Tang, S., Zhang, H.: Toward an RSU-unavailable lightweight certificateless key agreement scheme for VANETs. China Commun. **11**(9), 93–103 (2014)
4. Huang, D., Verma, M.: ASPE: attribute-based secure policy enforcement in vehicular ad hoc networks. Ad Hoc Netw. **8**, 1526–1535 (2009)
5. Kang, Q., Liu, X., Yao, Y., Wang, Z., Li, Y.: Efficient authentication and access control of message dissemination over vehicular ad hoc network. Neurocomputing **181**, 132–138 (2016)
6. Rao, Y.S., Dutta, R.: Efficient attribute based access control mechanism for vehicular Ad Hoc network. In: Lopez, J., Huang, X., Sandhu, R. (eds.) NSS 2013. LNCS, vol. 7873, pp. 26–39. Springer, Heidelberg (2013). https://doi.org/10.1007/978-3-642-38631-2_3
7. Vimercati, S.D.C.D.: Discretionary access control policies (DAC). Encycl. Crypt. Secur. 356–358 (2011)
8. Lawson, C., Wildy, H.: Mandatory access control (MAC) in virtual machines. Constr. Equipment (2014)
9. Ferraiolo, D.: Role-based access control (RBAC) (2004)
10. Ferraiolo, D., Cugini, J., Kuhn, D.R.: Role-based access control (RBAC): features and motivations (1995)
11. Hu, V.C., Kuhn, D.R., Ferraiolo, D.F.: Attribute-based access control. Computer **48**(2), 85–88 (2015)

System Building

Cryptanalysis of a Public Key Cryptosystem Based on Data Complexity Under Quantum Environment

Zhengjun Jing[✉], Chunsheng Gu, and Peizhong Shi

School of Computer Engineering, Jiangsu University of Technology,
ChangZhou, China
zhengjun_jing@163.com

Abstract. Shor presented a quantum algorithm to factor large integers and compute discrete logarithms in polynomial time. As a result, public key cryptosystems, such as RSA, ElGamal and ECC, which are based on these computational assumptions will become insecure with the advent of quantum computers. To construct a secure anti-quantum public-key cryptosystem, Wu et al. introduced the notion of data complexity under quantum environment. Based on the hardness of NP-complete problems and data complexity, they presented a new public key cryptosystem. Using Shor's quantum algorithm, we break their public key cryptosystem by directly solving the private key from the public key. Therefore, their public key cryptosystem is insecure in a quantum computer.

Keywords: Public-key cryptosystem · Data complexity ·
Quantum algorithm · Discrete logarithm · Integer factorization

1 Introduction

Public-key cryptography is indispensable in secure communications for an open networked environment such as the Internet. In 1976, Diffie and Helman introduced the notion of public-key cryptography in "New Directions in Cryptography" [1], and proposed a key exchange protocol based on discrete logarithms over an insecure channel. However, they did not present public-key cryptosystems in [1]. Subsequently, Rivest, Shamir, and Adleman [2] described a public-key encryption scheme and a signature scheme, called RSA, whose security depends on the difficulty of factoring. Afterwards, ElGamal [3] presented a public key cryptosystem and a signature scheme which are based on discrete logarithm assumption. Miller [4] discussed the use of elliptic curves in cryptography and

Supported by the National Natural Science Foundation of China (Nos. 61672270, 61602216, and 61702236), the Qing Lan Project for Young Researchers of Jiangsu Province of China (No. KYQ14004), and Jiangsu Overseas Research & Training Program for University Prominent Young & Middle-aged Teachers and Presidents.

J. Li et al. (Eds.): SPNCE 2019, LNICST 284, pp. 411–420, 2019.
https://doi.org/10.1007/978-3-030-21373-2_32

proposed an analogue of the Diffie-Hellman key exchange protocol. Furthermore, using the discrete logarithm on the elliptic curve, we can construct a public key encryption scheme and signature scheme similar to that of ElGamal. However, Shor [5] described a polynomial time quantum algorithm which is able to factor large integers and compute discrete logarithms. Consequently, the public-key cryptosystems RSA, ElGamal, and ECC, which are based on these computational problems become insecure with the advent of quantum computers.

The study in post-quantum cryptography has seen a series of activities that constructed many post-quantum public-key cryptosystems [6]. These schemes mainly include code-based public-key cryptosystems [7], lattice-based public-key cryptosystems [8–11], multivariate public-key cryptosystems [12,13], quantum public-key cryptosystems based on quantum physics [14,15], DNA-based public-key cryptosystems [16]. Although these schemes are believed to be resistant to quantum attacks, it is always better to provide more candidate post-quantum public-key schemes. Recently, Wu et al. [17] introduced the concept of data complexity to the public key cryptosystems under a quantum environment, and described a public key cryptosystem and a signature scheme based on the hardness of NPC problems and data complexity. They considered several possible quantum attacks for their schemes and claimed that their schemes are secure in a quantum computer. However, they did not provide any rigorous proof of security for their schemes. Therefore, it is necessary to further study the security of their schemes [17].

Our main contribution is to prove that the public key cryptosystem and signature scheme proposed by Wu et al. [17] are insecure on a quantum computer. Our key observation is that there exists a polynomial time quantum algorithm that transforms the public key of their schemes [17] into a system of linear equations. This is because the matrix operations $\odot, \otimes$ used by their schemes are both component-wise multiplication. Consequently, by the definitions of $\odot, \otimes$, we can generate a linear system of the private key for their schemes on a quantum computer. Then, applying the Gaussian elimination method, we can obtain the private key from solving this linear system. Therefore, the public key cryptosystem and signature scheme in [17] are not immune to quantum attacks.

The remainder of this paper is organized as follows. We first give some preliminaries in Sect. 2, and describe the public key cryptosystem (PKC) [17] in Sect. 3. We present the cryptanalysis of PKC in Sect. 4. Finally, in Sect. 5 we conclude this paper and provide some suggestions for improvement.

2   Preliminaries

In this paper, quantum algorithms are only used to decompose large integers and to compute discrete logarithms over a finite field, all other algorithms are classical ones. For simplicity, we use Shor's quantum algorithm as a black box algorithm, and do not define quantum computation in this paper.

Data complexity, that is used for the differential attack of DES, refers to an attack algorithm requires the number of plaintext-ciphertext pairs. Wu et al. [17]

introduced the notion of data complexity under a quantum environment to construct an anti-quantum public key cryptosystem. The data complexity of quantum Turing machine (QTM) defined by [17] means the sum of input data and processing data of an algorithm in QTM. Since we do not require data complexity in our cryptanalysis, consequently we do not provide the related definitions of data complexity for simplicity.

In the following, we first give some notations and definitions of the related operations in this paper. Then, we briefly review the discrete logarithm problems and the integer factorization problems, and present Shor's quantum algorithm with two lemmas.

2.1 Notations

Throughout this paper, let n be the security parameter. We write $[n] = \{1, 2, \cdots, n\}$. Let p be a prime, $\mathbb{Z}_p = \mathbb{Z}/p\mathbb{Z}$, and $\mathbb{Z}_p^* = \mathbb{Z}_p \setminus \{0\}$. By convention, vectors are in column form. We use bold lower-case letters like $\mathbf{a}$ to denote column vectors, and bold upper-case letters like $\mathbf{A}$ to denote matrices. We use the superscript T to denote the transpose of vector or matrix, e.g. $\mathbf{a}^T, \mathbf{A}^T$.

Given an element $g \in \mathbb{Z}_p^*$ and matrices $\mathbf{A} = (a_{i,j}), \mathbf{B} = (b_{i,j}) \in \mathbb{Z}_p^{*(m \times m)}$, we define some operations of matrices in $\mathbb{Z}_p^*$ that are used in this paper as follows:

$$g^{\mathbf{A}} = (g^{a_{i,j}})_{m \times m}, i, j \in [m],$$

$$\mathbf{A}^{-1} = (a_{i,j}^{-1})_{m \times m}, i, j \in [m],$$

$$\mathbf{A} \odot \mathbf{B} = (a_{i,j} b_{i,j})_{m \times m}, i, j \in [m],$$

$$\mathbf{A}^t = \underbrace{\mathbf{A} \odot \mathbf{A} \cdots \odot \mathbf{A}}_{t} = (a_{i,j}^t)_{m \times m}, i, j \in [m],$$

$$\mathbf{A} \otimes \mathbf{B} = \begin{pmatrix} a_{1,1}\mathbf{B} & a_{1,2}\mathbf{B} & \cdots & a_{1,m}\mathbf{B} \\ a_{2,1}\mathbf{B} & a_{2,2}\mathbf{B} & \cdots & a_{2,m}\mathbf{B} \\ \vdots & \vdots & \cdots & \vdots \\ a_{m,1}\mathbf{B} & a_{m,2}\mathbf{B} & \cdots & a_{m,m}\mathbf{B} \end{pmatrix} \in \mathbb{Z}_p^{*(m^2 \times m^2)}.$$

2.2 Discrete Logarithm Problem

The discrete logarithm problem defined in $\mathbb{Z}_p^*$ is computationally intractable for classic computers. That is, there is no polynomial time algorithm for the discrete logarithm problem on a classical computer. However, there exists an efficient quantum algorithm that solves the discrete logarithm problem.

A group G is cyclic if and only if there exists an element $g \in G$ such that for every element $a \in G$, there exists an integer x such that $g^x = a$. In this paper, we call g a generator of G.

Definition 1 (generator, [18]). Given a prime p, an integer $g \in \mathbb{Z}_p^*$ is called a generator of $\mathbb{Z}_p^*$ if $p - 1$ is the smallest positive integer such that $g^{p-1} = 1$ mod p.

Definition 2 (discrete logarithm problem, [18]**).** Given a prime p, a generator $g \in \mathbb{Z}_p^*$, and an integer $a \in \mathbb{Z}_p^*$, the discrete logarithm problem is to find an integer $x \in [p-1]$ such that $a = g^x \mod p$.

Lemma 1 (Shor, [5]**).** Given a prime p, a generator g, and any number $a \in \mathbb{Z}_q^*$, there exists a polynomial time quantum algorithm, which finds the exponent $\overline{a}$ such that $a = g^{\overline{a}} \mod p$.

2.3   Integer Factorization Problem

Integer factorization problem is a product of decomposing a composite number into smaller integers. The factorization is called prime factorization, if these smaller integers must be prime numbers. According to the fundamental arithmetic theorem, any integer greater than one has a unique prime factorization. Similarly, there is no polynomial time algorithm for the integer factorization problem for classical computers. But there exists an efficient quantum algorithm for the integer factorization problem.

Definition 3 (integer factorization problem, [18]**).** Given an integer $n \in \mathbb{Z}$, factor n into primes, namely, $n = \prod_{i=1}^{k} p_i^{e_i}, e_i \in \mathbb{N}$.

Lemma 2 (Shor, [5]**).** Given an integer n, there exists a polynomial time quantum algorithm, which factors n into primes, namely, $n = \prod_{i=1}^{k} p_i^{e_i}, e_i \in \mathbb{N}$.

3   Public Key Cryptosystem (PKC)

In this section, we adaptively describe the public key cryptosystem (PKC) in [17]. This public key scheme consists of three algorithms: KeyGen, Encryption, and Decryption.

KeyGen

(1) Choose a prime $p > 2^m p_1^{r_1} \cdots p_s^{r_s}$, where $p_1, \cdots, p_s$ are odd primes and $r_1, \cdots, r_s \in \mathbb{N}$.

(2) Randomly choose three different integers $t_1, t_2, t_3 \in [\varphi(p)]$, where $\varphi(p) = p - 1$ is the Euler function of p.

(3) Randomly choose three $m \times m$-dimensional matrices

$$\mathbf{A} = (a_{i,j})_{m \times m}, \mathbf{B} = (b_{i,j})_{m \times m}, \mathbf{D} = (d_{i,j})_{m \times m},$$

where $a_{i,j}, b_{i,j}, d_{i,j} \in \mathbb{Z}_p^*$.

(4) Compute $\mathbf{Y}_1, \mathbf{Y}_2, \mathbf{Y}_3$ as follows:

$$\begin{cases} \mathbf{Y}_1 = \mathbf{A}^{t_1} \odot \mathbf{B}^{t_2} \odot \mathbf{D}^{t_3} & \mod p, \\ \mathbf{Y}_2 = \mathbf{B}^{t_1} \odot \mathbf{D}^{t_2} \odot \mathbf{A}^{t_3} & \mod p, \\ \mathbf{Y}_3 = \mathbf{D}^{t_1} \odot \mathbf{A}^{t_2} \odot \mathbf{B}^{t_3} & \mod p, \end{cases}$$

such that $y_{1i,j}, y_{2i,j}, y_{3i,j} \geq 2^m, i, j \in [m]$. Otherwise, it returns to Step (3).

(5) Output a public key $pk = \{p, \mathbf{A}, \mathbf{B}, \mathbf{D}, \mathbf{Y}_1, \mathbf{Y}_2, \mathbf{Y}_3\}$ and a private key $sk = \{t_1, t_2, t_3\}$.

Encryption

(1) Given the public key pk, let $\mathbf{M} = (m_{i,j})_{m^3 \times m^3}$ with $m_{i,j} \in \mathbb{Z}_p^*$ be an m^6-dimensional plaintext.

(2) Randomly choose three different integers $s_1, s_2, s_3 \in [p - 1]$.

(3) Compute $\mathbf{U} = \mathbf{Y}_1^{s_1} \otimes \mathbf{Y}_2^{s_2} \otimes \mathbf{Y}_3^{s_3} \mod p$.

(4) Compute $\{\mathbf{C}, \mathbf{C}_1, \mathbf{C}_2, \mathbf{C}_3\}$ as follows:

$$
\begin{cases}
\mathbf{C} & = \mathbf{U} \odot \mathbf{M} \quad \mod p, \\
\mathbf{C}_1 & = \mathbf{A}^{s_1} \otimes \mathbf{B}^{s_2} \otimes \mathbf{D}^{s_3} \quad \mod p, \\
\mathbf{C}_2 & = \mathbf{B}^{s_1} \otimes \mathbf{D}^{s_2} \otimes \mathbf{A}^{s_3} \quad \mod p, \\
\mathbf{C}_3 & = \mathbf{D}^{s_1} \otimes \mathbf{A}^{s_2} \otimes \mathbf{B}^{s_3} \quad \mod p.
\end{cases}
$$

(5) Output a four-tuple ciphertext $ct = \{\mathbf{C}, \mathbf{C}_1, \mathbf{C}_2, \mathbf{C}_3\}$.

Decryption

(1) Given the private key sk, let $ct = \{\mathbf{C}, \mathbf{C}_1, \mathbf{C}_2, \mathbf{C}_3\}$ be a four-tuple ciphertext.

(2) Compute $\mathbf{V} = \mathbf{C}_1^{t_1} \odot \mathbf{C}_2^{t_2} \odot \mathbf{C}_3^{t_3} \mod p$.

(3) Output the plaintext $\mathbf{M} = \mathbf{V}^{-1} \odot \mathbf{C} \mod p$.

4   Cryptanalysis of PKC

In this section, we present a polynomial time quantum algorithm that finds the private key from the public key of PKC. As a result, the PKC in [17] is insecure on a quantum computer.

Our main idea is that, by the component-wise multiplication of matrix operation $\odot$ in the public key, we transform a system of exponential equations into a system of linear equations using the Shor's quantum algorithms, and solve the private key using Gaussian elimination.

To implement the above transformation, the key is how to efficiently find a generator g of $\mathbb{Z}_p^*$. In the following, we give three well-known lemmas to efficiently generate a generator g of $\mathbb{Z}_p^*$. Concretely speaking, Lemma 3 shows that $\mathbb{Z}_p^*$ has many generators, Lemma 4 gives a method of determining whether an element is a generator of $\mathbb{Z}_p^*$, and Lemma 5 describes a quantum polynomial time algorithm that produces a generator of $\mathbb{Z}_p^*$ using the quantum polynomial time algorithm of integer factorization in Lemma 2.

Lemma 3. Suppose that p is a prime, then there exist $\varphi(p - 1)$ generators in $\mathbb{Z}_p^*$.

Proof. According to Theorem 7.28 in [18] (or Theorem 2.18 in [19]), $\mathbb{Z}_p^*$ is a cyclic group for a prime p. Hence, $\mathbb{Z}_p^*$ has at least a generator.

Now, assume that g is a generator of $\mathbb{Z}_p^*$. Namely, $g^{p-1} = 1 \mod p$ and for any $1 \le k < p-1$, $g^k \ne 1 \mod p$. Therefore, if r and $p-1$ are relatively prime, then $g_1 = g^r$ is also a generator of $\mathbb{Z}_p^*$. This is because $p-1$ is the smallest positive integer such that $g_1^{p-1} = 1 \mod p$. Again since $\varphi(p-1)$ integers in $[p-1]$ are prime to $p-1$, the result follows.   □

Lemma 4. Suppose that p is a prime and $p - 1 = \prod_{i=1}^{k} p_i^{e_i}$ is the prime factorization of $p - 1$. Then g is a generator of $\mathbb{Z}_p^*$ if and only if for each $i \in [k]$, $g^{\frac{p-1}{p_i}} \ne 1 \mod p$.

Proof. It is easy to verify that if g is a generator of $\mathbb{Z}_p^*$, then for each $i \in [k]$, $g^{\frac{p-1}{p_i}} \ne 1 \mod p$.

Now, we show the opposite direction. Without loss of generality, let r be the smallest positive integer such that $g^r = 1 \mod p$. By contradiction, assume $r < p - 1$. Since p is a prime, $g^{p-1} = 1 \mod p$. If $r \nmid (p-1)$, then there exist two positive integers s, k such that $p - 1 = kr + s$ and $0 < s < r$. So, we have $g^s = 1 \mod p$. This contradicts that r is the smallest positive integer such that $g^r = 1 \mod p$. Hence, $r | (p-1)$. As a result, there exists a prime p_i which satisfies $r | \frac{p-1}{p_i}$. So, $g^{\frac{p-1}{p_i}} = 1 \mod p$. This contradicts the condition that for each $i \in [k]$, $g^{\frac{p-1}{p_i}} \ne 1 \mod p$. Thus, $r = p - 1$. Consequently, g is a generator of $\mathbb{Z}_p^*$.   □

Lemma 5. Given a prime p, there exists a probabilistic polynomial time quantum algorithm which finds a generator g of $\mathbb{Z}_p^*$.

Proof. Using the polynomial time quantum algorithm in Lemma 2, we factor $p - 1$ into primes. Without loss of generality, let $p - 1 = \prod_{i=1}^{k} p_i^{e_i}$.

According to Lemma 4, we can find a generator g of $\mathbb{Z}_p^*$ as follows.

(1) Randomly select $g \in \mathbb{Z}_p^*$.

(2) If $g^{\frac{p-1}{p_i}} \ne 1 \mod p$ for each $i \in [k]$, then g is a generator of $\mathbb{Z}_p^*$. Otherwise, repeat from (1).

Obviously, selecting and testing an element in the steps (1), (2) take polynomial time in n.

In order to find a generator, we analyze how many random elements need to be selected. By Lemma 3, the number of generators in $\mathbb{Z}_p^*$ is $\varphi(p-1)$. Again since $\varphi(p-1) > \frac{p-1}{6 \log \log (p-1)}$ by Theorem 15 in [20], the probability that a random element is a generator is about $\frac{1}{6 \log \log (p-1)}$. Therefore, we expect to have to select $O(\log \log p)$ random candidate elements for g to get a generator with overwhelming probability.

It is easy to verify that the above algorithm is a probabilistic polynomial time quantum algorithm.   □

By Lemma 5, we can efficiently compute a generator g of the cyclic group $\mathbb{Z}_p^*$. For simplicity, we assume that a generator g of $\mathbb{Z}_p^*$ is given in the following Lemmas 6 and 7.

Lemma 6. Given a prime p, a generator g, and a matrix $\mathbf{A} = (a_{i,j}) \in \mathbb{Z}_p^{*(m \times m)}$, there exists a polynomial time quantum algorithm, which finds the exponent matrix $\overline{\mathbf{A}}$ such that $\mathbf{A} = g^{\overline{\mathbf{A}}} \mod p$.

Proof. For each entry $a_{i,j}, i,j \in [m]$ in $\mathbf{A}$, we compute $\overline{a}_{i,j}$ using the quantum algorithm of discrete logarithm in Lemma 1 such that $a_{i,j} = g^{\overline{a}_{i,j}} \mod p$. Thus, $\overline{\mathbf{A}} = (\overline{a}_{i,j})_{m \times m}$ and $g^{\overline{\mathbf{A}}} = (g^{\overline{a}_{i,j}})_{m \times m} = (a_{i,j})_{m \times m} = \mathbf{A} \mod p$. The Lemma 6 follows. □

Lemma 7. Given a prime p, a generator g, and a matrix $\mathbf{A} = (a_{i,j}) \in \mathbb{Z}_p^{*(m \times m)}$, then $\mathbf{A}^t = g^{\overline{\mathbf{A}} \times t} \mod p$, where $\mathbf{A} = g^{\overline{\mathbf{A}}} \mod p$.

Proof. Given $\mathbf{A} = (a_{i,j})_{m \times m}, i,j \in [m]$, according to the definition of $\mathbf{A}^t$, we have

$$\mathbf{A}^t = \underbrace{\mathbf{A} \odot \mathbf{A} \cdots \odot \mathbf{A}}_{t}$$

$$= (a_{i,j}^t)_{m \times m}$$

$$= ((g^{\overline{a}_{i,j}})^t)_{m \times m}$$

$$= (g^{\overline{a}_{i,j} \times t})_{m \times m}$$

$$= g^{(\overline{a}_{i,j})_{m \times m} \times t}$$

$$= g^{\overline{\mathbf{A}} \times t} \mod p.$$

The Lemma 7 follows. □

We are now in a position to prove the main theorem.

Theorem 1. Given the public key $pk = \{p, \mathbf{A}, \mathbf{B}, \mathbf{D}, \mathbf{Y}_1, \mathbf{Y}_2, \mathbf{Y}_3\}$, there exists a probabilistic polynomial time quantum algorithm, which solves the secret key $sk = \{t_1, t_2, t_3\}$.

Proof. According to KeyGen, p is a prime. By Lemma 5, we can efficiently find a generator g of the cyclic group $\mathbb{Z}_p^*$.

Thus, given pk, we can compute $\overline{\mathbf{A}}, \overline{\mathbf{B}}, \overline{\mathbf{D}}, \overline{\mathbf{Y}}_1, \overline{\mathbf{Y}}_2, \overline{\mathbf{Y}}_3$ using Lemma 6 such that

$$\begin{cases} \mathbf{A} = g^{\overline{\mathbf{A}}} \mod p, \\ \mathbf{B} = g^{\overline{\mathbf{B}}} \mod p, \\ \mathbf{D} = g^{\overline{\mathbf{D}}} \mod p, \end{cases} \quad \begin{cases} \mathbf{Y}_1 = g^{\overline{\mathbf{Y}}_1} \mod p, \\ \mathbf{Y}_2 = g^{\overline{\mathbf{Y}}_2} \mod p, \\ \mathbf{Y}_3 = g^{\overline{\mathbf{Y}}_3} \mod p. \end{cases}$$

Since $\mathbf{A} = (a_{i,j})_{m \times m} = (g^{\overline{a}_{i,j}})_{m \times m}$, $\mathbf{B} = (b_{i,j})_{m \times m} = (g^{\overline{b}_{i,j}})_{m \times m}$, and $\mathbf{D} = (d_{i,j})_{m \times m} = (g^{\overline{d}_{i,j}})_{m \times m}$, then by Lemma 7, we get

$$\mathbf{A}^{t_1} = g^{t_1 \overline{\mathbf{A}}}$$

$$\mathbf{B}^{t_2} = g^{t_2 \overline{\mathbf{B}}}$$

$$\mathbf{D}^{t_3} = g^{t_3 \overline{\mathbf{D}}}$$

Consequently, we have

$$\mathbf{Y}_1 = \mathbf{A}^{t_1} \odot \mathbf{B}^{t_2} \odot \mathbf{D}^{t_3} = g^{t_1\overline{\mathbf{A}}+t_2\overline{\mathbf{B}}+t_3\overline{\mathbf{D}}} = g^{\overline{\mathbf{Y}}_1} \quad \bmod\ p.$$

Using same methods, we can obtain

$$\mathbf{Y}_2 = \mathbf{B}^{t_1} \odot \mathbf{D}^{t_2} \odot \mathbf{A}^{t_3} = g^{t_1\overline{\mathbf{B}}+t_2\overline{\mathbf{D}}+t_3\overline{\mathbf{A}}} = g^{\overline{\mathbf{Y}}_2} \quad \bmod\ p,$$

$$\mathbf{Y}_3 = \mathbf{D}^{t_1} \odot \mathbf{A}^{t_2} \odot \mathbf{B}^{t_3} = g^{t_1\overline{\mathbf{D}}+t_2\overline{\mathbf{A}}+t_3\overline{\mathbf{B}}} = g^{\overline{\mathbf{Y}}_3} \quad \bmod\ p.$$

Therefore, we can generate a system of linear equation as follows:

$$\begin{cases} t_1\overline{\mathbf{A}} + t_2\overline{\mathbf{B}} + t_3\overline{\mathbf{D}} = \overline{\mathbf{Y}}_1 \quad \bmod\ (p-1) \\ t_1\overline{\mathbf{B}} + t_2\overline{\mathbf{D}} + t_3\overline{\mathbf{A}} = \overline{\mathbf{Y}}_2 \quad \bmod\ (p-1) \\ t_1\overline{\mathbf{D}} + t_2\overline{\mathbf{A}} + t_3\overline{\mathbf{B}} = \overline{\mathbf{Y}}_3 \quad \bmod\ (p-1). \end{cases}$$

Since there exist $3\,m^2$ $(m \geq 1)$ linear equations in the above equation system, we can solve three unknown variables $t_1, t_2, t_3 \in [p-1]$.

It is not difficult to verify that the above computations take a polynomial time in quantum computers. $\qquad\square$

Furthermore, we can obtain the following result.

Theorem 2. Given the public key $pk = \{p, \mathbf{A}, \mathbf{B}, \mathbf{D}, \mathbf{Y}_1, \mathbf{Y}_2, \mathbf{Y}_3\}$ and a four-tuple ciphertext $ct = \{\mathbf{C}, \mathbf{C}_1, \mathbf{C}_2, \mathbf{C}_3\}$, then exists a polynomial time quantum algorithm, which recovers the plaintext $\mathbf{M}$ from the ciphertext ct.

Proof. Using Theorem 1, we can compute the private key sk from the public key pk. Then, we directly decrypt the ciphertext ct using the private key sk, and obtain the corresponding plaintext $\mathbf{M}$ in ct. $\qquad\square$

5   Conclusions

In this paper, we present a polynomial time quantum algorithm that finds the private key from the public key of PKC in [17]. Furthermore, we also provide a polynomial-time quantum algorithm to solve the private key of the signature scheme in [17]. Consequently, their public key cryptosystem is insecure in a quantum computer.

Our results show that there is still much work to be done to construct secure anti-quantum public key cryptosystem using data complexity. Since our attack mainly depends on component-wise multiplication in matrix operations $\odot, \otimes$, a possible improvement is to change matrix operations $\odot, \otimes$ to prevent attackers from generating discrete logarithm problems based on public keys.

Acknowledgements. This work was supported by the National Natural Science Foundation of China (Nos. 61672270, 61602216, and 61702236), the Qing Lan Project for Young Researchers of Jiangsu Province of China (No. KYQ14004), and Jiangsu Overseas Research & Training Program for University Prominent Young & Middle-aged Teachers and Presidents.

References

1. Diffie, W., Hellman, M.E.: New directions in cryptography. IEEE Trans. Inf. Theory **IT–22**, 644–654 (1976)
2. Rivest, R.L., Shamir, A., Adleman, L.M.: A method for obtaining digital signatures and public-key cryptosystems. Commun. ACM **21**(2), 120–126 (1978)
3. ElGamal, T.: A public key cryptosystem and a signature scheme based on discrete logarithms. In: Blakley, G.R., Chaum, D. (eds.) CRYPTO 1984. LNCS, vol. 196, pp. 10–18. Springer, Heidelberg (1985). https://doi.org/10.1007/3-540-39568-7_2
4. Miller, V.S.: Use of elliptic curves in cryptography. In: Williams, H.C. (ed.) CRYPTO 1985. LNCS, vol. 218, pp. 417–426. Springer, Heidelberg (1986). https://doi.org/10.1007/3-540-39799-X_31
5. Shor, P.W.: Polynomial-time algorithms for prime factorization and discrete logarithms on a quantum computer. SIAM J. Comput. **26**, 1484–1509 (1997)
6. Buchmann, J.A., Butin, D., Göpfert, F., Petzoldt, A.: Post-quantum cryptography: state of the art. In: Ryan, P.Y.A., Naccache, D., Quisquater, J.-J. (eds.) The New Codebreakers. LNCS, vol. 9100, pp. 88–108. Springer, Heidelberg (2016). https://doi.org/10.1007/978-3-662-49301-4_6
7. McEliece, R.J.: A public-key cryptosystem based on algebraic coding theory. Deep Space Network Progress Report 44, pp. 114–116 (1978)
8. Peikert, C.: Lattice cryptography for the internet. In: Mosca, M. (ed.) PQCrypto 2014. LNCS, vol. 8772, pp. 197–219. Springer, Cham (2014). https://doi.org/10.1007/978-3-319-11659-4_12
9. Stehlé, D., Steinfeld, R.: Making NTRU as secure as worst-case problems over ideal lattices. In: Paterson, K.G. (ed.) EUROCRYPT 2011. LNCS, vol. 6632, pp. 27–47. Springer, Heidelberg (2011). https://doi.org/10.1007/978-3-642-20465-4_4
10. Lyubashevsky, V., Peikert, C., Regev, O.: On ideal lattices and learning with errors over rings. In: Gilbert, H. (ed.) EUROCRYPT 2010. LNCS, vol. 6110, pp. 1–23. Springer, Heidelberg (2010). https://doi.org/10.1007/978-3-642-13190-5_1
11. Regev, O.: On lattices, learning with errors, random linear codes, and cryptography. In: STOC 2005, pp. 84-93 (2005)
12. Tao, C., Diene, A., Tang, S., Ding, J.: Simple matrix scheme for encryption. In: Gaborit, P. (ed.) PQCrypto 2013. LNCS, vol. 7932, pp. 231–242. Springer, Heidelberg (2013). https://doi.org/10.1007/978-3-642-38616-9_16
13. Petzoldt, A., Chen, M.-S., Yang, B.-Y., Tao, C., Ding, J.: Design principles for HFEv- based multivariate signature schemes. In: Iwata, T., Cheon, J.H. (eds.) ASIACRYPT 2015. LNCS, vol. 9452, pp. 311–334. Springer, Heidelberg (2015). https://doi.org/10.1007/978-3-662-48797-6_14
14. Bennett, C.H., DiVincenzo, D.P., Smolin, J.A., Wootters, W.K.: Mixed-state entanglement and quantum error correction. Phys. Rev. A **54**, 3824–3851 (1996)
15. Shi, J.J., Shi, R.H., Guo, Y., Peng, X.Q., Tang, Y.: Batch proxy quantum blind signature scheme. Sci. China Inf. Sci. **56**, 1–9 (2013). 052115
16. Lai, X.J., Lu, M.X., Qin, L., Han, J.S., Fang, X.W.: Asymmetric encryption and signature method with DNA technology. Sci. China Inf. Sci. **53**(3), 506–514 (2010)
17. Wu, W.Q., Zhang, H.G., Wang, H.Z., Mao, S.W., Jia, J.W., Liu, J.H.: A public key cryptosystem based on data complexity under quantum environment. Sci. China Inf. Sci. **58**, 1–11 (2015). 110102

18. Shoup, V.: A Computational Introduction to Number Theory and algebra, 2nd edn. Cambridge University Press, Cambridge (2008)
19. Goldwasser, S., Bellare, M.: Lecture Notes on Cryptography (2008). http://cseweb. ucsd.edu/mihir/papers/gb.html
20. Rosser, J., Schoenfield, L.: Approximate formulas for some functions of prime numbers. Ill. J. Math. **6**, 64–94 (1962)

A Design of the Group Decision Making Medical Diagnosis Expert System Based on SED-JD Algorithm

Na Zong[1,2], Wuyungerile Li[1,2]([✉]), Pengyu Li[1,2], Bing Jia[1,2], and Xuebin Ma[1,2]

[1] Inner Mongolia University, Hohhot 010021, Inner Mongolia, China
gerile@imu.edu.cn
[2] Inner Mongolia A.R. Key Laboratory of Wireless Networking and Mobile Computing, Hohhot 010021, China

Abstract. Medical expert system not only has a lot of medical professional knowledge, but also has inference ability. The inference engine is not only one of the cores of the expert system, but also the key to designing the expert system. We focus on inference engine. In order to improve the diagnostic accuracy of medical diagnostic expert system, we propose the Group Decision Making (GDM) medical diagnosis expert system based on the Standardized Euclidean Distance-Jaccard Distance (SED-JD) algorithm. The mainly research content of inference engine is similarity measurement algorithm (that is SED-JD) and inference engine rule scheme (that is GDM). In order to get more accurate diagnosis, data preprocessing was performed before our experiments. In the design of inference engine, the selection of the Group Decision Making Objects (GDMOs) depends on the maximum similarity distance (MaxDist). The final decision result depends on the average similarity distance of each subgroup. By comparing the similarity scheme and GDM scheme, the experimental results show that GDM scheme is more effective and accurate. By comparing the Standardized Euclidean Distance (SED) algorithm, the Jaccard Distance (JD) algorithm and SED-JD algorithm, the experimental results show that SED-JD algorithm is more accurate.

Keywords: Medical expert system · Group Decision Making · Similarity measurement

1 Introduction

Artificial Intelligence (AI) is a new kind of intelligence which its respond is similar to human intelligence. The expert system is one of the important branches of AI

Supported by the National Natural Science Foundation of China (Grants No. 61761035, 41761086, 61461037, 61661041) and "Scientific and Technological Innovation Project of Inner Mongolia Autonomous Region System Development and Product Application of Urban Flood Disaster Monitoring and Early-warning Management".

J. Li et al. (Eds.): SPNCE 2019, LNICST 284, pp. 421–432, 2019.
https://doi.org/10.1007/978-3-030-21373-2_33

application, and has a important directions that is medical expert system [1]. In this paper, an improved Group Decision Making (GDM) scheme, Subgroup-based Group Decision Making (SGDM), is proposed for inference engine. The expert system and GDM are introduced below.

1.1   Medical Expert System

Expert system is a computer (software) system that can solve difficult and complex problems like human experts [2]. Medical expert system has not only a lot of medical professional knowledge, but also inference ability. Therefore, medical expert system conducts medical diagnosis and medical related inference by simulating the process of analyzing problems in the medical field. Medical expert system, as the assistant of medical system, can lighten the burden of medical workers and make medical work more efficient.

The typical structure of medical expert system [3] is similar to general expert system, including man-machine interface, inference engine, explain module, knowledge base, dynamic database and knowledge base management system. The typical structural diagram of the medical expert system is shown in Fig. 1. Man-machine interface refers to the interaction interface between users and expert system. Inference engine refers to the realization of (generalized) inference procedures. Explain module is responsible for explaining the behavior and results of the expert system to users. Knowledge base refers to the set of knowledge which stored in computers. The knowledge base generally includes expert knowledge, domain knowledge and so on. Dynamic database stores initial evidences, inference results and so on. Knowledge base management system is the supporting software of knowledge base. The relationship between them is similar to the function of database management system on database.

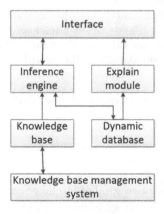

Fig. 1. The Structural diagram of expert system.

In the whole system, the most important modules are the inference engine and the knowledge base. Inference engine is the logical core of expert system.

Knowledge base is the foundation and support of expert system. We focus on the design of the inference engine and the knowledge base.

1.2 Group Decision Making

Science of Decision Making [4] is a comprehensive subject that takes decision making as the research object. That mainly studies the principle, procedure and method of decision making, and explores how to make correct decisions. Group Decision Making (GDM) [5] is a research field with a long history in Science of Decision Making. GDM was proposed by Duncan in 1948 [6]. Hwang gave a clear definition of GDM in 1987 [7] that GDM is decision scheme. Firstly, different members propose their own decision plans. Then form all the plans into a set. Finally form a consistent decision plan based on individual preferences and certain rules. The above is GDM connotation. Meanwhile, the people who participate in decision making constitute the decision making group. The simplest scenario of GDM is election.

For medical diagnostic expert system, it is not enough to diagnose according to similarity measurement only. We can think of each sickness as a group, and the boundaries between groups are not very clear, as shown in Fig. 2. According to the similarity measurement, the input sample is the most similar to a sample in class A and should be classified as class A. But in fact, class A is adjacent to class B. This lead to a miscalculation. In order to reduce or even eliminate sample classification errors on the boundary, GDM is introduced into the medical diagnostic expert system. The majority rule commonly [8] applied in GDM is that the preference of most people is the group preference.

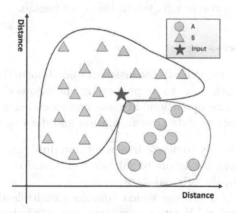

Fig. 2. Similarity judgement diagram.

In Sect. 2, we will introduce the work related to this research. In Sect. 3, we will introduce the system design, and in Sect. 4 implement the design and give the results. Finally, the conclusion and prospect is made in Sect. 5.

2 Related Work

The related work of this paper mainly involves medical expert system, data preprocessing, similarity measurement and GDM.

2.1 Medical Expert System

The inference model of expert system mainly includes prescription production inference model [9–11], fuzzy inference model [12–16] and machine learning inference model [17]. According to the application scenarios, the type of the expert system can be divided into diagnostic [18], explanatory [19], predictive [20], decision-making [21], design [22] and control [23]. And the type of the medical expert system can be divided into diagnostic, explanatory and predictive. According to the classification of output, the type of the expert system is mainly divided into analysis and design. And medical expert system is mainly analytical type. According to the classification of knowledge representation [24], the type of the expert system is mainly divided into production rule representation, predicate logic representation, frame representation, semantic Web representation and so on. Medical expert system is mainly production rule representation type. According to the classification of knowledge, the type of both expert system and medical expert system can be divided into precise inference and imprecise inference [25].

The inference mechanism of medical expert system [26] mainly includes simple production system inference engine, Bayesian theory-based inference engine, MYCIN inference model-based inference engine, fuzzy inference theory-based inference engine, machine learning theory-based inference engine. In this paper, we prefer to a simple production system inference engine.

2.2 Data Preprocessing

Incomplete (with missing values), inconsistent and abnormal raw data will bring obstacles to the research, so data preprocessing operations should be carried out before the research. The operations of data preprocessing mainly include data cleaning, data integration, data transformation and data specification [27].

- Data cleaning is mainly to delete irrelevant and duplicate data, smooth noise data, filter out data irrelevant to mining topics and deal with missing and abnormal values in the original data set.
- Data integration is a process which combines multiple data sources into a consistent data storage. Entity recognition and attribute redundancy should be considered in this process.
- Data transformation mainly carries on the standardization processing to the data. Its methods include the function transformation, the data standardization (normalization), the continuous attribute discretization, the attribute construction, the wavelet transformation and so on.

– Data specification can produce new data set which is smaller than the original data but retains the integrity of the original data. Data specification can reduce the impact of invalid and error data on mining, improve the accuracy, reduce the time of data mining, and reduce the cost of data storage.

2.3 Similarity Measurement

For medical diagnosis expert system, many inference engines are designed based on similarity measurement between medical samples. Similarity measurement [28] is a measurement that comprehensively judges the similarity between two things. The more similar two samples are, the more increased similarity measurement is. There are many kinds of methods for similarity measurement, which are usually selected according to practical problems. Similarity measurements which commonly used include correlation coefficient and similarity coefficient. Correlation coefficient measurements the degree of proximity between variables. Similarity coefficient measurements the degree of proximity between samples. The degree of similarity between samples can be expressed by the following functions.

(1) Similarity coefficient function: the range of similarity coefficient is $[0, 1]$, and the values are positively correlated with similarity. That is to say, the more similar the samples are, the closer the similarity coefficient value is to 1; the more dissimilar the samples are, the closer the similarity coefficient value is to 0.
(2) Distance function: each sample is regarded as a point in n-dimensional space. Distance is used to represent the similarity between samples and is negatively correlated with similarity.

2.4 Group Decision Making

Peng et al. [29] used similarity as the only selection factor for Group Decision Making Object (GDMO). In this scheme, a certain number of GDMO are set firstly. Then GDMOs according to similarity are selected. Finally the minority is subject to the majority.

3 The System Design

This section mainly introduces the main research content of this paper, including data preprocessing, similarity measurement algorithm (that is SED-JD), and GDM scheme (that is SGDM).

3.1 Privacy Data Preprocessing

In this paper, GDM is made based on similarity measurement. Therefore, samples need to be set up in advance for similarity measurement and GDM. Data preprocessing is very important, which is related to the correctness of the whole algorithm. We mainly did the following work.

- Data integration. We merge multiple data sources in this paper. The merge process takes the consultation number as the primary key and merges the data with the same consultation number into one piece of data.
- Data cleaning. We delete private data, irrelevant data, duplicate data, etc.
- Data transformation. We normalize the data, including the standardization of numerical values and the transformation of character values.

3.2   Proposed SED-JD Algorithm

In this paper, similarity measurement between samples is used as the first step of inference. For any sample to be diagnosed, the similarity will be calculated with all samples in the sample set. Due to the sample data of this paper there are both numeric values and character values, in this paper, the similarity measurement will combine the Standardized Euclidean Distance (SED) algorithm and the Jaccard Distance (JD) algorithm, called SED-JD algorithm. SED is used to calculate numeric values, and JD is used to calculate character values. Then combine the two results to get the final similarity.

SED Algorithm. SED is an improvement of the Euclidean Distance (ED). ED is the most commonly used distance calculation formula. Since ED measurements the absolute distance between samples in a multidimensional space, that is, the calculation is based on the absolute value of the characteristics of each dimension, so ED's calculation needs to ensure that all dimensional indicators are at the same scale level. Therefore, the values of each dimension should be standardized before calculation. The standardized formula is formula (1), and the standardized result is expressed by $x_i{}^*$, x_i refers to the ith value of a attribute, $\bar{x}$ is the mean of the attribute, and s is the standard deviation of the attribute.

$$x_i{}^* = \frac{x_i - \bar{x}}{s} \tag{1}$$

SED's calculation formula is formula (2), where $d(X, Y)$ represents the values between sample X and sample Y calculated by SED, n is the number of attributes, x_i is the ith value of sample X, y_i is the ith value of sample Y, s_i represents the standard deviation of the ith attribute.

$$d(X, Y) = \sqrt{\sum_{i=1}^{n} (\frac{x_i - y_i}{s_i})^2} \tag{2}$$

Since SED calculates the absolute distance between samples, the larger the value of $d(X, Y)$ is, the smaller the similarity is. When $d(X, Y) = 0$, it means that the two samples coincide exactly.

JD Algorithm. Jaccard Similarity Coefficient (JSC) is a kind of similarity measurement which mainly used for computing symbols or boolean value. Because the characteristics of the sample attributes are symbols or boolean, so the similarity between samples can only be measured by whether they are the same or not. Therefore, JSC only care about whether the common characteristics between samples are consistent. In short, the proportion of the intersection in the union of set A and set B, which is represented by the symbol $J(A, B)$. The formula is shown in formula (3).

$$J(A, B) = \frac{|A \cap B|}{|A \cup B|} \tag{3}$$

In contrast to JSC, the Jaccard Distance (JD) uses the proportion of different elements in two sets to all the elements to measure the divisibility of two sets. It is expressed in symbol $J_\sigma(A, B)$. The formula is shown in formula (4).

$$J_\sigma(A, B) = 1 - J(A, B) = \frac{|A \cup B| - |A \cap B|}{|A \cup B|} \tag{4}$$

Proposed SED-JD Algorithm. The similarity measurement used in this paper is represented by the symbol $D(X, Y)$, and the formula is shown in formula (5). And $d(X_E, Y_E)$ is the similarity value between sample X and sample Y which calculates by SED. $J_\sigma(X_J, Y_J)$ is the similarity value between sample X and sample Y which compare by JD. JD collect all character attributes as a set. Therefore, we treat $J_\sigma(X_J, Y_J)$ as the average distance of character attributes. SED calculates properties separately. So $d(X_E, Y_E)$ and $J_\sigma(X_J, Y_J)$ have different scales. To calculate the total distance, in this paper, the usual way to combine the two scales is to multiply a and $J_\sigma(X_J, Y_J)$, where a is the number of attributes which participate in JD calculation.

$$D(X, Y) = d(X_E, Y_E) + a \cdot J_\sigma(X_J, Y_J) \tag{5}$$

3.3   GDM Scheme

The GDM rule used in this paper is majority rule. The decision making process can be divided into the following steps.

(1) Set parameter that the number of GDMO that we call it Object_Number.
(2) Calculate the similarity between the input sample and the comparison sample, and put the comparison sample into the Group Decision Making Candidate Set (GDMCS) according to the similarity.
(3) If the similarity calculation between the input sample and all the comparison samples is completed, it will enter the next step; otherwise, it will enter (2).
(4) Select GDMOs. Select the 1st to the Object_Number elements in the GDMCS and put them into the Group Decision Making Object Set (GDMOS).
(5) Organize GDMOS. Calculate the number of elements of the same diagnosis result in GDMOS respectively.
(6) The diagnosis results were obtained. The result with the most elements selected is the diagnostic result.

See Fig. 3 for the flow chart of SGDM.

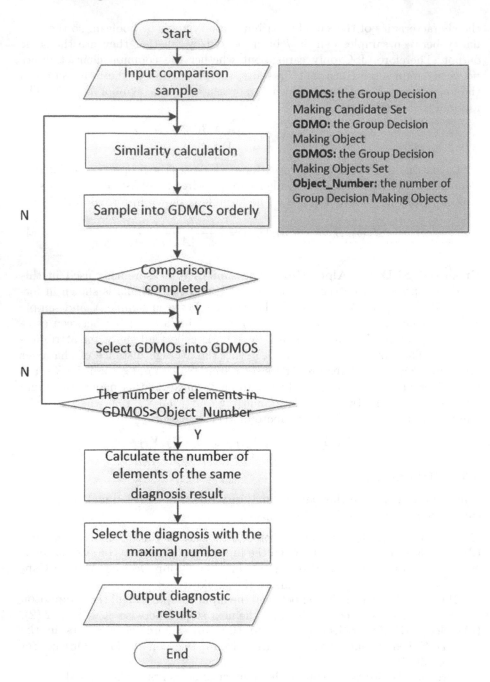

Fig. 3. The flow chart of GDM.

4   Experiment

We compare the accuracy and time consumption of two schemes and three algorithms. Two schemes are similarity scheme and GDM scheme. The three algorithms are SED algorithm, JD algorithm and SED-JD algorithm. At the same time, the accuracy of different Object_Number is compared.

4.1   Experimental Basis

All experiments were run on a Windows 8 64-bit system. The host configuration is as follows: Inter(R) Core(TM) i5-7300HQ CPU, 16 GB RAM.

The experimental data was derived from simulation data at https://github.com/synthetichealth/synthea. After preprocessing these data, we obtained 1066 samples. There were five symptoms in the samples and each with more than 100. We divide the processed samples into two parts, one as the sample set and the other as the test set.

4.2   Experimental Evaluation

Figure 4 is a comparison diagram of the results of the two schemes. SED-JD was used as the similarity measurement algorithm in the comparison. Meanwhile, in the GDM scheme, we select the result (based on accuracy) when Object_Number is 4. As can be seen from Fig. 4, although the two schemes have little difference in result, GDM scheme has better result than similarity scheme on the whole. When the number of samples is about 360, the result of the schemes is the best. This indicates that the selection of samples' number should be appropriate. In addition, the accuracy rate of both schemes has some twists and turns. This is because the samples are disordered, and the distribution of symptoms varies with the number of samples.

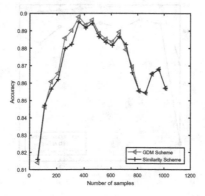

Fig. 4. Schemes comparison diagram.

Figure 5 is a comparison diagram of the three algorithms. GDM scheme that Object_Number is 4 is used in the comparison. As can be seen from Fig. 5, the accuracy of all three algorithms increases rapidly with the increase of the number of samples and then tends to be stable. Meanwhile, we can see that SED-JD algorithm is much better than the other two algorithms.

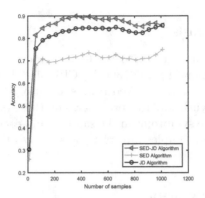

Fig. 5. Algorithms comparison diagram.

Figure 6 shows the selection of different Object_Numbers in the GDM scheme. As we can see from Fig. 6, the accuracy of all three algorithms increases with Object_Number and then decreases slightly. So we can know that the Object_Number selection should not either too large or too small, which means that the Object_Number selection should be appropriate. As can be seen from the figure, SED-JD algorithm and SED algorithm work best when Object_Number is 4, and JD algorithm works best when Object_Number is 3.

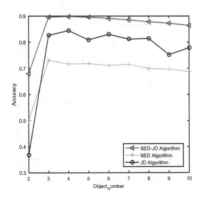

Fig. 6. The selection for Object_Number diagram.

5   Conclusion and Future Work

We mainly study two aspects: SED-JD algorithm and GDM scheme. We compare the accuracy of two schemes and three algorithms. Experimental results show that the SED-JD algorithm proposed in this paper is superior to the other two algorithms. GDM scheme is superior to similarity scheme, but the difference is not large. Therefore, how to optimize GDM scheme is the next step.

References

1. David, J.S., Rodney, C.G.F., Kate, B.: Assessment, criticism and improvement of imprecise subjective probabilities for a medical expert system. In: Machine Intelligence & Pattern Recognition, pp. 285–294 (1990)
2. Liao, S.: Expert system methodologies and applications—a decade review from 1995 to 2004. Expert Syst. Appl. **28**(1), 93–103 (2005)
3. Peiyu, W.: The medical expert diagnoses and analogous system. Jilin University (2008)
4. Si, L., Zijian, L., Tian, L.: Decision making research. J. Hubei Univ. Natl., 87–105 (1988)
5. Fubing, R., Lingling, L.: Advance of group decision making abroad research. J. Mod. Inf., 172–177 (2018)
6. Duncan, B.: On the rationale of group decision-making. J. Polit. Econ. **56**(1), 23–24 (1948)
7. Hwang, C.L., Lin, M.L.: Group Decision Making Under Multiple Critical. Springer, New York (1987). https://doi.org/10.1007/978-3-642-61580-1
8. Yuda, H.: Impossibility theorem and majority rule of group decision making. Science **56**(6), 50–52 (2004)
9. De Silva, N.T., Jayamanne, D.J.: Computer-aided medical diagnosis using Bayesian classifier-decision support system for medical diagnosis. Int. J. Multidiscip. Stud. (2016)
10. Mottalib, M.M., Rahman, M.M., Habib, M.T.: Detection of the onset of diabetes mellitus by Bayesian classifier based medical expert system. Trans. Mach. Learn. Artif. Intell. (2016)
11. Buntine, W.: Learning classification rules using Bayes. In: Proceedings of the Sixth International Workshop on Machine Learning, pp. 94–98 (1989)
12. Oad, K.K.: A fuzzy rule based approach to predict risk level of heart disease. Central South University (2014)
13. Dennis, B., Muthukrishnan, S.: AGFS: adaptive genetic fuzzy system for medical data classification. Appl. Soft Comput. **25**, 242–252 (2014)
14. Sanz, J.A., Galar, M., Jurio, A., Brugos, A.: Medical diagnosis of cardiovascular diseases using an interval-valued fuzzy rule-based classification system. Appl. Soft Comput. **20**, 103–111 (2014)
15. Reddy, P.V.S., Sadana, A.: Fuzzy medical expert systems for clinical medicine learning through the fuzzy neural network. Int. J. Clin. Med. Res. **2**(5), 54–60 (2015)
16. Agrawal, P., Madaan, V., Kumar, V.: Fuzzy rule-based medical expert system to identify the disorders of eyes, ENT and liver. Int. J. Adv. Intell. Paradig. **7**(3/40), 352–367 (2015)

17. Inbarani, H.H., Azar, A.T., Jothi, G.: Supervised hybrid feature selection based on PSO and rough sets for medical diagnosis. Comput. Methods Programs Biomed. **113**(1), 175–185 (2014)
18. Ying, X., Huailong, L., Haitao, W.: Design of diagnosis expert system for children's motor skill disorder. In: Modern Educational Technology, pp. 121–126 (2015)
19. Yunfeng, M.: Design and development of an interpretation expert system for the prevention and control of equine disease. Northeast Agricultural University (2016)
20. Lin, D., Wenru, L.: Biblimetrics analysis of experts system research for rice disease forecast. In: Digital Agricultural Machinery and Equipment, pp. 76–83 (2012)
21. Bo, H., Qing, C., Pengji, Y.: Research on fuzzy decision expert system. In: Mechanical Engineering (1991)
22. Lizhi, H., Zhonghai, Y.: Expert system of hydraulic wrench based on examples. In: Electronic Science and Technology, pp. 122–124+12 (2016)
23. Da, L., Jian, D., Gang, Q.: Control expert system and its application in power plants. In: Northeastern Electric Power Technology (1997)
24. Pan, Z., Bo, W., Xiaoxia, Q.: Integrated application of multiple knowledge representation methods in expert systems. In: Microcomputer Applications, pp. 4–5+18–4 (2004)
25. Zhao, W., Zhaoqing, Y.: Fuzzy expert system inference engine design. Wuhan Institute of Chemical Technology (2003)
26. Xin, Z., Yundou, W., Lijun, G.: Prospects and general methods of designing medical expert system inference machine. Chin. Med. Equip. J., 100–102+11 (2013)
27. Zhigang, G., Xu, J.: Research on data preprocess in data mining and its application. Appl. Res. Comput. **7**, 117–119 (2004)
28. Baosheng, L., Liping, Y., Donghua, Z.: Comparison of some classical similarity measures. Appl. Res. Comput. **23**, 1–3 (2006)
29. Peng, X., Na, L., Changqing, J.: A medical diagnosis expert system based on correlation analysis of features. In: Computer Engineering and Applications (2018)

Design and Implementation of a Lightweight Intrusion Detection and Prevention System

Xiaogang Wei[✉]

NARI Group Corporation/State Grid Electric Power Research Institute,
Nanjing 210003, China
andrew_wee@163.com

Abstract. While mobile internet brings convenience to people, it also introduces many security risks. For security protection of specific business, the technical means such as traffic analysis and illegal protocol identification can effectively detect network attacks, because of the simple business protocol and small business access. This paper proposes a lightweight intrusion detection and prevention method, based on nDPI, adopting common network packet capture means for design and implementation of a lightweight intrusion detection and prevention system. The test results show that the system can detect the abnormal protocol through the traffic and trace back to the corresponding terminal, so as to handle the abnormal terminal response and block the abnormal connection initiated from the terminal, thereby achieving the purpose of intrusion prevention.

Keywords: Intrusion detection · Intrusion prevention · Traffic analysis · Protocol identification

1 Introduction

With the wide application of mobile informationization technology, the number of mobile terminals is growing rapidly, and various mobile applications are emerging one after another, providing many conveniences for people's production and life. However, while providing convenience, mobile informationization technology also brings a lot of security risks, such as the risk of illegal terminals accessing the intranet. Attackers use legitimate terminals to carry out network attacks on the intranet system. There are many forms of cyber attacks, such as DOS attacks and port scan attacks. Such attacks can cause service rejection or service response delays. Abnormal traffic or excessive traffic will appear in the network data transmission. Therefore, through the analysis of network traffic and the intrusion detection and prevention, the network environment can be effectively managed [1], which is essential for the safe operation of mobile informationization business.

At present, the traffic and protocols of the power mobile business connected to the intranet are relatively simple, which is different from mobile internet business, using many and complex protocols. In view of this situation, this paper proposes lightweight intrusion detection and prevention method, based on nDPI (network Deep Packet Inspection) [2, 3], which analyze network traffic, identify the network protocol, and distinguish the abnormal network protocol of the power mobile business connected to the internal network, and on this basis, perform network redirection on the connection

J. Li et al. (Eds.): SPNCE 2019, LNICST 284, pp. 433–439, 2019.
https://doi.org/10.1007/978-3-030-21373-2_34

with the abnormal network protocol. The lightweight intrusion detection and prevention system is described in detail below.

2   System Design

2.1   Software Process Design

The lightweight intrusion detection and prevention system designed in this paper is mainly composed of three parts, which are composed of network traffic capture

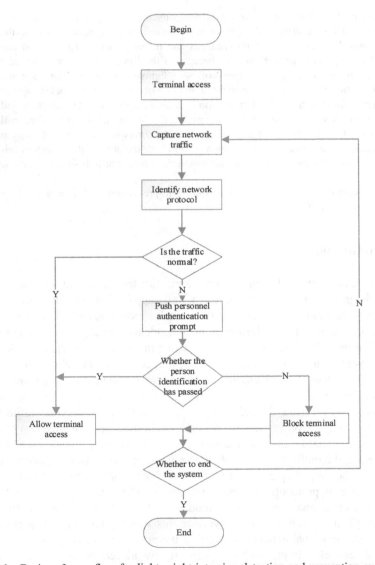

Fig. 1. Basic software flow for lightweight intrusion detection and prevention systems

module, protocol identification engine and response processing module. The basic software flow chart is shown in Fig. 1.

The capture module of network traffic captures the traffic generated after the terminal accesses the network according to certain rules. And the protocol analysis engine performs protocol analysis on the captured network traffic, and can distinguish the abnormal protocol in the business running process according to the established protocol. This method is especially effective for a single protocol and a simple process. After that the response handling module operates on network traffic with an abnormal protocol, and determines whether to allow the terminal to access the network according to the authentication result.

2.2   Deployment Architecture Design

The deployment architecture is shown in Fig. 2. All types of terminals, such as PCs, laptops, tablets, and mobile phones, access the application server deployed on the internal network by wireless network (such as a carrier network or a self-built WIFI network), passing through routers, application firewalls, access switches, and other network devices. Because the wireless network itself has a large number of security risks, in order to ensure that the internal network resources are not damaged or sniffed by attackers, network traffic passing through the terminal access process needs to be detected. The port mirroring function of the switch mirrors the traffic entering the application server to an idle port of the intrusion detection and prevention system for analysis.

Different from the general intrusion prevention system in the critical network path, the intrusion detection and prevention system designed in this paper adopts bypass work, which not only does not affect the data forwarding performance when the terminal accesses the application server, but also avoids node failure because of software defect. That directly causes the terminal to fail to access the application server.

Fig. 2. Overall deployment architecture

3   System Implementation

3.1   Capture Module of Network Traffic

Network traffic capturing is a prerequisite for traffic monitoring [4–6], and there are many ways to capture traffic. This article uses the libpcap library on Linux. Libpcap (Packet Capture Library) is a packet capture function library. It is a network packet capture function library under Unix/Linux platform. It is a system-independent user layer packet capture API interface, which provides a layer for network monitoring. Tcpdump, developed based on libpcap, is capture tool on Linux. The process of using libpcap in this paper is as follows.

(i)   Get network interface. Determine the network interface that needs to be monitored on the intrusion detection and prevention system. The interface can be specified or automatically selected by libpcap and he specific function is pcap_lookupdev().

(ii)   Open the network interface. After determining the network interface to be monitored, the interface need to be initialized and the specific function is pcap_open_live().

(iii)   Get the data packet. After opening the network interface, the interface has started to be listened. This is the core part of used process of the libpcap. The function pcap_dispatch() can be used to complete the task of obtaining the data packet.

(iv)   Release network interface. This function releases the interface after the completion of operation. The specific function is pcap_close().

3.2   Recognition Engine of Network Protocol

The purpose of capturing network traffic is to identify the network protocol, distinguish the abnormal protocol, and facilitate the subsequent response processing. This paper implements network anomaly protocol identification based on nDPI technology. nDPI is an extension library of OpenDPI [7–9] maintained by ntop. It has been developed from OpenDPI, solves many problems of OpenDPI, and has quite perfect application layer protocol recognition function [10–12], almost becoming the only choice in the DPI field. This system performs secondary development of the nDPI source code, and adds an identifiable protocol type to the power-specific service, and alerts the abnormal protocol, and notifies the subsequent response processing module to timely process the connection that generates the abnormal protocol. The specific process is shown as follows.

(i)   Initialize recognition engine. Call ndpi_init_detection_module() to initialize the detection module of the recognition engine.

(ii)   Set the protocol to be identified. Call ndpi_protocol_detection_bitmask2() to set the protocol mask, call ndpi_load_protocols_file() to load the protocol file, and specify which protocols are specifically identified by the protocol file.

(iii)   Identify protocol. ndpi_detection_process_packet() is used to obtain the specific information of the packet, including the protocol stream and the detailed information of the packet. During the running of the business, the system performs protocol matching according to the specified protocol. If the matching cannot be completed, the protocol is abnormal. For abnormal protocols, it can be traced back to specific terminals to facilitate subsequent response processing.

(iv) Statistics and analysis: The system performs statistics on the protocols identified during the operation of the business and visualizes the processing of the abnormal protocols.

3.3   Response Handling Module

The system response for the terminal (PC, notebook, tablet, mobile phone, etc.) that initiates the abnormal protocol is shown in Fig. 3. After the terminal initiates an access request to the application service, the intrusion detection and prevention system designed in this paper obtains and monitors the traffic on the network through the capture module of network traffic, and traces the terminal initiated by the abnormal protocol after the recognition engine detects the abnormal protocol. And the network redirection packet is sent to the terminal, then the access of the terminal is redirected to the authentication service. After the authentication service receives the request of the terminal, the authentication prompt is pushed for the terminal. And only the authenticated terminal is allowed to access the network.

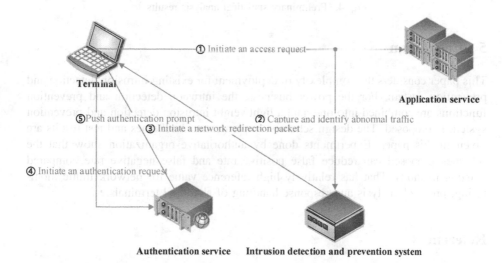

Fig. 3. Flow diagram of response and processing

4   System Tests

When setting the protocol file, you can specify the specific network protocol and port, or specify the IP address included in the specified protocol, or even specify the specific website name. The system can identify the corresponding protocol by string matching. Figure 4 shows one of the statistical analysis results after system detection. HTTP and

ICMP are the protocols specified in the protocol file, and 13.9% are unspecified protocols in the protocol file, then further analysis is required. Finally, 13.5% of the traffic is considered abnormal by the system, which should processed for subsequent response. In the actual power business, the protocol type is single. So it is easier to distinguish other protocols unrelated to the business through the system designed in this paper. The traffic carrying these unrelated protocols will be redirected by the system to further check whether the terminal users have Aggressive behavior.

Fig. 4. Preliminary statistical analysis results

5   Conclusion

This paper considers the complexity of deployment for existing intrusion detection and prevention system. For the power business, the intrusion detection and prevention functions are combined into one, and a lightweight intrusion detection and prevention system is proposed. The design schemes, implementation schemes and test results are given in this paper. Experiments done by authoritative organization show that the schemes proposed can reduce false positive rate and false negative rate compared existing methods. That has relatively high reference value for network traffic monitoring, protocol analysis and response handling of abnormal terminals.

References

1. Zhou, Y.: Application of protocol analysis technology in intrusion detection system. Comput. Syst. Appl. **20**(6), 161–164 (2011)
2. Yuan, C.-L., Ouyang, Z.-Y.: Research on experimental platform of traffic monitoring and analysis based on nDPI. Exp. Technol. Manag. **32**(3), 97–100 (2015)
3. Deri, L., Martinelli, M.: nDPI: open-source high-speed deep packet in spection. In: IWCMC 2014 (2014)
4. Su, J.-F.: Research and implementation of topology visualization in network measuring instrument. Xidian University (2012)
5. PCAP Next Generation Dump File Format [OL], May 2014. http://www.tcpdump.org/pcap/pcap.html

6. Song, X.-Y.: Research and design of an application layer network traffic monitoring system. Xi'an University of Science and Technology (2016)
7. Wei, Y., Zhou, Y.-F.: Analysis of message identification for OpenDPI. Comput. Eng. Supplement(1), 98–100 (2011)
8. L, Y.-M., W, Y.: Illegal business identification technology based on DPI and DFI. In: Software Guide, vol. 14, no. 12, pp. 177–179 (2015)
9. Zhuo, W.-H.: An improvement of NBOS S traffic identification module. Southeast University (2014)
10. Liu, A.X., Meiners, C.R., Norige, E., et al.: High-speed application protocol parsing and extraction for deep flow inspection. IEEE J. Sel. Areas Commun. 32(10), 1864–1880 (2014)
11. Zhuo, Z.-L.: Research on the key technologies of network tracing in the anonymous network. University of Electronic Science and Technology (2018)
12. Jing, P.: Implementation of deep packet inspection in integrated space and ground network. Beijing Jiaotong University (2017)

Reliability Analysis of Coupled Cyber-Physical Systems Under Different Network Types

Hao Peng[1,2], Zhe Kan[1], Dandan Zhao[1(✉)], Jianmin Han[1],
and Zhaolong Hu[1]

[1] College of Mathematics and Computer Science,
Zhejiang Normal University, Jinhua 321004, Zhejiang, China
ddzhao@zjnu.edu.cn
[2] Shanghai Key Laboratory of Integrated Administration Technologies
for Information Security, Shanghai 200240, China

Abstract. In this paper, the reliability performance analysis of coupled cyber-physical systems under different network types is investigated. To study the underlying network model, we propose a practical model for interdependent cyber-physical systems using network percolation theory. For different network models, we also study the effect of cascading failures effect and reveal mathematical analysis of failure propagation in such systems. The simulation results show that there exists a threshold for the proportion of faulty nodes and different system parameters, beyond which the cyber-physical systems collapse.

Keywords: Cyber-Physical systems · Percolation theory · Cascading failures · Interdependent network

1 Introduction

With the latest developments in communication and information technologies, the application of cyber-physical systems (CPS) [1–5] in our lives is becoming more and more extensive. Generally, the cyber-physical systems depend on two main networks: cyber layer network which provides control function or communication function and physical layer network which includes conventional power grid, smart grid. Communication network needs grid network to support power energy, while power stations are controlled by communication network. Thus, the two networks are connected and mutually interdependent. However, for interdependent system architecture, the failures in one network can lead to the cascading risk in another. Actually, the breakdown of a power station network [6–10] could result in the corresponding nodes failure in communication network. Especially, the further failures may even occur recursively between the interdependent CPS and then the cascading failures are big issues in such coupled CPS.

In order to improve the reliability of CPS, it is necessary to explore the cascading failures in actual interdependent CPS systems. Recently many researchers have paid more attentions in this research field. Currents research in smart gird systems [11–14] mainly focuses on failures about load balancing and load distribution. Most of these techniques rely on methods commonly used in distributed systems. Architecture for

J. Li et al. (Eds.): SPNCE 2019, LNICST 284, pp. 440–449, 2019.
https://doi.org/10.1007/978-3-030-21373-2_35

distributed generation way, which can help prevent cascading failures, is described in Ref. [15]. However, fault analysis and the impact of communication network on power grid were not mentioned. Optimization mechanisms have been used to balance demand and supply in Ref. [16]. Besides, the researcher has deeply investigated load distribution attack to provide effective prevention on false data injection [17]. Fault location method in cyber-physical has been investigated in Ref. [18]. Obviously, existing work on modelling smart gird systems is mainly about extracting properties from physical systems and assumed associated cyber system and matching with some physical network families. Toft and Maasoumy et al. [19] focused on the challenges of modeling cyber-physical systems that arise from the intrinsic heterogeneity and sensitivity to timing. However, the actual interdependent CPS systems are often different network types, so this paper will study the reliability of interdependent CPS systems under different network types.

The remainder of the paper is organized as follows: Sect. 2 introduces the system model of the CPS and the related definition. Sections 3 and 4 show the cascading process analysis when attack different type of networks. Theoretical solution and simulation analysis are introduced in Sect. 5. Then Sect. 6 is the conclusion.

2 System Model

In this section, we first introduce the network model of coupled CPS. According to the study and analysis of the coupled interdependent network, we establish a model that conforms to the characteristics of the coupled CPS in reality. From the research on the existing coupled CPS system [2–4, 6], we obtain that the coupling network is usually composed of multiple networks. Without loss of generality, we assume that the coupled network consists of two interdependent networks and the type of two interdependent networks is different. Thus we specify that the two networks that form the coupled network are the SF network and the ER network respectively.

Next, we will explain some basic concepts. There are two ways that connection mode of nodes in coupled network. One is the connection between the internals of the network that the link just between nodes in a single network. The other is the connection of the nodes connecting the two networks. When one network in the coupled network is attacked, only the functional nodes that satisfies the following two conditions in the network as follows:

(1) The node must belong to the giant connected component;
(2) The node must be connected to a functional node in internal network.

When a network in coupled network is attacked, the failure of the nodes in one network affects the function of the nodes in the other network. If none of the two networks fails or the two networks completely collapse, the network reaches steady state. This iterative failure process is called cascading failures. Cascading failures are a common failure process in coupled systems. If cascading failures are not controlled, cascading failures can cause severe damage.

3 Initial Failure in SF-Network A

The two networks that compose the coupled network one is SF network, the other is ER network. The generating function of the SF network is $G_{A0}(z) = \sum_k P_A(k) \cdot z^k$. Analogously, the generating function of the ER network is $G_{B0}(z) = \sum_k P_B(k) \cdot z^k$. Then the generating function of the underlying branching processes is

$$G_{A1}(z) = G'_{A0}(z)/G'_{A0}(1) \tag{1}$$

We denote the number of nodes remaining after the node has been removed as N'_{A1}, we know that $N'_{A1} = p \cdot N_A$. The fraction of the nodes belonging to the giant connected component to the number of nodes is

$$g_A(p) = 1 - G_{A0}[1 - p(1 - f_A)] \tag{2}$$

Where f_A is function of p. f_A and p satisfy the following equation

$$f_A = G_{A1}[1 - p(1 - f_A)] \tag{3}$$

3.1 Random Failure in Network A

We assume that after being attacked, the proportion of deleted nodes is $1\text{-}p$. So the number of remaining nodes in network A is

$$N'_{A1} = p \cdot N_A = \mu'_1 \cdot N_A \tag{4}$$

We denote the giant component as N_{A1}, then we can obtain

$$N_{A1} = g_A\left(\mu'_1\right) \cdot N'_{A1} = \mu'_1 \cdot g_A\left(\mu'_1\right) \cdot N_A = \mu_1 \cdot N_A \tag{5}$$

3.2 Impact of Cascading Failures on Network B

Owing to network A and network B depends on each other, nodes in network B will fail because of the failure of nodes in network A. We can calculate the number of nodes in network B that connect to nodes in network A:

$$N'_{B2} = \left[1 - (1 - \mu_1)^3\right] \cdot N_B = \left(\mu_1^3 - 3 \cdot \mu_1^2 + 3 \cdot \mu_1\right) \cdot N_B = \mu'_2 \cdot N_B \tag{6}$$

Then we will again apply the apparatus of generating functions and calculate the number of nodes in network B that belong to the giant connected component:

$$N_{B2} = g_B\left(\mu'_2\right) \cdot N'_{B2} = \mu'_2 \cdot g_B\left(\mu'_2\right) \cdot N_B = \mu_2 \cdot N_B \tag{7}$$

3.3   Further A-Nodes Cascading Failure Due to B-Node Failures

According to the random failure in Step 3.1, we can know that one node in network B may be connected to one, two or three nodes in network A, or it may not be connected to any node in network A. Here there is no relationship within or between networks, so the number of nodes with dependencies in network A is

$$N'_{A3} = \mu_2 \cdot N_B \cdot \frac{[C_3^1 \cdot \mu_1 \cdot (1 - \mu_1)^2 \cdot 1 +}{C_3^1 \cdot (1 - \mu_1) \cdot 2 + \mu_1^3 \cdot 3]} / \left[1 - (1 - \mu_1)^3\right] \tag{8}$$

From N_{A1} to N'_{A3}, we obtain

$$N_{A1} - N'_{A3} = \left(1 - g_B\left(\mu'_2\right)\right) \cdot N_{A1} \tag{9}$$

Since deleted nodes do not belong to N_{B2}, N_{A1}, and N'_{A3}, the proportion of nodes removed from N_{A1} is equal to the same proportion of nodes removed from N'_{A3},

$$N_{A1} - N'_{A3} = \left(1 - g_B\left(\mu'_2\right)\right) \cdot N_{A1} = \left(1 - g_B\left(\mu'_2\right)\right) \cdot N'_{A1} \tag{10}$$

The number of the giant component is

$$N_{A3} = \mu'_3 \cdot g_A\left(\mu'_3\right) \cdot N_A = \mu_3 \cdot N_A \tag{11}$$

3.4   Further Fragment of Network B

The nodes in network B will fail due to the failure of the nodes in network A because of the interdependence of the coupled networks. Similar to the second step, we can get the number of nodes with dependencies in the remaining nodes in network B:

$$N'_{B4} = \left[1 - (1 - \mu_3)^3\right] \cdot N_B = (\mu_3^3 - 3 \cdot \mu_3^2 + 3 \cdot \mu_3) \cdot N_B \tag{12}$$

From N_{B2} to N'_{B4}, we can obtain

$$N_{B2} - N'_{B4} = \left[1 - (\mu_3^3 - 3 \cdot \mu_3^2 + 3 \cdot \mu_3)/\mu_2\right] \cdot N_{B2} \tag{13}$$

The number of total removed nodes to the original network B is

$$1 - \mu'_2 + \mu'_2 \cdot \left[1 - (\mu_3^3 - 3 \cdot \mu_3^2 + 3 \cdot \mu_3)/\mu_2\right]$$
$$= 1 - \mu'_1 \cdot (\mu_3^2 - 3 \cdot \mu_3 + 3) \cdot g_A\left(\mu'_3\right) \tag{14}$$

The number of the giant component is

$$N_{B4} = \mu_4' \cdot g_B\left(\mu_4'\right) \cdot N_B \qquad (15)$$

According to the previous derivation process, we can obtain the following recursion relations

$$\begin{cases} \mu_{2i}' = \mu_1' \cdot \left(\mu_{2i-1}^2 - 3 \cdot \mu_{2i-1} + 3\right) \cdot g_A\left(\mu_{2i-1}'\right) \\ \qquad \mu_{2i+1}' = \mu_1' \cdot g_B\left(\mu_{2i}'\right) \end{cases} \qquad (16)$$

Where $\mu_1' = p$. Next we will analyze the iterative process of the coupled network when attacking the ER network.

4   Initial Failure in ER-Network B

Owing to the number and the type of two networks in the coupled CPS is different; the cascading failure process is different accordingly. Next, we will analyze the cascading failure process when the ER network B is attacked.

4.1   Initial Failure in Network B

Analogously, we assume that $(1-p) \cdot N_B$ nodes in network B are removed due to attack. The number of remaining nodes is

$$N_{B1}' = p \cdot N_B = \mu_1' \cdot N_B \qquad (17)$$

The number of the giant component is

$$N_{B1} = g_B\left(\mu_1'\right) \cdot N_{B1}' = \mu_1' \cdot g_B\left(\mu_1'\right) \cdot N_A = \mu_1 \cdot N_A \qquad (18)$$

4.2   Cascading Failures on Network A Due to B-Node Failures

The failure of nodes in network B will cause the nodes in network A to fail. According to the connection relationship between network A and network B, we can calculate the number of nodes in network A with dependencies. So

$$N_{A2}' = \mu_1 \cdot N_B \cdot 3 = \mu_1 \cdot N_A = \mu_2' \cdot N_A \qquad (19)$$

The number of the giant component is

$$N_{A2} = N_{A2}' \cdot g_A\left(\mu_2'\right) = \mu_2' \cdot g_A\left(\mu_2'\right) \cdot N_A = \mu_2 \cdot N_A \qquad (20)$$

4.3 Further Fragment on Network B

Network B will continue to fragment as cascading failures proceed. To calculate the number of nodes with dependencies in network B in the third step, we define a new variable, $q_1 = g_A(\mu'_2)$. The number of nodes in network B with dependencies is

$$N'_{B3} = \mu'_2 \cdot N_A \cdot \left[1 - (1 - q_1)^3\right]/3 = \mu'_2 \cdot (q_1^3 - 3 \cdot q_1^2 + 3 \cdot q_1) \cdot N_B \qquad (21)$$

So the fraction of remaining nodes is

$$\mu'_3 = p \cdot (q_1^3 - 3 \cdot q_1^2 + 3 \cdot q_1) \qquad (22)$$

Then the number of the giant component is

$$N_{B3} = \mu'_3 \cdot g_B\left(\mu'_3\right) \cdot N_B = \mu_3 \cdot N_B \qquad (23)$$

4.4 More Cascading Failures of Network A

Using the theory in Ref. [4], we get

$$N_{A2} - N'_{A4} = \left(1 - p \cdot g_A\left(\mu'_2\right) \cdot g_B\left(\mu'_3\right)/\mu_2\right) \cdot N'_{A2} \qquad (24)$$

Then the number of the giant component is

$$N_{A4} = \mu'_4 \cdot g_A\left(\mu'_4\right) \cdot N_A = \mu_4 \cdot N_A \qquad (25)$$

The fraction can be obtained by the recursion relations,

$$\begin{cases} \mu'_{2i+1} = p \cdot (q_i^3 - 3 \cdot q_i^2 + 3 \cdot q_i) \\ \mu'_{2i} = p \cdot g_B(\mu'_{2i-1}) \end{cases} \qquad (26)$$

Where $q_i = g_A(\mu'_{2i})$.

5 Theoretical Solution and Numerical Simulation

In this section, we analyze the iteration relation derived from the above model and find the corresponding theoretical solution.

5.1   Critical Threshold Solution

For the cascading failure of the coupled network, although we do not know which step the cascading failure will stopped, the network will not split again when the cascading failure stops. Thus we can get the following equations:

$$\begin{cases} \mu'_{2i} = \mu'_{2i-2} = \mu'_{2i+2} \\ \mu'_{2i+1} = \mu'_{2i-1} = \mu'_{2i+3} \end{cases} \tag{27}$$

In order to facilitate the analysis of iterative formulas for cascading failure, the variable x, y is defined to satisfy the following equations:

$$\begin{cases} y = \mu'_{2i} = \mu'_{2i-2} = \mu'_{2i+2} \\ x = \mu'_{2i+1} = \mu'_{2i-1} = \mu'_{2i+3} \end{cases} (0 \le x, y \le 1) \tag{28}$$

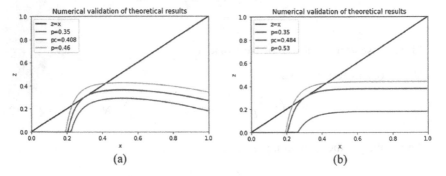

Fig. 1. Theoretical solution

Thus, Eq. (28) can be represented by the following equation set

$$\begin{cases} y = p \cdot \left((x \cdot g_A(x))^3 - 3 \cdot x \cdot g_A(x) + 3 \right) \cdot g_A(x) \\ x = p \cdot g_B(y) \end{cases} \tag{29}$$

Figure 1(a) and (b) show the cases that correspond to Eqs. (28) and (29) when attacking SF network and ER network, respectively. For the purpose of illustrate the graphical solution of Eq. (28), we plot Eqs. (28) and (29) for SF network with $\lambda = 2.8$ and ER network with $\alpha = 4$. Such as, in Fig. 1(a), the curve don't intersects with the straight line when $p < 0.408$, and the curve is tangent to the straight line when $p = 0.408$, the curve intersects with the straight line when p > 0.408. Thus from Fig. 1 (a), we can derive the critical threshold $p_{c-SF} = 0.408$ when attacking the SF network. Similarly, Fig. 1(b) shows that the critical threshold $p_{c-ER} = 0.484$ when attacking the ER network. We can see that the critical threshold when attacking the SF network is smaller than the critical value of the attack ER network.

5.2   Numerical Simulation

Next, we mainly verify the correctness of the theoretical results through numerical simulation. We create two networks according to the specified parameters. One is the SF network, the number of nodes is 30,000, and the other is the ER network, the number of nodes is 10000. Then according to the model described above, the two networks are connected together, that is, three nodes in the network A are randomly connected to one node in the network B, and the inter-network connection is completely random. So we have established a coupling network.

In Fig. 2, the blue curve shows the proportion of the remaining functional nodes in B and the red curve represents the proportion of the remaining nodes in network A after the cascading failure stops. We can see that the proportion of nodes in Network A is always lower than the proportion of nodes in Network B. In Fig. 2(b), although the network attack occurs in network B, the proportion of the remaining functional nodes in network B is still greater than the proportion of the functional nodes of network A. This phenomenon is caused by the connection relationship between network B and network A.

In order to further verify the correctness of the theory, we take multiple values near the critical threshold and find the probability of the existence of the giant connected component. In Fig. 3, the abscissa p represents the fraction of the nodes that were not

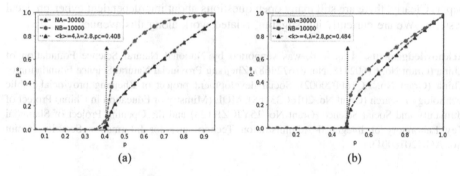

Fig. 2. The fraction of survival in both networks (Color figure online)

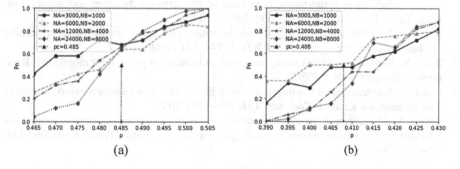

Fig. 3. Numerical validation of theoretical results

attacked to the number of nodes in the original network. The critical threshold is indicated by a black arrow. From Fig. 3(a) and (b), we can see that the number of nodes for the coupled system increases from small to large. As the number of nodes increases, the curve becomes steeper, and it is getting closer to the critical threshold. Therefore, we can infer that the curve will produce a first-order phase transition near the critical threshold, which is completely different from the second-order phase transition that characterizing percolation in a single network. Figure 3 also verifies the correctness of the conclusions from theoretical analysis.

6 Conclusion

This paper investigates the reliability performance of interdependent cyber-physical systems under different network types. Our findings demonstrate that there is always a critical threshold value. If the percentage of failing nodes is greater than the critical value, the interdependent smart gird systems will collapse. Our theory analysis and simulation experiment also show that, if both networks satisfy the same degree distribution, the system reliability does not have the direct connection with the system size. However, our proposed analysis model still has some limitations which could be our future work. For instance, the giant components could not always work in reality. It is also of interest to study models that are more realistic than the existing ones in this paper. Clearly, there are still many open questions about interdependent cyber-physical systems. We are currently investigating related work along this avenue.

Acknowledgements. This work was supported by National Natural Science Foundation of China (Grant No. 61602418, No. 61672468), Zhejiang Provincial Natural Science Foundation of China (Grant No. LQ16F020002), Social development project of Zhejiang provincial public technology research (Grant No. 2016C33168), MOE (Ministry of Education in China) Project of Humanity and Social Science (Grant No. 15YJCZH125) and the Opening Project of Shanghai Key Laboratory of Integrated Administration Technologies for Information Security (Grant No. AGK2018001).

References

1. Kurt, S.: Packet size optimization in wireless sensor networks for smart grid applications. IEEE Trans. Ind. Electron. **64**(3), 2392–2401 (2017)
2. Kamyab, F.: Demand response program in smart grid using supply function bidding mechanism. IEEE Trans. Smart Grid **7**(3), 1277–1284 (2016)
3. Zeng, X.: E-AUA: an efficient anonymous user authentication protocol for mobile IoT. IEEE Internet Things J. (99), 1 (2018)
4. Fadel, E.: Spectrum-aware bio-inspired routing in cognitive radio sensor networks for smart grid applications. Comput. Commun. **101**, 106–120 (2017)
5. Aktas, A.: Experimental investigation of a new smart energy management algorithm for a hybrid energy storage system in smart grid applications. Electr. Power Syst. Res. **144**, 185–196 (2017)

6. Khan, A.A.: Requirements, design challenges, and review of routing and MAC protocols for CR-based smart grid systems. IEEE Commun. Mag. **55**(5), 206–215 (2017)
7. Khazali, A.: A stochastic–probabilistic energy and reserve market clearing scheme for smart power systems with plug-in electrical vehicles. Energy Convers. Manag. **105**, 1046–1058 (2015)
8. Ouyang, M.: Resilience assessment of interdependent infrastructure systems: with a focus on joint restoration modeling and analysis. Reliab. Eng. Syst. Saf. **141**, 74–82 (2015)
9. Garvey, P.R.: Modeling and measuring the operability of interdependent systems and systems of systems: advances in methods and applications. Int. J. Syst. Syst. Eng. **5**(1), 1–24 (2014)
10. Bayram, I.S.: Electric power allocation in a network of fast charging stations. IEEE J. Sel. Areas Commun. **31**(7), 1235–1246 (2013)
11. Xu, G.: A novel efficient MAKA protocol with desynchronization for anonymous roaming service in Global Mobility Networks. J. Netw. Comput. Appl. **107**, 83–92 (2018)
12. Zhao, J.: Short-term state forecasting-aided method for detection of smart grid general false data injection attacks. IEEE Trans. Smart Grid **8**(4), 1580–1590 (2017)
13. Farraj, A.: A game-theoretic analysis of cyber switching attacks and mitigation in smart grid systems. IEEE Trans. Smart Grid **7**(4), 1846–1855 (2016)
14. Ozay, M.: Machine learning methods for attack detection in the smart grid. IEEE Trans. Neural Netw. Learn. Syst. **27**(8), 1773–1786 (2016)
15. Rampurkar, V.: Cascading failure analysis for Indian power grid. IEEE Trans. Smart Grid **7**(4), 1951–1960 (2016)
16. Tan, K.M.: Integration of electric vehicles in smart grid: a review on vehicle to grid technologies and optimization techniques. Renew. Sustain. Energy Rev. **53**, 720–732 (2016)
17. Li, S.: Quickest detection of false data injection attack in wide-area smart grids. IEEE Trans. Smart Grid **6**(6), 2725–2735 (2015)
18. Hartmann, T., Fouquet, F., Klein, J.: Generating realistic smart grid communication topologies based on real-data. In: 2014 IEEE International Conference on Smart Grid Communications, pp. 428–433. IEEE (2014)
19. Toft, M.B.: Responsible technology acceptance: model development and application to consumer acceptance of Smart Grid technology. Appl. Energy **134**, 392–400 (2014)

Invulnerability Assessment of Cyber-Physics Systems for Blockchain Environment

Hao Peng[1,2], Zhe Kan[1], Dandan Zhao[1(✉)], Zhonglong Zheng[1], and Feilong Lin[1]

[1] College of Mathematics and Computer Science, Zhejiang Normal University, Jinhua 321004, Zhejiang, China
ddzhao@zjnu.edu.cn
[2] Shanghai Key Laboratory of Integrated Administration Technologies for Information Security, Shanghai 200240, China

Abstract. Due to the decentralized nature and security attributes of blockchain, cyber-physical systems (CPS) emerge more and more interdependent. However, an important challenge of such interdependent CPS is the cascading failures. Thus, how to analyze the invulnerability of interdependent coupled CPS becomes critical and indispensable. In this paper, we have modeled the interdependent CPS in the blockchain environment, and analyzed the cascading failures process based on the network characteristics. Besides, based on simulation experiments, we analyze the main factor affecting the invulnerability of CPS.

Keywords: CPS system · Cascading failures · Invulnerability analysis · Blockchain

1 Introduction

In recent years, the global industrial Internet is in the critical period of undecided pattern [1–3], the window period of large-scale expansion, and the opportunity period to seize the dominant power. CPS (Cyber-Physical Systems) [4, 5] is the core architecture of the Industrial Internet, a multi-dimensional complex system for integrated computing, network and physical environments. It can make the Internet of things system more reliable, efficient and real-time collaborative.

With the widespread popularity and deep development of CPS systems, such as data exchange between isomerism networks will bring new security problems to cyber-physical systems [6–8]. Blockchain technology [9–11] provides a technical basis for building trusted and realizes peer-to-peer data sharing, coordination and communication based on decentralized credit. CPS systems based on blockchain technology [12, 13] are increasingly being applied to industrial Internet applications. Meanwhile, the CPS system based on blockchain technology has certain security attributes and security guarantees [14]. However, the CPS system for the blockchain environment is a decentralized highly distributed heterogeneous coupled system [15]. Each subsystem should work in coordination with each other through wired or wireless communication [16]. According to the computer security theory [17], any heterogeneous system that is

© ICST Institute for Computer Sciences, Social Informatics and Telecommunications Engineering 2019
Published by Springer Nature Switzerland AG 2019. All Rights Reserved
J. Li et al. (Eds.): SPNCE 2019, LNICST 284, pp. 450–458, 2019.
https://doi.org/10.1007/978-3-030-21373-2_36

not physically connected to the server is untrustworthy. Heterogeneous coupled CPS systems in a blockchain environment have certain vulnerabilities [18].

From the above, the existing CPS system invulnerability analysis mainly focuses on the invulnerability problem of a single CSP system and lacks the invulnerability analysis of the heterogeneous coupled CPS system oriented to the blockchain environment. In this study, we discuss the cascading failure process by modeling and analyzing the heterogeneous coupled CPS in the existing blockchain environment. And through the simulation and comparison experiments, we analyze the main influencing factors affecting the invulnerability of CPS in Blockchain scenario.

2 Related Models and Concepts

In this section, we model the coupled system by analyzing the relationship between multiple networks that make up the coupled CPS in Blockchain environment.

2.1 System Model

The coupled physical network is a coupled network composed of a communication network and a physical network by analyzing the characteristics of the coupled system and some examples of coupled systems in real life [8, 10, 13], and the number of nodes in the communication network is generally larger than the number of nodes in the physical network. In order to qualitatively study and analyze the coupled network, this paper assumes that the connections between the nodes of the two networks are equal connections. This paper specifies that both networks are Scale-Free networks through analyzing the nature of the interdependent CPS systems. The failure or attack of some networks generally occurs in communication networks, and the failure and attack of the network are generally random.

2.2 Basic Concept

When the communication network is attacked, only nodes that satisfy the following two conditions can maintain the function [18].

- A node in one network is connected to at least a node that maintains functionality in another network.
- The node must belong to the largest connected component.

In order to facilitate theoretical analysis, the communication network is represented by A, and the physical network is represented by B. The number of nodes of the communication network and the physical network is represented by N_A and N_B respectively. When a network in coupled network is attacked, the failure of the nodes in one network affects the function of the nodes in the other network. If none of the two networks fails or the two networks completely collapse, the network reaches steady state. This iterative failure process is called cascading failures. Cascading failures are a common failure process in coupled systems. If cascading failures are not controlled, cascading failures can cause severe damage.

3   Theoretical Analyses

In this section, the mathematical analysis of the cascading failures process is performed by using the generation function and percolation theory in network science [5–7]. The generation functions of network A is

$$G_{A0}(z) = \sum_k P_A(k) z^k \qquad (1)$$

Where $P_A(k)$ is the degree distribution of network A. According to the above description, network A is a scale-free (SF) network, so the degree distribution of network A is subject to a power law distribution. Its degree distribution is:

$$P_A(k) = c \cdot k^{-\lambda} \qquad (2)$$

The generating function of the underlying branching processes is

$$G_{A1}(z) = G_{A0}'(z)/G_{A0}'(1) \qquad (3)$$

When some nodes are randomly deleted, the degree distribution of the remaining nodes and the generation function of the degree distribution will change. After randomly deleting a node, the number of remaining nodes is $N_{A1}' = p * N_A$. The fraction of nodes that belong to the giant connected component is

$$g_A(p) = 1 - G_{A0}[1 - p(1 - f_A)] \qquad (4)$$

The same conclusion can be drawn in Network B.

3.1   Random Attack in Network A

Next, we analyze the change in the number of nodes in each step of the cascading failures process based on the above theory. We assumed that the fraction $(1 - p)$ of nodes fails due to random attack, so the number of remaining nodes is

$$N_{A1}' = p \cdot N_A = \mu_1' \cdot N_A \qquad (5)$$

Which μ_1' is the fraction of nodes that remaining $\mu_1' = p$. Then the fraction of nodes that belong to the giant component of network A is

$$N_{A1} = g_A\left(\mu_1'\right) \cdot N_{A1}' = \mu_1' \cdot g_A\left(\mu_1'\right) \cdot N_A = \mu_1 \cdot N_A \qquad (6)$$

3.2   Cascading Failure of Nodes in Network B

In the previous step, we have obtained the number of nodes that maintain the function after cascading failures. Since one node in network B is randomly connected with three nodes in network A, the number of nodes in network B can be obtained.

$$N'_{B2} = \left[1 - (1 - \mu_1)^3\right] \cdot N_B = \left(\mu_1^3 - 3 \cdot \mu_1^2 + 3 \cdot \mu_1\right) \cdot N_B = \mu'_2 \cdot N_B \tag{7}$$

The number of nodes belonging to the giant connected component in N'_{B2} is

$$N_{B2} = g_B\left(\mu'_2\right) \cdot N'_{B2} = \mu'_2 \cdot g_B\left(\mu'_2\right) \cdot N_B = \mu_2 \cdot N_B \tag{8}$$

3.3   More Cascading Failures in Network A Due to B-Node Failures

Since there is no relationship between intra-network connections and inter-network connections, the number of nodes in network A can be calculated as:

$$N'_{A3} = \mu_2 \cdot N_B \cdot \frac{[C_3^1 \cdot \mu_1 \cdot (1 - \mu_1)^2 \cdot 1 +}{C_3^1 \cdot (1 - \mu_1) \cdot 2 + \mu_1^3 \cdot 3]} \Big/ \left[1 - (1 - \mu_1)^3\right] \tag{9}$$

From N_{A1} to N'_{A3} we can get

$$N_{A1} - N'_{A3} = \left(1 - g_B\left(\mu'_2\right)\right) \cdot N_{A1} \tag{10}$$

Since the deleted nodes do not belong to N_{B2}, N_{A1} and N'_{A1}, the fraction of nodes removed from N_{A1} is equal to the removal of the same fraction of nodes from N'_{A1},

$$N_{A1} - N'_{A3} = \left(1 - g_B\left(\mu'_2\right)\right) \cdot N_{A1} = \left(1 - g_B\left(\mu'_2\right)\right) \cdot N'_{A1} \tag{11}$$

The fraction of total removed nodes is:

$$1 - \mu'_1 + \left(1 - g_B\left(\mu'_2\right)\right) \cdot \mu'_1 = 1 - \mu'_1 \cdot g_B\left(\mu'_2\right) \tag{12}$$

The number of nodes belonging to the giant connected component is

$$N_{A3} = \mu'_3 \cdot g_A\left(\mu'_3\right) \cdot N_A = \mu_3 \cdot N_A \tag{13}$$

3.4   Further Cascading Failures in Network B

In the third step, the failure of the A network will further fail the nodes in the network B. Then the number of nodes with dependencies in the remaining nodes is

$$N'_{B4} = \left[1 - (1 - \mu_3)^3\right] \cdot N_B = \left(\mu_3^3 - 3 \cdot \mu_3^2 + 3 \cdot \mu_3\right) \cdot N_B \tag{14}$$

Thus the total number of failed nodes in Network B is

$$1 - \mu'_2 + \mu'_2 \cdot \left[1 - \left(\mu_3^3 - 3 \cdot \mu_3^2 + 3 \cdot \mu_3\right)/\mu_2\right] = 1 - \mu'_1 \cdot \left(\mu_3^3 - 3 \cdot \mu_3 + 3\right) \cdot g_A\left(\mu'_3\right) \tag{15}$$

So

$$\mu'_4 = \mu'_1 \cdot \left(\mu_3^2 - 3 \cdot \mu_3 + 3\right) \cdot g_A\left(\mu'_3\right) \tag{16}$$

Based on the analysis of the cascading failures process in the previous steps, we can get the iterative relationship of the nodes that are deleted from the network at each stage, expressed by the following equation

$$\begin{cases} \mu'_{2i} = \mu'_1 \cdot \left(\mu_{2i-1}^2 - 3 \cdot \mu_{2i-1} + 3\right) \cdot g_A\left(\mu'_{2i-1}\right) \\ \mu'_{2i+1} = \mu'_1 \cdot g_B\left(\mu'_{2i}\right) \end{cases} \tag{17}$$

Which $\mu'_1 = p$, we will detailed analyze the Eq. (17) in the next section.

4   Experimental Simulations

The main content of this section is to solve the iterative equation obtained in the previous analysis process, and we will verify the theoretical results of the obtained theoretical results to ensure the correctness of the analysis conclusion.

4.1   Solution of Equation

Based on the previous analysis, we obtained the iterative relationship between the two networks in the coupled network during the cascading failures process. The network will not split again when the cascading failure stops, we can obtain

$$\begin{cases} \mu'_{2i} = \mu'_{2i-2} = \mu'_{2i+2} \\ \mu'_{2i+1} = \mu'_{2i-1} = \mu'_{2i+3} \end{cases} \tag{18}$$

To facilitate the analysis of iterative formulas for cascading failures, we define new variable $y = \mu'_{2i} = \mu'_{2i-2} = \mu'_{2i+2}$ and $x = \mu'_{2i+1} = \mu'_{2i-1} = \mu'_{2i+3}(0 \le x, y \le 1)$. So the Eq. (18) can be presented by the following equation. So

$$\begin{cases} y = p \cdot \left((x \cdot g_A(x))^3 - 3 \cdot x \cdot g_A(x) + 3\right) \cdot g_A(x) \\ x = p \cdot g_B(y) \end{cases} \tag{19}$$

For scale-free networks, this equation is difficult to solve, so we use the way of drawing to find an approximate solution. We define new equations $z = x$ and $z = p \cdot g_B \left[p \cdot \left((x \cdot g_A(x))^3 - 3 \cdot x \cdot g_A(x) + 3 \right) \cdot g_A(x) \right]$, then we will draw the two lines in the figure, where the two lines are tangent is the solution of the equation.

In Fig. 1, we use $\lambda_A = \lambda_B = 2.8$, and the value of the minimum degree in the network is 3. As the value of p increases, the two lines will be tangent, and the p-value at the time of tangency is the solution of Eq. (19). By calculating the nearest distance between the two lines, we can more accurately find the value of p when the two lines are tangent.

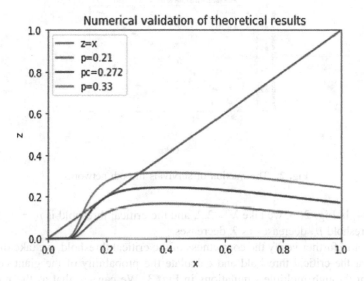

Fig. 1. Solution of equation

4.2 Experimental Verification

In order to verify the correctness of the critical threshold of cascading failures, we use the following simulation settings. Firstly, we construct two scale-free networks based on the specified minimum degree, number of nodes and parameter λ in the simulation experiment. Then, random attacks are represented by randomly deleted nodes. The simulation experiment simulates the process of cascading failure at each step.

In Fig. 2 we compare the variation of the fraction of the remaining nodes in the network when λ takes different values in the end of cascading failures. The black arrow indicates the critical threshold p_c. Meanwhile, the abscissa indicates the proportion of nodes that have not been attacked in the initial stage, and the ordinate indicates the proportion of remaining nodes in the network when the failures stop.

From Fig. 2(a) we see that the network will have the largest connected cluster when the value of p is greater than the critical threshold, which verifies the correctness of our mathematical analysis. In Fig. 2(b), we take $\lambda = 2.4$, and the critical threshold is

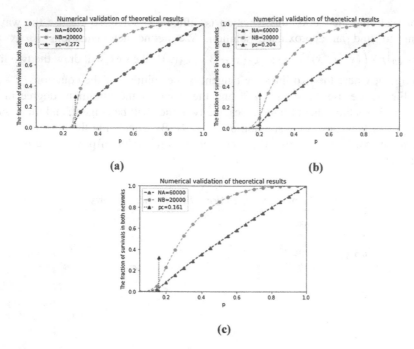

Fig. 2. The fraction of survivals in both networks

$p_c = 0.204$, In Fig. 2(c), we take $\lambda = 2.2$, and the critical threshold is $p_c = 0.161$. The critical threshold p_c decreases as λ decreases.

In order to further verify the correctness of the critical threshold, we take different p values near the critical threshold and calculate the probability of the giant connected component through multiple simulations in Fig. 3. We can see that as the number of

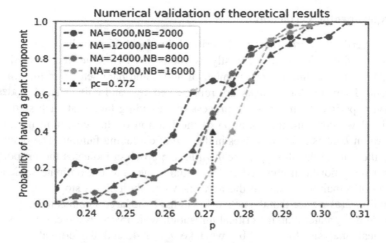

Fig. 3. Probability of having a giant component

nodes increases, the curve becomes steeper near the critical threshold p_c. This phenomenon indicates that the theoretical analysis results are correct. According to the trend of the curve, we can speculate that as the number of nodes increases, the trend of the curve near the critical threshold will become steeper, when the number of nodes is large enough, the network will produce a first-order phase change at the critical threshold. When the values of p and p_c are the same, there may be a maximum connected component or it may not exist. The probability of existence of the giant connected component and the probability of complete collapse are both 0.5.

5 Conclusions

In this paper, we first model the coupled heterogeneous CPS system in a blockchain environment. Then the principle of cascading failure process is analyzed. At the same time, the invulnerability of the system under random attack is compared and analyzed with the simulation process. At last, the analysis of existing research indicates the trend of future research. The invulnerability research of heterogeneous coupled CPS systems in the blockchain environment is still in the initial stage, and there are still many security issues that need further research and discussion.

Acknowledgements. This work was supported by National Natural Science Foundation of China (Grant No. 61602418), Zhejiang Provincial Natural Science Foundation of China (Grant No. LQ16F020002), Social development project of Zhejiang provincial public technology research (Grant No. 2016C33168), MOE (Ministry of Education in China) Project of Humanity and Social Science (Grant No. 15YJCZH125) and the Opening Project of Shanghai Key Laboratory of Integrated Administration Technologies for Information Security (Grant No. AGK2018001).

References

1. Al-Rubaye, S.: Industrial internet of things driven by SDN platform for smart grid resiliency. IEEE Internet Things J. **6**(1), 267–277 (2017)
2. Li, J.Q.: Industrial internet: a survey on the enabling technologies, applications, and challenges. IEEE Commun. Surv. Tutor. **19**(3), 1504–1526 (2017)
3. Mayer, S.: An open semantic framework for the industrial internet of things. IEEE Intell. Syst. **32**(1), 96–101 (2017)
4. Karnouskos, S.: Stuxnet worm impact on industrial cyber-physical system security. In: Conference on IEEE Industrial Electronics Society, pp. 4490–4494. IEEE (2011)
5. Jia, D.: A survey on platoon-based vehicular cyber-physical systems. IEEE Commun. Surv. Tutor. **18**(1), 263–284 (2017)
6. Colombo, A.W.: Industrial automation based on cyber-physical systems technologies. Comput. Ind. **81**(C), 11–25 (2016)
7. Wei, A.: Adaptive cyber-physical system attack detection and reconstruction with application to power systems. IET Control Theory Appl. **10**(12), 1458–1468 (2016)
8. Pasqualetti, F.: Attack detection and identification in cyber-physical systems – part I: models and fundamental limitations. IEEE Trans. Autom. Control **58**(11), 2715–2729 (2012)

9. Natoli, C.: The balance attack against proof-of-work blockchains: the R3 testbed as an example (2016)
10. Natoli, C.: The balance attack or why forkable blockchains are Ill-Suited for consortium. In: IEEE/IFIP International Conference on Dependable Systems and Networks, pp. 579–590. IEEE (2017)
11. Pass, R., Seeman, L., Shelat, A.: Analysis of the blockchain protocol in asynchronous networks. In: Coron, J.-S., Nielsen, J.B. (eds.) EUROCRYPT 2017. LNCS, vol. 10211, pp. 643–673. Springer, Cham (2017). https://doi.org/10.1007/978-3-319-56614-6_22
12. Dong, Z.: Blockchain: a secure, decentralized, trusted cyber infrastructure solution for future energy systems. J. Mod. Power Syst. Clean Energy 6(5), 958–967 (2018)
13. Cebe, M.: Block4Forensic: an integrated lightweight blockchain framework for forensics applications of connected vehicles (2018)
14. Kosba, A., Miller, A., Shi, E.: Hawk: the blockchain model of cryptography and privacy-preserving smart contracts. In: Security & Privacy, pp. 839–858. IEEE (2016)
15. Amin, S.: In quest of benchmarking security risks to cyber-physical systems. IEEE Netw. 27(1), 19–24 (2013)
16. Shin, D.H.: Cascading effects in interdependent networks. IEEE Netw. 28(4), 82–87 (2014)
17. Huang, C.: A study on web security incidents in China by analyzing vulnerability disclosure platforms. Comput. Secur. 58(C), 47–62 (2016)
18. Rungger, M.: A notion of robustness for cyber-physical systems. IEEE Trans. Autom. Control 61(8), 2108–2123 (2016)

Intrusion Detection System for IoT Heterogeneous Perceptual Network Based on Game Theory

Man Zhou, Lansheng Han[✉], Hongwei Lu, and Cai Fu

School of Computer Science and Technology,
Huazhong University of Science and Technology, Wuhan, China
{zhou_man,hanlansheng,luhw,fucai}@hust.edu.cn

Abstract. With the acceleration of the Internet of things (IoT) construction, the security and energy consumption of IoT will become an import factor restricting the overall development of the IoT. In order to reduce the energy consumption of the IoT heterogeneous perceptual network in the attack-defense process, the placement strategy of the intrusion detection system (IDS) described in this paper is to place the IDS on the cluster head nodes selected by the clustering algorithm called ULEACH, which we have proposed in this paper. Furthermore, by applying modified particle swarm optimization, the optimal defense strategy is obtained. Finally, the experiment results show that proposed strategy not only effectively detects multiple network attacks, but also reduces energy consumption.

Keywords: IoT security · Particle swarm optimization ·
Energy consumption · Intrusion detection system · Game model

1 Introduction

1.1 Current Research and Motivation

As the Internet of things (IoT) develops rapidly, its security faces serious challenges [2]. One of the major problems the perceptual layer of IoT faces is energy consumption [3]. In fact, many experts are currently proposing a variety of methods to optimize energy efficiency for the IoT [10]. Ozger [12] has proposed a totally new networking architecture, namely, Energy Harvesting Cognitive Radio Networking for Internet of Things-enabled Smart Grid. Luo [9] has analyzed energy consumption model and data relay model in WSN-based IoT, and then proposed the concept of "equivalent node" to select relay node for optimal data transmission and energy conservation. Unfortunately, all those studies in the field of energy optimization have focused only on the operation of the IoT system, while ignoring the energy consumption of the intrusion detection itself [1].

Most of the intrusion detection algorithms proposed can be divided into two categories: misuse detection algorithms (signature-based) and anomaly detection

© ICST Institute for Computer Sciences, Social Informatics and Telecommunications Engineering 2019
Published by Springer Nature Switzerland AG 2019. All Rights Reserved
J. Li et al. (Eds.): SPNCE 2019, LNICST 284, pp. 459–471, 2019.
https://doi.org/10.1007/978-3-030-21373-2_37

algorithms (behavior-based) [7]. Sedjelmaci has designed a new framework for intrusion detection in cluster-based wireless sensor networks (CWSN) [15]. In CWSN, all sensor nodes were clustered, and a cluster head (CH) was elected to manage the operation of its own cluster. However, those proposed hybrid technologies simultaneously activate intrusion detection on low energy IoT devices, and reduce the network performance.

To date, some proposed solutions have applied game theory to IoT security strategy in order to reduce energy consumption [8]. Senouci has proposed a game theoretic technique to activate anomaly detection technique only when a new attack's signature was expected to occur [14]. For the purpose of reducing energy consumption and ensuring high efficiency, Han has proposed an intrusion detection model based on game theory and an autoregressive model. Most of those papers do not consider the dynamic change of both parties' decision in the game process when solving the equilibrium solution of the model. As a result, we apply modified particle swarm optimization (PSO) to obtain model's mixed Nash equilibrium solution. As one of the most representative methods, PSO aims to generate computational intelligence by simulating collective behavior in nature. Therefore, it has the advantages of simple implementation, good performance and fast convergence speed.

1.2   IoT

IoT service systems are aimed at monitoring and controlling the behavior of the physical world using a vast interlinked network of devices such as sensors, gateways, switches, routers, computing resources, applications or services, and humans to link the digital world with the physical. Considering the technical architecture of the IoT, which could be divided into three layers: the perceptual layer, the network layer, and the application layer, as shown in Fig. 1.

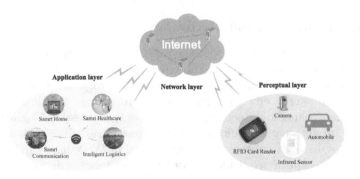

Fig. 1. The architecture of the IoT

The perceptual layer uses multiple sensors, sensor network, RFID, QR code and cameras, etc. to comprehensively sense physical world information. The layer mainly deals with information recognized and collected by the sensing devices. The collected information is then securely transmitted to the upper layer through the network layer to achieve remote control or direct communication between objects. The nodes of the perceptual layer are heterogeneous and simple. They have limited computing and storage capabilities and carry less energy, and often in an unattended environment without effective monitoring, which makes them more vulnerable.

With the increase in the number of IoT applications, the problem of cross-coverage of multiple networks has become an increasingly prominent issue. The perceptual layer of the IoT is composed of multiple heterogeneous nodes, and the performance of the nodes and density differ among themselves. In addition, a large number of sensor nodes are deployed in different scenarios and are responsible for collecting various information. There is also a great difference in energy consumption between nodes. Therefore, it is necessary to balance energy consumption of nodes and take comprehensive consideration of the nodes' heterogeneity to improve the traditional technology, and thus improve the quality and effectiveness of communications.

In terms of a single network, the Internet, mobile communication, etc. have established some effective mechanisms, but the research on the perceptual layer of the IoT is still in the initial stage. There are more and more attacks on the perceptual layer, including physical attacks, forgery, resource exhaustion attacks, privacy leakage threats and so on. At the same time, the communication capability, storage capacity, energy consumption rate, and residual energy of the nodes in the perceptual layer are diverse. For the purpose of balancing detection efficiency and the energy consumption of the IDS in heterogeneous perceptual network, we place the IDS on the CHs selected by proposed clustering algorithm ULEACH. Then build dynamic intrusion detection model and apply modified particle swarm optimization to obtain optimal defense strategy.

2   Non-uniform Clustering Algorithm ULEACH

Clustering improves the network lifetime and stability period and efficiently helps in solving congestion and collusion that have high drainage effect of the energy. CH aggregates and access as a relay by having the data from the members and send it to the BS. If a node with small density is selected as a CH, the network energy will be quickly depleted and the network will become paralyzed. In order to select the optimal CH and improve the utilization of the node, this paper improves the original LEACH protocol [6], and proposes a new clustering algorithm ULEACH which is suitable for the heterogeneous perceptual layer of the IoT.

In order to fully analyze the heterogeneity of the perceptual layer network, we define the following concepts and provide calculation formulas:

Definition 1 *Residual energy.* *In the first round of the data transmission step, a node reports its own position information and the current residual energy*

E_{re} to the Sink node, and the Sink node then calculates the average residual energy $\overline{E_{re}}$ of all nodes in the collection based on the received information. If E_{re} is lower than $\overline{E_{re}}$, it is ineligible to be a candidate CH. In the second round, in order to reduce the node's traffic, all nodes in the network send only their own current energy information to the Sink node and no longer send location information.

Definition 2 *Energy consumption rate.* The energy consumption rate represents the average energy consumption per round of the node and reflects the energy consumption during the operation. In fact, if a node is repeatedly selected as a CH, its average energy consumption is relatively high. Therefore, in the CH selection algorithm, the probability that a node with a higher energy consumption rate would be selected as a CH is smaller so as to maintain a balanced distribution of loads in the network. The energy consumption rate is evaluated as:

$$E_R = \frac{E_{init} - E_{re}}{r - 1}, \tag{1}$$

where E_{init} represents the initial energy of the node. Based on the information it receives, Sink node will calculate the average energy consumption $\overline{E_R}$ of all the nodes. If $\overline{E_R}$ is lower than E_R, it is ineligible to be a candidate CH.

Definition 3 *Overall performance.* The overall performance of the perceptual layer node includes both the communication and storage capabilities. The data transmission capabilities of different types are distinct, and the heterogeneous communication capability is mainly manifested in the data transmission rate. The specific formula is as follows:

$$B_c = (a * V_c + b * R_c)\triangle t_1, \tag{2}$$

where B_c, V_c, R_c, and $\triangle t_1$ respectively indicate communication capability, the transmission rate of heterogeneous data, the transmission rate of homogeneous data, and a period of time. Furthermore, a,b is the ratio of homogeneous and heterogeneous nodes.

The data processing is another important part of the node, and different monitoring application scenarios require different data processing capabilities. CHs possess greater data storage capabilities and stronger data fusion capabilities: that is, CHs generally player a more important role in the perceptual layer network. Therefore, the heterogeneous storage power includes both the data storage speed and the storage capacity and is calculated as follows:

$$B_s = T_s + \triangle t_2 * (a * V_s + b * R_s), \tag{3}$$

where B_s, T_s, V_s, R_s, and $\triangle t_2$ respectively represent the storage power, the total storage capacity, the storage speed of heterogeneous data, the storage speed of homogeneous data, and a period of time.

Combining both the communication capabilities Eq. (2) and storage capabilities Eq. (3), the overall performance of the perceptual layer nodes is defined as Eq. (4), where B and ξ_1 express the overall performance and the influence of communication capabilities on the overall performance, respectively.

$$B = \xi_1 * B_c + (1 - \xi_1) * B_s \tag{4}$$

In summary, for the purpose of maintaining the performance of the network, the nodes selected as CHs must possess the following characteristics: the residual energy is greater than the average energy of all nodes; the energy consumption rate is lower than the average energy consumption rate of all nodes; and overall performance is higher. Therefore, $P_i(t)$ of the LEACH clustering protocol [6] is adjusted as $P_i(t_{iso})$.

$$P_i(t_{iso}) = \begin{cases} \frac{p_{iso}}{1 - p_{iso} \times (r \bmod (1/p_{iso}))}, & (C_i(t) \in R) \cap (E_{re} \geq \overline{E_R}) \cap (E_R < \overline{E_R}) \\ 0, & others \end{cases} \tag{5}$$

where $p_{iso} = k/N * (1 + (B - B_{min})/(B_{max} - B_{min}))$, and B_{max}, B_{min} represent the highest and lowest overall performance of all nodes, respectively.

By optimizing the calculation method of the node threshold, the ULEACH clustering algorithm will comprehensively take the residual energy, energy consumption rate, and overall performance of the nodes into account. That will balance the energy consumption between nodes, and extend the lifetime of the perceptual layer network. The main steps of the ULEACH clustering algorithm are as Algorithm 1.

3   Intrusion Detection System

In the following, we will establish a dynamic intrusion detection model based on game theory to simulate the attack-defense process, and apply the improved PSO algorithm to obtain model's mixed Nash equilibrium solution between the attacker and IDS, in which a game mechanism is added to the fitness function.

3.1   Dynamic Intrusion Detection Model Based on Game Theory

As described above, the CHs possess more residual energy, a smaller energy consumption rate, and higher overall performance. For this reason, an attacker would select CHs to attack rather than cluster member nodes. In the same way, the IDS also tends to deploy the defense system on the CHs. Therefore, we declare that the establishment of the attack-defense process is based on the CHs.

The IoT intrusion detection model mainly includes two players: the attacker (A) and IDS (I). For the moment, the strategy space is recorded as S_A and S_I, and the payoff function is expressed as U_A and U_I. Therefore, at time t the status of each combat unit is defined as $G_i(t) = \{(I, A), (S_{Ii}(t), S_{Ai}(t)), (U_{Ii}(t), U_{Ai}(t))\}$ [5]. There is no point when an attacker or defender does not take

---

Algorithm 1. ULEACH clustering algorithm

Input: parameters E_{re}, E_R and B
Output: lifetime

1: Initialize the heterogeneous network of the perceptual layer
2: Set the basic information of the nodes and run round r=0
3: **while** lifetime **do**
4:    **if** r=0 **then**
5:       Obtain the location information
6:       Calculate $\overline{E_{re}}$, $\overline{E_R}$, and the overall performance
7:       Each node generates a random number between 0 and 1, and if this number is less than a certain threshold $P_i(t_{iso})$ shown as **Eq. (5)**, the node becomes a CH.
8:       The CH broadcasts the message that it has become a CH to all nodes
9:       The node that has not become a CH decides which cluster to join based on the strength of the received broadcast signal, and responses to the CH
10:      Set the running round $r = r + 1$
11:      liftime=lifetime_reducing( )
12:    **else**
13:       The cluster member nodes send their own information (E_{re}, E_R, and B) to the CH
14:       The CH sends the integrated information to the Sink node
15:       Select the node with more residual energy, a smaller energy consumption rate, and higher overall performance as CH
16:       The node that has not become a CH chooses a suitable cluster to join, and responds to the CH
17:      Set the running round $r = r + 1$
18:      liftime=lifetime_reducing( )
19:    **end if**
20: **end while**
21: **return** lifetime

---

action. Therefore, we only consider the situation when both the attacker and the defender take action at the same time.

According to the advantages and disadvantages of the two detection techniques and their complementarities [4], the paper coordinate the two detection methods and adopt one at each detection process. In this case we need to develop a strategy where the IDS chooses the optimal method at the right moment.

The attacker can either select the common means (P_{A1}), or new methods (P_{A2}). At the same time, the IDS can either use the anomaly detection method (M_{I1}), or the misuse detection method (M_{I2}). The strategies of the IDS and attacker are expressed as I_i and A_j, respectively, and their total utility function is each defined as B_I and B_A. We define $B_{ij}(I)$ and $B_{ij}(A)$ as the benefit to the IDS and attacker, respectively, when strategies I_i and A_j are chosen.

False alarm rate and missed report rate are two key metrics to measure IDS performance. Assume that, using the anomaly detection method, the missed report rate and the false alarm rate for common attacks are φ_1 and 0; the missed report rate and the false alarm rate for new methods of attack are 0 and ω_1. Similarly assume that, using the misuse detection method, the missed report rate and the false alarm rate for common attacks are 0 and ω_2; the missed report rate and the false alarm rate for new methods of attack are φ_2 and 0.

When the attacker chooses the common methods, and the IDS adopts the anomaly detection method. In this scenario, the missed report rate and false alarm rate are φ_1 and 0. Suppose that $\gamma_1 = \varphi_1 \alpha_i(t)\beta_i(t)$, $\gamma_2 = \omega_1 \alpha_i(t)\beta_i(t)$, $\gamma_3 = \omega_2 \alpha_i(t)\beta_i(t)$, and $\gamma_4 = \omega_2 \alpha_i(t)\beta_i(t)$. Obtaining the value of B_{ij} shown as Table 1.

Table 1. Benefit parameter B_{ij} and value

Parameter	Value
$B_{11}(I)$	$[\frac{1-\varphi_1}{\varphi_1}U_4(t) - \frac{1-\alpha_i(t)}{\alpha_i(t)}U_3(t)]\gamma_1$
$B_{11}(A)$	$[\frac{1-\alpha_i(t)}{\alpha_i(t)}U_3(t) - \frac{(2\varphi_1-1)\alpha_i(t)-\varphi_1}{\varphi_1\alpha_i(t)}L_{Ai}(t)]\gamma_1$
$B_{12}(I)$	$[\frac{1-\omega_1}{\omega_1}U_4(t) - \frac{1-\alpha_i(t)}{\alpha_i(t)}U_3(t)]\gamma_2$
$B_{12}(A)$	$[\frac{1-\alpha_i(t)}{\alpha_i(t)}U_3(t) - \frac{(2\omega_1-1)\alpha_i(t)-\omega_1}{\omega_1\alpha_i(t)}L_{Ai}(t)]\gamma_2$
$B_{21}(I)$	$[\frac{1-\omega_2}{\omega_2}U_4(t) - \frac{1-\alpha_i(t)}{\alpha_i(t)}U_3(t)]\gamma_3$
$B_{21}(A)$	$[\frac{1-\alpha_i(t)}{\alpha_i(t)}U_3(t) - \frac{(2\omega_2-1)\alpha_i(t)-\omega_2}{\omega_2\alpha_i(t)}L_{Ai}(t)]\gamma_3$
$B_{22}(I)$	$[\frac{1-\varphi_2}{\varphi_2}U_4(t) - \frac{1-\alpha_i(t)}{\alpha_i(t)}U_3(t)]\gamma_4$
$B_{22}(A)$	$[\frac{1-\alpha_i(t)}{\alpha_i(t)}U_3(t) - \frac{(2\varphi_2-1)\alpha_i(t)-\varphi_2}{\varphi_2\alpha_i(t)}L_{Ai}(t)]\gamma_4$

$$X' = \begin{bmatrix} B_{11}(I) & B_{12}(I) \\ B_{21}(I) & B_{22}(I) \end{bmatrix}, Y' = \begin{bmatrix} B_{11}(A) & B_{12}(A) \\ B_{21}(A) & B_{22}(A) \end{bmatrix} \tag{6}$$

The rows and columns in bivariate utility matrix (6) represent separately the IDS's and attacker's strategies.

Assuming that the attacker adopts the common means and the new methods with probability q and $1 - q$, respectively. Meanwhile the IDS uses the anomaly detection and the misuse detection methods with probability p and $1 - p$, respectively. By using bivariate utility matrix (6), we can gain the total utility function B_I and B_A of the IDS and attacker.

$$\begin{aligned} B_I &= pqB_{11}(I) + p(1-q)B_{12}(I) + (1-p)qB_{21}(I) + (1-p)(1-q)B_{22}(I), \\ B_A &= pqB_{11}(A) + p(1-q)B_{12}(A) + (1-p)qB_{21}(A) + (1-p)(1-q)B_{22}(A). \end{aligned} \tag{7}$$

Table 2. Alternate parameters and value

Parameter	Value
ε_1	$(1 - \varphi_1)\alpha_i(t)\beta_i(t)$
ε_2	$(1 - \omega_1)\alpha_i(t)\beta_i(t)$
ε_3	$(1 - \omega_2)\alpha_i(t)\beta_i(t)$
ε_4	$(1 - \varphi_2)\alpha_i(t)\beta_i(t)$
τ_1	$\varphi_1(2\alpha_i(t) - 1)\beta_i(t) - \alpha_i(t)\beta_i(t)$
τ_2	$\omega_1(2\alpha_i(t) - 1)\beta_i(t) - \alpha_i(t)\beta_i(t)$
τ_3	$\omega_2(2\alpha_i(t) - 1)\beta_i(t) - \alpha_i(t)\beta_i(t)$
τ_4	$\varphi_2(2\alpha_i(t) - 1)\beta_i(t) - \alpha_i(t)\beta_i(t)$

$B_{ij}(I)$ and $B_{ij}(A)$ in the matrices (6) are brought into Eq. (7), suppose that the parameters shown as Table 2. Obtaining:

$$
\begin{aligned}
B_I &= (\varepsilon_4 + pq(\varepsilon_1 + \varepsilon_3 - \varepsilon_2 - \varepsilon_4) + p(\varepsilon_2 - \varepsilon_4) + q(\varepsilon_3 - \varepsilon_4)) * (U_1(t) + U_2(t) - L_{Ii}(t)) \\
&\quad - (\gamma_4 + pq(\gamma_1 + \gamma_3 - \gamma_2 - \gamma_4) + p(\gamma_2 - \gamma_4) + q(\gamma_3 - \gamma_4)) * \frac{1 - \alpha_i(t)}{\alpha_i(t)} U_3(t), \\
B_A &= (\gamma_4 + pq(\gamma_1 + \gamma_2 - \gamma_3 - \gamma_4) + p(\gamma_2 - \gamma_4) + q(\gamma_3 - \gamma_4)) * \frac{1 - \alpha_i(t)}{\alpha_i(t)} U_3(t) \\
&\quad - (\tau_4 + pq(\tau_3 + \tau_4 - \tau_1 - \tau_2)).
\end{aligned}
\tag{8}
$$

Next, we need to find the value of (p,q) that makes the IDS obtain the most benefit at the game time.

3.2 PSO for Mixed Equilibrium Nash Solution

In the PSO algorithm, each particle represents potential solution (p, q), and the group consists of M particles $X = \{X_1, X_2, \cdots, X_M\}$ representing potential solutions [16]. In the 2-dimensional target search space, the solution represented by the particle is $X_i = \{x_{i1}, x_{i2}\}$, where $X_{ij} \subseteq [0, 1], j = 1, 2$. x_{i1} indicates the probability that a defender will perform an anomaly detection, and x_{i2} represents the probability that an attacker uses a common means.

All particles have no weight, no volume, and fly at a certain speed in the search space. In addition, each particle has a Fitness Function value determined by the optimization function, and both search optimal solution in a random way according to its own Fitness Function value. The position and velocity of the particle i at time t are expressed as: $S_i = (s_{i1}(t), s_{i2}(t), \cdots s_{iM}(t))$, $V_i = (v_{i1}(t), v_{i2}(t), \cdots v_{iM}(t))$.

In each search process, particle i constantly updates its velocity and position by tracking two extreme values. The first extreme value is the position of the particle with the best Fitness Function value found in the particle experience, usually called the individual extreme value, expressed as PS, where $PS_i = \{ps_{i1}, ps_{i2}, \cdots, ps_{iM}\}$. And the other extreme value is the position of the particle with the best Fitness Function value in the current population. For the global extremum, denoted by GS, where $GS(t) = (gs_1(t), gs_2(t), \cdots, gs_M(t))$, $GS(t) = G_g(t)$, $g \in \{1, 2, \cdots, M\}$, and g is the subscript of a particle with the best global position. The changes of particle swarm position and velocity are shown as Eq. (9).

$$v_{ij}(t+1) = \omega v_{ij}(t) + c_1 r_1(p_{ij}(t) - s_{ij}(t)) + c_2 r_2(p_{ij}(t) - s_{ij}(t))$$
$$s_{ij}(t+1) = p_{ij}(t) + s_{ij}(t) + v_{ij}(t+1) \ i = 1, 2, \cdots, N \ \ j = 1, 2 \tag{9}$$

where ω is called the inertia weight, and its value determines the inheritance degree of the current velocity, which makes the algorithm capable of development and exploration. The range of the ω is set as $[\omega_{\min}, \omega_{\max}]$, then, the ω of the ith iteration is shown in Eq. (10). i_{max} is the maximum number of iteration.

$$\omega_i = \omega_{\max} - \frac{\omega_{\max} - \omega_{\min}}{i_{\max}} \times i \tag{10}$$

c_1, c_2 are learning factors or acceleration factors, and are set to 2. Learning factors enable particles to self-satisfy and learn from the best individuals in the group, thus approaching their historical best within the group. And $r_1, r_2 \sim U(0, 1)$.

In addition, each particle has a Fitness Value determined by the optimization function, and conducts a certain random search in the solution space according to its own adaptive value. For the IDS, fitness function is MSE shown as Eq. (11).

$$
\begin{aligned}
MSE &= B_I - B_A \\
&= [(\varepsilon_4 + pq(\varepsilon_1 + \varepsilon_3 - \varepsilon_2 - \varepsilon_4) + s_{i1}(\varepsilon_2 - \varepsilon_4) + s_{i2}(\varepsilon_3 - \varepsilon_4)) * (U_1(t) + U_2(t) - L_{Ii}(t)) \\
&\quad - (\gamma_4 + pq(\gamma_1 + \gamma_3 - \gamma_2 - \gamma_4) + s_{i1}(\gamma_2 - \gamma_4) + s_{i2}(\gamma_3 - \gamma_4)) * \frac{1 - \alpha_i(t)}{\alpha_i(t)} U_3(t)] \\
&\quad - [(\gamma_4 + pq(\gamma_1 + \gamma_2 - \gamma_3 - \gamma_4) + s_{i1}(\gamma_2 - \gamma_4) + s_{i2}(\gamma_3 - \gamma_4)) * \frac{1 - \alpha_i(t)}{\alpha_i(t)} U_3(t) \\
&\quad - (\tau_4 + pq(\tau_3 + \tau_4 - \tau_1 - \tau_2)].
\end{aligned}
\tag{11}
$$

The main steps to find the value of (p, q) that makes the most profit for the IDS at the game time are shown in Algorithm 2.

Finally, the solution s_g represented by the particle at the optimal position is gained through the Algorithm 2, and the value of (p, q) that makes the IDS obtain the most benefit.

3.3   Model for Dynamic Intrusion Detection Based on Game Theory

The proposed dynamic intrusion detection game model combines anomaly detection with misuse detection to defend against both common attacks and new methods of attacks, as shown in the Algorithm 3.

Algorithm 2. Find the values of p and q based on PSO

Input: Randomly generated initial particles
Output: Particle value of (p, q)
1: Let $t = 0$, and initialize the position and velocity of the particles in the algorithm
   space
2: **while** $\left(\left| MSE_{s_i(t+1)} - MSE_{ps_i(t)} \right| > 0.001 \text{ or } t < 1000 \right)$ **do**
3:     Let $t = t + 1$
4:     Update the velocity of all particles
5:     Update the position of all particles
6:     Calculate the current Fitness Function value and compare it with the that of
       the previous iteration. If the current value is smaller than that of the previous
       iteration, update the current position of the particle according to the position
       of the particle. That is if $MSE_{s_i(t+1)} < MSE_{ps_i(t)}$, then $ps_i(t+1) = s_i(t+1)$.
7:     Calculate the current global optimal position g_{t+1} of the population
8:     Compare the current global optimal location with the previous iteration's global
       optimal location, if g_{t+1} is superior to g_t, then g_{t+1} is the global optimal position
       of the group
9:     Update $\omega, s_{ij}(t+1)$ according to Eq. (10), Eq. (9).
10: **end while**
11: **return** Particle value of (p, q) for the IDS to maximum the profit.

---

4   Simulation Experiment and Analysis

Due to the limitations of a real experimental environment, such as high cost,
and poor performance, we evaluate the proposed intrusion detection model in
the DeterLab platform [11]. The topology of three clusters in the model are
shown in Fig. 2. All of their initial energy was set to 10J, except for the Sink
node located in the center, which had no energy restriction. We set the alterable
number of the attack nodes per round to 5% to 15%, and the sum of the number
of the attack nodes and the common member nodes was stable. The number
of selected CH nodes in each round of the experiments were 5% to 10%. The
duration of each round of the attack-defense process was 50 s, the interval was
1 min, and the number of CHs selected per round was not fixed. The experimental
parameters are shown in Table 3.

In order to obtain more convincing results, we compared the game-based
intrusion detection model for IoT perceptual layer (GTULDS-Proposed) with the
current advanced algorithms. Rowayda has proposed a new hybrid heterogeneous
energy-aware IoT protocol (HHEDS) for complex IoT network with multiple
levels of heterogeneity located in different regions [13]. Sedjelmaci has proposed a
game theory based technique to activate anomaly detection technique only when
a new attack's signature is expected to occur(LHDS) [14]. Figure 3a shows the
intrusion detection rate of each intrusion detection algorithm when the number of
the attack nodes changes. The detection rate represents the ratio of the number
of attackers correctly detected to the total number of attackers.

According to Fig. 3a, the increase in the number of the attack nodes reduces
the detection rate and has roughly the same impact on the three algorithms.

Table 3. Simulative experimental parameters

Parameter	Value
Each round time/s	50
Node pause time/s	60
Node interface	IEEE 802.15.4
Network clustering protocol	ULEACH
Size of detection area/m	100^2
Number of sensor nodes	200
Number of attack nodes	From 5% to 15% of overall nodes
Initial energy of node/J	10

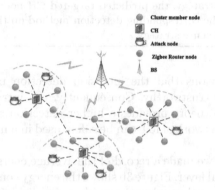

Fig. 2. The topology of three clusters in the model

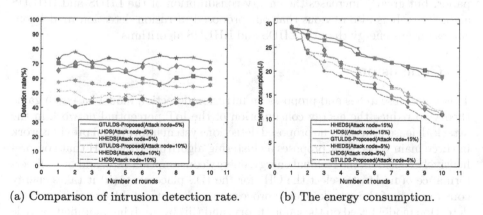

(a) Comparison of intrusion detection rate.   (b) The energy consumption.

Fig. 3. The intrusion detection rate and energy consumption of the algorithm.

Algorithm 3. Dynamic intrusion detection model based on game model

---

Input: parameters $U_1(t)$, $U_2(t)$, $U_3(t)$, $L_{Ii}(t)$, $L_{Ai}(t)$, $E_i(t)$, E_{max}, E_{min}, $\beta_i(t)$, and $\alpha_i(t)$

Output: Optimal defense strategy

1: Initialize heterogeneous network of the perceptual layer
2: Set the basic information of the nodes
3: With the clustering algorithm ULEACH, the CHs for the IDS placement strategy are selected
4: Construct dynamic intrusion detection model based on game theory to minimize energy consumption
5: According to Algorithm 2, the probability p of performing the anomaly detection method and the probability q of adopting the common means are obtained
6: Based on the value of p and q, the mixed utility of the IDS B_I and the attacker B_A are calculated to solve the mixed Nash equilibrium solution, and the optimal defense strategy that could balance the detection efficiency and energy consumption of the system is obtained
7: Using the defense strategy, the predicted targeted CH node, and attack time, the Sink node adopts the corresponding detection method on the targeted node
8: **return** Optimal defense strategy

In addition, it is obvious that the intrusion detection model built with the game theory is more trustworthy. Consequently, the intrusion detection algorithm based on game theory provides a higher detection rate and ensures that the perceptual layer network of IoT can be safely used in a more complex network environment.

In the simulation, we made a record of the average energy consumption of all nodes in the perceptual layer. Figure 3b shows the energy consumption of the three intrusion detection algorithms when the number of malicious nodes changes. It can be seen from Fig. 3b that the increase in the number of the attack nodes has little effect on the energy consumption of the intrusion detection model proposed in this paper, but greatly increases the energy consumption of the LHDS and HHEDS algorithms. It is also obvious that our proposed intrusion detection model consumes far less energy than the LHDS and HHEDS algorithms.

5   Conclusion

This paper researches and proposes an intrusion detection model based on game theory to reduce the energy consumption of the IoT perceptual network in the attack-defense process. The proposed detection system improves on previous work in three main ways: (i) it proposes a clustering algorithm ULEACH that comprehensively considers the residual energy, energy consumption rate, and overall performance of nodes, to select the CHs for the IDS placement; (ii) it takes energy consumption of the attack-defense process into account, establishes the intrusion detection model based on the game theory; and (iii) by applying modified particle swarm optimization, the optimal defense strategy that could balance the detection efficiency and energy consumption of the system is obtained.

Acknowledgment. This paper is supported by National Natural Science Fund NSF: 61272033 & 61572222.

References

1. Castiglione, A., Palmieri, F., Fiore, U.: Modeling energy-efficient secure communications in multi-mode wireless mobile devices. Comput. Syst. Sci. **81**, 1464–1478 (2015)
2. Bhunia, S.: Internet of things security: are we paranoid enough. In: 2018 IEEE International Conference on Consumer Electronics (ICCE), p. 1. IEEE (2018)
3. Caviglione, L., Merlo, A.: The energy impact of security mechanisms in modern mobile devices. Netw. Secur. **2012**(2), 11–14 (2012)
4. Hajisalem, V., Babaie, S.: A hybrid intrusion detection system based on ABC-AFS algorithm for misuse and anomaly detection. Comput. Netw. **136**, 37–50 (2018)
5. Han, L., Zhou, M., Jia, W., Dalil, Z., Xu, X.: Intrusion detection model of wireless sensor networks based on game theory and an autoregressive model. Inf. Sci. **476**, 491–504 (2018)
6. Heinzelman, W.R., Chandrakasan, A., Balakrishnan, H.: Energy-efficient communication protocol for wireless microsensor networks. In: Proceedings of the 33rd Annual Hawaii International Conference on IEEE, vol. 2, p. 10 (2000)
7. Henningsen, S., Dietzel, S., Scheuermann, B.: Misbehavior detection in industrial wireless networks: challenges and directions. Mobile Netw. Appl. **23**(5), 1330–1336 (2018)
8. Hossein, J.: Designing an agent-based intrusion detection system for heterogeneous wireless sensor networks: robust, fault tolerant and dynamic reconfigurable. Int. J. Commun. Netw. Syst. Sci. 4, 523–543 (2011)
9. Luo, J., Wu, D.: Optimal energy strategy for node selection and data relay in WSN-based IoT. Mobile Netw. Appl. **20**(2), 169–180 (2015)
10. Merlo, A., Migliardi, M., Caviglione, L.: A survey on energy-aware security mechanisms. Pervasive Mob. Comput. **24**, 77–90 (2015). special Issue on Secure Ubiquitous Computing
11. Michael Quick, T.R.D.: The deter project. https://www.isi.deterlab.net/index.php3
12. Ozger, M., Cetinkaya, O., Akan, O.B.: Energy harvesting cognitive radio networking for IoT-enabled smart grid. Mobile Netw. Appl. **23**(4), 956–966 (2018)
13. Sadek, R.A.: Hybrid energy aware clustered protocol for IoT heterogeneous network. Future Comput. Inform. J. **3**(2), 166–177 (2018)
14. Sedjelmaci, H., Senouci, S.M., Taleb, T.: An accurate security game for low-resource IoT devices. IEEE Trans. Veh. Technol. **66**(10), 9381–9393 (2017)
15. Sedjelmaci, H., Senouci, S.M., Feham, M.: New framework for a hierarchical intrusion detection mechanism in cluster-based wireless sensor networks. Secur. Commun. Netw. (2011)
16. Shi, Y., Eberhart, R.: A modified particle swarm optimizer. In: Proceedings of the IEEE Conference on Evolutionary Computation, pp. 69–73 (1998)

A Blockchain-Based Digital Advertising Media Promotion System

Yong Ding, Decun Luo, Hengkui Xiang, Chenjun Tang, Lingang Liu,
Xiuqing Zou, Shijie Li, and Yujue Wang[(✉)]

Guangxi Key Laboratory of Cryptography and Information Security,
Guilin University of Electronic Technology, Guilin 541004, China
yjwang@guet.edu.cn

Abstract. With the development of information technologies, digital media advertising (AD) based on the Internet has penetrated into every aspect of real life. Particularly, in recent years, the rapid development of modern digital media technology has brought huge opportunities to the Internet digital advertising (IDA), where many digital advertising media systems have been introduced. However, after these digital advertising media systems are released to the IDA market, some problems become increasingly prominent. For example, a large number of low-quality advertisements (ADs) have caused great troubles for Internet users, and the fake traffic has plunged the IDA market into a crisis of trust. It is necessary to rebuild the trust and suppress the spreading of low-quality ADs. To address this issue, we propose a blockchain-based digital advertising media system (B^2DAM). With the desirable features of blockchain such as decentralization, trust system, high autonomy and tamper resistance, our system is able to improve the experience of Internet users, purify the environment of IDA market, and further promote the sound development of the IDA market.

Keywords: Blockchain · AD token · AD media promotion system

1 Introduction

The advancement of Internet technology has driven the rapid development of IDA. Nowadays, Internet advertising media has been integrated into all aspects of the Internet, which has become an important driving force for the Internet economy and real economy [26]. However, behind the boom of IDA, there are some problems that cannot be ignored. On one hand, Internet users are gradually moving away from IDA [24], which are mainly caused by the irregularity of the IDA market. These irregularity phenomena include the imperfectness of supervision mechanism and the backward IDA market operation mechanism. On the other hand, IDA fraud [19] has angered advertisers, as a result, the IDA market is in a crisis of trust.

© ICST Institute for Computer Sciences, Social Informatics and Telecommunications Engineering 2019
Published by Springer Nature Switzerland AG 2019. All Rights Reserved
J. Li et al. (Eds.): SPNCE 2019, LNICST 284, pp. 472–484, 2019.
https://doi.org/10.1007/978-3-030-21373-2_38

As a new thing in the advertising ecosystem, its regulatory system has a lot of deficiencies, so that there are many unreasonable competition phenomena. Currently, the IDA always publishes pop-up ADs, spam emails, forced push ADs, etc. The proliferation of these ADs has brought poor and even unbearable experience to the Internet users. Some ADs may contain viruses, which induce users to click on viruses and implant them into the user devices, so as to steal the users' personal privacy data. These problems reflects that there lacks effective supervision mechanism for the IDA and the existing operation mechanism is outdated. In fact, most websites rely on click-through rate to earn AD revenue. Some advertisers may try to use fraudulent means to improve click-through rate, which is called "IDA fraud" [19]. Therefore, In the absence of regulatory and operating mechanism, it is vital to make AD market move towards a sound and healthy development path.

As an emerging technology in the Internet, the blockchain technology has caused great concern. Blockchain has the characteristics of decentralization, high reliability, anonymity, traceability and high security. Many blockchain-based application systems with autonomous property have been designed [3]. It is well-known that Bitcoin has been running steadily for ten years without any support of a management center. The blockchain is regarded as one of the most promising subversive Internet technologies. It makes many countries release various policies to support the landing of its applications. Thus, the blockchain technology can be employed to address the aforementioned issues in existing IDA media system.

1.1 Our Contributions

In this paper, we introduce a blockchain-based digital advertising media system (B^{2}DAM). The B^{2}DAM system using blockchain framework, which is named AD-chains. Based on the blockchain technology, It realize a AD-coins trading system, which is a type of virtual digital currency [7], to address the issues in the IDA ecosystem. Our system can be designed in a modular manner, where advertising coins (AD-coins) are employed to realize a reward mechanism and the interests of various roles are clarified in the decentralized system. The non-tamperable nature of the blockchain ensures that all the transactions of AD-coins are irreversible. The Ad-coin system provides interests as well as restrictive effects to the roles of AD market. With the revenue mechanism, users could be motivated to watch ADs more actively compared to that in existing IDA systems.

1.2 Related Works

The users' privacy exposure is a prominent problem in the IDA market. Budak et al. [5] found that the widespread use of AD-blocking softwares and the third-party platform tracking are the main causes of threats. To optimize the IDA strategy, Katsumata et al. [17] proposed a model for website classification using website content, so that AD agencies can understand the attributes and themes of each website. Estrada-Jiménez et al. [12] analyzed the potential privacy issues in IDA and further suggested privacy protection methods.

The public blockchain is the most characteristic part of the blockchain, which enjoys decentralized, highly reliable, and non-tamperable properties. In 2008, Nakamoto [25] is the first to proposed Bitcoin, which is known as the blockchain 1.0. Bitcoin uses "Proof of Work" (POW) as the consensus mechanism. However, the Bitcoin system does not have smart contract and there are many restrictions on the POW consensus mechanism.

Although Bitcoin provides the highest possible security, there is almost no scalability and its throughput rate is too small [16]. Wood [29] suggested that real-world applications should be able to run in any form, not just simple scripts restricted in Bitcoin [1]. The blockchain 2.0 era is represented by the typical technologies such as Ethereum. Compared to Bitcoin, Ethereum uses a POS consensus mechanism [18], where the analysis shows that its performance is better than Bitcoin on most technical indicators [27].

However, the current throughput and scalability of Ethereum does not meet the requirements of large-scale applications [8]. Thus, the *Block.one* corporation developed a new blockchain architecture, which is named EOS, to enable vertical and horizontal scaling of decentralized applications. Their blockchain architecture may ultimately scale to millions of transactions per second, eliminate user fees, and allow quick deployment and maintenance in decentralized applications (DApps), in the context of a governed blockchain [11].

In the Blockchain 3.0 era [31], the blockchain serves as an infrastructure platform for the Internet. People are able to create a wide variety of applications on this platform. The EOS blockchain framework using Delegated Proof of Stake (DPOS) consensus mechanism. The framework enjoys faster transaction processing speed and higher throughput rate, and it is seen as one of the most promising platforms for the development of the public blockchain platform [9].

Currently, Blockchain has been described as the key to the industry 4.0 era [2] and has been used to develop many secure application systems. Hjalmarsson et al. [15] designed a secure electronic voting system based on blockchain to ensure the fairness and privacy in voting. Yang et al. [32] built a decentralized public voting system based on the Ethereum. In [28], the blockchain is employed to address the management problem in supply chain. Li et al. [21] solved the privacy protection problem caused by the open transparency of blockchain, and proposed a secure blockchain-based energy transaction system in industrial Internet of Things.

1.3   Paper Organization

The remainder of this paper is organized as follows. In Sect. 2, we review some technical basis regarding the blockchain technology. We provide the system model of the IDA media promotion system and summarize design principles in Sect. 3. In Sect. 4, we describe the design details of each module of our construction. Finally, Sect. 5 concludes the paper.

2   Preliminaries of Blockchain

2.1   Technical Framework of Blockchain

A blockchain is defined as a chronological arrangement of data blocks in a form similar to a linked list structure. The cryptography technology and consensus mechanisms are employed to ensure that block data cannot be tampered with and forged, and to achieve decentralized ledger. Blockchain is highly related to some traditional technologies such as peer-to-peer network technology, asymmetric cryptography, consensus mechanism, and smart contracts [34].

2.2   Key Technologies of Blockchain

Blockchain technology uses a number of recent advances of cryptography and security technologies, especially for identity authentication and privacy protection technologies [33]. Some specific techniques include encryption algorithms, hash algorithms, digital signatures, digital certificates, PKI systems [22], Merkle trees [23], etc. Hash algorithm and digital signature scheme can ensure the integrity of blockchain structure. Digital signature and digital certificate guarantee non-repudiation of transactions. Merkle tree can organize transaction data in the block structure according to their hash values, which ensures that the transaction data cannot be maliciously falsified [10].

Blockchain can be regarded as a distributed ledger based on trust mechanism. Different nodes can be added to the blockchain network to implement synchronization and decentralization. Compared with traditional distributed storage technology, the blockchain system provides certain fault tolerance performance under the untrusted networks. With Byzantine fault tolerance [6], each node in an untrusted environment can only know that the majority of nodes in the entire network are honest, and all honest nodes can achieve consistence in the system.

The consensus mechanism in the blockchain system allows decentralized nodes to jointly maintain the consistency of the blockchain ledger. Many consensus mechanisms have been proposed, for example, Proof of Work (POW), Proof of Stake (POS) [4], Delegated Proof of Stake (DPOS), Byzantine fault tolerance (BFT). Among them, POW is a mechanism to obtain block construction permissions using computer computing power. POS allocates the accounting right according to the amount of assets held by nodes and the time of holding money. DPOS improves POS greatly in achieving a consensus mechanism of selects the block person through the voting mechanism to complete the trust operation.

Blockchain uses smart contract [20] to disseminate, verify, and enforce contracts in an informational manner, so as to achieve trusted transactions without third parties. Blockchain technology provides a trusted execution environment for smart contracts. A blockchain-based smart contract is essentially a piece of unchangeable computer code. Smart contacts ensure the security and efficiency of the system and greatly reduces the transaction cost.

3   System Model

The B^{2}DAM system consists of six modules, that is, the identity and Ad-coin account management module (IAAM), advertising delivery module (AD-DM), advertising recommendation module (AD-RM), advertising evaluation module (AD-EM), advertising prediction module (AD-PM), user feedback module (UFM). In B^{2}DAM, digital signature, time stamping and distributed consensus mechanism are used to implement decentralized peer-to-peer AD-coins trading. The underlying blockchain of the B^{2}DAM system can be realized using a open source multiple-chains framework, where AD-chains can be built.

3.1   System Framework

As shown in Fig. 1, the B^{2}DAM system mainly includes two layers, that is, blockchain layer and modules layer. The blockchain layer uses a multi-chains framework as a real-time blockchain services to the modules layer. The module layer is implemented through smart contracts and DApps. It is responsible for transaction and interaction between different roles in the B^{2}DAM system, which through the queries to the ledger and AD-coins transaction services provided by the blockchain layer.

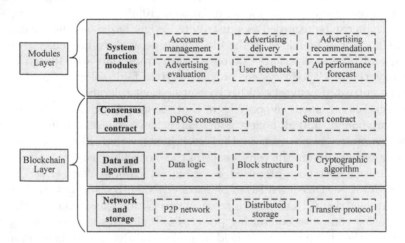

Fig. 1. B^{2}DAM system framework.

3.2   System Design Goals

To construct a high degree of autonomy and stable system, the B^{2}DAM system design must satisfy the following principles.

First, the amount of AD-coins must set a threshold. The stability of AD-chains depends on a large number of users' nodes. In the early stage of the

B^2DAM system, it is necessary to attract advertisers, AD publishers and Internet users. Therefore, a reward mechanism is needed. Each role in the system can be added to the AD-chains as a node. Once the amount of AD-coins reaches a threshold, the reward mechanism aborts. Users can only obtain AD-coins by watching ADs, which can be exchanged for AD watching rewards.

Second, users must be rewarded for watching ADs. As long as users complete the viewing of AD, both users and the AD publisher are reward with AD-coins. If users find a low quality AD, they can choose close, skip, or add comments after viewing this AD. Watching ADs is no longer a waste of time, but a way to earn money.

Third, the transactions of AD-coins must be verified. In order to prevent the proliferation of AD-coins, the amount of AD-coins are restricted in the system. The two roles of a transaction must have their own wallet address with enough AD-coins. The transaction records the transfer of Ad-coin from one wallet address to another. The entire transaction process needs to be verified by the blockchain consensus mechanism and completed by smart contracts. A secure consensus mechanism guarantees the security of currency transactions.

3.3   System Model

The B^2DAM system can be run as follows. The advertiser pays some AD-coins to put the AD-related information into the AD-chains. The AD-chains calls the AD-EM to evaluate the AD, and rank the AD-related information through the smart contract. The AD-EM reevaluates the AD after each user scoring the AD. The AD publisher calls the AD-RM to get the AD-related information. That is a kind of answering mechanism. In fact, the AD-RM will pushes suitable AD information to the AD publisher based on the quality score of the AD and the publisher's influence. The AD publisher delivers AD to users by their platforms, such as website, short videos platforms.

Users are able to obtain a part of the AD-coins of the advertiser after viewing the AD, and the other part is paid to the AD publisher. Users can redeem the rewards to the AD publisher after they have a enough AD-coins. In the early stage, the B^2DAM system can use the smart contract to set an incentive mechanism [13], so as to stimulate users to watch ADs. New users can earn additional AD-coins by watching ADs on the AD publisher platform constantly, while the AD broadcasting platform can also get rewards from advertisers for a certain amount of AD-coins.

4   Our B^2DAM system

Our B^2DAM system consists of six modules and a blockchain framework, including the identity and Ad-coin account management module (IAAM), advertising delivery module (AD-DM), advertising recommendation module (AD-RM), advertising evaluation module (AD-EM), advertising prediction module (AD-PM), user feedback module (UFM) and AD-chains. As shown in Fig. 2, these modules are invoked by three types of entities: advertisers, publishers, and users.

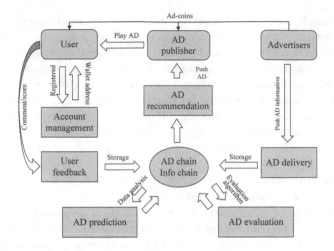

Fig. 2. A running procedure of B²DAM system.

4.1   System Blockchain Platform

As shown in Fig. 3, our B²DAM system employs the multi-chain technology, which is named AD-chains [30]. One of that is the parent-chain, which is a public blockchain that used for AD-coins transaction. The other is the sub-chain, which is used to store the AD-related information delivered by advertisers. Most important, considering the extensibility of our system, other subchains can be added to the parent-chain in future.

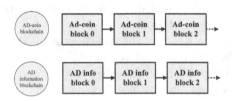

Fig. 3. AD-chains structure in the B²DAM system.

In the B²DAM system, AD-coins transactions records and AD-related information records cannot be deleted or changed, which is open to the public.

Our parent-chain is designed with the EOS blockchain framework, to ensure that all information such as AD quality score, users' scoring, and playing number are all cannot be tampered with. The incentive mechanism can award virtual currency to publishers, users and advertisers in the early system stage. Note that the total number of rewards is reduced year by year, and the reward is no longer provided after the platform is stable. In detail, the blockchain platform is implemented as follows.

The information chain includes the wallet address, the times of AD playing, the URL of AD, the amount of AD credit for promotion, and the initial AD quality value.

Using the DPOS consensus mechanism to construct the parent-chain and subchain's blocks, which has an unparalleled advantage over other consensus mechanisms. A voting mechanism is employed to filter low-quality AD. By eliminating advertiser which provide the low-quality ADs, we can ensure the a near 100% participation rate of the high-quality ADs provider. The DPOS algorithm has a high rate of blockout, which can confirm the transaction with 99.9% certainty within 1.5 s, thus ensuring that the transaction throughput in the service network meets the performance requirements.

To successfully deliver an AD, the advertiser need to freeze the required amount of AD-coins. The AD-coins obtained by the user for watching AD are realized by corresponding smart contracts. The smart contracts can divide and transfer AD-coins to the AD publisher and the user according to a predetermined proportion. Also, according to the AD-EM, AD quality score can be dynamically updated by implemented a specific smart contract.

4.2 Identity and Account Management Module

In this module, users must providing their personal information to complete the account registration. Then, all registered users would obtain valid wallet addresses respectively, which can be used for AD-coins transactions in the B²DAM system. Note that each user can only have one valid account at the same time. The management system also periodically checks these account members. If some users behaves abnormally, a penalty mechanism would be triggered, or their account would be forcibly logged off. If users' behaviors are illegal, the B²DAM system can inform AD publisher that he has registered, and deliver the evidence to pursue their legal actions.

Advertisers can also complete the registration by providing their information. Then this modular will set up a function for advertiser registration, where a amount of pre-stored AD-coins are deposited and the number of it can range from low to high. Due to the different investment capabilities of advertisers, they are allowed to choose the amount of pre-stored AD-coins. At the same time, the system will set a minimum pre-stored quota. If the minimum amount is not met, they cannot be registered as an advertiser.

4.3 Advertising Delivery Module

This module realizes AD delivery backend functionality through the smart contracts which written by the high-level programming language. DApps will be designed to call the smart contracts, in order to provide users with the function of AD delivery. Advertisers need to store ADs in a network server, and then the AD-related information will be delivered to the AD-chains through the DApps. The AD-related information that is published on AD-chains can be modified. However, all modifications are traceable to ensure that advertisers can modify the AD-related information according to the score of real-time evaluation by the AD-EM.

In the B^{2}DAM system, each registered advertisers can deliver his AD-related information to the information chain, under the condition that there must be enough pre-stored AD-coins met the quota. All advertisers have equal opportunities to compete. There will be no so-called "advertising giants", since the final result is determined by users and the AD-EM.

4.4   Advertising Recommendation Module

Currently, there are numerous AD publishers. To push AD to some large platforms, advertisers need to invest more money into a new AD for high-quality. They also pay a large amount of fees to the AD publisher, which means some capital-rich advertisers may be able to monopolize their AD. When the same types of AD are looped, the user feel tired for these types AD. In this module, a *first-responder* mechanism is designed to solve the current situation of unequal promotion opportunities of ADs. After an AD is delivered by the ad delivery module, the major AD publishers can select ADs from this system, that is, the AD publishers can *answer* the AD. When some publisher confirms that the AD-related information exists on the AD-chains, he can obtain the broadcasting right of this AD. Then, other publishers can continue to *answer*. These mechanism ensures the fairness of competition between publishers.

To avoid artificial manipulation and prevent the capital-rich advertisers from using the capital advantage to infinitely loop their ADs, we set a maximum times of broadcasting for each AD, such that each AD can only be allowed for a limit times of broadcasting. Then, the publisher continues to select AD and broadcast it to users.

4.5   User Feedback Module

This module is designed to improve the user's viewing experience in this system, so the user's evaluation results will affect the AD's value in real time. When some user completes the viewing of a whole AD on the AD publisher's platform, the system will hint the user to score this AD. The score will affect the total score from the AD-EM. To motivate the user to conduct scoring, this module provides a new mechanism. When the score given by a large number of users is close to the total score given by the AD-EM, these users would obtain more AD-coins. Then, this value will be fed back to the AD-EM in real time, and the AD-EM will update the AD quality score according to a certain proportion.

4.6   Advertising Evaluation Module

Some well-known AD publishers usually have a large appeal to users. They always occupied important position in the AD ecosystem, While smaller AD publishers are not. When an AD is played on a little-known publisher compared with a powerful AD publisher, the popularity and influence of playback are incomparable.

In this module, the quality of AD and the user revenues can be judged and evaluated. An AD's quality score is influenced by the scale of AD publisher, including the number of AD watched, the numbers of skipped, and the user's score of the AD. In detail, this module employs the following AD evaluation rules.

The size of the publisher's platform is used as a reference factor, which is positively related to the number of users. In fact, the scores provided by the large platform is better than that from small platforms. For the AD publishers that registered in our system, its score is based on the number of users, which can be divided into four grade. The grade is A, B, C, D. Let X_a, X_b, X_c, X_d be the proportion of platforms, and W_a, W_b, W_c, W_d be the AD quality score generated by each platform. The AD's total quality score can be calculated as follows

$$W = W_a \times X_a + W_b \times X_b + W_c \times X_c + W_d \times X_d$$

The number of AD skipped is negatively correlated with the quality score of AD in the system. Under the condition of paid viewing of AD, most AD that are expected to be skipped may have quality problems.

The evaluation score of some user for an AD is positively correlated with the quality score of AD in the system. When completed the watching of some ADs, the user is asked to scoring the AD to reflect the expected score. The user scoring is the expected of different platforms generated by the average value of the evaluation of each publisher's user. Let the average score be a, b, c and d, and the proportion of the publisher playing amount that produces the average score be $P(a)$, $P(b)$, $P(c)$ and $P(d)$. Then, we can compute an expect value as follows

$$E = a \times P(a) + b \times P(b) + c \times P(c) + d \times P(d)$$

The total score is generated by the sum above, and the average score will be affected by the total score, that is,

$$\text{total score} = \text{market price} \times \text{total score/average score}.$$

In the system, All the parameters are stored in the information chain.

According to the above four rules, each impact factor can be quantified, and the weighted average is the quality score of this AD in the system.

4.7   Advertising Prediction Module

The AD-PM uses a machine learning algorithm to predict the number of viewers and their revenues, and feeds the results back to advertisers and AD publishers [14]. According to the predicted-effect of AD, the advertiser can decide whether to continue the AD playing or not. If the AD does not bring enough revenue or the number of viewers is too small, the AD publisher will no longer play the AD and choose to answer another AD. In addition, the module also uses data mining algorithms to analyze the types of AD that users often watch, and combines the recommendations of the AD-RM with the user as much as possible.

5 Conclusion Remarks

Based on the current blockchain technology, this paper proposes an digital advertising media promotion system (B^2DAM) in the IDA media industry. The lack of supervision and effective operation mechanism leads to the proliferation of low quality AD, which means an efficient way is needed to maintain the healthy development of the IDA market. Thus, our B^2DAM is designed to improve the quality and effectiveness of advertising, enhance the enthusiasm of user participation, and enhance the user viewing experience. More importantly, the quality of AD in the advertising market could be improved, thus the problems in existing IDA ecosystem can be solved.

Acknowledgment. This research was supported in part by the National Natural Science Foundation of China under projects 61772150, 61862012, 61862011, and 61602125, the National Cryptography Development Fund of China under project MMJJ20170217, the Guangxi Key R&D Fund under project AB17195025, the Guangxi Natural Science Foundation under grant 2018GXNSFAA281232, the Guangxi Young Teachers' Basic Ability Improvement Program under grant 2018KY0194, and the open program of Guangxi Key Laboratory of Cryptography and Information Security under project GCIS201702.

References

1. Andrychowicz, M., Dziembowski, S., Malinowski, D., Mazurek, Ł.: Modeling Bitcoin contracts by timed automata. In: Legay, A., Bozga, M. (eds.) Formal Modeling and Analysis of Timed Systems, pp. 7–22. Springer, Cham (2014)
2. Aste, T., Tasca, P., Matteo, T.D.: Blockchain technologies: the foreseeable impact on society and industry. Computer **50**(9), 18–28 (2017). https://doi.org/10.1109/MC.2017.3571064
3. Beck, R.: Beyond Bitcoin: the rise of blockchain world. Computer **51**(2), 54–58 (2018)
4. Bentov, I., Lee, C., Mizrahi, A., Rosenfeld, M.: Proof of activity: extending Bitcoin's proof of work via proof of stake. SIGMETRICS Perform. Eval. Rev. **42**(3), 34–37 (2014). https://doi.org/10.1145/2695533.2695545
5. Budak, C., Goel, S., Rao, J., Zervas, G.: Understanding emerging threats to online advertising. In: Proceedings of the 2016 ACM Conference on Economics and Computation, EC 2016, pp. 561–578. ACM, New York (2016). https://doi.org/10.1145/2940716.2940787
6. Castro, M., Liskov, B.: Practical byzantine fault tolerance. In: Proceedings of the Third Symposium on Operating Systems Design and Implementation, OSDI 1999, pp. 173–186. USENIX Association, Berkeley (1999). http://dl.acm.org/citation.cfm?id=296806.296824
7. Chuen, D.L.K.: Handbook of Digital Currency: Bitcoin, Innovation, Financial Instruments, and Big Data. Academic Press, Cambridge (2015)
8. Dennis, R., Disso, J.P.: An analysis into the scalability of Bitcoin and ethereum. In: Yang, X.-S., Sherratt, S., Dey, N., Joshi, A. (eds.) Third International Congress on Information and Communication Technology. AISC, vol. 797, pp. 619–627. Springer, Singapore (2019). https://doi.org/10.1007/978-981-13-1165-9_57

9. Dhillon, V., Metcalf, D., Hooper, M.: Recent developments in blockchain. Blockchain Enabled Applications, pp. 151–181. Apress, Berkeley (2017). https://doi.org/10.1007/978-1-4842-3081-7_11

10. Dhumwad, S., Sukhadeve, M., Naik, C., Manjunath, K.N., Prabhu, S.: A peer to peer money transfer using SHA256 and Merkle tree. In: Annual International Conference on Advanced Computing and Communications (2017). http://eprints.manipal.edu/id/eprint/150090

11. EOS.IO: Technical white paper. Technical report (2017). https://github.com/EOSIO/Documentation/blob/master/TechnicalWhitePaper.md

12. Estrada-Jiménez, J., Parra-Arnau, J., Rodríguez-Hoyos, A., Forné, J.: Online advertising: analysis of privacy threats and protection approaches. Comput. Commun. **100**, 32 – 51 (2017).https://doi.org/10.1016/j.comcom.2016.12.016, http://www.sciencedirect.com/science/article/pii/S0140366416307083

13. Freund, D.A.: Economic incentives and blockchain security. J. Secur. Oper. Custody **10**(1), 67–76 (2018)

14. Goodfellow, I., Bengio, Y., Courville, A., Bengio, Y.: Deep Learning, vol. 1. MIT Press, Cambridge (2016)

15. Hjalmarsson, F.P., Hreioarsson, G.K., Hamdaqa, M., Hjalmtysson, G.: Blockchain-based e-voting system. In: 2018 IEEE 11th International Conference on Cloud Computing (CLOUD), pp. 983–986, July 2018.https://doi.org/10.1109/CLOUD.2018.00151

16. Karame, G.: On the security and scalability of Bitcoin's blockchain. In: Proceedings of the 2016 ACM SIGSAC Conference on Computer and Communications Security, CCS 2016, pp. 1861–1862. ACM, New York (2016). https://doi.org/10.1145/2976749.2976756

17. Katsumata, S., Motohashi, E., Nishimoto, A., Toyosawa, E.: The contents-based website classification for the internet advertising planning: an empirical application of the natural language analysis. Rev. Socionetw. Strat. **11**(2), 129–142 (2017). https://doi.org/10.1007/s12626-017-0007-0

18. Kiayias, A., Russell, A., David, B., Oliynykov, R.: Ouroboros: a provably secure proof-of-stake blockchain protocol. In: Katz, J., Shacham, H. (eds.) CRYPTO 2017. LNCS, vol. 10401, pp. 357–388. Springer, Cham (2017). https://doi.org/10.1007/978-3-319-63688-7_12

19. Kotila, M., Cuevas Rumin, R., Dhar, S.: Compendium of ad fraud knowledge for media investors. Technical report, WFA Global Transparency Group, Brussels, Belgium (2016)

20. Lauslahti, K., Mattila, J., Seppälä, T.: Smart contracts-how will blockchain technology affect contractual practices? Technical report, ETLA C The Research Institute of the Finnish Economy (2017)

21. Li, Z., Kang, J., Yu, R., Ye, D., Deng, Q., Zhang, Y.: Consortium blockchain for secure energy trading in industrial internet of things. IEEE Trans. Ind. Inform. **14**(8), 3690–3700 (2018). https://doi.org/10.1109/TII.2017.2786307

22. Markovic, M.: Data protection techniques, cryptographic protocols and PKI systems in modern computer networks. In: 2007 14th International Workshop on Systems, Signals and Image Processing and 6th EURASIP Conference focused on Speech and Image Processing, Multimedia Communications and Services, pp. 13–24, June 2007. https://doi.org/10.1109/IWSSIP.2007.4381086

23. Merkle, R.: Secrecy, authentication, and public key systems. Ph. D. thesis, Stanford University (1979)

24. Müller, L.: Transforming online advertising: a user centric approach to bridge the gap. In: Proceedings of the 2018 ACM SIGMIS Conference on Computers and People Research, SIGMIS-CPR 2018, pp. 181–182. ACM, New York (2018). https://doi.org/10.1145/3209626.3209632

25. Nakamoto, S.: Bitcoin: a peer-to-peer electronic cash system. Technical report (2008). https://bitcoin.org/bitcoin.pdf

26. PwC: Iab internet advertising revenue report - 2016 full-year results. Technical report, Interactive Advertising Bureau (IAB) and PricewaterhouseCoopers (PwC) (2017). https://www.iab.com/wp-content/uploads/2016/04/IAB_Internet_Advertising_Revenue_Report_FY_2016.pdf

27. Rouhani, S., Deters, R.: Performance analysis of ethereum transactions in private blockchain. In: 2017 8th IEEE International Conference on Software Engineering and Service Science (ICSESS), pp. 70–74, November 2017). https://doi.org/10.1109/ICSESS.2017.8342866

28. Saberi, S., Kouhizadeh, M., Sarkis, J., Shen, L.: Blockchain technology and its relationships to sustainable supply chain management. Int. J. Prod. Res., 1–19 (2018). https://doi.org/10.1080/00207543.2018.1533261

29. Wood, G.: Ethereum: a secure decentralised generalised transaction ledger. Ethereum Proj. Yellow Pap. **151**, 1–32 (2014)

30. WOOD, G.: Polkadot: vision for a heterogeneous multi-chain framework (draft 1). Technical report, Founder, Ethereum & Parity (2016)

31. Yang, W., Garg, S., Raza, A., Herbert, D., Kang, B.: Blockchain: trends and future. In: Yoshida, K., Lee, M. (eds.) PKAW 2018. LNCS (LNAI), vol. 11016, pp. 201–210. Springer, Cham (2018). https://doi.org/10.1007/978-3-319-97289-3_15

32. Yang, X., Yi, X., Nepal, S., Han, F.: Decentralized voting: a self-tallying voting system using a smart contract on the ethereum blockchain. In: Hacid, H., Cellary, W., Wang, H., Paik, H.-Y., Zhou, R. (eds.) WISE 2018. LNCS, vol. 11233, pp. 18–35. Springer, Cham (2018). https://doi.org/10.1007/978-3-030-02922-7_2

33. Yu, S., Wang, G., Liu, X., Niu, J.: Security and privacy in the age of the smart internet of things: an overview from a networking perspective. IEEE Commun. Mag. **56**(9), 14–18 (2018)

34. Zheng, Z., Xie, S., Dai, H., Chen, X., Wang, H.: An overview of blockchain technology: architecture, consensus, and future trends. In: 2017 IEEE International Congress on Big Data (BigData Congress), pp. 557–564. IEEE (2017)

Detecting Steganography in AMR Speech Based on Pulse Correlation

Jie Liu[1], Hui Tian[1(✉)], Xiaokang Liu[1], and Jing Lu[2]

[1] College of Computer Science and Technology, National Huaqiao University,
Xiamen 361021, China
{liujiecs,htian,xkliu}@hqu.edu.cn
[2] Network Technology Center, National Huaqiao University,
Xiamen 361021, China
jlu@hqu.edu.cn

Abstract. This paper presents a novel methodology to detect the steganography on the fixed codebook (FCB) of adaptive multi-rate (AMR) speech stream. We have found that correlations of pulses are influenced by the steganographic operation. Based on this, two categories of features are proposed to characterize the pulse correlations, namely subframe-level pulse correlation based on self-information and track-level pulse correlation based on mutual-information, whose feature dimension is only 1/5 of the state of the art. The proposed method employs the support vector machine as the classifier and is evaluated with a large quantity of AMR speech samples. The experimental results demonstrate that the propose method is effective and has a better detection performance than the state of the arts.

Keywords: Steganography · Steganalysis · Adaptive multi-rate speech ·
Pulse correlation · Self-information · Mutual-information

1 Introduction

Steganography is the art of covert communication by hiding secret information in digital media, such as image [1, 2], text [3, 4], audio [5, 6] and video [7, 8]. To prevent threats and damages caused by illegal uses of steganography, steganalysis, the countermeasure of steganography, has attracted increasing attention from researchers, which aims to detect the existence of secret information in digital media [9]. In recent years, as the fast development of the Internet, Voice over Internet Protocol (VoIP) has become a popular communication service over the Internet and mobile software, which drives researches on the VoIP-based steganography [10]. Compared with traditional carriers, there are many advantages of VoIP-based carriers, such as high steganographic bandwidth, instantaneity and flexible steganographic length [11].

In VoIP service, speech signals are encoded by VoIP codecs into digital information, which are then packetized, and transmission occurs as IP packets over the Internet [12]. In general, there are three types of VoIP codecs: waveform codec, such as ITU G.711; parametric codec, such as LPC-10; hybrid codec, such as adaptive multi-rate (AMR) codec. Because the hybrid codec has a high compression ratio while

Published by Springer Nature Switzerland AG 2019. All Rights Reserved
J. Li et al. (Eds.): SPNCE 2019, LNICST 284, pp. 485–497, 2019.
https://doi.org/10.1007/978-3-030-21373-2_39

keeping an acceptable speech quality, it is widely applied in VoIP scenarios. Moreover, AMR is a popular format of spoken audio, which has a widespread application in mobile devices. Therefore, AMR speech has become a hot spot of the VoIP-based steganography. To confront the challenges of the AMR-based steganography, the steganalysis of AMR speech streams is conducted in this paper.

For AMR codec, there are three suitable embedding domains including linear predictive coefficient (LPC) [13, 14], adaptive codebook (ACB) [15, 16], fixed codebook (FCB) [17, 18]. Compared with LPC and ACB, FCB accounts for a larger proportion in each frame, for example, the total bits of each frame for AMR narrow bandwidth (AMR-NB) with 12.2 kbit/s mode are 244 bits, while the total bits of FCB are 140 bits [19], which are more than a half. Furthermore, in AMR encoding process, the structure of FCB is based on the interleaved single-pulse permutation (ISPP) design and the search procedure of FCB is the depth-first tree. All the characteristics indicate that the steganography on FCB can be high-capacity and slightly perceptible. Based on this, there have been some steganographic methods on FCB, for example, Geiser and Vary [17] proposed a steganography by confining the second pulse position in the same track during the FCB search to create a covert channel, which can reach up to 2 kbit/s bandwidth with AMR-NB at 12.2 kbit/s mode. Miao et al. [18] presented an adaptive suboptimal pulse combination constrained method to embed secret information during FCB search, which further introduced a steganographic factor to control the embedding capacity.

In recent years, there have been some effective steganalysis methods to detect the above steganographic algorithms, for example, Miao et al. [20] proposed two methods to detect FCB-based steganography. One calculated the Markov transition probabilities of pulse positions in the same track as steganalysis features. The other utilized the joint entropy and conditional entropy to detect secret information. The experimental results show that both methods can detect the Geiser's [17] and Miao's [18] steganography methods, but the detection accuracy are not satisfied. Later, Ren et al. [21] studied the FCB search strategy of steganography and found that there exists a difference of the probability of the same pulse position between cover and steganographic samples. The probabilities of the same pulse position in each track are applied as steganalysis features whose dimension is only 7-dimension. Experiments show that Ren's [21] method outperforms Miao's [20] method. Recently, Tian et al. [22] proposed another effective detection method which has a better detection performance than Ren's [21] while the feature dimension is 498-dimension. In Tian's method [22], the Markov transition matrix of the pulse pairs in the same subframe and the joint probabilities of the pulse pairs in different subframe are calculated as steganalysis features. Thought Ren's method [21] has a low feature dimension, the detection accuracy is not satisfied; while Tian's method [22] is better, the feature is relatively high. To cover the shortages existing in the state of the arts [21, 22], we present a more accurate detection method based on the support vector machine by employing the correlation of pulses to fully capture the influence caused by steganography on FCB as the steganalysis features, namely subframe-level pulse correlation based on self-information and track-level pulse correlation based on mutual-information. The experimental results show that the proposed method is able to detect the steganography methods on the FCB and outperforms the state of the arts. The main contributions of this paper can be concluded as follow:

(1) This paper proposed two effective categories of steganalysis features. The proposed features are only 100 dimensional, which is 1/5 of that of the state of the art;
(2) A support vector machine based steganalysis scheme is presented;
(3) The proposed steganalysis scheme outperforms the state of the arts.

The rest of this paper is organized as follows. Section 2 introduces the standard encoding principle of the AMR codec, the steganography conducted AMR speech streams and the state of arts for steganalysis. The proposed features are described in Sect. 3. Section 4 presents the support vector machine based steganalysis method. Experiments and analysis are shown in Sect. 5. Finally, concluding remarks are given in Sect. 6.

2 Background and Related Work

This section first introduces the standard encoding principle of AMR codec, then reviews the steganography methods [17, 18] conducted on the FCB, finally, presents the state of the arts for steganalysis [21, 22].

2.1 Standard Encoding Principle of AMR Codec

The AMR codec [19] is a multi-mode codec which supports 8 narrow band encoding modes with bit rates ranging from 4.75 kbit/s to 12.2 kbit/s and 9 wide band encoding modes with bit rates between 6.6 kbit/s and 23.85 kbit/s. The encoding algorithm of the AMR codec is algebraic code-excited linear prediction whose main functions can be divided into three parts: LPC analysis, pitch delay search and FCB search. Because this paper concentrates on the steganography for FCB, only the search strategy of FCB is illuminated, which takes AMR-NB with 12.2 kbit/s mode as the example.

There are 10 non-zeros pulses in the innovation vector, where all the pulses have two amplitudes +1 or −1. In each subframe, there are 40 positions, which are divided into 5 tracks and each track locates two pulses as shown in Table 1. The FCB search aims at minimizing the mean square error between the weighted input speech and the weighted synthesized speech. Let $b(n)$ be the presetting amplitudes which is the sum of the normalized $d(n)$ vector and normalized long-term prediction residual $res_{LTP}(n)$:

Table 1. The FCB structure of AMR-NB with 12.2 kbit/s.

Track	Pulse	Position
0	i_0, i_5	0, 5, 10, 15, 20, 25, 30, 35
1	i_1, i_6	1, 6, 11, 16, 21, 26, 31, 36
2	i_2, i_7	2, 7, 12, 17, 22, 27, 32, 37
3	i_3, i_8	3, 8, 13, 18, 23, 28, 33, 38
4	i_4, i_9	4, 9, 14, 19, 24, 29, 34, 39

$$b(n) = \frac{res_{LTP}(n)}{\sqrt{\sum_{i=0}^{39} res_{LTP}(i)res_{LTP}(i)}} + \frac{d(n)}{\sqrt{\sum_{i=0}^{39} d(i)d(i)}}. \tag{1}$$

The pulse positions with the maximum absolute values of $b(n)$ are searched firstly for five tracks, then the global maximum value for all pulse positions is selected as the position of the first pulse i_0. Next, four iterations are conducted. The position of pulse i_1 is set to the local maximum of each track in each iteration. The pulse pairs $\{i_2, i_3\}$, $\{i_4, i_5\}$, $\{i_6, i_7\}$ and $\{i_8, i_9\}$ are searched by sequentially searching in the nested loops. All the pulse starting positions except i_0 are cyclically shifted in each iteration. Therefore, the pulse pairs are altered, and the pulse i_1 is located a local maximum of a different track. The remain pulses are searched for the other positions in the tracks. There exists at least one pulse in the position corresponding to the global maximum and one pulse in position corresponding to one of the 4 local maxima.

2.2 AMR-Based Steganography

Due to the FCB search is based on the depth-first tree, only a small subset of suitable positions is searched, which leads to a suboptimal codebook. Therefore, it is possible to modify the pulse position with an imperceptible degradation on speech quality to hiding information. The AMR-based steganographic algorithms [17, 18] embed secret information by modifying the FCB search strategy based on the above characteristics.

Geiser and Vary [17] proposed a steganography which restricted the admissible position of the second pulse in each track of AMR-NB with 12.2 kbit/s mode. In Geiser's method, 2 bits secret information is embedding in each track and the pules positions of $i_5, \ldots, i_9$ are selected two out of 8 possible values. Denote i_t and i_{t+5} as the first and the second pulse position in the same track respectively and $(m)_{i,j}$ as the bits at position i and j of the secret information m in binary representation. The restricted rule of can be expressed as

$$i_{t+5} = \begin{cases} g^{-1}\left(g\left(\lfloor\frac{i}{5}\rfloor\right) \oplus (m)_{2t,2t+1}\right) \cdot 5 + t \\ g^{-1}\left(g\left(\lfloor\frac{i}{5}\rfloor\right) \oplus (m)_{2t,2t+1} + 4\right) \cdot 5 + t \end{cases}, \tag{2}$$

where g and g^{-1} are Gray encoding and decoding by table lookup; "$\oplus$" is the bitwise exclusive disjunction (XOR); $\lfloor x \rfloor$ is the round down function. At the receiver end, the secret information is extracted by

$$(m)_{2t,2t+1} = \left(g\left(\left\lfloor\frac{i_t}{5}\right\rfloor\right) \oplus g\left(\left\lfloor\frac{i_{t+5}}{5}\right\rfloor\right)\right) \bmod 4. \tag{3}$$

Miao et al. [18] present another steganography to embed secret information in AMR speech by searching a suboptimal codevector to replace the cover one. Assume m_t as the secret information to be embedded and p_{ti} is the i-th pulse in the t-th track. The restricted rule of Miao's method is defined as follow

$$m_t = \left(\sum_{i=0}^{L_t} g\left(\left|\frac{p_{t_i}}{N}\right|\right) \right) \oplus \eta, \tag{4}$$

where g is Gray encoding by table lookup; N is the number of tracks; L_t is the number of non-zero pulses in track t; η is the embedding factor to control the embedding bits. Particularly, for AMR-NB with 12.2 kbit/s mode, η is usually set as 1, 2, 4. At the receiver end, the secret information is extracted by calculating Eq. (4) again.

2.3   The State of the Arts for AMR-Based Steganalysis

There have been some effective steganalysis methods to detect steganography on FCB of AMR speech streams. In this section, two of the best detection methods are introduced.

Ren et al. [21] presented a low dimension steganalysis based on the probabilities of same pulse positions. In the work, Ren et al. analyzed the impact of steganography on the pulse conditional probability in the t-th track (PCP_t), which is calculated by

$$PCP_t(i,j) = \frac{1}{N_S} \sum_{f=1}^{N_S} \delta(i_a(f,t) = i, i_b(f,t) = j), \tag{5}$$

where i, j are the possible positions and follow $0 \le i,j \le N_p - 1$; N_s is the number of subframes; f is the label of subframe and follows $0 \le f \le N_s$; i_a and i_b are the first and the second non-zero pulse position respectively. $\delta(R)$ is defined as

$$\delta(R) = \begin{cases} 1, & R \text{ is true} \\ 0, & else \end{cases}. \tag{6}$$

It is observed that $PCP_t(i, i)$, the probabilities of two pulses in the same position, are distinguishing between steganographic samples and cover samples. Therefore, in Ren's method, the average of $PCP_t(i, i)$ in all tracks are employed as steganalysis features.

However, if the steganography avoids modifying the pulse in the same positions, Ren's method [21] will be invalid. Motivated by the shortcoming of Ren's method, Tian et al. [22] proposed more complete features including long-term features of pulse pairs (LTFS), short-term features of pulse pairs (STFS) and track to track correlation features (TTFS). The LTFS is the probability distributions of the pulse pairs, which is given by

$$P(x,y) = \frac{\sum_{i=0}^{N_s-1} \left(\delta(p_{i,j} = x, p_{i,j+T} = y) \| \delta(p_{i,j} = y, p_{i,j+T} = x) \right)}{N_s}, \tag{7}$$

where N_s is the same as Eq. (5); $(p_{i,j}, p_{i,j+T})$ is the pulse pair for the j-th track in the i-th subframe. The STFS is the Markov transition matrix (MTM) of the pulse pairs of a track in the same subframe. Let p $((a, b) \mid (c, d))$ be the probability that the pulse pair (c, d) is followed by (a, b), so the MTM in the i-th track is described below

$$
M_i = \begin{bmatrix} P(u_{i,0}|u_{i,0}) & P(u_{i,0}|u_{i,1}) & \cdots & P(u_{i,R-1}|u_{i,R-1}) \\ P(u_{i,1}|u_{i,0}) & \ddots & & \\ \vdots & & \ddots & \\ P(u_{i,R-1}|u_{i,0}) & \cdots & \cdots & P(u_{i,R-1}|u_{i,R-1}) \end{bmatrix}, \tag{8}
$$

where R is the number of all potential pulse-position pairs for i-th track.

The TTFS is the joint probability matrix of pulse pairs, which can be written as

$$
J_{i,j} = \begin{bmatrix} P(u_{i,0}, u_{i,0}) & P(u_{i,0}, u_{i,1}) & \cdots & P(u_{i,R-1}, u_{i,R-1}) \\ P(u_{i,1}, u_{i,0}) & \ddots & & \\ \vdots & & \ddots & \\ P(u_{i,R-1}, u_{i,0}) & \cdots & \cdots & P(u_{i,R-1}, u_{i,R-1}) \end{bmatrix}. \tag{9}
$$

Although Tian's method [22] has a better detection performance, the feature dimension is quite high (498-dimensional). Given the shortcomings of the-state-of-the-art steganalysis methods, we present a high accurate detection method with a reasonable feature dimension.

3   The Proposed Steganalysis Features

In this section, we will introduce the proposed steganalysis features which include two categories: the subframe-level pulse correlation (SPC) based on self-information and the track-level pulse correlation (TPC) based on mutual information.

3.1   The Subframe-Pulses Features Based on Self-information

For AMR-NB with 12.2 kbit/s mode, each frame is divided into four subframes and in each subframe, there are 10 pulses. For the standard principle, the pulse pairs search order in a same subframe is: $\{i_0, i_1\}$, $\{i_2, i_3\}$, $\{i_4, i_5\}$, $\{i_6, i_7\}$ and $\{i_8, i_9\}$ as the blue line in Fig. 1 while for steganography, the search order is: $\{i_0, i_5\}$, $\{i_1, i_6\}$, $\{i_2, i_7\}$, $\{i_3, i_8\}$ and $\{i_4, i_9\}$ as the red line in Fig. 1.

The steganography modifies the search strategy of the pulse pairs in the subframe, and the encoding process is successive which means the latter pulse is related to the former pulse. Thus, the short-term stability of speech is destroyed by the steganographic operation. Therefore, the correlation among the pulses in the same subframe is affected by steganography. To describe the correlation of pulses in the same subframe, the SPC is calculated as steganalysis feature by the following equation:

$$
H(x,y) = -\log_2 \left(\frac{\sum_{i=0}^{L} \sum_{j=i}^{L} \left((\delta(l_i = x) \,\&\, \delta(l_j = y)) \,||\, (\delta(l_i = y) \,\&\, \delta(l_j = x)) \right)}{C_L^2} \right), \tag{10}
$$

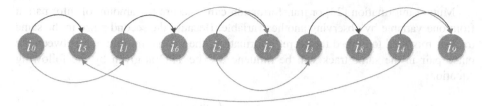

Fig. 1. The search strategy of pulse pairs between standard and steganographic principle. (Color figure online)

where L is the total of the pulse in a subframe; l_i is the i-th pulse in the subframe; x, y are the pulse positions. For AMR-NB 12.2 kbit/s mode, $L = 10$ and $x, y \in [0, 7]$. In steganalysis, the average SPC of all the subframe are applied as the steganalysis feature whose dimension is 36-D.

The comparison of SPC value between cover and steganographic sample is shown in Fig. 2. From Fig. 2 we can learn that (1) for both cover and steganographic sample, the SPC values are larger in different pulse positions than those in the same pulse positions; (2) the SPC values are influenced by steganography and the changes of SPC values in different pulse positions are more significant than those in the same pulse position.

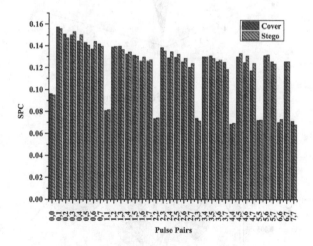

Fig. 2. The comparison of SPC between cover sample and steganographic sample at embedding rate of 100%

3.2 The Track-Pulses Features Based on Mutual Information

The SPC indicates the correlation of all the pulses in the subframe, while the steganography algorithms are implemented by modifying the second pulse position in the same track. To get the more precise correlation of the pulse pair in the same track, the TPC are proposed to capture the influence on the pulse pair in the same track.

Mutual information [23] or transformation can measure the amount of information from one variable by observing another variable. Because the second pulse in the same track is modified to embed the secret information, the mutual information between the pulse pair in the same track will be influenced. The TPC is given by the following equation:

$$I(x,y) = p(x,y) \log_2 \left(\frac{p(x,y)}{p(x)p(y)} \right), \tag{11}$$

where x, y are the first pulse position and the second pulse position in the same track; $p(x)$, $p(y)$ are the marginal probability distribution of x, y respectively; $p(x, y)$ is the

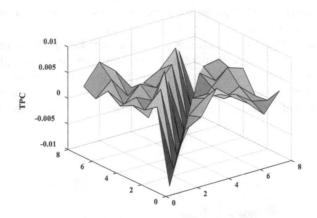

(a)   TPC of cover sample

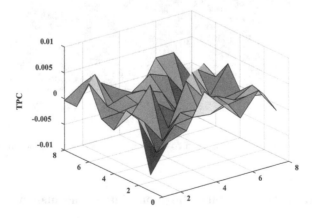

(b)   TPC of steganographic sample

Fig. 3. The comparison of TPC between cover samples and steganographic sample at embedding rate of 100%.

joint probability distribution of x and y. Similarly, the average of TPC of all track is employed in steganalysis whose dimension is 64.

The comparison of TPC between cover sample and steganographic sample is shown in Fig. 3, from which it can be concluded that the distribution of TPC of steganographic sample is more even than that of cover sample.

Thus, the proposed features include SPC with 36-dimensional and TPC with 64-dimensional, whose feature dimension is 100-dimensional. The proposed feature dimension is only 1/5 of Tian's feature dimension.

4   Steganalysis Scheme Based on Support Vector Machine

In this section, we present a steganalysis model based on support vector machine [24] (SVM), which contains a training process and detection process. Specifically, the training process consists of the following three steps:

Step 1: Samples preparation. Collect a quantity of speech samples and encoded them with the AMR codec and conduct steganography on them at different embedding rates.

Step 2: Features extraction. Extract the proposed features in Sect. 3 from both cover samples and steganographic samples.

Step 3: Model training. Train the SVM model with the features extracted in Step 2.

Similarly, the detection process includes two steps:

Step 1: Feature extraction. Extract the proposed features from the samples to be detected.

Step 2: Detection. Input the extracted features into the trained SVM and make detection decision according to the output of the model.

5   Experiments and Analysis

5.1   Experimental Setup

To evaluate the experimental without loss generality, we collect 4000 speech samples with length of ten second as the dataset, and all the samples are encoded with AMR-NB 12.2 kbit/s mode. There are four steganography methods are detected in the steganalysis experiments, including Geiser's method [17] and Miao's methods with $\eta = 1$, 2, 4 [18]. All the detection methods are implemented on Python 3.6 with sklearn.svm [25]. Moreover, accuracy (ACC), false positive rate (FPR) and false negative rate (FNR) are employed as the metrics in the steganalysis experiment.

5.2   Detection Performance and Analysis

The steganalysis experiments for ten second samples at different rates (from 0.1 to 1.0) are conducted in this section, and we compare the proposed method with the state of the arts [21, 22]. In each steganalysis experiment, half samples are used to trained the model and the remained samples are employed as the test set to evaluate the detection performance for each steganography. The experimental results are listed from Table 2, 3, 4 and 5.

Table 2. Detection performance for Geiser's method [17].

Embedding rate	Ren's method [21]			Tian's method [22]			The proposed method		
	ACC	FPR	FNR	ACC	FPR	FNR	ACC	FPR	FNR
10%	0.5690	0.4460	0.4160	0.5703	0.4585	0.4010	**0.6212**	0.3775	0.3800
20%	0.6623	0.3805	0.2950	0.7120	0.3055	0.2705	**0.7302**	0.2650	0.2745
30%	0.7378	0.3115	0.2130	0.8260	0.1820	0.1660	**0.8455**	0.1420	0.1670
40%	0.8103	0.2260	0.1535	0.9020	0.1050	0.0910	**0.9137**	0.0750	0.0975
50%	0.8692	0.1480	0.1135	0.9523	0.0425	0.0530	**0.9550**	0.0415	0.0485
60%	0.9035	0.1105	0.0825	0.9762	0.0245	0.0230	**0.9722**	0.0250	0.0305
70%	0.9340	0.0820	0.0500	0.9850	0.0145	0.0155	**0.9858**	0.0140	0.0145
80%	0.9453	0.0600	0.0495	0.9942	0.0065	0.0050	**0.9935**	0.0045	0.0085
90%	0.9553	0.0500	0.0395	0.9958	0.0040	0.0045	**0.9968**	0.0030	0.0035
100%	0.9655	0.0405	0.0285	0.9972	0.0025	0.0030	**0.9988**	0.0015	0.0010

Table 3. Detection performance for Miao's method with $\eta = 1$ [18].

Embedding rate	Ren's method [21]			Tian's method [22]			The proposed method		
	ACC	FPR	FNR	ACC	FPR	FNR	ACC	FPR	FNR
10%	0.5288	0.5070	0.4355	0.5350	0.4645	0.4655	**0.5537**	0.4590	0.4335
20%	0.5715	0.4700	0.3870	0.5998	0.4010	0.3995	**0.6415**	0.3580	0.3590
30%	0.5887	0.4130	0.4095	0.6937	0.3125	0.3000	**0.7208**	0.2860	0.2725
40%	0.6445	0.3955	0.3155	0.7520	0.2440	0.2520	**0.7947**	0.2045	0.2060
50%	0.6835	0.3515	0.2815	0.8193	0.1820	0.1795	**0.8472**	0.1515	0.1540
60%	0.7228	0.3220	0.2325	0.8748	0.1295	0.1210	**0.8965**	0.0975	0.1095
70%	0.7515	0.2730	0.2240	0.9115	0.0890	0.0880	**0.9325**	0.0640	0.0710
80%	0.7967	0.2335	0.1730	0.9440	0.0515	0.0605	**0.9540**	0.0415	0.0505
90%	0.8263	0.2000	0.1475	0.9647	0.0350	0.0355	**0.9720**	0.0215	0.0345
100%	0.8538	0.1740	0.1185	0.9792	0.0225	0.0190	**0.9782**	0.0175	0.0260

From the above tables, we can reach the following conclusions. Firstly, for each detection method, the detect accuracy is proportionate to the embedding rate while the FPR and FNR decrease according to the rise of embedding rate. Secondly, the detection performances for Miao's method $\eta = 4$ are better than the others, while detection performances for Miao's method $\eta = 1$ are the worst, which may be that the Miao's method $\eta = 4$ modifies the most pulse position and Miao's method $\eta = 1$ modifies the least pulse position. Thirdly, the proposed method outperforms the state of the arts especially at the low embedding rates. For Geiser's method, the proposed method

Table 4. Detection performance for Miao's method with $\eta = 2$ [18].

Embedding rate	Ren's method [21]			Tian's method [22]			The proposed method		
	ACC	FPR	FNR	ACC	FPR	FNR	ACC	FPR	FNR
10%	0.5735	0.4545	0.3985	0.5805	0.4360	0.4030	**0.6155**	0.3895	0.3795
20%	0.6583	0.3865	0.2970	0.7175	0.2975	0.2675	**0.7458**	0.2410	0.2675
30%	0.7418	0.3060	0.2105	0.8220	0.1785	0.1775	**0.8470**	0.1445	0.1615
40%	0.8103	0.2230	0.1565	0.9055	0.0920	0.0970	**0.9150**	0.0830	0.0870
50%	0.8705	0.1460	0.1130	0.9525	0.0540	0.0410	**0.9510**	0.0420	0.0560
60%	0.9077	0.0995	0.0850	0.9755	0.0240	0.0250	**0.9725**	0.0220	0.0330
70%	0.9380	0.0720	0.0520	0.9868	0.0125	0.0140	**0.9872**	0.0110	0.0145
80%	0.9470	0.0590	0.0470	0.9930	0.0060	0.0080	**0.9918**	0.0085	0.0080
90%	0.9515	0.0535	0.0435	0.9952	0.0030	0.0065	**0.9968**	0.0030	0.0035
100%	0.9643	0.0395	0.0320	0.9978	0.0020	0.0025	**0.9988**	0.0020	0.0005

Table 5. Detection performance for Miao's method with $\eta = 4$ [18].

Embedding rate	Ren's method [21]			Tian's method [22]			The proposed method		
	ACC	FPR	FNR	ACC	FPR	FNR	ACC	FPR	FNR
10%	0.6262	0.4130	0.3345	0.6470	0.3575	0.3485	**0.6847**	0.3240	0.3065
20%	0.7610	0.2890	0.1890	0.8270	0.1890	0.1570	**0.8353**	0.1665	0.1630
30%	0.8672	0.1480	0.1175	0.9240	0.0770	0.0750	**0.9253**	0.0705	0.0790
40%	0.9300	0.0820	0.0580	0.9725	0.0250	0.0300	**0.9722**	0.0255	0.0300
50%	0.9600	0.0460	0.0340	0.9880	0.0130	0.0110	**0.9882**	0.0105	0.0130
60%	0.9673	0.0330	0.0325	0.9938	0.0070	0.0055	**0.9950**	0.0050	0.0050
70%	0.9792	0.0225	0.0190	0.9960	0.0035	0.0045	**0.9980**	0.0015	0.0025
80%	0.9852	0.0150	0.0145	0.9988	0.0020	0.0005	**0.9982**	0.0015	0.0020
90%	0.9900	0.0120	0.0080	0.9992	0.0005	0.0010	**0.9995**	0.0005	0.0005
100%	0.9930	0.0075	0.0065	1.0000	0.0000	0.0000	**1.0000**	0.0000	0.0000

reaches over 60% accuracy when the embedding rate is only 10%, nearly the accuracy achieves more than 70% for Miao's method $\eta = 4$ at the same embedding rates, which indicates that although the proposed method has a low feature dimension the steganalysis is more effective than that of the state of the art.

6 Conclusion and Future Work

In this paper, the detection of AMR-based steganography on FCB is researched. The correlations among the pulse positions in the same subframe and in the same track are explored firstly and the self-information of the pulse-pair combinations in the same subframe and the mutual information of the two pulse in the same track are proposed to describe the correlation of pulse-position difference completely. Then, the two kind of features are applied as steganalysis features, whose feature dimension is only

100-dimensional. We proposed an SVM-based steganalysis scheme with the proposed features. The experimental results show that the detection performance of the proposed method is better than the state-of-the-art methods. In the future, we will try to employed some strategies to enhance the detection performance at low embedding rates.

Acknowledgements. This work was supported in part by National Natural Science Foundation of China under Grant Nos. U1536115 and U1405254, Natural Science Foundation of Fujian Province of China under Grant No. 2018J01093, Program for New Century Excellent Talents in Fujian Province University under Grant No. MJK2016-23, Program for Outstanding Youth Scientific and Technological Talents in Fujian Province University under Grant No. MJK2015-54, Promotion Program for Young and Middle-aged Teacher in Science & Technology Research of Huaqiao University under Grant No. ZQN-PY115, Program for Science & Technology Innovation Teams and Leading Talents of Huaqiao University under Grant No.2014KJTD13, Opening Project of Shanghai Key Laboratory of Integrated Administration Technologies for Information Security under Grant No. AGK201710.

References

1. Gaurav, K., Ghanekar, U.: Image steganography based on Canny edge detection, dilation operator and hybrid coding. J. Inf. Secur. Appl. **41**, 41–51 (2018)
2. El_Rahman, S.A.: A comparative analysis of image steganography based on DCT algorithm and steganography tool to hide nuclear reactors confidential information. Comput. Electr. Eng. (2016)
3. Majumder, A., Changder, S.: A novel approach for text steganography: generating text summary using reflection symmetry. Procedia Technol. **10**, 112–120 (2013)
4. Vidhya, P.M., Paul, V.: A method for text steganography using Malayalam text. Procedia Comput. Sci. **46**, 524–531 (2015)
5. Kar, D.C., Mulkey, C.J.: A multi-threshold based audio steganography method. J. Inf. Secur. Appl. **23**, 54–67 (2015)
6. Devi, R.R., Pugazhenthi, D.: Ideal sampling rate to reduce distortion in audio steganography. Procedia Comput. Sci. **85**, 418–424 (2016)
7. Dasgupta, K., Mondal, J.K., Dutta, P.: Optimized video steganography using genetic algorithm (GA). Procedia Technol. **10**, 131–137 (2013)
8. Kar, N., Mandal, K., Bhattacharya, B.: Improved chaos-based video steganography using DNA alphabets. ICT Express **4**, 6–13 (2018)
9. Cheng, J., Kot, A.C.: Steganalysis of halftone image using inverse halftoning. Signal Process. **89**, 1000–1010 (2009)
10. Mazurczyk, W.: VoIP steganography and its detection-a survey. ACM Comput. Surv. **46**, 1–21 (2013)
11. Tian, H., et al.: Optimal matrix embedding for voice-over-IP steganography. Signal Process. **117**, 33–43 (2015)
12. Kassim, M., Rahman, R.A., Aziz, M.A.A., Idris, A., Yusof, M.I.: Performance analysis of VoIP over 3G and 4G LTE network. In: IEEE, Kanazawa, Japan, pp. 37–41 (2017). http://ieeexplore.ieee.org/document/8298391/. Accessed 20 July 2018
13. Xiao, B., Huang, Y., Tang, S.: An approach to information hiding in low bit-rate speech stream. In: Proceedings of the IEEE GLOBECOM 2008 - 2008 IEEE Global Telecommunications Conference, pp. 1–5 (2008)

14. Liu, P., Li, S., Wang, H.: Steganography in vector quantization process of linear predictive coding for low-bit-rate speech codec. Multimedia Syst. **23**, 485–497 (2017)
15. Huang, Y., Liu, C., Tang, S., Bai, S.: Steganography integration into a low-bit rate speech codec. IEEE Trans. Inf. Forensics Secur. **7**, 1865–1875 (2012)
16. Nishimura, A.: Data hiding in pitch delay data of the adaptive multi-rate narrow-band speech codec. In: 2009 Fifth International Conference on Intelligent Information Hiding and Multimedia Signal Processing, pp. 483–486 (2009)
17. Geiser, B., Vary, P.: High rate data hiding in ACELP speech codecs. In: 2008 IEEE International Conference on Acoustics, Speech and Signal Processing, pp. 4005–4008 (2008)
18. Miao, H., Huang, L., Chen, Z., Yang, W., Al-hawbani, A.: A new method for covert communication via 3G encoded speech. Comput. Electr. Eng. **38**, 1490–1501 (2012)
19. Speech Codec Speech Processing Functions; Adaptive Multi-Rate—Wideband (AMR-WB) Speech Codec; Transcoding Functions (Release 6), document 3GPP TS 26.190 V6.1.1 (2005)
20. Miao, H., Huang, L., Shen, Y., Lu, X., Chen, Z.: Steganalysis of compressed speech based on Markov and entropy. In: Shi, Y.Q., Kim, H.-J., Pérez-González, F. (eds.) IWDW 2013. LNCS, vol. 8389, pp. 63–76. Springer, Heidelberg (2014). https://doi.org/10.1007/978-3-662-43886-2_5
21. Ren, Y., Cai, T., Tang, M., Wang, L.: AMR steganalysis based on the probability of same pulse position. IEEE Trans. Inf. Forensics Secur. **10**, 1801–1811 (2015)
22. Tian, H., et al.: Steganalysis of adaptive multi-rate speech using statistical characteristics of pulse pairs. Signal Process. **134**, 9–22 (2017)
23. Shannon, C.E.: A mathematical theory of communication. Bell Syst. Tech. J. **27**, 379–423 (1948)
24. Chang, C.-C., Lin, C.-J.: LIBSVM: a library for support vector machines. ACM Trans. Intell. Syst. Technol. **2**, 27:1–27:27 (2011)
25. Sklean source. https://github.com/scikit-learn/scikit-learn. Accessed 11 Nov 2018

State Consistency Checking for Non-reentrant Function Based on Taint Assisted Symbol Execution

Bo Yu⬭, Qiang Yang$^{(\boxtimes)}$ ⬭, and CongXi Song⬭

College of Computer, National University of Defense Technology,
Changsha 410073, China
290149807@qq.com

Abstract. Non-reentrant functions are commonly used in multi-thread programs, such as network services and other event-driven programs, to reserve some global states in a concurrent context. However, calling non-reentrant functions may bring several kinds of dangerous pointer dereference faults, and will lead to serious consequences such as program vulnerabilities. To beat this, this paper presents an approach to check state consistency against non-reentrant functions based on taint analysis and symbol execution technology. The proposed method records the program taint states and traces the data flow during the symbol execution process where some rules are specified to check the state consistency and exceptions such as null pointer reference, pointer double free and pointer use-after-free. We implement a proof-of-concept system SC2NRF based on the symbol execution framework *angr*. Further experiments show that our approach is able to effectively check state consistency of non-reentrant functions in binary programs.

Keywords: Binary program · State consistency · Non-reentrant function · Taint analysis · Symbol execution

1 Introduction

Non-reentrant functions have been widely used in large-scale real-life programs to provide user-friendly and smart functionality. There are usually referenced in a concurrent context a competing code sequences (e.g. threads or signal handlers) that may influence their states [1, 2]. If not carefully designed, the calling of programs with non-reentrant functions will lead to dangerous program state faults, and then introduce serious consequences, such as pointer dereference error. For clarity, we explain this problem using two CVEs with high scores, i.e. CVE-2018-0101 and CVE-2015-0291. In the first example, a buffer address in a non-reentrant function is assigned to a global pointer and a local buffer pointer. The local buffer pointer is freed in the tail of the function, while the global pointer still holds the buffer address. When the function is called again, a double-free vulnerability is triggered and a system crash will happen. In the another example CVE-2015-0291, there is a non-reentrant function in which the address of a local buffer *A* is assigned to another local pointer *B* and the length of buffer

J. Li et al. (Eds.): SPNCE 2019, LNICST 284, pp. 498–508, 2019.
https://doi.org/10.1007/978-3-030-21373-2_40

A is also assigned to another local variable *C*. When the function returned, local pointer *B* is set to NULL, but the local variable *C* is not processed accordingly. When this function is called again in a specified condition, the local pointer *B* remains there, but the value of local variable *C* holds the last time assignment, and the rest codes uses the value of *C* to access *B*, which leads to a null-pointer dereference vulnerability and results in process crash.

Both the two CVEs are exemplars about non-reentrant function problems, however, the issue cannot be avoided or resolved using existing thread safety techniques. The root cause is that the states of different variables are inconsistent in program semantics, and this inconsistency in a defect program implementation will cause serious software faults. Existing vulnerability detection technologies (e.g. double free checking and null-pointer checking techniques based on static and dynamic detection methods) cannot meet the requirements of checking such state inconsistency in non-reentrant function. Additionally, state inconsistencies also exist in block-chain applications such as smart contracts [3, 4]. The core problem of consistency checking is to find the relations of state variables and track the data flow of state variables in different execution paths. Based on the data flows in a non-reentrant function, existing defects in binary programs can be detected for further improvements.

According to above analysis of this inconsistency issue, we model it as a kind of consistency checking of program states between different program paths. The key factors to solve this issue are program state model, state analysis of program executions and dynamic consistency checking, and several techniques can be leveraged for this purpose. In general, both the static analysis and dynamic analysis can be used to analyze non-reentrant function. But static analysis solutions (e.g., [5]) usually have high false positives because many program states are dynamically generated [6], and arc only fit for small programs due to intrinsic challenge (i.e., alias analysis). Given a specific execution, the program state and data flow are deterministic, it is easier and more reliable to use dynamic analysis to check state consistency.

Several dynamic analysis techniques are widely adopted for program analysis, e.g., symbol execution [7], taint analysis [8] and information flow analysis [9]. Symbol execution could explore program paths thoroughly and discover program states in a more proactive way, but most solutions of symbol execution could not accurately analyze the relations of program states in different paths. Taint analysis can trace the taint propagation process and record the taint relation of program states, but existing solutions are not fine-grained enough for consistency checking. Current solutions based on information flow analysis include flow-insensitive, path-sensitive, and context-sensitive flow analysis [9–11], can build data flow in multi-grain levels. However, the disadvantages of these approaches are that the inter-process data flows are omitted, including call stack data flow and function return data flow, and data flows constructed are limited. Similar to heap overflow [12] and double-fetch [13, 14], state inconsistencies are root cause of program faults. Hence, a fine-grained state consistency analysis approach is necessary to solve this problem.

To address this issue, the data flow of non-reentrant function need to be constructed, and consistencies of data flow are modeled and checked in case of any non-consistencies in given non-reentrant function. Based on this idea, we present a state consistency checking method, and propose an inter-process data flow model for state consistency checking. Especially, we leverage symbol execution technology to construct multiple execution traces, together with the data flow constructed with taint analysis technique.

The main contributions of this paper include: (1) a state consistency checking framework (implemented as SC2NRF system) for constructing and analyzing inter-process data flow; (2) a symbol assisted taint analysis approach to trace data flow and build data flow relations; and (3) a rule-based state consistency checking algorithm to find data flow faults in program implementations.

The rest of this paper is organized as follows. In Sect. 2, the state consistency checking framework together with its working process and checking algorithm is discussed in detail. Section 3 describes the implementation and experiments of the SC2NRF system. Discussions and the conclusions are presented in Sect. 4.

2 State Consistency Checking Framework

We aim to discover state inconsistencies in program execution process with the combination of static control analysis and symbol execution. To achieve this goal, we define the data flow models of binary program in advance, and describe how to manually define consistency rules and automatically generate them based on heuristic algorithms.

Furthermore, to make the solution efficient and practical, we propose an approach which uses taint-assisted symbol execution methods to generate full data flow and detect potential inconsistencies of program states. At last we concrete values in path constraints and inconsistency constraints to speed up the checking process.

Figure 1 depicts the working flow of the proposed framework. Firstly, we analyze the target program with static analysis to construct the control flow graph and identify function call attributes. The program is run by taint assisted symbol execution and we will collect taint expressions and path constraints during each block's execution. Our analysis module then tries to build global data flow relations and checks any inconsistencies against given consistency rules. At last, inconsistency results are exported and identified for further analysis.

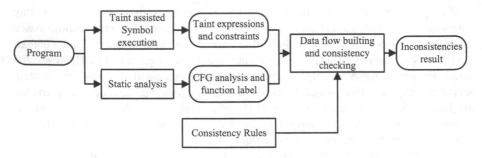

Fig. 1. Framework overview.

2.1   Information Flow Model for Code Block

A data flow shows how instructions correlate with each other with respect to the production and consumption of data. Efficiently generating a sound data flow for a binary slice has several challenges. First, program slicing requires a flow-sensitive and context-sensitive data flow analysis, which however has a run-time complexity exponential to the number of all possible paths in a program. Second, analyzing the data flow of binary programs poses some unique problems. Hence, we propose a data flow model upon a single code block of binary program to provide fine-grained data flow relations.

Definition 1. Given CFG_f the control flow graph of a non-reentrant function f and c a code block in CFG_f, we model the operation expressions list of block c as $I_c = \{y_i = op(x_i),$ for x_i in block $c\}$, where op is an algorithm operation or logic operation. Given two blocks in CFG_f namely c_1 and c_2, edge $e_{condition} = (c_1, c_2)$ records condition of block c_1 to block c_2 if data I_{c1} of c_1 flows to I_{c2} of c_2 under the *condition*.

Definition 2. We use DFR_c to denotes summary of data flow relation in block c. For each *dfr* in DFR_c, $dfr(y_i, y_j)$ means that there is a data flow relation between y_i and y_j. For example, if y_i is the buffer pointer of a input string, and yj is the string length of the input string, then $dfr(y_i, y_j)$ equals to $y_j = str\_length(y_i)$, where str_length is a typical kind of data flow relations. Other data flow relations include pointer aliasing, pointer repositioning, logic operations and so on.

We also define the typical data flow relations between code blocks as in Fig. 2. In Fig. 2(a), the fork flow model means that two data flows are forked by program execution conditions, and in Fig. 2(b), relation flow means that $flow_1$ and $flow_2$ are flowed to next code block with the relation r, and in Fig. 2(c), flow1 and flow2 are aggregated in one block by algorithm operation or logic operation. In our discussion, the three data flow relations are common in real-programs.

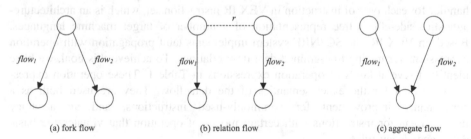

(a) fork flow   (b) relation flow   (c) aggregate flow

Fig. 2.   Three kinds of basic data flow relations.

Based on the data flow relations in Definitions 1 and 2, we model the fine-grained data flows along the execution traces of non-reentrant functions. However, data flow relations in real programs are complex and diverse, and the state consistency rules have to be defined based on data flow relations. To handle the issues mentioned above, our framework follows [15] to analyze data flow, which is an inter-procedural data flow analysis algorithm that uses *def-use* chains.

2.2 Taint-Assisted Symbol Execution Approach

To analyze a given non-reentrant function, we build the constraints between input bytes and the data flow relations of program code blocks by performing symbolic execution. However, existing symbol execution approaches are lack of support for fine-grained data flow analysis. We propose a new solution to mitigation this issue. More specifically, we tag data flows and taint them between code blocks. Based on the state-copy symbol execution techniques, we can calculate the overall data flow relationship in parallel, and check state consistency online. It is worthy that detecting state inconsistency between different program paths no matter there is any broken consistency rules.

The SC2NRF system tracks taint data flows of program paths. In general, it performs a fine-grained taint propagation analysis to track each value's source and data flow relation.

However, previous taint analysis solutions trace only the taint sources. The relation between different data flow and taint propagation process are not recorded. For example, programs may use *strlen* or other custom functions to infer some values (e.g., length) of the inputs, and then use them as size to allocate memory. In this case, operations upon the input buffer are indirectly affected by the inputs. Both the input buffer and variable that record the length of the buffer need to be record.

Classical dynamic taint analysis solutions usually do not propagate taint information for control dependencies [16], due to the concern of taint propagation efficiency. Instead, the SC2NRF system taints the symbol input, the data flow relation and their propagation by extending the symbol execution techniques to support fine-grained data flow taint. More specially, this system leverages the position of input bytes as taint attributes, and propagate these taint expressions along the trace.

For the generic instrumentation, we adopt a taint propagation policy based on the notion of data dependency [17–19]. If the output is a direct copy or transformation of the input, then it will be tainted if the input is tainted. This gives us a good coverage over all instructions and allows us to implement taint propagation without a special handler for each type of instruction in VEX IR instruction set, which is an architecture-agnostic, side-effects-free representation of a number of target machine languages. Based on VEX IR, the SC2NRF system implements taint propagation with operation expressions for tracing fine-grained data flow relations. To achieve this goal, we have identified several kinds of operation expressions in Table 1. These operation expressions account for the exact semantics of the data flow. They are used both as a performance improvement for commonly-used instructions, and an accuracy improvement for instructions with certain modes of operation that violates the basic data dependency rules.

To record the taint attributes and taint expression in symbol execution process, we have defined several kinds of set to aid analysis process. These recording set include store expression table $STORE_{REC}$, register expression table REG_{REC}, temp expression table TMP_{REC} and global taint label table $GLOBALTAINT_{REC}$, to record the memory store records, register writing records, local variables and immediate variables and global taint information in the symbol execution process.

Furthermore, the traces we collected only include user space instructions. Then some data flows will be missing when the system library functions are called. The

Table 1. Operation expression cases to generic data dependency propagation.

Instruction type	Reason and specific expression
Algorithm, logic and BITS wide transformation instructions	These instructions are recorded with the form of value = $op(EXP_{A1}, EXP_{A2},...)$, and new expression is built and inserted into TMP_{REC}, where op is a concrete instruction type and A_i is one of the arguments
System library call	These instructions are identified by function call graphs generated by static analysis, and are recorded with the form of value = $call(EXP_{A1}, EXP_{A2},...)$, and a new expression is built and inserted into TMP_{REC}, where $call$ is a concrete instruction type and A_i is one of the arguments
Memory store instructions	To identify the operation semantics of these instructions, both the target memory *address* and the *data* need to be checked before generating an expression. These writing data could be one of the memory store types, include arguments preparing for next function call with the form of $BP+positive\_immediate\_value$, local variable saving for temp results with the form of $BP-positive\_immediate\_value$ or $BP-negative\_immediate\_value$, reading return results from sub function call $SP-positive\_immediate$. Hence, the corresponding expression is inserted into $STORE_{REC}(address)$
Memory loading instructions	Similarly, the address of memory loading instructions could be one of the following types, namely loading immediate value with the form of $immediate\_value$, loading argument values from program stack with the form of $add(sp, positive\_immediate)$, loading temp results from program stack with the form of $add(bp, negative\_immediate)$, and so on, then an expression with the form is inserted into TMP_{REC}
Register writing instructions	In these register writing instructions, the written data should be one of the following types, immediate value with the form of $immediate$, or another temp result in TMP_{REC}. In all cases, the target register ID is checked to analyze the program semantic. For example, if the register ID is BP or SP, the instruction is going to preparing program stack for function call entry or function call exit. Otherwise, an expression is inserted into REG_{REC} to save the temp result
Register reading instructions	At first, if the register ID is in REG_{REC}, then get the operation expression from REG_{REC} and insert it into TMP_{REC}. Otherwise, we use the lazy initialization approach proposed in previous work to initialize the register and generate a temp expression and insert it into TMP_{REC}

SC2NRF system will check values of registers before and after the system call instructions (e.g., malloc). If the value of any register other than the destination operand has changed, a potential data flow missing is found. In this case, we will clean the taint attributes of the register to avoid false positives. Another choice is using summary information of syscalls to propagate the taint attributes for kernel execution.

The SC2NRF system leverages a lazy initialization policy to initialize registers in REG_{REC} and global memory in TMP_{REC}. As non-reentrant functions with initialization code that is responsible for setting various memory locations to initial values, setting up request handlers, and performing other housekeeping tasks cannot execute before analysis if some data structures are not initialized, superfluous paths based on normally infeasible environment conditions are introduced into the analysis. To mitigate this, SC2NRF system adopts a lazy approach to memory and register initialization. When the symbol execution engine encounters a memory read from uninitialized memory, it identifies other procedures that contain direct memory writes to that location, and labels them as initialization procedures. If an initialization procedure is identified, the state is duplicated: one state continues execution without modification, while the other one runs the initialization procedure before resuming execution. This allows the SC2NRF system to safely execute initialization code without the risk of breaking the analysis.

With the taint propagation process defined in Sect. 2.2, the SC2NRF system can build global information flow relations along the program traces in symbol execution. Let uses T_G for a global variable set and T_L as a local variable set, then the information flow of a non-reentrant function T_F can be built. Based on the taint expression and symbol execution, the information flow building process is shown as follows.

Let uses f as a non-reentrant function to be analyzed, CFG_f is the inter-process control flow graph of function f, c_i is a basic block in CFG_f's node set. Let uses $T_I = T_G \cup T_L \cup T_F$ to denote the variable set to be analyzed in code block $_c$, where $T_G = \{T_{g1}, T_{g2},..., T_{gm}\}$, $T_L = \{T_{l1}, T_{l2},..., T_{lm}\}$ and $T_F = \{T_{f1}, T_{f2},..., T_{fm}\}$. For each step in symbol execution, let uses c to the denote current code block executed. The following steps S1–S5 illustrate how to build the global information flow.

S1. Sets the arguments and global variables in function f as tainted variables;
S2. For each element $y_i = op(x_i)$ in I_c, The SC2NRF system uses the operation expression case to propagate the tainted variables and record the taint expression simultaneously.
S3. If y_i is an global variable in T_G, then we can search $STORE_{REC}$ using the key y_i and get $exp = STORE_{REC}[y_i]$, which is the information flow of y_i. Meanwhile, the taint label of y_i can be obtained by expression $GLOBALTAINT_{REC}[exp]$;
S4. If y_i is an local variable in T_I, then we can search TMP_{REC} using the key y_i and denote it as $exp = TMP_{REC}[y_i]$, which is the information flow of y_i. Also, the taint label of y_i can be obtained by expression $GLOBALTAINT_{REC}[exp]$;
S5. If y_i is an argument to a sub function in T_F, then it will be disposed according to the type. If y_i is a register argument, we search the REG_{REC} with expression y_i and denote it as $exp = REG_{REC}[y_i]$, which is the information flow of y_i, and the taint label of y_i is $GLOBALTAINT_{REC}[exp]$. Otherwise, the argument y_i is a stack argument, then we acquire the temp expression of y_i from $TMP_{REC}[y_i]$ and search the $STORE_{REC}$ with keyword $exp = TMP_{REC}[y_i]$, that is, we get $exp_1 = STORE_{REC}[exp]$,

which is the information flow of y_i. At last, the taint label of y_i can be expressed as $GLOBALTAINT_{REC}[exp_1]$.

2.3 State Consistency Checking Algorithm

To provide automated support for state consistency checking requirements, we have design an algorithm for analyzing the program states. The SC2NRF system checks the requirements of state consistency against a given consistency rules. Because the consistency rules describe the properties that non-reentrant functions must satisfy, the consistency rules by our algorithm are independent of a particular application.

Consistency rules defined in the SC2NRF system are expressed with condition lists. Meanwhile, the condition types include operation timing condition, space condition, other attribute condition, which usually are defined on function calls, value assignments, and memory positions and so on. For example, given a consistency rule of the case that a global buffer pointer and a local buffer pointer pointing to the same location, it follows a common operation list with the form of $R = <malloc, free, set\_to\_NULL>$ (otherwise double-free or use-after-free vulnerability will happen on this buffer).

Checking the consistency of program states is usually quite complex. We must follow different data flows of this buffer and check whether the common operation list is preserved during the execution process. To solve this issue, the SC2NRF system leverages a consistency checker to incrementally check program state when a new code block is executed. We design a checking algorithm to validate operation expressions of each code block's execution against current program states, which is show in Algorithm 1. To simplify the analysis process, we use function $get\_exp(x)$ to denote the retrieving of taint expression of variable x, $update\_state$ to denote the taint propagation and taint expressions computing.

Algorithm 1. Consistency checking algorithm for program state.	
Inputs	Consistency rules R; Code block c; Operation list $I_c=\{y_i=op(x_i)$, for x_i in block $c\}$; Current program state set S;
Outputs	Inconsistency results IR;

Step S0	Set $IR=\{\}$
	For each element $y_i=op(x_i)$ in I_c:
	    $exp=get\_exp(y_i)$
	    $S=update\_state(S, exp)$
	    For each state s in S:

Step S1	For each r in R:
	        If s_1.flow $\cap$ r.conditions $\neq \emptyset$ and p s_2.flow $\cap$ r.conditions $\neq \emptyset$:
	            $ir=<s_1, s_2, r.conditions>$
	            $IR.add(ir)$
	        End for
	    End for
	End for

Consistency rules are broken once their conditions are meet in two data flow, which is shown in Algorithm 1. Thus, this algorithm checks the program state from the angle of data flow relations, consistency conditions and new attributes in current code block c. It is easy to know that the computational complexity of this algorithm is $O(max(|R|) \times max(|S|) \times max(|I|))$, where the upper bound of $|I|$ is the max size of a code block size, and the upper bound of $|S|$ is the max number of paths in target non-reentrant function.

3   Implementation and Evaluations

In this section, we present the implementations and evaluation of the SC2NRF system. Our prototype implementation leverages *angr* as the symbol execution engine, which provides the state-copy path discovery and is suitable for our state management and consistency checking. In addition, the taint propagation and data flow relations are expressed in VEX immediate representation language. The taint analysis components takes about 1100 LOC of python codes, and this component is integrated with *angr*'s main code. Meanwhile, the *state* class of *angr* is also patched to support the taint expression computing.

The analysis environment is a 64-bit Ubuntu 16.04 system running on a computer of Intel Xeon (R) CPU E5-2630 v4 2.20 GHz and 64G RAM. As show in Table 2, 4 known vulnerabilities in 4 applications are validated in our experiment. During this test, three kinds of data were collected, including the number of code blocks, consumed time and the length of tainted instructions. The total number of code blocks in a tested function represents the workload of the analysis process, and the consumed time of each test is increased as the number of code blocks increases. The max length of tainted expressions in each function varies according to the computed data flow. Finally, the SC2NRF is able to discover all of them successfully. It is worth noting that, additional python codes are needed to analyze each function.

Table 2. Known state inconsistencies validated by SC2NRF system.

ID	Function	Code blocks	Consumed time (s)	Max length of tainted Exp.
CVE-2018-0101	sub_8079B40	895	4.12	29
CVE-2015-0291	sub_4406C0	1335	6.43	8
CVE-2015-8651	sub_996EC80	2006	8.02	24
CVE-2011-0073	sub_1046620E	720	3.94	76

For vulnerability CVE-2015-0327 in Openssl 1.0.2, it requires to invoke the *clinethello* message twice. During the execution process, different paths will check a common global pointer for reading and writing. Our solution can detect the inconsistencies in the two paths. Other samples also illustrate the effectiveness of our approach.

Actually, this solution in general will not generate false negatives since the rules are defined manually. The SC2NRF system can validate inconsistencies existing in known vulnerabilities but not all are not exploitable. Another disadvantage of SC2NRF is that the non-reentrant functions in binary program need to be identified manually by program analysis, which is a time-consume job.

4 Conclusions

State inconsistencies are the root cause of memory corruptions in non-reentrant functions. In this paper, we have proposed an approach for state consistency checking which based on consistency rules, and implemented a system called SC2NRF using famous symbol execution *angr*. The key components of SC2NRF system include taint assisted symbol execution module and consistency checking module. It is able to explore each program path in depth to find inconsistencies that are hard to detect and prone to miss by existing solutions. We also evaluated the SC2NRF system with several known CVEs, making our solution more practical. The experiment results show that this solution is effective.

References

1. Agre, J.R., Tripathi, S.K.: Modeling reentrant and nonreentrant software. In: Proceedings of the 1982 ACM Sigmetrics Conference on Measurement and Modeling of Computer Systems, pp. 163–178 (1982)
2. Wang, K., Chen, J.: Symmetry Detection for incompletely specified functions. In DAC Conference, pp. 434–437 (2004)
3. Kiffer, L., Rajaraman, R.: A better method to analyze blockchain consistency. In: Proceedings of the 2018 ACM SIGSAC Conference on Computer and Communications Security, pp. 729–744 (2018)
4. Tsankov, P., Dan, A., Drachsler Cohen, D., Gervais, A., Buenzli, F., Vechev, M.: Securify: practical security analysis of smart contracts. In: Proceedings of the 2018 ACM SIGSAC Conference on Computer and Communications Security, pp. 1–15 (2018)
5. Feist, J., Laurent, M., Potet, M.L.: Statically detecting use after free on binary code. J. Comput. Virol. Hacking Tech. **10**(3), 211–217 (2014)
6. Long, F., Sidiroglou-Douskos, S., Kim, D., Rinard, M.: Sound input filter generation for integer overflow errors. In: Proceedings of the 41st ACM SIGPLAN-SIGACT Symposium on Principles of Programming Languages, pp. 439–452 (2014)
7. Do, T., Fong, A.C.M., Pears, R.: Dynamic symbolic execution guided by data dependency analysis for high structural coverage. In: Maciaszek, L.A., Filipe, J. (eds.) ENASE 2012. CCIS, vol. 410, pp. 3–15. Springer, Heidelberg (2013). https://doi.org/10.1007/978-3-642-45422-6_1
8. Corin, R., Manzano, F.A.: Taint analysis of security code in the KLEE symbolic execution engine. In: Chim, T.W., Yuen, T.H. (eds.) ICICS 2012. LNCS, vol. 7618, pp. 264–275. Springer, Heidelberg (2012). https://doi.org/10.1007/978-3-642-34129-8_23

9. Bai, J.J., Wang, Y.-P., Lawall, J., Hu, S.: DSAC : effective static analysis of sleep-in-atomic-context bugs in kernel modules bugs in kernel modules. In: Proceedings of the 2018 USENIX Annual Technical Conference, pp. 587–600 (2018)

10. Yamaguchi, F., Maier, A., Gascon, H., Rieck, K.: Automatic inference of search patterns for taint-style vulnerabilities. In: Proceedings of the 2015 IEEE Symposium on Security and Privacy, pp. 797–812 (2015)

11. Xue, L., et al.: NDroid: towards tracking information flows across multiple android contexts. IEEE Trans. Inf. Forensics Secur. **14**(3), 814–828 (2019)

12. Jia, X., Su, P., Yang, Y., Huang, H., Feng, D.: Towards efficient heap overflow discovery. In: Proceedings of the 26th USENIX Security Symposium, pp. 989–1007 (2017)

13. Lu, K., Wang, P.-F., Li, G., Zhou, X.: Untrusted hardware causes double-fetch problems in the I/O memory. J. Comput. Sci. Technol. **33**(3), 587–602 (2018)

14. Wang, P., Lu, K., Li, G., Zhou, X.: A survey of the double-fetch vulnerabilities. Concurr. Comput. Pract. Exp. **30**(6), 1–20 (2018)

15. Tok, T.B., Guyer, Samuel Z., Lin, C.: Efficient flow-sensitive interprocedural data-flow analysis in the presence of pointers. In: Mycroft, A., Zeller, A. (eds.) CC 2006. LNCS, vol. 3923, pp. 17–31. Springer, Heidelberg (2006). https://doi.org/10.1007/11688839_3

16. Schwartz, E.J., Avgerinos, T., Brumley, D.: All you ever wanted to know about dynamic taint analysis and forward symbolic execution (but might have been afraid to ask). In: IEEE Symposium on Security and Privacy, pp. 317–331 (2010)

17. Daniel, M., Honoroff, J., Daniel, M., Charlie, M.: Engineering heap overflow exploits with Javascript. In: Proceedings of WOOT, pp. 1–6 (2008)

18. Duck, G.J., Yap, R.H., Carvallaro, L.: Stack bounds protection with low fat pointers. In: Network and Distributed System Security Symposium, pp. 1–20 (2017)

19. Neugschwandtner, M., Milani Comparetti, P., Haller, I., Bos, H.: The borg: nanoprobing binaries for buffer overreads. In: Proceedings of the 5th ACM Conference on Data and Application Security and Privacy, pp. 1–19 (2015)

SE Dots: A Sensitive and Extensible Framework for Cross-Region DDoS Processing

Li Su$^{(\boxtimes)}$, Meiling Chen, Jin Peng, and Peng Ran

China Mobile Research Institute, Beijing 100053, China
{suli, chenmeiling, pengjin, ranpeng}@chinamobile.com

Abstract. This paper proposed a SE Dots architecture and system with type awareness and high scalability to improve the ability to handle DDoS attacks across networks. Firstly, we designed a Dots protocol that includes attack type extensions, which enables accurate sensing of attack types. Then, the shunt capability module and adaptive matching module are extended in Dots framework to realize the adaptive selection of various disposal mechanisms, thus effectively extend the docking of different types of Mitigator to achieve a finer-grained cleaning effect. Technical verification shows that, under the same DDoS attack, the use of SE Dots scheme and architecture can improve the disposal efficiency by 17% and increase the user access success rate by 31.5% without increasing the cost of equipment. and it has strong advancement and practicability.

Keywords: Dots · DDoS attack · Attack linkage disposal · Flow cleaning

1 Background

Distributed Denial of Service (DDoS) is a type of resource-consuming attack, which exploits a large number of attack resources and uses standard protocols for attacking. DDoS attacks consume a large amount of target object network resources or server resources, so that the target object cannot provide network services normally. At present, DDoS attack is one of the most powerful and indefensible attacks on the Internet, and due to the extensive use of mobile devices and IoT devices in recent years, it is easier for DDoS attackers to attack with real attack sources (broilers). In 2018, the threat of DDoS attacks is still increasing. the traffic of DDoS reflection attack using memcached server vulnerabilities reached a peak of 1.7 Tbps. The opening ceremony of pyeongchang winter Olympics was subjected to DDoS attacks for up to 12 h. The industries affected by DDoS attack include banks, governments and games.

The current anti-DDoS modes mainly include three modes: one is single-point operation, such as self-built anti-DDoS equipment in the machine room [1]; the Second is cloud protection which achieve unified protection through flow lead; The third is joint prevention within an organization (called a domain) [2], such as anti-DDoS linkage processing and cloud cleaning centers. However, the current attack presents a distributed and large traffic trend, and the attack sources are spread all over the world. As far as the current situation is concerned, a certain range of defenses can no longer meet the anti-DDoS attack requirements, and comprehensive cross-network collaboration is required [3]. In order to shield operator differences from defending DDoS

J. Li et al. (Eds.): SPNCE 2019, LNICST 284, pp. 509–517, 2019.
https://doi.org/10.1007/978-3-030-21373-2_41

attacks across the entire network (global), the IETF working group proposed the DOTS framework [4], which is used to automate and standardize DDoS countermeasures and to shield differences in various anti-ddos solutions.

The existing DOTS implementation mechanisms have two problems: the first is that the mitigation request only defines the IP address, port range, protocol type, FQDN (fully qualified domain name), URI of the attacked target, but does not contain the attack type or bandwidth. As a result, the amount of information that is being attacked by the attacking target is insufficient. The second problem is that DOTS framework only uses BGP to process attack traffic. The near-source black hole operation will discard all traffic, which directly leads to the normal traffic loss of the attacked object. On the basis of DOTS, this paper proposes a flexible extended DOTS architecture that can perceive the attack types. Firstly, by extending the mitigation request method of signal channel and clarifying the attack type, the Mitigator can specifically handle the attack in the mitigation request; The second is to add request methods of the DDoS http mitigation and shunt policy module, which can adaptively select attack defense method according to the attack site, and improve the DDoS defense under the DOTS framework.

2   Existing Technologies and Shortcomings

At present, the main technologies of DDOS attack protection include: single point device protection, reverse proxy (cloud protection) and linkage defense.

Single point protection relies on the independent deployment of DDOS devices for protection. This method is simple to deploy, but due to the limited processing ability of a single device for attacks, it has insufficient capacity to deal with large traffic attacks that cause network congestion. Moreover, it is difficult to conduct uniform detection and disposal when different devices are deployed upstream and downstream in one network [5].

Reverse proxy, also known as cloud protection, is a dedicated cloud platform that implements DDOS attack detection and filtering. When the system detects abnormal traffic, it actively redirects traffic to the cloud acceleration server, and the cloud protection equipment will perform cleaning operation and then re-injected to the router of the business system [6]. The cloud protection method adopts centralized deployment, which is suitable for the cleaning needs of small and medium-sized enterprises or services; However, in the case of large-scale traffic attack, the cost of flow lead is huge and may cause new network congestion. Therefore, the cloud cleaning method is not suitable for large-scale traffic cleaning.

The linkage disposal technology is to construct a linkage system separately, analyze the data such as attack alarms issued by different anti-DDOS devices, coordinate and dispose of them. The advantage of adopting this mode is that it can deal with attacks in complex networks, especially in the case of attacks against large traffic, which can mobilize the processing capabilities of existing networks to achieve near-source distributed cleaning Under the premise of not adding new equipment, more effective cleaning of larger attack traffic can be realized, especially suitable for scenarios such as Metropolitan area network, IDC, customer business collaborative protection and so on [7].

DOTS is a cross-domain (cross-organization) processing framework for DDoS attacks defined by the IETF, and also is an implementation method of linkage processing technology. The DOTS establishes a general architecture, method and processing mechanism without considering specific attack disposal devices and means [8], which is very suitable for use in the scenarios of network operation and business operation separation. DOTS framework includes the following four parts: Attack Target, DOTS Client, DOTS Server and Mitigator.

The attack mitigation process of the DOTS framework is shown in Fig. 1.

The process is as follows:

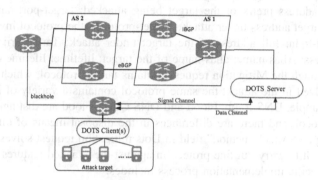

Fig. 1. DOTS framework diagram based on BGP mitigation mode

(1) Attack target is attacked by DDoS, then DOTS Client sent mitigation request to DOTS Server;

(2) Receiving requests, DOTS Server parses request packets to obtain attack details, such as IP address information, etc.;

(3) Using BGP to generate an optimal path through BGP neighbor relationships;

(4) Mitigator chooses one or more of the nearest routers for black holes based on BGP results.

There are two interfaces between DOTS client and DOTS server: Signal Channel [9] and Data Channel. Signal Channel [10] is used for client to seek attack mitigation from server and server to inform client of the state of the mitigation process. The Data Channel is used for related configuration and policy information exchange (between client and server).

There are two implementation shortcomings in the existing DOTS framework: first, only the message communication mechanism is defined, and the attack type transmitted is not defined, which will reduce the Mitigator's processing capability and efficiency. Second, the existing mechanism only supports mitigation notification through BGP, and the mitigation notification based on BGP can only reach the routing device for traffic lead, but cannot convey the attack type and mitigation mechanism, which is not conducive to timely attack disposal, making it difficult to meet the demand by using BGP traffic lead and disposal.

3   SE DOTS Technical Principle

SE DOTS is to add the definition of attack type in the existing DOTS framework, which can effectively improve the processing efficiency and accuracy of DOTS linkage. At the same time, extend the message communication mechanism based on HTTP to form the processing capability of classification and extension.

3.1   Attack Type Awareness

In the current mechanism, when the DOTS client detects a DDoS attack, it sends a mitigation request through the signal channel, which contains the following fields: target-prefix: address prefix of the target being attacked; target-port-range: the port range of the target address under attack; Target-protocol: the protocol involved in this attack; Target-fqdn: full address of the target under attack; Target-uri: URL of the attacked address; Alias-name: alias-name of the target; lifetime: lifetime of mitigation requests. Although the Mitigation request contains target-protocol, which refers to the protocol involved in the attack, the same protocol contains a variety of DDoS attack types. For example, DNS Reply Flood and DNS Query Flood are distinguished below the DNS protocol, and there are differences in the disposal means of different attack types. Adding an "Attack method" field in Dots mitigation request solves the problem that it is difficult to carry out fine protection against the attacked features of the attack target. The specific implementation process includes:

(1)   When Attack Target creates an identifier, add the "Target-attack-Type" field;
(2)   DOTS Client responds to requests and sends messages to DOTS Server according to existing processes;
(3)   DOTS Server parses the request and generates mitigation request messages according to the type requirements of Mitigator;

SE DOTS adds "target-attack-type" and "target-bandwidth" fields to the mitigation request, which belongs to the Signal message generated by the attack target and sent to DOTS Client.

For the target-DDoS-type field, we define it as a string Type, and define the two fields according to the attack method and extension name. Similar to other existing linkage disposal technologies, there may be problems in the actual network environment, that attack target and mitigator (such as cleaning equipment) belong to different models of different vendors, because different vendors have different definitions of Attack in understanding and implementation. When an attack occurs, some devices may not be considered as an attack, and the effect of linkage cleaning may not be achieved. It is also possible that the detection device considere it as A type attack, while the cleaning device consider it as B type attack. When performing the cleaning schedule, it will cause the problem of incorrect cleaning or over-cleaning. Both of these errors will cause the normal business to fail to link. Therefore, it is necessary to unify the attack definition, form a standard attack definition, and solve the problem of cleaning errors from the source. we give out a complete format for DDoS attacks as [protocol level] [protocol name] [message name/operation name/port] [attack methods feature description field 1] [attack methods feature description field 2] [attack methods describe the standard field], interval between each field operators use "," symbol or any other symbol agreed.

For example: HTTP Get Flood(CC) definition,we defined the target-Attack-Type field as:

```
{
"Attack-Name":" Application _Layer, HTTP, Get,,, Flood"
"Attack-Alias":"HTTP CC Flood"
}
```

Based on the perceptual extension, the DOTS Server can accurately inform Mitigator of the objects and attack types that need to be disposed when the mitigation instructions are delivered to the Mitigation, so that the Mitigator can be accurately disposed.

3.2   Disposal Capacity Expansion (Extensible)

DOTS framework currently implements DDoS attack mitigation notification using BGP. Under the existing mechanism, BGP mode mitigation includes two types of measures: First, the traffic is drained through the BGP mechanism, and the dedicated cleaning equipment/cleaning center handle the traffic. Second, black hole routing (discarding) is performed on the traffic through the BGP mechanism. However, there are some deficiencies in how to choose these two kinds of measures [11]: in the case of super-large traffic attack (occupying full bandwidth), it is difficult to schedule the traffic on a large scale in the BGP shunt mode; However, when the attack intensity is lower than the limit, the BGP black hole operation drops all the traffic, which directly leads to the loss of normal traffic of the attacked object.

In SE DOTS, the HTTP request handling module of DOTS framework is extended, and a traffic shunt policy module is added between the DOTS Server and the Mitigator to determine which mitigation method is adopted by the DOTS server. The DOTS system architecture diagram that extends the HTTP mitigation communication approach is shown in Fig. 2.

Cleaning equipment refers to the equipment specially used for DDoS attack traffic cleaning, including hardware and software. Cleaning center refers to a centralized cleaning equipments cluster.

The new process is as follows:

(1) Mitigation request issued by DOTS client;
(2) DOTS server receives the mitigation request, parses the request, transfers the mitigation parameters to the shunt policy module, and starts the shunt strategy to select the BGP or HTTP mitigation mode;
   (a) When BGP mode is selected, the processing flow is the same as Fig. 1;

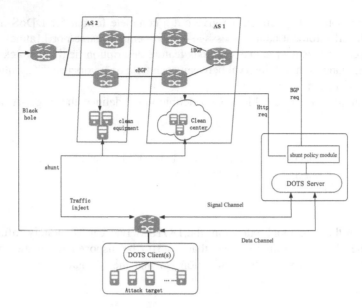

Fig. 2. The DOTS system architecture diagram extending the HTTP method

(b) When select HTTP mode, send the mitigation request to the corresponding cleaning equipment (or cleaning center). The cleaning equipment (or cleaning center) will trigger the flow lead. After processing, the normal business flow will be injected back into the attack target link.

The flow of the shunt policy module is shown in Fig. 3 below.

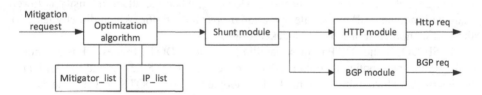

Fig. 3. Processing flow of shunt policy module

Among them, Mitigator_list is the list library of protection devices, and IP_list is the corresponding protection IP of the protection device. The main functions of the shunt strategy module are as follows:

(1) DOTS server parsers parameters, including: target-prefix, target-port-range, target-protocol, target-fqdn, lifetime, target-bandwidth, and target-attack-type;

(2) Take the parsed parameters as the input of the preferred algorithm:
  (a) Compare the target-prefix with the IP_list of the protection device to find the corresponding mitigation provider;
  (b) Select a cleaning device according to the target-protocol;
  (c) Match the bandwidth to the cleaning device capability, and the cleaning device is completely processed within the cleaning capability range. When the capacity is insufficient, the shunt part performs BGP processing. If the cleaning device is selected, select different cleaning devices according to the target-attack-type.
(3) According to the results of the preferred algorithm to select disposal method: when the cleaning device is used for protection, the HTTP module is used to construct an HTTP request, such as POST http://ip:port/traffic/...; when using BGP disposal, BGP request is sent using the BGP module construct.

4 SE DOTS Technical Advantages Analysis and Experiments

In SE DOTS, the Attack Target can report all the attacked situations to the DOTS Server through one message sending, while the DOTS Server can release different types of Attack disposal methods through the shunt module, reducing the communication overhead and improving the efficiency and accuracy of disposal.

Carry out simulation experiments to simulate the existing network in the following experimental network:

- The bandwidth of link A where the protection object resides: 10G;
- traffic model of protection objects: normal service traffic 500M, which are HTTP requests [12] (TCP SYN traffic is generated at the same time); The total limited bandwidth is 1G, and cleaning is performed when the bandwidth exceeds 1G;
- Total attack traffic: 0–10G, using hybrid attack traffic model; There are four types of attacks: UDP Flood (20%), MemCached Flood (25%), SYN Flood (30%) and HTTP Flood [13] (25%). MemCached is not included in UDP and the SYN generated by HTTP is not counted repeatedly.
- The total bandwidth of BGP traction link B: 20G, the use rate of the flow in this link accounts is 60% (simulates existing network), the maximum limitation is 90%, that means that the maximum drainage capacity is 6G;
- Cluster cleaning ability: about 90% of the shunted attack.

Attack Target pre-configured the threshold of SYN, UDP, MemCached, HTTP Attack [14], (assuming that attacks use these four types), perform joint cleaning experiment using environment parameters above [15]. The experimental results of black hole routing (dots-bgp-bhr), bgp-based shunted mode (dots-bgp-fc) and SE DOTS are shown in Figs. 4 and 5 below.

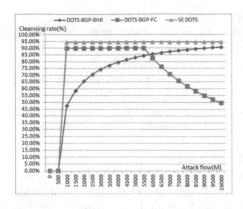 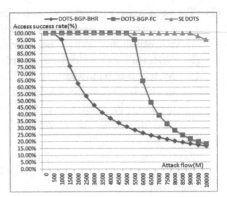

Fig. 4. Cleaning rate comparison during attack   **Fig. 5.** Comparison of access success rate

In the above scenario, DOTS-BGP-BHR mode can only be discarded according to the sett type. After the attack of the same type exceeds the normal threshold, it can only be discarded according to a certain proportion, so that the access success rate of normal users becomes lower. In the BGP-based DPS-BGP-PC mode, drainable traffic can be disposed. However, because the type of attack cannot be detected, all traffic need to be cleaned, resulting in a waste of network resources and cleaning capacity. Compare the main indicators of DOTS-BGP-BHR, DOTS-BGP-PC, and SE DOTS during the 0–10G attack and calculate the average value. The list is shown in Table 1.

Table 1. SE DOTS attack processing comparative analysis table.

	Cleaning rate	Normal flow rate of false cleaning	User access success rate
DOTS-BGP-BHR	80.0%	63.6%	36.4%
DOTS-BGP-FC	77.5%	31.9%	68.1%
SE DOTS	94.5%	0.4%	99.6%

The experimental results show that, under the same disposal mechanism, SE DOTS can effectively improve the cleaning capacity by 17.0% compared with the existing mechanism dots-bgp-fc, reducing the mis-cleaning traffic/increasing the user access success rate by 31.5%. This mechanism effectively cooperates with the protection capabilities of the existing network and protects the network smoothly and the healthy operation of the business.

5   Conclusion

In this paper, a comprehensive analysis of DDOS attack protection technology is carried out. Based on the DOTS mechanism of IETF, an SE DOTS framework with the capability of sensing and disposing protocol expansion is designed. Based on the analysis and experimental results, the SE DOTS linkage disposal technology can better identify and handle attacks, ensure the success rate of users accessing services. From the development of the industry, the DOTS linkage disposal technology will be further extended in the scenarios of operators and IDC service providers. It is necessary to further promote industry standardization in subsequent work and reduce the risks brought by DDOS attacks.

References

1. Akamai: How to Protect Against DDoS Attacks - Stop Denial of Service (2016). https://www.akamai.com/us/en/resources/protect-against-ddos-attacks.jsp. Accessed 10 Jan 2017
2. Rodrigues, B.B., Bocek, T., Stiller, B.: Multi-domain DDoS mitigation based on blockchains. In: IFIP International Conference on Autonomous Infrastructure Management and Security, June 2017
3. Rodrigues, B., Bocek, T., Lareida, A., Hausheer, D., Rafati, S., Stiller, B.: A blockchain-based architecture for collaborative DDoS mitigation with smart contracts. In: Tuncer, D., Koch, R., Badonnel, R., Stiller, B. (eds.) AIMS 2017. LNCS, vol. 10356, pp. 16–29. Springer, Cham (2017). https://doi.org/10.1007/978-3-319-60774-0_2
4. Mortensen, A., Andreasen, F., Reddy, T., Teague, N., Compton, R.: Draft-ietf-dots-architecture [EB/OL].https://tools.ietf.org/html/draft-ietf-dots-architecture-10
5. Dobbins, R., Migault, D., Fouant, S., Moskowitz, R., Teague, N.: Draft-ietf-dots-use-cases [EB/OL].https://tools.ietf.org/html/draft-ietf-dots-use-cases-16
6. Mortensen, A., Moskowitz, R., Reddy, T.: Draft-ietf-dots-requirements [EB/OL].https://tools.ietf.org/html/draft-ietf-dots-requirements-16
7. Steinberger, J., Kuhnert, B., Sperotto, A., Baier, H., Pras, A.: Collaborative DDOS defense using flow-based security event information. In: NOMS 2016–2016 IEEE/IFIP Network Operations and Management Symposium, pp. 516–522, April 2016
8. Grady, J., Christiansen, C.A., Price, C., Richmond, C.: Worldwide DDoS prevention products and services 2013–2017 forecast. IDC #239954e, vol. 1, March 2013
9. Reddy, T., Boucadair, M., Patil, P., Mortensen, A., Teague, N.: Draft-ietf-dots-signal-channel [EB/OL].https://tools.ietf.org/html/draft-ietf-dots-signal-channel-26
10. Boucadair, M., Reddy, T., Nishizuka, K., Xia, L., Patil, P.: Draft-ietf-dots-data-channel [EB/OL].https://tools.ietf.org/html/draft-ietf-dots-data-channel-24
11. Fayaz, S.K., Tobioka, Y., Sekar, V.: Bohatei: flexible and elastic DDoS defense. In: 24th USENIX Security Symposium, August 2015
12. Jiao, J., Ye, B.: Detecting TCP-based DDoS attacks in Baidu cloud computing data centers. In: IEEE 36th Symposium on Reliable Distributed Systems (SRDS) (2017)
13. Hong, K., Kim, Y., Choi, H., Park, J.: SDN-assisted slow HTTP DDoS attack defense method. IEEE Commun. Lett. **22**, 688–691 (2018)
14. Stevanovic, D., Vlajic, N.: Application-layer DDoS in dynamic web-domains: building defenses against next-generation attack behavior. In: IEEE Conference on Communications and Network Security, October 2014
15. Nagpal, B., Sharma, P., Chauhan, N., Panesar, A.: DDoS tools: classification, analysis and comparison. In: 2015 2nd International Conference on Computing for Sustainable Global Development (INDIACom) (2015)

Scheme, Model and Application for Data

A One-Way Variable Threshold Proxy Re-signature Scheme for Mobile Internet

Yanfang Lei[1], Mingsheng Hu[1](✉), Bei Gong[2], Lipeng Wang[1], and Yage Cheng[1]

[1] College of Information Science and Technology, Zhengzhou Normal University,
Zhengzhou 450044, China
hero_jack@163.com
[2] College of Computer Sciences, Beijing University of Technology,
Beijing 100124, China

Abstract. In recent years, the mobile Internet has been rapidly developed and widely used. Aiming at the problems of the weak computing power of mobile internet mobile terminal equipment, limited energy supply and high security requirements due to the complexity of mobile Internet environment, we proposes a secure and efficient server-assisted verification threshold proxy re-signature scheme, and the correctness of the program is verified. The proposed scheme includes a threshold proxy re-signature algorithm and a server-assisted authentication protocol scheme. Threshold proxy re-signature is a technique of proxy re-signature using threshold, which can decentralize the proxy's signature rights. In the scheme, the verifier and the server send the complex signature verification operation to a semi-trusted server through the protocol, which effectively reduces the computational load of the verifier. The security analysis results show that the new scheme is safe and it is proved that the scheme is safe under collusion attack and adaptive selection message attack under the standard model. The performance analysis results show that the new scheme proposed in this paper has shorter signature length, less computational cost, higher verification efficiency and better adaptability to the mobile Internet environment.

Keywords: Threshold proxy re-signature ·
Server-assisted authentication protocol · Secret sharing ·
Unforgeability · Robustness · Completeness

1 Introduction

With the advent of the information age and the rapid development of the information technology, the Internet has penetrated into all aspects of our daily

Supported by the National Natural Science Foundation of China (Grant No. U1304614, U1204703), Henan Province Education Science Plan General Topic "Research on Trusted Degree Certification Based on Block-chain" (Grant No. (2018)-JKGHYB-0279), Zhengzhou Innovative Science and Technology Talent Team Construction Project Fund Project (Grant No. 131PCXTD597), Henan Science and Technology Project (Grant No. 162102310238).

J. Li et al. (Eds.): SPNCE 2019, LNICST 284, pp. 521–537, 2019.
https://doi.org/10.1007/978-3-030-21373-2_42

lives. The development of mobile communication technology is changing with each passing day. Mobile terminals such as Ipad, smart phones, wireless sensors, and electronic keys have become an indispensable part of our lives and work. The further development of network technology has brought more convenience to our lives. The rise of e-commerce and e-government has brought people from the real material world into a convenient electronic age. Online shopping, stock operations, communication and access to network resources can be carried out anytime, anywhere via the Internet. However, due to the limitations of the mobile Internet terminal device itself, the computing power is generally weak, which makes it necessary for people to perform a large amount of time for verification in resource request and resource access. In addition, because the mobile Internet environment is more complicated, there are higher requirements for security. Therefore, it is necessary to design a scheme that can solve terminal computing power, limited energy supply and high security to be applied in the mobile Internet environment.

Quisquater et al. first proposed a server-assisted verification signature scheme in 2000, which included a standard signature system and a server-assisted verification protocol. The scheme assigned complex signature verification operations to a semi-trusted server for execution. It effectively reduced the amount of certifier calculations and adapts to low-end electronic devices such as smartphones, electronic keys, and wireless sensors. In 2005, Girault et al. presented a formal security model for server-assisted computing at the Asia-Pacific conference. In 2008, Girault et al. proposed a security definition for server-assisted verification signatures in [1]. In 2011, a provable secure server-assisted verification signature scheme was presented in [2], but this scheme could not effectively resist the collusion attack between the server and the signer. Later, combined with the aggregate signature and server-assisted verification signatures, Wu et al. [3] proposed a cryptosystem for server-assisted authentication of aggregated signatures. This system consisted of an aggregate signature system and a server-assisted authentication protocol. It aggregated the different signatures of multiple messages into one signature, which greatly saved broadband expenditure, saved verification time and improved verification efficiency.

Proxy re-signature is an important research direction in cryptography, and scholars who at home and abroad have devoted a lot of work to this direction. In [4], the security model of proxy re-signature was first proposed and given two schemes, and a strict security proof was given based on the random prediction model. In [5], the further definition of the security attribute definition of proxy re-signature was given, and a secure proxy re-signature scheme under a standard model was constructed based on the literature [6]. The defects of this scheme were presented and an improvement method was given in [7]. In [8], the author proposed a one-way multi-purpose proxy re-signature scheme, but the signature verification overhead increased linearly with the increase of the number of re-signature layers. In recent years, proxy re-signature has attracted much attention, and some proxy re-signature schemes with special properties have been proposed, such as identity-based proxy re-signature [9], lattice-based proxy re-signature [10,11]. Although the proxy re-signature scheme has a wide range of applications, it also has some defects. For example, once the re-signature key is compromised, the security of the solution will be compromised. In addition, the agent's rights are too concentrated and need to be decentralized in order to make the solution more reliable. Then there is the concept of threshold proxy re-signature. Threshold proxy re-signature is a technique for thresholding the proxy re-signature, and dispersing the signature right of the proxy. Between two signers, the original only one agent is set as n semi-trusted agents, and the re-signature key is distributed to each agent by secret sharing technology. The re-signature can only be synthesized when at least t agents send their valid verifiable signatures. Threshold proxy re-signature schemes could be used to reduce public key management overhead, space-saving specific path traversal certificates, and generate manageable weak group signatures [12–14].

With the rapid development of cloud computing and big data, cloud computing providers with powerful computing capabilities have become agents in proxy re-signing schemes, and low-end computing devices are very important cloud computing terminals [15]. These devices have weak computing power, limited energy supply and short response times. However, most of the current proxy re-signature signature verification algorithms require complex bilinear-parings operations and cannot be adapted to low-end computing devices with weak computing power. In addition, we consider that in theory, the trustee Alice should not bear any security risks, and the risks faced should be borne by the trustee Bob. In order to solve above problems, this paper combines the security attributes of server-assisted verification signature and threshold proxy re-signature, and proposes a formal model of one-way server-assisted verification variable threshold proxy re-signature, and constructs a one-way server-assisted verification variable threshold proxy re-signing scheme that can effectively resist collusion attacks. However, the one-way scheme can achieve two-way function through the conversion between the trustee Alice and the delegator Bob. The verifier completes the verification of the signature with a small computational cost by executing a server authentication protocol with the server, which improves the verification efficiency of the signature. The verification algorithm reduces complex bilinear-parings operations and has lower computational time overhead, so it can be better adapted to the mobile Internet environment.

2   Prerequisite Knowledge

2.1   Bilinear Pairings

Bilinear pairings function is a bilinear map between two cyclic groups. As all the points in elliptic curve gathered into a group, bilinear parings function applies just in elliptic curve. Let G_1 and G_2 be two cyclic groups of the prime order q, where q is a large prime number. Let g is a generator of G_1. Assume that the discrete logarithm problems in both G_1 and G_2 are hard to solve. Let $e : G_1 \times G_1 \longrightarrow G_2$ is a bilinear map that satisfies the following [16,17] properties:

a. Bilinear: For any $\tau_1, \tau_2 \in Z$, satisfy $e(\tau_1 g_1, \tau_2 g_2) = e(g_1, g_2)^{\tau_1 \tau_2}$ for all $g_1, g_2 \in G_1$.

b. Non-degenerate: There is $g_1, g_2 \in G_1$, such that $e(g_1, g_2) \neq 1$.

c. Computable: There is an efficient algorithm to compute $e(g_1, g_2)$, for any $g_1, g_2 \in G_1$.

2.2   Computational Diffie-Hellman (CDH) Problem and Corresponding Hypothesis

Based on the group, we can define the following hard cryptographic problem:

Definition 1 CDH problem [18]: Give a triple $(g, \tau_1 g, \tau_2 g) \in G_1^3$ for $\tau_1, \tau_2 \in Z_q^*$, find the elements $\tau_1 \tau_2 g$.

In order to obtain the following safety analysis results, we introduce the following hypothesis.

Definition 2 CDH Hypothesis [18]: There is no algorithm that can solve the CDH problem in group G_1 with a non-negligible probability in polynomial time.

2.3   Secret Sharing Model

Distribution Stage: Let q be a prime number and secret $s \in Z_q^*$ to be distributed. Suppose there is a threshold of (t, n): in a group with n members $P_i(i = 1, 2, ..., n)$, the secret s can be recovered when at least t members cooperate. The basic idea is: first randomly generate $\alpha_1, \alpha_2, ..., \alpha_{t-1}$ and generate the function $F(x) = s + \alpha_1 x + \alpha_2 x^2 + ... + \alpha_{t-1} x^{t-1}$, then calculate $X_i = F(i) \in Z_Q^*$ and issue (i, X_i) to each member P_i, note that we can get $X_0 = F(0) = s$ when $i = 0$.

Reconstruction Stage: Let $\Phi \subseteq 1, 2, ..., n$ and $|\Phi| \geq t$, where $|.|$ represents the order of the set Φ. Then, the function $F(x) = \sum_{j \in \Phi} \chi_{x_j}^{\Phi} x_j$ where parameter $\chi_{x_j}^{\Phi} = \prod_{k \in \Phi, k \neq j} \frac{x-k}{j-k}$ and note that $\chi_{x_j}^{\Phi} \in Z_q^*$ is the Lagrange interpolation polynomial coefficient [19]. Finally, we can recover the secret $s = F(0) = \sum_{j \in \Phi} \chi_{0_j}^{\Phi} x_j$ where $\chi_{0_j}^{\Phi} x_j = \prod_{k \in \Phi, k \neq j} \frac{0-k}{j-k}$.

3   Scenario Model and Security Definition

3.1   Model of Server Auxiliary Threshold Proxy Re-signature Scheme

The threshold proxy re-signature scheme is a tuple in a polynomial time (Setup, Keygen, Rekey, Sign, Resign, Verify, Server-setup, Sever-verify) contains the following eight algorithms.

Setup(1^k) $\rightarrow$ *cp*: Given a constant k, and runs the algorithm to generate a public parameter *cp*.

Keygen$(cp) \to (pk, sk)$: Given the system parameter cp, we obtain the signer's public and private keys (pk, sk).

Rekey(pk_A, sk_A, pk_B, sk_B): After inputting (pk_A, sk_A, pk_B, sk_B), generate a re-signature key $r_{A \to B}$. The re-signature key generation algorithm Rekey distributes the re-signature key $r_{A \to B}$ into n shares, and secretly distributes the n sub-keys $rk_{A \to B}^i$ to agents n for storage. The agent P_i can generate a re-signature sub-key $rk_{A \to B}^i$ and verifiable its public key $\nu k_{t,i}$ according to the provided threshold value t. It should be noted that the key sk_A is unnecessary here.

Sign (m, sk_A): Given a message m and the private key sk_A of the trustee Alice, an original signature $\sigma_{A(m)}$ of the message m corresponding to the public key pk_A is generated.

Resign: The Combiner collects partial re-signatures from each agent and confirms that when at least t are legal, the Combiner synthesizes them into a re-signature $\sigma_{B(m)}$ and outputs it.

Verify: Given the public key pk, the message m and the signature σ to be verified, if σ is the valid signature of the message m corresponding to the public key pk, output 1, otherwise, output 0.

Server-setup(cp): Given the parameter cp, a string Vst is generated for the verifier.

Server-verify(Vst, m, pk, σ): For the string Vst, the public key pk and the message signature pair (m, σ), if the server lets the verifier confirm that σ is a valid signature, output 1, otherwise, output 0.

Because the signer's computing power is limited, complex cryptographic operations cannot be performed. Therefore, a large computing task can be transferred to the server through an interaction protocol with the server, and the signature verification can be completed by using the server.

3.2 Security Definition

The security of the server-assisted verification threshold proxy re-signature includes at least the unforgeability and robustness of the threshold proxy re-signature and the completeness of the server-assisted authentication protocol $Server - verify$. Robustness and unforgeability means that even if an attacker colludes with $t - 1$ agents, the signature scheme will still work correctly, but the attacker cannot resign. This ensures that a legal signature of a new message cannot be generated in the case of a joint attack. The completeness of the server-assisted authentication protocol $Server - verify$ ensures that the server cannot convince the verifier that an illegal signature is legitimate.

Next, based on the definition of completeness given in document [20], this paper defines the completeness of server-assisted authentication protocol under joint attack and adaptive selection message attack by designing game rules between challenger and attacker.

In the Game1 below, since the attacker and the trustee Alice can be colluded, the attacker can obtain the trustee's private key and can generate the original signature of any message. By conducting a limited server-assisted verification challenge with the challenger, the attacker's goal is to convince the verifier that an illegal signature is legitimate. Also in Game2, since the server is allowed to collude with the agent, the attacker owns the agent's re-signature key and can convert the original signature of any message to the re-signature of the corresponding message. After a limited number of server-assisted verification queries with the challenger, the attacker's goal is to convince the verifier that an illegal re-signature is legitimate. The verifier's string Vst is secret to the attacker. If the attacker wins in Game1, the verifier cannot judge whether the original signature provided by the attacker is legal, indicating that the signature scheme cannot resist the joint attack between the server and the trustee Alice. Similarly, if the attacker wins in Game2, it means that the verifier cannot judge whether the re-signature provided by the attacker is legal, indicating that the signature scheme cannot resist the collusion attack of the server and the agent. Therefore, if the attacker wins in any of the games, the signature scheme is not complete. The specific implementation of the two games is as follows:

Game1: In this game, attacker A_1 has the private key pair (pk_A, sk_A) of the trustee Alice, which can represent the original signature of any message by the trustee Alice.

Establishment: Challenger C first runs $Setup, Keygen$ and $Server-setup$ three algorithms to obtain the system parameter cp, trustee Alice's public-private key pair (pk_A, sk_A) and string Vst, then cp and (pk_A, sk_A) are sent to attacker A_1.

Query: The attacker A_1 can adaptively perform q_c verification queries with the aid of the server. For each query(m_i, σ_i), Challenger C acts as the verifier, attacker A_1 acts as the server, A_1 and C first perform the server-assisted authentication protocol, and then return the output as a response to A_1.

Output: The attacker A_1 outputs a message m^* and a string σ^*. Let Γ_{m^*} is the set of all legal signatures of m^*, and σ^* is not in Γ_{m^*}. If $Verify(m^*, pk_A, \sigma^*) = 0$ is satisfied and $Server - verify(Vst, m^*, pk_A, \sigma^*) = 1$, it indicates that the attacker A_1 convinces the challenger C that σ^* is m^* corresponds to the legal signature of the public key pk_A, and the attacker A_1 wins in the game.

Game2: In this game, the attacker A_2 has the re-signature key $rk_{A \to B}$ between the trustee and the delegator, which can convert the original signature of the message to the re-signature corresponding to the same message on behalf of the agent.

Establishment: Challenger C runs $Setup, Keygen, Rekey$ and $Server - setup$ four algorithms to obtain the system parameter cp, public and private key pairs (pk_A, sk_A) and (pk_B, sk_B) of Alice and Bob, the re-signature key $rk_{A \to B}$, and the character string Vst, and send cp, pk_A, pk_B and $rk_{A \to B}$ to the attacker A_2.

Query: The attacker A_2 can adaptively perform the q_c server-assisted authentication query, which is the same as the response method in Game1.

Output: The attacker A_2 finally outputs a message m^* and a string σ^*. Let Γ_{m^*} is a set of all legal signatures corresponding to the public key pk_B of m^*, and σ^* is not in Γ_{m^*}. If $Verify(m^*, pk_B, \sigma^*) = 0$ and $Server-verify(Vst, m^*, pk_B, \sigma^*) = 1$, the attacker A_2 lets the challenger C be sure that σ^* is m^* legal signature, and attacker A_2 wins in this game.

The probability that an attacker wins the above game depends entirely on the probability of the coin toss of the challenger and the attacker.

Next, we give two definitions about security.

Definition 3: If the probability of an attacker winning in the above two games is negligible, then the server-assisted authentication protocol in the server-assisted verification proxy re-signing scheme is complete.

Definition 4: If a threshold proxy re-signature scheme has both unforgeability and robustness under adaptive selection message attack, and the server-assisted verification protocol is complete, the corresponding server-assisted verification threshold proxy re-signature scheme is said to be secure under collusion attack and selection message attack.

4 A New One-Way Server Auxiliary Verification Threshold Proxy Re-signature Scheme

In this part, we construct a one-way server-assisted verification variable threshold proxy re-signature scheme that is both secure and efficient and adapts to the mobile Internet environment. The participating entities of the new scheme include the delegator Bob, the trustee Alice, the verifier, the n semi-trusted agents and the server, where the trustee is responsible for generating the original signature of the message, and the semi-trusted agents convert the original signature into the re-signature of the principal, and the verifier completes the valid verification of the signature under the protocol of the semi-trusted server. The specific scheme is as follows:

Setup: Let q be a prime number of length k, G_1 and G_2 are two cyclic multiplication groups of order q, let g be the generator of group G_1, e : $G_1 \times G_1 \rightarrow G_2$ is a bilinear pairings, $H()$ is a public and anti-collision one-way hash function $H : {0,1}^* \rightarrow G_1$. Arbitrarily pick n positive integers $q_1 < q_2 < ... < q_{n-1}$ satisfying the condition $gcd(q_i, q_j) = 1$ and $gcd(q_i, q) = 1$, where $0 \leq i < j \leq n-1$, and let $F = q_0 q_1 ... q_{n-1}$, public system parameters $(cp) = (e, q, G_1, G_2, g, h, H, F, q_0, ..., q_{n-1})$.

Keygen: After entering the security parameter $cp = 1^k$, pick a random number x from Z_q and output the public key $pk = (pk^1, pk^2) = (g^x, h^{\frac{1}{x}})$ and private key $sk = x$.

Rekey: Given the public key of the trustee Alice $pk_A = (pk_A^1, pk_A^2) = (g^a, h^{\frac{1}{a}})$ and the private key of the principal Bob $sk_B = b$, then do the following:

a. Find two random numbers l_i, m_i arbitrarily in $[1, q-1]$ and calculate $\alpha_i = l_i m_i \prod_{j=0}^{i-1} q_j mod F$, $i = 0, 1, ..., n-1$. From the Chinese remainder theorem, $\alpha_0 \in Z_F$ can be obtained such that $\alpha_0 = sk_B = bmodq_i, i = 0, 1, ..., n-1$. Then construct a $n-1$ degree polynomial $f(x) = \alpha_0 + \sum_{i=0}^{n-1} \alpha_i x^i$. Given a positive integer $t(1 \leq t \leq n)$, there exists a $t-1$ degree polynomial $f_t(x) = f(x)modq_{t-1} = b + \sum_{i=1}^{t-1} \alpha_i x^i$.

b. Broadcast $X_j = g^{\frac{\alpha_j}{a}}$ and $Y_j = g^{\alpha_j}, j = 0, 1, ..., n-1$. By the Chinese remainder theorem, we can obtain the re-signature key $rk_{A \to B}^i \in Z_F$, namely $rk_{A \to B}^i = (pk_A^2)^{f_t(i)}modq_{t-1} = h^{\frac{f_t(i)}{a}}, t = 1, 2, ..., n$. Then, the information $(i, rk_{A \to B}^I)$ is secretly sent to the agent $P_i, i = 1, 2, ..., n$, where $X_0 = g^{\frac{b}{a}}, Y_0 = pk_B = g^b$.

c. The agent $P_i(1 \leq i \leq n)$ first calculates $rk_{A \to B}^{n,i} = rk_{A \to B}^i modq_{t-1}$, then determines whether the sub-key $rk_{A \to B}^i$ is valid by verifying whether the following two formulas are true.

$$e(rk_{A \to B}^{n,i}, g) = e(\prod_{j=0}^{n-1} X_j^{i^j}, h), \tag{1}$$

and

$$e(\prod_{j=0}^{n-1} X_j, pk_A^1) = e(\prod_{j=0}^{n-1} Y_j^{i^j}, g). \tag{2}$$

If the verifications are established, it indicates that the sub-key $rk_{A \to B}^i$ is valid. Given any positive integer $t(1 \leq t \leq n)$, the agent P_i can separately calculate $rk_{A \to B}^{t,i} = rk_{A \to B}^i modq_{t-1}$ by the initially obtained re-signature key $rk_{A \to B}^i$, and broadcast its verification public key $\nu k_{t,j} = g^{f_t(i)} = \prod_{j=0}^{t-1} Y_j^{i^j}$.

Sign: Given that the trustee's private key is a and a n_m bit long message $m = (m_1, m_2, ..., m_{n_m}) \in \{0, 1\}^{n_m}$, then pick a random constant t and let $r = h^t$, $s = a(H(m||r) + t)(modq)$, output the strong signature $\sigma = (r, s)$ and output a weak signature $\sigma = (r, h^s)$ that cannot be resigned.

Resign:

a. Partial key generation: Assuming the threshold is t, enter a threshold t, public key pk, message m, and signature σ_A, Verify this equation $Verify(pk_A, m, \sigma_A) = 0$, if it is established, enter the resigned sub-key $rk_{A \to B}^{t,i}$, and obtain the corresponding re-signature

$$\sigma_{B,i} = (r, s_i) = (r, (rk_{A \to B}^{t,i})^s) = (r, h^{f_t(i)(H(m||r)+t)}), \tag{3}$$

if it is not established, output 0.

b. Re-signature generation: After combiner obtains some partial re-signatures σ_{B,i_1}, verify the legality of partial signature by verifying whether the following equation

$$e(g, s_i) = e(\nu k_{t,i}, rh^{H(m||r)}), \tag{4}$$

is valid. If the composer obtains at least t legally partial duplicate signatures $(\sigma_{B,i_1}, ..., \sigma_{B,i_t})$, then its re-signature is where is the coefficient of Lagrange interpolation polynomial.

$$\sigma_B = (r, \prod_{i=1}^{t} s_i^{\chi_{0,i}}) = (r, \prod_{i=1}^{t} h^{\chi_{0,i}f(i)(H(m||r)+t)\sum_{i=1}^{t}\chi_{0,j}f(i)}) = (r, h^{b(H(m||r)+t)}),$$

(5)

where $\chi_{0,i}$ is the coefficient of Lagrange interpolation polynomial.

Verify: We input the public key $pk_A = (pk_A^1, pk_A^2)$, the message m and the signature σ to be verified (when σ is the signature under the weak key, let $s = h^s$), if the equation

$$e(g, s) = e(pk_B, rh^{H(m||r)})$$

(6)

is established, then output 1, otherwise output 0.

Server-setup: Given a system parameter cp, the verifier picks a random element x from Z_q^* to make the string $Vst = x$.

Server-verify: Given $Vst = x$, a public key pk and a signed message pair $(m, \sigma = (\sigma_1, \sigma_2))$, the server-assisted authentication interaction protocol between the verifier and the server is as follows:

  a. Firstly, the verifier calculates $\sigma' = (\sigma_1', \sigma_2') = ((\sigma_1)^x, (\sigma_2)^x) = (r^x, s^x)$. Then the verifier sends m, σ' to the server.
  b. The server calculates $\eta_1 = e(g, \sigma_1')$ and $\eta_2 = e(pk_B, \sigma_2' h^{H(m||r)})$, and sends η_1, η_2 to the verifier.
  c. The verifier through the calculation to verify whether the equation

$$\eta_1 = \eta_2$$

(7)

is established. If the equation is true, the verifier is convinced that σ is the legal signature of the message m, and outputs 1, otherwise, the verifier is convinced that σ is an invalid signature and outputs 0.

5   Correctness Analysis

Theorem 1. *When the threshold is t, if (1) and (2) are established, the obtained re-signature sub-key is valid.*

Proof. Because of $rk_{A\rightarrow B}^i = h^{\frac{f_t(i)}{a}}, t = 1, 2, ..., n$, Lagrange polynomial and the properties of bilinear mapping, we get

$$e(rk_{A\rightarrow B}^{n,i}, g) = e(h^{\frac{f_t(i)}{a}}, g) = e(h^{\sum_{j=0}^{n-1}\frac{\alpha_j i^j}{a}}, g) = e(h, g^{\frac{\sum_{j=0}^{n-1}\alpha_j i^j}{a}})$$

$$= e(h, \prod_{j=0}^{n-1}(g^{\frac{\alpha_j}{a}})^{i^j}) = e(h, \prod_{j=0}^{n-1}X_j^{i^j}).$$

Due to $A_j = g^{\frac{\alpha_j}{a}}$, we obtain

$$e(\prod_{j=0}^{n-1} X_j, pk_A^1) = e(\prod_{j=0}^{n-1} g^{\frac{\alpha_j}{a}}, g^a) = e(\prod_{j=0}^{n-1} g^{\alpha_j}, g) = e(\prod_{j=0}^{n-1} Y_j, g). \tag{8}$$

In addition, we have

$$rk_{A\to B}^{t,i} = rk_{A\to B}^i \, mod q_{t-1} = h^{\frac{f_t(i)}{i}}, \tag{9}$$

and

$$\nu k_{t,i} = \prod_{j=0}^{t-1} Y_j^{i^j} = \prod_{j=0}^{t-1} g^{\alpha_j^{i^j}} = g^{f_t(i)}. \tag{10}$$

Theorem 2. *When the threshold is t, if (4) is established, the partial re-signature is valid.*

Proof. From $s_i = h^{f_t(i)(H(m||r)+t)}$, $\nu k_{t,i} = g^{f_t(i)}$ and the properties of bilinear mapping, we obtain

$$e(g, s_i) = e(g, h^{f_t(i)(H(m||r)+t)}) = e(g^{f_t(i)}, h^{H(m||r)+t}) = e(\nu k_{t,i}, rh^{H(m||r)}). \tag{11}$$

Theorem 3. *When the threshold is t, if (6) is established, the re-signature is valid.*

Proof. From

$$s_i = h^{f_t(i)(H(m||r))}$$

and the properties of bilinear mapping, we have Displayed equations are centered and set on a separate line.

$$e(g, s) = e(g, \prod_{i=1}^{t} s_i^{\chi_{0,i}}) = e(g, \prod_{i=1}^{t} h^{\chi_{0,i} f(i)(H(m||r)+t)}) = e(g, h^{(H(m||r)+t)\sum_{i=1}^{t} \chi_{0,i} f_t(i)})$$

$$= e(g, h^{b(H(m||r)+t)}) = e(g^b, h^{H(m||r)+t}) = e(pk_B, rh^{H(m||r)}),$$

where $r = h^t$.

Theorem 4. *If the equation (7) is established, the verifier is convinced that σ is the legal signature of the message m.*

Proof. For the signature of the principal Bob $\sigma_B = (\sigma_{B1}, \sigma_{B2}) = (r, s)$ and the character string $Vst = x$, then we have Displayed equations are centered and set on a separate line.

$$\eta_1 = e(g, \sigma_{B1}') = e(g, (\prod_{i=1}^{t} s_i^{\chi_{0,i}})') = e(g, (\prod_{i=1}^{t} s_i^{\chi_{0,i}})^x)$$

$$= e(g, (\prod_{i=1}^{t} h^{\chi_{0,i} f(i)(H(m||r)+t)})^x) = e(g, (h^{(H(m||r)+t))\sum_{i=1}^{t} \chi_{0,i} f(i)})^x)$$

$$= e(g, (h^{b(H(m||r)+t)})^x) = e(g^{bx}, h^{H(m||r)+t}) = e((pk_B)^x, h^{H(m||r)+t})$$

$$= e((pk_B)^x, rh^{H(m||r)}) = e(pk_B, r^x h^{H(m||r)}) = e(pk_B, r' h^{H(m||r)}) = \eta_2.$$

Through the above derivation process, it can be proved that when the threshold is t, the re-signature sub-key, partial re-signature and re-signature verification algorithm are effective, and the correctness of the server-assisted verification protocol is obtained. Since the original signature is the same length as the re-signature, this scheme satisfies transparency and multi-purpose rows. In addition, since the trustee's private key, the principal's private key, and the agent's re-signature key are all elements in Z_q^*, the scheme satisfies the key optimality.

6   Security Analysis

The following is an analysis of the scheme proposed in this paper is non-forgeable and robust, and the server verification protocol $Servier - verify$ of the scheme satisfies the completeness. Therefore, in order to prove the security of the scheme, it is necessary to prove that the scheme satisfies the non-forgeable, robustness and completeness of the server-assisted verification protocol.

The third adversary who wants to forge the proxy re-signature of message m for the proxy signers and original signer must have the original signer's signature $\sigma_A(m)$, and it cannot be forged. Next, we will explain by the proof of the following Theorem that even if the third adversary knows the pair (r, s) sent by the original signer, he still cannot make a forgery signature on any other message. So he cannot make a forgery proxy signature on m either. On the other hand, the original signer cannot create a valid proxy re-signature, because the proxy re-signature is obtained by the proxy signers using the CDH signature scheme and the proxy signers' secret proxy $\{rk_{A \rightarrow B}^i\}$ shares which contain the private key of each proxy signer.

Theorem 5. *Assuming the third adversary has the* $\sigma_A(m) = (r, s)$, *our scheme is still secure.*

Proof. If we want to know the re-signature $\sigma_B = (r, h^{b(H(m||r)+t)})$ of message m, we must know Bobs private key $b, H(m||r)$ and t. Although he has known the signature $\sigma_A(m = (r, s))$, where $r = h^t, s = a(H(m||r) + t)(mod q)$, he still cannot get $H(m||r)$ and t, because this problem is equivalent to the discrete logarithm problem. Even he cannot get Bobs private key t. Thus, the scheme is still secure.

Theorem 6. *Under the standard model, when* $n \geq 2t - 1$, *our proposed scheme is robust to any attacker who can collude with the* $t - 1$ *agents.*

Proof. The compositor is able to verify the legitimacy of a partial re-signature and therefore can reject a malicious agent. Since there are at least t honest agents and each honest agent calculates a legal re-signature σ_i, the synthesizer Combiner can obtain the set Φ of the honest agent's serial number i and $|\Phi| \geq t$. Therefore, the compositor can always have a legal partial re-signature to calculate the re-signature of the message m. From this, we can get the scheme is strong when $n \geq 2t - 1$.

Theorem 7. *The server-assisted authentication protocol Servier − verify of the proposed scheme is complete under collusion attack and adaptive selection message attack.*

We prove this theorem by the following two lemmas.

Lemma 1. *Assuming that the attacker of the server and the trustee Alice is A_1, the probability that the attacker A_1 makes the challenger C convinced that an illegal original signature is legal is negligible.*

Proof. Let A_1 act as the server in the server's secondary authentication protocol, and C acts as the certifier in the protocol. Given the illegal original signature of a message, the goal of A_1 is to convince C that the illegal signature is legitimate. The interaction process between attacker A_1 and challenger C is as follows:

Establishment: Challenger C executes the initialization algorithm to generate the system parameter cp, randomly selects two elements $x^*, \gamma \in Z_q^*$, makes $Vst = x^*$, and calculates the public-private key pair of Alice $(pk_A, sk_A) = (e(g^\gamma, h^{\frac{1}{\gamma}}))$. Then it sends $\{cp, pk_A, sk_A\}$ to attacker A_1.

Query: Attacker A_1 can adaptively perform a limited number of server-assisted verification queries. For each inquiry (m_i, σ_i), Challenger C and attacker A_1 perform a server-assisted authentication protocol, and then return the output of the protocol as a response to attacker A_1.

Output: Finally, the attacker A_1 outputs the message m^* and the string $\sigma^* = (\sigma_1^*, \sigma_2^*)$. Let Γ_{m^*} be the set of all legal signatures of the message m^* corresponding to the public key pk_A, and σ^* is not in Γ_{m^*}. After the challenger C receives (m^*, σ^*), it uses Vst to calculate $(\sigma^*)' = ((\sigma_1^*)', (\sigma_2^*)') = ((\sigma_1^*)^{x^*}, (\sigma_2^*)^{x^*})$, and sends $(\sigma^*)' = ((\sigma_1^*)', (\sigma_2^*)')$ to attacker A_1. Then the attacker A_1 calculates $\eta_1^* = e(g, (\sigma_1^*)')$ and $\eta_2^* = e(pk_B, (\sigma_2^*)')$, and returns $\eta_1^* = \eta_2^*$ to Challenger C. The probability of the equation $\eta_1^* = \eta_2^*$ being established is $\frac{1}{q-1}$.

    a. Since $(\sigma^*)' = (\sigma^*)^{x^*}$ and $x^* \in_R Z_q^*$, Therefore, the probability that the attacker A_1 successfully forged $(\sigma^*)'$ by σ^* is $\frac{1}{q-1}$.

    b. Suppose the attacker A_1 returns (η_1^*, η_2^*) such that $\eta_1^* = \eta_2^*$, then $\eta_1^* = e(pk_B, r^{x^*} h^{H(m||r)}) = e(pk_B, rh^{H(m||r)})^{x^*}$. For the sake of writing, let $e(pk_B), rh^{H(m||r)} = M$. Through a simple calculation, we get

$$x^* = \log_M \eta_1^*. \tag{12}$$

Since x^* is an element that randomly selected from Z_q^*, the attacker finds x^* such that the probability that the above equation holds is $\frac{1}{q-1}$.

In summary, the attacker A_1 makes the challenger C convinced that the probability that the message (m^*, σ^*) is a legal signature is $\frac{1}{q-1}$. Since q is a large prime number, the attacker A_1 makes the challenger C convinced that the probability of (m^*, σ^*) being a legal signature is negligible.

Lemma 2. *Assuming that A_2 is an attacker colluded by the server and t agents, A_2 makes Challenge C believe that the probability that an illegal re-signature is legal is negligible.*

Proof. Let A_2 acts as the server role in the server-assisted authentication protocol, and C is the certifier role in the protocol. Given the illegal signature of a message, the goal of A_2 is to convince C that the illegal signature is legitimate. The interaction between the two is as follows:

Establishment: Challenger C runs the system initialization algorithm to get the system parameter cp, randomly selects the three elements in Z_q^* as x^*, α, β, and makes $V st = x^*$. The public-private key pairs of Alice and Bob are calculated as $(pk_A, sk_A) = (e(g^\alpha, h^{\frac{1}{\alpha}}), \alpha)$, $(pk_B, sk_B) = (e(g^\beta, h^{\frac{1}{\beta}}), \alpha)$ and the re-signature key $rk_{A \to B} = \beta/\alpha$. Send cp, pk_A, pk_B, and $rk_{A \to B}$ to attacker A_2.

Query: Same as the interrogation response process in Lemma 1.

Output: Attacker A_2 outputs message m^* and string $\sigma^* = (\sigma_1^*, \sigma_2^*)$. Let Γ_{m^*} be the set of legal signatures of message m^* corresponding to public key pk_B, and σ^* is not in Γ_{m^*}. Similar to the analysis process in Lemma 1, the attacker A_2 makes the challenger C convinced that (m^*, σ^*) is a legal signature with a probability of $1/(q-1)$, so the probability that the attacker A_2 convinced the challenger C that (m^*, σ^*) is a legal signature is negligible.

In summary, we get the one-way server-assisted verification threshold proxy re-signature scheme proposed in this paper is safe under collusion attack and adaptive selection message attack.

Next, we present a performance analysis of the server-assisted verification threshold proxy re-signature scheme.

7 Performance Analysis

The computational difficulty of the server-assisted verification threshold proxy re-signature scheme adapted to the mobile Internet proposed in this paper is equivalent to the CDH problem. In order to compare performance with the currently existing threshold proxy re-signature algorithm, the following symbols are defined in this paper. It should be noted that since the calculation amount of the addition, multiplication, HMAC algorithm and hash function is relatively small, we only consider the exponential operation and the bilinear pair operation with large calculation amount when considering the calculation overhead (Table 1).

Table 1. Calculation symbol representation

Symbol	Description
C_m	$Multiplication calculation$
C_n	$Addition calculation$
C_o	$HMAC algorithm calculation$
C_h	$Hash function calculation$
$|G_1|$	$The length of the element in G_1$
$|G_2|$	$The length of the element in G_2$
C_p	$Index calculation$
C_q	$Bilinear pairing calculation$

The following analysis will be carried out from four aspects: secret segmentation, signature algorithm, re-signature algorithm and signature verification. The re-signature algorithm includes two parts: partial re-signature algorithm and synthetic re-signature algorithm. The calculation amount of the server-assisted verification threshold proxy re-signature algorithm adapted to the mobile Internet is as shown in Table 2.

Table 2. Calculated amount of the program in this paper

Procedure	Calculated amount
$Rekey$	$(4 + 2t)C_p$
$Sign$	C_p
$Re - sign$	$2t(C_p + C_q)$
$Verify$	$2C_q$
$Server - verify$	$3C_p + 2C_q$

The literature [21] and [22] respectively propose the threshold proxy re-signature scheme. The server-assisted verification threshold proxy re-signature algorithm proposed in this paper is compared with the existing two algorithms based on its signature length and computational cost. The comparison results are as follows:

From the results of Table 3, it can be seen that compared with the literature [21, 22], the computational cost of the new scheme in this paper is much smaller than that of the literature [21, 22]. In the re-signature algorithm, the exponential operation of this scheme is only $2t$ operations, far less than other schemes, and the bilinear pairing operation in this procedure is a bit greater than that of the literature [21, 22]. However, in the verification procedure However, in the verification process of this scheme, through the interaction protocol between the verifier and the server, the bilinear pairing operation with high computational

Table 3. Calculation overhead of the threshold proxy re-signature algorithm

Scheme	Signature length	Re-signature generation	Verification
$Alg.in$ [21]	$4|G_1|$	$(4t+6)C_p + 5C_q$	$5C_q$
$Alg.in$ [22]	$3|G_1|$	$(3t+2)C_p$	$4C_q$
$Ours$	$|G_1|$	$2t(C_p + C_q)$	0

complexity is transferred to the server for execution, which reduces the computational burden of the verifier, thus saving the verification time and improving the efficiency of verification. In addition, the signature length of this article is much shorter than that of the literature [21,22], saving storage space. Therefore, the new algorithm proposed in this paper is more advantageous than the previous algorithm.

In the new scheme of this paper, the verifier transfers the complex bilinear pairing operation task to the server through the server-assisted verification protocol, so the signature verification does not need to perform a computationally intensive bilinear pairing operation. Therefore, the problem of limited computing power of mobile terminals in the mobile Internet environment is solved. In addition, under the standard model, the proposed scheme is non-forgeable under the adaptive selection message, and the server-assisted verification protocol process is complete. Therefore, the server-assisted verification threshold proxy re-signature scheme proposed in this paper is safe under collusion attacks and adaptive selective message attacks, so as to meet the requirements for high security requirements due to the complexity of the mobile Internet environment. In summary, this paper proposes that the server-assisted verification threshold proxy re-signature scheme can be better adapted to the mobile Internet environment.

8   Conclusion

At present, mobile Internet technology and its applications have been rapidly developed, and some low-end computing devices such as smart phones have been widely used. However, the corresponding information security mechanism issues and low-end computing power, limited energy supply, etc. problems have not yet found an effective solution. Aiming at these problems, this paper proposes a formal model of server-assisted verification threshold proxy re-signature, constructs a specific implementation scheme, and gives corresponding security proof. The scheme is based on threshold proxy re-signature and server-assisted authentication scheme. The threshold proxy re-signature algorithm can resist joint attacks and overcome various security defects. Verifiers and servers transfer complex bilinear pairing operations to servers through the interaction protocol between them, which greatly reduce the computational complexity of verifiers, improve the verification efficiency, and satisfy the needs of low-end computing devices with weak computing power and limited energy supply. The comprehensive analysis shows that the scheme can be well applied to the application environment of mobile internet.

References

1. Girault, M., Lefranc, D.: Server-aided verification: theory and practice. In: Roy, B. (ed.) ASIACRYPT 2005. LNCS, vol. 3788, pp. 605–623. Springer, Heidelberg (2005). https://doi.org/10.1007/11593447_33
2. Wei, W., Yi, M., Willy, S., et al.: Provably secure server-aided verification signatures. Comput. Math. Appl. **61**(7), 1705–1723 (2011)
3. Wu, H., Xu, C.X., Deng, J.: A server-aided aggregate verification signature scheme from bilinear pairing. In: Proceedings of INCS, China, Xi'an, pp. 503–506 (2013)
4. Ateniese, G., Hohenberger, S.: Proxy re-signatures: new definitions, algorithms, and applications. In: Proceedings of the 12th ACM CCS, Alexandria, USA, pp. 310–319 (2005). https://doi.org/10.1145/1102120.1102161
5. Shao, J., Cao, Z., Wang, L., Liang, X.: Proxy re-signature schemes without random Oracles. In: Srinathan, K., Rangan, C.P., Yung, M. (eds.) INDOCRYPT 2007. LNCS, vol. 4859, pp. 197–209. Springer, Heidelberg (2007). https://doi.org/10.1007/978-3-540-77026-8_15
6. Waters, B.: Efficient identity-based encryption without random Oracles. In: Cramer, R. (ed.) EUROCRYPT 2005. LNCS, vol. 3494, pp. 114–127. Springer, Heidelberg (2005). https://doi.org/10.1007/11426639_7
7. Kiiate, K., Ikkwon, Y., Secogan, L.: Remark on Shao et al.'s bidirectional proxy re-signature scheme in indocrypt'07. Int. J. Netw. Secur. **9**(1), 8–11 (2009). https://doi.org/10.6633/IJNS.200907.9(1).02
8. Libert, B., Vergnaud, D.: Multi-use unidirectional proxy re-signatures. In: Proceedings of the 15th ACM Conference on Computer and Communications Security, Alexandria, USA, pp. 511–520 (2008). https://doi.org/10.1145/1455770
9. Wang, W.P.: An identity-based blind proxy re-signature scheme. Comput. Appl. Softw. **29**(10), 308–313 (2012). https://doi.org/10.3969/j.issn.1000
10. Tian, M.M.: Identity-based proxy re-signatures from lattices. Inf. Process. Lett. **115**(4), 462–467 (2015). https://doi.org/10.1016/j.ipl.2014.12.002
11. Jiang, M.M., Hu, Y.P., Wang, B.C., et al.: Identity-based unidirectional proxy re-signature over lattice. J. Electron. Inf. Technol. **36**(3), 645–649 (2014). https://doi.org/10.3724/SP.J.1146.2013.00818
12. Hao, S.G., Zhang, L., Muhammad, G.: A union authentication protocol of cross-domain based on bilinear pairing. J. Softw. **8**(5), 1094–1100 (2013). https://doi.org/10.4304/jsw.8.5.1094-1100
13. Nguyen, T.C., Shen, W., Luo, Z., Lei, Z., Xu, W.: Novel data integrity verification schemes in cloud storage. In: Lee, R. (ed.) Computer and Information Science. SCI, vol. 566, pp. 115–125. Springer, Cham (2015). https://doi.org/10.1007/978-3-319-10509-3_9
14. Sun, Y., Chen, X.Y., Du, X.H.: A proxy re-signature scheme for stream switching. J. Softw. **26**(1), 129–144 (2015). https://doi.org/10.13328/j.cnki.jos.004553
15. Long, Z.H., Gong, J., Wang, B.: Energy efficiency study of clustered secure routing protocol secure communication method in wireless sensor networks. J. Electron. Inf. **37**(8), 2000–2006 (2015). https://doi.org/10.11999/JEIT141284

16. Boneh, D., Franklin, M.: Identity-based encryption from the weil pairing. In: Kilian, J. (ed.) CRYPTO 2001. LNCS, vol. 2139, pp. 213–229. Springer, Heidelberg (2001). https://doi.org/10.1007/3-540-44647-8_13

17. Long, Z.H., Gong, J., Wang, B., et al.: Energy efficiency study of secret communication method on clustering. J. Electron. Inf. Technol. **37**(8), 2000–2006 (2015). https://doi.org/10.11999/JEIT141284

18. Bao, F., Deng, R.H., Zhu, H.F.: Variations of Diffie-Hellman problem. In: Qing, S., Gollmann, D., Zhou, J. (eds.) ICICS 2003. LNCS, vol. 2836, pp. 301–312. Springer, Heidelberg (2003). https://doi.org/10.1007/978-3-540-39927-8_28

19. Shamir, A.: How to share a secret. Commun. ACM **22**, 612–613 (1979)

20. Wang, Z., Lu, W.: Server-aided verification proxy re-signature. In: Proceedings of Trust, Security and Privacy in Computing and Communications, Melbourne, Australia, pp. 1704–1707 (2013). https://doi.org/10.1109/TrustCom.2013.211.

21. Yang, X.D., Wang, C.F.: Flexible threshold proxy re-signature schemes. Chin. J. Electron. **20**(4), 691–696 (2011)

22. Li, H.Y., Yang, X.D.: One-way variable threshold proxy re-signature scheme under standard model. Comput. Appl. Softw. **12**, 307–310 (2014)

A New Signcryption Scheme Based on Elliptic Curves

Wen-jun Cui[1], Zhi-juan Jia[1], Ming-sheng Hu[1(✉)], Bei-Gong[1,2], and Li-peng Wang[1]

[1] College of Information Science and Technology,
Zhengzhou Normal University, Zhengzhou 450044, China
cui2361078314@163.com, 2361078314@qq.com
[2] Beijing University of Technology, Beijing 100124, China

Abstract. Based on the intractable problem of discrete logarithm in ECC and the intractability of reversing a one-way hash function, this paper presents a signcryption scheme with public verifiability and forward security. In the process of security proof, the unforgeability ensures that the attacker can't create a valid ciphertext. We verify the cipher text c instead of the plain text m in verification phase. We protect the plain text m, which makes the proposed scheme confidential. Thus, the proposed scheme has the property of public verification. And the scheme ensures that if the sender's private key is compromised, but the attacker can't recover original message m from cipher text (c, R, s). By the performance analysis, our proposed scheme mainly uses the model multiplication. Compared with Zhou scheme, the number of model multiplication has lost one time in signcryption phase, which leads to the significant increase in calculation rate. Moreover, the signature length has lost $2|n|$ compared with Zhou scheme. In other words, the minimum value of complexity is reached in theory. This makes the scheme have higher security and wider applications.

Keywords: Public verifiability · Forward security · Unforgeability · Model multiplication

1 Introduction

From the invention of public key cryptography to the 1990s, delivering an arbitrary length's message in a secure and authenticated way with an expense less than that required by signature-then-encryption seemed to have never been solved. Fortunately, Zheng discovered a new cryptographic primitive termed as "signcryption", which satisfied both the functions of digital signature and public key encryption in a logically single step simultaneously, and with a cost significantly smaller than that required by signature-then-encryption. The saving in cost growed proportionally to the size of security parameters [1]. Based on elliptic curve cryptosystems, a new signcryption was presented, and it saved the communication cost at least 1.25 times and enhanced computation cost 1.19 times over ECDSA-then-PSCE-1 [2]. The signcryption scheme, which can be verified by the third party after the specific recipient removed his key

© ICST Institute for Computer Sciences, Social Informatics and Telecommunications Engineering 2019
Published by Springer Nature Switzerland AG 2019. All Rights Reserved
J. Li et al. (Eds.): SPNCE 2019, LNICST 284, pp. 538–544, 2019.
https://doi.org/10.1007/978-3-030-21373-2_43

information, was a publicly verifiable scheme. Analysis showed that the proposed scheme is secure against the adaptive chosen ciphertext attack [2]. Combining digital signature and encryption functions, an efficient signcryption scheme based on elliptic curve was proposed [3]. The scheme takes lower computation and communication cost to provide security functions. It not only provides message confidentiality, authentication, integrity, unforgeability, and non-repudiation, but also forward secrecy for message confidentiality and public verification. And the judge can verify sender's signature directly without the sender's private key when dispute occurs [3].

A signcryption scheme with public verifiability and forward security was shown in [4]. An open problem on the design of signcryption was successfully solved. And the security properties of this scheme was proved in detail [4]. By using verifiable secret sharing and secure multi-party computation, the authors proposed a protocol for threshold generation of the signcryption [5]. Because point addition couldn't map coordinate addition directly, a linear sum of coordinates to reconstruct the private coordinate was introduced. And the complexity is less than the same schemes based on DLP (Discrete Logarithm Problem) [5]. An enhancement of the e-mail protocol using signcryption based on Elliptic curve was introduced, and it provided confidentiality, authenticity, integrity, unforgeability, non-repudiation, forward secrecy and public verifiability [6]. [7] highlighted limitations of the existing ECC based schemes using signcryption. These limitations include some missing security aspects as well as high computation power requirement, more communication overhead incurred and large memory requirements. Moreover, [7] proposed an efficient lightweight signcryption scheme based on HECC which satisfied all the security requirements. Compared with existing signcryption schemes, the scheme reduced significant amounts of computation, communication costs and message size [7].

New signcryption schemes based on elliptic curve cryptography were introduced [8]. The security of proposed schemes is based on elliptic curve discrete logarithm problem (ECDLP) and elliptic curve Diffie-Hellman problem (ECDHP). The proposed schemes provided various desirable security requirements like confidentiality, authenticity, non-repudiation and forward security as well as chosen ciphertext attack and unforgeability [8]. A public verifiable signcryption scheme with forward security was presented in [9]. In this scheme, the verification process didn't need the sender's private key, a parameter was hided in the index, so attacked who obtained the sender's private key wouldn't get any secret information between these participates before this communication. And furthermore, authentication and message recovery was not separated, but in the process of public verify, the message confidentiality won't be damaged [9]. An improvement scheme was proposed with public verifiability and forward security, the correctness and security were proved in [10]. The efficiency of the scheme was increased significantly compared with two existing schemes. Moreover, a new signcryption scheme based on elliptic curves was proposed with public verifiability and forward security. In the algorithm, both the numbers of model multiplication and model inverse were reached the minimum four times and zero times, the efficiency of the algorithm was increased significantly compared with the existing signcryption scheme [10]. The authors extended hybrid signcryption technique to the certificateless setting, and constructed a provably secure certificateless hybrid signcryption (PS-CLHS) scheme [11]. In the random oracle model, the authors proved that the proposed scheme satisfies the indistinguishability and unforgeability under the hardness of the bilinear Diffie-Hellman problem and computational Diffie-Hellman problem [11].

2   Preliminaries

For convenience of the readers, we will recall some basic facts and some useful properties. For more details, the readers can refer to [3, 12–14].

2.1   Elliptic Curve

An elliptic curve is defined as a nonsingular cubic curve over finite field in two variables, $f(x, y) = 0$, with a rational point (which may be a point at infinity) which satisfy the equation: $y^2 = x^3 + ax + b$. The field T is generally taken to be the complex numbers, reals, rationales, or a finite field.

2.2   Elliptic Curves Over $GF(p)$

Elliptic Curve Cryptography (ECC) was discovered in 1985 by Victor Miller (IBM) and Neil Koblitz as an alternative mechanism for implementing public-key cryptography based on elliptic curve over finite field.

An elliptic curve E over R (real numbers) is defined by a Weierstrass equation

$$y^2 + a_1 xy + a_3 y = x^3 + a_2 x^2 + a_4 x + a_6$$

where $a_1, a_2, a_3, a_4, a_6 \in T$. By performing the change of variables, we get one of the simplified Weierstrass equations

$$y^2 = x^3 + ax + b \text{ where } 4a^3 + 27b^2 \neq 0,$$

together with a special point 0 called the point at infinity. G is a generator of elliptic curve. n is the order of G, which satisfies $nG = 0$.

2.3   Elliptic Curve Discrete Logarithm Problem

ECC is based on discrete logarithm that is much more difficult to challenge at equivalent key lengths as compare to other public key cryptography.

Let P and Q be two points of an elliptic curve with order n and n is a prime. The point $Q = kP$ where $k < n$. Given these two points P and Q, find the correct k of Q. Up to now, it is computational infeasible to generate k from P and Q.

2.4   Hash Function

A hash function takes a group of characters and maps it to a value of a certain length called a hash value or message digest. The hash value is representative of the original string of characters, but is normally smaller than the original. Hash function is mainly used to generate a fixed length of string. Hash function can be divided into weak no-collision hash function and strong no-collision hash function.

Hash function is weak no-collision if a given an information x and there be an information which contents is unfeasible.

Hash function is strong no-collision if an information $x' \neq x$ which contents to $h(x) = h(x')$ is unfeasible.

3   The Proposed Scheme

Most of existing schemes can't simultaneously provide public verifiability and forward security. To solve this problem, based on the intractable problem of discrete logarithm in ECC and the intractability of reversing a one-way hash function, this paper presents a public verifiable signcryption scheme with forward security.

3.1   Initialization Phase

In this phase, we should select and publish some parameters as follows:

Set E is an elliptic curve over $GF(p)$, G is a generator of elliptic curve E. The sender A randomly selects an integer $x_A \in Z_n^*$ as her private key. Meanwhile, A computes her public key $y_A = x_A G$. Similarly, the recipient B also selects private key $x_B \in Z_n^*$ and public key $y_B = x_B G$, (E', D') is the secure encryption and decryption pair.

3.2   Signcryption Phase

The sender A randomly selects $r \in Z_n^*$, then $R = rG$, $K = ry_B = (k, l)$. Generating cipher text $c = E'_k(m)$. Computing Hash function value $e = h(c)$, Hamming weight $d = ham\,(e)$, $s = r + d + x_A \bmod n$. A Sends the signcrypted text (c, R, s) to B.

3.3   Unsigncryption Phase

B receives the signcrypted text (c, R, s). Computing $K = x_B R = (k, l)$, Hash function value $e = h(c)$, Hamming weight $d = ham\,(e)$, $t = (s - d) \bmod n$. Generating plain text $m = D'_k(c)$.

Verifying $tG - y_A$ is equal to R or not. If it is true then B accepts (c, R, s) which is sent by A.

The signcrypted text (c, R, s) is a valid one, its correctness is given below.

$$(s - d)G - y_A = (r + d + x_A - d)G - x_A G = rG = R.$$

4 Analysis of the Proposed Scheme

In this section, there is a discussion of the security aspects of the proposed scheme.

4.1 Security Proof

The proposed work not only provides unforgeability and non-repudiation (public verification) but also forward secrecy.

1. Unforgeability

Unforgeability ensures that the attacker can't create a valid ciphertext. In the proposed scheme, the attacker cannot create a valid (c, R, s) without the private key of the sender A. If an attacker forges a valid (c', R', s') from previous (c, R, s), the key is to generate a correct s'. Since $s = r + d + x_A$, the attacker must get random r and x_A, which the attacker can't get obviously. To obtain x_A from $y_A = x_A G$ and r from $R = rG$, then the attacker has to solve ECDLP firstly but it is computationally infeasible. Therefore, our proposed scheme satisfies unforgeability.

2. Non-repudiation

The proposed scheme provides the non-repudiation property. Namely, the proposed scheme has the property of public verifiability. When dispute occurs for the sender and recipient, the recipient can send (c, R, s) to the Third-party Trusted Center for settling whether the original cipher text c sent by the sender. During this process, the Third-party Trusted Center can determine whether the signature is generated by the sender, because only the sender can use her own private key x_A to generate correct signature s. Thus, the proposed scheme satisfies non-repudiation property.

Meanwhile, we verify the cipher text c instead of the plain text m in verification phase. We protect the plain text m, which makes the proposed scheme confidential. Therefore, the proposed scheme has the property of public verification.

3. Forward secrecy

The proposed scheme ensures that if the sender's private key is compromised, but the attacker can't recover original message m from cipher text (c, R, s). In the proposed scheme if the attacker tries to derive plain text m, he has to get the secret key k because of $m = D'_k(c)$. There are two ways to deduce k:

(1) We need know r because of $K = ry_B = (k, l)$. However, to obtain r from $R = rG$, then the attacker has to solve ECDLP firstly but it is computationally infeasible.
(2) We need know x_B because of $K = x_B R = (k, l)$. But as B's private key, x_B can't be got.

Therefore our proposed scheme provides forward secrecy.

4.2 Performance Analysis

We compare cost of our proposed work with some elliptic curve cryptography schemes and try to reduce the cost of computation. Recently, our proposed scheme and Zhou scheme [10] simultaneously provide public verifiability and forward security. Same as Zhou scheme [10], both the numbers of model index and model inverse are reached the minimum zero times. Compared with Zhou scheme [10], the number of model multiplication has lost one time in signcryption phase, which leads to the significant increase in calculation rate. Moreover, the signature length has lost $2|n|$ compared with Zhou scheme. In other words, the minimum value of complexity is reached in theory (Table 1).

Table 1. Performance Comparison

	Zhou scheme [10]		The proposed scheme	
	Signcryption phase	Unsigncryption phase	Signcryption phase	Unsigncryption phase
Model index	0	0	0	0
Model inverse	0	0	0	0
Model multiplication	2	1	1	1
Hash function	1	1	1	1
Signature length	$5|n|$		$3|n|$	

5 Conclusion

Based on the intractable problem of discrete logarithm in ECC and the intractability of reversing a one-way hash function, this paper presents a public verifiable signcryption scheme with forward security. In the process of security proof, the unforgeability ensures that the attacker can't create a valid ciphertext. We verify the cipher text c instead of the plain text m in verification phase. We protect the plain text m, which makes the proposed scheme confidential. Thus, the proposed scheme has the property of public verification. And the scheme ensures that if the sender's private key is compromised, but the attacker can't recover original message m from cipher text (c, R, s). By the performance analysis, our proposed scheme mainly uses the model multiplication. Compared with Zhou scheme [10], the number of model multiplication has lost one time in signcryption phase, which leads to the significant increase in calculation rate. Moreover, the signature length has lost $2|n|$ compared with Zhou scheme. In other words, the minimum value of complexity is reached in theory. This makes the scheme have higher security and wider applications.

References

1. Zheng, Y.L.: Digital signcryption or how to achieve cost(signature & encryption) ≪ cost (signature) + cost(encryption). In: Kaliski, B.S. (ed.) CRYPTO 1997. LNCS, vol. 1294, pp. 165–179. Springer, Berlin (1997). https://doi.org/10.1007/BFb0052234
2. Han, Y., Yang, X., Hu, Y.: Signcryption based on elliptic curve and its multi-party schemes. In: Proceedings of the 3rd International Conference on Information Security, pp. 216–217. ACM (2004)

3. Hwang, R.J., Lai, C.H., Su, F.F.: An efficient signcryption scheme with forward secrecy based on elliptic curve. Appl. Math. Comput. **167**(2), 870–881 (2005)
4. Qi, M.P., Chen, J.H., Fe, D.B.: Signcryption scheme with public verifiability and forward security. Appl. Res. Comput. **23**(9), 98–106 (2006)
5. Han, Y., Yang, X., Hu, J.: Threshold signcryption based on elliptic curve. In: 2009 International Conference on Information Technology and Computer Science, pp. 370–373. IEEE (2009)
6. Mohapatra, A.K., Kushwaha, J., Popli, T.: Enhancing email security by signcryption based on elliptic curve. Int. J. Comput. Appl. **71**(17), 28–30 (2013)
7. Ch, S.A., Sher, M., Ghani, A., et al.: An efficient signcryption scheme with forward secrecy and public verifiability based on hyper elliptic curve cryptography. Multimed. Appl. **74**(5), 1711–1723 (2015)
8. Nayak, B.: Signcryption schemes based on elliptic curve cryptography (2014)
9. Qi, M.P., Chen, J.H., He, D.B.: Signcryption scheme with public verifiability and forward security. Appl. Res. Comput. **31**(10), 3093–3094 (2014)
10. Zhou, K.Y.: Attack analysis and improvement on the signcryption scheme with public verifiability and forward security. J. Northwest Normal Univ. (Nat. Sci.) **51**(6), 50–53 (2015)
11. Yu, H.F., Yang, B.: Provably secure certificateless hybrid signcryption. Chin. J. Comput. **38**(4), 804–813 (2016)
12. Al-Somani, T.F., Ibrahim, M.K., Gutub, A.: High performance elliptic curve GF (2m) crypto-processor. Inf. Technol. J. **5**(4), 742–748 (2006)
13. Sun, Y., Chen, X.Y., Du, X.H., et al.: Proxy re-signature scheme for stream exchange. J. Softw. **26**(1), 129–144 (2015)
14. Johnson, D., Menezes, A., Vanstone, S.: The elliptic curve digital signature algorithm (ECDSA). Int. J. Inf. Secur. **1**(1), 36–63 (2001)

A Robust Reversible Watermarking Scheme for Relational Data

Ruitao Hou[1,2], Hequn Xian[1,2(✉)], Xiao Wang[3], and Jing Li[1,2]

[1] College of Computer Science and Technology, Qingdao University,
Qingdao 266071, China
xianhq@126.com
[2] State Key Laboratory of Integrated Services Networks, Xidian University,
Xi'an 710071, China
[3] Qingdao Ocean Shipping Mariners College, Qingdao 266071, China

Abstract. Reversible watermarking is widely used in copyright protection of relational data. It allows recovering the original data besides claiming copyright. In current schemes, watermarked data are either completely restored to the original version or kept unchanged. We present a robust and reversible watermark which allows arbitrary portion of the watermark to be removed. Experiments show the robust of the proposed algorithm is robust.

Keywords: Watermark · Reversible · Copyright · Relational data

1 Introduction

Reversible watermarking technique for relational data is an effective method to protect copyright which is developed from traditional watermarking technique for relational data [1, 2]. It allows the inversion of watermark embedding to recover the original data. However, existing reversible watermarking schemes for relational data still have some problems. Suppose Alice is the owner of some relational data, and embeds a watermark into her data with a reversible watermarking technique before distributing them to user Bob. If Bob finds out that the usability of the data does not meet his requirements, he can purchase relevant keys from Alice to perform the inverse operation of watermark embedding. Thus, Bob obtains the original data. After that, if Bob sells the recovered data to others without Alice's consent, Alice will not be able to claim copyright because there is no longer a watermark in the recovered data. In the above scenario, although usability can be enhanced via recovering the original data, the owner loses the ability to claim the copyright permanently. This problem mainly stems from the facts that existing schemes cannot control the extent of data recovery and all watermarks are removed during the data recovery process. Therefore, enhancing the usability of data while simultaneously preserving the copyright claim has become a new research focus.

In this paper, a robust reversible watermarking scheme for relational data named GRW is proposed. Quality grade is defined to describe the impact of watermark embedding on the usability of data. Four fundamental algorithms are designed to facilitate the processes of watermark embedding, data quality grade detection, watermark

J. Li et al. (Eds.): SPNCE 2019, LNICST 284, pp. 545–550, 2019.
https://doi.org/10.1007/978-3-030-21373-2_44

detection, and data quality grade enhancement. Reversibility can be achieved by upgrading watermarked data from a low data quality grade to higher grades.

2 Related Work

The first reversible watermarking scheme for relational data were proposed by Zhang et al. [3]. In this scheme, a histogram with difference values is used to achieve watermark reversibility. Gupta and Pieprzyk proposed a reversible watermarking scheme (DEW) [4]. They used difference expansions to achieve the reversibility of the watermark. However, this scheme is less robust to tuple alteration attacks. Combining genetic algorithms and difference expansion, Jawad and Khan considered the watermarking problem as a constrained optimization problem and applied difference expansion to achieve reversibility (GADEW) [5]. Franco-Contreras proposed a robust reversible watermarking scheme based on circular histogram transforms [6]. In this scheme, a circular histogram transform was constructed, and relative angular positions of some attribute values were changed to implement watermark embedding. Iftikhar et al. utilized genetic algorithms and a data analysis method in information theory to deal with the watermarking problem (RRW) [7]. They used genetic algorithms to generate the optimal watermark to minimize data distortion. However, the generation of an optimal watermark requires heavy computation, and the efficiency is unsatisfactory when processing very large volumes of data. Farfoura et al. converted a recognizable image into a bit stream, which was embedded into the least significant bits of attribute values (PEEW) [8]. They utilized prediction error expansion of integers to achieve reversibility of the watermark. Imamoglu designed a reversible watermarking method using the firefly algorithm and difference expansion [9]. The firefly algorithm was used to select the optimal attribute pairs, which were then embedded as the watermark. Jiang et al. divided relational data into blocks, and a watermark was embedded into the wavelet domain of these data blocks. The wavelet transform was used to implement watermark reversibility [10]. Although data recovery can be achieved using the above schemes, they do not allow control of the extent of data recovery. GRW is proposed in this work to solve this problem.

3 GRW Scheme

GRW consists of four procedures: (1) watermark partition embedding; (2) data quality grade detection; (3) watermark detection; and (4) data quality grade enhancement.

3.1 Quality Grade

Definition 1. Quality grade, QD, is the quantified value of data usability under the impact of watermark embedding. $QD \in [0, \lambda - 1], QD \in N$, where λ indicates the number of data partitions.

According to Definition 1, the owner can divide the data into λ partitions. When QD equals 0, all data partitions contain watermarked tuple. When QD is equal to $\lambda - 1$, there is no watermark. When the value QD is q, the number of partitions containing watermarked tuple is $\lambda - 1 - q$.

3.2 Watermark Partition Embedding

Before the watermark is embedded into the original data, the watermark and an auxiliary string S need to be created. The data owner can convert some identification information into a binary sequence. S is created randomly, but the length of it is equal to the length of the watermark. S has auxiliary roles in data quality grade detection, watermark detection, and data quality grade enhancement.

The watermark partition embedding algorithm is shown as Algorithm 1.

Algorithm 1. Watermark partition embedding
Input: original data, data partition key, watermark embedding key, watermark, auxiliary string
Output: watermarked data, auxiliary data
1   **for** each tuple in the original data **do**
2   Calculate the data partition of the tuple
3   **if** (the tuple is supposed to contain watermark bit) **then**
4   Calculate the location the watermarked bit;
5   Calculate the watermark bit $W[l]$
6   Calculate the corresponding bit in auxiliary string $S[l]$;
7   Calculate the auxiliary data bit;
8   Store he auxiliary data bit in storage structure of auxiliary data;
9   Obtain the watermark bit with $W[l]$ xor $S[l]$;
10   Calculate the original bit in the tuple;
11   Update the tuple and set the value of wat
12   Update the original bit in the tuple with $W[l]$ xor $S[l]$
13   **end if**
14   **end for**
15   Return the data watermarked and the auxiliary data

3.3 Quality Grade Detection

Quality grade detection is the preliminary procedure of watermark detection and data quality grade enhancement. Its purpose is to confirm data partitions watermarked. The data quality grade detection algorithm is shown in Algorithm 2.

Algorithm 2. Quality grade detection

Input: watermarked data, storage structure of auxiliary data, data partition key, watermark embedding key, auxiliary string
Output: quality grade
1   Initialize data quality grade QD
2   **for** each tuple in the watermarked data **do**
3   Determine which data partition the tuple belongs to;
4   **if** (the tuple contains watermark bit) **then**
1   Locate the watermarked bit;
2   Select a bit from the corresponding auxiliary string;
3   Calculate the auxiliary data bit;
5   Store the auxiliary data bit in a temporary data structure
6   **end if**
7   **end for**
8   **for** each data partition **do**
9   **if**(the bit in temporary data structure matches the bit in auxiliary data for current data partition **then** QD ++;
10   Return QoD;

3.4   Watermark Detection

The watermark detection algorithm is shown as Algorithm 3. We use the majority voting mechanism [2] to improve the accuracy of detection.

Algorithm 3. Watermark detection

Input: watermarked data, storage structure of auxiliary data, data partition key, watermark embedding key, auxiliary string , quality grade
Output: watermarked data
1   Determine which data partitions are supposed contain the watermark according to the value of quality grade;
2   **for** each tuple in the watermarked data **do**
3   Determine which data partition the tuple belongs to;
4   **if** (data partition is supposed to have watermark) **then**
4   **if** (the tuple is supposed to carry watermark) **then**
5   Locate the watermarked bit;
6   Select a bit from the corresponding auxiliary string;
5   Get the auxiliary data bit;
6   Calculate the watermark bit $W_D[I]$
7   Use majority voting mechanism to obtain the watermark bit;
      end if
      end for
8   Count the voting result for the intended watermark
9   Return the detection result W_D

3.5 Quality Grade Enhancement

The purpose of quality grade enhancement is to reverse the watermark embedded in some data partitions. The algorithm is shown as Algorithm 4.

Algorithm 4. Data quality grade enhancement
Input: watermarked data, storage structure of auxiliary data, part of data partition key, Watermark embedding keys, quality grade
Output: relational data after enhancing data quality grade
7   **for** each tuple in watermarked data **do**
8   **if** (the tuple belongs to a watermarked partition) **then**
9   **if** (the tuple contains watermark bit) **then**
10   Locate the watermarked bit;
11   Select a bit from the corresponding auxiliary string;
12   Calculate the auxiliary data bit;
13   Obtain the watermark bit with xor calculation;
14   Calculate the original bit in the tuple;
15   Update the tuple and set the value of watermark bit to the original bit
end if
16   Return the data after quality grade enhancement

4 Experiments

To verify the robustness of GRW, we simulated tuple deletion attack on watermarked data. An adversary randomly deletes some tuples from watermarked data with intention to destroy the watermark. The setting of the experiments are as follows: 200000 tuples, 20 data partition, 1 water marked tuple in 4, 53 attributes capable for watermark. We compared GRW with DEW [4], GADEW [5], RRW [7], and PEEW [8].

Watermark Detection. As shown in Fig. 1, the detection accuracy of GRW and RRW remained at 100% when up to 90% tuples were attacked. When a large proportion of tuples were deleted, the detection accuracy of other schemes decreased.

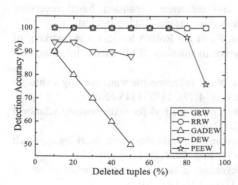

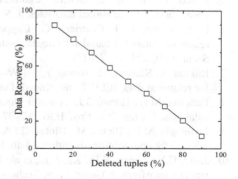

Fig. 1. Watermark detection accuracy after tuple deletion attacks

Fig. 2. Data recovery accuracy after tuple deletion attacks

Data Recovery. As shown in Fig. 2, when 50% of tuples were deleted, 48.81% watermarked tuples could be recovered to the original data as 51.19% watermarked tuples were deleted by the adversary. All remaining watermarked tuples could be successfully recovered.

5   Conclusions

Existing reversible watermarking schemes remove all watermarks in the data and do not allow control of the extent of data recovery. Once the original data is recovered, the owner loses the protection of copyright. A robust reversible watermarking scheme for relational data is proposed in this paper. The quality grade can be enhanced incrementally by removing arbitrary portions of the watermark. Experiments showed that the proposed scheme has high robustness against tuple deletion attack.

Acknowledgment. This research is supported by the Open Project Program of The State Key Laboratory of Integrated Services Networks (ISN19-14), Hequn Xian is the corresponding author.

References

1. Agrawal, R., Kiernan, J.: Watermarking relational databases. In: Proceedings of the 28th International Conference on Very Large Data Bases, pp. 155–166. VLDB Endowment (2002)
2. Sion, R., Atallah, M., Prabhakar, S.: Rights protection for categorical data. IEEE Trans. Knowl. Data Eng. **17**(7), 912–926 (2005)
3. Zhang, Y., Yang, B., Niu, X.-M.: Reversible watermarking for relational database authentication. J. Comput. **2**(17), 59–65 (2006)
4. Gupta, G., Pieprzyk, J.: Reversible and blind database watermarking using difference expansion. In: Proceedings of the 1st International Conference on Forensic Applications and Techniques in Telecommunications, Information, and Multimedia and Workshop, pp. 24–29. ICST (Institute for Computer Sciences, Social-Informatics and Telecommunications Engineering) (2008)
5. Jawad, K., Khan, A.: Genetic algorithm and difference expansion based reversible watermarking for relational databases. J. Syst. Softw. **11**(86), 2742–2753 (2013)
6. Franco-Contreras, J., Coatrieux, G., Cuppens, F., et al.: Robust lossless watermarking of relational databases based on circular histogram modulation. IEEE Trans. Inf. Forensics Secur. **9**(3), 397–410 (2014)
7. Iftikhar, S., Kamran, M., Anwar, Z.: RRW—a robust and reversible watermarking technique for relational data. IEEE Trans. Knowl. Data Eng. **4**(27), 1132–1145 (2015)
8. Farfoura, M.E., Horng, S.J.: A novel blind reversible method for watermarking relational databases. J. Chin. Inst. Eng. **1**(36), 87–97 (2013)
9. Imamoglu, M.B., Ulutas, M., Ulutas, G.: A new reversible database watermarking approach with firefly optimization algorithm. Math. Probl. Eng. **2017**(2), 1–14 (2017)
10. Jiang, C.X., Cheng, X.H., Xu, X.L., et al.: Reversible database watermark based on integer wavelet transform. J. Guilin Univ. Technol. **37**(1), 191–195 (2017)

BL-IDS: Detecting Web Attacks Using Bi-LSTM Model Based on Deep Learning

Saiyu Hao[1], Jun Long[1(✉)], and Yingchuan Yang[2]

[1] College of Computer, National University of Defense Technology, Changsha, China
{haosaiyu17,junlong}@nudt.edu.cn
[2] Institute of Atmospheric Physics, Chinese Academy of Sciences, Beijing, China

Abstract. Current anomaly-based network attack detection methods face difficulties such as unsatisfied accuracy and lack of generalization. The Rule-based Web attack detection is difficult to combat against unknown attacks and is relatively easy to bypass. Therefore, we propose a new method to detect Web attacks using deep learning. The method is based on analyzing HTTP request, where only some preprocessing is required, and the automatic feature extraction is done by the Bi-LSTM itself. The experimental results on the dataset HTTP DATASET CSIC 2010 show that the Bi-LSTM has good performance. This method has achieved state-of-the-art results in detecting Web attacks, and has a high detection rate while maintaining a low false alarm rate.

Keywords: Web attacks · Deep learning ·
Bidirectional long-short term memory

1 Introduction

Web applications play an extremely important role in people's daily lives. It brings great convenience to people. They can use Web applications for shopping, office, learning, entertainment and so on. However, the security of Web applications has long existed. Hackers can steal user's private data by attacking Web applications, disabled Web services, steal sensitive user information, and bring serious financial loss to both service providers and users.

However, it's hard to protect Web applications from attack. Even though developers and researchers have developed many solutions, like Web application firewalls (WAF), Web intrusion detection systems (Web IDSs), penetration testing, to protect Web applications, Web attacks remain a major threat. Generally, There are two approaches to detect Web attacks, one is the signature-based [1], another is the anomaly-based [2]. The signature-based method establish the detection model from known attacks and any behavior having the same attack signatures is identified as an attack. Contrarily, the anomaly-based method

Supported by the National Natural Science Foundation of China (Grant No. 61105050).

J. Li et al. (Eds.): SPNCE 2019, LNICST 284, pp. 551–563, 2019.
https://doi.org/10.1007/978-3-030-21373-2_45

establishes a profile from normal behaviors and any violation is identified as an attack. The signature-based method is accepted and adopted more wildly than the anomaly-based method because generally the signature-based one has lower false alarm rate and achieves higher accuracy. Although it is effective, the rule-based method is still problematic. On the one hand, It is just as good as the range of the rule set, which means it is unable to identify attacks which are not in its signature dataset. On the other hand, bypassing WAF can be done easily if they replace keywords of existing malicious requests or encode themselves multiple times [3,4].

Here, based on the BRNN [5] (Bidirectional recurrent neural networks) with the Bi-directional Long-Short Term Memory (Bi-LSTM) unit, we put forward a new anomaly detection method to detect Web attacks. Our model takes Uniform Resource Locators (URLs) and request body in the HTTP POST requests (only URLs for HTTP GET requests) as the input. After the URLs are tokenized, they will be mapped to vectors. Then the Bi-LSTM will learn from the normal request patterns. And then a trained neural network based on the output of the Bi-LSTM to judge whether given requests are anomalous. Our method has achieved state-of-the-art results in detecting Web attacks, the experimental results show that BL-IDS has a high detection rate and maintains a low false alarm rate.

The rest of the paper is organized as follows: Sect. 2 is introduction of Some related works. Section 3 is description of the method based on deep learning to detect Web attacks. Section 4 is experimental results and discussions. Section 5 is conclusion of this paper.

2   Related Works

Many machine learning techniques are used to detect Web attacks, Kruegel et al. have presented a multi-model method to detect Web attacks in [6]. The method analyzes HTTP requests and uses some different models built on different features, like attribute length, attribute character distribution, structural inference, invocation order and so on. Abou-Assaleh et al. [7] explored the idea of automatically detecting new malicious code using the collected dataset of the benign and malicious code which is based on N-gram. Moh et al. [8] have put forward a multi-stage log analysis architecture, which combines both pattern matching and supervised machine learning methods. It uses logs produced by the application during attacks to detect detecting SQL injection attacks effectively. Cao built a system which can avoid false negatives and enhance the efficiency of detecting work by using a prevailing machine learning algorithm called Adaboost in [9].

In recent years, deep learning, a branch of machine learning, has become increasingly popular and has been used in the field of information security. Cui et al. [10] propose an improved NIDS using word embedding-based deep learning (WEDL-NIDS), which first reduces the dimension of a packets payload via word embedding and learns the local contentful features of network traffic using deep convolutional neural networks (CNNs) [11], followed by adding the head features and learning global temporal features using long short-term memory (LSTM) [12] networks. The result they got was quite well. Fredrik Valeur et al. [13] had developed an anomaly-based system that learns the profiles of the normal database access performed by Web-based applications using a number of different models. These models allow for the detection of unknown attacks with reduced false positives and limited overhead. Zhang et al. [14] have put forward a deep learning method to detect Web attacks which is using a specially designed CNN. Similar to our work, the difference is the network architectures, they use the Convolutional Neural Network while we use the Bi-LSTM based on Bidirectional recurrent neural network [5]. And the method we have proposed has better performance.

3 BL-IDS

BL-IDS aims to detect Web attack from HTTP request to improve the accuracy of IDS. Bi-LSTM can be trained using all available input information in the past and future of a given period of time, word2vec can output high-quality word vectors from huge dataset and maintain the similarity of semantic words, so we combine the advantages of both. The implementation schemes are illustrated in Fig. 1.

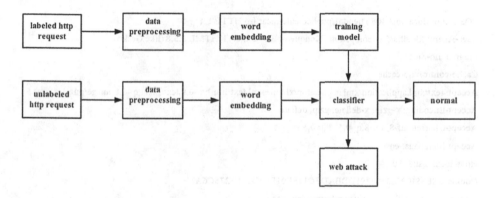

Fig. 1. The implementation schemes of Bi-LSTM

The different stages of BL-IDS are described as follows:

- **Data Preprocessing**: We decode HTTP request, then we split the decoded HTTP request, the Segmentation character includes /, & and so on.
- **Word embedding**: We map each word into a word vector using word2vec [15], The mapped word vectors are used as an input to a model based on a neural network.
- **Training model and detect Web attack**: We use the labeled word vectors to train a model based on neural network. Then use the trained model to classify the new HTTP request as Web attack or normal.

3.1 Data Preprocessing

In this section, We decode HTTP request, then we split the decoded HTTP request, the Segmentation character includes /, &, +, ?, =, @ and so on.

The process of this section is shown as Fig. 2.

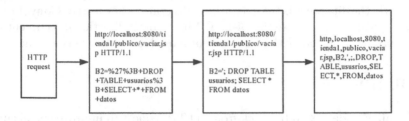

Fig. 2. The process of data preprocessing

The following is a HTTP request between a user and a Web application (Fig. 3):

POST http://localhost:8080/tienda1/publico/autenticar.jsp HTTP/1.1

User-Agent: Mozilla/5.0 (compatible; Konqueror/3.5; Linux) KHTML/3.5.8 (like Gecko)

Pragma: no-cache

Cache-control: no-cache

Accept: text/xml,application/xml,application/xhtml+xml,text/html;q=0.9,text/plain;q=0.8,image/png,*/*;q=0.5

Accept-Encoding: x-gzip, x-deflate, gzip, deflate

Accept-Charset: utf-8, utf-8;q=0.5, *;q=0.5

Accept-Language: en

Host: localhost:8080

Cookie: JSESSIONID=23391DBBADEC19FE01E02D201F278C6A

Content-Type: application/x-www-form-urlencoded

Connection: close

Content-Length: 60

modo=entrar&login=caria&pwd=egipciaca&remember=off&B1=Entrar

Fig. 3. A POST request message example by users

This is a request message based on HTTP. The HTTP request consists of three parts: the request line, headers and request body. The request line is the first line of the HTTP request message, and its format is as follows:

Method   Request-URI   HTTP-Version

Method represents the request method; Request-URI is a uniform resource identifier; HTTP-Version represents the requested HTTP protocol version. There are many kinds of methods. The two common methods are as GET and POST. GET request to get the resource identified by the Request-URI, POST appends new data to the resource identified by the Request-URI. The format of the Request-URI is as follows:

$$\text{http://host[}"\text{:"}\text{port][abs\_path]}$$

HTTP indicates that the network resource is located through the HTTP protocol; Host indicates the legal Internet host domain name or IP address; Port specifies a port number, and if it is empty, the default port 80 is used; Abs_path specifies the URI of the requested resource. HTTP/1.1 is a version of the protocol version. Headers is the additional information that the client passes the request to the server and the information of the client itself. The request body is usually the form content submitted by the user in the POST mode. The HTTP request between the hacker and the server may be like Fig. 4, and the main difference of the HTTP request between the hacker's and the user's has been bolded.

POST http://localhost:8080/tienda1/publico/vaciar.jsp HTTP/1.1

User-Agent: Mozilla/5.0 (compatible; Konqueror/3.5; Linux) KHTML/3.5.8 (like Gecko)

Pragma: no-cache

Cache-control: no-cache

Accept: text/xml,application/xml,application/xhtml+xml,text/html;q=0.9,text/plain;q=0.8,image/png,*/*;q=0.5

Accept-Encoding: x-gzip, x-deflate, gzip, deflate

Accept-Charset: utf-8, utf-8;q=0.5, *;q=0.5

Accept-Language: en

Host: localhost:8080

Cookie: JSESSIONID=71D6797908C1D911A839D8BD161473AA

Content-Type: application/x-www-form-urlencoded

Connection: close

Content-Length: 77

B2=%27%3B+DROP+TABLE+usuarios%3B+SELECT+*+FROM+datos

Fig. 4. A POST request message example by hackers

The main difference between the two is in the url part of the request line and the request body part (for the GET method, the main difference is in the url part), and the rest of the information we do not pay attention to. The reason for this is as follows: Most Web attacks are implemented by modifying the URL and request body, and doing so is convenient. Taking the HTTP request message of Fig. 2 as an example, our attention is:

http://localhost:8080/tienda1/publico/vaciar.jsp
B2=%27%3B+DROP+TABLE+usuarios%3B+SELECT+*+FROM+datos

First, the contents of our concern is URL decoding, We can get the following:

http://localhost:8080/tienda1/publico/vaciar.jsp
B2='; DROP TABLE usuarios; SELECT * FROM datos

After that, use some special characters to divide, these special characters include:,/, &, =, +, etc.

The split data is as follows:

http, localhost, 8080, tienda1, publico, vaciar.jsp,
B2, ', ;, DROP, TABLE, ususrios, SELECT, *, FROM, datos.

3.2 Word Embedding

The effective representation of words in HTTP request is a critical step. In this section, we map each word into a word vector using Word2Vec [15]. Word embedding is a key technique in the field of natural language processing, which maps words into a vector. The mapped word vector can usually be used as an input to a neural network. Nowadays, more and more people adopt distributed representations of words in a vector space, because it can help learning algorithms to achieve better performance in natural language processing tasks by grouping similar words. Word2Vec is a excellent toolkit based on distributed representations of words and phrases. Word2Vec can output high-quality word vectors from huge data sets. At the same time, it can also maintain the similarity of semantic words, that is, the distances after similar words are mapped into vectors are similar. Therefore, in this paper, we adopt the model based on Skip-Gram. As shown in Fig. 5, the preprocessed HTTP request is mapped to a vector by Word2Vec.

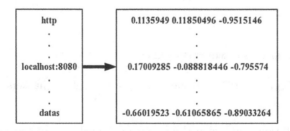

Fig. 5. The preprocessed HTTP request is mapped to a vector

Two popular implementations of Word2Vec are CBoW model and Skip-Gram model. In this paper, we adopt Skip-gram model. The difference between CBoW and Skip-Gram is that for a given context, the CBoW predicts input word,

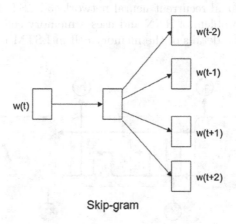

Fig. 6. The architecture of Skip-Gram model [15]

while Skip-Gram predicts the context for a given input word. The architecture of Skip-Gram model is shown in Fig. 6.

The Skip-Gram model is actually divided into two parts. The first part is to build a model, and the second part is to get embedded word vectors through the model.

3.3 Training Model and Detecting Web Attack

We treat the preprocessed sequence in Sect. 3.1 as a word, map it to a vector using word2vec as an input of model. And then we train model based on neural network use train sample. When the model is trained, it can be a classifier to detection Web attack or normal request. The neural network architecture is shown as Fig. 7.

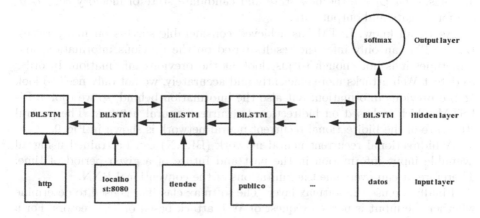

Fig. 7. The neural network architecture

The neural network model we adopted is Bi-LSTM. Bi-LSTM is based on LSTM and bidirectional recurrent neural network [5]. LSTM aims to overcome vanishing gradient problem of RNN and uses a memory cell to present the previous timestamp. The details of the memory cell in LSTM is shown in Fig. 8.

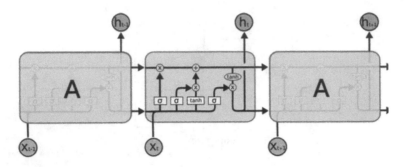

Fig. 8. The memory cell in LSTM.

Current improved LSTM usually consists of three gates in each cell: input, forget, and output. They are calculated as follows:

$$i_t = \sigma(W_i \cdot [h_{t-1}, x_t] + b_i) \tag{1}$$

$$\tilde{C}_t = \tanh(W_c \cdot [h_{t-1}, x_t] + b_C) \tag{2}$$

$$f_t = \sigma(W_f \cdot [h_{t-1}, x_t] + b_f) \tag{3}$$

$$C_t = f_t \cdot C_{t-1} + i_t \cdot \tilde{C}_t \tag{4}$$

$$o_t = \sigma(W_o \cdot [h_{t-1}, x_t] + b_o) \tag{5}$$

$$h_t = f_t \cdot \tanh(C_t) \tag{6}$$

where x_t is the input at time t, W_i, W_C, W_f, W_b are weight matrices, b_i, b_C, b_f, b_o are biases, $C_t, \tilde{C}_t$ are the new state and candidate state of memory cell, f_t, o_t are forget gate and output gate.

As we all know, LSTM has achieved considerable success on many issues. But LSTM can only infer the results based on the previous information, and sometimes it is not enough to just look at the previous information. In order to detect Web attacks more efficiently and accurately, we not only need to look at the previous information, but also the information behind, so we took a Bi-LSTM which is based on bidirectional recurrent neural network. The general structure of the bidirectional recurrent neural network is shown in Fig. 9.

A bidirectional recurrent neural network (BRNN) can be trained using all available input information in the past and future of a given period of time. Therefore, it can overcome the limitations of the conventional RNN.

Finally, we use the softmax layer. The softmax classifier is used to determine whether the input is normal request or Web attack based on the vectors. For a

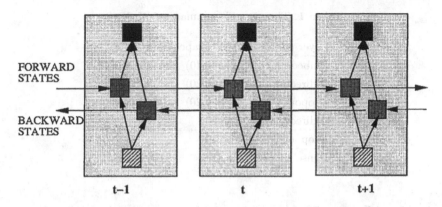

Fig. 9. General structure of the bidirectional recurrent neural network (BRNN) shown unfolded in time for three time steps [5]

list z, z_j, means the j-th element in z, and we set the output function as Softmax function:

$$\sigma(z)_j = \frac{e^{z_j}}{\sum_{k=1}^{K} e^{z_k}} \tag{7}$$

where K denotes the numbers of different labels.

4 Experimental Results and Discussion

This section we conducted various experiments on the dataset HTTP DATASET CSIC 2010 [16] to evaluate the performance of our proposed method for detecting Web attacks.

4.1 Dataset

The HTTP dataset CSIC 2010 includes thousands of automatically generated Web requests which can be used to test Web attack protection systems. It was developed at the Information Security Institute of CSIC (Spanish Research National Council). The HTTP dataset CSIC 2010 includes the generated traffic targeted to an e-Commerce Web application. The dataset includes 36,000 normal requests and more than 25,000 anomalous requests. The HTTP requests are labeled as normal or anomalous.

4.2 Experiment

Experiment Setup. Our experiment software platform uses the Keras (using tensorflow as backend), all the experiments run on a server machine, whose operating system is Ubuntu 14.04. The batch size is 128 and training time is about 10 epochs. The network summary is shown in Table 1. The number of total params is 2060442, all of them is trainable.

Table 1. The network summary of BL-IDS

Layer (type)	Output shape	Param
Embedding	(None,56,40)	2053840
Bidirection	(None,56,20)	4080
Dropout	(None,56,20)	0
Bidirection	(None,20)	2480
Dropout	(None,20)	0
Dense	(None,2)	42

Evaluation Metrics. There are five metrics used to evaluate the performance of BL-IDS detecting Web attacks method: the detection rate, the false alarm rate, the accuracy, the precision and F1 score. According to the commonly used concepts in machine learning methods, we use TP, FP, TN and FN to express the number of true positive, false positive, true negative and false negative respectively. The binary confusion matrix is shown in Table 2. Detection rate (also known as recall rate) and Precision are used to evaluate the system's performance in detecting abnormal HTTP requests. False alarm rate is used to evaluate the misclassifications of normal HTTP requests. Accuracy is used to evaluate the overall performance of the system. The F1 score is used to evaluate the performance of every class of HTTP request, taking into account both precision and detection rate of the classification model. The five criteria formulas are presented below.

Table 2. Binary confusion matrix

	Actual class:abnormal	Actual class:normal
Predicted class:abnormal	TP	FP
Predicted class:normal	FN	TN

$$Detcction\ rate = \frac{TP}{TP + FN} \tag{8}$$

$$Precision = \frac{TP}{TP + FP} \tag{9}$$

$$False\ alarm\ rate = \frac{FP}{FP + TN} \tag{10}$$

$$Accuracy = \frac{TP + TN}{TP + FP + TN + FN} \tag{11}$$

$$F_1\ score = 2 \cdot \frac{precision \cdot detection}{precision + detection} \tag{12}$$

4.3 Results and Discussions

We used batch training methods to train the Bi-LSTM for 10 epochs. The batch size is set as 128 and the validation_split is set as 0.1. We Train on 43966 samples and validate on 4886 samples. The training accuracy and loss and the validation accuracy and loss every one epoch are recorded. The trends of the metrics are

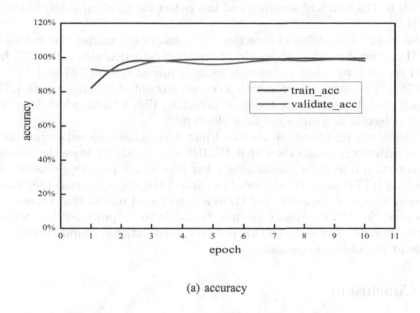

(a) accuracy

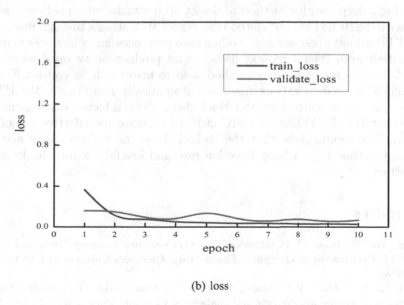

(b) loss

Fig. 10. Accuracy and loss in the training stage

presented in Fig. 10. Figure 10(a) shows the accuracy trends, where the orange curve represents the validation accuracy and the dark cyan represents the training accuracy. It shows that after about 7 epochs of training, both the training and validation accuracies have achieved above 98%. Figure 10(b) shows the loss trends, where the orange curve represents the validation loss and the dark cyan represents the training loss. Clearly, both the training and validation losses decrease rapidly towards 0. The trends of accuracy and loss reflect the good capability of the Bi-LSTM.

We evaluate its ability of detecting Web attacks by running the trained Bi-LSTM on test data after 10 epochs of training, detection rate is 98.17%, false alarm rate is 1.40%, test accuracy is 98.35%, precision is 99.00% and F_1 score is 98.58%. This illustrates that with a certain amount of training, the Bi-LSTM has achieved state-of-the-art results in detecting Web attacks, which have both a high detection rate and a low false alarm rate.

Compared with Zhang [14]'s method, our method has achieved better results. Our experimental results show that BL-IDS can greatly improve the accuracy and detection rate while maintaining a low false alarm rate. Our analysis suggests that HTTP requests are more like natural languages, because they can all be considered as a sequence, and there is a temporal relationship between the sequences. So HTTP requests are more suitable to be processed by recurrent neural networks such as Bi-LSTM. However, convolutional neural networks are better at processing image tasks.

5   Conclusion

Exploring a deep learning method to detect Web attacks, which is based on the RNN with the Bi-LSTM. The method can detect Web attacks through inspecting the HTTP request packets. First, studing data preprocessing, which selects useful information from HTTP request packets and produce many word sequences. Second, studing the embedding method used to map words to vectors. Finally, a Bi-LSTM is used to extract features automatically and classify the HTTP request packets to normal or abnormal class. We conducted experiments on the dataset HTTP DATASET CSIC 2010 to evaluate the effectiveness of the method. The results show that the Bi-LSTM can be trained easily and the detection method have a high detection rate and low false alarms in detecting Web attacks.

References

1. Axelsson, S.: Research in intrusion-detection systems: a survey. Technical report 98–17, Department of Computer Engineering, Chalmers University of Technology (1998)
2. Garcia, T.P., Diaz, V.J., Macia, F.G., et al.: Anomaly-based network intrusion detection: techniques, systems and challenges. Comput. Secur. **28**(1), 18–28 (2009)
3. OWASP. https://www.owasp.org/index.php/SQL_Injection_Bypassing_WAF

4. Lupták, P.: Bypassing Web application firewalls. In: Proceedings of 6th International Scientific Conference on Security and Protection of Information, pp. 79–88 (2011)
5. Schuster, M., Paliwal, K.K.: Bidirectional recurrent neural networks. IEEE Trans. Signal Process. **45**(11), 2673–2681 (1997)
6. Kruegel, C., Vigna, G., Robertson, W.: A multi-model approach to the detection of web-based attacks. Comput. Netw. **48**(5), 717–738 (2005)
7. Abou-Assaleh, T., Cercone, N., Keselj, V., Sweidan, R.: N-gram-based detection of new malicious code. In: Proceedings of the 28th Annual International Computer Software and Applications Conference, COMPSAC 2004, vol. 2, pp. 41–42. IEEE (2004)
8. Moh, M., Pininti, S., Doddapaneni, S., Moh, T.S.: Detecting Web attacks using multi-stage log analysis. In: IEEE International Conference on Advanced Computing, pp. 733–738 (2016)
9. Cao, L.C.: Detecting web-based attacks by machine learning. In: 2006 International Conference on Machine Learning and Cybernetics, pp. 2737–2742. IEEE (2006)
10. Cui, J., Long, J., Min, E., Mao, Y.: WEDL-NIDS: improving network intrusion detection using word embedding-based deep learning method. In: Torra, V., Narukawa, Y., Aguiló, I., González-Hidalgo, M. (eds.) MDAI 2018. LNCS (LNAI), vol. 11144, pp. 283–295. Springer, Cham (2018). https://doi.org/10.1007/978-3-030-00202-2_23
11. Krizhevsky, A., Sutskever, I., Hinton, G.E.: ImageNet classification with deep convolutional neural networks. In: Advances in Neural Information Processing Systems, pp. 1097–1105 (2012)
12. Hochreiter, S., Schmidhuber, J.: Long short-term memory. Neural Comput. **9**(8), 1735–1780 (1997)
13. Valeur, F., Mutz, D., Vigna, G.: A learning-based approach to the detection of SQL attacks. In: Julisch, K., Kruegel, C. (eds.) DIMVA 2005. LNCS, vol. 3548, pp. 123–140. Springer, Heidelberg (2005). https://doi.org/10.1007/11506881_8
14. Zhang, M., Xu, B., Bai, S., Lu, S., Lin, Z.: A deep learning method to detect web attacks using a specially designed CNN. In: Liu, D., Xie, S., Li, Y., Zhao, D., El-Alfy, E.-S.M. (eds.) ICONIP 2017. LNCS, vol. 10638, pp. 828–836. Springer, Cham (2017). https://doi.org/10.1007/978-3-319-70139-4_84
15. Mikolov, T., Sutskever, I., Chen, K., Corrado, G.S., Dean, J.: Distributed representations of words and phrases and their compositionality. In: Advances in Neural Information Processing Systems, pp. 3111–3119 (2013)
16. HTTP DATASET CSIC 2010. http://www.isi.csic.es/dataset/

An Static Propositional Function Model to Detect Software Vulnerability

Lansheng Han, Man Zhou[✉], and Cai Fu

School of Computer Science and Technology,
Huazhong University of Science and Technology, Wuhan, China
{hanlansheng,zhou_man1125}@hust.edu.cn

Abstract. Due to lacking proper theory to accurately describe characteristics of vulnerability, the existing static detection models are designed for specific vulnerability is hard to be expanded and the latter often encounters the state space explosion and with higher false positive rate. This paper proposes a static detection model of a five-tuple $(n_0; F; S; P; Q)$: the vulnerability initial nodes set, program state space, Vulnerability Syntax Rules, preconditions of vulnerability, and post-conditions of vulnerability are accurately described. We design a testing prototype system for the static detection model and carry out experiments to evaluate the results with the vulnerabilities disclosed by NIST. Our model find more vulnerabilities of Wireshark than published by NIST and shows higher detection efficiency than that of FindBugs. Formal accurately description is prerequisite of auto-detection of vulnerability.

Keywords: Software vulnerability · Propositional function ·
Static analysis · State space explosion

1 Introduction

With the advent of information society and the popularization of software applications, more security problems of computer are arising from software vulnerabilities. Software vulnerability is weakness in software systems that may cause the application crash or be exploited by a threat to gain unauthorized access to information [1,2]. So software vulnerability detection has been a research focus of information security in recent years [3]. And various detection approaches are put forward [4,5].

1.1 Motivation and Contributions

All these existing approaches are falling into three main categories: static, dynamic, and integrated analysis systems. But due to lacking proper theory to accurately describe characteristics of vulnerability, they are imprecise, resulting

© ICST Institute for Computer Sciences, Social Informatics and Telecommunications Engineering 2019
Published by Springer Nature Switzerland AG 2019. All Rights Reserved
J. Li et al. (Eds.): SPNCE 2019, LNICST 284, pp. 564–575, 2019.
https://doi.org/10.1007/978-3-030-21373-2_46

in a large amount of false positives. Dynamic analysis systems, such as "fuzzers", can provide conditional inputs. However, they suffer from exhaustive test cases.

Current researches agree that every software vulnerability is caused by some flaws or defects of the software [3]. Most software defects and flaws are parts of software inherent attributes and they always occur regularly [6]. So we believe that software vulnerabilities follow certain patterns and can be identified by them if the patterns are accurately be described [7].

Many years of the research on the vulnerabilities detection make us believe false positives are caused by suspicion or misunderstanding, the both are due to the lack of an accurate formal description of the vulnerability especially for some high speed detecting tools.

In this paper, we propose a vulnerability static detection model by abstracting the characteristics of a variety of vulnerabilities in form of propositional function. We focus on software source code detection and try to formalize patterns of vulnerability. If there is a violation of patterns in a program, there will be software vulnerability. We discriminate and describe a variety of software vulnerabilities formally by this model.

1.2 Related Work

In the following, we briefly review the prior work most closely related to our model in two groups: theoretical approaches and mature tools.

Clarke proposed a formal software vulnerability testing technology which can judge whether a given program meets the pre-defined characteristics or not by traversing the state space [8]. Obviously, there will be a state space explosion when it is used to detect large-scale programs.

Describing vulnerability characters appropriately is a critical step for its detection. Wilander proposed a generic way to model the security characteristics of codes by vulnerability dependency graph [9].

B. Liang and K.K. Hou proposed an expanded finite-state machine model which can traverse the possible executable paths in a program statically and identify the current operation. This model reduces the false positives to some extent, but all possible executable paths in the program need to be traversed, so the detect efficiency still needs to be improved [10].

Compass is a static analysis tool for checking source code designed by ROSE Team [11]. It does not describe the characteristics of vulnerabilities in depth.

Some lightweight approaches include Rats [12], Prefast [13] as well as Splint [14], they can not find deep layer vulnerabilities and also require manual annotations. FindBugs is a static analysis tool to find defects in Java code but not a style checker.

There are some other tools, like Coverity, Fortify, CodeSonar, and IBM Security AppScan Source (formerly Rational). Due to the auto scanning, those tools can make thorough analysis with configurable rule sets. Lack of formal description of vulnerability, thorough scanning need long run time and the false positive rate is still high [15].

2   Static Detection Model Based on Propositional Function

CFG (Control Flow Graph) and PDG (program dependency graph) are two important useful data structures for program static analysis [16,17]. A CFG is a directed graph that shows all paths might be traversed through a program during its execution, whose edges represent possible flow of control between statements [18]. Amed at describing vulnerability conveniently by the propositional function, we define the related concepts in CFG and PDG at first.

2.1   Related Definitions in CFG

Let n_i and n_j be two nodes on CFG:

Definition 1. *In a CFG, if there is sequence $p = <n_0, ..., n_m>$ which meets $(n_{i-1}, n_i) \in E$, where $i = 1, 2...m$. Then there is an executable path between n_0 and n_m, denoted by $EP(n_0, n_m)$. The set of all the executable paths in program denoted by EP.*

Definition 2. *If there is an executable path $EP(n_i, n_j)$ between n_i and n_j, then n_i is the predecessor node of n_j, denoted by $Pred(n_i, n_j)$; n_j is the successor node of n_i, denoted by $Succ(n_i, n_j)$. Let n be a sentence, and the set of all its predecessor nodes called the precursor node set of n, denoted by $Pred(n)$. The set of all its successor nodes is called the successor node set of n, denoted by $Succ(n)$.*

Definition 3. *In a CFG, n_i is post-dominated by n_j if every directed path from n_i to $Exit$(not including n_i) contains n_j, denoted by $PD(n_j, n_i)$. It should be noted that n_i is not the post-dominator of itself. Let n be a sentence, and the set of all its post-dominator is called the post-dominator set of n, denoted by $PD(n)$.*

Definition 4. *There is an executable path $EP(n_i, n_j)$. n_j is data dependent on n_i, denoted by $DD(n_j, n_i, v)$ if*

(1) there is a variable v, the value of v at n_i has been used during execution of n_j.
(2) v is not redefined on $EP(n_i, n_j)$.

Definition 5. *There is an executable path between n_i and n_j. n_j is control dependent on n_i, denoted by $CD(n_i, n_j)$ if*

(1) each node on $EP(n_i, n_j)$ from n_i to n_j (except n_i and n_j) is post-dominated by n_j.
(2) n_i is not post-dominated by n_j.

2.2   Vulnerability Static Detection Model Based on Propositional Function

Following the above definitions, we can construct our detection model based on propositional function.

Definition 6. *The detection model is defined as a five-tuple denoted as Vulnerability = $\{n_0, F, S, P, Q\}$. It includes the vulnerability initial nodes set, program state space, Vulnerability Syntax Rules, preconditions of vulnerability, and post-conditions of vulnerability. The followings are the detailed description of the five-tuple.*

Vulnerability initial nodes set n_0. n_0 is the initial characteristic nodes of vulnerability which is the entrance node of vulnerability detection. For a program M, its sentence is finite. So, the vulnerability initial nodes set n_0 is finite and certain.

Program state space F. F is the program state space extracted from source code, CFG and PDG. It contains the EP in program, control dependency and data dependency among nodes. F is an Intermediate Representation which contains all necessary information for vulnerability detection, and it can not be empty.

Vulnerability Syntax Rules set S. S is a set of vulnerability syntax rules which are state transition rules between vulnerability initial nodes set n_0 and vulnerable nodes set N on EP.

Precondition P. P is Precondition which means that any node $n(n \in N)$ must meet these state conditions before executing, where N is the set of nodes related to vulnerabilities. Otherwise, there will be a vulnerability.

Post-conditions Q. Q is Post-conditions which means that any node n in N must meet these rules after executing. Otherwise, there will be a vulnerability.

With the model above, the complete process of vulnerability detection can be described as $F : \{P\}n_0 \xrightarrow{s} N\{Q\}$. This process has two steps:

Step 1. Locate vulnerabilities roughly. $n_0 \xrightarrow{s} N$ means that we find the vulnerable node which conforms to the Vulnerability Syntax Rules set S from n_0 on EP. For any $EP_i(EP_i \in F)$, if there is a node n_1 conforms to $n_0 \xrightarrow{s} n_1$, n_1 is a vulnerability related node, $n_1 \in N$.

Step 2. Locate vulnerabilities precisely. $\{P\}N\{Q\}$ means that we detect the vulnerable nodes set N by Precondition P and Post-conditions Q. For any $EP_i(EP_i \in F)$, if there is node n_2 conforms to $n_1 \xrightarrow{p} n_2$ before n_1 executing, and there is node n_3 conforms to $n_1 \xrightarrow{Q} n_3$ after n_1 executing, the detection result is TRUE, and n_1 does not have a vulnerability. Before n_1 executing, if $\neg \forall n_2$ conforms to $n_1 \xrightarrow{p} n_2$, or after n_1 executing, $\neg \forall n_3$ conforms to $n_1 \xrightarrow{Q} n_3$, detection result is FALSE and n_1 has a vulnerability.

Next we will use propositional function to describe some types of software vulnerabilities.

2.3   Formal Description of Software Vulnerability Based on Propositional Function

In this paper, we focus on describing and detecting nine software vulnerabilities in four types with CWE number which are the most prone to general programs, as shown in Table 1. Before formulating these software vulnerabilities, we also need some definitions in the form of propositional function.

Table 1. Software vulnerabilities

Vulnerability	CWE number
Null Pointer Dereference	CWE-476; CWE-690
Buffer Overflow	CWE-119; CWE-120
Uncontrolled Format String	CWE-134
Resource Relation Flaws	CWE-401; CWE-404; CWE-415; CWE-416

Definition 7. *The way to use variable v can be described as definition-use-check relationships. $DEF(v, n)$ means the statement, definition or assignment of v at sentence n; $USE(v, n)$ means v is used or cited on node n; $CHECK(v, n, Statement)$ means detect the statement of v on node n. For example, $CHECK(v, n, Null)$ means detecting whether the statement of v on n is Null or not, and the check result will be True or False.*

Definition 8. *The type of a parameter in program M can be described by corresponding propositional functions. For example: pointer variable $v = \{v | \exists v \in M, type\ of\ v\ is\ Pointer\}$ is denoted by $Pointer(v)$; function f is denoted by $Function(f)$, etc.*

Definition 9. *Use the $ResourceAllocateFunctionList$ to denote the function set related to resource allocation. In C Programming Language the common resource allocation functions are malloc(), fopen(), calloc(), new(), etc. The $ResourceAllocateFunctionList(n)$ denotes resource allocation functions on node n, abbreviated as $RAF(n)$. $ResourceRelease(n)$ means to release resources related to resource allocation functions $RAF(n)$ on node n, abbreviated as $RR(n)$.*

Definition 10. *The format functions are denoted by $FormatFunctionList$. In C Programming Language common format functions include printf(), strncpy(), fwprintf(), snwscanf(), fprint(), printf(), etc. $FormatFunction(n)$ means format function which is called on node n, abbreviated as $FF(n)$.*

Definition 11.
The buffer related functions are denoted by $BufferFunction(n)$. The common buffer related API functions include memcpy(), strcpy(), sprint(), vsprintf(), gets(), scanf(), strcat(), etc.

Definition 12. *Propositional function CallFunction(n) means the information of functions called on node n.*

Definition 13. *Propositional function SharedResource(v, n) means shared resources on node n in program v. Propositional function SharedResource(v) means the set of all shared resources in program v.*

Definition 14. *Propositional function $IsIn(n_1, n_2)$ means $n_1 \subseteq n_2$ and propositional function $\neg IsIn(n_1, n_2)$ means $n_1 \not\subseteq n_2$.*

With these formal definition we can present formal propositional function for software vulnerability. We summarize the characteristics of these vulnerabilities and achieve its propositional function.

(1) Null Pointer Dereference. For a target program M, the set of sentence n which defines or declares pointers in M is vulnerability initial nodes set denoted by n_0. Its propositional function is:

$$n_0 = \{n | \exists n \in M \wedge DEF(Pointer(v), n)\}. \tag{1}$$

On any executable path $EP_i(EP_i \in EP)$, if there is a successor node n_1 of n_0 which calls $Pointer(v)$ and is data dependent on n_0 with $Pointer(v)$, n_1 is a vulnerable node s. Its propositional function is:

$$S = Succ(n_1, n_0) \wedge DD(n1, n0, Pointer(v)) \wedge USE(Pointer(v), n_1). \tag{2}$$

On this executable path $EP_i(EP_i \in EP)$, if there is a node n_2 which is data dependent on n_0 with $Pointer(v)$ and vulnerable node n_1 is control dependent on n_2, and $Pointer(v)$ is Null on n_2, n_1 does not have any vulnerability. Otherwise, n_1 has vulnerabilities. Its propositional function is:

$$P = DD(n_2, n_0, Pointer(v)) \wedge CD(n_2, n_1) \wedge CHECK(Pointer(v), n_2, NotNull), \tag{3}$$

Q on NPD is Null.

(2) Buffer overflow. For a target program M, the set of sentence n which calls the buffer related functions is vulnerability initial nodes set denoted by n_0. Its propositional function is:

$$n_0 = \{n | \exists n \in M \ wedge CallFunction(n) \subseteq Buffer FunctionList\}. \tag{4}$$

On any executable path $EP_i(EP_i \in EP)$, if n_0 is data dependent on $Buffer(v_1)$ which is defined on the predecessor node n_1 of n_0, n_0 is a vulnerable node. Its propositional function is:

$$S = DD(n_0, n_1, Buffer(v_1, n_0)) \wedge DEF(Buffer(v_1), n_1) \wedge Pred(n_1, n_0). \tag{5}$$

On this executable path $EP_i(EP_i \in EP)$, if there is a node n_2 that n_0 is control dependent on, and n_1 is the postdominator of n_2, and both buffer size and input data length are matching, n_2 does not have vulnerability. Otherwise, n_2 has vulnerabilities. Its propositional function is:

$$P = CD(n_2, n_0) \land PD(n_2, n_1) \land CHECK(buffer(v_1), input(v_2), n_1, Size) \cup$$
$$CHECK(buffer(v_1), input(v_2), n_0, Size),$$
(6)

Q on Buffer Overflow is null.

(3) Uncontrolled Format String. For a target program M, the set of sentence n which calls $FormatFunctionList$ is vulnerability initial nodes set. Its propositional function is:

$$n_0 = \{n | \exists n \in M \land CallFunction(n) \subseteq FormatFunctionList\}. \quad (7)$$

On any executable path $EP_i(EP_i \in EP)$, if n_0 is data dependent on variable v defined on its predecessor node n_1, n_0 is a vulnerable node. Its propositional function is:

$$S = Succ(n_1, n_0) \land DEF(v, n_1) \land DD(n_0, n_1, v). \quad (8)$$

On this EP_i, if both the type and the number of parameters in a format string function are matching on node n_0, the result is TRUE, which means n_0 does not have vulnerability. Otherwise, n_0 has vulnerabilities. Its propositional function is:

$$P = CHECK(FF(n_0), n_0, Parameter), \quad (9)$$

and Q is null.

(4) Resource Related Flaws. In target program M, the set of sentence n which defines or declares a variable v belonging to resource allocation functionlist is a vulnerability initial nodes set n_0. Its propositional function is:

$$n_0 = \{n | \exists n \in M \land DEF(v, n) \subseteq ResourceAllocateFunctionList\}. \quad (10)$$

On any executable path EP_i, if node n_1 which is the successor node of n_0 calls resource allocation functions on n_0 denoted by $RAF(n_0)$ and is data dependent on n_0 which is the precursor node of n_1 with $RAF(n_0)$, n_1 is a vulnerable node. Its propositional function is:

$$S = USE(RAF(n_0), n_1) \cup Succ(n_1, n_0) \land DD(n_1, n_0, RAF(n_0)). \quad (11)$$

On this EP_i, if there is not resource release operation $RR(n_2)$ corresponding resource allocation functions $RAF(n_0)$ on node n_2 which is the precursor node of n_1, the precondition P is True. Its propositional function is:

$$P = Pred(n_2, n_1) \land IsIn(RR(n_2), RAF(n_0)). \quad (12)$$

On this EP_i, if there is node n_3 which is the post-dominator of n_1 and is data dependent on its predecessor node n_0 with $RAF(n_0)$, and there is resource release operation $RR(n_1)$ or $RR(n_3)$ corresponding $RAF(n_0)$, the post-conditions Q is True. Its propositional function is:

$$Q = PD(n_3, n_1) \wedge DD(n_3, n_1, RAF(n_0)) \wedge (IsIn(RAF(n_0), RR(n_3))$$
$$\cup IsIn(RAF(n_0), RR(n_1))). \tag{13}$$

We must consider the case that if n_0 can not deduce n_1 by the vulnerability syntax rules set S, the variables or functions defined on n_0 belong to redundant code.

3 Detection Algorithm

Based on this model, we design a static detection process for software vulnerability analysis, as shown in Fig. 1. It includes: basic information analysis and rules.

3.1 Basic Information Analysis

The basic information analysis module is used to generate and extract some basic static information from target program, as shown in Fig. 1.

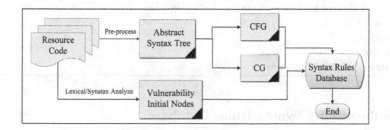

Fig. 1. Basic processing module flow chart

Firstly, use lexical and syntax analysis to extract vulnerability initial nodes set n_0 from target program source code. Secondly, use compiler front-end (such as GCC, java compiler) to generate abstract syntax tree AST, and construct CFG and CG (call graph).

3.2 Solution of Vulnerable Nodes Set N

Vulnerable nodes set N is a set of nodes which may contain vulnerabilities. Solving N is the coarse locating process of vulnerability analysis which we described in Sect. 3.2. Steps of Solving N are as follows:

Step 1. Search the program state space F starting from vulnerability initial nodes set n_0.

Step 2. Insert the nodes which conform to vulnerability syntax rules S into vulnerable nodes set N.

Algorithm 1 is shown as follow:

Algorithm 1. The algorithm of solving vulnerable nodes set N

1: **Input**: space F
2: **Output**: vulnerable nodes set N_{EPSi}
3: Initialization: $N_{EPSi} = \{\emptyset\}$
4: **for** each $n \in EPSi$, except n_0 **do**
5:    **if** $(Relation(n_0, n) \subseteq F\&\&Relation(n_0, n) == Si)$ **then**
6:       $N_{EPSi} = N_{EPSi} \bigcup n$
7:    **end if**
8: **end for**
9: **return** N_{VEPSi}

Algorithm 2. The algorithm of discriminating vulnerability

1: **Input**: space F, N_{EPS_i}, preconditions P, post-conditions Q
2: **Output**: Vulnerable Nodes
3: Initialization: Vulnerable Nodes= $\{\emptyset\}$
4: **for** each $n \in N_{EPS_i}$ **do**
5:    **for** each $m \in EPS_i, m \neq n$ **do**
6:       **if** $(Relation(n, m) \subsetneq F)$ **then**
7:          Vulnerable Nodes=Vulnerable Nodes $\bigcup n$
8:       **else if** $(Relation(n, m) \in F\&\&(Relation(n, m)! = P||(Relation(n, m)! = Q))$ **then**
9:          Vulnerable Nodes=Vulnerable Nodes $\bigcup n$
10:      **end if**
11:   **end for**
12: **end for**
13: **return** Vulnerable Nodes

3.3 Vulnerability Syntax Rules Database

Vulnerability rules database is a database which includes vulnerability syntax rules set S, vulnerability preconditions P and vulnerability post-conditions Q. It also contains some API functions, such as $ResourceAllocation$ $FunctionList, FormatFunctionList, BufferFunctionList$, and so on.

According to Definitions 2–5 in Sect. 2.1, Definition 6 in Sect. 2.2 and Definitions 7, 12, 14 in Sect. 2.3, we summarize the vulnerability syntax rules for S, P, Q in Table 2.

4 Experiments and Evaluation

To evaluate the effectiveness of our approach, we proceed to evaluate our method by carrying on experiments from Sep., 2013 to May, 2016 on 4 open resource software and contrast of detection on CWE-476($Tomcat$4.0) of our method with FindBug 3.0.1.

We have verified and confirmed the vulnerabilities of 4 open source projects which was disclosed by NIST, shown as Table 3.

Table 2. Vulnerability syntax rules S, P, Q of the four types of vulnerability

Vulnerability types	Syntax rules for S, P, Q
Null Pointer Dereference	$S = Succ(n_1, n_0) \wedge DD(n1, n0, Pointer(v)) \wedge USE(Pointer(v), n_1)$ $P = DD(n_2, n_0, Pointer(v)) \wedge CD(n_2, n_1) \wedge CHECK(Pointer(v), n_2, NotNull)$ $Q = \emptyset$
Buffer Overflow	$S = DD(n_0, n_1, Buffer(v_1, n_0)) \wedge DEF(Buffer(v_1), n_1) \wedge Pred(n_1, n_0)$ $P = CD(n_2, n_0) \wedge PD(n_2, n_1) \wedge CHECK(buffer(v_1), input(v_2), n_1, Size)$ $\cup CHECK(buffer(v_1), input(v_2), n_0, Size)$ $Q = \emptyset$
Uncontrolled Format String	$S = Succ(n_1, n_0) \wedge DEF(v, n_1) \wedge DD(n_0, n_1, v)$ $P = CHECK(FF(n_0), n_0, Parameter)$ $Q = \emptyset$
Resource Flaws	$S = USE(RAF(n_0), n_1) \cup Succ(n_1, n_0) \wedge DD(n_1, n_0, RAF(n_0))$ $P = Pred(n_2, n_1) \wedge IsIn(RR(n_2), RAF(n_0))$ $Q = PD(n_3, n_1) \wedge DD(n_3, n_1, RAF(n_0)) \wedge (IsIn(RAF(n_0), RR(n_3))$ $\cup IsIn(RAF(n_0), RR(n_1)))$

Table 3. Verify and confirm the vulnerabilities disclosed by NIST

Vtype		NPD	BF	UFS	RRF
Chrome 5.0	NISTnum	0	1	0	5
	FOLBnum	0	1	0	5
Wireshark1.8	NISTnum	1	43	1	0
	FOLBnum	1	40	1	0
ABM1.0	NISTnum	0	58	8	9
	FOLBnum	0	49	8	8
Asterisk10.2	NISTnum	5	14	0	0
	FOLBnum	5	14	0	0
The accuracy of FOLB^EPS		100%	88.9%	100%	92.8%

Notation: The accuracy of FOLB^EPS = FOLBnum/NISTnum

As shown in Table 3, the open source projects that we test covering all types of vulnerabilities we describe in this paper. Results show that resource operations flaws, null pointer dereference and format string have high detection accuracy. And buffer overflow has low false positives rate and false negatives rate. Therefore, the method that we propose can be applied to detect most of vulnerabilities.

A Java project tomcat 4.0 is a real software system widely used as serverlet container, whose vulnerabilities are also disclosed by $NIST$. Here we use our method to detect $Null\ Pointer\ Dereference(CWE\text{-}476)$ and compare the result with that of FindBugs 3.0.1. Although FindBugs has been around for a long time, due to its universality and openness, we select the newer FindBugs 3.0.1 as the experiment tool. The result is shown in Table 4.

Table 4. Null Pointer Dereference (CWE-476) detection results contrast on Tomcat 4.0 between FindBugs 3.0.1 and FOLB^EPS

Detection tools	Detection result	Confirmed	Confirmed as false positives number	Can't confirmed	False positives rate	Detection rate
FindBugs	36	2	22	12	61.1%	5.6%
FOLB^EPS	42	13	21	8	50%	30.9%

The result shows that the detection rate of our method is higher than that of FindBugs and the False positives rate is also lower than that of FindBugs.

5   Conclusions and Future Work

In this paper, we proposed a static vulnerability detection model based on propositional function. Firstly, we defined and described the existing preconditions, characteristics and properties of vulnerabilities, and gave corresponding discriminant formula in terms of propositional function. Then constructed our detection model with a five-tuple. Then we designed a static detection process according to the new model, and used propositional function to described four types of disclosed software vulnerabilities in CWE. Finally, we carried out experiments, to verify that our model based on the propositional function realized more accurate description of vulnerability, improved detection rate and reduced the false alarm rate.

Acknowledgement. This work was supported in part by the National Natural Science Foundation of China under Grant (No. 61272033, 61272045, 61572222); and the National Grand Fundamental Research 973 Program Foundation of China (No. 2014CB340600). We also thank students of class 2013, 2014 and 2015 majoring information security in our university for their hard work of analysis and collecting vulnerability information of many $C/C++/Java$ open sources. They filtered 7,168 vulnerabilities and achieved 1,761 vulnerabilities, patches and attribute information see the attachment1.

References

1. Martins, E., Morais, A., Cavalli, A.: Generating attack scenarios for the validation of security protocol implementations. In: The 2nd Brazilian Workshop on Systematic and Automated Software Testing (SBES 2008 -SAST), Brazil, October 2008
2. Du, W., Mathur, A.: Vulnerability testing of software system using fault injection. In: Proceeding of the International Conference on Dependable Systems and Networks (DSN 2000), Workshop on Dependability Versus Malicious Faults (2000)
3. Chen, Z.Q., Zhang, Y., Chen, Z.R.: A categorization framework for common vulnerabilities and exposures. Comput. J. Arch. **53**(5), 551–580 (2010)
4. Perl, H., Dechand, S., Smith, M., et al.: VCCFinder: finding potential vulnerabilities in open-source projects to assist code audits. In: ACM SIGSAC Conference on Computer and Communications Security, pp. 426–437. ACM (2015)
5. Czibula, G., Marian, Z., Czibula, I.G.: Software defect prediction using relational association rule mining. Inf. Sci. **264**(183), 260–278 (2014)
6. Li, P., Cui, B.J.: A comparative study on software vulnerability static analysis techniques and tools. In: IEEE International Conference on Information Theory and Information Security, pp. 521–524. IEEE Press, Beijing (2010)
7. Zeng, F.P., Chen, A.Z., Tao, X.: Study on software reliability design criteria based on defect patterns. In: Proceedings of the 8th International Conference on Reliability, Maintainability and Safety (ICRMS 2009), pp. 723–727. IEEE, Chengdu (2009)
8. Clarke, E., Grumberg, O., Peled, D.: Model Checking. MIT Press, Cambridge (1999)
9. Wilander, J.: Modeling and visualizing security properties of code using dependence graphs. In: Proceedings of 5th Conference on Software Engineering Research and Practice in Sweden, pp. 65–74. ACM Press, Vasteras (2005)
10. Meland, P., Spampinato, D., Hagen, E., Baadshaug, E., Krister, K., Velle, K.: SeaMonster: providing tool support for security modeling. In: National Conference on Information Security, NISK 2008, November 2008
11. Quinlan, D., Panas, T.: Source code and binary analysis of software defects. In: 5th Annual Workshop on Cyber Security and Information Intelligence Challenges and Strategies, pp. 1–4. AMC Press, New York (2009)
12. Rough Auditing Tool for Security (RATS). https://code.google.com/p/rough-auditing-tool-for-security/. Accessed Jan 2015
13. PREfast Analysis Tool. https://msdn.microsoft.com/enus/library/ms933794.aspx. Accessed Jan 2015
14. Splint Annotation-Assisted Lightweight Static Checking. http://splint.org/. Accessed Jan 2015
15. Coverity Scan — Static Analysis. https://scan.coverity.com/. Accessed Aug 2015
16. Allence, F.E.: Control flow analysis. ACM SIGPLAN Not. **5**(7), 1–19 (1970)
17. Ferrante, J., Ottenstein, K.J., Warren, J.D.: The program dependence graph and its use in optimization. ACM Trans. Program. Lang. Syst. **9**(3), 319–349 (1987)
18. Horwitz, S., Reps, T., Binkley, D.: Interprocedural slicing using dependence graphs. In: ACM/SIGPLAN88 Conference on Programming Language Design and Implementation, pp. 26–60. ACM Press, Atlanta (1988)

Design of ZigBee-Based Energy Harvesting Wireless Sensor Network and Modeling of Solar Energy

Yingcong Liu, Wuyungerile Li[✉], Baoyintu, and Bing Jia

Inner Mongolia University, Hohhot 010000, China
gerile@imu.edu.cn

Abstract. Traditional wireless sensor networks rely on battery power to operate, but when the node's energy is exhausted, the node loses its ability to operate. To enable wireless sensor networks to achieve continuous working, researchers have turned their attention to energy harvesting wireless sensor networks. The energy harvesting wireless sensor network has the advantages of energy renewable, low maintenance cost, etc., and can achieve permanent use of nodes to a certain extent. However, the energy collected by nodes in such networks will change with the change of environment and time, so the survival of energy-gathering wireless sensor networks in environmental detection needs further study and research. In view of the above problems, we designed a solar energy harvesting wireless sensor network in this paper, and designed energy harvesting and energy consumption related experiments to record the energy and network characteristics under different weather and time, collected under different conditions, and model the solar energy collected under different circumstances, so as to provide basic data for the further research of network reliability and other characteristics.

Keywords: Zigbee · EH-WSN · Energy model

1 Introduction

As a low-cost, small-sized wireless communication computer network, Wireless Sensor Networks (WSNs) can be placed in ridiculous areas for environmental monitoring for a long time [1]. Since the battery energy of wireless sensor networks is limited [2], research on wireless sensor networks is now focused on how to improve the efficiency of energy utilization and extend the service life of nodes [3]. In addition, there are batteries in the wireless sensor network. In a harsh environment, the battery may leak, which is serious for environmental pollution and is not suitable for large-scale deployment [4]. In contrast, energy harvesting wireless sensor networks can collect energy from the environment, enable energy in the battery to be recycled, and use energy sources such as solar, wind, and vibration energy [5]. After the node dies, the energy harvesting

© ICST Institute for Computer Sciences, Social Informatics and Telecommunications Engineering 2019
Published by Springer Nature Switzerland AG 2019. All Rights Reserved
J. Li et al. (Eds.): SPNCE 2019, LNICST 284, pp. 576–584, 2019.
https://doi.org/10.1007/978-3-030-21373-2_47

equipment collects energy from the environment, fills the energy storage device, and restarts the node, achieving the permanent work of the node to a certain extent [6]. In this paper, solar panels are used to collect solar energy and convert it into electrical energy. After the maximum power is tracked, the charging management module supplies power to the rechargeable battery of the wireless sensor node. However there are still some unavoidable problems in energy harvesting wireless sensor networks. The randomness and uncertainty of energy collection seriously restrict the development of energy harvesting wireless sensor networks. How to adjust the working state of nodes based on the collected uncertain energy has become an urgent problem to be solved. In this paper, we mainly design and implement the solar illuminance collection experiment, to collect the illuminance data and model the illuminance data of different time and different weather for the future solar energy collection wireless sensor network.

2 EH-WSN Overall Structural Design

For the whole system, the energy-gathering wireless sensor network platform designed in this paper is composed of solar energy-gathering wireless sensor nodes [7], sink nodes and upper computer (as shown in Fig. 1). Among them, the solar collector wireless sensor node monitors the surrounding environment information as the terminal node and the routing node. The collected information is simply processed and uploaded to the coordinator node. Finally, the coordinator node uploads the information to the host computer through Rs485. In terms of energy use, terminal nodes and routing nodes collect solar energy through solar panels, and the energy comes from clean and pollution-free solar energy in the environment. The power supply of the sink node is supplied by the upper computer without considering the energy loss. ZigBee communication is used between each node. The whole platform realizes the functions of data acquisition, processing, transmission and display.

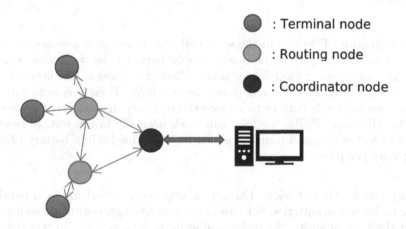

Fig. 1. Energy harvesting type wireless sensor overall structure.

2.1   System Hardware Design

The energy harvesting wireless sensor hardware mainly includes the design of terminal nodes, routing nodes and aggregation nodes. For the ZigBee wireless sensor network, it mainly includes the design of routers, coordinators and terminal devices. Among them, the number of terminal devices is the largest, which is an important information collection device and the network component in the whole system. The router device is set as a node with both acquisition and routing functions. The hardware design is the same as the terminal device, and the software configuration is different. The overall hardware design of the terminal node and the router node is shown in Fig. 2. It is mainly composed of a solar energy collection module, an energy storage device, a sensor module, a microprocessor (MCU) module, and a ZigBee communication module. Since the energy harvesting wireless sensor network is adopted in this paper, this paper focuses on the energy harvesting module and energy storage part of the sensor node.

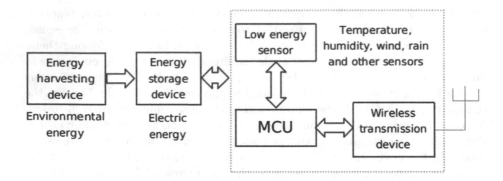

Fig. 2. EH-WSN node.

Energy Storage Device. In the solar collector type wireless sensor network, the most important part is the power supply part. Unlike traditional wireless sensor networks, power modules for solar-collected wireless sensor networks can collect energy from the environment and recycle it [8]. Therefore, in this article, we use a rechargeable battery to replace the ordinary dry battery. Considering that the MCU and ZigBee modules can work normally in the voltage range of 3.7 V to 7 V, the designed terminal uses a rechargeable lithium battery of 3.7 V to 4.2 V for the power supply.

Energy Harvesting Device. This article selects 6 V polysilicon solar panels to charge rechargeable batteries. Since the solar panel voltage output varies depending on the light intensity, the rechargeable battery cannot be directly charged. This paper designs the use of maximum power tracking (MPPT) technology to power rechargeable batteries and other modules. The overall design is shown in Fig. 3. The MPPT controller can detect the generated voltage of the solar panel in real time and track the highest voltage and current values (VI). To allow the system to charge the battery with maximum power output. It is the brain of photovoltaic system used in solar photovoltaic systems to coordinate the work of solar panels, batteries and loads.

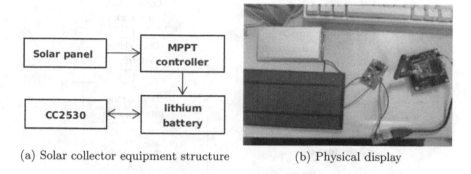

(a) Solar collector equipment structure   (b) Physical display

Fig. 3. Energy harvesting equipment

Microprocessor (MCU) Module. This paper uses a microprocessor module that is an enhanced 8051 integrated on the CC2530 chip, with lower power consumption, 8 kB of RAM, and optional 32/64/128/256 KB flash. Since the ZigBee stack Z-Stack is required to run, 256 KB of flash memory is selected.

Sensor Module. The sensor module is mainly responsible for collecting information such as ambient temperature, humidity and illuminance, directly using digital sensors or converting analog quantities into digital quantities by A/D conversion.

2.2   System Software Design

The software used in this paper uses the Z-Stack protocol stack provided by TI. The Z-Stack protocol stack is a polling task scheduling management system, using OSAL (Operating System Abstraction Layer) [9]. ZigBee protocol stack is a communication protocol formed by ZigBee Alliance, which standardizes the network layer and application layer on the physical layer and media access control layer defined by IEEE802.15.4. In order to make each layer of the protocol stack work independently, a hierarchical structure is adopted, the protocol stack is modified appropriately, and the application layer is programmed to meet the different needs of users. In this paper, the coordinator and terminal nodes respectively design software programs according to the Z-Stack protocol stack (see Fig. 4), which realizes the networking requirements of the system.

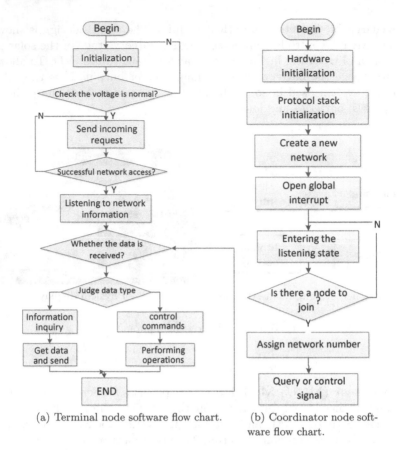

(a) Terminal node software flow chart.

(b) Coordinator node software flow chart.

Fig. 4. Software flow chart.

3 Network Experiment and System Test

This paper uses a PC, a coordinator and two terminals to form a star network for temperature acquisition networking experiments. The coordinator receives the data of each node, and the serial port is connected with the host computer, and the accepted data is displayed through the upper computer, and the power is supplied by the upper computer USB port. The terminal equipment is distributed in the area that needs to be collected and monitored. The energy collection type equipment designed in this paper is used for power supply, which is responsible for collecting data and transmitting it through wireless radio frequency signals. The terminal sends a data to the coordinator every 20S, and the experimental data is as shown in the Fig. 5.

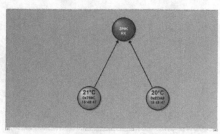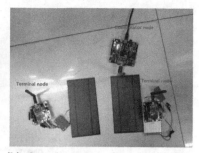

(a) Terminal node software flow chart. (b) Coordinator node software flow chart.

Fig. 5. Software flow chart.

4   Solar Illuminance Collection Experiment

The collection efficiency of solar energy is affected by many factors, such as geographical location, different seasons, different time of day, the placement of solar panels, etc. According to the formula for calculating the solar altitude angle [10]:

$$sinh = sin\phi sin\delta + cos\phi cos\delta cos\omega. \tag{1}$$

Where h is the solar elevation angle, ϕ is the time angle under the system of the local star, δ is the current solar declination, and ω is the local latitude. According to the formula, regions at different latitudes will have different solar elevations in different seasons. The higher the angle of the sun is, the more solar energy is collected. Therefore, in the same latitude area of the Northern Hemisphere, the solar energy height angle is large in summer, and the solar radiation collected is the largest, while in winter, the opposite is true. During different periods of the day, the amount of radiation collected during the day is large, and at night the solar radiation is basically 0. In addition, weather is also one of the factors affecting solar energy collection. Cloud thickness, haze and strong wind will affect the collection efficiency of sensor-less nodes. Therefore, the energy supply of solar energy harvesting wireless sensor networks are very unstable. We need to study the law of solar energy collection under different conditions. We use the CC3200 and B-LUX-V30B environmental light sensors as shown in the Fig. 5 to collect the illumination information under direct sunlight, and upload the AP to the cloud through the WiFi module on CC3200, and draws a line graph. The experimental site was selected as Hohhot City, with a latitude of 40.48° north latitude, 111.40° east longitude and an altitude of 1023 m. The climate type is mid-temperate and semi-arid with a collection interval of 50 s.

We measured solar illuminance for different weather in August and December, respectively. In Fig. 6, we measure solar illuminance data for two types of weather on a sunny day and a cloudy day in August, and use the method of changing the position of the sensor to simulate the data after the illuminance

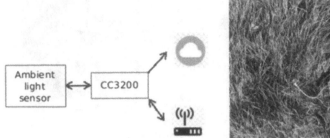

(a) Illumination data collection experiment design structure

(b) Physical display

Fig. 6. CC3200 collects illuminance data

sensor is blown by the wind. From the figure, we can see that on a sunny day, the illuminance value starts to rise from the morning, and reaches about 10000 Lux around noon. As the sunlight shifts, the illuminance value drops again, and after sunset, the illuminance value drops to zero. On cloudy days, the illuminance data is relatively stable. It floats between 20000 Lux and 40,000 Lux after 8:00 in the morning. The highest value of the data appears at 12 noon, and the illuminance value drops to 0 after sunset. On a sunny day, we changed the angle of the sensor so that the sensor angle was facing east. It was found that the illuminance reached a maximum of 90000 Lux at the beginning of 9 o'clock. The illuminance was slightly higher than the normal sunny day, and it began to drop after 11 o'clock. At 12 o'clock, the illuminance is similar to that in the case of cloudy days, and then the illuminance data is similar to that collected on cloudy days. In general, in the sunny summer of Hohhot, the average maximum illuminance per hour can reach 10WLux, while on cloudy days, from 7:00 am to 4:00 pm, the illuminance fluctuates between 2 W and 4WLux, the specific illuminance value not only related to time, but also related to the thickness of the clouds. When the clouds are thick, the illuminance is low, and when the clouds are thin, the illuminance is high. The illuminance data is similar to that on a cloudy day when the sensor is not obscured and the illuminance is greatest when it is perpendicular to the sun. When the sensor is in shadow, the illuminance data is similar to that on a cloudy day.

In December, due to the continuous sunny days, we collected data for three consecutive days of sunny days, as shown in Fig. 7. It can be seen that in winter, the solar irradiance data starts from 8:00 in the morning and reaches a maximum of 60,000 Lux at noon. Lower, gradually drop to 0 after 5 pm. In the clear summer, the light level reached 60,000 Lux at 9:00 am and 60,000 Lux above 3 pm. Also in the clear winter, it did not reach 60,000 Lux when the light was the highest at 1 pm, and the winter illuminance data were significantly lower than the summer. On the whole, on the one hand, the solar irradiance intensity in December is lower than that in August. On the other hand, solar energy can be collected in December shorter than August.

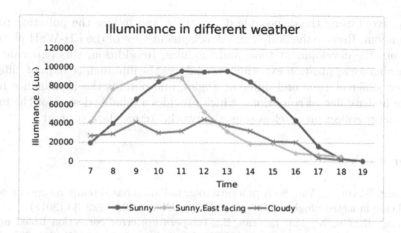

Fig. 7. Illuminance data for different weather in August.

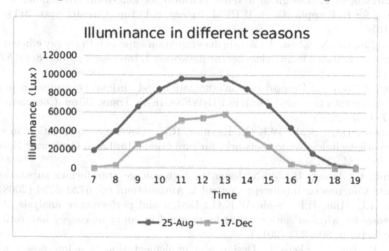

Fig. 8. Illumination data for sunny days under different months.

In summary, solar energy collection has great instability, which is very different in different weather and seasons. In the subsequent research process, we need to adopt different energy management and transmission schemes in different seasons and weather to ensure the reliability of the entire wireless network (Fig. 8).

5   Conclusion

This paper introduces the design and implementation of a solar collector type wireless sensor network based on ZigBee. The designed node has low cost, low power consumption, and can collect energy from the environment. The use time is long, and the node can be charged after the sleep, complete the recycling of energy, avoid using the disposable dry battery, and reduce the pollution to the environment. Reduce the design and development time of the EH-WSH platform with versatile development tools and modules. In addition, this paper designs an illuminance acquisition experiment, analyzes the illuminance data of different weather, different time and different angles, and obtains the illuminance information under different conditions, which provides a reliable design for the future solar energy collection wireless sensor network. Actual data support.

References

1. Wang, B., Gu, X., Yan, S.: A practical solar radiation based temperature correction scheme in meteorological WSN. Int. J. Sens. Netw. **28**(1), 22–33 (2018)
2. Wang, B., Gu, X., Ma, L., Yan, S.: Temperature error correction based on BP neural network in meteorological WSN. Int. J. Sens. Netw. **23**(4), 265–278 (2017)
3. Lazarescu, M.T.: Design of a WSN platform for long-term environmental monitoring for IOT applications. IEEE J. Emerg. Sel. Top. Circuits Syst. **3**(1), 45–54 (2013)
4. Wang, B., Gu, X., Zhou, A.: Acode dissemination approach to energy efficiency and status surveillance for wireless sensor networks. J. Internet Technol. **8**(4), 877–885 (2017)
5. Tang, S., Tan, L.: Reward rate maximization and optimal transmission policy of EH device with temporal death in EH-WSNs. IEEE Trans. Wirel. Commun. **16**(2), 1157–1167 (2017)
6. Harrison, D.C., Seah, W.K.G., Rayudu, R.K.: Coverage preservation in energy harvesting wireless sensor networks for rare events. In: Local Computer Networks, pp. 181–184 (2015)
7. Qiang, G., Wang, H.: WSN design in high-voltage transformer substation. In: World Congress on Intelligent Control & Automation, pp. 6720–6724 (2008)
8. Zhi, A.E., Tan, H.P., Seah, W.K.G.: Design and performance analysis of MAC schemes for wireless sensor networks powered by ambient energy harvesting. Ad Hoc Netw. **9**, 300–323 (2011)
9. Wu, F., Hu, X., Shen, J.: Design and implementation of a low power wireless sensor network data acquisition system. In: International Conference on Intelligent Computation Technology & Automation (2009)
10. Duffie, J.A., Beckman, W.A.: Solar Engineering of Thermal Processes. A Wiley-Interscience, Hoboken (1980)

Application of Big Data Technology in JD

Ning Shi$^{(\boxtimes)}$ and Huwei Liu

Beijing Wuzi University, Beijing, China
398807172@qq.com, 591878845@qq.com

Abstract. The arrival of the era of big data has brought about changes
and impacts on human life, work, and thinking. With the rapid development of the scale and number of e-commerce in China, the e-commerce
marketing requires continuous innovation. Big data can tap and utilize
the underlying business value behind the data to achieve more precise
positioning and marketing. This article analyzes the big data theory and
method, discusses the three major challenges of data holding, data processing and data security brought by e-commerce in the era of big data.
The era of big data analyzes and accurately updates and changes the target audience. A case study of JD e-commerce company was conducted
again to analyze JD's big data platform and the application and practice
of marketing based on the platform. Inspired by the case study, we found
weaknesses and made suggestions.

Keywords: Big data · JD · Butterfly Festival

1 Research Background

Nowadays, with the widespread use of the Internet and the development of the
Internet of Things, information is increasingly large. Behind these data information, important information and commercial value are hidden. Because of
technological innovations and applications such as cloud computing, data that
was originally difficult to collect for storage and use began to reflect its value
and was easily used. With the explosion of information and the breakthrough
of modern technology, big data will bring about tremendous changes to life and
business. Big data will gradually create more value for humanity. In recent years,
big data has been increasingly sought after by various industries.

On the Internet, the use of big data can completely describe the trajectory
of each individual's life, and can completely capture the main behavior of each
individual or consumer. Big data on the Internet carries the most extensive
intentions and needs of consumers. Every search, click, browse, and comment in
life is a real life moment that can directly reflect their personality, preferences,
and wishes. Using data mining and other technologies to describe the data on

Supported by the Beijing Great Wall Scholar (No. CIT & TCD20170317), and the
Collaborative Innovation Center.

J. Li et al. (Eds.): SPNCE 2019, LNICST 284, pp. 585–595, 2019.
https://doi.org/10.1007/978-3-030-21373-2_48

the Internet to describe consumers' habits, etc., can find and use the commercial value behind the data and achieve more precise positioning and marketing.

On January 31, the China Internet Network Information Center (CNNIC) released the 41st "Statistical Report on China's Internet Development" in Beijing. As of December 2017, the number of Internet users in China reached 772 million, and the penetration rate reached 55.8% [1]. Modern people have become more and more dependent on the Internet. The web pages and websites we have browsed are all recorded in the form of data. This is the source of big data.

2   The Concept of Big Data

Big data is one of the hottest words in the world. What is big data?

The Gartner Research Institute believes that after an effective processing model, big data has special values such as better decision-making capabilities, process optimization capabilities, and insight capabilities [2]. Big data has information assets that are diversified in type, have high-speed data growth, and have a quantity of Shanghai characteristics.

Big data has the following four characteristics that summarize big data: Volume (large quantity), Variety (variety), Velocity (high frequency speed), and Value (high value) [3].

Volume refers to the huge amount of data, and the measurement unit of big data cannot be measured in GB at all. It rises from GB to TB, and TB quickly rises to PB.

Variety mainly represents the rich and diversified characteristics of data types. The types of big data include a large amount of unstructured data (pictures, videos, texts, geographic locations, audio files, etc.), different types of data derived from sensors, recorded data of mobile terminals, search browsing data on the Internet, and other real-time online data, etc.

Velocity refers to processing speed. The recording of large amounts of data, etc. imposes higher requirements on the processing technology of big data. It requires faster and more efficient data distribution and discrete technology processing. This is precisely the difference from the traditional nature of data mining technology [4]. The high-speed and high-accuracy data mining processing of massive data can only exert its huge commercial value on the results of processing.

Value refers to the low density of value and high value in business. The 21st century is an era of information. With the use of cloud computing and the production of massive data, the use and use of data in the society will become increasingly dependent in the future. Many industries and companies have been keenly aware of the business opportunities and value. However, due to the inadequacies and limitations of the era and knowledge and technology, the value of big data could not be fully tapped and used.

3   Big Data Application in JD

3.1   JD Introduction

On March 2nd, 2018, JD released the financial statements for the fourth quarter and the full year of fiscal year 2017. The data shows that in 2017, JD net revenue was RMB 362.3 billion (approximately US$55.7 billion), an increase of 40.3% year-on-year; net profit was RMB 116.8 million (approximately US$ 18 million) [5]. JD is currently China's largest B2C e-commerce company, accounting for more than half of China's self-operated e-commerce market share.

In 2017, JD established a strategy for unbounded retail. At the beginning of this year, JD made major adjustments to its organizational structure and established three major business groups, namely the Fast Consumer Business Group, the Electronic Entertainment Group, and the Lifestyle Business Group. At the cooperation conference of the consumer products division of the Fast Forward Business Group, JD Supermarkets announced the establishment of a "brand value community" together with its brand name. They upgraded their past cooperation to a "symbiotic cooperation" model and evolved toward the integration of "people, goods, and field" driven by big data and artificial intelligence. And to achieve data sharing, category construction, user win-win situation, scene symbiosis, and truly realize the symbiosis with the brand business, cooperation and win-win.

3.2   JD Big Data Platform and Application Framework

JD big data platform is divided into four major modules, namely customer modules, tool product modules, model modules, and technology modules. As shown in Fig. 1.

In the customer big data module, the source of customer big data mainly includes the general consumer, JD partners, and JD internal customer data. One of the partners with JD is data from merchants, data from suppliers, and data from other partners, such as Tencent. The data from the JD Group mainly comes from four parts: customer data from JD Mall, data from JD Finance, data from international business and patting network. From JD customer big data module, it can be seen that JD's acquisition of big data comes mainly from external data on the one hand, and JD's internal data on the other hand.

In the tool product module, it mainly includes the data compass of professional analysis such as recommendation system, search engine, JD hui. There is also JD independent innovation R&D dispatching platform, data integration development platform, data knowledge management platform, JD analyst platform, data mining platform, and data quality monitoring platform. The data compass can be divided into seller version, industry version and so on. Through the recommendation system, search engine, JD, etc., the data of ordinary consumers in the customer big data module is processed and applied.

The model module mainly includes user portrait, sales forecast, credit model, merchant rating, distribution grid and wind control model. The user's portrait is

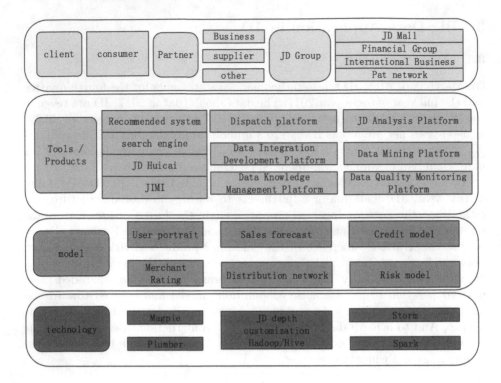

Fig. 1. JD big data platform four modules map.

a combination of experienced business staff and engineers after analyzing a large amount of data, and describes the consumer characteristics of a user group or a single customer with similar attributes and characteristics. Through the analysis of the user, the attributes of the user's portraits are tagged, and the users in the same tag can use the recommendation system to promote the products in a unified manner. User portraits are the most important part of achieving accurate marketing. The rating of the store and the results of the system are displayed on the front page of the business rating system and the back office system. Users and operators can quickly and easily find what they need, and both parties share information. The user clearly understands the performance and level of service, merchandise and timeliness of the stores in front of him. Rich and clear quantitative information provides efficient and objective data support for his decision to enter stores and shopping. The result of the rating is a report card submitted by the operator. The transcripts detail the good and bad shops, help operators find their own strengths and weaknesses, and promote their continued efforts to learn. This will not only improve the operational dead ends, but also attract more users and improve operational results through better rating results, creating a virtuous circle. The sales forecast is JD forecasting of the monthly, or even the entire year's sales of JD after analyzing the situation and data of warehousing and distribution, so as to facilitate the preparation and planning of cargo warehousing and marketing of JD in the next month or year. Risk control is through the analysis of user behavior and words and actions to identify the malicious user, then the corresponding shield and reduce the risk of the mall, which is the application of big data in risk control.

In the technology module, technologies such as Magpie, Plumber, Storm, Spark, and JD's deeply customized version of Hadoop are included [6]. The technology module in the big data platform is the basic framework of the big data platform, and JD has many innovations in this technology. Through in-depth study of Hadoop distributed technology, many innovations are realized in the localization deployment process, such as:

(1) Directional development, support for index creation based on HDFS;
(2) Directional transformation, combining small files at the Map level, saving resource consumption;
(3) Support dynamic allocation of resource queues;
(4) Control of the task runtime and HDFS read and write support through parameters;
(5) Self-developed calculation functions applicable to JD Big Data Service Platform;
(6) Optimize and improve Hadoop storage performance, support more types of data storage formats, etc.

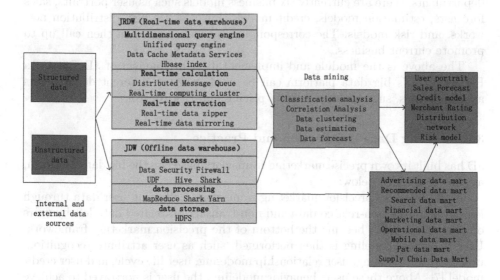

Fig. 2. JD big data platform implementation mechanism.

In addition to the four major modules of JD Big Data, the implementation mechanism and basic architecture of JD Big Data Platform are shown in Fig. 2. First, collect internal data of the company. The data is mainly divided into structured data and unstructured data. Due to the characteristics of big data to be processed in real time, JD has a large number of users who generate a large amount of data online every day. In order to obtain real-time data processing, maximum value can be obtained for timely processing and recommendation. Therefore, the data is divided into real-time data warehouses and ideal data warehouses to extract, calculate, and query real-time data. For historical data or offline data, it is also necessary to use HDFS for data storage, and use Map Reduce, spark, Yarn and other technologies for data processing, and then perform data access. In order to better serve enterprises and departments, JD has established a data mart, which is a line-oriented data production environment based on JDW. Provides application services for each line, including dozens of departments such as advertising, recommendation, search, finance, marketing, operations, BDA, mobile, pat, and supply chain, and thousands of users provide data services. Compared with the general data warehouse, data marts are more professional and easy to use. In fact, whether it is a real-time data warehouse or an offline data warehouse or a data mart, all the data are pre-processed and analyzed. Data mining is mainly achieved through classification analysis, correlation analysis, data clustering analysis, data estimation, and data prediction analysis. It faces big data. JD conducts sampling through distributed computing, iterates through memory calculations, and abstracts and simplifies common processes to lower the threshold. After a series of data mining, the data is returned to the data mart for use, or stored directly. Faced with the needs of different business departments, there are currently six business models such as user portraits, sales forecasts, estimation models, credit models, business ratings, distribution networks, and risk models. The corresponding business units can then call up to promote current business.

The above is the module and implementation mechanism of JD Big Data Platform. JD's big data platform can be used in many different departments and businesses, such as supply chain, pricing and risk control.

3.3   JD Big Data Application and Practice

JD has built its own precise marketing framework based on the big data platform, as shown in Fig. 3 below:

In JD big data precision marketing framework, collecting user data through log data, transaction-related data and non-transaction-related data left by users on the Internet has become the bottom of the precision marketing framework. User behavior modeling is then performed, such as user attribute recognition, user interest modeling, user relationship modeling, user life cycle, and user credit model [7]. Above these users behavior modeling, the user is portrayed to achieve user marketing value and user risk rating assessment, and is provided as the underlying data to various marketing systems. Finally, after knowing the portrait of the user, it uses EDM, SMS, APPPUSH, and product packaging advertisements to promote and achieve accurate marketing. Based on precision marketing on big data platforms, marketing methods are cross-platform, cross-terminal, and

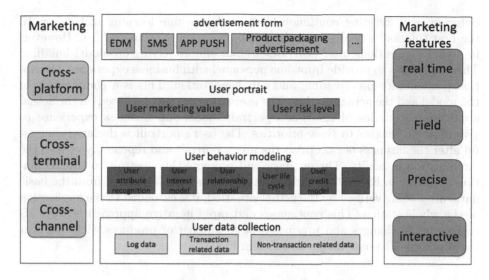

Fig. 3. Marketing structure.

cross-channel, with real-time, on-site, accurate, and interactive marketing features. Big data precision marketing is a dynamic and cyclical process. Continuous precision marketing is implemented before, during, and after implementation [8].

Among them, the user portrait is the most important foundation and part of big data precision marketing [9]. After the user's portrait is an analysis of a large amount of data, the data is used to describe the individual user as a basis or prediction of sales or product recommendation, which is also a solution for converting data into commercial value. Users' long-term behaviors such as page views and shopping are all multi-dimensional and huge data measured in terabytes, and these data constitute the basic data of user portraits. The data of user portraits can be roughly divided into three major parts. One is the basic demographic attributes, including natural attributes and social attributes such as age, gender, occupation, income, and life stage. The other is behavioral preference. This data mainly comes from the user's behavior when browsing the page to infer its preferences, such as the personal attention field. The last one is the data purchased by the user, the purchased goods, unit price, return rate, and evaluation feedback. The user's basic data and behavioral preferences are excavated with data and labeled with different labels to characterize the user's personal characteristics. In addition, by analyzing the crowd of the same tag, or by analyzing the user behavior preference characteristics in different dimensions of different business scenarios, the data is directly converted into the user image. A user may be portrayed by a 3000+ tag to match between the product and the user. The prediction of the user's future behavior leads to the user's behavior so as to obtain a huge business opportunity.

Logically speaking, JD portraits of users are mainly based on the data mining and analysis of massive data, forming a benchmark learning method or criterion, and iterating continuously through machine learning methods until the best solution is finally formed, and the program is promoted [10]. However, in actual applications, user portraits are not simply relying on model building. The final step is to provide front-line personnel with business experience description portraits for proofreading and supplementation. This is a combination of the model and the actual market. The user's portrait will be based on the actual application scenarios of the user's portrait model and business experience to give different weights to show priorities. The user's portrait is declared successful after the business person takes the user's portrait and repeatedly verifies the modification in reality. The engineer will promote this portrait to the JD station application. Extracting and summarizing the user's portrait from the basic data, after being verified by the actual situation, it is extended to the application of the whole station. This continuous and rapid iterative approach enables JD to face up to changes and produce a large number of products with excellent performance. The user image is shown in Fig. 4.

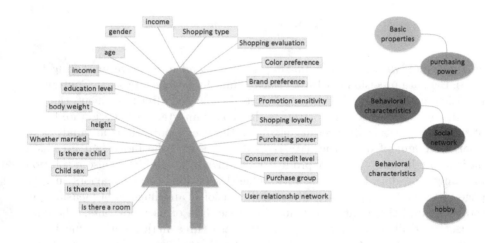

Fig. 4. User portraits.

Through the big data platform's acquisition and analysis of big data, JD will give each user a different label. Each user will have a lot of labels and images, and these labels will be dynamically updated according to the user's browsing and trading behavior. In this way, the user can be recommended for the product that the user is interested in, and the recommendation effect can be obtained from the user's feedback after the transaction, and the tag is updated again.

After applying big data, JD can get a variety of consumer shopping habits and preferences, find similar people and potential customers, and forecast and launch popular products in the market. Compared with traditional e-commerce providers, JD advantages are obvious, and it also reflects the extremely high value of big data technology. According to JD big user data [11], over the past five years, the number of female online shopping users has grown by more than 200%, making JD more focused on women's shopping habits. In the past five years, the transaction volume of the JD platform has grown by a factor of 10, from RMB 86.9 billion in 2012 to RMB 939.2 billion this year. In addition to the success of brand building and the purchasing power of users, big data has played a big role.

Through the analysis of big data, corresponding accurate marketing strategies and personalized services are provided. Take JD Beauty-Butterfly Festival data as an example to analyze.

According to the latest JD Big Data, the sales volume of JD Beauty Cosmetics Co., Ltd. increased by 102% year-on-year.. In 2011–2017, the penetration rate of online beauty and makeup consumption continued to increase, and the online shopping habits of products have been formed. The proportion of online sales of major cosmetics groups has increased substantially.

The consumption growth index for each tier-one city in 2016 (the index reflects the relative level of each tier-level region and does not reflect the absolute value of growth) shows that in 2016, the "value-added consumption" in the Five-line area region grew fastest, reaching 203% year-on-year. The year-on-year growth of the six-wire region and the year-on-year growth of the fourth-line region were as high as 186% and 160% respectively. In contrast, the first-tier regions, second-tier regions and third-tier regions maintained rapid growth in 2016 compared with the same period in 2015, but the growth was only 100%, 118% and 139% respectively.

In 2017, consumers' skin care and beauty awareness increased significantly. In terms of specific categories, as consumption upgrades continue to ferment, from January to April 2017, from the perspective of year-on-year sales growth, the number of make-ups occupied four, and the "beauty of the eyebrows" category was highly favored. It is well known that the outbreak of makeup is closely related to the degree of economic development.

With the rise of "Men Color" era, men are also becoming one of the main consumers of beauty makeup. According to the comparative analysis of 2015–2016 big data, in the aspect of skin care beauty, the per capita consumption gap between male users and female users has decreased from 26.6 RMB in 2014 to 13.7 RMB.

According to the "Fine Beauty User Map", Guangdong, Beijing, and Jiangsu are the largest gathering places for young people (ages 19–25) who are keen on value-for-money consumption, ranking the top three. In addition, big data also shows that white-collar workers have become the main force of the "Appearance Association", and over 29% of users come from white-collar workers and general staff. It is worth noting that in 2016, both male and female users, facial skin care products accounted for more than 50%.

The big data analysis based on user evaluation found that the cost-effectiveness and service have become the most important factor for online beauty consumers, and the proportion of perception evaluation is over 70%. In addition, presenting a beauty care product is becoming a way of expressing family care. The role of the wife is very important. Among the top five keywords, "wife likes" and "wife bought" occupy the top two.

4   Conclusion

In the context of big data, consumers can be divided into multiple groups. For each group, they can provide targeted services. The increase in the amount of data such as consumer behavior can provide a certain basis for e-commerce users to accurately screen and consume. Through the big data window, e-commerce companies can carry out more personalized and intelligent ad-push services, and can create more accurate business models. In addition, e-commerce through big data, can also better increase the viscosity of users to better carry out new product development and service, and ultimately reduce operating costs.

E-commerce providers can better drive and operate data. For internal links, companies can use data to analyze and evaluate them, and then use these data views for management. Taking JD as an example, it integrates its resources such as JD Mall, JD, and JD Logistics, and then uses these data resources to accurately target customer groups and consumer behavior. At the same time, it also elevates the competition for e-commerce from a simple price war to a differentiated competition. At present, JD has formed a data platform product, such as Data Cube and Quantum Hengdao, which includes operations analysis of stores, product analysis and buyer behavior analysis, industry analysis, financial analysis, and supply chain analysis.

In the context of big data, data assets have become a consensus and have become a relatively core industrial trend. In the future of enterprise competition, it is a competition of scale and activity. The economic benefits and effects of data generation have become more important for companies, and thus have spawned various data-related businesses. Data assets are a kind of capital manifestation of the current Internet ubiquity. Its role in the Internet is not only reflected in the service itself, but also has a certain degree of financial value. The data function not only reflects the use value in the product, but also can grow into a kind of real value. Currently, leaders of data assets, such as Apple, Google, etc., are using different forms of software development to better collect different types of data and better play the commercial value of big data. This new type of integration will eventually form a four-in-one pan-Internet company with "terminal + application + platform + data", which can better survive in the fierce big data competition.

References

1. China Internet Information Center, October 2017. http://tech.sina.com.cn/i/2018-01-31/doc-ifyrcsrv9714983.shtml. Accessed 31 Jan 2018
2. Li, B.W.: E-commerce Big Data. Publishing House of Electronics Industry, Beijing (2014)

3. Ma, J.G.: The concept, characteristics and application of big data. Natl. Def. Sci. Technol. **10**(17), 10–17 (2013)
4. Meng, X.: Big data management: concepts, techniques, and challenges. Comput. Res. Dev., 146–169 (2013)
5. Speedway.   http://finance.jrj.com.cn/tech/2018/03/02184824186090.shtml. Accessed 02 Mar 2018
6. JD R&D System: JD Technology Decryption. Publishing House of Electronics Industry, Beijing (2014)
7. Chen, X.: Discussion on business model of big data business. E-commerce, 16–17 (2013)
8. Wang, X.: Application of big data technology in precision marketing. Inf. Commun. Technol., 21–26 (2014)
9. Huang, S.: The deconstruction and reconstruction of marketing system under the background of "big data". Mod. Commun. (J. Commun. Univ. China), 13–20 (2012)
10. Zhang, D.: The opportunities and challenges of electronic commerce development in the era of big data. Foreign Trade, 85–86 (2014)
11. China   Economic   Net.   http://finance.ce.cn/rolling/201803/02/t20180302_28318714.shtml. Accessed 02 Mar 2018

A Trusted International Settlement Solution Based on Cross Check of CDRs

Peng Ran[✉], Jin Peng, Bo Yang, Li Su, Xiaoyong Hang,
and Junzhi Yan

China Mobile Research Institute, Beijing 100053, China
ranpeng@chinamobile.com

Abstract. This paper proposes a trusted international settlement solution based on Cross Check of CDRs, improving the credibility and verification efficiency of international settlement, and preventing fraud and tampering. Based on the distributed settlement architecture of blockchain and cloud database, the solution confirm the CDRs of home operator, roaming operator, transit operator, third-party operator and user to form a trusted consensus. Based on smart contract reducing the duplication check of CDRs and bills, the solution improve the operational efficiency. Using cloud database and blockchain deposits technology, the solution solve the data storage capacity limitation and data tampering problem of blockchain. The solution effectively solves the problems of CDRs fraud, data tampering and disclosure, CDRs/bill duplication check in the existing international settlement service of operators. Experiment proves that the settlement efficiency of the single operator in the solution can be improved to hour level to realize the fully automation of settlement process.

Keywords: Settlement · Blockchain · CDRs

1 Background

With the continuous advancement of globalization, exchanges between countries and personnel exchanges has become more and more frequent, and operators' international settlement business has become more and more arduous. Taking an operator as an example, it has international roaming services with nearly 400 foreign operators and nearly billion CDRs service per day, which requires a lot of manpower and resources to carry out CDRs and account confirmation.

Blockchain technology is an integrated innovation of P2P (peer to peer) network, consensus algorithm, cryptographic algorithm, and smart contract. Telecom operators can use blockchain technology to establish mutual trust and cooperation between operators, communication industry. They also can try to apply blockchain technology to roaming settlement [1], security, IoT, electronic payment, copyright protection and many other fields [2].

© ICST Institute for Computer Sciences, Social Informatics and Telecommunications Engineering 2019
Published by Springer Nature Switzerland AG 2019. All Rights Reserved
J. Li et al. (Eds.): SPNCE 2019, LNICST 284, pp. 596–604, 2019.
https://doi.org/10.1007/978-3-030-21373-2_49

2 Existing Technologies and Shortcomings

In the scenario (as shown in Fig. 1) of existing international settlement business (including user visiting/visited SMS, telephone service, traffic service, etc.): David of home operator (Operator A) visits country B and uses roaming operator(Operator B) service of country B. David calls Emma of third-party operator (Operator C) in country B. In this scenario, the settlement parties include home operator, roaming operator, third-party operator, transit broker 1 between home operator and roaming operator, and transit broker 2 between roaming operator and third-party operator.

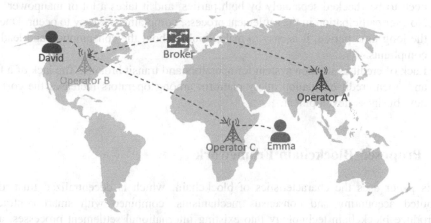

Fig. 1. Roaming call scenario

According to the contract, home operator shall pay roaming charges to roaming operator, third party operator, transit broker 1, and transit broker 2 within the contract period. The existing international roaming settlement process is as follows:

(1) Roaming operator and third-party operator create a roaming CDRs of home operator.
(2) Submit CDRs to home operator daily or monthly.
(3) Home operator performs the CDRs format check according to CDRs standard of GSMA (whether the format meets the standard, whether the logical correlation between the CDRs values is correct, etc.), returns confirmation if the verification succeed. If there is an objection, roaming operator and third-party operator performs step 1 again to generate the revised CDRs.
(4) According to the contract, roaming operator and third-party operator generate a bill based on the CDRs, then send the bill to home operator.
(5) Home operator validate the bill according to the previously confirmed CDRs and agreements. If there is any objection to the statement, roaming operator and third-party operator are sent a report, and step 4 is executed to generate the revised bill; if there is no objection, the confirmation would be sent.

(6) After receiving the confirmation, roaming operator and third-party operator shall generate the amount bill based on bill receivable and bill payable.
(7) Home operator performs payment with other operators and the transit brokers.

In the existing international settlement process, the main problems are as follows:

- The CDRs is provided by a roaming operator, and the CDRs is easy to be distorted. If the system of roaming operator has a clock inconsistency failure or the data flow process is artificially modified, the CDRs data will be distorted
- Duplication check of CDRs/bills consumes a lot of manpower. Home operator check the CDRs, bills which provided by roaming operator. Both CDRs and bills need to be checked separately by both parties, and it takes a lot of manpower.
- No user participation in the settlement process, complaints are easy to occur. Due to the long time period, it is easy to make doubts about the consumption and lead to complaints.
- Lack of credit evaluation system for operators and transit brokers. The lack of a fair and open credit evaluation query platform among operators increases the cost of new business development.

3   Proposed Blockchain Framework

This paper uses the characteristics of blockchain, which is decentralized trust, distributed accounting and consensus mechanisms, combined with smart contracts, introduce blockchain technology into existing international settlement processes, and provide an efficient and reliable blockchain platform solution for international settlement business [3, 4]. The overall architecture of the solution is shown below (Fig. 2).

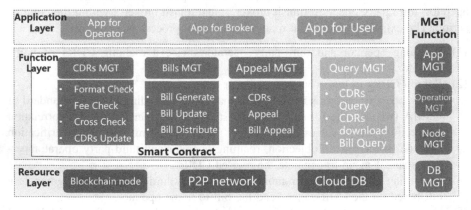

Fig. 2. Architecture

The solution is based on the consortium blockchain. Each participant (home operator, roaming operator, third-party operator, transit broker, user) participates in the blockchain platform to implement the CDRs Cross Check, Bill Output, Credit Evaluation and display through the blockchain platform.

The key processes of this solution are: (1) Smart Contract Maintenance, (2) CDRs Format Check, (3) simple CDRs Generation, (4) CDRs Upload, (5) CDRs Cross Check, (6) Unified Bill Output, (7) International Settlement, (8) Credit Rating Evaluation, (9) Credit Inquiry.

(1) Smart Contract Maintenance

Maintenance word of Credit Rating Evaluation smart contract, Billing smart contract, CDRs Cross Check smart contract in the process [5].

Billing smart contract is mainly used for the generation of unified bills. It is prepared by home operator according to the contract signed between operators and transit brokers, and is confirmed to be stored in the blockchain by the roaming operators and transit brokers. Home operator updates the smart contract synchronously when the billing contract is updated.

Credit Rating Evaluation smart contract calculates the credit rating according to the format check, the tariff rate check, the false CDRs, the timely settlement rate, and the user complaint rate of the international roaming participants.

(2) CDRs Format Check

Roaming operator, home operator, third-party operator need to perform format check by format standard of GSMA.

(3) Simple CDRs Generation

Roaming operator, home operator, third-party operator will generate the original CDRs to simple CDRs (including the necessary fields for generating bills, such as the calling number, called number, home operator code, duration, etc.) in accordance with format standard of GSMA, and fields of simple CDRs of all operators should be consistent.

Home operator, roaming operator, and third-party operator will perform the simple CDRs generation according to the following rules [6].

- Simple CDRs of roaming operator. The original CDRs are classified according to the operator ID of the calling number, and then classified again by operator ID of called number.
- Simple CDRs of home operator. The original CDRs are classified according to the operator network identification used by the calling number.
- Simple CDRs of third-party operator: The original CDRs are classified according to the operator ID and the operator network ID used by the calling number.

(4) CDRs Upload

Roaming operator, home operator, third-party operator upload the original CDRs and the simple CDRs into the cloud database every 30 min (the time period can be set, such as 30 min, 1 h).

Roaming operator, home operator, third-party operator upload access URLs, hash value of original CDRs and simple CDRs into the blockchain.

(5) CDRs Cross Check

The CDRs Cross Check smart contract validates the hash value of simple CDRs uploaded by home operator, roaming operator, third-party operator in 5 min after every 30 min CDRs uploaded. If the hash value is consistent, the user's CDRs are valid; if the hash value is inconsistent, the CDRs need to be reprocessed (Fig. 3).

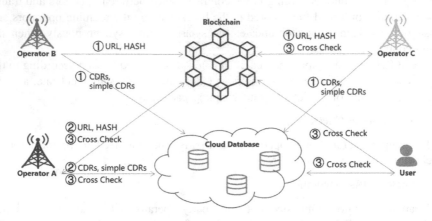

Fig. 3. CDRs cross check model

(6) Unified Bill Generate

After the agreed period (such as one month), Billing smart contract generates a unified bill for the previous month, and records the bill in the blockchain.

(7) International Settlement

The international roaming participants (home operator, roaming operator, third-party operator, transit broker 1, transit broker 2) perform offline settlement based on the generated unified bill. Operators and transit brokers shall submit the settlement vouchers to the system.

(8) Credit Rating Evaluation

According to the format check, tariff rate check, CDRs authenticity, settlement status (settlement certificate) and user complaint rate of the stakeholders during the settlement process, Credit Rating Evaluation smart contract carry out credit rating of international roaming participants [7, 8].

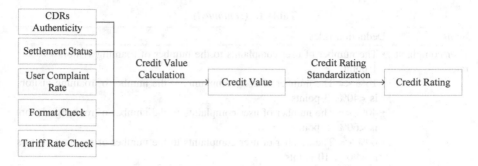

Fig. 4. Credit rating evaluation model

The credit scores in the model (as shown in Fig. 4) are calculated as follows:

$$Credit\ score\ =\ base\ score - a * CDRs\ authenticity - b * settlement\ status - c * user$$
$$complaint\ rate - d * format\ check - e * tariff\ rate\ check$$

$$(a > 0;\ b > 0;\ c > 0;\ d > 0;\ e > 0;\ a+b+c+d+e = 1)$$

The five parameters a, b, c, d, and e in the formula are configurable.

Credit score: Calculated by Credit Rating Evaluation smart contract on a daily basis, the value range of the credit score is (0, 100). When the lower or upper limit is reached, the score is no longer deducted or increased.

Base score: The base score of the participant is divided into 80 points. When the participant of the node has no deduction in one day, add 0.1 to the original base score. If there is a serious deduction (the deduction of 10 points (including more than 10 points)), the base score will remain at 80 points in the calculation period of the current month and the next month (Table 1).

Table 1. Deduction rules of credit rating evaluation

Items	Deduction rules
CDRs authenticity	• Found 1 false CDRs record, 10 points; • Each additional false CDRs record, 10 points
Settlement status	International roaming participants shall complete all fee settlements according to the bill within the agreed time; • Settlement exceeded time <5 days, 2 points • 5 days <= settlement exceeded time <10 days, 5 points • 10 days <= settlement exceeded time <30 days, 10 points • Settlement exceeded time >= 30 days, 20 points

(continued)

Table 1. (*continued*)

Items	Deduction rules
User complaint rate	• The number of user complaints to the number of roaming visitors <10%, 1 point • 10% <= The number of user complaints to the number of roaming visitors is <40%, 3 points • 40% <= The number of user complaints to the number of roaming visitors is <60%, 5 points • 60% <= The number of user complaints to the number of roaming visitors is <90%, 10 points
Format check	• The number of CDRs with incorrect format check: 5–20, 1 point • The number of CDRs with incorrect format check: 21–50, 3 points • The number of CDRs with incorrect format check: 51–100, 5 points • The number of CDRs with incorrect format check: more than 100, 10 points
Tariff rate check	• The number of CDRs with incorrect tariff rate check: 5–20, 1 point • The number of CDRs with incorrect tariff rate check: 21–50, 3 points • The number of CDRs with incorrect tariff rate check: 51–100, 5 points • The number of CDRs with incorrect tariff rate check: more than 100, 10 points

(9) Credit Inquiry

Participants of the blockchain platform can query the credit status of each node in the system, as a reference for launching new services; users can also query the operator's credit status through the system as a reference for selecting operators.

4 Advantages Analysis and Experiment

In this paper, the trusted international settlement solution based on Cross Check of CDRs can reduce duplication check and the risk of user complaints, improve the settlement efficiency of roaming services, and provide a unified, open and transparent credit evaluation platform.

- Home operators, roaming operators, third-party operators and users are involved to contribute to CDRs, with cross check to enhance the trustiness. The validated CDRs are recorded in the blockchain to prevent tampering.
- The user provides CDRs data and participates in cross check to reduce user complaint behavior.
- Only hash value of the simple CDRs is stored in the blockchain platform, which can prevent the risk of the original CDRs leakage, protect the user's data privacy and solve the problem of data storage capacity limit in blockchain.
- Credit Rating Evaluation smart contract achieve a unified credit rating method in the blockchain system. Participants in blockchain can query the credit rating, which prevent the information leakage.

In the experiment, based on the Hyperledger Fabric platform, 4 operators were selected to carry out experiments. All 4 operators have international roaming services with each other and carry out roaming settlement at monthly. The offline contracts should be transferred to the smart contract, and the CDRs of all operators and users should be uploaded to the cloud database and blockchain for automatic processing. CDRs Cross Check, Billing smart contract check the CDRs and generate bills automatically.

Assuming that international settlement is carried out at monthly, it takes an average of 4.5 days to complete the clearing and settlement of a single operator with the current processing method. In the experiment, the clearing and settlement can be improved to the hourly level, which greatly reduces the manual checking workload and improves the clearing and settlement efficiency of roaming services (Fig. 5).

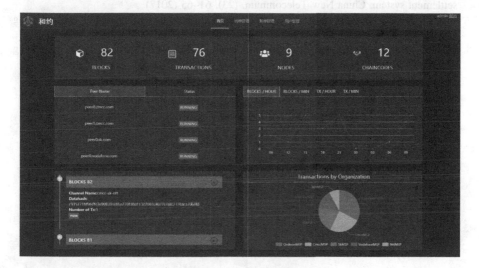

Fig. 5. Prototype of solution

5   Conclusion

This paper introduces the blockchain technology into international settlement business, and the characteristics of distributed network architecture, cryptographic algorithm, consensus mechanism, smart contract of the blockchain technology with cloud database. It provides an efficient and reliable blockchain platform solution for the international settlement business between operators.

Based on the analysis and experimental results, it is shown that the clearing and settlement of international roaming service based on CDRs Cross Check can reduce the duplication check, improve the clearing and settlement efficiency of roaming service, reduce the risk of user complaints, and provide open and transparent credit evaluation platform for all operators.

References

1. Hyvärinen, H., Risius, M., Friis, G.: A blockchain-based approach towards overcoming financial fraud in public sector services. Bus. Inf. Syst. Eng. **59**, 441–456 (2017)
2. Zhu, X., He, Q., Guo, S.: On the role of blockchain technology in supply chain finance. China Bus. Market **32**(3), 111–119 (2018)
3. Wang, Z.-P., Wu, Q.-H.: Design of blockchain for clearing and settlement. J. Cryptol. Res. **5**(5), 538–545 (2018)
4. Li, B., et al.: Transaction system and key technologies of multi-energy system based on heterogeneous blockchain. Autom. Electr. Power Syst. **42**(4), 183–193 (2018)
5. Lu, J., Song, B., Xiang, W.-H., Zhou, Z.-M.: Smart contract for electricity transaction and charge settlement based on blockchain. Comput. Syst. Appl. **26**(12), 34–50 (2017)
6. Kong, C.Y., Liu, Y.F., Zhang, X.D.: A heterogeneous data conversion method for roaming settlement system. China New Telecommun. (23), 61–65 (2017)
7. Li, C., Dai, B., Zhao, X., Wang, X.: Design and implementation of digital credit trading system based on blockchain technology. Mod. Comput. (27), 74–78 (2018)
8. Ju, C., Zou, J., Fu, X.: Design and application of big data credit reporting platform integrating blockchain technology. Comput. Sci. **45**(z2), 522–526,552 (2018)

Fog-Enabled Smart Campus: Architecture and Challenges

Chaogang Tang[1], Shixiong Xia[1], Chong Liu[2], Xianglin Wei[3(✉)], Yu Bao[1], and Wei Chen[1]

[1] School of Computer Science and Technology,
China University of Mining and Technology, Xuzhou 221000, China
[2] The George Washington University, Washington, D.C. 20052, USA
[3] Nanjing Telecommunication Technology Research Institute,
Nanjing 210000, China
wei_xianglin@163.com

Abstract. In recent years, much attention has been paid on the design and realization of smart campus, which is a miniature smart city paradigm consisting of its unique infrastructures, facilities, and services. Realizing the full vision of smart campus needs an instrumented, interconnected, and intelligent cyber physical system leveraging ICTs and physical infrastructures in the campus. Moreover, the study of a smart campus could pave a way for studying smart cities. In a smart campus, heterogeneous big data is continuously generated by the different functional sensing devices. This poses great challenges on the computation, transmission, storage, and energy consumption of traditional sensor-to-cloud continuum, which typically incurs huge amount of network transmission, high energy consumption, and long (sometimes intolerable) processing delay. Based on these observations, we propose a fog-enabled smart campus to enhance the real-time service provisioning. An architecture of smart campus is put forward, in which multiple fog nodes are deployed to guarantee the real-time performance of services and applications by performing tasks at the network edge. Furthermore, a lot of open research issues regarding to this architecture are discussed in hope to inspire to expand more research activities in this field.

Keywords: Smart campus · Fog computing · Architecture · Internet of Things

1 Introduction

1.1 A Subsection Sample

Sensor-cloud (SC), i.e. the sensor-to-cloud continuum, has received increasing attention recently, which integrates WSN and Cloud Computing and aims to enable the processing of sensed data with a variety of types in the remote cloud centers [1, 2]. The development of Internet of Things (IoT) and the Information and Communication Technology (ICT) help accelerate the development of Sensor-cloud. IoT defines a new connection paradigm, where people and things can connect and communicate at any-time, in anyplace, and with anything as well as anyone, ideally using any network and any services [3]. The development of IoT gives rise to great changes in the Information

J. Li et al. (Eds.): SPNCE 2019, LNICST 284, pp. 605–614, 2019.
https://doi.org/10.1007/978-3-030-21373-2_50

and Communication Technology (ICT), which can provide services to greatly promote the living standards of urban residents. As an application of SC, the concept of smart cites was proposed by different researchers in the past few years, which utilizes ICT as well as physical infrastructures (e.g., IoT devices and sensors) to fulfill the vision of an instrumented, interconnected, and intelligent city [4, 5].

Smart cities include many areas, such as smart homes, smart vehicles, smart campuses, smart factories, and smart offices. Of all these areas, the idea of smart campuses is the most similar to that of smart cities because in essence a smart campus is a relatively smaller ecosystem of a smart city in terms of population and engaged activities. Many researchers who study smart cities starts with smart campuses, since the smart campus research can directly apply to other territorial initiatives, such as smart cities and smart factories. On the other hand, smart campuses also have their own characteristics. For instance, the actors are mainly students, teachers and office staffs, and the engaged activities are mainly teaching activities. To the best of our knowledge, there is still no a widely accepted definition of smart campuses, but as far as we are concerned, the smart campus can be described as follows: As a small-scale, but self-contained model of a smart city, a smart campus aims to provide intelligent, humanized, convenient services for students, teachers and staffs with daily activities in a campus community via ICT and physical infrastructures.

Note that the activities facilitated by services delivered by a smart campus are not restricted to academic aspects, other nonacademic activities, such as smart parking, smart grid management, and smart alarm systems, are also involved. All these intelligent services cannot be realized without the use of IoT devices/sensors which collect and transmit data for further processing and analysis.

The amount of data generated from time to time by these sensing devices is significantly large (e.g., the surveillance cameras), which poses issues such as the costs on latency, storage, and energy consumption for communication. SC cannot guarantee the efficiency when coping with these big data, especially for some latency-sensitive services/applications (e.g., real-time incidents warnings) [6]. Based on these observations, we in this paper propose a fog computing based architecture of a smart campus with regards to service provisioning and application management.

Fog computing paradigm, also known as edge computing, is considered as one of the key enablers of IoT and big data applications [7, 8]. It brings computation and storage resources to the edge of a network, enabling the execution of highly demanding applications while meeting strict delay requirements. It usually acts as an intermediate layer between cloud data centers and IoT devices/sensors; it brings cloud-based services closer to IoT devices [9]. Thus, data can be processed in real-time and the efficiency of service provisioning can be guaranteed.

2   Related Works

Since an amount of the similarity exists between a smart city and a smart campus, we in this section review some existing works about smart campuses as well as smart cities. A smart campus offers an integrated, comfortable, intelligent environment for working, study and living via ICTs, IoT, mobile internet, and cloud computing. A smart campus involves many subareas such as smart parking, smart building, smart teaching, smart learning, and smart energy grid [10–12]. We in this section mainly focus on the architecture design and techniques to implement a smart campus as well as a smart city. A number of papers paid attention to the concept of a smart city and a smart campus and proposed the corresponding architectures as well as the domain applications [13–16]. Since huge quantity of data is generated continuously in a smart city and green city, how to manage these big data is crucial to the fulfillment of a smart city. Wei et al. have applied ant colony optimization for the task scheduling optimization problem in the mobile cloud computing scenarios [13].

Perera et al. have surveyed the application of fog computing in smart cities, and reviewed existing approaches proposed to tackle challenges in fog computing domain [3]. In addition, they identified major functionalities that fog computing platform can support, with the purpose of shedding light on further directions on fog computing based smart cities. Newaz et al. have proposed a web-based energy cloud platform framework for analyzing energy consumption behavior of campus environment, and predicting energy demand in the future [17].

To improve the educational environment and the comprehensive management level of universities, Bi et al. have constructed a smart campus system based on Building Information Modeling and 3D Geographic Information System platform [18]. A 3D visualization campus information system called "smart campus" was constructed, which provides feasible solutions for constructing smart campus. Bates et al. have discussed big data in the smart city by a case study which uses the existing IoT infrastructure to create a campus-scale "living laboratory." This kind of living laboratory can promote energy savings [19]. Atif et al. have constructed a ubiquitous learning model in the context of a pervasive smart campus [20]. They defined a model of a smart campus, and advocated learning practices in the light of new paradigms such as context-awareness, ubiquitous learning, and pervasive environment. A progress report about China's smart city is given in [21]. Liu et al. have constructed an architecture of China's smart city with four layers, i.e., sensing layer, transmission layer, processing layer and application layer, respectively.

For latency-sensitive tasks and applications, a cloud computing based smart campus does not provide a satisfactory solution due to the latency related tasks/applications uploading. To the best of our knowledge, very few work that brings fog computing into the smart campus research. In this paper we propose a fog computing-based architecture of a smart campus, where some time-critical tasks/applications can be deployed and utilized efficiently in a smart campus.

3 Architecture

In a smart campus, various types of data are collected by sensors employed widely all the time. The large volumes of data are then processed and analyzed, with the purpose of benefiting teachers and students in both daily teaching and leisure activities. For some latency-sensitive services in smart campuses, the response time of data processing in campus cloud data center may not be fast enough due to the limited bandwidth and many concurrent accesses to the cloud center. Therefore, fog computing, as an intermediate layer in between cloud data centers and IoT devices, is introduced to facilitate data collection, processing and analysis so that time-sensitive services can be performed in real-time.

3.1 Fog Computing in Smart Campus

To illustrate the application of fog computing in a smart campus, an example is presented in Fig. 1. While in reality, varieties of smart devices with computational capabilities deployed at the edge of network (e.g., gateways, routers) can serve as fog nodes, we recommend those special servers with appropriate computational capabilities as fog nodes in this paper. This is because services with different goals usually have different requirements for fog nodes in terms of computational and storage capabilities.

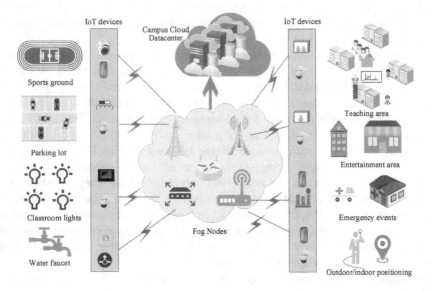

Fig. 1. An example of applying fog computing based smart campus.

In Fig. 1, we list enumerate eight typical application scenarios where fog computing is employed for decision making. For instance, from the view point of energy savings in a smart campus, lights in classrooms should be controlled automatically– they can be turned off automatically when classrooms are empty. This is an essential part of functionalities which a smart building is supposed to have. Another interesting observation is that sometimes classrooms are not empty, but occupied by only a few students studying. In such case, the power consumption is still not negligible. Interestingly, this case has been becoming the main cause of unnecessary electricity wastes compared to the former case for most universities in China. However, with fog computing introduced in smart campus, we can avoid this situation and greatly reduce unnecessary power consumption. For instance, the fog nodes gather the information collected by various sensors such as surveillance cameras in each classroom and analyze it with suitable algorithms to decide which classroom(s) the lights should be turned off. Then students in the classroom with lights being turned off can be guided to specific classrooms with lights on. Thus, the power consumption can be reduced to a great extent. In essence, this student reallocation problem is a special 0/1 multiple knapsack problem, and it is known that this combinatorial optimization problem is NP-hard.

Similarly, fog computing can also be used to control the air condition in each classroom based on temperature and the humidity of a classroom detected by sensors. By doing this, the carbon dioxide emission can be reduced and thus meaningful steps can be taken for environment protection, which at the same is also aligned with the major purpose of applying campus smart grid. In addition, in emergency events like car collision or persons injured in sports facilities, the fog nodes can start an emergency preplan and sometimes initiate direct communication with the campus rescue center for further assistance.

Due to space limitation, we do not dwell on other applications one by one here. However, in the section of case studies, we study three scenarios in more details to underline the necessity of applying fog computing to smart campus.

3.2 Architecture Design in Smart Campus

Figure 2 presents an architecture of fog computing based smart campus proposed in this paper, which consists of four layers – cyber physical layer, data management layer, data processing layer, and domain application layer. Note that we separate data processing and data management for the sake of information sharing and resource reuse.

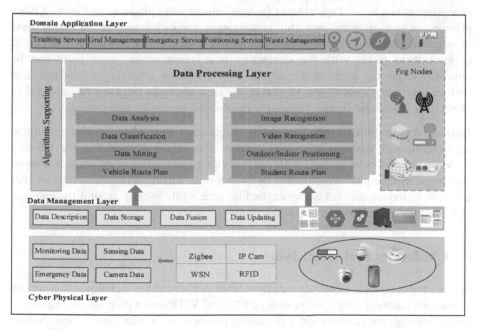

Fig. 2. The architecture of fog computing based smart campus proposition.

Cyber Physical Layer. In a smart campus, various types of information can be leveraged to improve the teaching and study environments and the living environments with the help of ICT and physical infrastructure. The cyber physical layer is composed by a densely distributed ecosystem which covers various sensors. Thus data from multiple sources can be sensed and collected, e.g., by surveillance cameras, GPS, RFID tags, etc. The core technology in the cyber physical layer is IoT, which enables direct interactions among various entities (e.g., sensors, routers, gateways).

Data Management Layer. Enormous amount of information is continuously collected by the cyber physical layer. To make data processing more efficient in the next stages, we add an intermediate layer called data management layer in between the cyber physical layer and the data processing layer. Data management layer is responsible for data preprocessing such as data description, data fusion. The same event can be captured by sensors of different types while data from different sensors usually have a variety of formats. Thus, redundancy of data may exist when storing them. To manage data efficiently, it is necessary to process the sensed data in advance, such as redundancy removing. In addition, data fusion is also an essential part in data management layer, which integrates data from multiple sources to provide much more consistent, accurate and meaningful information than that provided by any individual data source.

Data Processing Layer. Data processing layer is the core of the fog computing based architecture in a smart campus; it integrates the application of fog computing and remote campus cloud data centers. This layer is in charge of processing the sensed data of different types via fog computing. Many time-sensitive services and tasks can be processed in this layer. Typical tasks include vehicle route planning and student route planning which requires powerful computation capacities and at the same time demands a real-time response. It is sometimes very difficult for a single IoT device to perform these tasks. With fog computing based architecture, these tasks can be uploaded to the fog nodes at the edge of networks, thus achieving almost real-time performance and requirements. Moreover, the data and tasks can even be uploaded to cloud data centers for further processing in case fog nodes are overloaded.

Domain Application Layer. The domain application layer offers specific intelligent applications and services in a smart campus. For example, regarding the learning activities, students can be guided to suitable classrooms with vacant seats in a smart campus, thus saving the classroom/seats finding time. Smart parking service is another example to reduce the parking space finding time while cycling around the campus, especially for newcomers.

4   Challenges and Open Issues

While a fog computing based smart campus leverages several key techniques that are still in the early stages of development such as V2V and V2I in smart parking, smart gird and smart building, we can envision a promising prospect in the near future. Nonetheless, there still exist many challenges and open issues about this fog computing based architecture. In this section, we present and discuss some challenges and open issues, with the purpose of serving as an inspiring guidance for future research within this field.

4.1 Quick Decision Making for Fog Computing

Bringing fog computing into a smart campus is intended to guarantee the real-time performance of time-sensitive applications deployed in a smart campus. For instance, for smart parking in campus, the key to maintaining the real-time response is to perform most of computations locally. Specifically, a parking slots allocation scheme is computed by fog nodes based on some objective function. The campus cloud center would start to function when the performance of fog nodes degrades due to overheads or increasing need for coordination among fog nodes. As a result, designing suitable thresholds below which the uploading is activated, for various applications, is very important to ensure the real-time performance. In addition, how to make efficient strategies and deploy algorithms at the fog nodes for time-sensitive applications also affects the quality of service.

4.2 Deep Learning Based Middleware Design

Deep learning has been widely adopted for supporting many applications in the data processing layer of our smart campus architecture, such as image/video recognition, route planning, and data mining. Compared with traditional methods, deep learning-based algorithms perform much better but require much more computation capacity and energy consumption. An efficient way to incorporate deep learning into the smart campus architecture is to design a deep learning-based middleware and leverage it to support the applications. The challenge here is how to design a middleware that can support heterogeneous applications at the same time.

4.3 Efficient Security Enhancement and Privacy Protection

Smart applications are supported by information sharing and processing among diverse sensing and processing devices located at one or multiple trust zones in a timely manner. It is worth noting that many identity, location, and health related data will also involve in this process. Many security concerns may arise in this process. The major challenges include how to ensure that only authenticated users can acquire particular data, and how to fulfill users' privacy requirements, on the condition that the energy consumption and processing latency are still acceptable for the whole system.

4.4 Cooperation Between Fog Nodes and Campus Cloud Nodes

Cooperation between fog nodes and cloud nodes is also an import issue. There is a tradeoff between fog node computation offloading and transmission latency. On one hand, to overcome the resource constraints in fog computing, computation offloading mechanism is often adopted for the computation-intensive tasks, in which some computing modules of the application are offloaded to powerful nodes in a campus cloud center. On the other hand, since task offloading results in transmission latency, computation should be performed locally in fog nodes as much as possible. Therefore, the key to cooperation between fogs and clouds is that there should exist a tradeoff between fogs and clouds, where the fog nodes should decide which behaviors at what granularity level under what conditions should be offloaded to the cloud computing.

4.5 Data Fusion in Smart Campus

With the rapid development of ICTs and increasing application of various sensors deployed for smart campuses, sensed data with a variety of types and formats will show an explosive growth. How to integrate these data from multiple sources to generate more consistent, accurate, and meaningful information is very important in smart campuses. Data fusion techniques should be applied to supporting better service provisioning in smart campuses.

4.6 Campus Smart Grid

To respond to increasing demands for energy saving –including renewable energy and environments protection, smart grid in campuses aims to reduce the total overall energy while satisfy more campus' energy demands by innovating the current electrical power system via ICTs. However, a few issues still need to be addressed concerning the campus smart grid. For instance, there is still no clear consensus on smart grid design methodology in smart campuses. On another hand, how to develop efficient strategies and algorithms which is capable of analyzing and processing the sensed data from smart grid devices is crucial to achieve the expected goals of campus smart grid.

4.7 Testbed Construction

To realize a practical fog computing based smart campus architecture requires a significant investment on the deployment, operation and maintenance at both fog computing and cloud computing center. Accordingly, it is necessary and cost effective to design and develop a testbed before implementing the full-scale architecture. A testbed allows various data reduction, data fusion, task offloading, and service optimization algorithms to be deployed and tested, and various domain applications to be evaluated and characterized.

5 Conclusions

Smart campuses offer an integrated, comfortable, intelligent environment for working, study and living via incorporating Information Communication Technologies, Internet of Things, mobile internet, and cloud computing paradigms. However, traditional sensor-to-cloud continuum may incur long transmission delay, high energy consumption, and privacy leakage when the tasks/applications are uploaded to a campus cloud for execution. To break this stalemate, we propose a fog computing based smart campus architecture, in which a few fog nodes are deployed to process the data near the data source. Furthermore, a few challenges and open research issues are outlined in hope to inspire more future research activities within this field.

References

1. Fan, J., Wei, X., Wang, T., Lan, T., Subramaniam, S.: Deadline-aware task scheduling in a tiered IoT infrastructure. In: GLOBECOM 2017-2017 IEEE Global Communications Conference, pp. 1–7. IEEE, December 2017
2. Wang, T., Wei, X., Liang, T., Fan, J.: Dynamic tasks scheduling based on weighted bi-graph in mobile cloud computing. Sustain. Comput. Inform. Syst. **19**, 214–222 (2018)
3. Perera, C., Qin, Y., Estrella, J., Reiff-Marganiec, S., Vasilakos, A.: Fog computing for sustainable smart cities: a survey. ACM Comput. Surv. **50**(3), 1–43 (2017). https://doi.org/10.1145/3057266
4. Tang, C., Hao, M., Wei, X., Chen, W.: Energy-aware task scheduling in mobile cloud computing. Distrib. Parallel Databases **36**(3), 1–25 (2018)
5. Taleb, T., Dutta, S., Ksentini, A., Iqbal, M., Flinck, H.: Mobile edge computing potential in making cities smarter. IEEE Commun. Mag. **55**(3), 38–43 (2017)
6. Wang, T., Wei, X., Tang, C., Fan, J.: Efficient multi-tasks scheduling algorithm in mobile cloud computing with time constraints. Peer-to-Peer Netw. Appl. **11**(4), 793–807 (2018)
7. Bonomi, F., Milito, R., Zhu, J., Addepalli, S.: Fog computing and its role in the internet of things. In: Edition of the Mcc Workshop on Mobile Cloud Computing, pp. 13–16 (2012)
8. Tang, C., Wei, X., Hao, M., Zhu, C., Wang, R., Chen, W.: Traffic signal phase scheduling based on device-to-device communication. IEEE Access **6**, 47636–47645 (2018)
9. Wei, X., Fan, J., Lu, Z., Ding, K.: Application scheduling in mobile cloud computing with load balancing. J. Appl. Math. **2013**, 409539:1–409539:13 (2013)
10. Chuling, L., Xie, Z., Peng, P.: A discussion on the framework of smarter campus. In: 2009 Third International Symposium on Intelligent Information Technology Application, Shanghai (2009)
11. Nie, X.: Research on smart campus based on cloud computing and Internet of Things. Appl. Mech. Mater. **380–384**, 1951–1954 (2013)
12. Liu, Y.L., Zhang, W.H., Dong, P.: Research on the construction of smart campus based on the Internet of Things and cloud computing. Appl. Mech. Mater. **543–547**, 3213–3217 (2014)
13. Wei, X., Fan, J., Wang, T., Wang, Q.: Efficient application scheduling in mobile cloud computing based on MAX–MIN ant system. Soft. Comput. **20**(7), 2611–2625 (2016)
14. Liu, X.: A study on smart campus model in the era of big data. In: International Conference on Economics, Management Engineering and Education Technology, pp. 919–922 (2017)
15. Yin, C., Zhang, X., Hui, C., Wang, J.Y., Cooper, D., David, B.: A literature survey on smart cities. Sci. China Inf. Sci. **58**(10), 100102:1–100102:18 (2015). https://doi.org/10.1007/s11432-015-5397-4
16. Wei, X., Fan, J., Lu, Z., Ding, K., Li, R., Zhang, G.: Bio-inspired application scheduling algorithm for mobile cloud computing. In: 2013 Fourth International Conference on Emerging Intelligent Data and Web Technologies, pp. 690–695. IEEE, September 2013
17. Newaz, S.H.S., et al.: A web based energy cloud platform for campus smart grid for understanding energy consumption profile and predicting future energy demand. In: International Conference on Information and Communication Technology Convergence, pp. 173–178. IEEE (2014)
18. Bi, T., Yang, X., Ren, M.: The design and implementation of smart campus system. J. Comput. **12**(6), 527–533 (2017)
19. Bates, O., Friday, A.: Beyond data in the smart city: repurposing existing campus IoT. IEEE Pervasive Comput. **16**(2), 54–60 (2017). https://doi.org/10.1109/MPRV.2017.30

20. Atif, Y., Mathew, S.S., Lakas, A.: Building a smart campus to support ubiquitous learning. J. Ambient. Intell. Hum. Comput. **6**(2), 223–238 (2015)
21. Liu, P., Peng, Z.: China's smart city pilots: a progress report. Computer **47**(10), 72–81 (2014). https://doi.org/10.1109/MC.2013.149

An Ant Colony Optimization Fuzzy Clustering Task Scheduling Algorithm in Mobile Edge Computing

Jianwei Liu[1], Xianglin Wei[2(✉)], Tongxiang Wang[1],
and Junwei Wang[1]

[1] Army Engineering University of PLA, Nanjing 210007, China
[2] Nanjing Telecommunication Technology Research Institute,
Nanjing 210007, China
wei_xianglin@163.com

Abstract. Mobile edge computing has always been a key issue in the development of the mobile Internet and the Internet of things, how to efficiently schedule tasks has gradually become the focus of mobile edge computing research. Task scheduling problem belongs to the NP-hard optimization problem. Many traditional heuristic algorithms are applied to deal with the task scheduling problem. For improving the problem that ant colony algorithm has slow convergence speed, an ant colony optimization fuzzy clustering algorithm is proposed in this paper. In this algorithm, the fuzzy clustering algorithm is used to reduce the search space range in order to reduce the complexity of the scheduling algorithm and the number of iterations. And the optimal solution of the scheduling is found using the strong global search ability of ant colony algorithm. The simulation results show that the performance of the ant colony optimization fuzzy clustering algorithm is better than that of the First-Come-First-Served algorithm and the traditional ant colony optimization algorithm.

Keywords: Mobile edge computing · Task scheduling ·
Ant colony optimization algorithm · Fuzzy clustering algorithm

1 Introduction

With the rapid development and popularization of mobile Internet and the Internet of things (IoT), various applications such as augmented reality (AR) and virtual reality (VR) has greatly expanded the functions of mobile devices. Meanwhile, IoT businesses such as smart city, environmental monitoring, and intelligent agriculture are emerging. However, due to the limited storage, computing and perceived capabilities of mobile devices, mobile applications face many challenges in quality of service (QoS), mobility management and security. In this case, a new computing paradigm, i.e. Mobile Edge Computing (MEC), has been paid much attention by researchers due to its wide employment in several scenarios, such as IoT and Vehicular Network.

© ICST Institute for Computer Sciences, Social Informatics and Telecommunications Engineering 2019
Published by Springer Nature Switzerland AG 2019. All Rights Reserved
J. Li et al. (Eds.): SPNCE 2019, LNICST 284, pp. 615–624, 2019.
https://doi.org/10.1007/978-3-030-21373-2_51

A typical mobile edge computing architecture consists of MEC servers and mobile devices [1, 2]. Compared to mobile devices, MEC servers are deployed at the edge of the network and have more available resources, which can process some computation-intensive, storage-intensive or latency tolerant tasks. And mobile devices can reduce their own computing load and energy consumption by offloading some tasks to MEC servers. Therefore, it is very important to design an efficient task scheduling strategy under MEC architecture. Previous works have investigated heuristic algorithms to deal with scheduling problem in MEC such as genetic algorithm and ant colony optimization (ACO) algorithm. However, traditional heuristic algorithms have some shortcomings such as high complexity, long iteration time and local optimum. When a large number of tasks need to be processed, the traditional scheduling algorithm is used to iterate for too long and cannot meet the requirements of tasks' deadline, which affecting mobile device user's quality of experience (QoE). Moreover, When the traditional task scheduling algorithm selects the resource, its target is the total service resource, which does not consider the characteristics of the resource itself and the preferences of the user or task, which leads to the large cost of the resource selection and the blind interest. Therefore, it is important to find a suitable method to reduce the resource selection range, thereby reducing the task scheduling spending.

Inspired by the above motivations, an ant colony optimization and fuzzy clustering (ACOFC) algorithm is proposed in this paper. Firstly, according to the tasks' preference for resources, the fuzzy clustering algorithm is used to divide the resources in order to reduce the space of the resource search and the complexity of the algorithm. Afterwards, the ACO algorithm is used to find the optimal scheduling solution in the divided spaces. At last, a series of numerical tests are conducted to illustrate the performance of the ACOFC algorithm is better than that of the First-Come-First-Served algorithm (FCFS) and the ACO algorithm.

The rest of paper is organized as follow. Section 2 overviews related studies on task scheduling. the system model is presented and, the joint scheduling problem is formulated in Sect. 3. The calculations of collision probability and access delay are discussed in Sect. 4. Section 5 presents a series of numerical test. Finally, the contributions of this paper are concluded in Sect. 6.

2 Related Work

In the previous work, Wei et al. formulated the joint scheduling problem as a 0-1 knapsack problem for the deadline-constraint tasks and the ACO-based method was employed to maximize the profits for the service providers [3]. In [4], They put forward a scheduling algorithm based on MAX–MIN Ant System (MMAS) considering multi-dimensional resources. Then, the load balancing of mobile devices was considered when scheduling the results [5]. Later, Wang et al. modified the algorithm while taking the types of tasks with deadline-constraint into consideration [6].

Although amounts of heuristic traditional scheduling algorithms have been proposed to scheduling problems with different targets, how to improve the traditional algorithm to solve scheduling problem is rarely studied in the MEC system. In [9], Wang et al. proposed an improved genetic algorithm method where the min-min and max-min algorithm are used to boost the search efficiency. For improving ACO algorithm's shortcomings in task scheduling, a task scheduling algorithm based on simulated annealing ant colony Algorithm is put forward in [10]. In this algorithm, the local optimal solution is constructed by ACO algorithm, the strong local search ability of simulated annealing algorithm (SA) is utilized to avoid algorithm trapped in local optimum at a certain probability.

3   System Model and Problem Formulation

3.1   MEC System Model

Before introducing the scheduling problem, our system model is presented in Fig. 1. The service providers, including MEC servers and mobile devices, can run the tasks concurrently. MEC servers are attached to the access point of the mobile devices to achieve low response latency, and mobile devices can offload tasks to the mobile servers. Both mobile devices and MEC servers have limited resources. MEC servers have more available resources than mobile device so that the processing time for task on MEC servers is shorter. Assume that each task cannot be further partitioned. The general working process is as follow:

- Each mobile device sends offloading requests to the decision maker in MEC servers by the wireless access network.

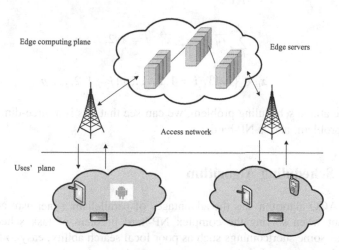

Fig. 1. System model

- According to the collected offloading requests of all the mobile devices and the property of each task, the decision maker executes the scheduling algorithm to decide where should the tasks be processed (in the mobile device locally or in the MEC server).
- The mobile devices offload the chosen tasks to the MEC servers.
- The MEC servers handle the tasks received and send their results to the mobile devices.

3.2   Problem Formulation

Assume that the resource dimension is three dimensions the resource for each MEC server i can be represented as a vector $\vec{c}_i = (c_i^{comp}, c_i^{stor}, c_i^{comm})$, where c_i^{comp}, c_i^{stor} and c_i^{comm} represents computing resources, storage resources and communication resources respectively. The set of tasks to be scheduled is represented as $I = \{1, 2, \ldots, n\}$, the value of each task in I is expressed as $(p_1, p_2, \ldots, p_n)$. And when the task i is running on the MEC server j, the resource that it consumes is represented as a vector $\vec{r}_{ij} = (r_{ij}^{comp}, r_{ij}^{stor}, r_{ij}^{comm})$. Assuming that all the task scheduling requests reach the decision maker at the same time and each task can only be offloaded to one MEC server. Under the constraints of the resources of each MEC server, the scheduling goal is to maximize the total profits, namely:

$$\text{Maximize} \sum_{j=1}^{n} \sum_{i=1}^{m} p_j \times x_{ij} \tag{1}$$

$$\text{Subject to:} \sum_{j=1}^{n} x_{ij} \leq 1, \ i = 1, 2, \ldots, m \tag{2}$$

$$\sum_{i=1}^{m} \vec{r}_{ij} \times x_{ij} \leq \vec{c}_i, \ j = 1, 2, \ldots, n \tag{3}$$

$$x_{ij} \in \{0, 1\}, \ i = 1, 2, \ldots, m; j = 1, 2, \ldots, n \tag{4}$$

From the above scheduling problem, we can see that this is a three-dimensional 0-1knapsack problem, and is NP-hard.

4   Tasks Scheduling Algorithm

The simple ACO algorithm has the advantages of parallelism, synergism and positive feedback, but when solving the complex NP-hard problem of task scheduling, the algorithm has some shortcomings such as poor local search ability, easy to fall into the local optimal solution and slow convergence speed.

For solving this NP-hard scheduling problem, we propose an ACOFC algorithm, which can be widely utilized to solve this kind of combinational optimization problem. At first, fuzzy clustering algorithm is used to divide the tasks to be scheduled can be divided into three categories by tasks' preference for resources: computational task set, bandwidth task set, and storage task set. Similarly, MEC servers can be divided into three categories: computational server set, bandwidth server set and storage server set. By using fuzzy clustering algorithm, the tasks and the MEC servers are divided respectively, which reduces the spatial space of the search and the complexity of the algorithm. Afterwards, Because of the strong global search ability of ACO algorithm, the ACO algorithm is used to find the optimal scheduling solution in the space of task set and MEC server set with the same resource preference.

4.1 Resource Fuzzy Clustering

Fuzzy c-means clustering method (FCM) is a data clustering method based on the optimization of objective function. Given the data set $X = \{x_1, x_2, \ldots, x_n\}$, the objective of FCM algorithm is to find a fuzzy partition cluster $U_{c \times n}$ of the data set, that is, divide the original data into c fuzzy groups, and minimize the non-similarity index between each group of samples and its clustering center. The general definition of clustering objective function is as follows.

$$J(U, c_1, \cdots, c_c) = \sum_{i=1}^{c} J_i = \sum_{i=1}^{c} \sum_{j}^{n} u_{ij}^a d_{ij}^2 \tag{5}$$

where U_{ij} represents the membership degree of data j to fuzzy group i, the value of U_{ij} is between 0 and 1. c_i is the clustering center of fuzzy group i, and $d_{ij} = ||c_i - x_j||$ is the Euclidean distance between the i clustering center and the j data point. $a \in [1, \infty)$ is a weighted index.

4.2 ACO Tasks Scheduling Algorithm

After fuzzy clustering of tasks and MEC servers, the task set and MEC server set, which have the same resource preferences, are respectively taken as tasks to be scheduled and service providers for ACO algorithm.

The basic principle of ACO algorithm is to release pheromones on the path of the natural ants, and the following the concentration of the remaining pheromones in the path of the left pheromones is higher, and the higher the concentration of the remaining pheromones, the greater the probability of selecting the path, which gradually converts to the process of the optimal solution of the entire company.

Local Heuristic Information and Path Selection.
In the ACO algorithm, the path can be determined by pheromone concentration and local heuristic values. Resource consumption is an important factor influencing the

scheduling goals. Therefore, the local heuristic value can be determined by the remaining resources. This means that the corresponding path of a host with a larger remaining resource has a higher priority. ACOFC algorithm considers the task profit and the resource consumption of the task, and defines the local heuristic information as

$$\eta_i(t) = \frac{h_i}{\sum_{j=1}^{m} |\frac{\vec{c_i}}{\vec{c_i} - \vec{r_{ij}}}|} \tag{6}$$

where h_i represents the profit of task i. And the probability that ant q selects the next task i is

$$P_{ij}^q = \begin{cases} \frac{[\tau_{ij}(t)]^\alpha [\eta_{ij}(t)]^\beta}{\sum_{k \in allowedq(t)} [\tau_{ik}(t)]^\alpha [\eta_{ik}(t)]^\beta} \\ 0, \qquad\qquad\qquad otherwise \end{cases} \tag{7}$$

where α and β are the weighted factors of the pheromone and heuristic value. $\tau_{ij}(t)$ presents the pheromone concentration on the path from i to j at time t.

Pheromone Update.
After each cycle of ACO algorithm, the pheromone needs to be updated according to the partial solutions. At first, the pheromone applied on the link would decline at a certain rate according to the volatile characteristics of pheromone. Besides, the solutions will increase its value for the ants. Assume that $\tau_{ij}(t)$ will be updated to be $\tau_{ij}(t+1)$ at time $t+1$.

$$\tau_{ij}(t+1) = (1-\rho)\tau_{ij}(t) + \Delta\tau_{ij}(t) \tag{8}$$

where ρ represents the evaporation rate of the ant. $\Delta\tau_i(t)$ is the increment of the pheromone, which can be determined according to the partial solution. The calculation of $\Delta\tau_j(t)$ is:

$$\Delta\tau_{ij}(t) = \sum_{q=1}^{Q} \Delta\tau_{ij}^q(t) \tag{9}$$

where Q is the ants' number. $\Delta\tau_{ij}^q(t)$ is determined by the partial solution at time t:

4.3   Algorithm Description

Algorithm: ACOFCalgorithm

1: **For** *tasks and MEC servers*

2: *Set the number of clusters c, the maximum number of iterations T, accuracy of convergence*
   ε and initialize the membership matrix U_0

3:    **If** *the current iteration number $t \leq T$ and $\|U_t - U_{t-1}\| \leq \varepsilon$*

4:       *Calculate the distance between the centroid and the data point;*

5:       *Calculate the FCM objective function;*

6:       *Update the membership matrix U_t;*

7:    **End**

8: **End**

9: *According to the obtained membership matrix, the task and MEC servers are divided into*
   different categories

10: **For** *each group of the task set and MEC server set which have the same resource*
       preference.

11:      **For** *each cycle of ACO*

12:         **For** *each ant*

13:            *Determine the available links between tasks and MEC servers according to the*
               resource's consumption;

14:            *Place pheromone on paths based on the path's priority;*

15:            **If** *there is at least one path*

16:               *Calculate local heuristic value for each path;*

17:               *Choose the path with highest selection probability;*

18:               *Add the path to the partial solution;*

19:               *Update the paths set and remaining resource of hosts;*

20:            **End**

21:            *Calculate the profit of the partial solution;*

22:            *Update the best value of the solution;*

23:            *Update the pheromone of each path;*

24:         **End**

25:      **End**

       End

26: **Return** the total optimal value.

---

5   Numerical Tests

In this section, we conduct a series of numerical tests to analyze the ACOFC algorithm by MATLAB simulator. In order to better evaluate the performance of the ACO algorithm, two typical scheduling algorithms, i.e. FCFS algorithm and ACO algorithm are utilized to compare with our proposed algorithm under different experimental settings.

In this simulation, the dimension of the resource is three, which represents computing resources, communication resources, and storage resources. There are m MEC servers and n tasks in the MEC system. Assume that these tasks arrive at the same time and each task has a large demand for a certain resource. The task's consumption of three-dimensional resources is in the range $[a_1, a_2]$ on a MEC server. And the three-dimensional resource capacity of MEC servers is evenly distributed within the interval $[a_3, a_4]$. The profit of the task is subject to uniform distribution $[a_5, a_6]$ within the interval. The number of loops is set to 5. The main parameters employed in the simulation process are illustrated in Table 1.

Table 1. Related parameters

Parameters	Value	Parameters	Value
α	1	a_2	50
β	1	a_3	50
n	100	a_4	100
m	20	a_5	10
ρ	0.3	a_6	40
a_1	10		

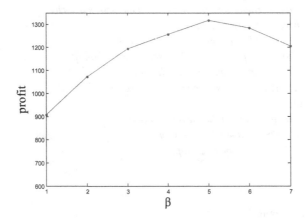

Fig. 2. Comparison of total profit for different β

Figure 2 shows the impact of β, which is defined as the local heuristic value in the path section process, on the result of ACOFC algorithm. The x-coordinates are the β, and the y-coordinates are the total profit. As β increases, the total profit increases with it linearly. While total profit is little reduced when β is larger than 5.

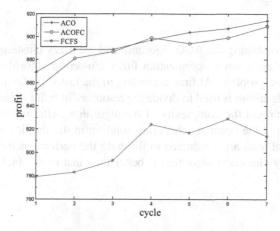

Fig. 3. The total profit varies with cycle for ACO, ACPFC and FCFS

The performance of ACOFC algorithm is illustrated in Fig. 3. by comparing with ACO algorithm and FCFS algorithm. the x-coordinate represents the cycles and the y-coordinate represents the total profit. From the figure, we can see that the total profit of ACOFC algorithm is close to that of ACO algorithm.

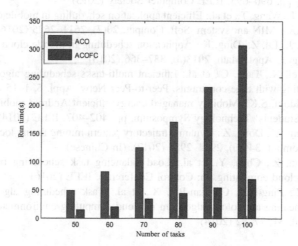

Fig. 4. Comparison of run time for different number of tasks

In Fig. 4, the x-coordinates are the number of tasks, and the y-coordinates are the run time. We compare the run time of ACPFC algorithm with that of ACO algorithm under different number of tasks. We can see that the running time of ACOFC algorithm is much shorter than ACO algorithm, especially in the case of a large number of tasks to be scheduled

6 Conclusion

In this paper, by combining the ACO algorithm and the fuzzy clustering algorithm, we have proposed an ant colony optimization fuzzy clustering algorithm to deal with a NP-hard scheduling problem. At first, according to the tasks' preference for resources, fuzzy clustering algorithm is used to divide the resources in order to reduce the space of the resource search and the complexity of the algorithm. Afterwards, the ACO algorithm is used to find the optimal scheduling solution in the divided spaces. At last, a series of numerical tests are conducted to illustrate the performance of the ant colony optimization fuzzy clustering algorithm is better than that of the FCFS algorithm and the ACO algorithm.

References

1. Mao, Y., You, C., Zhang, J., et al.: A survey on mobile edge computing: the communication perspective. IEEE Commun. Surv. Tutor. **19**(4), 2322–2358 (2017)
2. Abbas, N., Zhang, Y., Taherkordi, A., et al.: Mobile edge computing: a survey. IEEE Internet Things J. **PP**(99), 1 (2017)
3. Wei, X., Fan, J., Lu, Z., et al.: Bio-inspired application scheduling algorithm for mobile cloud computing. In: Fourth International Conference on Emerging Intelligent Data and Web Technologies, pp. 690–695. IEEE Computer Society (2013)
4. Wei, X., Fan, J., Wang, T., et al.: Efficient application scheduling in mobile cloud computing based on MAX—MIN ant system. Soft. Comput. **20**(7), 2611–2625 (2016)
5. Wei, X., Fan, J., Lu, Z., Ding, K.: Application scheduling in mobile cloud computing with load balancing. J. Appl. Math. **2013**(3), 337–366 (2013)
6. Wang, T., Wei, X., Tang, C., et al.: Efficient multi-tasks scheduling algorithm in mobile cloud computing with time constraints. Peer-to-Peer Netw. Appl. **5**, 1–15 (2017)
7. Ravi, A., Peddoju, S.K.: Mobility managed energy efficient Android mobile devices using cloudlet. In: Students' Technology Symposium, pp. 402–407. IEEE (2014)
8. Deng, J., Wang, Y., Dong, Z.: Dynamic trajectory pattern mining facing location prediction. Appl. Res. Comput. **34**(10), 2984–2988 (2017). (In Chinese)
9. Wang, T., Liu, Z., Chen, Y., et al.: Load balancing task scheduling based on genetic algorithm in cloud computing. In: Control Conference. IEEE (2016)
10. Hao-Rong, Z., Ping-Hua, C., Jian-Bin, X., et al.: Task scheduling algorithm based on simulated annealing ant colony algorithm in cloud computing environment. J. Guangdong Univ. Technol. **31**, 77–82 (2014)

Mechanism and Method in New Computing

A Posted Pricing Mechanism
Based on Random Forests
in Crowdsourcing Market

Lifei Hao[1,2], Bing Jia[1,2(✉)], and Chuxuan Zhang[1,2]

[1] College of Computer Science, Inner Mongolia University, Hohhot 010021, China
jiabing@imu.edu.cn
[2] Inner Mongolia A.R. Key Laboratory of Wireless Networking and Mobile
Computing, Hohhot 010021, China

Abstract. With the rapid development of the Internet, the combination of outsourcing and Internet has produced an overturning mode for labor cooperation – crowdsourcing. Crowdsourcing outsource the work that used to be done by internal staffs of a company or organization to non-specific people in a free and voluntary way, which concentrates the wisdom of public to solve difficult problems, greatly optimizes the rational allocation of human resources and thus improves the social productivity. In the environment of crowdsourcing market, how to set an "appropriate" price to recruit workers to complete a given task at a reasonable quality and cost is a key problem which restricts the development of it. Therefore, this paper proposes a posted pricing method based on the Random Forests (RF) algorithm in crowdsourcing market. The proposed mechanism is described theoretically and the actual crowdsourcing date is acquired from Taskcn by python spider firstly. Then, based on these empirical data, serval typical machine learning methods have been compared, which proves that RF is a very suitable method for posted pricing in crowdsourcing market. Finally, extensive experiments have been conducted and analysed for optimizing the parameters in RF and a set of parameters suitable for posted pricing in crowdsourcing is given to construct the corresponding RF model.

Keywords: Crowdsourcing · Pricing mechanism · Random Forests ·
Machine learning · Web spider

1 Introduction

In recent years, as the rapid development of Internet technology and combing with outsourcing, a innovative mode of labor cooperation – crowdsourcing [7] has emerged, which means that the work previously performed by employees in a company or institution can be outsourced to non-specific mass groups in a free and voluntary way through Internet technology. In practice, whether in domestic or abroad, there are many crowdsourcing platforms, thus the crowdsourcing

© ICST Institute for Computer Sciences, Social Informatics and Telecommunications Engineering 2019
Published by Springer Nature Switzerland AG 2019. All Rights Reserved
J. Li et al. (Eds.): SPNCE 2019, LNICST 284, pp. 627–636, 2019.
https://doi.org/10.1007/978-3-030-21373-2_52

market formed. Currently, crowdsourcing has been applied on a large scale and there are still unlimited market opportunities to be explored by the further developing of it.

A typical crowdsourcing structure [13] universally consists of three subjects: the requester, the worker, and the crowdsourcing platform, as shown in Fig. 1. Requester is the initiator of a specific crowdsourcing activity, which mainly releases the task and provides rewards. Workers who complete tasks and receive rewards are the group composed of individuals or teams to solve problems. As an intermediary, the crowdsourcing platform hosts the rewards and connects requesters and workers. In the whole process of crowdsourcing, rewards is the most important incentive approach to enable workers completing tasks on time and with a high quality.

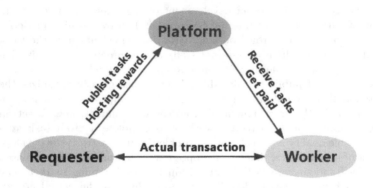

Fig. 1. The typical structure of crowdsourcing.

If the pricing for rewards is too low, the number of workers involved in the task will be insufficient, which will affect the completion of the task or make the quality lower. On the contrary, it will cause the waste of economic resources, increase the cost of employers and platforms, and thus reduce their benefits. Therefore, how to set an appropriate price to recruit groups to complete the task at a reasonable quality and cost, namely the crowdsourcing pricing problem, is the core issue restricting the development of crowdsourcing [4,5].

To solve the problem of posted pricing, [5] proposed a posted pricing mechanism based on quality-aware Bayesian model (assuming that the cost and completion quality of workers can be obtained from the probability distribution of historical data) in crowdsensing. [10] proposed a multi-parameter posted pricing mechanism based on collection-behavior by applying all-payment auction. [11] studied the using of autoregressive method with market sentiment indicators to predict American oil prices, and concluded that autoregressive method was not strong in predicting, so that the Machine Learning (ML) method should be considered to solve such problems. [8] converted the posted pricing problem into MAB (multi-armed bandit) problem to solve, and designed an optimal algorithm to exploit the unique features of microtask crowdsourcing. This paper adopted the actual data of Amazon MTurk platform. Since a crowdsourcing platform will generate a large amount of historical data after running for a period of time, we can use ML to make empirical price prediction. Obviously, although each of the above methods proposed innovation to solve the posted pricing problem, ML method was not taken into account for such a typical price prediction problem (although mentioned in [11], not implemented). Therefore, this paper proposes a posted pricing mechanism based on the Random Forests (RF) [2] which belongs to an ensemble ML method in the crowdsourcing market.

The rest of paper is organized as follows. Section 2 discusses the theory of RF. Section 3 obtained the actual history transaction data in a crowdsourcing platform by using python spider technology. In Sect. 4, on the one hand, RF and other ML methods in price predicting are compared by means of data mining. On the other hand, RF is adjusted and optimized via experiments, and appropriate parameters are given. The final section summarizes the full paper and outlooks future work.

2   Random Forest

2.1   Basic Concepts

As a new rising, highly flexible ML algorithms, the Random Forests (RF) have a broad application prospects, e.g. it can be used to simulate marketing, analyze customer source, retention and loss, and also to predict the risk of disease as well as susceptibility. In recent years, the using of RF by participants in international and domestic competitions have been quite high.

RF's basic unit is Decision Tree (DT) and it is an algorithm that integrates multiple DTs by the idea of ensemble learning, a large branch of machine Learning. There are two key words in the name of RF. One is "random" and the other is "forests". "Forests" represents many DTs to be generated in the algorithm, while "random" represents random sampling and random selecting features. Intuitively, each DT is a regressor or classifier, so that n trees will have n regression or classification results for an input sample. The RF integrates all the regression results or voting results and calculates the mean value or specifies the category with the most votes as the final output.

For a DT in RF, in order to determine the order of feature selection, the concepts of Information (I), Entropy (E) and Information Gain (IG) need to be introduced. If there is a group of things waiting for classified that can be divided into a number of categories, the information of a certain class x_i can be defined by Formula (1). Where $p(x_i)$ is the probability when x_i occurs.

$$I(X = x_i) = -\log_2 p(x_i) \tag{1}$$

In information theory and probability theory, entropy is a measure of random variables' uncertainty. Combined with the information above, entropy is the expected value of information, which can be denoted as follow.

$$E(X) = \sum_{i=1}^{n} p(x_i)I(x_i) = -\sum_{i=1}^{n} p(x_i)\log_2 p(x_i) \tag{2}$$

IG is an indicator used to select features in DT algorithm. The larger the IG is, the better the selectivity of this feature will be. In the probability theory, it is defined as the difference between the entropy of the set to be classified and the conditional entropy of a selected feature, as in the Formula (3).

$$IG(Y|X) = E(Y) - E(Y|X) \tag{3}$$

where

$$E(Y|X) = \sum_{x} p(x)E(Y|X = x) \tag{4}$$

2.2 The Algorithm

In the RF, the generation rules of each DT are as follows:

- **Step1** : For each DT, if the size of training set is n, n training samples are randomly and reversely (known as bootstrap sampling) extracted from the training set as the specific training set for this DT;
- **Step2** : If the dimensions of each sample are M, specify a constant $m < M$, and randomly select m features in M as subset. Each time the DT dividing, select the optimal one of the m features;
- **Step3** : Each DT grows to its maximum extent and there is no pruning process.

It can be seen that the training set of each DT is different and contains repeated training samples. Therefore, the classification effect (error rate) of RF is related to two factors: the greater the correlation between any two DTs in the forest, the greater the error rate; the stronger the classification ability of each DT in the forest, the lower the error rate of the whole forest. If the number of feature selection m is reduced, the relevance and classification ability of each DT will be reduced correspondingly and vice verse. So it is a key issue how to choose the optimal m. At the same time, increasing the number of DT in RF can improve the precision and regression results, but the algorithm efficiency will be reduced.

In addition, the Minimum Number of Sample Leaves (MNSL) of a DT, i.e. the minimum number of end nodes in a DT, will have an important impact on its prediction effect. This is because smaller MNSL will make it easier for the model to capture the noise in the data, which will result in the problem of over-fitting. In the same way, the maximum depth of DT can cause similar problems if not limited. Therefore, we will adjust and optimize these four parameters in the experiment (Sect. 4).

3   Data Acquisition

In this paper, the python spider [12] technology is used to acquire the historical transaction data from the crowdsourcing platform Taskcn [1], one of the earliest crowdsourcing platforms in China. The program flow of python spider used for this work is shown in Fig. 2. First, we have made a deep analysis to the source code of target site's webpage, identified URL format and the structure of each label. Secondly, the directory list of all completed tasks is traversed, and the URL to be visited is spliced by task ID. Then, regular expression and the third-party open source library Beautiful Soup [3] are used to parse the webpage and obtain the content of it. Finally, each transaction data acquired is processed into CSV format and stored on the hard disk. In addition, in the process of web page parsing, the spider also handle the issues such as messy code, task deleted, content confidential etc.

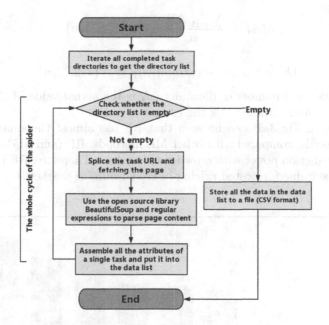

Fig. 2. The program flow chart of python spider.

Finally, after a period of crawling, 35, 622 transaction data of all completed reward tasks on Taskcn from year 2006 to 2018 had been gotten. Each piece of data contains 18 attributes such as task ID, task category, requester's credit, task price etc. After data preprocessing such as data cleaning, useless attribute deleting and abnormal data eliminating, 34, 805 pieces of valid data were finally obtained, and each had 11 available attributes.

4 Experiment

4.1 The Comparison of Machine Learning Methods

For the task data from the above section, each task contains multiple attributes (such as category, time limit, workload etc.). The ML methods can be used to predict its price by its attributes. Since the price is a continuous value, this is a typical regression problem, and we use the general process of data mining [9] to research.

The open source machine learning and data mining software Weka [6] had been used to compare the predicting results of some ML methods (e.g., M5 Model Tree (M5MT), Artificial Neural Network (ANN), k-Nearest Neighbour (KNN), Linear Regression (LR), etc.) that are suitable for dealing with regression problem. Mean Absolute Error (MAE) is used as the evaluation index, which defined as Formula (5). The verification method adopts k-fold cross validation and $k = 10$.

$$MAE = \frac{\sum_{i=1}^{n} AE_i}{n} \quad i \in \{1, 2, ..., n\} \tag{5}$$

where

$$AE_i = |actual_i - estimated_i| \quad i \in \{1, 2, ..., n\} \tag{6}$$

where n is the total number of data, $actual_i$ is the actual value of the ith data in the test set, and $estimated_i$ is the estimated value.

As shown in Fig. 3, it can be seen that RF has almost the smallest MAE. In another words, compared with other ML methods, RF (and M5MT) has the best price prediction power with crowdsourcing data. Therefore, RF is a method that is very suitable for posted pricing in crowdsourcing market.

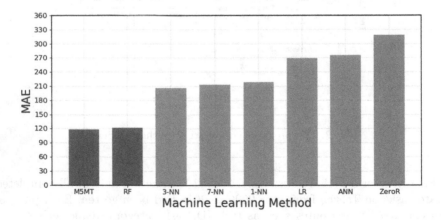

Fig. 3. The comparison between ML methods for price prediction in crowdsourcing.

4.2 Parameter Adjusting for Random Forests

In order to study the influence of four parameters (tree number n, the number of feature selection m, the minimum number of sample leaves l, the maximum depth of each DT d) discussed in Sect. 2.2 on regression results, this section specially designed two experimental schemes, using MAE of k-fold cross validation and

Table 1. The parameter setting in two experiment schemes.

Parameters	Scheme-A	Scheme-B
n	$\{5, 10, 15, ..., 60\}$	40
m	$\{1, 2, ..., 7\}$	5
l	2	$\{10, 20, 30, 40\}$
d	∞	$\{3, 6, 9, ..., 30\}$

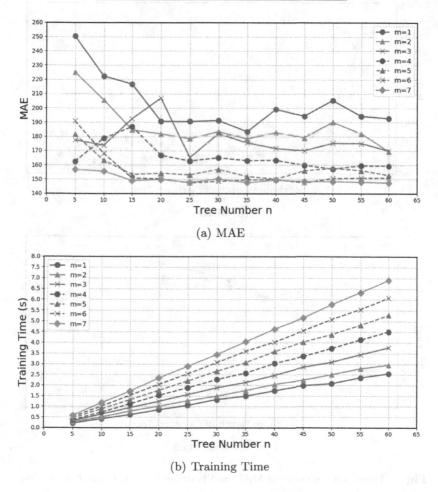

(a) MAE

(b) Training Time

Fig. 4. The changing curve of MAE and training time as m and n increasing.

evaluating the training time of all data (34, 805). Both schemes are implemented by python on a PC with i5 CPU, 8 GB RAM and Win-7 (64 bit) operating system and designed via the control variable method, as shown in Table 1. In Scheme-A, $\{l, d\}$ are fixed values and $\{m, n\}$ changes, while in Scheme-B reversed.

When m increases gradually, MAE decreases (see Fig. 4(a)), while m increases to a certain value, MAE does not change significantly ($m = 5$, $m = 6$, $m = 7$ almost overlap). When m is large, the value of n has little influence on the prediction error. Both m and n have a linear effect on the training time (see Fig. 4(b)). Therefore, the prediction ability and training time of RF are contradictory corresponding to the setting of m and n. It should be tried to use smaller m and n when ensuring that MAE meets the requirements.

Then turn the lens to how l and d for a single DT affect the overall performance of RF. As can be seen from Fig. 5, when d is relatively small, the curve

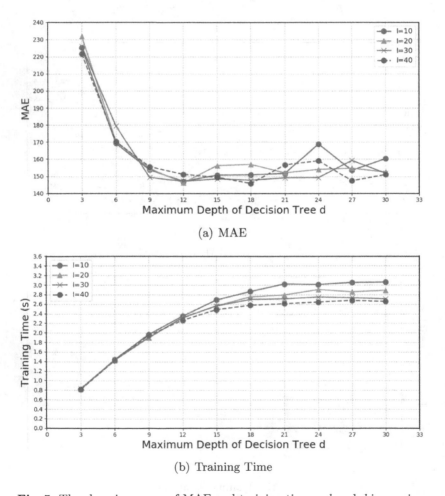

(a) MAE

(b) Training Time

Fig. 5. The changing curve of MAE and training time as l and d increasing.

of MAE and training time almost overlapped, which is because l and m have a conflict. Due to the limiting for the maximum depth of DT, DT cannot be further divided, so only m works. When m becomes larger, l starts to act and thus the curve starts to differ. In Fig. 5(a), when m is about 10, MAE reaches the minimum. When $m < 10$, MAE curve is steep and training time curve is relative slow and MAE is not changing after $m > 10$. Besides, l has little effect on MAE and training time. In summary, $\{m, n, l, d\} = \{5, 40, 40, 10\}$ is a relative better setting of parameters in the case talked in this paper.

5   Conclusions

At present, the development speed of crowdsourcing is extremely rapid, from the traditional task crowdsourcing to the emerging mobile crowdsensing. However, rewards pricing as the most important incentive factor in crowdsourcing is the core issue that restricts its development. This paper firstly analyzed the impact of higher or lower pricing, and then investigated and summarized the posted pricing methods for crowdsourcing proposed so far. Secondly, aiming at solving the pricing problem for crowdsourcing, this paper innovatively adopted a machine learning method – Random Forests, and made a detailed theoretical description with in-depth analysis of the four parameters that affect the performance of this algorithm. Python spider technology had been used to acquire real crowdsourcing transaction data. In the final experiment, the actual effects of 8 ML methods in price prediction had been compared, and it can be confirmed that RF almost has the best pricing possibility. In order to adjust and optimize the RF model, two additional experimental schemes is designed, and a comparison between the algorithm's pricing results and training times for modeling with four parameters is made. Finally, by in-depth analysis of the experimental results, a parameter setting suitable for the case in this paper is given. What's more, although it is feasible to solve posted pricing problems with RF, the posted method's results are slightly unsatisfactory. In the future, we will try to regard posted pricing as a classification problem and hope it can perform well in the accuracy of predicting recommended price range.

Acknowledgement. This work was supported by a grant from the National Natural Science Foundation of China (No. 41761086).

References

1. Taskcn (2006). http://www.taskcn.com/
2. Breiman, L., Cutler, A.: Random forests (1999). https://www.stat.berkeley.edu/%7Ebreiman/RandomForests/cc_home.htm
3. Chunmei, Z., Guomei, H., Zuojie, P.: A study of web information extraction technology based on beautiful soup. J. Comput. **10**(6), 381–387 (2015). https://doi.org/10.17706/jcp.10.6.381-387

4. Han, K., Huang, H., Luo, J.: Quality-aware pricing for mobile crowdsensing. IEEE/ACM Trans. Networking **26**(4), 1728–1741 (2018). https://doi.org/10.1109/TNET.2018.2846569
5. Han, K., Huang, H., Luo, J.: Posted pricing for robust crowdsensing. In: ACM International Symposium on Mobile Ad Hoc Networking and Computing (Mobi-Hoc 2016), Paderborn, Germany, pp. 261–270, July 2016. https://doi.org/10.1145/2942358.2942385
6. Holmes, G., Donkin, A., Witten, I.H.: WEKA: a machine learning workbench. In: Proceedings of ANZIIS 1994 - Australian New Zealand Intelligent Information Systems Conference, pp. 357–361, November 1994. https://doi.org/10.1109/ANZIIS.1994.396988
7. Howe, J.: Crowdsourcing: why the power of the crowd is driving the future of business. J. Consum. Mark. **26**(4), 305–306 (2009). https://doi.org/10.1108/07363760910965918
8. Hu, Z., Zhang, J.: Optimal posted-price mechanism in microtask crowdsourcing. In: Proceedings of the Twenty-Sixth International Joint Conference on Artificial Intelligence, IJCAI 2017, pp. 228–234 (2017). https://doi.org/10.24963/ijcai.2017/33
9. Kantardzic, M.: Data-Mining Concepts, Chap. 1, pp. 1–25. Wiley, Hoboken (2011). https://doi.org/10.1002/9781118029145.ch1
10. Sun, J., Ma, H.: Collection-behavior based multi-parameter posted pricing mechanism for crowd sensing. In: 2014 IEEE International Conference on Communications (ICC), pp. 227–232, June 2014. https://doi.org/10.1109/ICC.2014.6883323
11. Tariq, S.: Developing market sentiment indicators for commodity price forecasting using machine learning. Master thesis, The University of Manitoba (2018)
12. Xiaojuan, Z.: Application of crawler technology based on python. Office Informatization (2018)
13. Yan, J., Liu, R., Liu, H.: A literature review of domestic and foreign crowdsourcing research. Forum Sci. Technol. China **1**(8), 59–68, 151 (2017)

A Reverse Auction Incentive Mechanism Based on the Participant's Behavior in Crowdsensing

Tao Zhou[1,2], Bing Jia[1,2(✉)], and Wuyungerile Li[1,2]

[1] Inner Mongolia A.R. Key Laboratory of Wireless
Networking and Mobile Computing, Hohhot 010021, China
jiabing@imu.edu.cn

[2] College of Computer Science, Inner Mongolia University, Hohhot 010021, China

Abstract. Crowdsensing has been integrated into many aspects of human life. Compared with the general mode of perception which need to arrange a large number of sensors in advance, crowdsensing uses the idea of crowdsourcing to distribute tasks to participants carrying mobile sensing devices with them, which can save the cost of deploying sensing nodes. Therefore, how to make people actively participate in perception has become a hot issue. The existing incentives mainly include bonus incentives, game entertainment incentives, and social relationship incentives. This paper proposes a reverse auction incentive mechanism based on the participant's behavior. Specifically, we analyze the user's behavior and build a model of participant competency assessment firstly; then, according to the above analysis, each user is scored and the reward is distributed using the improved reverse auction algorithm. The experimental results show the effect of the proposed method.

Keywords: Crowdsensing · Incentive mechanism ·
The participant's behavior · Privacy protection

1 Introduction

With the development of wireless communication and smart mobile devices, life is becoming more and more intelligent. From smart homes to smart cities, Internet of Things (IoT) technology has been integrated into all aspects of human life. Crowdsensing is also a new perception mode of IoT. Crowdsensing is a way which uses people carrying mobile sensing devices with them as the basic unit of perception. Compared with the general mode of perception, crowdsensing need arrange a large number of sensors in advance. The crowdsensing system assigns the task to the participants. Participants upload their own sensing data with the mobile devices and act as sensors. The most important thing in crowdsensing is how to improve the enthusiasm of user participation. In the crowdsensing system, there are many different incentives. It can be divided into money-based

© ICST Institute for Computer Sciences, Social Informatics and Telecommunications Engineering 2019
Published by Springer Nature Switzerland AG 2019. All Rights Reserved
J. Li et al. (Eds.): SPNCE 2019, LNICST 284, pp. 637–646, 2019.
https://doi.org/10.1007/978-3-030-21373-2_53

incentives and non-money-based incentives. Krontiris, Lee and Rula et al. have proposed some incentives for bonus incentives [1–3] and the money-based incentive mainly to encourage participants to participate through the payment of rewards. The monetary incentive is the auction mechanism which is to complete the quotation of the perceived data by the participants and select the subset of participants with lower payment cost. And the remuneration payment incentives is the main incentive currently [4]. Non-money-based incentives mainly include entertainment game incentives, social relationship incentives and virtual point incentives. Entertainment game motivation refers to the use of the game's entertainment and attraction to motivate users to complete the perception task by introducing the game strategy into the group perception system such as Kawajiri et al. proposed Steered crowdsensing: incentive design towards quality-oriented place-centric crowdsensing [5] and Han et al. proposed an enhancing motivation in a mobile participatory sensing project through gaming [6]. Social relationship incentives refer to a certain social network relationship built by the existing or server platform in which the participant is located [7,8]. The participants are motivated to maintain a sense of belonging in the social relationship. The virtual point incentive means that the participant will In the perceived task, virtual points are rewarded [9,10]. The real money converted from virtual points, some kind of physical object or the virtual reward sent by it will encourage users to participate in the perception task. However, many scholars have ignored the issue of user behaviour and user privacy. In this paper, we propose a reverse auction incentive mechanism based on the participant's behavior which consider the user privacy.

The rest of the paper is organized as follows. Section 2 construct the model of participant competency assessment. Section 3 presents a reverse auction incentive mechanism based on participant's behavior. Section 4 describes the experiment and results. Finally, we conclude our work in Sect. 5.

2   The Model of the Competency Assessment of the Participant

2.1   Evaluate the Participant's Positional Participation Ability

Dividing the Area. When the crowdsensing system plans to perceive the data, the first thing that needs to be done is the determination of the geographic location. Most researchers use GPS positioning to determine the geographic location of a participant. However, the GPS positioning is accurate, which poses a threat to the participant's location privacy, thus affecting the participants' enthusiasm for participation. In this paper, we considers the characteristics of the above situation to divide the geographical location into regions. When the region is divided, the adjustment parameters can be modified to arbitrarily enlarge and reduce the region, which is more flexible than the traditional division method.

Calculate the number of longitude partitions ($longitude_{zone}$) and latitude partitions ($latitude_{zone}$) based on the measuring range. The method is defined as follows:

$$longitude_{zone} = \frac{longitude_{max} - longitude_{min}}{\alpha}, \tag{1}$$

$$latitude_{zone} = \frac{latitude_{max} - latitude_{min}}{\beta}. \tag{2}$$

Where, the $longitude_{min}, longitude_{max}, latitude_{min}, latitude_{max}$ is the maximum and minimum values of the measurement range. α, β is the parameter of partition.

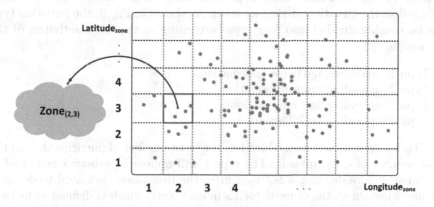

Fig. 1. Divided area.

As shown in Fig. 1, the partitioning formula can be obtained from the partitioning formula $latitude_{zone} \times longitude_{zone}$. Record the partition as $Zone_{i,j}, i \in [0, latitude_{zone}], j \in [0, longitude_{zone}]$, and calculate the area where the participant is located according to the coordinates of the participants. Methods as below:

$$Zone_j = \frac{lo - longitude_{min}}{\alpha}, \tag{3}$$

$$Zone_i = \frac{la - latitude_{min}}{\beta}. \tag{4}$$

Where lo is the longitude of the location where the participant uploaded the data and la is the longitude of the location where the participant uploaded the data. α, β is the parameter of partition.

Hot Spot Area. The crowdsensing task requires participants to collect information about each location. The more participants and the more data collected by the participants, the more data the server gets, and the better the data needed for the location. In this paper, we define the participant's location activity ability according to the distance between the participant's data area and the hot spot area. The farther away the participant is from the hotspot area, the more meaningful it is for data users, and the stronger the participant's positional activity ability. Most of the participants will collect the data which from hotspots. So, the closer the participant is to the hot spot area, the more meaningless it is for data users, and the weaker the participant's positional activity ability. It will encourage more participants to collect data in remote locations. It is also possible to collect as much data as possible from remote areas to more realistically reflect the situation at that location. As shown in Fig. 2, the partition type can be roughly divided into four types according to the daily activities of the participants:

Type 1: uploading intensive information.
Type 2: uploading more information.
Type 3: uploading less information.
Type 4: uploading no information.

The hot spot area is area which has the most number of participants and the most number of data uploads. The type 1 will appear in sub-area and the hot spot area. Before defining a hot spot area, the first thing that need to define is the participation status of participants in each area, which is defined as follows:

$$Zone(i, j) = \frac{N\_Zone_{(i,j)}}{N\_all} + \frac{NU\_Zone_{(i,j)}}{NU\_all}, \tag{5}$$

Where N_all is the number of data uploaded by all users of a task. $N\_Zone_{(i,j)}$ is the number of data in the area numbered (i, j) for all users in the area. NU_all is the number of users participating in a task. $NU\_Zone_{(i,j)}$ is the number of users participating in the task in $Zone_{i,j}$.

Calculate the $Zone(i, j)$ value for each region and define the maximum value in $Zone_{i,j}$ as $max(i, j)$. Usually there is only one hot spot area which named as $ZoneHot_{i,j}$, we define the maximum value in $Zone_{i,j}$, that is, $max(i, j)$ as the hot spot area. However, it does not rule out that there is a case where the maximum value and the next largest value of $Zone_{i,j}$ are extremely small. In this case, it is obviously inappropriate to define a hot spot area, so both the maximum value and the sub-value area are defined as hotspot areas. By analogy, multiple hot spot areas ($ZoneHot_{i,j}$) can be set, but depending on the size of the area, the hot spot area is limited in number. The specific definition is as follows:

$$Zone_{hot}(i, j) \in \{Zone(i, j) | max(i, j) - Zone(i, j) \leq a\}, \tag{6}$$

Where a is the difference between $max(i, j)$ and $Zone(i, j)$, and all regions in which the difference is within this range are defined as hot spot regions, $Zone_{hot}(i, j)$ is the $Zone(i, j)$ value of the hot spot area ($ZoneHot_{i,j}$).

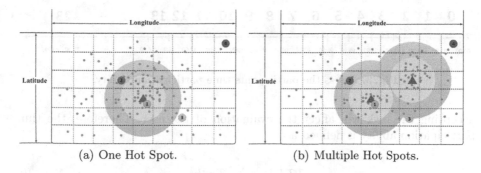

(a) One Hot Spot.   (b) Multiple Hot Spots.

Fig. 2. Hot spot area. (Color figure online)

Assessment Method. According to the regional hot spot [11], the participant's positional activity ability can be defined by calculating the distance between the participant and the hot spot area. As shown in Fig. 2(a), the hot spot area (the area marked by the triangle in the figure) is the center of the circle. In this study, the farther away from the center of the circle (hot spot), the more active the participants are, and the more information is collected. value. When there is only one hot spot area, since the blue circle is farther away from the hot spot area than the yellow circle, it is considered that the positional activity ability of the participants in the blue circle is stronger than the positional activity of the participants in the orange circle. As shown in Fig. 2(b), when there are multiple hot spot areas, the average distance between the area where the point is located and the hot spot area is taken. Commonly used methods for calculating distance include Euclidean distance, Manhattan distance, standardized Euclidean distance, cosine distance, and Chebyshev distance. In this study, the area measured by the task is divided into equal-sized areas. This structure is closer to the definition of Chebyshev distance [12], so the participant's position activity ability is defined as follows:

$$PZone = \frac{\sum_{m=1}^{n_{hot}} |Zone_{i,j} ZoneHot_{i,j}|}{n_{hot}} \times \tau, \qquad (7)$$

$$|Zone_{i,j} ZoneHot_{i,j}| = max\{|i - i_{hot}|, |j - j_{hot}|\}, \qquad (8)$$

where τ is the capability parameter and n_{hot} is the number of hot spots.

2.2   Evaluate the Participant's Time Participation Ability

In the crowdsensing task, the time the participants spend on the task is also an important indicator to measure the ability of the participants. The longer the participation time, the stronger the participant's time participation ability. Every task posted by the server has an expiration date. As shown in the Fig. 3, this article divides 24 time zones into 24 time zones. The time the participant participates in the task and the amount of information the user uploads after

Fig. 3. Assess the participants time participation ability.

accepting the task will affect the evaluation of the user. Therefore, the time participation ability is defined as:

$$TTPR = \sum_{i=1}^{e} Task_i, \tag{9}$$

$$Task = \frac{Actask}{Atask} \times \chi, \tag{10}$$

where $AcTask$ represents the actual participation time of each user. $ATask$ indicates the time of a task. Task is the proportion of time each user participates in the task, and χ is the adjustment parameter. e is the number of times collected by the user.

2.3   The Competency Assessment of the Participant

According to the above description, the participant's ability is mainly divided into the participant's time participation ability and the participant' s positional activity ability, which are defined as follows:

$$Capacity = \theta \times \frac{\sum_{i=1}^{n} PZone_i}{n} + \mu \times TTPR_i, \tag{11}$$

where $TTPR_i$ is the participant's time participation ability, $PZone_i$ is the participant's position participation ability, n is the number of data collected by the participant in a certain task, and θ, μ are adjustment parameters which $\theta + \mu = 1$.

3   A Reverse Auction Incentive Mechanism Based on the Participant's Behavior

3.1   The Participant's Comprehensive Ability Value

In the reverse auction incentive mechanism based on participant behavior, the participants' comprehensive capabilities are defined as the average comprehensive ability value of all participants is taken as the threshold value of the bonus, which is defined as follow,

$$Threshold = \frac{\sum_{i=1}^{N} Capacity_i}{N \times \varphi}, \tag{12}$$

where Threshold is the critical value, N is the total number of participants, and $Capacity_i$ is the comprehensive ability of each participant. φ is the adjustment parameter.

3.2 An Incentive Mechanism Based on the Participant's Capacity

The reward given by the crowdsensing task is ω. When the participant's capacity is lower than the threshold value, the participant does not receive the bonus. When the participant's capacity is above the threshold, the participant's bonus will be paid. The higher the participant's total ability value, the more the reward W_i the task pays to the participant. The relationship is as shown in the following formula.

$$W_i = \frac{Capacity_i}{\sum_{j=1}^{k} Capacity_i} \times \omega, \tag{13}$$

where W_i is the bonus paid to the participant i for the task. k is the number of participants whose comprehensive ability is higher than the threshold. $Capacity_i$ is the comprehensive ability of each participant. ω is the total compensation of the participants given by the task.

4 Experiment and Result Analysis

4.1 Set Up

In this paper, we use the Gowalla data set which is a location-based social networking website where users share their locations by checking-in and consists of 196,591 nodes to analyze the experiment [13]. It have collected a total of 6,442,890 check-ins of these users over the period of Feb. 2009–Oct. 2010. In experiment, we selected two groups of data which user number is 0–49. The one is the data in 8. Oct. 2010–10. Oct. 2010 interval named $Task_1$, the other is the data in 1. Oct. 2010–31. Oct. 2010 interval named $Task_2$. The experimental parameters are set as Table. 1. Then, we divide latitude and longitude partitions and mark the user point in the partition which are shown in the Figs. 4 and 5. Figure 4 is the distribution of users in $Task_1$ and Fig. 5 is the distribution of users in $Task_2$.

Table 1. The simulation parameters

No	Parameter	Value	No	Parameter	Value
1	α	0.5	7	m	1
2	β	2	8	n	50
3	a	5	9	θ	0.5
4	τ	0.1	10	μ	0.5
5	χ	100	11	φ	1
6	n_{hot}	2,4	12	ω	1000

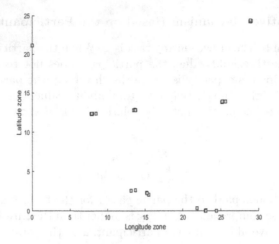

Fig. 4. Latitude and longitude partition of Task1.

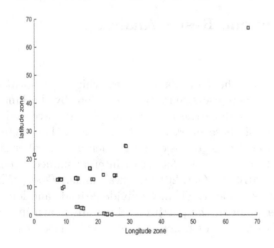

Fig. 5. Latitude and longitude partition of Task2.

4.2   Result Analysis

By the data set in the experiment, we can not accurately evaluate the user participation, so we only evaluate the user bonus. As shown in Fig. 6 that the benefits obtained by the two tasks are similar for each user. However, the total number of bonuses in $Task_2$ is much less than the total number of bonuses in $Task_1$. Figure 7 shows the average bonus and number of participants for $Task_1$ and $Task_2$ users. $Task_1$ has more bonuses than $Task_2$, but $Task_1$ has fewer participants than $Task_2$. It can be seen that the more participants, the better the incentive effect, the more the number of bonuses can be reduced.

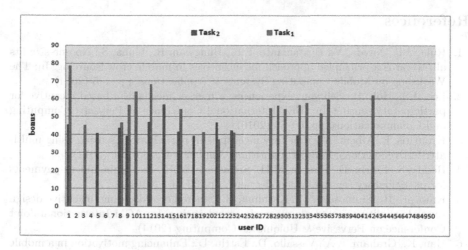

Fig. 6. Bonus analysis.

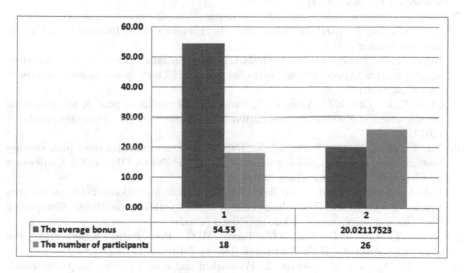

Fig. 7. The average bonus & number of participants.

5   Conclusion and Future Work

In general, reverse auction incentive mechanism based on the participant's behavior proposed in this paper has certain effects on user incentives. The current experiment is mainly based on the data set. Then we will collect the data in the field for experimentation and add the contrast experiment to reflect the excitation effect.

References

1. Rula, J.P., Navda, V., Bustamante, F.E., Bhagwan, R., Guha, S.: No one-size fits all: towards a principled approach for incentives in mobile crowdsourcing. In: The Workshop on Mobile Computing Systems & Applications, pp. 1–5 (2014)
2. Lee, J.S., Hoh, B.: Sell your experiences: a market mechanism based incentive for participatory sensing. In: IEEE International Conference on Pervasive Computing and Communications, pp. 60–68 (2010)
3. Krontiris, I., Albers, A.: Monetary incentives in participatory sensing using multi-attributive auctions. Parallel Algorithms Appl. **27**(4), 317–336 (2012)
4. Reddy, S., Estrin, D., Hansen, M.H., Srivastava, M.B.: Examining micro-payments for participatory sensing data collections, pp. 33–36 (2010)
5. Kawajiri, R., Shimosaka, M., Kashima, H.: Steered crowdsensing: incentive design towards quality-oriented place-centric crowdsensing. In: ACM International Joint Conference on Pervasive & Ubiquitous Computing (2014)
6. Han, K., Graham, E.A., Vassallo, D., Estrin, D.: Enhancing motivation in a mobile participatory sensing project through gaming. In: IEEE Third International Conference on Privacy (2011)
7. Luo, T., Kanhere, S.S., Tan, H.P.: SEW-ing a simple endorsement web to incentivize trustworthy participatory sensing. In: Eleventh IEEE International Conference on Sensing (2014)
8. Bigwood, G., Henderson, T.: IRONMAN: using social networks to add incentives and reputation to opportunistic networks. In: IEEE Third International Conference on Privacy (2012)
9. Chou, C.M., Lan, K.C., Yang, C.F.: Using virtual credits to provide incentives for vehicle communication. In: International Conference on Its Telecommunications (2013)
10. Yu, T., Zhou, Z., Da, Z., Wang, X.: INDAPSON: an incentive data plan sharing system based on self-organizing network. In: IEEE INFOCOM - IEEE Conference on Computer Communications (2016)
11. Balachandran, A., Bahl, P., Voelker, G.M.: Hot-spot congestion relief in public-area wireless networks. In: Proceedings Fourth IEEE Workshop on Mobile Computing Systems and Applications, 2002, pp. 70–80 (2002)
12. Kløve, T., Lin, T.T., Tsai, S.C., Tzeng, W.G.: Permutation arrays under the Chebyshev distance. IEEE Trans. Inf. Theory **56**(6), 2611–2617 (2010)
13. Cho, E., Myers, S.A., Leskovec, J.: Friendship and mobility: friendship and mobility: user movement in location-based social networks. In: ACM SIGKDD International Conference on Knowledge Discovery and Data Mining (KDD) (2011)

A General Hardware Trojan Technique Targeted on Lightweight Cryptography with Bit-Serial Structure

Yijun Yang[1,2], Liji Wu[1,2(✉)], Ye Yuan[1,2], and Xiangmin Zhang[1,2]

[1] Institute of Microelectronics, Tsinghua University, Beijing 100084, China
lijiwu@mail.tsinghua.edu.cn
[2] Tsinghua National Laboratory for Information Science and Technology,
Tsinghua University, Beijing 100084, China

Abstract. Lightweight ciphers have a wide range of applications such as IoT, anti-counterfeiting labels, and passive RFID, which drawing loads of attention in recent years. Obviously, the most significant metric of lightweight cryptography is the area. To implement the smallest area lightweight cipher, to the best of our knowledge, the bit-serial structure is used. However, the bit-serial provides a possible access for the small area occupied hardware Trojan to steal key information at the same time, which makes lightweight ciphers vulnerable to Trojan attack. In this paper, we introduce a general hardware Trojan scheme targeted on ciphers based on bit-serial technique, which can leakage secret key through only one flip-flop at least with ease. This paper will alert cryptographic designers not implement the ciphers only based on design specifications, without taking hardware security into account.

Keywords: Hardware Trojan · Hardware security · Lightweight cryptography · Bit-serial

1 Introduction

The integrated circuit (IC) foundries are now wilder-distributed. As the perplexity of third-party companies and vendors involved increased, hardware security is facing more serious safety threats from various malicious attacks and modifications in terms of Hardware Trojans. A Trojan is usually embedded into a very small part of the circuit from all design phases, such as layout level, gate level and register-transfer level (RTL) and any parts of an untrusted IC supply chain. Additional, avoiding been detected by circuit test technique easily, the hardware Trojan may always-on or be activated by hard conditions or rare signals. Due to the concealment of those malicious circuits, the detection of hardware Trojan is a tricky issue [12–17].

Subsequent paragraphs, however, are indented.

A directly common idea to hunt for hardware Trojan is to relay on the very-large-scale integration (VLSI) test architectures, whose main idea is to run different test patterns and observe the output and behavior of the circuit, since circuit faults are similar to hardware Trojans in some degree. However, this VLSI testing scheme can

J. Li et al. (Eds.): SPNCE 2019, LNICST 284, pp. 647–655, 2019.
https://doi.org/10.1007/978-3-030-21373-2_54

work well for defects detection but not for ingenious hardware Trojan. The reasons for that are concluded as follow: (1) hardware Trojan has no uniform Trojan models as defects' fault models; (2) to enhance target circuit's testability i.e. controllability together with observability, structured Design for Test (DFT) are widely used to control and observe the internal states of circuits, whereas DFT itself can induce potential safety hazard [3]. In addition, traditional automatic test pattern generation (ATPG) algorithm either general Random testing strategy are not effective for Trojan, especially for sequential Trojan activation and detection, cause the sequential testing is extremely time- consuming with low fault coverage rate [8].

In general, Trojan designers may pursuit Trojan area as small as possible, on one hand, the actual spare space of the target chip is always limited, on the other hand, a smaller Trojan inducing weaker side-channel physical parameter information, such as power, time delay, electromagnetic emission and so forth [4], can avoid been detected by side-channel analysis (SCA) based hardware Trojan detection method. Since SCA based detection may be strongly influenced by fabrication variations or measurement errors i.e. sensitive to noise and errors.

In order to cause damage influence leakage key information, hardware Trojan trends to attack all sorts of crypto hardware, especially lightweight ciphers, which are universally employed in both commercial and military applications. For instance, Internet of Things (IoT), which will have 4 billion connected users, anti-counterfeiting, RFID tags, sensor networks, distributed control systems, etc. are increasingly providing convenience and service for our daily life [1]. And those successful working smart devices aforementioned highly depend on lightweight ciphers to provide secure and private communication. Therefore, the research on lightweight cipher's hardware security issue is very valuable and necessary [5, 6].

Considering the requirements for both low cost and security application background, lightweight ciphers have already obtained more attention in the past few years. In general, a lightweight cipher contains a single encryption function or both encryption and decryption function based on either Feistel structure or Substitution-Permutation Network (SPN) to ensure the security [9]. The significant criteria for lightweight cipher contain reliability, cost i.e. chip area, and throughput [9]. A natural idea to reduce area is to limit the data path. In 2017, Jean, Moradi et al. propose the first strategy called bit-sliding, with which the authors first implement the smallest implementation of AES-128 to date [9]. Nevertheless, bit-sliding structure aforementioned can be applied to other lightweight cryptography like PRESENT and SKINNY, without loss of its generality [9]. However, the hardware aspect security issue of bit-sliding was overlooked by its authors. Note that our hardware Trojan technique is just targeted on this state of art structure, revealing its potential hardware security weakness.

2 Preliminaries

In this section, we first use AES hardware implement as an example cipher circuit to clarify the difficulties encountered by hardware Trojan insertion. And then we cover the core idea of bit-sliding techniques designed for state-of-art lightweight ciphers. Next, a few main metrics of a practical hardware Trojan are presented so as to address the craftiness of our hardware Trojan.

2.1 The Bit-Serial Implementation Strategy

In general, to reach small area occupation desire, cipher designers trend to cut the data path, but that is really tough to make the data path smaller than the Sbox size. The bit-sliding strategy that we mentioned here, make the extremely small bit-serial Application Specific Integrated Circuit (ASIC) implementations of SPN based ciphers come true and the strategy could reduce the data path to a single bit, in the case throughout allows.

The conducting idea of the bit-sliding technique is to serially implement the SPN-based cryptographic algorithms instead of parallel implementing in order to decrease the data path to only one bit and replace scan flip-flop by regular flip-flop, since the scan flip-flop is more about 25% area expensive than regular flip-flop. Here, we just recall the 1-bit-serial implementation, but this strategy also supports other data-path like 2-bit or 4-bit.

Moreover, the overview of the bit-serial data path architecture for AES-128 is shown in Fig. 1 [9], in which the white block indicates regular flip-flop, the scan flip-flop is highlighted by green, black arrows refer to data flow direction and the blue ones represent shift direction during ShiftRows operations. As we know, AES contains KeyExpansion, SubBytes, MixColumns, ShiftRows, and AddRoundKey steps [11]. Under bit-serial architecture, KeyExpansion, AddRoundKey, ShiftRows together with plaintext input step are performed in a bit serial style. In [9], the authors introduce the details of the timing control of the circuit, so for the sake of space, we will not present them here. Note that both the serial form of KeyExpansion and AddRoundKey step bring hidden dangers to hardware security, and our Trojan is aimed the KeyExpansion step exactly to steal the secret key.

2.2 The Bit-Serial Implementation Strategy

First, it should be remarked that a hardware Trojan usually consists of two parts, trigger, and payload [15]. The payload is the action or the damage which a hardware Trojan will do when it is activated [16]. And the trigger refers to the singles or the special condition that could activate the hardware Trojan [16].

In order to hide from being discovered by detection algorithms and achieve damages, a well-designed hardware Trojan should have the following metrics.

Controllability. This characteristic is used to measure whether a hardware Trojan is able to be activated at a desired time and at a presupposed position. From the Trojan designer point of view, we want the Trojan has good controllability.

Concealment. We hope that the insertion of hardware Trojan will make as small as possible changes to the host circuit, no matter at the functional level or back-end layout level. In this case, a hardware Trojan with good concealment can avoid being detected by logic test algorithms, SCA-based detection algorithms easier.

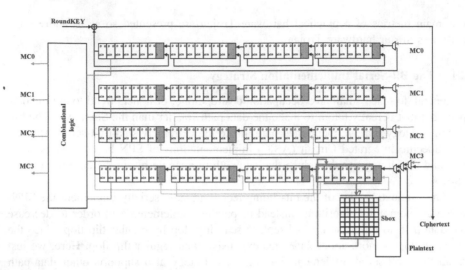

RoundKEY

MC0
MC1
MC2
MC3

Combinational logic

MC0
MC1
MC2
MC3

Sbox

Ciphertext

Plaintext

Fig. 1. The data path architecture based on bit-serial technique [9]. (Color figure online)

Rare Trigger Condition. If the trigger condition of the hardware Trojan is too easy to satisfy, then the hardware Trojan is more likely to be found during functional test or ATPG based logic test as we have mentioned in the Introduction section. In this regard, to make the hardware Trojan better hidden, the selection of trigger signals and timing control are crucial issues.

Destructiveness. The implantation of hardware Trojans has special purposes, which are often destructive. Generally, the destructiveness of hardware Trojans can be summarized as the following three aspects [7].

(1) Stealing confidential information or sensitive internal signals to attackers.
(2) Disturbing or interrupting the normal function of the chip, and causing errors during the execution.
(3) Maliciously leaking battery energy to shorten system life or even havocking the whole system directly or indirectly.

Taking into account the malicious nature of hardware Trojan, a powerful hardware Trojan may have as much damage as possible.

It should be noticed that the above four hardware Trojan metrics are often contradictory, and the Trojan designer should make a trade-off according to the actual situation.

3 Trojan Design

Our Trojan design technique is a general strategy targeted on bit-serial structure lightweight ciphers. And the objective of the hardware Trojan is the task of stealing the RoundKey or the secret key directly of the lightweight cryptographic algorithm in the KeyExpansion circuit bit by bit. It is noteworthy that, using the RoundKey, the attacker can easily obtain the secret key of the lightweight cryptography [11]. Both the trigger theory and the payload implementation details are presented, respectively.

3.1 Mechanism of Trojan Payload

To explain clearly we use the bit-sliding architecture proposed in [9] to illustrate our Trojan approach. The overview architecture of our Trojan scheme is shown in Fig. 2 [9], where the host circuit is the KeyExpansion block, and the Trojans are highlighted in red, the victim flip-flop is highlighted in yellow, and the green blocks indicate the scan flip-flop same to Fig. 1.

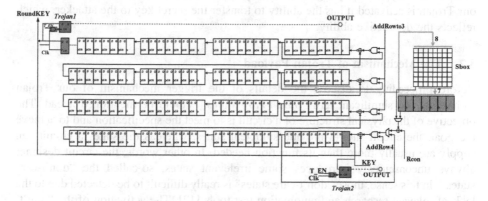

Fig. 2. The mechanism of hardware Trojan architecture based on [9].

First, we will focus on *Trojan1* shown in the top left of Fig. 2. The Trojan payload working process can perform as follows. In this case, during the first 128 clock cycle 128-bit plaintext is shifted in the registers which are illustrated in Fig. 1, at the same time the first round has been generated bit by bit serially per clock cycle based the bit-serial architecture as shown in Fig. 2. In order words, after 128 clock cycles, the first round RoundKey is already prepared and registered in the flip-flops. Next operation is AddRoundKey, which is carried out serially as well. Simultaneously, the Trojan enable signal T_EN is tied to 1, that is to say, the Trojan is triggered.

The main circuit structure of the hardware Trojan is a drop edge triggered D-type flip-flop, which takes the output of the victim flip-flop, highlighted in yellow, as its input and uses the ciphertext output port that is idle during the AddRoundKey encryption process as its output. Note that the area of the Trojan according to manu-facturing process, and might be further reduced for the using of back-end layout design strategy Therefore, while the RoundKey is shifted bit by bit to complete the AddRoundKey operation, our hardware Trojan accurately propagate the RoundKey serially to the output port and leaks the key information to the attacker cat likely without disturbing the normal encryption operation.

Note that, it is easy to see that the hardware Trojan can be implanted on any of the 128 flip-flops and any round through the key path indiscriminately, as long as the correct trigger signal *T_EN* is given in time. Therefore, from a practical point of view, the designer of hardware Trojan can implant the Trojan to a more reasonable place after considering the actual situation, whether space is enough or the routing resource is sufficient, of the physical layout. In this sense, our hardware Trojan scheme has some flexibility. Furthermore, Trojan2 is another example of our Trojan scheme. As shown in Fig. 2, Trojan2 use the secret Key signal as its input directly, so, in this case, to obtain the Key, the *T_EN* needs to be tied to logic 1 during the first 128 clock cycle.

We remark that our Trojan payload contains only one register and one NAND gate, and it does not affect the normal operation of the host circuit during either activated mode or unactivated mode, i.e. it has ideal concealment characteristics. In addition, the security of a cryptography algorithm totally depends on its secret key. However, once our Trojan is activated it has the ability to transfer the secret key to the attacker, which reflects the destructive ability.

3.2   The Mechanism of Trojan Payload

Before proceeding to discuss the details of the trigger mechanism of our Trojan technique, one significant term *"don't-care states"* should be mentioned ahead. The objective of the physical structure of a circuit is to meet the specification and to achieve the goal, the circuit should provide sufficient states, whereas the states a circuit can supply are usually more than its function needed. In other words, the circuit designer always unconsciously introduces some irrelevant states, so-called the "don't-care states". In this sense, those "don't-care states" is really difficult to be detected due to the lack of relevant research and automation test tools [12]. The activation of the "don't-care states" always along with illegal operations, which the customs rarely touch when the circuit system is normally executed. As a result, it would then be beneficial to attempt to use those "don't-care states" as the trigger signals for hardware Trojans, by which the rare trigger condition metric of the hardware Trojan can be dramatically improved.

The trigger signals of our hardware Trojan take advantages of "don't-care states" aforementioned. As for our Trojan trigger mechanism, the hardware Trojan is activated when the last three digits of the input 128-bit plaintext equal to "110" and the plaintext input port has high-level illegal signals within two clock cycles after the end of the plaintext stream input.

The circuit of trigger circuit could be realized in various forms, and Fig. 3 illustrates a simple implementation consisting of host circuit's control logic, to simplify the description, which is abstracted as an 8-bit counter highlighted in blue recording the encryption timing process, and the trigger cone. First, in the process of plaintext feeding, when the 126th clock cycle arrives, G1 outputs a high level that is connected to one input pin of G4. Simultaneously, the other pin of G4 is always monitoring the input port of plaintext, hence if the 127th plaintext bit equals to "1", G4 will supply a pulse through a 4–input OR gate, G8, to the 3bit-Counter illustrated in Fig. 3, and the counter will plus one. Subsequently, during the 128th clock cycle, once the plaintext bit is "1", G5 will carry out a plus to the 3bit-Counter, and the counter plus one again. In the same way, when the 128th plaintext bit equals to "0", the 3bit-Counter will reach "011".

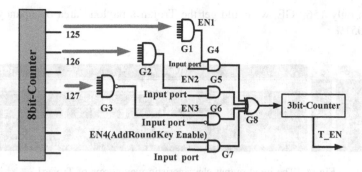

Fig. 3. The trigger mechanism architecture.

So far, the process of plaintext input is completed, and then the lightweight cipher will perform the step of AddRoundKey whose internal control signal EN4 acts as the enable signal of G7. To put it differently, in the next 128 clock cycle, the plaintext input IO port is idle. Therefore, in the first two clock cycles of the AddRoundKey operation, if two logic 1 are continuously fed to the plaintext input port, the 3-bit counter will reach to "101", next then the hardware Trojan enable signal T_EN will turn to logic 1 i.e. the Trojan payload will be activated, nor the 3-bit counter will be reset and waiting for next possible trigger change. Note that, in this example implementation, to obtain the two bits external off-chip trigger signal, we have to lose the first two digits of the RoundKey, but that does not matter since we can recover the complete 128-bit key by the exhaustive method. To emphasize that, since the trigger signals including internal signal and external signal and "don't-care states", and related to sequential circuit implementation, we say that our Trojan has rare trigger condition.

4   Verification

In order to verify the effectiveness of our hardware Trojan technique, we have embedded the hardware Trojan into the key path of AES-128 bit-serial architecture [9], which is an extremely small area lightweight cipher architecture, according to the mechanisms we presented in Sect. 3. It is to be noted that, due to intellectual property reasons, we did not get the implementation detail of its AES-128 control logic in [9], but this does not affect our analysis of the area of our Trojan, by synthesizing the Trojan as a separate module.

Taking the implantation of *Trojan1*, which is highlighted in red in Fig. 2, as an example. Plotted in Fig. 4, the input-output characteristic waveforms of the Trojan circuit displays that the payload part of *Trojan1* could steal the RoundKey bit by bit once it was triggered by the Trojan trigger enable signal *T_EN*. Furthermore, we synthesized Trojan payload circuit with the GSMC 180 nm Mixed-Signal 1P7M process, and from the cell report provided by the synthesizer, we can find that only one register, i.e. 8 GE (Gate Equivalent), is required to achieve the stealing function. In addition, using the data reported in [9], the smallest implementation of AES-128 encryption only 1560 GE, we could get the Trojan's payload area occupancy ratio is about 0.0051%.

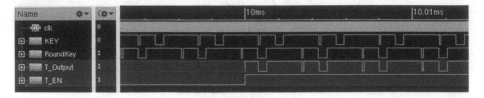

Fig. 4. The input-output characteristic waveforms of Trojan1.

In the light of the mechanism of trigger signals introduced in Sect. 3 plotted in Fig. 3, we have implemented the Trojan trigger cone circuit, and we have synthesized the cone circuit with the GSMC 180 nm Mixed-Signal 1P7M process as well. From the cell report supplied by the synthesizer the whole cone needs 49 GE, so its area occupancy ratio over the lightweight cipher is around 3.04%. Therefore, the total area occupancy ratio of our Trojan is 3.0451%. We have to emphasize that the area of the hardware Trojan is related to the process, and can be further reduced by the choice of the cells and superb layout design skills.

5   Conclusion and Discussion

In this paper, we introduce a general hardware Trojan design technique targeted on lightweight ciphers which are based on bit-serial structure such as SKINNY, PRESENT, AES and so forth. And four main metrics a sophisticated hardware Trojan should be equipped with have been discussed briefly. The function of this Trojan is to steal the RoundKey/Key serially and leak it to the attacker without causing any malfunction of the host circuit. The payload circuit of the hardware Trojan can be constructed by only one register and a NAND gate. As for the trigger signals of the hardware Trojan, we take advantage of the "don't-care states" of the host circuit, in the same time internal logic control wires are utilized to shrink the changes of the host circuit. To put it differently, we use both internal and external signals together to activate the hardware Trojan, which helps the Trojan avoiding been detected by the traditional functional or structural testing techniques. Moreover, though the examples in this paper are targeted on the 1-bit-serial scenario, this Trojan scheme can tackle 2-bit serial cipher easily as well. In order to demonstrate the effectiveness of this Trojan scheme, we inserted our Trojan into the key path of a lightweight cipher and the results are in line with expectations. We hope that through the introduction of this general hardware Trojan technique, we can alert the chip designer to the consideration of hardware security.

Acknowledgement. The authors would like to thank Professor Hu He for early discussions. And we would like to thank Amir Moradi et al. for sharing their SKINNY codes. This work was supported by the National Science and Technology Major Project of China under Grant 2017ZX01030301.

References

1. http://www.rcrwireless.com/20160628/0pinion1reality-check-50b-iot-devices-connected-2020-beyond-hype-reality-tag10
2. Da Rolt, J., Di Natale, G., Flottes, M., Rouzeyre, B.: New security threats against chips containing scan chain structures. In: 2011 IEEE International Symposium on Hardware-Oriented Security and Trust, San Diego CA, p. 110 (2011)
3. Rostami, M., Koushanfar, F., Rajendran, J., Karri, R.: Hardware security: threat models and metrics. In: Proceedings of the International Conference on Computer-Aided Design (ICCAD 2013), Piscataway, NJ, USA. IEEE Press, pp. 819–823 (2013)
4. Kelly, S., Zhang, X., Tehranipoor, M., et al.: Detecting hardware Trojans using on-chip sensors in an ASIC design. J. Electron. Test. **31**(1), 11–26 (2015)
5. Qu, G., Yuan, L.: Design things for the internet of things: an EDA perspective. In: Proceedings of the 2014 IEEE/ACM International Conference on Computer-Aided Design (ICCAD 2014), pp. 411–416. IEEE Press (2014)
6. Gao, M., Wang, Q., Arafin, M.T., Lyu, Y., Qu, G.: Approximate computing for low power and security in the Internet of Things. Computer **50**(6), 27–34 (2017)
7. Jin, Y., Kupp, N., Makris, Y.: Experiences in Hardware Trojan design and implementation. In: 2009 IEEE International Workshop on Hardware-Oriented Security and Trust, Francisco, CA, pp. 50–57 (2009)
8. Wang, X., Tehranipoor, M., Plusquellic, J.: Detecting malicious inclusions in secure hardware: challenges and solutions. In: 2008 IEEE International Workshop on Hardware-Oriented Security and Trust, Anaheim, CA, pp. 15–19 (2008)
9. Jean, J., Moradi, A., Peyrin, T., Sasdrich, P.: Bit-sliding: a generic technique for bit-serial implementations of SPN-based primitives. In: Fischer, W., Homma, N. (eds.) CHES 2017. LNCS, vol. 10529, pp. 687–707. Springer, Cham (2017). https://doi.org/10.1007/978-3-319-66787-4_33
10. Beierle, C., et al.: The SKINNY family of block ciphers and its low-latency variant MANTIS. In: Robshaw, Matthew, Katz, Jonathan (eds.) CRYPTO 2016. LNCS, vol. 9815, pp. 123–153. Springer, Heidelberg (2016). https://doi.org/10.1007/978-3-662-53008-5_5
11. Stallings, W.: Cryptography and Network Security: Principles and Practice. Pearson, Upper Saddle River (2017)
12. Lv, Y.Q., Zhou, Q., Cai, Y.C., et al.: Trusted integrated circuits: the problem and challenges. J. Comput. Sci. Technol. **29**(5), 918–928 (2014)
13. Zhang, J., Yuan, F., Xu, Q.: DeTrust: defeating hardware trust verification with stealthy implicitly-triggered hardware Trojans. In: Proceedings of the 2014 ACM SIGSAC Conference on Computer and Communications Security, pp. 153–166. ACM (2014)
14. Zhang, J., Xu, Q.: On hardware Trojan design and implementation at register-transfer level. In: 2013 IEEE International Symposium on Hardware-Oriented Security and Trust (HOST), pp. 107–112. IEEE (2013)
15. Jin, Y., Makris, Y.: Hardware Trojan detection using path delay fingerprint. In: 2008 IEEE International Workshop on Hardware-Oriented Security and Trust HOST, pp. 51–57 (2008)
16. Wolff, F., Papachristou, C., Bhunia, S., et al.: Towards Trojan-free trusted ICs: problem analysis and detection scheme. In: Design, Automation and Test in Europe, pp. 1362–1365. IEEE (2008)
17. Wang, Q., Wang, A., Qu, G., Zhang, G.: New methods of template attack based on fault sensitivity analysis. IEEE Trans. Multi-Scale Comput. Syst. **3**(2), 113–123 (2017)

Identification and Trust Techniques Compatible with eIDAS Regulation

Stefan Mocanu[1(✉)], Ana Maria Chiriac[2], Cosmin Popa[2],
Radu Dobrescu[1], and Daniela Saru[1]

[1] University Politehnica of Bucharest, Splaiul Independentei 313, Bucharest,
Romania
stefan.mocanu@upb.ro
[2] Ingenios.ro, George Constantinescu 2C, Bucharest, Romania

Abstract. This study presents the current situation (starting with January 2015) related to EU Regulation eIDAS. eIDAS represents the latest EU initiative to build a common framework for electronic identification and trust services. It was the intention of European Council to elaborate and impose a minimal legislation which should guarantee compatibility and interoperability of national identification and trust systems while still allowing the existence of local legal flavors. It is expected that eIDAS will offer safer interactions between various entities (such as private enterprises, public enterprises, citizens, administration) thus contributing to the growth of European market and the improvement of cross-border transactions. Exposure of the current state is combined with suggestions and discussions about improvements to the former eID resulting from the new regulation. A section on the implementation of interoperability framework in some member states gives a first insight into the work which will be required in the next few years for completing the implementation. This paper presents a thorough review of the main identification and trust techniques in eIDAS and the differences to previous or more local similar frameworks.

Keywords: eIDAS · eID · Trust · User identification · Interoperability ·
Electronic signature · Remote signing

1 Introduction

1.1 What Is eIDAS?

The EU eIDAS (Electronic ID and Trust Services) regulation [1] has been developed to support the existence of a single European market and secure electronic commerce. For organizations making online transactions with European citizens, the Regulation brings not only significant opportunities but also raises many new requirements.

EIDAS imposes standards for electronic identity, authentication and electronic signature. The main purpose is to encourage and support e-commerce by introducing measures to increase its security. EIDAS replaces an old European Commission directive. It is the 1999/93/EC Directive which regulates the electronic signature and has been implemented in many EU countries. As a result, all national implementations related to the electronic signature need to be re-evaluated in order to comply with

J. Li et al. (Eds.): SPNCE 2019, LNICST 284, pp. 656–665, 2019.
https://doi.org/10.1007/978-3-030-21373-2_55

eIDAS. Unlike the Directive governing the use of electronic signatures, eIDAS has been developed in the form of a Single Regulation, which implies the existence of a single set of rules applicable to all EU countries [1, 2].

The European Council requested the Commission to create a digital single market [9, 13] by 2015, with the aim of rapid progress in the digital economy, but also because legal certainty is absolutely necessary for both citizens and businesses before they interact digitally. Figure 1 presents an overview of eIDAS framework.

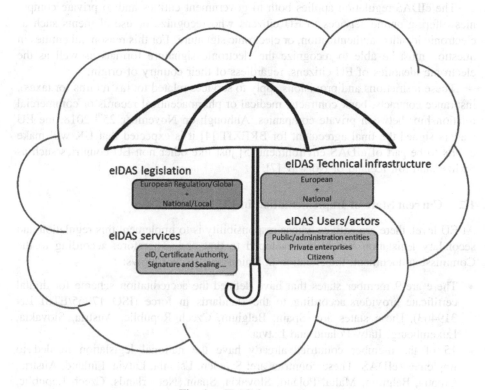

Fig. 1. eIDAS framework

In the previous figure, one can identify the most important components of eIDAS environment. The Regulation itself along with other European normative acts will ensure the compatibility and interoperability of all local or national subsystems. At this level, other mandatory aspects are decided. It is the case of building and maintaining a global list of trust service providers (or TSPs) or issuing technical infrastructure requirements (for example: the format of the electronic signature or the functionality of hardware devices used for generating signatures or seals). It is also the case of amending and/or adopting various standards elaborated by industry or R&D entities to cover the requirements of the Regulation. Another component of the eIDAS legislation is given by national/local legislation. The restrictions, in this case, demand that national requirements cannot be lower than global ones if the interaction with a fully compliant eIDAS entity is aimed.

The Digital Single Market features digital identification (eID) and e-Trust Services (eTS). The old directive has led to a confusing situation with regard to the multiple types of signatures of individuals and their verification methods when dealing with the issue of interaction with other parts of each Member State of the European Union.

Thus, the purpose of the regulation is that both individuals and legal entities can use their national electronic identity (eID) in any of the EU Member States to access various government services and to be able to make secure electronic transactions, taking advantage of their rights in all Member States [3].

The eIDAS regulation applies both to government entities and to private companies offering online services to EU citizens who recognize or use elements such as electronic identity, authentication, or electronic signature. For this reason, all entities in question must be able to recognize the electronic signature formats as well as the electronic identities of EU citizens, regardless of their country of origin.

These restrictions and provisions apply to services related to: tax returns (or taxes), insurance contracts, bank contracts, medical or pharmaceutical records or commercial relationships between private companies. Although on November 25th 2018, the EU leaders signed the final agreement for BREXIT [4] it is expected that UK will make efforts to be part of eIDAS environment [5] just like other non-EU countries such as Switzerland [6], Iceland or Norway [7].

1.2   Current State of Implementation in EU

At EU level, there are entities whose responsibility is to implement this regulation and secondary legislation has been developed to that end. Therefore, according to the Commission document, the situation at Union level is as follows:

- There are 9 member states that have defined the accreditation scheme for digital certificate providers according to the standards in force (ISO 17065/ETSI EN 319403). These states are: Spain, Belgium, Czech Republic, Austria, Slovakia, Luxembourg, Italy, Poland and Latvia.
- 15 of the member countries already have the national legislation needed to implement eIDAS. These countries are: Sweden, Estonia, Latvia, Finland, Austria, Croatia, Belgium, Malta, Poland, Slovakia, Spain, Netherlands, Czech Republic, Italy and Slovenia
- Among the member countries, 3 are in the process of developing the necessary legislation: Luxembourg, Lithuania and Germany
- Instead, Romania (along with Portugal, Greece, Bulgaria, Hungary and Ireland) is among the 6 countries where there is no detailed information on the implementation stage of eIDAS.

Although the Regulation does not require a national law to adopt the legislative decision, there are certain responsibilities that each member state of the Union has, responsibilities that need to be achieved by internal legislation. These include setting means for identifying citizens, defining sanctions and appointment of a supervisory body that will define how to check the providers and help cooperation with other Member States.

2 Essentials of eIDAS

There are two essential aspects of eIDAS Regulation. The first part is related to the identification services of an entity and deals with the electronic identification schemes. The second part addresses the requirements for eIDAS trust services, including e-signature, web authentication and other e-mail services.

Much of the eIDAS Regulation is focused on requirements for electronic signatures, as set out in Directive 1999/93/EC. A simplified eIDAS architecture is presented in Fig. 2.

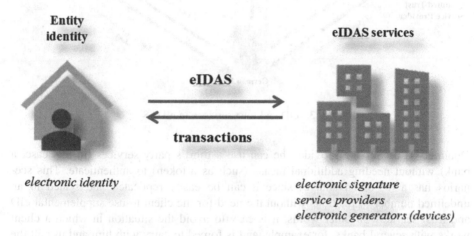

Fig. 2. Simplified eIDAS architecture

As depicted in the previous figure, there are 3 key elements related to the eIDAS working environment [8]. First is related to electronic signature and aims to define a structure and the format of the electronic signature as well as the means to place the signature in various document formats. The second is related to Trust Service Providers (TSPs) which are certified entities that can provide the necessary information to develop and support trust services. The third is related to various hardware devices (hardware security module - HSM) that will be used to generate secure electronic signatures. Since these devices will be manipulated by regular users, they must be reliable, easy to use and user friendly.

Figure 3 presents a possible scenario for integrating eID with trust services as presented in eIDAS.

Figure 3 describes the following situation: Ion is a Romanian citizen that is using the services of a German bank. When logging on the e-banking application, Ion's e-identity must be confirmed. After this, Ion can fill banking documents but, in order for these to become effective, they must be signed via a Qualified Trust Service Provider. Based on Ion's interactions with the National Identity Provider and the

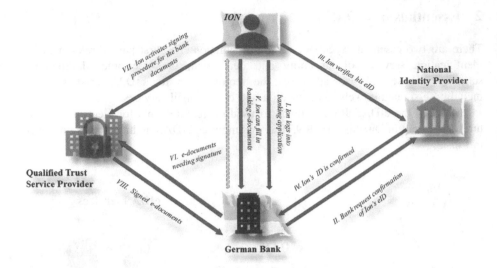

Fig. 3. eID and trust services in eIDAS

Qualified Trust Service Provider, he can use a third's party services (in this case, a bank) without needing additional means (such as a token) to authenticate. This scenarios has a lot of advantages since it can be easily replicated and scaled to an undefined number of relations without the need for the client to use supplemental eID and trust services. In other words, it is easy to avoid the situation in which a client works with several banks, for example, and is forced to carry with him and use all the time many tokens. This is very close to "one size fits all" philosophy.

2.1   User Identification and Trust in eIDAS

Electronic Identification (e-Identification or eID)

With the increase of online services now available even in remote regions, methods of uniquely identifying users had to be developed. It is the case of eID which must ensure secure access to online services and electronic transactions made by each individual. eID maps the virtual presence of a person to his or her physical identity so this will be allowed to use various online services. Until now, existing eIDs across Europe could not be used in other countries but the one they were issued in. Lack of an unitary legislation framework obstructed or, at least, did not facilitate cross border transactions, banking or healthcare transactions or other similar processes between entities located in different countries [9]. eIDAS Regulation comes to fix this problem by giving the eIDs the legal validity for cross-border transactions [11, 12] and allowing them to have the same legal status as traditional paper-based processes.

Previous aims and scopes of eIDs are not only preserved but also extended in eIDAS. The user must benefit from a fast, easy and secure access to electronic services regardless of their supplier (that can be local or national administrative entities [18], public or private enterprises, individuals etc.) under a strict protection of his personal data. The extensions refer to accessing transnational services that may include: European wide identity (which will improve frequent border crossing based transactions), European travel or health insurance (which will reduce time wasting and formalities in case of critical events), banking (as presented in Fig. 3), business and many other situations in which various short or long term exchanges and transactions. Let's take, for example, the case of students that are involved in programs like ERASMUS. Today, in many European countries, for these students temporary local ID cards are issued. Once eIDAS will be fully operational, these formalities will no longer be necessary, saving a lot of time and resources. In this respect, a survey [2] was initiated by the European Commission in May 2017.

Although the electronic identification of the citizen musts be done by their national authority, eIDAS Regulation imposes that electronic IDs of all EU citizens must be recognized in all EU countries, regardless their place of issue. In this respect, eIDAS regulation does not aim to level national standards on identity management so it allows different eID methods as long as they are interoperable. These provisions will apply to government services and any other services that rely on identities issued by national authorities. For these reasons, there is more pressure on the public entities and less to the private entities since the latter will only need to use information not generate it.

There are three levels of safety of eIDAS identification schemes: low, substantial and high. All EU entities must accept the level of safety considered by the issuing authority. This will generate the possibility of giving individual access to services that require a certain level of safety.

Prior to eIDAS, several similar initiatives were carried, some of their ideas being imported into eIDAS. One of the projects, STORK (Secure idenTity acrOss boRders linked [10, 11], failed to be implemented due to the lack of legislative support. With the lesson learnt, eIDAS came not only with the technical aspects necessary for the implementation of cross-border identification but also the necessary legal framework. There are reports [14] which reveal the fact that some national eID systems are already classified as "high" on the safety scaled of eIDAS.

Web Authentication
With web authentication, eID users can be recognized anywhere when they need certain services. The Regulation stipulates the use of verification and validation certificates for website authentication, as means to guarantee a trust service [1, 16].

Online services dedicated to integrating digital security providers, managers and consumers at high levels of security must, in turn, meet certain standards of identity certification. In this regard, we investigated several studies conducted by the European Network and Information Security Agency (ENISA) on Qualified Web Authorization Certificates [16, 17]. These specifications are an integral part of the eIDAS Regulation and provide standards on which Digital Identity Providers can qualify for TLS (SSL) identity as well as the security conditions that a website has to meet to qualify as provider of secure online services.

Electronic Signature (eSignature)
User identification, electronic or physical, is, most of the times, not enough for guaranteeing that a transaction or agreement is valid and will be carried out without

problems. For this reason, the handwritten signature is applied on paper documents and an electronic equivalent is needed for electronic documents.

The use of electronic signatures has grown steadily in electronic transactions, both in the governmental/local administration and private environments. As presented in [8] the usage of electronic signature had an increase rate of 2.5 from 2012 and 2014 (interval for which certain data is available) and is estimated to have an increase rate of 4 (between 2012 and 2015) and of about 6 (between 2012 and 2016). By the moment this study was elaborated, no certain data for 2015, 2016 and 2017 were published. Other statistics reveal that, in present, over 43.3% of private companies use electronic signature,

The electronic signature must fulfill two functions:

– Authenticate signer
– Offer the guarantee that a document was not been modified in any ways after the signature was inserted.

The signature itself (container and content) can be presented in various forms: email signature, scan or picture of a written signature, signature generated by a dedicated device or application. For a higher level of trust, eIDAS brings two new types of electronic signature: Advanced Electronic Signature (AES) and Qualified Electronic Signature (QES).

The advanced electronic signature must meet the demands of a regular electronic signature by uniquely identifying the signer and guarantying that the signed document was not altered after the signing but also it must guarantee that the signer himself was in control of the signing process. Simply put, the AES must exceed a simple electronic signature by containing elements capable to eliminate identity theft.

The qualified electronic signature is a particular case of advanced electronic signature. The QES must be supported by a qualified creation device and, in addition, by a qualified "public key" certificate issued by a TSP. It has been mentioned before that TSP and the generator devices list is managed at global level so they must undergo a sever assessment process before being invested as "qualified". The qualified electronic signature is the only type of electronic signature that will have the same legal value with the written signature so it will not be subject of a potential legal dispute. The other types of electronic signatures may have the same functionality but they are not as strong so a possible legal dispute related to a signed document must be settled in a court of law.

Remote Signature

eIDAS allows the use of remote signing services. In the case of a local signature, the user will create it by using a security hardware device. Remote signing is an alternative to local signature creation by providing a remote signature creation mechanism. For this to be possible, the signing keys are no longer on a portable device but are provided remotely via a service that simulates a physical HSM. Thus, the user is no longer dependent on a physical device that can be lost, stolen, or deteriorated. Currently, this approach appears to be largely preferred by the general public.

The general idea is to replace the physical HSMs with an online service provided by a TSP where the user's signing keys are held. A similar idea was presented in [15].

The signature functionality and recognition by third parties is totally the same but the signing process can be done by using a smartphone or computer with a minimal web-browser. This novelty approach introduced by eIDAS is highly supporting the online transactions which exhibit continuous growth. Another important help is coming from the high degree of penetration and use of smartphones which eliminate any constraints when it comes to mobile access of web services.

A remote signing procedure is presented in Fig. 4. As one can see, the procedure is simple and requires very few resources from the user. The TSP receives requests from the users via a safe channel (for example, HTTPS), is generating electronic signatures and sends them back to the users. The generation process is based on the users' signing keys stored on the HSMs hosted by the TSP. Upon request, each user is activating his own signing key based on some secure credentials. Since the entire signature generation process is at the TSP level, it is mandatory that a high level of security is implemented on site. Users' devices (smartphones or computers) must have multiple layers of security when are being used for remote signing purposes. For example, the access for regular non-critical applications (phone, Waze, weather etc.) can be granted based on a simple PIN but the access for credentials should require stronger security (longer passwords, biometric features etc.).

Remote Signing procedure

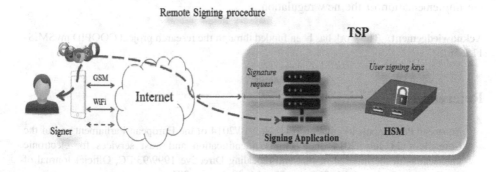

Fig. 4. eIDAS remote signing procedure

Depending on the security of the signature request and signing key activation, eIDAS refers to 2 levels of remote signing. In fact, this is related to the entity where signing key activation is done at the TSP. In case of Level 1 remote signing, the key activation is made inside the signing application (see Fig. 4). This makes the signing application the only entity where user's activation request is received, processed and executed. Level 1 remote signing does not impose special restrictions to HSMs which can be any certified module. This approach may raise some questions or suspicions related to the fact that TSP's signing application obtains the user's activation key. Higher level of security is granted by Level 2 remote signing. In this case, the signature activation is done by the HSMs (see Fig. 4), whilst the signing application only receives and passes the user's activation data without executing it. This way, the risk of compromising the user's data is reduced to minimum.

3   Conclusions

In this paper, an investigation over the electronic identification and trust techniques from eIDAS is presented. The eIDAS Regulation seeks to create a unique and safe EU market for government agencies, public and private enterprises and online service providers.

Prior to eIDAS adoption, the heterogeneity of national or local electronic identity and trust systems prevented any efforts of making them compatible and interoperable. The solution for these problems came under the form of a mandatory legislative act issued by EU for harmonizing electronic identification and trust services.

The functionality and philosophy behind eIDAS are presented together with the stages of implementation in various countries of EU. The main electronic identification techniques and differences to the former ones are analyzed and presented in detail. Trust aspects related to the user, as individual, are also presented under various forms of electronic signature.

Although eIDAS aims to unite the European legislation in its field, it must be pointed that eIDAS will not enforce a common, unique identification system but will ensure the compatibility and interoperability of national systems. This should be totally transparent to the end user which should only benefit from the advantages derived from the implementation of the new regulation.

Acknowledgement.   The work has been funded through the research project COOPID mySMIS-115656.

References

1. European Parliament: Regulation (EU) No 910/2014 of the European Parliament and of the Council of 23 July 2014 on electronic identification and trust services for electronic transactions in the internal market and repealing Directive 1999/93/EC, Official Journal of the European Union, OJ L 257, pp. 73–114, 28 August 2014
2. European Comission. https://ec.europa.eu/digital-single-market/en/news/feasibility-study-cross-border-use-eid-and-authentication-services-eidas-compliant-support-0
3. European Commission. https://ec.europa.eu/digital-single-market/en/trust-services-and-eid
4. European Council: Special meeting of the European Council (Art. 50), 25 November 2018. https://www.consilium.europa.eu/en/meetings/european-council/2018/11/25/
5. ComputerWeekly: EU sees eIDAS regulation come into full force, September 2018
6. KPMG Switzerland: Swiss companies must comply with eIDAS for digital access to EU markets. https://blog.kpmg.ch/swiss-companies-must-comply-eidas-digital-access-eu-markets/
7. Norwegian Communication Authority. https://eng.nkom.no/technical/trust-services/eidas/eidas-regulation
8. Thales: The Impact of the European eIDAS Regulation. www.thales-esecurity.com
9. European Comission. https://ec.europa.eu/digital-single-market/en/e-identification
10. Leitold, H., Zwattendorfer, B.: STORK: architecture, implementation and pilots. In: ISSE 2010 Securing Electronic Business Processes, pp 131–142 (2010)

11. Sideridis, Alexander B., Protopappas, L., Tsiafoulis, S., Pimenidis, E.: Smart cross-border e-Gov systems and applications. In: Katsikas, Sokratis K., Sideridis, Alexander B. (eds.) e-Democracy 2015. CCIS, vol. 570, pp. 151–165. Springer, Cham (2015). https://doi.org/10. 1007/978-3-319-27164-4_11
12. Secure ID News. https://www.secureidnews.com/news-item/eidas-digital-id-finds-use-in-cross-border-european-banking/
13. European Comission. https://ec.europa.eu/digital-single-market/en/news/questions-answers-trust-services-under-eidas
14. Federal Office for Information Security: eIDAS Notification of the German eID. https://www.bsi.bund.de/EN/Topics/ElectrIDDocuments/German-eID/eIDAS-notification/eIDAS_notification_node.html
15. Zwattendorfer, B., Tauber, A.: Secure cloud authentication using eIDS. In: Proceedings of IEEE CCIS2012 (2012)
16. ENISA: Qualified Website Authentication Certificates, December 2015. https://www.enisa.europa.eu/
17. ENISA: Security guidelines on the appropriate use of qualified website authentication certificates, December 2016. https://www.enisa.europa.eu/
18. Pimenidis, E., Georgiadis, C.K.: Can e-Government applications contribute to performance improvement in public administration? Int. J. Oper. Res. Inf. Syst. 5(1), 48–57 (2014)
19. European Commission. https://ec.europa.eu/digital-single-market/en/news/questions-answers-trust-services-under-eidas

Gathering Pattern Mining Method Based on Trajectory Data Stream

Ying Xia[1($\boxtimes$)], Lian Diao[1], Xu Zhang[1], and Hae-young Bae[2]

[1] School of Computer Science and Technology,
Chongqing University of Posts and Telecommunications, Chongqing, China
{xiaying, zhangx}@cqupt.edu.cn,
S160201017@stu.cqupt.edu.cn
[2] Department of Computer Engineering, Inha University, Incheon, South Korea
hybae@inha.ac.kr

Abstract. Moving object gathering pattern refers to a group of incident or case that are involved large congregation of moving objects. Mining the moving object gathering pattern in massive and dynamic trajectory data streams can timely discover the anomalies in the group moving model. This paper proposes a moving object gathering pattern mining method based on trajectory data stream, which consists of two stages: clustering and crowed mining. In the clustering stage, the MR-GDBSCAN clustering algorithm is proposed. It uses the grid to index moving objects and uses the grid as a clustering object and determines the center of each cluster. In the crowed mining phase, the sliding time window is used for incremental crowed mining, and the cluster center is used to calculate the distance between different clusters, thereby improving the crowed detection efficiency. Experiments show that the proposed moving object gathering pattern mining method has good efficiency and stability.

Keywords: Gathering pattern · Trajectory data streams · Clustering · Crowed · Sliding time window

1 Introduction

In recent years, with the development of mobile positioning, Internet, cloud computing, big data technology and the popularity of smart terminals. Location-based information services are increasingly enriched, and moving object trajectory data is continuously concentrated in many information service platforms, such as website check-in data, mobile signaling data, vehicle-mounted GPS data, RFID data, etc. The moving object gathering pattern mining of massive and dynamic trajectory data can timely find some moving object groups that are close to each other and move together [1], and provide services for traffic dispatching, public safety and other fields.

Many researchers have studied the moving object gathering pattern, such as flock [2, 3], moving cluster [4], convoy [5, 6], swarm [7], companion [8]. As the research progresses, its conditional constraints are more in line with human behavior patterns. Zheng et al. [1] proposed a gathering pattern, which consists of clusters of at least n time slices, and requires at least m_p participator in each cluster. This method firstly establishes

© ICST Institute for Computer Sciences, Social Informatics and Telecommunications Engineering 2019
Published by Springer Nature Switzerland AG 2019. All Rights Reserved
J. Li et al. (Eds.): SPNCE 2019, LNICST 284, pp. 666–676, 2019.
https://doi.org/10.1007/978-3-030-21373-2_56

a grid index on the trajectory data, then clusters the moving objects on each time slice, and proposes a closed crowed concept to detect the moving object gathering pattern. The concept of participator proposed makes the pattern more suitable for the behavior patterns of moving objects in real life. Zhang et al. [9] proposed a gathering pattern mining method based on spatio-temporal graph. It finds the largest complete subgraph that satisfies the spatiotemporal constraints in the spatio-temporal graph composed of clusters, and then mines the gathering pattern at a given time or position. Zhang et al. [10] considered that the gathering pattern is defined based on the "co-occurrence" pattern. It has a "parking problem", and the mining results are mixed with a large number of non-moving aggregated objects. To solve this problem, a converging pattern based on group motion process modeling is proposed. Yang et al. [11] used a quadtree to index data in the DBSCAN clustering algorithm to improve the mining efficiency of the converging pattern.

It can be seen that the moving object gathering pattern mining method is continuously improved with the change of data characteristics such as static data, dynamic data, big data, and streaming big data. Therefore, how to conduct efficient gathering mode mining in big data and streaming environment is the current research hotspot. This paper focuses on trajectory big data with streaming features, and relies on the Spark Streaming [12] framework to efficiently mine the gathering pattern of moving objects from the trajectory data stream. In the streaming environment, data is continuously received and gathering results are continuously output. If only the closed-crowed [1] is found, it often requires a large delay to obtain the gathering result, and it is not well adapted to the service requirements with high timeliness such as road condition analysis and route planning.

The main contributions of this article are: (1) A grid-based clustering algorithm is proposed. The algorithm first maps each moving object into a unique grid, and records the number of moving objects in the grid as weight, and then clusters the weighted grid to improve the efficiency of clustering. (2) An incremental open crowed detection algorithm based on sliding time window is proposed. First, set the sliding time window width and the window sliding distance, then cluster each time window data in the sliding time window, and then mine the crowed in the sliding time window. With the newly arrived time window data, the crowed detection result of the last sliding time window is multiplexed to update the crowed detection result of the current sliding time window.

The remainder of the paper is organized as follows. The relevant definitions of the moving object gathering pattern are given in Sect. 2. A gathering pattern mining method based on trajectory data stream is described in detail in Sect. 3. We evaluate the efficiency and scalability of the method in Sect. 4, and summarize the full text in Sect. 5.

2 Definition

For the convenience of description, the related concepts and symbols are first defined.

2.1 Snapshot Trajectory

Given the moving object database O_{DB} and the time domain of database T_{DB}, the snapshot trajectory $Sli_i = \{(o_i, t_i)|o_i \in O_{DB}, t_i \in T_{DB}\}$, Sli_i is the snapshot trajectory of the moving object o_i in the t_i time slice. It belongs to a subset of the snapshot trajectory set Sli.

2.2   Core Grid

Given the distance threshold σ, and the cluster density threshold m_c, the $grid_{(x,y)}$ is a core grid when any of the following conditions are satisfied:

1. The number of moving objects in the grid $grid_{(x,y)}$ is more than m_c.
2. The grid in the neighborhood of the grid $grid_{(x,y)}$ contains more moving objects than m_c.

2.3   Snapshot Cluster

Let the set $c_i = \{o_1, o_2, \ldots, o_i\}$ be a set of moving objects of a time slice i ($1 \leq i \leq k$). For a given cluster density threshold m_c, and a distance threshold σ. c_i is a snapshot cluster when the following conditions are satisfied:

1. $size(c_i) \geq m_c$.
2. The distance between the members of c_i in the grid g_k and g_p is not greater than σ, $Dist(g_k, g_p) \leq \sigma$.

2.4   Crowed

Given the moving object database O_{DB}, the cluster density threshold m_c, the distance threshold σ, and the lifetime threshold k_c, a crowed C_r is a sequence of snapshot clusters at consecutive timestamps, i.e., $C_r = (c_{t_a}, c_{t_{a+1}}, \ldots, c_{t_b})$. The following conditions need to be satisfy [1]:

3. The lifetime of C_r is defined as $C_r.\tau$, is not less than k_c, i.e., $C_r.\tau = b - a + 1 \geq k_c$.
4. There are at least m_c objects at any time, i.e., $\forall a \leq i \leq b, |c_{i_i}| \geq m_c$.
5. The distance between two consecutive snapshot clusters is not greater than 2σ, i.e., $d_H(c_{t_i}, c_{t_{i+1}}) \leq 2\sigma, \forall a \leq i \leq b - 1$.

2.5   Participator

In crowed C_r, a moving object can be referred to as a participator, which appears at least k_p times in the crowed [1].

2.6   Gathering

A crowed is a gathering, which has at least m_p participator in each snapshot cluster [1], i.e., $\forall c_t \in C_r, |\{o|o(t) \in c_t, o \in Par(C_r)\}| \geq m_p$.

Figure 1 is an example of the movement trajectory of seven moving objects in seven time slices. By definition, o_1, o_2, o_3, o_4 form a gathering, and o_5, o_6, o_7 form an another gathering. The symbols used in this paper are listed in Table 1.

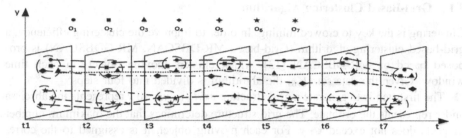

Fig. 1. Moving object gathering pattern.

Table 1. Table of notations.

Notation	Definition	Notation	Definition
O_{DB}	Moving object database	$d_H(c_i, c_j)$	Distance between clusters c_i, c_j
T_{DB}	Time domain of database	k_c	Lifetime threshold of a crowed
t_i	A time point in T_{DB}	m_c	Cluster density threshold
o_i	A moving object	$\text{Par}(C_r)$	Participator set of a crowed C_r
Sli_i	A snapshot trajectory at time t_i	k_p	Lifetime threshold of a participator
c_i	A snapshot cluster at time t_i	m_p	Support threshold of a gathering
C_r	A crowed	σ	Distance threshold
$C_r.\tau$	The lifetime of a crowed		

3   Gathering Pattern Mining Method Based on Trajectory Data Stream

In the streaming environment, the trajectory data is continuously received, we continuously cluster in each time window, and perform crowed detection in the sliding time window. If the crowed is detected in turn for each time window in each sliding time window, the efficiency is often unsatisfactory. Therefore, it is considered to use the incremental detection method to perform crowed mining on the real-time arrival time window. The structural framework of the method described in this paper is shown in Fig. 2, which mainly includes two parts: moving object clustering and crowed detection.

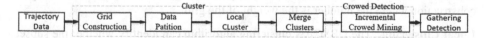

Fig. 2. Spark Streaming-based trajectory data stream gathering pattern mining method framework.

3.1   Grid-Based Clustering Algorithm

Clustering is the key to crowed mining. In order to improve the clustering efficiency, a grid-based clustering algorithm (Grid-based MR-DBSCAN, MR-GDBSCAN) is proposed based on MR-DBSCAN [13], which clusters moving objects in each time window. Given the data set O_{DB}, the algorithm is divided into four steps:

The first step is to generate a grid structure $grid_{(x,y)}$, where x represents the abscissa and y represents the ordinate. The grid structure determines that the maximum number of grids does not exceed $x * y$. For each moving object, it is assigned to the corresponding grid according to its latitude and longitude coordinates.

The second step is data partitioning. In the distributed environment, data partitioning may make the results of clustering inaccurate, especially those that are close to the partition boundaries. For example, the objects o_1, o_2, o_3 belong to c_i, but if the data is partitioned, o_1, o_2 are partitioned in the same partition, but o_3 is in another partition. It causes the clustering results in the partition to be inconsistent with the clustering results on the entire snapshot cluster, but it is less efficient if all the data is clustered on one partition. Therefore, the partitioning method in the MR-DBSCAN algorithm is used for processing.

The third step is local clustering. Using grids as clustering objects instead of moving objects can greatly improve clustering efficiency.

The fourth step is to merge clusters. Using the MR-DBSCAN algorithm, the clusters in each partition are combined to obtain the global clustering result.

Grid Construction. Given a data set O_{DB}, each point has its own grid. It is calculated as follows:

$$\left(x = \left\lceil \frac{x - x_{min}}{\partial} \right\rceil, y = \left\lceil \frac{y - y_{min}}{\partial} \right\rceil \right) \tag{1}$$

where ∂ is the length of the grid, the value is half of σ, x_{min} and y_{min} are the minimum longitude and minimum latitude of O_{DB}. We define n_{xy} to represent the weight of $grid_{(x,y)}$, which is the number of moving objects contained in the grid. Once all the data has been mapped to the corresponding grid, the weight of the grid can be determined. Then, the average value of the latitude and longitude is calculated by the coordinates of all the moving objects of the grid as new grid coordinates, so that the grid coordinates change with the distribution of the objects in the grid. The final data format looks like this: $\langle newgrid, time, oldgrid, n_{xy} \rangle$, where newgrid represents the grid id (including x coordinate and y coordinate), which is the average calculated grid coordinate, time indicates the time slice number, oldgrid indicates the old grid id. Figure 3 is an example of a grid construction where the number is the weight of the grid.

Local Clustering. The DBSCAN clustering algorithm can identify whether the subset is a cluster based on the subset density of a data set, and can identify cluster clusters of arbitrary shapes, but its time complexity $O(n^2)$ is unacceptable when clustering

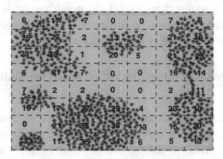

Fig. 3. Grid construction

massive amounts of data. In the process of local clustering, using the grid as the clustering object instead of using the point as the clustering object makes the clustering efficiency greatly improved. Figure 4 shows an improved local clustering algorithm.

The algorithm starts from any unvisited grid p in the dataset and traverses in order. Second find all the grids in the neighborhood of the grid p as its neighbor grid, and then sum the weight of its neighbor grids. If the sum is smaller than the parameter Minpts, the grid p is marked as a noise grid, and then turn to next grid. Otherwise p is a core grid, build cluster c_p based on grid p, and then perform the same detection and expansion on its neighbor grid.

Algorithm 1 : Local clustering	
Input:	Dataset D, Radius *Eps*, Density threshold *Minpts*
Output:	Cluster C
1.	$C \leftarrow \emptyset$
2.	**for** each unvisited grid p in D **do**
3.	Mark p as visited
4.	NG = getNeighbourGrid(p, Eps) // find the neighbor grid
5.	*pointInNG* = Sum(N) // count the weight of the neighbor grid
6.	**if** *pointInN* < *MinPts* **then**
7.	Mark p as Noise
8.	**else**
9.	C = next cluster
10.	ExpandCluster(p, NG, C, Eps, MinPts)
11.	**Return** C

Fig. 4. Local clustering algorithm

The time complexity of the algorithm is $O(\sum_{i=1}^{partition}(|S_i| * \text{getNeighbor-Grid}()))$ where partition is the number of partitions, $|S_i|$ is the number of grids in each partition, and GetNeighborGrid() is the time to get its neighbor grids. Therefore, the time complexity of the algorithm depends on the number of partitions, the number of grids in the partition, and the time it takes to find its neighbors.

3.2   Incremental Crowed Mining Algorithm Based on Sliding Time Window

In the detection process of the crowed, the concept of sliding time window is used, and the crowed is mined in the sliding time window. When the new time window arrives, it will reuse the crowed mining result of the last sliding time window to update the crowed result of the current time window, which saves space and reduces the amount of calculation. Figure 5 is a sliding time window model, which uses three times windows as the calculation window of the sliding time window, and slides one time window distance. Figures 6 and 7 briefly describe the *func* function and the *invFunc* function for incremental mining crowed that rely on the *reduceByKeyAnd Window (func, invFunc, windowLength, interval)* functions of the Spark Streaming framework, where *windowLength* represents the length of the sliding time window, *interval* represents the sliding distance.

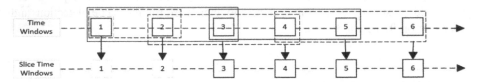

Fig. 5. Sliding time window model

Relying on the *reduceByKeyAndWindow* function, it will call the *func* function to perform crowed mining for each time window. When the sliding time window size is equal to its set value, the mining result of the current sliding time window will be output. When the fourth time window comes, the *invFunc* function is called to process the candidate crowed result of the last sliding time window, which will get a new crowed candidate set. Then, this new crowed candidate set will be combined with the cluster in the current time window to expand into a new crowed.

In daily life, a large gathering, parade and other activities, the flow of people is often very slow, gradual, rather than mutated [1], the shape and size of the population changes relatively slowly. Therefore, the cluster center can often represent the position of the cluster and can be used to calculate the distance between the cluster and the cluster, which can improve the calculation efficiency.

Algorithm 2 : *func (CC, CW)*	
Input:	Crowed candidate set for the current sliding time window CC
	Cluster set of the next time window CW
Output:	Crowed set within the current sliding time window CS
1.	$CS \leftarrow \emptyset$
2.	$addClaster \leftarrow \emptyset$
3.	**for** each crowed candidate *cc* in *CC* **do**
4.	$Cr' \leftarrow$ FindCluster(*cc, CW*) //find the set if clusters that are within 2σ distance to cc.
5.	$addClaster \leftarrow addClaster \cup Cr'$
6.	**if** $Cr' = \emptyset$ **then**
7.	$CS \leftarrow CS \cup cc$
8.	**else**
9.	**for** each *c* in *Cr'* **do**
10.	$cc \leftarrow cc \cup c$
11.	$CS \leftarrow CS \cup cc$
12.	$CS \leftarrow CS \cup$ notAddedCluster(*addCluster, CW*) //the clusters cannot be appended to any current crowed camdidate will become new crowed camdidate.
13.	**return** CS

Fig. 6. Crowed detection algorithm

Algorithm 3: *invFunc (CC, CW)*	
Input:	Crowed mining results from the last sliding time window *CC*
	The cluster in Time window that is discarded in the current sliding time window *CW*
Output:	Duplicate crowed set *DC*
1.	$DC \leftarrow \emptyset$
2.	**for** each window *w* in *CW* **do**
3.	**for** each cluster c in w **do**
4.	$DC \leftarrow$ updateCrowed(*c, CC*) //find the cluster in the Crowed and delete it in the Crowed.
5.	**return** *DC*

Fig. 7. Update crowed algorithm

4 Experiment

The experiment used data provided by Datacastle's Traffic Line Time Prediction Competition [1], which contains more than 1.4 billion GPS records for more than 14,000 taxis in Chengdu. The data is recorded from August 03, 2014 to August 30, 2014, and the upload interval is one minute. We attach a time attribute to the car id to bring all the data to one day. In this experiment, we generate 3 sets of data, D1 has up to 250,000 moving objects, D2 has up to 600,000 moving objects, and D3 has up to 1 million moving objects. As shown in Fig. 8, the amount of data processed in each time window in each data set simulates a business activity, with a flow of people from more to less. In the data stream, we send data to Kafka at intervals of 1 min, and then read the data through Spark Streaming for processing. The experimental cluster consists of four hosts. Its CPU is 4-core Intel(R) Xeon(R)E2430@2.2 GHz, 8G memory, running Linux operating system, building Hadoop 2.60 and Spark1.60 distributed cluster.

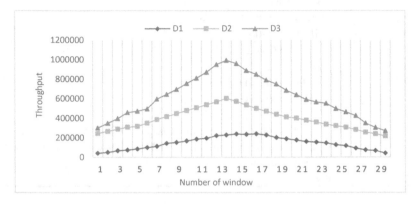

Fig. 8. The amount of data processed in each time window

4.1 Efficiency Evaluate

Given the data set D1, the time database $|O_{DB}|$ contains 30 time slices, First set the cluster density threshold $m_c = 10$, sliding time window = 6 min, window sliding distance = 1 m, time threshold = 4 min, distance threshold σ take GPS coordinate interval = 0.002, the distance is about 200 m, crowed clustering distance threshold $\mu = 2\sigma$. Figure 9 shows the gathering pattern mining processing time in which the sliding time window has six-time windows and the sliding distance is one time window. The processing time is obtained by observing the Spark UI. As can be seen from the figure, as the amount of data in each time window increases, the change of the mining time of the gathering pattern based on the MR-DBSCAN algorithm and the Crowed-TAD algorithm (abbreviated as Crowed-TAD) is consistent with the change of the data amount. It has good mining efficiency when the amount of data is small. However, with the change of data volume, the processing time of the gathering pattern detection method (abbreviated as Proposed) based on MR-GDBSCAN algorithm and incremental open crowed detection algorithm based on sliding time window remains stable, and the gathering pattern mining is more efficient.

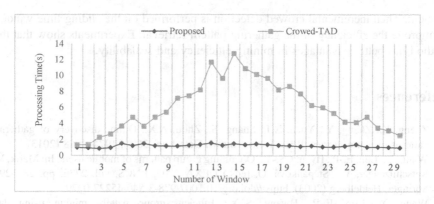

Fig. 9. Gathering pattern mining processing time

4.2 Scalability Evaluate

On the datasets with different data volumes, the Proposed method is evaluated for scalability, and its parameters use the parameter settings in the efficiency evaluation. As can be seen from Fig. 10, as the amount of data in the data set continues to increase, although the detection time increases, the gathering pattern mining efficiency remains within an acceptable range.

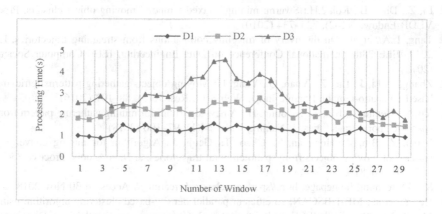

Fig. 10. Processing Time evaluate of different data sets

5 Conclusion

Moving object gathering pattern is a research hotspot in mobile object pattern mining. In order to adapt to the efficient gathering pattern mining requirements in big data and streaming environment, this paper proposes a moving object gathering pattern mining method based on trajectory data stream. The method first optimizes the traditional DBSCAN clustering algorithm, which uses grids to cluster and make clustering more efficient. Then incremental crowed detection is performed on the sliding time window to improve the efficiency of the gathering pattern retrieval. Experiments show that this method has better advantages in mining efficiency and scalability.

References

1. Zheng, K., Zheng, Y., Yuan, N.J., Shang, S., Zhou, A.X.: Online discovery of gathering patterns over trajectories. IEEE Trans. Knowl. Data Eng. **26**(8), 1974–1988 (2013)
2. Wang, Y., Lim, E.-P., Hwang, S.-Y.: On mining group patterns of mobile users. In: Mařík, V., Retschitzegger, W., Štěpánková, O. (eds.) DEXA 2003. LNCS, vol. 2736, pp. 287–296. Springer, Heidelberg (2003). https://doi.org/10.1007/978-3-540-45227-0_29
3. Wang, Y., Lim, E.-P., Hwang, S.-Y.: Efficient group pattern mining using data summarization. In: Lee, Y., Li, J., Whang, K.-Y., Lee, D. (eds.) DASFAA 2004. LNCS, vol. 2973, pp. 895–907. Springer, Heidelberg (2004). https://doi.org/10.1007/978-3-540-24571-1_78
4. Kalnis, P., Mamoulis, N., Bakiras, S.: On discovering moving clusters in spatio-temporal data. In: Bauzer Medeiros, C., Egenhofer, M.J., Bertino, E. (eds.) SSTD 2005. LNCS, vol. 3633, pp. 364–381. Springer, Heidelberg (2005). https://doi.org/10.1007/11535331_21
5. Jeung, H., Yiu, M.L., Zhou, X., Jensen, C.S., Shen, H.T.: Discovery of convoys in trajectory databases. Comput. Sci. **1**(1), 1068–1080 (2009)
6. Aung, H.H., Tan, K.-L.: Discovery of evolving convoys. In: Gertz, M., Ludäscher, B. (eds.) SSDBM 2010. LNCS, vol. 6187, pp. 196–213. Springer, Heidelberg (2010). https://doi.org/10.1007/978-3-642-13818-8_16
7. Li, Z., Ding, B., Rol, J.H.: Swarm: mining relaxed temporal moving object clusters. Proc. VLDB Endow. **3**(1–2), 723–734 (2010)
8. Tang, L.A., et al.: On discovery of traveling companions from streaming trajectories. In: 2012 IEEE 28th International Conference on Data Engineering. IEEE Computer Society (2012)
9. Zhang, J., Li, J., Liu, Z., Yuan, Q., Yang, F.: Moving objects gathering patterns retrieving based on spatio-temporal graph. Int. J. Web Serv. Res. **13**(3), 88–107 (2016)
10. Yu, Y., Genlin, J., Bin, Z., Xiaoting, H.: A new algorithm for mining gathering pattern from spatio-temporal trajectories. J. Nanjing Univ. **54**(1), 97–106 (2018)
11. Yifan, Z., Bin, Z., Hongyan, S., Chao, T., Genji, J.: Algorithm for mining converging patterns of moving objects from spatiotemporal trajectories. J. Data Acquis. Process. **33**(3), 487–495 (2018)
12. SparkStreaming homepage. http://spark.apache.org/streaming/. Accessed 30 Nov 2018
13. He, Y., et al.: MR-DBSCAN: an efficient parallel density-based clustering algorithm using MapReduce. In: 2011 IEEE 17th International Conference on Parallel and Distributed Systems, pp. 473–480 (2011)

Travel Modes Recognition Method Based on Mobile Phone Signaling Data

Ying Xia[1], Jie Tang[1($\boxtimes$)], Xu Zhang[1], and Hae-young Bae[2]

[1] School of Computer Science and Technology,
Chongqing University of Posts and Telecommunications, Chongqing, China
{xiaying, zhangx}@cqupt.edu.cn,
S160201056@stu.cqupt.edu.cn
[2] Department of Computer Engineering, Inha University, Incheon, South Korea
hybae@inha.ac.kr

Abstract. With the acceleration of urbanization and motorization, the characteristics and rules of residents' travel are constantly changing. Analysis of this information provides reference and guidance for transportation planning, urban management and residents' travel. With the development of mobile positioning and wireless communications, GPS signals, mobile phone signaling data and other data have established the foundation for obtaining wide-area travel information. This paper proposes a travel mode recognition method based on mobile phone signaling data. In the data preprocessing stage, the method effectively identifies and processes exceptions such as "ping-pong switching" effect and "data drift" effect through time-space threshold filtering, and accurately recognizes key points in the trajectory segmentation stage through feature analyses. In the recognition stage, this method utilizes the road network constraints to improve the calculation of features. The experimental results show that the method can effectively recognize the mode of residents' travel according to the mobile phone signaling data.

Keywords: Travel mode recognition · Mobile phone signaling ·
Clustering analysis · Data preprocessing · Road network constraints

1 Introduction

Travel mode analysis is one of the important categories in traffic analysis. It provides reference and guidance for traffic planning, urban management and residents' travel. Travel mode refers to a group of vehicles or means used by residents to complete a trip, such as walking, bicycles, motorcycles, cars, taxis, buses and rail transit. GPS signals and mobile phone signaling are the main data sources for travel trajectory analysis. Some researches extract position information from mobile phone GPS and other modules to calculate characteristic parameters, and use machine learning and other methods to recognize modes [1–3]. However, not all mobile devices have enabled GPS module in real time, and such methods are less robust to the analysis of residents with larger time spans and spatial extents.

© ICST Institute for Computer Sciences, Social Informatics and Telecommunications Engineering 2019
Published by Springer Nature Switzerland AG 2019. All Rights Reserved
J. Li et al. (Eds.): SPNCE 2019, LNICST 284, pp. 677–688, 2019.
https://doi.org/10.1007/978-3-030-21373-2_57

The signaling data reflects the user's communication information such as mode, time and location. The location information is obtained by collecting a cell identification number or by a cellular positioning technology. Since the signaling data can reflect the location information in a wide range of time and space, it is widely used in urban computing, especially in the field of travel analysis.

On the other hand, the current methods for analyzing the travel modes use the research framework made up of trajectory data preprocessing, trajectory segmentation and recognition models [2]. But there are still several problems. Firstly, the data anomalies are not fully considered in the preprocessing. The second is that it's not comprehensive enough in the trajectory segmentation, so that only one travel mode is adopted for a single travel. This is often not practical enough. The third is that the feature calculation method needs to be improved to enhance the accuracy of recognition. Therefore, based on the existing methods, this paper improves these three steps of data preprocessing, trajectory segmentation and mode recognition respectively to improve the accuracy of travel mode recognition.

This paper consists of four sections. Section 1 is an introduction. Section 2 states the problem, expounding the necessity of steps such as data preprocessing and trajectory segmentation, and roughly introduces the solutions. Section 3 proposes the recognition framework and proposes the solutions for each stage. Section 4 demonstrates the effectiveness of the recognition method through experimental analysis. Section 5 makes a summary.

2 Statement of Problem

Mobile phone signaling data cannot be directly used for analysis, since it is affected by factors such as terrain fluctuations, building distribution and multipath effects during propagation. And the uneven distribution of base stations makes the signaling data low in positioning accuracy and poor in quality. Therefore, in this paper, data preprocessing, trajectory segmentation and recognition models need to pay special attention to the problems caused by these effects.

2.1 Mobile Phone Signaling Data

The signaling data includes fields such as *MSID*, *Data_time*, *CELL_ID*, etc. The *MSID* is the unique identification number of the mobile phone user; *Data_time* indicates the generated time of current signaling; The *CELL_ID* is the connected base station number. The location of the base station is determined when the base station is planned and constructed. Each base station number uniquely determines its coordinates, so the user's location information is hidden in the *CELL_ID*. Therefore, a single piece of signaling data can be defined as Eq. 1.

$$signaling = \; <MSID, Data\_time, CELL\_ID, \dots > \tag{1}$$

A set of signaling data for a user can be represented as Eq. 2, where the signaling sequence is arranged in chronological order of *Data_time*.

$$userDATA = \{signaling_1, signaling_2, signaling_3, \ldots\} \tag{2}$$

2.2 Track Definition

The mobile phone user number (*id*) can be determined by the *MSID* and stored in the *users*, which contains the *MSID*s of all mobile phone users, so the user number set definition is as shown in Eq. 3.

$$users = \{id | id \in MSID\} \tag{3}$$

The location *point* of a single user corresponding to a single piece of signaling data. The location *point* definition is as shown in Eq. 4, where *lng* and *lat* respectively represent the longitude and latitude of the location point corresponding to the piece of signaling data, and *t* represents the signaling generated time, that is, $t \in Data\_time$. The *s* is the velocity of each *point*. Use *P* to collect all *points*.

$$point = <id, lng, lat, t, s> \tag{4}$$

A trajectory is a sequence of a series of position *points* of a single user stringed up by time. The trajectory is defined as *track*, shown in Eq. 5. Where $point_i \in P$, $point_i.t > point_{i+1}.t$, and $point_i.id = point_{i+1}.id$.

$$track = \{ <point_1, point_2, \ldots, point_i, \ldots, point_n> \} \tag{5}$$

The sub-track is defined as *travel* in Eq. 6, which contains the sequence of the sub-track *points* of the corresponding user.

$$travel \subseteq track \tag{6}$$

2.3 Data Preprocessing

Due to factors such as uneven distribution of base stations and obvious terrain differences, the original signaling data has exceptions such as "data drift", "ping-pong switching", and backtracking during recording [4]. It is necessary to accurately identify these exceptions in the data preprocessing stage and properly handle them to guarantee the data quality for subsequent operations.

2.4 Track Segmentation

"A trip" of a resident usually corresponds to multiple modes of travel [5], such as the order of "walking" – "transit" – "railway" – "walking". The different modes are connected by "staying" or "transferring". Therefore, it is necessary to identify these "key points" (stay points and transfer points) in advance, and then divide the travel trajectory into several sub-tracks. Because different travel modes have large differences in speed change and time consumption, it can be identified by means of travel distance and travel time.

2.5   Travel Mode Recognition

In the study of travel mode recognition, the choice of travel feature variables has a great influence on the accuracy. Literature [6] uses the sensor data collected by the spiral instrument module in the mobile phone to analyze whether the user is in the bus or in the car. Literature [7] selects two travel feature variables, travel distance and maximum acceleration, to identify the four modes of travel including walking, bicycle, bus and car. Through analyzing the historical trajectories and similar research results, it is found that there are obvious differences on 5 feature variables such as travel distance, average speed, median speed, 95% quantile speed and low speed rate in each travel mode [8]. Therefore, the above five eigenvalues of each sub-track are calculated separately, and the SVM, C4.5 decision tree, BP neural network, convolutional neural network and other methods can be used to identify better results [8–10]. In addition, some researches have used the swarm intelligence algorithm such as particle swarm optimization to optimize the recognition mode to solve the problems of local optimum and precocity [8, 11]. On the other hand, most of the above identification methods use the labelled data to train the recognition model and then identify the unknown data. This supervised machine learning approach requires a lot of up-front work to label the mode of travel and lacks adaptability to signaling data in other regions.

Therefore, this paper considers the five travel features as the input variables of the recognition model, which are travel distance, average speed, median speed, 95% quantile speed and low speed rate. And recognize four travels modes of "walking", "rail transit", "buses" and "cars". At the same time, it is considered to use the less-cost unsupervised machine learning method to recognize the travel mode, conducting a cluster analysis to divide the sub-tracks of different travel modes by the internal differences of the travel data, to achieve the purpose of travel mode recognition.

3   Overall Process Design

Based on the above analysis, the overall process of recognize the travel modes of residents using signaling data is designed as shown in Fig. 1.

It mainly includes two stages: data preparation and travel mode recognition. The data preparation stage includes two steps of data preprocessing and track segmentation, and the travel mode recognition stage recognize the travel mode by cluster analysis of the travel feature data.

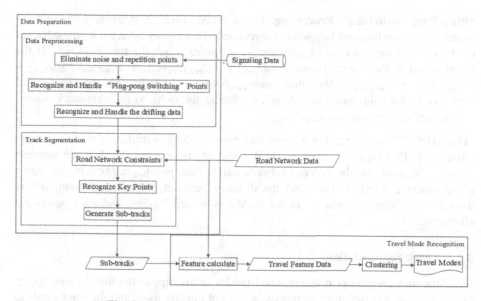

Fig. 1. The overall process of travel mode recognition

3.1 Data Preprocessing

The data preprocessing firstly uses the user number to divide all the signaling data into users and integrates them into the user track data set. Then the time and space thresholds are used to sequentially remove noise points, repetition points, "ping-pong switching" points, and "data drift" points for each user.

User Division. The user division step generates the signaling trajectory data set *userDATA* for each user, using all the given signaling sets, according to the user number *id*. In this process, the signaling data of all users is firstly sorted in ascending order according to the *id*, and it's arranged in the order of time stamp *Data_time* in the same *id* group. After that, the first signaling is read and a trajectory data set *userDATA* belonged to the user is created, then each subsequent signaling will be traversed in turn through the loop: if the user trajectory set of the next signaling does not exist yet, the user's *userDATA* will be created and the current signaling will be added; if it already exists, adds this signaling to the user's *userDATA*. When the next signaling is empty, the loop ends, and finally the *userDATA* collection of different users is generated. The single user's trajectory dataset *userDATA* is defined as the travel trajectory *track* for this user, and each signaling in is defined as a *point*.

Removing Duplicate Points. For a given user trajectory sequence *track*, the repeated points *point** in the set are deleted, as defined by Eq. 7.

$$point* = \{point | point_i.lng = point_{i-1}.lng, \text{ AND } point_i.lat = point_{i-1}.lat\} \quad (7)$$

"Ping-Pong Switching" Processing. For a given *track*, if there is a "ping-pong switch", only the first and last *point*s are retained. That is, any adjacent k time-adjacent track *point*s in the *track*, $point_{i+1}$, $point_{i+2}$, ..., $point_{i+k}$, set the threshold thr_1. If the travel speed of the k track *points* $s = (d_{i+1,i+2} + d_{i+2,i+3} + ... + d_{i+k-1,i+k}) / (t_{i+1,i+2} + t_{i+2,i+3} + ... + t_{i+k-1,i+k}) > thr_1$, then $point_{i+1}$, $point_{i+2}$, ..., $point_{i+k}$ is the sequence of track *point*s for "ping-pong switching", excluding the $i+2$th to $i+k-1$th track *point*s, leaving only $point_i$ and $point_{i+k}$.

"Data Drift" Processing. For a given user *track*, if there is drift data, such *point*s are eliminated. That is, for a given *track*, if $point_i$ exists, making the distance between $point_{i+1}$ and $point_i$ and the distance between $point_{i+1}$ and $point_{i+2}$ are both bigger than a given distance threshold thr_2, and the distance between $point_{i+2}$ and $point_i$ is less than $2 * thr_2$, then the $point_{i+1}$ in the middle is a "drift" point, and such *point*s are eliminated.

3.2   Track Segmentation

Since the user may adopt multiple travel modes in his trip, in the travel mode recognition, the user's *travel*, after preprocessing, is not directly used, and the *track* needs to be converted into segments (sub-tracks). This process is to find the key points in the travel trajectory first, then use them to segment a series of continuous data track points and divide the user track into several travel segments indicating different travel modes.

Road Network Constraints. In the communication system, the precise location of the user needs to be estimated using multiple pieces of signaling data and various positioning algorithms. In general, users travel on the road, so the user's travel distance is measured by calculating the road network distance of the travel.

First, use the coordinate generation function to generate the latitude and longitude coordinates of the specified two points as A (*lat, lng*), B (*lat, lng*). Then use the road network data to solve routes between the two points $path_1$, $path_2$, $path_3$ ... $path_n$, and the distances corresponding to each route. Since the adjacent two track points A and B in the travel trajectory are not far apart from each other, the solved distances of the navigation paths of the n paths between A and B are not significantly different, so the shortest navigation route among the n paths is extracted as the road network distance of the two track points. This function's input is the latitudes and longitudes of the two points, and the output is the road network distance of the two points, defined as function d ().

Key Points Recognition. The definition s represents the instantaneous velocity of each point, and d () represents the distance function between adjacent points. The speed calculation of the $i+1$th point is defined as shown in Eq. 8.

$$s_{i+1} = d(point_i, point_{i+1}) / (point_{i+1}.t - point_i.t) \tag{8}$$

Key points are not exactly one point, but a set of points in a continuous time range. The speed of the stay points is closed to 0, and the speed before and after the stay range is not closed to 0. So the stay points are defined as any adjacent k time-adjacent points $point_{i+1}, point_{i+2}, \ldots, point_{i+k}$ in the *track*, if $point_{i+1}.s = point_{i+2}.s = \ldots = point_{i+k}.s = 0$, and the time spans between $i + 1_{th}$ and $i + k_{th}$ exceeds th_3, all points from $i + 1$ to $i + k$ are stay points.

Another type of key points is the transfer points. Transfer is a form of transition from one mode to another. There are two situations when transferring. One is to transfer to another mode without waiting, such as taking a taxi immediately after walking or getting off the bus. The another needs to wait in its place, such as waiting for a bus after walking or recruiting taxis. The first transferring may not have points with a speed of 0, but there are adjacent points i and $i+1$, and the difference between the average velocity before i and the average velocity after $i+1$ is bigger than thr_4. The second transferring has points where the speed is 0, and the continuous time does not exceed the time of thr_5, and the difference of average speed before and after the transfer range exceeds thr_4.

Sub-track Generation. After recognizing a certain set of key points, the *track* can be divided into two different *travels* by the first key point and the last key point. Therefore, the user's travel *track* is divided into several segments of *travel* using key points. Then users' travel segment set T is generated, which contains the all chronological sorted users' sub-tracks. The definition is as shown in Eq. 9. And each sub-track *travel* is unique numbered by $tID = id\_i$, that is, a combination of user number and sequence number. The set T contains all the travel sub-tracks of all users and is distinguished by tID. The five features of each *travel* are calculated and included in the set.

$$T = <travel_1, travel_2, travel_3, \ldots, travel_n > \qquad (9)$$

3.3   Travel Mode Recognition

Feature Calculation. The travel distance is calculated by using the cumulative method, which is the sum of the road network distances between the two points. The travel distance D is calculated as shown in Eq. 10.

$$D = \sum_{i=1}^{n} d(i+1, i) \qquad (10)$$

Since the speed of travel is not evenly distributed, the average speed cannot be calculated by dividing the total travel distance by the total travel time, but the average of the speeds between adjacent sets of track points. The calculation method of the average travel speed $\bar{S}$ is as shown in Eq. 11.

$$\bar{S} = \frac{1}{n}\sum_{i=1}^{n} \frac{d(i+1, i)}{t_{i+1} - t_i} \qquad (11)$$

The speed set S of travel is arranged as S_N from small to large, and the median speed takes the middle number of the speed set S_N. When the number is even, the median speed takes the average of the middle two speeds. The 95% quantile speed takes the speed stands at the 95% position of the speed set S_N. The low speed rate takes the ratio of the speed less than 30 km/h in the set S. Therefore, the data set T is a table of n rows and 6 columns, each row represents a *travel*, and each column represents the feature value of the corresponding *travel* as the *travel* number *tID*, the travel distance *tTLen*, the average speed *tAvS*, the median speed *tMdS*, and the 95% quantile speed *tNFS* and low speed rate *tLSR*.

Recognition Method. The core of the recognition model is to use the inherent differences of the data to divide the data T into four different categories, each representing different modes of travel, namely walking, cars, buses and rail transit. Due to the improvement of feature extraction and eigenvalue calculation, T has significant differences in the five feature values. Therefore, the data set T can be effectively divided. In this paper, K-means clustering algorithm is used to divide the data T to reflect the rationality of the data preprocessing and data preparation process. Then, based on the analysis of the characteristics of the travel segments in the clusters, the travel mode can be inferred.

4   Experiments

The signaling data used in the experiment was provided by Chongqing Transport Planning and Research Institute. It contains 11587 records as signaling information of 14 users during the week from May 11 to May 17, 2015. The experiment was performed on the MATLAB platform. This paper uses three fields: *MSID*, *Data_time* and *CELL_ID*.

Data Preprocessing. After data preprocessing, exceptions are eliminated. The results are shown in Fig. 2. The Fig. 2(a) is the trajectory point of a user on the day of May 12, 2015. Figure 2(b) is the user's trajectory connected with the points that removes the repeated positioning and drift points, and Fig. 2(c) is the user's trajectory after removing the "ping-pong switching". Through data preprocessing, the user trajectory is smoother and clearer without losing the spatial distribution information of the location, and the real travel route is more effectively expressed.

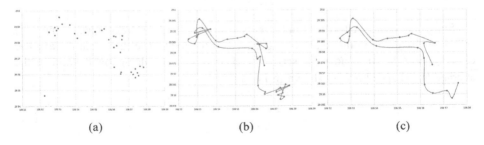

(a)   (b)   (c)

Fig. 2. The preprocessing results

Road Network Constraints. The distance between two location points is calculated by calling the Baidu Map API's calculation method (*RouteMatrix* API). Firstly, the interface address of the Baidu Map API is accessed. The latitudes and longitudes of the two points, the return text type, the user's AK are transmitted and request a response. Then, the required distance data is extract according to the returned text result. The system automatically calculates the nearest route between the two points. The returning distance is the road network distance between the two points, and the time consuming is the time required for a corresponding travel mode.

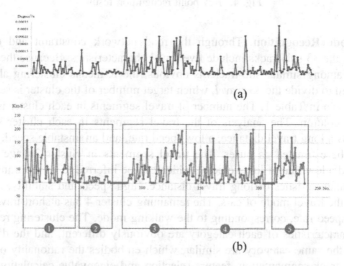

(a)

(b)

Fig. 3. The speed change after road network constraints

Figure 3 shows the change of the track speed of the user 4 before and after the road network constraint. Figure 3(a) shows the velocity distribution generated by directly calculating the Euclidean distance using the coordinates of the user, and Fig. 3(b) shows the speed distribution of the user after utilizing the road network constraint. The two distributions consistently have a similar trend in the speed change, but the distance calculation method is improved by the road network constraint in the Fig. 3(b), getting a better reflection of the difference of different travel modes in the speed distribution, and the key points can be more intuitively reflected in Fig. 3(b).

Track Segmentation. Figure 3(b) above shows the user's travel trajectory divided into five sub-tracks using indicators such as speed. Figure 4 below shows the trajectory segmentation process and results for User 1. The velocity turning occurs in the area in the red circle in Fig. 4(b) and the leftmost point's velocity approaches zero, so this point is recognized as a key point. As shown in Fig. 4(c), the key points split the track into two sub-tracks. The original data contains 14 users' signaling data, segmented resulting in 33 sub-tracks.

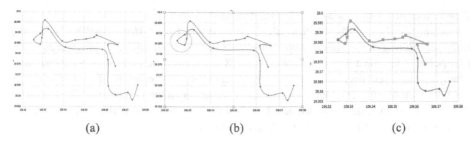

(a)   (b)   (c)

Fig. 4. Key point recognition result

Travel Mode Recognition. Through the road network constraint and eigenvalue calculation, the 33 sub-tracks include five travel characteristics. Because the difference of features among similar sub-tracks is obvious, the K-means clustering algorithm is implemented to divide the 33 *travel*, which target number of the cluster is set as 4. The result is shown in Table 1. The number of travel segments in each cluster is shown in the second column. The analysis of the travel segments in each cluster shows that cluster 1 has a long travel distance, a low speed rate, and an unstable speed. The travel mode can be estimated as buses. The travel segments in cluster 2 have a uniform velocity and a low rate of low velocity, which can be inferred to be rail transit. Cluster 3 has the characteristics of long travel distance, high speed and stability, and can be inferred to the travel mode of cars. The remaining cluster 4 has a short travel distance and a low speed rate, corresponding to the walking mode. The clustering results show that the characteristics of each category are obviously different, and the data characteristics of the same category are similar, which embodies the rationality of data preprocessing, track segmentation, feature selection and eigenvalue calculation.

Table 1. Numbers in each cluster

Cluster number	Number of travels
1	5
2	1
3	26
4	1
Total	33
Missing	0

Through cluster analysis, the 33 users travel segments include 5 bus travel, 26 travel by car, 1 travel by walking and 1 travel left by rail transit, which embodies the effectiveness of the method of clustering and analyzing travel modes. Table 2 shows the recognition result of 14 users' signaling data by using the travel mode recognition method proposed in this paper.

Table 2. Recognition Result for 14 users

User number	Travel modes	User number	Travel modes
01	Bus-Car-Car-Bus-Car	08	Car
02	Walking	09	Car
03	Car-Car-Bus	10	Bus
04	Car	11	Car
05	Car-Rail Transit-Car	12	Car
06	Car	13	Car
07	Car	14	Bus-Car

5   Conclusion

This paper proposes a travel mode recognition method based on mobile phone sig-naling data. In order to solve the data quality problems caused by uneven distribution of base stations and terrain differences, this method firstly recognizes and processes the exceptions in the data preprocessing stage through time and space threshold screening. In order to compensate for the calculation error caused by the inaccurate positioning of the base station, it is proposed to improve the feature calculation method by using the road network constraint, to improve the accuracy of the distance and speed. At the same time, the key points are accurately recognized through feature analysis, and the trajectory is segmented by using these key points to solve the "One Travel, One Mode" problem in traditional travel analysis. Finally, this paper uses the unsupervised machine learning method to cluster the sub-tracks after segmentation and combine the indicators of the data samples to recognize the travel modes. The experimental results show that the method can effectively recognize the travel mode according to the mobile phone signaling data. Due to the limited data samples, the modes are mainly recognized through the combination of unsupervised learning and empirical analysis. Subsequent research will conduct col-lecting volunteer data sets to validate the proposed method.

References

1. van Dijk, J.: Identifying activity-travel points from GPS-data with multiple moving windows. Comput. Environ. Urban Syst. **70**, 84–101 (2018)
2. Fang, Z., Jian-yu, L., Jin-jun, T., et al.: Identifying activities and trips with GPS data. IET Intell. Transp. Syst. **12**(8), 884–890 (2018)
3. Shafique, M.A., Hato, E.: Use of acceleration data for transportation mode prediction. Transportation **42**(1), 163–188 (2015)
4. Liu, Z., et al.: Traffic travel mode recognition method based on mobile phone grid data, CN108171973A (2018)
5. Wang, L., Zuo, Z.Y., Fu, J.H.: Travel mode character analysis and recognition based on SVM. J. Transp. Syst. Eng. Inf. Technol. **14**(3), 70–75 (2014)
6. Heydary, M.H., Pimpale, P., Panangadan, A.: Automatic identification of use of public transportation from mobile sensor data. In: Green Technologies Conference (GreenTech), pp. 189–196. IEEE (2018)

7. Zheng, Y., Liu, L., Wang, L., et al.: Learning transportation mode from raw GPS data for geographic applications on the web. In: Proceedings of the 17th International Conference on World Wide Web, pp. 247–256. ACM (2008)
8. Linlin, W.U., Biao, Y., Peng, J.: Research on travel mode identification of university students based on IPOS-SVM. Comput. Eng. **44**(1), 193–198 (2018)
9. Xiao, G., Juan, Z., Zhang, C.: Travel mode detection based on GPS track data and Bayesian networks. Comput. Environ. Urban Syst. **54**, 14–22 (2015)
10. Dabiri, S., Heaslip, K.: Inferring transportation modes from GPS trajectories using a convolutional neural network. Transp. Res. Part C: Emerg. Technol. **86**, 360–371 (2018)
11. Li, Z., Bo, C., Sun, J., et al.: Travel mode recognition based on particle swarm optimization and support vector machine. Appl. Res. Comput. **33**(12), 1–5 (2016)

Two-Level Feature Selection Method
for Low Detection Rate Attacks
in Intrusion Detection

Chundong Wang[1,2], Xin Ye[1,2($\boxtimes$)], Xiaonan He[3], Yunkun Tian[3],
and Liangyi Gong[1,2]

[1] Key Laboratory of Computer Vision and System, Ministry of Education,
Tianjin University of Technology, Tianjin 300384, China
306187260@qq.com
[2] Tianjin Key Laboratory of Intelligence Computing and Novel Software Technology,
Ministry of Education, Tianjin University of Technology, Tianjin 300384, China
[3] Tianjin E-Hualu Information Technology Co., Ltd., Tianjin 300350, China

Abstract. In view of the fact that some attacks have low detection
rates in intrusion detection dataset, a two-level feature selection method
based on minimal-redundancy-maximal-relevance (mRMR) and information gain (IG) was proposed. In this method, irrelevant and redundant
features were filtered preliminarily to reduce data dimension by using
mRMR algorithm, and highly correlated features to low detection rate
attacks were obtained based on the calculation of information gain, and
finally these features were integrated together to get final feature subset. The experimental results showed that the classification result of the
feature subset filtered by this method had a better classification performance than the current filtering methods and improved the testing
results of some attacks with low detection rates effectively.

Keywords: Feature selection · Information gain · mRMR ·
Intrusion detection

1 Introduction

Network security is more and more prominent with the rapid expansion of Internet and computer technology. In recent years, intrusion detection system (IDS),
which plays an increasingly important role in the network security engineering,
has been widely studied. As a key technology of network security active defense
system, intrusion detection can detect the malicious of network users without

Our work is supported by NSFC: The United Foundation of General Technology and
Fundamental Research (No. U1536122), the General Project of Tianjin Municipal Science and Technology Commission under Grant (No. 15JCYBJC15600), the Major
Project of Tianjin Municipal Science and Technology Commission under Grant (No.
15ZXDSGX00030).

© ICST Institute for Computer Sciences, Social Informatics and Telecommunications Engineering 2019
Published by Springer Nature Switzerland AG 2019. All Rights Reserved
J. Li et al. (Eds.): SPNCE 2019, LNICST 284, pp. 689–696, 2019.
https://doi.org/10.1007/978-3-030-21373-2_58

compromising the security of host and network [1]. It is a classifier designed to detect and classify network and host behaviors to identify whether they are normal or abnormal, and sent corresponding alerts. Therefore, improving the detection speed and accuracy is the key problem to be solved in IDS.

However, most of the results show that when there is a better whole detection rate, the detection rates of each classes may have great differences. This may cause the existence of low detection rate attack (LDRA). There are two reasons for LDRA: one is that the class distribution is nonuniform, the samples of lower detection rate classes are not enough and they are overwhelmed by other classes, so that these classes with a large sample size are dominant. This problem can be solved through increasing the number of their samples, but when there is a great disparity between samples sizes of each classes, this method may increase a great number of samples in the dataset, which can reduce the efficiency of the classifier; The other reason is that the selected features are not relevant to the low detection rate classes. To solve this problem, the most relevant feature subset should be found by improving the feature filtering method [2].

In order to prevent LDRA in intrusion detection from being ignored and having a tendency to give rise to security threat, a feature selection method for LDRA was proposed in this paper to improve their detection rates. In this method, irrelevant and redundant features were filtered preliminarily to reduce data dimension by using mRMR algorithm; in order to obtain the features most relevant to LDRA, we gathered them into a small dataset, then calculated the information gain in it and select some features greater than a given threshold. Finally these features were unioned together to get final feature subset. Experimental results show that our method can improve the detection rate of these classes effectively without affecting the overall and other class detection rates.

The rest of this article is divided into the following sections: Sect. 2 describes the related works; Sect. 3 introduces the feature selection method for LDRA; Sect. 4 reports the experiment and its results and Sect. 5 is the conclusion.

2   Related Work

In intrusion detection, reducing data dimension is an indispensable step in data preprocessing, so feature selection has become the focus of current research. Feature selection algorithms can be classified into 2 modes: filter and wrapper. The filter mode doesn't consider the learning algorithm and has a small computation. It can remove the noise and redundant features effectively. Information gain, mutual information, chi square distribution and mRMR [3] are the common filter method. The wrapper mode needs to determine the classification algorithm in advance, and then use the classifier to evaluate feature sets, which tends to a better classification performance, but has a higher computational cost. Aggarwal et al. [4] conducted a further research on the familiar intrusion detection dataset KDD 99, divided its features into 4 different classes according to the content and experimented with each combinations in classes to find the most influential combining class on detection rate and false alarm rate; Wu et al. [5] combined the two modes, filtrated noise and irrelevant features by Fisher score and information gain respectively, then use the sequential backward selection algorithm to select feature subset; Cui et al. [6] proposed a feature selection method based on RS-PSO-SVM which can shorten time consumed greatly. However, the above methods just divided the dataset into 2 classes: normal or abnormal. They only thought about a better whole detection rate but made no comparison with each classes. If there are an obvious gap to the detection rates of each classes, it means that the whole detection rate cannot represent detection levels of each attack so that the whole detection rate should not be the main reference and evaluating standard.

In that case, Tang et al. [7] screened features through information gain and established an intrusion detection model with FCM clustering algorithm to improve its detectability; Huang et al. [8] proposed an intrusion detection method based on principal component analysis (PCA) increase its efficiency; Jia et al. [9] put forward a K-means based feature reduction method and reduced feature attributes by multiple clustering iterations; Mao et al. [10] integrated filter and wrapper methods. The filter method based on mutual information was firstly used to remove irrelevant attributes and the wrapper method based on improved adaptive genetic algorithm and improved evaluation function is used to select optimal attribute subset. For some situation that low detection rate classes are caused by the imbalance dataset, Feng et al. [11] combined SMOTE and GBDT algorithms, which were used to balance the dataset and make the classification respectively. These approaches took into account and improved the detection rates of each classes and had a better experimental results.

This paper makes some improvements based on the above researches, proposing a two level selection method based on mRMR and information gain for the lower detection rate attacks. The experimental results show that the method has better detection rates than other methods whether in whole dataset or each class.

3 Two-Level Feature Selection Method

A good feature selection method can improve the performance of machine learning algorithm, simplify the model and increase the speed. A common feature selection method is to maximize the correlation between the feature and the classification variable, which is to select the first k variables with the highest correlation to the classification variables. However, in feature selection, the combination of these features does not improve the performance of the classifier, because it is possible that features are highly correlated with each other, and these features are redundancy features. Therefore, feature selection filters not only the unrelated features but also the redundant features [12]. The mRMR algorithm is used to remain the maximum relevance feature as well as filter the redundancy features.

3.1   Minimal-Redundancy-Maximal-Relevance

Minimal-Redundancy-Maximal-Relevance (mRMR) is a filter feature selection method based on mutual information, aiming at obtaining a subset contains features that are highly correlated with the class vector and uncorrelated with other features. Mutual information is a concept in information theory which is used to express the relationship and measure the correlation between features. Suppose there are two random variables x and y, their mutual information is defined as Eq. 1.

$$I(x;y) = \iint P(x,y) \log \frac{P(x,y)}{P(x)P(y)} dxdy \tag{1}$$

Maximal-relevance is the measure of selecting features correlated with class and its computation is based on the mutual information between individual feature and class vector; Minimal-redundancy is the criterion of screen out redundancy features which is based on the mutual information between two features. Suppose the feature subset is S and C is the classification variable, the two formulas are Eqs. 2 and 3.

$$max\, D(S,c)\,; \quad D = \frac{1}{|S|} \sum_{x_i \epsilon S} I(x_i;c) \tag{2}$$

$$min\, R(S)\,; \quad R = \frac{1}{|S|^2} \sum_{x_i,x_j \epsilon S} I(x_i,x_j) \tag{3}$$

Define $\Phi(D,R)$ as the mRMR value of feature which is used to screen features, the formula is Eq. 4.

$$max\, \Phi(D,R)\,; \quad \Phi = D - R \tag{4}$$

3.2   Information Gain

Information gain is an important index of feature selection, which is defined as the amount of information that a feature can bring to the classification system. The more information it brings, the more important it is, the greater its information gain value is. In order to improve the accuracy of LDRA, we gather them into a new dataset and obtain the most important features to these classifications by calculating information gain of each features in this dataset.

Entropy represents the uncertainty of a feature. Suppose there are n classes in dataset, and class set $C = \{C_1, C_2, \cdots, C_i, \cdots, C_n\}$, $|C_i|$ is the number of samples of class Ci, $|D|$ implies sample size of dataset, $P(C_i)$ indicates the probability that class is C_i. We use H to represent entropy and the formula is Eq. 5.

$$H(C) = -\sum_{i=1}^{n} P(x_i) \log_2 P(x_i) = -\sum_{i=1}^{n} \frac{|C_i|}{|D|} \log_2 \frac{|C_i|}{|D|} \tag{5}$$

If feature T has m different values, divide the dataset into m subsets according to these values, that is $T = \{T_1, T_2, \cdots, T_k, \cdots, T_m\}$. Define $|T_k|$ as the number of subsets T_k and $|T_{kc_i}|$ as the number of class C_i in T_k. The conditional entropy satisfies Eq. 6.

$$H(C|T) = -\sum_{k=1}^{m} \frac{|T_k|}{|D|} H(T_k) = -\sum_{k=1}^{m} \frac{|T_k|}{|D|} \sum_{i=1}^{n} \frac{|T_{kc_i}|}{|T_k|} log_2 \frac{|T_{kc_i}|}{|T_k|} \quad (6)$$

Make the subtraction to get the information gain value according to Eq. 7.

$$IG(T) = H(C) - H(C|T) \quad (7)$$

3.3   Two-Level Feature Selection Method

The flow diagram of the two-level feature selection method presented in this paper is shown in Fig. 1. The method is mainly divided into 4 stages, they are: preparation stage, execution stage, selection stage and integration stage. Detailed procedures for each stages are described as below:

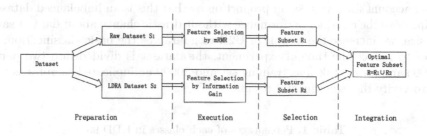

Fig. 1. The method flow diagram

- Preparation stage: define raw dataset as S_1 and duplicate LDRA classes from S_1 to a new dataset, namely the LDRA dataset S_2. Then quantize, normalize and discretize the data in dataset.
- Execution stage: mRMR feature selection method is used to select the features of the data in S_1 and calculate the mRMR values of each features; Information gain is used to select the features of the data in S_2 and calculate the entropy values of each features in LDRA. Both of the two values are sorted in descending order.
- Selection Stage: The results of the previous stage are further selected. Features whose mRMR value is greater than 0 are put into the feature subset R_1, which can guarantee the great reduction of data dimension; Features whose entropy value is greater than the specified threshold are put into the feature subset R_2, which can select out the features have high correlations with classification in LDRA.
- Integration stage: Integrate R_1 and R_2 as the final feature subset R. $R = R_1 \cup R_2$.

4   Simulated Experiment

4.1   Data Preprocessing

The dataset used in the experiment is the KDD 99 [13]. It contains 5 million network connection records and is composed of 41 features. Each connection is labeled as normal or abnormal. As for abnormal class, 39 types of attacks are summarized into four categories:

- DoS: Denial of Service.
- Probe: Monitor and other detection activities.
- R2L: Remote to Local. Illegal accesses from remote machines.
- U2R: User to Root. Unauthorized accesses to local superuser privilege by ordinary users.

The data distribution of dataset is shown in Table 1. From Table 1, the ratio of normal to abnormal is 1:4, but in abnormal class, DoS attack account for nearly 80% of the entire dataset and the remaining attack classes (especially R2L and U2R) account for a very small proportion so that this is an imbalanced dataset. To improve the classifier performance without drastic change about dataset sample size, we increase the sample of U2R to guarantee the basic classification. In order to reduce the time of experiment, the dataset is divided into two parts, 50000 samples are taken as training set and 30000 unduplicated samples as test set to verify the experimental results.

Table 1. Percentages of each classes in KDD 99

Class	Normal	DoS	Probe	R2L	U2R
Percentage	19.69	79.24	0.83	0.23	0.01

4.2   Results and Analysis

According to the classification results before feature selection, Probe, R2L, U2R has a relatively low detection rate, so we gather the three types into a new training set DR_Train. Then utilize mRMR to screen out the features into the feature subset mRMR_Sub and select the features in DR_Train through the calculated information gain values to the feature subset IG_Sub, at that time we can obtain the final optimal feature subset Final_Sub. Features contained in each subsets are shown in Table 2.

Our method is compared with the methods of literature [5,6,10] and the 41 attributes without any feature selection in the same experimental environment. The results will be considered not only in part but also in whole so the detection rates of each types of attacks and abnormal will be focused on. For the reason that the approaches we compare with are based on SVM, LibSVM was used

Table 2. Features contained in each subsets

Feature subset	Number of features	Features contained in subset
mRMR_Sub	15	3,24,12,32,31,37,6,23,1,2,40,38,5,39,36
IG_Sub	8	3,5,4,35,2,12,40,33
Final_Sub	19	1,2,3,4,5,6,10,12,23,24,31,32,33,35,36,37,38,39,40

Table 3. Comparison of feature selection methods

Methods	Normal	Dos	Probe	R2L	U2R	Abnormal
Literature [5]	99.8	99.9	86.6	78.1	50.8	99.60
Literature [6]	99.8	99.4	81.6	51.6	24.6	98.95
Literature [10]	99.7	100	73.9	50	70.5	99.51
All features	100	100	89.3	68.8	68.9	99.75
Our method	99.9	99.9	93.1	81.3	83.6	99.78

as the classification and testing algorithm and experiments were conducted on Weka. The results of the experiment are shown in Table 3.

Table 3 shows the validity and accuracy of our method. Compared with literature [5], literature [6] and literature [10], our method has good classification effect both from whole and part. Compared with all features, class probe, R2L and U2R classes have significant improvements. Therefore, our method wipes out the redundancy while preserves the correlation features, reduces the dimension and keeps the detection rate at the same time.

In order to test the stability of the method, define the abnormal detection rate, accuracy, false report rate (FNR), false alarm rate (FAR) and modeling time as evaluating criteria for further comparative testing. The experimental results are shown in Table 4. As can be seen from Table 4, though the methods of literature [5] and literature [10] have the smaller feature dimension and the shorter modeling time, their accuracy rate is low and FNR and FAR are also higher than our method, which shows that the number of features is not the less the better. Compared with all features, it maintains the detection rate of abnormal. Although the FAR has increased, the accuracy hold the level with all features in the case of shortening nearly 50% of the time, and it reduce the FNR, so our method is more stable.

Table 4. Comparison of stability of feature selection methods

Method	Number of features	Detection rate	Accuracy	FNR	FAR	Modeling time
Literature [5]	13	99.60	99.61	0.5	0.19	8.45
Literature [6]	17	98.95	99.08	1.04	0.22	16.22
Literature [10]	7	99.51	99.52	0.45	0.27	9.82
All features	41	99.75	99.76	0.27	0.03	17.5
Our method	19	99.78	99.77	0.2	0.1	10.1

5   Conclusion

Feature selection can effectively reduce the data dimension and improve the efficiencies of classifiers. However, the detection rates between categories may have great difference in a dataset. In this paper, a two-level feature selection method based on mRMR and information gain is proposed for LDRA in intrusion detection. The method uses mRMR to filter irrelevant features, reduces the data dimension, and improves some classes detection rates by information gain calculation, and finally combine these features together. Finally, the validity and expansibility of the method are proved.

References

1. Li, X., Yao, Y.: Master and use Snort tools for intrusion detection. Comput. Appl. Softw. **23**(3), 123–124 (2006)
2. Zhang, Y., Yang, A., Xiong, C., et al.: Feature selection using data envelopment analysis. Knowl. Based Syst. **64**, 70–80 (2014)
3. Peng, H., Long, F., Ding, C.: Feature selection based on mutual information: criteria of max-dependency, max-relevance, and min-redundancy. IEEE Trans. Pattern Anal. Mach. Intell. **27**(8), 1226–1238 (2005)
4. Aggarwal, P., Sharma, S.K.: Analysis of KDD dataset attributes - class wise for intrusion detection. Procedia Comput. Sci. **57**, 842–851 (2015)
5. Wu, X., Peng, X., Yang, Y.: Two-level feature selection method based on SVM for intrusion detection. J. Commun. **36**(4), 19–26 (2015)
6. Cui, W., Meng, X., Li, J.: Feature selection based on RS-PSO-SVM. Microelectron. Comput. **1**(3), 120–123 (2015)
7. Tang, C., Liu, P., Tang, S.: Anomaly intrusion behavior detection based on fuzzy clustering and features selection. J. Comput. Res. Dev. **52**(3), 718–728 (2015)
8. Huang, J., Chen, G., Ling, X.: Intrusion detection based on principal component analysis. J. China Jiliang Univ. **18**(3), 221–224 (2007)
9. Jia, F., Yan, Y., Zhang, J.: K-means based feature reduction for network anomaly detection. J. Tsinghua Univ. (Sci. Technol.) **58**(2), 137–142 (2018)
10. Mao, L., Yao, S., Hu, C.: A new hybrid attribute selection method and its application in intrusion detection. Trans. Beijing Inst. Technol. **28**(3), 218–221 (2008)
11. Feng, H., Li, M., Hou, X.: Study of network intrusion detection method based on SMOTE and GBDT. Appl. Res. Comput. **34**(12), 3745–3748 (2017)
12. Bolón-Canedo, V., Sanchez-Marono, N., Alonso-Betanzos, A.: Feature selection and classification in multiple class datasets: an application to KDD Cup 99 dataset. Expert Syst. Appl. **38**(5), 5947–5957 (2011)
13. Zhang, X., Cao, H., Jia, L.: Research of intrusion detection system dataset KDD CUP99. Comput. Eng. Des. **31**(22), 4809–4812 (2010)

A Novel Wireless Sensor Networks Malicious Node Detection Method

Hongyu Yang[✉], Xugao Zhang, and Fang Cheng

School of Computer Science and Technology,
Civil Aviation University of China, Tianjin 300300, China
hyyang@cauc.edu.cn

Abstract. This paper proposed a malicious node detection model based on reputation with enhanced low energy adaptive clustering hierarchy (Enhanced LEACH) routing protocol (MNDREL). MNDREL is a novel algorithm, which is aimed at identifying malicious nodes in the wireless sensor network (WSN) more efficiently. Cluster-head nodes are first selected based on the enhanced LEACH routing protocol. Other nodes in WSN then form different clusters by selecting corresponding cluster-head nodes and determine the packets delivery paths. Each node then adds its node number and reputation evaluation value to the packet before sending it to the sink node. A list of suspicious nodes is then formed by comparing the node numbers, obtained through parsing with the packets by the sink node, with the source node numbers. To determine the malicious nodes in the network, the ratio of the suspect value to the trusted value of each node is further calculated and compared with a predefined threshold. The simulation experiments show that the proposed algorithm in this paper is more efficient in detecting malicious nodes in WSN with lower false alarm rate than other state-of-the-art methods.

Keywords: Wireless sensor network · Network security · Malicious node · Reputation evaluation · Cluster-head node

1 Introduction

In recent years, Wireless Sensor Networks (WSN) [1, 2, 10] has been widely used in surveillance of military operations, medical secure, construction and other fields. Due to the special working environment, WSN is vulnerable to threats as the internal nodes of it may be controlled as malicious nodes. Therefore, the detection of the malicious nodes in the Wireless Sensor Networks (WSN) has become a research hotspot.

This section addresses the existing related literatures on wireless sensor malicious node detection. Prathap et al. [3] have presented a scheme of Catching Packet Modifiers with Trust Support (CPMTS). In CPMTS scheme, the identity of the node and the reputation value of the parent node were added into the packet, which was encrypted and transferred to the base station, as a tag and the reputation value obtained by analyzing the information decrypted from the packet which was received by the base station was compared with the threshold to identify the malicious node. Though the scheme improved the detection rate of malicious nodes to an extent, the consumption of

J. Li et al. (Eds.): SPNCE 2019, LNICST 284, pp. 697–706, 2019.
https://doi.org/10.1007/978-3-030-21373-2_59

the node energy was too excessive during data transmission. Althunibat et al. [4] have proposed an algorithm for detecting the malicious nodes in wireless sensor networks regardless of the type and the number of the nodes. To identify malicious nodes in networks, the algorithm used the real report of the node to master the intelligent behavior of malicious nodes. With the high complexity of the algorithm, the detection effect is unsatisfactory when there are more malicious nodes. Cui et al. [5] have presented a detection method based on reputation with a voting mechanism for wireless networks. The method gave suspect voting on neighbor nodes by analyzing the behavior of neighbour nodes forwarding packets and the malicious node was judged according to the suspect value. However, when the bad mouthing attack frequently comes to the same normal node, the method will fail.

Though research into malicious nodes detection has achieved some results, the efficiency of above methods is still unsatisfactory. Further research needs to be carried on. Thus, the major contribution of our work will be:

- We proposed a Malicious Node Detection algorithm based on Reputation with Enhanced LEACH [6], MNDREL. To improve the detection efficiency, the model will combine the Enhanced LEACH routing protocol with a reputation evaluation mechanism and identify the malicious nodes in WSN effectively.
- We compared the efficiency of MNDREL, FMATM and HRTM methods through a series of simulation experiments and demonstrated that the proposed method in this paper stands out with higher detection rate and lower false alarm rate.

The remainder of the paper is organized as follows. Section 2 discusses the related work on malicious node detection. Section 3 shows the whole structure of the MNDREL model. In Sects. 4, 5 and 6, the sub-modules, which are the cluster construction module, the packet forwarding module and the malicious node detection module, are illustrated separately. The proposed model is compared with other two methods through the experiment in Sect. 7. Finally, Sect. 8 summarizes the conclusion.

2   Related Work

2.1   Fuzzy Logic Based Multi-attribute Trust Model

Because of the uncertainty of the decision taken according to some specific behavior of a node, a fuzzy logic based multi-attribute trust model (FMATM) [9] was proposed to improve the trust based security model. The final trust value of a node is calculated with fuzzy computational theory based on four trust metrics: message success rate (MSR), elapsed time at node (ETN), correctness (CS) and fairness (FS). The final trust value is classified as low (l), medium (m) and high (h). According to the simulation results, the FMATM model is more efficient in detecting malicious nodes than the Hierarchical Trust Management Protocol (HTMP).

2.2 High-Reliability Trust Evaluation Model

Gong et al. proposed a high-reliability trust evaluation model (HRTM) [1] for secure routing to refine the trust evaluation result of a node and improve the related routing trust evaluation model. The HRTM evaluated the trust of routing nodes according to the inner states of a node and the outside interaction behaviors between nodes. With high detection efficiency and fast responding, the HRTM was able to defense internal and external attacks on a router.

The above two methods are relatively efficient in identifying the behavior of a node, however, the information of a node considered is not enough, so we utilize the FMATM and the HRTM to detect malicious nodes in WSN and compare the simulation results with the model proposed in this paper. Details of the comparison are discussed in Sect. 7.

3 Model Structure Design

The MNDREL model consists of a Clusters Construction (CC) module, a Packets Forwarding (PF) module, and a Malicious Nodes Decision (MND) module, which contains two sub-modules, the packet analysis sub-module and the integrated decision sub-module (as shown in Fig. 1).

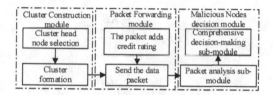

Fig. 1. MNDREL model structure

Firstly, the CC module determines the Cluster-Head node (CH) and divides the network into clusters to form a transmission path of packets; Secondly, the PF module transmits the packet containing the reputation value of the parent node evaluated by the current node to the Sink Node (SN); Finally, the MND module analyses the reputation value in the packet to determine the malicious node.

In the MNDREL model, the detection steps for the malicious nodes of the network are designed as follows:

Step 1. According to the remaining capacity of the node, the distance to the sink point, the signal strength and other conditions, a number of cluster heads from the network nodes are selected;

Step 2. The selection results of the cluster-head are broadcast by each cluster-head to notify the remaining nodes. With the distance of each node to each cluster-head calculated separately, one round of clustering is completed after the nodes join the cluster with the minimum distance;

Step 3. In way of sharing the key with the sink node, each node adds the reputation evaluation value of its parent node to the data packet and encrypts the data information;

Step 4. The packet is transmitted from the cluster nodes to the cluster-head by one or several hops, thus forwarded to the sink node by the cluster-head.

Step 5. After the sink point receives the data packet, the data packet analysis sub-module of the MND module will extract parameters such as the node number and the reputation value of the parent node in the packet. The suspicious node list is constructed by comparing the node number and the source node number and the reputation value from the packet and the reputation value calculated by other nodes are combined as the input of the integrated decision sub-module;

Step 6. The reputation value of various nodes is calculated by the integrated decision sub-module and it is compared with the threshold to determine whether there are malicious nodes in the network.

4   Cluster Construction Module

4.1   Cluster Head Node Selection

The approach of cluster-head selection is defined as follows:

$$RB_{avg} = \frac{\sum_{i=1}^{n} RB_i}{n} \tag{1}$$

$$DB_{avg} = \frac{\sum_{i=1}^{n} DB_i}{n} \tag{2}$$

$$P_i = w \times \frac{RB_i}{RB_{avg}} \times \frac{DB_{avg}}{DB_i} \tag{3}$$

where RB_{avg} represents the remaining power of all nodes, DB_{avg} represents the average distance of each node and the sink node in WSN, RB_i denotes the current remaining power of node i, DB_i represents the distance of node i and the sink node, n represents the number of live nodes at present time, P_i represents the probability that node i becomes a cluster-head.

Formula (3) satisfies the condition $(RB_i/RB_{avg}) > 1$, $(DB_{avg}/DB_i) > 1$ and $SB_i > SB_{Th}$. SB_i is the quantized value of the signal strength of node i; SB_{Th} is the critical value of the signal strength, which is assigned as the value of the weakest intensity of signal strength of the nodes that the sink node could sense. w is a fixed constant greater than 1.

4.2   Clustering Process

The clustering process is as follows:

Step 1. The cluster-head node notifies other nodes of Head_Msg;

Step 2. After receiving the Head_Msg, the non-cluster-head node chooses the cluster in which it expects to join. According to the distance from different cluster-head and the received signal strength of a cluster-head, the non-cluster-head node sends the Join_Clu_Msg to the cluster-head. The Join_Clu_Msg includes the number of the node that sends the application and the number of the specified cluster-head number.

Step 3. Each cluster-head summarizes the Join_Clu_Msg and determines the nodes that can join the corresponding cluster based on the maximum transceiver capacity of the cluster-head, thus forming different clusters of WSN;

Step 4. The packet is transmitted from the cluster nodes to the cluster-head by one or several hops, thus forwarded to the sink node by the cluster-head, thereby determining the routing path of the packet in the network.

5   Packet Forwarding Module

5.1   Packet Delivery

With the division of clusters in WSN finished, the sink node sets the time slice length of the packet transmission and notifies other nodes in the network and the nodes in each cluster forward the packet to the cluster-head within the specified time slice.

The process of packet transmission is shown in Fig. 2. When the source node P sends data, P creates the packet $m_1 = <P_{id}, M_{id}, T_Q, D>$, and the packet m'_1 is then generated by encrypting m_1 using the key P_{key} shared between the packet and the cluster-head node CH_1. Where P_{id} is the number of node P, M_{id} is the number of packet m_1, T_Q is the reputation value evaluated by node P for its parent node Q and D is the data get by source node P.

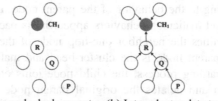

(a) Cluster node deployment   (b) Intra-cluster data transfer

Fig. 2. Process of packet transmission

Node Q generates packet m_2 by adding the node number, the packet number and the reputation evaluation value of the parent node R into packet m'_1 and it generates packet m'_2 by encrypting m_2 with the shared Q_{key} of node Q and CH_1. Following the similar process, CH_1 finally gets the packet, encrypts it and sends it to the sink node within the specified time slice.

5.2   Reputation Evaluation

The process of reputation evaluation is designed as follows:

Step 1. Each node records the number of the parent node to which it forwards the packet. The sink point establishes a tree topology including all parent-child node relationships according to the information collected from each node and decrypts the data packet based on the topology to detect the malicious node in the network;
Step 2. After the network node is deployed, each node adds a reputation evaluation table to the parent node in the data packet, and the reputation evaluation value for the parent node calculated by the child node includes the credibility evaluation value and the suspicion evaluation value (as shown in Table 1), the credibility evaluation value and the suspicion evaluation value are initialized to 0. k represents the node number in the network, $k = 1, 2, ..., n$; n represents the number of nodes participating in the packet transmission;

Table 1. Parent node reputation evaluation table

Parent node number	k
Credible evaluation value	0 or 1
Suspect evaluation value	0 or 1

Step 3. After the parent node receives the packet from the child, the behavior of the packet forwarding by the parent node within the pre-set time slice will determine the credibility evaluation value and the suspicion evaluation value of the parent node. If malicious behaviors such as the packet dropping, packet modification, packet misrouting or packet delay appear in the parent node, the child node sets the suspicion evaluation value to 1 and the credibility evaluation value to 0. Conversely, the credibility evaluation value is set to 1 and the suspicion evaluation value is set to 0;
Step 4. After a round of packet delivery, the child node can perform corresponding operations according to the behavior of the parent node: If the parent node is not the cluster-head and malicious behaviors appear in its packet forwarding process, the child node notifies the neighbor one-hop node of the malicious behavior by broadcast. If the parent node is the cluster-head and malicious behaviors appear in its packet forwarding process, the child node joins other clusters in the next round of selection and deletes the original parent node number from the node number list.

6   Malicious Node Decision Module

The malicious node decision module is combined of two parts: the packet analysis sub-module and the integrated decision sub-module.

6.1   Packet Analysis Sub-module

When packet m is passed to the sink point, the analyzing step for m is designed as follows (the packet analysis process is shown in Fig. 3):

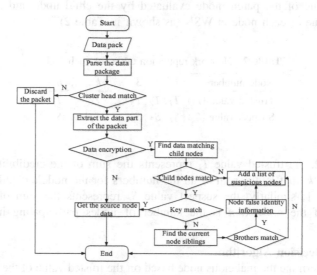

Fig. 3. Packet analysis flowchart

Step 1. The sink point encrypts packet m on the basis of the key shared with the cluster-head and produces packet m';

Step 2. Parse packet m' and remove the node number, packet number and the reputation evaluation value of the cluster-head, if other data in the packet is unencrypted, then m' is from the source node;

Step 3. If the data of packet m' is partly encrypted, then backtrack the upstream node according to the routing path of packet m', and decrypt the data packet through the upper layer shared key until the data of the source node is obtained;

Step 4. If the information of all the child nodes of a parent node does not match the packet information, illustrating that malicious packet modification appears in the parent node or any corresponding child node, then the parent node and all the child nodes are added to the suspicious node list;

Step 5. If the node number in the packet does not match the decryption key number in the decryption process, check the sibling node of the current node to see if there is a matching one and determine whether the identity of the sibling node is impersonated by the current node. If the impersonation exits, add the current node to the suspicious node list.

6.2 Integrated Decision Sub-module

Node Reputation Value

When the data packet has been delivered, the sink point parses the packet, gets the reputation value of the parent node evaluated by the child node and generates the reputation value of each node in WSN (as shown in Table 2).

Table 2. Network reputation table for each node

Node number	1	2	3	...	k	...	n
Trusted value (T_k)	T_1	T_2	T_3	...	T_k	...	T_n
Suspect value (S_k)	S_1	S_2	S_3	...	S_k	...	S_n

In Table 2, the trusted value T_k represents the sum of the credibility evaluation value of node k, that is, the sum of all the numbers for the node's credibility evaluation value of 1; similarly, the suspect value S_k represents the sum of the suspect evaluations of the node k; n is the number of nodes participating in the packet transfer.

Reputation Decision Algorithm

In order to determine the malicious node based on the trusted value of the node and the behavior of the node in the process of data packet transmission, this paper proposes a reputation decision algorithm. The algorithm determines the malicious node by analyzing the suspect value and the trusted value of each node and comparison with the detection threshold.

According to the literature [4], the detection rate is higher and the false alarm rate is lower with the detection threshold set as 1.2. Therefore, the detection threshold R_{Th} is set to 1.2 in this paper. Calculate the ratio R_k (k is the node number, $k = 1, 2, ..., n$) of suspect value to trusted values for all nodes:

$R_k \geq R_{Th}$, if node k is in the suspicious node list, determine k as a malicious node; if node k is not in the suspicious node list and no impersonation of the identity of other nodes appears, node k will be added to the suspicious node list, waiting for the next round of detection.

$R_k < R_{Th}$, if node k is in the suspicious node list, retain it and wait for the next round of detection; if node k is not in the suspicious node list and no impersonation of the identity of other nodes appears, then k is determined as a normal node.

In the above process: If node k is determined to be malicious, the sink node will broadcast its number and the nodes with a forwarding relationship with it will delete its number from the parent node list. If node k is added into the suspicious node list after a round of detection, however, it satisfies the relation of $R_k < R_{Th}$ in several other rounds of detection, then move it out of the suspicious node list and use it as a normal node in packet delivery activity.

7 Experiment and Analysis

The experiment was conducted on the OPNET (opnet-14.5) platform. The MAC layer adopts the 802.11 wireless communication protocol, and the network layer adopts the Enhanced LEACH routing protocol. The number of nodes in the network simulation experiment is 50, 100, …, 400, and the number of malicious nodes generated randomly is 5, 10, …, 40. The source node generates a data packet of 4000B every 100 ms to be transmitted to the cluster-head through the parent node, and then sent to the sink node by the cluster-head. Based on the experimental conclusions of [7] and [8], the network simulation time of this experiment is set to 50 s, and the time slice length of data packet transmission is set to t = 2 s. After the OPNET sends the packet based on the Enhanced LEACH routing protocol, the experimental data is processed through MATLAB programming by which the algorithm and the module function mentioned above are realized.

In the same environment, we compared efficacy of the MNDREL detection model, the Fuzzy logic based Multi-Attribute Trust Model (FMATM) [9] and the High-reliability Trust evaluation Model (HRTM) [1]. The number of nodes is set to 50, 100, …, 400, and the number of malicious nodes generated randomly is set to 5, 10, …, 40. The detection rate and the false alarm rate are shown separately in Fig. 4.

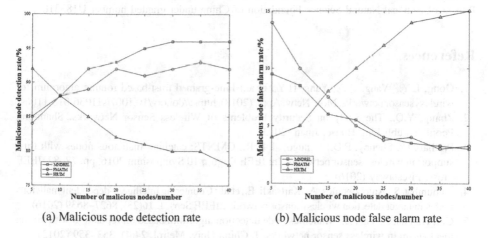

(a) Malicious node detection rate   (b) Malicious node false alarm rate

Fig. 4. Detection comparison of MNDREL, FMATM and HRTM

It can be seen from Fig. 4(a) and (b) that with the increase of the number of malicious nodes, the detection rate of malicious nodes in HRTM method decreases, the false alarm rate increases while the detection rate of MNDREL model and FMATM model increases and the false alarm rate decreases. Compared with FMATM, the detection rate and the false alarm rate of the MNDREL model is more stable.

The experimental results show that the MNDREL model can maintain a high detection rate and a low false alarm rate when the number of malicious nodes in the network changes. The reason is that the MNDREL model is based on the Enhanced LEACH routing protocol. With the relatively fixed routing path of the packet, the malicious node in the network is easier to be tracked and located, thus leading to high detection efficiency. In addition, the MNDREL model judges the suspicious node generated during the process of packet transmission and with the increasing of nodes and packets, the information extracted from the reputation evaluation is more, so the malicious node is easier to be found, thus leading to gradual rising of the detection rate and the gradual descending of the false alarm rate.

8   Conclusions

To improve the effect of malicious nodes detection, we proposed a novel algorithm, MNDREL. The malicious nodes can be effectively identified according to the suspect value and the trusted value evaluated by MNDREL. Simulation experiments proved that the MNDREL model outperformed in detecting malicious nodes in WSN with lower false alarm rate than FMATM and HRTM. However, the real time performance of the MNDREL model has to be improved. By adding time stamps into the model, we will monitor the dynamic changing situation of malicious nodes in WSN, moreover, the distribution of malicious nodes within a certain time can be predicted.

Acknowledgement. This research was funded by the Civil Aviation Joint Research Fund Project of National Natural Science Foundation of China under granted number U1833107.

References

1. Gong, L.Y., Wang, C.D., Yang, H.Y., et al.: Fine-grained trust-based routing algorithm for wireless sensor networks. Mob. Netw. Appl. (2018). https://doi.org/10.1007/s11036-018-1106-z
2. Zhang, Y.Q.: The Study on Security Problems of Wireless Sensor Networks. Shandong People's Publishing House, Jinan (2013)
3. Prathap, U., Shenoy, P.D., Venugopal, K.R.: CMNTS: catching malicious nodes with trust support in wireless sensor networks. In: IEEE Region 10 Symposium 2016, pp. 77–82. IEEE Press, Piscataway (2016)
4. Althunibat, S., Antonopoulos, A., Kartsakli, E., et al.: Countering intelligent-dependent malicious nodes in target detection wireless sensor networks. IEEE Sens. J. **16**(23), 8627–8639 (2016)
5. Cui, H., Pan, J., Yan, D.: Malicious node detection algorithm based on reputation with voting mechanism in wireless sensor networks. J. China Univ. Metrol. **24**(4), 353–359 (2013)
6. Das, S., Das, A.: An algorithm to detect malicious nodes in wireless sensor network using enhanced LEACH protocol. In: International Conference on Advances in Computer Engineering and Applications 2015, pp. 875–881. IEEE Press, Piscataway (2015)
7. Liu, H.B., Cui, J.M., Dai, H.J.: Multivariate classification-based malicious detection for wireless sensor network. Chin. J. Sens. Actuators **24**(5), 771–777 (2011)
8. Hui, L.L., Pan, J.L., Cui, H.: A reputation-based method for detecting malicious nodes in WSNs. J. China Univ. Metrol. **23**(1), 41–47 (2012)
9. Prabha, V.R., Latha, P.: Fuzzy trust protocol for malicious node detection in wireless sensor networks. Wirel. Pers. Commun. **94**(4), 1–11 (2016)
10. Belhajem, I., Maissa, Y.B., Tamtaoui, A.: Improving vehicle localization in a smart city with low cost sensor networks and support vector machines. Mob. Netw. Appl. **23**(4), 854–863 (2018)

Grid Partition and Agglomeration for Bidirectional Hierarchical Clustering

Lei Wu[1], Hechang Chen[1,2], Xiangchun Yu[1], Sun Chao[1],
Zhezhou Yu[1(✉)], and RuiTing Dou[1]

[1] College of Computer Science and Technology, Jilin University,
Changchun, China
yuzz@jlu.edu.cn
[2] Key Laboratory of Symbolic Computation and Knowledge Engineering,
Ministry of Education, Changchun, China

Abstract. Clustering is an important data processing tool, which can be used to reveal the distribution structure of unfamiliar domain data, or as preprocess methods to magnify data object to accelerate subsequent processing or simplify models. However, the distribution of many real-world data in feature space is very complex or uneven. Besides, the similarity/distance is not easy to be properly defined in feature space with different dimensional quantity. Therefore, many existing clustering algorithms are not stable in real datasets, and better performance of different datasets relies on artificial special design, such as scale normalization. In this paper, we propose a bidirectional hierarchical clustering (BHC) algorithm with two phases. In the first phase (Top-down), based on the probability density function of data in different dimensions, the feature space is divided into over-segmented grids to adapt to the complex distribution of data. In the second phase (Bottom-up), based on statistical information, a robust distance instead of geometrical distance is defined to agglomerate the grids into a dendrogram. Compared with the individual data points, grids created in the first phase can carry more statistical information, and the magnified processing objects can accelerate the clustering process. The second phase enhances the algorithm's ability by the ability of recognize arbitrary shape data clusters. The effectiveness of BHC is compared with 20 popular or recent clustering algorithms on 8 artificial datasets and 6 real-world datasets. And the results show that our algorithm can achieve good results on most datasets. In particular, BHC surpasses all the comparison algorithms involved in the experiment on all real-world datasets. In addition, in order to test the efficiency of the algorithm, we design an experiment which can test the influence of dimension and data size on the operation time.

Keywords: Hierarchical clustering · Grid-based clustering · Top-down · Bottom-up

J. Li et al. (Eds.): SPNCE 2019, LNICST 284, pp. 707–722, 2019.
https://doi.org/10.1007/978-3-030-21373-2_60

1 Introduction

As an unsupervised learning tool, without additional label information, clustering has a wide range of applications, such as biological gene classification [1–3], chemical molecular structure [4, 5], astrophysics [6–8] and business market analysis [9]. It can be used to demonstrate the inherent structure of spatial distribution of data, helping people explore unfamiliar areas from the perspective of data distribution. In addition, in the computer field, clustering technology is often used as a preprocessing method to reduce the complexity of subsequent processing or models [10]. Since a variety of data with different types and sizes are constantly generated, clustering algorithm has always been a hot research topic. At present, the research of clustering algorithm mainly focuses on three aspects: overcoming the effects of high-dimensional data and big data on experimental effect and efficiency [11, 12], processing complex data clusters [13–16] and reducing the dependence of algorithms on user-specified parameters [17, 18].

However, most of the above studies are lopsided without an integrated manner, which may lead to two problems: (1) Clustering algorithms using global partition strategy cannot process data with complex and uneven distribution. For example, the DBSCAN [19] algorithm can handle clusters of arbitrary shapes. But it cannot perform well when encountering data with uneven distribution. (2) Considering different dimensional quantity, it is very difficult to define a reasonable point-to-point distance, especially in high-dimensional data. For example, DPC [13] algorithm and its improved algorithms [14–16], which need to calculate the distance between points, are not robust on real-world datasets.

In this paper, we propose a bidirectional hierarchical clustering algorithm called BHC. As the point-to-point distance definition is unreliable and the data distribution is complex and uneven, we can divide the data into over-segmented subsets, where data points in a subset have the same spatial distribution and statistical information. That is the basic idea of BHC. Leveraging the statistical information of subsets to calculate robust distance between subsets, those over-segmented subsets can be re-agglomerated into a dendrogram. Accordingly, our bidirectional clustering algorithm consists of two opposite-directional phases: Top-down and Bottom-up. In the first phase, based on OptiGrid [20] algorithm, a coarse grid partition is performed recursively in dividing the feature space into non-interfering grids. Even if the data distribution is uneven or complex, the points in a grid have the same distribution characteristics. In the second phase, through the statistical information shared by the data points in the grid, a grid-to-grid distance is defined. And grids are agglomerated successively according to the order of the number of points in grids. Although the grids in the first stage are simple rectangles, the algorithm can handle clusters of arbitrary shapes through the second phase. The benefit of Top-down process is that a robust distance can be defined regardless of data size, dimension and distribution. In addition, statistical information in grids can be applied to identify outliers and noise. The major contributions of this paper are summarized as follows:

1. We proposed a spatial grid partition method based on data distribution, where points in same grids have the same distribution characteristics. In this method, performing coarse grid partition recursively results in over-segmented grids while the validity of segmentation is guaranteed. In addition, feature compositor is applied to select features that have more contributions to the formation of a particular cluster.

2. We defined a robust distance between grids that can be used to agglomerate the divided grids into dendrogram. This distance is calculated from the statistical information of the data points in the grid instead of the geometric information, thus avoiding the effects of high dimensional quantity.

3. We benchmark BHC with 20 popular or recent clustering algorithms on 8 artificial datasets and 6 real-world datasets, and our algorithm achieves the best result far superior to the comparison algorithms on all real-world datasets, which proves the stability and superiority of our algorithm in dealing with practical problems. What' more, our algorithm is less affected by the data size and data dimension in the efficiency experiment. An example of BHC flow is shown in Fig. 1.

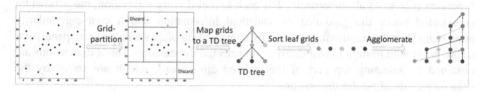

Fig. 1. An example of BHC flow

2 Methodology

In this section, we will introduce BHC with two component phases which are in opposite directions: Top-down and Bottom up. These two phases are respectively described in detail in Sects. 2.1 and 2.2.

2.1 Top-Down for Grid Partition

Partitioning the feature space into grids is a feasible strategy for big data, as magnified processing objects can accelerate the clustering process. Additionally, grids can carry more statistical information than individual data points. Therefore, this strategy is robust against outliers, since grids containing outliers are highlighted as their data points are relatively less. Besides, in BHC, the statistical information is used to define a robust distance between grids.

In this process, the feature space is partitioned recursively by the Top-down approach into multilevel coarse-grained grids to form a Top-Down (TD) tree structure, (see Fig. 2). However, axes-parallel partitions are not suitable for high-dimensional data due to data sparseness problem. Namely, the number of data points in each grid is so few that it may lose statistical significance. Hence, we adopt as wide a bandwidth as possible in one-dimensional Gaussian kernel estimation to promise a robust grid partition. And each partitioning is performed in some particular dimensions, which are selected from all dimensions according to their contribution of individual dimensions to the formation of a particular region or grid. Through recursive partitioning, an over-segmented grid set is created, while the validity of segmentation is guaranteed.

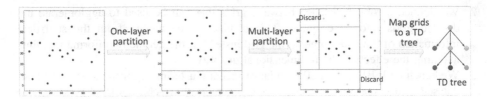

Fig. 2. An example of Top-down flow

Specifically, for a partition processing, based on OptiGrid [20] algorithm, the kernel density function is applied in the training set to calculate the probability density functions (PDFs) of all dimensions. For each kernel density estimation, the bandwidth is selected under the guidance of statistical information and a coarse-granularity approach. Then the partitioning is done by some cutting planes which are perpendicular to the point with minimal point densities in selected dimensions. These dimensions are obtained by selecting top part of the ordered dimensions, which are sorted by the difficulty of dividing the dimensions.

One-Layer Coarse-Grained Partitioning

OptiGrid provides a powerful framework for grid-partitioning by optimal cutting planes which are located at the minimal density points of PDFs in the corresponding contracting projection. In BHC, contracting projections are specifically referred to as axes projection.

For a dataset $D = \{X_1, X_2, ..., X_n\}$ with n d-dimensional points and $X_k = \{x_{k,1}, x_{k,2}, ..., x_{k,d}\}$, the PDF of D in the i-th dimension can be approximated by the one-dimensional Gaussian kernel $g(x_{k,i}, \lambda_i)$ respect to the bandwidth λ_i:

$$f_i(D, \lambda_i) = \frac{1}{n} \sum_{k=1}^{n} g\left(x_{k,i}, \lambda_i\right) = \frac{1}{\sqrt{2\pi} n \lambda_i} \sum_{k=1}^{n} \exp\left(\frac{(x - x_{k,i})^2}{2\lambda_i^2}\right) \tag{1}$$

When data points spread sparsely in a dimension, a number of spikes (maxima) would appear in the PDF (see the top two graphs in Fig. 4). Obviously, such PDFs is not what we want as too many minimal density points for cutting planes. In DENCLUE [21] and OptiGrid, a threshold is defined to cut the impact of spikes, where the spikes with a density below the threshold would not be taken into account.

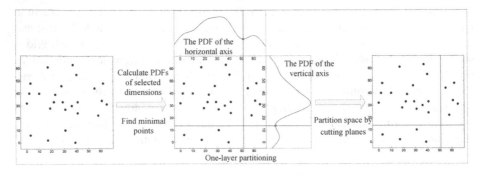

Fig. 3. One-layer partitioning processing

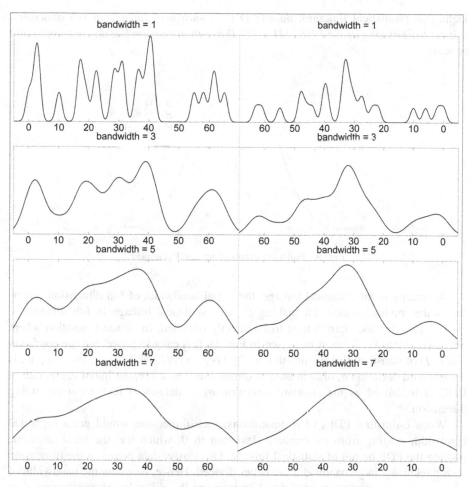

Fig. 4. PDFs with different bandwidth of two dimension of data points in Fig. 3

As shown in Fig. 4, with the increase of the bandwidth, the curve of the PDF becomes smooth and a number of useless spikes disappear. Hence, a larger value of bandwidth can filter the impact of sparse data. In this method, we attempt to use coarse-grained bandwidth to alleviate the existence of spikes. When estimating PDF, the value of the bandwidth decreased from one initial bandwidth, until more than one peak appears in the PDF. Determining cutting plane by fewer density peaks, the grids are more robust since fewer bad partitions would be done. As shown in Fig. 3, a one-layer partitioning is performed to divide a grid into four sub-grids by two cutting planes. Especially, over-segmentation is guaranteed by performing partitioning recursively.

A key problem in our method is the preset of the initial bandwidth. When setting a large value, a lot of computation is invalid; when setting a small value, the bandwidth cannot filter the impact of sparseness. To determine a proper initial bandwidth, we introduce a definition: statistical linkage.

Definition (**statistical linkage**): *dataset D is of statistical linkage in i-th dimension respect to λ_i as long as the PDF $f_i(D, \lambda_i)$ of D in i-th dimension has one maximal point at most.*

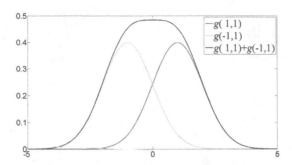

Fig. 5. Function graph of an ideal situation

According to the statistical linkage, the initial bandwidth of i-th dimension can be set as the minimal bandwidth making D is of statistical linkage in i-th dimension. However, such bandwidth is hard to be directly obtained. In an ideal situation where only two points X_1, X_2 exist in D (see in Fig. 5), it is easy to prove that the condition makes D of statistical-linkage in i-th is $\lambda_i \geq (x_{2,i} - x_{1,i})/2$, while $\lambda_i \geq (x_{2,i} - x_{1,i})/2$ is the standard deviation σ_i of D in the i-th dimension. Therefore, the initial bandwidth in BHC is initialized as the standard deviation σ_i of dataset D in the corresponding dimension.

When estimating PDFs of d dimensions, each dimension would get a separated bandwidth ranging from its standard deviation to 0, which has the maximal value making the PDF be not of statistical linkage. Obviously, data points in the dimension with a relatively large bandwidth are better divided. Hence, based on the bandwidth of a dimension, a variate can be defined to measure the difficulty of partitioning data points in this dimension.

Definition (**partitioning degree**): *A partitioning degree for the i-th dimension of the dataset D is defined as follows:*

$$degree_i^D = \arg\max H(d) \quad 0 < d \leq M \tag{2}$$

$$H(d) = \begin{cases} d, & \text{if } f_i\left(D, \frac{d}{M}\sigma_i\right) \text{has two or more maxima} \\ 0, & \text{else} \end{cases} \tag{3}$$

where an interval $[0, \sigma_i]$ is divided into M segments and the bandwidth of the i-th dimension λ_i is assigned to $\sigma_i \, degree_i/M$. Figure 6 shows the calculation order of partitioning degree.

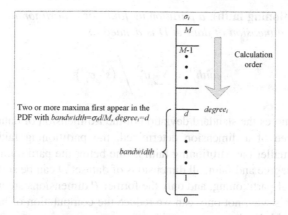

Fig. 6. Calculation order of partitioning degree.

As for how to find the minima in PDFs, a stride detection approach is applied in our method, where the stride is set as half of the bandwidth (see Fig. 7). For two adjacent detection points x_k, x_{k+1}, if the first derivative of point x_{k+1} is less than or equal to 0 while the first derivative of x_k is bigger than 0, a minimum between x_k and x_{k+1} is approximated as follows:

$$x_{min} = \frac{x_{k+1} + x_k}{2} + \frac{\lambda^2}{x_{k+1} + x_k} \cdot \ln\left(\frac{y_{k+1}}{y_k}\right) \tag{4}$$

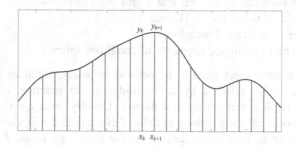

Fig. 7. Minima detection through stride detection approach

Dimension Sorting

When a coarse-grained partitioning is done in dataset D, each dimension gets a partitioning degree, which can be used to measure the contribution of individual dimensions to the formation of a particular sub-grid. According to the partitioning degree, part of dimensions is selected to reduce the impact of high dimensions. Since the partitioning degree is an integer within a certain range $(0, M]$, there may be a number of equal degrees over dimensions, which results in a confusion of selecting dimensions. Hence, an extra variate is defined as supplementary.

Definition (**partitioning faith**): *a partitioning faith for a partitioning set {D_1, D_2, ..., D_s} over the i-th dimension of dataset D is defined as:*

$$faith_i^D = \sum_j^s \sigma_i^{D_j} \bigg/ \left(s \cdot \sigma_i^D\right) \tag{5}$$

Where σ_i^D denotes the standard deviation of the i-dimension of dataset D. After the partitioning degree of a dimension determined, the partitioning faith is confirmed. Obviously, the smaller the partitioning faith is, the better the partitioning performs. By the partitioning degree and faith, all dimensions of dataset D can be sorted according to the performance of partitioning, and only the former P dimensions are involved in grid-partitioning. In this way, not only can we reduce the computation of high dimensional data, but also avoid the data sparse problem.

Recursive Partitioning

One-layer partitioning processing is not enough to separate points belonging to different data clusters into different grids. Therefore, we need to partition data space recursively to guarantee data points in a grid have similar distribution characteristics, while different dimensions would be selected in each partition. Recursively partitioning stops for a sub-grid if the data points in this grid are below a threshold *max_data* or the depth of this node in TD tree is above a threshold *L*. A sub-grid is discarded if the data points in this grid are below a threshold *min_data* to alleviate the effect from outliers and noise. Hence, a total of five parameters need to be confirmed by the user:

- *max_data*: the maximal data points that a grid can contains
- *min_data*: the minimal data points that a grid need contains
- *L*: the threshold of the depth of TD tree
- *P*: the number of selected dimensions
- *M*: the number of partitioned segments of candidate interval

Although five parameters need to be defined by users, all those parameters are integers and are easily selected by cross-validation. In practice, the selection of *min_data* and *max_data* rely on the test dataset. Usually, *max_data* is less than the minimal number of data points belong to defined clusters and *min_data* is determined by the proportion of outliers in the dataset. As for parameter L and P, if we select a relatively large P and a small L can guarantee the precision of grid-partitioning, and algorithm runs faster; if we select a relatively small P and a large L can guarantee the precision, and algorithm is more robust. Therefore, we need to make a tradeoff between the running speed and the robustness of the algorithm when we preset L and P. The selection of M is usually unwarranted, while a range [5, 30] can be taken as a reference.

2.2   Bottom-Up for Grid Agglomeration

In this process, the leaf nodes in the TD tree created in the Top-down phase are agglomerated successively by the Bottom-up approach to form a hierarchical structure. In many multilevel grid-based clustering algorithms such as STING [22], grids that belong to different parent grids cannot be merged directly, so that may result in error accumulation. In addition, the traditional 4/8-collection strategy is not suitable for coarse-grained and feature-selected grids in our algorithm. Hence, in BHC, a robust statistical-based distance of any two grids is proposed, so that any leaf grids can be merged. Besides, adopting the corresponding strategy in the DPC, the agglomerative sequence of grids is sorted according to the number of data points in the grids.

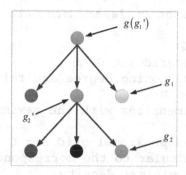

Fig. 8. An example of TD tree

For any two leaf grids g_1, g_2 in the TD tree (see in Fig. 8), g is the lowest common ancestor of g_1 and g_2, and the distance of g_1 and g_2 is defined as follows:

$$dis(g_1, g_2) = \sum_{i=1}^{d} \frac{degree_i^g}{faith_i^g} \cdot F_i(g_1, g_2) \tag{6}$$

where $F_i(g_1, g_2)$ is a discriminant function that determines if g_1 and g_2 are linked in the i-th dimension. The criterion of $F_i(g_1, g_2)$ in the i-th dimension is whether the distance between the centers μ_i^{g1}, μ_i^{g2} of g_1 and g_2 is greater than the sum of the bandwidth $\lambda_i^{g1'}$, $\lambda_i^{g2'}$ of their parent nodes of their parent $g1'$ and $g2'$ instead of g:

$$F_i(g_1, g_2) = \begin{cases} 1, & \text{if } \left| \mu_i^{g1} - \mu_i^{g2} \right| \geq \lambda_i^{g1'} + \lambda_i^{g2'} \\ 0, & \text{else} \end{cases} \tag{7}$$

In DPC, an attractive idea is of a novel definition of the nearest point: the nearest neighbor of a node is defined as a node with the nearest distance and a higher density concurrently. Besides, data points in DPC are agglomerated in ascending order of their local density, which provides a novel agglomerative chain. This agglomerative chain is more robust in the result than that of the traditional definition of the nearest neighbor chains [26], since more typical data centers are detected.

Based on DPC, in our method, the nearest grid of g_i is defined as a grid g_t with the nearest distance and more data points:

$$t = \underset{j:num(g_j) > num(g_i)}{\arg\min} \left(dis(g_j, g_i) \right) \tag{8}$$

where $num(g_j)$ denotes the number of points in grid g_j. In BHC, leaf grids are agglomerated in ascending order of the number of data points in grids. In other words, the smaller gird agglomerates with its nearest center first, since the effect of mis-agglomeration of smaller grids is more acceptable than that of larger grids. With the grid-partitioning and the agglomerative chain, we are now able to describe BHC generally.

Partitioning (dataset D, layer, min_data, max_data, L, P, M)

Output: grid set G;
1. Initialize the grid set $G \leftarrow \phi$;
2. Calculate partitioning degree and faith of all dimension of dataset D;
3. Determine P dimensions with the maximum degree and smaller faith;
4. Construct a P-dimensional grid set G' by cutting planes perpendicular to the corresponding dimension at the point with minimal density;
5. Map all data points $x \in D$ into G' and delete the grid with the number of data points less than min_data;
6. For each grid $g \in G'$ do
    i. If $num(g) > max\_data$ and layer$<L$ Then
        a. partitioning (g, layer+1, min_data, max_data, L, P, M);
    ii. Else
        a. insert g into G;

BHC (dataset D, min_data, max_data, L, P, M)
1. $G \leftarrow$ Partitioning (D, 0, min_data, max_data, L, P, M);
2. Foreach pair of grids g_1 and $g_2 \in G$ do
    i. Calculate the distance of g_1, g_2;
3. Ascending sort grids in G according to the number of data in grids: g_1, g_2, ... g_k;
4. For $i=1$ To $k-1$ do
    i. Find the nearest grid g_t of g_i according to (8);
    ii. Aggregate the two clusters that g_i and g_t belong;

3   Experiments

We designed three experiments to demonstrate the superiority of our proposed method. We first benchmark the algorithm on 8 artificial datasets. Then 6 real-world datasets from UCI datasets [23] are tested. At last, we test the efficiency of our method in datasets *Dim-sets* [25] with different sizes and dimensionalities. The concentrated introductions of above test datasets can be found in [24]. Each experiment is compared with several well-known clustering algorithms. Note that the results of unstable clustering algorithms whose clustering results are different with each clustering, including K-means [31], K-medoids [32], K-medians [33], are the averages of the results of repeated 50 times.

3.1 Experiment on Artificial Datasets

In this part, we benchmark the algorithm on 8 artificial datasets, and the results are presented in Fig. 9. The accuracies of our method and 20 well-known clustering algorithms for 8 artificial datasets are shown in Table 1. In Table 1, the corresponding database for each column are *aggregation, compound, pathbased, spiral, D31, R15, jain* and *flame*; the corresponding clustering algorithms for each row are Single [26], Complete [26], UPGMA [26], WPGMA [26], Ward [26], UPGMC [26], WPGMC [26], Rock [27], Chameleon [28], Cure [29], Birch [30], K-means [31], K-medians [33], K-medoids [32], DBSCAN [19], DPC [13], PERCH [11], DSets-DBSCAN [17], SNN-DPC [16], KNN-DPC [14], and our method BHC.

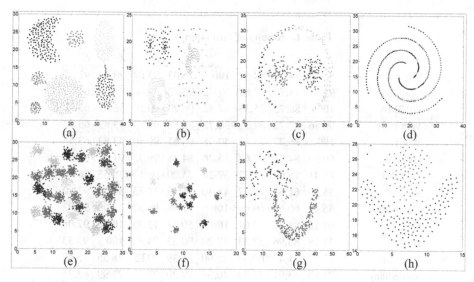

Fig. 9. Results of artificial datasets: (a) *aggregation*, (b) *compound*, (c) *pathbased*, (d) *spiral*, (e) *D31*, (f) *R15*, (g) *jain* and (h) *flame*

In the first column in Table 1 for dataset *aggregation* (see Fig. 9(*a*)) with 7 clusters of different shapes and varying size, UPGMA (100%), UPGMC (100%), KNN-DPC (99.23%) and our method (99.23%) can handle the dataset very well. Database *compound* (see Fig. 9(*b*)) contains 6 clusters of different shapes, sizes, and densities, where the lower-left ring-like cluster encircles another cluster, and the upper-right corner has two compounded clusters of different density. Due to its complex distribution structure, no algorithm can handle database *compound* well, and DSets-DBSCAN (93.98%), BHC (89.72%) perform best. Dataset *pathbased* (see Fig. 9(*c*)) and *spiral* (see Fig. 9

(*d*)) has non-convex clusters with large curvature, which are not what our method can deal with. Only SNN-DPC can cluster *pathbased* well and Single, Chameleon, Cure, DBSCAN, DPC and SNN-DPC perform well in dataset *spiral*. For dataset *D31* (see Fig. 9(*e*)) and *R15* (see Fig. 9(*f*)) with data points located with high overlap, our method successfully divides data points into correct clusters. Similar to *pathbased* and *spiral*, Dataset *jain* (see Fig. 9(g)) and *flame* (see Fig. 9(h)) also has non-convex clusters, while our method achieves considerable performance over those two datasets.

In Table 1, we can find that in artificial datasets with unified dimensions, DPC and its improved algorithms performed stable, which proves their ability to handle complex-shaped clusters. Due to the distortion caused by axes-parallel grid-partitioning, our algorithm cannot achieve best accurate results over test cases. This distortion is more likely to be an inherent defect of grid-partitioning, which can be released by increasing the depth of TD tree. However, a TD tree with a huge depth will reduce the number of data points in the leaf nodes to lose statistical significance, which may affect the precision of grid distance. Even though BHC is not the strongest algorithm when dealing with complex-shaped clusters, our algorithm achieves competitive results on all datasets except *spiral*.

Table 1. Results of artificial datasets

Method	A	C	P	S	D	R	J	F
Single	83.88	84.46	80.67	**100**	76.03	95.67	99.73	91.25
Complete	91.37	78.70	72.67	39.42	95.42	99.00	86.06	63.75
UPGMA	**100**	86.72	75.33	37.82	96.23	99.50	86.06	63.75
WPGMA	90.86	87.72	67.33	38.78	88.58	98.83	93.83	65.42
Ward	**100**	86.72	73.33	40.38	96.61	99.50	93.83	63.75
UPGMC	86.55	84.21	67.67	35.26	84.48	99.33	91.15	63.75
WPGMC	85.41	75.69	73.33	37.20	75.00	99.17	78.55	96.00
Rock	55.20	61.65	71.67	48.40	11.45	18.33	85.52	92.50
Chameleon	85.41	60.65	69.00	**100**	**97.68**	**99.67**	73.99	97.92
Cure	94.16	88.47	92.67	**100**	50.45	73.33	**100**	97.08
Birch	77.28	85.96	37.33	37.20	90.23	74.83	**100**	93.33
K-means	77.92	71.43	69.33	35.90	81.39	7332	78.55	75.42
K-medians	71.57	63.91	73.33	40.38	79.29	77.17	73.99	63.75
K-medoids	73.85	79.45	65.00	40.38	80.61	81.17	73.99	63.75
DBSCAN	95.18	81.45	68.67	**100**	77.97	97.33	92.49	96.67
DPC	89.72	88.22	78.00	**100**	78.10	99.33	95.17	98.33
Perch	75.29	66.04	69.03	44.70	84.61	95.65	67.86	67.04
DSets-DBSCAN	82.49	**93.98**	94.33	55.77	82.54	72.33	92.76	97.92
SNN-DPC	97.84	86.21	**97.67**	**100**	97.39	**99.67**	87.67	98.75
KNN-DPC	99.23	86.71	65.33	69.87	96.38	**99.67**	70.78	**100**
BHC	99.23	89.72	82.00	59.29	94.74	99.16	95.97	98.33

3.2 Experiment on Real-World Datasets

To illuminate the performance of our method on real-world problems, 6 real-world datasets from UCI datasets: *iris*, *wine*, *glass*, *breast cancer*, *yeast*, *thyroid*, are chosen to verify the effectiveness of BHC. The accuracy of our method and the compared algorithms on those datasets are shown in Table 2. It is obvious in Table 2 that our method is superior to all compared algorithms on all test datasets. Especially in dataset *wine* and *glass*, our algorithm achieved 97.19% and 51.75% clustering accuracy, while the second-best results of rest algorithms were 93.26% (Chameleon, Birch) and 58.88% (K-means) respectively. It proves the advantage of our method to deal with real-world problems. Besides, among these algorithms shown in Table 2, Single, Rock and DBSCAN have the worst performance, even Single and DBSCAN achieved good results on artificial datasets.

Considering Tables 1 and 2 together, we can find that many algorithms that performed well on artificial datasets performed poorly on real-world datasets. For DCP algorithm and its improved algorithm SNN-DPC, KNN-DPC, they achieved considerable results in all artificial datasets due to their ability of handling complex-shaped clusters. However, the dimensions of artificial datasets are simple and uniform in size. So, when applied in real-world datasets, those algorithms needing distance matrix, such as DPC, K-means, performed poorly, as point-to-point distance is difficult to be properly measured. In addition, for DBSCAN and other algorithms that use the global

Table 2. Results of real-world datasets

Method	I	W	B	Y	G	T
Single	82.67	55.05	63.09	31.94	43.46	77.67
Complete	96.00	89.89	79.61	36.05	42.52	85.12
UPGMA	96.67	89.33	91.39	41.37	48.60	81.86
WPGMA	96.00	86.52	92.44	41.51	50.47	69.77
Ward	96.67	84.83	91.39	44.74	43.46	87.44
UPGMC	96.00	88.20	89.81	41.85	47.20	87.44
WPGMC	96.00	65.73	85.59	38.48	45.79	82.79
Rock	66.67	59.55	78.91	34.37	43.46	70.70
Chameleon	96.67	93.26	93.32	43.94	57.48	83.26
Cure	96.67	91.01	91.74	43.80	55.14	92.09
Birch	**97.33**	93.26	91.92	43.16	56.54	88.84
K-means	94.00	92.13	92.27	38.41	58.88	86.98
K-medians	94.00	92.69	92.62	40.78	46.73	93.02
K-medoids	96.00	86.46	92.41	37.69	50.00	84.65
DBSCAN	84.00	60.67	62.92	31.94	45.79	77.67
DPC	96.00	91.01	91.74	37.40	51.40	88.37
Perch	80.13	60.28	74.48	34.47	50.93	57.81
DSets-DBSCAN	96.00	78.88	68.19	48.88	32.24	71.63
SNN-DPC	**97.33**	73.03	90.68	42.72	48.60	78.61
KNN-DPC	96.67	64.04	82.60	37.06	57.01	63.25
BHC	**97.33**	**97.19**	**94.20**	**51.75**	**62.62**	**94.42**

partitioning strategy, stable results can be obtained only when the data is evenly distributed. From Table 2, a conclusion can be drawn that BHC is robust and effective in processing real-world datasets.

3.3 Efficiency Analysis

To demonstrate the efficiency of our method, we performed analysis in datasets with different sizes and dimensionalities. We first test the clustering algorithms in dataset *Dim-sets* with six kind of dimensionalities: 32, 64, 128, 256, 512, 1024. We then draw several various-size datasets by copying the 1024-dimensional data points in *Dim-sets*. Figure 10 shows the running time of clustering algorithms versus dimensionality and data size. Note the run time is recorded when the algorithm obtains a 100% accuracy rate on the dataset.

As shown in Fig. 10(a), the running time has linear dependency with the increase of dimensionality, and Birch have a relatively small growing rate. The reason that the growth rate of running time of our method is higher than Birch, is our method takes a more time-consuming process in each dimension to perform grid-partitioning. As shown in Fig. 10(b), the running time of SINGLE, CHAMELEON, DBSCAN and DPC increases with the size of datasets by exponential growth; the running time of our method and Birch has been kept at a very low level. In addition, with the increase of data size, the running time of Birch exceeds our algorithm gradually.

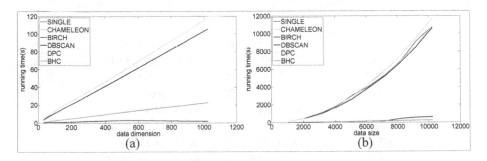

Fig. 10. Running time comparison: (a) with different data dimension, (b) with different data size

Generally, our method and Birch are both good at handling high-dimensional data and big data, while our method is better at big data and Birch is better at high-dimensional data.

4   Conclusions

In this paper we proposed a bidirectional hierarchical clustering algorithm called BHC where the Top-down and Bottom-up processes are performed to form a dendrogram. Through the strategy of over-segmentation and the definition of distance between grids, BHC can process complex and uneven data and avoid the influence of unstable geometric distance. Our method is good at large-scale and high-dimensional data, and is robust to outliers and noise. Experiment results verified the superiority of our method in efficiency and effectiveness over common clustering algorithms. However, one limitation of our algorithm is distortion caused by grid-partition. As a follow-up work, we will develop the kernel function as the projection to deal with nonlinear problems.

Acknowledgment. This work was supported by the Science and Technology Developing Project of Jilin Province No. 20150204007GX, the Key Science-Technology Project of the National Education Ministry of China under Grant No. 02090, the National Natural Science Foundation of China (Nos. 61472159), Project of Guizhou High-level Study Abroad Talents Innovation and Entrepreneurship (2018.0002), and Guangdong Natural Science Foundation (2018A030313339).

References

1. Lin, X., Stur, E., Ekrem, T.: Exploring genetic divergence in a species-rich insect genus using 2790 DNA barcodes. PLoS ONE **10**, e0138993 (2015)
2. Khaldi, N., Wolfe, K.H.: Evolutionary origins of the fumonisin secondary metabolite gene cluster in Fusarium verticillioides and Aspergillus niger. Int. J. Evol. Biol. **2011**, 423821 (2011)
3. Cimermancic, P., et al.: Insights into secondary metabolism from a global analysis of prokaryotic biosynthetic gene clusters. Cell **158**, 412–421 (2014)
4. Yan, C., Zou, X.: Predicting peptide binding sites on protein surfaces by clustering chemical interactions. J. Comput. Chem. **36**, 49–61 (2015)
5. Chu, C.W., Holliday, J.D., Willett, P.: Combining multiple classifications of chemical structures using consensus clustering. Bioorg. Med. Chem. **20**, 5366–5371 (2012)
6. Reddick, R.M., Tinker, J.L., Wechsler, R.H., Lu, Y.: Cosmological constraints from galaxy clustering and the mass-to-number ratio of galaxy clusters: marginalizing over the physics of galaxy formation. Astrophys. J. **783**, 118 (2014)
7. Krumholz, M.R.: The big problems in star formation: the star formation rate, stellar clustering, and the initial mass function. Phys. Rep. **539**, 49–134 (2014)
8. Anderson, L., et al.: The clustering of galaxies in the SDSS-III Baryon Oscillation Spectroscopic Survey: baryon acoustic oscillations in the Data Releases 10 and 11 Galaxy samples. Mon. Not. R. Astron. Soc. **441**, 24–62 (2013)
9. Li, Z., Wang, W., Yang, C., Ragland, D.R.: Bicycle commuting market analysis using attitudinal market segmentation approach. Transp. Res. Part A Policy Pract. **47**, 56–68 (2013)
10. Ramirez, I., Sprechmann, P., Sapiro, G.: Classification and clustering via dictionary learning with structured incoherence and shared features (2010)
11. Kobren, A., Monath, N., Krishnamurthy, A., Mccallum, A.: A hierarchical algorithm for extreme clustering. In: ACM SIGKDD International Conference on Knowledge Discovery and Data Mining, pp. 255–264 (2017)
12. Elankavi, R., Kalaiprasath, R., Udayakumar, D.R.: A fast clustering algorithm for high-dimensional data. Int. J. Civ. Eng. Technol. **8**, 1220–1227 (2017)
13. Rodriguez, A., Laio, A.: Clustering by fast search and find of density peaks. Science **344**, 1492–1496 (2014)
14. Du, M., Ding, S., Jia, H.: Study on density peaks clustering based on k-nearest neighbors and principal component analysis. Knowl.-Based Syst. **99**, 135–145 (2016)

15. Wu, B., Wilamowski, B.M.: A fast density and grid based clustering method for data with arbitrary shapes and noise. IEEE Trans. Ind. Inform. **PP**, 1 (2016)
16. Liu, R., Wang, H., Yu, X.: Shared-nearest-neighbor-based clustering by fast search and find of density peaks. Inf. Sci. (NY) **450**, 200–226 (2018)
17. Hou, J., Gao, H., Li, X.: DSets-DBSCAN: a parameter-free clustering algorithm. IEEE Trans. Image Process. **25**, 3182–3193 (2016)
18. Yang, X.-H., et al.: Parameter-free Laplacian centrality peaks clustering. Pattern Recogn. Lett. **100**, 167–173 (2017)
19. Ester, M., Kriegel, H.P., Sander, J., Xu, X.: A density-based algorithm for discovering clusters in large spatial databases with noise. In: International Conference on Knowledge Discovery and Data Mining, pp. 226–231 (1996)
20. Hinneburg, A., Keim, D.A.: Optimal grid-clustering: towards breaking the curse of dimensionality in high-dimensional clustering. In: Proceedings of the International Conference on Very Large Data Bases, pp. 506–517 (1999)
21. Keim, D.A., Hinneburg, A.: An efficient approach to clustering in large multimedia databases with noise. In: International Conference on Knowledge Discovery and Data Mining, pp. 58–65 (1998)
22. Wang, W., Yang, J., Muntz, R.R.: STING+: an approach to active spatial data mining. In: Proceedings of the International Conference on Data Engineering, pp. 116–125 (1999)
23. Dheeru, D., Karra Taniskidou, E.: UCI Machine Learning Repository. http://archive.ics.uci.edu/ml. Accessed 29 Nov 2018
24. Fränti, P., Sieranoja, S.: K-means properties on six clustering benchmark datasets. J. Appl. Intell. **48**, 4743–4759 (2018)
25. Fränti, P., Virmajoki, O., Hautamaki, V.: Fast agglomerative clustering using a k-nearest neighbor graph. IEEE Trans. Pattern Anal. Mach. Intell. **28**, 1875–1881 (2006)
26. Murtagh, F., Contreras, P.: Algorithms for hierarchical clustering: an overview. Wiley Interdiscip. Rev. Data Min. Knowl. Discov. **2**, 86–97 (2012)
27. Guha, S., Rastogi, R., Shim, K.: ROCK: a robust clustering algorithm for categorical attributes. Inf. Syst. **25**, 345–366 (2000)
28. Karypis, G., Han, E.-H., Kumar, V.: Chameleon: hierarchical clustering using dynamic modeling. Computer (Long. Beach. Calif) **32**, 68–75 (1999)
29. Guha, S., Rastogi, R., Shim, K.: CURE: an efficient clustering algorithm for large databases. ACM SIGMOD Rec. **27**, 73–84 (1998)
30. Zhang, T., Ramakrishnan, R., Livny, M.: BIRCH: an efficient data clustering method for very large databases. ACM SIGMOD Rec. **25**, 103–114 (1996)
31. MacQueen, J., et al.: Some methods for classification and analysis of multivariate observations. In: Proceedings of the Fifth Berkeley Symposium on Mathematical Statistics and Probability, vol. 1, pp. 281–297 (1967)
32. Kaufman, L., Rousseeuw, P.: Clustering by Means of Medoids. North-Holland, Amsterdam (1987)
33. Bradley, P.S., Fayyad, U.M., Reina, C., et al.: Scaling clustering algorithms to large databases. In: KDD 1998, pp. 9–15 (1998)

A Non-repudiable Dynamic Provable Data Possession

Jun-Feng Tian[1,2], Rui-Fang Guo[1,2(✉)], and Xuan Jing[1,2]

[1] School of Cyberspace Security and Computer Institute, Hebei University,
Baoding 071000, China
grf.skzxc@gmail.com
[2] Hebei Key Laboratory of High Confidence Information Systems,
Hebei University, Baoding 071000, China

Abstract. With the widespread popularity of cloud storage, cloud storage security issues have also received much attention. A provable data possession (PDP) scheme can effectively help users to verify the integrity of data stored remotely in the cloud. For this reason, the client's PDP scheme is constantly improving and developing. In view of the problem that the existing PDP scheme pays less attention to the clients deceiving the cloud server, a non-repudiable dynamic PDP scheme based on the Stern-Brocot tree (SB-NR-DPDP) is proposed. We put forward a dynamic storage structure and dynamic operation algorithm based on the Stern-Brocot tree, so that it can satisfy the client's dynamic data operations and realize the non-repudiation feature of the scheme. This scheme can resist hash value attacks, delete-insert attacks and tamper with cloud return value attacks. The theoretical analysis shows that the proposed scheme has less computing and storage overhead than other schemes.

Keywords: Cloud storage · Provable data possession · Stern-brocot · Dynamic operation

1   Introduction

As cloud storage can provide users with high-quality data storage and computing services [1], cloud storage has gradually gained wide popularity among users. Cloud storage not only provides convenience for users but also raises serious security problems for them. Cloud storage not only makes users relinquish physical control of the data but also increases the risk of data being leaked by, tampered with and deleted by cloud service providers. In addition, the security of cloud storage is threatened by external attackers, hardware failures and other factors. Therefore, research on the integrity verification of users' cloud data is urgently needed.

A provable data possession (PDP) scheme can effectively help users to verify the integrity of data stored remotely in the cloud. However, research on PDP has paid little attention to user deception by cloud service providers. For example, a user once issued an order to delete a certain piece of data to the cloud service provider, but the user denied that order when authenticating the integrity and blamed the cloud service provider, resulting in disputes between the user and the cloud service provider. For this

J. Li et al. (Eds.): SPNCE 2019, LNICST 284, pp. 723–730, 2019.
https://doi.org/10.1007/978-3-030-21373-2_61

reason, by introducing the Stern-Brocot tree type of dynamic data structure, this paper proposes a non-repudiable dynamic provable data possession scheme (SB-NR-DPDP).

2 Related Work

To solve the problem of users checking cloud data integrity, researchers have proposed a provable data possession (PDP) scheme. In 2007, Ateniese et al. [2] first proposed the PDP scheme. To support user dynamic operations and to improve the scheme's flexibility of the scheme, the researchers proposed dynamic PDP scheme. For example, [1, 3, 4]. To eliminate complex key and certificate management and to improve PDP scheme efficiency, Zhao et al. [5] proposed the first identity-based PDP scheme in 2013. To solve the problem of user unreliability and improve the credibility of both parties in a PDP scheme, in 2014, Mo et al. [6] proposed a non-repudiation PDP scheme based on the Merkle hash tree and timestamps. Feng [7] et al. found that the existing dynamic data structure could not satisfy the non-repudiation feature of the PDP scheme very well. By introducing a logical index table (ILT), they proposed the non-repudiation and identity-based, non-repudiable dynamic PDP scheme (ID-NR-DPDP) in cloud storage.

3 The System Model

An SB-NR-DPDP scheme model contains four primary entities: the private key generator (PKG), the data owner (User), the cloud server provider (CSP), and the unbiased judge. As shown in Fig. 1, their functions are as follows.

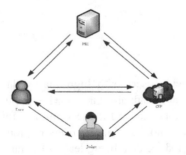

Fig. 1. SB-NR-DPDP scheme model

- PKG: A trusted third party, which is called the private key generator. It can help users generate private keys.
- User: The data owner who uses cloud storage services to outsource data to remote clouds.

- Cloud server: A semi-trusted entity that stores and processes the user's data. It can prove data integrity to clients, but sometimes the cloud server can destroy data integrity and trick clients into believing that the data are still intact in the cloud.
- Judge: A trusted third party that resolves disputes when they arise between the user and the cloud service provider.

4 The Dynamic Operation Algorithm of the Stern-Brocot Tree

The Stern-Brocot tree [8] is a binary tree used to construct a set consisting of all non-negative minimal fractions. It was discovered independently by German mathematician Moritz Stern and French watchmaker Achille Brocot. The dynamic operation algorithm in the Stern-Brocot tree includes an insert, delete and modify algorithm. Users and the cloud server initialize the tree: the root node is $\frac{1}{1}$ and is used to form a tree structure that is symmetric to the root node. The left child of the root node is $\frac{N}{M}$, which is the seed node. The right child is $\frac{M}{N}$. Using a seed, a Stern-Brocot tree with a symmetric root node can be established. As shown in Fig. 2, all the fractions in the tree are in the simplest form.

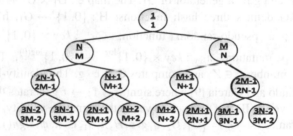

Fig. 2. Partial Stern-Brocot tree with seed (N, M)

The algorithm calculates the height of the tree that needs to be established according to the number of seeds and the number of data blocks n. Each leaf node in the tree corresponds to a unique pointer variable, and each pointer variable points to the user's corresponding data block F_{wx}.

Insert algorithm: When data blocks F_{wx} need to be inserted, an update from the most recent operation starts after the largest leaf node. The pointer variable wx corresponding to the appropriate insert block position is found. It then points to the file block F'_{wx}. The number of blocks is updated at the same time.

Deletion algorithm: To delete the correspondence between pointer variables and file blocks, it needs to delete the wx pointer to F_{wx}, and let wx = 1 as failure node that is to add wx as a global pointer variable for the dynamic operation algorithm. Finally, update the number of blocks at the same time, n = n − 1. The purpose of marking the failure node is that when the tree is built again, wx conflicts with the global variable value, indicating that the position is the failure position. Continue to look for the insertion position, so as to prevent the deletion - insertion attack. If the deleted position is at the last block, a new block will be inserted after the newly deleted position to avoid the delete - insert attack. When there are not enough leaves in the tree, a row will be generated again and the global variable will be cleared after initialization.

Modify algorithm: First, it removes the relationship between the pointer variable wx and the file block F_{wx}, and makes pointer variable value wx $= 1$. It then adds wx as a global pointer variable for the dynamic operation algorithm. Then, it follows the insertion algorithm to find pointer variable wx$'$ corresponding to the insertion location, and points to modify the file.

5 Details of the SB-NR-DPDP Scheme

The SB-NR-DPDP scheme include six algorithms: Setup, Extraction, Tagging, Processing, Proof, and Judgement, which are described in detail in the following sections.

5.1 Setup

This algorithm is executed by the PKG. Let G_1, G_2 be a cyclic multiplication groups with prime order, and g be a generator of G_1. The map $e : G_1 \times G_1 \rightarrow G_2$ is a bilinear pairing. The PKG defines three hash functions: $H : \{0,1\}^* \rightarrow G_1$, $h : \{0,1\}^* \rightarrow Z_q^*$, $h_1 : \{0,1\}^* \rightarrow Z_q^*$; a pseudo-random function: $\emptyset_{key} : key \times \{0,1\}^* \rightarrow Z_q^*$; and a pseudo-random permutation: $\pi_{key} : key \times \{0,1\}^{\log(\theta)} \rightarrow \{0,1\}^{\log(\theta)}$. The PKG then selects a random number $c \in Z_q^*$ and computes $C = c \cdot g$. The identity-based signature algorithm of Galindo and Garcia [9] where $sign(sk_{ID}, f) \rightarrow \ell$ generates the signature for the message, and verify(ID, f, ℓ) is used to verify the signature validity. PKG publishes the public parameters $G_g = \{G_1, G_2, q, g, e, H, h, h_1, C, \pi, \phi, sign(), verify()\}$ and keeps the msk $= c$ secret.

5.2 Extraction

The PKG selects a random number $j \in_R Z_q^*$ and computes $R = j \cdot g$, $Z = j + c \cdot h(ID||R) \mod q$; therefore, $sk_{ID} = (R, Z)$. The PKG uses this algorithm to generate the client's secret key, sk_c, or the cloud server's secret key, sk_s.

5.3 Tagging

Given an F, the client chooses a random file name NI from some large domain and splits the file into n blocks, $F = F_1||F_2||\ldots F_n$, given $F_x, 1 \leq x \leq n, F_x = F_{x1}||F_{x2}||\ldots F_{xs}$. Then, the client selects s random values $u_1, u_2, \ldots u_s \in G_1, U = (u_1, u_2, \ldots u_s)$, and then initializes the tree by the dynamic operation algorithm of the Stern-Brocot tree to obtain wx. It then calculates the signature ℓ_c and label T_{wx}, where $\ell_c = sign(sk_c, NI||U||n||(N, M))$ and $T_{wx} = Z_c \cdot \left(H(NI||wx||U) + \sum_{K=1}^{S} F_{wx,k} \cdot u_k \right)$. Then, the client uploads

$\{F_{wx}, T_{wx}, NI, U, n, (N,M)\}$ to the cloud server. Next, the cloud server uses equations
$e\left(\sum_{x=1}^{n} T_{wx}, g\right) = e\left(\sum_{x=1}^{n} H(NI||wx||U) + \sum_{K=1}^{s}\left(\sum_{x=1}^{n} F_{wx}\right) \cdot u_k, R_c + h(ID_c||R_c) \cdot C\right)$
and $1 = verify(ID_c, NI||U||n||(N,M), \ell_C)$ to check the validity of T_{wx}, $(1 \le x \le n)$ and
ℓ_c. If one of them does not hold, the operation stops. Otherwise, the cloud server stores
them, computes the signature $\ell_s = sign(ID_s, \ell_c)$, and returns ℓ_s as a receipt to the client.
The client receives the receipt from the cloud server, and then checks the validity of the
receipt ℓ_s by using the equation $1 = verify(ID_s, \ell_s, \ell_c)$. If it is invalid, the operation stops.
Otherwise, the client stores $\{NI, n, (N,M), \ell_s, \ell_c\}$ and deletes data blocks and tags from
local storage.

5.4   Processing

- **Insert**

The client wants to insert a new block F'. First, the client obtains the pointer variable wx'
corresponding to the new insertion location and the number of file blocks n by using the
dynamic operation algorithm. Then, the file F' is divided into s sections, $F' = \left(F'_1||F'_2||\ldots F'_s\right)$. The client computes the new label T'_{wx} and signature ℓ'_c, by using the
equations $T'_{wx} = Z_c \cdot \left(H(NI||wx'||U) + \sum_{k=1}^{s} F'_k \cdot u_k\right)$ and $\ell'_c = sign(sk_c, IN||NI||wx'||n)$. Next, the client uploads $\{IN, F', T'_{wx}, U, n, \ell'_c\}$, to the cloud server. Then, the
cloud server checks the validity T'_{wx} and ℓ'_c, by using the equations $1 = verify(ID_c, IN||U||wx'||n, \ell'_c)$ and $e\left(T'_{wx}, g\right) = e(H(NI||wx'||U) + \sum_{k=1}^{s} F'_k \cdot u_k, R_c + h(ID_C||R_c) \cdot C)$. If one of them does not hold, the operation stops; otherwise, the cloud
server updates n, ℓ'_c. Then, the signature $\ell'_s = sign(ID_s, \ell'_c)$ is computed and ℓ'_s is
returned as a receipt to the client. The client receives the receipt from the cloud server and
then checks the validity of the receipt ℓ'_s by using the equation $1 = verify(ID_s, \ell'_s, \ell'_c)$. If it
is invalid, the operation stops; otherwise, the client updates n, ℓ'_c, ℓ'_s, and deletes F', T'_{wx}
from local storage.

- **Delete**

The client wants to delete block F_{wx}. First, the client obtains the pointer variable wx
corresponding to the delete location, and the number of file blocks n by using the
dynamic operation algorithm. The client computes the signature ℓ'_c, by using the
equation $\ell'_c = sign(sk_c, NI||U||wx||n)$. Then, the client uploads $\{NI, U, n, wx, \ell'_c\}$ to the
cloud server. Next, the cloud server checks the validity by using the equation
$1 = verify(ID_c, NI||U||wx||n, \ell'_c)$. If it holds, the cloud server updates n, ℓ'_c. Then, the
signature $\ell'_s = sign(ID_s, \ell'_c)$ is computed and ℓ'_s is returned as a receipt to the client. The
client receives the receipt from the cloud server and then checks the validity of the
receipt ℓ'_s by using the equation $1 = verify(ID_s, \ell'_s, \ell'_c)$. If it is invalid, the operation
stops; otherwise, the client updates n, ℓ'_c, ℓ'_s.

- **Modify**

The client wants to modify the file block value into F'. First, the client obtains the pointer variable wx' corresponding to the new insertion location of the new block by using the dynamic operation algorithm. Then, the file F' is divided into s sections - $F' = (F'_1||F'_2||\ldots||F'_S)$. The client computes the new label T'_{wx} and signature ℓ'_c, by using the equations $T'_{wx} = Z_c \cdot (H(NI||wx'||U) + \sum_{k=1}^{s} F'_k \cdot u_k)$ and $\ell'_c = sign(sk_c, NI||U||wx'||n)$. Then, the client uploads $\{F', T'_{wx}, NI, U, wx', n, \ell'_c\}$ to the cloud server. The cloud server checks the validity T'_{wx} and ℓ'_c, by using the equations $1 = verify(ID_c, NI||U||wx'||n, \ell'_c)$ and $e(T'_{wx}, g) = e(H(NI||wx'||U) + \sum_{k=1}^{s} F'_k \cdot u_k, R_c + h(ID_c||R_C) \cdot C)$. If one of them does not hold, the operation stops; otherwise, the cloud server updates ℓ'_c. Then, the signature $\ell'_s = sign(ID_s, \ell'_c)$ is computed and ℓ'_s is returned as a receipt to the client. The client receives the receipt from the cloud server and checks the validity of the receipt ℓ'_s by using the equation $1 = verify(ID_s, \ell'_s, \ell'_c)$. If it is invalid, the operation stops; otherwise, the client updates ℓ'_c, ℓ'_s, and deletes the file block and its labels.

5.5 Proof

The client wants to verify the integrity of the file NI. First, the client selects a random number i, where $1 \leq i \leq n$ and $s_1, s_2 \in_R Z^*_q$. The client computes $S_2 = s_2 \cdot g, \hat{\ell}_c = sign(sk_c, NI||s_1||S_2||i)$ and sends the challenge $chal = \left(i, s_1, S_2, NI, \hat{\ell}_c\right)$ to the cloud server. Upon receiving the challenge, the cloud server stops the dynamic operations of this file, selects $s_3 \in_R Z^*_q$, computes $S_3 = s_3 \cdot g$, $S = s_3 \cdot S_2$, $Y = \{y(\pi_{s_1}(\rho))|1 \leq \rho \leq i\}$, $a_y = \phi_S(y)$, $y \in Y$, $\hat{F}_k = \sum_y a_y F_{yk}$, $1 \leq k \leq s$, $T = \sum_{y \in Y} a_y \cdot T_y$, $\hat{\ell}_s = sign(sk_s, S_3||n||(N, M)||\hat{F}_1||\hat{F}_2||\ldots||\hat{F}_S||\hat{T})$, and sends $re = \{S_3, n, (N, M), \hat{F}_1, \hat{F}_2, \ldots \hat{F}_s, \hat{T}, \hat{\ell}_s\}$ to the client as a response. Then, the client computes $S = s_2 \cdot S_3$, $Y = \{y(\pi_{s_1}(\rho))|1 \leq \rho \leq i\}$, $a_y = \phi_S(y)$, and $y \in Y$, and then checks the validity of response by using the equations $e(\hat{T}, g) = e\left(\sum_{y \in Y} a_y \cdot H(NI||y||U) + \sum_{k=1}^{s} \hat{F}_k \cdot u_k, R_c + h(ID_c||R_c) \cdot C\right)$ and $1 = verify\left(ID_s, S_3, n, (N, M), \hat{F}_1, \hat{F}_2, \ldots \hat{F}_s, \hat{T}, \hat{\ell}_s\right)$. When the equations are true, the data are proven to be complete.

5.6 Judgement

When there is a dispute between the client and the cloud server, they each send the latest data information to the judge. The cloud server sends the latest $chal = \left(i, s_1, S_2, NI, \hat{\ell}_c\right)$ and response $re = \{S_3, n, (N, M), wx', \hat{F}_1, \hat{F}_2, \ldots, \hat{F}_s, \hat{T}, \hat{\ell}_s\}$, s_3, ℓ_c to the judge. Then, the judge checks the validity of ℓ_s. If it is invalid, the cloud server is the winner. Otherwise, the judge checks the validity of ℓ_c and re. If one of them is winner, the client is the winner.

6 Efficiency Analysis

We perform an efficiency analysis of the storage and computational overhead of the scheme, and compare it with two of the best alternative schemes. Let $T_H, T_{add}, T_{mul}, T_p, T_{exp}$ denote the running time of a hash function instruction, an addition instruction in G_1, a multiplication instruction, a bilinear pairing instruction, and an exponentiation instruction. The PRF, PRP and other operations are omitted in our evaluation, because their computational costs are negligible. Suppose the data are split into n blocks. Each block of data is divided into s parts, and the number of challenge blocks is c. Table 1 presents the comparisons between our scheme and two other schemes [1, 7].

From Table 1, we can see that our scheme's computational overhead is the same as scheme [7], so the computational cost is mainly compared with scheme [1]. Our scheme is more efficient because we use a bilinear pairing operation with less computational overhead instead of using exponential operations, and the time expended by $T_H, T_{add}, T_{mul}, T_p$ is less than T_{exp}. On the other hand, we can see that when the value of n is fixed, the computational cost of the two schemes is linear with the number of s. Moreover, as the s grows, the growth rate of tag generation computational overhead in scheme [1] is significantly higher than ours. Though comparison, we found that the computational overhead of our scheme is reduced, so our scheme is more efficient. Since both schemes [1, 7] need to maintain the table structure, the scheme, the clients and cloud server do not need to maintain the table structure, and the storage overhead is fixed. Only the number of data blocks n and the seed of the tree can be stored, and the storage overhead is independent of the file size. For this reason, the storage overhead of our scheme is significantly lower than that of the schemes [1, 7], which reduces the storage overhead of the clients and the cloud server.

Table 1. Comparison with other schemes.

Schemes		Ref. [7]	Ref. [1]	Ours
Computational cost in tag generation phase	Client side	$(ns+2)T_{mul} + nsT_{add}$ $+ (n+1)T_{Hash}$	$nsT_{mul} + nT_{Hash}$ $+ n(s+1)T_{exp}$	$(ns+2)T_{mul}$ $+ nsT_{add} + (n+1)T_{Hash}$
Computational cost at generates proof	Cloud side	$(2c+4)T_{mul} + (c-1)T_{add}$ $+ T_{Hash}$	$(2c-1)T_{mul}$ $+ (c-1)T_{add} + cT_{exp}$	$(2c+4)T_{mul}$ $+ (c-1)T_{add} + T_{Hash}$
Computational cost at verifying the proof	Client side	$(c+s+4)T_{mul} + (c+s+2)T_{add}$ $+ 3T_{Hash} + T_p$	$(c+s-1)T_{mul} + cT_{Hash}$ $+ (c+s+1)T_{exp}$	$(c+s+4)T_{mul}$ $+ (c+s+2)T_{add} + 3T_{Hash} + T_p$
Storage cost		ITL list	ORT list	Fixed

7 Summary

The scheme enables the clients and the cloud server to dynamically manipulate outsourced files, making the PDP solution more suitable for practical application. The program supports identity authentication, enabling the PDP solution to eliminate complex certificate management. The program supports non-repudiation and solves the disputes between the client and the cloud server. the proposed scheme has less computing and storage overhead than other schemes. As such, it has high efficiency.

References

1. Yan, H., Li, J., Han, J., et al.: A novel efficient remote data possession checking protocol in cloud storage. IEEE Trans. Inf. Forensics Secur. **12**(1), 78–88 (2017)
2. Ateniese, G., Burns, R., Curtmola, R., et al.: Provable data possession at untrusted stores. In: ACM Conference on Computer and Communications Security, pp. 598–609. ACM (2007)
3. Yang, K., Jia, X.: An efficient and secure dynamic auditing protocol for data storage in cloud computing. IEEE Trans. Parallel Distrib. Syst. **24**(9), 1717–1726 (2013)
4. Barsoum, A.F., Hasan, M.A.: Provable multicopy dynamic data possession in cloud computing systems. IEEE Trans. Inf. Forensics Secur. **10**(3), 485–497 (2017)
5. Zhao, J., Xu, C., Li, F., et al.: Identity-based public verification with privacy-preserving for data storage security in cloud computing. IEICE Trans. Fundam. Electron. Commun. Comput. Sci. **96**(12), 2709–2716 (2013)
6. Mo, Z., Zhou, Y., Chen, S., et al.: Enabling non-repudiable data possession verification in cloud storage systems. In: IEEE, International Conference on Cloud Computing, pp. 232–239. IEEE, (2014)
7. Wang, F., Xu, L., Wang, H., et al.: Identity-based non-repudiable dynamic provable data possession in cloud storage. Comput. Electr. Eng. **69**, 521–533 (2017)
8. Graham, R., Knuth, D., Patashnik, O.: Specific Math: A Foundation for Computer Science. Posts & telecom press, Beijing (2013)
9. Galindo, D., Garcia, F.D.: A Schnorr-like lightweight identity-based signature scheme. In: Proceedings of Second International Conference on Cryptology in Africa (AFRICACRYPT 2009), 21–25 June, pp. 135–148 (2009)

Zone Based Lossy Image Compression Using Discrete Wavelet and Discrete Cosine Transformations

Nafees Ahmad[1], Khalid Iqbal[2], Lansheng Han[1(✉)], Naeem Iqbal[2], and Muhammad Adil Abid[3]

[1] School of Computer Science and Technology, Huazhong University of Science and Technology, Wuhan 430074, Hubei, People's Republic of China
{nafees, hanlansheng}@hust.edu.cn

[2] Department of Computer Science, COMSATS University Islamabad, Attock Campus 43600, Islamabad, Pakistan
khalidiqbal@cuiatk.edu.pk,
fa15-rcs-015@ciit-attock.edu.pk

[3] Department of Computer Science and Technology, Shandong University, Jimo, Qingdao 266237, People's Republic of China
emadilabid.bl22@mail.sdu.edu.cn

Abstract. Due to the huge volume of image data generation in numerous domains, image compression has got the attention of researchers to minimize redundant image contents for efficient handling and transmission. However, a small region of interest (ROI) in the whole image is a major challenge in image compression. In this perspective, lossless image compression techniques have a low compression rate, and lossy image compression approaches, like JPEG, JPEG2000 and HD Photo, slightly loose data with high compression ratio. High compression ratio of lossy image compression helps in saving storage and fast transfer of data. In this paper, we proposed new DWT based zoning technique in combination with DCT for image compression. DWT divides an image into LL, LH, HL and HH frequencies and Zoning is further dividing these images into four parts as an input to DCT one after another. The output of DCT on each zone is then combined into a compressed bitstream image. Extensive experimentation is performed on various common images to compare the results with JPEG, JPEG2000 and HD Photo methods. Our ZDD methods remarkably performed better than the aforementioned techniques.

Keywords: Lossy image compression · Discrete Cosine Transform · Discrete Wavelet Transform

1 Introduction

Rapid growth of multimedia applications and increasing of the high-resolution images on a large scale create the problem of storage and transferring of data [1–3]. Compression techniques are the application of image processing that deals with the reduction of bits to represent the image. Attractive part of image compression is the

J. Li et al. (Eds.): SPNCE 2019, LNICST 284, pp. 731–742, 2019.
https://doi.org/10.1007/978-3-030-21373-2_62

resolution of the image. Nowadays, it plays a leading role in many application i.e., quality improvement in satellite images [4], enhancement of resolution in a video [5] and feature computation [6]. Generally, two kinds of resolution methods exist in image processing, single image super-resolution and multi-image super-resolution method. The algorithms [7–9] of multiple-image super-resolution accept the low-resolution images of same scene in the form of input and perform registration technique to transform images for their size reduction. The output information is then combined with the distorting constraints of low-quality input images to develop a high-quality framework for showing the output of the high-resolution image. For appropriate working of super-resolution image algorithm, the smaller pixels in low-resolution images should be repositioned. It is very crucial to reposition the smaller pixels; these pixels can be repositioned by registration techniques. The repositioning of pixels in objects like a model of a human being is more complex.

Perhaps, algorithms in [10] achieve high-quality output; though, the enhancement aspects are constraint by factors near to 2. The algorithms [11–13] for single-image super-resolution cannot relocate smaller pixels due to the only input. In replacement, these algorithms make the learning model on the basis of low resolution and high-resolution images counterpart through training. Consequently, in the later stage, these models predict the missing pixels of the low-resolution image. Indeed, based on trained features between high-quality and low-quality images, the tested output of these algorithms is much better to enhance compression of the input image. Therefore, the reduction and regeneration of high-quality images are very essential. In compression of an image, there is a very vital part of information theory. Importantly, the dimension of the data i.e. histogram can be decreased by using information theory [14, 15]. Lossy and Lossless are the two methods for compressing the image [16, 17]. In lossy compression technique, the compressed image cannot be restored to its original image because of losing some information due to compression while on the other hand in lossless compression method, the compressed image can be restored to its original image. Lossy image compression technique is renowned for compression; it gives higher compression than lossless compression. Lossless compression technique considers risk with an aim to avoid loss of information, for example in medical image processing, high information required related patient to identify the disease. The primary purpose of this technique is to decrease the image size as much as possible without losing the content of the image [18]. However, in case of lossy compression, loss of information is acceptable within the boundary.

Wavelets importantly involved in Internet-based applications. It deals with the image compression and signal processing. Usually, this method compressed image in a large manner than other techniques like JPEG [11, 19]. In Discrete Wavelet Transform (DWT), initially, an operation performed on the row of the image to get the input value and then used on the columns. This procedure is called two-dimension wavelet breakdown of the image [20, 21]. This procedure accomplishes the image into four smaller bands including High-High (HH), Low-Low (LL), High-Low (HL) and Low-High (LH). The frequency of the original image is wrapped completely by the frequency of the smaller bands.

In this work, we proposed a new way of lossy image compression technique, named as ZDD, which is based on DWT and Discrete Cosine Transform (DCT) by performing zoning on result of DWT. The objective of the ZDD method is to improve the PSNR while compressing an image. In our research work, the basic ingredient is zoning that helps in recognizing the deep parts of the image and that can be focused more accurately for better and efficient results. The goal of ZDD is to reduce the size of original image to make more space for storage of a variety of images. The quantitative and visual results prove that the proposed methodology is more helpful for lossy compression of an image. Our lossy image compression method can be used as it leads better results in comparison to the existing ones. We used benchmark dataset contains 15 colour based images for experimental purpose. On the basis of PSNR values, the results are evaluated to validate our proposed research. DCT decreases the psychovisual dismissals of any image and the DCT lossy compression image is a quantization method [22, 23]. The quality of the decompressed picture can be improved by using DWT. While DCT works with the boundary points and for producing accurate calculation results cosine is used instead of sine. It takes different frequencies and makes a flow for data points and then summing those points by using cosine. Furthermore, DCT works better for smaller high-frequency bands [24]. Therefore, DCT is chosen to get the input of DWT based four zones with deep information.

2 Related Work

This section introduces the background information and related work of image compression technology. Many states of the art image compression techniques are available, such as Wavelet Compression Technique (WCT) [19], Discrete Wavelet Transform (DWT) [4] etc. All of these techniques play an important role in many image processing applications.

2.1 Wavelet Compression Technique (WCT)

Wavelet Compression Technique is often used in many image processing applications. It is specifically used for resolution enhancement-based applications.

Different authors have proposed different image enhancement models based on wavelet transform. In [25], the author proposes a technique to improve image resolution by interpolating the high sub-bands of SWT and DWT. Initially, SWT was used to improve the boundary of the image. Then, DWT is used in parallel with SWT to decompose the image into four sub-bands. After that, the input image plus high-frequency bands are interpolated and the estimated high-frequency sub-bands are generated through SWT high sub-bands. Lastly, the inverse of discrete cosine transformation (IDWT) is used to combine all sub-bands to produce a new high- quality image. The block diagram of [25] is illustrated in Fig. 1.

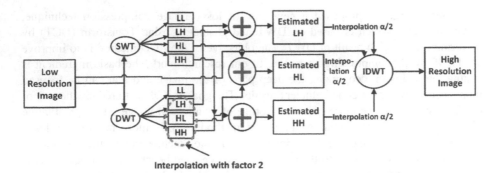

Fig. 1. The framework proposed in [25]

2.2   Discrete Wavelet Transform (DWT)

In order to obtain a high-resolution image using DWT, a new learning-based technique is proposed [26]. This method's novelty comes in the domain of wavelet-based specific application design. Initially, super-resolution image approximation is achieved by filter coefficients and high-frequency wavelet information in the wavelet domain (WD). On this basis, the regularization framework based on sparse distribution is used to degrade the image. Finally, output image is calculated from initial super-resolution and wavelet coefficients. The one advantage of this algorithm is; it learns from initial approximation rather than using registered image. Moreover, this method uses sparse priority to preserve neighbourhood dependencies. Another advantage of the method is to use wavelet coefficients to present the best point range function to simulate the achievement process of the image.

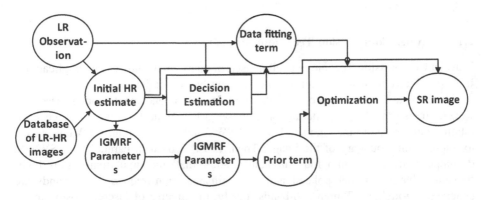

Fig. 2. The framework of Discrete wavelet transform in [27]

A learning-based approach is presented in Fig. 2 proposed by [28]. This method takes a database of low-resolution and high-resolution images as input. Initially, authors acquired the high-frequency sub-bands from database images by using DWT. Using high-frequency details, an initial high-resolution image was destroyed and then images were modelled with aliases and noise. In the next step, the original image and test image was used to determine the aliasing entries. The early model of the super-resolution image was selected as an In-homogeneous Gaussian Markov Random Field (IGMRF). At the final stage, maximum posterior (map) approximation method was applied in order to get the minimum cost function.

In article [29], authors used DWT to divide the image into four sub-bands (HH, HL, LH, and LL). They used DWR to compress the Low-Low (LL) subband and SVD to compress high-frequency subbands (HH, HL, and LH). The proposed approach has been validated in a number of well-known images, including airfields, peppers, Lena and boats. The results were compared with WDR and JPEG2000. This technique showed improvement in term of PSNR and visual result than these existing methods.

2.3   Zoning

This technique refers to divide the image into N parts which can grab discriminative depth detail of image as much as possible. Suppose I is an image, zoning method generally divide the image into N zones i.e., $Z1$, $Z_2 \ldots Z_n$ (N > 1). Each zone provides depth information of an image. Zoning is not only useful for the lossy type of image compression but also useful in medical image compression when each pixel is critically essential. In medical imaging, initially zones defined the depth location of an image and then further operation has been performed over those zoned areas. When compression technique is applied then zones can neglect the most irrelevant information, the useful information still remains there. Hence, it is a more useful technique in many lossy image compression applications. Different authors have proposed zoned based models for different problems such that character recognition, identifying facial expressions from the images. Jin et al. [28] divided the image 4×4, 4×9, 4×16, 8×8 and 10×10 zones in recognition of Chinese characters. They computed the directional features from those separated grids. One more study [29] has also done on Chinese character recognition through zoning. In this work Liu et al. used a direct decomposition method on 4×4 grids. Pal and Chaudhuri et al. [30] presented their work on character recognition on the base of zone information. In this work, the authors suggested the Indian language for their character recognition on the base of zoning. In [31], authors worked on the recognition of car plates. They divided the car plate image into 4×4 zones to compute pixel depth feature. In [6], the authors proposed a zone-based model for identifying the facial expressions from an image. In this work, authors fetched the required information from the marked regions or zones and then apply their proposed technique to recognize facial expression. Authors in [14] proposed a model to the visual objects within an image based on the frequency domains and the region-based zones. In this work, a hybrid model is presented to visualize objects within an image. For this, the authors divided an image into two different parts such that frequency domains and region-based zones. Firstly, the authors applied frequency domain features on the grids; secondly, a region-based part was highlighted. They made more clear visualization among the various images which were tested and utilized in their research work. Hence the zone-based approach makes work more easily with high accuracy comparatively.

2.4   Discrete Cosine Transform (DCT)

DCT plays a vital role in lossy image compression. DCT actually works with the boundary points, to get accurate results cosine is used instead of sine. It takes different frequencies, makes a flow for data points, and then sums those points by using sum function of cosine. If there is a need to skip smaller high-frequency sub-bands then DCT works better and that is the reason to choose DCT in proposed research work.

The DCT for 2D image I of size M × N can be calculated from below equation:

$$D_{ct} = \beta_c \beta_t \sum_{i=0}^{M-1} \sum_{j=0}^{N-1} I_{ij} \cos\frac{\pi(2i+1)c}{2M} \cos\frac{\pi(2j+1)t}{2N} \begin{cases} 0 \le c \le M-1 \\ 0 \le t \le N-1 \end{cases} \quad (1)$$

Where

$$\beta_c = \begin{cases} \frac{1}{\sqrt{M}}, & c = 0 \\ \sqrt{\frac{2}{M}}, & 0 \le c \le M-1 \end{cases} \quad \beta_t = \begin{cases} \frac{1}{\sqrt{N}}, & t = 0 \\ \sqrt{\frac{2}{N}}, & 0 \le t \le N-1 \end{cases}$$

The original image can get by using the inverse of DCT, the following equation can calculate IDCT:

$$I_{ij} = \sum_{i=0}^{M-1} \sum_{j=0}^{N-1} \beta_c \beta_t D_{ct} \cos\frac{\pi(2i+1)c}{2M} \cos\frac{\pi(2j+1)t}{2N} \begin{cases} 0 \le c \le M-1 \\ 0 \le t \le N-1 \end{cases} \quad (2)$$

Where

$$\beta_c = \begin{cases} \frac{1}{\sqrt{M}}, & c = 0 \\ \sqrt{\frac{2}{M}}, & 0 \le c \le M-1 \end{cases} \quad \beta_t = \begin{cases} \frac{1}{\sqrt{N}}, & t = 0 \\ \sqrt{\frac{2}{N}}, & 0 \le t \le N-1 \end{cases}$$

Authors [24] proposed a lossy image compression technique based on DCT, in which an image is divided bases of frequencies, where the low frequencies are discarded. The authors applied proposed technique on various images like pepper image with quantization. Landge et al. [15] proposed a comparison technique based on DCT, in which only grayscale images of different sizes (256 × 256, 64 × 64 and 8 × 8) were taken. Their method achieved compressed image less in size than the original one. In this work, they used the MATLABXILINX-MATLAB methodology for their proposed compression technique. The reconstruction was done by using inverse of DCT to get the original image. Uma et al. [32] used the DCT method for the 2-D grayscale image to increase the storage space for saving more images at a time. They used VLSI architecture for parallel computation of images with the DCT and report satisfactory results. The authors mentioned that DCT is a moderate and best technique for image compression in terms of parallel programming.

3   Proposed Methodology

Our presented method, i.e. ZDD, compresses images with losses to save storage space as well as to transfer image files.

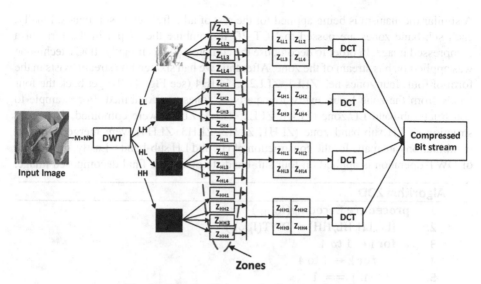

Fig. 3. Encoding framework of proposed work

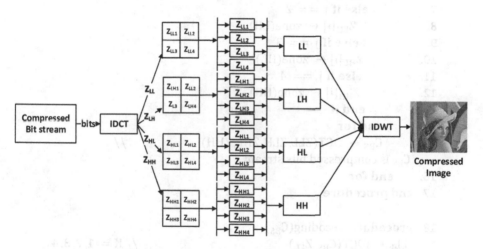

Fig. 4. Decoding framework of proposed work

For better understanding, encoding block diagram is shown in Fig. 3 and decoding block diagram is presented in Fig. 4. It is obvious from Fig. 3, Discrete Wavelet Transform (DWT) is applied on the input image to decompose an image into four equal parts on basis of their frequency sub-bands. The four-equal frequency sub-bands consist of high-high (HH), high-low (HL), low-high (LH) and low-low (LL). These four images are then saved into a folder with their names as LL, LH, HL, HH gained through DWT. In the next step, each frequency sub-bands decomposed into four chunks, for example sub-band LL is divided into zone low low 1 (ZLL_1), zone low low 2 (ZLL_2), zone low low 3 (ZLL_3), and low low 4 (ZLL_4) respectively as shown in Fig. 3. Similarly, remaining three sub-bands are divided into four zones each. Then, DCT 2D were applied to each zone, as we had 2D images, therefore we applied DCT 2D instead of 1D.

A similar mechanism is being applied for the rest of all 3 frequency sub-bands. Finally, each sub-band zones are passed to DCT 2D to combine the output in the form of a compressed image. In order to decompose the compressed bits initially, IDCT technique was applied on bits stream of the zone. After this, we had sixteen bits stream exists in the form of four, four zones i.e., ZLL1, ZLL2 … ZHH4 (see Fig. 4). To get back the four bands from the zone layer, every four parts of zones are combined. For example to construct sub-band LL zone (ZLL1, ZLL2, ZLL3, ZLL4) were combined, for reconstruction of LH sub-band zone (ZLH1, ZLH2, ZLH3, ZLH4) were merged. Similar combinations are made for the construction of HL and LH sub-bands. Lastly, the inverse of DWT operation is applied on four sub-bands to obtain the final decomposed image.

Algorithm ZDD

1. **procedure** Encoding($I_{M \times N}$)
2. $[LL, LH, HL, HH] \leftarrow DWT(I_{M \times N})$
3.   **for** $i \leftarrow 1$ *to* 4
4.   **for** $k \leftarrow 1$ to 4
5.   **if** j == 1
6. $Z_{LL}[i] \leftarrow zone(LL)$
7.   **else if** j == 2
8. $Z_{LH}[i] \leftarrow zone(LH)$
9.   **else if** j == 3
10. $Z_{HL}[i] \leftarrow zone(HL)$
11.   **else if** j == 4
12. $Z_{HH}[i] \leftarrow zone(HH)$
13.   **end if**
14.   **end for**
15. $C_{BS} \leftarrow DCT(ZLL, ZLH, ZHL, ZHH)$ //
      C_{BS} is compressed bits stream
16.   **end for**
17. **end procedure**

18. **procedure** Decoding(C_{BS})
19. $LL_k \leftarrow IDCT(C_{BS}.Z_{LL})$ // K = 1, 2, 3, 4
20. $LH_k \leftarrow IDCT(C_{BS}.Z_{LH})$
21. $HL_k \leftarrow IDCT(C_{BS}.Z_{HL})$
22. $LH_k \leftarrow IDCT(C_{BS}.Z_{HH})$
23. $LL \leftarrow \{LL[1]\ LL[2]; LL[3]\ LL[4]\}$ //Reconstruct sub − band LL
24. $LH \leftarrow \{LH[1]\ LH[2]; LH[3]\ LH[4]\}$
25. $HL \leftarrow \{HL[1]\ HL[2]; HL[3]\ HL[4]\}$
26. $HH \leftarrow \{HH[1]\ HH[2]; HH[3]\ HH[4]\}$
27. $D_{M \times N} \leftarrow IDWT(LL, LH, HL, HH)$
28.   **output** $D_{M \times N}$ //$D_{M \times N}$ genrate decompressed image
29. **end procedure**

---

4   Experimental Results and Discussions

Our proposed methodology consists of two parts. First, Encoding is used to reduce the bandwidth for quick transfer of data. Second, Decoding is the inverse process of encoding. The encoding and decoding of the ZDD method is implemented by the algorithm as presented in the previous section.

In this section, we presented the effectiveness of our proposed ZDD methodology results for lossy image compression. We used real-world images for experimental purpose as shown in Table 1. All the results are compared with the standard state of the art of previous techniques such as JPEG, JPEG 2000 and HDR photos. The fundamental concept of JPEG technique was to eliminate the unnecessary information from an image. Generally, in JPEG compression, the visual appearance of an image can be seen different from its original image. However, it does not lose any useful information. Moreover, a tradeoff exists between the quality of image and storage size. Second, JPEG2000 is used to compare results with the ZDD method. This technique was developed on the basis of JPEG, and the aim of JPEG2000 was to obtain more accurate compression. The comparisons were made on the state-of-the-art images used in JPEG, JPEG 2000 and HDR photos to ensure the consistency of results. Our methodology (ZDD) showed competitive results with well-known JPEG, JPEG2000 and HDR Photos. Quantitative comparisons were made for the analysis by using PSNR values and can be computed by Eq. 3. PSNR refers to Peak Signals to Noise Ratio, precisely it depicts the quality of regenerated compressed matrix with respect to the original images. Thus, Mean Square Error (MSE), as computed by Eq. 4, is the total squared error between the input image and the compressed image while PSNR measures the peak error

$$PSNR = 10 \log_{10} \frac{r^2}{MSE} \tag{3}$$

$$MSE = Sum(I_1(m, n) - I_2(m, n))^2 \tag{4}$$

In Eq. 4 while calculating MSE, $I_1(m, n)$ is the matrix to represent the original image, $I_2(m, n)$ represents a compressed matrix, m and n describe the dimensions of image and r in Eq. 3 depicts the maximum value of the matrix image. The detailed PSNR values for compression ratio 20:1 of ZDD method is mentioned in Table 1 along with other proposed techniques (JPEG, JPEG2000, and HD) with respect to PSNR values. In comparison with JPEG 2000, results were improved on 9 images out of 15 tested images as shown in Table 1. However, the results of 7 images out of 15 images by ZDD are found better than JPEG. For visual results, we compared the compressed image with the original image as shown in Fig. 5. We have compared our work with existing methods and gained better results as that of previous ones on the basis of PSNR values. The PSNR values and visual results clearly show that our method performed better than existing methods.

Table 1. Represents the comparative evaluation of the ZDD method with existing methods

Image	Method			
	JPEG PSNR	JPEG 2000 PSNR	HD photo PSNR	ZDD method PSNR
big_building.jpg	34.7226	25.266	21.7518	34.5036584
Big_tree.jpg	32.166	34.839	27.2198	34.6955269
bridge.jpg	32.1607	34.452	26.2629	32.5471716
Cathedral.jpg	34.3605	33.218	28.2349	37.7619170
Deer.jpg	31.7454	47.1979	36.6806	36.0143370
Fireworks.jpg	40.7422	37.1857	32.4577	40.3344634
Floer_foveon.jpg	37.8429	35.4603	29.1615	35.6577277
hdr.jpg	39.6114	39.0162	34.7	35.8046278
leaves_iso_200	35.6442	26.9464	22.6741	33.7354433
leaves_iso_1600	35.3111	39.0855	31.6836	33.6628123
Nightshot_iso_100	40.4402	40.4049	34.959	36.4697993
Nightshot_iso_160	35.1703	41.9129	38.2821	36.9412316
Spider_web.jpg	36.1093	35.1134	28.691	33.4924241
Zartificial.jpg	39.3692	23.2222	20.7011	34.1076934
Zone_plate.jpg	36.4246	42.4073	39.8255	35.1559657

(a)   (b)

Fig. 5. (a). Original Image (b). ZDD method compressed image

5   Conclusion

In this research paper, new lossy image compression technique, named as ZDD is presented. ZDD compresses the images with an objective to reduce the image size for transmission of lossy images. ZDD is composed of DWT and DCT for image compression. DWT based bands are divided into zones to get the deep knowledge of pixels. Each band of DWT is decomposed into zones and then passed to DCT by combining all zones into a compressed image. After compressing input images, image is decompressed by using IDCT, applied on zone bitstream. Zones bit streams were merged in order to get the four DWT sub-bands (LL, LH, HL and HH). These frequency sub-bands are then transformed into a single by using IDWT. Experimental results of ZDD performed better and competitive to existing technologies such as JPEG, JPEG2000 and HD photos. However, DWT describes the frequency and spatial picture of an image with low energy on lower frequency sub-bands and edges and texture on high-frequency sub-bands. Therefore, we intend to consider edges and texture at high sub-bands including energy concentrated on lower sub-bands of images for better image compression.

Acknowledgment. This paper is supported by National Natural Science Fund NSF: 61272033 & 61572222.

References

1. Fujii, B.T., et al.: Digital cinema and content distribution on optical high-speed networks, vol. 101, no. 1 (2013)
2. Qian, A.: High-definition image processing algorithm and digital platform design, pp. 1–3 (2012)
3. Chen, T., et al.: High definition image pre-processing system for multi-stripe satellites' image sensors. IEEE Sens. J. **12**(9), 2859–2865 (2012)
4. Demirel, H., Anbarjafari, G.: Discrete wavelet transform-based satellite image resolution enhancement. IEEE Trans. Geosci. Remote Sens. **49**(1), 1997–2004 (2011)
5. Anbarjafari, G., Izadpanahi, S.: Video resolution enhancement by using discrete and stationary wavelet transforms with illumination compensation, December 2012
6. Paper, C., Direkoglu, C., Ozkaramanli, H., Demirel, H.: Region-based super-resolution aided facial feature extraction from low- resolution sequences, April 2005
7. Liu, C., Sun, D.: On Bayesian adaptive video super resolution. IEEE Trans. Pattern Anal. Mach. Intell. **36**(2), 346–360 (2014)
8. Polatkan, G., Zhou, M., Carin, L., Blei, D.: A Bayesian nonparametric approach to image, pp. 1–30 (2018)
9. Rasti, P., Demirel, H.: Arade ğ erleme ve Ardından Geri İ teratif Projeksiyon Kullanarak İ mge Çözünürlü ğ ü Geli ş tirme Image Resolution Enhancement by Using Interpolation Followed by Iterative Back Projection (2013)
10. Glasner, D., Bagon, S., Irani, M.: Super-resolution from a single image (2009)
11. Anbarjafari, G., Demirel, H.: Image super resolution based on interpolation of wavelet domain high frequency subbands and the spatial domain input image. ETRI J. **32**(3), 390–394 (2010)

12. Dong, C., Loy, C.C., He, K., Tang, X.: Learning a deep convolutional network for image super-resolution, September 2014
13. Zhu, Y., Zhang, Y., Yuille, A.L.: Single image super-resolution using deformable patches (2014)
14. Demirel, H., Anbarjafari, G.: Data fusion boosted face recognition based on probability, vol. 2009 (2009)
15. Landge, A.D., Bagal, S.A., Lichade, S.M.: Grayscale image compression using discrete cosine transform, vol. 4, no. 2, pp. 1359–1366 (2016)
16. Zhang, X.: Lossy compression and iterative reconstruction for encrypted image. IEEE Trans. Inf. Forensics Secur. 6(1), 53–58 (2011)
17. Hussain, F., Jeong, J.: Efficient deep neural network for digital image compression employing rectified linear neurons, vol. 2016 (2016)
18. Wahba, W.Z., Maghari, A.Y.A.: Lossless image compression techniques comparative study, February 2016
19. Karami, A., Yazdi, M.: Compression of hyperspectral images using discerete wavelet transform and tucker decomposition, April 2012
20. Paper, C., Demirel, H., Anbarjafari, G., Izadpanahi, S.: Video resolution enhancement by using complex wavelet transform, September 2011
21. Ghazel, M., Freeman, G.H., Vrscay, E.R.: Fractal-wavelet image denoising revisited. IEEE Trans. Image Process. 15(9), 2669–2675 (2006)
22. Khedr, W.M., Abdelrazek, M.: Image compression using DCT upon various quantization. Int. J. Comput. Appl. 137(1), 11–13 (2016)
23. Katharotiya, A., Mahesh, G.M.: Comparative analysis between DCT & DWT techniques of image compression, January 2011 (2014)
24. Raid, A.M., Khedr, W.M., Ahmed, W.: JPEG image compression using discrete cosine transform - a survey, vol. 5, no. 2, pp. 39–47 (2014)
25. Demirel, H., Anbarjafari, G.: IMAGE resolution enhancement by using discrete and stationary wavelet decomposition, vol. 20, no. 5, pp. 2010–2012 (2011)
26. Patel, R.C., Joshi, M.V.: Super-resolution of hyperspectral images: use of optimum wavelet filter coefficients and sparsity regularization. IEEE Trans. Geosci. Remote Sens. 53(4), 1728–1736 (2015)
27. Gajjar, P.P., Joshi, M.V.: New learning based super-resolution: use of DWT and IGMRF prior. IEEE Trans. Image Process. 19(5), 1201–1213 (2010)
28. Jin, L., Wei, G.: Handwritten chinese character recognition with directional decomposition cellular features. J. Circuits Syst. Comput. 08(04), 517–524 (1998)
29. Liu, C.-L., Eim, I.-J., Kim, J.H.: High accuracy handwritten Chinese character recognition by improved feature matching method. In: Proceedings of the Fourth International Conference on Document Analysis and Recognition, vol. 2, pp. 1033–1037 (1997)
30. Chaudhuri, B.B., Pal, U.: Indian script character recognition: a survey. Pattern Recogn. 37(9), 13 (2004)
31. Xiang, P., Xiuzi, Y., Sanyuan, Z.: A hybrid method for robust car plate character recognition. Eng. Appl. Artif. Intell. 18, 963–972 (2005)
32. Uma, R.: FPGA implementation of 2-D DCT for JPEG image compression. Int. J. Adv. Eng. Sci. Technol. (IJAEST) 7, 1–9 (2011)

Author Index

Abid, Muhammad Adil   731
Ahmad, Nafees   731
Aïmeur, Esma   141

Bae, Hae-young   666, 677
Bao, Yintu   333
Bao, Yu   605
Baoyintu   576
Bei-Gong   538
Björkman, Mats   311

Chao, Sun   707
Chen, Bing   226
Chen, Hechang   707
Chen, Meiling   509
Chen, Pengyuan   96
Chen, Wei   605
Chen, Wenqi   378
Chen, Zhenyu   125
Cheng, Fang   697
Cheng, Ya-ge   15
Cheng, Yage   521
Chiriac, Ana Maria   656
Cui, Wen-jun   538
Cui, Xiaoqing   268

Diao, Lian   666
Ding, Yong   246, 268, 472
Dobrescu, Radu   656
Dou, RuiTing   707

Fan, Kefeng   246
Fotouhi, Hossein   311
Fu, Cai   459, 564
Fu, Shaojing   210, 318

Gao, Jiqiang   46, 73
Gao, Zhiqiang   246
Gong, Bei   3, 15, 521
Gong, Liangyi   689
Gu, Chunsheng   411
Guo, Rui-Fang   29, 723
Guo, Xiaojie   73
Guo, Yue   46

Han, Jianmin   114, 440
Han, Lansheng   459, 564, 731
Han, Shengqiang   178, 198
Hang, Xiaoyong   596
Hao, Lifei   342, 627
Hao, Saiyu   551
He, Xiaonan   298, 689
He, Yuan   226
Hou, Ruitao   545
Hu, Ming-sheng   3, 538
Hu, Mingsheng   521
Hu, Zhaolong   114, 440

Iqbal, Khalid   731
Iqbal, Naeem   731

Jia, Bing   342, 421, 576, 627, 637
Jia, Jingyu   46
Jia, Nan   210
Jia, Zhi-juan   15, 538
Jia, Zhi-Juan   3
Jing, Xuan   29, 354, 723
Jing, Zhengjun   411

Kan, Zhe   114, 440, 450
Kennington, Casey   152

Lei, Yan-fang   15
Lei, Yanfang   521
Li, Jing   545
Li, Kongbo   298
Li, Min   46
Li, Pengyu   421
Li, Shijie   472
Li, Shuyu   58
Li, Wuyungerile   333, 421, 576, 637
Li, Xiang   282
Li, Zhen   354
Lin, Feilong   450
Liu, Chong   605
Liu, Huwei   585
Liu, Jiachen   333
Liu, Jianwei   615
Liu, Jie   282, 485

Liu, Lingang   472
Liu, Nan   401
Liu, Xiaokang   282, 485
Liu, Yangyang   198
Liu, Yingcong   333, 576
Liu, Zheli   73
Long, Jun   551
Lu, Hongwei   459
Lu, Jing   282, 378, 485
Luo, Decun   472

Ma, Xuebin   421
Mehdy, Nuhil   152
Mehrpouyan, Hoda   152
Meng, Qingyu   362
Mo, Xiuliang   96
Mocanu, Stefan   656
Mu, Baoying   198

Niu, Xiaxia   38

Peng, Fang   378
Peng, Hao   114, 440, 450
Peng, Jin   46, 509, 596
Popa, Cosmin   656

Ran, Peng   46, 509, 596

Sahnoune, Zakaria   141
Saru, Daniela   656
Shao, Tong   354
Shao, Xuebin   178
Shi, Ning   585
Shi, Peiji   178, 198
Shi, Peizhong   411
Song, CongXi   498
Su, Li   509, 596
Sun, Mengyao   73

Tang, Chaogang   605
Tang, Chenjun   472
Tang, Jianchao   210, 318
Tang, Jie   677
Tang, Shijie   246
Tian, Hui   282, 378, 485
Tian, Jun-Feng   29, 723
Tian, Tian   388
Tian, Yuechi   354
Tian, Yunkun   298, 689

Vahabi, Maryam   311

Wang, Chundong   96, 105, 298, 689
Wang, Han   58
Wang, Huiyong   246, 268
Wang, Jia   378
Wang, Jianing   96
Wang, Jigang   388
Wang, Jing   73
Wang, Junwei   615
Wang, Kaiyu   401
Wang, Liming   388
Wang, Li-peng   15, 538
Wang, Li-Peng   3
Wang, Lipeng   521
Wang, Tongxiang   615
Wang, Xiao   545
Wang, Xinyu   125
Wang, Yujue   246, 268, 472
Wei, Xianglin   605, 615
Wei, Xiaogang   433
Wu, Guowei   125
Wu, Lei   707
Wu, Liji   647
Wu, Qiyu   362
Wu, Yuduo   46

Xia, Shixiong   605
Xia, Ying   666, 677
Xian, Hequn   545
Xiang, Hengkui   472
Xiu, Jiapeng   401
Xu, Jian   226, 362
Xu, Ming   210, 318
Xu, Zhen   388

Yan, Junzhi   596
Yang, Bo   596
Yang, Hongyu   697
Yang, Jing   388
Yang, Qiang   498
Yang, Yijun   647
Yang, Yingchuan   551
Yang, Zhengqiu   401
Yao, Lin   125
Ye, Xin   689
Yin, An-Sheng   87
Yin, Mingxin   73
Yu, Bo   498
Yu, Xiangchun   707

Yu, Yanbo   362
Yu, Zhezhou   707
Yuan, Ye   647
Yue, Xiaohan   226

Zhang, Chuxuan   342, 627
Zhang, Jia-lei   3
Zhang, Jianzhong   73
Zhang, Qi   210
Zhang, Shun-Yi   87
Zhang, Xiangmin   647
Zhang, Xu   666, 677
Zhang, Xugao   697

Zhang, Yanan   178, 198
Zhao, Chunhui   105
Zhao, Dandan   114, 440, 450
Zhao, Yan   38
Zheng, Jia   198
Zheng, Wenbai   105
Zheng, Zhonglong   450
Zhong, Stevenyin   178
Zhou, Fucai   362
Zhou, Man   459, 564
Zhou, Tao   637
Zong, Na   421
Zou, Xiuqing   472

Printed in the United States
By Bookmasters